Praise for the Reformation Commentary on Scripture

"Protestant reformers were fundamentally exegetes as much as theologians, yet (except for figures like Luther and Calvin) their commentaries and sermons have been neglected because these writings are not available in modern editions or languages. That makes this new series of Reformation Commentary on Scripture most welcome as a way to provide access to some of the wealth of biblical exposition of the sixteenth and seventeenth centuries. The editor's introduction explains the nature of the sources and the selection process; the intended audience of modern pastors and students of the Bible has led to a focus on theological and practical comments. Although it will be of use to students of the Reformation, this series is far from being an esoteric study of largely forgotten voices; this collection of reforming comments, comprehending every verse and provided with topical headings, will serve contemporary pastors and preachers very well."

Elsie Anne McKee, *Archibald Alexander Professor of Reformation Studies and the History of Worship, Princeton Theological Seminary*

"This series provides an excellent introduction to the history of biblical exegesis in the Reformation period. The introductions are accurate, clear and informative, and the passages intelligently chosen to give the reader a good idea of methods deployed and issues at stake. It puts precritical exegesis in its context and so presents it in its correct light. Highly recommended as reference book, course book and general reading for students and all interested lay and clerical readers."

Irena Backus, *Professeure Ordinaire, Institut d'histoire de la Réformation, Université de Genève*

"The Reformation Commentary on Scripture is a major publishing event—for those with historical interest in the founding convictions of Protestantism, but even more for those who care about understanding the Bible. As with IVP Academic's earlier Ancient Christian Commentary on Scripture, this effort brings flesh and blood to 'the communion of saints' by letting believers of our day look over the shoulders of giants from the past. By connecting the past with the present, and by doing so with the Bible at the center, the editors of this series perform a great service for the church. The series deserves the widest possible support."

Mark A. Noll, *Francis A. McAnaney Professor of History, University of Notre Dame*

"For those who preach and teach Scripture in the church, the Reformation Commentary on Scripture is a significant publishing event. Pastors and other church leaders will find delightful surprises, challenging enigmas and edifying insights in this series, as many Reformational voices are newly translated into English. The lively conversation in these pages can ignite today's pastoral imagination for fresh and faithful expositions of Scripture."

J. Todd Billings, *Gordon H. Girod Research Professor of Reformed Theology, Western Theological Seminary*

"The reformers discerned rightly what the church desperately needed in the sixteenth century—the bold proclamation of the Word based on careful study of the sacred Scriptures. We need not only to hear that same call again for our own day but also to learn from the Reformation how to do it. This commentary series is a godsend!"

Richard J. Mouw, *President Emeritus, Fuller Theological Seminary*

"Like the Ancient Christian Commentary on Scripture, the Reformation Commentary on Scripture does a masterful job of offering excellent selections from well-known and not-so-well-known exegetes. The editor's introductory survey is, by itself, worth the price of the book. It is easy to forget that there were more hands, hearts and minds involved in the Reformation than Luther and Calvin. Furthermore, encounters even with these figures are often limited to familiar quotes on familiar topics. However, the Reformation Commentary helps us to recognize the breadth and depth of exegetical interests and skill that fueled and continue to fuel faithful meditation on God's Word. I heartily recommend this series as a tremendous resource not only for ministry but for personal edification."

Michael S. Horton, *J. G. Machen Professor of Systematic Theology and Apologetics, Westminster Seminary, California*

"The Reformation was ignited by a fresh reading of Scripture. In this series of commentaries, we contemporary interpreters are allowed to feel some of the excitement, surprise and wonder of our spiritual forebears. Luther, Calvin and their fellow revolutionaries were masterful interpreters of the Word. Now, in this remarkable series, some of our very best Reformation scholars open up the riches of the Reformation's reading of the Scripture."

William H. Willimon, *Professor of the Practice of Christian Ministry, Duke Divinity School*

"The Reformation Scripture principle set the entirety of Christian life and thought under the governance of the divine Word, and pressed the church to renew its exegetical labors. This series promises to place before the contemporary church the fruit of those labors, and so to exemplify life under the Word."

John Webster, *Professor of Divinity, University of St. Andrews*†

"Since Gerhard Ebeling's pioneering work on Luther's exegesis seventy years ago, the history of biblical interpretation has occupied many Reformation scholars and become a vital part of study of the period. The Reformation Commentary on Scripture provides fresh materials for students of Reformation-era biblical interpretation and for twenty-first-century preachers to mine the rich stores of insights from leading reformers of the sixteenth century into both the text of Scripture itself and its application in sixteenth-century contexts. This series will strengthen our understanding of the period of the Reformation and enable us to apply its insights to our own days and its challenges to the church."

Robert Kolb, *Professor Emeritus, Concordia Theological Seminary*

"The multivolume Ancient Christian Commentary on Scripture is a valuable resource for those who wish to know how the Fathers interpreted a passage of Scripture but who lack the time or the opportunity to search through the many individual works. This new Reformation Commentary on Scripture will do the same for the reformers and is to be warmly welcomed. It will provide much easier access to the exegetical treasures of the Reformation and will hopefully encourage readers to go back to some of the original works themselves."

Anthony N. S. Lane, *Professor of Historical Theology and Director of Research, London School of Theology*

"This volume of the RCS project is an invaluable source for pastors and the historically/biblically interested that provides unparalleled access not only to commentaries of the leading Protestant reformers but also to a host of nowadays unknown commentaters on Galatians and Ephesians. The RCS is sure to enhance and enliven contemporary exegesis. With its wide scope, the collection will enrich our understanding of the variety of Reformation thought and biblical exegesis."

Sigrun Haude, *Associate Professor of Reformation and Early Modern European History, University of Cincinnati*

"The Reformation Commentary on Scripture series promises to be an 'open sesame' to the biblical exegesis, exposition and application of the Bible that was the hallmark of the Reformation. While comparisons can be odious, the difference between Reformation commentary and exposition and much that both preceded and followed it is laid bare in these pages: whereas others write about the Bible from the outside, Reformation exposition carries with it the atmosphere of men who spoke and wrote from inside the Bible, experiencing the power of biblical teaching even as they expounded it. . . . This grand project sets before scholars, pastors, teachers, students and growing Christians an experience that can only be likened to stumbling into a group Bible study only to discover that your fellow participants include some of the most significant Christians of the Reformation and post-Reformation (for that matter, of any) era. Here the Word of God is explained in a variety of accents: German, Swiss, French, Dutch, English, Scottish and more. Each one vibrates with a thrilling sense of the living nature of God's Word and its power to transform individuals, churches and even whole communities. Here is a series to anticipate, enjoy and treasure."

Sinclair Ferguson, *Senior Minister, First Presbyterian Church, Columbia, South Carolina*

"I strongly endorse the Reformation Commentary on Scripture. Introducing how the Bible was interpreted during the age of the Reformation, these volumes will not only renew contemporary preaching, but they will also help us understand more fully how reading and meditating on Scripture can, in fact, change our lives!"

Lois Malcolm, *Associate Professor of Systematic Theology, Luther Seminary*

"Discerning the true significance of movements in theology requires acquaintance with their biblical exegesis. This is supremely so with the Reformation, which was essentially a biblical revival. The Reformation Commentary on Scripture will fill a yawning gap, just as the Ancient Christian Commentary did before it, and the first volume gets the series off to a fine start, whetting the appetite for more. Most heartily do I welcome and commend this long overdue project."

J. I. Packer, *Retired Board of Governors Professor of Theology, Regent College*

"There is no telling the benefits to emerge from the publication of this magnificent Reformation Commentary on Scripture series! Now exegetical and theological treasures from Reformation era commentators will be at our fingertips, providing new insights from old sources to give light for the present and future. This series is a gift to scholars and to the church; a wonderful resource to enhance our study of the written Word of God for generations to come!"

Donald K. McKim, *Executive Editor of Theology and Reference, Westminster John Knox Press*

"Why was this not done before? The publication of the Reformation Commentary on Scripture should be greeted with enthusiasm by every believing Christian—but especially by those who will preach and teach the Word of God. This commentary series brings the very best of the Reformation heritage to the task of exegesis and exposition, and each volume in this series represents a veritable feast that takes us back to the sixteenth century to enrich the preaching and teaching of God's Word in our own time."

R. Albert Mohler Jr., *President, The Southern Baptist Theological Seminary*

"Today more than ever, the Christian past is the church's future. InterVarsity Press has already brought the voice of the ancients to our ears. Now, in the Reformation Commentary on Scripture, we hear a timely word from the first Protestants as well."

Bryan Litfin, *Professor of Theology, Moody Bible Institute*

"I am delighted to see the Reformation Commentary on Scripture. The editors of this series have done us all a service by gleaning from these rich fields of biblical reflection. May God use this new life for these old words to give him glory and to build his church."

Mark Dever, *Senior Pastor, Capitol Hill Baptist Church, and President of 9Marks.org Ministries*

"Monumental and magisterial, the Reformation Commentary on Scripture, edited by Timothy George, is a remarkably bold and visionary undertaking. Bringing together a wealth of resources, these volumes will provide historians, theologians, biblical scholars, pastors and students with a fresh look at the exegetical insights of those who shaped and influenced the sixteenth-century Reformation. With this marvelous publication, InterVarsity Press has reached yet another plateau of excellence. We pray that this superb series will be used of God to strengthen both church and academy."

David S. Dockery, *President, Trinity International University*

"Detached from her roots, the church cannot reach the world as God intends. While every generation must steward the scriptural insights God grants it, only arrogance or ignorance causes leaders to ignore the contributions of those faithful leaders before us. The Reformation Commentary on Scripture roots our thought in great insights of faithful leaders of the Reformation to further biblical preaching and teaching in this generation."

Bryan Chapell, *Chancellor and Professor of Practical Theology, Covenant Theological Seminary*

"After reading several volumes of the Reformation Commentary on Scripture, I exclaimed, 'Hey, this is just what the doctor ordered—I mean Doctor Martinus Lutherus!' The church of today bearing his name needs a strong dose of the medicine this doctor prescribed for the ailing church of the sixteenth century. The reforming fire of Christ-centered preaching that Luther ignited is the only hope to reclaim the impact of the gospel to keep the Reformation going, not for its own sake but to further the renewal of the worldwide church of Christ today. This series of commentaries will equip preachers to step into their pulpits with confidence in the same living Word that inspired the witness of Luther and Calvin and many other lesser-known Reformers."

Carl E. Braaten, *Cofounder of the Center for Catholic and Evangelical Theology*

Reformation Commentary on Scripture

New Testament

IXa

1 Corinthians

Edited by
Scott M. Manetsch

General Editor
Timothy George

Associate General Editor
Scott M. Manetsch

IVP Academic
An imprint of InterVarsity Press
Downers Grove, Illinois

To my parents,
Thomas Jerome† and Edna Elise Manetsch,
with my profound gratitude and love

InterVarsity Press
P.O. Box 1400, Downers Grove, IL 60515-1426
www.ivpress.com
email@ivpress.com

InterVarsity Press® is the book-publishing division of InterVarsity Christian Fellowship/USA®, a movement of students and faculty active on campus at hundreds of universities, colleges and schools of nursing in the United States of America, and a member movement of the International Fellowship of Evangelical Students. For information about local and regional activities, visit intervarsity.org.

Design: Cindy Kiple
Images: Wooden cross: iStockphoto
The Protestant Church in Lyon: The Protestant Church in Lyon, called "The Paradise" at Bibliotheque Publique et Universitaire, Geneva, Switzerland, Erich Lessing/Art Resource, NY

ISBN 978-0-8308-2972-9 (print)
ISBN 978-0-8308-9173-3 (digital)

Printed in the United States of America ♾

green press INITIATIVE *As a member of the Green Press Initiative, InterVarsity Press is committed to protecting the environment and to the responsible use of natural resources. To learn more, visit greenpressinitiative.org.*

Library of Congress Cataloging-in-Publication Data

Names: Manetsch, Scott M, editor.
Title: 1 Corinthians / edited by Scott M. Manetsch.
Other titles: 1 Corinthians (2017) | First Corinthians
Description: Downers Grove : IVP Academic, [2017] | Series: Reformation commentary on Scripture. New Testament ; IXa | Includes bibliographical references and indexes.
Identifiers: LCCN 2016059618 (print) | LCCN 2017000139 (ebook) | ISBN 9780830829729 (hardcover : alk. paper) | ISBN 9780830891733 (digital) | ISBN 9780830891733 (eBook)
Subjects: LCSH: Bible. Corinthians, 1st—Commentaries.
Classification: LCC BS2675.53 .A156 2017 (print) | LCC BS2675.53 (ebook) | DDC 227/.20709031—dc23
LC record available at https://lccn.loc.gov/2016059618

P 26 25 24 23 22 21 20 19 18 17 16 15 14 13 12 11 10 9 8 7 6 5 4 3 2 1
Y 40 39 38 37 36 35 34 33 32 31 30 29 28 27 26 25 24 23 22 21 20 19 18 17

Reformation Commentary on Scripture Project Staff

InterVarsity Press

Publisher
Jeff Crosby

Associate Publisher, Director of Editorial
Cindy Bunch

Associate Publisher, Director of IVP Academic
Daniel G. Reid

CONTENTS

ACKNOWLEDGMENTS

There are many people who deserve my heartfelt gratitude for their encouragement and practical assistance in the completion of this volume. In particular, I wish to thank friends and faculty colleagues John Woodbridge, Douglas Sweeney, Eckhard Schnabel, D. A. Carson, and Timothy George for their enthusiasm for this project and their faithful support over the last several years. Your friendship and partnership in Christian ministry mean so much to me. I am also indebted to John Thompson for his kindness in reading an early version of this manuscript and offering valuable suggestions for its improvement. In addition, I am grateful for the fine graduate assistants at Trinity Evangelical Divinity School who have lent a hand in this project by tracking down sources and reading drafts of my work, including David Anderson, David Barshinger, Philip Cox, Justin Dunton, Jeffrey Fisher, Andre Gazal, Jihoon Jin, Ethan McCarthy, Timothy Padgett, Thomas Parfitt, Matt Shrader, and John Simons. My thanks also to the administration of Trinity Evangelical Divinity School for granting me a sabbatical in the spring semester of 2014, which allowed me to devote focused time to this commentary. Over these past years, it has been a special pleasure to work closely with the excellent editorial team at InterVarsity Press responsible for the Reformation Commentary on Scripture series. Andy Le Peau, Dan Reid, Brannon Ellis, David McNutt, David Hooper, and Todd Hains: thank you for your professionalism, your hard work, and your extraordinary patience, which have made this volume possible. Of all these talented and generous colleagues, I owe a special debt of gratitude to the assistant project editor (and my student), Todd Hains, for his unflagging enthusiasm for the RCS, his remarkable knowledge of German sources, and his assistance in translating them.

In addition, I would like to say a special thank you to my family. I am most grateful for the gracious support, encouragement, and love that my dear wife, Catherine, and my daughters, Hannah and Melissa, have shared with me during the course of this writing project. Thank you so much—each one of you is so precious to me. Finally, I wish to acknowledge with profound gratitude my parents Thomas Jerome (†) and Edna Elise Manetsch, who first shared the glad tidings of God's Word with me, and who have been God's instrument of grace, guidance, and spiritual inspiration through the course of my life. This book is dedicated to them with my deepest respect and enduring love.

Scott M. Manetsch

ABBREVIATIONS

ANF	The Ante-Nicene Fathers. 10 vols. Edited by Alexander Roberts and James Donaldson. Buffalo, NY: Christian Literature, 1885–1896. Available online at www.ccel.org.
ASD	Opera Omnia Desderii Erasmi Roterodami. Amsterdam: Elsevier, 1969–.
BoC	*The Book of Concord: The Confessions of the Evangelical Lutheran Church*. Edited by Robert Kolb and Timothy J. Wengert. Translated by Charles Arand et al. Minneapolis: Fortress, 2000.
BRN	*Bibliotheca Reformatoria Neederlandica*. 10 vols. Edited by S. Cramer and F. Pijper. The Hague: Martinus Nijhoff, 1903–1914. Digital copies online at babel.hathitrust.org.
BSLK	*Die Bekenntnisschriften der evangelisch-lutherischen Kirche*. 12th ed. Göttingen: Vandenhoeck & Ruprecht, 1998.
CHB	*Cambridge History of the Bible*. 3 vols. Cambridge: Cambridge University Press, 1963–1970.
CNTC	*Calvin's New Testament Commentaries*. 12 vols. Edited by D. W. Torrance and T. F. Torrance. Grand Rapids: Eerdmans, 1959–1972.
CO	*Ioannis Calvini Opera quae supersunt omnia*. 59 vols. Corpus Reformatorum 29-88. Edited by G. Baum, E. Cunitz and E. Reuss. Brunswick and Berlin: C. A. Schwetschke, 1863–1900. Digital copy online at archive-ouverte.unige.ch/unige:650.
Creeds	Philip Schaff. *The Creeds of Christendom: With a Critical History and Notes*. 3 vols. New York: Harper & Row, 1877. Reprint, Grand Rapids: Baker, 1977. Accessible online at ccel.org.
CRR	Classics of the Radical Reformation. 12 vols. Waterloo, ON, and Scottdale, PA: Herald Press, 1973–2010.
CTS	Calvin Translation Society edition of Calvin's commentaries. 46 vols. Edinburgh, 1843–1855. Several reprints, but variously bound; volume numbers (when cited) are relative to specific commentaries and not to the entire set. Available online at www.ccel.org.
CWE	*Collected Works of Erasmus*. 86 vols. projected. Toronto: University of Toronto Press, 1969–.
DMBI	*Dictionary of Major Biblical Interpreters*. Edited by Donald K. McKim. Downers Grove, IL: IVP Academic, 2007.
E^2	*Dr. Martin Luther's sämmtliche Werke*. 2nd ed. 26 vols. Frankfurt and Erlangen: Heyder & Zimmer, 1862–1885. Digital copies online at babel.hathitrust.org.

EEBO	Early English Books Online. Subscription database, eebo.chadwyck.com.
LCC	Library of Christian Classics. 26 vols. Edited by John Baillie et al. Philadelphia: Westminster, 1953–1966.
LCL	Loeb Classical Library. Edited by Jeffrey Henderson. Cambridge, MA: Harvard University Press, 1911–. Digital copy online at www.loebclassics.com.
LW	*Luther's Works [American edition]*. 82 vols. projected. St. Louis: Concordia; Philadelphia: Fortress, 1955–1986, 2009–.
MO	*Philippi Melanthonis Opera quae supersunt omnia*. 28 vols. Corpus Reformatorum 1-28. Edited by C. G. Bretschneider. Halle: C. A. Schwetschke, 1834–1860. Digital copies online at archive.org and books.google.com.
OER	*Oxford Encyclopedia of the Reformation*. 4 vols. Edited by Hans J. Hillerbrand. New York: Oxford University Press, 1996.
NPNF	A Select Library of the Nicene and Post-Nicene Fathers of the Christian Church. 28 vols. in two series, denoted as NPNF and NPNF[2]. Edited by Philip Schaff et al. Buffalo, NY: Christian Literature, 1887–1894. Several reprints; also available online at www.ccel.org.
PG	Patrologia cursus completus. Series Graeca. 161 vols. Edited by J.-P. Migne. Paris, 1857–1866.
PL	Patrologia cursus completus. Series Latina. 221 vols. Edited by J.-P. Migne. Paris: Migne, 1844–1864.
PMR	*The Peter Martyr [Vermigli] Reader.* Edited by John Patrick Donnelley and Joseph C. McLelland. Kirksville, MO: Truman State University Press, 1999.
PRDL	Post Reformation Digital Library. Online database at prdl.org.
r, v	Some early books are numbered not by page but by folio (leaf). Front and back sides (pages) of a numbered folio are indicated by *recto* (r) and *verso* (v), respectively.
RCS	Reformation Commentary on Scripture. 28 vols. projected. Edited by Timothy George and Scott M. Manetsch. Downers Grove, IL: IVP Academic, 2011–.
WA	*D. Martin Luthers Werke, Kritische Gesamtausgabe: [Schriften]*. 73 vols. Weimar: Hermann Böhlaus Nachfolger, 1883–2009. Digital copies online at archive.org.
WADB	*D. Martin Luthers Werke, Kritische Gesamtausgabe: Deutsche Bibel.* 12 vols. Weimar: Böhlaus Nachfolger, 1906–1961.
WATR	*D. Martin Luthers Werke, Kritische Gesamtausgabe: Tischreden*. 6 vols. Weimar: Hermann Böhlaus Nachfolger, 1912–1921. Digital copies online at archive.org.

BIBLE TRANSLATIONS

CEB	Common English Bible
ESV	English Standard Version
KJV	King James Version
LXX	Septuagint
NASB	New American Standard Bible
NIV	New International Version
NKJV	New King James Version
NRSV	New Revised Standard Version
Vg	Vulgate

A GUIDE TO USING THIS COMMENTARY

Several features have been incorporated into the design of this commentary. The following comments are intended to assist readers in making full use of this volume.

Pericopes of Scripture

The scriptural text has been divided into pericopes, or passages, usually several verses in length. Each of these pericopes is given a heading, which appears at the beginning of the pericope. For example, the first pericope in this commentary is 1 Corinthians 1:1-3, "Paul greets the Corinthians." This heading is followed by the Scripture passage quoted in the English Standard Version (ESV). The Scripture passage is provided for the convenience of readers, but it is also in keeping with Reformation-era commentaries, which often followed the patristic and medieval commentary tradition, in which the citations of the reformers were arranged according to the text of Scripture.

Overviews

Following each pericope of text is an overview of the Reformation authors' comments on that pericope. The format of this overview varies among the volumes of this series, depending on the requirements of the specific book(s) of Scripture. The function of the overview is to identify succinctly the key exegetical, theological and pastoral concerns of the Reformation writers arising from the pericope, providing the reader with an orientation to Reformation-era approaches and emphases. It tracks a reasonably cohesive thread of argument among reformers' comments, even though they are derived from diverse sources and generations. Thus, the summaries do not proceed chronologically or by verse sequence. Rather, they seek to rehearse the overall course of the reformers' comments on that pericope.

We do not assume that the commentators themselves anticipated or expressed a formally received cohesive argument but rather that the various arguments tend to flow in a plausible, recognizable pattern. Modern readers can thus glimpse aspects of continuity in the flow of diverse exegetical traditions representing various generations and geographical locations.

Topical Headings

An abundance of varied Reformation-era comment is available for each pericope. For this reason we have broken the pericopes into two levels. First is the verse with its topical heading. The reformers' comments are then focused on aspects of each verse, with topical headings summarizing the essence of the individual comment by evoking a key phrase, metaphor or idea. This feature provides a bridge by which modern readers can enter into the heart of the Reformation-era comment.

Identifying the Reformation Authors, Texts and Events

Following the topical heading of each section of comment, the name of the Reformation commentator is given. An English translation (where needed) of the reformer's comment is then provided. This is immediately followed by the title of the original work rendered in English.

Readers who wish to pursue a deeper investigation of the reformers' works cited in this commentary will find full bibliographic detail for each Reformation title provided in the bibliography at the back of the volume. Information on English translations (where available) and standard original-language editions and critical editions of the works cited is found in the bibliography. The Biographical Sketches section provides brief overviews of the life and work of each commentator, and each confession or collaborative work, appearing in the present volume (as well as in any previous volumes). Finally, a Timeline of the Reformation offers broader context for people, places and events relevant to the commentators and their works.

Footnotes and Back Matter

To aid the reader in exploring the background and texts in further detail, this commentary utilizes footnotes. The use and content of footnotes may vary among the volumes in this series. Where footnotes appear, a footnote number directs the reader to a note at the bottom of the page, where one will find annotations (clarifications or biblical cross references), information on English translations (where available) or standard original-language editions of the work cited.

Where original-language texts have remained untranslated into English, we provide new translations. Where there is any serious ambiguity or textual problem in the selection, we have tried to reflect the best available textual tradition. Wherever current English translations are already well rendered, they are utilized, but where necessary they are stylistically updated. A single asterisk (*) indicates that a previous English translation has been updated to modern English or amended for easier reading. We have standardized spellings and made grammatical variables uniform so that our English references will not reflect the linguistic oddities of the older English translations. For ease of reading we have in some cases removed superfluous conjunctions.

GENERAL INTRODUCTION

The Reformation Commentary on Scripture (RCS) is a twenty-eight-volume series of exegetical comment covering the entire Bible and gathered from the writings of sixteenth-century preachers, scholars and reformers. The RCS is intended as a sequel to the highly acclaimed Ancient Christian Commentary on Scripture (ACCS), and as such its overall concept, method, format and audience are similar to the earlier series. Both series are committed to the renewal of the church through careful study and meditative reflection on the Old and New Testaments, the charter documents of Christianity, read in the context of the worshiping, believing community of faith across the centuries. However, the patristic and Reformation eras are separated by nearly a millennium, and the challenges of reading Scripture with the reformers require special attention to their context, resources and assumptions. The purpose of this general introduction is to present an overview of the context and process of biblical interpretation in the age of the Reformation.

Goals

The Reformation Commentary on Scripture seeks to introduce its readers to the depth and richness of exegetical ferment that defined the Reformation era. The RCS has four goals: the enrichment of contemporary biblical interpretation through exposure to Reformation-era biblical exegesis; the renewal of contemporary preaching through exposure to the biblical insights of the Reformation writers; a deeper understanding of the Reformation itself and the breadth of perspectives represented within it; and a recovery of the profound integration of the life of faith and the life of the mind that should characterize Christian scholarship. Each of these goals requires a brief comment.

Renewing contemporary biblical interpretation. During the past half-century, biblical hermeneutics has become a major growth industry in the academic world. One of the consequences of the historical-critical hegemony of biblical studies has been the privileging of contemporary philosophies and ideologies at the expense of a commitment to the Christian church as the primary reading community within which and for which biblical exegesis is done. Reading Scripture with the church fathers and the reformers is a corrective to all such imperialism of the present. One of the greatest skills required for a fruitful interpretation of the Bible is the ability to listen. We rightly emphasize the importance of listening to the voices of contextual theologies today, but in doing so we often marginalize or ignore another crucial context—the community of believing Christians through the centuries. The serious study of Scripture requires more than the latest

Bible translation in one hand and the latest commentary (or niche study Bible) in the other. John L. Thompson has called on Christians today to practice the art of "reading the Bible with the dead."[1] The RCS presents carefully selected comments from the extant commentaries of the Reformation as an encouragement to more in-depth study of this important epoch in the history of biblical interpretation.

Strengthening contemporary preaching. The Protestant reformers identified the public preaching of the Word of God as an indispensible means of grace and a sure sign of the true church. Through the words of the preacher, the living voice of the gospel (*viva vox evangelii*) is heard. Luther famously said that the church is not a "pen house" but a "mouth house."[2] The Reformation in Switzerland began when Huldrych Zwingli entered the pulpit of the Grossmünster in Zurich on January 1, 1519, and began to preach a series of expositional sermons chapter by chapter from the Gospel of Matthew. In the following years he extended this homiletical approach to other books of the Old and New Testaments. Calvin followed a similar pattern in Geneva. Many of the commentaries represented in this series were either originally presented as sermons or were written to support the regular preaching ministry of local church pastors. Luther said that the preacher should be a *bonus textualis*—a good one with a text—well-versed in the Scriptures. Preachers in the Reformation traditions preached not only about the Bible but also from it, and this required more than a passing acquaintance with its contents. Those who have been charged with the office of preaching in the church today can find wisdom and insight—and fresh perspectives—in the sermons of the Reformation and the biblical commentaries read and studied by preachers of the sixteenth century.

Deepening understanding of the Reformation. Some scholars of the sixteenth century prefer to speak of the period they study in the plural, the European Reformations, to indicate that many diverse impulses for reform were at work in this turbulent age of transition from medieval to modern times.[3] While this point is well taken, the RCS follows the time-honored tradition of using *Reformation* in the singular form to indicate not only a major moment in the history of Christianity in the West but also, as Hans J. Hillerbrand has put it, "an essential cohesiveness in the heterogeneous pursuits of religious reform in the sixteenth century."[4] At the same time, in developing guidelines to assist the volume editors in making judicious selections from the vast amount of commentary material available in this period, we have stressed the multifaceted character of the Reformation across many confessions, theological orientations and political settings.

Advancing Christian scholarship. By assembling and disseminating numerous voices from such a signal period as the Reformation, the RCS aims to make a significant contribution to the ever-growing stream of Christian scholarship. The post-Enlightenment split between the study of the Bible as an academic discipline and the reading of the Bible as spiritual nurture was foreign

[1]John L. Thompson, *Reading the Bible with the Dead* (Grand Rapids: Eerdmans, 2007).
[2]WA 10,2:48.
[3]See Carter Lindberg, *The European Reformations*, 2nd ed. (Malden, MA: Wiley-Blackwell, 2010).
[4]Hans J. Hillerbrand, *The Division of Christendom* (Louisville, KY: Westminster John Knox, 2007), x. Hillerbrand has also edited the standard reference work in Reformation studies, *OER*. See also Diarmaid MacCulloch, *The Reformation* (New York: Viking, 2003), and Patrick Collinson, *The Reformation: A History* (New York: Random House, 2004).

to the reformers. For them the study of the Bible was transformative at the most basic level of the human person: *coram deo.*

The reformers all repudiated the idea that the Bible could be studied and understood with dispassionate objectivity, as a cold artifact from antiquity. Luther's famous Reformation breakthrough triggered by his laborious study of the Psalms and Paul's letter to the Romans is well known, but the experience of Cambridge scholar Thomas Bilney was perhaps more typical. When Erasmus's critical edition of the Greek New Testament was published in 1516, it was accompanied by a new translation in elegant Latin. Attracted by the classical beauty of Erasmus's Latin, Bilney came across this statement in 1 Timothy 1:15: "Christ Jesus came into the world to save sinners." In the Greek this sentence is described as *pistos ho logos,* which the Vulgate had rendered *fidelis sermo,* "a faithful saying." Erasmus chose a different word for the Greek *pistos—certus,* "sure, certain." When Bilney grasped the meaning of this word applied to the announcement of salvation in Christ, he tells us that "immediately, I felt a marvellous comfort and quietness, insomuch as 'my bruised bones leaped for joy.'"[5]

Luther described the way the Bible was meant to function in the minds and hearts of believers when he reproached himself and others for studying the nativity narrative with such cool unconcern:

> I hate myself because when I see Christ laid in the manger or in the lap of his mother and hear the angels sing, my heart does not leap into flame. With what good reason should we all despise ourselves that we remain so cold when this word is spoken to us, over which everyone should dance and leap and burn for joy! We act as though it were a frigid historical fact that does not smite our hearts, as if someone were merely relating that the sultan has a crown of gold.[6]

It was a core conviction of the Reformation that the careful study and meditative listening to the Scriptures, what the monks called *lectio divina,* could yield transformative results for *all* of life. The value of such a rich commentary, therefore, lies not only in the impressive volume of Reformation-era voices that are presented throughout the course of the series but in the many particular fields for which their respective lives and ministries are relevant. The Reformation is consequential for historical studies, both church as well as secular history. Biblical and theological studies, to say nothing of pastoral and spiritual studies, also stand to benefit and progress immensely from renewed engagement today, as mediated through the RCS, with the reformers of yesteryear.

Perspectives

In setting forth the perspectives and parameters of the RCS, the following considerations have proved helpful.

Chronology. When did the Reformation begin, and how long did it last? In some traditional accounts, the answer was clear: the Reformation began with the posting of Luther's Ninety-five

[5]John Foxe, *The Acts and Monuments of John Foxe: A New and Complete Edition,* 8 vols., ed. Stephen Reed Cattley (London: R. B. Seeley & W. Burnside, 1837), 4:635; quoting Ps 51:8; cited in A. G. Dickens, *The English Reformation,* 2nd ed. (University Park, PA: The Pennsylvannia State University Press, 1991), 102.

[6]WA 49:176-77, quoted in Roland Bainton, "The Bible in the Reformation," in *CHB,* 3:23.

Theses at Wittenberg in 1517 and ended with the death of Calvin in Geneva in 1564. Apart from reducing the Reformation to a largely German event with a side trip to Switzerland, this perspective fails to do justice to the important events that led up to Luther's break with Rome and its many reverberations throughout Europe and beyond. In choosing commentary selections for the RCS, we have adopted the concept of the long sixteenth century, say, from the late 1400s to the mid-seventeenth century. Thus we have included commentary selections from early or pre-Reformation writers such as John Colet and Jacques Lefèvre d'Étaples to seventeenth-century figures such as Henry Ainsworth and Johann Gerhard.

Confession. The RCS concentrates primarily, though not exclusively, on the exegetical writings of the Protestant reformers. While the ACCS provided a compendium of key consensual exegetes of the early Christian centuries, the Catholic/Protestant confessional divide in the sixteenth century tested the very idea of consensus, especially with reference to ecclesiology and soteriology. While many able and worthy exegetes faithful to the Roman Catholic Church were active during this period, this project has chosen to include primarily those figures that represent perspectives within the Protestant Reformation. For this reason we have not included comments on the apocryphal or deuterocanonical writings.

We recognize that "Protestant" and "Catholic" as contradistinctive labels are anachronistic terms for the early decades of the sixteenth century before the hardening of confessional identities surrounding the Council of Trent (1545–1563). Protestant figures such as Philipp Melanchthon, Johannes Oecolampadius and John Calvin were all products of the revival of sacred letters known as biblical humanism. They shared an approach to biblical interpretation that owed much to Desiderius Erasmus and other scholars who remained loyal to the Church of Rome. Careful comparative studies of Protestant and Catholic exegesis in the sixteenth century have shown surprising areas of agreement when the focus was the study of a particular biblical text rather than the standard confessional debates.

At the same time, exegetical differences among the various Protestant groups could become strident and church-dividing. The most famous example of this is the interpretive impasse between Luther and Zwingli over the meaning of "This is my body" (Mt 26:26) in the words of institution. Their disagreement at the Colloquy of Marburg in 1529 had important christological and pastoral implications, as well as social and political consequences. Luther refused fellowship with Zwingli and his party at the end of the colloquy; in no small measure this bitter division led to the separate trajectories pursued by Lutheran and Reformed Protestantism to this day. In Elizabethan England, Puritans and Anglicans agreed that "Holy Scripture containeth all things necessary to salvation: so that whatsoever is not read therein, nor may be proved thereby, is not to be required of any man" (article 6 of the Thirty-Nine Articles of Religion), yet on the basis of their differing interpretations of the Bible they fought bitterly over the structures of the church, the clothing of the clergy and the ways of worship. On the matter of infant baptism, Catholics and Protestants alike agreed on its propriety, though there were various theories as to how a practice not mentioned in the Bible could be justified biblically. The Anabaptists were outliers on this subject. They rejected infant baptism altogether. They appealed to the example of the baptism of Jesus and to his final words as recorded in the Gospel of Matthew (Mt 28:19-20): "Go therefore, and make disciples of all nations, baptizing them in the name of the Father, and of the Son, and of the Holy Spirit, teaching them to observe all that I have commanded you." New Testament Christians, they argued, are to follow not only the commands of Jesus in the Great Commission, but also the exact order in which they were given: evangelize, baptize, catechize.

These and many other differences of interpretation among the various Protestant groups are reflected in their many sermons, commentaries and public disputations. In the RCS, the volume editors' introduction to each volume is intended to help the reader understand the nature and significance of doctrinal conversations and disputes that resulted in particular, and frequently clashing, interpretations. Footnotes throughout the text will be provided to explain obscure references, unusual expressions and other matters that require special comment. Volume editors have chosen comments on the Bible across a wide range of sixteenth-century confessions and schools of interpretation: biblical humanists, Lutheran, Reformed, Anglican, Puritan and Anabaptist. We have not pursued passages from post-Tridentine Catholic authors or from radical spiritualists and antitrinitarian writers, though sufficient material is available from these sources to justify another series.

Format. The design of the RCS is intended to offer reader-friendly access to these classic texts. The availability of digital resources has given access to a huge residual database of sixteenth-century exegetical comment hitherto available only in major research universities and rare book collections. The RCS has benefited greatly from online databases such as Alexander Street Press's Digital Library of Classical Protestant Texts (DLCPT) as well as freely accessible databases like the Post-Reformation Digital Library (prdl.org). Through the help of RCS editorial advisor Herman Selderhuis, we have also had access to the special Reformation collections of the Johannes a Lasco Bibliothek in Emden, Germany. In addition, modern critical editions and translations of Reformation sources have been published over the past generation. Original translations of Reformation sources are given unless an acceptable translation already exists.

Each volume in the RCS will include an introduction by the volume editor placing that portion of the canon within the historical context of the Protestant Reformation and presenting a summary of the theological themes, interpretive issues and reception of the particular book(s). The commentary itself consists of particular pericopes identified by a pericope heading; the biblical text in the English Standard Version (ESV), with significant textual variants registered in the footnotes; an overview of the pericope in which principal exegetical and theological concerns of the Reformation writers are succinctly noted; and excerpts from the Reformation writers identified by name according to the conventions of the *Oxford Encyclopedia of the Reformation*. Each volume will also include a bibliography of sources cited, as well as an appendix of authors and source works.

The Reformation era was a time of verbal as well as physical violence, and this fact has presented a challenge for this project. Without unduly sanitizing the texts, where they contain anti-Semitic, sexist or inordinately polemical rhetoric, we have not felt obliged to parade such comments either. We have noted the abridgement of texts with ellipses and an explanatory footnote.

While this procedure would not be valid in the critical edition of such a text, we have deemed it appropriate in a series whose primary purpose is pastoral and devotional. When translating *homo* or similar terms that refer to the human race as a whole or to individual persons without reference to gender, we have used alternative English expressions to the word *man* (or derivative constructions that formerly were used generically to signify humanity at large), whenever such substitutions can be made without producing an awkward or artificial construction.

As is true in the ACCS, we have made a special effort where possible to include the voices of women, though we acknowledge the difficulty of doing so for the early modern period when for a variety of social and cultural reasons few theological and biblical works were published by women. However, recent scholarship has focused on a number of female leaders whose literary remains show us how they understood and interpreted the Bible. Women who made significant contributions to the Reformation include Marguerite d'Angoulême, sister of King Francis I, who supported French reformist evangelicals including Calvin and who published a religious poem influenced by Luther's theology, *The Mirror of the Sinful Soul*; Argula von Grumbach, a Bavarian noblewoman who defended the teachings of Luther and Melanchthon before the theologians of the University of Ingolstadt; Katharina Schütz Zell, the wife of a former priest, Matthias Zell, and a remarkable reformer in her own right—she conducted funerals, compiled hymnbooks, defended the downtrodden and published a defense of clerical marriage as well as composing works of consolation on divine comfort and pleas for the toleration of Anabaptists and Catholics alike; and Anne Askew, a Protestant martyr put to death in 1546 after demonstrating remarkable biblical prowess in her examinations by church officials. Other echoes of faithful women in the age of the Reformation are found in their letters, translations, poems, hymns, court depositions and martyr records.

Lay culture, learned culture. In recent decades, much attention has been given to what is called "reforming from below," that is, the expressions of religious beliefs and churchly life that characterized the popular culture of the majority of the population in the era of the Reformation. Social historians have taught us to examine the diverse pieties of townspeople and city folk, of rural religion and village life, the emergence of lay theologies and the experiences of women in the religious tumults of Reformation Europe.[7] Formal commentaries by their nature are artifacts of learned culture. Almost all of them were written in Latin, the lingua franca of learned discourse well past the age of the Reformation. Biblical commentaries were certainly not the primary means by which the Protestant Reformation spread so rapidly across wide sectors of sixteenth-century society. Small pamphlets and broadsheets, later called *Flugschriften* ("flying writings"), with their graphic woodcuts and cartoon-like depictions of Reformation personalities and events, became the means of choice for mass communication in the early age of printing. Sermons and works of devotion were also printed with appealing visual aids. Luther's early writings were often accompanied by drawings and sketches from Lucas Cranach and other artists. This was done "above all for the sake of children and simple folk," as Luther

[7]See Peter Matheson, ed., *Reformation Christianity* (Minneapolis: Fortress, 2007).

put it, "who are more easily moved by pictures and images to recall divine history than through mere words or doctrines."[8]

We should be cautious, however, in drawing too sharp a distinction between learned and lay culture in this period. The phenomenon of preaching was a kind of verbal bridge between scholars at their desks and the thousands of illiterate or semiliterate listeners whose views were shaped by the results of Reformation exegesis. According to contemporary witness, more than one thousand people were crowding into Geneva to hear Calvin expound the Scriptures every day.[9] An example of how learned theological works by Reformation scholars were received across divisions of class and social status comes from Lazare Drilhon, an apothecary of Toulon. He was accused of heresy in May 1545 when a cache of prohibited books was found hidden in his garden shed. In addition to devotional works, the French New Testament and a copy of Calvin's Genevan liturgy, there was found a series of biblical commentaries, translated from the Latin into French: Martin Bucer's on Matthew, François Lambert's on the Apocalypse and one by Oecolampadius on 1 John.[10] Biblical exegesis in the sixteenth century was not limited to the kind of full-length commentaries found in Drilhon's shed. Citations from the Bible and expositions of its meaning permeate the extant literature of sermons, letters, court depositions, doctrinal treatises, records of public disputations and even last wills and testaments. While most of the selections in the RCS will be drawn from formal commentary literature, other sources of biblical reflection will also be considered.

Historical Context

The medieval legacy. On October 18, 1512, the degree *Doctor in Biblia* was conferred on Martin Luther, and he began his career as a professor in the University of Wittenberg. As is well known, Luther was also a monk who had taken solemn vows in the Augustinian Order of Hermits at Erfurt. These two settings—the university and the monastery—both deeply rooted in the Middle Ages, form the background not only for Luther's personal vocation as a reformer but also for the history of the biblical commentary in the age of the Reformation. Since the time of the Venerable Bede (d. 735), sometimes called "the last of the Fathers," serious study of the Bible had taken place primarily in the context of cloistered monasteries. The Rule of St. Benedict brought together *lectio* and *meditatio*, the knowledge of letters and the life of prayer. The liturgy was the medium through which the daily reading of the Bible, especially the Psalms, and the sayings of the church fathers came together in the spiritual formation of the monks.[11] Essential to this understanding was a belief in the unity of the people of God throughout time as well as space, and an awareness that life in this world was a preparation for the beatific vision in the next.

[8]Martin Luther, "Personal Prayer Book," LW 43:42-43* (WA 10,2:458); quoted in R. W. Scribner, *For the Sake of Simple Folk: Popular Propaganda for the German Reformation* (Cambridge: Cambridge University Press, 1981), xi.

[9]Letter of De Beaulieu to Guillaume Farel (1561) in *Theodor Beza nach handschriftlichen und anderen gleichzeitigen Quellen*, ed. J. W. Baum (Leipzig: Weidmann, 1851), 2:92.

[10]Francis Higman, "A Heretic's Library: The Drilhon Inventory" (1545), in Francis Higman, *Lire et Découvire: la circulation des idées au temps de la Réforme* (Geneva: Droz, 1998), 65-85.

[11]See the classic study by Jean Leclercq, *The Love of Learning and the Desire for God* (New York: Fordham University Press, 1961).

The source of theology was the study of the sacred page *(sacra pagina)*; its object was the accumulation of knowledge not for its own sake but for the obtaining of eternal life. For these monks, the Bible had God for its author, salvation for its end and unadulterated truth for its matter, though they would not have expressed it in such an Aristotelian way. The medieval method of interpreting the Bible owed much to Augustine's *On Christian Doctrine*. In addition to setting forth a series of rules (drawn from an earlier work by Tyconius), Augustine stressed the importance of distinguishing the literal and spiritual or allegorical senses of Scripture. While the literal sense was not disparaged, the allegorical was valued because it enabled the believer to obtain spiritual benefit from the obscure places in the Bible, especially in the Old Testament. For Augustine, as for the monks who followed him, the goal of scriptural exegesis was freighted with eschatological meaning; its purpose was to induce faith, hope and love and so to advance in one's pilgrimage toward that city with foundations (see Heb 11:10).

Building on the work of Augustine and other church fathers going back to Origen, medieval exegetes came to understand Scripture as possessed of four possible meanings, the famous *quadriga*. The literal meaning was retained, of course, but the spiritual meaning was now subdivided into three senses: the allegorical, the moral and the anagogical. Medieval exegetes often referred to the four meanings of Scripture in a popular rhyme:

> The letter shows us what God and our fathers did;
> The allegory shows us where our faith is hid;
> The moral meaning gives us rules of daily life;
> The anagogy shows us where we end our strife.[12]

In this schema, the three spiritual meanings of the text correspond to the three theological virtues: faith (allegory), hope (anagogy) and love (the moral meaning). It should be noted that this way of approaching the Bible assumed a high doctrine of scriptural inspiration: the multiple meanings inherent in the text had been placed there by the Holy Spirit for the benefit of the people of God. The biblical justification for this method went back to the apostle Paul, who had used the words *allegory* and *type* when applying Old Testament events to believers in Christ (Gal 4:21-31; 1 Cor 10:1-11). The problem with this approach was knowing how to relate each of the four senses to one another and how to prevent Scripture from becoming a nose of wax turned this way and that by various interpreters. As G. R. Evans explains, "Any interpretation which could be put upon the text and was in keeping with the faith and edifying, had the warrant of God himself, for no human reader had the ingenuity to find more than God had put there."[13]

With the rise of the universities in the eleventh century, theology and the study of Scripture moved from the cloister into the classroom. Scripture and the Fathers were still important, but they came to function more as footnotes to the theological questions debated in the schools and brought together in an impressive systematic way in works such as Peter Lombard's *Books of Sentences* (the standard theology textbook of the Middle Ages) and the great scholastic *summae* of the

[12]Robert M. Grant, *A Short History of the Interpretation of the Bible* (New York: Macmillan, 1963), 119. A translation of the well-known Latin quatrain: *Littera gesta docet/Quid credas allegoria/Moralis quid agas/Quo tendas anagogia.*

[13]G. R. Evans, *The Language and Logic of the Bible: The Road to Reformation* (Cambridge: Cambridge University Press, 1985), 42.

thirteenth century. Indispensible to the study of the Bible in the later Middle Ages was the *Glossa ordinaria*, a collection of exegetical opinions by the church fathers and other commentators. Heiko Oberman summarized the transition from devotion to dialectic this way: "When, due to the scientific revolution of the twelfth century, Scripture became the *object* of study rather than the *subject* through which God speaks to the student, the difference between the two modes of speaking was investigated in terms of the texts themselves rather than in their relation to the recipients."[14] It was possible, of course, to be both a scholastic theologian and a master of the spiritual life. Meister Eckhart, for example, wrote commentaries on the Old Testament in Latin and works of mystical theology in German, reflecting what had come to be seen as a division of labor between the two.

An increasing focus on the text of Scripture led to a revival of interest in its literal sense. The two key figures in this development were Thomas Aquinas (d. 1274) and Nicholas of Lyra (d. 1340). Thomas is best remembered for his *Summa Theologiae*, but he was also a prolific commentator on the Bible. Thomas did not abandon the multiple senses of Scripture but declared that all the senses were founded on one—the literal—and this sense eclipsed allegory as the basis of sacred doctrine. Nicholas of Lyra was a Franciscan scholar who made use of the Hebrew text of the Old Testament and quoted liberally from works of Jewish scholars, especially the learned French rabbi Salomon Rashi (d. 1105). After Aquinas, Lyra was the strongest defender of the literal, historical meaning of Scripture as the primary basis of theological disputation. His *Postilla*, as his notes were called—the abbreviated form of *post illa verba textus*, meaning "after these words from Scripture"—were widely circulated in the late Middle Ages and became the first biblical commentary to be printed in the fifteenth century. More than any other commentator from the period of high scholasticism, Lyra and his work were greatly valued by the early reformers. According to an old Latin pun, *Nisi Lyra lyrasset, Lutherus non saltasset*, "If Lyra had not played his lyre, Luther would not have danced."[15] While Luther was never an uncritical disciple of any teacher, he did praise Lyra as a good Hebraist and quoted him more than one hundred times in his lectures on Genesis, where he declared, "I prefer him to almost all other interpreters of Scripture."[16]

Sacred philology. The sixteenth century has been called a golden age of biblical interpretation, and it is a fact that the age of the Reformation witnessed an explosion of commentary writing unparalleled in the history of the Christian church. Kenneth Hagen has cataloged forty-five commentaries on Hebrews between 1516 (Erasmus) and 1598 (Beza).[17] During the sixteenth century, more than seventy new commentaries on Romans were published, five of them by Melanchthon alone, and nearly one hundred commentaries on the Bible's prayer book, the Psalms.[18] There were two developments in the fifteenth century that presaged this development and without which it

[14]Heiko Oberman, *Forerunners of the Reformation* (Philadelphia: Fortress, 1966), 284.
[15]Nicholas of Lyra, *The Postilla of Nicolas of Lyra on the Song of Songs*, trans. and ed. James George Kiecker (Milwaukee: Marquette University Press, 1998), 19.
[16]LW 2:164 (WA 42:377).
[17]Kenneth Hagen, *Hebrews Commenting from Erasmus to Bèze, 1516–1598* (Tübingen: Mohr, 1981).
[18]R. Gerald Hobbs, "Biblical Commentaries," *OER* 1:167-71. See in general David C. Steinmetz, ed., *The Bible in the Sixteenth Century* (Durham: Duke University Press, 1990).

could not have taken place: the invention of printing and the rediscovery of a vast store of ancient learning hitherto unknown or unavailable to scholars in the West.

It is now commonplace to say that what the computer has become in our generation, the printing press was to the world of Erasmus, Luther and other leaders of the Reformation. Johannes Gutenberg, a goldsmith by trade, developed a metal alloy suitable for type and a machine that would allow printed characters to be cast with relative ease, placed in even lines of composition and then manipulated again and again, making possible the mass production of an unbelievable number of texts. In 1455, the Gutenberg Bible, the masterpiece of the typographical revolution, was published at Mainz in double columns in gothic type. Forty-seven copies of the beautiful Gutenberg Bible are still extant, each consisting of more than one thousand colorfully illuminated and impeccably printed pages. What began at Gutenberg's print shop in Mainz on the Rhine River soon spread, like McDonald's or Starbucks in our day, into every nook and cranny of the known world. Printing presses sprang up in Rome (1464), Venice (1469), Paris (1470), the Netherlands (1471), Switzerland (1472), Spain (1474), England (1476), Sweden (1483) and Constantinople (1490). By 1500, these and other presses across Europe had published some twenty-seven thousand titles, most of them in Latin. Erasmus once compared himself with an obscure preacher whose sermons were heard by only a few people in one or two churches while his books were read in every country in the world. Erasmus was not known for his humility, but in this case he was simply telling the truth.[19]

The Italian humanist Lorenzo Valla (d. 1457) died in the early dawn of the age of printing, but his critical and philological studies would be taken up by others who believed that genuine reform in church and society could come about only by returning to the wellsprings of ancient learning and wisdom—*ad fontes*, "back to the sources!" Valla is best remembered for undermining a major claim made by defenders of the papacy when he proved by philological research that the so-called Donation of Constantine, which had bolstered papal assertions of temporal sovereignty, was a forgery. But it was Valla's *Collatio Novi Testamenti* of 1444 that would have such a great effect on the renewal of biblical studies in the next century. Erasmus discovered the manuscript of this work while rummaging through an old library in Belgium and published it at Paris in 1505. In the preface to his edition of Valla, Erasmus gave the rationale that would guide his own labors in textual criticism. Just as Jerome had translated the Latin Vulgate from older versions and copies of the Scriptures in his day, so now Jerome's own text must be subjected to careful scrutiny and correction. Erasmus would be *Hieronymus redivivus*, a new Jerome come back to life to advance the cause of sacred philology. The restoration of the Scriptures and the writings of the church fathers would usher in what Erasmus believed would be a golden age of peace and learning. In 1516, the Basel publisher Froben brought out Erasmus's *Novum Instrumentum*, the first published edition of the Greek New Testament. Erasmus's Greek New Testament would go through five editions in his lifetime, each one with new emendations to the text and a growing section of annotations that expanded to include not only technical notes about the text but also theological comment. The influence of Erasmus's Greek New

[19]E. Harris Harbison, *The Christian Scholar in the Age of the Reformation* (New York: Charles Scribner's Sons, 1956), 80.

Testament was enormous. It formed the basis for Robert Estienne's *Novum Testamentum Graece* of 1550, which in turn was used to establish the Greek *Textus Receptus* for a number of late Reformation translations including the King James Version of 1611.

For all his expertise in Greek, Erasmus was a poor student of Hebrew and only published commentaries on several of the psalms. However, the renaissance of Hebrew letters was part of the wider program of biblical humanism as reflected in the establishment of trilingual colleges devoted to the study of Hebrew, Greek and Latin (the three languages written on the *titulus* of Jesus' cross [Jn 19:20]) at Alcalá in Spain, Wittenberg in Germany, Louvain in Belgium and Paris in France. While it is true that some medieval commentators, especially Nicholas of Lyra, had been informed by the study of Hebrew and rabbinics in their biblical work, it was the publication of Johannes Reuchlin's *De rudimentis hebraicis* (1506), a combined grammar and dictionary, that led to the recovery of *veritas Hebraica*, as Jerome had referred to the true voice of the Hebrew Scriptures. The pursuit of Hebrew studies was carried forward in the Reformation by two great scholars, Konrad Pellikan and Sebastian Münster. Pellikan was a former Franciscan friar who embraced the Protestant cause and played a major role in the Zurich reformation. He had published a Hebrew grammar even prior to Reuchlin and produced a commentary on nearly the entire Bible that appeared in seven volumes between 1532 and 1539. Münster was Pellikan's student and taught Hebrew at the University of Heidelberg before taking up a similar position in Basel. Like his mentor, Münster was a great collector of Hebraica and published a series of excellent grammars, dictionaries and rabbinic texts. Münster did for the Hebrew Old Testament what Erasmus had done for the Greek New Testament. His *Hebraica Biblia* offered a fresh Latin translation of the Old Testament with annotations from medieval rabbinic exegesis.

Luther first learned Hebrew with Reuchlin's grammar in hand but took advantage of other published resources, such as the four-volume Hebrew Bible published at Venice by Daniel Bomberg in 1516 to 1517. He also gathered his own circle of Hebrew experts, his *sanhedrin* he called it, who helped him with his German translation of the Old Testament. We do not know where William Tyndale learned Hebrew, though perhaps it was in Worms, where there was a thriving rabbinical school during his stay there. In any event, he had sufficiently mastered the language to bring out a freshly translated Pentateuch that was published at Antwerp in 1530. By the time the English separatist scholar Henry Ainsworth published his prolix commentaries on the Pentateuch in 1616, the knowledge of Hebrew, as well as Greek, was taken for granted by every serious scholar of the Bible. In the preface to his commentary on Genesis, Ainsworth explained that "the literal sense of Moses's Hebrew (which is the tongue wherein he wrote the law), is the ground of all interpretation, and that language hath figures and properties of speech, different from ours: These therefore in the first place are to be opened that the natural meaning of the Scripture, being known, the mysteries of godliness therein implied, may be better discerned."[20]

The restoration of the biblical text in the original languages made possible the revival of scriptural exposition reflected in the floodtide of sermon literature and commentary work. Of even

[20]Henry Ainsworth, *Annotations upon the First Book of Moses Called Genesis* (Amsterdam, 1616), preface (unpaginated).

more far-reaching import was the steady stream of vernacular Bibles in the sixteenth century. In the introduction to his 1516 edition of the New Testament, Erasmus had expressed his desire that the Scriptures be translated into all languages so that "the lowliest women" could read the Gospels and the Pauline epistles and "the farmer sing some portion of them at the plow, the weaver hum some parts of them to the movement of his shuttle, the traveler lighten the weariness of the journey with stories of this kind."[21] Like Erasmus, Tyndale wanted the Bible to be available in the language of the common people. He once said to a learned divine that if God spared his life he would cause the boy who drives the plow to know more of the Scriptures than he did![22] The project of allowing the Bible to speak in the language of the mother in the house, the children in the street and the cheesemonger in the marketplace was met with stiff opposition by certain Catholic polemists such as Johann Eck, Luther's antagonist at the Leipzig Debate of 1519. In his *Enchiridion* (1525), Eck derided the "inky theologians" whose translations paraded the Bible before "the untutored crowd" and subjected it to the judgment of "laymen and crazy old women."[23] In fact, some fourteen German Bibles had already been published prior to Luther's September Testament of 1522, which he translated from Erasmus's Greek New Testament in less than three months' time while sequestered in the Wartburg. Luther's German New Testament became the first best-seller in the world, appearing in forty-three distinct editions between 1522 and 1525 with upward of one hundred thousand copies issued in these three years. It is estimated that 5 percent of the German population may have been literate at this time, but this rate increased as the century wore on due in no small part to the unmitigated success of vernacular Bibles.[24]

Luther's German Bible (inclusive of the Old Testament from 1534) was the most successful venture of its kind, but it was not alone in the field. Hans Denck and Ludwig Hätzer, leaders in the early Anabaptist movement, translated the prophetic books of the Old Testament from Hebrew into German in 1527. This work influenced the Swiss-German Bible of 1531 published by Leo Jud and other pastors in Zurich. Tyndale's influence on the English language rivaled that of Luther on German. At a time when English was regarded as "that obscure and remote dialect of German spoken in an off-shore island," Tyndale, with his remarkable linguistic ability (he was fluent in eight languages), "made a language for England," as his modern editor David Daniell has put it.[25] Tyndale was imprisoned and executed near Brussels in 1536, but the influence of his biblical work among the common people of England was already being felt. There is no reason to doubt the authenticity of John Foxe's recollection of how Tyndale's New Testament was received in England during the 1520s and 1530s:

---

[21]John C. Olin, *Christian Humanism and the Reformation* (New York: Fordham University Press, 1987), 101.

[22]This famous statement of Tyndale was quoted by John Foxe in his *Acts and Monuments of Matters Happening in the Church* (London, 1563). See Henry Wansbrough, "Tyndale," in *The Bible in the Renaissance*, ed. Richard Griffith (Aldershot, UK: Ashgate, 2001), 124.

[23]John Eck, *Enchiridion of Commonplaces*, trans. Ford Lewis Battles (Grand Rapids: Baker, 1979), 47-49.

[24]The effect of printing on the spread of the Reformation has been much debated. See the classic study by Elizabeth L. Eisenstein, *The Printing Press as an Agent of Change* (Cambridge: Cambridge University Press, 1979). More recent studies include Mark U. Edwards Jr., *Printing, Propaganda and Martin Luther* (Minneapolis: Fortress, 1994), and Andrew Pettegree and Matthew Hall, "The Reformation and the Book: A Reconsideration," *Historical Journal* 47 (2004): 1-24.

[25]David Daniell, *William Tyndale: A Biography* (New Haven: Yale University Press, 1994), 3.

> The fervent zeal of those Christian days seemed much superior to these our days and times; as manifestly may appear by their sitting up all night in reading and hearing; also by their expenses and charges in buying of books in English, of whom some gave five marks, some more, some less, for a book: some gave a load of hay for a few chapters of St. James, or of St. Paul in English.[26]

Calvin helped to revise and contributed three prefaces to the French Bible translated by his cousin Pierre Robert Olivétan and originally published at Neuchâtel in 1535. Clément Marot and Beza provided a fresh translation of the Psalms with each psalm rendered in poetic form and accompanied by monophonic musical settings for congregational singing. The Bay Psalter, the first book printed in America, was an English adaptation of this work. Geneva also provided the provenance of the most influential Italian Bible published by Giovanni Diodati in 1607. The flowering of biblical humanism in vernacular Bibles resulted in new translations in all of the major language groups of Europe: Spanish (1569), Portuguese (1681), Dutch (New Testament, 1523; Old Testament, 1527), Danish (1550), Czech (1579–1593/94), Hungarian (New Testament, 1541; complete Bible, 1590), Polish (1563), Swedish (1541) and even Arabic (1591).[27]

Patterns of Reformation

Once the text of the Bible had been placed in the hands of the people, in cheap and easily available editions, what further need was there of published expositions such as commentaries? Given the Protestant doctrine of the priesthood of all believers, was there any longer a need for learned clergy and their bookish religion? Some radical reformers thought not. Sebastian Franck searched for the true church of the Spirit "scattered among the heathen and the weeds" but could not find it in any of the institutional structures of his time. *Veritas non potest scribi, aut exprimi,* he said, "truth can neither be spoken nor written."[28] Kaspar von Schwenckfeld so emphasized religious inwardness that he suspended external observance of the Lord's Supper and downplayed the readable, audible Scriptures in favor of the Word within. This trajectory would lead to the rise of the Quakers in the next century, but it was pursued neither by the mainline reformers nor by most of the Anabaptists. Article 7 of the Augsburg Confession (1530) declared the one holy Christian church to be "the assembly of all believers among whom the Gospel is purely preached and the holy sacraments are administered according to the Gospel."[29]

Historians of the nineteenth century referred to the material and formal principles of the Reformation. In this construal, the matter at stake was the meaning of the Christian gospel: the liberating insight that helpless sinners are graciously justified by the gift of faith alone, apart from any works or merits of their own, entirely on the basis of Christ's atoning work on the cross. For Luther especially, justification by faith alone became the criterion by which all other doctrines and

[26]Foxe, *Acts and Monuments,* 4:218.

[27]On vernacular translations of the Bible, see *CHB* 3:94-140 and Jaroslav Pelikan, *The Reformation of the Bible/The Bible of the Reformation* (New Haven: Yale University Press, 1996), 41-62.

[28]Sebastian Franck, *280 Paradoxes or Wondrous Sayings,* trans. E. J. Furcha (Lewiston, NY: Edwin Mellen Press, 1986), 10, 212.

[29]BoC 42 (BSLK 61).

practices of the church were to be judged. The cross proves everything, he said at the Heidelberg disputation in 1518. The distinction between law and gospel thus became the primary hermeneutical key that unlocked the true meaning of Scripture.

The formal principle of the Reformation, *sola Scriptura,* was closely bound up with proper distinctions between Scripture and tradition. "Scripture alone," said Luther, "is the true lord and master of all writings and doctrine on earth. If that is not granted, what is Scripture good for? The more we reject it, the more we become satisfied with human books and human teachers."[30] On the basis of this principle, the reformers challenged the structures and institutions of the medieval Catholic Church. Even a simple layperson, they asserted, armed with Scripture should be believed above a pope or a council without it. But, however boldly asserted, the doctrine of the primacy of Scripture did not absolve the reformers from dealing with a host of hermeneutical issues that became matters of contention both between Rome and the Reformation and within each of these two communities: the extent of the biblical canon, the validity of critical study of the Bible, the perspicuity of Scripture and its relation to preaching, and the retention of devotional and liturgical practices such as holy days, incense, the burning of candles, the sprinkling of holy water, church art and musical instruments. Zwingli, the Puritans and the radicals dismissed such things as a rubbish heap of ceremonials that amounted to nothing but tomfoolery, while Lutherans and Anglicans retained most of them as consonant with Scripture and valuable aids to worship.

It is important to note that while the mainline reformers differed among themselves on many matters, overwhelmingly they saw themselves as part of the ongoing Catholic tradition, indeed as the legitimate bearers of it. This was seen in numerous ways including their sense of continuity with the church of the preceding centuries; their embrace of the ecumenical orthodoxy of the early church; and their desire to read the Bible in dialogue with the exegetical tradition of the church.

In their biblical commentaries, the reformers of the sixteenth century revealed a close familiarity with the preceding exegetical tradition, and they used it respectfully as well as critically in their own expositions of the sacred text. For them, *sola Scriptura* was not *nuda Scriptura.* Rather, the Scriptures were seen as the book given to the church, gathered and guided by the Holy Spirit. In his restatement of the Vincentian canon, Calvin defined the church as "a society of all the saints, a society which, spread over the whole world, and existing in all ages, and bound together by the one doctrine and the one spirit of Christ, cultivates and observes unity of faith and brotherly concord. With this church we deny that we have any disagreement. Nay, rather, as we revere her as our mother, so we desire to remain in her bosom." Defined thus, the church has a real, albeit relative and circumscribed, authority since, as Calvin admits, "We cannot fly without wings."[31] While the reformers could not agree with the Council of Trent (though some recent Catholic theologians have challenged this interpretation) that Scripture and tradition were two separate and equal sources of divine revelation,

[30]LW 32:11-12* (WA 7:317).
[31]John C. Olin, ed., *John Calvin and Jacopo Sadoleto: A Reformation Debate* (New York: Harper Torchbooks, 1966), 61-62, 77.

they did believe in the coinherence of Scripture and tradition. This conviction shaped the way they read and interpreted the Bible.[32]

Schools of Exegesis

The reformers were passionate about biblical exegesis, but they showed little concern for hermeneutics as a separate field of inquiry. Niels Hemmingsen, a Lutheran theologian in Denmark, did write a treatise, *De methodis* (1555), in which he offered a philosophical and theological framework for the interpretation of Scripture. This was followed by the *Clavis Scripturae Sacrae* (1567) of Matthias Flacius Illyricus, which contains some fifty rules for studying the Bible drawn from Scripture itself.[33] However, hermeneutics as we know it came of age only in the Enlightenment and should not be backloaded into the Reformation. It is also true that the word *commentary* did not mean in the sixteenth century what it means for us today. Erasmus provided both annotations and paraphrases on the New Testament, the former a series of critical notes on the text but also containing points of doctrinal substance, the latter a theological overview and brief exposition. Most of Calvin's commentaries began as sermons or lectures presented in the course of his pastoral ministry. In the dedication to his 1519 study of Galatians, Luther declared that his work was "not so much a commentary as a testimony of my faith in Christ."[34] The exegetical work of the reformers was embodied in a wide variety of forms and genres, and the RCS has worked with this broader concept in setting the guidelines for this compendium.

The Protestant reformers shared in common a number of key interpretive principles such as the priority of the grammatical-historical sense of Scripture and the christological centeredness of the entire Bible, but they also developed a number of distinct approaches and schools of exegesis.[35] For the purposes of the RCS, we note the following key figures and families of interpretation in this period.

Biblical humanism. The key figure is Erasmus, whose importance is hard to exaggerate for Catholic and Protestant exegetes alike. His annotated Greek New Testament and fresh Latin translation challenged the hegemony of the Vulgate tradition and was doubtless a factor in the decision of the Council of Trent to establish the Vulgate edition as authentic and normative. Erasmus believed that the wide distribution of the Scriptures would contribute to personal spiritual renewal and the reform of society. In 1547, the English translation of Erasmus's *Paraphrases* was ordered to be placed in every parish church in England. John Colet first encouraged Erasmus

[32]See Timothy George, "An Evangelical Reflection on Scripture and Tradition," *Pro Ecclesia* 9 (2000): 184-207.

[33]See Kenneth G. Hagen, "'*De Exegetica Methodo*': Niels Hemmingsen's *De Methodis* (1555)," in *The Bible in the Sixteenth Century*, ed. David C. Steinmetz (Durham: Duke University Press, 1990), 181-96.

[34]LW 27:159 (WA 2:449). See Kenneth Hagen, "What Did the Term *Commentarius* Mean to Sixteenth-Century Theologians?" in *Théorie et pratique de l'exégèse*, eds. Irena Backus and Francis M. Higman (Geneva: Droz, 1990), 13-38.

[35]I follow here the sketch of Irena Backus, "Biblical Hermeneutics and Exegesis," *OER* 1:152-58. In this work, Backus confines herself to Continental developments, whereas we have noted the exegetical contribution of the English Reformation as well. For more comprehensive listings of sixteenth-century commentators, see Gerald Bray, *Biblical Interpretation* (Downers Grove, IL: InterVarsity Press, 1996), 165-212; and Richard A. Muller, "Biblical Interpretation in the Sixteenth and Seventeenth Centuries," *DMBI* 22-44.

to learn Greek, though he never took up the language himself. Colet's lectures on Paul's epistles at Oxford are reflected in his commentaries on Romans and 1 Corinthians.

Jacques Lefèvre d'Étaples has been called the "French Erasmus" because of his great learning and support for early reform movements in his native land. He published a major edition of the Psalter, as well as commentaries on the Pauline Epistles (1512), the Gospels (1522) and the General Epistles (1527). Guillaume Farel, the early reformer of Geneva, was a disciple of Lefèvre, and the young Calvin also came within his sphere of influence.

Among pre-Tridentine Catholic reformers, special attention should be given to Thomas de Vio, better known as Cajetan. He is best remembered for confronting Martin Luther on behalf of the pope in 1518, but his biblical commentaries (on nearly every book of the Bible) are virtually free of polemic. Like Erasmus, he dared to criticize the Vulgate on linguistic grounds. His commentary on Romans supported the doctrine of justification by grace applied by faith based on the "alien righteousness" of God in Christ. Jared Wicks sums up Cajetan's significance in this way: "Cajetan's combination of passion for pristine biblical meaning with his fully developed theological horizon of understanding indicates, in an intriguing manner, something of the breadth of possibilities open to Roman Catholics before a more restrictive settlement came to exercise its hold on many Catholic interpreters in the wake of the Council of Trent."[36] Girolamo Seripando, like Cajetan, was a cardinal in the Catholic Church, though he belonged to the Augustinian rather than the Dominican order. He was an outstanding classical scholar and published commentaries on Romans and Galatians. Also important is Jacopo Sadoleto, another cardinal, best known for his 1539 letter to the people of Geneva beseeching them to return to the Church of Rome, to which Calvin replied with a manifesto of his own. Sadoleto published a commentary on Romans in 1535. Bucer once commended Sadoleto's teaching on justification as approximating that of the reformers, while others saw him tilting away from the Augustinian tradition toward Pelagianism.[37]

Luther and the Wittenberg School. It was in the name of the Word of God, and specifically as a doctor of Scripture, that Luther challenged the church of his day and inaugurated the Reformation. Though Luther renounced his monastic vows, he never lost that sense of intimacy with *sacra pagina* he first acquired as a young monk. Luther provided three rules for reading the Bible: prayer, meditation and struggle *(tentatio)*. His exegetical output was enormous. In the American edition of Luther's works, thirty out of the fifty-five volumes are devoted to his biblical studies, and additional translations are planned. Many of his commentaries originated as sermons or lecture notes presented to his students at the university and to his parishioners at Wittenberg's parish church of St. Mary. Luther referred to Galatians as his bride: "The Epistle to the Galatians is my dear epistle. I have betrothed myself to it. It is my Käthe von Bora."[38] He considered his 1535 commentary on Galatians his greatest exegetical work, although his massive commentary on Genesis

[36]Jared Wicks, "Tommaso de Vio Cajetan (1469-1534)," *DMBI* 283-87, here 286.

[37]See the discussion by Bernard Roussel, "Martin Bucer et Jacques Sadolet: la concorde possible," *Bulletin de la Société de l'histoire de protestantisme français* (1976): 525-50, and T. H. L. Parker, *Commentaries on the Epistle to the Romans, 1532–1542* (Edinburgh: T&T Clark, 1986), 25-34.

[38]WATR 1:69 no. 146; cf. LW 54:20 no. 146. I have followed Rörer's variant on Dietrich's notes.

(eight volumes in LW), which he worked on for ten years (1535–1545), must be considered his crowning work. Luther's principles of biblical interpretation are found in his *Open Letter on Translating* and in the prefaces he wrote to all the books of the Bible.

Philipp Melanchthon was brought to Wittenberg to teach Greek in 1518 and proved to be an able associate to Luther in the reform of the church. A set of his lecture notes on Romans was published without his knowledge in 1522. This was revised and expanded many times until his large commentary of 1556. Melanchthon also commented on other New Testament books including Matthew, John, Galatians and the Petrine epistles, as well as Proverbs, Daniel and Ecclesiastes. Though he was well trained in the humanist disciplines, Melanchthon devoted little attention to critical and textual matters in his commentaries. Rather, he followed the primary argument of the biblical writer and gathered from this exposition a series of doctrinal topics for special consideration. This method lay behind Melanchthon's *Loci communes* (1521), the first Protestant theology textbook to be published. Another Wittenberger was Johannes Bugenhagen of Pomerania, a prolific commentator on both the Old and New Testaments. His commentary on the Psalms (1524), translated into German by Bucer, applied Luther's teaching on justification to the Psalter. He also wrote a commentary on Job and annotations on many of the books in the Bible. The Lutheran exegetical tradition was shaped by many other scholar-reformers including Andreas Osiander, Johannes Brenz, Caspar Cruciger, Erasmus Sarcerius, Georg Maior, Jacob Andreae, Nikolaus Selnecker and Johann Gerhard.

The Strasbourg-Basel tradition. Bucer, the son of a shoemaker in Alsace, became the leader of the Reformation in Strasbourg. A former Dominican, he was early on influenced by Erasmus and continued to share his passion for Christian unity. Bucer was the most ecumenical of the Protestant reformers seeking rapprochement with Catholics on justification and an armistice between Luther and Zwingli in their strife over the Lord's Supper. Bucer also had a decisive influence on Calvin, though the latter characterized his biblical commentaries as longwinded and repetitious.[39] In his exegetical work, Bucer made ample use of patristic and medieval sources, though he criticized the abuse and overuse of allegory as "the most blatant insult to the Holy Spirit."[40] He declared that the purpose of his commentaries was "to help inexperienced brethren [perhaps like the apothecary Drilhon, who owned a French translation of Bucer's *Commentary on Matthew*] to understand each of the words and actions of Christ, and in their proper order as far as possible, and to retain an explanation of them in their natural meaning, so that they will not distort God's Word through age-old aberrations or by inept interpretation, but rather with a faithful comprehension of everything as written by the Spirit of God, they may expound to all the churches in their firm upbuilding in faith and love."[41] In addition to writing commentaries on all four Gospels, Bucer published commentaries on Judges, the Psalms, Zephaniah, Romans and Ephesians. In the early years of the Reformation, there was a great deal of back and forth between Strasbourg and Basel, and both

[39]CNTC 8:3 (CO 10:404).

[40]*DMBI* 249; P. Scherding and F. Wendel, eds., "Un Traité d'exégèse pratique de Bucer," *Revue d'histoire et de philosophie religieuses* 26 (1946): 32-75, here 56.

[41]Martin Bucer, *Enarrationes perpetuae in sacra quatuor evangelia*, 2nd ed. (Strasbourg: Georg Ulrich Andlanus, 1530), 10r; quoted in D. F. Wright, "Martin Bucer," *DMBI* 290.

were centers of a lively publishing trade. Wolfgang Capito, Bucer's associate at Strasbourg, was a notable Hebraist and composed commentaries on Hosea (1529) and Habakkuk (1527).

At Basel, the great Sebastian Münster defended the use of Jewish sources in the Christian study of the Old Testament and published, in addition to his famous Hebrew grammar, an annotated version of the Gospel of Matthew translated from Greek into Hebrew. Oecolampadius, Basel's chief reformer, had been a proofreader in Froben's publishing house and worked with Erasmus on his Greek New Testament and his critical edition of Jerome. From 1523 he was both a preacher and professor of Holy Scripture at Basel. He defended Zwingli's eucharistic theology at the Colloquy of Marburg and published commentaries on 1 John (1524), Romans (1525) and Haggai–Malachi (1525). Oecolampadius was succeeded by Simon Grynaeus, a classical scholar who taught Greek and supported Bucer's efforts to bring Lutherans and Zwinglians together. More in line with Erasmus was Sebastian Castellio, who came to Basel after his expulsion from Geneva in 1545. He is best remembered for questioning the canonicity of the Song of Songs and for his annotations and French translation of the Bible.

The Zurich group. Biblical exegesis in Zurich was centered on the distinctive institution of the *Prophezei,* which began on June 19, 1525. On five days a week, at seven o'clock in the morning, all of the ministers and theological students in Zurich gathered into the choir of the Grossmünster to engage in a period of intense exegesis and interpretation of Scripture. After Zwingli had opened the meeting with prayer, the text of the day was read in Latin, Greek and Hebrew, followed by appropriate textual or exegetical comments. One of the ministers then delivered a sermon on the passage in German that was heard by many of Zurich's citizens who stopped by the cathedral on their way to work. This institute for advanced biblical studies had an enormous influence as a model for Reformed academies and seminaries throughout Europe. It was also the seedbed for sermon series in Zurich's churches and the extensive exegetical publications of Zwingli, Leo Jud, Konrad Pellikan, Heinrich Bullinger, Oswald Myconius and Rudolf Gwalther. Zwingli had memorized in Greek all of the Pauline epistles, and this bore fruit in his powerful expository preaching and biblical exegesis. He took seriously the role of grammar, rhetoric and historical research in explaining the biblical text. For example, he disagreed with Bucer on the value of the Septuagint, regarding it as a trustworthy witness to a proto-Hebrew version earlier than the Masoretic text.

Zwingli's work was carried forward by his successor Bullinger, one of the most formidable scholars and networkers among the reformers. He composed commentaries on Daniel (1565), the Gospels (1542–1546), the Epistles (1537), Acts (1533) and Revelation (1557). He collaborated with Calvin to produce the *Consensus Tigurinus* (1549), a Reformed accord on the nature of the Lord's Supper, and produced a series of fifty sermons on Christian doctrine, known as *Decades,* which became required reading in Elizabethan England. As the *Antistes* ("overseer") of the Zurich church for forty-four years, Bullinger faced opposition from nascent Anabaptism on the one hand and resurgent Catholicism on the other. The need for a well-trained clergy and scholarly resources, including Scripture commentaries, arose from the fact that the Bible was "difficult or obscure to the unlearned, unskillful, unexercised, and malicious or corrupted wills." While forswearing papal claims to infallibility, Bullinger and other leaders of the magisterial Reformation saw the need for a kind of Protestant magisterium as a check against the tendency to read the Bible in "such sense as everyone shall be persuaded in himself to be most convenient."[42]

Two other commentators can be treated in connection with the Zurich group, though each of them had a wide-ranging ministry across the Reformation fronts. A former Benedictine monk, Wolfgang Musculus, embraced the Reformation in the 1520s and served briefly as the secretary to Bucer in Strasbourg. He shared Bucer's desire for Protestant unity and served for seventeen years (1531–1548) as a pastor and reformer in Augsburg. After a brief time in Zurich, where he came under the influence of Bullinger, Musculus was called to Bern, where he taught the Scriptures and published commentaries on the Psalms, the Decalogue, Genesis, Romans, Isaiah, 1 and 2 Corinthians, Galatians and Ephesians, Philippians, Colossians, 1 and 2 Thessalonians, and 1 Timothy. Drawing on his exegetical writings, Musculus also produced a compendium of Protestant theology that was translated into English in 1563 as *Commonplaces of Christian Religion.*

Peter Martyr Vermigli was a Florentine-born scholar and Augustinian friar who embraced the Reformation and fled to Switzerland in 1542. Over the next twenty years, he would gain an international reputation as a prolific scholar and leading theologian within the Reformed community. He lectured on the Old Testament at Strasbourg, was made regius professor at Oxford, corresponded with the Italian refugee church in Geneva and spent the last years of his life as professor of Hebrew at Zurich. Vermigli published commentaries on 1 Corinthians, Romans and Judges during his lifetime. His biblical lectures on Genesis, Lamentations, 1 and 2 Samuel, and 1 and 2 Kings were published posthumously. The most influential of his writings was the *Loci communes (Commonplaces)*, a theological compendium drawn from his exegetical writings.

The Genevan reformers. What Zwingli and Bullinger were to Zurich, Calvin and Beza were to Geneva. Calvin has been called "the father of modern biblical scholarship," and his exegetical work is without parallel in the Reformation. Because of the success of his *Institutes of the Christian Religion* Calvin has sometimes been thought of as a man of one book, but he always intended the *Institutes*, which went through eight editions in Latin and five in French during his lifetime, to serve as a guide to the study of the Bible, to show the reader "what he ought especially to seek in Scripture and to what end he ought to relate its contents." Jacob Arminius, who modified several principles of Calvin's theology, recommended his commentaries next to the Bible, for, as he said, Calvin "is incomparable in the interpretation of Scripture."[43] Drawing on his superb knowledge of Greek and Hebrew and his thorough training in humanist rhetoric, Calvin produced commentaries on all of the New Testament books except 2 and 3 John and Revelation. Calvin's Old Testament commentaries originated as sermon and lecture series and include Genesis, Psalms, Hosea, Isaiah, minor prophets, Daniel, Jeremiah and Lamentations, a harmony of the last four books of Moses,

[42]Euan Cameron, *The European Reformation* (Oxford: Oxford University Press, 1991), 120.

[43]Letter to Sebastian Egbert (May 3, 1607), in *Praestantium ac eruditorum virorum epistolae ecclesiasticae et theologicae varii argumenti*, ed. Christiaan Hartsoeker (Amsterdam: Henricus Dendrinus, 1660), 236-37. Quoted in A. M. Hunter, *The Teaching of Calvin* (London: James Clarke, 1950), 20.

Ezekiel 1–20, and Joshua. Calvin sought for brevity and clarity in all of his exegetical work. He emphasized the illumination of the Holy Spirit as essential to a proper understanding of the text. Calvin underscored the continuity between the two Testaments (one covenant in two dispensations) and sought to apply the plain or natural sense of the text to the church of his day. In the preface to his own influential commentary on Romans, Karl Barth described how Calvin worked to recover the mind of Paul and make the apostle's message relevant to his day:

> How energetically Calvin goes to work, first scientifically establishing the text ("what stands there?"), then following along the footsteps of its thought; that is to say, he conducts a discussion with it until the wall between the first and the sixteenth centuries becomes transparent, and until there in the first century Paul speaks and here the man of the sixteenth century hears, until indeed the conversation between document and reader becomes concentrated upon the substance (which must be the same now as then).[44]

Beza was elected moderator of Geneva's Company of Pastors after Calvin's death in 1564 and guided the Genevan Reformation over the next four decades. His annotated Latin translation of the Greek New Testament (1556) and his further revisions of the Greek text established his reputation as the leading textual critic of the sixteenth century after Erasmus. Beza completed the translation of Marot's metrical Psalter, which became a centerpiece of Huguenot piety and Reformed church life. Though known for his polemical writings on grace, free will and predestination, Beza's work is marked by a strong pastoral orientation and concern for a Scripture-based spirituality.

Robert Estienne (Stephanus) was a printer-scholar who had served the royal household in Paris. After his conversion to Protestantism, in 1550 he moved to Geneva, where he published a series of notable editions and translations of the Bible. He also produced sermons and commentaries on Job, Ecclesiastes, the Song of Songs, Romans and Hebrews, as well as dictionaries, concordances and a thesaurus of biblical terms. He also published the first editions of the Bible with chapters divided into verses, an innovation that quickly became universally accepted.

The British Reformation. Commentary writing in England and Scotland lagged behind the continental Reformation for several reasons. In 1500, there were only three publishing houses in England compared with more than two hundred on the Continent. A 1408 statute against publishing or reading the Bible in English, stemming from the days of Lollardy, stifled the free flow of ideas, as was seen in the fate of Tyndale. Moreover, the nature of the English Reformation from Henry through Elizabeth provided little stability for the flourishing of biblical scholarship. In the sixteenth century, many "hot-gospel" Protestants in England were edified by the English translations of commentaries and theological writings by the Continental reformers. The influence of Calvin and Beza was felt especially in the Geneva Bible with its "Protestant glosses" of theological notes and references.

During the later Elizabethan and Stuart church, however, the indigenous English commentary came into its own. Both Anglicans and Puritans contributed to this outpouring of biblical studies.

[44]Karl Barth, *Die Römerbrief* (Zurich: TVZ, 1940), 11, translated by T. H. L. Parker as the epigraph to *Calvin's New Testament Commentaries*, 2nd ed. (Louisville, KY: Westminster John Knox, 1993).

The sermons of Lancelot Andrewes and John Donne are replete with exegetical insights based on a close study of the Greek and Hebrew texts. Among the Reformed authors in England, none was more influential than William Perkins, the greatest of the early Puritan theologians, who published commentaries on Galatians, Jude, Revelation and the Sermon on the Mount (Mt 5–7). John Cotton, one of his students, wrote commentaries on the Song of Songs, Ecclesiastes and Revelation before departing for New England in 1633. The separatist pastor Henry Ainsworth was an outstanding scholar of Hebrew and wrote major commentaries on the Pentateuch, the Psalms and the Song of Songs. In Scotland, Robert Rollock, the first principal of Edinburgh University (1585), wrote numerous commentaries including those on the Psalms, Ephesians, Daniel, Romans, 1 and 2 Thessalonians, John, Colossians and Hebrews. Joseph Mede and Thomas Brightman were leading authorities on Revelation and contributed to the apocalyptic thought of the seventeenth century. Mention should also be made of Archbishop James Ussher, whose *Annals of the Old Testament* was published in 1650. Ussher developed a keen interest in biblical chronology and calculated that the creation of the world had taken place on October 26, 4004 B.C. As late as 1945, the Scofield Reference Bible still retained this date next to Genesis 1:1, but later editions omitted it because of the lack of evidence on which to fix such dates.[45]

Anabaptism. Irena Backus has noted that there was no school of "dissident" exegesis during the Reformation, and the reasons are not hard to find. The radical Reformation was an ill-defined movement that existed on the margins of official church life in the sixteenth century. The denial of infant baptism and the refusal to swear an oath marked radicals as a seditious element in society, and they were persecuted by Protestants and Catholics alike. However, in the RCS we have made an attempt to include some voices of the radical Reformation, especially among the Anabaptists. While the Anabaptists published few commentaries in the sixteenth century, they were avid readers and quoters of the Bible. Numerous exegetical gems can be found in their letters, treatises, martyr acts (especially *The Martyrs' Mirror*), hymns and histories. They placed a strong emphasis on the memorizing of Scripture and quoted liberally from vernacular translations of the Bible. George H. Williams has noted that "many an Anabaptist theological tract was really a beautiful mosaic of Scripture texts."[46] In general, most Anabaptists accepted the apocryphal books as canonical, contrasted outer word and inner spirit with relative degrees of strictness and saw the New Testament as normative for church life and social ethics (witness their pacifism, nonswearing, emphasis on believers' baptism and congregational discipline).

We have noted the Old Testament translation of Ludwig Hätzer, who became an antitrinitarian, and Hans Denck that they published at Worms in 1527. Denck also wrote a notable commentary on Micah. Conrad Grebel belonged to a Greek reading circle in Zurich and came to his Anabaptist convictions while poring over the text of Erasmus's New Testament. The only Anabaptist leader with university credentials was Balthasar Hubmaier, who was made a doctor of theology (Ingolstadt, 1512) in the same year as Luther. His reflections on the Bible are found in his numerous

[45]*The New Scofield Reference Bible* (New York: Oxford University Press, 1967), vi.

[46]George H. Williams, *The Radical Reformation*, 3rd ed. (Kirksville, MO: Sixteenth Century Journal Publishers, 1992), 1247.

writings, which include the first catechism of the Reformation (1526), a two-part treatise on the freedom of the will and a major work *(On the Sword)* setting forth positive attitudes toward the role of government and the Christian's place in society. Melchior Hoffman was an apocalyptic seer who wrote commentaries on Romans, Revelation and Daniel 12. He predicted that Christ would return in 1533. More temperate was Pilgram Marpeck, a mining engineer who embraced Anabaptism and traveled widely throughout Switzerland and south Germany, from Strasbourg to Augsburg. His "Admonition of 1542" is the longest published defense of Anabaptist views on baptism and the Lord's Supper. He also wrote many letters that functioned as theological tracts for the congregations he had founded dealing with topics such as the fruits of repentance, the lowliness of Christ and the unity of the church. Menno Simons, a former Catholic priest, became the most outstanding leader of the Dutch Anabaptist movement. His masterpiece was the *Foundation of Christian Doctrine* published in 1540. His other writings include *Meditation on the Twenty-fifth Psalm* (1537); *A Personal Exegesis of Psalm Twenty-five* modeled on the style of Augustine's *Confessions; Confession of the Triune God* (1550), directed against Adam Pastor, a former disciple of Menno who came to doubt the divinity of Christ; *Meditations and Prayers for Mealtime* (1557); and the *Cross of the Saints* (1554), an exhortation to faithfulness in the face of persecution. Like many other Anabaptists, Menno emphasized the centrality of discipleship *(Nachfolge)* as a deliberate repudiation of the old life and a radical commitment to follow Jesus as Lord.

Reading Scripture with the Reformers

In 1947, Gerhard Ebeling set forth his thesis that the history of the Christian church is the history of the interpretation of Scripture. Since that time, the place of the Bible in the story of the church has been investigated from many angles. A better understanding of the history of exegesis has been aided by new critical editions and scholarly discussions of the primary sources. The *Cambridge History of the Bible*, published in three volumes (1963–1970), remains a standard reference work in the field. The ACCS built on, and itself contributed to, the recovery of patristic biblical wisdom of both East and West. Beryl Smalley's *The Study of the Bible in the Middle Ages* (1940) and Henri de Lubac's *Medieval Exegesis: The Four Senses of Scripture* (1959) are essential reading for understanding the monastic and scholastic settings of commentary work between Augustine and Luther. The Reformation took place during what has been called "le grand siècle de la Bible."[47] Aided by the tools of Renaissance humanism and the dynamic impetus of Reformation theology (including permutations and reactions against it), the sixteenth century produced an unprecedented number of commentaries on every book in the Bible. Drawing from this vast storehouse of exegetical treasures, the RCS allows us to read Scripture along with the reformers. In doing so, it serves as a practical homiletic and devotional guide to some of the greatest masters of biblical interpretation in the history of the church.

The RCS gladly acknowledges its affinity with and dependence on recent scholarly investigations of Reformation-era exegesis. Between 1976 and 1990, three international colloquia on the

[47]J-R. Aarmogathe, ed., *Bible de tous les temps*, 8 vols.; vol. 6, *Le grand siècle de la Bible* (Paris: Beauchesne, 1989).

history of biblical exegesis in the sixteenth century took place in Geneva and in Durham, North Carolina.[48] Among those participating in these three gatherings were a number of scholars who have produced groundbreaking works in the study of biblical interpretation in the Reformation. These include Elsie McKee, Irena Backus, Kenneth Hagen, Scott H. Hendrix, Richard A. Muller, Guy Bedouelle, Gerald Hobbs, John B. Payne, Bernard Roussel, Pierre Fraenkel and David C. Steinmetz (1936–2015). Among other scholars whose works are indispensible for the study of this field are Heinrich Bornkamm, Jaroslav Pelikan, Heiko A. Oberman, James S. Preus, T. H. L. Parker, David F. Wright, Tony Lane, John L. Thompson, Frank A. James and Timothy J. Wengert.[49] Among these scholars no one has had a greater influence on the study of Reformation exegesis than David C. Steinmetz. A student of Oberman, he emphasized the importance of understanding the Reformation in medieval perspective. In addition to important studies on Luther and Staupitz, he pioneered the method of comparative exegesis showing both continuity and discontinuity between major Reformation figures and the preceding exegetical traditions (see his *Luther in Context* and *Calvin in Context*). From his base at Duke University, he spawned what might be called a Steinmetz school, a cadre of students and scholars whose work on the Bible in the Reformation era continues to shape the field. Steinmetz served on the RCS Board of Editorial Advisors, and a number of our volume editors pursued doctoral studies under his supervision.

In 1980, Steinmetz published "The Superiority of Pre-critical Exegesis," a seminal essay that not only placed Reformation exegesis in the context of the preceding fifteen centuries of the church's study of the Bible but also challenged certain assumptions underlying the hegemony of historical-critical exegesis of the post-Enlightenment academy.[50] Steinmetz helps us to approach the reformers and other precritical interpreters of the Bible on their own terms as faithful witnesses to the church's apostolic tradition. For them, a specific book or pericope had to be understood within the scope of the consensus of the canon. Thus the reformers, no less than the Fathers and the schoolmen, interpreted the hymn of the Johannine prologue about the preexistent Christ in consonance with the creation narrative of Genesis 1. In the same way, Psalm 22, Isaiah 53 and Daniel 7 are seen as part of an overarching storyline that finds ultimate fulfillment in Jesus Christ. Reading the Bible with the resources of the new learning, the reformers challenged the exegetical conclusions of their medieval predecessors at many points. However, unlike Alexander Campbell in the nineteenth century, their aim was not to "open the New Testament as if mortal man had never seen

[48]Olivier Fatio and Pierre Fraenkel, eds., *Histoire de l'exégèse au XVIe siècle: texts du colloque international tenu à Genève en 1976* (Geneva: Droz, 1978); David C. Steinmetz, ed., *The Bible in the Sixteenth Century* [Second International Colloquy on the History of Biblical Exegesis in the Sixteenth Century] (Durham: Duke University Press, 1990); Irena Backus and Francis M. Higman, eds., *Théorie et pratique de l'exégèse. Actes du troisième colloque international sur l'histoire de l'exégèse biblique au XVIe siècle, Genève, 31 août–2 septembre 1988* (Geneva: Droz, 1990); see also Guy Bedouelle and Bernard Roussel, eds., *Bible de tous les temps*, 8 vols.; vol. 5, *Le temps des Réformes et la Bible* (Paris: Beauchesne, 1989).

[49]For bibliographical references and evaluation of these and other contributors to the scholarly study of Reformation-era exegesis, see Richard A. Muller, "Biblical Interpretation in the Era of the Reformation: The View From the Middle Ages," in *Biblical Interpretation in the Era of the Reformation: Essays Presented to David C. Steinmetz in Honor of His Sixtieth Birthday*, ed. Richard A. Muller and John L. Thompson (Grand Rapids: Eerdmans, 1996), 3-22.

[50]David C. Steinmetz, "The Superiority of Pre-Critical Exegesis," *Theology Today* 37 (1980): 27-38.

it before."[51] Rather, they wanted to do their biblical work as part of an interpretive conversation within the family of the people of God. In the reformers' emphatic turn to the literal sense, which prompted their many blasts against the unrestrained use of allegory, their work was an extension of a similar impulse made by Thomas Aquinas and Nicholas of Lyra.

This is not to discount the radically new insights gained by the reformers in their dynamic engagement with the text of Scripture; nor should we dismiss in a reactionary way the light shed on the meaning of the Bible by the scholarly accomplishments of the past two centuries. However, it is to acknowledge that the church's exegetical tradition is an indispensible aid for the proper interpretation of Scripture. And this means, as Richard Muller has said, that "while it is often appropriate to recognize that traditionary readings of the text are erroneous on the grounds offered by the historical-critical method, we ought also to recognize that the conclusions offered by historical-critical exegesis may themselves be quite erroneous on the grounds provided by the exegesis of the patristic, medieval, and reformation periods."[52] The RCS wishes to commend the exegetical work of the Reformation era as a program of retrieval for the sake of renewal—spiritual réssourcement for believers committed to the life of faith today.

George Herbert was an English pastor and poet who reaped the benefits of the renewal of biblical studies in the age of the Reformation. He referred to the Scriptures as a book of infinite sweetness, "a mass of strange delights," a book with secrets to make the life of anyone good. In describing the various means pastors require to be fully furnished in the work of their calling, Herbert provided a rationale for the history of exegesis and for the Reformation Commentary on Scripture:

> The fourth means are commenters and Fathers, who have handled the places controverted, which the parson by no means refuseth. As he doth not so study others as to neglect the grace of God in himself and what the Holy Spirit teacheth him, so doth he assure himself that God in all ages hath had his servants to whom he hath revealed his Truth, as well as to him; and that as one country doth not bear all things that there may be a commerce, so neither hath God opened or will open all to one, that there may be a traffic in knowledge between the servants of God for the planting both of love and humility. Wherefore he hath one comment[ary] at least upon every book of Scripture, and ploughing with this, and his own meditations, he enters into the secrets of God treasured in the holy Scripture.[53]

Timothy George
General Editor

[51] Alexander Campbell, *Memoirs of Alexander Campbell*, ed. Robert Richardson (Cincinnati: Standard Publishing Company, 1872), 97.
[52] Richard A. Muller and John L. Thompson, "The Significance of Precritical Exegesis: Retrospect and Prospect," in *Biblical Interpretation in the Era of the Reformation: Essays Presented to David C. Steinmetz in Honor of His Sixtieth Birthday*, ed. Richard A. Muller and John L. Thompson (Grand Rapids: Eerdmans, 1996), 342.
[53] George Herbert, *The Complete English Poems* (London: Penguin, 1991), 205.

INTRODUCTION TO 1 CORINTHIANS

The biblical books of 1 and 2 Corinthians were situated along the fault line of theological controversy and religious change in sixteenth-century Europe. The seismic impact of the message of these apostolic letters is illustrated in two poignant scenes from the Reformation era. One of these scenes is well-remembered; the other is almost entirely forgotten. One scene set the trajectory of early modern religious history; the other decisively altered the course of one man's life.

The first scene occurred in the autumn of 1529, in the castle of the Landgrave of Hesse in the German city of Marburg. For three days leading Protestant theologians from Germany and Switzerland met in Marburg to debate the nature of Christ's presence in the Eucharist, in hopes of achieving theological consensus that would foster a united political front against the Catholic emperor. The Lutheran delegation, represented by such luminaries as Martin Luther, Philipp Melanchthon, Justus Jonas and Caspar Cruciger, insisted that Scripture taught the corporeal presence of Christ's body in, with, and under the sacramental elements. On the other side of the table, the Reformed delegation, represented by Huldrych Zwingli, Johann Oecolampadius, Martin Bucer, and Caspar Hedio, rejected this Lutheran interpretation and insisted instead that Christ's resurrected body remained in heaven, that the bread and wine were ordinary elements that symbolized Christ's death for sinners. During this protracted debate, Luther repeatedly pushed Zwingli to consider the full import of Jesus' words of consecration, recorded in 1 Corinthians 11. To make his point, he inscribed with chalk on the conference table the words *Hoc est corpus meum* ("This is my body"; 1 Cor 11:24) as biblical proof of the doctrine of corporeal presence. In the end, the religious parties were unable to find common ground on this contested point, and Luther refused to accept Zwingli's offer of the right hand of Christian fellowship. Their disagreement over four biblical words—*Hoc est corpus meum*—was decisive in formalizing a theological rupture that remains to this day.[1]

The second scene occurred twelve years later in Naples and involved the religious conversion of Galeazzo Caracciolo (1517–1586), the marquis of Vico. Caracciolo was born to one of the most powerful and influential Catholic families in Italy, related (through his mother) to archbishops and cardinals, including Gian-Pietro Carafa, the future Pope Paul IV (r. 1555–1559). As a young man Caracciolo was sent to the imperial court to serve as a page and cupbearer to Emperor Charles V. At age twenty, he contracted a brilliant marriage to Vittoria Carafa, the daughter of

[1]See Martin Brecht, *Martin Luther*, trans. James L. Schaaf (Minneapolis: Fortress, 1994), 2:325-39; W. P. Stephens, *The Theology of Huldrych Zwingli* (Oxford: Clarendon, 1986), 218-59.

the Duke of Naecera, with whom he lived happily for fourteen years and fathered four sons and two daughters. Despite the trappings of wealth, prestige and power, the Marquis of Vico, while still in his early twenties, experienced deep spiritual restlessness that moved him to join a circle of Catholic reformers in Naples known as the *Spirituali*, who were committed to the pursuit of religious truth and personal holiness. In late 1541, as a member of this circle, Caracciolo attended a memorable sermon on 1 and 2 Corinthians preached by the humanist and theologian Peter Martyr Vermigli. The message of this sermon proved to be life-changing for Caracciolo, who quietly resolved to disavow the world and its pleasures, and embrace the evangelical faith. A decade later, at the age of thirty-four, Caracciolo renounced the Catholic religion and departed Naples, leaving behind his wife, six children, possessions and aristocratic titles, and immigrated to the Reformed city of Geneva, where he spent the rest of his life for the sake of the Christian gospel.[2] For Caracciolo, the message of 1 and 2 Corinthians spoke to his spiritual hunger and was instrumental in his religious conversion.

Reformation and Sacred Scripture

Historians have sometimes compared the Protestant Reformation of the sixteenth century to a religious and social revolution. And there is something to that. The Reformation brought about vast, fundamental and lasting changes in church and society in Europe that are still recognizable to this day. The Reformation divided Western Christendom by challenging the Roman Church's dominance in the West. It awakened German nationalism and permanently shaped German language and culture. It introduced new conceptions of vocation, family life and divorce that became commonplace in the modern world. It challenged traditional Catholic piety and devotional practices, promoting instead a more simplified Word-centered spirituality. It created rival confessional churches that, unwittingly, contributed to the rise of Europe's modern nation-states.[3]

It would be wrong, however, to think of Protestant leaders such as Luther, Zwingli, Melanchthon, and John Calvin primarily as religious agitators or social revolutionaries. For though they attacked the medieval church and rejected many of her institutions and teachings, their chief concern was not to dismantle the Christian church but to repair or reform it according to the Word of God. In other words, the Protestant reformers were *not* attempting to create a new church; they were attempting to restore to her pristine condition the one holy universal church. Calvin emphasized this very point in his letter to the Catholic bishop Jacopo Sadoleto in 1539: "Our agreement with antiquity is far closer than yours. . . . In all these points, the ancient church is clearly on our side."[4]

[2]For Caracciolo and his conversion, see Benedetto Croce, *Galéas Caracciolo, Marquis de Vico* (Geneva: Droz, 1965), 12-13. Robert Kingdon's study *Adultery and Divorce in Calvin's Geneva* (Cambridge, MA: Harvard University Press, 1995) devotes a chapter to Caracciolo's prolonged (and successful) efforts to divorce his Catholic wife on the grounds of abandonment.

[3]For considerations of the Reformation's long-term impact, see Steven Ozment, *Protestants: The Birth of a Revolution* (New York: Doubleday, 1993); Heinz Schilling, "Confessional Europe," in *Handbook of European History 1400–1600*, ed. Thomas Brady, Heiko A. Oberman and James Tracy (Leiden: Brill, 1994), 1:641-81.

[4]John Calvin, "Reply to Sadoleto," in *John Calvin–Jacopo Sadoleto: A Reformation Debate*, ed. John Olin (repr.; Grand Rapids: Baker, 1987), 62, 74.

The Protestant reformers agreed that true spiritual reformation would occur only as the church submitted to the authority of Scripture. They insisted that the Scripture, as God's holy Word, must be the *norma normans*—the ruling authority for Christian faith and practice. As Luther stated in 1519, "The church is captive to the authority of Scripture and does not teach anything but the Word of God."[5] For first-generation reformers such as Luther and Zwingli, this conviction was not an abstract commitment to biblical authority but reflected their own personal encounter with the Scripture. Zwingli's career as a reformer commenced when, as the newly appointed people's priest at Grossmünster Church in Zurich on January 1, 1519, he began to preach verse by verse through the Gospel of Matthew. Over the next six years, Zwingli's daily expositions of Scripture served as a kind of wrecking ball that demolished the Catholic institutions and traditional beliefs of the city church. The Word of God, Zwingli once wrote, "will as surely have its way as the Rhine [River], which you can stem for a while, but not stop." With good reason a biographer of Zwingli has claimed that "the Bible was at the heart of Zwingli's reformation."[6] The same can be said of Luther, who discovered the Christian gospel—and found peace for his tormented conscience—as he took up the doctor's cap at the University of Wittenberg and began lecturing in 1513 through the books of Psalms, Romans, and Galatians. As he studied and taught the Scripture, as he unleashed the Word of God, the evangelical message spread like wildfire throughout the German empire and beyond. With only a bit of hubris, Luther remembered it this way: "I simply taught, preached and wrote God's Word; otherwise I did nothing. And then while I slept or drank Wittenberg beer with my friends Philip [Melanchthon] and [Nicholas von] Amsdorf, the Word so greatly weakened the papacy that no prince or emperor ever inflicted such losses upon it. I did nothing; The Word did everything."[7]

Protestant biblical scholarship in the sixteenth century was in large part the beneficiary of a pedagogical program known as northern humanism, which prioritized the mastery of the humane letters (*studia humanitatis*), the cultivation of eloquence, the recovery of ancient texts, and the careful study of the Christian Scriptures in their original languages of Hebrew and Greek. During the late fifteenth and early sixteenth centuries Catholic humanist scholars such as Lorenzo Valla, Johannes Reuchlin, Jacques Lefèvre d'Étaples, and Desiderius Erasmus forged new paths as they undertook rigorous philological study of the Bible in its original languages and produced essential study tools such as Greek and Hebrew grammars and lexicons, commentaries on Scripture, and improved Latin translations of the Greek and Hebrew text. Protestant reformers such as Luther, Zwingli, Melanchthon, Bucer, and Calvin were heirs of this humanist intellectual tradition. They believed that the careful study of the Christian Scriptures, in their original languages, was necessary for recovering the Christian gospel and achieving the reformation of the church. As Luther put it famously, "Let us be sure of this: we will not long preserve the gospel

[5]First Psalms Lectures, LW 10:29. For development of this theme in Luther's writings, see Mark Thompson, *A Sure Ground on Which to Stand: The Relation of Authority and Interpretive Method in Luther's Approach to Scripture* (Eugene, OR: Wipf & Stock, 2006), 276-82.

[6]W. P. Stephens, *Zwingli: An Introduction to His Thought* (Oxford: Oxford University Press, 2001).

[7]"Second Sermon after Invocavit" (1522), LW 51:77.

without the languages."[8] Like their humanist predecessors, the reformers produced a variety of exegetical aids, concordances, commentaries, and dictionaries to elucidate the meaning of the sacred text. So too, they promoted curricular reforms at the University of Wittenberg and other Protestant gymnasia, academies, and universities that gave priority to the study of sacred philology and the biblical languages. Within a generation or so, Protestant pastors were expected to be *homines trilinguarum*—knowledgeable in Latin, Hebrew, and Greek—to ensure that they rightly handled God's Word in their preaching and teaching.[9] The Protestants were also committed to making God's Word more accessible to the laity through Bible translation. During the sixteenth century, Protestant scholars produced new (and improved) versions of the Bible in Arabic, Czech, Dutch, English, French, German, Italian, Latin, Portuguese, and Spanish.[10] Around 200,000 copies of Luther's German Bible (1534) were printed in Wittenberg before 1620.[11] Similarly, more than eighty editions of the French Bible were produced in Geneva alone between 1550 and 1600.[12]

The priority Protestant leaders gave to sacred philology and intensive Scripture study is illustrated in the career of a long-forgotten professor named Jean Ribit, who taught theology at the Reformed Academy of Lausanne from 1547 to 1559. In 1549, Ribit drafted his weekly schedule, which included this Scripture-saturated program of study for Tuesdays:

- Rise at 4:00 a.m. Give thanks to God for his protection through the night, and solicit his continued strength for the new day. Prepare the morning's theological lecture and memorize relevant biblical texts.

- At 5:00 a.m., commit theological and biblical insights to writing.

- At 6:00 a.m., attend the daily sermon in Lausanne's church. Following the sermon, make final preparations for the morning lecture.

- At 9:00 a.m., present theological lecture at the Academy. The class session will proceed as follows: recite introductory prayer; read aloud the biblical text in Hebrew or Greek, followed by the French translation; provide a careful exposition of the biblical passage, explaining the words or clauses that are unclear and examining textual variants; introduce the exegetical judgments of ancient and modern commentators; present a detailed discussion of the theological topics found in the biblical text as well as principal points of application. The goal is to "explain as carefully as possible . . . the mind of the [biblical] author," for in doing so one "instructs the church both in private and public."

- At 10:00 a.m., eat lunch and spend time in prayer.

[8] LW 45:360.

[9] There was, of course, significant difference between the ideal and the reality. In his study of Protestant clergy in the Palatinate between 1555 and 1619, Bernard Vogler concludes that by the end of the sixteenth century almost all the ministers knew Latin, two-thirds knew Greek, but only a few had facility reading Hebrew. See Vogler, *Le Clergé Protestant Rhénan au Siècle de la Réforme (1555–1619)* (Paris: Éditions Ophrys, 1976), 228.

[10] Jaroslav Pelikan, *The Reformation of the Bible, the Bible of the Reformation* (New Haven, CT: Yale University Press, 1996), 49-62.

[11] M. H. Black, "The Printed Bible," in *CHB* 3:432.

[12] Bettye Thomas Chambers, *Bibliography of French Bibles: Fifteenth- and Sixteenth-Century French-Language Editions of the Scriptures* (Geneva: Droz, 1983).

- At 11:00 a.m., attend to domestic duties, write personal correspondence or attend student sermons at the Academy.

- At noon, study the Hebrew text of Scripture, page through a Hebrew dictionary and recite the Psalms and Proverbs.

- At 1:00 p.m., listen to wife read the Bible and follow along in either the Greek or Hebrew text.

- At 2:00 p.m., read three chapters of the Bible and commit parts of it to memory.

- At 3:00 p.m., study the passage of Scripture that will be examined in the *Congregation* of the city pastors the following day. Consult relevant commentaries, including those of Nicholas of Lyra, Augustine Steuchus, Jerome, Sebastian Münster, Augustine, Huldrych Zwingli, Origen, Basil the Great, and Ambrose. Spend time meditating on the passage for personal edification.

- At 5:00 p.m., read three chapters of the New Testament.

- At 6:00 p.m., eat dinner.

- At 7:00 p.m., assist children with their school work and oversee their catechism lessons.

- At 8:00 p.m., lead household through family prayers and confession of sins.[13]

Obviously most Protestant ministers and laity in the sixteenth century did not possess the educational background, the time, or the motivation to devote such careful attention to the biblical languages and interpretation as did Ribit. Nevertheless, Ribit's example points to the Protestants' conviction that the renewal of the Christian church was closely tied to the recovery, study, and exposition of God's Word. For reformers such as Luther, Calvin, and Ribit, biblical scholarship was not an end in itself; rather, it was intended to equip preachers to proclaim God's gospel through sermons, sacraments, and catechisms. It is with good reason, then, that historian Irena Backus has argued that biblical exegesis became "the chief purveyor" of Protestant doctrine—and, we might add, a crucial agent of religious change.[14]

Commentaries, Commentators, and Paul's Corinthian Correspondence

Humanistic biblical scholarship was transmitted to evangelical pulpits primarily through biblical commentaries. This could happen in several ways. First of all, professors in Protestant universities and academies relied on biblical commentaries as they trained future pastors in Bible and theology. This was illustrated in the teaching ministry of Jean Ribit. It was also witnessed in the career of the reformer Wolfgang Musculus, whose biblical lectures to students at the municipal secondary school in Bern drew extensively from biblical commentaries both ancient and modern.[15] Second, parish ministers also depended on biblical commentaries as essential tools in preparing

[13]This remarkable text is found in Henri Meylan, "Professeurs et Étudiants, Questions d'Horaires et de Leçons," in *La Réforme et l'éducation*, ed. Jean Boisset (Toulouse: Privat, 1974), 70-71.

[14]Irena Backus, "Bible: Biblical Hermeneutics and Exegesis," in *OER* 1:154.

[15]See Scott M. Manetsch, "(Re)constructing the Pastoral Office: Wolfgang Musculus's Commentaries on 1 and 2 Corinthians," in *On the Writing of New Testament Commentaries*, ed. Stanley Porter and Eckhard Schnabel (Leiden: Brill, 2013), 253-66.

sermons and catechetical lessons. Thus, for example, an inventory of the personal libraries of Reformed and Lutheran pastors in the Palatinate from 1580 to 1585 reveals that 12.2 percent of the books were devoted to Old Testament exegesis, and 17.4 percent treated New Testament exegesis.[16] Another example is seen in the personal library of a rural pastor from Geneva named Jean de Brunes. At his death in 1603, de Brunes's library contained 549 titles, including the Hebrew Bible, the Greek New Testament, Greek and Hebrew dictionaries, grammars, concordances, harmonies of the Gospels, and commentaries on every book of the Bible.[17]

A minor episode from Calvin's career illustrates the strategic importance of commentaries in Protestant religious culture.[18] When Calvin returned to Geneva from Strasbourg in 1541, he had recently completed his commentary on Romans, and had begun commenting on 1 and 2 Corinthians. Unfortunately the demands of pastoral ministry along with incessant polemical battles made it impossible for Calvin to make progress on his exegetical writing—and his friends became increasingly worried and impatient. When Guillaume Farel urged his colleague to return to his commentaries, Calvin responded, "I only wish I had more time and better health."[19] In November 1545, Calvin received a long, urgent letter from his friend Valeran Pullain:

> All the learned, whenever they meet, ask me when those commentaries will finally be ready. Let me tell you something: You are not being very wise when you allow Satan to draw you away to other projects which, although they are not to be despised, are nevertheless not as useful as the treatment of Scripture. . . . Look, my father, I am speaking in this fashion because I am convinced that it is for the glory of Christ and the up-building of his church. For, Calvin, I wish that you would resolve once for all never to rest until you have written commentaries on all the epistles of Paul, then on the Prophets, then on the rest of the sacred books. Gracious God! How they would help the church! How much they would do for the glory of Christ![20]

The long-awaited commentary on 1 Corinthians finally appeared in January 1546, to the delight of Calvin's friends in Strasbourg. John Hooper, the future bishop of Gloucester, was less enthusiastic, however. In a letter to Bucer, he complained, "Calvin's commentary on 1 Corinthians displeased me exceedingly"—no doubt due to Calvin's explanation of the Lord's Supper in his comments on 1 Corinthians 11.[21] As this brief vignette indicates, biblical commentaries were highly valued by early Protestants, who depended on them for edification, biblical understanding, and polemical advantage.

[16]Vogler, *Le Clergé Protestant Rhénan*, 254.

[17]M. Puyroche, "La bibliothèque d'un Pasteur à la fin du XVIe siècle," *Bulletin de la société de l'histoire du Protestantisme français* 21 (1872): 327-37. Jean de Brunes served the Genevan church from 1598 to 1601, and then transferred to the Reformed church in Lyons, where he died in 1603. Lutheran pastors' libraries also contained a substantial number of volumes devoted to biblical exegesis. See, for example, Gerald Strauss, "The Mental World of a Saxon Pastor," in *Reformation Principle and Practice*, ed. Peter Newman Brooks (London: Scolar Press, 1980), 161-70.

[18]This incident is reported in T. H. L. Parker, *Calvin's New Testament Commentaries*, 2nd ed. (Louisville, KY: Westminster John Knox, 1993), 18-19.

[19]Farel to Calvin, October 1546, in CO 12:391.

[20]Pullain to Calvin, November 1545, CO 12:216.

[21]Hastings Robinson, ed. *Original Letters Relative to the English Reformation* (Cambridge: Cambridge University Press, 1846), 44-48.

Calvin was in no way unique among the reformers in writing commentaries. During the sixteenth and early seventeenth centuries, Protestant and Catholic scholars produced hundreds of biblical commentaries, interpreting every verse of the Scripture canon. These commentaries were not intended to supplant the authority of holy writ; rather, their purpose was to clarify the meaning of the biblical text, usually in conversation with Christian interpreters both ancient and modern. Commentaries during the Reformation era appeared in a variety of literary forms and genres, spanning a continuum from brief philological comments with little theological content to extensive theological reflection with minimal attention paid to grammar or syntax. Exegetical treatments of Scripture were variously titled commentaries (*commentarii*), paraphrases (*paraphrases*), annotations (*annotationes, annotatiunculae*), explanations (*enarrationes, explicationes*), expositions (*expositiones*), sermons (*sermones*), and homilies or sermon outlines (*postille*)—though as we shall see shortly such nomenclature never constituted hard-and-fast literary categories in the sixteenth century.[22]

Reformation commentaries on 1 and 2 Corinthians illustrate the variety and versatility of these literary genres. More than fifty different Protestant and pre-Tridentine Catholic authors wrote commentaries on 1 Corinthians before 1660. Another forty-five commentaries were produced on 2 Corinthians during the same period.[23] Pre-Tridentine Catholic commentators on 1 and 2 Corinthians included the brilliant biblical scholar Jacques Lefèvre d'Étaples; the Dominican theologian, and Luther's opponent at the Diet of Augsburg, Cardinal Tomasso de Vio Cajetan; and the Dutch humanist Desiderius Erasmus. John Colet, the dean of St. Paul's Church in London, also produced a manuscript copy of a commentary on 1 Corinthians.

A significant number of Lutheran churchmen also published sustained interpretations of 1 and 2 Corinthians, whether in the form of commentaries, annotations, sermon collections, or sermon outlines. Chief among these interpreters were the Wittenberg humanist and reformer Philipp Melanchthon, the Wittenberg preacher and pastor Johannes Bugenhagen, the pastor of Nordhausen and Eisleben Johann Spangenberg, and Gnesio-Lutheran theologians Tilemann Hesshus and David Chytraeus. Martin Luther never produced a comprehensive study of either 1 Corinthians or 2 Corinthians, but he did publish brief expositions of 1 Corinthians 7 and 1 Corinthians 15 as well as postils on select passages from the Corinthian correspondence.

In a similar fashion, Reformed authors on the Continent and in England found Paul's Corinthian correspondence to be rich soil for interpretation and comment. During the sixteenth and early seventeenth centuries, noteworthy studies of 1 and 2 Corinthians were produced by the Zurich theologian Huldrych Zwingli and his successor Heinrich Bullinger. Peter Martyr Vermigli's massive study of 1 Corinthians became the gold standard for Reformed commentaries on that epistle. In Geneva, the reformer John Calvin, his colleague Theodore Beza, and their successor Giovanni Diodati all wrote commentaries or annotations on 1 and 2 Corinthians—as did

[22]See Kenneth Hagen, "What Did the Term *Commentarius* Mean to Sixteenth-Century Theologians?," in *Théorie et pratique de l'exégèse: Actes du troisième colloque international sur l'histoire de l'exégèse biblique au XVIe siècle*, ed. Irena Backus and Francis Higman (Geneva: Droz, 1990), 13-38; Irena Backus, "Bible: Hermeneutics and Exegesis," in *OER* 1:158.

[23]These figures include commentaries on the entire the entire Bible, commentaries on the New Testament, commentaries on the Pauline epistles, and discrete commentaries on 1 and 2 Corinthians.

the Bernese biblical scholar Wolfgang Musculus and the Dutch theologian Andreas Hyperius. In addition, the Strasbourg reformer Martin Bucer and Genevan pastor Simon Goulart penned theological discourses that included extensive comment on select passages from these Pauline letters. A generation later, Protestants in England also published popular exegetical studies on 1 and 2 Corinthians, as seen in the commentaries of David Dickson and John Trapp, the sermons of John Donne, and the marginal notes that appeared in the *English Annotations* (1645).

Despite this impressive inventory of commentators, there are relatively few so-called Radical Protestant and Anabaptist authors. As has frequently been noted, few Radical and Anabaptist leaders had either the humanistic training or the unhurried leisure and physical safety to produce substantial exegetical works. Nevertheless, in their polemical and catechetical writings, Anabaptist and Radical church leaders such as Balthasar Hubmaier, Andreas Bodenstein von Karlstadt, Hans Denck, and Menno Simons offered occasional comments on passages in 1 and 2 Corinthians that related to their particular theological or practical concerns, such as believers' baptism, pacifism, the Lord's Supper, and free church ecclesiology. Likewise, while a number of Protestant women interacted vigorously with Scripture (including texts from 1 and 2 Corinthians) and produced a variety of implicitly exegetical commentary in the course of defending not only the Reformation per se but also collateral issues such as the propriety of clergy marriage and the imperative for women to speak and bear testimony, there remain relatively few focused comments on the Corinthian correspondence from women of the period. Fortunately, a few exceptions may be found from the likes of Argula von Grumbach, Marie Dentière, and Katharina Schütz Zell, and these will appear below.[24]

While Reformation commentaries on 1 and 2 Corinthians appeared in a variety of literary genres and styles, four major categories were especially popular. Biblical commentaries known as *paraphrases* were made famous by Erasmus, who published his *Paraphrases* on the New Testament from 1517 to 1524. In Erasmus's hands, the paraphrase provided a continuous exposition and explanation of the New Testament intended to simplify and clarify its meaning for ordinary readers. Paraphrasing was "the art of saying things differently, without saying different things."[25] When his opponents accused him of tampering with Scripture, Erasmus defended his work by insisting that he had elucidated Paul's meaning by "bridging gaps, smoothing rough passages, bringing order out of confusion and simplicity out of complication, untying knots, [and] throwing light on dark places."[26] In the century after their publication, Erasmus's *Paraphrases* were translated into several languages for use in local parish ministry.[27]

[24] For more information, see for example Marion Ann Taylor, ed., *Handbook of Women Biblical Interpreters* (Grand Rapids: Baker Academic, 2012); Merry E. Wiesner-Hanks, *Women and Gender in Early Modern Europe* (Cambridge: Cambridge University Press, 2008); Kirsi Stjerna, *Women and the Reformation* (Oxford: Blackwell, 2008); and John L. Thompson, "Rules Proved by Exceptions: The Exegesis of Paul and Women in the Sixteenth Century," in *A Companion to Paul in the Reformation*, ed. R. Ward Holder (Leiden: Brill, 2009), 501-40.

[25] Cited in Cornelis Augustijn, *Erasmus: His Life, Works, and Influence*, trans. J. C. Grayson (Toronto: University of Toronto Press, 1991), 101.

[26] CWE 42:xv. Erasmus is speaking specifically here of his *Paraphrases* on Paul's letter to the Romans.

[27] Augustijn, *Erasmus*, 101. In England, for example, it was mandated in 1547 that every parish church possess a copy of Erasmus's

Annotations—a broad and malleable genre—were a second popular form of Reformation commentary. Of all Erasmus's publications, the *Novum Instrumentum* (1516) was arguably his greatest achievement. In this work, Erasmus presented his reader with the Greek text of the New Testament (drawn from the best available Greek manuscripts), a fresh Latin translation from the Greek text, and extensive exegetical notes or annotations to justify his new translation. In subsequent editions, these annotations were expanded considerably, creating a full-blown philological and exegetical commentary on the New Testament; hence, the work thereafter became known as the *Annotationes*. In the decades that followed, Protestant exegetes such as Beza and Diodati produced their own annotations, which provided extensive philological notations on the Greek text—often in conversation with Erasmus—in defense of a Protestant reading of the New Testament.[28] And yet, not all commentaries bearing the title *annotations* were studies in philology and textual criticism. Melanchthon's *Annotationes* on 1 Corinthians (1522), for example, paid little attention to Greek grammar or syntax, adopting instead a rhetorical approach that explained the meaning of select passages or topics that were of theological and pastoral concern for early evangelicals. Passages that did not contribute to Melanchthon's theological purpose were treated cursorily, or even ignored.[29] Most examples of Protestant annotations, however, fell somewhere in between the divergent approaches adopted by Erasmus and Melanchthon. Thus, for example, the *English Annotations*, commissioned by the English parliament in the early 1640s, presented its readers with detailed exegetical and doctrinal notes on nearly every verse in 1 and 2 Corinthians so as to confirm the Reformed theological perspective on display at the Westminster Assembly.[30]

Not surprisingly, many Reformation commentaries on 1 and 2 Corinthians bore the title *commentarius* (sometimes called *explicationes* or *expositiones*), but once again this classification allowed for different interpretive styles. Calvin's commentaries on the Corinthian correspondence were characterized by lucid brevity (*perspicua brevitate*) as he provided a concise philological and theological exposition of each verse of the biblical text. Calvin intended that longer, more detailed theological topics (*loci communes*) be treated in his *Institutes of the Christian Religion*.[31] Musculus's commentaries on 1 and 2 Corinthians, by contrast, were far more detailed, as they interpreted each biblical pericope in successive steps that included a fresh Latin translation, general remarks

Paraphrases.

[28]See Jan Krans, *Beyond What Is Written: Erasmus and Beza as Conjectural Critics of the New Testament* (Leiden: Brill, 2006).

[29]Thus Melanchthon devotes only a couple of pages of his *Annotationes* to 1 Corinthians 7–8, and entirely ignores 1 Corinthians 16. See Melanchthon, *Annotations on the First Epistle to the Corinthians*, ed. and trans. John Patrick Donnelly (Milwaukee: Marquette University Press, 1995), 16-17. For more on Melanchthon's rhetorical method, see Timothy J. Wengert, "The Rhetorical Paul: Philip Melanchthon's Interpretation of the Pauline Epistles," in Holder, *A Companion to Paul in the Reformation*, 129-64; and Wengert, "Philip Melanchthon's 1522 Annotations on Romans and the Lutheran Origins of Rhetorical Criticism," in *Biblical Interpretation in the Era of the Reformation*, ed. Richard Muller and John Thompson (Grand Rapids: Eerdmans, 1996), 124-38.

[30]See Randall Pederson, *Unity in Diversity: English Puritans and the Puritan Reformation, 1603–1689* (Leiden: Brill, 2014), 120-23. The first edition of the *English Annotations* was for the most part a revision and update of the notes from the *Geneva Bible* (1560). Subsequent editions in 1651 and 1657–1658 witnessed a significant augmentation of the textual notes.

[31]For Calvin's exegetical method, see especially John Thompson, "Calvin as a Biblical Interpreter," in *The Cambridge Companion to John Calvin*, ed. Donald K. McKim (Cambridge: Cambridge University Press, 2004), 58-73.

on the passage, philological analysis of key terms, and finally moral and dogmatic observations on the passage.[32] Vermigli's massive commentary on 1 Corinthians adopted this same approach, though it contained more extensive interaction with early Christian commentators and provided the reader with lengthy theological excurses on topics such as marriage and divorce, the *imago Dei*, faith and works, Christian freedom, purgatory, and soul sleep. A very different style of commentary-writing is seen in Colet's manuscript on 1 Corinthians, which exposited the biblical text chapter by chapter, examining select passages that were especially conducive to his Neoplatonic vision for moral improvement and union with God.[33] Yet another approach is found in Trapp's *A Commentary or Exposition* (1656), which presented a pastiche of terse commentary, moral exempla, and memorable quotations, drawn from the writings of several dozen Reformation authors, including Beza, Calvin, John Foxe, Luther, Melanchthon, Oecolampadius, Richard Sibbes, Girolamo Zanchi, and Zwingli.

A fourth popular style of commentary literature on 1 and 2 Corinthians during the Reformation era was the postils. The postils were different from other Reformation commentaries in that most of them were compiled by Lutheran or Catholic churchmen, most were written in German (rather than Latin), and most followed closely the calendar of liturgical readings.[34] In the sixteenth century, Lutheran postils could take different forms: some were expositions of Scripture in the form of brief homilies, while others functioned more as sermon outlines, providing brief summaries and exegetical notes on the text. The postils of prominent Lutheran pastors such as Johann Spangenberg, Veit Dietrich, and David Chytraeus were widely read, but Luther's postils were far and away the most popular, appearing in ten separate sermon collections during the sixteenth century. When his *Sommerpostille* appeared in 1544 (thanks to the careful editorial work of his friend Caspar Cruciger), Luther enthused, "In these the epistle and gospel readings throughout the year are clearly and merrily handed to us, or, as I would say, are chewed for us as a mother chews mash for her little baby."[35] So popular were these postils that laypeople in the countryside sometimes requested that they be read aloud in place of their pastor's Sunday sermon.[36] Postils having been long neglected, historians now recognize this postil literature to have been crucial in the dissemination of religious ideas in Germany during the age of the Reformation.[37]

A Guide to Reading 1 Corinthians

Protestant exegetes in the early modern period found 1 Corinthians to be especially relevant to their religious situation. Although it could not compare to the epistle of Romans in terms of

[32]See Craig S. Farmer, *The Gospel of John in the Sixteenth Century: The Johannine Exegesis of Wolfgang Musculus* (New York: Oxford University Press, 1997); and Farmer, "Wolfgang Musculus," in *DMBI* 765-69.

[33]J. Arnold, "John Colet," in *DMBI* 321-24.

[34]See John M. Frymire, *The Primacy of the Postils: Catholics, Protestants, and the Dissemination of Ideas in Early Modern Germany* (Leiden: Brill, 2010); and Todd R. Hains, "Luther and the Bound Conscience in His German Church Postils" (MA thesis, Trinity Evangelical Divinity School, 2007), 47-62. Because postils usually followed the liturgical cycle, only a handful of the postils treat passages from 1 and 2 Corinthians.

[35]Cited in Hains, "Luther and the Bound Conscience," 60 (WA 21:201; cf. LW 77:8). For a modern edition of Luther's Summer Postils, see LW 77–79.

[36]Strauss, "Mental World of a Saxon Pastor," 163.

[37]Frymire argues this point in his *Primacy of the Postils*, 1.

theological content and systematic argument, Paul's first epistle to the church at Corinth nevertheless addressed a variety of theological and practical issues that were at the forefront of Protestant concerns in the sixteenth century. The Protestant reformers found within the epistle theological ammunition to attack Catholic teaching regarding purgatory, transubstantiation, Roman primacy, good works, clerical celibacy, and religious images. More positively, Lutheran, Reformed, and Anabaptist leaders mined Paul's letter for practical wisdom on such topics as pastoral leadership, church discipline, marriage and divorce, preaching, gender roles, lawsuits, and spiritual gifts. In addition, 1 Corinthians addressed key theological themes that were of central importance to the Protestants such as law-gospel, justification by faith alone, the Lord's Supper, and the future resurrection. In all these ways, then, sixteenth- and seventeenth-century interpreters looked to 1 Corinthians as a kind of theological and practical blueprint for restoring contemporary church and society. It was with good reason, then, that Vermigli dedicated his commentary on 1 Corinthians to Edward VI, the king of England, with the hope that the young king would consult this biblical book as he endeavored to reform the English church.[38]

Pre-Tridentine Catholic and Protestant commentators accepted traditional interpretations regarding the authorship and provenance of this biblical letter. They agreed that 1 Corinthians was written by the apostle Paul to the Corinthian church several years after he had visited and planted a church in the city, as recorded in Acts 18. Protestant exegetes insisted that Paul had sent this letter from Ephesus—contrary to an inscription in the Vulgate that identified Philippi as the epistle's place of origin.[39] Located on an isthmus between the Aegean and Ionian Seas, the ancient city of Corinth was a commercial center and gathering place for traders and merchants from throughout the Mediterranean world. The city was also home to the famous temple dedicated to the goddess Venus and with it the hundreds of temple prostitutes who plied their trade among townspeople and visitors. For Protestant and pre-Tridentine Catholic exegetes, cosmopolitan Corinth was emblematic of ostentatious wealth, spiritual pride, and sexual license, a "groundswell of every sin, iniquity, and vice" as Johann Spangenberg observed.[40] Tragically, the church in Corinth had assimilated many of these sinful attitudes and practices and had become characterized by disorders, divisions, scandals, and corruption—filled with "mad saints," "immature know-it-alls," and pseudo-apostles. As they described this woeful state of affairs, many Protestant commentators saw parallels between the Corinthian church and the church in their own day. As Luther noted, "These Corinthians may well be an example for our people in these days, who also certainly need an epistle of this kind."[41]

Modern readers will no doubt find material in this present volume that is insightful and challenging, edifying and mystifying. Here we briefly explore six key themes related to the interpretation and doctrine of 1 Corinthians.

[38]See Peter Martyr Vermigli, *In Selectissimam S. Pauli Priorem ad Corinth. Epistolam . . . Commentarii doctissimi* (Zurich: Christoph Froschauer, 1551), *3v.

[39]See below comments on 1 Cor 16:9.

[40]Johann Spangenberg, *Der Apostel Geschichte: Kurtze auslegung Fur die jungen Christen inn Frage verfasset* (Wittenberg: Georg Rhau, 1545), 158v-159r.

[41]Preface to 1 Corinthians, LW 35:380-81.

The character of premodern exegesis. The Protestant and pre-Tridentine Catholic commentators whose writings are found in this volume were by and large traditional in their approach to Scripture. To be sure, most early modern commentators were beneficiaries of the humanist program of biblical scholarship that accented philology and rhetorical analysis, and rejected the monopoly of the Vulgate translation. So too, Protestant commentators regularly denounced patristic and medieval exegetes for their fanciful allegorical readings of Scripture and their inattention to the literal meaning of the sacred text. But in most other ways, Reformation exegetes shared the core assumptions and convictions of the Christian interpretive tradition. They recognized the divine origin of Christian Scripture, and assumed the unity of the biblical canon by virtue of its divine authorship and purpose. They believed that right understanding of God's Word was dependent on the Holy Spirit's gift of illumination. They taught that the meaning of a particular passage was located in the text itself, which was to be understood in light of the larger purpose and meaning of Scripture as a whole (the *analogia Scripturae*).[42] They assumed that fruitful biblical interpretation must be conducted in conversation with Christian interpreters from the past and present. Finally, Reformation commentators insisted that the Bible's authoritative message was intended for the church of their own day as well as for the first-century church. For Luther and his colleagues, then, Scripture was not a book to be criticized, doubted, deconstructed, or treated as a mere artifact of antiquarian interest; rather, it was God's timeless and authoritative Word, worthy of Christians' careful study and reverent obedience.

Literal and spiritual interpretation. Reformation commentators routinely criticized the allegorical or spiritual approach to biblical interpretation as it was practiced by the majority of medieval Catholic interpreters. Bucer spoke for most of his Protestant colleagues when he maligned fanciful allegories as a "blatant insult to the Holy Spirit," contrived by Satan to "lure us away from the true and efficacious teachings and examples of Christ."[43] Instead, the reformers championed the grammatical or literal sense of the text as the surest way to discern the intention of the biblical author and the mind of the Holy Spirit—a move that Jaroslav Pelikan has called a "Copernican Revolution" in hermeneutics.[44] But this does not mean that Protestant exegetes advocated a bare literalism as they read the sacred text. Reformation commentators such as Luther, Zwingli, Bucer, and Calvin recognized that the literal or natural sense of Scripture often contained various layers of meaning or significance that spoke of Christ, Christian morality, and Christian hope to believers of their own day.[45] Paul's assertion in 1 Corinthians 10:11 that historical events recorded in the Old Testament were "written down for our instruction" demonstrated the ongoing spiritual significance of these ancient texts. Paraphrasing this passage, Zwingli noted, "It is not at all true

---

[42]This explains why Reformation commentators frequently inserted biblical cross-references to illustrate or explain the passage under consideration. What modern readers might take for "proof-texting" was rather the authors' demonstration of the fundamental unity and coherence of the biblical canon.

[43]Cited in David Wright, "Martin Bucer," in *DMBI* 249.

[44]Pelikan, *Reformation of the Bible*, 29.

[45]In so doing, the reformers were folding the interpretive senses of the ancient *quadriga* (literal, allegorical, moral, anagogical) back into the literal meaning of the text.

that these events do not pertain to you, because they were written chiefly for your benefit."[46] In addition to timeless moral lessons, Protestant exegetes believed that the Old and New Testaments contained various types, figures, symbols, and allegories that pointed to Christ, the church, and the last things. In a postil on 1 Corinthians 13, Luther indicated that Paul's statement in verse 2—"If I . . . understand all mysteries"—referred to the discernment of the "hidden, secret meaning beneath the superficial meaning of the narrative."[47] And what was this secret meaning? For Luther, the spiritual or mystical meaning of Scripture was just this: Jesus Christ and his gospel. Thus, "if you would interpret well and confidently, set Christ before you, for he is the man to whom all [of Scripture] applies, every bit of it."[48]

Reformation-era commentators on 1 Corinthians navigated the straits between literal and spiritual exegesis in various ways. Some interpreters such as Cajetan, Bucer, Calvin, Beza, and Diodati employed a more restrained hermeneutic that prioritized grammar, philology, and theological analysis, indulging in spiritual exegesis only sparingly. With good reason, the title of Cajetan's commentary included the words "interpreted according to the literal sense."[49] Other interpreters such as Colet, Lefèvre d'Étaples, Luther, Zwingli, Musculus, and Trapp displayed greater freedom in drawing from Scripture spiritual and mystical meanings that elucidated christological, moral, and eschatological themes. Thus, for example, in treating Paul's typological treatment of Israel's exodus in 1 Corinthians 10:1-6, Lefèvre d'Étaples explained its christological significance in this manner:

> The Jews are a figure of the people of Christ; the clouds a figure of the Holy Spirit; the sea a figure of baptism; Moses a figure of Christ as law-giver; manna a figure of the body of Christ as heavenly bread and life-giving food; water flowing from the rock a figure of the blood of Christ as life-giving drink; the rock a figure of Christ, pierced on the cross; the desert a figure of the world; the Promised Land a figure of the heavenly kingdom; the serpents a figure of demons; the destroyer a figure of the righteousness of God; the various punishments a figure of the different eternal penalties.[50]

In a similar fashion, Luther concluded that Paul's statement that he was "untimely born" in 1 Corinthians 15:8 referred to the fact that his spiritual mother—namely, the Jewish synagogue or Judaism—had given birth to him prematurely, unbaptized, and that as a "dead child" he had "persecuted Christ and his Christendom."[51] Yet another example of this penchant for spiritual exegesis is found in Trapp's treatment of 1 Corinthians 11:8, where he expands on a

[46]Zwingli, *Annotatiunculae . . . ex ore Zvinglij* (Zurich: Christoph Froschauer, 1528), 76. For more on Zwingli's exegetical approach, see Stephens, *Zwingli*, 40-42.

[47]Church Postil: Epistle for Quadragesima Sunday, WA 17,2:163. Johann Spangenberg interpreted this verse in a similar fashion. See his *Postilla Teütsch: Für die iungen Christen Knaben und Meidlin in Fragstuck verfasset Von dem fürnembsten Festen durch das gantze Jar* (Augsburg: Valentin Othmar, 1547), 4:128v.

[48]Luther, "Preface to the Old Testament," LW 35:247.

[49]Cardinal Cajetan, *Epistolae Paul et Aliorum Apostolorum. Ad graecam veritatem castigate, & per reverendissimum dominum Thomam de vio, Caietanum, Cardinalem sancti Xisti, iuxta sensum literalem enarratae. Recens in lucem editae* (Paris: Jean Petit, 1540).

[50]Jacques Lefèvre d'Étaples, *Commentariorum in Epistolas Beati Pauli . . . Liber Secundus* (Cologne: Eucharii, 1531), 115v-116r.

[51]LW 28:83.

traditional motif explaining why Eve was drawn from Adam's rib: "Woman was made from [Adam's] bone, but of one bone. . . . It was a bone from his side, not his head (she is not to be his mistress); nor his foot (she is not to be his handmaid); but his side, to show that she is a companion to her husband. It was a bone from under the arm, to remind the man to protect and defend the woman. It was a bone not far from his heart, to remind the man to love and cherish the woman."[52]

All of these Reformation-era commentators were in agreement, however, that the spiritual sense of the text must in some way be governed by the letter, lest Scripture become (as Bucer put it) little more than a wax nose that could be tweaked this way and that.[53] Protestant exegetes agreed that allegorical or spiritual readings of Scripture were not to be used to establish points of doctrine; their value lay in elucidating or illustrating Christian truth. So too, Luther and his colleagues insisted that all interpretation—literal and spiritual—must always accord with the analogy of faith (*analogia fidei*), that is, the broader message of Scripture and Christian teaching. In his exegesis of 1 Corinthians 9:9 ("You shall not muzzle an ox") William Perkins summarized these principles as follows: "But [allegories] are to be used with these caveats: let them be used sparingly and soberly; let them not be farfetched, but fitting to the matter in hand; they must be quickly dispatched; they are to be used for the instruction of the life and not to prove any point of faith."[54] On the other hand, mystical or spiritual readings were recognized as especially appropriate when the literal meaning of the biblical text conflicted with sound doctrine and morality or produced readings that were false or absurd.[55] Musculus employed this criterion negatively when he argued that Paul's statement that he "fought with beasts in Ephesus" (1 Cor 15:32) must be taken literally, rather than figuratively, since "metaphorical interpretations ought not to be rashly foisted on the plain message of a passage unless one is forced to do so by absurdity, by impossibility or by the clear error of the plain meaning."[56] In summary, these hermeneutical principles demonstrate that while Protestant interpreters remained committed to the literal sense of sacred Scripture, they also recognized that philology and grammatical analysis alone could not capture the rich christological, doctrinal, moral, and eschatological message that the Holy Spirit wished to communicate to his church through it. Though they may have vilified the medieval *quadriga* and allegorical exegesis, they never entirely abandoned it.

Exegesis and the Christian tradition. Early modern scholars who commented on 1 Corinthians were indebted to the exegetical tradition of the early Christian church. The Protestant reformers looked to patristic sources to achieve two strategic purposes: to understand better the biblical text and to demonstrate that Protestant interpretation was faithful to Scripture and in

[52]John Trapp, *A Commentary or Exposition upon all the Books of the New Testament* (London: Ekins, 1656), 686.

[53]Wright, "Martin Bucer," 250.

[54]William Perkins, *The Art of Prophesying*, in *The Work of William Perkins*, ed. Ian Breward (Appleford, UK: Sutton Courtenay Press, 1970), 84.

[55]This principle was explicitly set forth in Matthias Flacius Illyricus's book *Clavis Scripturae S. seu de Sermone Sacrarum Literarum* (Basel: Ioannes Oporinus, 1567). See Pelikan, *Reformation of the Bible*, 35.

[56]Wolfgang Musculus, *In Ambas Apostoli Pauli ad Corinthios Epistolas Commentarii* (Basel: Johannes Herwagen, 1566), 672-73.

line with the orthodox teaching of the Christian tradition. [57] Reformation commentators frequently cited with approval early Christian authors such as Tertullian (died c. 230), Athanasius (d. 373), Augustine (354–430), John Chrysostom (d. 407), Ambrosiaster (fl. 366–384), and Theophylact[58]—with Chrysostom and Augustine being the most popular. Protestant exegetes praised the Greek bishop Chrysostom for his clear and faithful exposition of the text of Scripture. As Calvin noted, it was Chrysostom's "supreme concern never to turn aside even to the slightest degree from the genuine, simple sense of Scripture and to allow himself no liberties by twisting the plain meaning of the words."[59] Augustine too was held up as a model to be emulated—not so much for his method of interpretation as for his forceful articulation of the doctrines of sin and grace. Accordingly, Lutheran exegetes Chytraeus and Hesshus listed Augustine in the ranks of Luther and the apostle Paul as Christian leaders who possessed unique endowments of spiritual wisdom and Christian knowledge.[60] At the same time, a number of Protestant commentators did not hesitate to criticize what they saw as Augustine's overly subtle exegesis and his theological errors, especially his defense of infant Communion and his disparaging words regarding sexual intercourse within marriage.[61]

Reformation commentators regularly looked to early Christian authors for help when they encountered Scripture's most difficult passages. Invariably, they did their exegetical work in conversation with the church's interpretive tradition. An illustration of this is seen in the reformers' treatment of one of the most perplexing passages in Paul's epistles, namely, the reference to "being baptized on behalf of the dead" in 1 Corinthians 15:29. A number of thorny problems present themselves: What is meant by the words "baptized" (*baptizontai*) and "dead" (*nekrōn*)? How should one translate the Greek preposition *hyper* ("on behalf of")? And, does Paul approve of these baptisms or not? In their commentaries, the reformers considered a variety of interpretations proposed by traditional exegetes: The heretic Marcion (died c. 160) appealed to this verse to justify the practice of baptizing the corpses of his dead followers. Tertullian and Ambrose argued that this verse alluded to the practice of vicarious baptisms, performed by living believers for the dead. Cyprian (d. 258) suggested that the verse spoke of the practice of deferring baptism until death was imminent. Chrysostom and Theophylact concluded that the verse pointed to the symbol of baptism itself, namely, that believers are baptized into death, even as they await

[57]Richard Muller and John Thompson are certainly correct to argue that early Protestant biblical interpretation was never "a conversation between a lonely exegete and a hermetically sealed text" (Muller and Thompson, "The Significance of Precritical Exegesis: Retrospect and Prospect," in Muller and Thompson, *Biblical Interpretation in the Era of the Reformation*, 342).

[58]Theophylact was the eleventh-century bishop of Ochryda, Bulgaria, who wrote influential commentaries (largely dependent on John Chrysostom) on the Gospels, the book of Acts, the Pauline epistles, and the Minor Prophets. Reformation commentators mistook him for an early church father.

[59]Preface to Chrysostom's Homilies, CO 9:835. See John McIndoe, "John Calvin: Preface to the Homilies of Chrysostom," *Hartford Quarterly* 5 (1965): 23.

[60]See David Chytraeus, *Dispositio epistolarum, quae diebus dominicis et aliis in ecclesia usitate populo proponi solent* (Wittenberg: Johannes Crato, 1563), 382-83; Tilemann Hesshus, *Explicatio Prioris Epistolae ad Corinthios & proposita piae iuuentuti in Academia Ienensi* (Jena: Ernst von Gera, 1573), 11v.

[61]See Calvin, CO 9:835; Bullinger, *The Decades of Henry Bullinger*, ed. Thomas Harding (Grand Rapids: Reformation Heritage Books, 2004), 3:398; Peter Martyr Vermigli, *In Selectissimam Priorem ad Corinthios Epistolam . . . Commentarii* (Zurich: Christoph Froshouer, 1551), 152v.

the future resurrection. Reformation commentators rehearsed, assessed, and critiqued these various interpretive options, and sometimes proposed new ones of their own. Calvin and Donne followed Cyprian's explanation that the "dead" were those who were facing imminent death.[62] Zwingli agreed with Tertullian that this passage was an allusion to vicarious baptisms of Christians on behalf of deceased believers. Luther and Melanchthon departed from these traditional interpretations, arguing instead that Paul was speaking of an early (undocumented) Christian custom in which believers were baptized in cemeteries among the graves of the dead, as a vivid testimony of the future resurrection.[63] Bullinger argued that the passage referred to an ancient pagan ritual in which corpses were washed or sprinkled before internment.[64] The editors of the *English Annotations* concluded that Paul was employing the word *baptism* as a metaphor for persecution; hence, the hope of the resurrection was demonstrated by believers suffering on behalf of Christ and the martyrs.[65] Hesshus, after reviewing in detail the traditional interpretations of this verse, concluded with agnosticism—and then launched into an attack on the Catholic practice of sprinkling holy water on graves.[66] Although it is not always clear whether the reformers had direct or indirect access to patristic commentaries, their exegetical work nevertheless took seriously the Christian tradition and engaged in a lively conversation with it.

The Lord's Supper. It is not surprising that Reformation debates over the meaning and practice of the Eucharist found clear expression in commentaries on 1 Corinthians. Paul's treatment of the Lord's Supper in 1 Corinthians 10:3-4, 16-22; and 11:17-34 served as spiritual instruction—and apologetic ammunition—for early modern exegetes who sought to explain the wonder and mystery of believers' participation with Christ in this sacred meal. As this present volume demonstrates, pre-Tridentine Catholic, Lutheran, Reformed, and Anabaptist exegetes contested nearly every square inch of this biblical terrain, exploring central questions regarding the nature and efficacy of Holy Communion: In what sense does the Jewish Passover find fulfillment in the Christian Eucharist (1 Cor 10:3-4)? What does Paul mean when he describes the Lord's Supper as "participation" (*koinōnia*) in the body and blood of Christ (1 Cor 10:16)? How should one interpret Jesus' words of consecration in 1 Corinthians 11:24—"This is my body which is for you. Do this in remembrance of me"? What exactly does Paul mean when he calls the Corinthians to self-examination and warns them against partaking of the supper in an unworthy manner (1 Cor 11:27)? In their interpretation of these passages, Protestant commentators sharply criticized Catholic eucharistic theology of their day. Luther, Zwingli, Calvin, and their followers rejected the Catholic teaching that the sacrament of the Eucharist was a bloodless sacrifice or a re-presentation of Christ for sinners, since Scripture taught that "Christ died once for all" on the cross for sinners (Heb 7:27). They also excoriated Catholic canon law for forbidding the cup to

[62]CNTC 9:329-30; John Donne, *The Sermons of John Donne*, ed. George Potter and Evelyn Simpson (Berkeley: University of California Press, 1953–1962), 7:206-9.
[63]LW 28:149-51.
[64]Heinrich Bullinger, *In Priorem ad Corinthios Epistolam Commentarius* (Zurich: Christoph Froschauer, 1549), 246-47.
[65]John Downame, ed., *The English Annotations*, 2nd ed. (London: John Legatt, 1651), EE4v-EE5r.
[66]Hesshus, *Explicatio Prioris Epistolae ad Corinthios*, 668.

the laity in the Eucharist. And also they disavowed the Catholic teaching that sacraments were efficacious by virtue of their performance alone, as long as no obstacle was present (*ex opere operato*); rather, the Protestants insisted, it was by faith that Christians received the benefits presented in the holy sacraments.

The most contentious issue, of course, was how to interpret Jesus' words of consecration recorded in 1 Corinthians 11:24, *Hoc est corpus meum*. The Fourth Lateran Council in 1215 had established as Catholic dogma the teaching of transubstantiation, that when the priest consecrates the bread and wine, the elements are changed substantially into the very body and blood of Jesus Christ.[67] Though Protestant exegetes rejected the doctrine of transubstantiation, seeing it as the bastard child of Aristotle's philosophy rather than the offspring of apostolic teaching, they nevertheless disagreed sharply among themselves as to the nature of Christ's presence in the sacramental meal. Luther rejected the Catholic teaching of transubstantiation for the first time in 1520 and proposed instead Christ's corporeal presence in the sacramental elements: "For my part, if I cannot fathom how the bread is the body of Christ, yet I will take my reason captive to the obedience of Christ (2 Cor 10:5) and, clinging simply to his words, firmly believe not only that the body of Christ is in the bread, but that the bread is the body of Christ."[68] This conclusion was later enshrined in Lutheran doctrinal standards such as the Augsburg Confession (1530) and the *Book of Concord* (1580). By the mid-1520s, however, a number of interpreters began to propose alternative, more spiritual readings of this passage. In 1524, Karlstadt parted company from his former colleague Luther by denying the bodily presence of Christ in the sacrament; he argued instead that the supper was a recollection or a remembrance of Christ's death.[69] The following year, Zwingli in Zurich published Cornelis Hoen's "Most Christian Letter," which argued that the word "is" (*est*) in the phrase "This is my body" should be understood as a figurative expression or trope that meant "signifies."[70] Zwingli thereafter defended and promoted this symbolic view in treatises aimed against Luther and his followers. For Zwingli, the Lord's Supper was a rite whereby believers commemorated and celebrated Christ's sacrificial death; they did not actually feed on Christ's body, however, for Christ's ascended body was in heaven, not on earth, although Christ was spiritually present among the body of believers.[71] A more strictly memorialist view was espoused by Anabaptist leaders such as Balthasar Hubmaier, Michael Sattler, and Menno Simons.

Following the disastrous conclusion of the Marburg Colloquy in 1529, Protestant leaders in Germany and Switzerland attempted to find a mediating position between Luther's doctrine of corporeal presence and Zwingli's symbolic view. At the Wittenberg Concord in 1536, for example,

[67]See Norman P. Tanner, ed., *Decrees of the Ecumenical Councils* (Washington, DC: Georgetown University Press, 1990), 1:230.

[68]LW 36:34.

[69]See Andreas Bodenstein von Karlstadt, "Proving from Holy Scripture That Christ Is in the Sacrament," in *The Eucharistic Pamphlets of Andreas Bodenstein von Karlstadt*, ed. Amy Nelson Burnett (Kirksville, MO: Truman State University Press, 2011), 137-38. In her book *Karlstadt and the Origins of the Eucharistic Controversy* (New York: Oxford University Press, 2011), Burnett demonstrates that Karlstadt's eucharistic theology was influenced in part by the writing of Cornelis Hoen.

[70]See Heiko A. Oberman, *Forerunners of the Reformation* (New York: Holt, Rinehart and Winston, 1966), 252-53.

[71]Stephens, *The Theology of Huldrych Zwingli*, 94-110. See also LCC 24: 230, 254, 257-58.

Melanchthon and Bucer reached a consensus that the body and blood of Christ are truly and substantially present, offered and received *with* (rather than *in*) the sacramental bread and wine.[72] A similar approach was taken by Calvin, who defended what has been called Christ's real spiritual presence in the Eucharist. In Calvin's view, the Lord's Supper is more than a memorial service: the symbols of bread and wine communicate to believers that which they signify, namely, the very substance of Christ's body. However, since Christ has ascended and his body is now located in heaven (not on earth), it is there that believers feed on the life-giving flesh of Christ and are united with him through the agency of the Holy Spirit.[73] In the end, efforts like these to find middle ground between Luther and Zwingli's doctrine of the Lord's Supper failed to heal the breach between Protestant churches. Sixteenth- and early seventeenth-century commentaries on 1 Corinthians illustrate the fact that the eucharistic controversy continued to produce its toxic fallout well after Luther and Zwingli were gone from the scene.

Marriage and family life. Reformation-era commentators discovered a gold mine of theological insight and practical wisdom regarding singleness, marriage, divorce, and family life in Paul's first letter to the Corinthians. Here the divide between pre-Tridentine Catholic and Protestant interpretation was especially pronounced. While affirming marriage as an inviolable sacrament of the church, Catholic biblical scholars taught that human sexuality and marriage were obstacles to Christian spirituality and inferior to a celibate life devoted to Christian service and prayer. In his exegesis of 1 Corinthians 7:1, Cajetan bluntly stated, "Marriage is a hindrance to the spiritual life."[74] Similarly, Lefèvre d'Étaples concluded that celibate priests, monks, and nuns were "follow[ing] the example of virginity of the Son of God who wished to be born of a virgin and honored virginity above marriage."[75] Protestant exegetes like Luther, Zwingli, and Calvin challenged this traditional viewpoint at every turn. They denied that the celibate life was a superior human estate or worthy of God's special merit—after all, had not most of the first apostles been married men? (The reformers disagreed with one another, however, whether Paul had ever been married.[76]) The reformers insisted that it was God's intention and calling for most men and women to marry, bear children, and raise a family. "Marriage does not hinder godliness," Hesshus observed; "rather, it is the school of the Holy Spirit."[77] In their comments on 1 Corinthians 7 Protestant authors regularly enumerated the primary purposes for marriage: it is a remedy for fornication; it allows for the propagation and nurture of children; and, some believed, it provides companionship and mutual support to husbands and wives. According to Farel, God intended for husbands and wives to exercise this "holy institution for his honor and glory, and for the edification of [their] neighbor."[78]

[72]Martin Greschat, *Martin Bucer: A Reformer and His Times*, trans. Stephen E. Buckwalter (Louisville, KY: Westminster John Knox, 2004), 136-38; See also *OER* 4:286-87.

[73]See Calvin's comments on 1 Cor 11:24 and *Institutes* 4.17.1-50; see also, Brian Gerrish, *Grace and Gratitude: The Eucharistic Theology of John Calvin* (Minneapolis: Fortress, 1993), 122.

[74]Cardinal Cajetan, *In Sacrae Scripturae expositionem reperiuntur* (Lyons: Jean & Pierre Prost, 1639), 5:105.

[75]Lefèvre d'Étaples, *Commentariorum in Epistolas Beati Pauli . . . Liber Secundus*, 111r. At the same time, Lefèvre d'Étaples acknowledged that the estates of virginity, marriage, and widowhood were all "good."

[76]See comments on 1 Cor 9:4-5.

[77]Hesshus, *Explicatio Prioris Epistolae ad Corinthios*, 115r-v.

[78]Guillaume Farel, "Summary and Brief Exposition," in *Early French Reform: The Theology and Spirituality of Guillaume Farel*, ed.

Protestant exegetes derived a variety of practical conclusions from their understanding of Paul's teaching on marriage. They defended clerical marriage and encouraged priests, monks, and nuns to renounce their vows of celibacy and seek married life. They warned parents not to prevent their adult daughters from seeking husbands. They also recognized the rights of widows and widowers to pursue remarriage if they should choose. At the same time, even as they praised Christian marriage as a holy and honorable estate, Protestant commentators believed that 1 Corinthians 7:10-16 provided biblical warrant for divorce—a practice strictly forbidden in Catholic canon law. Though there were differences of opinion, most Protestant exegetes believed that Scripture allowed for the dissolution of marriage in cases of adultery, abandonment, or (as Luther suggested) hatred. In the final analysis, however, singleness and marriage belonged to the category of Christian freedom and both should be considered sacred vocations through which men and women express their faith in Christ. Thus, as Luther noted, "St. Paul considers no single estate blessed except this one—the estate of being a Christian; the others are free in the sense that they cannot in themselves further our salvation or damnation."[79]

Pastoral formation and spiritual direction. Readers of this present volume may well be surprised how frequently the commentators address matters related to pastoral life and practice. There are good reasons for this. Nearly all of the scholars who commented on 1 Corinthians were also parish ministers with extensive pastoral experience. Moreover, a significant number of Protestant commentaries on 1 Corinthians had their genesis in the lecture hall, as the reformers instructed future generations of ministers and civil servants on Paul's message and its implications for church and society. As a result, many commentaries functioned as virtual ministerial handbooks, communicating detailed advice to pastoral candidates on such topics as the minister's personal character, pastoral duties, the qualities of good preaching, the nature of pastoral care and church discipline, and the inevitable challenges encountered by faithful ministers.[80] These precious pastoral gems appear throughout the reformers' comments on 1 Corinthians, but especially in passages where Paul treated topics such as human eloquence and wisdom (1 Cor 1:18–2:16), Christian leadership (1 Cor 3:1–4:21), church discipline (1 Cor 5:9-13), vocation (1 Cor 7:17-24), the apostles' authority (1 Cor 9:1-27), the sacraments (1 Cor 10:14-22; 11:17-34), spiritual gifts (1 Cor 12:1-31), and prophecy (1 Cor 14:1-40). Thus, for example, in his comments on 1 Corinthians 9:26 ("So I do not run aimlessly"), Chytraeus defined the role of a pastor this way: "The ends of the ministry of the gospel are to teach rightly the true doctrine of the gospel, to administer the sacraments and to perform the other parts of their office faithfully for the glory of God and that many people might be saved."[81]

Though Reformation commentators praised pastoral ministry as a high and holy calling, they nevertheless recognized it to be a difficult and dangerous vocation. Tilling the hard soil of men and women's souls was strenuous work and required fortitude and courage. Faithful pastors

Jason Zuidema and Theodore Van Raalte (Burlington, VT: Ashgate, 2011), 170.

[79]LW 28:40.

[80]This is particularly evident in Wolfgang Musculus's commentaries. See Manetsch, "(Re)constructing the Pastoral Office," 253-66.

[81]Chytraeus, *Dispositio epistolarum*, 93.

would invariably be ignored, resented, even hated. Zwingli highlighted this fact in his comments on 1 Corinthians 2:4 ("my message [was] . . . in demonstration of the Spirit and of power"): "Here we learn that those who preach the gospel of Christ crucified without fear and trials do not at all aim at the target—as if it were possible to preach the cross without the cross."[82] Clearly Reformation commentaries on 1 Corinthians served as an important resource for shaping pastoral identity and guiding Protestant ministers in their work of preaching and pastoral care.

At the same time Reformation interpreters had a broader readership in view, for their ultimate goal was to provide biblical instruction, consolation, and warnings to the men and women who belonged to their churches. Thus Reformation commentaries on 1 Corinthians pulsate with practical advice and encouragement for ordinary Christians traveling their earthly pilgrimages. Commentators reflected on the nature of confession and Christian assurance; they analyzed the pathology of spiritual blindness and the joys of life in the Spirit; they warned against the dangers of wealth and pride, while extolling the virtues of generosity and humility; they offered sage advice for citizens, husbands, wives, parents, and children; they described God's purposes in suffering and the glorious hope of heaven. The theme of Christian hope is particularly prominent in this literature, running as a leitmotif throughout and achieving a final, triumphant crescendo in Paul's treatment of the future resurrection of the saints in 1 Corinthians 15. Hesshus's commentary on 1 Corinthians 15:22 is typical in the hope, joy, and supreme confidence it conveys; it serves as a most appropriate conclusion to the introduction of this volume.

At that time, God will no longer reign in the church through the ministry of the gospel and sacraments, but his divinity will impart heavenly blessings directly; he will fill us with his penetrating light; he will adorn us with complete righteousness; he will drench us with pure joy; he will raise us up to eternal life. . . . Seeing God will be our highest goodness, our greatest happiness, our eternal joy. . . . "O Lord Jesus, when we will have happily finished the race that you ordained for us, with the help of your Spirit, guide us to this highest and singular happiness and eternal joy, so that the fruit of your death might also shine forth in us, and that we might love you forever, Eternal Father, Son, and Holy Spirit, and never grow weary of worshiping you. Amen."[83]

Scott M. Manetsch

[82]Zwingli, *Annotatiunculae . . . ex ore Zvinglij*, 18-19.
[83]Hesshus, *Explicatio Prioris Epistolae ad Corinthios*, 342v-343r.

COMMENTARY ON 1 CORINTHIANS

Overview: As a general rule, Reformation commentators begin their treatment of this epistle by describing the location and dismal moral condition of the ancient city of Corinth, and summarizing the various theological and practical issues that Paul addresses throughout the letter. Unlike Paul's letter to the Romans, the letter of 1 Corinthians does not contain a systematic statement of Christian doctrine; rather, as with familiar correspondence, it addresses in turn a variety of practical issues affecting the Corinthian church, including division among believers, lawsuits, principles for marriage, church discipline, dietary regulations, public worship, and spiritual gifts. In the midst of these instructions, Paul forcefully reminds the Corinthians not to ignore the glorious gospel of grace, achieved through the death and resurrection of Jesus Christ. Several Reformation commentators insist that the message of 1 Corinthians holds particular relevance for their contemporary audience: the vices of wealth, luxury, and pride that once infected the Corinthian church continue to threaten contemporary society and undermine the gospel of grace, producing the same toxic results in self-promotion, ambition, and division among Christians. Yet, despite all of these problems, the apostle Paul still addresses the assembly of Christians in Corinth as a "church," which serves as an important reminder that, in the present age, the church of Jesus Christ will never be perfect. Rather, as Calvin argues, a true church is present where the gospel is faithfully proclaimed, the sacraments properly celebrated, and Jesus Christ worshiped.

Prolegomena: Introduction to 1 Corinthians

An Exhortation to Unity in Faith and Love. Martin Luther: In this epistle St. Paul exhorts the Corinthians to be one in faith and love, and to see to it that they learn the chief thing, namely, that Christ is our salvation, the thing over which all reason and wisdom stumbles. . . .

[Paul] had taught his Corinthians Christian faith and freedom from the law. But then the mad saints came along, and the immature know-it-alls. They broke up the unity of the doctrine and caused division among the believers. One claimed to belong to Paul, the other to Apollos; one to Peter, the other to Christ. One wanted circumcision, the other not; one wanted marriage, the other not; one wanted to eat meat sacrificed to idols, the other not. Some wanted to be outwardly free; some of the women wanted to go with uncovered hair, and so on. They went so far that one man abused his liberty and married his father's wife, some did not believe in the resurrection of the dead, and some thought lightly of the sacrament. In short, things got so wild and disorderly that everyone wanted to be the expert and do the teaching and make what he pleased of the gospel, the sacrament, and faith. Meanwhile they let the main thing drop—namely, that Christ is our salvation, righteousness, and redemption—as if they had long since outgrown it. This truth can never remain intact when people begin to imagine they are wise and know it all.

That is exactly what is now happening to us. Now that we, by God's grace, have opened the gospel to the Germans, everyone claims that he is the top expert and alone has the Holy Spirit—as if the gospel had been preached in order that in it we should show our cleverness and reason, and strive for a reputation. These Corinthians may well be an example for our people in these days, who also certainly need an epistle of this kind. But this is the way things have to go with the gospel; mad saints and immature know-it-alls have to create disturbances and offenses, so that those who are "tested," as St. Paul also says here, may be revealed. Preface to the First Epistle of Saint Paul to the Corinthians.[1]

Differences Between Paul's Letters to the Romans and Corinthians. Philipp Melanchthon: The epistle to the Romans is didactic, teaching what the gospel is and where justification comes from. It is like a summation of the whole of Scripture and consists wholly of one topic: from where does justification come? The topics of this epistle to the Corinthians are various; some of them deal with laws, others with the gospel. Therefore it cannot be understood as a continuous argument on one common subject. Rather several things are gathered within it, as usually happens in familiar correspondence. The epistle to the Romans is a coherent argument. Here in 1 Corinthians there is no argument, but different things are brought up consecutively. Annotations on 1 Corinthians.[2]

Corinth Was a Wicked City. Johann Spangenberg: Corinth is the capital of the district of Achaia. It has two ports—one toward Asia, the other toward Italy—and so it was a powerful trading center. People from every part of the world, traders and merchants, gathered there. Now usually wherever there is great wealth there is also great splendor, haughtiness, and everything in abundance. Also where many people from different lands and nations come together, numerous strange sins, iniquities, and vices are found. And so too was the case here in Corinth. For we read that in Corinth there was a temple of the goddess Venus, in which more than a thousand women—fashioned in the image of Venus—lived in open sin. Satan led the Corinthians into such blindness that they considered rampant shame a service to God. Thus the city of Corinth was a groundswell of every sin, iniquity, and vice. Brief Exegesis of Acts 18:1.[3]

Moral Corruption Was Rife in Corinth. Desiderius Erasmus: So then, although the Corinthians had long since received instruction in the gospel through the preaching of Paul, nevertheless their natural qualities and some of the vestiges of their former life still remained so that there was danger that they might be separated from the purity of Christ, with philosophers alluring them to despise the preaching of the cross as insignificant and naive, and with false apostles alluring them to embrace Judaism. For it is a difficult thing to be transformed from the state in which you were born and accustomed to live for a long time, into a different person. Preface to Paraphrases on 1 Corinthians.[4]

Paul's Purpose for Writing This Epistle. David Dickson: Corinth is a famous market town of Achaia, in the narrow straights of the Peloponnese, situated between the Aegean and Ionian Seas. The apostle Paul taught in this city a year and a half, where he founded a church with great difficulty. Satan endeavored in many ways to rend, infect, and corrupt this church. Recognizing the crafty plans of Satan, the apostle wrote this epistle to the Corinthians so that he might produce a seasonable remedy to these great evils. Exposition of 1 Corinthians.[5]

The Corinthians Were the Seal of Paul's Apostleship. John Calvin: From its inception, the Corinthian church was justly renowned, both on account of its great size and the outstanding

[1]LW 35:380-81; citing 1 Cor 3:13.
[2]Melanchthon, *Annotationes in Epistolam priorem ad Corinthios*, 28.
[3]Spangenberg, *Der Apostel Geschichte*, 158v-159r.
[4]Erasmus, *Paraphrases*, 193.
[5]Dickson, *Exposition of St. Paul's Epistles*, 39*.

gifts with which they had been endowed, as well as by the gross and shameful vices with which it struggled. Moreover, Luke demonstrates how much effort and how many dangers and difficulties Paul endured to win them to Christ. It is well known how populated of a city Corinth was, how wealthy it was on account of its fame as a trading center, and how addicted it was to pleasures. Indeed, the old proverb "It is not granted to everybody to go to Corinth" testifies to how expensive and full of debauchery it was. When Paul enters that city, what success, I ask you, can he have hoped for? He is a little, unknown man, lacking in eloquence or brilliance, exhibiting neither wealth nor power. The fact that his confidence and zeal for proclaiming the gospel were not swallowed up by that huge abyss shows that he was equipped with the extraordinary power of the Spirit of God, and at the same time that God was working through his effort in a heavenly—rather than human—fashion. Accordingly, it is not for nothing that Paul boasts that the Corinthians are the "seal of his apostleship." Commentary on Acts 18:1.[6]

Paul Needed to Battle Factionalism in Corinth. Giovanni Diodati: After St. Paul had founded the church of Corinth (as reported by St. Luke in Acts 18), the devil very quickly sowed discord in it by several disorders, divisions, scandals, and corruptions, in doctrine as well as in church government, in private morality as well as in communal life. This is what prompted the apostle in his zeal and fatherly concern to bring prompt remedy to it by this epistle. In the beginning of this letter, he very sharply censures the Corinthians for their factions, with some people supporting one of the pastors and other people supporting another. This factionalism resulted from the Corinthians' diverse evaluation of the knowledge and seasoned eloquence of each of the pastors, with whom they were dazzled, with a vain admiration. Paul goes on to attack such vain affection and ambition in the preachers as the cause of the depravity and division of the church, the debasement of the simple and effectual truth of the gospel, the weakening of the power of the Holy Spirit (who is the only author of faith), and the contempt of Paul's holy example. And especially, the Corinthians' pursuit of their own honor and the applause of the world led to the degradation of the glory of God. And because those proud, worldly preachers had heaped scorn on the apostle's manner of preaching as low and vulgar, Paul wishes the Corinthians to examine their own weaknesses, which had prevented him from imparting more sublime doctrine to them. Preface to Annotations on 1 Corinthians.[7]

The Authority of Scripture. Peter Martyr Vermigli: Before I begin to explain the meaning of this letter it is appropriate to begin by saying a few things about the sacred writings, by which we may be encouraged to study them and helped somewhat in pursuing this aim. . . .

In the first place, speaking about the dignity and usefulness of holy Scripture, I would provide this definition of it, although it is rather dull and unimaginative (for it is easy to define something exactly and perfectly that is not divine). Here it is, therefore: *a certain expression of the wisdom of God, inspired by the Holy Spirit, and thereafter sealed in writings by faithful people as a remembrance.* Peter attests to this same incitement for our salvation and renewal inspired by the Holy Spirit, in chapter one of his second epistle, saying: "For, in times past, prophecy was not produced by the will of men, but being moved by the Holy Spirit, holy men spoke from God." The greatest honor is ascribed to it because Christ as well as his apostles, the holy fathers, and pure councils have made use of its testimony in proving those things that were determined. Nor should any of those traditions be judged necessary for salvation that are not included there firmly and solidly. . . .

[6]CO 48:423-24 (cf. CTS 37:179-80); citing Acts 18; 1 Cor 9:2. The proverb "It is not granted to everybody to go to Corinth" is attributed to Horace (Epistle 17; LCL 194:362-63).

[7]Diodati, *Pious Annotations*, Ll*.

Therefore the first principle according to which all theological truths are determined ought to be this: "The Lord has spoken" [*Dominus dixit*]. Moreover, this clarity is not to be sought from the light of human understanding or our reason, but from the light of faith, which should be most persuasive to us, and which is contained in the sacred writings. Preface to Commentary on 1 Corinthians.[8]

Satan's Strategy Against the Corinthian Church. John Calvin: Paul, after teaching in Corinth for a year and a half (as Luke mentions in Acts 18), was forced at length by the wickedness of the Jews to sail from there into Syria. During Paul's absence false apostles had crept in, not to disturb the church openly with wicked doctrines (in my judgment), nor intentionally to undermine sound doctrine. But, priding themselves in the splendor and magnificence of their oratory, or rather, being puffed up with their empty and pompous speech, they held in contempt Paul's simplicity, and even the gospel itself. Then, because of their ambition, they contributed to the church being split into various factions. And last of all, they considered everything unimportant, provided only they were highly esteemed, and attempted to promote their own reputation, rather than Christ's kingdom and the people's welfare.

Again, since those vices were popular at Corinth with which mercantile cities are usually infested—luxury, arrogance, vanity, pleasures, insatiable covetousness, and ambition—these vices had penetrated into the church itself so that discipline had greatly deteriorated. In fact, purity of doctrine had already begun to collapse, so that the chief article of religion—the resurrection of the dead—was called into question. Nevertheless, amid so much corruption of every sort, the Corinthians were pleased with themselves, as though all their affairs were in the best possible condition. These are Satan's usual tricks: if he cannot obstruct the path of doctrine, he creeps forward secretly to attack it; if he cannot suppress it by manifest lies, so as to prevent it from coming into the open, he digs secret pits to destroy it. Finally, if he cannot alienate people's minds from it all at once, he causes them to depart from it gradually. Preface to Commentary on 1 Corinthians.[9]

[8]Vermigli, *In Selectissimam Priorem ad Corinthios Epistolam . . . Commentarii*, 1r-v; citing 2 Pet 1:21.

[9]CO 49:297-98 (cf. CTS 39:37-38).

1:1-3 PAUL GREETS THE CORINTHIANS

Paul, called by the will of God to be an apostle of Christ Jesus, and our brother Sosthenes,
[2]To the church of God that is in Corinth, to those sanctified in Christ Jesus, called to be saints together with all those who in every place call upon the name of our Lord Jesus Christ, both their Lord and ours:
[3]Grace to you and peace from God our Father and the Lord Jesus Christ.

Overview: Paul, along with Sosthenes, introduces his first letter to the Corinthian church by asserting his apostolic authority and greeting them in the Lord's grace and peace. As our Reformation commentators note, before chastising the Corinthians for the many problems that are affecting this body of believers, Paul appeals to his apostolic office and their discipleship to Christ, who is Lord over all.

Thanksgiving to Teaching. Tilemann Hesshus: Now in each chapter, Paul usually treats a single theme. Paul begins his epistle with thanksgiving in which he commends the blessing of God toward the Corinthian Church, which he has adorned and furnished with the most excellent of gifts. Paul not only congratulates the Corinthians for so many distinguished gifts of wisdom, faith, eloquence, and knowledge of God, but he also comforts them, declaring the constancy of God's goodwill toward them and that God in his kindness will confirm them in this faith. Now, Paul intentionally begins with this congratulation so as to demonstrate that he is not censuring the Corinthians because he is envious of their gifts, but rather so that he might teach, motivate, and warn them to use their gifts rightly and that these gifts might be increased and strengthened in them. Next, Paul implores the Corinthians to a sincere zeal for peace and concord so that they might avoid disagreement and schisms. And since the source and root of all divisions, schisms, and contention in the church is the pride of human nature, the admiration of one's own wisdom, eloquence, teaching, and similar sorts of gifts, Paul, in order to extract this root, condemns with a most severe judgment the darkness of the human mind and shows how no true wisdom exists in men and women without the illumination of the Holy Spirit (for the human mind is so blind that it cannot know God through its own strength). So too he shows that God is opposed to the counsel of the wise and has revealed teaching that is altogether contrary to the judgment of the wise. For God chooses for himself in the church the weak, the foolish, and the unimportant, so that he might shame whatever the world considers exalted so that there might be no reason for anyone to boast or praise themselves before God. Instead, all the boasting of wisdom, righteousness, and life should belong to our Lord Jesus Christ alone. Preface to Explication of 1 Corinthians.[1]

Calm Before Rebuke. John Calvin: Paul begins by congratulating the Corinthians, which serves as an exhortation that they should go on as they have begun, and in this way he softens them beforehand so as to make them more teachable. But immediately he proceeds to rebuke them, reminding them of the dissensions that were troubling their church. Desiring to cure this evil, he calls them to exchange arrogance for humility. He overthrows all the wisdom of the world, so that he might encourage the preaching of the cross alone. At the same time, he also humbles them individually by urging them to consider the kinds of people the Lord has adopted, for the most part, as members of his flock. Preface to Commentary on 1 Corinthians.[2]

[1]Hesshus, *Explicatio Prioris Epistolae ad Corinthios*, 2v-3r.
[2]CO 49:299-300 (cf. CTS 39:40-41).

1:1-3 *Greetings*

Paul Called to the Apostolic Office. Wolfgang Musculus: "Called to be an apostle." This is not the same thing as Paul saying "I have been named or designated an apostle," or "I am the one called an apostle." Rather he has been called to the apostolic office (as Erasmus translates it in Romans 1). For what is named or appointed by men is not strongly recommended. But Paul always emphasizes the function to which God has called him. For in this way he commonly presented the authority of his gospel teaching to show that he was not running to and fro but had been called and sent by God. It is proposed concerning the false prophets that they were running about, without a calling or a commission, and so they had not been prophesying from God. And thus, in order to persuade his readers that his doctrine is from God, Paul defends his apostolic calling against the false apostles at the very beginning of his letter. Commentary on 1 Corinthians 1:1.[3]

The Identity of Sosthenes. Jacques Lefèvre d'Étaples: We learn from the Acts of the Apostles that this Sosthenes was the chief ruler of the synagogue who, having disregarded the honor of his office, embraced the eternal kingdom of Christ and became a companion with Paul for the gospel of Christ. All the Jews of Corinth rose up against him before the tribunal of Gallio, proconsul of Achaia, on account of Christ. Commentary on 1 Corinthians 1:1.[4]

Corinthian Believers Are United in Christ. John Colet: Since, then, the divine mind of Paul is thinking of this sort of composite unity consisting of God and humanity—one Christ from a very great number of anointed—we may therefore easily understand what is meant by those forms of expression frequently found in Paul: "through Christ," "in Christ," "with Christ," "through him," "from him," "in him," "in God with Christ," "in God through Christ." For all who are in this mystical composite are in God, who, beginning his deification in humanity taken from Mary, through him as through a head, has thereafter distributed to the rest for the fashioning of the whole. And all who are in this composite and perfect man and Christ are also in God, the life-giving soul through Christ the head—for they are in that Christ who is both God and human.

And since the Corinthians were thus in Christ—as they wished themselves to be considered and professed themselves to be—Paul wisely begins by drawing attention to whatever is praiseworthy in them, and gives thanks because of the good they manifest and because they continue to hold to the foundation of the faith and of the church. He does this so as to draw them on by this gentle and touching introduction to read the rest of the letter, and cause them to hear more readily what he is going to criticize in their conduct. . . .

And so now, since by letter he must correct in the Corinthians a great many things that have gone wrong since his departure, he begins with what will be more acceptable, and makes as it were an easy approach to the other and rather bitter words he is forced to use, so that the Corinthians may willingly accept and drink down the cup of saving medicine, its rim coated with sugar. Exposition of 1 Corinthians 1.[5]

Paul Identifies Corinthian Believers as a "Church." John Calvin: It may perhaps appear strange that Paul should give the name "the church of God" to a group of people who were infested with so many vices that Satan ruled over them rather than God. It is certain that he did not mean to flatter the Corinthians, for he speaks under the direction of the Spirit of God, who is not accustomed to flatter. But in the midst of such filth, what appearance of a church is any longer evident? . . . This passage ought to be carefully

[3]Musculus, *Comm. 1 Cor.*, 1.

[4]Lefèvre d'Étaples, *Commentariorum in Epistolas Beati Pauli . . . Liber Secundus*, 102r-v; citing Acts 18:17.

[5]Colet, *Enarratio*, 75.

observed, so that we do not require the church, while in this world, to be free from every wrinkle and stain, or that we hastily take away this name "church" from every assembly that does not meet our standards. For it is a dangerous temptation to think that there is no church where perfect purity is not seen. . . .

On what basis, then, did Paul recognize a church at Corinth? It was this: that he saw among them the evangelical doctrine, baptism, the Lord's Supper—the marks by which a church ought to be determined. . . . To be sure, some faults had crept into the administration of the Supper; discipline and decency of behavior had largely collapsed. Despising the simplicity of the gospel, the Corinthians had given themselves over to pretense and pomp. And due to their ministers' ambition, they were divided into various parties. Nevertheless, because they held on to the fundamental teaching—the one God was worshiped among them and invoked in the name of Christ; they were trusting on Christ for salvation; and they had not altogether corrupted the ministry—for this reason a church remained among them. Hence, wherever the worship of God is unimpaired and the fundamental teachings remain (as I have said), there we judge without difficulty that a church exists. Commentary on 1 Corinthians 1:2.[6]

Definition of the Church. Wolfgang Musculus: Here Paul explains in a roundabout manner what he understands by the church of God. There was a Jewish synagogue in Corinth, as Acts 18 demonstrates. The Jews took pride in being the people of God and also the church of God. That is why Paul decided not to write "to the synagogue of the Jews," but instead he wrote "to the church of God that is in Corinth." In doing this, he set forth a specific definition of that Christian church, saying, "to those sanctified in Christ Jesus, called to be holy." With these words, he makes clear what the church of God is, namely, the multitude of saints called and made holy through Christ Jesus. . . . Paul makes the same proposition against the factious people because he is mindful that sanctification and the calling to holiness come through Christ. Chrysostom understood by the notion of "sanctification" the water of baptism, in which we are made holy by Christ; that is, we are set apart from the profane world into the faith and worship of God. And since this sanctification and this calling to holiness do not take place in the name of some minister or teacher or baptizer, but in the name of Christ, therefore Paul appropriately calls them "those sanctified in Christ Jesus and called to be saints" (as it is in the Greek) against the zeal of the factious people.

Now Paul beautifully commends the grace of God, because he does not simply call them holy, which God alone is capable of, but rather he calls them "sanctified" and "called to be holy," that is, called to the holiness and grace of God. For the merit of the faithful is not proclaimed here, but rather the grace of God in Christ. For the title and declaration that we are called holy or sanctified does not attest to our virtue, but to divine grace. . . .

It must be noted, therefore, that even though the Corinthian church was so wretchedly corrupt and divided, the apostle still called it the church of God, sanctified and called to be saints. In the same way, Christ said in Acts 18: "Do not be afraid, etc. since I have many people in this city." Although this church was very corrupt, nevertheless in it were still those genuine and tested believers for whom the gift of this title was appropriate. Commentary on 1 Corinthians 1:2.[7]

The Church Errs When It Loses the Word of God. Heinrich Bullinger: For as in the church of Israel the Lord reserved to himself a remnant, I mean Moses, Joshua, and undoubtedly many more . . . so there is no doubt that although many do err in the church the Lord by his mercy preserves to himself a certain number who both understand aright and by whose faith and diligence errors are destroyed and the wandering

[6]CO 49:307 (cf. CTS 39:50-52).

[7]Musculus, *Comm. 1 Cor.*, 3-4; citing Acts 18:9-10.

flock of the Lord are brought back again into the holy fold.

Therefore the church is said to err when a part of it has lost the Word of God and errs. And it does not err wholly or altogether, for certain remnants (by the grace of God) are reserved, by whom the truth can flourish again and be spread abroad again in every place. St. Paul called the churches of the Corinthians and the Galatians the holy churches of God; yet these erred greatly in doctrine, in faith, and in manners: but who doubts that among them there were many who were most sincere followers of the pure doctrine preached by St. Paul? Therefore that holy church erred insofar as it did not continue steadfastly in true doctrine, and it did not err in so far as it did not depart from the truth delivered by the apostles. Decades.[8]

All Things Are Given Through Christ. Philipp Melanchthon: Paul makes mention of both the Father and Christ so as to show not so much that Christ is God, but that all things are given through Christ. He speaks of Christ's human nature to establish and strengthen faith because we would more certainly believe what we hear through Christ as being acceptable, whose name is not as terrifying as the name of God. Annotations on 1 Corinthians 1:3.[9]

Grace and Peace. Tilemann Hesshus: Grace signifies the free favor, mercy, and compassion of God, by which he freely pardons sins without our contribution of good works, accepts us ungrateful sinners, and proclaims us righteous and heirs of eternal life. Peace signifies spiritual and physical blessings; certainly, it includes the gift of the Holy Spirit, peace of conscience, renewed righteousness and life, gladness in God, and the inheritance of eternal life. Further, it includes protection, sustenance, guidance, consolation, and every good thing that we need, both in this present life and in the life to come. Explication of 1 Corinthians 1:3.[10]

[8]LCC 24:316-17.

[9]Melanchthon, *Annotations on the First Epistle to the Corinthians*, 31.

[10]Hesshus, *Explicatio Prioris Epistolae ad Corinthios*, 10r.

1:4-9 THANKSGIVING

4I give thanks to my God always for you because of the grace of God that was given you in Christ Jesus, 5that in every way you were enriched in him in all speech and all knowledge— 6even as the testimony about Christ was confirmed among you— 7so that you are not lacking in any gift, as you wait for the revealing of our Lord Jesus Christ, 8who will sustain you to the end, guiltless in the day of our Lord Jesus Christ. 9God is faithful, by whom you were called into the fellowship of his Son, Jesus Christ our Lord.

Overview: Paul expresses gratitude for the Christians in Corinth, noting in particular that God, who has graciously endowed them with speech and knowledge and every other spiritual gift, will faithfully sustain them until the Lord's return. Reformation commentators recognize in this brief passage important themes that will reappear throughout the remainder of the letter, including the nature of grace, the inestimable value of the gospel, the substance of spiritual knowledge, the function of spiritual gifts in the church, and the glorious return of Jesus Christ. They agree that grace is found in Christ alone, and that the gospel of Jesus Christ is the heart's true treasure. Why Paul singles out the gifts of speech and knowledge, and what these gifts entail, however, elicits discussion and some disagreement. While several commentators believe that "speech and knowledge" points to speaking in tongues and miraculous words of knowledge, others suggest that Paul is referring to preaching and wise leadership, gifts essential for a healthy church. Whatever the case, the carnal behavior of Christians in Corinth proves that possessing spiritual gifts does not make a person "spiritual" or mature in Christ. For Reformation commentators, the Christian's hope is found not in the endowment of gifts but in the sure hope of Christ's second coming and God's faithfulness to sustain his people to the end. Alert to the pastoral issues at stake, the reformers insist that Scripture warrants Christians' assurance that God will protect and sustain their faith and bring them to eternal glory.

1:4-7 *The Abundant Grace of God*

Paul's Thanksgiving. John Trapp: Thus Paul begins most of his epistles. Thanks to God was always in Augustine's mouth, who had Paul's spirit. Every gracious person is a grateful person. The same Greek word signifies both "grace" and "thanks." Only those of Abraham's seed who are "as the stars of the heaven" can in their courses sing a song of praise to God. . . . Wicked people cannot say, "I give thanks to God," for they have no true notion of God; rather, they are his enemies, and therefore all their words of thanks are but as music at funerals. Commentary on 1 Corinthians 1:4.[1]

Paul Begins by Complimenting the Corinthians. David Dickson: Because Paul was about to reprove many vices among the Corinthians, here in these verses of the preface he commends what was good in them, confirming their faith in God, lest they should faint by his sharp reproofs. Throughout, he shows what opinion he had of them, and his goodwill toward them, whereby he might better achieve the outcome he desired. Exposition of 1 Corinthians 1:4.[2]

Grace Received *in* Christ Jesus. Wolfgang Musculus: Chrysostom renders the Greek *en Christō Iēsou* as "by Christ Jesus." Although this does not displease me, I am more satisfied if we read it as it is in the Greek, "in Christ Jesus." For we

[1]Trapp, *A Commentary or Exposition*, 658*.
[2]Dickson, *Exposition of St. Paul's Epistles*, 40*.

are instructed and enriched in the gifts of the grace of God not only through Christ but also in Christ, that is, when we are incorporated in him. . . . To be alive, to be human, to be healthy, to be wealthy, to be wise—all of these come from the grace of God. For the earth is full of the goodness of God. And those who obtain the grace of God of this sort ought to recognize it and give thanks for it. But the apostle is not speaking about this kind of grace in this passage. Therefore, he makes clear what he is talking about by means of an explanation when he says: "which was given to you through Christ, or in Christ." That is, "which you, who believe, have received in Christ." Although they were rich and had been endowed with worldly wisdom, nevertheless Paul mentions none of these things. Rather, he commends only those things that they had received by faith in Christ. And he does this for good reason. For what are all these remaining things compared to this grace? Commentary on 1 Corinthians 1:4.[3]

The Christian's True Treasure. Heinrich Bullinger: The majority of people think that true riches are those things produced from the earth—but they are completely wrong. In truth, riches are those heavenly things that cannot be lost or corrupted. For in Christ, who is the living bread coming down from heaven, is hidden all the treasures and wisdom and knowledge of God. Therefore, the heart's treasure is the Lord Christ, the pledge of grace, in whom the heavenly Father has given us all things. Paul explains still more clearly these heavenly riches by making a distinction: "in all speech and all knowledge (or learning)"—a distinction that encompasses all reality that is eternal and heavenly. What follows from this he immediately explains with these words: "If indeed the testimony about Christ was confirmed in you, so that you are not lacking in any gift." And so, by "speech" and "knowledge" Paul includes all the very precious gifts of God. Commentary on 1 Corinthians 1:5-6.[4]

Enriched in Speech and Knowledge. Philipp Melanchthon: In his usual way, [Paul] employs the terms "speech and knowledge" for the evangelical knowledge of Christ or the gospel and the spiritual knowledge of Christ, just as in nearly all his other epistles he desires the brothers to experience a fuller knowledge of Christ. Naturally, Paul is anticipating those who would obscure the doctrine of faith with doctrines of works, who would attribute justification to works rather than to Christ, who would preach Christ as lawgiver and not as Savior. . . . The knowledge of Christ is the knowledge of the greatness and mercy and grace of God, which is poured out through Christ. Isaiah 53:11 speaks of this: "In his knowledge he will justify many"; also 2 Corinthians 3: "Beholding the glory of God in the face of Christ." So to know Christ means to know God by knowing the mercy poured out through Christ; that is, the works of God are known in us. And we shall learn to trust God, love God, and be prepared for all his wishes. Annotations on 1 Corinthians 1:5.[5]

Speech and Knowledge Are Precious Gifts of the Spirit. Tilemann Hesshus: Grace in this passage does not only signify the gracious favor and mercy of God by which God pardons the sins of believers on account of Christ, but it also encompasses the other benefits of Christ and the gifts of the Holy Spirit. Thus Paul explains himself by identifying the *charismata*, that is, the gifts, as speech and knowledge. For those whom God justifies by grace through faith in Christ, he also bestows on them the Holy Spirit. The Spirit is neither a poor nor indifferent guest, but brings with him a multitude of gifts, and confers to his host a new and marvelous knowledge of God and his will, understanding of holy Scripture, the ability to

[3]Musculus, *Comm. 1 Cor.*, 9-10. For Chrysostom's treatment of this passage, see his *Homilies on 1 Corinthians* (homily 2), in NPNF 12:6.

[4]Bullinger, *In Priorem ad Corinthios Epistolam Commentarius*, 9.

[5]Melanchthon, *Annotationes in Epistolam priorem ad Corinthios*, 32; citing Is 53:11; 2 Cor 3:18.

preach the gospel, wisdom in governing the church, constancy in confessing the truth when facing dangers, diligence, keenness in judging things of the Spirit, dexterity in refuting errors, as well as other gifts, by which the church of Christ is built up and adorned. What Paul here calls *logon kai gnōsin* (speech and knowledge), Christ calls *stoma kai sophian* (mouth and wisdom) in Luke. These two excellent gifts are especially necessary for teaching and governing the church, so that those who have been furnished with the gift of speaking might be able to teach, warn, and reproach others, and refute those who are erring; and second, so that those who have been gifted with true wisdom might be able to discern what is true from what is false, understand the mysteries of God, and apply the discretion of the Spirit through their ministry. Athanasius, Augustine, and Luther were endowed with both speech and knowledge, as their writings demonstrate. Explication of 1 Corinthians 1:5.[6]

Enriched in Every Way. Giovanni Diodati: Paul means specifically the miraculous gifts of tongues and the knowledge of the mysteries of the Christian faith, infused in those days by the Holy Spirit into various people, both for the confirmation of the faith and for the speedy provision of capable persons either for founding churches or for continuing to build those churches that were already founded by the apostles. Annotations on 1 Corinthians 1:5.[7]

Rich, but Carnal? Martin Luther: Here you might ask why St. Paul boasts so jubilantly about the Corinthians—how they are so rich in everything that they do not lack a single thing, etc.—since he himself later acknowledges that they had hordes and sects.... All right, here we must remember what I have often said: Christianity can never be so pure that there aren't also some false and wicked people mixed in, just as there will always be weeds, cheatgrass, corncockles, wild mustard along with pure grain. And so whoever wants to examine the church only to find what's broken or impure among the whole lot of Christians will miss the church—even the gospel and Christ—and will never find or encounter the church at all. So, this is said to us as a comfort: if we keep the gospel pure, we have the treasure that God gives his church, so that we lack nothing.

But it's still not so strong and perfect that those who hear it have totally and completely grasped it or are pure in faith and in life; rather there are always some who do not believe and some who are still weak and imperfect. Nevertheless the treasure and riches of doctrine and knowledge are surely present.... To sum up, where the word remains, there the church certainly remains also. Church Postil (1544): Epistle for the Eighteenth Sunday After Trinity.[8]

Spiritual Gifts Do Not Make One Spiritual. Wolfgang Musculus: The Greek word here is *charisma*, that is, what is given out of gracious affection. Hence, many people translate the word as "gift." Paul does not mean any gift whatsoever, but, as I have said, those gifts that he mentions in chapter 12 below.... Some people (including Chrysostom) have asked how it was that the Corinthians, who were lacking in none of the gifts of the Spirit, were able to be carnal. For Paul will say of them a little later: "Are you not carnal?" And he also says: "I cannot speak to you as spiritual people, but as carnal." Several commentators suggest here that there were two factions within this church. One faction included people who remained good; they are mentioned in chapter 11.... The other faction included people who were dishonorable. Those people whom Paul corrected and scolded belonged to this latter faction, it is suggested. Along with this explanation, Chrysostom gives other reasons why Paul praised the Corinthians for possessing spiritual gifts and yet criticized them for many things. He suggests that

[6]Hesshus, *Explicatio Prioris Epistolae ad Corinthios*, 11r-v; citing Lk 21:15.
[7]Diodati, *Pious Annotations*, Ll2*.
[8]WA 22:309.

the Corinthians had practiced such spiritual gifts in the beginning (enriched in all speech and knowledge) when they had first received these gifts, but afterward, when apathy had rendered them more indulgent, they had lost the power of the Spirit and had begun to be carnal once again. But Paul's expression of gratitude for the Corinthians, and what he says later in chapters 12 and 14, do not favor this conclusion. Or, Chrysostom suggests, perhaps the apostle has spoken these things hyperbolically inasmuch as we are accustomed to make something bigger than it truly is by employing a figure of speech that enlarges the point. . . .

I will say what seems best to me: These gifts that Paul attributes to the Corinthians are of such a kind that nothing would prevent Paul, at the same time, from judging the Corinthians as carnal. For those miraculous gifts of the Spirit—that were flourishing in the apostles' churches as a confirmation of the gospel—do not make a person spiritual. Rather, it is spiritual regeneration that comes by faith, by which the heart is cleansed, that finally makes a spiritual person out of a carnal one. Yes indeed, it is completely impossible that these gifts, however miraculous, should by themselves make a spiritual person out of a carnal one. In fact, if regeneration by the Spirit of Christ is absent, the gifts are more inclined to make a person haughty and proud, as the apostle says a little later: "Knowledge puffs up, love builds up." Commentary on 1 Corinthians 1:7.[9]

The Promised Revelation of Christ Provides Consolation. Philipp Melanchthon: "Awaiting the revelation." For Paul this is the most powerful consolation against all adversities. It's as if he were saying: "Granted, the world now threatens and confronts us with every hardship. But just wait, the time is very short before Christ will come and glorify you, and you will reign with him." According to Hebrews 10: "He who is coming will come and not delay." Moreover, to draw closer to Paul's use of "awaiting," it's as if he were saying: "Granted, sin weighs you down; granted, despair is tugging at you, but just wait for the revelation of Christ. For at present, nothing appears except sin. Righteousness and life are hidden in Christ, if you believe. And when he will appear, your life and your righteousness shall appear at the same moment" (Col 3). . . .

Thus you see it makes sense why we should not despair, why we should anticipate the day of Christ. But what if I cannot do this? Paul answers, "You can indeed." How? By my own strength? By no means! Rather, Paul says, "Christ will give you the strength," and "the Spirit will help our weakness" (Rom 8). But how do I know that he is going to give me strength? Listen: "God is faithful," etc. It's as if he were saying: "He is not only good and kind and inclined to bring help, but faithful and truthful; he has bound himself with his promise." There is no doubt that he carries through what he has promised. He has promised to be our father and our shepherd. Annotations on 1 Corinthians 1:7.[10]

The Corinthians' Hope. Tilemann Hesshus: Here Paul describes the end of the whole Christian religion, and by what hope the Corinthians should sustain themselves. The Corinthians had been reconciled to God through faith in Jesus Christ and were recipients of the Holy Spirit, who was conferring on them every kind of gift. Nevertheless, they were carrying around weaknesses and sins, from which saints desire to be liberated. They also desired more knowledge of God, wisdom, strength, faith, and similar kinds of gifts. Therefore Paul teaches them that these things are going to be restored on the day of the revealing of Jesus Christ, when, with the dead being raised, Jesus Christ along with all his angels and the elect will appear in the clouds, and will adorn his faithful people with eternal glory. Explication of 1 Corinthians 1:7.[11]

---

[9]Musculus, *Comm. 1 Cor.*, 12-13; citing 1 Cor 3:1; 11:19; 8:1. For Chrysostom's treatment of this passage, see his *Homilies on 1 Corinthians* (homily 2), in NPNF 12:6-7.

[10]Melanchthon, *Annotationes in Epistolam priorem ad Corinthios*, 32, 34; citing Heb 10:37; Col 3:3; Rom 8:26; 1 Cor 1:9.

[11]Hesshus, *Explicatio Prioris Epistolae ad Corinthios*, 12v.

1:8-9 *God's Unwavering Faithfulness*

God Sustains His People to the End. David Chytraeus: Perseverance is to remain in a true confession of Christ and in constant and perpetual faith until the last breath of life. Now since Christ says, "The one who endures to the end will be saved," and since our nature is so weak, and since we face so many perils and assaults of the devil, and since we can easily slip and fall, godly minds may become distressed and ask how they can persevere in the true confession and faith to the end. Saul fell, though he had previously been approved of God and had been indwelt by the Holy Spirit. The apostle Judas fell. Our first parents, who were created in the image of God, fell. Finally, there are innumerable examples throughout life [of people falling away from God]. Therefore, so that we might be steadfast in faith, let us always fix our eyes on these words of sweetest comfort, 1 Corinthians 1: "Christ will strengthen you to the end, so that you might be guiltless in the day of our Lord Jesus Christ." Luke 22: "I have prayed for you Peter, that your faith may not fail." Now Christ prays not only for Peter and the apostles but for all who believe their preaching. First Corinthians 10: "God is faithful, and he will not let us be tempted beyond our strength, but with the temptation he will also provide a way of escape, that we may be able to endure it." John 14: "I will ask my Father to send you another comforter, who will be with you forever."

Strengthened with these sweetest of promises, let the minds of the godly fight against wavering and doubt, remain diligent in fervent prayer, and be circumspect and watchful in avoiding all occasions for falling and all of the devil's snares and dangers. Let faith be their shield; let prayer be their piercing arrow, and God's Word their sword; and let them depend on Christ alone. He will strengthen us to the end so that, even though sin still remains in us, we may be blameless on the day of our Lord Jesus Christ, who was made sin and a curse for us, so that we might be set free from the condemnation of the law, and be made the righteousness of God in him. Postil on the Eighteenth Sunday After Trinity.[12]

The Name of the Lord Jesus Christ. John Trapp: Eleven times in these ten verses (as Chrysostom well observes) the apostle mentions the Lord Jesus Christ, who was to him—and should be to us—honey in the mouth, music in the ear, and joy in the heart. The Jews used to cast to the ground the book of Esther before they read it, because the name of God is not in it. This was wrong for them to do. But it is recorded that Augustine—quite properly—cast aside the writings of Cicero (though he otherwise found them very delightful) because he did not find in them that mellifluous name of Jesus. Commentary on 1 Corinthians 1:8.[13]

God Is Faithful to His People. Martin Luther: What Christ has begun in you and gladly given you, he will certainly sustain in you until the end, indeed forever, so long as you don't fall from it or cast it away from you through unbelief. For his word or promise given to you and his work that he effects in you are not mutable, like human words and works, but sure, certain, divine, immovable truth. Now because you have such a divine calling, you should comfort yourself in it and firmly depend on it. Church Postil (1544): Epistle for the Eighteenth Sunday After Trinity.[14]

Christians Experience Fellowship with the Son. John Calvin: Erasmus renders this passage "into partnership" [*in consortium*]. The Vulgate translated it "society" [*societatem*]. I have preferred the translation "into the fellowship" [*in communionem*] because this brings out better the force of the Greek word *koinōnias*. For the

[12]Chytraeus, *Dispositio epistolarum*, 448-49; citing Mt 10:22; Lk 22:32; 1 Cor 10:13; Jn 14:16.

[13]Trapp, *A Commentary or Exposition*, 658*. For Augustine's view of Cicero, see Augustine Curley, "Cicero, Marcus Tullius," in *Augustine Through the Ages*, ed. Allan Fitzgerald (Grand Rapids: Eerdmans, 1999), 190-93.

[14]WA 22:310-11.

purpose of the gospel is that Christ may become ours, and that we may be engrafted into his body. Now when the Father gives him to us as a possession, he also communicates himself to us in him; and thus we come to share in every blessing. This, then, is Paul's argument: "Since you have been brought into fellowship with Christ through the gospel, which you received by faith, you have no reason to fear the danger of death, since you have been made partakers of him who rose as conqueror over death." In sum, when Christians look at themselves, they find only reason for trembling, or rather despair; but because they have been called into fellowship with Christ, they ought to think of themselves (as far as assurance of salvation is concerned) in no other way than as members of Christ, recognizing all the blessings of Christ as their own. And so, they will take hold of an unwavering hope of final perseverance (as it is called), if they consider themselves as Christ's members, who cannot possibly fall away. Commentary on 1 Corinthians 1:9.[15]

The Mystery of Fellowship with the Son. John Calvin: What I say is that the moment we receive Christ by faith as he offers himself in the gospel, we become truly members of his body, and life flows into us from him as from the head. For in no other way does he reconcile us to God by the sacrifice of his death than because he is ours and we are one with him. That is how I interpret the passage in which Paul says that believers are called into the *koinōnia* of Christ (1 Cor 1:9). The words "company" or "fellowship" do not seem adequate to convey his thought: it suggests to me the sacred unity by which the Son of God engrafts us into his body, so as to communicate to us all that is his. Thus we draw life from his flesh and blood, so that they are not undeservedly called our "food." How it happens, I confess, is far above the measure of my intelligence. Hence I adore the mystery rather than labor to understand it. . . . Believers come into this communion on the very first day of their calling. But insofar as Christ's life grows in them, he offers himself every day to be enjoyed by them. Letter to Peter Martyr Vermigli.[16]

[15]CO 49:313 (cf. CTS 39:60-61). For Erasmus's use of the Latin word *societatem* to translate the Greek word *koinōnias*, see *Erasmus' Annotations on the New Testament*, ed. Anne Reeve and M. A. Screech (Leiden: Brill, 1990), 438.

[16]Calvin to Vermigli, 8 August 1555; CO 15:722-23.

1:10-17 DIVISIONS IN THE CHURCH

[10]I appeal to you, brothers,[a] by the name of our Lord
Jesus Christ, that all of you agree, and that there be
no divisions among you, but that you be united in the
same mind and the same judgment. [11]For it has been
reported to me by Chloe's people that there is
quarreling among you, my brothers. [12]What I mean is
that each one of you says, "I follow Paul," or "I follow
Apollos," or "I follow Cephas," or "I follow Christ." [13]Is
Christ divided? Was Paul crucified for you? Or were
you baptized in the name of Paul? [14]I thank God that
I baptized none of you except Crispus and Gaius, [15]so
that no one may say that you were baptized in my
name. [16](I did baptize also the household of Stepha-
nas. Beyond that, I do not know whether I baptized
anyone else.) [17]For Christ did not send me to baptize
but to preach the gospel, and not with words of
eloquent wisdom, lest the cross of Christ be emptied of
its power.

a Or *brothers and sisters.* In New Testament usage, depending on the context, the plural Greek word *adelphoi* (translated "brothers") may refer either to *brothers* or to *brothers and sisters;* also verses 11, 26

Overview: Paul's forceful appeal for Christian unity is a major theme in this epistle, necessitated by the numerous divisions and controversies that afflicted the Corinthian church. Most Reformation commentators believe that the false apostles mentioned by Paul were not heretics per se, but schismatic teachers who opposed Paul's authority and sought disciples for themselves—even naming factions after themselves (not unlike the ancient Donatists and Novatianists). Because God is one, Christians are commanded to reflect his unity by living together in peace, harmony, and mutual affection. For Anabaptist communities, unity is more than an ideal to be pursued; it is necessary for their very survival. Because many of the false apostles are "stamping" their disciples with their own baptism, Paul insists that he is free from such partisanship, having baptized only a handful of disciples when he was at Corinth, including the household of Stephanas. This reference to household baptisms triggers much discussion, particularly among Anabaptist commentators, who reject the supposition that small children were baptized as a part of these households. Other interpreters focus on Paul's statement "Christ did not send me to baptize" to insist that pastors must prioritize preaching the gospel over baptizing people. Indeed, they contend that celebration of the sacraments is worthless without God's Word accompanying it.

1:10-11 *The Need for Unity*

Unity and Schism. Tilemann Hesshus: This is the chief purpose of the whole letter, whereby Paul encourages the Corinthian church, torn by various sects and factions, to strive for wholesome concord and Christian unity. For God is not a God of disorder and disagreement, but of peace and harmony. And Christ has not called us to quarrels, but to mutual affection and love. Therefore one and the same Spirit is poured out on God's people that the Spirit might unite them to God the Father and Son, as well as to one another, so they might be one in God. For this reason, Christ says, "In this way they will know that you are my disciples, if you have love for one another" (John 13).... Therefore it is the responsibility of all Christians to strive with the greatest of effort to avoid disagreements and quarrels and support concord and the unity of the Spirit....

But heresy and schism are not the same thing. Heresy is an error against an article of faith, which overturns the foundation of religion, and is defended stubbornly contrary to Scripture. The errors of Samosata, Nestorius, and Pelagius were all heresies. Schism is quarreling that is aroused by stubbornness or a zeal for arguing on account of different ceremonies or certain kinds of actions—but without corruption of the articles of faith. Thus Donatus stirred up schism when he accused Caecilian of handing over the sacred writings, and did not wish to acknowledge him as a true member of the church. EXPLICATION OF 1 CORINTHIANS 1:12.[1]

SURVIVAL DEPENDS ON UNITY. DIRK PHILIPS: The congregation . . . will be called a city, because like a city it must be united; the citizens need to be firmly attached to each other, living and walking according to one kind of policy, law, and statutes so long as the city wants to remain standing. Thus it must also take place in the congregation. There must be unity in spirit and faith (1 Cor 1:10; 10:21); there one must walk according to one rule of the divine Word; there one must maintain harmoniously the divine policy that this city has received from God. THE CONGREGATION OF GOD.[2]

THE NATURE OF UNGODLY DIVISIONS. WOLFGANG MUSCULUS: "There should not be divisions among you." . . . Paul now declares the inverse of what he said earlier, "that all of you agree." Therefore, being divided into factions is the opposite of everyone proclaiming the same thing and professing together the same doctrine. Thus those people are schismatic who do not proclaim the same thing among themselves, who do not agree whether Christ is the sole author of salvation . . . and who do not profess the same doctrines. For to assert the one thing is to exclude the other thing. Thus it is surely absurd and impossible for people not to be schismatic who do not proclaim, teach, or profess the same thing among themselves. Is that not the case with those who consider themselves Augustinians, Benedictines, Franciscans more than Christians? Is that not also the case with those Thomists, Scotists, Albertists, etc. who disagree among themselves with various opinions? Or again, is that not the case with the nominalists and realists? They do not wish to be considered schismatic, even though they do not proclaim the same things among themselves. COMMENTARY ON 1 CORINTHIANS 1:10.[3]

IDENTITY OF CHLOE. HEINRICH BULLINGER: Now, so that he might not seem deluded by groundless suspicion, Paul says plainly . . . that he has learned about this disagreement from the household of Chloe. Most people think Chloe is the name of a woman. Ambrosius writes that certain people thought it was the name of a place. It appears in fact that this was a woman of spiritual prominence. Paul mentions the name of this household out of admiration or as proof of his discretion. For it is necessary that his report be specific (but with the name of men suppressed) lest we ascribe to them any sort of jealousy. COMMENTARY ON 1 CORINTHIANS 1:11.[4]

1:12-13 *The Dangers of Partisanship*

PAUL ADDRESSES THE PROBLEM OF SCHISM. DAVID DICKSON: Now Paul comes to the matter of schism. The Corinthians are arguing over their teachers, preferring some before others, as if they were more perfect, naming themselves after them,

[1]Hesshus, *Explicatio Prioris Epistolae ad Corinthios*, 14r-v; citing Jn 13:35. Paul of Samosata (bishop of Antioch from 260 to 268) was condemned for teaching the ancient heresy of adoptionism, that Jesus was adopted as God's Son at his baptism. Nestorius (patriarch of Constantinople from 428 to 431) was condemned as a heretic for refusing to endorse the Virgin Mary as *Theotokos* ("bearer of God" or "mother of God"), and for teaching (it was believed) that the human and divine natures were not united in the one person of Christ. The British monk Pelagius (born c. 360) was confronted by Augustine and condemned by the Synod of Carthage (418) for rejecting the doctrine of original sin and affirming instead that human beings possess unhindered free will and are able to achieve salvation without God's grace. Donatus (died c. 355) was the leader of a schismatic Christian group that denied the sacramental power and authority of Catholic church leaders such as Felix of Aptunga, who had betrayed the faith during persecution. Felix later returned to ecclesiastical office and ordained Caecilian as bishop.
[2]CRR 6:377.

[3]Musculus, *Comm. 1 Cor.*, 17-18. Protestant apologists regularly pointed to the divisions and schisms among the various religious orders and philosophical schools in the Roman Catholic Church. Here Musculus distinguishes between the theological traditions of the Dominican Thomas Aquinas (1225–1274), the Franciscan Duns Scotus (c. 1266–1308), and the Dominican Albert the Great (1193–1280). Medieval theologians fiercely debated the metaphysical question of whether universals (e.g., "dog" or "table") existed *before* a particular thing (realism), *in* a particular thing (conceptualism), or *after* a particular thing (nominalism).
[4]Bullinger, *In Priorem ad Corinthios Epistolam Commentarius*, 11.

with envy and contempt for each other. Paul does not identify these teachers; by leaving them unnamed, he pacifies the minds of the schismatic so that these divisions might more easily be laid aside. And by way of example, he names himself, Apollos, and Cephas, although in the following chapters of the epistle it is clear that the authors and promoters of the schism were their own vain babbling teachers. These same teachers also heaped contempt on Paul before the Corinthians, so that he could scarcely maintain his place among them. Exposition of 1 Corinthians 1:12.[5]

Followers of Peter and Christ? Wolfgang Musculus: What should we say about the followers of Peter and Christ? Why did some people say that they were followers of Cephas, when we do not read that he ever came to Corinth? I think that the false apostles were opposing the authority of Peter to Paul in an attempt to introduce foreign doctrine under his name and to promote themselves. Thus they called their faction "Cephists" out of hatred for Paul. . . .

What should be said about those who called themselves the followers of Christ? Were they also schismatic? Ambrose understands them to be those who were persevering in the truth and faith of Christ, who renounced all those disputes. But why then does the apostle mention them along with the schismatic? Chrysostom says that . . . Paul criticizes them for considering themselves true followers of Christ. But why does he say this only to this one group when he should have said it to all of them?

In agreement with other interpreters, it seems to me possible for people who call themselves followers of Christ to be no less schismatic than if they were to call themselves followers of Paul or Peter. How so? If they do this in a contentious and perverse manner, as when people break the unity and peace with the name of Christ, and employ the name of Christ to defend some perverse opinion, and exclude from Christ other people who hold different opinions and separate themselves from them. People who do this wrongly call themselves followers of Christ, although being a true follower of Christ is a good thing. In the same way, it is good and appropriate for all Christians to call themselves evangelical. But if people, in the name of the gospel, separate themselves from the rest of the community of Christians, having become perversely puffed up against others because of some difference of opinion poorly understood, are they not violating charity and dividing the body of Christ? Commentary on 1 Corinthians 1:12.[6]

Christians Have Long Struggled for Unity. John Jewel: [Catholics accuse us of having] fallen into various sects, whereby some of us are called Lutherans, some of us Zwinglians, and that we cannot yet completely agree among ourselves regarding the whole substance of our doctrine. But what would they have said if they had been in the first times of the apostles and holy fathers, when one said "I hold to Paul"; another, "I hold to Cephas"; another "I hold to Apollos"? When Paul sharply rebuked Peter? When, after a falling out, Barnabas departed from Paul? . . . When also Theophilus, Epiphanius, Chrysostom, Augustine, Rufinus, Jerome—all of whom were Christians, church fathers, and catholics—strove against one another with the most bitter and unending contentions? . . . And yet what a stir and uproar [the Catholics] now make regarding those two poor names, Luther and Zwingli! Because these two men are not yet in complete agreement on a certain point of doctrine, they would have us think that both of them are deceived; that neither of them had the gospel; and that neither of them taught the truth aright. . . . Surely it is no new thing that men are but men, although they are called by the name of Christians. Apology.[7]

Christ Must Have Preeminence in the Church. John Calvin: Therefore Paul condemns as the most pernicious enemies of our faith

[5]Dickson, *Exposition of St. Paul's Epistles*, 40*.

[6]Musculus, *Comm. 1 Cor.*, 24-25.

[7]Jewel, *Apology of the Church of England*, 44, 45, 50*.

those people who draw away disciples after themselves so as to split the church into parties. For this reason, therefore, he does not allow humans to have preeminence in the church so that they usurp Christ's supremacy. He does not allow them to be held in such honor as to take away even in the slightest amount from Christ's dignity. Ministers of Christ must have their due honor, of course, and they are masters in their own way. But this provision must always be kept in view, that what belongs to Christ must in no way be diminished—that he is the one and only Master, and valued as such. For that reason good ministers have the following aims: to serve Christ together in common, ascribing power, authority, and glory to him alone; to fight under his banner; to obey him alone; and to bring other people into subjection to his lordship. Those who are influenced by ambition are winning disciples for themselves, not for Christ. This then is the source of all evils; this is the most destructive of all plagues; this the deadly poison of all churches—when ministers are devoted to their own interests rather than to Christ. Commentary on 1 Corinthians 1:12.[8]

Divisions in the Body of Christ. The English Annotations: The first reason why schisms ought to be eschewed is because Christ seems by that means to be divided and torn into pieces. Christ cannot be the head of two different and disagreeing bodies, since he is but one.... Another reason is because people cannot, without causing God great injury, depend on ordinary human beings as on Christ. This is what they were doing when ... they allowed the gospel to be uttered by one man but rejected that same gospel when it was uttered by another; and so these factions were called by the names of their teachers. Now St. Paul here sets down his own name, not only to avoid offense, but also to show that he was not pleading his own cause.... The third reason [why schisms should be eschewed] is taken from the form and end of baptism, wherein we make a promise to Christ, calling also on the name of the Father and the Holy Ghost. Therefore, even if persons do not fall from the doctrine of Christ, yet if they wholly depend on certain teachers—and despise others—they forsake Christ. For if they consider Christ as their only master, they will listen to his teaching from whomever speaks it. Annotations on 1 Corinthians 1:13.[9]

1:14-17 *Baptism and Christian Unity*

Paul Avoids Using Baptism to Promote Factionalism. Wolfgang Musculus: It is clear that the false apostles were using baptism in a contentious manner in order to incite and strengthen their faction, just as what is read more fully in the last chapter of Galatians concerning the teachers of circumcision: "They force you to be circumcised so that they may boast in your flesh." And the false apostles were baptizing people as adherents of their teaching, stamping them with the name of their faction. At the same time, they viewed with contempt those who had been baptized by others. For this was no doubt the trick of Satan, that his servants might misuse this symbol of baptism, by which the Holy Spirit wished to seal the children of God into one body, for the destruction of the body of Christ. Both Ambrose and Augustine perceived this same party spirit among the Donatists and Novatianists. For these men defended the power of baptism of their faction alone, and did not admit into their fellowship anyone who had been baptized by others. And in our own day, the Anabaptists have renewed this same plague. Because this perverse party spirit for baptizing was now prevailing among the Corinthians, so that in their baptism the false apostles were stamping people as their own initiates, for their own glory and not for Christ, ... the apostle demonstrates and shows in this passage that he is far from this party spirit, and thus he writes in this fashion: "I give thanks

[8]CO 49:317 (cf. CTS 39:66-67).

[9]Downame, *Annotations*, CC3v-4r*.

to God that I baptized none of you." Commentary on 1 Corinthians 1:14.[10]

Household Baptisms No Doubt Included Infants. John Calvin: Now, everyone may see that infant baptism was by no means fashioned by humankind, resting as it does on such firm approbation of Scripture. Nor is their silly objection plausible that there is no evidence of a single infant ever being baptized by the hands of the apostles! For even if this is not expressly related by the Evangelists, still, because infants were not excluded when mention is made of a family being baptized, who in his senses can reason from this that they were not baptized? If such arguments were valid, women should similarly be barred from the Lord's Supper, since we do not read that they were admitted to it in the apostolic age (Acts 16:15, 32); but here we are content with the rule of faith. For when we weigh what the institution of the Supper implies, it is also easy to judge from this to whom the use of it ought to be granted. We observe this also in baptism. Indeed, when we pay attention to the purpose for which it was instituted, we clearly see that it is just as appropriate to infants as to older persons. For this reason, infants cannot be deprived of it without open violation of the will of God, its author. Institutes.[11]

Household Baptisms Did Not Include Infants. Menno Simons: Paedobaptists object quite foolishly, saying that the apostles baptized whole households, as the household of Cornelius (Acts 10:48); the household of Stephanas (1 Cor 1:16); the household of Lydia and the jailer (Acts 16:15, 33); included in which they say it may be presumed that there were also small children. From this argument, beloved brethren, they show how unwittingly that they cannot produce Scriptures to prove that infants should be baptized. For wherever mere presumption is followed, there evidently no proof is available. Christian Baptism.[12]

Neither Peter nor Paul Baptized Infants. Balthasar Hubmaier: Note here that this text cannot be applied to young children, because they do not say or boast that Peter or Paul had baptized them. They are not able to speak but only cry miserably. Beyond that, it is not even certain that there were children there. Let that be proved first. On the Christian Baptism of Believers.[13]

Christians Are Not Baptized on Another's Faith. Balthasar Hubmaier: Some of you speak to me of the foreign faith of father and mother, others of the faith of the godparents, while others speak of the faith of the church, and that without any basis in Scripture. For if the children are baptized in the faith of their father and mother, why then are fathers and mothers forbidden to sponsor their children for baptism? If it is done by virtue of the faith of the godparents or the church, then people would be saved by the faith of another. All of which is totally contradictory to the Scripture. For the righteous one will live by his own faith, Hab 2:4; Rom 1:17. Whoever believes and is baptized is saved, not the one for whom one believes, Mark 16:16. On Infant Baptism.[14]

Paul's Priority Was Preaching the Gospel. Huldrych Zwingli: How can Paul say he was not sent to baptize, since Christ gave his disciples the command to consecrate through baptism those to whom they preached the gospel? Now, two of Christ's teachings are stated here: first and foremost, to preach the gospel to all

[10]Musculus, *Comm. 1 Cor.*, 28-29; citing Gal 6:12-13. Donatus (c. 355) was the leader of a schismatic Christian group that denied the sacramental power and authority of Catholic church leaders such as Felix of Aptunga, who had betrayed the faith during persecution but later returned to ecclesiastical office. The Donatists were opposed in their views by Augustine, who appealed to the need for church unity and pointed out the sinfulness of all Christians and the need for God's grace. Novatian (d. c. 258), a presbyter in the Roman church, and his followers formed rival churches to protest the lenient policies adopted by orthodox churches toward Christians who lapsed during times of persecution.

[11]LCC 21:1331 (*Institutes* 4.16.8).

[12]Simons, *Complete Writings*, 281.

[13]CRR 5:133-34.

[14]CRR 5:289-90.

nations and, second, to engraft those same people, who had learned of Christ through the disciples, into the people of God through the sign of baptism. Therefore Paul himself does not totally deny being sent to baptize (for he baptized the household of Stephanas as well as Gaius and Crispus); however, he does say he was chiefly sent to preach the gospel; he was under the threat of penalty if he did not clearly preach the gospel. Indeed, he was very attentive to this responsibility to complete the remaining work that was unfinished. ANNOTATIONS ON 1 CORINTHIANS 1:17.[15]

APOSTLES USUALLY DELEGATED BAPTIZING TO ORDINARY PASTORS. GIOVANNI DIODATI: It is likely that Paul employed Silas and Timothy in the act of baptizing the great number of people who believed and were baptized when he was at Corinth (Acts 18:5, 8).... In Matthew 28:19, the apostles were sent out equally both to preach and baptize. Therefore the meaning here is that the apostles' charge was chiefly to lay the foundation of churches by preaching, without the responsibility of baptizing all the believers one by one, with individual instruction and examination. This was left to the care of the ordinary pastors that were established by the apostles in the churches, by means of those previously mentioned miraculous gifts that made them capable of this calling in an instant. ANNOTATIONS ON 1 CORINTHIANS 1:14, 17.[16]

PAUL COMPARES PREACHING AND BAPTISM. WOLFGANG MUSCULUS: In this comparison of preaching and baptism we see the clear value of preaching the gospel and how it excels the responsibility to baptize people. And the task of preaching imposed on the apostles and evangelists was so important that [Paul said] it was woe to them if they did not preach the gospel—he did not say it was woe to them if they did not baptize per se....

Therefore Paul acknowledges, or rather he defends his calling to preach with simple words, even though the false apostles reproached him for it. And he is not at all ashamed of this calling, since he says that he was not only sent to preach the gospel, but he was sent to proclaim as simply as possible the message of the cross of Christ to the Gentiles, having rejected the eloquent arrangement of words and reliance on the power of all worldly wisdom. And Paul does this by means of negation when he says "not with words of wisdom"—that is, "with simple words." COMMENTARY ON 1 CORINTHIANS 1:17.[17]

SACRAMENTS ARE WORTHLESS WITHOUT GOSPEL PREACHING. TILEMANN HESSHUS: Paul here shows what the chief part of his ministry is: He does not say that it is to baptize people, since this could be done by other ministers of the church whose gifts were inferior to Paul's; rather, it is to proclaim the gospel and explain the mysteries of the divine Word. The commandment to baptize people had been enjoined on every one of the apostles, including Paul. For Christ said, "Go, baptize everyone," etc. The administration of the sacraments and the preaching of the gospel must not be separated. To be sure, the sacraments are a seal of the promise, but the greatest priority must be given to preaching and exposition of the Word, for without the preaching of the Word the sacraments are worthless performances, void of all fruit. And too, it involves far more effort and work to teach the people concerning God and the blessings of the Mediator than to administer the sacraments. EXPLICATION OF 1 CORINTHIANS 1:17.[18]

OUTWARD BAPTISM NOT ESSENTIAL. HANS DENCK: Where the outward baptism is administered in this covenant it is good. Where there is not the case, [baptism] is of no avail for the reasons given. Outward baptism is not essential to salvation. Thus St. Paul says that he had not been sent to baptize (which was not essential) but rather to preach the gospel (which was essential). CONFESSION ADDRESSED TO THE CITY COUNCIL OF NUREMBERG.[19]

[15]Zwingli, *Annotatiunculae . . . ex ore Zvinglij*, 9-10.
[16]Diodati, *Pious Annotations*, Ll1*.
[17]Musculus, *Comm. 1 Cor.*, 31.
[18]Hesshus, *Explicatio Prioris Epistolae ad Corinthios*, 20r-v.
[19]Denck, *Selected Writings*, 20.

Paul Is Not Condemning Eloquence Per Se. John Calvin: But what if someone in our day speaks in a rather elegant fashion, and uses eloquence to explain gospel teaching? Should that person be rejected on this account, as if he spoiled the gospel, or obscured the glory of Christ? I answer first that eloquence is not at all contrary to the simplicity of the gospel when, without snobbishness, it not only gives the gospel first place and is subject to it, but also serves it as a slave girl serves her mistress. For, as Augustine says, "He who assigned Peter to be a fisherman, also assigned Cyprian to be an orator."[20] By this he means that both men were from God, although the one, who is far superior in authority, lacked any attractiveness of speech, while the other, who sits at his feet, was famous for his outstanding eloquence. Thus we must not condemn or reject the kind of eloquence that does not aim at distracting Christians with an outward luster of words so as to intoxicate them with empty amusements, tickle their ears, or cover up the cross of Christ with its ostentation. Instead, true eloquence aims at calling us back to the original simplicity of the gospel so that, of its own accord, it extols only the preaching of the cross and finally performs the duty of a herald as it were to obtain a hearing for those fisherman and unlearned people who have nothing to recommend them except the power of the Spirit. Commentary on 1 Corinthians.[21]

The Difference Between Gospel Teaching and Philosophy. Philipp Melanchthon: [Paul] seized the opportunity to describe the method of evangelical teaching. And thus he digresses in a most splendid passage to discuss the difference between the wisdom of the flesh and the wisdom of the spirit, and the difference between gospel teaching and philosophical teaching. First, he says he preached not with the wisdom of words, that is, not with agreeable and likely arguments conceived by human reason. For this is his meaning: he simply preached the gospel, not philosophy. The two are so much in conflict with each other that when philosophy is allowed in, the gospel is at once clouded over and Christ is obscured. Hence Paul says, "lest the cross of Christ be emptied of its power," because philosophy attributes everything to our own power and works, whereas the gospel takes away everything and teaches that there is no other justification except by believing in Christ. Annotations on 1 Corinthians 1:17.[22]

Rhetoric Must Be Free from Ostentation. John Trapp: "Not with words of eloquence"—even though Paul could have done this as well as anyone else. . . . But he did not want to put the sword of the Spirit into a velvet scabbard, lest it not pierce. . . . Augustine repented (as well he ought) that when he was young he had preached more to please than to profit. And Luther was known to say that he is the best preacher who preaches commonly, popularly [*trivialiter*] and especially to the people's capacity. It is not unlawful to use rhetoric in sermons, as long as it is free from ostentation. Commentary on 1 Corinthians 1:17.[23]

[20]See Augustine, *Tractates on John* 7.17 (NPNF 7:54).
[21]CO 49:321-22 (cf. CTS 39:76-77).
[22]Melanchthon, *Annotationes in Epistolam priorem ad Corinthios*, 38.
[23]Trapp, *A Commentary or Exposition*, 659*.

1:18-31 CHRIST THE WISDOM AND POWER OF GOD

[18]For the word of the cross is folly to those who are
perishing, but to us who are being saved it is the
power of God. [19]For it is written,
"I will destroy the wisdom of the wise,
and the discernment of the discerning I will
thwart."
[20]Where is the one who is wise? Where is the
scribe? Where is the debater of this age? Has not God
made foolish the wisdom of the world? [21]For since, in
the wisdom of God, the world did not know God
through wisdom, it pleased God through the folly of
what we preach[a] to save those who believe. [22]For Jews
demand signs and Greeks seek wisdom, [23]but we
preach Christ crucified, a stumbling block to Jews and
folly to Gentiles, [24]but to those who are called, both
Jews and Greeks, Christ the power of God and the
wisdom of God. [25]For the foolishness of God is wiser
than men, and the weakness of God is stronger than
men.
[26]For consider your calling, brothers: not many of
you were wise according to worldly standards,[b] not
many were powerful, not many were of noble birth.
[27]But God chose what is foolish in the world to shame
the wise; God chose what is weak in the world to
shame the strong; [28]God chose what is low and
despised in the world, even things that are not, to
bring to nothing things that are, [29]so that no human
being[c] might boast in the presence of God. [30]And
because of him[d] you are in Christ Jesus, who became
to us wisdom from God, righteousness and sanctifica-
tion and redemption, [31]so that, as it is written, "Let
the one who boasts, boast in the Lord."

a Or *the folly of preaching* **b** Greek *according to the flesh* **c** Greek *no flesh* **d** Greek *And from him*

Overview: Because the false apostles in Corinth were taking pride in their eloquence and learning, Paul now contrasts God's wisdom and power with the worldly wisdom sported by the proud Corinthians. In general, Reformation commentators do not reject human philosophy or eloquence outright. But they are keen to show the many ways in which the message of Christ's cross appears offensive and foolish to unbelievers who depend on human reason or good works. Reason cannot conceive of a crucified Son of God, or of a Savior who submits to death on a cross, or of salvation based on grace rather than human performance. So too, human wisdom finds repulsive the sorry cast of characters that God calls to preach the gospel and populate the church. Throughout salvation history, God consistently works in power through faithful people who are weak, uneducated, poor, and despised. Thus the glorious foolishness of the cross demolishes all human pretension and boasting. At the end of the chapter, Protestant interpreters find special significance in Paul's description of Christ as the believers' "wisdom, righteousness, sanctification, and redemption." This statement serves as a beautiful summary of Christian proclamation and faith, highlighting the fact that salvation is by God's grace alone through Christ alone. It also reminds believers that only Christ deserves praise and glory in his church.

1:18-19 *The Cross Is Foolish Yet Powerful to Save*

The Power and Wisdom of Christ and His Cross. Jacques Lefèvre d'Étaples: Those who wish to be saved should meditate on the cross of Christ, they should cling to the cross, they should carry their cross, mortifying their bodies (that is, concupiscence), and they should follow Christ in this world, who was once in the world. And now that he lives in eternity, they should follow him outside this world to live in eternity. And this is the singular and most true theorem of all religion: either we remain in this world, or we flee the world. The wisdom of worldly philosophy does not proclaim this; nor do the commentaries of the philosophers contain this. . . .

For now Christ is no other than God and the most blessed Son of God in eternity. He was crucified for us, and then and now he was all-powerful and all-knowing. In him alone people ought to place all their wisdom, strength, and glory; they should boast in him alone. And thus God chooses things that are foolish, impotent, ignoble, contemptible, and things that are not, lest people think that they might boast in wisdom, power, nobility, and honor. But they should ascribe the only cause for boasting to God alone, and pay attention to him alone. Commentary on 1 Corinthians 1:18-25.[1]

The Foolishness of the Cross. Wolfgang Musculus: How is it that the word of the cross seems to be foolishness to those perishing? For there must be something in it that unbelievers judge to be foolish. Jesus, a crucified man, was proclaimed by the apostle to be the Son of God as well as the Savior of the world. Now both of these statements represented the greatest foolishness to the wisdom of the world: either to believe that he was the Son of God, since he endured crucifixion (and was even able to be crucified), or to believe that a man who submitted in weakness to the cross was able to be a savior of other people when he refused to save himself. So the Jews were also saying: "He saved others, but he is not able to save himself." Therefore that word of the cross was completely offensive to unbelievers, the wise people of the world, both in proclaiming that a crucified man is the Son of God, and in affirming that he is the Savior of the world. If Jesus is God, they ask, how could he appear more foolish? If it was God hanging on a cross, why was he unable to free himself from the hands of mere mortals? And if he is a man so weak that he was unable to flee the cross, what could possibly be more foolish than this, to believe that this crucified man is able to save mortal human beings—even if he was a very righteous man—since he was unable to be the savior of himself? Commentary on 1 Corinthians 1:18.[2]

Three Descriptions of the Gospel. Philipp Melanchthon: Those who are humble and acknowledge their sin are raised up with the gift of Christ's righteousness, and just as the gospel is a terror to the proud and unbelieving, so it is a consolation to the humble. This passage cannot be understood unless one has compared the pattern of the cross to the pattern of human wisdom. Now Paul attributes three names to the gospel: he calls it the "word of the cross," in that it offends and mortifies the flesh. Second, he calls it the "foolishness of the cross" because it fights against the wisdom of the flesh. And also Paul calls it "God's power," which is the instrument by which God empowers those who believe. Annotations on 1 Corinthians 1:18.[3]

The Wisdom of the Cross. Dirk Philips: Christ Jesus is such a master and his Word is of such nature and power that whoever receives and keeps it with a believing heart shall find in the simplicity of the teaching of Christ the unspeakable counsel of heavenly wisdom. They shall, in the words of the cross that in the first glimpse appears simplistic and despised (1 Cor 1:18), see and observe much that far surpasses all human cleverness, no matter how high and wonderful it may appear. The Enchiridion: Concerning the True Knowledge of Jesus Christ.[4]

The Cross Is Foolishness to the World. Huldrych Zwingli: In this prophecy Isaiah compares human wisdom and understanding to what is seen in the dreams of people who are asleep. Paul adapts this image beautifully, as if he were saying: "In the matter of the gospel all the wisdom of the world is rejected and empty, since it is able neither to see nor to learn the mystery of the cross. Indeed, worldly wisdom is so unfit for achieving anything of this that it is altogether rejected. For

[1]Lefèvre d'Étaples, *Commentariorum in Epistolas Beati Pauli . . . Liber Secundus*, 101v-102r.

[2]Musculus, *Comm. 1 Cor.*, 35.

[3]Melanchthon, *Annotationes in Epistolam priorem ad Corinthios*, 40.

[4]CRR 6:167.

what scribe or otherworldly investigator will be able to be wise here? Ever since God tied salvation to the cross alone, he made the wisdom of this world foolishness. Truly, do you not see that all the wisdom of this world is foolishness, for God brought salvation to the world through his only Son, who was crucified?" Annotations on 1 Corinthians 1:19.[5]

Paul Preserves the Intention of Isaiah's Prophecy. John Calvin: A great difficulty emerges here, because whereas the terms *wisdom* and *discernment* are taken by Isaiah in a positive sense, Paul cites this passage for a contrary purpose, as if human wisdom is condemned by God as perverse, and human discernment is rejected as a mere vanity. I confess that this is the usual interpretation, but since it is certain that the apostle did not twist the prophecies of the Holy Spirit into other meanings, I prefer to depart from the common opinion rather than accuse Paul of error. And in other respects the genuine meaning of the prophet does not fit badly with Paul's intention. For if even the wisest of persons becomes a fool when the Lord removes the right spirit, how much confidence will be placed in human wisdom? . . . Now we see how appropriately Paul uses this testimony. Isaiah declares that God's punishment will be on all those who honor God with their fanciful wisdom so that "wisdom would perish from their wise men." Paul makes use of the testimony of Isaiah in order to prove that the wisdom of this world perishes and is nothing when it vaunts itself against God. Commentary on 1 Corinthians 1:19.[6]

1:20-21 *God's Wisdom and the World's Wisdom*

Dangers of Human Wisdom. Martin Luther: St. Paul most severely rebukes and condemns this shameful wisdom, and makes these connoisseur saints out to be fools. He says outright that they know nothing of Christ, or of the Spirit and gifts of God given to us in Christ, and that they had better begin to learn. It takes spiritual folk to understand this. The desire to be wise and the pretenses of cleverness in the gospel are the very things that really give offense and hinder the knowledge of Christ and God, and create disturbances and contentions. This clever wisdom and reason can well serve to make for nothing but mad saints and wild Christians. Yet such people can never know our Lord Christ, unless they first become fools again and humbly let themselves be taught and led by the simple word of God. Preface to 1 Corinthians.[7]

God Did Not Use Those Considered "Wise" to Build Up the Church. David Dickson: God in the calling of his church rejected the works and persons of the wisest among the Jews and Gentiles, allowing the greatest part of the wise politicians, the scribes (that is, interpreters of the law), and the disputers of this world (that is, philosophers) to walk in their own ways. Indeed, he permitted almost the whole multitude of the wise of this world to wallow like fools in the mire and dirt, along with their worldly wisdom and learning, outside the boundaries of his church, or the kingdom of heaven. In making this argument, the apostle alludes to the prophecy of Isaiah 29:14. For if you ask, "Where are the wise?"—they are not found in the church, for their wisdom does not lead them to the true knowledge of their misery, and they count as foolishness the belief that their only remedy is Christ. This is the force of Paul's argument: "In the calling and building up of the church, God did not use the wise of this world, nor their eloquence. Therefore, it is no wonder that Christ sent me to preach not with wisdom of words." Exposition of 1 Corinthians 1:20.[8]

The Foolish Plan of the Wise God. Philipp Melanchthon: Thus this world did not know God as wise. While we seek after the wise God, his wisdom estranges us from him because it

[5]Zwingli, *Annotatiunculae . . . ex ore Zvinglij*, 10-11. Paul is here quoting Is 29:14.
[6]CO 49:323-24 (cf. CTS 39:79-80); citing Is 29:14.

[7]LW 35:381-82.
[8]Dickson, *Exposition of St. Paul's Epistles*, 41*.

is not understood. For what is more incomprehensible than the wondrous administration of the world? Do those who fix their eyes on the many evils in the world and on so many events that appear pure chance comprehend nothing less than a wise God? By contrast, spiritual persons know a foolish God through folly. How is God foolish? Because they grasp in the foolishness of God's goodness and mercy: for what is more foolish than for God to become flesh, that is, sin and cursed through his folly and mortification, that is: contrary to the sense and judgment of the flesh? Annotations on 1 Corinthians 1:21.[9]

General and Special Knowledge of God. Wolfgang Musculus: Someone may perhaps ask why the apostle says that "the world did not know God through wisdom," when the same apostle says in Romans 1 that God's wisdom is known through his visible works. Here we must note that the knowledge of God is twofold. First, there is that general knowledge available to everyone from God's most illustrious creation. Paul speaks about this sort of knowledge in Romans 1. It does not save, although it renders people without excuse. Second, there is this special knowledge, which is the knowledge of the divine will in Christ that leads to salvation. Certainly this is the sort of knowledge that, in the wisdom of God, the world through its wisdom did not know about, as Paul says here in this passage. Commentary on 1 Corinthians 1:21.[10]

1:22-25 *Jews and Greeks Find God's Wisdom Incomprehensible*

The Jews Seek a Sign. Philipp Melanchthon: To seek a sign is to want to be certain according to the capacity of human judgment, as Psalm 4 says, "Who will show us a good sign?" It's as if Paul were saying, "When I command you to be confident amid adversities, you say: 'Behold, look how every sign that happens to us turns out contrary to what we hoped for; I cannot hope for life when I have death placed before my eyes; I cannot hope for salvation when I have sin placed before my eyes. If God would have shown me a sign that he wanted to save me, I would have gladly believed in him. But how can I believe when every sign is different from what I was hoping for?'" Thus the Jews do not believe when they hear that Christ is Savior yet nevertheless abandons his people to be killed and condemned (which are signs contrary to salvation). Therefore they demand signs by which to be certain of salvation according to their own judgment; and when the signs do not happen, they lose hope. Thus in Matthew 16, Jesus says "An adulterous generation seeks a sign." Annotations on 1 Corinthians 1:22.[11]

The Difference Between Jews, Gentiles, and Christians. John Colet: For Paul, there are three kinds of people: the Jews, the Gentiles, and those called from among these to be Christians. Among the Jews there was blindness from perversity of their wills; among the Gentiles there was wickedness arising from their ignorance. Stupidity prevailed over the Gentiles, arising from their own wisdom, and they wished Christ ill. Among the Jews, a dark and wretched blindness crept from their malice. For if they had known the Lord of glory, they would never have crucified him. But Christ, as I have just now said, is the strength of God and the wisdom of God. Those who have been summoned by the warm rays of his divinity to cling to him in fellowship are that third kind of person, whom Paul speaks of as those called and chosen into that glory. Their minds are enlightened by the presence of the divinity, and their wills straightened. By faith they behold clearly the wisdom of Christ, and by love they take firm grasp of his power. . . . For these in the free choice of God are lifted by his gracious gift from the darkness of the Gentiles into the light of faith, from the cold of

[9]Melanchthon, *Annotationes in Epistolam priorem ad Corinthios*, 42.
[10]Musculus, *Comm. 1 Cor.*, 40.
[11]Melanchthon, *Annotationes in Epistolam priorem ad Corinthios*, 44; citing Ps 4:6; Mt 16:4.

the Jews into the warmth of love, so that they may see in Jesus Christ the truth of God, and may be joyful in his goodness and power. Exposition of 1 Corinthians 1.[12]

But We Preach Christ! John Trapp: We not only preach *of* Christ, but we *preach* Christ; we give what we preach. It is the special office of the ministry to lay Christ open, to hold up the tapestry, to unfold the hidden mysteries of Christ. The Holy Ghost who is within them takes that which is Christ's and shows it to men and women. Commentary on 1 Corinthians 1:23.[13]

The Scandal of the Cross. Peter Martyr Vermigli: Paul calls the cross of Christ a stumbling block [*scandalum*] to the Jews because he saw that, when they heard it mentioned, they became agitated and tried to block the advance of the gospel. And since the Jews were so opposed to it that they recoiled from the Christian faith, their feelings of displeasure are called a stumbling block. . . . For the Greeks, the word of Christ seemed to be nothing other than foolishness. For this reason when Paul was explaining the mysteries of Christ among the Athenians, he was called a babbler,[14] and Festus said of him, "Your great learning has driven you insane!" Commentary on 1 Corinthians 1:23.[15]

God Calls His People. Wolfgang Musculus: Understand this statement: "Christ, the wisdom and power of God" to refer to the crucified Christ, his cross and death. For as Jerome reminds us regarding this passage, Paul is not speaking about the divinity of Christ, but about the mystery, administration, and power of the cross, which the Jews found offensive and the Greeks foolishness. But believers find the cross to be the wisdom and power of God, namely for salvation. When Paul says, "to those who are called, Jews as well as Greeks," he makes a distinction between those peoples who disbelieve and those who believe, so that we should not think that entire nations have been condemned. He calls believers "those who are called." Although he wished all people in general to be called, nevertheless Christ himself had said: "Many are called, but few are chosen." From this we learn that not everyone who has been called comes to faith in Christ. Paul understands "those who are called" in this passage to be those whom God has destined to salvation, whom God wished to be called into his kingdom by special grace, just as we read in Romans 8: "those whom he predestined, he also called; and those whom he called, he also justified." Commentary on 1 Corinthians 1:24.[16]

God's Wisdom Defies Human Understanding. Tilemann Hesshus: The greatness of divine wisdom, which is imparted to us in Christ, is illustrated by a comparison of dissimilar things. *For the foolishness of God*—that is, what seems to us to be absurd, tasteless, and foolish. Thus God commanded Abraham, when he was ninety-nine years old, to circumcise the flesh of his foreskin. God commanded Ezekiel to eat a scroll. God commanded Moses along with the people to go into the desert and the sea. God hurled Joseph into a pit, drove him into exile, and cast him into prison, although he had decided to make him the lord of Egypt. God chose fishermen, common and uncultured people, and the poor to be apostles so that by them he might call the world to repentance. When establishing his kingdom, God passed over the wise and powerful, and chose instead the lame, deaf, blind, lepers, and paupers. God commanded his only-begotten Son to suffer death on the cross. These and innumerable other things seem absurd and foolish to our reason. But God expressed his exceptional wisdom to his people through these things, which surpassed by far all of the wisdom of human intellect. For in all these things, the

[12]Colet, *Enarratio*, 81, 85; citing 1 Cor 2:8.

[13]Trapp, *A Commentary or Exposition*, 662*.

[14]Literally "a seed-picker."

[15]Vermigli, *In Selectissimam Priorem ad Corinthios Epistolam . . . Commentarii*, 25; citing Acts 17:18; 26:24.

[16]Musculus, *Comm. 1 Cor.*, 42; citing Mt 22:14; Rom 8:30. For Jerome's statement, see his "Letter to Paulinus," in NPNF 6:98.

righteousness, wisdom, and power of God are seen. Explication of 1 Corinthians 1:25.[17]

1:26-28 *God's Unlikely Children*

God Chose Simple People to Preach the Gospel. Huldrych Zwingli: From this it is not difficult to recognize that Jesus chose ignorant and simple fishermen to preach the gospel instead of the many who were wise or able to speak eloquently. And through the preaching of those men, however simple they may have been, Christ subjected to himself the most important people of this world, indeed, the entire world, for he was able to make the strength of tyrants nothing as well as the learning of philosophers. Consider then the condition of those who believed (for he is able to do so much more through preaching than believers realize). At the beginning, when the gospel was first preached, not many powerful people, not many of noble birth submitted to the yoke of faith. For who from among the leaders and the Pharisees believed in him? Consequently, it was the simple that were entrusted with preaching the gospel. Similarly, it was simple people who believed this teaching. Therefore, nothing is to be attributed to human wisdom and strength, for all power is God's alone. Annotations on 1 Corinthians 1:26.[18]

God Uses Ordinary People to Declare His Gospel. Wolfgang Musculus: "For consider your calling, brothers, not many of you were wise." Paul demonstrates what he said earlier concerning the condition of those who had been called, that is, those who believed in Christ. He gives a twofold explanation. First, he explains what sort of condition characterized the ministers of the gospel, namely, that they were ignorant men. In the eyes of the world, they were unlearned, weak, common men. But through their ministry and teaching they declared salvation and eternal life, bringing about the conversion of a great number of people to faith in Christ. No one can doubt that, without any persuasiveness of human wisdom or power of human strength, these ministers brought about such great things throughout the world that neither the power nor wisdom of the world could resist them. This serves, therefore, as a striking proof of divine wisdom and power being declared in the cross of Christ. Quadratus has shown how the foolishness of God is wiser than humans, and how the weakness of God is stronger than humans in his most beautiful example of a certain philosopher who, when he could not be led to faith in Christ with arguments and carefully devised syllogisms, came to faith through the simple preaching of the gospel of Christ by a certain ignorant bishop....

These words describe not only the condition of ministers but also the quality of Christians in general whom God has called: people who were ignorant, poor, common, weak, and nothing in the eyes of the world compared to those wise, powerful, and noble people who were especially struggling against the truth of the gospel. And with this expression, the apostle beautifully resolved the scandal that the believers were suffering because of their low and simple condition (and the splendor of their opponents' condition) since he shows how things appeared to God, that he especially chooses these kinds of people through whom he might declare his wisdom and power by the foolishness of gospel preaching. Commentary on 1 Corinthians 1:26.[19]

The Church Established Through Poor, Despised People. Simon Goulart: Poverty has built cities, discovered the arts and useful occupations, created the laws and government necessary for human life. Those great men and women were poor whom God appointed to build and maintain his church. I see poverty as patience in Jacob, moderation in Joseph, kindness in Moses,

---

[17] Hesshus, *Explicatio Prioris Epistolae ad Corinthios*, 28r-v; citing Gen. 17, Ex 12-13, Ezek 3:1.
[18] Zwingli, *Annotatiunculae . . . ex ore Zvinglij*, 14.
[19] Musculus, *Comm. 1 Cor.*, 42-43. Quadratus was a second-century Christian apologist. His account is found in Eusebius's *Ecclesiastical History* 10.3.

undaunted courage in David, full of mystery in the prophets, apostles, and in a very large number of doctors in the ancient church. I see poverty more fervent than even the passion of the martyrs and confessors of the truth of the gospel, whom one can name the poor of Jesus Christ. Now it has pleased God (as Paul said, who himself was a wise and blessedly poor man) to choose the lowly and despised things of this world, indeed even things that are nothing, to nullify things that are, so that no fleshly human being might glorify himself before him (1 Cor 1:28).... It is in poverty and in contempt for perishable things that the luster of the church is seen. When religion gave birth to an abundance of earthly goods, the daughter suffocated her mother. When early Christian bishops were made of gold, their crosses were made of wood. But bishops became like wood when their crosses appeared as gold. The more that there was simplicity in the administration of the Word of God and the sacraments, the more that pastors were small and humble in the eyes of the world, and the church had fewer troubles. And who can dare to despise poverty in a faithful servant of God in the presence of the prophets, apostles, confessors and martyrs, and Jesus Christ himself—who were all poor? On Poverty.[20]

No One Has Reason for Pride. John Calvin: Furthermore, it would be absurd for anyone to infer from this that God has overthrown the glory of the flesh so as to preclude the great and noble people of the world from any hope of salvation. There are some foolish people who not only use [Paul's words here] as an excuse to insult the great, as if they were abandoned by God, but also to despise them when comparing themselves to them. But let us remember that Paul is saying these things to the Corinthians, who, although they had no great standing in the world, nevertheless were still proud, though without reason. Therefore, in casting down the powerful, wise, and great, God does not thereby raise up the weak, unlearned, and despised to a position of pride; rather, he humbles all people equally. Therefore let those who are contemptible in the eyes of the world reflect on this fact: "How unassuming we should be when even those who are most illustrious in the eyes of the world are left with nothing. If the radiance of the sun is covered up, what then is to happen to the stars? And, if the light of the stars is extinguished, what is to happen to things shrouded in darkness?" Commentary on 1 Corinthians 1:26-27.[21]

Knowledge of God's Truth Sanctifies Human Studies. Richard Baxter: It is one thing to know the creatures as Aristotle, and another thing to know them as a Christian. None but a Christian can read one line of his *Physics* so as to understand it rightly. It is a high and excellent study, and of greater use than many apprehend; but it is the smallest part of it that Aristotle can teach us.... Your study of physics and other sciences is not worth a rush if it be not God that you seek after in them. To see and admire, to reverence and adore, to love and delight in God, as exhibited in his works—this is the true and only philosophy; the contrary is mere foolery, and is so called again and again by God himself. This is the sanctification of your studies, when they are devoted to God, and when he is the end, the object, and the life of them all. Reformed Pastor.[22]

1:29-31 *No Grounds for Boasting*

God Rejects Human Wisdom and Righteousness. Wolfgang Musculus: It should be noted here how the apostle indicates with the words "human flesh" and "boasting" that all that wisdom, power, righteousness, and piety, and all those strengths that are outside of Christ are intolerable to God. Accordingly, the whole of our righteousness and piety is nothing other than fleshly filth, the whole of our strength and virtues nothing but fleshly weakness, indeed detestable

[20]Goulart, *Seconde partie des Discours Chrestiens*, 240-42.

[21]CO 49:329 (cf. CTS 39:90-91).

[22]Baxter, *Reformed Pastor*, 57, 58.

boasting . . . that obscure the glory of God. For in Christ, God rejects all such wisdom, piety, and righteousness; in fact, he rejects whatever we pretend with words or outward appearance. Commentary on 1 Corinthians 1:29.[23]

Because Believers Are in Christ They Become Godlike. John Colet: In their own nature, human beings are wicked, unwise, impure, nothing. God, on the other hand, is being-itself, purity-itself, wisdom-itself, goodness-itself. There is, however, a mediator between God and human beings, Jesus Christ, who in a wondrous way united within himself divinity and humanity. Being God himself, he made humans godlike. In him we are born again so that we may exist, may be made pure, may be enlightened, and may be justified, to the end that we may be holy, wise, and good, and being made like God, may become gods. Exposition of 1 Corinthians 1:30.[24]

The Church Is the Home of Sinners. Martin Luther: May a merciful God preserve me from a Christian church in which everyone is a saint! I want to be and remain in the little flock and that church where there are the fainthearted, the feeble, and the ailing, who feel and recognize the wretchedness of their sins, who sigh and cry to God incessantly for comfort and help, who believe in the forgiveness of sin, and who suffer persecution for the sake of the Word, which they confess and teach purely and without adulteration. Satan is a cunning rogue. Through his fanatical activity he wants to trick the simpleminded into the belief that the preaching of the gospel is useless. "Greater effort is necessary," they say. "We must lead a holy life, bear the cross, and endure persecution." By such a semblance of self-styled holiness, which runs counter to the Word of God, many a person is misled. But Christ is our righteousness and our holiness. In him, not in ourselves, we have perfection (Col 2). I find comfort in and cling to the words of St. Paul in 1 Corinthians 1, that Christ "became for us wisdom from God, and righteousness and sanctification and redemption." Sermons on John 1.[25]

Jesus: Our Wisdom, Righteousness, Sanctification, and Redemption. Huldrych Zwingli: "Whom God made our wisdom." Naturally, God by his nature not only renews all things but also guides them. Jesus was sent to us from the Father to teach us true, real, heavenly wisdom. In him all the treasures of wisdom and knowledge are hidden. He is the brightest light that disperses and drives out all of the darkness of sins and errors. "Righteousness." Now all of us are [declared] righteous, though none of us is truly righteous. He opened up the path of righteousness for us by becoming our righteousness before God. In this way, he satisfies God's righteousness, because he offers himself as a sacrifice to the Father for us. By this means he has brought us to God. Now this has happened so that we might not trust in our own wisdom or righteousness, but might learn from divine wisdom what work was needed. We rest in divine righteousness since our own righteousness is filthier than menstrual rags. "Sanctification." That is, we are made truly holy through him, as seen in John 17. "Redemption." Truly, when we had been sold under sin by the prince of this world and had become the most shameful slaves, Christ liberated us from this servitude, not with gold or silver, but with his own blood, bringing us into his kingdom. He himself became the price of our redemption. His innocence washed away our guilt. His death granted us life. His blood washed away our filth. Annotations on 1 Corinthians 1:30.[26]

Jesus Christ Is Our Treasure. John Calvin: Since there are many people who, although they do not wish deliberately to renounce

[23]Musculus, *Comm. 1 Cor.*, 45.
[24]Colet, *Enarratio*, 86.
[25]LW 22:55; citing Col 2:10; 1 Cor 1:30.
[26]Zwingli, *Annotatiunculae . . . ex ore Zvinglij*, 15-16; citing Is 64:6 and John 17:17.

God, nevertheless look for things apart from Christ (as if he alone did not comprise all things in himself), Paul lists in passing what and how great a treasure is found in Christ and, at the same time, states that our entire mode of existence is found in him. . . . First, Paul says, Christ has been made our wisdom. By this he means that we find absolute perfection of wisdom in him, because in him the Father reveals his fullness to us, that we might not desire to know anything except him. . . . Second, Paul says, Christ has been made our righteousness. By this he means that in his name we have been accepted by God because he has expiated our sins by his death, and his obedience has been imputed to us for righteousness. For since the righteousness of faith consists in the forgiveness of sins and gracious acceptance, we obtain both through Christ. Third, Paul calls Christ our sanctification. By this he means that we, who by nature are unholy, are born again by his Spirit into holiness so that we might serve God. From this we also gather that it is not possible for us to be justified freely through faith alone without at the same time living in holiness. For these graces are joined together as if by an inseparable bond, so that anyone who attempts to separate them, at the same time, tears Christ apart. . . . Fourth, Paul says that Christ has been given to us for redemption. By this he means that we are delivered by his goodness from all bondage to sin, and from all the miseries that flow from it. And so, redemption is the first gift of Christ that is begun in us, and the last to be perfected. For salvation begins when we are rescued from the labyrinth of our sin and death, but in the meantime we groan for the day of final resurrection, yearning for our final redemption. Commentary on 1 Corinthians 1:30.[27]

The Blessings Conferred by Christ on the Church. The English Annotations: Having nothing at all of yourselves, God has given you all in Christ, according to the decree he made that he should be the source and the root of all the spiritual blessings conferred on the church. These blessings are wisdom, by the revelation of the mystery of salvation; righteousness, by his satisfaction and perfect obedience for our justification; sanctification, by the gift of the Spirit of regeneration; and redemption both of body and soul from all evil and misery, by the last and glorious resurrection in virtue of our mystical union with him. Annotations on 1 Corinthians 1:30.[28]

God Demolishes the Boasting of the Flesh. Wolfgang Musculus: "As it is written, 'Let the one who boasts,'" etc. Paul adds this conclusion for the purpose of countering the false apostles, who were seeking in this world their own knowledge and righteousness outside the glory of Christ. Now Paul recalls the passage of the prophet Jeremiah, chapter 9[:23]: "Thus the Lord says, 'Let not the wise man boast in his wisdom,'" etc. And so the apostle has concisely stated in this brief conclusion a summary of our preaching and faith when he says, "whom God made our wisdom, righteousness, sanctification, and redemption." Because he demolishes all boasting in the flesh and he will wage war against the learned, the wise and the powerful of this world . . . until the consummation of the world. Because those who wish to be wise, powerful, righteous, and holy cannot be partners with Christ and the wisdom of God has no place in them. Commentary on 1 Corinthians 1:30-31.[29]

Our Greatest Hope Comes from Christ Alone. Desiderius Erasmus: There is no comparison between divine and human things. For although in the judgment of the world you are contemptible and worthless, nevertheless, out of the goodness of God the Father, you have acquired true and great worth. For the Father adopted you into the fellowship of his Son, and through him all things have been bestowed on you, things of a different sort than what was falsely promised by

[27]CO 49:331 (cf. CTS 39:92-94).

[28]Downame, *Annotations*, CC4r*.

[29]Musculus, *Comm. 1 Cor.*, 47; citing Jer 9:23.

the lofty people of this world. You experienced true and salvific wisdom through Christ, so that there is no need of philosophy. You experienced innocence through Christ, so that you now require no help from the Mosaic law. You experienced a sanctified life through Christ, so that no one may reckon it from their merits. We experienced freedom through Christ, so that we might be redeemed by his blood from the tyranny of corruption. In brief, according to the Father's purpose, we owe our greatest happiness to Christ alone. And so, what Jeremiah wrote has occurred: "Let not the wise find pleasure in their wisdom; let not the powerful trust in their strength; let not the rich place their confidence in their riches, for these things provide no happiness. But if anyone wishes to boast, let them boast in this, namely that they know God, the author and source of all good things." PARAPHRASE ON 1 CORINTHIANS 1.[30]

[30]Erasmus, *Paraphrases*, 215; citing Jer 9:23-24.

2:1-5 Proclaiming Christ Crucified

And I, when I came to you, brothers,[a] did not come proclaiming to you the testimony[b] of God with lofty speech or wisdom. [2]For I decided to know nothing among you except Jesus Christ and him crucified. [3]And I was with you in weakness and in fear and much trembling, [4]and my speech and my message were not in plausible words of wisdom, but in demonstration of the Spirit and of power, [5]so that your faith might not rest in the wisdom of men[c] but in the power of God.

a Or *brothers and sisters* **b** Some manuscripts *mystery* (or *secret*) **c** The Greek word *anthropoi* can refer to both men and women

Overview: Paul reminds the Corinthians that during his visit with them, his preaching ministry had depended on neither eloquence nor human wisdom, but had focused on Jesus Christ and his cross. Reformation commentators find in Paul's words important lessons for gospel preaching in their own day. Preachers must proclaim the central and basic truth of Christianity, namely that Christ's death and resurrection defeated the power of Satan and achieved salvation, reconciliation, and liberation for sinners. Near-universal condemnation is directed toward anyone who might muddle this gospel message by extolling human works, flaunting human philosophy, or showing off human eloquence. The fact that some commentators defend a modest use of rhetoric in the service of the gospel, while others (including Anabaptist authors) criticize the pompous sermons of their confessional opponents, indicates that there was never complete agreement on the proper use of the art of persuasion in Protestant homiletics. Paul's surprising admission that his ministry was characterized by weakness and fear also invites discussion as to the role of hardship and suffering in Christian ministry. Zwingli is hardly unique among the Protestant reformers when he observes that the minister who preaches the cross will also suffer the cross.

Divine Strength and Wisdom in Preaching. Wolfgang Musculus: This chapter is divided into two parts. First, the apostle reminds the Corinthians how he did not come to them equipped with worldly eloquence and wisdom, and how he acted among them, namely, with weakness and trembling. Second, he defends the preaching of the gospel from the disgrace of foolishness, claiming that it is the wisdom of God, unrecognized and incomprehensible to unspiritual persons. Such wisdom is known only to spiritual persons by the Spirit of God. Commentary on 1 Corinthians 2.[1]

Divine Foolishness. Tilemann Hesshus: In the second chapter Paul teaches by means of his own example that neither human wisdom nor eloquence should be seen in gospel ministry, and that the Word of God should not be preached in an agreeable style so as to win applause and serve human greed, but should be preached with all humility. For human reasoning knows nothing of divine matters; and the gospel of Christ is the word of the cross, far removed from carnal judgment and from all external splendor. And here in this passage Paul shows the difference between the wisdom of the Spirit and the opinions or imaginings of the world. He teaches how terribly depraved is the whole nature of human beings, for it is shrouded in the darkest shadows of ignorance and the gloomiest fog of foolishness so that it understands nothing of those matters that pertain to the Spirit. Thus human nature cannot know God, but considers the entire Word of God as foolishness; but that wisdom which the Holy Spirit reveals in the Word is celestial. Explication on Introduction to 1 Corinthians.[2]

[1]Musculus, *Comm. 1 Cor.*, 47.
[2]Hesshus, *Explicatio Prioris Epistolae ad Corinthios*, 3r-v.

2:1-2 The Message of Paul's Minstry

Paul's Situation in Coming to Corinth. Jacques Lefèvre d'Étaples: When Paul was disputing at Athens with the Jews and with the Epicurean and Stoic philosophers, he converted to the righteousness of faith Dionysius and Damaris his wife, along with their household and many others. He came to Corinth, where he was received hospitably by Aquila and Priscilla. And he suffered much opposition from the Jews and was threatened even to the point of death. This account is reported in the Acts of the Apostles. Paul reminds the Corinthians of all this when he says, "When I came to you brothers." Commentary on 1 Corinthians 2:1.[3]

Testimony—or Mystery—of God? Theodore Beza: [The Greek reads] *to martyrion tou theou*, that is the gospel, by which God reveals himself to human beings, of which God is both the author and witness. . . . Now Ambrose reads *mystērion* (mystery) instead of *martyrion* (testimony), which is also found in two ancient Greek manuscripts. This reading seems especially fitting, particularly since the Syrian interpreter also reads it in this fashion. Annotations on 1 Corinthians 2:2.[4]

The Ineffectiveness of Evangelical Preachers. Dirk Philips: Oh, how many pride themselves now at the present time that they have received the gospel out of the grace of God and yet do so little, yes, nothing according to it! They want to be great masters in the Scripture and be called evangelical preachers, but Christ Jesus and him crucified they know not (1 Cor 2:2). The Enchiridion: The Sending of Preachers.[5]

There Is No Room for Boasting. Menno Simons: By the grace of God I am not minded like those who, in their imagination, soar above the clouds and want to be like unto the Most High. But, I repeat, I am a poor, miserable sinner who must daily fight with the flesh, the world, and the devil, and daily seek the mercy of the Lord, and who with the holy Paul boasts of nothing but Christ Jesus alone and that he was crucified for us. Why I Do Not Cease Teaching and Writing.[6]

Human Teaching about Works Is Pernicious. Philipp Melanchthon: Paul says in 2 Corinthians 4: "He himself has shone in our hearts to give the light of the knowledge of God in the face of Christ," that is, that they might be illuminated by the knowledge of God's glory shining in the face of Christ. The apostle alludes to this here when he says that he knows nothing except Jesus Christ and him crucified. It's as if he were saying, "just as I was knowing nothing except Christ, so any teaching other than about Christ is pernicious." All doctrines of works or human satisfaction hide Christ. But to have known Christ crucified and to see the most foolish image of Christ made a sin and a curse—these are the images that serve as testimonies to the divine mercy expressed toward us. Annotations on 1 Corinthians 2:2.[7]

The Knowledge of Christ Crucified. Wolfgang Musculus: When Paul mentions the knowledge of Christ crucified, he does not simply mean the historical account of Christ's resurrection, which unbelieving Jews also certainly knew about and could see. Rather, he means the mystery of the cross, concealed from all unbelievers, in which have been hidden all the treasures of the wisdom and knowledge of God. At first appearance, these

[3]Lefèvre d'Étaples, *Commentariorum in Epistolas Beati Pauli . . . Liber Secundus*, 102v; citing Acts 18:1-17.

[4]Beza, *Annotationes Maiores*, 160. Scholars continue to debate whether the superior Greek reading of this verse is *martyrion* or *mystērion*. See Fee, *1 Corinthians*, 88 n. 1. Ambrose (Ambrosiaster) treats this verse in his *Comment. in Epist. ad Cor*, in PL 17:202-3. Though long attributed to the fourth-century bishop of Milan, St. Ambrose, Reformation-era exegetes (including Erasmus) demonstrated that the commentary had been written by a different, unknown author who was later named "Ambrosiaster."

[5]CRR 6:214.

[6]Simons, *Complete Writings*, 311*.

[7]Melanchthon, *Annotationes in Epistolam priorem ad Corinthios*, 46, 48; citing 2 Cor 4:6.

words seem to belittle the gifts that Paul had spoken about, as if it was of little or no importance to know Christ Jesus and him crucified. But in fact, Paul's words boast of an infinite amount of wisdom and knowledge inasmuch as the whole world could never equal God's wisdom. It is just as if, in the audience of the wealthiest and most powerful aristocrats, he were to say, "Today, I have determined to proclaim nothing among you except divine riches, which are infinite and eternal." And if, standing among the powerful of this world ... he were to say "I have determined that I can do nothing among you except all things through God who strengthens me." And when in the presence of the wise, he were to say, "I have determined to know nothing among you wise people except the most hidden purposes of God that the whole world is unable to understand." This, in fact, is precisely what ... Paul says here: "I have determined to know nothing among you except Jesus Christ, and him crucified," that is, nothing except the Son of God, Savior of the world, the Lord of heaven and earth; the one who has achieved the victory over death, Satan, and hell; the redemption and liberation of the whole of humanity; the reconciliation with God and restoration of all things in heaven and on earth; in sum, the recovery of true and eternal happiness. For all these things are included in this knowledge of Christ and him crucified. Commentary on 1 Corinthians 2:2.[8]

Priority of Preaching Christ Crucified. John Calvin: This little clause is added by way of enlargement (*auxesin*) with the view of galling so much more those arrogant masters, by whom Christ was next despised, as they were eager to gain applause by being renowned for a higher kind of wisdom. This is a beautiful passage. From it we learn both what faithful ministers ought to teach, and what we must be learning throughout our whole lives, compared to which every thing else is to be considered dung. This is a beautiful passage. From it we learn both what faithful ministers ought to teach, and what we must be learning throughout our whole lives, compared to which everything else is to be considered dung. Commentary on 1 Corinthians 2:2.[9]

2:3-5 *The Method of Paul's Ministry*

God's Saints Are Often Terrified—for Good Reason. Tilemann Hesshus: Paul is not ashamed to admit his weakness, fear, and trembling, so that he might teach us not to engage in ministry for our own praise, but for the salvation of the church. The apostle was often greatly troubled in his mind and scared to death, as he several times admits.... Now God afflicted the apostles as well as the prophets with such terrors for many reasons: First, so that they might recognize for themselves the magnitude of God's anger against the wretchedness of sin, and get a small taste of it. Second, so that they might better experience the immense benefit of the Son of God, who set us free from such terrors of conscience by his blood. Third, so that they might not become conceited with those great gifts that God had given them, nor trust in themselves. Fourth, so that they might be aroused within themselves to put to death the old Adam, and desire all the more eagerly for eternal life. Fifth, so that, by their example, they might provide comfort to other members of the church who are weaker. For since many people within the church are overwhelmed by panics and fears of this sort, certainly they cannot conclude that these are signs of God's wrath if they see that the apostles, prophets, and church fathers experienced similar terrors. Sixth, so that in this way, the power of God might be more evident and all the praise might redound to him who has gathered his church and destroyed the kingdom of Satan. The pious mind should think about these things when it reads about the intense terrors of the greatest of men, such as Abraham, Jacob, Moses, Joshua, David, Hezekiah, and Paul. Explication of 1 Corinthians 2:2.[10]

[8]Musculus, *Comm. 1 Cor.*, 50.

[9]CO 49:333-34 (cf. CTS 39:97).

[10]Hesshus, *Explicatio prioris epistolae ad Corinthios*, 35v-36r.

Paul's Weakness and Fear. The English Annotations: Paul asserts his weakness against the power of eloquence and excellence of words. And he therefore joined with it fear and trembling, which are companions of true modesty. He is not speaking of the kind of fear and trembling that terrifies the conscience or indicates guilt, but the kind that is contrary to vanity and pride. Annotations on 1 Corinthians 2:3.[11]

Christian Preachers Must Cloak Human Wisdom. William Perkins: In the promulgation [of the sermon] two things are required: the hiding of human wisdom and the demonstration or showing of the Spirit. Human wisdom must be concealed, whether it be in the matter of the sermon or in the setting forth of the words, because the preaching of the word is the testimony of God and the profession of the knowledge of Christ and not of human skill: and again, because the hearers ought not to place their faith in the gifts of human beings, but in the power of God's Word (1 Cor 2:1-2, 5).

If people think that by this means barbarism should be brought into pulpits, they must understand that the minister may, yes, and must, privately use at his liberty the arts, philosophy, and variety of reading while he is framing his sermon, but he ought in public to conceal all these from the people and not make the least ostentation. *Artis etiam celare artem*: it is also a point of art to conceal art.

The demonstration of the Spirit is when the minister of the Word as he preaches behaves in such a way that all, even ignorant persons and unbelievers, may judge that it is not so much he that is speaking, as the Spirit of God in him and by him (1 Cor 2:4; 14:24-25; 4:19-20; Mic 3:8). This makes the ministry to be lively and powerful (Luke 11:27). The Art of Prophesying.[12]

Paul Employed the Most Excellent Form of Preaching. David Dickson: Paul is saying, "My speech and preaching never glittered with the acuteness of wit or human philosophy, nor with fineness of words fitted for persuasion, but in the evidences of Scripture and sound truth. Through these the Spirit demonstrated his power and worked in your hearts. Therefore this kind of preaching is most excellent." Exposition of 1 Corinthians 2:4.[13]

Paul's Reason for Plain Speech. The English Annotations: Paul gives here a reason why he concealed all art and eloquence, and used such plain speech in his preaching. It was for their great profit, not only that they might better understand him and more fully comprehend the mysteries he taught, but also so that they might thereby manifestly know that the gospel was from heaven. Therefore he privately rebukes them because in seeking vain ostentation and the show of human wisdom and eloquence, they willingly deprived themselves of the greatest help of their faith, the plain evidence of the Spirit. Annotations on 1 Corinthians 2:4.[14]

The Source of Paul's Power. Huldrych Zwingli: I know that the ancients and many other interpreters have understood the word "power" (*dynamis*) to mean the working of miracles. However, it seems to me that Paul generally understands *dynamis* to refer to that faith, devotion, and fervor with which those who are stimulated by the Spirit of God are endowed, both those who proclaim the Word of God diligently and effectively and those who hear the gospel proclaimed and believe. Indeed, people who behave and perform all things feebly and apathetically are a type of doubter. In fact, Paul boasts that he preached "in demonstration," that is, giving evidence "of the Spirit's power," as if he were saying: "Inasmuch as I was poor and weak, offering nothing of wisdom or eloquence, you easily recognized that I accomplished among you only that which the Spirit empowered me to do."

[11]Downame, *Annotations*, CC4r*.
[12]Perkins, *The Works of William Perkins*, 345*.
[13]Dickson, *Exposition of St. Paul's Epistles*, 43*.
[14]Downame, *Annotations*, CC4r*.

Here we learn that those who preach the gospel of Christ crucified without fear and trials do not at all aim at the target—as if it were possible to preach the cross without the cross. Therefore those who trust in human wisdom and power achieve nothing. Annotations on 1 Corinthians 2:4.[15]

God's Power Seen in Paul's Preaching. John Calvin: Now if the apostle's preaching had been dependent on the power of eloquence alone, it could have been overthrown by superior eloquence; moreover, no one would call something to be solid truth that rested on the brilliance of oratory. Truth may be helped by eloquence, but it must not rest on it. Now it is necessary for the most powerful things to stand by themselves, without any props. That is why this passage is an exceptional commendation of Paul's preaching, because heavenly power shone so clearly in it that it prevailed against so many obstacles, while receiving no support from the world. It follows, therefore, that the Corinthians must not allow themselves to be separated from his teaching, which they recognize rested on God's authority. Commentary on 1 Corinthians 2:5.[16]

Simple Evangelical Teaching Is Certain and Immovable. Wolfgang Musculus: It is as if Paul were saying: "so that your faith is not built on sand, but on a rock. It is not doubtful and uncertain, but firm, sure and immovable." This especially refers to a building that is supported by a foundation so that it is not subject to ruin. . . . Now who are those who are inclined to trust in persuasive words of human wisdom other than those who establish their faith on human wisdom? Now how is it possible for that wisdom to be unwavering and to withstand and endure the attack of the flesh, along with its human reasoning, the world, and Satan?

See how effectively Paul attacks the zeal for human wisdom and commends the simplicity of evangelical teaching. Earlier he said: "Lest the cross of Christ be emptied." Thus human wisdom empties the cross of Christ, while evangelical simplicity maintains the glory of the cross of Christ. Then, "So that no one might boast before God in their flesh." Again, "Let those who boast, boast in the Lord." Therefore human wisdom gives glory to the flesh and takes it away from God. Whereas the simplicity of evangelical teaching takes glory away from the flesh and ascribes it to God. And now, in this passage, Paul says: "so that your faith might not rest in human wisdom but in the power of God." Therefore persuasive human words establish faith on the sands of human wisdom, where it will soon be ruined, while the simplicity of the apostolic teaching, built on the rock of divine power, will continue unmoved amid all the temptations and supernatural attacks of Satan, the world, and the flesh. Commentary on 1 Corinthians 2:5.[17]

---

[15]Zwingli, *Annotatiunculae . . . ex ore Zvinglij*, 18-19.
[16]CO 49:335-36 (cf. CTS 39:101).
[17]Musculus, *Comm. 1 Cor.*, 54-55; citing 1 Cor 1:17, 29, 31.

2:6-16 Wisdom from the Spirit

[6]*Yet among the mature we do impart wisdom,*
although it is not a wisdom of this age or of the rulers
of this age, who are doomed to pass away. [7]*But we*
impart a secret and hidden wisdom of God, which
God decreed before the ages for our glory. [8]*None of*
the rulers of this age understood this, for if they had,
they would not have crucified the Lord of glory. [9]*But,*
as it is written,

> *"What no eye has seen, nor ear heard,*
> *nor the heart of man imagined,*
> *what God has prepared for those who love him"—*

[10]*these things God has revealed to us through the*
Spirit. For the Spirit searches everything, even the
depths of God. [11]*For who knows a person's thoughts*
except the spirit of that person, which is in him? So
also no one comprehends the thoughts of God except
the Spirit of God. [12]*Now we have received not the*
spirit of the world, but the Spirit who is from God,
that we might understand the things freely given us by
God. [13]*And we impart this in words not taught by*
human wisdom but taught by the Spirit, interpreting
spiritual truths to those who are spiritual.[a]

[14]*The natural person does not accept the things of*
the Spirit of God, for they are folly to him, and he is
not able to understand them because they are
spiritually discerned. [15]*The spiritual person judges all*
things, but is himself to be judged by no one. [16]*"For*
who has understood the mind of the Lord so as to
instruct him?" But we have the mind of Christ.

a Or *interpreting spiritual truths in spiritual language,* or *comparing spiritual things with spiritual*

Overview: Paul insists that God's glorious plan of salvation through Jesus Christ so defies human wisdom that only spiritual people, endowed with the Holy Spirit, are able to comprehend it. In light of a medieval tradition that associated spiritual maturity with sacred office, Protestant commentators emphasize that the phrase "spiritual persons" refers to all Christians in general, that is, those who have been reconciled to God through faith and have received the Holy Spirit, who makes known to them the hidden wisdom of God. Whereas spiritual persons understand the mystery of Christ's death and resurrection, unregenerate "natural persons" continue to despise Christ and his cross because they trust only in their human wisdom and natural affections. The Holy Spirit not only reveals heavenly wisdom but also applies Christ's salvation to believers by assuring them that they are justified before God and secure as God's beloved children. Finally, Paul's startling statement that the "the Lord of glory" was crucified (1 Cor 2:8) invites Reformation commentators to consider the profound mystery regarding the communication of Christ's human and divine natures in the unity of his person, and to explore whether one can properly speak of God suffering on the cross.

2:6-9 *God's Wisdom Is Not of This Age*

Paul Continues His Defense of Gospel Preaching. Wolfgang Musculus: This verse begins the second part of the chapter, where Paul defends the preaching of the gospel from the insults and ignominy of foolishness, describing it as divine wisdom, even though it is hidden. Indeed, this wisdom is hidden from people of this age, but is known to those who are spiritual. Paul has acknowledged the humility of his words and person; but, in him, this humility had been joined to the power of the Holy Spirit. Yes indeed, he has acknowledged that the world views the preaching of the gospel as foolishness; yet this preaching contains a hidden wisdom that wise persons are unable to comprehend. Therefore he has defended from ridicule the humility of his person, the weakness of his physical nature, and the simplicity of his words by the statement "in demonstration of the Spirit and of power." Now, here also he defends the glory of this message that he proclaims concerning the cross of Christ through the gospel when he says: "We speak wisdom among the mature," etc. He focuses on two themes to the end of the chapter: first, that this wisdom, concealed in mystery and unknown to the world and to the princes of this world, cannot be apprehended through natural human understanding; second, that this wisdom is revealed through the Spirit of God to those who believe and are spiritual. Commentary on 1 Corinthians 2:6.[1]

What Does Paul Mean by "Mature"? John Calvin: Lest Paul seem to despise wisdom (as do those unlearned and ignorant people who condemn learning with a kind of barbarian ferocity), he adds that he is not devoid of that true wisdom that is deemed as such by suitable judges. He calls "mature," not those who have attained full and complete wisdom, but those who possess a sound and right judgment. For Greek interpreters always translate the Hebrew word *tôm* with the Greek word *teleion*, which means complete or mature. Commentary on 1 Corinthians 2:6.[2]

The Light of God's Truth. John Trapp: [The wisdom of this age] is like the labor of moles, which dig dexterously underground but are blind above ground, and never open their eyes (according to Pliny) until the pangs of death are upon them. Do we cry to Christ, as the blind man in the Gospel did, who when Jesus asked him "What do you want?" said "Lord, that my eyes might be opened"? Philosophers observe that light is the vehicle of inspiration; light begets the flower in the field, the pearl in the sea, the precious stone in the earth. Thus the foundation of all renovation is illumination. O cry aloud to the Father of lights, "to give the light of the knowledge of the glory of God in the face of Jesus Christ!" This will occur when the wisdom of this world . . . comes to nothing. Commentary on 1 Corinthians 2:6[3]

Tyrants as Rulers of This Age. Wolfgang Musculus: Now Paul calls them "rulers of this age" not "those foolish tyrants." For he is not speaking about those powerful tyrants that are more beasts than human, but about the wise people of this age: the wise and prudent among the Gentile philosophers as well as the Jewish priests, scribes, and Pharisees. For the principle and requirement for governing demands either that philosophers rule or that rulers and princes philosophize. Certainly, in our day, this passage does not fit very well, except perhaps insofar as he says that the rulers of this age do not possess the knowledge of the wisdom of God, which is proclaimed in Christ. Commentary on 1 Corinthians 2:6.[4]

Evil Spirits and Magistrates as Rulers of This Age. The English Annotations: By the "rulers of this age" some understand the evil spirits, who rule in the air, and are called elsewhere *kosmokratoras* (Eph 6:12), that is, rulers of the darkness of this world who were the authors of pagan practice and religion. Others, by "rulers of this age," understand the kings and emperors of the earth, who dictated their laws out of the principles of human wisdom. But the words seem rather to carry a larger sense and extend to all those who have great power and authority over others, who esteem the statecraft that they use in their government the greatest and only wisdom in the world. Annotations on 1 Corinthians 2:6.[5]

The Hidden Wisdom of God. John Colet: In Jesus Christ is that miracle which must be adored and worshiped, that God himself should enter into union with human nature. This Being, composite of God and man, whom the Greeks call

[1]Musculus, *Comm. 1 Cor.*, 55.
[2]CO 49:336 (cf. CTS 39:102).

[3]Trapp, *A Commentary or Exposition*, 662*; citing Mk 10:51-52; 2 Cor 4:6. Pliny the Elder (c. 23/24–79) was a Roman scholar who composed *Natural History*, a work that sought to collate all ancient knowledge on the physical world.
[4]Musculus, *Comm. 1 Cor.*, 57.
[5]Downame, *Annotations*, CC4v*.

the God-man [*theanthrōpos*] lived here on earth and dwelt with humans for their salvation, that he might call them back and reconcile them to God the Father. He was steadfast in testing, in displaying virtue, and in defending justice all the way to death, even death on the cross. Then when he had conquered death, routed the devil, and ransomed humankind, so that he might have unfettered power of electing for himself (without the adversary having any grievance) those whom he wished, might call whom he would, and might justify those he called—when he had thus, I say, vanquished and laid low death and the author of death—he arose alive from death, and showed himself alive to many, and confirmed the fact with many proofs. Then, finally, as his disciples looked on, he ascended on high in his divinity and humanity to the Father, to oversee thence from heaven the progress and perfection of the work he had begun on earth, and continue to assist it to the extent appropriate. And then finally, after all these things, at the right time, when all has reached its fullness, when the principles contrary to God have been scattered afar and banished from his creatures . . . then at last, I say, when the warfare and battle everywhere between the light and the darkness will have lasted long enough, he shall come again, as God and the angels look on, the same Leader and Lord of hosts who first brought war against the enemy and who was the first to engage the enemy in hand-to-hand combat, winning victory by his patience and his death. He will come to aid his own people, in great light and power, so that, after driving wickedness and folly to flight, he may enlighten all things and make them good, and may at the end of all, by raising the dead to life, conquer death and swallow it up into immortality. Those who are to live he shall carry off with him into heaven; those who are to die he shall scatter into everlasting death far from himself, into that outer darkness, so that thenceforward, in a world formed anew, only life may reign forever in wisdom and justice.

This is that great and wonderful and astounding miracle in Jesus Christ; through him, the incarnate Son of God, the whole dispensation of God is wisely and powerfully accomplished. This, I say again, is the miracle we must believe with all faith and must love with all love, the miracle full of grace and truth, the miracle hidden in mystery, predestined before time for our glory, and at the appropriate time brought into reality and effect, and made manifest and revealed to humanity. Exposition of 1 Corinthians 2.[6]

God's Hidden Plan. Huldrych Zwingli: To expand [on Paul's words]: The wisdom of God, which until now was secret and hidden, we publicly declare and make known to all people. Indeed, God established from eternity his plan for the creation, fall, and renewal of humanity; however, it was hidden, not from God, but from us. By the covenant it was revealed only to a very few. Annotations on 1 Corinthians 2:7.[7]

The Mystery of God's Wisdom. Wolfgang Musculus: God's infinite wisdom appears everywhere to the eyes of mortals as they consider the creation around them. But Paul indicates that he is speaking not about what is seen but about things that are more hidden. And so, when he said in general terms "the wisdom of God," he added more specifically (so that grace might be discerned even more) "in mystery," etc. The word "mystery" is used not only in our religion but also in many others to designate a special and very holy secret that is thought to be disseminated to the general public by virtue of propitiatory sacrifice. Now, [many interpreters] wish the Greek word *mystērion* to mean . . . something that ought to be kept secret and remain hidden from within. By contrast, Paul uses the word this way: one thing is seen and heard or perceived with the senses, but something else is believed. . . . The preaching of the cross of Christ is a mystery, for it was not clear what was displayed in it, and on the surface it was not clear what was to be believed. Jews see human weakness in the

[6]Colet, *Ennaratio*, 91, 93. The Greek word *theanthrōpos* was coined by Origen to express the close union of the two natures of Christ.
[7]Zwingli, *Annotatiunculae . . . ex ore Zvinglij*, 20.

cross and death of Christ, and thus they are offended. But Christians believe the cross and death of Christ are the power of God, and thus they are saved. Accordingly, the sacraments of baptism and the Eucharist are called mysteries of the new covenant, for the unbeliever fails to recognize the meaning of the water, the bread, and the wine; whereas the believer understands by faith, and adores. Thus, as one ancient author has put it: "Believers recognize what is tasted here." Commentary on 1 Corinthians 2:7.[8]

Wisdom of the Gospel Different from Human Philosophy. David Dickson: The wisdom of the gospel is the wisdom of the living and eternal God, because it was wisely ordained by God and because in it the wonderful wisdom of God is revealed, touching the salvation and redemption of human beings.... Human philosophy is common and obvious to everyone who has the gifts of nature, but the wisdom of the gospel is a mystery, a hidden wisdom, because it is not understood by natural reason, as with human philosophy, but by supernatural revelation. Expositions of 1 Corinthians 2:7.[9]

The Lord of Glory Suffered. Tilemann Hesshus: Paul proves that the wisdom of the gospel is unknown to the rulers of this world by a most clear sign of their ignorance, along with its effect: since they crucified the Lord of glory, the only-begotten Son of God, the Redeemer and Savior of humanity. And those who did this were not common people, nor heathens ignorant of God, but the most powerful rulers and priests among the people of God. The Messiah had been promised to them before others. They were constantly hearing the preaching of the prophets concerning the coming of the Messiah and his spiritual kingdom. They were rulers among the people of God, holding tightly to the law and the promises concerning the Messiah, and they were seeking to instruct the whole world. Even though these people heard the heavenly preaching of Christ and saw with their own eyes his incredible miracles, nevertheless, with a terrible insanity and fury, together with the Roman prefect Pilate, they crucified the Lord of glory, the Prince of life, the Founder of the church....

[Let us now examine] the doctrine of the communication of Christ's attributes,[10] how it is related to this statement, and in what manner one should speak piously and cautiously concerning our Lord Jesus Christ as God and man, so as not to divide the one person nor confuse the natures. The divine nature of Christ did not suffer, was not crucified, did not die—for it is immutable. Nevertheless, God is called the Logos, the Lord of glory, the Son of God who suffered, was crucified, died, and was buried. For a property belonging to one nature is attributed to the whole person together [*in concreto*] on account of the hypostatic union. Both natures retain their essential properties and attributes, which nevertheless communicate together [*in concreto*] to express the personal union. This is not a worthless debate concerning words or phrases; rather, this topic is certainly of the greatest importance so that the hypostatic union of the two natures of Christ might be affirmed. When Polycarp is injured, God doesn't suffer, does he? For even if the Holy Spirit indwells the heart of Polycarp, God and Polycarp are not one person. But when the man Jesus Christ was crucified, the Lord of glory himself was crucified, because Jesus Christ is one person, both God and man. Explication of 1 Corinthians 2:8.[11]

[8]Musculus, *Comm. 1 Cor.*, 58.

[9]Dickson, *Exposition of St. Paul's Epistles*, 43*.

[10]Hesshus here addresses an ancient christological controversy over how the properties of Christ's human and divine natures communicate in the unity of his person. This controversy was revisited by Lutheran and Reformed theologians in the sixteenth century, in large part as it related to Christ's corporal presence in the Lord's Supper. See Richard A. Muller, *Dictionary of Latin and Greek Theological Terms: Drawn Principally from Protestant Scholastic Theology* (Grand Rapids: Baker, 1985), 72-74.

[11]Hesshus, *Explicatio Prioris Epistolae ad Corinthios*, 39r-v. Polycarp, the Bishop of Smyrna, was burned to death for his Christian faith in the mid-second century.

Christ Did Not Suffer in His Divine Nature. Peter Martyr Vermigli: I strongly deny that Christ suffered in his divine nature. I would grant that God was born, suffered and died, and was crucified because Christ as one person is indivisible; he thus has the two natures conjoined in himself, but not confused or mixed. Hence this Christ, who is truly God and man, is believed to have suffered, been crucified, and to have died. But if it is asked: by virtue and reason of both natures? The response will be by virtue of the human nature; since when Paul says the Lord of glory was crucified he attributes to the whole Christ what applies to him because of the condition of the one part. Letter to the Polish Lords and Ministers.[12]

The Incomprehensible Blessings of the Future Life. Wolfgang Musculus: It is customary to appeal to this passage here concerning the enormous blessings of the future life, that they cannot be grasped and are incomprehensible to the human mind. And with good reason. For although we have perceived in many ways the value of those blessings by faith in Christ, nevertheless we have not perceived all of them. Or rather we have not perceived the most dazzling among them, but instead still see everything obscurely and in riddles. But how great and precious these blessings are is indicated by what is inferred from this statement, that the grandest and most splendid things that we see and hear, and that our hearts comprehend on earth, are inferior to those future, heavenly blessings. And that is true not only because these blessings have been hidden but also because they are infinite in their magnitude, number, and duration. It is impossible for human beings to apprehend these blessings—not even those who are otherwise most capable of discernment. For what is more receptive and voracious than the desire of the heart (to say nothing about the intellect)? Nevertheless, the heart is not sufficient either to understand or desire the greatness of heavenly blessings. Now truly the blessings we read about in Scripture, that we hear through the preaching of the gospel, that we as believers comprehend by faith—these blessings are very great. And yet, someday, when we come to possess them, not partially but completely, it will be like what is read concerning the queen of Sheba, who, when she saw that Solomon's wisdom was far greater than reported, was amazed and said in shock: "The report was true that I heard in my own land about your words and your wisdom, but I did not believe the reports until I came and saw it with my own eyes. And I now know that not the half was reported to me. Your wisdom and prosperity far surpass the report that I heard." But there is an important difference between earthly blessings and heavenly blessings: the more intensely we desire earthly blessings when they are absent, the more quickly they become worthless when they are present, because in themselves they are worthless. . . . But with heavenly blessings, the more we desire them when they are absent, the more we love them when we possess them, and thus we do not loathe them, because they provide more when we possess them than was promised when we did not. Commentary on 1 Corinthians 2:9.[13]

The Christian's Glorious Inheritance. Balthasar Hubmaier: I also believe and confess eternal life that you, my God and Lord, shall give to your believers and elect ones after this miserable life, endowing them with certain, bright, and joyous contemplation of your divine countenance, and satisfy all their desires with eternal rest, eternal peace, and eternal blessedness, which joy, rapture, and delight no man can express or conceive here on earth. For no eye has seen, no ear has heard, and it has never entered into the heart of man what God has prepared for those who love him. Twelve Articles of the Christian Faith.[14]

[12]Peter Martyr Vermigli to the Polish Lords & Ministers, in *Peter Martyr Vermigli*, 5:151.

[13]Musculus, *Comm. 1 Cor.*, 61-62; citing 1 Kings 10:6-7.

[14]CRR 5:240.

The Joy of the Saints. John Trapp: As God prepared paradise for Adam, so he prepared heaven for all of his children. Yet he does not reserve everything for the life to come, but gives a few grapes of Canaan in this wilderness. And so this text is to be understood of gospel-joy and those present comforts that the saints have here on earth, that reward before the reward. For not only in the future but even "in the doing of God's will there is great reward," such as the natural eye has not seen, nor the ear heard. The stranger does not interfere with this joy. It is the sparkle of that white stone; it is that new name known to none but those who have it; it is a comfort confined to the communion of the saints. Commentary on 1 Corinthians 2:9.[15]

2:10-13 *The Spirit Reveals God's Thoughts*

Paul Directs These Words Against the False Prophets. Heinrich Bullinger: What follows was written specifically against the false apostles for the sake of declaring and confirming what was said earlier. For the apostle discloses the method God uses to reveal that heavenly wisdom to his saints. From this we glean from what instructor, or by what method, saving wisdom is learned. One doesn't learn it from philosophers, teachers, or those philosophical guides, nor from those champions of free will or eloquence—as the false apostles believed—but through the Spirit of God. Commentary on 1 Corinthians 2:10.[16]

The Holy Spirit Reveals God's Secrets. Desiderius Erasmus: God reveals his secrets to those of us who are his friends, not by means of human teaching, but by the secret breath of his Spirit. For the Spirit, who is divine and proceeds from God, lays bare the most hidden and obscure secrets of God, which human curiosity cannot penetrate. It is easy to discern the facial appearance of other people. But no mortal being can perceive what is hidden in the secret recesses of their minds. The Spirit alone knows this; he alone knows what goes on in people's minds. And so, people contemplate hidden things and several of them investigate them, but no one knows those things that are concealed in the divine mind and counsel except the eternal Spirit, who is most intimate with God and knows all things on account of him. People share their secret thoughts with other people in soft whispers. God shares his judgments with the pious through the Spirit of God—not through human spirits, which are able to convey nothing except human things. That is what the Spirit is like, and that is what he teaches. Paraphrases on 1 Corinthians 2.[17]

God Alone Instructs Through His Spirit. Huldrych Zwingli: "For who knows a person's thoughts?" Paul proves his point with a comparison. No one knows what is in a person's heart, except the person himself. Therefore, who is able to know the secret of God except God himself? Now, since you recognize that this plan of God is secret—the plan by which he has freed you from death through his Son—it is necessary that you be instructed by God alone. With these words, Paul shows that faith in God comes through Christ, not from human beings, but from God alone. It is as if he were to say: "Do you understand? Do you believe? Therefore you have received this understanding and revelation from God." Notice here that Paul implicitly criticizes the false apostles, who were flattering themselves before the Corinthians with seductive words and certain elaborate questions. It is as if he were saying: "In no way did I act like this among you, but I came in humility. And, nevertheless, you are mighty in faith and in the understanding of God. Thus you see that this happened by the power of God alone." Annotations on 1 Corinthians 2:11.[18]

[15]Trapp, *A Commentary or Exposition*, 662*; citing Ps 19:11; Rev 2:17.
[16]Bullinger, *In Priorem ad Corinthios Epistolam Commentarius*, 24.
[17]Erasmus, *Paraphrases*, 220 [*sic* 219].
[18]Zwingli, *Annotatiunculae . . . ex ore Zvinglij*, 21.

Christian Preachers Are Ministers of God's Spirit. Wolfgang Musculus: First, it should be noted here that the power of human free will can accomplish nothing of the things of God and that human reason is blind to the knowledge of the truth of God that is in Christ Jesus. Thus Christ said to Peter in Matthew 16: "Flesh and blood has not revealed this to you, but my Father who is in heaven." And John 6: "No one comes to me unless my Father draws him." . . . Thus no knowledge, no wisdom, no diligence of human reason whatsoever will be able to understand the will of God unless the revelation of God is added—Paul is mindful of this here. For if no human being, not even the wisest among them, can discern the thoughts of even a very stupid person unless they receive it by revelation, how can anyone discern the thoughts of God unless the revelation of God is added? From this, however, we should not conclude that the ministry of the Word is useless due to the fact that it is administered by human preachers. For it has been established by God that faith comes by hearing, and that ministers of the Word are ministers of God's Spirit and dispensers of those mysteries. And so Paul was appointed to bring light to the Gentiles. For this reason he strove to bring the Galatians to Christ. And Christ sent his apostles into the world so that they might teach all nations. And in John 17 he prayed: "I do not ask for these only, but also for those who will believe in me through their word." There is great usefulness in the ministry of the Word, through which the foolish are brought to saving faith. . . .

It should also be noted that the apostle is speaking about the true and living knowledge of God, not that which comes through mere study of the Scriptures without separate revelation. This kind of Scripture study is more opinion than sure knowledge, it lasts only for a time, it is uncertain and changes. Hence it is ineffective, unable to change the heart or transform the life; it does not bring about faith, love of God or neighbor, or fear of God. But that knowledge which comes through the revelation of God brings about all these things through itself, that is, through the inspiration of the Spirit of God. Therefore to the study of the Scriptures one must join earnest prayers, a humble mind, and a desire for righteousness. For the Spirit of God rests on those who are humble and fear God. Commentary on 1 Corinthians 2:11.[19]

The Spirit Testifies to Our Justification. Philipp Melanchthon: The Holy Spirit brings it about that we know the gifts given by Christ. Note how effectually the Spirit teaches that grace and truth have been given through Christ; that is, the Spirit brings it about that you steadfastly believe that you are justified through Christ without any regard for works. That passage of John 14, "he will teach you all things," pertains here. Annotations on 1 Corinthians 2:12.[20]

The Spirit Assures the Elect of Their Salvation. John Calvin: This passage very clearly refutes that diabolical teaching of the sophists which keeps believers in constant uncertainty. For they prescribe that all believers should doubt whether they are in God's grace, and they allow no assurance of salvation except that which hangs on moral or probable conjecture. But in this way they overturn faith in two respects. For they want us to doubt whether we are in a state of grace, and afterward they throw us into doubt regarding final perseverance. But here the apostle declares in general terms that the elect have been given the Spirit, by whose testimony they know with certainty that they have been adopted to the hope of eternal salvation. Certainly, if the sophists wish to defend their doctrine, they must either deprive the elect of the Spirit of God, or make even the Spirit subject to uncertainty. Both ideas are clearly at odds with Paul's teaching. Therefore we know that this is the nature of faith: that the conscience has from the Holy Spirit a sure testimony of God's goodwill toward it, so that with confidence it does

[19]Musculus, *Comm. 1 Cor.*, 65; citing Mt 16:17; Jn 6:44; 17:20.
[20]Melanchthon, *Annotationes in Epistolam priorem ad Corinthios*, 50; citing Jn 14:26.

not doubt to call on God as Father. Commentary on 1 Corinthians 2:12.[21]

The Content and Form of Paul's Teaching. Wolfgang Musculus: After discussing the knowledge of God, which is through the Spirit of God, Paul turns his attention to the ministry of teaching. . . . He considers two things. First, the nature of Paul's teaching, which the world did not understand and judged to be foolishness when he was preaching that redemption is through the cross of Christ. This is what Paul means when he says: "what we impart." As if to say: "What do we declare other than what is imbued by God's Spirit and what we have obtained through the knowledge of those things given to us by God? This is exactly what we proclaim by the Spirit of God. Now we do not proclaim the wisdom of this world but the wisdom that God has given us, so that we might know the generosity of his gifts." We should speak in a similar way about these things. Therefore this is the teaching of the gospel: to speak about what God has given us. Whoever does not pass on this primary teaching in no way behaves like a gospel teacher.

Second, the apostle commented about his teaching, that it was not communicated with persuasive words of human wisdom but with plain and simple words, which people who delighted in flowery speech and syllogisms found worthless and contemptible. For they ignored the precious nature of what Paul was teaching since the attractiveness of the apostle's plain words resembled the most beautiful of all things. He considers this when he says, "in words not taught by human wisdom, but taught by the Spirit." It's as if he were saying: "The reason our preaching is not flavored with human reason is because we have been imbued with the Spirit of God, not the world. For the Spirit is not only the illuminator and teacher of our heart, but the governor of our mouth and the instructor of our words." People devoted to worldly wisdom have their formulas for speaking well, which they employ carefully. But is it not insanity to require those who speak by the Spirit of God to adopt a pattern of speaking that accords with the spirit of the world? Commentary on 1 Corinthians 2:13.[22]

Expressing Spiritual Things with Spiritual People. The English Annotations: The phrase "expressing spiritual things with spiritual" allows a double translation and interpretation. If we read the phrase as expressing spiritual things with *other spiritual things*, then the meaning is that we apply spiritual terms and manners of propounding and expressing to spiritual matters and subjects. . . . For example, if the question is whether Christ rose the third day, we bring a confirmation and illustration out of the prophet Jonah. The word used in this text is rightly translated "to judge together," that is, by comparing texts of holy Scripture and setting spiritual things one against the other, we can make a more certain judgment of them (as when mirrors opposite one another cast mutual light one on the other). But if we read this phrase as "expressing spiritual things with *spiritual persons*," then the meaning is clearly this: that we are to confer with the faithful about points of faith, and communicate spiritual mysteries to other spiritual persons, not to those who are still carnal and mere worldlings, for to do so would be to cast pearls before swine. This latter interpretation agrees well with the following verse, where the apostle distinguishes natural persons from spiritual persons, and affirms that natural persons do not perceive the things of the Spirit of God. Annotations on 1 Corinthians 2:13.[23]

2:14-16 *Spiritual Discernment*

The Light of God's Wisdom Reaches More Noble People First. John Colet: But

[21]CO 49:342 (cf. CTS 39:112-13). Calvin usually employs the term *sophists* to refer to medieval Catholic theologians and members of the theological faculty at the University of Paris (the Sorbonne) whom he believed had distorted the Christian gospel.

[22]Musculus, *Comm. 1 Cor.*, 68-69.

[23]Downame, *Annotations*, CC4v*. The former rendering is Origen's. See Mark Sheridan, *Language for God in Patristic Tradition: Wrestling with Biblical Anthropomorphism* (Downers Grove, IL: IVP, 2014), 34, 229-332.

if God himself is essential nobility, wisdom, and power, who does not see that Peter, John, James, and the rest of the apostles, even before God's truth had shed its light on the earth, were as far superior in wisdom and strength as they were removed from the foolishness and the weakness of those other people. So it should be not at all surprising if God . . . chose people considered stupid and weak, since in reality they were more noble than all the world, were more separate from the worthlessness of the world, and had a loftier stature. Just as at sunrise the higher reaches of the earth are first and more easily touched by the rays of light, so likewise when the light came forth which was to enlighten every human being coming into this world, it first shone on those who stood taller among the human race and soared like mountains out of the valleys of humankind. More slowly, however, do the rays of divine light penetrate to other people, who are in the depths, and in the cold regions, enshrouded in their own foggy wisdom. In those lower regions the rays of divine light enlighten people with more difficulty, and abandon them more quickly, unless it should happen that those rays disperse the cloud with more penetrating beams of light and so enlighten them, enabling them to cast off all that they have and rise up to Christ. . . . No one should doubt, therefore, that God really did choose for himself the nobility and the wisdom and the power of the human race, although they were not considered such, and that he began to enlighten humanity's cloud in its purer part, so that thence the rays of light might pierce to thickest blackness. Exposition of 1 Corinthians 2.[24]

Spiritual Things Are Inaccessible to Natural Reason. Jacques Lefèvre d'Étaples: Among spiritual persons there are many levels. Those who perceive the gifts of the Holy Spirit are certainly spiritual, but they are less spiritual than those whom the Holy Spirit indwells. And although soul and reason are united in human beings, it happens that the rational person does not attain the mysteries and hidden things of God by means of reason. For the hidden things are foolishness to the rational person, in the same manner that mathematics is foolishness to the nonmathematician. For a person judges it foolishness if someone says that the sun is more than a hundred times larger than the earth, or that the moon is two thousand four hundred and seventy-four (that is 2,474) times smaller than the sun, because these matters are decided and disproved and examined by means of mathematics. And nonmathematicians are not able to understand the things of mathematics. So too it is with those matters pertaining to the Spirit of God. Commentary on 1 Corinthians 1:14.[25]

The Identity of the Unspiritual Man. Philipp Melanchthon: In this passage Paul called persons "natural" to mean that aspect of human beings we commonly call "rational"—the best part of human nature—since the natural person lives by means of the mind, not according to crass bodily pleasure. . . . Socrates or Zeno or Paul before his conversion can be identified as men of this sort. Such are all those who are just and wise without having the spirit of Christ. In other passages Paul calls humans "flesh" according to the whole of their nature. Here he describes them as "natural" for the important reason that he wishes to emphasize that he is speaking especially about humans according to their higher faculties. In so doing, he is opposing the sophists, who falsely assign the flesh to only part of humankind, namely the body. He calls it "natural" here, so as to make it clear that he is talking not just about human emotions but also about human reason. Annotations on 1 Corinthians 2:14.[26]

---

[24]Colet, *Ennaratio*, 95, 97; citing Jn 1:9.

[25]Lefèvre d'Étaples, *Commentariorum in Epistolas Beati Pauli . . . Liber Secundus*, 103v. In fact, the sun is approximately 109 times larger than the earth, and 416 times larger than the moon.

[26]Melanchthon, *Annotationes in Epistolam priorem ad Corinthios*, 52.

The Identity of the Natural Person. Tilemann Hesshus: Paul identifies the "natural person" as the entire person, soul and body, together with all the capacities of the mind, the will, and the heart—insofar as we have been naturally generated from our parents, but not yet regenerated by the Holy Spirit. For spiritual things oppose natural things. That is why things left in their original condition are called natural. Of such kind are not only the heathen and all those outside the church but also all those within the church who have not yet been converted by the Holy Spirit. Therefore, regardless of whether men and women are powerful in wisdom, erudition, intellect, strength, or practical knowledge of things, if they have not been regenerated and illuminated by the Holy Spirit, they are "natural persons" and do not at all understand the things of the Spirit. In the same sense, sacred Scripture elsewhere calls "carnal" what in this passage Paul refers to as the "natural person." . . . However gifted with wisdom the heathen were—Themistocles, Solon, Plato, Xenophon, Scipio, Lelius, Augustus—they were still "natural persons." The Pharisees Gamaliel and Nicodemus (before his conversion) and all who were destitute of the light of the Holy Spirit were "natural persons." After all, Christ says: "Unless a person has been born again by water and Spirit, he will not see the kingdom of God"—Paul is teaching the same thing here. Explication on 1 Corinthians 2:14.[27]

The Natural Person Is Not a Block of Wood. Heinrich Bullinger: Natural persons (that is, persons not yet regenerate by the Holy Spirit) are not blocks altogether without all sense or feeling: for if they were utterly without all the discourses of reason, then how should the preaching of the gospel seem like foolishness to them? By the gift of God, natural persons hear and understand the words and sense of the holy Scripture. But because of their natural corruption they are not touched by them; they do not rightly judge them; they judge them as folly. Nor do natural persons perceive that the [truths of Scripture] must be discerned spiritually, because they are not regenerate, and are still without the true light of God's most Holy Spirit. Decades.[28]

Teachers Must Be Taught by the Spirit. Dirk Philips: Those who do not have the Spirit of the Lord do not understand the Word of the Lord and do not experience what is spiritual. How should they then be able to teach God's Word correctly or correctly distribute the gifts of the Spirit (1 Cor 2:14)? Therefore all should well see to it that they do not accept the office of teacher before the teachers themselves have been taught by God and been enlightened with the Holy Spirit, through whom they may speak God's Word correctly. The Enchiridion: The Sending of Preachers.[29]

Natural Persons Cannot Be Trusted in Spiritual Matters. Wolfgang Musculus: When natural persons try to attain to the knowledge of Christ's kingdom, their efforts are in vain. When they debate concerning matters of the spirit, they talk nonsense. When they express their opinion, they lie. When they establish a religious practice, it is done very rashly. When they teach, they seduce. When they win a group of converts, they lead them astray. Why? Because they are unable to learn. Therefore, why should we trust those who employ natural judgment (or, sometimes, even carnal judgments) in conducting the Christian faith? Commentary on 1 Corinthians 2:14.[30]

The Holy Ghost Makes God Known. John Donne: People can teach us ways to find out things: the pilot how to find land; the astronomer how to find a star. People can [also] teach us ways to find God: the natural person through the book of creatures; the moral person through an exemplary life; the Jew in the law; the Christian in the gospel. But . . . only the Holy Ghost enables us to

[27]Hesshus, *Explicatio Prioris Epistolae ad Corinthios*, 44v-45r; citing Jn 3:5.

[28]Bullinger, *Decades*, 1:99*.

[29]CRR 6:206.

[30]Musculus, *Comm. 1 Cor.*, 73.

find God so as to make him our own, and to enjoy him. Sermon Preached upon Whitsunday.[31]

Natural Men and Women Are Limited by Their Natures. John Trapp: The water rises no higher than the spring from whence it came. So natural men and women can ascend no higher than nature. If unreasoning creatures could draw a picture of God, Xenophanes said, they would certainly paint him like themselves, because they can think of nothing above themselves. Commentary on 1 Corinthians 2:14.[32]

Two Ways of Judging the Spirits. Martin Luther: What we say is this: the spirits are to be tested or proved by two sorts of judgment. One is internal, whereby through the Holy Spirit or a special gift of God anyone who is enlightened concerning themselves and their own salvation judges and discerns with the greatest certainty the dogmas and opinions of all human beings. Of this it is said in 1 Corinthians: "The spiritual person judges all things, but they themselves are judged by no one." This belongs to faith and is necessary for every individual Christian. We have called it above "the internal clarity of holy Scripture." . . . [The second is] an external judgment, whereby with the greatest certainty we judge the spirits and dogmas of all human beings, not only for ourselves, but also for others and for their salvation. This judgment belongs to the public ministry of the Word and to the outward office, and is chiefly the concern of leaders and preachers of the Word. We make use of it when we seek to strengthen those who are weak in faith and confute opponents. This is what we earlier called "the external clarity of Scripture." Bondage of the Will.[33]

Spiritual Judgment. Wolfgang Musculus: No natural person is able to judge, evaluate, and understand the spiritual person. As John 3 says: "The Spirit blows where he wishes, and you hear his sound, but you do know where he comes from or where he goes. So it is with everyone born of the Spirit." For this kind of spiritual life, characterized by spiritual understanding and living spiritually, cannot be understood by the judgment of reason. And thus, this kind of spiritual life is not common to all people; it is understood only by those who have received these things, who are spiritual. "The world," John says, "has not known you, because it has not known God." Some interpreters explain these words in a different fashion. Ambrose understands the word "judge" as the equivalent of "condemn." . . . Thus spiritual persons judge all things; that is, by their example unbelievers are condemned. And too, the spiritual person is judged and condemned by no one. Jerome also interprets the passage in this way. Commentary on 1 Corinthians 2:15.[34]

This Passage Does Not Refer to Popes. John Trapp: Papists will argue that "this spiritual person that judges all things, but is himself to be judged by no one" refers to the pope. But when this epistle was written, there was no such thing as a pope, and no such doctrine that the pope is infallible and must not be contradicted even if he speaks blasphemy or heresy—indeed, even if he draws thousands of souls after him to hell (as the canonists teach). Commentary on 1 Corinthians 2:15.[35]

Believers Have the Mind of Christ. Philipp Melanchthon: When Paul says, "we have the mind of Christ," it is the same as what he

[31]Donne, *Sermons of John Donne*, 6:129*.

[32]Trapp, *A Commentary or Exposition*, 663*. Xenophanes (c. 570–475 BC) was an ancient Greek philosopher and poet.

[33]LCC 17:159* (cf. p. 112); citing 1 Cor 2:15.

[34]Musculus, *Comm. 1 Cor.*, 73; citing Jn 3:5; 1 Jn 3:1. Ambrose (Ambrosiaster) treats this passage in his *Comment. in Epist. I ad Cor.*, PL 17:207.

[35]Trapp, *A Commentary or Exposition*, 663*. The doctrine of papal infallibility (*ex cathedra*, on matters of faith and morals) wasn't officially adopted until Vatican I (1869–1870). However, theories of papal infallibility were in currency in the Western church from the fourteenth century. See Eamon Duffy, *Saints and Sinners: A History of the Popes* (New Haven, CT: Yale University Press, 1997) and Brian Tierney, *Origins of Papal Infallibility, 1150–1350: A Study on the Infallibility, Sovereignty, and Tradition of the Middle Ages* (Leiden: Brill, 1972).

said above, "God has revealed to us through his Spirit." That is, he made us believe the gospel, which otherwise offends the sanctimonious and is mocked by the wise.... Because we know Christ, we know the will of the Father in Christ. And knowing the will of the Father we can judge spiritually concerning God's works both within us and outside us. For Christ is displayed before us as a sort of exemplar or mirror in which we can contemplate both the image of sin and the image of life. In his dying we see the wrath of God toward sin. In his coming back to life, we see his mercy. Again, in his dying we see that the path to life goes through death and that it is therefore God's good purpose; because we are mortified, we see the Son has been glorified through death. Therefore his death is an act of mercy or of God's favor.... Therefore he says, "we have the mind of Christ"; that is, we see what is the will of God, both in his being merciful and being wrathful in Christ. And so, Christ is the image of his will. It therefore follows that those who know this image judge spiritually. Thus John says: "The only-begotten Son, who is in the bosom of the Father, has made him known to us." Annotations on 1 Corinthians 2:16.[36]

God's Purposes in Christ. Tilemann Hesshus: Paul proves the previous statement that spiritual things cannot be discerned by carnal persons from the testimony of the prophet Isaiah, drawn from chapter 40. For the prophet witnesses to the fact that the secret purposes of God regarding the gathering of the church and the governance of the world are known to no human being apart from heavenly revelation. Therefore the natural person, who is not illuminated by the light of the Holy Spirit, cannot discern the mystery of the gospel, which involves God's secret purposes concerning the gathering of the church. However, we Christians, who have been reconciled to God by faith and given the Holy Spirit, possess the mind of Christ. That is, we understand the purpose and plan of the eternal God, which he decreed concerning the redemption of humanity through his Son. We understand the purpose of Jesus Christ for gathering the church. We know who God is and how he wishes to be worshiped. We know that God, in his law, sternly condemns the sins of all human beings. We know that, in the gospel, grace is offered to all who repent—the remission of sins, righteousness, the Holy Spirit, and life eternal. We know for what purpose Christ endured the cross, and why he subjects the church to the cross. We know how we are to pray to God and what in fact will be given to believers in eternal life. Explication of 1 Corinthians 2:16.[37]

[36]Melanchthon, *Annotationes in Epistolam priorem ad Corinthios*, 54, 56; citing Jn 1:18.

[37]Hesshus, *Explicatio Prioris Epistolae ad Corinthios*, 48r; citing Is 40:13.

3:1-23 Divisions in the Church

But I, brothers,[a] *could not address you as spiritual people, but as people of the flesh, as infants in Christ.* [2]*I fed you with milk, not solid food, for you were not ready for it. And even now you are not yet ready,* [3]*for you are still of the flesh. For while there is jealousy and strife among you, are you not of the flesh and behaving only in a human way?* [4]*For when one says, "I follow Paul," and another, "I follow Apollos," are you not being merely human?*

[5]*What then is Apollos? What is Paul? Servants through whom you believed, as the Lord assigned to each.* [6]*I planted, Apollos watered, but God gave the growth.* [7]*So neither he who plants nor he who waters is anything, but only God who gives the growth.* [8]*He who plants and he who waters are one, and each will receive his wages according to his labor.* [9]*For we are God's fellow workers. You are God's field, God's building.*

[10]*According to the grace of God given to me, like a skilled*[b] *master builder I laid a foundation, and someone else is building upon it. Let each one take care how he builds upon it.* [11]*For no one can lay a foundation other than that which is laid, which is Jesus Christ.* [12]*Now if anyone builds on the foundation with gold, silver, precious stones, wood, hay, straw—* [13]*each one's work will become manifest, for the Day will disclose it, because it will be revealed by fire, and the fire will test what sort of work each one has done.* [14]*If the work that anyone has built on the foundation survives, he will receive a reward.* [15]*If anyone's work is burned up, he will suffer loss, though he himself will be saved, but only as through fire.*

[16]*Do you not know that you*[c] *are God's temple and that God's Spirit dwells in you?* [17]*If anyone destroys God's temple, God will destroy him. For God's temple is holy, and you are that temple.*

[18]*Let no one deceive himself. If anyone among you thinks that he is wise in this age, let him become a fool that he may become wise.* [19]*For the wisdom of this world is folly with God. For it is written, "He catches the wise in their craftiness,"* [20]*and again, "The Lord knows the thoughts of the wise, that they are futile."* [21]*So let no one boast in men. For all things are yours,* [22]*whether Paul or Apollos or Cephas or the world or life or death or the present or the future—all are yours,* [23]*and you are Christ's, and Christ is God's.*

a Or *brothers and sisters* **b** Or *wise* **c** The Greek for *you* is plural in verses 16 and 17

Overview: Because the Corinthians are judging by means of the flesh—and have entirely too high a view of themselves—they are mere babes in Christ and have been overtaken by jealousy and factionalism, which misses the heart of the gospel. The Reformation commentators identify similar problems present in the church of their own day and, with Paul, warn their contemporaries of the dangers of divisions that disrupt Christian unity, promote one Christian leader above fellow ministers (and even above Christ), and defile the holy temple of God. This chapter invites extensive discussion of theological and practical themes that were at the forefront of many of the reformers' critiques of the medieval church, including the evils of ecclesiastical hierarchy, the fable of purgatorial fire, and the danger of elevating human wisdom over divine grace. At the same time, the reformers attempt to resolve several conundrums in this chapter: Why does Paul speak of "wages" in 1 Corinthians 3:8 when Christians are justified by grace through faith alone? What precisely is the "foundation" that Paul laid in Corinth? (Is it the message of Christ? Or Christ's gospel? Or justification by faith?) What does Paul mean when, in 1 Corinthians 3:21, he writes that Christians possess "all things," when human experience seems to contradict this at every turn? Although Protestant commentators do not give identical answers to these various questions, they share the central conviction that Christian ministers, as servants of Christ and his church, must humbly proclaim his gospel, while recognizing that God alone provides the spiritual harvest.

What Dignity Should Be Given to Ministers. John Calvin: In the beginning of the third chapter, Paul applies what has just been said to the Corinthians. For he complains that, since they are carnal, they are scarcely capable of learning even the most basic teachings of the gospel. In this way he demonstrates that the distaste which they had for the Word did not come from any defect in the Word itself, but from their own ignorance. At the same time, he subtly warns them that their minds must be renewed for them to begin to evaluate things rightly. Afterward, Paul shows what dignity should be given to ministers of the gospel: namely, that it should in no way detract from the glory of God. For there is only one Lord, and all ministers are his servants. They are simply his instruments. God alone possesses the power, and all the results proceed from him. At the same time, Paul shows that the building up of the church should be their main purpose. He takes the opportunity to explain the true and correct method of effective building, namely, that Christ should be the only foundation and that the whole structure should coincide with the foundation. And in passing, having testified that he was a wise master builder, he warns those coming after him to conform the end of the work to the beginning. Paul also urges the Corinthians not to permit their minds to be defiled by false teaching, since they are the temples of God. And he again reduces the pride of human wisdom to nothing, so that only the knowledge of Christ might be displayed among the believers. Introduction to 1 Corinthians.[1]

Ministers Are God's Instruments. Tilemann Hesshus: In chapter three, Paul continues his description of the weakness of the Corinthians. For they are not only weighed down by the ignorance and errors of nature, but they are also indulging in their carnal affections. That is why they should not strut about proudly, but instead should modestly and humbly acknowledge the weakness of their nature and continually call on God for an increase in gifts. Next, Paul teaches on what the power of God and the gift of salvation depend: certainly not in the excellent gifts of the minister, nor by the eloquence, cunning, dignity, or position of the minister; rather it is by the potency of the all-powerful God. Paul advises ministers only to be instruments that God uses for gathering the church; for it is God who ignites light and life, and works salvation in the heart, through the voice of ministers or apostles or prophets or bishops. And so, they are not governors, but should be dependent on God. And lest anyone disturb the church of Christ by his pride or stubbornness, Paul points out that the elect are the temple of the Holy Spirit. Introduction to 1 Corinthians.[2]

The Strategy of the False Apostles. Wolfgang Musculus: Paul returns in this chapter to the subject that he began in the first so as to correct the Corinthians who were promoting dissensions among themselves. Not only was Paul's doctrine exposed to the calumnies of the false apostles, but also the humility of his person and the uncultured manner of his speaking; for the false apostles were elevating the teaching of foolishness even as they were discrediting Paul's words as uncultured and despicable—the calumny that Paul successfully opposed in chapter 2. Out of their contempt for the cross of Christ and apostolic humility . . . the false apostles were ingratiating themselves to the minds of the Corinthians. And in the name of wisdom and eloquence, they were alluring disciples to themselves and dividing the church of Christ while despising the teaching of the simple cross of Christ. Commentary on 1 Corinthians 3:1.[3]

[1]CO 49:300 (cf. CTS 39:41-42).

[2]Hesshus, *Explicatio Prioris Epistolae ad Corinthios*, 4r.

[3]Musculus, *Comm. 1 Cor.*, 75.

3:1-4 *Baby Christians*

The Nature of Spiritual Food. John Colet: These foods that are harder and more difficult to digest (except of course, for more excellent souls) are those highest truths and purest principles, divine and spiritual, that have as their consequences the most complete and perfect ways of living. They are suitable only for those who are powerful of soul, those who are focused altogether into oneness, who, having despised the world and the body, stand firm in the loftiest part of their minds, in unity and in an indivisible center. These people are so powerful and malleable that they accept with a strong mind whatever truth is given from above, however solid and simple it be and however much it surpasses reason, holding it with a firm faith, to digest it with an efficacious love, to turn it to the best, to venerate and worship it. . . .

In conclusion, then, Paul wishes them to know that he did not impart to the Corinthians the highest principles of reality and the Christian religion, but matters more fit for their minds, which still adhered more to the world than to God. Among the perfect he spoke wisdom; for the imperfect, he accommodated things in a manner foolish, lower, and less refined. This was why he tolerated for a time less complete and less perfect ways of behavior, indulging the Corinthians with gentleness as much as he could. He looked not to how much he was permitted, but to how much something would benefit others, and he thought less about what he could do than what was best for the Corinthians, and the extent to which they could take it in, tolerate it, digest it, and turn it into good nourishment for the soul—lest, through lack of consideration, he might kill those very people whose salvation was his goal. Exposition of 1 Corinthians 3.[4]

Paul Employs a Gentle Rebuke. Huldrych Zwingli: Consider Paul's remarkable wisdom here. First, he addresses them tenderly. Next, he shows them their faults openly, though with gentleness, by employing here a metaphor from the education of children. . . . With these words, Paul indirectly reproaches those who had come to teach the Corinthians after him, as if he were saying: "Who made you children a second time? No one, except those who came to you after my departure." Paul is always on guard lest those who had come to Christ out of Judaism should thrust the ceremonies of the law and the principles of the world on believers. Whenever this happens, the Word of God and faith in Christ are extinguished simultaneously. Annotations on 1 Corinthians 3:1.[5]

All True Christians Are Spiritual. Dirk Philips: Thus the Christians are now one spirit with God, out of whom they are born. But now some have an objection here, namely, that Paul wrote to the Corinthians (who were also Christians), "I have not been able to speak to you as spiritual but as of the flesh." Out of these words of Paul, some persons wish to assert that the weak and young Christians are the carnal children of God and should be so called. But we say that one may not thus understand the words of the apostle. For the reason Paul called the Corinthians "carnal" happened on this account: they were quarrelsome and partisan and also in part carnally minded, as James says, "From where does quarreling and warfare come among you? Is it not out of the lusts that fight in your members?" (James 4:1).

Now since the passionate desire of the flesh and ignorance were still found among the Corinthians, and also in part had the upper hand over the Spirit, therefore the apostle called them carnal. Nevertheless, they were also spiritual according to the new birth, after they had through faith received the gift of the Holy Spirit, according to the previously quoted words of the Lord: "What is born out of the Spirit, that is spirit" (John 3:6). Again, "he who is united to the Lord becomes one spirit with him" (1 Cor 6:17). Again, you are spiritual, that is, if the spirit of Christ dwells in you. Again, "whoever does

[4]Colet, *Enarratio*, 109, 111; citing 1 Cor 2:16.

[5]Zwingli, *Annotatiunculae . . . ex ore Zvinglij*, 24.

not have the spirit of Christ does not belong to him" (Rom 8:9). Out of all this it is easily understood that all Christians are spiritual even though they may indeed still be tempted by the flesh, yes, indeed may become overrun and surprised with human frailties and mistakes. The Enchiridion: Tabernacle of Moses.[6]

Two Meanings of "People of the Flesh." Wolfgang Musculus: How can Paul call the Corinthians "people of the flesh" when later in chapter 4 he says: "I bore you in Christ Jesus through the gospel," and in this present passage: "as children of Christ, I fed you with milk"? If they had been born in Christ through the gospel, and thus were children in Christ, they certainly had the Holy Spirit. . . . Now what does it mean to be people of the flesh, than not to be spiritual and to live and be influenced by the flesh? We answer that the term "people of the flesh" is used in two ways. First, people are said to be "of the flesh" who live completely according to the flesh, who have not yet been regenerated and fully experienced the Spirit of Christ and the grace of God, but are still completely established in the sins of the flesh. This type of "fleshly person" is described by Paul in Romans 8: "Those who are carnal, are concerned about fleshly things." Again, "Those who are in the flesh cannot please God. You, however, are not in the flesh if in fact the Spirit of God lives in you." Second, people are also called "fleshly" who, even though they have been regenerated in Christ, are nevertheless still weak and infants in Christ both with respect to knowledge and with respect to putting to death the desires of the flesh. That was the condition of the Corinthians in this passage, who were called by that name because fleshly concerns were still predominant. Commentary on 1 Corinthians 3:1.[7]

Pastors Must Be Wise in Nourishing God's People. Theodore Beza: It is the duty of pastors to accommodate themselves to the capacity of the people whom they wish to nourish so as to never offer poison in place of milk. For though milk and solid food are each beneficial, they differ in form and in the way they should be introduced. Annotations on 1 Corinthians 3:1.[8]

Paul Gave the Corinthians Spiritual Milk. The English Annotations: "I fed you with milk," that is, as Clement of Alexandria wrote in his *Paedagogus* . . . "I have catechized you in Christ with simple, true, and nourishing food that was wholesome and easy to digest. For such is milk to children." The apostle's charity in condescending to the capacity of his hearers and feeding them, as sucklings in Christ, with the sincere milk of the Word is discussed by St. Ambrose and St. Chrysostom, when they discuss the miracle that occurred when Paul suffered martyrdom. For when Paul was beheaded, some of the ancient writers affirm that . . . milk issued from him instead of blood. Annotations on 1 Corinthians 3:2.[9]

The Danger of Factions. Richard Baxter: It is a great and a common sin throughout the Christian world to take up religion in the way of faction; and instead of a love and tender care of the universal church, to confine that love and respect to a party. . . . Yet it has been found, by long experience, that concord is a sure friend to piety, and piety always moves to concord; while, on the other hand, errors and heresies are bred by discord, as discord is bred and fed by them. We have seen, to our sorrow, that where the servants of God should have lived together as one—of one heart and one soul and one lip—and should have promoted each other's faith and holiness, and

[6]CRR 6:281

[7]Musculus, *Comm. 1 Cor.*, 77-78; citing 1 Cor 4:15; Rom 8:5, 8-9.

[8]Beza, *Annotationes Maiores*, 166.

[9]Downame, *Annotations*, DD1*. Chrysostom discusses this passage in his *Homilies on 1 Corinthians* (homily 8), in NPNF 12:43-48. For Clement's statement, see ANF 2:218. For the tradition that Paul bled milk, see Pseudo-Chrysostom, *In principes Apostolorum Petrum et Paulum*, 2 (PG 59:494); Acts of Paul 14.5 (Richard I. Pervo, *The Acts of Paul: A New Translation with Introduction and Commentary* [Cambridge: James Clarke, 2014], 38).

admonished and assisted each other against sin, and rejoiced together in the hope of future glory, we have, on the contrary, lived in mutual jealousies. We have drowned holy love in bitter contentions, and studied to disgrace and undermine one another, and to increase our own parties by right or wrong. We who used to boast of our love for the brethren as a mark of our sincerity in the faith have now turned it into the love of a party only; and those who are against that party have more of our spleen and envy and malice than our love. I know that this is not so with all, nor prevalently with any true believer, yet it is so common that it may cause us to question the sincerity of many who are thought by themselves and others to be most sincere. Reformed Pastor.[10]

The Source of Divisions. Wolfgang Musculus: It ought to be observed in this passage where factions and divisions in the church come from. First, from the flesh, because divisive persons, although they seem to be the most spiritual, nonetheless live in a fleshly fashion. And in particular, factions and divisions come from jealousy and rivalry, when one person is jealous of another. For contentions arise when people desire to elevate another person, in whom they boast, all the way to heaven, while at the same time casting everyone else down to hell. And when this is disputed, factions and divisions are immediately born so that the unity of the body of Christ is torn apart. Accordingly, the apostle is concerned here to remove that first stirring of rivalry because he knows that when that has happened, the Corinthians can quickly be called back to harmony. Commentary on 1 Corinthians 1:3.[11]

Ministers of the Gospel Are Equal. David Chytraeus: Ministers that rightfully and faithfully perform these [pastoral] duties are all equal and they are peers as related to the efficacy and power of the ministry; no one is any greater or superior to another. For they together are neither the governors of doctrine nor the lords of the church, but Christ's ministers . . . and stewards—stewards, that is, not of their own possessions, but of the gospel and Christ's benefits. Therefore let no one vaunt himself above others in the church, or stir up debate and strife regarding the authority and power of the teacher or minister from whom they receive doctrine. Let us banish from the church and congregation statements like these: "I follow Paul; I follow Peter; I follow Apollos." But let everyone esteem themselves as members of one Christ and ministers of equal standing who, as they fulfill their duties, allow God to judge privately who has excelled whom. And those ministers who have performed their duties aright, let them not seek . . . human judgment or the rash and poisonous verdicts of other mortals, whereby they are judged either inferior or superior to others. Rather, let them be content with the witness of their good conscience.

Now the fact that, afterward, ministers were distinguished from one another by degrees—this was a human contrivance for the sake of order. Jerome, in his letter to Evangelus, addresses this matter at length, arguing that priests and bishops are the same office; and that though afterward one was chosen to be above the rest, this was done to avoid schism. "Wherever there is a bishop, whether he be at Rome or at Engubium or at Constantinople or at Rhegium or at Alexandria or at Thanis, his dignity is one and his priesthood is one. Neither the abundance of riches nor the lowliness of poverty makes him more or less a bishop; all alike are the successors of the apostles." Postil on the Third Sunday in Advent.[12]

3:5-9 *Paul and Apollos—God's Fellow Workers*

Who Was Apollos? Jacques Lefèvre d'Étaples: Paul left Apollos behind in Corinth

[10]Baxter, *Reformed Pastor*, 157, 160-61*.

[11]Musculus, *Comm. 1 Cor.*, 81.

[12]Chytraeus, *Dispositio epistolarum*, 535-36. The citation is from Jerome to Evangelus, in NPNF 6:289. Chytraeus has replaced the city Thanis for Zoan in this citation.

when he returned to Jerusalem via Ephesus. This arrangement is described in the Acts of the Apostles. Now it happened that while Apollos was in Corinth, Paul, after traveling to regions in the north, came to Ephesus. . . . Apollos was a Jew by birth, from Alexandria, a man eloquent and powerful in the Scriptures. Commentary on 1 Corinthians 3:5.[13]

Ministers Win Disciples for Christ, Not for Themselves. John Calvin: Here Paul begins to address how we should view ministers and for what purpose they have been set apart by the Lord. Now, he names himself and Apollos rather than other people so as to avoid grounds for jealousy. "For what else are all ministers appointed," he asks, "except to lead you to faith through their preaching?" From this Paul concludes that there should be no boasting in human beings; faith allows of no boasting except in Christ alone. Hence, those who praise human beings beyond measure strip away their true dignity. For the chief thing of all is that they are ministers of the faith, that is, that they acquire disciples not for themselves but for Christ. Now, although he seems to depreciate the dignity of ministers in this way, he does not however deprive it of its proper value. For Paul is saying a great deal when he says that we obtain faith through their ministry. Commentary on 1 Corinthians 3:5.[14]

The Apostles Were Servants, Not Lords. Wolfgang Musculus: Here is how the apostles should be assessed: they are servants, not lords. For it is not the role of servants to attract disciples to themselves, and it is not permissible for anyone to identify themselves as their disciples since there is only one Lord, who is head and chief of all the elect. Thus, in chapter 4 below, Paul says: "This is how one should judge us, as servants of Christ." *Through whom you believed.* Not, "in whom you believed." Not, "the one who brought you to faith." But, "through whom you believed," that is, "through whose ministry God brought you to faith in his Son." . . . The honor for this kindness is due, not to the servant, but to the one who generously bestowed it. Commentary on 1 Corinthians 3:5.[15]

Christ Superior to the Apostles in Every Way. Tilemann Hesshus: The vast distance that separates Jesus Christ from the apostles or other saints must always be kept in mind. (1) Christ is both man and all-powerful God; the apostles are weak human creatures. (2) The church prays to Christ in every need; it is wicked to pray to the apostles. (3) Jesus Christ is completely free from all sin; the apostles and saints are all sinners, conceived and born in sin. (4) Christ is the Mediator, Savior, and Lord of the church; but the apostles are not redeemers, rather they themselves administer redemption and are servants of the church. (5) Through the Word, Christ is powerful to illumine minds, transform wills, persuade hearts, inspire faith, and bring about life and comfort; the apostles are only ministers of the Word and sacraments. (6) Christ pours out and bestows the Holy Spirit; the apostles only baptize with water. (7) Christ is always everywhere present with his church and with each individual believer; the apostles were serving only some members of the church in a certain place for a limited time, until they finished their earthly lives. Explication on 1 Corinthians 3:5.[16]

Ministers Announce God's Message of Salvation. The English Annotations: After Paul sufficiently reproached the ambitious teachers and their foolish fawners, he now shows how true ministers are to be esteemed so that we attribute to them neither more nor less than what we ought. Therefore he teaches us that they are those by whom we are called to faith and salvation. Yet they are ministers of God, and as such they do nothing

[13]Lefèvre d'Étaples, *Commentariorum in Epistolas Beati Pauli . . . Liber Secundus*, 105r-v; citing Acts 18:24-28.
[14]CO 49:349 (cf. CTS 39:125).
[15]Musculus, *Comm. 1 Cor.*, 82-83; citing 1 Cor 4:1.
[16]Hesshus, *Explicatio Prioris Epistolae ad Corinthios*, 51r-v.

of themselves, but God works in them as it pleases him to furnish them with gifts. Annotations on 1 Corinthians 3:5.[17]

Ministers Plant and Water Souls. Wolfgang Musculus: This analogy of planting and watering is the most beautiful of all analogies. . . . First, Paul declares the reason for the ministry of the Word, why ministers of Christ are necessary, when he attributes to them planting and watering, thus making them the farmers of his garden and cultivators of the kingdom of heaven, which are their twin functions. For either they plant, that is they remove what is in the wild, such as a select shoot from a wild olive tree, and engraft it into an olive tree, or they water what has been planted, that is they nurture and guide it so that it might bear fruit that is useful to the Lord. The same thing holds true for the ministry of the Word. For ministers of Christ engraft into the kingdom of Christ those souls (like shoots) that have been removed from the kingdom of Satan. And they do this, first, by leading unbelievers to faith through the preaching of this Word. And then, just as with watering, they nurture and guide sinners . . . through repentance to an innocent life, while with admonitions and exhortations they strengthen them in the faith, hope, love, and patience of Christ, so that they might not slide back and be overcome by sin and, withering, be lost. The entire ministry is comprised in these two functions, and ministers must be engaged in them constantly. Now let us think about how much diligence, striving, and tiresome effort is required to tend a garden or vineyard so that from this we might appreciate the sense of care, duty, and attention required to plant and water souls. Commentary on 1 Corinthians 3:6.[18]

God Alone Gives Spiritual Growth. Heinrich Bullinger: Paul expresses very clearly through a parable what he has already said, that all boasting for the success of the gospel does not belong to ministers, but entirely to God. Now he draws his allegory from the cultivation of gardens and from rural farm life. People labor in vain when they plant a small tree and water it so that it isn't scorched much by the heat or doesn't die from lack of water, if a certain mystery of nature (that is, the power of God) doesn't also occur. Accordingly, its success . . . is not due to the planting or cultivation, but more to the heavenly power invigorating it. Let us now add the second and more obscure part of this parable that Paul lays out. In this same way, a person labors in vain who scatters the seed of God's Word in the field of the heart unless the power of the Most High touches the heart and makes it capable of receiving the seed and bearing fruit. Again, a person labors in vain who, by means of holy warnings and private consolation, seeks to refresh a troubled conscience, unless the secret power of the Spirit penetrates within and transforms the mind. And thus the conclusion follows: the person who plants is nothing, nor is the one who waters; but God is the one who gives the growth. Commentary on 1 Corinthians 3:7.[19]

Spiritual Growth Is God's Work. John Trapp: This verse made Cyril conclude in his preface to his catechism, "I may teach, and you hear, but God must do the deed when all is done." Otherwise, we may preach and pray . . . to no more purpose than Bede did when he preached to a heap of stones. Commentary on 1 Corinthians 3:7.[20]

What Does Paul Mean by Wages? Peter Martyr Vermigli: Of course, left to ourselves we perform evil works not good works, and we are not at all capable of good works (as has already been explained) unless we are prompted by the spirit and grace of Christ. Nevertheless, we do not deny that the term *wages* is sometimes employed for eternal life and even for salvation. Nevertheless, let us add that Paul does not employ the term in

[17]Downame, *Annotations*, DD1r*.

[18]Musculus, *Comm. 1 Cor.*, 84.

[19]Bullinger, *In Priorem ad Corinthios Epistolam Commentarius*, 29-30.

[20]Trapp, *A Commentary or Exposition*, 664*. See Cyril, "Procatechesis," NPNF 7:5.

the sense of a debt or obligation that is collected according to the worthiness of the labor, but only according to the will and mercy of God alone. Now it is perhaps appropriate for Paul to call them "wages" because this term speaks of something that is rewarded and refers approvingly to the quality and condition of the works; so too, because good works are afterward rewarded with eternal life, just as wages follow from the good works themselves as well as from the efficaciousness of the promise—although not from the worth of the works themselves. And finally, there is the additional fact that believers are granted salvation, even as wages are guaranteed to those who have fully deserved them. Commentary on 1 Corinthians 3:8.[21]

God Will Reward Faithful Pastors.

Tilemann Hesshus: [Paul's meaning is that] whether one teaches the gospel of Jesus Christ to the ignorant for the first time, or whether one more fully instructs, consoles, and admonishes people already established in Christ, they are both ministers of the same rank and experience the same reward when they have devoted themselves to Christ. Thus ministers such as Timothy and Titus were as helpful for the church as the apostle Paul. And each one receives his reward for his labor. Preachers should impress this most excellent promise upon the minds of the pious. The labors that godly pastors experience in the ministry are great and difficult. And the world is not only ungrateful but even vicious toward them, paying back good with many evils. In the face of so much human insecurity, pastors are often fearful lest all their labors and strivings and exertions and trials are in vain. But here, Paul emphasizes that God, according to the standard of his justice, will repay each person according to their labor. For there is no good work so small, when performed in faith and in view of the Mediator, that will not be compensated with a very great reward both in this life and especially in the life to come. Witness the words of Christ in Matthew 10, "Truly I say to you, those who give a cup of cold water to one of the least of these in my name will not lose their reward."

The apostle also teaches here that the power of ministry does not depend on the worthiness of ministers, but on the power of Christ, just as whatever material a king's seal is made from, whether gold or steel, nevertheless it imprints the same image into wax. And so, in a similar way, regardless of whether ministers are well-educated or ignorant, whether they are apostles or deacons, whether they are godly or hypocrites, when they proclaim the pure Word of God and administer the sacraments to us, there is no doubt that it will be efficacious for our salvation—provided we believe it to be the Word of Christ. Explication of 1 Corinthians 3:8.[22]

God Judges the Labor of Ministers.

Wolfgang Musculus: It should be noted here that Paul does not say that people will receive their wages according to the fruit that they produce, but according to their labor. The prophets labored mightily, but produced little fruit because of the great wickedness of the people. Wages, therefore, are reckoned not according to the quantity of fruit but according to labor. . . . People should not distinguish between ministers of God and judge them according to their differences. For it is God, not they, who judges how much faith, enthusiasm, labor, and diligence a minister employs. God alone discerns the hearts of all people and knows what he should give to a person, and how much. Therefore people who distinguish between ministers of Christ act in a way contrary to God himself. Paul will admonish the Corinthians about this later in chapter 4, when he says: "Therefore, do not pronounce judgment before its time, before the Lord comes." Commentary on 1 Corinthians 3:8.[23]

---

[21]Vermigli, *In Selectissimam Priorem ad Corinthios Epistolam . . . Commentarii*, 71.

[22]Hesshus, *Explicatio Prioris Epistolae ad Corinthios*, 51v-52r; citing Mt 10:42.

[23]Musculus, *Comm. 1 Cor.*, 87; citing 1 Cor 4:5.

God's Fellow Workers. John Calvin: Here is the best argument: We are employed in the Lord's work, and it is to him that we have devoted our labors. Therefore, since he is faithful and just, he will not disappoint us by withholding our reward. That is why those who look to other people or depend on them for remuneration are deceived. This is an exceptional commendation of the ministry, that although God is able to work by himself, he nevertheless invites us puny mortals to be his assistants and he makes use of us as his instruments. As for those papists, who pervert this statement to establish their "free will"—nothing could be more ridiculous. For Paul teaches here, not what humans can accomplish through their natural powers, but what the Lord accomplishes through them by means of his grace. Commentary on 1 Corinthians 3:9.[24]

3:10-15 *Building on the Foundation*

Humility Is Necessary to Build Christ's Church. John Colet: The humble ministers whom God uses in building and perfecting his work are the apostles, namely, those people who are faithful to God. They press on in what God has begun, relying on God himself and his Spirit for guidance; not depending on their own ingenuity, but drawing on the divine Spirit; not trusting themselves for anything, but God alone. Clearly these ministers expertly build up people in both wisdom and good conduct in a manner befitting the foundation—that is on the true and firm Christ—and through their building they achieve a lasting and most beautiful structure, with stones of gold, silver, and precious jewels all cemented together. Because of this patient constancy, the building will fear no harm from its adversaries, and in its illustrious beauty, it will please both God and God's friends.

By contrast, those who rely on their own ingenuity and think they can of themselves bring some new thing into the church are actually building a structure that is out of proportion to and unworthy of the foundation (that is, Christ), and is displeasing to God and dishonorable to the church. This is a building of wood, hay, and stubble; it is a building false, fragile, and perishable. The attacks of the enemy easily shatter it and, on the Day of the Lord, that testing fire of God will demolish it. Exposition of 1 Corinthians 3.[25]

The Different Fruit of True and False Apostles. Johann Spangenberg: What are the fruits of true apostles? They serve God for the betterment of people. Indeed, for their faithful service and holy exhortation they desire nothing in the world than afflictions, the cross, misery, suffering, and persecution. Hungry and in need, they barely even have stale bread. That is their reward, as all the prophets and apostles are rewarded.

What are the fruits of the false apostles? They serve themselves at the cost of many people. Indeed, in exchange for their lies and human spittle they desire from the world majestic dignity, great bishoprics, fat loans and benefices, goods, riches, and whatever their hearts lust for. That is their temporal reward; their eternal reward will come also. Epistle for the Third Sunday in Advent.[26]

The Work of Apostolic Imposters Will Be Judged. Huldrych Zwingli: Paul eloquently symbolizes his teaching by architecture, commending his work, that is, his "building," while at the same time reproaching those apostolic imposters who came after him. "Concerning the foundation," he says, "what I laid down was solid. Those apostles of yours do not disagree with me. For I know that no one can set down any other foundation than the one I set down—that is Jesus Christ. People will see what they are building on, however, for if they build on the proper foundation, their work will endure. But whatever has been built on Jewish ceremonies and the principles of this world will collapse. Though they now ignore and

[24]CO 49.352 (cf. CTS 39:131).

[25]Colet, *Enarratio*, 105.

[26]Spangenberg, *Postilla Teütsch*, 4:22r-v.

avoid both my judgment and the judgment of others, nevertheless, this clear foolishness and wickedness will be evident as soon as the day dawns and the fire burns." Annotations on 1 Corinthians 3:10.[27]

Paul's Gospel Was the True Foundation. Giovanni Diodati: "I laid a foundation." [Paul is saying:] "I have taught by the infallible guide of the Holy Spirit, the first, most certain, indubitable, and fundamental truth of the gospel, on which all the doctrine of those who come after me should be established and determined. For the foundation bears the weight of the building and by its dimensions regulates the design and construction thereafter; and its soundness and firmness determines the material with which it is to be built." Annotations on 1 Corinthians 3:10.[28]

Christ Is the True Foundation of the Church. Wolfgang Musculus: Therefore Paul emphasizes two things in this passage. First, that Christ is the foundation of the church. See Ephesians 2, 1 Peter 2, and Isaiah 28. Second, that no one can lay a foundation other than Christ, on which this building of God rests. For there is no other name under heaven given to men and women that they might be saved.... Moreover, Christ is the foundation of the church when people believe in him with sincere and firm faith, that he is the living Son of God and the only Savior of the world. Commentary on 1 Corinthians 3:11-12.[29]

The Foundation of Justification Is Faith in Christ. Philipp Melanchthon: The foundation of justification is nothing other than faith in Christ, that is: justification is nothing else except to believe in Christ.... The works that come from faith endure. Such was that work of David when he spared Saul. The person whose work does not rest on a solid foundation, that is, does not come from faith, is condemned. Such was the work when David took a census of the people. But how shall people be saved when their work is condemned? I answer: as much as the work is condemned, the people themselves will not be condemned provided that they rest on the foundation of faith. Thus David, even though he sinned, was still saved because justification is from faith and not from works. But he was saved "as through fire," that is, through the pangs of conscience. Annotations on 1 Corinthians 3:11.[30]

Gold, Silver, and Precious Stones. John Calvin: It would be insufficient to have constructed the foundation if its whole superstructure did not correspond to it. For even as it would be absurd to build a structure of worthless materials on a foundation of gold, so it is wicked to cover over Christ with contrary doctrines. Therefore Paul uses the terms "gold" and "silver" and "precious stones" to refer to doctrine that is worthy of Christ and that is a superstructure compatible with its foundation.... And it follows on the other hand that the terms "wood, hay, and stubble" designate doctrine that does not conform to the foundation, the sort of thing fabricated in the human brain that is then thrust forward as an oracle of God. For God wishes to establish his church through the pure preaching of his own Word, not through human fictions. These are the sorts of things that do nothing for edification, such as those curious questions that often contribute more to ostentation or to a passion for foolishness than to the salvation of men and women. Commentary on 1 Corinthians 3:12.[31]

Wood, Hay, Straw. John Trapp: [These are] rhetorical strains, philosophical fancies, that tend not to edification. Along with the gold, silver, and ivory of sound and savory truths there are also (as was the case on Solomon's ships) apes and peacocks, conceits and crotchets. Now, if persons

[27]Zwingli, *Annotatiunculae ... ex ore Zvinglij*, 25-26.
[28]Diodati, *Pious Annotationes*, L12v*.
[29]Musculus, *Comm. 1 Cor.*, 90; citing Acts 4:12.
[30]Melanchthon, *Annotationes in Epistolam priorem ad Corinthios*, 58. Citing Rom 3:23 and 1 Sam 24:4-15.
[31]CO 49:355 (cf. CTS 39:136-37); citing 1 Tim 1:4.

who forge the king's coin deserve punishment, what do they deserve who, in place of the tried silver of divine truths, stamp the name and character of God on their own base and brazen stuff? Commentary on 1 Corinthians 3:12.[32]

Meaning of "the Day." Huldrych Zwingli: I understand the word "day" as either that time of divine judgment or divine vengeance when the Lord will come down with vengeance and punishment, as is often mentioned in Isaiah, or it is that time when all things are revealed in this light, which is Christ (as John 8 and 12 report), according to the light of divine knowledge and truth. Annotations on 1 Corinthians 3:13.[33]

Different Levels of Builders and Buildings. Jacques Lefèvre d'Étaples: Among the people of God, there are builders and buildings. The first builders were the apostles, who laid the foundation. Many others succeeded them, building on their foundation with doctrine that was holy and pure, just as gold, silver, and precious stones are pure and untainted. Others built with wicked teachings and poisonous seductions, which are described as wood, hay, and straw (all of which are combustible). All of these are pronounced builders. The buildings are those people and commonwealths who receive either pure doctrine or the poison of pernicious teaching. And just as there are various levels of builders, represented by the distinction of gold, silver, and gems, so there are various levels of holiness and purity in the building of the builders of Christ. And some among the holy buildings will shine more brightly than others, just as gold or silver outshine other metals, and some stones are more precious than others. Similarly, the apostle teaches us through the reference to wood, hay, and straw that there are various levels of evil and wicked buildings just as there are various levels of wicked builders. Commentary on 1 Corinthians 3:13-15.[34]

Paul Is Referring to Purgatory. Cardinal Cajetan: So that you do not make the mistake of thinking that by the statement "but he will be saved" Paul meant that the work of a curious or conceited teacher, when examined, would be found acceptable and the teacher avoid punishment, Paul adds *how* he will be saved, namely, "but only as through fire." This statement, according to the plain and pleasing literal sense, signifies the punishment of purgatory after this life. From this passage, one finds proof of what is spoken about the time of that future day when the work of each person will be revealed. For that day will be after this life. And on that day, Paul says, not only will the work of people be examined, but those whose work does not survive the fire will be saved, but nevertheless as if they were passing through the fire to salvation. . . . Now Paul uses the word "fire" to signify the most rigorous test of divine judgment in the next life. And he broadens the meaning of this word to signify the actual punishment inflicted by this judgment. Commentary on 1 Corinthians 3:15.[35]

The Fiction of Purgatory. Wolfgang Musculus: Paul gives the grounds by which people's works will be made manifest. Things that are revealed are revealed by light, just as things that are hidden are hidden by darkness, as Paul notes in Ephesians 5. All those things that are faulty will be exposed by the light. Paul understands the word "day" to mean that light by which God will make all things clear. And by the word "fire" he means the power of examining and testing so as to make clear the value of something, whether it is gold, silver, etc. Thus, in Scripture, the word "fire" means temptation, test, and proof. . . .

The obscurity of this passage has badly tricked foolish Christians and has resulted in the opinion that has prevailed far and wide concerning the purgatorial fire by which venial sins are cleansed after death so that, by it, the souls of dead men and women fly to heaven just as gold is purified by the

[32]Trapp, *A Commentary or Exposition*, 665*. Conceits and crotchets are fancy articles and needlework.
[33]Zwingli, *Annotatiunculae . . . ex ore Zvinglij*, 26.
[34]Lefèvre d'Étaples, *Commentariorum in Epistolas Beati Pauli . . . Liber Secundus*, 104v.
[35]Cajetan, *In Sacrae Scripturae expositionem*, 5:95.

fiery furnace. How far this fiction is from the apostle's meaning will be abundantly clear when we consider carefully his words and argument.

First, Paul is not speaking about fire in a physical sense, the sort that is said to be in purgatory, but in a metaphorical sense, that is testing. For he is not speaking about physical gold, silver, precious stones, wood, hay, stubble, but about doctrine. And in the same way, he is not speaking about fire in a physical sense, but about the testing that fire represents. Thus, just as "gold" etc. ought to be understood figuratively, so also the term "fire" should be taken figuratively. . . .

Second, Paul is not speaking about physical testing, nor is his concern with good and bad works but with teaching, which he distinguishes as either pure or defiled. And he foretells that pure teaching will survive and receive God's praise, but that defiled teaching will be burned up and condemned by the heavenly builder. What does this have to do with the fiction of venial sins being cleansed in the purgatorial fires?

Third, it should be especially clear that Paul does not say that God will test with fire what sort of works "certain people have done," but "each person has done." Therefore, not only the works of the false apostles, but also the works of Paul and Peter are exposed to that fire. But Catholics do not dare hand the apostles over to purgatory, to whom they only assign venial sins. Nor do they commit the works of the wicked to this fire. But for Paul, the fire will test all people in every way.

Fourth, Paul does not say "the fire will cleanse," but "the fire will test." Who does not see that cleansing something is different from testing something? All things will be tested, but not all things will be cleansed.

Fifth, the apostle gives to fire the power of making visible and revealing, clearly those things that are hidden in this age. But how this corresponds with calling purgatorial fire "a revealer of sins" they alone can see. . . .

Now see how many different interpretations there are of this passage, and how the Catholic view does not agree with the church fathers. By *building* Jerome and Ambrose understand teachers and doctors. Augustine and Chrysostom understand each and every Christian. Or rather, on second thought, Chrysostom flatly denies that this word can be understood to mean teachers and doctors. Jerome interprets the phrase "gold, silver, precious stones, wood, hay, and stubble" to refer to auditors or disciples, or good or evil people. Augustine believes it refers to those who care about either God or the world. Chrysostom and Theophylact interpret the phrase to mean either good works or bad works. Jerome, Chrysostom, and Theophylact take the word "day" to mean the final day of judgment. Augustine understands the "day" to be the time of this present age. . . . By "fire" Jerome understands the testing of the future judgment. Augustine understands "fire" to refer to the temptations of the present time. Chrysostom and Theophylact explain it as the eternal fire of hell, a viewpoint that Ambrose nevertheless openly rejects. Behold, these are the conclusions of the church fathers, who interpret this passage in so many ways that each rejects the interpretation of the other. Why such a diversity of opinion? It is due to the obscurity of this passage, from whence the Catholics wish to fortify their very recent fiction of purgatorial fire—an interpretation that the fathers themselves did not teach. Commentary on 1 Corinthians 3:13-14.[36]

Paul Is Not Teaching Purgatory. The English Annotations: Contrary to what the Roman divines teach, Paul's reference to fire here does not mean purgatory. First, because it cannot be proved from Scripture that there is any such purgatory fire as they imagine that purges those who die with venial sins. Second, because in this passage *every* work is tried by the fire, but accord-

[36]Musculus, *Comm. 1 Cor.*, 92-95. Theophylact, archbishop of Ohrid, was a prolific biblical commentator in the eleventh century. His commentaries on the Gospels, Acts, and the Pauline epistles, which drew extensively from Chrysostom's exegetical work, had a significant influence on Erasmus's *Annotationes*. Theophylact's treatment of this verse is found in his *Expositio in Epist. I ad Cor.*, in PG 124:603-6. For Chrysostom, see his *Homilies of 1 Corinthians* (homily 9), in NPNF 12:49-53.

ing to Roman doctrine good works are not tried in the purgatorial fire. Third, the works described here are doctrines (as is clear from what comes before and follows), and several kinds of preaching—things which would be absurd to say that they should be tried by material fire, which our adversaries believe, that those who die with venial sins are tormented in purgatory. Annotations on 1 Corinthians 3:13.[37]

Gospel Preaching Involves Fiery Trials. David Dickson: But if anyone mingles with his preaching philosophical speculations, the hay of human wisdom or the stubble of wordy eloquence, or if he adds any other contrivances of his own, which cannot endure the sentence of divine judgment, he will experience the loss of all his labors. But the preacher shall be saved, "but only as through fire," that is, when he is able to endure the fiery and exact trial of God whereby he accurately separates sincere people from the hypocrites, as the fire purges the rust from metal. Here is the sum of the matter: the preacher himself shall be saved, if otherwise he is found sincere in the faith of Christ. Exposition of 1 Corinthians 3:15.[38]

3:16-17 *The Temple of God*

Paul Delights in the Temple Metaphor. Philipp Melanchthon: The apostle took singular delight in the figure of the temple of God so that he uses it so many times, as below in 1 Corinthians 6:19, 2 Corinthians 6:16, and likewise in Ephesians 2:21. Moreover, "the temple of God," "the tabernacle of God," and "the holy place of God" and similar terminology are never employed without great emphasis and stand for all those things being done in the Spirit, which used to be done physically in the temple. Just as the term "children of God" signifies favor and grace, so the term "temple of God" signifies God's presence and governance etc. Ezekiel 37:27 states, "My tabernacle shall be in them, and I will be their God and they will be my people." Annotations on 1 Corinthians 3:16.[39]

God's Temple Must Not Be Defiled by Pride or Quarreling. Tilemann Hesshus: Basing his argument on the outstanding worth of the saints, the authority of the Holy Spirit, and the terrifying prospect of divine judgment, Paul warns the Corinthians not to disturb the church with empty boasts or other quarrels concerning wisdom or gifts. Instead, with true humility and a sincere zeal for harmony, they should nourish, console, build up, and enlarge the church. The most holy temple of the almighty God should not be destroyed, disturbed, nor profaned, but rather built up and guarded in holiness. Even those heathen idolaters who were ignorant of God believed that the temples of their idols should be scrupulously revered, and they thought that people who plundered temples were punished by the gods. So too, the Jews, by God's command, defended the temple in Jerusalem with great zeal, and did not allow it to be defiled. It was not lawful for uncircumcised Gentiles to even go into the temple. How much more should the spiritual temple of God, where God himself dwells, be scrupulously revered! For God does not dwell in a temple made by human hands. But you saints and elect, you are the temple of the most high God. For he said: "I will live in you." Therefore it is a serious act of sacrilege to disturb or defile this sacred temple through pride or quarreling. Explication of 1 Corinthians 3:16.[40]

The Divinity of the Holy Spirit. John Calvin: In this passage we have a clear testimony for affirming the divinity of the Holy Spirit. For if he were a created being, or simply God's gift to us, his dwelling in us would not cause us to be temples of God. At the same time, we learn in what way

[37]Downame, *Annotations*, DD1r*.

[38]Dickson, *Expositions of St. Paul's Epistles*, 45*.

[39]Melanchthon, *Annotationes in Epistolam priorem ad Corinthios*, 60.

[40]Hesshus, *Explicatio Prioris Epistolae ad Corinthios*, 59v-60r.

God communicates himself to us and by what chain we are bound to him—namely, his pouring into us the power of his Spirit. Commentary on 1 Corinthians 3:16.[41]

Let Us Cleanse Our Defiled Souls. John Trapp: Next to the love of Christ indwelling our nature, we may wonder at the love of the Holy Ghost who dwells in our defiled souls. Let our care be to wash the pavement of this temple with our tears, to sweep it by repentance, to beautify it with holiness, to perfume it with prayers, to deck it with humility, to hang it with sincerity. The Spirit of God is a delicate being. The Holy Ghost will dwell in a poor, but pure house. Commentary on 1 Corinthians 3:16.[42]

True Temples and Their Adornment. Peter Martyr Vermigli: The temples of Christians, although they ought not to be adorned with so many external decorations and so much effort as God commanded in the Old Testament, nevertheless are dedicated to divine worship in the same way as the Old Testament temple. That is why if ever a church building is constructed among us, it is fitting to give thanks to God who has given his people a place where they can gather to fulfill their sacred obligations. And they should add their prayers for maintaining the proper and right use of this place. But now they have introduced into the consecration of churches incense, painted crosses, burning candles, oil, salt, and propitiatory water; and they draw in the dust letters in both Greek and Hebrew; and they add almost countless other signs for which they can provide no solid justification. Almost anyone can see, I think, how very superstitious all these things are; but they must be discredited if we wish to embrace pure religion. The ceremonies that adorn our temples, while they are few in number, are superior in value to all other ceremonies, for chief among them are praises to God, then confession of sins, the proclamation of sacred doctrine, prayers, the administration of the sacraments, the exercise of church discipline, and offerings for poor people. And so, it is possible to establish an argument from the lesser good, for if there exists so much dignity in the outward appearance of the Jewish temple or of our temples, then what should be said concerning the true, living, and genuine temple of God—which is who we are? It is clear that the apostle has rightly said, "He who destroys this temple of God, God will destroy him." Commentary on 1 Corinthians 3:17.[43]

God Will Severely Punish Those Who Disrupt the Church. Tilemann Hesshus: Here Paul adds a very serious threat that should strongly motivate us to guard against disrupting the church with our scandals and disputes. If anyone, in his wickedness, were to harm violently the palace of a great prince or emperor, he would be punished with the severest of punishments. In a similar fashion, know that God will punish most severely those who profane the most holy temple of the eternal God. Human beings can only kill the body; they cannot kill the soul. But God, when he has decided to damn a human being, hurls both body and soul into the eternal fire. This most serious punishment of all should motivate all pious people not to disturb the church. Explication of 1 Corinthians 3:17.[44]

3:18-23 *No Grounds for Boasting in Human Wisdom*

The Crux of the Corinthians' Problem. John Calvin: Here Paul puts his finger on the sore itself, since the entire problem derived from the fact that they thought too highly of their own wisdom. Therefore he warns them not to deceive

[41]CO 49.358 (cf. CTS 39:143).

[42]Trapp, *A Commentary or Exposition*, 665*. Trapp is quoting from Richard Sibbes's comments on Ephesians 4:30 in *A fountain sealed: or, The duty of the sealed to the Spirit, and the worke of the Spirit in sealing Wherein many things are handled about the Holy Spirit* (London, 1637).

[43]Vermigli, *In Selectissimam Priorem ad Corinthios Epistolam Commentarius*, 46.

[44]Hesshus, *Explicatio Prioris Epistolae ad Corinthios*, 60v.

themselves with a false belief by boasting of their own wisdom. By this he means that all who insist on their own understanding are deceiving themselves. Now, in my view, he is addressing those who were taught as much as the teachers. For they were more sympathetic and willing to listen to those ambitious teachers. And because they were so fastidious, the simplicity of the gospel did not appeal to their taste. The teachers, wanting to be highly esteemed, were concerned only to make a show. Therefore Paul warns both of them not to flatter themselves on their own wisdom; rather, those who think themselves wise should become fools in this world. . . . Moreover, the apostle does not require by these words that we completely renounce that insight that is innate to our nature or acquired from long experience, but only that we subject it in obedience to God so that all our wisdom comes from his Word. Commentary on 1 Corinthians 3:18.[45]

The Wisdom of the World. John Calvin: This is an argument taken from opposites, for to affirm the one is to overturn the other. Since, therefore, the wisdom of the world is foolishness with God, it follows that we cannot be wise in the sight of God unless we are fools according to the world. Now, we have already explained what Paul means by the wisdom of the world: for natural insight is the gift of God. The natural arts and all the sciences by which wisdom is acquired are gifts of God. But they are confined within their limits, and cannot penetrate into God's heavenly kingdom. Accordingly, they must be handmaidens and not mistresses. Or rather, they must be looked on as empty and worthless until they are completely subject to the Word and the Spirit of God. But if they set themselves against Christ, they are a noxious plague, and if they maintain that they are capable of anything in themselves, they should be judged as the worst of hindrances. Therefore, for Paul, the wisdom of the world is that which usurps authority for itself and refuses to be ruled by the Word of God or brought to submission so as to be completely subject to him. Commentary on 1 Corinthians 3:19.[46]

Paul Seeks to Turn Corinthians Away from False Wisdom. Wolfgang Musculus: Those who boast about their wisdom before other people are not at all concerned about God's judgment, for they do not seek after true wisdom. For them it is enough if they are considered to be wise, however God might judge them. But pious people would prefer to be considered fools in this age while, in fact, being wise before God, than the opposite. Therefore the apostle here attempts to call the Corinthians away from the pride of the false apostles. For he knew such a step was necessary in this matter so that the Corinthians might cease in their wrong-headed admiration of those men, turn away from their desire to emulate them, and return to ecclesiastical unity. Commentary on 1 Corinthians 3:19.[47]

God Will Catch the False Apostles. Huldrych Zwingli: "He catches." By this phrase Paul frightens greatly the false apostles. It is as if he were saying: "Guard yourselves, lest you fall into the Lord's judgment. However much you try to hide, you will not be able to conceal your plans from the Lord. The Lord knows that your intentions are vain and worthless, and in your craftiness he will catch you." Annotations on 1 Corinthians 3:19.[48]

The Craftiness of the Wicked Will Ultimately Be Thwarted. John Trapp: When [the wicked] have eviscerated themselves like spiders, tried all conclusions, beaten their brains, searched the devil's skull for new ideas, done all that they could to affect their designs, God lets them carry the ball on the foot until they are almost at the goal; he allows them to go to the end of their tether—and then he pulls them back, with shame enough to their task. He dealt this way with

[45]CO 49:359 (cf. CTS 39:143-45).

[46]CO 49:359-60 (cf. CTS 39:145).

[47]Musculus, *Comm. 1 Cor.*, 99.

[48]Zwingli, *Annotatiunculae . . . ex ore Zvinglij*, 28.

Sennacherib, Haman, Herod, and others. Commentary on 1 Corinthians 3:19.[49]

Paul Fortifies His Argument with Two Old Testament Texts. John Calvin: Paul supports what he has said by two texts from Scripture. The first of these is taken from Job 5:13. There the wisdom of God is exalted because in its presence no earthly wisdom can stand its ground. There is no doubt that in that context the prophet is speaking about the cunning and the designing. But since human wisdom is always like that when it is divorced from God, Paul quite rightly adapts it to mean that however much wisdom people acquire by themselves it counts for nothing in God's sight. The second text is from Psalm 94:11, where, after David claimed for God the function of and the authority for teaching all, he adds that "he knows the thoughts of all to be empty." Therefore no matter how highly they are valued by us they are futile in God's judgment. This is an excellent passage for bringing down the confidence of the flesh, for here God declares from above that whatever the mind of humankind conceives and purposes is simply nothingness. Commentary on 1 Corinthians 3:20.[50]

No Boasting in Human Beings. Tilemann Hesshus: Paul explicitly testifies here that neither the apostles nor any ministers are lords of the church, but rather the church is the mistress over all ministers, whether prophets and apostles or bishops and pastors. Therefore the Roman pontiff, cardinals, bishops, and prelates all exercise tyranny as they elevate themselves over the church, as they try to control it with their laws, as they prescribe dogmas of belief to it, as they snatch the power of judgment from it, as they impose unwelcome burdens apart from the Word of God, as they demand obedience from it on matters that don't relate to their ministry. This is the tyranny, therefore, that was condemned by Christ's statement: "The kings of the Gentiles exercise lordship; but not so with you" (Luke 22:25-26). Explication of 1 Corinthians 3:21.[51]

All Things Are Yours. Huldrych Zwingli: For the words of Christ are of themselves clear enough, when he says: "the Sabbath is made for man and not man for the Sabbath." . . . Now if it is true that the Sabbath that God established is to be subject to us, how much more then the time that human beings have imposed on us. Indeed, not only the time but also the persons that have thus fixed and established these particular times are none other than the servants of Christ and coworkers in the secret things of God, not revealed to men or women. And these same coworkers should not rule Christians, commanding as overlords, but should be ready only for their service and for their good. Therefore Paul says . . . "All things are yours; whether Paul or Apollos or Peter or the world or life or death or things present or things to come; all are yours." Here you see that all things are intended for humans or for the service of humans, not for their oppression, yes, the apostles themselves are for humans, not humans for the apostles. Liberty Respecting Food in Lent.[52]

The Kingdom of Christ. Philipp Melanchthon: This passage pertains to the kingdom of Christ. Now the kingdom of Christ causes injury to no creature nor can believers be wounded by sin. No law, not even the divine law, is able to condemn the consciences of believers: Romans 8:32, "He who did not spare his own Son etc., will he not also give us all things with him?" Annotations on 1 Corinthians 3:22.[53]

In What Sense Do Christians Have All Things? Tilemann Hesshus: Here we must consider the extraordinary wealth of the saints and

[49]Trapp, *A Commentary or Exposition*, 666*. See 2 Kings 19:37; Esther 7:1-10; and Acts 12:19-23.
[50]CO 49:360 (cf. CTS 39:146).
[51]Hesshus, *Explicatio Prioris Epistolae ad Corinthios*, 63v.
[52]In Jackson, *Ulrich Zwingli's Early Writings*, 81-82; citing Mk 2:27.
[53]Melanchthon, *Annotationes in Epistolam priorem ad Corinthios*, 62.

believers in Christ. Paul testifies that "all things are ours," not only all gold and silver, not only the dominion of the Turks and the kingdom of the French, but the entire world, and finally life and death itself and all creatures. This is the reason why nothing is more conceited than to boast in this. Now what group in the world is more burdened with want and poverty than Christians? They are exposed to the hatred of everyone and never have a sure residence. They travel about in the world as the most wretched of exiles. Nevertheless, what Paul asserts here is very true, for to believe in Christ is to believe he is Lord of the whole world. The possession of the world, which was lost through Adam, has been restored to us through Christ. And every creature is subject to the dominion of the Son of God. And all things work together for our salvation. And Christians do not need to worry about lacking anything, for they can obtain all things from the eternal Father though prayer. "Whatever you ask from the Father in my name," Christ said, "he will give it to you" (John 16:23). Again, Psalm 34: . . . "Those who fear the Lord lack no good thing." . . . Psalm 23: "God is my shepherd, I shall lack nothing." So too, Paul in Romans 8: "If God is for us, who can be against us? He who did not spare his own Son, but gave him up for us, how will he not give us all things with him?" Explication on 1 Corinthians 3:21.[54]

Christians Possess All Things in Christ. Martin Luther: Therefore, among Christians, nobody need complain that he is too poor or in too humble a station. Beloved, do you not have as much as a king or sovereign prince—a golden crown, power, goods, honor? After all, you have the same God, Creator of heaven and earth, the same Christ, the same baptism, and his whole heavenly kingdom; as St. Paul says of the Christians, they have nothing and yet possess everything, for as he says in 1 Corinthians 3, "all things are yours; and you are Christ's; and Christ is God's." Therefore under this Lord you are rich and blessed enough, so that even an emperor cannot have more than you. But remain in your station and be content, whether you sit above or below, and guard against this scrambling up higher, so that you will not think: "Because I am a prince, because I am noble, learned, powerful, I alone must be respected and elevated." But rather say: "Defend me, heavenly Father, from pride, for I know that the humblest plowman can be better in your sight than I." Sermon at Torgau Castle Church.[55]

Christian Attitudes Toward Life and Death. Wolfgang Musculus: "Whether life or death." Jerome understands this verse to refer to the life and death of Christ. Chrysostom applies it to the life and death of Christian ministers, as the apostle says: "If we live, we live for your benefit, if we die, we die for your encouragement." Ambrose understands the verse to refer to the life and death of Christians themselves. It is simpler for us to interpret this passage to mean the life and death of all of these persons together, whether Christ or ministers or whoever else or even we ourselves. Thus it is as if Paul were saying: "All things are yours, whether living or dying, whether in the present or in the future."

Now we see here that the experience of death is a wonderful thing, and that it is numbered among the blessings of God's sons and daughters. Truly, if you consider death to come from God, from whom we receive all things through Christ, and if you reflect on how all things are arranged to work for the good of the elect whether in life or in death, then you will not be surprised that Paul lists death among the blessings of the elect. Commentary on 1 Corinthians 3:22.[56]

Christians Belong to God Through Christ. Huldrych Zwingli: The apostles were not sent so that you might belong to them, but so

[54]Hesshus, *Explicatio Prioris Epistolae ad Corinthios*, 63v-64r; citing Ps 34:9; 23:1; Rom 8:31-32.

[55]LW 51:350*.

[56]Musculus, *Comm. 1 Cor.*, 104. Chrysostom's treatment of this passage is found in his *Homilies on 1 Corinthians* (homily 10), NPNF 12:55.

that they might belong to you, that is, so that they might serve you. By their labors you were lead to Christ. Therefore you are neither Paul's nor Apollos's, but Christ's. That is why it is proper for people to boast in the name of Christ. Now, Christ is God's. Therefore, if you belong to Christ, you also belong to God through Christ. Annotations on 1 Corinthians 3:22-23.[57]

As Mediator, Christ Unites Us to His Father. John Calvin: "Christ is God's." This subjection refers to Christ's humanity, for in taking on our flesh, he assumed the form and condition of a servant, so that he might make himself obedient to his Father in all things. And certainly in order for us to adhere to God through him, it is necessary that Christ have God as his head. But we should note the reason Paul added this. For he reminds us that our fullest happiness consists in being united to God, who is the greatest good, and this happens when we are gathered together under the head the heavenly Father has appointed for us. In the same sense Christ said to his disciples, "You ought to rejoice that I am going to the Father, for the Father is greater than I" (John 14:28), for there he set himself as the Mediator through whom believers come to the original source of all blessings. It is certain that those who depart from the unity of the head are deprived of such a great blessing. Commentary on 1 Corinthians 3:23.[58]

[57]Zwingli, *Annotatiunculae . . . ex ore Zvinglij*, 29.

[58]CO 49:361 (cf. CTS 39:148).

4:1-21 The Ministry of Apostles

This is how one should regard us, as servants of
Christ and stewards of the mysteries of God. 2More-
over, it is required of stewards that they be found
faithful. 3But with me it is a very small thing that I
should be judged by you or by any human court. In
fact, I do not even judge myself. 4For I am not aware
of anything against myself, but I am not thereby
acquitted. It is the Lord who judges me. 5Therefore do
not pronounce judgment before the time, before the
Lord comes, who will bring to light the things now
hidden in darkness and will disclose the purposes of
the heart. Then each one will receive his commenda-
tion from God.

6I have applied all these things to myself and
Apollos for your benefit, brothers,[a] that you may learn
by us not to go beyond what is written, that none of
you may be puffed up in favor of one against another.
7For who sees anything different in you? What do you
have that you did not receive? If then you received it,
why do you boast as if you did not receive it?

8Already you have all you want! Already you have
become rich! Without us you have become kings! And
would that you did reign, so that we might share the
rule with you! 9For I think that God has exhibited us
apostles as last of all, like men sentenced to death,
because we have become a spectacle to the world, to
angels, and to men. 10We are fools for Christ's sake,
but you are wise in Christ. We are weak, but you are
strong. You are held in honor, but we in disrepute.
11To the present hour we hunger and thirst, we are
poorly dressed and buffeted and homeless, 12and we
labor, working with our own hands. When reviled,
we bless; when persecuted, we endure; 13when
slandered, we entreat. We have become, and are still,
like the scum of the world, the refuse of all things.

14I do not write these things to make you ashamed,
but to admonish you as my beloved children. 15For
though you have countless[b] guides in Christ, you do
not have many fathers. For I became your father in
Christ Jesus through the gospel. 16I urge you, then, be
imitators of me. 17That is why I sent[c] you Timothy,
my beloved and faithful child in the Lord, to remind
you of my ways in Christ,[d] as I teach them every-
where in every church. 18Some are arrogant, as though
I were not coming to you. 19But I will come to you
soon, if the Lord wills, and I will find out not the talk
of these arrogant people but their power. 20For the
kingdom of God does not consist in talk but in power.
21What do you wish? Shall I come to you with a rod,
or with love in a spirit of gentleness?

a Or *brothers and sisters* **b** Greek *you have ten thousand* **c** Or *am sending* **d** Some manuscripts add *Jesus*

Overview: Paul continues to describe the qualities of a true apostle, while at the same time defending his ministry and message among the Corinthians and exposing the spiritual pride of their false apostles. Reformation commentators find in this chapter precious details as to the primary responsibilities of faithful Christian bishops and pastors. In particular, commentators call attention to the fact that ministers are servants (not lords) of Christ's church; that they proclaim the "mysteries of God" (which Protestant interpreters understand to mean the gospel message—not merely the sacraments); and that they exercise fatherly care over their spiritual "children," providing guidance and correction with an attitude of gentleness and loving concern. Though few Protestant ministers will suffer as intensely as the apostle Paul did, all faithful ministers should expect to be treated as contemptible by a world that celebrates human wisdom and eloquence and despises the simplicity of the gospel. Throughout these verses, Reformation commentators instruct their readers through the example of the apostle Paul of the importance of being submissive to

God's Word (which has supreme authority in the church) possessing a character worthy of imitation, appraising their gifts in a spirit of humility and gratitude, and being attentive to the divine will in fulfilling their particular stations in life.

True Apostles. John Calvin: In the beginning of the fourth chapter Paul explains the nature of the true apostolic office. And since the corrupt judgment of the Corinthians stood in the way of recognizing him as such, he rejects it and appeals to the Day of the Lord. Then, since he appeared contemptible to them on account of his humble appearance, he teaches them that this ought to be considered more to his honor than to his disgrace. He goes on from there to give examples which show that he was not concerned for his own glory, or for satisfying his appetites, but had faithfully performed the work of Christ and nothing else. Finally, he concludes by showing how the Corinthians should honor him. At the end of the chapter, Paul commends Timothy to them until he himself comes. And at the same time, he warns that on his arrival he will make it clear that he puts no value in that vacuous boasting by which the false apostles were promoting themselves. Introduction to 1 Corinthians.[1]

Cross-Bearing of Ministers. Tilemann Hesshus: In the fourth chapter, Paul teaches how wretched and full of troubles is the condition of apostles and all pious pastors in this world, and what dangers, calamities, exiles, and troubles accompany their ministries. For the Corinthians, who took pride in the gift of eloquence, were chasing after worldly glory from the ministry and preferred one person over another, just as if Christ had died, and the Spirit had established the ministry, so that human beings might have a reason for boasting and brashly exalting themselves over others. Therefore the apostle reminds them that the purpose for ministry is far different; for, of course, it is united with the greatest troubles, miseries, poverty, contempt, and dangers. Whereby those who perform the more lofty duties in the church must necessarily endure the more painful calamities, struggles, and dangers. This is why the apostle says that in this world they would be treated like scum and refuse (1 Cor 4:13). Now by such hardship and training, Christ wanted to fortify the apostles and pastors, lest they fight among themselves out of ambition or run after the delights of this world, or focus on civil domination. Introduction to 1 Corinthians.[2]

4:1-5 *God's Judgment Is What Matters*

All Christians Are Priests. Martin Luther: Now we, who have been baptized, are all uniformly priests in virtue of that very fact. The only addition received by the priests is the office of preaching, and even this with our consent. If the Romanists had to grant this point, they would have to admit that they had no right to lord it over us, except insofar as we, of our own free will, allowed them to do so. Thus it says in 1 Peter 2: "You are an elect race, a royal priesthood, and a priestly kingdom." It follows that all of us who are Christian are also priests. Those whom we call priests are really ministers of the Word, and chosen by us; they fulfill their entire office in our name. The priesthood is simply the ministry of the word. So in 1 Corinthians 4 it says: "Let a man so account of us as of ministers of Christ and stewards of the mysteries of God." Pagan Servitude of the Church.[3]

What Does This Epistle Reading Teach Us? Johann Spangenberg: Three things. First, what apostles, bishops, and preachers are, namely, servants not lords—not servants of Satan or of the world, but of Christ. As St. Paul says here, "This is how everyone should regard us, namely, as Christ's servants," etc. Second, what such service consists of,

[1] CO 49:300-301 (cf. CTS 39:42).

[2] Hesshus, *Explicatio Prioris Epistolae ad Corinthios*, 4r-v.

[3] In Dillenberger, *Martin Luther: Selections from His Writings*, 345-46 (cf. LW 36:112-13); citing 1 Pet 2:9.

namely, they must be faithful stewards of God's mysteries. That is, they are to lift up the gospel—in which the divine goods, graces, and gifts are hidden—before the people and to distribute the holy sacrament as Christ has ordained. Therefore Paul says here, "We seek nothing else from stewards than that they would be found faithful." Third, that devout bishops and preachers should not allow themselves to stray from such faithful service. Whether the world judges, convicts, damns them for it, they must diligently attend to their office and conduct themselves faithfully. They must commend their affairs to Christ, the highest Judge, who is not distant. He certainly will discover such untimely splinter judges and log carriers. That is what Paul is saying by, "To me it is a very small thing that I should be judged by you," etc. Epistle for Third Sunday in Advent.[4]

Bishops Are Servants of God's People. Philipp Melanchthon: The second topic of the epistle describes the office of bishops in which two things deserve the most attention. First, the names and traditions of bishops have nothing to do with piety, which is what the apostle intends when he says in 1 Corinthians 3:21, "So let no one boast of men," etc. And so it is not right for bishops to command or establish religious regulations, because the function of bishops in Matthew's last chapter is to teach what the Lord commands. Therefore the gospel does not grant bishops the authority to establish traditions. Thus Paul here calls bishops "stewards of the mysteries of God," that is, of the gospel.... That is, these ministers are yours. They do not have the right to bind you in some servitude; you are free; you are not their servants, rather they are your servants.... The second point to be noted is that all bishops are equal, for Paul makes them equivalent when he says in 1 Corinthians 4:6, "I have applied all this to myself and Apollos for your benefit; brethren, that you may learn in us lest anyone try to go beyond what is written," that is, lest any of the bishops think he is anything more than a minister and dispenser of the gospel. Annotations on 1 Corinthians 4:1.[5]

What Is a "Steward"? Johann Spangenberg: A "steward" is the person in charge of a master's house, along with his children and servants. He supplies them with food, clothes, and other basic needs, as now hospital superintendents, almoners, advocates, wardens, and the like do. These are true deacons. Why does Paul call himself and [other] preachers "stewards of God"? God also has a house, the Christian church, the assembly of Christians, over which he has established apostles, bishops, and preachers as stewards and wardens to care for the church, supplying them with good food and nourishment for their souls. So that we do not understand this care to be physical, St. Paul distinguishes these spiritual stewards of God from all other physical stewards through the little word *mysteriorum*, "mysteries." It is as if he wanted to say: "Human stewards are in charge of children and servants according to the body, and they give them physical food and nourishment. But God's stewards are in charge of the soul alone; they give spiritual food, that is, they preach the gospel and administer the precious sacraments according to Christ's command." Epistle for Third Sunday in Advent.[6]

Stewards of God's Mysteries. Wolfgang Musculus: The ministry of Christ is to be a steward of the mysteries of God. Now by the "mysteries of God," Paul means the grace of the new covenant accomplished by the blood of Christ and apprehended by faith for salvation and eternal life. It is too narrow to explain this only in regards to baptism and the Lord's Supper, since it relates to the apostolic dispensation in general. Paul is speaking about the stewardship of all those things that are connected with the grace of the kingdom

[4]Spangenberg, *Postilla Teütsch*, 4:17-18; referring to Mt 7:1-5.

[5] Melanchthon, *Annotationes in Epistolam priorem ad Corinthios*, 62, 64.

[6] Spangenberg, *Postilla Teütsch*, 4:20r-v.

of Christ. Because none of these things can be grasped by human reason, but are perceived entirely by revelation of the Holy Spirit, Paul rightly calls them "mysteries." The proclamation of the gospel is the stewardship of this grace. For by it, the remission of sins and eternal life is dispensed to believers. Thus Paul has already said, "It pleased God through the folly of preaching to save those who believe." This stewardship does not reside in the power of the minister, as if he multiplies the grace of God through his various sacrifices, but it is in the will and power of God, who gives the growth and opens the hearts of those who hear. Commentary on 1 Corinthians 4:1.[7]

The Mysteries of God and the Devil. Johann Spangenberg: There are two kinds of mysteries: God's and the devil's. What are the mysteries of God? Everything that we confess in faith, that we teach in the gospel and divine Scripture. Namely, Christ—God's Son—became man, was born, died, buried, rose again from the dead and ascended into heaven, etc. And all this was for our sake. These are great mysteries and secrets, which the world neither knows nor believes; yes, they consider them a mockery and foolishness, as Christ says. Now those who distribute and preach these mysteries are true apostles and stewards of Christ.

What are the mysteries of the devil? Everything that someone teaches and preaches aside from Scripture and God's Word, trying to aid others' souls. Like how some teach that human works and merits save; the pope is the head and cornerstone of the Christian church; the Mass is a sacrifice; monastic life is a new baptism; [holy] water, salt, palm branches, and incense scare away the devil, and so on—things that John saw written on the great Babylonian whore's forehead. Now those who distribute and preach this mystery are true apostles and stewards of Satan. Epistle for Third Sunday in Advent.[8]

God Equips Ministers. Martin Bucer: And in all this these ministers of the church are servants of Christ and stewards of the secret things of God, that is, of Christ's salvation and of the Holy Spirit, not merely of the letter. They take the elect of God and raise them up into the new eternal covenant, which has been established through the blood of our Lord Jesus Christ with all God's elect throughout the whole world. They also serve the Lord in ministering the holy gospel to his elect, teaching and admonishing them and also administering the holy sacraments, so that people might come to him, Christ our Lord, and be saved. . . .

But this they certainly do not accomplish by their own powers, but through the power and work of the Lord. Of themselves they could not even think of doing such a thing, but God equips them for the ministry. To that end the Lord gives them his Spirit and understanding of the Scriptures. His Spirit speaks through them; it is his power, his Spirit, and his work. It is he who gives success. True Care of Souls.[9]

The Ministry of the Gospel. David Chytraeus: Concerning the ministry of the gospel: God gathers for himself, from out of humanity, an everlasting church by the preaching of his Word, in which he has revealed himself, and by which alone (and not otherwise) he converts men and women to himself and endues them with true knowledge, righteousness, and everlasting salvation. As it is said in Acts 11: "He will declare to you a message by which you will be saved, you and your whole household." For this reason, out of his wonderful goodness and wisdom, he has sent out and ordained certain persons to preach and spread abroad the gospel by public ministry—even since the beginning of the world. The first preacher was the Son of God himself in Paradise. After him, there followed the fathers, prophets, apostles, and other ministers.

Now, a minister of the gospel is a person called of God, either mediately or immediately, to teach

[7] Musculus, *Comm. 1 Cor.*, 105-6; citing 1 Cor 1:21.
[8] Spangenberg, *Postilla Teütsch*, 4:21r-v; citing Mt 11:27; Rev 17:5.

[9] Bucer, *Concerning the True Care of Souls*, 21-22.

Christ's gospel faithfully, to distribute his sacraments, and to perform with diligence, faithfulness, and constancy all other duties belonging to the ministry of the gospel. By this ministry Christ himself works mightily and imparts true knowledge of God, righteousness, and eternal salvation to all people. Postil on the Third Sunday in Advent.[10]

Servants of Christ Need to Be Wise and Trustworthy. Wolfgang Musculus: There are two excellent gifts for a good servant: wisdom, by which he is able to manage everything, whatever the situation, in a convenient and helpful way on behalf of the household; then trustworthiness, by which he looks after the master's affairs rather than his own. The servant who possesses both of these gifts together is most recommended. Now, because in that age it was more important to boast about prudence and wisdom than about trustworthiness, the false apostles preferred to have a reputation for wisdom among the Corinthians than be approved by God for the probity of their trustworthiness. The apostle seems to highlight this when he says: "It is required of servants that they be found trustworthy." Not only is trustworthiness required of servants of Christ, but also, at the same time, wisdom, as Christ observes in Matthew 24: "Who, do you think, is the faithful and wise servant whom his master has set over his household, to give them their food at the proper time?" The trustworthiness that the apostle demonstrated in his ministry was considered of no importance; but the reputation for wisdom alone dominated among the false apostles. Thus it is with good reason that the apostle warns that faithfulness is required in this stewardship. Commentary on 1 Corinthians 4:2.[11]

Good Stewards Are Faithful. The English Annotations: [Paul means here] that they keep nothing back from the people of God, but reveal to them his whole counsel, that they deal faithfully with them in everything so that they might render a good account of their stewardship at the Great Audit. Now although there are other virtues required in a steward, such as skill, industry, and providence, yet the apostle only names the virtue of "faithfulness" because that is the chief virtue, and because it best served his purpose to beat down the pride of the Corinthians' teachers, who boasted of the goods committed to them, as if they were their own and not their Master's. Annotations on 1 Corinthians 4:2.[12]

Four Characteristics of a Faithful Minister. Tilemann Hesshus: "It is required that the minister be faithful." It's as if Paul were saying, "It is not necessary for ministers to be instructed in all things equally or to have the greatest gifts; but this alone is necessary, that they are faithful and invest to good use the talent they have received from the Lord." Now four things pertain to such faithfulness: First, it is necessary that ministers be people who hold tightly to the doctrine of the church. Let them be able to teach and be mindful of the church's struggles. And let them be zealous for learning and exploring heavenly truth, for those who are ignorant are not able to teach. People who profit from performing medical procedures that they have never learned are imposters and are justly punished for treachery. In a similar way, when people have not learned church doctrine, when they have not read the prophetic or apostolic writings—and yet undertake the office of pastor of the church—they are treacherous imposters.

Second, it is necessary that they labor diligently, in good faith and conscience. Let them not disregard the duties of their vocation. Let them not flee from annoyances. Let them not shrink from conflicts. Let them not play around with sophistic illusions. Let them not cloak their opinions in ambiguous generalities. Let them not trick the ignorant rabble. Rather, let them teach, confess, and do all things

[10]Chytraeus, *Dispositio epistolarum*, 532-33; citing Acts 11:14.
[11]Musculus, *Comm. 1 Cor.*, 107; citing Mt 24:45.
[12]Downame, *The English Annotations*, DD1v*.

faithfully, sincerely, and with pure conscience. Pelagius, because he played around with tricks and generalities, was not a faithful teacher.

Third, constancy is required, so that ministers do not allow themselves to be lured away from the profession of the truth and the righteous dispensation of mysteries by any money, any dangers, any adversities. Let them reproach the sins of everyone in equal measure. Let them offer the free remission of sins to everyone in equal measure and always fulfill the responsibilities of their office.

Fourth, piety is required of faithful ministers, so that everything in their ministries is related to the glory of eternal God and the salvation of the church. Let us not seek our own profit or our own honor, lest we detract from a respectable life, character, or doctrine or cause even a small offense to our hearers. When ministers of the Word exhibit this faithfulness, nothing more can be required from them. Explication of 1 Corinthians 4:2.[13]

Paul Does Not Judge Prematurely. Jacques Lefèvre d'Étaples: People who judge themselves to be good and worthy servants of God usurp for themselves the judgment of God—and this is pride. In doing this, they are evil and unworthy servants. As it is written: "God opposes the proud." Now those who do what they ought to do and what they are able to do, who do not judge themselves either good nor bad, but leave judgment to God—these people recognize the degree to which God has knowledge of all things. For God knows things about them that they themselves do not know. In this way the humble are prepared for grace. As it is written: "He gives grace to the humble." Paul encourages his readers to strive for humility and flee premature judgment, saying, "Do not pronounce judgment before the time." Commentary on 1 Corinthians 4:3-5.[14]

Why Is Paul Exempt from Human Judgment? John Calvin: But it might be asked what right Paul had not only to reject the judgment of one church but also to exempt himself from the judgment of people in general. For this is a condition common to all pastors: that they are to be judged by the church. I answer that it is a mark of good pastors to allow both their doctrine and their lives to be examined by the judgment of the church, and it is a sign of a good conscience not to avoid the light of inspection. In this respect, no doubt, Paul was prepared to submit himself to the judgment of the Corinthian church, and to be called to give an account of his life as well as doctrine—if there had been a right means of inquiry. Indeed, Paul often confers this power on them, and of his own accord demands that they be willing to judge aright. But when a faithful pastor sees that he is pressed down by unfair and perverse factionalism, and that there is no room for equity or truth, he ought to appeal to God and flee to his judgment seat, and not concern himself with human opinion. This is especially true when he cannot secure a true and proper hearing. Commentary on 1 Corinthians 4:3.[15]

God Alone Will Judge the Quality of Human Work. Desiderius Erasmus: "Since God alone knows these things, I consider him alone worthy to judge my labors." Therefore we should leave all judgment of hidden things to him, whose eyes perceive all things clearly; he will pronounce judgment on each person when the right time appears. Likewise, you ought to be careful lest—as servants—you anticipate the judgment of the Lord, judging things before their time. For the time of pronouncing judgment concerning these matters will not take place until the Lord returns to judge things in heaven, on earth, and under the earth. At that time he will bring to light those things that are now hidden in darkness, and he will make visible to the eyes of everyone those things that escape the notice of

[13]Hesshus, *Explicatio Prioris Epistolae ad Corinthios*, 67v-68r.
[14]Lefèvre d'Étaples, *Commentariorum in Epistolas Beati Pauli . . . Liber Secundus*, 105v; citing 1 Pet 5:5.

[15]CO 49:363 (cf. CTS 39:152).

human consciousness, which are hidden in the deepest recesses of the human heart. At that time people will receive the reward they deserve from him whose judgments are sure. Those who have sincerely performed their duty will receive eternal praise from God, even if they received little commendation from humans. Those who have not performed their duty will be shamed and punished, condemned by God, even if they were held in high esteem among humans. Paraphrase on 1 Corinthians 4.[16]

The Judgments of Wicked People Are Meaningless. John Trapp: A good minister who is reviled may reply as a steward once did when his outraged master called him a knave, etc.: "Your honor may speak as you please, but I believe not a word that you say; for I know myself to be an honest man." . . . Politian once said: "Some men flatter me and others slander me, yet I think neither the better nor the worse of myself for that; no more than I think myself taller or shorter when my shadow is longer in the morning and shorter at noon." Beza said, "A Spanish Jesuit disputing with us about the Eucharist called us foxes, apes, serpents, etc. My answer was that we believed it no more than we believed transubstantiation." Commentary on 1 Corinthians 4:3.[17]

Paul Was Not Righteous Before God. Huldrych Zwingli: "I am aware of nothing against myself." By these words, Paul does not consider himself completely innocent and free from all sin (for in another passage he does not hesitate to call himself the greatest of sinners and a persecutor of the church), but instead he is only indicating that he is free from treachery. It is as if he were saying, "As for me, I have not at all condemned myself, since I am aware of nothing against myself. Nevertheless, I am by no means justified, for it is the Lord who judges me. I commit my cause to him whose judgment is so pure and true that no one is able to stand before him as righteous." Annotations on 1 Corinthians 4:4.[18]

Papists Provide No Assurance for Faith. John Calvin: Let us note that Paul here is not speaking about his entire life, but only about his office as apostle. For if he was conscious of nothing wrong in himself, the complaint he makes in Romans 7:15 would not be true, where he mourns that he does the evil that he doesn't want to do, and that he is prevented by sin from giving himself completely to God. Therefore Paul was mindful of sin dwelling in him and confessed it. But with respect to his apostleship, which Paul is discussing here, he had conducted himself with so much integrity and faithfulness that his conscience did not accuse him in any way. . . .

Papists abuse this passage so as to shake the assurance of faith. And, to be sure, if one accepts their teaching, we could do nothing but tremble miserably our entire lives. For what tranquility would our minds experience if it were determined by our works whether we are pleasing to God? Therefore I confess that the only thing which follows from the main foundation of the papists is a perpetual disturbance of conscience. And accordingly we teach that we must take refuge in the gracious promise of mercy, which is offered to us in Christ, so that we might know with certainty that we are reckoned righteous by God. Commentary on 1 Corinthians 4:4.[19]

God's Judgment. Wolfgang Musculus: The Lord alone judges. Thus Paul shows that he is not concerned about the judgment of a human court, because he is eager to please God alone, before whom all his inmost thoughts are revealed. So much

[16]Erasmus, *Paraphrases*, 232.

[17]Trapp, *A Commentary or Exposition*, 666*. Angelo Ambrogini (1454–1494), also known as Politian, was an Italian humanist and poet. Theodore Beza's defense was delivered at the Colloquy of Poissy (1561), in response to a speech of Diego Lainez (1512–1565), general of the Society of Jesus, in which Lainez likened the Reformed to apes, foxes, and serpents.

[18]Zwingli, *Annotatiunculae . . . ex ore Zvinglij*, 30. Zwingli here alludes to Paul's description of himself in 1 Tim 1:13.

[19]CO 49:365 (cf. CTS 39:155-56).

so that Paul says: "It is the Lord who judges me." And, "The Lord knows who I am, the state of my heart and that faith with which I minister. I labor with this awareness, not at all concerned how other people judge me." But, I ask, how will we be safe in the sight of the Lord when everything rises or falls, not on our knowledge of these things but on his judgment? Thus we will say with David: "Do not enter into judgment with your servant, O Lord." . . .

Paul is once again pointing toward the false apostles who were seeking praise from people in a human court, with no consideration of God's judgment. Now he threatens them with the coming of the Lord, who will one day bring to light those deeds that they had practiced in darkness and had hidden from the knowledge of mortal creatures. "Thus the Lord will come," Paul says, "who will bring to light the things hidden in darkness and disclose the purposes of the heart." At that time, he says, different outcomes will be apparent. Those who are now held in contempt, if they are found to be faithful before God, will be glorious and illustrious. On the other hand, those who are now held in high esteem, if they are discovered to be treacherous before God, will be completely humbled. Commentary on 1 Corinthians 4:4-5.[20]

God Is the Final Judge of Our Ministry. David Dickson: The secret intentions of the heart and the hidden purposes of those in ministry shall not be made clear before the judgment day. Nor can anyone pass judgment on the excellence of a person's ministry but God alone, who on the judgment day will dispense to each one either praise or blame according to what is deserved. Therefore we are to beware of comparing people on the basis of their gifts. Exposition of 1 Corinthians 4:5.[21]

4:6-7 *No Reason for Boasting*

Paul Argues with Clarity and Consistency. Heinrich Bullinger: This clause [in verse 6] is interpretive. For with these few words, Paul explains with clarity the principle, scope, and summary of all that he has discussed so far from chapter 1, and at the same time he discloses why so far he has proposed all these matters under his own name and the name of Apollos. He raises this matter with the choice word *meteschēmatisa*, which means "I have transformed," that is (as Erasmus says), "I have applied the identity of other people to the two of us, and we have spoken about the purveyors of evil through the example of our own selves so as not to offend anyone." For it was the false apostles, not the apostles themselves, who were the cause of factions. . . . Therefore with this statement Paul has avoided naming those persons, etc. But for what purpose does he do all this? First, so that everyone might measure themselves by his standard and follow his example, and so that they might not evaluate these matters beyond what has been written (namely, because the words preached by the minister are not the words of the Lord). Second, so that, united together in gospel simplicity, you might continue to cling to Christ only, and not be puffed up with a partisanship where people support and oppose various leaders. See, dear reader, how wrong they are who say that the Scriptures have a diffuse goal. For you yourself can see that for our Paul, no argument, no sentence, no period—not even a word—is mentioned by chance. All things are found to be in complete agreement and related to a single goal. Commentary on 1 Corinthians 4:6.[22]

Church History Is Full of Examples of Self-Pride. Tilemann Hesshus: Because Paul holds out real hope for correcting those very proud teachers who were praising themselves, he spares them and does not make unfavorable mention of them by name. Rather he proposes everything by way of figures so as to explain through the example of Apollos and himself how teachers in the church

[20]Musculus, *Comm. 1 Cor.*, 110; citing Ps 143:2.
[21]Dickson, *Exposition of St. Paul's Epistles*, 46*.
[22]Bullinger, *In Priorem ad Corinthios Epistolam Commentarius*, 39. Bullinger is citing from Erasmus's *Annotations* on 1 Cor 4:6. See *Erasmus' Annotations on the New Testament*, 449.

should conduct themselves, namely, that no one should exalt themselves over others; no one should be puffed up; no one should exhibit a lofty and proud spirit against and over others. The false apostles, however, yield to no one but prefer themselves and their own opinions. Paul of Samosata was puffed up against Firmilian. John of Antioch was puffed up against Cyril. Dioscorus was against Flavian. Chrysostom was against Epiphanus. Rufinus was against Jerome. Jerome was against Augustine. And so, innumerable are the examples of this sort of very serious sin in the church, which have given birth to the most bitter of divisions. Therefore Paul warns that all people should view themselves with modesty; they should not proudly exalt themselves; they should not stubbornly defend their opinions when other people more clearly demonstrate the truth. EXPLICATION OF 1 CORINTHIANS 4:6.[23]

WE CANNOT BOAST IN GOD'S GIFTS. HULDRYCH ZWINGLI: "What makes you different?" That is, who teaches that you should consider yourself different from others? That you should place yourself higher than others? That you should force others to be subordinate to you? Of course, you may be more learned, more eloquent, and more righteous than other people. Why are you puffed up? Why are you proud of someone else's gift? If God considered you worthy of his gifts before others, there is nothing you can credit to yourself, there is nothing that you can boast about. For what you have you have not received from yourself, but you have received it from God. ANNOTATIONS ON 1 CORINTHIANS 4:7.[24]

NO PLACE FOR PRIDE. WOLFGANG MUSCULUS: Two things should be noted in this passage. First, no person has anything they have not received from God, whether directly or through the ministry of others, whether angels, humans, or animals. For human beings lack every good thing, etc. Second, it is improper to boast in someone else's good. For a person ought to boast in whom and from whom and by whom all things come. And so Paul says: "If then you received it, why do you boast as if you did not receive it?" . . . Paul notes the shamelessness of this sort of pride, as if he were to say: "How in the world do you, under the pretext of reason, . . . boast about something that is not yours, but that you received from someone else?" . . . Now see how foolish, ridiculous, absurd, and (in the sight of God) wicked it is to boast about the goods that you have, which you have nevertheless received from another. What should be concluded about those who hypocritically pretend to have certain things to ingratiate themselves in the estimation of others? COMMENTARY ON 1 CORINTHIANS 4:7.[25]

GOD APPOINTS EACH PERSON TO THEIR STATION. JOHN CALVIN: The sense is this: "Let him come forward, whoever he is, who is eager for preeminence and disturbs the church with his ambition. I will inquire of him who it is that makes him superior to others, that is, who has given him this right to be called out from among others and made superior to them?" Now this whole argument depends on the arrangement that the Lord has established in the church, that members of the body of Christ should be interdependent, with everyone being content with their own place, their own rank, their own office, and their own honor. If one member wishes to leave his own place so as to leap

[23]Hesshus, *Explicatio Prioris Epistolae ad Corinthios*, 71r-v. As bishop of Caesarea Mazaca, Firmilian (died c. 269) led the opposition against the heretic Paul of Samosata. During the Nestorian controversy, Cyril of Alexandria (c. 376–444) excluded Bishop John of Antioch from the Council of Ephesus (431). Archbishop Flavian of Constantinople (d. 449) and the patriarch Dioscorus of Alexandria (d. 454) sharply disagreed over the condemnation of the heretic Eutyches, who asserted that Christ's divinity absorbed his humanity, resulting in one nature. The Latin theologian Jerome (c. 347–420) and Rufinus of Aquileia (c. 350–410) engaged in a sharp pamphlet war over their translations and assessments of Origen's writings. The bishop of Hippo Augustine (354–430) objected to Jerome's decision to create a new Latin translation of the Old Testament, based on the Hebrew text.

[24]Zwingli, *Annotatiunculae . . . ex ore Zvinglij*, 31-32.

[25]Musculus, *Comm. 1 Cor.*, 116.

over to someone else's place and take over his office, what would happen to the body as a whole? Let us know, therefore, that the Lord has gathered us together in the church and appointed each person to his or her own station so that we might be of mutual benefit to one another under one head. Let us know also that we have been endowed with various gifts so that we might serve the Lord with modesty and humility and be zealous for his glory, for he has conferred on us all that we have. This, therefore, was the best solution for correcting the ambition of those who were wishing to be superior: to call them back to God so that they might recognize that none were created great or humble by their own choice, but that this was the choice of God alone. Commentary on 1 Corinthians 4:7.[26]

The Boasts of the "Theologians of Glory." John Trapp: "For who makes you." Paul directs his speech to those theologians of glory, as Luther usually called them, that is, those vainglorious, self-ascribing pastors at Corinth who sought to undermine Paul's authority, and would not answer when he asked "Who taught you?" . . . "And what have you received," etc. There are those who would hammer out their own happiness, like the spider climbing by the thread of its own weaving, who live according to the motto, "I owe everything to myself alone." "Why do you boast?" This is folly as great as for the groom to be proud of his master's horse, the stage actor of his borrowed robes, or the mud wall of the sunshine. Of all the good that is in us, we may well say as the young man did of his hatchet, "Alas, master, it was but borrowed." Commentary on 1 Corinthians 4:7.[27]

4:8-13 *The Harsh Trials Endured by the Apostles*

The Corinthians Should Have Followed Paul, Not Despised Him. John Colet: The officers in Christianity are all ministers, not masters, of the church. It is the duty of ministers, however, to be diligent in action and to seek praise not from people but from God alone, and not in this life, but in the life hereafter; it is their duty also to acknowledge that they do not have effectiveness in their ministry by their own strength, but by a power received from God. And so people must boast not of their ministers, but only of God.

Because the apostles were despised and ill-treated by the world, for that reason perhaps they began to be considered worthless in the eyes of the Corinthians, and to have no more esteem than the pagans had for those condemned men who were marked for death and cast to the beasts in the arena.

Although being aggrieved by their blindness, the apostle almost laughs with irony and pretends to praise them and give them a place above his own, so that they may recognize—especially those who wished to be seen as teachers among the Corinthians—their own folly and presumption, and be ashamed for despising the apostles, their own parents in Christ, for their harsh lives. Instead they should set the lives of the apostles and their "father" Paul before them as an example, and recognize that the most important thing for them to do is what the apostles consistently do; and they should eagerly follow the footsteps of those who set them in the right path. But if they become lost and deviate from the way of the apostles, what leader do they have to follow? It is necessary, therefore, for them to keep their eyes focused on him who goes before them and is their forerunner. This is especially true when the road is poorly traveled, and no footprints are seen except those of the one who has gone before them. Then you must watch the trail with all the more care, lest, if you wander from it, you return to the right path either too late or never. The Corinthians, however, had wandered from the footsteps of Paul; so he sent Timothy there to show them the way and lead the stragglers back to the path. Exposition of 1 Corinthians 4.[28]

[26]CO 49:366-67 (cf. CTS 39:158-59).
[27]Trapp, *A Commentary or Exposition*, 667*; citing 2 Kings 6:5.
[28]Colet, *Enarratio*, 113.

The Dangers of Ingratitude and Self-Indulgence. Philipp Melanchthon: The apostle reproves the Corinthians for being disgusted with and ungrateful for God's gifts, as if he were saying: "You are already filled up, and you therefore are disgusted with and scorn God's gifts." Or the passage can be taken ironically, as Ambrose reads it, namely, "Are you already fed up with the good things of the Spirit? Do you already scorn the good things of the Spirit that you have barely tasted? Has your hunger for the good things of the Spirit already been taken away? Do you already consider yourselves just and holy? You have made a beginning of being justified and sanctified by these first steps; you must go forward, not jump back nor come to a stop."

Consider the surprising way of the proud. Their first opinion—that they are better people—the apostle destroys when he says, "Who sees anything different in you?"; that is, in whose judgment are you superior to another? A second opinion follows this one: that the things we have belong to us because they have been given to us due to our merit, and we use these things against other people. And so, Paul says, "What do you have that you did not receive?" Last, because they are consumed by the flesh, their hunger for the things of the Spirit dies, and it seems that the flesh is abounding, not needing any further justification, and at the same time the hunger for spiritual things is scorned and destroyed, the fear of God perishes, God is scorned, and people return to their vomit.... Such are those people who, when they have once felt consolation, afterward return to their vomit having almost destroyed the fear of God by their self-indulgence. Annotations on 1 Corinthians 4:8.[29]

Paul Employs Irony to Shame the Corinthians. The English Annotations: The apostle continues his irony, and his meaning is this: "You are indeed in a far happier case and more excellent condition than we poor apostles who are distressed, persecuted, and despised of the world. We have good reason to wish to be partakers of your blessings and comforts, given that we live like miserable prisoners who anticipate every hour to be called to execution, after we have been ignominiously led about through the darkest places, and made public spectacles of misery and scorn." Annotations on 1 Corinthians 4:8-9.[30]

Paul Was a Spectacle to the World. Wolfgang Musculus: Paul makes evident, nevertheless, how he *is* superior: by being the most humbled of all people, and being rejected and afflicted to an astonishing degree. He declares, although very subtly, that God has not determined that his people who follow Christ will be honored and held as superior in this age. And he proves it by inferring from his own example. For he contrasts the striving and good fortune of the false apostles (whom he accuses of insincerity because they did not care and trouble themselves with the things of Christ, but were seeking their own benefit and considered it most important that they were famous and ruled with honor) with his own situation, given that he was weak, despised, and treated like a fool because of his faithfulness to Christ....

Why does he say that he is like a man whom God has sentenced to death and for what purpose does he assert it? "Because we have become a spectacle to the world, to angels, and to human beings." That is, "The only way we are superior in the world is that we are discredited, humbled, and treated as criminals, and thus we suffer public disgrace." It was customary at that time for criminals to be punished by means of a public spectacle, exposed to the disgrace of everyone. And Paul considers his disgrace all the greater, because he says that he had become a spectacle not for one city or another, but for the whole world, for both angels and human beings. Commentary on 1 Corinthians 4:9.[31]

[29]Melanchthon, *Annotationes in Epistolam priorem ad Corinthios*, 66; referring to Prov 26:11. For the reference to Ambrose (Ambrosiaster), see *Commentarius ad 1 Cor.*, in PL 17:217.

[30]Downame, *English Annotations*, DD1v*.

[31]Musculus, *Comm. 1 Cor.*, 118.

Like the Apostles, All Christians Will Suffer Hardships. Tilemann Hesshus: Paul demonstrates by the example of the apostles that the church cannot yet boast of a completed victory or of a kingdom won. To be sure, we have won a partial victory, and the heavenly kingdom is being prepared for us by Christ. But we have not yet achieved this glorious end through our power. We are still running in a race and have not yet won the prize. We must continually struggle with the flesh, with the world, with sin, with Satan, with an evil conscience, and with all sorts of disasters. Thus we should not take pride in the flesh as if we had vanquished all dangers and the snares of Satan. For by his counsel, the most wise and merciful God sends innumerable calamities and difficulties on his church so that we might not become proud nor give in to carelessness nor take pride in our spiritual gifts, but rather live in the constant fear of God. To illustrate this idea Paul draws on the example of the apostles, and proves that more than all other men the apostles struggled with the greatest troubles, distresses, dangers, and calamities in the world. Aside from our Lord Jesus Christ, who, after suffering in this world, died on a most cruel cross, no human beings were so roughly treated and harassed in this world as the apostles—as the history of Paul in the book of Acts testifies. Someone might wonder why it is that God allows his dearest children and most faithful servants to be treated so cruelly in this world. But the answer is easy: It is the will of God that those whom he has called into the fellowship of eternal life should be conformed to the image of his Son. And so, everyone enters into the kingdom of heaven through many trials. Explication on 1 Corinthians 4:9.[32]

Why Does Paul Call Himself Foolish, Weak, and Insignificant? Peter Martyr Vermigli: Paul sharply criticizes the Corinthians with this ironical statement, since (though he was their teacher and father) he calls himself a fool, weak, and insignificant—while they were boasting to be the exact opposite. Whence Chrysostom says: "If the apostle had simply said, 'You who pursue fame and wisdom: you are deceived, you have been tricked, you are completely mistaken since the Lord has determined these things far otherwise,' he would have spoken the complete truth. But he would not have made as great an impression on their minds as he did by using this kind of irony." Paul is saying, "you are wise in Christ, and yet you wish to join the gospel and Christianity with the wisdom of this world" (something the Corinthians would not have admitted). Here Paul means by the word "wisdom" that wisdom of the flesh which is death and at enmity toward God, since it refuses to be subject to him, as Paul says in Romans. Paul calls himself and the other apostles "fools," because this is what the world considered them to be, since it observed that Paul chased after neither wealth nor pleasures nor honor, but rather treated all these things that the masses sought after as contemptible for the sake of Christ. Paul writes that he is weak, because he did not associate with the powerful people of this world. He also calls himself ignoble and insignificant because he was not eloquent, nor was he considered among the chief of the apostles. Commentary on 1 Corinthians 4:10.[33]

The Corinthians Judge Paul Unfairly. David Dickson: Paul compares his afflictions with the Corinthians' prosperity, and he shows their unbalanced opinion of themselves and the apostle in three particulars. First, in wisdom (Paul says) we are accounted as fools, both by the world and by you, because we endure so many dangers for the sake of Christ. You think that you and others are wise, because you enjoy the gospel and are prosperous. Second, in strength, we appear weak, broken with distress, while you seem strong and powerful, living out of reach of any of the arrows of tribulation. Third, in honor, you shine

[32]Hesshus, *Explicatio Prioris Epistolae ad Corinthios*, 73r-v.

[33]Vermigli, *In Selectissimam Priorem ad Corinthios Epistolam . . . Commentarii*, 106v-107r. See Chrysostom, *Homilies on 1 Corinthians* (homily 13), in NPNF 12:72-73.

forth in glory and authority, while in the meantime we are ignominious and despised by you and others. Exposition of 1 Corinthians 4:10.[34]

Paul's Present Circumstance. John Calvin: The apostle here portrays his own condition, as if in a painting, so that by his example the Corinthians might learn to lay aside their proud spirit and embrace, as he did, the cross of Christ with a meek spirit. He shows consummate skill, for in reminding them of those things that had rendered him contemptible, he was confirming his unparalleled faithfulness and indefatigable zeal for the advancement of the gospel. And in turn he was subtly criticizing his rivals who, although they had not furnished any such evidence, nevertheless wished to be considered superior. Commentary on 1 Corinthians 4:11.[35]

Christians and Suffering. Wolfgang Musculus: What then? Is it impossible for people to be true and genuine ministers of Christ who are not taken for fools, who are not despised, who are not afflicted, who are not hungry and thirsty, who are not naked, who do not wander about without a home nor provide for themselves by working with their own hands? I answer: True Christian ministry and faithfulness to Christ are not found in these things. As a general rule, however, many ministers who are harassed ought to be considered honorable, while one finds that oftentimes the worst good-for-nothings are treated well. But the concern of ministers of Christ and other believers should be this: first that they seek the kingdom of God before all things from their hearts; and second that they are prepared to endure every circumstance for the sake of the name of Christ. Now if it happens that they are held in high esteem and experience peace, that's okay. For even Paul knew not only hunger, but also abundance and plenty. But if the Christian faces the cross, persecution, and contempt on account of Christ, this also should be borne and endured in the faith and love of Christ. Commentary on 1 Corinthians 4:11-13.[36]

Paul Willingly Endured Persecution and Humble Work. John Calvin: When Paul says that he endures persecution patiently and prays for those who malign him, he indicates not only that he is afflicted and humbled by God through the cross, but also that he is endowed with a disposition to humble himself willingly. In this way, perhaps, he is striking at the false apostles, who were so weak and soft that they could not bear being touched by even the smallest finger. In speaking about their work Paul adds "with our own hands" to express more clearly how contemptible his occupation was. It's as if he were saying: "Not only do I make a living through my own labor, but it is dirty, manual labor." Commentary on 1 Corinthians 4:12.[37]

The Meaning of "Scum." Theodore Beza: "Off-scouring" (*perikatharmata*), that is, refuse, dregs, dross, or filth that, on account of being ghastly, is purged from something. In short whatever is completely useless and left over when something is refined. For this reason Erasmus translates this word as "excrement." But I have retained the etymology found in the Greek dictionaries. Annotation on 1 Corinthians 4:13.[38]

Scum and Refuse of the World. Tilemann Hesshus: People are called "expiations and refuse" who by some horrible crime have offended God to such an extent that he is angry at an entire nation or even the whole world and cannot be placated without the offering of a propitiatory sacrifice or expiation. Thus Oedipus, Adratus, and others were considered as objects of divine wrath among the nations. In 2 Samuel 21, when a severe famine afflicted the land of Judea, David consulted the Lord and the seven sons of Saul were identified as guilty of murder and considered as sacrifices of expiation—and once they had been executed,

[34]Dickson, *Exposition of St. Paul's Epistles*, 47*.
[35]CO 49:370 (cf. CTS 39:164-65).
[36]Musculus, *Comm. 1 Cor.*, 121.
[37]CO 49:370 (cf. CTS 39:165).
[38]Beza, *Annotationes Maiores*, 173.

God was reconciled to the land of Judea. Therefore Paul points out that the world considers the apostles as contemptible sacrifices and objects of divine wrath, who cause God to be angry at the whole human race, because the apostles are prohibiting pagan worship and introducing into the world a new kind of teaching. It's as if, because of the apostles and their teaching, God was sending all sorts of calamities, wars, fires, blights, seditions, the ruin of the Roman Empire, destructions, plagues, famines, and every other sort of disaster. They thought that God could not be placated unless the apostles and their teaching were eliminated from the world. Therefore, since the world's opinion of the apostles was so severe, it is easy to understand why the apostles could neither seek nor hope for empty glory and applause in the world. The disciples of the apostles, therefore, also ought to discard completely the love of worldly glory; instead they should make up their minds to bear patiently and with good cheer the severest hatred and most extreme insults on account of the apostles' teaching. Explication of 1 Corinthians 4:13.[39]

The Dung of the World. John Trapp: The word signifies the dung cart (according to one commentator) that goes through the city, into which everyone brings and casts their filth. Everyone had some filth to cast on Paul and the apostles. Constantine, a citizen of Rouen, along with three others, having been condemned to be burned at the stake for their defense of the gospel, was put into a dung cart. In response, they began to rejoice, saying that although they were considered here the excrement of the world, yet their death would be a sweet aroma unto God. Commentary on 1 Corinthians 4:13.[40]

[39]Hesshus, *Explicatio Prioris Epistolae ad Corinthios*, 75r-v. Oedipus, king of Thebes, and Adratus, king of Argos, were tragic heroes in Greek mythology.

[40]Trapp, *A Commentary or Exposition*, 668*. The account of Constantine's martyrdom is reported in Foxe, *Acts and Monuments* 4.398.

4:14-21 *Paul's Personal Appeal*

Advice for Those Who Care for Souls. Philipp Melanchthon: [This passage] deals with the method of correction lest the harshness of a rebuke drive a person to despair. Thus Paul says here, "I do not write this to make you ashamed," that is, not to drive you to despair. This method of correction should be carefully preserved among those who are repentant, as Isaiah 42:3 says of Christ, "A bruised reed he will not break" etc. and "a dimly burning wick he will not quench" etc. Psalm 50 [51], "a contrite heart" etc. and 2 Corinthians 2:6-11, "For this person, this punishment by the majority is enough; so you should rather turn to forgive and comfort him, or he may be overwhelmed by excessive sorrow." Note how the apostle takes care that there is a limit to the punishment lest it provide an occasion for despair. Let those who hear confessions and direct consciences follow his example. Annotations on 1 Corinthians 4:14.[41]

Paul's Purpose for Admonition. John Calvin: But what is the purpose of this admonition? Namely, that the Corinthians, who were puffed up with their bombastic ideas, might learn to glory along with Paul in the lowliness of the cross and might no longer despise him for that which he was rightfully most honorable before God and the angels. In short, that, laying aside their former haughtiness, they might place greater value on those marks[42] of Christ that he bore than the vain and spurious ostentation of the false apostles. Let teachers infer from this that they must always administer moderation in their corrections so as not to wound people's minds with excessive harshness and so as not (as the popular proverb states) to mix honey or oil with vinegar. But most of all they should beware lest they seem to gloat over those whom they reprove or delight in

[41]Melanchthon, *Annotationes in Epistolam priorem ad Corinthios*, 70.

[42]Literally *stigmata*.

shaming them. No! And more than that, they must endeavor to make it plain that they are out for nothing other than the promotion of their welfare. For what will the teacher gain by his shouting, if (as I have said) he does not season the sharpness of his rebuke with moderation? Thus if we wish to produce any benefit in correcting people's faults, it is important to show them that our corrections come from a friendly heart. Commentary on 1 Corinthians 4:14.[43]

Paul's Approach with His Spiritual Children. Tilemann Hesshus: The apostle has delivered a strong and sharp rebuke in which he has reproached the Corinthians for their quarreling, lack of trust, and arrogance. And at the same time he pulled out their belief in human wisdom as the root of all these evils. Now, so as to soothe somewhat their minds after this sharp correction, Paul tells them of the affection with which he did it. Paul did not want to shame or to disgrace the Corinthians, but to advise them as sons what is just, healthy, pious, holy, and pleasing to God. Then he testified that he embraced his hearers with paternal love so that he might beget them as children in Christ through the gospel. That is, by preaching the gospel he had guided them to this happy condition where they were changed from being sons of Satan into sons of God. And just as Abraham was called the father of many nations, Paul calls himself their father, namely, in doctrine, ministry, instruction, and example.

Paul also explains how he sent his advice to them, namely, through his colleague Timothy. Paul does this, no doubt, so as to bring back to their memory the teachings they had received from him and the customs, lifestyle, and habits that Paul had cultivated in all the churches. And he especially encouraged them to hold on to the purity of doctrine, and then to rehearse and practice the apostles' teaching as well as to keep in view constantly the example of the whole apostolic life and practice. Thereupon Paul promises that he will come to Corinth and will publicly reprove and restrain those haughty teachers, who in Paul's absence were disturbing the church and abusing it with their show of erudition. Explication on 1 Corinthians 4:14-19.[44]

Spiritual Parents Are Different from Spiritual Guides. Wolfgang Musculus: Paul demonstrates the right basis for his judgment of the false apostles by making a comparison, showing that he is different from those teachers just as a parent is different from a school instructor. First, there is a great deal of difference between an instructor and a parent. It is possible that a school instructor is good for a boy for a time and has some authority over him. But this in no way diminishes the advantage of the parent and his control over the boy. However, in this fashion the false apostles were striving to be like instructors in Christ over the Corinthians. Second, the school instructor cannot achieve the trust and sweetness of the parental affection. Third, instructors change, so that it is possible for a boy over time to have a number of different instructors. But that is not the case with a parent, who alone is the boy's parent forever. This is certainly not the way the false apostles were viewing the Corinthians, and they were so shameless in assigning to themselves the title of "instructor" that the "boys" often forgot that Paul was their true spiritual father in Christ. And they treated Paul with loathing, and even contempt. Paul accuses them of foolishness when he says: "For though you have a thousand instructors in Christ, you do not have many fathers." Commentary on 1 Corinthians 4:15.[45]

The Word Begets Life. John Trapp: The Word of God is accompanied by a regenerating power. Exhortations from the Word are operative and effective means of sanctification, as when God said, "Let there be light," or Christ said, "Lazarus, come forth!" The Spirit makes the seed of the

[43]CO 49:371-72 (cf. CTS 39:168).

[44]Hesshus, *Explicatio Prioris Epistolae ad Corinthios*, 76r-v.

[45]Musculus, *Comm. 1 Cor.*, 122-23.

Word prolific and generative. And hence ministers are likened to *fathers*, as Moses was father to Aaron's children, who are therefore in that passage called *his* generation. As the philosopher said, "it is the most proper work of every living thing to beget its like." So also here. Commentary on 1 Corinthians 4:15.[46]

Corinthians Must Imitate Paul's Fatherly Example. Heinrich Bullinger: Now here, in passing, Paul inserts a charming comparison for the sake of amplification. Although you have ten thousand (that is, countless) teachers, nevertheless, you have few fathers. Although the false apostles are asserting their right to dominate and rule among you, nevertheless they lack fatherly affection toward you. In this way I far surpass them, since I birthed true godliness among you (if indeed you are in Christ Jesus) through the preaching of the gospel. Paul adds this by inference: "I urge you to be imitators of me." From this we learn first of all that a teacher is not a true teacher unless he has fatherly affection for his disciples. Anyone can take for himself the office of instructor, but not everyone possesses true fatherly affection. Second, we learn that the church is birthed from the Word of Truth. Hence, today, those people are false teachers who believe that the church's authority has priority over the Word of Truth, that is, the Scripture. For the church is not the lord of Scripture, but rather subjects itself to the Scripture and in all its decisions acts according to its precepts. Commentary on 1 Corinthians 4:15-16.[47]

Imitation Has Its Limits. John Calvin: But to what extent Paul wishes them to be imitators of him, he indicates elsewhere when he adds, "as I am in Christ." We must always hold to this imitation so that we don't follow any human teachers, except insofar as they lead us to Christ. We know what Paul intends here. The Corinthians were not only running away from the lowliness of the cross, but they were also despising their [spiritual] father because, having forgotten earthly glory, he was instead boasting in the disgrace of Christ. And the Corinthians considered themselves and others fortunate since they avoided things that were contemptible according to worldly standards. Therefore Paul admonishes them that, following his example, they should devote themselves to Christ by enduring all things with patience. Commentary on 1 Corinthians 4:16.[48]

Timothy Was Like a Faithful Son to Paul. Huldrych Zwingli: Out of love Paul calls Timothy his son, because he had given birth to him in Christ. Additionally he was obedient to Paul in all things, like a son to a father, imitating the faith and diligence of his father in preaching the gospel. Such faithfulness is especially required in a minister of the Word, so that he might properly rule the people and family of God, and so that he might remove all wickedness and unrighteousness from them. Otherwise, he risks calling down the wrath of God on himself, as Luke 12 warns those who are treacherous. Annotations on 1 Corinthians 4:17.[49]

Unlike the Corinthians, Timothy Follows Paul's Example. Desiderius Erasmus: But so that you don't forget anything of our teaching (since it is not yet possible for me to come to you), I am sending Timothy to you in my place. He is my son—not by virtue of his birth, of course, but by virtue of his faithfulness to God—for he first embraced Christ through my influence and has never separated himself from my fatherly example. He will remind you of my way of life: that I follow Jesus Christ and am devoted to his example, proclaiming Christ not only to you, but to many different churches. Just as Christ is the common author of us all, so we should all follow the same pattern of life. The legitimate son is he

[46]Trapp, *A Commentary or Exposition*, 668*; citing Jas 1:18; Gen 1:3; Num 3:1.

[47]Bullinger, *In Priorem ad Corinthios Epistolam Commentarius*, 43.

[48]CO 49:374 (cf. CTS 39:173); citing 1 Cor 11:1.

[49]Zwingli, *Annotatiunculae . . . ex ore Zvinglij*, 33.

who performs his duty, not out of fear of evil, but with a sincere heart. But there are some among you who, in my absence, have thrown off all shame and are conducting themselves in an insolent manner, as if I am never going to return. But they are wrong. For very soon I will come, if the Lord allows it, and then I will find out how powerful those haughty people really are in this matter, not in their words, but in their deeds. For the power of the gospel does not reside in magnificent speaking . . . but in power and heavenly potency, demonstrated in patience in the face of evil, harmony, innocence of the whole of life, and miracles. PARAPHRASES ON 1 CORINTHIANS 4.[50]

PAUL IS CHIEFLY CONCERNED WITH RIGHT TEACHING. WOLFGANG MUSCULUS: We are advised here about teaching the Word. When Paul says, "be imitators of me," and when he reports that he had sent Timothy "to remind you of my ways," the apostle is thinking especially (if not entirely) about right teaching. For the error of the Corinthians rested not just in certain practices of the church, but especially in that teaching of the cross of Christ, which the false apostles were changing by their love for philosophy. . . . It should be noted from this passage the path in Christ we should follow if we wish to perceive and practice the way of the apostolic and universal church; namely, that message that the apostle of Christ taught everywhere and constantly in all the churches. And the message of his teaching is witnessed in his writings. This same message that Paul gave to Timothy he gives to us. COMMENTARY ON 1 CORINTHIANS 4:17.[51]

THE IMPORTANCE OF WORD AND EXAMPLE. JOHN TRAPP: It is of excellent use to know what good people, especially ministers, do as well as what they say. Ministers' lives should be a transcript of their sermons, or so many sermons on the life of Christ. COMMENTARY ON 1 CORINTHIANS 4:17.[52]

PAUL WILL SOON COME TO CORINTH AND SILENCE HIS CRITICS. HEINRICH BULLINGER: Now since Paul did not come [to Corinth] but had sent Timothy instead, the false apostles were hurling false accusations at him: If he was a father, then why didn't he himself visit his sons?—suggesting no doubt that he had given up on the Corinthians. But they were wrong. For, [Paul writes,] "I will come very soon, if the Lord permits. To be sure, I know how much those teachers of yours are arrogant and boastful, but I know what is going to happen one day. I will not worry myself with the talk and sarcastic words of those men; I will examine their power." Paul challenges the power of their words. Now power resides in this: namely in righteousness, innocence, and faith. Paul adds this beautiful statement: "For the kingdom of God does not consist in talk, but in power." A similar—but even more beautiful—statement is found in Romans 14. So then, the false apostles are hypocrites who eloquently discuss Christ and the gospel, but in their life and behavior, they differ not at all from the wicked. COMMENTARY ON 1 CORINTHIANS 4:18-19.[53]

IF THE LORD WILLS. JOHN CALVIN: The clause "if the Lord wills" indicates that we should not promise anything to other people regarding the future, nor make any personal plans, unless we have added this provision, "insofar as the Lord permits." Hence, James with good reason laughs at the rashness of those people who plan out what they are going to do in ten years, when they cannot be certain of life for even a single hour. Now although we are not required constantly to use such forms of expression, nevertheless, it is a good idea to accustom ourselves to them so that we might continually train ourselves with this thought: that all our plans must be subject to the will of God. COMMENTARY ON 1 CORINTHIANS 4:19.[54]

---

[50]Erasmus, *Paraphrases*, 236-37.
[51]Musculus, *Comm. 1 Cor.*, 126.
[52]Trapp, *A Commentary or Exposition*, 668*.
[53]Bullinger, *In Priorem ad Corinthios Epistolam Commentarius*, 44; citing Rom 14:17.
[54]CO 49:375 (cf. CTS 39:174-75); citing Jas 4:15.

The Gospel Is Preached with Faith and Power. Huldrych Zwingli: The preaching of the gospel does not depend on eloquence or clever words. For Christ did not entrust such preaching to those who were trained in eloquence and wise in this world so that (as we clearly see) it might be founded on faith, a kind of passion and power. As Matthew says about Christ, "he was teaching with power," that is, with great might, vivacity, and energy. Annotations on 1 Corinthians 4:20.[55]

The Spiritual Power of Paul's Message Disarms the False Apostles. Philipp Melanchthon: This second passage deals with speech and power. "Speech" does not mean the elegance of an oration but plausible philosophical arguments, including even an understanding of the gospel devoid of the Spirit. "Power" means the efficacy or energy of the Spirit. Now the apostle says he is not going to waste time with either the philosophy or the theology of the false apostles, but will be investigating the Spirit. The Spirit is manifest in both teaching and life. Indeed, nobody who does not have the Spirit and does not live by the Spirit is able to teach spiritual things. Jeremiah 23:21, "I did not send the prophets, yet they ran," and Christ, in Matthew 7:29, "He taught them as one who had authority, and not as their scribes and Pharisees." . . . Therefore, just as the apostle was going to pass judgment on the Corinthians, so now judgment is passed on scholastic doctrine. Annotations on 1 Corinthians 4:20.[56]

Identifying the True Church. Dirk Philips: One reads holy Scripture and observes therein the signs by which the congregation is purified and set before our eyes, let us measure ourselves according to this true plumb line, and test ourselves with this touchstone (2 Cor 10:13). Then it shall be seen and discovered whether we or our opponents are closer to the truth. Yes, if we then or they shall be held as the Christian congregation. If the kingdom of God were to exist in high-sounding words, in false idle boasting, and not in power and truth, in righteousness, peace, and joy in the Holy Spirit (1 Cor 4:20), then the false prophets and false Christians would always have won the game. An Apology or Reply.[57]

God's Power Transforms People. Hans Hut: For the kingdom of God does not consist of talk or an exterior thing, but of power. Thus the gospel is not a speech but a power of God (1 Cor 2 and 4), which is given only by God and which completely renews the person, from their mouth to their heart, and in all their conduct and behavior. Therefore it is a very bad gospel that the world and learned preachers down to our age are involved with, and that does not improve people but only aggravates them. This I leave to all Christian brothers to judge. But blessed are they who hear the word and preserve it. On the Mystery of Baptism.[58]

Paternal Love Is Expressed Through Gentleness as Well as Discipline. Wolfgang Musculus: Paul intends that the threat and anxiety of his coming should cause terror among not only the haughty babblers but also among the other wrongdoers to such an extent that, when he arrives, he might bring about the correction of the rest of their vices. . . . Now these words clearly show Paul's paternal affection. For surely it is the father's role to discipline with a rod his disobedient sons so that they are not ruined, even as he embraces obedient sons with gentleness, kindness, and love. Paul shows that he is prepared to do either. Now with respect to love, we should not think that the rod has nothing to do with paternal love, since it is out of love itself that a father employs the rod on sons whom he loves so as to save them from ruin. But Paul employs the word "love" here for the paternal goodness and kindness

[55]Zwingli, *Annotatiunculae . . . ex ore Zvinglij*, 34; citing Mt 7:29.
[56]Melanchthon, *Annotationes in Epistolam priorem ad Corinthios*, 70, 72.
[57]CRR 6:178*.
[58]Hut in Baylor, *The Radical Reformation*, 163-64; citing 1 Cor 2:4.

that he shows toward obedient sons. Now Paul seems to be speaking here from the perspective of those who are reproached and disciplined harshly. For they do not feel the love of the father when they are being flogged, but when they are being treated pleasantly and kindly. Commentary on 1 Corinthians 4:21.[59]

Paul's Father-like Severity. The English Annotations: "Shall I come to you with a rod?" Paul might have said "with a sword," that is, of excommunication, which he brandishes in the next chapter, where he cuts off the incestuous Corinthian [from the church]. But since he has previously presented himself as their father, and he bore the tender affection of a father toward them, he instead expresses the severity he was to use among them by the metaphor of a rod, with which a father chastens his son in order to break him of some ill quality or misdeed, rather than of the sword or some other harsher punishment. Annotations on 1 Corinthians 4:21.[60]

[59]Musculus, *Comm. 1 Cor.*, 128.

[60]Downame, *English Annotations*, DD2r*.

5:1-13 Sexual Immorality Defiles the Church

It is actually reported that there is sexual immoral-
ity among you, and of a kind that is not tolerated
even among pagans, for a man has his father's wife.
2 And you are arrogant! Ought you not rather to
mourn? Let him who has done this be removed from
among you.
3 For though absent in body, I am present in spirit;
and as if present, I have already pronounced
judgment on the one who did such a thing. 4 When
you are assembled in the name of the Lord Jesus and
my spirit is present, with the power of our Lord Jesus,
5 you are to deliver this man to Satan for the destruc-
tion of the flesh, so that his spirit may be saved in the
day of the Lord.[a]
6 Your boasting is not good. Do you not know that
a little leaven leavens the whole lump? 7 Cleanse out
the old leaven that you may be a new lump, as you
really are unleavened. For Christ, our Passover lamb,
has been sacrificed. 8 Let us therefore celebrate the
festival, not with the old leaven, the leaven of malice
and evil, but with the unleavened bread of sincerity
and truth.
9 I wrote to you in my letter not to associate with
sexually immoral people— 10 not at all meaning the
sexually immoral of this world, or the greedy and
swindlers, or idolaters, since then you would need to
go out of the world. 11 But now I am writing to you not
to associate with anyone who bears the name of
brother if he is guilty of sexual immorality or greed, or
is an idolater, reviler, drunkard, or swindler—not
even to eat with such a one. 12 For what have I to do
with judging outsiders? Is it not those inside the
church[b] *whom you are to judge? 13 God judges*[c] *those*
outside. "Purge the evil person from among you."

a Some manuscripts add *Jesus* **b** Greek *those inside* **c** Or *will judge*

Overview: The fact that the church in Corinth has turned a blind eye to the shocking sin of incest committed by one of its members causes the apostle Paul to demand the expulsion of the sinner from the congregation and to offer clear guidelines for the practice of excommunication. Believing that Paul's instructions were also normative for their day, Protestant commentators emphasize the importance of church discipline for the health of the church and describe in detail the purposes and proper bounds for its use. Most interpreters see church discipline achieving three primary purposes, namely, encouraging the repentance of the sinner, preserving the purity of Christ's church, and protecting Christians from bad examples. Nearly all agree that Paul's warning to the Corinthian Christians "not to associate with sexually immoral people" refers to moral offenders within the church rather than in the world at large. Even so, commentators disagree as to whether excommunication entails merely excluding the sinner from the religious community or requires more radical social and even familial ostracism. Regardless of its specific application, the reformers agree that discipline should be motivated by brotherly love rather than a vindictive spirit; it should seek the healing, not the destruction, of the wayward Christian; it is intended to be medicine—not poison—for sinners.

The Right Way to Discipline. Martin Luther: In chapter 5, [the apostle Paul] rebukes the gross unchastity of the man who had married his stepmother, and would put him under the ban and give him over to the devil. Thus he shows the right way of using the ban; it must be laid on open vice, with the consent of the believing congregation, as Christ also teaches in Matthew 18. Preface to the First Epistle of Saint Paul to the Corinthians.[1]

[1] WML 6:464; citing Mt 18:15-17.

Paul's Censure. Wolfgang Musculus: In this entire chapter Paul censures the Corinthians for an act of fornication committed among them, or rather because they did not punish it. Then he urges them by means of arguments that they should remove the person who has committed this sin and expel him from their community, and hand him over to Satan. In this chapter Paul makes three points. First, he asserts the enormity of the sin that has been committed. Second, he censures the Corinthians because they did not reprove the fornicator. Third, he prescribes his judgment on what should be done with this man in their assembly. Commentary on 1 Corinthians 5.[2]

Paul Now Turns to Specific Moral Problems in the Corinthian Church. Tilemann Hesshus: Throughout this letter, Paul has undertaken to reproach and correct the confusion, errors, wickedness, and blunders of the Corinthians. Hence in the previous chapter he stopped up the source of all the evils, divisions, and confusion by condemning the pride of human nature as well as the presumption and conceit of wisdom. Now he addresses examples of some remaining sins. In this chapter Paul reproaches the Corinthians for their habit of fornication and incest, and he excommunicates and hands over to Satan a man who had taken his stepmother. Then he urges the Corinthians to drive blatant evildoers out of the church and to worship God in purity and truth. Next he explains that people who profess that they are members of the church together with them, yet defile themselves with blatant sins, should not be admitted to their meals nor allowed to have any fellowship with them. This sad example of moral failing in the Corinthian church demonstrates that we should not imagine that there is any church on earth that is altogether free from stain; nor are there churches noteworthy for being free from all wickedness, scandal, or division. For Satan plots against God's holy assembly in this fashion especially, attempting to deform it and render it suspicious to all. And he is eager to provoke God's wrath against it. Explication on 1 Corinthians 5:1.[3]

5:1-2 *Incest and Arrogance*

Pastors Must Address the Sins of Their Flock. Jacques Lefèvre d'Étaples: To be a pastor is to know the evils arising from the petulance of the flock and the diseases of the sheep. The apostle writes to the teachers of the Corinthians concerning such a matter, telling them that they should be shocked by a stepson having sexual intercourse with his stepmother. Commentary on 1 Corinthians 5:1.[4]

The Gravity of the Sin Described. Wolfgang Musculus: Paul does not say that "a man has his stepmother." Rather by describing the stepmother as "his father's wife" . . . Paul expresses the shamefulness of this wicked deed. Thus Leviticus 18 says that it is shameful for you to have your father's wife. For a man to have one and the same wife with his father is not only against God's law, but it is contrary to nature and contradicts and is inconsistent with common notions of decency. . . .

Paul does not say, "he knew his father's wife" but "he has his father's wife." It is one thing to commit a wrong once through foolishness and afterward refrain from it through repentance; it is another thing to engage continuously in sinful behavior. Here, what is even worse, the man publicly cohabits with his father's wife in a legal state of marriage. Such an act of whoring incest not only violates the honor of the father (which is what we read that Reuben did in Genesis 35), but it also wickedly allows the sanctity of marriage to be covered in the greatest wickedness. Certainly with the phrase "he *has* his father's wife" Paul is especially reproaching the imprudence of the fornicator as well as the rest of the Corinthians. Commentary on 1 Corinthians 5:1.[5]

[2]Musculus, *Comm. 1 Cor.*, 129.

[3]Hesshus, *Explicatio Prioris Epistolae ad Corinthios*, 78v-79r.

[4]Lefèvre d'Étaples, *Commentariorum in Epistolas Beati Pauli . . . Liber Secundus*, 107r.

[5]Musculus, *Comm. 1 Cor.*, 130; citing Lev 18:8.

The False Teachers Were Not Pastors, but Imposters. Huldrych Zwingli: [Paul's sense is this:] "Who does not see how far removed you are from the pursuit of true piety when you do not expel such great evil from among you! Where is the faithfulness and zeal of your teachers? Do you not see the truth of what I have said above, that they are so puffed up and swollen with pride that despite such rebukes they still do not strive after an innocent life? What? Is it not abundantly clear from this outrage that they teach only to satisfy their stomachs rather than for your improvement? If they were true fathers and true pastors, they would have seen to it that both this outrage, and the one who committed this outrage, were removed from your midst—they would not have spared anyone." Therefore we see in this passage that those false teachers permitted sins openly to fester. Those who boasted in the name of "pastor" deserved rather to be called "imposters." Annotations on 1 Corinthians 5:2.[6]

The Sin of One Person Brings Disgrace on the Whole Church. John Calvin: Paul had previously asserted that even the most excellent gifts provided no cause for boasting, since men and women possess nothing of their own, but they excel by the grace of God alone. Now, however, he attacks the Corinthians in a different way. "You are," he says, "covered with disgrace. What then is the basis for your pride or haughtiness? For you display incredible blindness in boasting when you are surrounded by disgraceful conduct, which is contrary to angels and human beings."

When Paul says, "should you not rather mourn," he is arguing from contrasts, for when people are mourning, all their boasting ceases. Now someone might ask, "Why should they mourn someone else's sin?" I answer that there are two reasons. First, because of the communion that exists among members of the church, it was proper that all the members should be wounded by such a deadly failing of the one. And, second, when a disgraceful act of this sort is perpetrated in a particular church, the guilt affects not only the author, but the entire assembly is polluted to a certain extent. For just as God humbles the head of a household when his wife or children act indecently, and the entire household is affected by the disgrace of one of its members, so every church should recognize that it is tainted by a disgraceful stain whenever any wicked crime is perpetrated in its midst. Commentary on 1 Corinthians 5:2.[7]

5:3-5 *The Punishment of the Offender*

The Nature of Ecclesiastical Judgment. Philipp Melanchthon: Besides other things, this passage is also to be noted regarding ecclesiastical judgment: first, the form of judgment (that is, who has the power to judge); second, what is the power of excommunication; last, what are the grounds for excommunication. Paul describes and teaches the form of judgment, who has the power to judge, when he commands those who have assembled together to pronounce etc. Therefore the right to lay down regulations and pass judgment does not belong to bishops alone etc. A similar form of judgment is also described in Matthew 18:16-20, "If he does not listen to you, tell it to the church, and if he refuses to listen even to the church, let him be to you as a Gentile and a tax collector." The grounds for excommunication are public faults, as listed here in the text. Likewise Matthew 18:15, "If your brother sins against you," that is, if he has sinned by committing an offense against you, either by sinning with scandal or with your knowledge. So Christ is talking about public crimes. This practice exists in the church so as to prevent such crimes.

Communion is twofold. First, there is the internal communion of the spirit of godly people; such is the communion in the church, namely, in those matters that pertain to the spirit. We do not lose this communion except through a sin of wickedness, and since you are righteous on

[6]Zwingli, *Annotatiunculae . . . ex ore Zvinglij*, 35.

[7]CO 49:378 (cf. CTS 39:180-81).

account of faith, it is impossible for any power, human or infernal, to strip this communion away because of sin. [Second], there is external communion, that is, the ordinary practice of the sacraments of the church—ecclesiastical excommunication cuts one off from that. Therefore excommunication is only an external punishment, the barring of a person from social ties or external interaction, as Paul says here, "Do not even eat with that fellow." The excommunication of those who have not lost internal communion is a blessing, as in . . . Matthew 5:11, "Blessed are you when men . . . utter all kinds of evil against you." Because nobody is rightly excommunicated who has not first lost internal communion. Annotations on 1 Corinthians 5:1-3.[8]

Discipline Is Indispensable for a Healthy Church. John Calvin: But because some persons, in their hatred of discipline, recoil from its very nature, let them understand this: if no society, indeed, no house that has even a small family can be kept in proper condition without discipline, it is much more necessary in the church, whose condition should be as ordered as possible. Accordingly, as the saving doctrine of Christ is the soul of the church, so does discipline serve as its sinews, through which the members of the body hold together, each in its own place. Therefore all who desire to remove discipline or to hinder its restoration—whether they do this deliberately or out of ignorance—are surely contributing to the ultimate dissolution of the church. For what will happen if each is allowed to do what they please? Yet that would happen, if to the preaching of doctrine there were not added private admonitions, corrections, and other aids of the sort that sustain doctrine and do not let it remain idle. Therefore discipline is like a bridle to restrain and tame those who rage against the doctrine of Christ; or like a spur to arouse those of little inclination; and also sometimes like a father's rod to chastise mildly and with the gentleness of Christ's Spirit those who have more seriously lapsed. . . . Now this is the sole remedy that Christ has enjoined and the one that has always been used among the godly. Institutes.[9]

The Purpose of the Ban. Menno Simons: These words of the apostle teach us three things. First, the great love that the faithful servant, Paul, had toward his disciples and children; for although he was not present there, yet as present in spirit, he cared for them in a fatherly fashion, and always taught, admonished, and advised them the very best things.

Second, we learn in whose name, how, and by whom this expulsion is to be effected; namely, in the name, that is, by the command and ordinance of our Lord Jesus Christ. For Paul did not presume to do anything that he had not first received of Christ, as he says. Yes, if Christ had not first instructed Paul to do so, he would not have dared to command the Thessalonians, in the name of our Lord Jesus Christ, that they should separate themselves from every brother who walked in a disorderly way, and not according to his ordinances. For this may properly be called doing things in the name of Christ, when it is done in conformity with his holy Word and will. Also it is to be done by the church, that is, no one shall ban by themselves or at their own pleasure. It shall be done by the congregation of God, after proper admonition; it shall be done in love, diligence, and faithfulness, with the power of Christ, that is, with the binding or closing key of the Word of God and the Holy Spirit. For if it be done without the Word and Spirit, without love and brotherly diligence, but through bitterness, anger, or a false report, not conformable to the Word, or for reasons not deserving the ban, then it is not a work of God. It is no medicine to the soul nor fruit of pure love, but a satanic contention, a corruption and pestilence to the soul, and an evident fruit of the flesh; in short, a curse, abomination, and stench before God. Let every person

[8]Melanchthon, *Annotationes in Epistolam priorem ad Corinthios*, 72, 74.

[9]LCC 21:1229-30 (*Institutes* 4.12.1).

reflect at length on these words of Paul, and they will by the grace of God see how rigidly this expulsion is commanded in the Scriptures, and how solemnly it should be practiced in the church, with the power of the Word and the Spirit of Christ.

Third, we learn that we should deliver an unrepentant transgressor unto Satan. Not, brethren, that he was not Satan's possession before the expulsion. As soon as he turned his heart away from the Lord and became ungodly, he became the property of Satan, even as a penitent sinner is the property of Christ. But now with audible voice through the church he is told that he is rejected from the communion of Christ and his church, and he is told that he is now Satan's own until he brings forth true fruits of repentance before God and his church. This is done that his adulterous, avaricious, refractory, and idolatrous flesh may be halted, and he may become ashamed and repentant by such declaration and the shunning by the pious; that he may go down and under as to his flesh, that is, his fleshly lusts, so that he may by these means be brought to repentance and his soul saved in the day of the Lord Jesus. A Clear Account of Excommunication.[10]

Paul Is Present in Spirit. John Calvin: Since the Corinthians were negligent in their duty, after Paul has condemned their laziness, he now instructs them in what they must do: namely, in order to remove this stain, that incestuous man must be excluded from the fellowship of believers. Thus Paul prescribes the cure for the disease to be excommunication, which the Corinthians had sinned in putting off for such a long time. When Paul says that he has pronounced this judgment "while absent in the body," he is thereby sharply reproaching the laziness of the Corinthians, for there is an implied contrast underlying his words. It's as if he were saying: "You who were present in Corinth should have cured this disease long ago, since it occurred constantly before your very eyes—but you did nothing. But I who am absent cannot put up with it." Lest anyone complain that Paul made a rash judgment based on rumors, given he was so far from Corinth, he asserts that he is "present in spirit," indicating by this that the path of duty was no less clear to him than if he were in their presence and witnessed the whole affair with his own eyes. Commentary on 1 Corinthians 5:3.[11]

Delivering the Sinner Over to Satan. Wolfgang Musculus: Now the apostle's judgment has two parts in which he prescribes what must be established concerning such a shameful fornicator. First, he indicates the action that must be taken, and second the goal to which condemnation of this disgraceful act should be directed. People interpret this passage in various ways. For Ambrose, the phrase "deliver this man over to Satan for the destruction of the flesh" means that he is to be cast out of the church and completely condemned. The phrase "destruction of the flesh" he understands as the destruction and condemnation of the body of the man. By the statement "so that his spirit might be saved in the day of the Lord" he believes refers to the Holy Spirit, not the spirit of the fornicator. The Holy Spirit here, he says, ought to be understood as the Spirit of the church, which is preserved when it is not lost.... Therefore Ambrose thinks that Paul desires the destruction of this fornicator to occur so that the Holy Spirit of the church of the Corinthians ... might be found safe in the day of judgment.... Ambrose's interpretation does not seem to express the mind of the apostle, who has placed here "flesh" and "spirit" by way of antithesis to refer to the corruption of the same person not different persons.

Chrysostom explains the phrase "hand the fornicator over to Satan" to refer to some disease or a serious injury, as seen in the case of Job. Although Job was afflicted in the flesh (though for a different reason), he avoided the eternal punishment of hell in the day of the Lord. Augustine ... gives a similar

[10]Simons, *Complete Writings*, 469-70*; citing 2 Thess 3:6.

[11]CO 49:379 (cf. CTS 39:182).

explanation in *Contra Parmenianus*, where he writes: "What then is the apostle doing when the man was handed over to Satan for the destruction of his flesh, if not to pass judgment for the purpose of saving him, so that either by punishment or corporal death (just as when Ananias and his wife fell dead at the feet of the apostle Peter) he might be rescued from the wicked lust of his flesh." That is what Augustine says. . . .

Thus we see here that even Satan is a minister of the church for the purpose of saving those whom he corrupts. In this way the apostle writes in 1 Timothy 1 that he has handed Hymenaeus and Alexander over to Satan so that they might not perish, but so that they might learn not to blaspheme. But we might ask, how is it that the spirit is saved in the day of the Lord through the destruction of the flesh? Is it only through the punishment of the flesh that the spirit can be saved? . . . It is safer for us to understand the phrase "destruction of the flesh" to refer to what happens when an offender is brought to repentance and his spirit made safe through either an attendant or a servant of Satan, whose intervention is capable of bringing about the forgiveness of sins and a spirit of grace. Commentary on 1 Corinthians 5:5.[12]

A Very Severe Judgment. Tilemann Hesshus: To "deliver the man over to Satan for the destruction of his flesh" is to give official notice that the unrepentant man has nothing in common with the church of Christ, does not participate in the benefits of Christ, has no hope of eternal life, is not a son of God. Rather he is trapped in sin and subject to the power and tyranny of Satan, whose cruelty he must fearfully ponder every single moment. And so this phrase teaches that the judgment of legitimate excommunication is the most severe and serious judgment of all. For what could be called more serious than that a person, by the authority of the church, be handed over to the power and tyranny of Satan and excluded from all God's protection and participation in the kingdom of Christ? And since God himself asserts that "I will curse those whom you curse and bless those whom you bless"—this shows that he will pour out his wrath on those who are separated from the fellowship of the church.

History does not report whether the Corinthian man guilty of incest was soon stricken by a serious illness. But Paul's second letter to the Corinthians reports that the man experienced enormous sadness. And so that phrase "to deliver the man over to Satan for the destruction of his flesh" indicates that the judgment of excommunication is not powerless in exciting terror, as some people think. Rather experience demonstrates that many very serious bodily punishments result from this very severe judgment of the church. Explication of 1 Corinthians 5:3.[13]

The Church Has the Right to Excommunicate Wrongdoers. John Trapp: How fiercely does the learned Erastus contend with Calvin and Beza about excommunication, denying the church any such power. The Jews had their three sorts of excommunication. The heathen also had theirs. Among the ancient Gauls, if people did not obey the decrees of their druids or priests, they were forbidden their sacrifices, and thereafter shunned by all as wicked persons; they gained no benefit from their laws, nor was any respect given to them. Commentary on 1 Corinthians 5:3.[14]

In the Name and Power of the Lord. John Trapp: This passage creates a high threshold to be rightly excommunicated. Indeed, it may happen that Jonah is cast out of the ship, while

[12]Musculus, *Comm. 1 Cor.*, 135-36; citing Acts 5:1-11; 1 Tim 1:20. Chrysostom's treatment of this verse is found in his *Homilies on 1 Corinthians* (homily 15), in NPNF 12:85. For Ambrose (Ambrosiaster), see his *Comment. in Epist. I ad Cor.*, in PL 17:219-20. For Augustine, see his *Contra Parmenianus* 3.1.

[13]Hesshus, *Explicatio Prioris Epistolae ad Corinthios*, 81r-v; citing Gen 12:3.

[14]Trapp, *A Commentary or Exposition*, 669*. Against Calvin and Beza, Thomas Lüber (known as Erastus; 1524–1583) argued that civil magistrates should hold jurisdiction over both the state and church (including the authority to excommunicate sinners). See *OER* 2:456-57.

Ham shall be reserved in the ark. "Your brothers who hate you and cast you out for my name's sake have said, 'Let the Lord be glorified, that we may see your joy'; but it is they who shall be put to shame" (Is 66:5). When the sentence of excommunication was read against a certain martyr, beginning with the words "In the name of the Lord," he cried out (as well he might), "You begin in the wrong name." And another of them, together with his five fellow sufferers, formally excommunicated their persecutors. By the abuse of this ordinance in those corrupt times, it became a common proverb: "In the name of the Lord he begins every evil." Commentary on 1 Corinthians 5:4.[15]

Delivering the Sinner to Satan. The English Annotations: The Lord explains what it is to be delivered to Satan when he says, "Let him be unto thee as a heathen and a tax collector" (Mt 18:17), that is to say, to be disenfranchised and put out of the right and liberty of the city of Christ, which is the church. This manner of expression was used in the past of major excommunication, and it seems to be taken from 1 Samuel 16:14, where Saul, being rejected of God, was caught and troubled by an evil spirit. In the early years of the church, after this major excommunication (as one of the ancients affirms), there followed great terrors in the persons excommunicated, agonies of spirit, indeed, even torments of body. God permitted these afflictions, not for the utter and irrevocable destruction of sinners, but for their correction and amendment, that their souls might be saved, though their bodies suffer. Annotations on 1 Corinthians 5:5.[16]

True Pastors Are Diligent in Discipline. Martin Bucer: Therefore, when there are true shepherds and physicians of souls in the church and the churches are well and properly ordered, they will never remain silent concerning these hurts and wounds to the inner being, which they learn of in the sheep of Christ, letting them carry on without penance, but when gentleness does not move such people to repent, they will like St. Paul no longer spare them, but will show the power of Christ and employ drastic measures to bring about the humiliation and mortification of the sinful flesh and require some significant proof of sorrow and intention to mend their ways. For such shepherds and caregivers of souls are true servants of Christ in the care of souls and the pastoral ministry, and are recognized as such by the churches. Will not the Spirit of Christ therefore work and act in them as well as he worked and acted in St. Paul, and as he also ordered and commanded his ancient and coarser people? True Care of Souls.[17]

Excommunication Is A Work of Charity. Dirk Philips: Evangelical excommunication is principally a work of charity, because by it the church of Jesus Christ is preserved and maintained in healthy doctrine, in good order, in divine unity, in Christian peace, and in obedience of faith. And also by it transgressors are corrected (1 Cor 5:4-5), if in any way they wish to be.

That is why no Christian church can subsist without evangelical excommunication. For the Lord Jesus Christ did not give the keys of the kingdom of heaven to his church in vain, the power of binding and loosing, of pardoning sins and retaining them (Mt 18:18). . . . If thus the church does not judge otherwise than as the Word and the Spirit of God testify and teach, it therein acts justly and its judgment is the judgment of God. But if the church does not judge and punish sins in conformity to the Word of God, in that it is disobedient to the Word and makes itself a participant in the sin of the other. Thus by a little leaven the whole dough is soured (1 Cor 5:6). . . .

[15]Trapp, *A Commentary or Exposition*, 669*. Trapp is referring to the martyrdom of Robert Smith. See Foxe, *Acts and Monuments*, 7:355

[16]Downame, *English Annotations*, DD2r*.

[17]Bucer, *Concerning the True Care of Souls*, 122. By "coarser people," Bucer is referring to the ancient Israelites.

Furthermore, the first thing that is required in fraternal love is that we search, with a benevolent heart and with all our power, the salvation of our neighbor by the means toward this ordained by God. If thus a brother has fallen away from the truth and cannot be helped by any instruction or Christian exhortation, there is nothing more fitting for his soul than evangelical excommunication (which is a bitter medicine, but always very profitable for the members who are on the way to spoiling) by which he may be shamed, so that the exterior person be destroyed in order that the interior can be saved in the day of the Lord Jesus (1 Cor 5:5). After this separation from the church, nothing can serve him better than a fraternal exhortation. Evangelical Excommunication.[18]

5:6-8 *Cleanse the Church of "Old Leaven"*

Sin Can Infect a Church Like Yeast in Bread. Philipp Melanchthon: How does a fornicator taint a particular church? First by scandal since his example draws others to the same wickedness or to blaspheming God's name. Second there is this too, that the sin of a single person is imputed to the whole group and defiles the whole group: Joshua 7, which treats the sin of Achan, because he stole consecrated items. Annotations on 1 Corinthians 5:6.[19]

An Evil Example Infects the Entire Church. Wolfgang Musculus: This, therefore, is the second reason Paul gives why he wishes the fornicator to be cast out from the fellowship of the church. Previously he said "so that he might be handed over to Satan for the destruction of the flesh, so that he might be saved in the day of the Lord"—a reason that focused on the salvation of the man who was corrupt and needed to be cast out. Here he adds an additional reason that pertains to the preservation of the purity of the church, which Paul places before our eyes through the example of yeast. For the power and destruction of a single person's bad example is like scabies that infect an entire flock of little lambs, or like yeast that leavens a whole lump of dough. The reasons for the contagious nature of sin are as follows. First, insofar as the nature of an evil example is so efficacious that it spreads, occupies, and corrupts easily and quickly; this is not the case with good things, which do not extend their influence as easily.... Second, an evil example receives a great deal of support from the strength and power of the sin that comes from the corruption of our flesh, which renders us more inclined toward receiving and imbibing evil.... Third, the location of the contagion is as important as its function. Even when we are by ourselves we sink into wickedness owing to our natural corruption. Should we not then be concerned when we are in close proximity to evil people? Commentary on 1 Corinthians 5:6.[20]

God's Truth Must Never Be Compromised. Martin Luther: This is a striking saying and a serious exhortation, that we should guard and watch ourselves with all diligence, so that we should let nothing false or strange commingle with or creep into the teaching of the gospel. God's word, faith, and conscience are very delicate things. ... Just like good malmsey[21] or expensive medicine—the more precious and pure they are, the more easily they can be tainted and become harmful, even if only a droplet of poison or some impurity is added—God's word and matters cannot tolerate any additives. It must be totally pure and clear, otherwise it's already tainted and no longer useful. And here's the worst part: it spreads and sticks so strongly that it cannot be removed again, just as leaven, however small the quantity, added to a lump of dough, permeates it so that soon enough it's all leavened—no one can stop it or make it unleavened again.

[18]CRR 6:601-2, 604*.

[19]Melanchthon, *Annotationes in Epistolam priorem ad Corinthios*, 74, 76.

[20]Musculus, *Comm. 1 Cor.*, 138-39.

[21]A strong, sweet Greek wine that was highly valued.

Therefore it's wrong and useless, that now some sham sages want to mediate and strike a compromise between us and our papal opponents. Sure, they would let the gospel be preached; however, they would still retain papal abuses along with it, saying that for the sake of the weak, we must not censure and quash everything, and for the sake of peace and unity, we must restrain ourselves somewhat and close ranks, so that each faction yields something to the other and bears patiently with the other. . . . No! It can't be so. For in this passage you hear that St. Paul doesn't want this, and God has solemnly forbidden it—to commingle a little leaven in with the good dough, for it permeates the whole lump and ruins it completely. If in just one point we commingle pure teaching with human additives, then damage is done. Through this the truth is obscured and souls are led astray. Therefore, in Christianity it's not to be tolerated, when someone wants to make such a mixture and patchwork in doctrine. Church Postil (1544): Epistle for Easter Sunday.[22]

Paul Elucidates Old Testament Types. Huldrych Zwingli: "Do not think that the disgrace of one person does not extend to the entire church. You are members of one body: therefore be warned lest in this way you give an opening to vices and wicked deeds, so that the whole body be infected by the contagion of one. Do you not see that a little yeast leavens and affects the entire lump of dough?" As a general rule Paul draws metaphors from visible things, which were certainly familiar and well-known to the Jews. In this way he elucidates the types of the Old Testament, while also showing that both the Jewish people and the Gentiles are the same church so that the Jews might not become arrogant and haughty, and the Gentiles not judge themselves to be inferior to the Jews (because they do not have the ceremonies of the Jews). Annotations on 1 Corinthians 5:6.[23]

The Nature of the Christian Passover. John Colet: Our Paschal victim, that spotless lamb in whom there was found no guile, the pure unleavened bread without the leaven of malice, has been offered up in sacrifice. And this is Christ, who must be eaten by us, not only by way of the sacrament, but also by way of imitation, so that taught by him and assuming his form we may become like him and may be (as far as is possible and grace permits) so pure and simple, in the sincerity and purity of justice, as to have no admixture of the opposite.

For in life itself and in action there ought to be all candor and simplicity, and (as far as it is given) a reflection of Christ in deed and in acts. This is what makes a truly Christian Passover where, under Christ's leadership, we depart the Egypt of this world and travel toward the heavenly Jerusalem. The whole of Christendom should constantly strive toward this goal and be continually engaged in the celebration of the Passover. . . .

And so let us feed on the purity of Christ; let us imitate him and walk as he walked, wisely, simply, with justice and innocence, so that we may arrive where he has arrived, and may rest on that mountain that no one ascends except those who approach without spot and with works of righteousness. And just as no one ascends there to God, the highest peak, unless they be true and just, neither does God come down here nor dwell with people so as to draw them on high to himself, unless there be in them truth, sincerity, and righteousness. And such a fellowship of people one wicked person can overthrow. Exposition of 1 Corinthians 5.[24]

We Must Follow the Spotless Lamb, Christ. Jacques Lefèvre d'Étaples: If the sons of Israel departed Egypt under the figure of sacrificing a lamb, how much more should we, who have the true Passover, depart this world and follow our spotless lamb into the mountains of eternity, where he feeds among the lilies of paradise, living

[22]WA 21:205-6 (cf. LW 77:14-15).
[23]Zwingli, *Annotatiunculae . . . ex ore Zvinglij*, 38.
[24]Colet, *Ennaratio*, 116, 118; citing Ps 24:3; 15:1.

in eternal daylight. We are able to follow this lamb only by works of the Spirit, not by works of the flesh. Commentary on 1 Corinthians 5:7-8.[25]

Christ Is Our Passover Lamb. Philipp Melanchthon: Just as there are two testaments, so there are two passing-overs and two Passover lambs. The first testament is the law, and the first Passover is the passing over from Egypt to the Promised Land. The Passover lamb of that first Passover is a sign of redemption, as in Exodus 13: "It shall be to you as a sign on your hand and as a memorial between your eyes." The second testament is the gospel or promise of grace, and the second Passover is the passing over from sin and death. The Passover lamb of that second Passover is Christ, the sure sign of our redemption. Jeremiah 16 describes those two Passovers: "Let it no longer be said, 'The Lord lives, who brought up the people of Israel out of the land of Egypt,' but, 'The Lord lives who brought up the people of Israel out of the north country.'" For the prophet himself was clearly speaking there about Christ. And this other Passover lamb Paul here describes as "our Passover lamb." Annotations on 1 Corinthians 5:7.[26]

Ways the Passover Lamb Prefigures Christ. The English Annotations: Christ is termed our Passover, either by a metonymy . . . or by a metaphor in regard to the many similarities between Christ and the Paschal lamb. First, as the lamb was without blemish, so Christ was without any spot of sin. Second, as no bone of the lamb was to be broken, so neither any bone of Christ was broken at his passion. Third, as the lamb was offered to God as a type of reconciliation and sanctification, so was Christ offered for the true reconciliation of all his elect and for the sanctification of all their sins. Fourth, as the Paschal lamb was to be eaten, so we feed on Christ by faith. Fifth, as the Paschal lamb was to be eaten with bitter herbs, so Christ's flesh is to be eaten in the sacrament with the sour and bitter remembrance of our sins, and Christ's painful suffering for them. Sixth, as the Paschal lamb was to be eaten with unleavened bread, so all who eat Christ must purge out of their consciences all leaven of maliciousness. Seventh, as that lamb was called *hapasah* in Exodus 12, which signifies a passing over, so Christ's death, in which he was sacrificed for us, might be called a *phase* or transition or passage, because by it he passed from the world to his Father. Finally, just as the doorposts and lintels were sprinkled with the blood of the lamb so that the family might escape the stroke of the destroying angel, so also those whose consciences are sprinkled by faith with the blood of Christ, the lamb of God who takes away the sins of the world, shall escape eternal destruction. Annotations on 1 Corinthians 5:7.[27]

Keeping the Feast. Wolfgang Musculus: The Jewish holiday of Passover was held for seven continuous days, during which the Jews observed solemn feasts, eating bread without yeast. Now, the apostle says, since the Passover lamb has been sacrificed for us, we too should celebrate this festival. Now, first of all, that mystical celebration of the feast consists in freedom from the works of death, that is to say, in spiritual rest devoted to the Lord. Second, it consists in public joy, for to keep the feast is a symbol for common gladness. And in his words of gratitude, Paul did not say, "Christ has been killed," but "Christ our Passover lamb has been sacrificed for us." Thus Paul signals the change from the type to the actual thing, from the type of the sacrificial lamb to the true sacrificed lamb, from the type of captivity in Egypt to the liberation of those who were once held captive under the tyranny of Satan. Certainly the memory of these things, which bring gladness to the hearts of godly people, should dwarf the solemn remembrance of the liberation of the people of Israel. Third, the festival of Passover consists in

[25]Lefèvre d'Étaples, *Commentariorum in Epistolas Beati Pauli . . . Liber Secundus*, 107v.

[26]Melanchthon, *Annotationes in Epistolam priorem ad Corinthios*, 76, 78; citing Ex 13:9; Jer 16:14-15.

[27]Downame, *English Annotations*, DD2r*.

unleavened meals and the throwing away of the old leaven. The apostle makes this point clear when he says: "Not with the old leaven, the leaven of malice and deceitfulness, but with the unleavened bread of sincerity and truth." Thus by "old leaven" he understands malice and deceitfulness, and by "unleavened bread" he understands sincerity and truth. Now the kingdom of heaven does have leaven, but not the old leaven, rather the new leaven, namely, the commencement of the gospel, by which the entire world is leavened. Christ's parables in Matthew 13 speak concerning this. The Pharisees also possess this old leaven, namely, hypocrisy (Luke 12) and perverse doctrine (Matthew 16). Commentary on 1 Corinthians 5:8.[28]

The Christian Life Is a Perpetual Banquet. John Trapp: The benefits we receive by means of Christ should crown the calendar of our lives with continual festivals. Yes, [they should] make us everlastingly merry at our perpetual banquet of a good conscience. Diogenes could say "that a good man keeps every day a holiday." And the Jews were bound to rejoice at all their feasts. As Ecclesiastes 9:7 states: "Eat your bread with joy, and drink your wine with gladness, for God now accepts your works." Commentary on 1 Corinthians 5:8.[29]

God Purifies Us Through Word and Spirit. Martin Luther: We should know that Christ's office and governance is in his church: through the word and faith he fully grants us his purity all at once; on top of that, through the Holy Spirit he makes our hearts new. However, he doesn't complete the work of our renewal and purification all at once, rather daily he works on us and cleanses us—the whole time we continue to grow in purity. He executes and effects this work through the office of the word by exhorting, rebuking, correcting, strengthening—as he did to the Corinthians through St. Paul—as well as through cross-bearing and suffering, etc.

He didn't come and do his work—suffering and rising again, etc.—to find a fully pure and holy people in us. He certainly accomplished his work perfectly in his person—since he was perfect and without any sin from his incarnation on—and he shares this purity with us fully, without any fault, and he lets us enjoy it, as long as faith clings to him. But for that same purity to follow in us still requires daily work until he perfects us too, just as he in himself is pure and without fault. On top of that he gave his word and Spirit, through which we should execute and effect the purgation of the old leaven that's leftover, so that we remain in this newly begun purity and not fall from it again and so that we can keep the faith, the Spirit, and Christ. This doesn't happen if we yield to the old carnal nature and don't resist it. . . .

Here's one thing this text teaches us: even in the saints, weakness, impurity, and sin still remain. These things have to be purged and yet won't be imputed to them, because the saints are in Christ and purge such leaven. Church Postil (1544): Epistle for Easter Sunday.[30]

Christians Must Put Away the Leaven of Their Former Lives. David Dickson: In this passage Paul infers his concluding argument, namely, that malice and wickedness should be put away both from themselves and from the church, and with the incestuous person being excommunicated they might worship and serve the Lord cheerfully with holiness in sincerity and truthfulness. The force of the argument is this: we cannot live in a holy and righteous manner (which the sign of the Paschal feast requires of us) unless the leaven of our former life and our wicked practices be purged from us and the house of God (i.e., the church), and unless we endeavor to preserve sincerity and truth in ourselves and the church. Therefore the offender is to be excommunicated. Exposition on 1 Corinthians 5:8.[31]

[28]Musculus, *Comm. 1 Cor.* 140-41.

[29]Trapp, *A Commentary or Exposition*, 670*. Diogenes, the founder of the Cynics, lived in Greece nearly four hundred years before the birth of Christ. This statement was attributed to him in Plutarch's *De Tranquillitate Animi*.

[30]WA 21:209-10 (cf. LW 77:17-18).

[31]Dickson, *Exposition of St. Paul's Epistles*, 48*.

5:9-13 *Church Discipline Is for Christians—Not Outsiders*

Paul's Previous Letter to the Corinthians No Longer Extant. The English Annotations: The letter referred to [in verse 9] is not now extant, for this present letter is Paul's first letter to the Corinthians that is found in the New Testament. Although piety leads us to acknowledge that this previous letter was written by divine inspiration (in the same way that we recognize the inspiration of the books of Nathan, Gad, Ahijah, Iddo, Shemaiah, and others mentioned in the Old Testament, which are now lost), yet it does not thus follow that the canon of the Scriptures is imperfect, as the Romanists would infer. For as the principal contents of those former books are believed to be found in the books of Chronicles and Kings, so it is likely that all points necessary for salvation, which were set down in that former letter to the Corinthians, are either contained in these two epistles that we have or some other books of holy Scripture. Annotations on 1 Corinthians 5:9.[32]

Paul Does Not Forbid All Interaction with Ungodly People. Tilemann Hesshus: The apostle Paul wrote the Corinthians that they should completely avoid dealing with those people who were defiling themselves with wicked deeds against their conscience. Moreover that neither they nor other vulnerable brothers and sisters should be defiled by the disease of wickedness. But the Corinthians did not correctly understand Paul's intention, for they were thinking that Paul desired that pious people abstain from all interaction with wicked and godless people, as if keeping company with godless people defiles us and renders us detestable to God. Therefore Paul clearly sets forth his meaning, namely, that he wasn't speaking about the sexually immoral, idolaters, blasphemers, and robbers *outside* the church. For if godly people were required to flee from all interaction with wicked people, it would be necessary for them to leave the world—for the whole world is mired in wickedness, and we encounter wicked and unclean people everywhere—and so godly people would not be able to transact business with anyone in the world, since they could not live with anyone. And, moreover, godly people cannot know whether a person is free from wickedness. Therefore Paul reminds the Corinthians that he was speaking about the sexually immoral, greedy, idolaters, and blasphemers who bore the name of Christians and wished to enjoy the benefits of the sacraments as members of the body of Christ, yet in the meantime were defiling themselves by destroying their conscience with wicked deeds. In so doing, these people demonstrate that they are devoid of all faith and feigning godliness with shameful hypocrisy. With this sort of people, who only bring disgrace to the church, one should not have any interaction and not even share a meal with them. Explication on 1 Corinthians 5:9-12.[33]

What Does Paul Mean by "Do Not Associate"? Jacques Lefèvre d'Étaples: But, you ask, what kind of "association" is Paul speaking of? Do you associate with persons when you speak to them, or when you happen to drink or eat with them? No. For even our Lord ate with publicans and sinners. But he was not associating with them or (as Paul uses the word) he was not commingling with them. In the same way the apostles associated with the Gentiles. Therefore to associate or commingle with them is to give one's consent to their behavior, becoming a partner that mingles and mixes and participates with them. Truly, when a church decides that such persons should be removed from its midst, then it should share neither drinking nor eating nor hardly even conversation with them (unless they are words of holy exhortation or correction). Commentary on 1 Corinthians 5:9.[34]

[32]Downame, *English Annotations*, DD2r*. The extracanonical books of Nathan, Gad, Ahijah, Iddo, and Shemaiah are mentioned in 1 Chron 29:29; 2 Chron 9:29; 12:15; 13:22.

[33]Hesshus, *Explicatio Prioris Epistolae ad Corinthios*, 86r-v.

[34]Lefèvre d'Étaples, *Commentariorum in Epistolas Beati Pauli . . .*

The Ban Applies to People in the Church. Menno Simons: From these words of the apostle we learn that he had on a former occasion admonished the Corinthians, in an epistle, that they should shun the fornicators, the covetous, etc., but that they had understood it as referring to the fornicators of this world. Therefore Paul admonishes them in this epistle that this was not his meaning at all; for if they should shun these and avoid them, they must needs go out of the world. But he means those who are called brethren; as he shows in his plain language, saying, If any man that is called a brother be a fornicator or covetous, etc., with such a one do not eat—just as the Jews did not eat with the Gentiles and manifest sinners at the time of Christ, nor keep their company. For Christ and Paul are one and not divided. A Clear Account of Excommunication.[35]

Excommunication Must Be Severe but Not Cruel. John Calvin: "Do not even eat with such a person." First of all, we must know whether Paul's commandment is binding on the entire church or simply on individuals. I answer: this commandment pertains to individuals, though nevertheless it depends on the discipline of the whole fellowship. For the power of excommunication is not given to each particular member, but to the entire body. Yet individual believers should not have friendly relations with a person whom the church excommunicates. For otherwise, the authority of the church would become worthless, if individual members invited to their own tables those persons who had been excluded from the Lord's Table. By sharing of food Paul means here either living together or familiar association at meals. For if I enter an inn and see an excommunicated person sitting there, nothing prohibits me from eating together with him, for I have no power to exclude him. But Paul means that, as far as it pertains to us, we must avoid social ties with those whom the church has cut off from its fellowship.

Not satisfied with this severity, the Roman Antichrist has burst forth with its interdicts, prohibiting anyone from helping an excommunicated person with food, warmth, drink, or other necessities of life. Now such rigor is not discipline, but tyrannical and barbarous cruelty that is completely contrary to Paul's intention. For he wants us to consider the excommunicated person "not as an enemy, but as a brother," and we place this public mark of disgrace on him so that, filled with shame, he might repent. Commentary on 1 Corinthians 5:11.[36]

Do Not Even Associate with Them. John Trapp: The rivers of Peru, after they have run into the main sea—indeed, some report even twenty or thirty miles—keep themselves unmixed with the salt water, so that people can drink fresh water when they are far out at sea as if they were near the land. So too, at Belgrade in Hungary, where the Danube and Sava (two great rivers) meet, their waters mingle no more than water and oil, etc. In the same way, we must associate with the wicked in such a way that we do not hold needless society with them, that is, with one called a brother who belies his profession. Yet to those who are excommunicated, we must still perform our responsibility of charity, natural and civil duties, as those of parents toward their children, of children toward their parents, and the like. But do not come near such stinking stuff, unless you have the stomach for it. Commentary on 1 Corinthians 5:11.[37]

Principles of Church Discipline. Wolfgang Musculus: A treatment of this chapter requires that we note some principles regarding church discipline. First, the nature of excommunication is seen in this passage. Paul wants believers not only to deny table fellowship to the person who is excommunicated, but even more, to deny them fellowship in the mysteries of God. This is a kind of separation that completely denies all social

Liber Secundus, 107v.
[35]Simons, *Complete Writings*, 472-73*.
[36]CO 49:386 (cf. CTS 39:194-95); citing 2 Thess 3:15.
[37]Trapp, *A Commentary or Exposition*, 670*.

ties and communication with the shameful person. I know that some people think excommunication should not cut a person off from human relationships but only from religious fellowship. But I think this badly restricts the apostle's intention here, especially because of what he says [in verse 11]. For clearly in many cases . . . religious separation is completely ineffective when a person is not denied fellowship in the rest of life.

Second, we see in this chapter who has the power of excommunication. It belongs not only to the bishop, not only to the people, but to both the bishop and the people—that is, to the whole church. "When you are assembled together," Paul says, "and my spirit is with you." Those who transfer this power to superintendents alone, not only cause harm to the church, but also render this medicine powerless.

Third, we are admonished here of the kind of faults that should receive the sentence of excommunication. Not all faults in the church should be punished with this rod, but only those that, because of their seriousness, exclude a person from the kingdom of God. . . . All other faults should either be corrected with gentleness or endured with patience. But today faults that should be endured aren't, and faults that deserve excommunication are tolerated.

Fourth, we are also carefully taught in this chapter the purposes and use of excommunication, which are three: The first purpose is so that those of ill repute might be removed from the church and from the profession of the name of Christ. Paul introduced this concern immediately at the beginning of this chapter when he said, "It is actually reported that there is sexual immorality among you," etc. Therefore those faults are subject to the rod of excommunication that taint the good people of the church with the stinking odor of disgrace among outsiders. The second purpose is so that those who have sinned dangerously might be corrected. Paul says, "so that his spirit might be saved in the day of the Lord." Therefore people ought to be excommunicated who have sinned grievously and have completely ruined their salvation, so that they might repent and be brought back to their senses. The third purpose is so that the purity of the church might be preserved from infection, so that a little leaven will not spread through the entire lump of dough. These are the purposes of excommunication for those who have responsibility for it. But if people ignore these purposes, then excommunication is useless, or rather very pernicious and should not be employed. Commentary on 1 Corinthians 5:9-13.[38]

The Nature of Christians' Separation from the Ungodly. Martin Bucer: For when the holy apostle writes, "You are not to have anything to do with them or eat with them," he only wishes to forbid that association in eating and other activities that are voluntary, not that which is required by the general needs of nature, citizenship, or domestic relationships.

Thus all honorable people will relinquish and avoid anything approaching real friendship with those belonging to them who defile the relationship with ignominious stains by their dissolute morals. However, such honorable people and relatives will still have dealings with those whom otherwise they avoid in those things that are required by civil society and general human needs, and join with them in doing those things generally required of them by authority, even though it means eating with them, dealing with other things, making, buying and selling, and helping them in case of need. But apart from this they do not maintain friendly relations with them or have anything to do with them, avoid their company, and show in everything displeasure and disapproval of their dissolute and dishonorable ways. And this is how Christians are also to behave toward those who have been excluded from the church of God. . . . Therefore this avoiding in itself has no other purpose than that such unchristian people should be sooner ashamed of themselves and moved to repentance; for in other ways they experience from believers all fairness, love, and

[38]Musculus, *Comm. 1 Cor.*, 145-46.

goodwill, except in that one thing: that they can have no pleasure in their ungodliness, but must be filled with sorrow and abhorrence, because the Lord Christ is and means everything to them. True Care of Souls.[39]

How to Treat an Unrepentant Sinner. Huldrych Zwingli: Paul names certain great and shocking sins for which a brother or sister must be avoided, for in other respects all of us err in many ways. A brother or sister must not be blindly avoided or cast out, therefore, on account of just any sin, but only for these sins that Paul enumerates here, or other sins that are of similar gravity or even worse. Cases of banning people, which we call excommunication, should be handled in this manner. Inasmuch as Paul teaches that all Christians should be innocent, pure, and holy, set apart from the rest of the world not only in name but also in innocence and purity of life, therefore, they ought to exclude from the fellowship of believers those who are infected with such shocking scandals, lest the rest of the flock be poisoned or destroyed by their infection. But if the church is so negligent that it does not exclude people who sin publicly and refuse to repent, then the magistrates should exercise the sword against the guilty so as to check the behavior. All private citizens should refrain from social ties with wicked and foolish people, lest it seem that they support their shameful behavior or become defiled by their wickedness—especially if there is no hope of repentance. Therefore whether a person ought to avoid a brother or associate with him, follow the rule of charity and you will never err. Annotations on 1 Corinthians 5:13.[40]

Evangelical Excommunication. Dirk Philips: There is a difference between the excommunication of the law and that of the gospel: to wit, that by the excommunication of the law, several sins and transgressions were judged and punished by death. But by that of the gospel, the transgressors and sinners are segregated from the Christian church (1 Cor 5:13), in the name and power of our Lord Jesus Christ. For the church of God must be pure and the Lord's own and particular people. Evangelical Excommunication.[41]

---

[39]Bucer, *Concerning the True Care of Souls*, 186-87.

[40]Zwingli, *Annotatiunculae . . . ex ore Zvinglij*, 41.

[41]CRR 6:597*.

6:1-11 Lawsuits Among Believers

When one of you has a grievance against another,
does he dare go to law before the unrighteous instead
of the saints? [2]Or do you not know that the saints will
judge the world? And if the world is to be judged by
you, are you incompetent to try trivial cases? [3]Do you
not know that we are to judge angels? How much
more, then, matters pertaining to this life! [4]So if you
have such cases, why do you lay them before those
who have no standing in the church? [5]I say this to
your shame. Can it be that there is no one among you
wise enough to settle a dispute between the brothers,
[6]but brother goes to law against brother, and that
before unbelievers? [7]To have lawsuits at all with one
another is already a defeat for you. Why not rather
suffer wrong? Why not rather be defrauded? [8]But you
yourselves wrong and defraud—even your own
brothers![a]

[9]Or do you not know that the unrighteous[b] will
not inherit the kingdom of God? Do not be deceived:
neither the sexually immoral, nor idolaters, nor
adulterers, nor men who practice homosexuality,[c]
[10]nor thieves, nor the greedy, nor drunkards, nor
revilers, nor swindlers will inherit the kingdom of
God. [11]And such were some of you. But you were
washed, you were sanctified, you were justified in the
name of the Lord Jesus Christ and by the Spirit of
our God.

a Or *brothers and sisters* **b** Or *wrongdoer* **c** The two Greek terms translated by this phrase refer to the passive and active partners in consensual homosexual acts

Overview: Paul's strong rebuke of the Corinthians' litigiousness and his warning that "the unrighteous will not inherit the kingdom of God" (1 Cor 6:9) invite much discussion among Protestant commentators. Most magisterial reformers (including Melanchthon here) defend the role of Christian magistrates to wield the sword and execute public justice, even as they warn Christians against pursuing their rights at court or taking legal action against fellow Christians. Better to be wronged than to bring disgrace to the name of Christ in civil courts! By contrast, Anabaptist interpreters read Paul's injunctions through the lens of Jesus' teaching in the Sermon on the Mount as a universal prohibition against Christians participating in any form of civil justice, whether as magistrates, judges, lawyers, or litigants. (The attitude of Anabaptist leader Balthasar Hubmaier provides a singular exception to this restrictive view of the sword.) In their comments on the final verses of this section, Reformation commentators emphasize that the "unrighteous" are those who refuse to repent of their wickedness. Christians are forgiven people, not perfect people. Rather than focusing on Paul's expansive list of Corinthian vices, most interpreters describe and celebrate God's abundant grace by which sinners are washed, sanctified, and justified through the death of Jesus Christ.

Rebuking Public Disputes. Martin Luther: In chapter 6 Paul rebukes contention and disputing in the courts, especially before heathen and unbelievers. He teaches them that they should settle their cases among themselves, or suffer wrong. Preface to 1 Corinthians.[1]

Condemnation of Lawsuits and Abuses. Tilemann Hesshus: In chapter 6, Paul condemns the lawsuits and quarrels of the Corinthians, which they were disputing in court before a Gentile judge, instead of settling their differences peacefully among themselves. Next, Paul condemns those who, under the pretext of freedom, were openly seeking out prostitutes and were

[1]LW 35:382*.

defiling themselves with various wicked deeds. And he hands down the principle that no one is an heir of eternal life who defiles himself with wicked deeds, such as lust, unrighteousness, idolatry, theft, drunkenness, and other such things. Introduction to 1 Corinthians.[2]

6:1-8 *The Church Should Judge Disputes Between Believers*

The Corinthians Have Not Imbibed the Gospel. Huldrych Zwingli: It seems that the Corinthians were more curious about the gospel than imbibing its piety. So it happened that very few of them actually changed with respect to their way of life. For there were some among them who were so wicked that they were unjustly trying to drag their brothers and sisters to court. Or, at the very least, they were so lacking in self-control that they were unable to endure patiently even the smallest offense. Now the apostle shows that they are sinning in two ways. First, because there are still those among them who violently and wickedly harm their neighbors. Second, because those who have suffered these offenses do not obtain support. And this happens in matters of *biōtikois*, that is, in trivial matters regarding daily sustenance. Therefore Paul rebukes them for suing various people in court over matters essential and necessary for physical life. What is even more shameful is that they do this before a worldly judge! Annotations on 1 Corinthians 6:1.[3]

Lawsuits Are Like a Public Illness. Jacques Lefèvre d'Étaples: When there are many physicians in a city, this is a sign of much illness. So too, when there are many lawsuits being arraigned in the courts, this is a sign (as it is said) of much injustice. And frequently it happens that a just person who initiates a case or is summoned to court returns from court unjust. Commentary on 1 Corinthians 6:7-9.[4]

The Church Loses When It Sues for Its Rights. John Colet: But these lost little men—and our age is full of their sort (which should never be the case), churchmen and those who are given preeminence in the church—these men, I say, who are almost entirely ignorant of the teachings of the Gospels and the apostles, ignorant of divine justice and of Christian truth, commonly say that they must defend the cause of God, the right of the church, the heritage of Christ, the property of the priesthood, and that it would be a sin not to defend these things.

Oh, the narrowness, the blindness, the wretchedness of these men! When they undertake a legal case, they lose not only these worldly goods but also those eternal blessings, and even while they lose all these things, they imagine that they are acquiring them, defending them, and saving them. Despite what has happened everywhere in the church, these men (whose eyes are blinder than fishes) do not see how their wranglings and litigations have resulted in loss to religion, including the lessening of their authority, the neglect of Christ, and the blasphemy against God. Nor do they see, finally, how every day, little by little and subtly, they are either losing (or barely maintaining) those very things they call "church property," which they think they are keeping or recovering by their lawsuits. . . .

Without doubt the method for preserving in the church the things once given her is the same as the method by which they were first gained: love for God and neighbor, a desire for heavenly things, contempt for this world, true godliness, religion, charity, kindness toward others, simplicity, patience, the acceptance of misfortunes, an eagerness always to do good to all people, so that evil might be conquered by continual goodness. When people saw that in churchmen there was no greed and no abuse of people's generosity, this aroused the hearts of men and women everywhere to think well of the church of Christ, to be well-disposed toward it, to love it, to be generous and openhanded toward it,

[2]Hesshus, *Explicatio Prioris Epistolae ad Corinthios*, 4v.
[3]Zwingli, *Annotatiunculae . . . ex ore Zvinglij*, 42.
[4]Lefèvre d'Étaples, *Commentariorum in Epistolas Beati Pauli . . . Liber Secundus*, 108v.

and to give continually, heaping gift upon gift. Exposition of 1 Corinthians 6.[5]

Christians Must Not Be Parties in Lawsuits. Philipp Melanchthon: A major question is whether it is lawful to participate in civil trials. First, it is lawful for magistrates to conduct such trials, but it is extremely unlawful to be party to such suits.

Just as the law "you shall not kill" regulates the right to punish a capital crime, so too the law "Let the person taking your coat have your cloak as well" regulates the same right to punish, since trials and laws are part of the sword, that is the civil administration. Thus they do not sin who administer the sword when they kill the guilty, as seen in Romans 13:5, "Therefore one must be subject, not only to avoid punishment, but also for the sake of conscience." Thus the magistrates who lay down the law do not sin, nor do the lawyers employed and called in by the magistrates. Thus Paul allows here the choosing of lawyers and judges when he says, "You should be ashamed because you set up in the church as judges those whom you treat with contempt, namely, the Gentiles. Far better, if you want to have a trial, to choose wise men as arbiters who can pronounce judgment."

Now on the roles of litigants. It is not right to go to court to vindicate your own case, Matthew 5:40, "And if anyone would sue you and take your coat, let him have your cloak as well." Note also this passage: "To have lawsuits at all with one another is defeat for you." . . . In the case of a defendant or accused person who has been wronged, it is lawful to answer in a trial about the charge. First, the person who initiates the case causes an injury; this is to be treated according to the principle "If any one forces you to go one mile, go with him two." . . . Second, the nature of a lawsuit, which belongs to the sword, demands that the defendant defend their case, that they should not lie but put forward their case honestly, as it is, but without striving for and seeking victory. The case must be pleaded, because the sword commands those summoned to court to speak up. But it is not right to pursue one's own cause.

It is not right to level accusations, even if justice seems to stand on your side, except when somebody with a godly spirit warns a magistrate of his duty, seeking the public good rather than their own interest. For bishops and teachers have a special duty in such cases, and regardless of who they are, they should without scandal oppose an injury, not to themselves, I say, but to others. Jeremiah 21 says, "Execute justice in the morning and deliver the oppressed from the hand of the accuser, lest my wrath go forth like a fire." Isaiah 1 also says, "Defend the fatherless, plead for the widow."

Lawyers do not sin when they have been commissioned by the magistrate to handle cases, because they are part of the sword, nor do professors of law in the schools sin, nor do they sin at all who act thus to protect the oppressed, because this is their duty, even though they are not expressly appointed by the magistrates. Thus St. Augustine defended his church in court. [But] agents hired by the parties in a civil case do sin because they make themselves party to the litigants, because they stir up litigation and for the most part employ the sword for gain. Annotations on 1 Corinthians 6.[6]

Paul's Three Concerns. Wolfgang Musculus: The apostle scolds the Corinthians in this matter for three reasons. For the sin that they were committing here was not single, but threefold. First, it was altogether ridiculous that a Christian was calling another Christian to a heathen court. Paul cuts off this evil activity as if it were an evil root. Second, it was wrong that those who were injured were not doing what was appropriate for Christians, but were pursuing a judicial charge in a law court. Paul attacks this second in this passage. Third, since they were doing what they thought had been forced on them by the people harming them, Paul also reproves them, showing that there

[5]Colet, *Ennaratio*, 120, 122.

[6]Melanchthon, *Annotationes in Epistolam priorem ad Corinthios*, 80, 82; citing Mt 5:21, 40, 41; Jer 21:12; Is 1:17.

is no place for wicked people in the kingdom of God. COMMENTARY ON 1 CORINTHIANS 6:1-9.[7]

CHRISTIANS MUST NOT JUDGE OR PUNISH THE WICKED. THE SCHLEITHEIM ARTICLES: Now many who do not recognize what Christ wills for us will ask whether a Christian may also use the sword against evil people for the sake of protecting the good or for the sake of love. Our unanimous answer is as follows: Christ teaches us to learn from him that we should be mild and of humble heart, and in this way we will find rest for our souls. Now Christ says to the woman taken in adultery, not that she should be stoned according to the law of his Father . . . but that she should be dealt with in mercy and forgiveness and with a warning to sin no more. . . . We should also hold to this in our laws, according to the rule about the ban.

Second, it is asked about the sword, whether a Christian may pass judgment in worldly quarrels and conflicts at law such as unbelievers have with one another. This is the answer: Christ did not want to decide or judge between brother and brother concerning an inheritance, and he refused to do so. Then we should do likewise.

Third, it is asked about the sword, whether a Christian may hold a position of governmental authority if he is chosen for it. This is our reply: Christ should have been made a king, but he rejected this and did not view it as ordained by his Father. We should do likewise and follow him. In this way we will not walk into the snares of darkness. . . .

Last, it should be pointed out that it is not fitting for a Christian to be a magistrate for these reasons: the authorities' governance is according to the flesh, but the Christian's is according to the spirit. Their houses and dwellings remain in this world, but the Christian's are in heaven. Their citizenship is of this world, but the Christian's is in heaven. Their weapons of conflict and war are carnal and only directed against the flesh, but the Christian's weapons are spiritual and directed against the fortifications of the devil. Worldly people are armed with spikes and iron, but Christians are armed with the armor of God—with truth, with justice, with peace, faith, and salvation, and with the word of God. ARTICLE 6: CONCERNING THE SWORD.[8]

CHRISTIANS MAY JUDGE AND PUNISH THE WICKED. BALTHASAR HUBMAIER: Here, here listen to Paul, you dear brothers and sisters, and see. If ever Christians want to bring suit against each other over nourishment, that is, for temporal goods, which already is wrong, then it should nonetheless happen before a Christian and not before an unbelieving judge. Note here, brothers and sisters: This you have skipped, that if Christians ever want to dispute with each other and are not at peace with one another, that they sin even more, yes indeed they sin in a twofold way if they carry out such dispute before an unbelieving judge and not before a Christian. That is why Paul mocks the Corinthians and says that if they ever want to bring suit against each other, they should take the most despised ones among themselves as judges. That he said to their shame, as if they had no righteous and wise Christians among themselves who might judge between them, but they have to run to get an unbelieving judge. For that they should really be ashamed.

Here even a blind person can see that a Christian may very well and with good conscience sit in court and council and may judge and decide also in temporal matters. Although the wranglers and quarrelers are sinning, they would sin even more if they would carry out their cases before unbelieving judges. If then a Christian, by power of the divine Word, may and should be a judge with the mouth, he may also be a protector with the hand of the one who wins justice and may punish the unjust. For of what use would the law, court, and judge be if one were not allowed to carry out and enforce the punishment of evildoers? Of what use would a

[7]Musculus, *Comm. 1 Cor.*, 148.

[8]In Baylor, *The Radical Reformation*, 177-78; Jn 8:11; Lk 12:13; Jn 6:15.

shoe be if one were not allowed to put it on? See, dear brothers and sisters, that council, court, and law are not wrong. That also the judge may and should be a Christian, although the quarreling parties are sinning because they do not prefer to be taken advantage of. Consequently, a Christian may also, according to God's order, carry the sword in God's place over the evildoer and punish them. Because of the evil ones it is ordered in this way by God for protection and shielding the godly. . . .

You say, "But is it not so that one should not judge?" (Mt 7:1). Yes. Nor should one do injustice to anyone. But should it ever happen among Christians, a Christian judge should be appointed immediately who will administer justice for residents and foreigners. This must happen or Scripture must break to pieces. As far as I am concerned, no human being can overthrow that. On the Sword.[9]

How Will the Saints Judge the World? Wolfgang Musculus: But one might ask, how is it that Christian believers are going to judge the world and angels, when the Father has given all judgment to his Son, and he alone has been established as the judge of the living and the dead? Clearly, as Ambrosius explains it, because the treachery of the world will be condemned by the example of the faith of believers. Thus the twelve apostles, chosen from Israel, were condemning the treachery of Israel. In the same way, in Matthew 12, the Ninevites and the queen of the South were condemning the unbelieving nation. Rich soil, by virtue of its fertility, condemns barren soil, since barren soil does not benefit in the same way from cultivation and rain. The ignorant person who doesn't benefit from a teacher is rightly condemned by other students with the same teacher who advance far beyond him. And so, clearly, the world is justly condemned by believers, because it has despised that heavenly grace demonstrated in Christ, which believers themselves have embraced. Nevertheless, one interpreter explains this passage as follows: the saints are judging the world because they are assistants of the supreme judge, as one finds in Matthew 19: "When the Son of Man will sit on his glorious throne, you also will sit on twelve thrones, judging the twelve tribes of Israel." There is no contradiction here, since both interpretations are valid. Commentary on 1 Corinthians 6:2.[10]

Saints Will Judge Both This World and Satan. Tilemann Hesshus: Paul adds to his rebuke two very weighty reasons drawn from the argument of greater things. He says, "The saints will judge the world"—how much more are they capable of settling disputes regarding earthly possessions? Again, "The saints will judge the angels" (i.e., unclean spirits)—then why should they not judge disputes over physical property? The fact that the saints, along with Christ, will one day be judges of the world and Satan is clear from Christ's words in Matthew 19: "You will sit on thrones judging the twelve tribes of Israel" (19:28) and again . . . "The Son of Man, together with the multitude of angels and the elect. . . ." Certainly the supreme judge of the world is Christ. But the saints will assist Christ, and together they will condemn wicked people and unclean spirits according to the Word of God.

Therefore there is an extraordinary reversal of things. For in this world, the saints are the most despised and miserable of all people, condemned to all sorts of punishments by the judgment of cruel and wicked men. But in the final judgment, the saints will sit on judgment seats and will condemn the world to eternal death with the severest of judgments. [Emperor] Decius [*sic*] condemned with a cruel judgment [St.] Lawrence to the flames. But in the final judgment, Lawrence will stand at the side of the judge, Christ, and pass the judgment of eternal condemnation on Decius. Therefore godly people fortify themselves with this extraordinary consolation, especially when they are handed over to the judgment seat and condemned to death with cruel judgments.

[9]CRR 5:502-3*.

[10]Musculus, *Comm. 1 Cor.*, 150; citing Mt 12:41-42; 19:28.

The second argument is that the saints will judge Satan along with all of his angels. For they are kept for judgment, and Christ will surrender Satan under our feet. How much more, then, are the saints able to judge disputes pertaining to earthly things and to this life! Explication of 1 Corinthians 6:2-3.[11]

By "Angels" Paul Means Demons. Huldrych Zwingli: I think that in this passage, by synecdoche, "angels" should be understood as "demons," that is, wicked angels. For there are also good angels. But how will human beings judge demons? As we have said above: by a contrast. An angel is pure spirit; a human being is composed of both flesh and spirit. Therefore, since a demon would consider a human, standing firm in the faith, as nothing more than a mass of flesh, subject to sin and corruption, how will he not acknowledge himself to be condemned by the righteous judgment of God? For even though the demon is pure spirit and possesses nothing [of flesh] to separate him from God, nevertheless, he will fail. But the human who continually clings to God is rightfully blessed, despite the many ways he fails. Annotations on 1 Corinthians 6:3.[12]

Believers Will Judge Angels. John Calvin: This passage is taken in various ways. Chrysostom reports that some people understood it as referring to priests, but this is too forced. Others explain this passage as referring to angels in heaven, in the sense that angels are subject to the judgment of the Word of God, and if need be, they can be judged by us through this Word. Galatians 1:8 is cited in this regard: "If an angel from heaven were to announce any other gospel, let him be accursed." On the face of it, this interpretation does not seem to be out of line with Paul's argument: for if all whom God has enlightened with his Word are endowed with such authority so that, through the Word, they judge not only humans but even angels, then how much more will they judge matters that are trivial and contemptible? But, since Paul speaks here in the future tense as if meaning the very last day, and his words convey the idea of actual judgment (as the saying goes), it is better in my opinion to understand these as apostate angels. For the argument will not be any less conclusive if taken in this sense: "The demons who came from so noble an origin, and even now, despite their fall from their lofty position, are immortal creatures superior to this corruptible world—we will judge. What then? Shall those things that are subject to our physical appetites be exempt from our judgment?" Commentary on 1 Corinthians 6:3.[13]

When We Wrong Other Christians, We Wrong Christ. Tilemann Hesshus: Paul vehemently rebukes going to court before the political magistrates, because as judges the magistrates are not at all preferable to brothers belonging to the same religion and because disputes between avowed Christians should be settled privately and without outrage. But in particular Paul severely criticizes the authors of outrages and disputes and warns them to avoid injustice lest they condemn their neighbors, fall from grace, and thereby be deprived of the inheritance of eternal life. For blatant injustice cannot coexist with faith. "It would be better," he says, "for you to suffer wrong, keeping the matter secret and committing your cause to God. For the Christian religion requires this. But you accuse some people of injury and charge others with damage. . . . And your sin is all the more serious because you charge your brothers with injury, whom you are duty bound to help. For the person who harms his brother harms Christ. As the Son of God testifies: 'Whatever you did, either good or evil, for one of the least of these, you did it for me' (Mt 25:40). Indeed, no one should cause injury to

---

[11]Hesshus, *Explicatio Prioris Epistolae ad Corinthios*, 90v-91r. St. Lawrence, one of the chief deacons of the church in Rome, was martyred during the reign of Emperor Valerian in 258 when he refused to hand over the church's poor funds to the authorities.
[12]Zwingli, *Annotatiunculae . . . ex ore Zvinglij*, 44-45.

[13]CO 49:389 (cf. CTS 39:201). Chrysostom's treatment of this verse is found in his *Homilies on 1 Corinthians* (homily 16), in NPNF 12:91-92.

anyone, but those who harm a brother sin more grievously than those who cause injury to a Gentile or Turk." Explication of 1 Corinthians 6:5-8.[14]

The Absurdity of Civil Lawsuits. Wolfgang Musculus: Paul emphasizes the absurdity of this evil. They should have settled their dispute through the judgment of arbitrators. But instead of doing that, brothers dare to pursue lawsuits against their brothers, and that before unbelievers. Hitherto, Paul has declared the first part of this sin, which he also shows is not single, but threefold. First, that they chose arbitrators from outside the fellowship, which they did out of contempt for the church. Second, that a brother was going to court in a judicial case against his brother. Third, that they were doing this before judges who were unbelievers. It is as if householders were not allowing a dispute to be settled by other members of the household, but were pursuing a judicial case from the outside against one of their own. Now observe that Paul says "before unbelievers." Earlier [in verse 1] he called these pagan judges "the unrighteous." Here, he calls them *apistous*, that is, "unbelievers." Now there is a twofold sense intended with the Greek word *apistoi*. First, that they are incredulous unbelievers, foreign to faith in Christ. Second, that they are untrustworthy and unfaithful. Commentary on 1 Corinthians 6:6.[15]

Brother Against Brother. John Trapp: Still Satan is busy, and Christians are thus malicious. As if they lacked other enemies, they fly in one another's faces, as did Epiphanius and Chrysostom, Luther and Zwingli, Hooper and Ridley, Taylor and Lambert, those English exiles at Frankfurt in Queen Mary's day and Knox, etc. Commentary on 1 Corinthians 6:6.[16]

Better to Suffer Wrong Than to Initiate a Lawsuit. John Colet: Let us plainly conclude, therefore, that it is not appropriate for Christians to dispute at law before any judge about any matter, whether of property or of person, or to seek their own rights, since for a Christian there can be no greater justice, nothing more equitable, than to suffer and put up with wrongs. In this patience we will possess our souls. But if we should wish to identify something in this world as our own and demand it and strive for it in court of law and waste our time in lawsuits—although it is completely incompatible with the sincerity of love—is it not abundantly clear that then we are acting unworthily and unjustly, and in our impatience losing our souls? Exposition of 1 Corinthians 6.[17]

True Christians Avoid All Violence and Litigation. Anabaptists of Trieste: All defense and physical resistance; all warring, fighting, insurrection, and resisting evil; and all litigation in worldly courts and quarrelling over temporal goods are excluded. Christ clearly forbids killing or angry resentment (Mt 5). To this we add Paul who says: "Do not avenge yourselves, my beloved, but give place to God's wrath" (Rom 12). Going to law with one another is a defeat for you. Why do you not rather suffer injustice (1 Cor 6)? We and all true Christians accept and obey this. Following the command of Christ, we will not aid any injustice, nor whatever serves warring, murder, rebellion, and disunity. Confession.[18]

Jewish Commentators Agree with Paul. The English Annotations: The Greek word *hēttēma* . . . signifies "to have the worst" in a conflict or combat. Whereby the apostle implies that the flesh was too strong for the spirit of those Corinthians who, out of covetousness, malice, or desire for revenge, dragged their fellow Christians before the tribunals of the heathens. And even if their cases before the law courts might be superior, yet in fact they . . . receive thereby greater damage to their souls than they receive in damages. In a fashion similar to that of the apostle, Moses

[14]Hesshus, *Explicatio Prioris Epistolae ad Corinthios*, 92r-v.
[15]Musculus, *Comm. 1 Cor.*, 153.
[16]Trapp, *A Commentary or Exposition*, 671*.
[17]Colet, *Enarratio*, 126; citing Lk 21:19.
[18]CRR 10:267; citing Mt 5:38-40; Rom 12:19.

Gerundensis and Rabbi Salomon in their discourses on the discipline of the Hebrews, condemn the practice of those Jews who went to law against their fellow Jews in the courts of the infidels. For they say, "He who brings an Israelite before the tribunal of the Gentiles to have his case tried despises the name of God and commits idolatry." Annotations on 1 Corinthians 6:7.[19]

6:9-11 *The Unrighteous Will Not Inherit God's Kingdom*

Two Motivations for Purity. Philipp Melanchthon: There are two arguments by which Paul exhorts us against impurity. The first is taken from the punishment, namely, that the impure will not inherit the kingdom of God, describing the terrible punishment in restrained terms. For just as the term *heir* or *son* is the name for the mercy or grace of God, so to be excluded from the inheritance is the name for the divine wrath and curse and fury. . . .

The second is an argument based on the gospel, and it is drawn from God's favor. Paul is accustomed to arguing this way very often, as if he were saying: "Get busy, brothers and sisters, God's abundant and great favor requires that you mortify your flesh. You have been justified. You have been enrolled among the children of God. Why, then, do you not do the will of God?" Thus Romans 12, "I appeal to you by the mercies of God to present your bodies," etc., and 2 Corinthians 7, "Since we have these promises, let us cleanse ourselves from every iniquity. . . ." Annotations on 1 Corinthians 6:9, 11.[20]

Christians Struggle with Sins but Aren't Controlled By Them. Tilemann Hesshus: In this second part of the chapter, Paul shifts from a particular sin to general kinds of sin, and he shows the final reason why we ought to abstain not only from disputes and insults but from all wicked deeds: namely, so that we might not be cut off and deprived from inheriting the kingdom of heaven. For it is impossible that people who possess a conspicuous faith that embraces the benefits of the Mediator should defile themselves by destroying their consciences with wickedness. "Faith pertains to consolation," Bernard says, "but that person does not experience consolation who rejoices when he does wrong and exults in evil, for without faith it is impossible to please God." Therefore those who ruin their consciences by acting wickedly can cherish no hope of inheriting eternal life. The prophets and apostles often repeat this view so that we don't fool ourselves in imagining that we will be participants of the kingdom of heaven, even if we sin against our conscience—as the libertines shamelessly imagine. John says: "He who sins is from the devil." And Paul states in Romans 8: "If you will live according to the flesh, you will die." Again, "the mind of the flesh is death." Again, in Galatians 5: "Now the works of the flesh are evident: sexual immorality, adultery, idolatry, etc. . . . Those who do such things cannot possess the kingdom of God." . . . Therefore this very serious threat should always be kept before us so that we don't lapse into sin against our conscience.

The first thing to be gleaned from this teaching is that people who pollute themselves with outward wickedness are not living members of the church, and have no part in the kingdom of God. When David defiles himself with adultery and murder, he is not a son of God; rather, he is exposed to eternal condemnation. Similarly, the incestuous Judah, the murderer Joab, the thief Achan are not living members of Christ. Second, one should note the difference between those sins that remain in Christian saints and those sins that destroy faith. There are a variety of sins in saints, who nevertheless hold on to faith, please God, and are heirs of eternal life. On the other hand, those people who are controlled by sin and live according to the flesh are not heirs of life, but are exposed to

[19]Downame, *English Annotations*, DD2v*. Moses Gerundensis (b. 1194), also known as Nachmanides, and Rabbi Shlomo Yitzchaki (1040–1105), better known as Rashi, were medieval Jewish scholars known for their learned commentaries on the Talmud.

[20]Melanchthon, *Annotationes in Epistolam priorem ad Corinthios*, 84; citing Rom 12:1; 1 Cor 7:1.

eternal condemnation. Therefore the sin that is pardoned or covered in saints and believers is called original sin. All sorts of vices that originate in the mind, will, and heart are imparted by this original sin, such as negligence of duty, careless words, lapses in judgment, sins of ignorance, impure affections, love of self, pride, jealousy, love of money, fear of rejection, love of revenge, and similar faults. Godly people deplore these faults and fight against them as much as they can with the assistance of the Holy Spirit, and they continually seek from God pardon for these sins. Concerning these weaknesses, Scripture says: "Everyone who is godly will pray to you for this" (Psalm 32:6). Again: "If we say that we are without sin, we deceive ourselves and the truth is not in us" (1 John 1:8). EXPLICATION OF 1 CORINTHIANS 6:9-11.[21]

EVIL PEOPLE MUST NOT BE TOLERATED IN CHURCH. DIRK PHILIPS: These words give us to understand sufficiently that the transgressors and despisers of godly teaching and the saving grace of our Lord Jesus Christ shall much less escape the punishment of God than those escaped who sinned against the law of Moses. Now, therefore, for that reason also evil and carnal people may not be tolerated in the congregation of the Lord, just as the apostles expressly testify. For Paul writes thus to the Corinthians, "Do you not know that the unrighteous shall not inherit the kingdom of God?" THE BAN.[22]

THE MEANING OF "UNRIGHTEOUS." JOHN CALVIN: By "unrighteousness" we are to understand that which is opposed to strict morality. Therefore unrighteous persons are those who inflict injury on their brothers and sisters, who defraud or cheat others, who, in short, are intent on their own advantage to the injury of others. Such unrighteous persons will not possess the kingdom of God. However, it goes without saying that the term "unrighteous"—such as adulterers, thieves, the covetous, and revilers—refers to people who do not repent from their wickedness, but obstinately persevere in their sins. And the apostle himself states this explicitly, when he says that the Corinthians were once such as these. Wicked people thus *do* obtain the kingdom of God, but only if they have been first converted to the Lord in true repentance and in this way have abandoned their wickedness. For although conversion is not the cause of our pardon, nevertheless we know that none are reconciled to God unless they repent. COMMENTARY ON 1 CORINTHIANS 6:9.[23]

THE KINGDOM OF THE DEVIL AND THE KINGDOM OF GOD. MARTIN LUTHER: There are two kingdoms. The first kingdom is a kingdom of the devil. In the Gospel the Lord calls the devil a prince or king of this world, that is, of a kingdom of sin and disobedience. . . . Now all of us dwell in the devil's kingdom until the coming of the kingdom of God. However, there is a difference. To be sure, the godly are also in the devil's kingdom, but they daily and steadfastly contend against sins and resist the lusts of the flesh, the allurements of the world, the whisperings of the devil. After all, no matter how godly we may be, the evil lust always wants to share the reign in us and would like to rule us completely and overcome us. In that way God's kingdom unceasingly engages in combat with the devil's kingdom. And the members of the former are preserved and saved because they . . . fight against the devil's kingdom in order to enlarge the kingdom of God. . . .

The other kingdom is that of God, namely, a kingdom of truth and righteousness, of which Christ says, "Seek first the kingdom of God and his righteousness." What is God's or his kingdom's righteousness? It is the state when we are free from sin, when all our members, talents, and powers are subject to God and are employed in his service, enabling us to say with Paul, "I live, but it is no longer I but Christ who lives in me." . . . That

[21]Hesshus, *Explicatio Prioris Epistolae ad Corinthios*, 92v-93v; Bernard of Clairvaux, *Sermon on the Annunciation* (PL 183:394); citing Heb 11:6 (in Bernard); 1 Jn 3:8; Rom 8:13, 6; Gal 5:19.
[22]CRR 6:245.

[23]CO 49:392-93 (cf. CTS 39:207-8).

comes to pass when we are ruled not by sin but only by Christ and his grace. Thus God's kingdom consists only of peace, discipline, humility, chastity, love, and every other virtue and is devoid of wrath, hatred, bitterness, unchastity, and every other vice. Now let all persons test themselves to see whether they are inclined in this or in that direction, and they will know to which kingdom they belong. An Exposition of the Lord's Prayer.[24]

Unrepentant Sinners Will Not Inherit God's Kingdom. Wolfgang Musculus: It is an error to think that Christianity is nothing more than the profession of an empty title and a religion of external ceremonies. That is the opinion of the pagans, but not of true Christians, from whom firm piety and true righteousness are required in order to inherit the kingdom of God. . . . Those people whom Paul has called "unrighteous" he now describes with specific examples. He in no way enumerates all the kinds of unrighteousness, but only those types of sins to which he knew the Corinthians and the rest of those coming out of paganism were especially exposed. These sins included sexual immorality, idolatry, adultery, effeminacy, homosexual activity, theft, greed, drunkenness, abusive language, and rapacity. . . . This passage seems to some people a little bit too harsh, because Paul combines certain vices, which seem to be less severe, with more serious ones, and he subjects them to the same punishment (namely, the deprivation of the kingdom of heaven), even though it is certain that there are levels of sins, with some more serious than others, and that there are also levels of punishments. Inasmuch as simple fornication is not of the same seriousness as adultery, effeminacy, and homosexual activity; and, again, those sins are not as serious as the worship of idols, which is a sin against the first table of the law. . . . It should be recognized, therefore, that the apostle here is not describing what punishments will be meted out for those sins in the future, but in this way he announces that all these kinds of sinners are deprived from the kingdom of God. And once deprived of the kingdom of God, different punishments await different people. Commentary on 1 Corinthians 6:9.[25]

No Happiness Without Holiness. John Trapp: It is an undefiled inheritance, 1 Peter 1:4. No dirty dog ever trampled on that golden pavement, Rev 22:15. Heaven spewed out the angels; shall it lick up the unrighteous? The serpent could slither himself into paradise, but no wicked person could ever get into heaven. There is no happiness to be had without holiness. Commentary on 1 Corinthians 6:9.[26]

Carnal Sinners Must Be Banned from the Church. Menno Simons: We are, in the power of the holy Word, to exclude from the holy church of the Lord all offensively carnal sinners, such as fornicators, adulterers, drunkards, etc., and that without foregoing public admonition, which adds to the mortification and public rebuke of their sins and godless conduct, so inciting them to do penance. Instruction on Excommunication.[27]

Christians Have Been Cleansed from Their Previous Wickedness. Desiderius Erasmus: It is not enough to be washed in the [baptismal] water; nor is it enough to be engrafted into Christ, unless the whole life corresponds to the teaching of Christ. Therefore, being removed from the world, you have been united into the

[24]LW 42:38-40; citing Jn 16:11; Mt 6:33; Gal 2:20. Luther's doctrine of the two kingdoms underwent development throughout his career as a reformer. See Paul Althaus, *The Ethics of Martin Luther* (Minneapolis: Fortress, 2007), 43-82; and William J. Wright, *Martin Luther's Understanding of God's Two Kingdoms: A Response to the Challenge of Skepticism* (Grand Rapids: Baker Academic, 2010).

[25]Musculus, *Comm. 1 Cor.*, 157. In the Greek text, the words "effeminate persons" (*malakoi*) and "homosexual offenders" (*arsenokoitai*) refer to the passive and active partners in a consensual homosexual relationship. The ESV translates the two words with the phrase "men who practice homosexuality."

[26]Trapp, *A Commentary or Exposition*, 671*.

[27]Simons, *Complete Writings*, 975.

body of Christ so that hereafter the whole of your life corresponds to Christ, its head. Does it escape you that those who live wickedly—even though they're baptized—are to be excluded from inheriting the kingdom of heaven? Lest anyone fool themselves, I say it again and again—and I say it also to you—that neither the sexually immoral nor idol worshipers nor adulterers nor the effeminate (who, acting like eunuchs, submit to the lust of their schoolmasters) nor those who wickedly abuse other men nor thieves nor the greedy nor drunkards nor those who curse nor those who seize others' goods by force are partakers of the kingdom of God. Nothing will come from your new title if your life is contaminated by old vices, or rather, if by your offenses Christ is turned into a pretext for the most grievous condemnation. And these disgraceful things that I have just now brought up counted against you formerly, before you had been born again through Christ. I am not reproaching you for what you were, only warning you not to revert to that same behavior. You have been washed from your previous offenses; out of gratitude for this cleansing, watch out lest you be defiled again. And not only did the cleansing with his blood restore your innocence, but on the other hand it conferred holiness and righteousness, not by virtue of the law or your merits, but through Jesus Christ, in whose name you have been baptized, and through the Spirit of our God, through whose secret breath the church's sacraments are effectual. Paraphrase on 1 Corinthians 6.[28]

Boast in Christ. Martin Luther: I believe in one holy Christian church. We are all saints, and cursed be the one who does not boast and call himself a saint. If you believe the word of Christ, then you are just as much a saint as St. Peter and every other saint! Here's why: Christ certainly won't lie to you. If you don't say, "I have as much as St. Peter, and I'm just as holy as St. Peter," then you're ungrateful to your Lord Christ. . . . Such boasting is not arrogance, but humility and thankfulness. And whoever doesn't boast blasphemes Christ and baptism. For baptism is a work of God. And it's holy. Christ is holy too; his body and his blood are also holy. How could I imagine—if he gives and grants this to me—that I too should not be holy? That'd be like saying: "Christ is not holy." We are totally overwhelmed with holiness and with such a holiness. Heaven and earth are too small to grasp it, and nevertheless they doubt right away whether we too are holy. . . . Friends, it's not a joke, but a very dangerous thing to talk about the communion of saints. We honor Christ, not ourselves, when we boast about this holiness: because we are knit into his holiness and suffering, we too become holy.

Is it not true if a rich man who had been bequeathed a thousand *gulden* nevertheless wanted to say that he is poor and has nothing, that he is a fool? The same is true here. That I acknowledge myself to be a sinner, I do well, as far as it concerns my own person. But because I am no longer Adam's child, but God's child, so then I am truly holy! And so we must distinguish carefully: as far as I am a human and Adam's child, I belong in hell—even if I were a Carthusian,[29] still there I would humbly belong. But that's not what those who strut around with their works do. They turn the whole thing upside down and pride themselves on their works. But if you believe that you have been baptized into such a brotherhood and sonship, then say: "Now I am no longer Adam's child, no longer a sinner, so long as I am in this brotherhood." If you can brag about it, then do it. I'm still learning this, for it's very difficult for a sinner to say: "I have a seat in heaven next to St. Peter." And yet we must praise and boast about this holiness—that alone is the golden brotherhood. Sermon on the Thursday after Easter (April 21, 1530).[30]

[28]Erasmus, *Paraphrases*, 247-48.

[29]The Carthusians were known for their strict ascetic monastic rules: they were only allowed to eat one meal a day except during high festivals of the church, and their diet consisted chiefly of vegetables, bread, and water.

[30]WA 32:92-93.

Washed, Sanctified, Justified. John Calvin: Paul uses three words to express the same thing so that he may the more effectively deter them from returning again to the condition they had once escaped. Therefore, although these three words aim at the same thing, nevertheless their variety lends great force to what he says. For there is an implied antithesis between washing and filth, sanctification and pollution, justification and guilt. His point is that having been justified, they must not call down guilt on themselves anew; having been sanctified, they must not pollute themselves again; having been washed, they must not disgrace themselves with new defilements. On the contrary, they should pursue purity, persevere in true holiness, and detest the filthy habits of their former life. From this we understand the end for which God reconciles us to himself by the gracious remission of our sins.

Although I have said that the three words express one and the same thing, I do not believe by this that there is no difference in their meaning. For, properly speaking, God justifies us when he frees us from condemnation by not imputing our sins to us. God cleanses us when he washes away the remembrance of our sins. Thus the only difference between these two is that one is straightforward while the other is metaphorical. For in fact the metaphor is found in the word "washing," because Christ's blood is compared to water. Moreover, he sanctifies by reforming our sinful nature by his Spirit; thus sanctification relates to regeneration. But in this passage, the apostle's only purpose was to magnify with various expressions of praise the grace of God, which has freed us from our bondage to sin, so that we might learn from this how much we should abhor all things that provoke the wrath and vengeance of God against us. Commentary on 1 Corinthians 6:11.[31]

The Grace of the Triune God. Wolfgang Musculus: The triune majesty of God is expressed in this passage, through whom washing, cleansing, sanctification, and justification are given to the person who believes in Christ. For Paul is mindful of first our God, second the Lord Jesus, and third the Holy Spirit. And this is because we have been baptized in the name of the Father and the Son and the Holy Spirit. Let us note here the magnitude of heavenly grace, which washes away our grave shame and by which grace is restored. Commentary on 1 Corinthians 6:11.[32]

[31]CO 49:394-95 (cf. CTS 39:211-12).
[32]Musculus, *Comm. 1 Cor.*, 158.

6:12-20 FLEE SEXUAL IMMORALITY

12“All things are lawful for me,” but not all things are
helpful. “All things are lawful for me,” but I will not
be dominated by anything. 13“Food is meant for the
stomach and the stomach for food”—and God will
destroy both one and the other. The body is not meant
for sexual immorality, but for the Lord, and the Lord
for the body. 14And God raised the Lord and will also
raise us up by his power. 15Do you not know that your
bodies are members of Christ? Shall I then take the
members of Christ and make them members of a
prostitute? Never! 16Or do you not know that he who
is joined[a] to a prostitute becomes one body with her?
For, as it is written, “The two will become one flesh.”
17But he who is joined to the Lord becomes one spirit
with him. 18Flee from sexual immorality. Every other
sin[b] a person commits is outside the body, but the
sexually immoral person sins against his own body.
19Or do you not know that your body is a temple of
the Holy Spirit within you, whom you have from
God? You are not your own, 20for you were bought
with a price. So glorify God in your body.

a Or *who holds fast* (compare Genesis 2:24 and Deuteronomy 10:20) **b** Or *Every sin*

Overview: Concerned that the Corinthians are using their freedom in Christ as an excuse to indulge in fornication, the apostle Paul takes this occasion to explain the limits of Christian liberty, warn of the dangers of sexual immorality, and remind his readers that their bodies are holy temples consecrated to the Lord. While Protestant commentators heartily endorse the Pauline principle that Christian liberty in “indifferent matters” must be subordinate to the general welfare of the church and to God’s glory, at the same time they criticize the medieval church for undermining Christian liberty through various unbiblical regulations (such as the restriction of eating meat during Lent). More than one commentator reminds readers that the Christian’s greatest freedom is found in service to Jesus Christ and his church. In their treatment of Paul’s injunction against fornication, Reformation interpreters provide sizeable lists of the unique dangers of the sin of fornication. More positively, in this context they also discuss at length the beautiful mystery of the believer’s spiritual union (in soul *and* body) with Jesus Christ and the inestimable privilege of being called “temples of the Holy Spirit.” Because Christians are God’s holy people, united to Christ by faith, they must live lives of moral purity, offering their worship and mundane labor as spiritual sacrifices to God.

6:12-14 *Christian Liberty and Fornication*

Christians Must Seek the Common Good. John Colet: The Corinthians thought that they could go to law to claim what was theirs, that without sin they could participate in the banquets of idolaters, that without fear, relying on the boldness of their consciences, they could openly feast on things offered to idols. They were too thoughtless and were not aware of the demands made by the church’s welfare. They had not learned that the only things permitted are those things that are beneficial and useful for the public welfare. They did not remember that the whole church of Christ is like a body, in which all should live and do all things, not for themselves, but for the whole body, not for their own advantage, but for the benefit of the entire community, and with a far-reaching regard for the consequences of present acts. Everyone must be constantly aware that their own personal advantage depends on the common good, because their personal advantage lessens to the extent that the common benefit decreases, in whatever way this happens. Now [the common welfare] consists chiefly and foremost in unity, concord, love, peace, and joy in the Holy Spirit. . . .

Therefore, if you love the public welfare and the unity and beauty of the Christian society (which ought to be your first and only love), but even if you love yourself and your own advantage . . . never consider anything more important than Christ himself, in whom you live as a member, not by your own strength, but by his.

Do not seek, then, what is yours, but only what is Jesus Christ's. Use all things for the benefit of Christ alone. And do not abuse yourself, since you no longer belong to yourself, but to Christ. You are a member of Christ; you have been bought into his body with a great price, the price of his most sacred and holy blood, to serve him alone, to depend on him, to do all things by him—not for yourself, I say, but for him. Exposition of 1 Corinthians 6.[1]

The Corinthians Employed Christian Liberty to Justify Their Sin. John Calvin: Interpreters expend a lot of effort to understand the connection of these verses [to what has come before] since they appear somewhat incongruous to the apostle's intentions. For my part, I will omit a summary of these various interpretations, and say what, in my judgment, is most appropriate. It is likely that the Corinthians even up to that time retained much of their previous licentiousness and still reeked of the customs of the city. Now when vices prowl about with impunity, custom is taken for law, and then afterward vain pretexts are devised by way of excuse. Such was the case here, as the Corinthians were seeking refuge in the shadow of Christian liberty so as to justify almost everything they did. They were wallowing in great luxury, which was mixed with much pride (as usually happens). Since this was an outward matter, they did not think they were sinning. Indeed, it appears from Paul's words that their abuse of liberty extended all the way to fornication. Now, then, most appropriately, after he had spoken about their vices, Paul criticizes the perverse excuses by which they were flattering themselves in outward sins. Commentary on 1 Corinthians 6:12.[2]

Christians Are Free from Dietary Restrictions. Huldrych Zwingli: Paul writes to the Corinthians (1 Corinthians 6:12), "All things are lawful unto me, but all things are not expedient. . . . Meats for the belly and the belly for meats: but God shall destroy both it and them." That is, all things are free for me, although some things are rather to be avoided, in case they offend my neighbor too much. . . . And therefore no one can take from me my freedom and bring me under his authority. Food is taken into the belly to sustain life. As now the belly and food are both to be destroyed, it makes no difference what one eats or wherewith one nourishes his mortal body. Liberty Respecting Food in Lent.[3]

The Nature of Christian Freedom. Tilemann Hesshus: "All things are lawful for me." No doubt the fornicators at Corinth were flaunting and abusing their freedom. And not only did they interpret such freedom to relate to indifferent things (as the apostles had taught), but they transferred it even to sins. Thus Paul is restraining them. " . . . but not all things are useful." What must be considered and reflected on is not only what is permitted but also what is useful, what enhances the glory of God and the edification of the church. The first clause teaches that it is completely lawful for us to accept things that are neutral and indifferent. The second clause teaches that we must consider not only what is permitted to us but also what is useful for the church. It was lawful for Paul to forego circumcising Timothy, but it was not useful for the church. Therefore Paul circumcised him.

"All things are lawful for me, but I will not be dominated by anything." That is, in the case of liberty, we must not abuse it so that the lusts of the flesh drive us back into servitude. Instead we must

[1] Colet, *Enarratio*, 128, 130.

[2] CO 49:396 (cf. CTS 39:213-14).

[3] In Jackson, *Ulrich Zwingli's Early Writings*, 74-75.

make use of the freedom of the Spirit, which Christ has procured for us, so that we might bridle and repress the lusts of the flesh and give ourselves in service, serving Christ and profiting our neighbor. For the greatest freedom is to serve Jesus Christ and his bride, the church. Therefore Paul teaches here that true liberty is that spiritual freedom, which always has control over lusts and the carnal affections. Explication of 1 Corinthians 6:12.[4]

Unlike Eating Meat, Fornication Is Not an Indifferent Matter. David Dickson: The second part of this chapter . . . concerns avoiding simple fornication (as it is called), which the Corinthians considered an indifferent matter, as did other Gentiles. Paul proceeds to the reproof by undercutting the apology they were preparing to make. The Corinthians might say, "All indifferent things are lawful for us; fornication, like eating meat, is also indifferent; therefore it is also lawful for us." First, Paul answers in general terms by limiting the major premise. For all indifferent things are lawful only insofar as they are appropriate and lawful, so that we are not brought into the bondage of our passions by the intemperate use of our liberty. For under such circumstances a person sins in using indifferent things.

Furthermore, Paul answers the secondary argument in specific terms, showing the difference that exists between eating meats and practicing fornication. Paul grants that it is lawful to eat any kind of meat, because God has ordained the goodness of the natural order in which meat is designed for the stomach, and the stomach for meat. But Paul adds this provision: that as God will one day destroy meat, so he will also one day destroy the stomach; hence, we should not endanger our eternal salvation or the salvation of others by causing offense for the sake of our stomachs. As far as fornication is concerned, Paul denies that it is permissible like eating meat; rather fornication is sin and must be avoided. Exposition of 1 Corinthians 6:12-13.[5]

Human Reliance on Food Will End. Wolfgang Musculus: In Colossians 2, the apostle emphasizes the powerlessness of foods so as to belittle them (since when they are eaten they perish and are corrupted), speaking of those who were devoting a lot of religious scruples to these corruptible things. Now Paul says here that God himself will equally destroy the stomach and food. Although, of course, this will happen universally at the end of the world, we nevertheless see it happen daily through death, but we don't think a lot about it. Therefore it is as much the work of God to destroy and ruin the stomach and food as it is to create them. And what is spoken about the stomach and food should also be applied to all other kinds of pleasures. However, note that Paul is not saying that the body is to be destroyed by God in the same way as the stomach. For the body will remain, but the stomach, which is used in this life, will be destroyed. Commentary on 1 Corinthians 6:13.[6]

Eating and Fornication. The English Annotations: [Paul is saying that] food and drink are indifferent things, but fornication is not of the number of such things. For although both eating food and fornication are bodily acts, yet the quality of the food has no moral relation to the soul, either in its present sanctification or its future glorification. So too, eating food leaves behind no impression on the soul (Mt 15:11, 17), but is only for the sustenance of this life, and after our passage to the next life, the use of food and the stomach and belly that digest it will be abolished. Whereas, on the other side, all sexual activity—except that in marriage—is expressly prohibited by God and is destructive and repugnant to the right end and use of our bodies. For our bodies are to be consecrated to Christ (belonging as members to him) and to be governed and employed by him to serve him in holiness and purity, and by that means to be made partakers of his glory in the final resurrection. Annotations on 1 Corinthians 6:13.[7]

[4]Hesshus, *Explicatio Prioris Epistolae ad Corinthios*, 95r-v.
[5]Dickson, *Exposition of St. Paul's Epistles*, 49-50*.
[6]Musculus, *Comm. 1 Cor.*, 162; citing Col 2:16-23.
[7]Downame, *English Annotations*, DD2v*.

Unlike the Stomach, the Body Will Not Be Destroyed. Wolfgang Musculus: "But God raised the Lord." Paul opposes this statement to what he has said concerning the stomach and food, namely, that "God will destroy both one and the other." Now someone might say: "But not only our stomachs but our entire bodies will be destroyed." Thus Paul answers by saying: "Indeed, our bodies will die, but then they will be raised up by God." Now he praises the dignity of our bodies in several ways: First, by their union with Christ, an argument that he will soon address in what follows. Second, by the eternal and glorious resurrection in the future. Thus he says: "But God raised the Lord, and he will raise us also." Commentary on 1 Corinthians 6:14.[8]

6:15-18 *Flee from Sexual Immorality!*

Extinguish Lust by Delighting in Christ. John Colet: Restrain and extinguish lust by the desire of that inextinguishable delight that Christ will at last infuse into his people. Beware of adultery; beware of fornication; beware of misusing your own body, which is no longer your own, but a member of Christ. For when you dishonor your own body, you violate the body of Christ and the temple of the Holy Spirit; you sacrilegiously take what belongs to Christ's sacred holiness and give it to a harlot for shameful dishonoring, besmirching and debasing your own body—indeed, Christ's body in you—since in that union it happens that a person is made one with the body of the prostitute, as that ancient testimony teaches: "They shall be two in one flesh." . . .

Will you shamefully subject to a harlot for everlasting damnation that which should serve Christ and the Spirit in beauty and honor for life unending? Is not the whole of a person drawn in the direction to which one part inclines? If then this inferior bodily part plays the harlot by being joined to a prostitute, must not the soul also at the same time be torn away and divorced from God? And if, too, this higher, spiritual part should cling entirely upward to God and be made one spirit with him, will it not raise up with it the body into a spiritual state? Exposition of 1 Corinthians 6.[9]

What Does It Mean That Our Bodies Are Members of Christ? John Calvin: This passage is an explanation, or, if you prefer, an amplification of the previous sentence. For that expression "the body is for the Lord" could be somewhat obscure due to its brevity. Hence, by way of explanation Paul says that Christ is so closely bound to us and we to him that we are united with him in one body. Thus, if I unite myself with a prostitute, I tear Christ apart limb by limb (as much as it is in my power) because it is impossible that I should drag him into communion with so great a pollution. Now since the very thought of this should be abhorrent to us, Paul uses the expression that he often employs when speaking of things absurd: "Never!" It should be noted that the spiritual unity we share with Christ pertains not only to the soul but also the body, so that we are flesh of his flesh, etc. Otherwise our hope of resurrection would be feeble, if our union were not of such a nature, that is, complete and firm. Commentary on 1 Corinthians 6:15.[10]

The Dangers of Fornication. Simon Goulart: In chapter 6, the apostle says that fornicators and adulterers are shut out of the kingdom of God. Therefore that we may have a part in the inheritance of the saints, who are sanctified and justified in the name of the Lord Jesus, and by the Spirit of God, we must remember first that our bodies are not for fornication, but for the Lord, and the Lord for the body. Second, seeing that our bodies shall rise again, not to ignominy and pollution, but to glory and holiness, it is necessary to keep them pure and unpolluted, for they are members of Christ, and consequently it is a horrible sacrilege to make them members of

[8]Musculus, *Comm. 1 Cor.*, 162-63.

[9]Colet, *Explicatio*, 132; citing Gen 2:24.

[10]CO 49:397-98 (cf. CTS 39:216-17).

a prostitute. Third, that being members united to the Lord, and made one spirit with him, it is in no way appropriate to join them to a prostitute, with whom we are made one body. Fourth, that fornication ought to be detested above all other sins: for whatever sin a person commits, it is outside their body, but the person who commits adultery sins against their own body. Fifth, that our bodies are the temples of the Holy Spirit, which is in us, which we have from God. Sixth, that we are not our own to live as we wish, for we have been bought and redeemed with a price, that is, by the precious blood of Christ, as a Lamb without spot and blemish, as St. Peter describes him. For these strong and compelling reasons, St. Paul frames a holy exhortation to all people, especially to old wise persons, whom it most concerns, who before all others are bound to think and be mindful of it. Glorify then God in your body and in your soul, which belong to God. The Wise Vieillard.[11]

The Christian's Body Belongs to the Lord. Dirk Philips: We establish this as an immoveable basis of truth that the apostle said: "Do you not know that your bodies are the temples of the Holy Spirit, which you have received from God, and you are not fully in control of yourselves?" (1 Cor 3:16). And again, "Do you not know that your members are members of Jesus Christ?" (1 Cor 6:15). From this it then follows powerfully that a Christian has no power over their own body in order to take that which belongs to the Lord and give it to an unbeliever. For since a Christian's body belongs to the Lord and is a temple of the Holy Spirit, how can it be given to an unbeliever outside of Jesus Christ, outside his word and will and outside his congregation?

That a Christian's body is the Lord Jesus Christ's body, that the aforementioned words of the apostle clearly testify, and from this is also certainly evident and plain that it is united and married to the Lord through faith, just as many beautiful histories, figures, and sayings tell and witness in both testaments with great clarity. Three Admonitions.[12]

Oil and Water Cannot Mix. John Trapp: Scipio, when he was offered a harlot, said, "I would, if I were not a general." So too, we should say "If I were not a Christian." . . . A saint cannot indeed be made the member of a harlot, said a reverend man, because he cannot be glued or knit to any sin. Though a member of Christ and sin may fall one on another and touch each other, they are of an incompatible nature and will not cleave together. Water and oil violently shaken together may seem to mix, but will not continue so for long; there is no coalition, because they are of diverse natures; the one remains water still and the other oil. Commentary on 1 Corinthians 6:15.[13]

The Meaning of "One Flesh." Wolfgang Musculus: The proof is taken from Genesis 2, where it is written that Adam said: " 'This at last is bone of my bones and flesh of my flesh; on that account, she shall be called Woman, because she was taken out of Man.' Therefore a man shall leave his father and mother and hold fast to his wife, and they shall become one flesh." The apostle quotes this latter phrase ("and they shall become one flesh") . . . to serve as a proof in this present passage. Now it might seem surprising that, from this passage, he proves that a man and a prostitute become one flesh, since Adam spoke those words not about fornication but about the legitimate union of a man and his wife. Since there is such great difference between prostitutes and legitimate spouses, how can both be capable of the same meaning? First, because there is no difference as regards the sex of both partners. There is a man and a woman in both the act of fornication as well as marital union. Second, because there is also no difference as regards the joining and physical union. . . . Thus it is possible to

[11]Goulart, *Wise Vieillard*, 68-69*; citing 1 Pet 1:19.

[12]CRR 6:564.

[13]Trapp, *A Commentary or Exposition*, 672*. Scipio Africanus (263–183 BC) was a prominent Roman general and consul, famous for his strict morality and courageous leadership.

say of fornicators as well as of legitimate spouses that the two shall become one flesh. However, the blessing of God, "Be fruitful and multiply, and fill the earth," is certainly addressed only to legitimate spouses. But that multiplication of the human race through the union of a man and a woman happens as much when they are united illegitimately as when they are united in true and lawful marriage. Commentary on 1 Corinthians 6:16.[14]

Does Marriage Separate Us from Christ? Tilemann Hesshus: Paul brings up the testimony of Genesis 2, "and the two shall become one flesh," because this passage speaks about the closest and most indissoluble covenant of marriage union. Now Paul applies it to fornication so as to warn the fornicator of the fact that he becomes one flesh with the prostitute. For this reason this wicked act should be abhorred among Christians. Now if someone asks whether physical intercourse in marriage tears a person's body from Christ, one must respond that a faithful Christian husband is not bodily separated from Christ, even if he discharges the marital debt to his wife. For marriage is honorable in every way, and the cohabitation of husbands and wives has been divinely ordained. Thus, when spouses in good conscience devote themselves to procreating children according to the commandment of God, they are not driving out the Holy Spirit, nor are they tearing themselves from the spiritual body of Christ.

"He who is joined to the Lord, is one Spirit." Paul shows how we become and continue to be members of the body of Christ, namely, through the Holy Spirit, whom the Son of God pours into us and whom we receive by faith. And as a result he unites us very closely with God and showers on us righteousness, love of God, eternal life, and joy. We are one spirit, that is, one spiritual body, and all of us are directed and sanctified by one and the same Spirit. Explication of 1 Corinthians 6:16-17.[15]

[14]Musculus, *Comm. 1 Cor.*, 165-66; citing Gen 2:23-24; 1:28.
[15]Hesshus, *Explicatio Prioris Epistolae ad Corinthios*, 97r-v; citing Gen 2:24.

Fornication Defiles the Body in Unique Ways. John Calvin: Having treated honorable conduct, Paul now shows how much we should abhor fornication, presenting the enormity of its wickedness and ugliness. Now he develops this by comparing it to other sins, stating that fornication alone of all sins puts a mark of disgrace on the body. The body, it is true, is also defiled by theft, murder, drunkenness, as Scripture testifies: "your hands are polluted with blood" (Isaiah 1:15); "You have presented your members as instruments of iniquity for sin" (Romans 6:19), and similar verses. Some people, in order to avoid this inconsistency, have interpreted the clause "his own body" to mean "those who are united to Christ." But for me, this interpretation is not at all convincing.... Thus my explanation is that Paul does not completely deny that there are other sins which dishonor and bring disgrace to our body, but he simply means that the sin of fornication defiles our body in a different manner than with other sins. My hand, indeed, is stained by theft or murder; my tongue by slander or perjury; my whole body by drunkenness. But fornication leaves behind a stain impressed on the body unlike other sins. According to this comparison, or rather, on the basis of this argument of greater-lesser, other sins are said to be outside the body, though not because they have no effect whatsoever on the body. Commentary on 1 Corinthians 6:18.[16]

The Dangers of Fornication. Wolfgang Musculus: Paul sums up the difference between fornication and other sins with two points. First, he asserts that every other sin that a person commits is outside the body. Second, he adds that the person alone who commits fornication sins against their own body. It is necessary to understand the difference between sinning against one's own body and sinning outside one's body. I will say what I think. To sin against one's own body is to allow it to be injured and to defile its chastity. For the honor of our body is its purity and chastity. To be defiled by sinning is when a sinful action transgresses against the body itself. On the other

[16]CO 49:399 (cf. CTS 39:219-20).

hand, the sin that is outside the body is that action which does not defile the body of the sinner, but extends to those things that are outside of it. Although we sin when we misuse our body's members by stealing, kidnapping, deceiving, bearing false testimony, murdering, etc., nevertheless this sinful action does not affect the whole body, but only certain members, and it relates to external matters and causes injury to other people. But a sin against one's own body is where a person's chastity and honor are defiled by some filthy action. Such is the case with fornication. Therefore fornication differs from all other sins in this way, that while other sins are performed outside the body, fornication sins against one's own body. Commentary on 1 Corinthians 6:18.[17]

Christians Must Flee Fornication. The English Annotations: Here the apostle uses various arguments to discourage the Corinthians from fornication. First, because it stains the body with a peculiar kind of filth. Second, because a fornicator is guilty of sacrilege, since our bodies are consecrated to God as his temples (verse 19). Third, because we are not our own to give our bodies to another, much less to Satan and the flesh, seeing that God himself has bought us at such a great price for the purpose of serving him in body and soul. By employing the word "fleeing" here, Paul implies that whereas other vices are conquered by struggling and striving with them, the best way to subdue the vice of fornication is to fight with it after the manner of the Parthians, who fought by fleeing. Annotations on 1 Corinthians 6:18.[18]

6:19-20 *Your Body Is a Holy Temple*

Believers Belong to Christ and Are Called to Holiness. Huldrych Zwingli: This is a strong exhortation to live out their faith in a way that focuses singularly on what pleases Christ. It is as if Paul were saying: "If you are faithful, your faithfulness comes from the inspiration of God. Therefore God dwells in you. Therefore you are a temple of God, made holy by his Spirit. Thus you cannot claim to have personal rights since you have been purchased at great price. Why, therefore, do you say that the Lord is unwilling to help you with your moral filth and lust?" Paul says the same thing in his letter to the Romans: "Do not let sin reign in your mortal body." Therefore, since you are fully in Christ, do not defile yourself with wickedness and outrage, neither in body nor in soul. Instead be pure and holy so that Christ may be glorified in you.

The phrase "your bodies" means "you." This is a Hebrew figure of speech, as seen in 1 Samuel 21, "the vessels of the young men are holy," that is, the young men themselves are holy. Those from among the Gentiles who came to faith in Christ believed that it was lawful to frequent prostitutes. It appears that Paul said these things for that reason. In a similar fashion, the apostles were forced to declare that the Gentiles must guard themselves against fornication. Annotations on 1 Corinthians.[19]

Body and Spirit Must Be Separated from All Ungodliness. Dirk Philips: One must praise God, both with the body and the spirit, which belong to God (1 Cor 6:20). And if one will know, hear the words of Paul to wit: "What comparison has God's temple with the temple of idols? Therefore depart out of the middle of it, separate and do not touch anything impure," etc. (2 Cor 6:16-17). To understand this rightly, one must notice his actual meaning, namely, that he said thus: "You are the temple of the living God," as God spoke (1 Cor 3:16), "I will dwell in them and walk in them, and they shall be my people, and I will be their God." And at another place (1 Cor 6:19), "Do you not know that your bodies are the temples of the Holy Spirit, which you have

[17]Musculus, *Comm. 1 Cor.*, 169.

[18]Downame, *English Annotations*, DD3r*. The Parthians, who ruled an empire between the Euphrates and Indus Rivers in the third century BC, were known for shooting volleys of arrows as they fled the line of battle.

[19]Zwingli, *Annotatiunculae . . . ex ore Zvinglij*, 51-52; citing Rom 6:12; 1 Sam 21:5; Acts 15:29.

received from God, and you yourselves have no power." Again, "and do you not know that your members are Christ's members?" From this it is easy to measure and clearly to understand how one must separate oneself not only with the spirit and the heart but also with the body from idolatrous temples, from all godless preachers who stand in the pulpit and falsify the Lord's Word, and from all false religious services. Three Admonitions.[20]

How Can the Body Be a Temple of the Holy Spirit? Wolfgang Musculus: But one might inquire from this passage how our dull and corruptible bodies are able to be the temple of the Holy Spirit. Above, in chapter 3, Paul said: "Do you not know that you are the temple of God, and that the Spirit of God dwells in you?" Here he says: "Do you not know that your body is the temple of the Holy Spirit?" Does the Spirit of God dwell in our bodies? Would it not be more appropriate for our hearts to be described as the dwelling place of the Holy Spirit? Certainly I think so. Thus that expression is metaphorical that describes the dwelling place of God by the analogy of a temple made of stone, because God promised to administer his grace especially in the holy of holies and at the seat of propitiation within the temple, although otherwise neither heaven nor earth could contain him. And so, clearly, our bodies are the temple of the Holy Spirit when they constitute a sacred shrine because of the holiness of our hearts (which is by the Spirit of God), for the very reason that those gifts and moral qualities of the Holy Spirit especially achieve their work among them. For who is so absurd as to think that the incomprehensible Spirit of God, who is infinite, is enclosed in either our hearts or bodies? Commentary on 1 Corinthians 6:19.[21]

Bringing Glory to God Through Our Daily Labor. Tilemann Hesshus: No one should make use of those things that are forbidden for the purpose of their own lust, nor should they apply them to foul purposes. Our bodies do not belong to us by right or power, but they belong to God. For it is evident that God redeemed our bodies through the precious blood of his only-begotten Son. Therefore it is not permissible for us to use our freedom to abuse our bodies, but they should serve the will and glory of God. Paul points out many things here. He reminds us at what a great price we have been redeemed: to be sure, with the precious blood of Jesus Christ. Therefore we should strive mightily to render honor to him with our bodies. He warns us not to demand our rights. Therefore, in our every activity and endeavor, we should consider the will of the all-powerful God. What a great comfort it is when we employ the body according to the will of God; as Paul says, "may the all-powerful God be glorified in our spirit and body." Therefore the labors and hard work of the saints in all their various vocations are pleasing sacrifices to God, whether you are plowing or digging or cutting wood or cleaning the house—whatever works we perform in faith, according to the Word of God. The most pleasing sacrifice is when we oppose with our bodies the dangers and tyranny of wicked people for the sake of God's truth and glory. Explication of 1 Corinthians 6:20.[22]

The Gospel Is Worthless Apart from Union With Christ. Valentin Weigel: In this coming everything is given to us. Namely, we are in him and he remains in us. That he is born from the Virgin would be useless for us if he did not make his dwelling place in us. And that he rode into Jerusalem and entered the temple is useless for us if he is not also in us. Yes, all his suffering and dying would be wasted on us if he did not live in us. Gospel for the First Sunday in Advent.[23]

[20]CRR 6:394.
[21]Musculus, *Comm. 1 Cor.*, 172; citing 1 Cor 3:16.
[22]Hesshus, *Explicatio Prioris Epistolae ad Corinthios*, 98v-99r.
[23]Weigel, *Sämtliche Schriften*, 12,1:8.

7:1-16 Principles of Marriage

Now concerning the matters about which you wrote:
"It is good for a man not to have sexual relations
with a woman." [2]But because of the temptation to
sexual immorality, each man should have his own
wife and each woman her own husband. [3]The
husband should give to his wife her conjugal rights,
and likewise the wife to her husband. [4]For the wife
does not have authority over her own body, but the
husband does. Likewise the husband does not have
authority over his own body, but the wife does. [5]Do
not deprive one another, except perhaps by agree-
ment for a limited time, that you may devote
yourselves to prayer; but then come together again,
so that Satan may not tempt you because of your
lack of self-control.
[6]Now as a concession, not a command, I say
this.[a] [7]I wish that all were as I myself am. But each
has his own gift from God, one of one kind and one
of another.
[8]To the unmarried and the widows I say that it is
good for them to remain single, as I am. [9]But if they
cannot exercise self-control, they should marry. For it
is better to marry than to burn with passion.
[10]To the married I give this charge (not I, but the
Lord): the wife should not separate from her husband
[11](but if she does, she should remain unmarried or else
be reconciled to her husband), and the husband
should not divorce his wife.
[12]To the rest I say (I, not the Lord) that if any
brother has a wife who is an unbeliever, and she
consents to live with him, he should not divorce her.
[13]If any woman has a husband who is an unbeliever,
and he consents to live with her, she should not
divorce him. [14]For the unbelieving husband is made
holy because of his wife, and the unbelieving wife is
made holy because of her husband. Otherwise your
children would be unclean, but as it is, they are holy.
[15]But if the unbelieving partner separates, let it be so.
In such cases the brother or sister is not enslaved. God
has called you[b] to peace. [16]For how do you know, wife,
whether you will save your husband? Or how do you
know, husband, whether you will save your wife?

a Or *I say this:* **b** Some manuscripts *us*

Overview: Having addressed the problem of fornication among the Corinthian Christians, Paul turns his attention in 1 Corinthians 7 to the related issues of marriage, celibacy, separation, and divorce. For Reformation commentators, few portions of Scripture trigger as much discussion and heated controversy as these verses, raising important questions as to the nature of human sexuality, the purposes of marriage, the advantages (or dangers) of the celibate life, and the warrants for divorce. The rehearsed opinions of ancient church leaders such as Augustine and Jerome frequently serve as ammunition for defending or assailing the teachings of the medieval church. While Catholic interpreters affirm the sacramental nature of marriage, many of them present human sexuality and marriage as a hindrance to the spiritual life, championing instead a celibate life devoted to Christian service and prayer. By contrast, Protestant commentators find in Paul's words a clear testimony of the goodness of marriage and identify various God-ordained purposes for it: marriage is a remedy for fornication; marriage allows for the propagation and nurture of children; and, some believe, marriage provides companionship and mutual support to husbands and wives. Protestant interpreters are not in complete agreement as to whether sexual intercourse, even in the bounds of marriage, is ever completely free from the sin of lust. Nevertheless, they share a deep distrust of Catholic notions of celibacy, which, they believe, leaves many monks and nuns vulnerable to the "burning" desire of the flesh. The concluding verses of this passage focus on a final set of controversial issues related to divorce and separation. Whereas Catholic canon law prohibited all divorce (and remarriage), Protestant commentators defend divorce for innocent spouses in cases of adultery, and most of them also find justification for divorce in the advice Paul gives here to Christians deserted by an unbelieving spouse. Lutheran and Reformed interpreters are sharply divided, however, as to the meaning of Paul's mysterious words that unbelieving husbands and wives (and their children) are "made holy" by virtue of their connection to a Christian spouse or parent. For Reformed interpreters like John Calvin and Theodore Beza, the passage provides a clear justification for the baptism of the infant children of Christian believers.

In Praise of Chastity and Virginity. Martin Luther: In chapter 7, [the apostle Paul] gives instruction concerning chastity and married life. He praises chastity and virginity, saying that these are helpful in allowing closer attentiveness to the gospel, as Christ also teaches in Matthew 19 concerning celibates who are chaste for the sake of the gospel or the kingdom of heaven. But Paul wills that it be practiced without force or compulsion, or the risk of greater sin; otherwise, marriage is better than chastity that is continually aflame with passion. Preface to the First Epistle of Corinthians.[1]

Paul Now Responds to Specific Questions Regarding Marriage. John Calvin: Since he has spoken about fornication, Paul now appropriately proceeds to discuss marriage, which is a remedy for avoiding fornication. Now it appears that despite the great desolation that persisted in the church of Corinth, they still retained some respect for Paul since they were consulting him on uncertain matters. What precisely their questions were is not clear, except insofar as we can guess from his reply. This much, however, is well known, that immediately after the beginning of the church, superstition had crept in by Satan's cunning whereby a large number of people began to despise the sacred state of marriage out of a foolish admiration for celibacy. Many of these [early Christians] abhorred marriage as if it were some profane thing. Perhaps this infection had also spread among the Corinthians; or at least there were some very lazy spirits, who by immoderately extolling celibacy were endeavoring to alienate the minds of godly people from marriage. At the same time, as the apostle treats various other topics, he indicates that he had been consulted on many other questions. It is especially important that we listen to his teaching on each of them. Commentary on 1 Corinthians 7.[2]

Paul's Discussion of Sexual Ethics. Wolfgang Musculus: After having censured the filthy sin of fornication, the apostle now appropriately brings up the subject of marriage . . . lest anyone think that he condemned marriage along with fornication or lest that perception of fornication should not be recognized as erroneous. Now it seems that among the Corinthians there was some disagreement about marriage, such that some people thought it should be avoided for the sake of the Christian religion, and other people had separated themselves from their spouses out of religious devotion, especially those who were married to unbelievers. Good and pious men had written to the apostle concerning these matters, whence Paul says, "Concerning the matters about which you wrote," etc. And so in this chapter, he first treats the subject of marriage, then of unmarried persons, and third of virginity. Paul does this so clearly and distinctly, and with such great caution (lest he set a snare for anyone), that it is astonishing that certain ancient writers and learned men have not seen the light of this chapter. But this was necessary to fulfill the apostle's prophecy where he predicted that, in the future, the teaching of demons would arise in which marriages would be prohibited (see 1 Tim 4). Now, concerning marriage, he first teaches that it is permissible for

[1]LW 35:382; citing Mt 19:12.

[2]CO 49:400 (cf. CTS 39:221-22).

Christians to marry. Second, that all married persons should render their conjugal duty. Third, that married persons should not separate from one another. Fourth, Paul adds advice concerning married persons of different religious faith. Commentary on 1 Corinthians 7.[3]

7:1-7 *Husbands and Wives*

Paul Distinguishes Between Counsel, Command, Indulgence, and Prohibition. John Colet: Let us go back . . . to see what Paul teaches the Corinthians regarding counsel, command, indulgence, and prohibition. I shall say in advance, briefly and in general terms, . . . only what difference there is between these four things: to counsel, to command, to indulge, to prohibit. The latter two are always concerned with evil, the former two with good. For you *counsel* when you propose what is best and what each person should follow. You *command* when you instruct each person to follow that good as much as he or she can. You *indulge* someone when, against your will, you concede an evil that someone cannot avoid due to weakness. And you *prohibit* when you completely forbid someone from falling down and sliding back . . . into those sins that are appointed for death, for which there is no pardon, unless you rise again and repent of your fall. And so with *counsel* it is a matter of what you should do even if you cannot; with *prohibition* it is a matter of what you should not do even if you can; with *command* it is a matter of the good that each person can do; with *indulgence* it is a matter of the evil that each person cannot avoid. . . .

But now finally, with these matters set forth . . . let us draw nearer to our Paul. The Corinthians asked him what those who professed Christ were to do about marriage. His first wish in this matter was that all people should be as he was and be celibate, so that they might serve God with greater chastity and peace (for God himself is Chastity and Peace). For he wished all people—as much as they were able—to be as perfect as they could be, dedicated to God alone in Christ, devoted to as simple a life as possible. Wherefore he urges unmarried persons that, if a woman is a virgin, she should not marry; and if she is a widow, she should not remarry, so that she may devote herself to God in holiness and prayers more single-mindedly and more simply.

But although Paul wished and especially desired this best form of life for the Corinthians, yet, since he did not know the strength and the extent of each person's virtue, he did not dare to command for everyone a complete abstinence from marriage, lest this be an obligation that exceed their ability, and they break [God's] law and transgress the bounds prescribed. Therefore, acting with indulgence toward the Corinthians, and taking into account their weakness, he readily permitted that the man who knew himself to be too weak to live a celibate life should marry and take for himself in legitimate marriage one woman as a remedy for the fire of passion. In this way, the man who could not abstain from all women might still abstain from all but one. And this one woman is conceded to him lest his proneness to fleshly lust break out in some crime more detestable. Exposition of 1 Corinthians 7.[4]

Marriage Is a Hindrance to the Spiritual Life. Cardinal Cajetan: [By the phrase] "it is good for a man not to touch a woman" Paul means "not to get married." Paul is not in opposition to the Word of God, where it is written in Genesis 2, "it is not good for man to be alone," since that statement is speaking about a man according to nature. For it is not good for *natural* man to be alone, since this does away with natural propagation. Now, Paul is speaking here of man in relation to the *spiritual* life, in which it is not good for a man to get married. For marriage is a hindrance to the spiritual life. Commentary on 1 Corinthians 7:1.[5]

[3]Musculus, *Comm. 1 Cor.*, 174; citing 1 Tim 4:3.

[4]Colet, *Enarratio*, 186, 188.

[5]Cajetan, *In Sacrae Scripturae expositionem*, 5:105; citing Gen 2:18.

The Beautiful Fruit of Marriage. Guillaume Farel: When marriage is purely guarded, the two are but one body in true charity and love. Notice also what care mothers and fathers have for their children who come of a loyal marriage. In such a family the father knows that his children are his own and the mother never loved another or ever abandoned herself to anyone else, but was always loyal to her husband. What offices or works of true charity are not found in this holy state? . . . In the holy state of marriage the works of charity are practiced visibly and there is no manner of living where charity has so many occasions to flourish at all times and at every hour. For he who is charity established this state, honored it, and commanded it. And he who is the devil, being full of hatred, ruined it, dishonored it, and forbade it as much as he could.

Husbands, love your wives and live with them to avoid fornication. Be grounded in the Word of God and not in the murmurings and dreams of monks and priests. Understand the dignity of your state; in it lived all the holy patriarchs, prophets, and apostles of which Scripture speaks. You must acknowledge and respect marriage and not some vain dreams. Wives, obey your husbands and be subject to them in all as to our Lord, for the husband is the head and the wife is under his power. Take caution when you are separate from each other so that you do not fall into incontinence. Keep faithfulness and loyalty, for every wife who breaks her marriage must be condemned to die with the wicked (Lev 20). Summary and Brief Exposition.[6]

Vows of Celibacy Are Not Binding. Martin Luther: This then would be the first conclusion: that whoever does not feel that he has that precious quality[7] but rather is inclined to fornication, he is commanded to marry. And this commandment is to be received as coming not from a human being but from God. From this it follows that nobody can vow to be chaste, nor should he keep such a vow but rather break it if he finds or feels that he does not have that precious quality but is inclined to fornication; for such a vow is really made contrary to God's command. But one cannot vow anything against God's command, and even if the vow were made, still he is condemned who keeps it. . . .

Wherever there is not present this grace to live a celibate life by choice and desire, there it is better to marry. There is no other means to help there except marriage. Therefore if one cannot have the happy days of celibacy, then one must accept the evil days of marriage, for it is better to suffer evil days without sin in marriage than happy days without marriage in sin and unchastity. Commentary on 1 Corinthians 7:1.[8]

Early Church Fathers Erred Who Condemned Marriage. Philipp Melanchthon: The first topic of this chapter is whether it is lawful to contract marriage. Jerome dealt with this same matter in his writing *Against Jovinianus* and in his letters to Pammachius where he superstitiously exalted virginity. He cites in his letters to Pammachius the statement of the Greek writer Piérius, who spoke regarding this passage ("I wish that all were as I am"): "In saying this Paul clearly beyond question is preaching *agamia*, that is, celibacy." He calls Jovinianus a Christian Epicurus because he seems so strongly in favor of marriage. There are many passages of this sort in Jerome that are more superstitious than devout. Scripture approves of marriage, as in Matthew 19: "Not all men can receive this teaching"; and 1 Timothy 4 calls the teaching that forbids marriage "deceitful spirits and doctrines of demons." And when it was predicted that the vices of the flesh would reign above all in the last times, celibacy was by no means as popular as it is now. Neither virginity nor marriage is commanded, but they are left to each person's choice in that whichever is chosen is without sin. For marriage is certainly commanded

[6]In Zuidema and Van Raalte, *Early French Reform*, 167.
[7]That is, the gift to live a celibate life.
[8]LW 28:9, 12.

to those who are aflame with passion. To be aflame with passion is not to suffer from just any desires of the flesh, for none of the most holy virgins completely lacked fleshly flames, but those flames that cannot be quenched short of immoral behavior. I say that marriage is commanded for those who are so aflame with passion. Ambrose says: "Being aflame with passion is when the will consents to the heat of the flesh." Annotations on 1 Corinthians 7:1.[9]

We Must Be Wary About Marriage. John Trapp: Now since the fall, it is good, that is, convenient [not to have sexual relations] . . . on account of the many troubles of the married estate. It is not evil to marry, but good to be wary, lest marriage prove to be a "mar-age." Commentary on 1 Corinthians 7:1.[10]

Parents Should Encourage Their Children to Get Married. Huldrych Zwingli: Paul says in 1 Corinthians 7:2: "On account of unchastity shall each man take a wife for himself, and each woman a husband." From these words the following conclusion is drawn: Each man, without exception . . . if he feels he cannot get along without sexual intercourse, shall have a spouse of his own and be satisfied with his own. This ought to teach us fairly, that each father should say to his sons: "Dear sons, live pure lives. And if you ever feel that desire is overcoming you, tell me, and I will give you wives of your own." This same should each mother say to her daughters. In that case there would be many fewer prostitutes, many fewer bastards; and if one married, much less adultery. Besides it often happens that our children choose their own mates; and if they are not married according to their choice, their feelings and thoughts as to their spouses appear to them as heads on an imperial coin. But in case the above-mentioned regulation should be followed, they could not contradict or quarrel; for they would have been so reared from childhood that they might tell their needs. Now if the priest is troubled with desires, Paul tells him to take a wife; for he has excepted no one. Priests to Preach and to Marry.[11]

Marriage Is Holy and Honorable. John Jewel: We say that matrimony is holy and honorable in all sorts and states of persons, as in the patriarchs, in the prophets, in the apostles, in holy martyrs, in the ministers of the church, and in bishops, and that it is an honest and lawful thing (as Chrysostom says) for a man living in matrimony to take on himself the dignity of a bishop. And, as Sozomen says of Spyridion, and as Nazianzus says of his own father, we say that a good and diligent bishop does serve in the ministry never the worse for that he was married, but rather the better, and with more ability to do good. Further, we say that the same law which forcibly takes away this liberty from men and compels them against their wills to live single is "the doctrine of devils," as Paul states; and that, ever since the time of this law, a terrible uncleanness of life and manners in God's ministers and various horrible enormities have followed. Apology.[12]

Marriage Is for Procreation and to Prevent Fornication. Wolfgang Musculus: We see in this passage that the purpose of marriage is not only to procreate children but also for the purpose of preventing fornication. Therefore they err greatly who think that a marriage is

[9] Melanchthon, *Annotationes in Epistolam priorem ad Corinthios*, 92; citing Mt 19:11; 1 Tim 4:1-5. For Jerome's *Adversus Iovinianum*, see PL 23:221-354. Jerome's two letters to Pammachius (Letters 48-49) are found in PL 22:493-511; 511-12. Jerome cites Piérius (a priest in Alexandria during the second half of the third century) in his second letter to Pammachius, PL 22:511-12. Melanchthon's citation of Ambrose [Ambrosiaster] is from his *Commentarius in Epistolam 1 ad Corinthios*, in PL 17:229.

[10] Trapp, *A Commentary or Exposition*, 673*.

[11] In Jackson, *Ulrich Zwingli's Early Works*, 180* (ZSW 1:229-30).

[12] Jewel, *Apology of the Church of England*, 29*; citing 1 Tim 4:1-3. See Chrysostom, *In epist. ad Titum* 1.2. For the statement of the fifth-century church historian Sozomen, see his *Ecclesiastical History* 1.11. For the statement of the fourth-century bishop Gregory of Nazianzus, see his *Oratio XVIII, Funebris in patrem, praesente Basilio*, sec. 18.

not legitimate unless the partners are fertile, as if there is no longer any justification for marriage among those who are infertile, whether because of age or a natural defect. Here preventing fornication is a reason given for marriage. Now this sin of fornication must be feared and avoided, not only among those who are young and fertile, but also among those who are infertile and of advanced age. For this reason, the apostle does not permit widows to be supported in the church unless they have reached sixty years of age. It is certain therefore that marriage is completely justified both among the infertile and those of more advanced age. Commentary on 1 Corinthians 7:2.[13]

Marriage Has Several Purposes. Tilemann Hesshus: The chief and final reasons for the institution of marriage are, first, so that by the legitimate union of husbands and wives the human race might be propagated in an orderly and chaste fashion; second, so that the man might enjoy fellowship and have a companion who helps him with all his cares, endeavors, and labors. And Paul adds a third reason here, namely, for avoiding lust. For after human beings fell into sin and their natures were corrupted, marriage became the remedy so that they might be able to maintain self-control and protect purity of conscience. Therefore it is permitted for people to contract marriage who, because of their advanced age, have no hope for bearing offspring. Explication of 1 Corinthians 7:2.[14]

Conjugal Rights Have Been Established by God's Law. Peter Martyr Vermigli: Having established marriage as a thing necessary for the Corinthians (as we recounted previously), Paul now explains the laws by which married persons should live. Some people interpret this "marital kindness" generally: that marriage partners should show themselves prepared to perform all the duties of friendship to each other. Others conclude (and I think this is the better interpretation) that it speaks of conjugal rights, and Paul's words that follow indicate this. In some matters the man is placed before the woman. In Genesis it says: "Your desire will be for your husband and he shall rule over you." And Paul instructs husbands to love their wives, and by contrast he commands wives to respect their husbands and be subject to them. But, yet, they are considered as equals with respect to marital rights—this obligation arises from the divine law. For it is said: "The two are in one flesh." For that reason, [sexual intercourse in marriage] should be considered a healthy thing and no one should mistrust it as sinful, because it has its origin in divine law. And so, we should read with caution Augustine, in his book *On the Good of Marriage* and other works, when he writes that the conjugal duty is only free from sin when it is practiced for the sake of bearing children, because Paul here commands its use to avoid fornication. If you dare to say, "but it induces you to sin," even Augustine acknowledges that it is a light and venial sin, which is either not imputed or pardoned on account of the marriage bond. But I would say it is not a sin at all, since it is commanded by God. Commentary on 1 Corinthians 7:3.[15]

The Mutuality of the Marriage Covenant. Tilemann Hesshus: When Paul says that the husband does not have authority over his body, nor the wife over her body, he reminds [the Corinthians] how closely they have been bound together in the marriage covenant, and that the marriage covenant cannot be dissolved by the wishes or the vows that either party makes. But just as both parties entered into marriage by agreement, so neither has any authority over his or her body, except by mutual consent. This passage should be understood to relate not only to conjugal rights and vows, but also to adultery and desertion. For it is not permissible for someone to assert

[13]Musculus, *Comm. 1 Cor.*, 176-77; referring to 1 Tim 5:9.
[14]Hesshus, *Explicatio Prioris Epistolae ad Corinthios*, 101v.
[15]Vermigli, *In Selectissimam Priorem ad Corinthios Epistolam . . . Commentarii*, 152v; citing Gen 3:16. For Augustine's *On the Good of Marriage (De Bono Conjugali)*, see NPNF 3:397-413.

authority over their body against the matrimonial bond. And it is not permissible for a spouse to wander about here and there, without the agreement of the other spouse. The fact that Paul says that the husband does not have authority over his body, but the wife, indicates that the covenant is mutual, that the husband is strongly attached to his spouse, and the wife is strongly attached to her husband. Explication of 1 Corinthians 7:4.[16]

Equal Condition. John Calvin: But it may be asked why the apostle here makes [husbands and wives] equal and does not demand obedience and subjection from the wife. I answer that it was not Paul's intention to discuss all their duties, but the mutual obligation that pertains to the marriage bed. In other matters, therefore, the husband and wife differ as to their duties and rights; but in this respect, they share an equal condition, that is, in maintaining marital fidelity. For this reason polygamy is again condemned. For if this is a universal law of marriage, that a husband surrenders the authority over his body and gives it to his wife, then how could he afterward join himself to another wife, as if he were free? Commentary on 1 Corinthians 7:4.[17]

Laying Aside the Conjugal Right for Prayer. Martin Luther: St. Paul has very little confidence in their chastity because he well knows the devil and his tricks and the weakness of the flesh too. Here you see that married people are so bound up in one another that one cannot withdraw from the other even to fast or pray without the agreement of the partner; St. Paul would rather see prayer and fasting be relaxed than that one should so rule his body as to deny it to the marriage partner. Yet prayer is indeed a precious good work, and that it must give way before what seems to be such a trivial work, this is all the result of the law of love in which they are bound. Commentary on 1 Corinthians 7:5.[18]

[16]Hesshus, *Explicatio Prioris Epistolae ad Corinthios*, 102v.
[17]CO 49:403 (cf. CTS 39:225-26).
[18]LW 28:14.

Satan Tries to Use Sexual Abstinence. Huldrych Zwingli: "You should come together again as one." [It is as if Paul were saying:] "Seeing that . . . you cannot perpetually keep yourself free from fasting and abstinence, and since the passions of the flesh (to which people are naturally inclined) are violent, I want you both to agree on a time when you will once again share sexual intimacy. Otherwise, it may happen that you succumb to your lust. I am not giving you a command, but advice, because I am fully aware of Satan's cunning. He is setting traps for you all around, that he might in this way easily throw you down headfirst into wickedness." Annotations on 1 Corinthians 7:5.[19]

Marriage Is *Only* Given as a Concession for Evil. John Colet: Even in a marriage contracted because of the intensity of our sexual desire rather than our own wish, we must always demonstrate a commitment to live chastely rather than loosely, and therefore we shall indulge ourselves with our spouse as little as possible. In this way marriage will be for us—as it ought to be—a remedy for involuntary lust, not a resort for sexual delight for its own sake. Jerome speaks in this fashion: "The man who acts too passionately toward his wife is an adulterer." Those people, then, are surely to be held as contemptible who deliberately and intentionally practice sexual intercourse in marriage to fulfill in it their mutual lusts, since they are using marriage (which ought to be as chaste as weakness permits) to indulge in harlotry in a disgraceful and shameful fashion.

Let everyone here beware of thinking that Paul allows marriage for any other reason than one's inability to restrain oneself. And for this reason he grants by concession not only a first marriage, but a second also—even a third, if you should wish it. But if there is no reason of this kind, persuade yourself that you are not allowed even a first; because marriage has no goodness in it except insofar as it is a necessary remedy for evil. In this

[19]Zwingli, *Annotatiunculae . . . ex ore Zvinglij*, 53-54.

sense it is a good thing, since by means of the exchange of assistance, married men are restrained from fornicating promiscuously with many women. At one time, however, in the beginning, it was useful for the procreation of offspring so that the world might be filled with numerous descendants of the human race. And there was likewise a certain sacramental meaning to it, with regard to Christ and his bride, the church. Christ was born of a virgin, so that Christians might be born of the church, both virgin and mother. . . . But now that the Bridegroom has come, and the spiritual truth of marriage has been fulfilled, there is no reason why marriage should remain any longer as a figure of what is to come. And in Christianity the propagation of children no longer demands sexual relations in marriage, since our begetting is not a generation, but a regeneration in God. . . . In short, then, both Christian men and women ought to strive as much as they can for angelic chastity, before marriage, in marriage itself, and after marriage. Exposition of 1 Corinthians 7.[20]

Sexual Intercourse in Marriage Is Pure, Honorable, and Holy. John Calvin: Foolish zealots for celibacy abuse both parts of this verse. For because Paul says that he speaks "as a concession," they conclude from this therefore that sexual intercourse in marriage is wrong. For sin is present when one needs pardon. Moreover, from Paul's statement that he is speaking "not as a command," they infer that it is therefore a sign of greater holiness to give up the married state and go back to celibacy.

My answer to the former is as follows: since there is, I acknowledge, inordinate excess in all human affections, I do not deny that in sexual intercourse there is a lack of discipline that is corrupt—I concede this. More than that, I grant that this affection is exceptionally uncontrollable and almost bestial. But, on the other hand, I also maintain that whatever is corrupt or disgraceful in it is so covered by the honorable nature of marriage that it ceases to be corrupt, or, at least, God no longer reckons it as such. This is how Augustine beautifully treats the matter in his book *On the Good of Marriage*, and often elsewhere. You may summarize it this way: sexual intercourse between a husband and a wife is pure, honorable, and holy, because it is an undefiled institution of God. The uncontrollable passion with which people burn is a fault arising from the corruption of human nature; but for believers marriage is like a veil that covers this corruption so that it no longer appears before God. Commentary on 1 Corinthians 7:6.[21]

Marriage a Divine Gift That Teaches Faith. Martin Luther: Now that we are at the place where Paul praises matrimony so highly, calling it a divine gift, let us look a bit further and show that matrimony is the most religious state of all, and that it is unjust and wrong to refer to certain other "religious orders" while calling marriage a "secular order." It should be just the reverse, that marriage should be called the real religious order, as in truth it is, and these other orders should be called the real secular orders, which in truth they are. . . .

Now consider the religious orders so famous up to our time. The first thing you notice is that they are most securely provided with all the necessities of the body. A guaranteed income, food, clothing, shelter, and all sorts of other things they have in superfluity, earned by the work and care of others and given to them, so that they are not endangered in any way nor wish to be. . . . But if you take a wife and are married, this is the first shock: How are you going to support yourself, your wife and child? And this will go on for your whole life. Therefore the state of marriage is by nature of a kind to teach and compel us to trust in God's hand and grace, and in the same way it forces us to believe. For we can see that where there is no faith in marriage,

[20]Colet, *Enarratio*, 190, 192, 196. The quotation from Jerome, which appears in the margin of Colet's *Enarratio*, comes from his *Adversus Jovinianum*, in which he states his approval of Sextus's statement that "he who ardently loves his own wife is an adulterer" (see NPNF 1:386).

[21]CO 49:405-6 (cf. CTS 39:230-31).

there it is a most miserable institution, full of worry, fear, and hard work. On the other hand, the less faith these famous religious orders have, the better they get along, for their stomachs are filled gratis, and they need not look to God's hand nor await his goodness. Commentary on 1 Corinthians 7:7.[22]

Paul's Example Does Not Mandate Celibacy. Huldrych Zwingli: "For I wish that all people were as I am." The apostle's office required him to be gone from his wife for long periods of time; very rarely was he able to have sex with her. The apostle recognized that this gift had not been granted to everyone. Thus he was trying to say: "Would that all who were eager to be chaste were able to control themselves as I do. For it has turned out that, with this special gift from God, I do not experience so much the passions of the flesh when I am agitated by dangers, worries, and cares. But I know that this gift has been given only to a very few people. I know how vulnerable the flesh is. I know that only a small number of people are enabled to adhere to these counsels that surpass the law of God." I say, therefore, that people must measure their strength according to the diversity of God's gifts, lest they chase after that which is denied them and renounce with great sacrifice that which is permitted them. For we should not think that Paul's vow here necessitates [celibacy], because otherwise humanity would cease to exist, which would necessarily happen if no one had a wife. What fools they are who try to argue such things, using this passage as proof! Annotations on 1 Corinthians 7:7.[23]

Christian Marriage Can Promote Holiness. Martin Bucer: God has created the woman to be a help to the man that they might live godly lives together. Therefore, when marriage has been entered on and continued in the Lord, the wife does not separate her husband from the Lord. And when the wife is also zealous for the kingdom of God, her husband will please her more not by neglecting the work of God, but by carrying it out faithfully and well. In marriage of itself there is nothing unholy, nothing which is not ordained and blessed by God. Therefore of itself it will not in any way hinder holiness and well-doing, but rather promote it; always provided that the marriage is in the Lord, which is particularly appropriate and necessary in the case of ministers of the church.

This means that all those who abstain from marriage without being called to do so by the Lord are not thereby made more free of worldly affairs and attached more devotedly and freely to Christ the Lord, but rather sink even more into worldly affairs and are estranged from Christ the Lord; this is something that, sadly, we have seen only too grossly in the case of our so-called priests.

In time the dear [church] fathers came to understand Paul's word, in which he praises chastity outside marriage so highly, in far too broad a sense, and in a way to shun marriage itself, just as if of itself it hindered holiness, which cannot be the case: because it is a work and blessing of God, ordained in Paradise, so that sin could not render it impure of itself.

But the dear ancient fathers did not consider this sufficiently, allowing themselves to think that in marriage there was too much carnality, and that therefore it was inappropriate to the ministry of the church, or indeed to any really zealous Christian life. This is why they then praised virginity and widowhood so highly, while on the other hand showing such an aversion to marriage. True Care of Souls.[24]

God Gives Good Gifts to Everyone. Wolfgang Musculus: Divine goodness and generosity toward humankind ought to be noted in this, that God has bestowed gifts not only on some but on all mortals. For Paul does not say, "Some people have their own gift," but "Each person has their own gift from God." Therefore no one can complain of being deprived of divine kindness;

[22]LW 28:17, 18.

[23]Zwingli, *Annotatiunculae . . . ex ore Zvinglij*, 54.

[24]Bucer, *Concerning the True Care of Souls*, 48-49.

rather, all people have divine gifts, for which they should glorify God. Commentary on 1 Corinthians 7:7.[25]

7:8-9 *The Single Life*

The Celibate Life Is More Holy and Spiritual Than Marriage. Jacques Lefèvre d'Étaples: Both the celibate life and the life spent shunning carnal relations (which was how Paul lived in holiness)—whether for the man who does not take a wife, or for women who do not marry husbands, or even for men or women who are married who renounce carnal relations—ought to be preferred by far to marriage since it is more holy, more pure, and more spiritual. But this should not prohibit men who wish to marry a wife, or women who wish to enter marriage. This is not sin. Commentary on 1 Corinthians 7:8-9.[26]

Paul's Example Allows for Clerical Marriage. Martin Luther: His speaking in this way must indicate either that St. Paul's wife had died when he wrote this epistle and indicated that he was a widower or else that he must have put her from him with her consent and did not take her with him and therefore lived chastely with her in the state of matrimony, as stated in chapter 9. Whatever the case may be, whether his wife was dead or had consented to live separately from him for the sake of the gospel, one thing is certain: that he was living as a widower at that time and had been a married man. . . . Why have you not read this text and given it due consideration? Does it not say here clearly that a priest may marry? For even if I concede that St. Paul was a virgin or a widower, still he says that he has the right to be accompanied by a wife. Tell me, was St. Paul at that time not an apostle, a bishop, and a priest? How dare he presume to have the right and authority to marry? And since the high order of the apostles permitted a person to marry or stay married, why should not the lesser order of priests permit both remaining married and being married? Commentary on 1 Corinthians 7:8.[27]

Paul Is Giving Advice, Not a Command. Wolfgang Musculus: "But I say." It is clear from the clarification that follows what the apostle intends to say here. He is not prescribing or commanding, but giving advice. Christ employs this phrase in a different sense in Matthew 5: "I say to you, love your enemies," etc. In that context, Christ used the phrase "I say" in the sense of prescribing rather than giving advice. Commentary on 1 Corinthians 7:8.[28]

Advice to Widows. Tilemann Hesshus: Paul repeats his previous statement that, if someone has the gift of continence, it is a good and permissible thing to remain single. Widows shouldn't be afraid that they are sinning if they avoid remarriage. For it is lawful—but not required by command—to marry. But widows should examine whether their nature has been furnished with the gift of continence, and if they sense that they don't have it, then they should marry again. "For it is better to marry than to burn," that is, even if they experience many afflictions and troubles in marriage, yet these things can be endured with a better conscience than those persons who constantly struggle with flaming lusts and who make vows of continence that are incompatible with their natures. For that burning does not leave without the conscience being defiled and wounded. Countless examples show how unhappily it has turned out for those who obeyed the advice of monks and nuns and took vows of perpetual chastity (having rejected the advice of Paul): not only those people who, being overcome by the flesh, have slipped into foul lusts, but also those who refrained from all prostitution and adultery [but] experienced the gnawing pain of conscience as they were unable to repress their

[25] Musculus, *Comm. 1 Cor.*, 188.

[26] Lefèvre d'Étaples, *Commentariorum in Epistolas Beati Pauli . . . Liber Secundus*, 110r.

[27] LW 28:22, 23*; citing 1 Cor 9:5-6.

[28] Musculus, *Comm. 1 Cor.*, 189; citing Mt 5:44.

burning lust. Therefore this advice of Paul's is beneficial: it is better to be married and enter marriage according to the demands of nature than to consign oneself to continual burning lusts. . . .

At the same time Paul responds to a third question, namely, that second marriages are permitted. For he grants that widows may marry a second time. Therefore Tertullian and others who condemn second marriages are seriously deluded on this matter, and their teachings contradict the Holy Spirit. From this passage, people usually conclude that Paul had a wife previously, but when she died, he had remained a widower so that he could serve the kingdom of Christ without hindrance. They base this conclusion on the fact that Paul, in this passage, lists himself along with the widows and wants other people to imitate him. Explication on 1 Corinthians 7:8-9.[29]

Paul Gives One Primary Reason for Marriage. Martin Luther: Here St. Paul has piled all the reasons for marrying in one heap and set the goal for all chastity when he says: "But if they cannot exercise self-control, they should marry." This is as much to say: Necessity orders that you marry. . . . There are many other reasons why people marry. Some marry for money and property. Many people marry because of sheer immaturity, to seek sensual pleasure and satisfy it. Some marry to beget heirs. But St. Paul gives but this one reason, and I know of none fundamentally stronger and better, namely, need. Need commands it. Nature will express itself, fructify and multiply, and God does not want this outside of marriage, and so everyone because of this need must enter into marriage if he wants to live with a good conscience and in favor with God. If this need were not there, all the other reasons taken together would make very poor marriages. This is particularly true of that smart immaturity which leads fools to take lightly such a serious, needful, godly estate; but it is not long until they realize what they have done to themselves. . . . Truly it can be said: for every chaste person there should be more than a hundred thousand married people. Commentary on 1 Corinthians 7:9.[30]

The Meaning of "Burning." John Calvin: Nevertheless, we must define what is meant by "burning," for many people are stung by their fleshly desires, who nevertheless do not immediately need to find recourse in marriage. And in order to retain Paul's metaphor, it is one thing to burn, and another to feel the heat. Hence, what Paul here calls "burning" is not a mere titillation, but a boiling with lust that you can't resist. Yet since there are some people who flatter themselves in vain by thinking that they are absolved from all blame if they do not give into impure desire, we should make note of three levels of temptation. First, sometimes the assaults of impure desire are so strong that the will is overcome. This is the worst kind of burning, when the heart is aflame with lust. Second, sometimes we are pricked by the sting of the flesh so that we fight back vigorously; we do not allow the true love of sexual purity to be driven away from us, but rather we abhor all disgraceful and filthy desires. Hence, all people must be warned, and especially young people, that whenever they are assailed by their fleshly desires, they should oppose temptations of this sort by means of the fear of God, destroy every opportunity for unchaste thoughts, pray that God will give them the strength to resist, and apply themselves with all their might to extinguish the flames of lust. . . . Third, between these two levels there is a kind of temptation when persons do not indeed give full assent of their minds to lust, but yet burn with a blind passion, and are harassed in such a way that they are not able to call on God with a peaceful conscience. Such a temptation, therefore, which impedes a pure invocation of God and disturbs the

[29]Hesshus, *Explicatio Prioris Epistolae ad Corinthios*, 104r-v. The Latin church father Tertullian condemned the remarriage of widows, describing it as serial polygamy. See his treatises *De exhortatione castitatis* and *De monogamia*, found in ANF 4:50-58, 59-73, as well as two letters on the subject to his wife, at ANF 4:39-49.

[30]LW 28:26, 27, 28.

peacefulness of conscience, is a burning that cannot be extinguished except by marriage. Commentary on 1 Corinthians 7:9.[31]

Marriage as a Remedy for Burning. The English Annotations: Some interpret this "burning" to refer to the burning of hellfire for those who are incontinent, and no question the apostle's words are true in that sense. But because Paul does not specify this "burning" as either hellfire or eternal, nor does the biblical context look that way, the natural interpretation of the text seems to be this: It is better to marry than to burn with lust by forcing ourselves to live a single life, when we do not have the gift of continence. For either the will yields to the temptation of lust, or else we cannot call on God with a good conscience. Persons are not said to burn that feel the heat of the fire, for in that case even the most continent persons might be said to burn. Rather, Paul is speaking of persons who are singed and scorched thereby, who are so assaulted with the temptation of lust that they are in some way wounded and hurt in conscience. Annotations on 1 Corinthians 7:9.[32]

Marriage as Medicine for Lust. John Trapp: There is no lust so hot and violent that God's medicines rightly applied will not cool and heal them. Only remember that it is not the having—but the loving—of a wife that keeps a man chaste and clean. Commentary on 1 Corinthians 7:9.[33]

7:10-16 *Marriage, Divorce, and Mixed Marriages*

Honoring Marriage. Guillaume Farel: All of you who do not have the special gift (given only to a few) to control your heart, action, and will, take up this holy and honorable state [of marriage]. Enter into it in all fear of God. Use his holy institution for his honor and glory, and for the edification of your neighbor. Persevere in this state, fleeing all the separations that humans have invented. For as long as the wife is his wife and the husband her husband, the marriage cannot be broken or separated, except for the reason of adultery alone when the wife breaks faithfulness and loyalty promised to her husband.

Such is holy marriage that if one of the partners is a believer, she can live with the partner who is not a believer, as the unbeliever can remain with his believing partner. This does not block the good of marriage; it is still according to God, and the children are also holy and good as if both parents were believers. But all this has been trampled underfoot to slander and dishonor holy marriage, which our Lord wants to put back in its rightful place and to honor as he instituted it. Summary and Brief Exposition.[34]

Rules for Divorce and Separation. David Dickson: The second thing that the Corinthians inquire about relates to divorce, and they raise two questions. The first question deals with two believers: is it lawful for married Christians to divorce one another, unless adultery has occurred? Paul answers that it is not lawful; he states that his prohibition is not anything new, nor has it come from special revelation, but he is repeating an old command made by the authority of the Lord, who in the institution of marriage established that married persons should be one flesh, and therefore separation and divorce is not lawful.

But if the wife (claiming a necessary cause for separation, such as the endangerment of life) does depart, Paul commands either that she be reconciled to her husband or that she abstain from a new marriage (and thus from fornication).... In the meantime, Paul commands the husband not to put his wife away, or give her cause to depart.

The second question that Paul addresses deals with married persons where one is an unbeliever. Is divorce lawful for them? Paul says that he will

[31]CO 49:408-9 (cf. CTS 49:236-37).
[32]Downame, *English Annotations*, DD3r*.
[33]Trapp, *A Commentary or Exposition*, 673*.
[34]In Zuidema and Van Raalte, *Early French Reform*, 170.

answer this question from the authority of special revelation, because God has not stated in his law what Christians should do in that case. . . . First, Paul forbids the Christian man from putting away his unbelieving spouse, if she does not desire to leave him. . . . Second, if the unbelieving party will not remain in the marriage, Paul declares in this case that the marriage is void and the believer is free. Exposition of 1 Corinthians 7:10-15.[35]

Hatred Is Grounds for Divorce. Martin Luther: Here the apostle concedes that husband and wife may separate, provided that they do not marry again. In so doing he repeals the law of Moses according to which the man could send away his wife if he were displeased with her or tired of her and take another. And she, too, could take another, according to Deuteronomy 24:1-4. Now although Moses gave such a law to the Jews, to people who were hardheaded and heathenish, still such actions are not fitting for a Christian, and therefore Christ himself revoked it in Matthew 19:8-9. . . .

The apostle refers to one cause of divorce: anger—when a man and his wife cannot live together in harmony but only hatred and dispute, so that they can neither pray nor do any other good work. The text clearly states this by admonishing them either to be reconciled and not separate or to live without marriage if they cannot be reconciled and wish to separate. Where reconciliation is recommended, there anger and disharmony are indicated. The apostle certainly permits such separations by being lenient over against weaknesses of Christians when two people simply cannot get along together. In all other cases everyone is obligated to carry the burden of the other and not to separate from him. Commentary on 1 Corinthians 7:10-11.[36]

Adultery Only Grounds for Divorce. Philipp Melanchthon: Except for the case of adultery it is never lawful for a spouse to separate from a spouse. One can separate from an adulterer, as Matthew 19 shows. But the question remains: Whether it is lawful afterward for the other partner to marry? I answer: Unless it is lawful to remarry, it is not divorce. But what about Paul, who here commands her to remain unwed? I answer: Since Paul is not thinking about cases of adultery, he seems to be speaking only to cases aside from adultery. For the Gentiles and Jews repudiated their wives for any reason at all. Annotations on 1 Corinthians 7:10-11.[37]

Legitimate Reasons for Separation. Wolfgang Musculus: Even in legitimate marriages, there are some exceptional cases when separation from one's spouse is permissible. Although Paul states that "the wife should not separate from her husband, and the husband should not send away his wife," there are some occasions when it is permissible to do what is here prohibited. First, when the profanation of the marriage oath occurs through adultery. In this case, certainly, it is not only permissible for innocent partners to send away their adulterous spouses, but they would be judged foolish if they continued to live with them. Wherefore, in Proverbs 18 we read: "He who clings to an adulteress is foolish and unwise." The example of Joseph in Matthew 1 is well-known; because he was a righteous man, though he did not reckon to expose Mary's offense in public, nevertheless he decided that he should be separated from her.

Second, if the man is incurably impotent from birth so that he is not able to perform as a husband and so does not consummate the marriage, surely in this case it will be permissible for the wife to separate from him.

Moreover, if the husband either forces his wife to commit idolatry or clearly plots against the life of his wife, it will be permissible for the faithful and innocent spouse to be separated from him. And the apostle himself adds a religious reason

[35]Dickson, *Exposition of St. Paul's Epistles*, 51*.
[36]LW 28:31, 32.
[37]Melanchthon, *Annotationes in Epistolam priorem ad Corinthios*, 94; citing Mt 19:3-9.

when it is permissible for a wife to separate from her husband. So too, in Matthew 5 and 19, Christ makes an exception in the case of adultery. So then, what the apostle states here must be understood to refer to those various cases (which one cannot fully enumerate) concerning the separation of spouses that dissolve the bonds of marriage and separate those whom God has conjoined. Commentary on 1 Corinthians 7:10.[38]

Separation and Divorce. Wolfgang Musculus: This passage is cited by people who contend that it is completely illicit for spouses who separate from their lawful husbands or wives with whom they previously lived to marry a second time. Paul approves of divorce in the church in certain cases, they say, but thereafter both parties must remain either unmarried or be reconciled. And for this purpose they apply the words of Christ in Matthew 5 and 19, where the man who divorces his wife and the man who marries a divorced woman are condemned for adultery. We respond as follows: Neither Christ nor Paul is speaking about divorce that has been undertaken for the sake of adultery. Rather Christ spoke in this way because the Jews were saying that divorce was permissible for any reason whatsoever, arguing from both the tradition of the Jews and the law of Moses. Their question indicates this, when they were asking: "Is it lawful to divorce one's wife for any cause?" (Mt 19:3). The apostle here is also speaking about the sort of divorce that occurs on account of disagreement and enmity, as is plain from his statement, "or be reconciled to her husband."

Now in these passages Christ and Paul were not addressing a different kind of divorce, which was then practiced by both the Gentiles and the Jews, where spouses separated in such a way that they were permitted to remarry. Christ was also very much mindful of this kind of divorce: he addressed it and rejected it, except in cases where adultery had occurred. The sort of divorce recently invented by the popes, where neither the husband nor wife is given the freedom to remarry when the marriage ends because of adultery, reflects neither the custom of the Gentiles nor the Jews. This kind of "papal divorce" is a divorce more in name than in fact. Commentary on 1 Corinthians 7:11.[39]

Paul Distinguishes His Words from God's Words. Huldrych Zwingli: "But to the rest I say (I, not the Lord). . . ." The apostle states that the Lord is speaking when he teaches what is clearly stated in God's Word and law. Now Paul says that he himself is giving these instructions that, even if they are not explicitly stated by the Lord, are nevertheless dictated by faith and suggested by charity. So Paul acts with fear and reverence in all things, and thus in good faith he seeks the counsel given by the Spirit. Since these instructions [here in this passage] were not commanded by God, Paul says that they are his own words, not God's, so as to prevent his words—no matter how good—from being mistaken for God's words. For we should not mix or spoil divine commands with human instructions, nor should we force our opinions on other people as if they were God's. Annotations on 1 Corinthians 7:12.[40]

Marriage to an Unbeliever. Martin Luther: Because St. Paul here bears witness that these words are not from the Lord but from himself, he indicates that these things are not commanded by God but are left to the individual to choose in one way or another. For he distinguishes his own words from the word of the Lord, that the Lord's word is to be a commandment, but his own words advice. . . .

This is what St. Paul means when he says, "and she consents to live with him," etc., that is, if the non-Christian is content and willing to stay with the Christian spouse and allows him to do all things proper to a Christian. For marriage is an

[38]Musculus, *Comm. 1 Cor.*, 195; citing Prov 18:22 (LXX); Mt 1:19. For text-critical discussion, see Michael V. Fox, *Proverbs 10–31*, Anchor Bible 18b (New Haven, CT: Yale University Press, 2009), 1020.

[39]Musculus, *Comm. 1 Cor.*, 196.

[40]Zwingli, *Annotatiunculae . . . ex ore Zvinglij*, 55-56.

outward, physical thing that neither promotes nor hinders faith, and the one partner may well be a Christian and the other non-Christian, just as a Christian may eat with a heathen, Jew, or Turk, or drink, buy from them, and have all ordinary commerce with them. In the same way one marriage partner may now be a true devout Christian and the other an evil false Christian; still it is not necessary to dissolve the marriage because of piety or malice.

But if the non-Christian should not let his spouse be a Christian and live a Christian life and should hinder and persecute him, then it would be time to keep these words of Christ also physically: "He who loves wife or child more than me is not worthy of me" (Mt 10:37). Then divorce is in order; but once the divorce is effected, then there must either be reconciliation or that partner must remain unmarried who will not be reconciled, while the other is permitted to change his status. Commentary on 1 Corinthians 7:12-13.[41]

A Believer Must Never Marry an Unbeliever. Dirk Philips: Our adversaries allege that Paul permitted to the Corinthians that a believer may live with an unbeliever as long as the unbeliever consents to live with the believer in peace, that is, that the conscience of the believer remains clear (1 Cor 7:12-13), and that the unbeliever is sanctified through the believer. Hereby they want to compare it to a situation where a Christian brother or sister takes an unbeliever and unites with them—that the unbeliever and Christian will both be sanctified at that time when the Christian recognizes their apostasy and stubbornness against the Word of God and the congregation, shows sorrow, and promises improvement. We oppose this as a false basis and argue that the evidence and proof shows that the apostle was writing about a different situation, namely: If two persons, a man and woman, in the time of ignorance and unbelief had come together, promised each other to marry, and had lived together as married persons with each other, that these, on account of the gospel and faith, shall not separate nor break the promise they had made the one to the other (although in unbelief), still always with the aforementioned condition. But that anyone who lets themselves be called brother or sister in the congregation of the Lord accepts an unbelieving person in the world, that is far from the apostle Paul's original word and meaning. For what happens in ignorance, that God accounts to ignorance. But when the acknowledged and accepted truth is thereafter mishandled and stubbornly sinned against, that is an abomination before him. We think that no one is so ignorant that they do not understand and know this. About the Marriage of Christians.[42]

Living with a Nonbeliever. David Joris: Paul says: "This I say, not the Lord" (1 Cor 7:12). This is always regarded as less than what the Holy Spirit thinks fit to do at the time, and has therefore perished. It stands inferior to the greater. Do not think to follow your own spirit. Do not aim at your own will or knowledge. But see what is said here. . . . For this reason, I say that what was the good advice of Paul was not a command of the Lord in this matter. It was, however, good for the situation at the time. Why? Paul laid the foundation, Christ, as a wise carpenter. No one lays this in any other way, nor can preach another gospel than what was preached there (1 Cor 3:10-11). . . .

Furthermore, I mentioned before that Paul said that they were still fleshly children in understanding. They lived in much fornication and whoredom. Against them Paul had the wisdom to proceed with them, as is written, namely, as with unspiritual people (1 Cor 3:1-3). . . . For this reason it was good and needful for edification at that time, but not now. But Paul permitted it. . . . Understand that this did not mean the believer with the unbeliever, for the unbeliever would rule or command or forbid what is proper, holy, or edifying for the believer (1 Cor 7:12-13). No, not in this way. Therefore watch what you are opposing

[41]LW 28:33-34.

[42]CRR 6:570-71*.

and what it is that you are commanding. But practice modesty according to the time. Behold. Response to Hans Eisenburg.[43]

Living with Unbelieving Relatives. Martin Bucer: If anyone has relatives living with them who have been excluded from the church of God, so that they have a non-Christian spouse, parents, child, or some other relative, no believer can avoid such in eating, drinking, or other outward activities; rather the believing spouse is to behave and show themselves toward the unbelieving partner in the whole relationship of marriage, which is the highest of all human activities, in the friendliest way, so that they will be more likely to win their unbelieving spouse to the Lord (1 Cor 7). In the same way everyone is to behave toward their relations in all the various blood and family relationships. What God has joined together in this or other callings, let no one put asunder. True Care of Souls.[44]

Faithful Christians Won't Be Harmed by Non-Christian Spouses. Martin Luther: This is spoken in the Hebrew way and according to the manner of St. Paul, to the effect that all things are holy to the one who is holy. Thus he says in Titus 1:15: "To the pure all things are pure"; or in Romans 8:28: "We know that in everything God works for good with those who love him," which is to say: A Christian spouse may not be divorced but can live with a non-Christian mate and even conceive and raise non-Christian children. The reason is this: if the non-Christian spouse does not prevent the Christian mate from leading a Christian life, then faith is such a mighty thing that no hurt will come from living with a non-Christian; it will make no difference whether he associates with religious or irreligious people, for even death, that most terrible thing of all, is still a holy thing for a Christian. Commentary on 1 Corinthians 7:14.[45]

[43]CRR 8:165*.
[44]Bucer, *Concerning the True Care of Souls*, 187*.
[45]LW 28:34-35.

Unbelieving Husbands Are Sanctified by Their Believing Wives. Huldrych Zwingli: "For the unbelieving husband is sanctified by his wife." There are two possible meanings. First, it could happen that through daily interaction the unbelieving husband might be persuaded by the believing wife to convert to the faith. With this hope in view, the wife shall not separate from her husband. The second meaning is that the unbeliever is sanctified, that is, he is counted as part of the family and people of God, so long as the other spouse embraces the faith. On account of this, their children are also sanctified, that is, counted as part of the people of God, for the offspring follow the better half. Thus, as far as believers are concerned, all are equal in the old and new covenants. But for those who are not believers, things are not the same: for in the new covenant the wife is equal to the husband, but not in the old covenant, so that the gift of grace might everywhere abound.

"Your children are holy." If one spouse were to separate from the other, the children given to the unbelieving spouse would be unclean, that is, outside the church of God. . . . But if the believer remains with the unbelieving spouse, then the children are counted as part of the church of God. Annotations on 1 Corinthians 7:14.[46]

Marriage Is Not a Sacrament. Wolfgang Musculus: Some people who defend the view that there are seven sacraments in the church and attempt to prove this from the Scripture seize on this present passage to defend the sacrament of marriage. They ask why the unbelieving husband is sanctified and the children of such a marriage deemed holy, unless marriage is a sacrament? But those people should recognize that the matter under debate is not regarding the nature of the mysteries, but concerning the sacraments of the church and the new covenant. If marriage is a sacrament of the new covenant, they must acknowledge either that it was not a legitimate

[46]Zwingli, *Annotatiunculae . . . ex ore Zvinglij*, 56-57.

sacrament before the time of the new covenant, or (if they don't grant this) that pagans and unbelievers partake with us in the sacraments of the church. Second, these people should explain how the definition of a sacrament, which they draw from the theologian Augustine, is applicable to marriage. For Augustine says: "A sacrament consists of a word conjoined to a [physical] element." By "word" he understands the promise and words of institution of Christ made visible through the physical elements, which are the likeness of the thing signified, as is seen in baptism and the Eucharist. Commentary on 1 Corinthians 7:14.[47]

Children of Believers Are Made Holy from the Womb. John Calvin: This is an argument from effect: "If your marriage were unclean, then the children born of your union would also be unclean; but they are holy. Therefore your marriage is also holy. Therefore, just as the ungodliness of one parent does not prevent the children from being born holy, so it does not prevent the marriage from being pure." Some interpreters explain this passage as referring to civil sanctification, whereby the children are considered to be legitimate under law. But the same thing could be said of the condition of unbelievers. Therefore that explanation cannot be correct. Moreover, it is certain that Paul here wished to ease troubled consciences, so that people would not think that they incur defilement, as I have already said. Therefore this passage is a remarkable one, drawn from the most profound theology. For Paul teaches that the children of godly parents are set apart from other children by a certain privilege, so as to be reckoned holy in the church.

But how is this sentence consistent with what Paul teaches in Ephesians 2:3, that "we are all by nature sons of wrath"? Or with the statement of David: "Behold, I was conceived in sin," etc. (Ps 51:7)? I answer that there is a universal propagation of sin and condemnation through the seed of Adam. Every single person, therefore, is included under this curse, whether they are the offspring of believers or the ungodly. And believers do not give birth to children according to the flesh in such a way that they are regenerated by the Holy Spirit. Therefore all human beings are in the same natural condition, so that they are subject to sin and eternal death. But the fact that the apostle attributes here a special privilege to the children of believers derives from the blessing of the covenant, by which the curse of nature is overcome; and those who were by nature unholy are consecrated to God by grace. For this reason, Paul argues in Romans 11:16 that all of Abraham's descendants are holy, because God has made a covenant of life with them. "If the root is holy," he says, "so too are the branches." And God calls all who descended from Israel his sons. Now that the dividing wall has been broken down, the same covenant of salvation that was initiated with the seed of Abraham is imparted to us. But if the children of believers are exempt from the common destiny of human beings so as to be set apart to the Lord, why should we prevent them from receiving the sign [of the covenant]? If the Lord admits them to his church by his Word, why should we refuse them the sign? Commentary on 1 Corinthians 7:14.[48]

Children of Believers Are Not Made Holy from the Womb. Tilemann Hesshus: Paul says that the unbelieving husband is made holy by his believing wife. One should not understand sanctification in this passage to refer to the reconciliation and renovation that comes through the Holy Spirit. The unbeliever is not made holy by the believing spouse in this sense, for "the righteous lives by his faith," and "on that day, there will be two people in one bed, one will be taken and the other left behind" (Lk 17:34). Therefore one must understand these phrases to refer to legal or civil sanctification. . . . For it is permissible for a believer, without harm to his or her conscience, to live with an unbeliever; the

[47]Musculus, *Comm. 1 Cor.*, 204.

[48]CO 49:412-13 (cf. CTS 39:243). The "sign of the covenant" that Calvin speaks of here is the sacrament of baptism.

believer need not fear and is not defiled by the unbeliever. All things are pure for those who are pure. And all created things are sanctified for believers through the Word and prayer, which is the legitimate and holy use of these things.

Paul proves this statement by an argument from effect: since the children of those who differ regarding religion are made holy by their marriage. If the marriage were impure on account of differences in religion, then the children would be unclean, that is, illegitimate. But Paul considers the children as holy, or legitimately born; therefore such a marriage is legitimate and holy. It is clear in this passage, therefore, what Paul is calling permissible, legitimate, pure, lawful [is the marriage of a believer and an unbeliever].... John Calvin violently misconstrues this statement of Paul, since he interprets it to refer to spiritual sanctification and the removing of the curse. And he argues that the children of believers are made holy from the womb, that is, exempt from the curse, because they possess a unique privilege as children of saints, based on the promise "I will be God to their seed." But this interpretation is very far from Paul's intention, and does not accord with the analogy of faith. For the whole of sacred Scripture testifies that all children of both the saints and the wicked are born slaves to sin and under the curse of the law. "We were all by nature sons of wrath"; and John 3: "Unless a person has been born anew from water and Spirit, he cannot enter the kingdom of God." And John the Baptist says: "Do not say, 'We have Abraham as our father.' For God is able to awaken from these rocks sons of Abraham." Again, "... those who were born, not of blood, nor of the will of the flesh, nor of the will of a husband, but of God." And David, though born of very holy parents, said of himself: "Behold, I was brought forth in iniquity and in sins my mother conceived me." Therefore Paul does not intend by this promise "I will be your God and the God of your seed" that the children of saints are made holy from the womb. Explication of 1 Corinthians 7:14.[49]

The Children of Believers Belong to God's Covenant and Should Be Baptized. Theodore Beza: Paul concludes ... that the marriage union of a believer and unbeliever is also holy because children born from this union are judged to be in the covenant of God—the argument here is drawn from the effects to the cause. But what if someone should deny this? Or rather, no one can deny it, since it corresponds to the [divine] promise in which the seed is also included. And there is no other reason why we should admit the children of saints to baptism than because they are holy, that is, included in the covenant from the time they are in the womb—this much, indeed, we are able to conclude and determine from what God has revealed from his hidden judgment. This passage not only refutes the Anabaptists, who reject infants from baptism as unclean, but also those who consider baptism the doorway to salvation, and then exclude from salvation all who have not been baptized, even when no contempt for baptism is present. So too this passage refutes those people (whoever they may be) who have invented the case of "absolute necessity" (as they call it), which is a terrible abuse of baptism, as well as those who admit all infants to baptism indiscriminately—a practice never done and unheard of throughout the entire ancient church. In any event, this passage shows that it is necessary for all unbelieving adults to first be catechumens before being baptized. Annotations on 1 Corinthians 7:14.[50]

The Catholic Church Falsely Uses This Verse to Justify Infant Baptism. Anabaptists of Trieste: All human flesh has a sinful inclination and desire for what is wrong, but whoever has Christ's Spirit does not perform the

[49]Hesshus, *Explicatio Prioris Epistolae ad Corinthios*, 106r-107r; citing Eph 2:3; Jn 3:5; Lk 3:8; Jn 1:13; Ps 51:5.

[50]Beza, *Annotationes Maiores*, 189; referring to Gen. 17:7. According to Catholic canon law and Lutheran custom, emergency baptisms (i.e., baptisms of "absolute necessity") could be performed outside of the church by clergy or laity when a newborn infant's life was in jeopardy. The practice of emergency baptisms was rejected by most Reformed churches.

works of the flesh. Children also enjoy this grace as Paul says: the unbelieving person is made holy through his believing wife otherwise, the children would be unclean. But now they are holy (1 Cor 7). Godly parents raise up, teach, and direct their children to godliness and do not allow them to nourish sin in their flesh. Rather, they bring them up in the fear and admonition of the Lord according to the command of God.

The Antichrist insists on washing the sin away with water, but this does not change them; the inclination is there as before and remains in them as long as they are on earth. But God does not charge those with sin who do not consent to it or do it, for it is written that God judges the thought. The inclination to sin that is not consented to in the heart is no sin before God. It is not living in sin but is sin resisted. The dear Paul in his gospel includes the children in grace and Christian righteousness.

The sum of the matter is that Antichrist has no Scripture, example, or command of God or his holy apostles, not a single letter of Scripture for the baptism and chrism of children and other invented rituals used with small children. [The Antichrist] wants to grant them salvation with magic, otherwise they would be unredeemed. It is as though only through him could the children receive grace and be justified. This is to mock the precious suffering of Christ. Confession.[51]

Children of Christian Parents Are Holy. The English Annotations: If the marriage were not to some degree sanctified, then children born from the marriage would not be comprised from birth within the covenant that God made with the fathers and their children (see Gen 17:7). Nor would these children be endued with the Spirit of sanctification, nor should the church hold them capable of baptism until grown up to the age when they might be received into the church on account of their own faith. But Paul says that they are now holy, that is, comprised in the outward covenant of God, having access and right to the signs and seals of his grace, and this is also the case for all those who are born of both believing parents. By "holy," then, Paul means sanctified to God in baptism, made members of the church and partakers of the grace of regeneration according to their measure and condition. Annotations on 1 Corinthians 7:14.[52]

Remarriage Permitted in Cases of Desertion. Tilemann Hesshus: Paul now instructs consciences on a second situation: If the unbelieving partner does not wish to live with the believing spouse on account of religion and he or she separates and dissolves the marriage, what then should be done by the believing and innocent spouse? Paul answers: the brother or sister in this situation "is not enslaved." It's as if he were saying: "believing partners are not thereby sacrificing religious devotion, and they shouldn't be fearful for their consciences, as if they were being held captive in this situation. For you are free. . . . Christ has claimed us as his own, and in no situation is it possible for believers to be snatched away. Therefore partners who have been deserted are not guilty, and if they need to remarry for the sake of their consciences, it is permissible for innocent and believing partners to contract another marriage." Paul thus announces that innocent spouses are free. But people who desert their spouses by their own decision should not assume that they are released and free to contract another marriage. Instead, they ought to seek forgiveness from the ecclesiastical consistory or the ministry or the civil magistrates. On the basis of Paul's principle, it is clear that ecclesiastical or political judges can in good conscience grant remarriage to innocent spouses who have been deserted, as long as those who deserted them defiantly violated the law. However, deserted and innocent spouses must wait for a time period defined by law [before remarriage]. Explication of 1 Corinthians 7:15.[53]

[51]CRR 10:265-66.

[52]Downame, *English Annotations*, DD3r-v*.

[53]Hesshus, *Explicatio Prioris Epistolae ad Corinthios*, 107r-v.

God Has Called Us to Peace. Martin Luther: We should live peaceably with one another. Therefore a Christian spouse should not quarrel with their non-Christian mate concerning belief or unbelief nor separate from their mate if that non-Christian mate permits them to lead a Christian life. Each one should leave the other to their faith and commend the whole matter to God. For no one can be driven or forced to believe; instead, God must draw them in grace, and we should teach, admonish, and supplicate, not force. And so a Christian spouse should conduct the outward forms of the married state peaceably with their non-Christian mate and not threaten or defy their partner either with running away or turning him away. For God is not a God of dissension but a God of peace. Commentary on 1 Corinthians 7:15.[54]

God Can Convert Unbelieving Spouses. John Calvin: In my opinion, this word of encouragement is drawn from the benefit to be gained, for it is a great and excellent blessing when a wife wins over her husband. Now unbelievers are not in so hopeless a condition that they cannot be brought to the faith. They are dead, it is true, but God is able to raise the dead. Therefore, as long as there remains some hope of progress, and the godly wife cannot tell but that she may, through her holy life, be able to bring her husband to the right path, she ought to try every means before leaving him. For as long as a person's salvation is uncertain, we ought to be all the more disposed toward optimism. However that may be, Paul's statement that the wife is able to save her husband is certainly incorrect, since he is ascribing to humans what properly belongs to God—but there is nothing absurd in this. For since God works efficaciously by means of the instruments he uses, he imparts his power to them to a certain extent, or, at least, he connects it with their ministry so that what is achieved, he says is done by them. And so God has sometimes ascribed to [human instruments] the honor that belongs to him alone. Let us remember, however, that we are able to do nothing on our own, except insofar as we are directed by him as instruments. Commentary 1 Corinthians 7:16.[55]

[54]LW 28:38*; citing 1 Cor 14:33.

[55]CO 49:413 (cf. CTS 39:244-45).

7:17-24 Live as You Are Called

17 Only let each person lead the life[a] that the Lord has
assigned to him, and to which God has called him.
This is my rule in all the churches. 18 Was anyone at
the time of his call already circumcised? Let him not
seek to remove the marks of circumcision. Was
anyone at the time of his call uncircumcised? Let him
not seek circumcision. 19 For neither circumcision
counts for anything nor uncircumcision, but keeping
the commandments of God. 20 Each one should
remain in the condition in which he was called.
21 Were you a bondservant when called? Do not be
concerned about it. (But if you can gain your freedom,
avail yourself of the opportunity.) 22 For he who was
called in the Lord as a bondservant is a freedman of
the Lord. Likewise he who was free when called is a
bondservant of Christ. 23 You were bought with a
price; do not become bondservants of men. 24 So,
brothers,[b] in whatever condition each was called,
there let him remain with God.

a Or *each person walk in the way* **b** Or *brothers and sisters*

Overview: Having established the principle that the gospel does not require Christian converts to change their marital status, Paul now applies this same principle to circumcision and human servitude: as a general rule, Christians should remain in the state to which God has called them. Reformation commentators construct a rich theology of vocation on the basis of these verses. God has assigned to each Christian an order and manner of living in the world for the purpose of bringing glory to God and serving the common good. This calling encompasses family roles (e.g., husband-wife, father-mother, parent-child), human occupations (e.g., magistrate, minister, tailor, farmer, servant), and even place of residence. Calling is the domain in which Christian men and women daily express their faith in Christ and live out their discipleship. Most commentators acknowledge that, under certain circumstances, God permits Christians to change their occupations or residence; yet, at the same time, they emphasize that Christians must beware of the common impulse to abandon their God-given responsibilities because of troubles and dangers or out of idleness and sloth. In treating the subject of circumcision and servitude, the interpreters agree that these human conditions are external and do not render a person holy or unholy, nor are they hindrances to Christian faith. Faith makes everyone equal before God.

7:17 *Being Faithful to God's Calling*

Living with Diversity in the Church. John Colet: Among the Corinthians, therefore, since there was great diversity and difference of persons—some celibate, others married; some virgins, others widows; some of them circumcised, others uncircumcised; some masters, others slaves—Paul recommends peace and tranquility as a general rule, urging that no one become agitated and change their position, but that everyone, according to their calling, walk in the role and quality in which they have been called. For God is no respecter of persons. Indeed, there is only one person who pleases him, and that is the person of Christ; and through the person of Christ he is building up for himself every sort of person without discrimination, until at last Christ is fully perfected in them.

In his great wisdom, then, Paul wishes that everyone remain in that place and persevere in that position to which they have been called: Jews, Gentiles, masters, slaves, virgins, married persons; not looking down their noses at the differences between people, which are nothing, but upholding and pledging all obedience to the one person of Christ, so that, once all the former differences have been abolished, everyone might put on the new and single and pure form of Christ. Then, coming together in renewal of spirit and in newness of person, they might be united in love, with no remembrance ever again of that former difference that was the chief cause of people's being at variance and in disagreement. Exposition of 1 Corinthians 7.[1]

Christians Are Free in Christ. Huldrych Zwingli: "Each person should continue in his own vocation." If a Gentile comes to you, it is not necessary for him to be circumcised. If a Jew comes to you, he does not need to be uncircumcised. A servant should not be dissatisfied with his position and condition, for his status means nothing to God; indeed, he is God's freedman. For even though he serves his master according to the flesh, nevertheless in his mind and conscience he is free. Paul says these things to console [the Corinthians], not to defend those people who promote a false religion of sects and factions. On the contrary, people who are called free are not at all superior in this respect, for, with their flesh already conquered, they ought to be dead in Christ, so that they live for Christ and not themselves. Annotations on 1 Corinthians 7:17.[2]

Faith Renders All Human Estates Blessed. Martin Luther: This verse concludes the part dealing with the state of matrimony. Its meaning is this: Faith and the Christian life are so free in essence that they are bound to no particular order or estate of society, but they are to be found in and throughout all orders and estates. Therefore you need not accept or give up any particular estate in order to be saved. On the contrary, the estate in which faith and the gospel find you, there you may stay and find your salvation. Therefore it is not necessary that you give up marriage and leave your non-Christian spouse for the sake of your faith or salvation. On the other hand, it is not necessary for you to be married, either to a Christian or a non-Christian spouse, for the sake of faith or salvation. And finally, if you are married, whether to a Christian or non-Christian, a virtuous or evil mate, you are not on that account either saved or condemned. All this is free, free. But if you are a Christian and remain one, then you will be saved; and if you remain unchristian, then you will be condemned. . . .

You see from this that St. Paul considers no single estate blessed except this one—the estate of being a Christian; the others are free in the sense that they cannot in themselves further our salvation or damnation. All of them, however, can become blessed through faith or damnable through unbelief, even though in themselves they be well maintained. Commentary on 1 Corinthians 7:17.[3]

We Must Not Transgress the Limits of Our Calling. John Calvin: The Lord bids each one of us in all life's actions to look to his calling. For he knows with what great restlessness human nature flames, with what fickleness it is borne hither and thither, how its ambition longs to embrace various things at once. Therefore lest through our stupidity and rashness everything be turned topsy-turvy, he has appointed duties for every person in his or her particular way of life. And that no one may thoughtlessly transgress their limits, he has named these various kinds of living "callings." Therefore each individual has their own post so that they may not heedlessly wander about throughout life. Institutes.[4]

Callings Are Great Gifts of God. Martin Luther: Age, sex, and callings differ greatly in this life. One teaches the church; another serves the government; still another instructs the youth; a mother busies herself with the care and upbringing of children; and the husband is concerned with providing an honest living. In the opinion of the world these are not very grand and impressive works. But if you look at the Word, that heavenly adornment and divine glory, why should you not

[1]Colet, *Enarratio*, 198; citing Acts 10:34.
[2]Zwingli, *Annotatiunculae . . . ex ore Zvinglij*, 57.
[3]LW 28:39-40.
[4]LCC: 20:724; cf. *Institutes*, 3.10.6.

act proudly over against Satan, and why should you not give thanks to God for such great gifts? For these are not bare works; they are adorned with the Word of God, since they have been enjoined on you by God. Lectures on Genesis 13:14-15.[5]

God Is the Author and Source of Every Calling. William Perkins: Now in every calling we must consider two causes: first, the efficient and author thereof; second, the final and proper end. The author of every calling is God himself: and therefore Paul says, "As God has called every person, let them walk" (v. 17). And for this reason, the order and manner of living in this world is called a vocation, because everyone is to live as he or she is called of God. . . . In a clock made by human art and handiwork there are many wheels, and each one has its several motions—some turn this way, some that way, some go softly, some apace, and they are all ordered by the motion of the watch. This is a notable likeness to God's special providence over humankind, which is the watch of the great world, allotting to all persons their motion and calling, and in those callings their particular office and function. Therefore it is true when I say that God himself is the author and beginning of callings. This overthrows the ungodly opinion of those who think that the particular condition and state of people in this life comes by chance, or by the bare will and pleasure of people themselves. . . .

The final cause or end of every calling I note in the last words of this description, "for the common good," that is, for the benefit and good estate of humankind. In everyone's body there are various parts and members, and each has its particular use and office, which it performs not for itself but for the good of the whole body; as the office of the eye is to see, of the ear to hear and the foot to go. Now all human societies are bodies. A family is a body, and so is every particular church a body and so too the commonwealth: and in these bodies there are several members who are people walking in various callings and offices, the execution of which must tend to the happy and good estate of the rest, indeed, of everyone, everywhere, as much as it is possible .

The common good of human beings stands in this: not only that they live but also that they live well, in righteousness and holiness and consequently in true happiness. And to attain this, God has ordained and disposed all callings, and in his providence designed persons to bear them. A Treatise of the Vocations of Men.[6]

Remaining Content in Our Station of Life. John Trapp: Even if you cannot save your spouse, still keep your station; be content with your condition in life and adorn it (1 Pet 3:1-2). It is the duty of a Christian, Luther said, to believe things invisible, to hope for things deferred, and to love God when he shows himself contrary to us. Commentary on 1 Corinthians 7:17.[7]

Paul Gives the Same Rule for All the Churches. John Calvin: I think Paul has added this phrase "and thus in all the churches" in order to counteract the calumnies of certain people who were alleging that he was asserting more authority for himself among the Corinthians than he dared among other people. However, it might be possible to see a different purpose, namely, that this teaching might carry greater weight when the Corinthians understood that it had already been publicized among all the churches. For we more easily embrace what we are told we share with all godly people. The Corinthians, on the other hand, would have found it annoying to be bound with a tighter chain than other people. Commentary on 1 Corinthians 7:17.[8]

7:18-20 *The Condition of Circumcised or Uncircumcised*

Christians Live by Faith and Love. Martin Luther: But here the Jews might say to Paul: "You say that circumcision is nothing, but

[5]LW 2:356.

[6]Perkins, *The Works of William Perkins*, 447-49*.
[7]Trapp, *A Commentary or Exposition*, 674*.
[8]CO 49:414 (cf. CTS 39:246).

only keeping God's commandments. Now circumcision has been strictly commanded to us by God; how could it then be nothing?" . . . Briefly, all the laws in the book of Moses were given until Christ should come; when he came, he was to teach and bring faith and love. Where these are, there all the commandments are fulfilled and annulled and set free, so that after the coming of Christ no more commandments are needed, except those of faith and love. If love commands it, then I should be circumcised; if not, then I should let it be. When love demands anger, then I should get angry; when it does not, I should forget it. When love demands an oath, then I should swear an oath; when it does not, then I should not. And so one is to deal with regard to all the commandments of God and men. COMMENTARY ON 1 CORINTHIANS 7:19.[9]

THE REQUIREMENT OF CIRCUMCISION ABOLISHED BY CHRIST. JOHN CALVIN: Since this was one of the commandments, so long as the church was bound to ceremonies of the law, we see that it is taken for granted that circumcision was abolished with the coming of Christ. Consequently the ignorant and weak were permitted to use it, but there was absolutely no benefit from it. For Paul speaks of it here as being of no significance. It is as if he were saying: "Since these are outward things, do not let them get in your way. Instead devote yourself to godliness and to the duties that God requires, which is the only thing he cares about."

But it is childish for the papists to allege this passage to destroy justification by faith. For Paul here is not discussing the grounds of righteousness, or how we might attain it, but only the effort with which believers should apply themselves. It is as if he were saying: "Do not waste your energy on worthless things, but instead keep busy with your responsibilities, which is pleasing to God." COMMENTARY ON 1 CORINTHIANS 7:19.[10]

KEEPING GOD'S COMMANDMENTS IS MORE IMPORTANT THAN EXTERNAL CEREMONIES. TILEMANN HESSHUS: Paul now applies this general principle to specific cases, namely, that persons should not be concerned whether they were called in a state of uncircumcision or circumcision. "If anyone," he says, "was circumcised when he was called, he should not seek to be uncircumcised." He should not think that he would be more suitable for the kingdom of God or better able to gain the benefits of Christ if he were a Gentile. The Jew should remain a Jew; he should not take on Gentile customs. On the other hand, Gentiles should not think they would have better access to the kingdom of God if they were circumcised. Rather, they should remain in their condition and estate and strenuously pursue godliness. "For neither circumcision nor uncircumcision counts for anything." That is, such things neither help nor hinder people from reaching the kingdom of God. For the kingdom of God does not consist in external ceremonies like these, but in "keeping the commandments of God." I understand this to mean the whole of apostolic teaching, not merely the legal requirements of the Ten Commandments. For the commandments of God are, first, "Turn to me and I will turn to you." And, "Here is my beloved Son, listen to him." Those who obey these divine commandments are suitable for the kingdom of heaven and participants by faith in all of his benefits. Therefore those external things should not be of great concern to us; rather we should work strenuously to fulfill the divine will. EXPLICATION OF 1 CORINTHIANS 7:18-19.[11]

PEOPLE USE THE IDEA OF CALLING TO DISOBEY CHRIST. HANS DENCK: Woe, woe, thrice woe on those perverse people who know the mind of their Lord yet do not do it and who still want to be justified. Oh, it shall be far more unbearable for them than for those from whom it was partly hidden. Is it not shame upon shame that we desire

[9]LW 28:42.
[10]CO 49:415 (cf. CTS 39:247-48).
[11]Hesshus, *Explicatio Prioris Epistolae ad Corinthios*, 110r-v; citing Mal 3:7; Mt 17:5.

to know Christ yet hold on to our godless nature nonetheless? We even excuse ourselves with the saying of Paul who bid everyone remain in the calling to which he was called. The sense would be as follows: If the Lord were to call one [who lives] in adultery, he should remain in it. Why then did Matthew not stay in the customs house? Indeed, in our opinion the fishermen were wrong when they left their work. This is what happens to us when we pick up fragments of Scripture and mend the old coat with a new patch. What Paul intended to say about married and single people we like to apply to our useless handiwork, our marketing, usury, and offices. This cannot be. Whether God Is the Cause of Evil.[12]

Is it Lawful for Us to Change Our Vocation? Tilemann Hesshus: In whatever vocation or situation the Lord calls us, we must remain there and faithfully serve, and not desert or make a change under the pretext of religion. People often dispute here whether it is lawful for us to change our vocation and move from one place to another, and even whether we are permitted to undertake a different kind of life. Many people in the mechanical arts, becoming impatient with their poverty and lack of success, abandon their vocation and promptly change their life situation—but frequently for the worse. Many people abandon their homes out of impatience, but as they run from winter, they are covered with snow. Therefore holy Scripture in many places (such as the Proverbs of Solomon, in Psalm 37, in Ecclesiastes, and elsewhere) advises and urges each of us to remain in that vocation and position; to endure patiently our troubles, dangers, and difficulties; and to commit every outcome to God. "Hope in the Lord and do good; dwell in the land and enjoy safe pasture." Again, "Turn from evil and do good, and live forever." Therefore we must repress the impulse toward impatience and not rashly change our life situation or leave our homes. But, to be sure, if you are confronted by some grave necessity—as when, in the work of ministry, the hearers don't want to provide adequate support (when they could) for you to sustain your household in an honorable fashion; when you are not able to enjoy a place because of poor health; when some people are trying to oppress your conscience; and especially when the hearers don't want to listen to you or have been persecuting you—then it is perfectly permissible to change your home and life situation. For Christ says, "If they have persecuted you in one city, flee to another." Or rather, if God himself has called you to another city and he has presented you with an opportunity so that your change in location brings great fruit to the church and you perceive it to be the kind will of God that you transfer to another city, then you act in a godly fashion, if you follow the calling of God. But beware lest you are motivated by greed. And do not focus on your wealth and honor; rather, focus on the glory of God, the salvation of the church, and offending no one. Do nothing contrary to godliness and justice. Explication of 1 Corinthians 7:20.[13]

People Must Remain Within the Boundaries of Their Vocation. William Perkins: Now before I treat the topic of special kinds of callings, there are two general rules that we must learn that belong to every calling. First, that whatever people attempt or do, either in word or deed, they must do it by virtue of their callings, and must keep themselves within the boundaries, limits, or precincts of it. This rule is laid down in the words of the apostle, "Let each person remain in the condition in which he was called," the intent of which is to bind people to their callings and to teach them to perform all their actions in accordance with them (Heb 11:6). Whatever is not done within the boundaries of a calling is not of faith, because people must have some warrant and word from God to assure them of their calling to do this or that thing before they can do it in faith....

The second general rule that must be remembered is this: that everyone must perform the duties of their calling with diligence.... There are

[12] Denck, *Selected Writings*, 206-7.

[13] Hesshus, *Explicatio Prioris Epistolae ad Corinthios*, 111r-v; citing Ps 37:3; 1 Pet 3:11; Mt 10:23.

two reasons for such diligence: First, the purpose for which God bestows his gifts on us is so that we might employ them in his service and for his glory in this life. . . . Second, to those who employ their gifts, more is given; but those who do not employ their gifts, what they have is taken from them. For work in a calling is as precious as gold and silver. For that reason, the person who maims another and disables them from doing the work of his calling is, by God's law, bound to give the value of their labor (Ex 21:19). In a similar fashion, our people have a common saying, that an occupation is as good as land, because land may be lost, but skill and work in a good occupation is profitable to the very end because it will provide help when the land fails.

On the other side, we must take heed of two damnable sins that are contrary to this diligence. The first is idleness, whereby we neglect or ignore the duties of our callings and the opportunity to glorify God. The second is sloth, whereby we perform our duties in a slack or careless manner. . . . Sloth and negligence in fulfilling the duties of our callings disrupt that pleasant order which God has established in human societies, both in the church and commonwealth. And, indeed, idleness and sloth are the causes of many damnable sins. The idle body and the idle brain are workshops of the devil. The sea that remains still putrefies, and the body that does not move becomes infected with disease. Now idle and slothful persons are a sea of corruption; and when they are idle, Satan is least idle, for then he is most busy to draw people to many different sins. A Treatise of the Vocations of Men.[14]

7:21-24 *The Condition of Slave or Free*

Servants and Free Persons. Desiderius Erasmus: What has been said about marriage and circumcision, the same thing should be thought concerning servitude. Evangelical teaching understands that those under the obligation of servitude should endure with patience their lot in life, and not think themselves liberated from the authority of their masters; rather, they have been liberated from the tyranny of wickedness. On the other hand, those free persons who have been called to Christ should not wish to change their state of life and cast themselves into servitude. But if it should happen that the opportunity presents itself, servants should eagerly seize their liberty and leave behind their servitude. If masters, out of hatred of Christ, reject their servants, then there is no reason why the servants should seek new masters. There is no reason why servants should be displeased at being free from their masters, since they have Christ as their patron, having been transformed from servants to his free men and women. By contrast, those persons who are freeborn, who have been reborn through baptism, there is no reason why they should be either dissatisfied or satisfied with their status, since by their baptism they have become servants of Christ. Paraphrase on 1 Corinthians 7.[15]

The State of Servitude and Marriage Are Not Impediments to Faith. Martin Luther: Now, just as a marriage partner is to conduct themselves toward their mate, to whom they are bound in body, so a slave should conduct themselves toward their master, whose bodily possession they are. . . . And what Paul here says concerning a slave, the same is to be said of all paid servants, maids, day laborers, workers, and domestics in their relations to their masters and mistresses. It should also be said of all vows, associations, corporations, or of any tie by which one person is related or obligated to another: in all these matters service, loyalty, and duty are to be maintained, regardless of whether the one party is Christian or non-Christian, good or bad, so long as they do not hinder faith and justice and allow you to live your Christian life. For all such estates are free and are not impediments to the Christian faith; and if the king of Poland or Hungary allies

[14]Perkins, *The Works of William Perkins*, 449-51*.

[15]Erasmus, *Paraphrases*, 264.

himself with the Turks, he should hold to it and say, as St. Paul here teaches us, "God calls us to peace." Commentary on 1 Corinthians 7:20.[16]

In Christ, All Christians Are Free. The English Annotations: No calling, however lowly, prevents one from being Christ's free person and a child of God by adoption and grace. All are redeemed from bondage to Satan and the servitude of sin, whether they are in an outward condition of bondage of liberty are Christ's free people. Annotations on 1 Corinthians 7:21.[17]

Faith Makes Everyone Equal Before God. Martin Luther: It is the same for God whether you are free or in bondage, just as circumcision and uncircumcision are the same; neither hinders faith and salvation. It is the same as when I say: It makes no difference to faith whether you are poor or rich, young or old, beautiful or ugly, learned or ignorant, layman or priest. For the one who is called in poverty is rich before God. The one who is called in riches is poor before God. The one who is called in youth is old before God. The one who is called in age is young before God. The one who is called in ugliness is beautiful before God. The one who is called as a layman is a priest before God. All this is true because faith makes us all equal before God and no difference of person or status will count. Commentary on 1 Corinthians 7:22.[18]

Spiritual Freedom in Christ. Giovanni Diodati: Paul confirms the exhortation made to servants, that they should bear their condition with mildness, finding comfort from their spiritual freedom from the curse of God, sin, the devil, and death—all through Jesus Christ. . . . [For free persons] are not the masters of themselves, nor of their wills and actions. They are subject to Christ their Lord. So in Christ all servants and other distressed persons have reason for comfort, and those who are free and live at ease have reason to be humble and submissive. Annotations on 1 Corinthians 7:22.[19]

Freedom and Servitude. Tilemann Hesshus: Paul exhorts us from the value of the resulting cause and the great worth of our freedom, so that we might guard the freedom that we possess in Christ. He says, "You were redeemed with a great price." Peter says, "Not with gold or silver, but with the precious blood of the only-begotten Son of God." It is right, therefore, that we strenuously guard this blessing purchased at such a price. And Paul instructs that we should not give ourselves to people in servitude or bind ourselves to them in such a way that we live for their pleasure. For people's affections fluctuate, and their desires are very fickle. Therefore we should be careful lest we are forced to serve the will of human beings, thereby wounding our conscience. But those who sell their labor to a particular master or to a particular church are not servants of people, but ministers of God. And the most pleasant and noble freedom is to serve Jesus Christ. When Paul orders us to remain in our calling before God, he is warning us always to be casting our eyes on God and considering his will lest we attempt anything contrary to it. Explication of 1 Corinthians 7:23.[20]

Do Not Be Blind Servants of Human Beings! John Trapp: [This verse refers to] when people command you to believe things forbidden by Christ, or when they would tyrannize over your conscience, as do the Jesuits, who require blind obedience. Cardinal Tolet says, "People may receive merit at God's hand in believing heresy, if their teacher propounds it, for their obedience is meritorious." "If a priest teaches it," says Stapleton, "be it true or false, take it as God's oracle." "If the church should approve and authorize Arianism or Pelagianism," says Erasmus, "I would do so too."

[16]LW 28:42, 43*.

[17]Downame, *English Annotations*, DD3v*.

[18]LW 28:43-44.

[19]Diodati, *Pious Annotations*, Ll4v*.

[20]Hesshus, *Explicatio Prioris Epistolae ad Corinthios*, 113r-v; citing 1 Pet 1:18-19.

But wise people would not do this. Commentary on 1 Corinthians 7:23.[21]

Christ Rules His People Through the Ministry of the Word. Martin Bucer: There is nothing that Christians on earth should more diligently guard against than that anyone should place a strange yoke on them in the name of Christ. We have been purchased by Christ our Lord, and therefore we are to make sure that we do not become the slaves of men, 1 Corinthians 7. By this purchase we are Christ's lambs, we are his one church and congregation, and therefore we must also have the Lord's teachers and ministers, whom we listen to in his name and follow with great humility, obedience, and submissiveness. This is because it is the Lord's will to rule among us through his appointed ministry. . . .

This is why Christians are first of all to ask the Lord with great earnestness to grant them faithful ministers, and to watch diligently in choosing them to see that they walk in accordance with their calling and serve faithfully; and when these ministers come to warn, punish, teach, or exhort in the Lord's name, not to dismiss it thoughtlessly and despise this ministry, as sadly many are wont to do today. True Care of Souls.[22]

[21]Trapp, *A Commentary or Exposition*, 674-75*.

[22]Bucer, *Concerning the True Care of Souls*, 195-96.

7:25-40 The Unmarried and the Widowed

*25Now concerning[a] the betrothed,[b] I have no com-
mand from the Lord, but I give my judgment as one
who by the Lord's mercy is trustworthy. 26I think that
in view of the present[c] distress it is good for a person
to remain as he is. 27Are you bound to a wife? Do not
seek to be free. Are you free from a wife? Do not seek
a wife. 28But if you do marry, you have not sinned,
and if a betrothed woman[d] marries, she has not
sinned. Yet those who marry will have worldly
troubles, and I would spare you that. 29This is what I
mean, brothers: the appointed time has grown very
short. From now on, let those who have wives live as
though they had none, 30and those who mourn as
though they were not mourning, and those who rejoice
as though they were not rejoicing, and those who buy
as though they had no goods, 31and those who deal
with the world as though they had no dealings with it.
For the present form of this world is passing away.*

*32I want you to be free from anxieties. The
unmarried man is anxious about the things of the
Lord, how to please the Lord. 33But the married man
is anxious about worldly things, how to please his wife,
34and his interests are divided. And the unmarried or
betrothed woman is anxious about the things of the
Lord, how to be holy in body and spirit. But the
married woman is anxious about worldly things, how
to please her husband. 35I say this for your own
benefit, not to lay any restraint upon you, but to
promote good order and to secure your undivided
devotion to the Lord.*

*36If anyone thinks that he is not behaving properly
toward his betrothed,[e] if his[f] passions are strong, and
it has to be, let him do as he wishes: let them
marry—it is no sin. 37But whoever is firmly estab-
lished in his heart, being under no necessity but
having his desire under control, and has determined
this in his heart, to keep her as his betrothed, he will
do well. 38So then he who marries his betrothed does
well, and he who refrains from marriage will do even
better.*

*39A wife is bound to her husband as long as he
lives. But if her husband dies, she is free to be married
to whom she wishes, only in the Lord. 40Yet in my
judgment she is happier if she remains as she is. And
I think that I too have the Spirit of God.*

a The expression *Now concerning* introduces a reply to a question in the Corinthians' letter **b** Greek *virgins* **c** Or *impending* **d** Greek *virgin* **e** Greek *virgin* **f** Or *her*

Overview: In response to their questions, Paul gives additional instructions to the Corinthians regarding celibacy and marriage, emphasizing that virgins and widows face fewer hardships in life and have greater freedom to serve the Lord than married persons. Protestant commentators agree that Paul's teaching on marriage is timeless, divine truth; at the same time, they seek to correct various ways in which (in their view) traditional church leaders have misunderstood or misapplied his instructions. Commentators reject the notion that the celibate state has intrinsic spiritual value or is deserving of God's special merit. Instead, they insist once again that God's intention is that most adults get married and participate in family life—which is a kind of schoolhouse for Christian sanctification. Paul gives men and women complete freedom to choose their marital state—and church authorities should do likewise. Protestant interpreters advise fathers to be especially sensitive to the needs and dispositions of their daughters, neither forcing marriage on daughters who are endowed with the gift of celibacy, nor preventing marriage to mature daughters who desire to take a husband. So too the commentators reject church traditions that discourage or prevent widows from remarriage. This is the larger principle that must always be kept in view: whether single or married,

Christians are called to live as pilgrims on earth, mindful of the brevity of life, thankful for the blessings of this world without being encumbered or ensnared by them.

7:25-28 *Advice for Virgins*[1]

The Excellence of Virginity. Jacques Lefèvre d'Étaples: The state of virginity is intrinsically good (that is, pure and holy), whether the virgin be a man, a eunuch, or a woman who remains celibate for the sake of the kingdom of heaven. They follow the example of virginity of the Son of God, who wished to be born of a virgin and honored virginity above marriage. The state of virginity is also good because of the "present urgency of life." For in the state of marriage there are many urgent concerns, there is a lot of work, there are a lot of worries to oversee one's wife and children, along with the servants, maids, and other dependents of the household. The state of virginity has none of these responsibilities. And this state of virginity was especially urgent in the time of the apostles. For those who were called to Christ were poor folk and destitute of all things because of Christ. Indeed, if they possessed any wealth, unbelievers would steal from those who were known to be Christians. For this reason, virginity was especially necessary for them. Many of those who had wives, children, and households to provide for were dragged off to execution as martyrs, with the result that their tender wives, infants, children, and household members—deprived and afflicted—could either be dragged away or were supported less freely. But the state of virginity is not intended for everyone; for God has released some people from this obligation. But there are virgins, there are married people, there are widows who remain celibate and continent—all these states are good. Commentary on 1 Corinthians 7:25-26.[2]

The Freedom of Virginity Is Better Than the Servitude of Marriage. Desiderius Erasmus: Now concerning the matter about which you asked, whether Christians should give their virgin daughters in marriage, or, as was the case with Christ, to keep them at home in a perpetual state of virginity so that they might serve him more freely, although I do not have a command from the Lord by which I might answer you with certainty, nevertheless I have some advice to recommend that seems best to me. I do not think my advice is going to exasperate you, since I too have been assigned apostolic authority and I too (as undeserving as I am) have been granted divine favor to faithfully and usefully impart wisdom from the mind of God—not looking to my own benefit, but what is useful for you. Therefore, for the sake of freedom, I judge it to be best if a virgin does not betroth herself to anyone except Christ. I say this, not because I deny that marriage is a holy and honorable estate, but because marriage brings with it a lot of misery and worries due to the marriage relationship and concerns about raising children. The person who abstains from marriage avoids these demands, which are a kind of servitude. Therefore it is preferable to embrace freedom if it is either blameless or prudent. It is not blameless for those people who have already bound themselves in marriage. Nor is it prudent for those people who are unable to control themselves. Paraphrases on 1 Corinthians 7.[3]

Paul's Opinion Has God's Authority Behind It. Heinrich Bullinger: The Paraphraser[4] thinks that the Corinthians had asked Paul whether Christians should give their virgin daughters in marriage or whether they should keep them at home in a state of perpetual virginity as holy vessels devoted to Christ so that they might serve him more freely. Paul, therefore, now answers them here. Ambrose concludes the same thing. Theophylact has written rather differently

[1]The Greek word *parthenos* (in verses 25, 28, 34, 36, 37, 38) is best translated "virgin." Here, the ESV renders the word "betrothed" or "betrothed woman."

[2]Lefèvre d'Étaples, *Commentariorum in Epistolas Beati Pauli . . . Liber Secundus*, 111r.

[3]Erasmus, *Paraphrases*, 266-67.

[4]That is, Erasmus.

concerning Paul, saying, "Since Paul has amply discussed the matter of continence and sufficiently reproved the Corinthians regarding it, he now passes over to the subject of virginity, which is far superior to other states." Holding the same view, a schoolman explains the phrase "concerning virgins" as a change of words in view of the fact that it is really "concerning virginity." For hitherto, Paul has treated the subject of chastity in marriage; now he proceeds also to discuss virginity. Paul says here that no law exists for preserving virginity. For the Lord said nothing other than this: "Not everyone can receive this teaching, but only to those whom it is given. Let the one who is able to receive it, receive it."

In like manner, Paul writes *gnōmēn de didōmi*, that is, "I give my opinion" or "I say what seems best to me." In other words, "I am expressing my opinion concerning this matter." And lest his readers disregard his opinion, he adds that he has obtained this from the divine mercy to speak concerning that matter what seemed best. Now Paul is speaking about his calling to the apostolic office and that the Lord had given him this by the Holy Spirit. Therefore, although no law concerning virginity exists in the divine Scriptures, the teachings that Paul brings forward here are not human, but have originated from the Holy Spirit of God. Commentary on 1 Corinthians 7:25.[5]

Paul's Words Do Not Support "Evangelical Counsels." Tilemann Hesshus: Paul now responds to another question of the Corinthians, namely, what should be established concerning virgins, whether daughters should be betrothed or whether they should be permanently provided for at home outside of marriage. Paul, with moderation, first distinguishes between advice, which communicates good faith, and a command of the Lord. For when the Lord commands something, it must be obeyed with a ready spirit without any evasion or deliberation. But in the case of human advice, we are not bound, but it is left to our free will whether we wish to follow it or consider something else. The pontiffs shamefully abuse this distinction, for they imagine that there are different kinds of divine commands: that some divine commands have been prescribed for everyone, and other divine commands have been given as "counsels" for achieving perfection. Thereupon they imagine those commands such as "If anyone says to his brother 'Raca,' he is liable to judgment" or again, "You shall not take an oath at all," or again, "If anyone divorces his wife, he makes her commit adultery," or again, "If anyone strikes you on the right cheek, turn to him the other also" have not been commanded to each and every person, but that they are "counsels" intended for the perfect. This error completely obscures the spiritual judgment of the law, which requires inner, spiritual, and absolute obedience from every person, no matter their position. How far this is from the mind of Paul, who says "the law is spiritual" about each of the Lord's commandments! Explication of 1 Corinthians 7:25.[6]

Family Life May Impede Gospel Ministry. Huldrych Zwingli: "Because of the present distress," that is, if you consider the troubles and tribulations of this life. "Given the troubles with which we are now pressured and afflicted on account of our faith in the gospel, I permit whatever estate that is advantageous and peaceful. If someone is not married, let him remain so. For having a wife or children is no small hindrance and can cause a person to be more hesitant to undertake the office of apostle or evangelist. I myself know this from experience." Annotations on 1 Corinthians 7:26.[7]

Christians Endure Difficulties in Every Age. John Calvin: [Paul's] meaning is this:

[5]Bullinger, *In Priorem ad Corinthios Epistolam Commentarius*, 173; citing Mt 19:11-12. Ambrose's (Ambrosiaster's) treatment of this verse is found in his *Comment. in Epist. I ad Cor.*, in PL 17:233. For Theophylact, see his *Expositio in Epist. I ad Cor.*, in PG 124:650.

[6]Hesshus, *Explicatio Prioris Epistolae ad Corinthios*, 113v-114r; citing Mt 5:22, 34, 32, 39.

[7]Zwingli, *Annotatiunculae . . . ex ore Zvinglij*, 60-61.

"Because of the difficulty that always presses on the saints in this life, I think that the best solution is that everyone should enjoy the freedom and convenience of celibacy, since this would be profitable for them." There are some interpreters, however, who view the term "difficulty" as referring to the apostle's own age, which was undoubtedly very troublesome for godly people. But to me it seems that Paul instead wished to indicate the distress with which the saints are perpetually harassed in this present life. And so Paul's words apply to all ages. And, indeed, I understand this passage in this way, that the saints in this world are often driven this way and that, and they are exposed to many and various storms, so that their condition would seem not at all conducive to marriage. Commentary on 1 Corinthians 7:26.[8]

The Present Distress. Wolfgang Musculus: When Paul, in his apostolic letters, refers to his own judgment, this doesn't mean that he is expressing matters of opinion of which he is uncertain. The advice Paul gives is certainly good. And so he adds a fuller explanation, for otherwise it would appear that he was opposing the teaching of Scripture, where God says: "It is not good for man to be alone. . . ." For that reason, Paul says, "in view of the present distress." What was that distress? Nearly everyone understands the "distress" to be the troubles of this age and the worries of this life. Ambrose expressly identified this "distress" as the troubles surrounding childbirth and raising children. To be sure, innumerable are the inconveniences of married life, and those who abstain from marriage are freed from many troubles. But, in my judgment, the apostle is not speaking here about those sorts of difficulties that are not peculiar to Christians, which they hold in common with all married persons, Jews and Greeks alike. . . . Rather, Paul is speaking here about a particular difficulty, which was especially oppressing and pressuring Christians at that time, when he says: "in view of the present distress." That distress was the persecution by which spouses were separated because they were Christians, with children also being torn from their parents; this persecution tempted even the strongest of them to abandon their faith in Christ out of their love for their spouses and their affection for their children. Commentary on 1 Corinthians 7:26.[9]

Marriage Is the School of the Holy Spirit. Tilemann Hesshus: Paul does not say that celibacy is a holier kind of life than marriage. Not at all. Rather, he says that celibate persons have fewer troubles and bodily afflictions. He gives this advice to the church, therefore, in view of the great difficulty of the time. But lest someone should seek in this a pretext for dissolving their marriage, Paul forbids everyone from separating from their spouses, to whom they are bound in an indissoluble covenant. The one who is married should remain in that state. For marriage does not hinder godliness; rather, it is the school of the Holy Spirit. But for those who are freed from marriage, they should not seek a spouse; they should enjoy the freedom and convenience that comes from this state. But the weakness and inconstancy of the human will is so great that it regrets whatever is its lot in life. And so, those whom God has given a companion in life, they desire to be freed from the marriage bond; and those who are unmarried think they are thereby more unhappy than others. Paul reproaches this fickleness and points out that our present state should be considered good and, as the opportunity allows, it should be employed with excellence in a suitable fashion. And we should not employ our present state in such a way that, indulging our desires, we exaggerate our miseries. Explication of 1 Corinthians 7:27.[10]

The Married Life Harder Than the Celibate Life. Wolfgang Musculus: "And I would spare you that," no doubt, due to their weakness. . . . Why then do [Roman Catholics]

[8]CO 49:418 (cf. CTS 39:253).

[9]Musculus, *Comm. 1 Cor.*, 223; citing Gen 2:18. For Ambrose's (Ambrosiaster's) treatment of this verse, see his *Comment. in Epist. I ad Cor.*, in PL 17:233.

[10]Hesshus, *Explicatio Prioris Epistolae ad Corinthios*, 115r-v.

claim that people who aspire to such a difficult vow of virginity and celibacy deserve the special approval of God on account of their (supposed) austerity of life? If they judge correctly, why then does the apostle recommend virginity to the Corinthians so as to spare them? Who does not see that to follow Christ with a sincere heart, more strength is required from those who are married than from virgins? Who does not understand that celibate persons live more calmly and peacefully than married persons? Yes indeed, countless numbers of so-called celibate persons . . . take up the celibate life so as to avoid the cares and countless worries of the married state. Likewise, if the more difficult and more worrisome kind of life deserves special reward, that life would be the married one, not the celibate one. But that's not how things work, because the eyes of God look on the sincerity of the heart whatever the state of this life (as long as it is not unlawful). Commentary on 1 Corinthians 7:28.[11]

Paul's Advice Is a Treasure. John Trapp: "But I would spare you that"—no more than that, and yet I will show you a means of escape, or at least a way to mitigate those troubles of the flesh. Thus, this first epistle to the Corinthians, though the weight of its argument is far inferior to the preceding epistle to the Romans, yet in a variety of things it should be judged equal to it, and in order of time before the other. As Erasmus said of Pliny's *Natural History*: "Surely it is a treasure, yes, a very world of things most worthy to be understood." Commentary on 1 Corinthians 7:28.[12]

7:29-31 *Living in View of the Urgency of the Times*

Christians Must Hold Loosely to the Things of This World. Martin Luther: This is a general teaching for all Christians, that they should treasure that eternal blessing which is theirs in the faith, despising this life so that they do not sink too deeply into it either with love and desire or suffering and boredom, but should rather behave like guests on earth, using everything for a short time because of need and not for pleasure. This would mean having a wife as though I did not have one, when in my heart I would rather remain unmarried but in order to avoid sin have found it necessary to have one. But he who seeks not necessity but also desire, he does not have a wife but is himself possessed by a wife. A Christian should hold to this principle also in all other things. He should only serve necessity and not be a slave to his lust and nurture his old Adam. Commentary on 1 Corinthians 7:29-31.[13]

The Time Is Short. John Calvin: All the things that aim toward the enjoyment of life are sacred gifts from God, but we spoil them and abuse them. If we look for the reason why, it is because we always dream that we will live forever in this world. The result is that those things which should be supports for our earthly journey become shackles to enchain us. Therefore it is with good reason that the apostle, in order to shake us from this stupor, calls us to consider the brevity of this life, and he infers from this that we ought to use all the things of this world as if we were not using them. For people who consider themselves to be pilgrims in this world use the things of this world as if they belonged to someone else—that is, as things that are lent to us for a single day. The main point is this: the mind of a Christian should not be occupied with earthly things or seek satisfaction in them. For we should live as if we were going to depart this life at any moment. Commentary on 1 Corinthians 7:30.[14]

Living in View of Eternity. Tilemann Hesshus: The apostle shows the goal that godly

[11]Musculus, *Comm. 1 Cor.*, 225.

[12]Trapp, *A Commentary or Exposition*, 675*. In 1525, Erasmus dedicated to the bishop of Olmutz an edition of Pliny's *Natural History* that the Dutch humanist had restored from ancient manuscripts.

[13]LW 28:52.

[14]CO 49:420 (cf. CTS 39:257).

people should always have before their eyes whenever they think about these worldly things: reflecting on the fact that this time that we spend in this world is brief and meager [and] we must depart from here. Thus our whole heart should not be distracted by concerns of worldly things, but should prepare us daily for eternal intimacy with God, and we should constantly serve the glory of God. Those who focus on this goal live in the world as if they are not in the world, for their mind and commonwealth are in heaven. And whether they gain or lose worldly possessions, their affection for religion remains yet the same, and in all things they sustain themselves on the hope of eternal life. "Those who have wives, as though they had none." It's as if Paul were to say: "They do not place their greatest happiness in marriage, that they have a pleasing life partner. Instead they reflect on the fact that someday they are going to be separated from their spouse and children. And so they readily serve the Lord, as if they do not have spouses." They place love of God before their love for their spouse. "Those who mourn, as though they were not mourning"; that is, they are not completely crushed by sorrow on account of the death of a husband or wife or relatives or children. But their griefs are moderated by the hope of the future resurrection, and that they will be forever victors in the presence of the Lord in heaven. "Those who rejoice, as though they were not rejoicing"; that is, those who are experiencing happiness should accept these blessings from God and rejoice in them. They do not place their greatest happiness in this momentary felicity, but know that it will change shortly and that various troubles here are to be expected. And so, even in rejoicing, God should be feared and humbly petitioned lest he allow us to fall. "Those who buy," Paul says, "as those who possess nothing." We are not able to be without business dealings while we are in this life. But Christians ought to use these dealings in such a way that they do not allow themselves to be completely occupied with buying and selling, nor should they place their chief happiness in the possession of earthly goods, but they should think constantly that they must depart from this place and leave behind everything. Therefore, people should use and enjoy the riches given to them by God with gratitude; and they should always be prepared to leave these things behind. Explication of 1 Corinthians 7:29-30.[15]

Mind the Sails. John Trapp: The Greek term means "contracted and rolled up," as sails used to be by mariners when the ship drew near to the harbor. Others say it is a metaphor from a piece of cloth rolled up, only a little left at the end. So God has rolled up all his works, yet has left only a little at the end, and then all his glory shall appear. The time is short, says the apostle, and you have business enough to complete; therefore let other things (such as courtship and commerce etc.) pass and mind the sails. . . . Some people, as they lay dying, would have given a world for more time. . . . Let us therefore use all speed and diligence, lest (as with children who have torn their books) we have ended our lives before we have learned our lessons. Commentary on 1 Corinthians 7:29.[16]

The Married State Is Ephemeral. John Trapp: They should not be excessively distracted by their wives, since they know not how soon God may take their spouses from them, as he did from Ezekiel, the delight of their eyes, their dearest spouses. The Jews today have a custom, when a couple are married, to break the glass from which the bridegroom and bride drank, thereby to admonish them of their dying condition, and that there must be a parting again before long. Commentary on 1 Corinthians 7:29.[17]

Four Dangers of Wealth. Wolfgang Musculus: The dangers of wealth are fourfold: First, the souls of those who possess wealth can become proud. As we Germans say: Abundance makes one bold.[18] Second, wealth can enchain the hearts of wealthy persons and cause them to trust in their wealth. David warns of this: "If riches

[15]Hesshus, *Explicatio Prioris Epistolae ad Corinthios*, 116r-117r.
[16]Trapp, *A Commentary or Exposition*, 675*.
[17]Ibid.; citing Ezek 24:18; Luke 16:19-31.
[18]In German, *Guot macht muot.*

increase, set not your heart on them!" Third, wealth can furnish the material and present the opportunity for luxury. This is observed in the wealthy man described in the Gospel. Fourth, having many things can flame greed and idleness, as it is said: "When money increases, the love of money also grows."

The souls of Christians are free from all these dangers. . . . They will not become proud; they will not place their trust in wealth; they will not give in to luxury; and they will not be greedy for many things, but will be so content with their wealth that they will be nothing less than moderate, generous of heart, temperate, and content with their present condition. Commentary on 1 Corinthians 7:30.[19]

The Form of This World Is Passing Away. Tilemann Hesshus: If some people, having undertaken a journey to the happy and blessed fatherland, should along the way come on an inn that is not altogether unpleasant, they are wise to enjoy it with a glad heart and give thanks to God and, in a certain way, refresh their limbs exhausted from the journey. But if they delight so much in the foreign inn that they forget that most pleasant and blessed fatherland, alas, they would be completely foolish! In a similar way, we are as pilgrims in this world: if wealth and other pleasant things in life come our way, and if we are granted a comfortable residence, we should enjoy these blessings granted to us by God. But we should beware lest we permit our hearts to be encumbered by the wealth and pleasant things of this life so that we forget eternal life. Christ's rule should always be in view for us: "Beware that your hearts are not weighed down with care from the necessities of this life. But be watchful and pray continually so that, escaping all these things, you might be worthy and able to stand before the Son of Man." And, along with Paul, we should always pray: "I desire to depart and be with Christ." In sum, we should place our greatest good and happiness, not in the perishable and transitory blessings of this world, but in the permanent happiness of eternal life. For the "form" [of this world]—that is, the glory, image, wealth, conveniences, and whatever in the world is dear to the flesh—is passing away; nothing is stable, nothing is permanent. Therefore the "form" is not the greatest good. Explication of 1 Corinthians 7:31.[20]

We Must Not Set Our Minds on This World. The English Annotations: It is a horrible wickedness, Saint Augustine says, to use those things that we ought only to enjoy or to enjoy those things that we ought only to use, to use God and heavenly things that we ought to enjoy and to enjoy the world and earthly things that we ought only to use. . . . Or, as others have expounded, we should not abuse things by an inordinate use of the same or by doting too much on them and cleaving to them.

Paul shows how ill-becoming and unworthy a thing it is for Christians to set their hearts on the things of this world, given that they are vain and transitory. Indeed, they are rather reflections and shadows of things, rather than true things in themselves (Prov 23:5). Just as in a pageant, mask, or comedy many persons are called up one after another onto the stage or scene, but at last both they and the scene are taken away, so it is with this present world, with one person succeeding another, and one generation another, until not only do they all die and fall away, but even the stage of this world on which they all acted their parts, vanishes away like a shadow, along with its glory. Annotations on 1 Corinthians 7:31.[21]

7:32-35 *Living Free of Anxiety*

Single Persons Are Entirely Free to Serve Christ. Desiderius Erasmus: I say these things because I want you to be distracted by

[19]Musculus, *Comm. 1 Cor.*, 230; citing Ps 62:10.

[20]Hesshus, *Explicatio Prioris Epistolae ad Corinthios*, 117v-118r; citing Lk 21:36; Phil 1:23.

[21]Downame, *English Annotations*, DD3v*.

as few worldly cares as possible and to embrace this most excellent kind of life that involves as few profane affairs as possible. In this regard, it is better to be celibate than in a condition of marriage. For a celibate man is not distracted by various concerns—how to satisfy his father-in-law or mother-in-law, how to satisfy other relatives, how to satisfy his wife or children, how to provide sustenance for his family that is growing by the day, how to come up with a dowry—but he is entirely free for Christ and has fulfilled the greatest of vows if he pleases Christ alone. On the other hand, the man who takes a wife, although he is partly free to serve the Lord, nevertheless owes a certain part of himself to his wife and to his wife's affairs. And the same thing is true for the wife. Since the wife does not have complete right to herself, she is not entirely free for Christ, but she is divided by various cares, half of her serving Christ and half of her serving her husband. Again, the virgin or the woman who is otherwise celibate cares for one thing only: to please her spouse Christ, whom she pleases by keeping herself completely chaste and undefiled, not only in body but also in mind. But for married persons, they consider it necessary to be divided between Christ and the world, and so they have trouble pleasing Christ as their spouse, to whom they owe obedience and whom they should please. Paraphrase on 1 Corinthians 7.[22]

Married Persons Need to Be Forewarned. John Calvin: Paul returns to that advice which he had spoken of [in verse 25] but had not yet fully explained, and (as is his custom) he begins by commending celibacy, and then afterward allows everyone the freedom to choose whatever they deem best for themselves. It is not, however, without good reason that he returns so often to praising the benefits of celibacy, for he saw that the burdens of marriage are far from light. Persons who are able to exempt themselves from these burdens should not overlook such a blessing. And it is helpful for those who resolve to get married to be forewarned concerning those troubles, so that afterward, when they experience them unexpectedly, they will not become depressed. This is what we observe happens to many people, for when they have promised themselves pure honey, when this expectation is frustrated, they are easily overwhelmed by the slightest mishap. Therefore let them know in good time what they should expect, that they may be prepared to endure everything patiently. Commentary on 1 Corinthians 7:32.[23]

Married Persons Are Divided. Martin Luther: The apostle does not want to condemn the married estate on this account. For he does not say that a married man is anxious only about the affairs of this world, or is separated from God. He says only that he is divided and is anxious about many affairs and cannot constantly pray or attend to the Word of God; although his work and care are good, still it is much better to be free to pray and attend to God's Word. In so doing the unmarried person is of much use and comfort to many people, yes, to all of Christendom, and this reason is great and noble enough to keep everyone from marrying who has the grace to remain single. But our monastics, who neither pray nor learn God's Word but torture themselves with the regulations of men and murmur and howl in the choir, they would do better to tend pigs as married people. Commentary on 1 Corinthians 7:32-34.[24]

Reasons Singleness Is to Be Preferred. David Dickson: Paul gives two reasons for his counsel regarding avoiding marriage. First, so that the Corinthians might be freed from trouble, which married people were likely to experience out of fear of persecution and the present condition. Second, because the unmarried person is at greater leisure for divine ministries, or to practice religious activities, and more directly to please God. But married persons are forced by their calling to spend

[22]Erasmus, *Paraphrases*, 269.

[23]CO 49:421 (cf. CTS 39:258-59).

[24]LW 28:53.

much of their time in earthly business and household cares. The husband's proper concern to please his wife, which is an act of obedience when it is performed in the fear of God, is not as direct an obedience and as near to God as religious activities. Exposition of 1 Corinthians 7:33.[25]

Wives Should Seek to Please Their Husbands. Wolfgang Musculus: It is not a sin for a woman to please her husband, as long as she especially pleases Christ. If it pertains to a married women to love her husband, to be prudent, chaste and sober, to take care of her home, to be kindhearted and submissive, then how will it be evil if she pleases her husband by doing these things (as it is commanded in Titus 2)? The apostle Peter urges married women to win their difficult and unbelieving husbands to the Lord through their righteous and honorable conduct. This is certainly not possible unless a woman pleases her husband. Commentary on 1 Corinthians 7:34.[26]

Paul Intends to Restrain No One. Tilemann Hesshus: Paul has interjected a necessary exception so that those who are examining themselves might be able to receive his advice without wounding or endangering their conscience. Paul is well aware that few people in this world have been equipped with the gift of chastity. The apostle is also aware of what kinds of lusts are excited in the wretched and corrupt human nature, what are the snares of the devil, and how great is their unconcern and dullness in prayer. And so, though he has set forth his advice with exceptional honesty regarding maintaining chastity, nevertheless, since everyone cannot receive this word (as Christ says), he clearly testifies that he would not place a restraint on consciences. He is not pushing either virgins or widows to bind themselves with a vow of chastity, as those raving, filthy, and wicked Roman popes do. Rather, he leaves them in complete freedom as to whether they wish to marry or abstain from marriage. But he has set before them only a good order of life and that persons who have been endowed with the gift of permanent chastity are able to be devoted to the Lord without distraction. Explication of 1 Corinthians 7:35.[27]

7:36-38 *Treatment of Virgins*[28]

Fathers Have Authority over Their Virgin Daughters—but Not Virginity Itself. Heinrich Bullinger: Paul makes clear by means of examples what he has said previously, so that there might be no obscurity in his meaning. It is permissible to explain the word "virgin" in terms of the person as well as the state of virginity itself. Here is Paul's meaning: If anyone has a virgin daughter who has reached maturity and is marriageable to a man . . . and she has a strong desire to be married . . . so that the father fears that she is going to attempt and risk something dishonorable in secret if she is not allowed to marry him—the father does not sin if he gives her to the man. . . . The second example is this: If anyone has a virgin daughter, that is, she is endowed with the gift of virginity, and he has firmly resolved in his heart (that is, not compelled by force but from the power of his own will) and has determined on the basis of this to preserve her virginity, he does well. For this attaches her soul even more firmly to God, and the father in no way sins against what is honorable. However, my explanation here has to do with virginity itself, because the virginity of a daughter has nothing to do with the will of the father, for it comes from her own affections, rather than the affections of her father or other people. And Paul tempers these examples so as to demonstrate that we

[25]Dickson, *Exposition of St. Paul's Epistles*, 52*.

[26]Musculus, *Comm. 1 Cor.*, 235-36; citing Tit 2:5; 1 Pet 3:1.

[27]Hesshus, *Explicatio Prioris Epistolae ad Corinthios*, 119r-v.

[28]Reformation commentators interpret this passage to refer to a father's treatment of his virgin daughter, rather than (as seen in the ESV) a man's treatment of the woman to whom he's betrothed. For modern commentators who disagree over the best rendering of these verses, compare Robertson and Plummer, *1 Corinthians*, 158-62 to Fee, *1 Corinthians*, 349-55.

should carefully consider whether something is advantageous or disadvantageous, honorable or dishonorable with respect to persons and circumstances. Now we learn from this discussion that it is the responsibility of parents to give their daughters in marriage. For among the ancients, marriage contracts were not ratified without parental authority. Commentary on 1 Corinthians 7:36.[29]

Children Must Not Contract Their Own Marriages. John Calvin: Now this passage serves to strengthen the authority of the father, which ought to be held sacred, since it derives from the universal law of nature. Now if in other matters of lesser importance no freedom is permitted to children without parental authority, how much less freedom should be given to children in contracting marriage? And this, to be sure, has been carefully promulgated in civil law, and especially in the Law of God.... Let us recognize, therefore, that in the giving of children in marriage the authority of parents is especially important, provided they do not tyrannically abuse it, as even the civil laws restrict it. And the apostle, in requiring that there be no necessity, was indicating that the deliberation of the parents should be influenced by what is best for the children. Let us therefore remember this balance to be the proper rule, that children should allow themselves to be governed by their parents, and that parents, on the other hand, not drag their children into something against their will, but have no other goal for their authority than their children's advantage. Commentary on 1 Corinthians 7:37.[30]

Fathers Should Allow Their Grown Daughters to Marry. David Dickson: The fourth matter about which the Corinthians inquire of Paul concerns the duty of parents who have power over the marriage status of their daughters, whether they should give their virgin daughters in marriage or not. The answer has two parts: The first rests on a threefold supposition: (1) If a father is suspected of detaining his daughter from marriage longer than is appropriate; (2) if his daughter has passed the flower of her age, that is, is at least twenty-years old, and is beginning to be more ripe of years; (3) if he sees that his virgin daughter is inclined toward marriage, then the father should follow the will of the virgin and his own. Let the daughter and the son-in-law, whom the father shall choose, be joined in marriage. In doing so, the parent does not sin.

The other part of the answer also rests on a threefold supposition: (1) If the father is confident that he is not wronging his daughter in withholding her from marriage; (2) if his daughter has the gift of continence.... (3) If he wishes to keep his virgin daughter unmarried, then the father has done well, Paul says, and has acted in the best interest of his daughter. Exposition of 1 Corinthians 7:36-37.[31]

Freedom to Serve God. John Calvin: "And so, he who gives in marriage...." This is the conclusion to both parts of this section, in which Paul states, in a few words, that parents are free from blame if they give their daughters in marriage. Nevertheless, he testifies that it is better if they keep their daughters at home unmarried. You should not understand by this, however, that celibacy is here preferred to marriage, except in the case previously noted. For if the girl does not have the power, the father acts badly when he tries to prevent his daughter from marriage. In such a case he is no longer acting as a father, but as a cruel tyrant. The sum of the whole discussion amounts to this: (1) That celibacy is better than marriage because with it there is greater freedom for people more readily to serve God; (2) yet that no necessity should be imposed to keep people from marrying, if they think it proper; (3) moreover, that marriage is the remedy designated by God for our weakness,

[29]Bullinger, *In Priorem ad Corinthios Epistolam Commentarius*, 175-76.
[30]CO 49:425-26 (cf. CTS 39:267-68).
[31]Dickson, *Exposition of St. Paul's Epistles*, 52*.

which everyone should use who has not been given the gift of continence. COMMENTARY ON 1 CORINTHIANS 7:38.[32]

7:39-40 *Advice for Widows*

BEST FOR WIDOWS NOT TO REMARRY. WOLFGANG MUSCULUS: This passage makes clear the apostle's concern. He says nothing here that he has not stated before, but by way of summary, he says three things: First, the wife is said to be bound when her husband is alive. Second, she is free to marry whom she wishes after her husband dies. Third, in Paul's judgment, she is nevertheless more blessed if she remains a widow. Paul has already addressed all these topics earlier, so why does he think it necessary to repeat himself? He returns to this subject out of his great concern, indeed anxiety, that he has not explained himself adequately; not in order to inject further subtlety to the discussion. COMMENTARY ON 1 CORINTHIANS 7:39.[33]

ADVICE TO WIDOWS. MARTIN LUTHER: Paul says the same thing in Romans 7:2-6, using a spiritual metaphor that he states here and elaborates on there. But it is the conclusion of this chapter that marriage is a bound thing in this world but free before God, just as he says above that a slave is a freedman before the Lord, even though he be a slave in this world. Those who live without marriage are free and unbound, both before God and in this world. Therefore he terms [the widow's] estate more blessed than the married estate, not in the sense of eternal blessedness, in which only faith will be greater or count for more according to its quality, but in the sense of this life, in which that estate has less trouble, worry, danger, and work. COMMENTARY ON 1 CORINTHIANS 7:40.[34]

WIDOWS MAY REMARRY, BUT ONLY "IN THE LORD." PETER MARTYR VERMIGLI: This passage pertains to widows, and it contains a twofold judgment. The first is to permit marriage to Christian widows, and the reason is added: because they are no longer subject to their husbands when they die. Paul makes one exception: that they marry "in the Lord." The second judgment is that the widows' condition will be happier if they remain unmarried. Next, so as to obtain authority for his teaching, he attests that he has the Spirit of God. When he writes that a woman is bound to her husband as long as he lives, this exception ought to be added (which Christ made): unless adultery occurs. And certainly also, as Paul himself has indicated, if an unbelieving spouse does not wish to remain in the marriage. But Paul here mentions only the dissolution [of marriage] that occurs through death, because it is the more general sort. For there are countless marriages in which, by the grace of God, neither of the causes for divorce ever occur. And when Paul says, "only in the Lord," it means either "you should determine concerning the marriage partner whether he is of the same religion," or "you should display a reverence and modesty worthy of Christians in the fear of the Lord—and not be like those shaken by unbridled lust as horses and mules." COMMENTARY ON 1 CORINTHIANS 7:39-40.[35]

PAUL ALLOWS WIDOWS TO REMARRY. TILEMANN HESSHUS: Just as Paul did not take away from virgins the freedom of marriage (although he communicated his advice regarding celibacy) lest he place a snare on their consciences, so he also does not place any law on widows to prohibit them from getting remarried if they crave marriage. "As long as her husband lives, she is bound by law." That is, the covenant of marriage remains indestructible, as long as both parties are alive. But when the

[32]CO 49:425-26 (cf. CTS 39:268-69).
[33]Musculus, *Comm. 1 Cor.*, 241.
[34]LW 28:55.
[35]Vermigli, *In Selectissimam Pauli Priorem ad Corinth. Epistolam . . . Commentarii*. 195-96. The Montantists were a second-century Christian movement named after their leader, Montanus. Known for its appeal to the Holy Spirit, its ascetic lifestyle, its affirmation of women in the ministry of the church, its belief in the role of dreams and visions, and the fact that Tertullian joined their ranks, the movement was later deemed heretical.

husband is taken from this life, the widow is completely free. "She can marry whom she wishes, but only in the Lord." That is, in the fear of the Lord and with earnest prayer to the Son of God, Jesus Christ. For without the blessing of Jesus Christ, marriage does not result in happiness. Here Paul very clearly approves—without any obscurity—second marriages. It is for this reason that Tertullian, Jerome, and others, who condemned or attacked second marriages, have hallucinated and sinned in this matter, because they have contradicted the teaching of the Holy Spirit.

When the apostle says that the widow will be happier if she remains as she is, this should not be understood to mean that she will be more acceptable to God, that she merits greater grace before God, or that she is closer to the kingdom of Christ—which is how the monks corrupt this passage of Paul. Rather, he is speaking of earthly and bodily happiness. "She will be happier"; that is, she will have fewer troubles; she will undergo fewer dangers; she will enjoy greater tranquility; she will be able to pursue godliness without constraint. And so she acts wisely if she holds on to this happiness given to her. But if she feels that she desires to marry a husband, Paul also decrees with certainty that she does not sin. So that godly people do not reject Paul's advice as proceeding from the wisdom of the flesh, he testifies that he has the Spirit of God, because he is an apostle of Jesus Christ. Explication of 1 Corinthians 7:39-40.[36]

Widows Are Free to Remarry. John Trapp: The Montanists (and with them Tertullian in his old age) were in error when they condemned second marriages, and said that it was no better than fornication. Nevertheless, that statement of Jerome is not to be disliked: "Think daily of death; and that will be enough to forbid the bans of second marriage." Commentary on 1 Corinthians 7:39.[37]

[36]Hesshus, *Explicatio Prioris Epistolae ad Corinthios*, 121r-v. For Jerome's view of second marriages and widowhood, see his *Against Jovinianus* (especially chapters 3-14), and his letter to Furia, in NPNF 6:102-8. For Tertullian's view on second marriages, see above at 1 Cor. 7:8-9.

[37]Trapp, *A Commentary or Exposition*, 677*.

8:1-13 FOOD OFFERED TO IDOLS

Now concerning[a] food offered to idols: we know that
"all of us possess knowledge." This "knowledge" puffs up,
but love builds up. 2 If anyone imagines that he knows
something, he does not yet know as he ought to know.
3 But if anyone loves God, he is known by God.[b]
4 Therefore, as to the eating of food offered to idols,
we know that "an idol has no real existence," and that
"there is no God but one." 5 For although there may be
so-called gods in heaven or on earth—as indeed there
are many "gods" and many "lords"— 6 yet for us there
is one God, the Father, from whom are all things and
for whom we exist, and one Lord, Jesus Christ, through
whom are all things and through whom we exist.
7 However, not all possess this knowledge. But some,
through former association with idols, eat food as
really offered to an idol, and their conscience, being
weak, is defiled. 8 Food will not commend us to God.
We are no worse off if we do not eat, and no better off
if we do. 9 But take care that this right of yours does
not somehow become a stumbling block to the weak.
10 For if anyone sees you who have knowledge eating[c]
in an idol's temple, will he not be encouraged,[d] if his
conscience is weak, to eat food offered to idols? 11 And
so by your knowledge this weak person is destroyed,
the brother for whom Christ died. 12 Thus, sinning
against your brothers[e] and wounding their conscience
when it is weak, you sin against Christ. 13 Therefore, if
food makes my brother stumble, I will never eat meat,
lest I make my brother stumble.

a The expression *Now concerning* introduces a reply to a question in the Corinthians' letter **b** Greek *him* **c** Greek *reclining at table* **d** Or *fortified;* Greek *built up* **e** Or *brothers and sisters*

Overview: In this chapter, Paul gives detailed instructions for the use of food that has previously been sacrificed to false gods in pagan temples. Reformation commentators emphasize that Paul is in no way condoning idolatry, but is providing general advice for how Christians should employ their freedom with respect to "neutral" or "indifferent" matters. Two principles are primary: the Christian's conscience must be governed by the Word of God; and Christian freedom must be regulated by the principle of love as believers seek the good of their neighbors. With these principles in view, Protestant interpreters warn their contemporaries against a careless use of spiritual freedom that wounds the consciences of weak and uneducated people, while at the same time criticizing various Catholic ceremonies (for example, Lenten fasts) that restrict believers' God-given freedom. The commentators find an especially important articulation of the doctrine of the Trinity here. Paul affirms that God is one, that the persons of the Father and Son are distinct, and that this one God is the source and sustainer of all that exists.

Do Not Despise the Weak. Martin Luther: In chapters 8 to 12 [the apostle Paul] discusses many different ways in which weak consciences are to be guided and regarded in external matters such as eating, drinking, apparel, and receiving the sacrament. Everywhere he forbids the strong to despise the weak, since he himself, even though he is an apostle, has refrained from many things to which he really had a right. Moreover the strong may well be afraid, because in ancient Israel so many were destroyed, all of whom had been led out of Egypt by miracles. Besides this, he makes several digressions into worthwhile teachings. Preface to the First Epistle to the Corinthians.[1]

The Flow of Paul's Argument. John Calvin: Paul now moves on to another question, which he had only touched on in chapter 6, without fully explaining it. For when he had

[1] LW 35:382-83.

spoken about the greed of the Corinthians and had concluded that discussion with this statement—"neither the greedy nor extortioners nor fornicators etc. will inherit the kingdom of God"—he had briefly mentioned there the matter of Christian freedom, saying, "all things are lawful for me." This gave him the opportunity to go on to discuss the subject of fornication and then marriage. Now, therefore, he describes in detail what he had only touched on regarding "neutral things," namely, how freedom should be regulated in "neutral things." By "neutral things" I mean those things that are neither good nor bad in themselves, but indifferent, which God has placed in our power. Now we ought to practice moderation in their use, so that there might be a difference between freedom and license. Commentary on 1 Corinthians 8.[2]

On Christian Liberty. Tilemann Hesshus: In chapter 8, the apostle treats a new subject, for he instructs the Corinthians about the true use of Christian freedom, and he criticizes its inappropriate use when it causes offense to one's neighbor. The Corinthians had understood from the teaching that Paul had given them concerning Christian freedom that the conscience of Christians was captive to no law, that idols were nothing, that all worldly things were clean. But they misused this knowledge and freedom to cause offense to their neighbors rather than to provide consolation to their consciences and build up the church. Therefore Paul criticizes this abuse and teaches with what godliness, modesty, love of neighbor, and concern for the pious they ought to use their freedom and knowledge of spiritual things. The divine law had prohibited the children of Israel from eating at feasts devoted to idols, that is, eating food that had been sacrificed to idols. And that law had very weighty reasons. For God demands a pure confession. He prohibits the approval of idols. He warns that we should abstain from idols and idolatry, lest we be attracted to ungodly worship. Thus it was customary in the church for both the Jewish and Gentile Christians to avoid sacrifices and abstain from idol worship. But various situations often occurred where Gentiles, who had been converted to the Christian faith, were invited by pagan acquaintances to dinner parties where they were served food that had been offered to idols. So too, a godly wife of a pagan husband was forced by her husband to attend these dinner parties. For this reason, various arguments, controversies, and questions were stirred up. Paul therefore instructed them on the idea of freedom, that the whole world belongs to the Lord and that all earthly things are pure. And thus there is no need for a tedious investigation as to what has been offered to idols and what has been brought from the market. But because certain people were proudly abusing this freedom, Paul restricts this freedom and subjects it to the rule of love, which, like a banner, ought to guide the whole practice of virtue. And so, this is the summary of Paul's opinion and the entirety of chapter 8: idols are completely nothing, and the food offered to idols is nothing; all the things of this world are clean, and Christians are permitted to use all the things God has created with thanksgiving. For that reason no scruple should be placed on our consciences. But when we notice that our brother or sister could be injured or offended by our action, we should not proudly boast in our knowledge nor brashly use our freedom, but rather we should consider our neighbor's weakness and be careful not to offend them. For the salvation of our neighbor ought to be more important to us than the free use of external things. Explication of 1 Corinthians 8.[3]

Indebted to Our Siblings in Christ. John Calvin: In the eighth chapter, Paul prohibits the Corinthians from having fellowship with idolaters in their filthy sacrifices, or practicing anything whatsoever that might wound weak consciences. And since they were making excuses for themselves under the pretext that, when they were associating with idolatry, they did so without any perverse

[2]CO 49:428 (cf. CTS 39:271-72).

[3]Hesshus, *Explicatio Prioris Epistolae ad Corinthios*, 123r-v.

thoughts (since in their hearts they acknowledged one God and they considered idols as lifeless images), Paul breaks apart the excuse on this principle: that each person should have regard for their brothers and sisters and that there are many weak people whose faith might be undermined by such dissimulation. Preface to Commentary on 1 Corinthians.[4]

Christian Freedom. Simon Goulart: From what has been said above we can know what Christian freedom is, which begins in this life and is perfectly accomplished in heaven. For thus Christian freedom is a spiritual deliverance, acquired by Jesus Christ, offered by the doctrine of the gospel in the name of Jesus Christ. On the one hand, the merit of Christ's death and obedience delivers believers from sin, the wrath of God, the curse of the law, eternal death, the ceremonies of Moses, human traditions, and suffering the consequences of divine justice. On the other hand, he gives believers the Holy Spirit, who seals in them the freedom of adoption, and turns their hearts to sincere obedience toward God, which enables them to begin to feel and taste the joys of eternal life. On Christian Liberty.[5]

8:1-3 *Knowledge Puffs Up but Love Builds Up*

Food Offered to Idols. Giovanni Diodati: "Now concerning [food offered to idols]." This was the meat used in pagan sacrifices, where, after some of it was consecrated and offered to idols, the rest was sold in the open market (1 Cor 10:25) or used at private feasts without any professed relation to the idol (1 Cor 10:27) or used in public feasts in honor of the idols and in their temples or shrines (1 Cor 8:10; 10:20-21). And the apostle, having been asked whether it is lawful to eat such meat, treats this subject in the present chapter only in this respect: namely, that although this is an indifferent matter, yet Christians should not do it to the scandal of their neighbors, who are weak in the faith, for fear of inducing them to do anything that may be against their consciences. However, in 1 Corinthians 10:19, Paul speaks of this matter in a more weighty consideration, in respect to communicating with the idol. Annotation on 1 Corinthians 8:1.[6]

Paul Anticipates the False Apostles' Arguments. Huldrych Zwingli: "All of us possess knowledge." The false apostles of Corinth were challenging Paul in this way: "Why do you forbid us from eating food sacrificed to idols, since no food is prohibited to us?" Anticipating their argument, Paul responds to them very appropriately, saying, "Truly, I am not talking about food in general, but about idolatrous feasts since they cause the weak to stumble. It is only because you do this so recklessly that I condemn you." It is also possible that the phrase "all of us possess knowledge" should be taken ironically. Annotations on 1 Corinthians 8:1.[7]

Paul Mimics the Corinthians' Boasts. Tilemann Hesshus: Paul here mimics the proud words with which the Corinthians boasted: "All of us are enlightened; all of us have been taught by the Lord; and thus all of us have knowledge that an idol is nothing." Now, even if it is true that all Christians are enlightened by God and that excellent gifts are evident among the saints, nevertheless there is a great difference among godly people. Some have more light and others less light. And the majority of people in the church are always the weaker part—and thus they should not be so proud in their boasts. Explication on 1 Corinthians 8:1.[8]

Knowledge Puffs Up. John Trapp: Paul employs here a metaphor from a pair of bellows, blown up and filled with wind. The French thus call fools *fols*, from the Latin word for bellows

[4]CO 49:301* (cf. CTS 39:44).
[5]Goulart, *Seconde partie des Discours Chrestiens*, 194-95.
[6]Diodati, *Pious Annotations*, MM1*.
[7]Zwingli, *Annotatiunculae . . . ex ore Zvinglij*, 64-65.
[8]Hesshus, *Explicatio Prioris Epistolae ad Corinthios*, 124r.

(*follis*), which contain nothing except air. Such are all proud fools. . . . Pride swells us above measure, unless humility, laid on us as a weight, keeps us down and charity regulates our knowledge for the good of others. . . . But how foolish were those whom Augustine mentioned who neglected the means of knowledge, because knowledge puffs up, and thus would be ignorant so as to be humble, and lack knowledge so that they might avoid pride? This was similar to Democritus, who plucked out his eyes in order to avoid the danger of uncleanness. Commentary on 1 Corinthians 8:1.[9]

Knowledge and Love. Wolfgang Musculus: "Knowledge puffs up." First, understand that this is true because of our corrupt nature and not because of any defect in knowledge. For we are so perverse that, what is good and profitable in itself becomes harmful because of our wickedness. In the same way, riches are good, yet they also lead to pride. Thus we Germans say: Abundance makes one bold.[10] This happens, nevertheless, not because riches are intrinsically wicked, but because *we* are wicked. Otherwise God who is the richest of all beings would also be the proudest of all beings. If knowledge were itself the cause of pride, then the more learned people became, the prouder they would be. But one can see countless numbers of ignorant folk who are far more prideful than those who are educated. Why? Because it is not knowledge itself that puffs up, but the exalted opinion of one's own knowledge that causes pride. . . . Second, understand that things turn out differently if love is missing. For just as riches do not lead to pride when love is present, and the law does not kill when it is undertaken with a gracious spirit (which gives life), so clearly knowledge does not puff up when love is present. Commentary on 1 Corinthians 8:1.[11]

[9]Trapp, *A Commentary or Exposition*, 677*. Tertullian reports the legend that the Greek philosopher Democritus (460 bc) blinded himself to prevent lusting after women. See his *Apology*, in ANF 3:51.

[10]In German, *Guot macht muot*.

[11]Musculus, *Comm. 1 Cor.*, 246.

The Nature of True Knowledge. John Calvin: "If anyone imagines." . . . Those who think they know something, who are delighted in the knowledge they think they possess, and who despise others from on high. Now Paul does not condemn knowledge here, but rather that ambition and haughtiness which profane people produce from it. On the other hand, he is not exhorting us to be skeptics who are always hesitating and suspended in doubt; nor does he approve of a false and artificial modesty, as if it is a good thing to believe that we are ignorant of things that we in fact know. Therefore "the person who imagines that he knows something"—that is, who becomes proud in what he thinks he knows so that he prefers himself to others and is self-conceited—"does not yet know what he ought to know." For the foundation of all true knowledge is personal knowledge of God, which produces in us humility and submission; indeed, rather than raising us up, it completely brings us low. For where pride is, there is ignorance of God. This is a beautiful passage that I wish everyone would learn by heart so that they might hold to the rule of right knowledge. Commentary on 1 Corinthians 8:2.[12]

Knowledge and Ignorance. John Trapp: "This one thing I know, that I know nothing," said Socrates. "Neither know I this yet, that I know nothing," said another. "Though I know myself ignorant of many things," said a third, yet I dare boldly profess with Origen that "I am not ignorant that I am ignorant." The greatest part of our knowledge is but the least part of our ignorance. And yet how apt we are to think we know all that's knowable, as in the case of Alcibiades, where, in his army, all would be leaders, none learners. Epicurus said that he was the first man who ever discovered truth, and yet in many things he was blinder than a beetle. Aratus the astrologer vaunted that he had counted the stars, and written of them all. . . . Wine is good when it goes to the heart to cheer it; but when it fogs up the head, it makes it giddy. So too

[12]CO 49:429 (cf. CTS 39:274).

does knowledge. Nestorius the heretic bragged that he alone understood the Scriptures, and that, until his time, all the world was benighted. He afterward fell into horrid blasphemy, and died in banishment. Commentary on 1 Corinthians 8:2.[13]

True Knowledge of God. Philipp Melanchthon: The expression "He is known by him" is a figure of speech over which interpreters disagree. Some understand "He is known by him" as meaning "accepted." From my perspective, however, it seems that Paul is speaking in his usual way with a change of grammatical relationship: "He is known by him" means "he knows God." For the very order of the sentence demands that we understand this statement as referring to *our* knowledge or understanding, not to our divine reception. Thus in Galatians 4 Paul writes "Formerly, when you did not know God, you were enslaved to beings that by nature are no gods. But now that you have come to know God, or rather to be known by God. . . ." Therefore this is the meaning: There is a twofold knowledge of the gospel. There is a literal meaning, that is, a fleshly understanding that is without the Spirit; that knowledge, however great it may be, is nothing but ignorance because the heart does not know with certainty what things are, and does not believe what is taught. In the last chapter of 1 Timothy, Paul calls this sort of knowledge "what is falsely called knowledge." . . . The other kind of knowledge is spiritual understanding, that is, what the Spirit writes on our heart. It belongs to those who know with certainty and believe in their heart what they teach and profess. In such an understanding there is "sincere faith," as 1 Timothy 1:5 puts it. Therefore a person loves God and so serves God in serving all creatures. Therefore Paul says here, "If one loves God, one is known by him," that is: "this person has the spirit of knowing God." Annotations on 1 Corinthians 8:3.[14]

External Book Knowledge Promotes Pride. Jörg Haug: The Scriptures give only an outer witness of a true life, but they cannot create a new being in me. For this reason one cannot rely on books or learned persons, because books do not produce Christians, for they tend to lead the reader outward rather than inward. Note that at the time of Christ and the apostles there were few books but many good Christians. Back then, divine knowledge was not stolen from books as is the practice now; back then, it was not a matter of moving from external to internals, which is like carrying water to the well. Book learning merely puffs up and produces arrogant persons who think highly of themselves and are forever learning but never arriving at an understanding of the truth. . . . But the true Christian life comes from God and begins in the depth of the soul, as is witnessed by the Scriptures and the creatures.

One should take from books only what concerns and witnesses to a true life, and one should let the book and the teacher go once they have given witness. One must await the power of God in the heart, for all writing and preaching is in vain if God does not give understanding. . . . I must test the witness of the Scriptures to see if it is true in me. But if I am of a different mind and have a wrong understanding, it will hinder me and hold me back from a true, divine understanding. A Christian Order of a True Christian.[15]

8:4-6 *There Is Only One God*

Corinthians Wrongly Applying Correct Doctrine. John Calvin: Paul now returns to that statement with which he began [this chapter], and he speaks more plainly concerning the excuse

[13]Trapp, *A Commentary or Exposition*, 677-78*. Alcibiades (d. 403 BC) was an Athenian military leader during the Peloponnesian War (431–404 BC). Greek philosopher Epicurus (c. 342–271 BC) taught that happiness, known through infallible sense perception, was the object of human life. The writings of Greek poet Aratus (c. 315–c. 245) describe astronomical phenomena and their influence on the weather.

[14]Melanchthon, *Annotationes in Epistolam priorem ad Corinthios*, 96; citing Gal 4:8-9; 1 Tim 6:20.

[15]CRR 10:18*.

the Corinthians were making. For, since the whole trouble took root from this evil—that they were pleased with themselves and despising others—he condemns in general that arrogant knowledge that was not founded in love. Now, however, he explains more specifically what sort of knowledge they were boasting about, namely, that an idol is an empty figment of the human brain, and thus should be considered as nothing. Accordingly consecration that is performed in the name of an idol is a foolish imagination and meaningless. Therefore Christians, who have no reverence for an idol, are not defiled when they eat food offered to idols. That is how they were justifying themselves—and Paul does not reject what they say as false, for it contains excellent doctrine. But Paul rejects it because they were making wrong use of it, violating the principle of love. Commentary on 1 Corinthians 8:4.[16]

Idols Have No Intrinsic Power. The English Annotations: Diverse popish writers, in order to distinguish their image worship from idolatry, expound these words thus: an idol is nothing in the world, that is, nothing formally or representatively, because though it is something materially (i.e., wood, gold, or silver or the like), yet it is nothing formally, because it does not represent any real deity. Whereas, on the other side, an image is the representation of something that has true existence in nature, such as the three persons [of the Trinity], angels, and departed saints. But this distinction of theirs, together with their gloss on this text, is evidently false. For many of the idols of the heathen—such as Baal, Diana, Dagon, as well as the bronze serpent the Jews made into an idol—were images of things that truly existed in nature. For Baal was the image of the sun; Diana or Lucina was the image of the moon; Dagon was the image of a fish; the bronze serpent was the image of the fiery serpents that really stung the Israelites. And God, in the second commandment, expressly forbids bowing down to or worshiping the image of anything that is in heaven above or in the earth beneath or the waters under the earth. But the apostle's true meaning in this passage is that . . . "an idol is nothing," that is, of no worth, having no power or strength within it to profane or hallow the meats offered to it. Annotations on 1 Corinthians 8:4.[17]

Idolaters Worship Different Kinds of Gods. Wolfgang Musculus: It appears that the Gentiles worshiped two kinds of gods, namely, heavenly gods and earthly gods. Some interpreters understand the term "earthly" to also include the gods of the underworld; other interpreters argue that there should be three kinds of Gentile gods. The phrase "whether in heaven" Jerome understands to refer to the angels, that is, heavenly spirits. Chrysostom, Theophylact, and Ambrose understand it to mean the sun, moon, and other stars, to which the Gentiles erroneously ascribed a certain amount of divinity.

The phrase "or on earth" Jerome understands to refer to the saints living on earth, about whom that scriptural passage speaks: "I said, 'You are gods, sons of the most high, all of you.'" Ambrose and Chrysostom understand it to mean those humans who have been considered among the number of the gods, such as Apollo, Aesculapius, Hercules, and Minerva. Nevertheless it seems to me that a more sound conclusion is this: that "on earth" ought not to be understood to refer to dead human beings whom the Gentiles worship with divine honor, but ought to be understood to refer to living human beings of this world, namely, all those princes who, while alive, believed (and wanted others to believe) that they had the power of being transformed from the rank of humans to that of gods. And I think that the same thing pertains to that which Paul adds—"just as there are many gods and many lords"—so that by the word "lords" we should understand the power of human authorities and anything they demand for the sake of mastery. Thus Roman emperors were called "lords." Commentary on 1 Corinthians 8:5.[18]

[16]CO 49:430 (cf. CTS 39:275).

[17]Downame, *English Annotations*, DD4r*.

[18]Musculus, *Comm. 1 Cor.*, 250; citing Ps 82:6. Prominent among

This Passage Teaches Several Important Doctrines. Tilemann Hesshus: Paul eloquently distinguishes between the knowledge of God in the church and that imaginary religious devotion whereby false divine powers are worshiped among the heathen. One should carefully observe, therefore, this important difference between the true church and other sects: the church recognizes the true God made manifest in the church as the one God, through whom all things exist. The heathen outside the church worship various divine powers that are nothing, and are neither able to help nor harm. (1) Moreover, the heathen outside the church are ignorant of the compassionate will of God revealed in the gospel. And thus they can place no hope in God. But the church recognizes the very compassionate will of God, which, because of Christ, wishes to pardon the sins and give grace to those who repent. (2) Paul also hands down the doctrine that the persons in the Godhead are distinct: God the Father, by whom all things exist, and the Son of God, Jesus Christ. (3) In this passage, the doctrine of creation is also touched on, since all things that have been made have been made through the Son. (4) The doctrine concerning the end established for human beings is set before us. Certainly the principle end of human beings is that they should live in service to the praise and glory of the divine, and celebrate forever the wisdom, justice, and all-powerful character of God. Explication of 1 Corinthians 8:4-6.[19]

Both the Father and Son Are God. Wolfgang Musculus: Paul first describes in general terms the divinity of the one, true God and then, more specifically, how that divinity has been demonstrated to believers. The general description is stated thus: "The Father from whom all things come." For Paul ascribes to God that he is the author and source of all things, when he says that all things come from him. . . . Paul then shows how his divinity pertains to believers, when he says: "in whom we live." The "we" here refers to those who believe in Christ, for whom God is one. The statement "in whom we live" relates to the fact that we are his people. Even so, it is not absurd if we follow the older interpreters in reading this Greek phrase *eis auton* as pertaining to the general providence of God, by which, even as we are from God, so we are also sustained and animated by him and live in him, as is stated in Acts 17. . . .

And this passage here should not be misunderstood to mean that the Son does not share the same divinity with the Father, for Paul calls Jesus "Lord," and says that through him "are all things." This passage should instead be employed to demonstrate that the Son is of the same power and divinity with the Father. For just as Paul does not take away from the Father when he ascribes lordship to the Son (as if the Father were not Lord of all!), so he does not detract from the Son's divinity by calling God "Father." . . . Now it appears that Paul calls Christ "Lord" to emphasize the fact that he is the only-begotten of God, who possesses everything with the Father, into whose hand the Father has given all things. Commentary on 1 Corinthians 8:6.[20]

Paul Here Affirms the Full Divinity of the Son. Heinrich Bullinger: [The Corinthians who possessed knowledge] were concluding the following: Heathen gods are nothing; therefore, neither idols nor the sacrifices of the gods are anything. Hence, the preceding argument was also approved, that there is only one God; therefore, there are not many gods. Paul no doubt explains this proposition in greater detail so as to protect the unity of God, lest the divine persons be mixed together. Accordingly, he ascribes equality to both the Father and the Son, that all things exist equally

the Roman gods were Apollo (god of the sun, divination, archery, healing, poetry, and music), Aesculapius (god of medicine), Hercules (son of the god Jupiter), and Minerva (goddess of wisdom and of the arts and sciences). Pseudo-Jerome treats this in *Expositio in Primam Epistolam ad Corinthios*, in PL 30:772 (1865 ed.). For Chrysostom, see his *Homilies on 1 Corinthians* (homily 20), in NPNF 12:113-14. For Theophylact, see his *Expositio in Epist. I ad Cor.*, in PG 124:658-59. For Ambrose (Ambrosiaster), see his *Comment. in Epist. I ad Cor.*, in PL 17:239.

[19]Hesshus, *Explicatio Prioris Epistolae ad Corinthios*, 125r.

[20]Musculus, *Comm. 1 Cor.*, 251-52; citing Acts 17:28.

through both of them, and that we exist through him—that is, the Father and Son, who is one God. Everything holds together by him, who is the author and source of all good things. And, of course, we have been created in him and have been set apart for his glory and worship. The Paraphraser[21] has explained those two members as follows: "For us, there is one God alone, whom we call Father (with respect to Jesus), the founder and author of the universe, the one who bestows all things on us, and whom alone we are required eagerly to please with godly worship. Likewise, the one God is the Lord Jesus Christ, through whom the Father confers all things on us, and by whose kindness alone we recognize the true God," etc. Now Paul has called Christ "Lord" for no other reason than this: that although the prophets called him God, they also frequently called him Lord. Although the ascription "Lord" (when this title is ascribed to Christ) is another name for God in the Scripture, it nevertheless refers even more to the mystery of the incarnation, by which he has liberated us from bondage to Satan (so that Satan now ceases to be our Lord), and Christ instead, who has purchased us with his blood, has begun to be our Lord. We read about this in Psalm 109:[22] "The Lord said to my Lord: 'Sit at my right hand.'" … It's as if the author were saying: "God said to my Lord." For in the first position, he employs the name Yahweh for God, in the second position the name Adonai. Moreover, Christ proved his divinity to the Jews from this same passage in Matthew 22. Accordingly, this passage of Paul clearly demonstrates the unity of God and the distinction of the persons. This is not a human invention, it is the testimony of God.

Moreover, he clearly proves that the Father and the Son, our Lord Jesus Christ, possess the same power, strength, and glory, and also the same kingdom and dominion. Therefore, dear brothers and sisters, let us not allow that wicked book titled *Concerning the Errors of the Trinity* to disturb us. Let us recognize that no error in the confession of the Trinity has ever arisen except those most extreme blasphemies thought up by Arius, Samosata, and Sabellius, together with the unlearned and wicked multitude of people. But the context requires one thing for Paul, and something different for godly people after Tertullian, Athanasius, Hilary, and Augustine had additionally defended the mystery of the Trinity once the scriptural canon was established. And though we cite their writings, we rest on divine authority rather than human authority, for they defended everything from the testimony of Scripture. Commentary on 1 Corinthians 8:5-6.[23]

The Spirit Is Not Excluded Here! Girolamo Zanchi: [Some sophists argue:] "But there's no mention of the Spirit. Therefore the apostle intimates that the Holy Spirit is included among this phrase 'all things.' But all things are made through the Son; therefore the Holy Spirit is a creature." …

I respond. By the name of the Father and of the one God, the Holy Spirit is not excluded—according to the above rule.[24] For … the persons

[21]That is, Erasmus.

[22]*Sic*, Ps 110:1.

[23]Bullinger, *In Priorem ad Corinthios Epistolam Commentarius*, 179; citing Mt 22:41-45. Bullinger is referring to Michael Servetus's book *De Erroribus Trinitatis* (1531), which shocked not only Reformed Protestants in Switzerland but Christians throughout Europe. The Alexandrian presbyter Arius (c. 250–336) argued that the Son was neither coessential nor coeternal with the Father, but was rather preeminent among God's creatures. The third-century priest Sabellius taught that God was indivisible, with Father, Son, and Holy Spirit being different modes of one divine person. The theological perspectives of Arius, Samosata, and Sabellius, which were challenged by orthodox theologians such as Tertullian (c. 155–c. 240), Athanasius (c. 296–373), Hilary of Poitiers (c. 300–c. 368), and Augustine, were formally condemned at the Council of Nicaea (325). Paul of Samosata, a bishop of Antioch during the second half of the third century, was accused of distinguishing between "Christ" as the Logos and Jesus, a mere man.

[24]"It should be noted that wherever mention is made only of the Father and the Son … there usually by the name of the Father is to be understood the person of the Father; by the name of Christ, the person of the Son. But the fact is that the Holy Spirit is never excluded: the Spirit is with both [the Father and the Son] and proceeds from both [the Father and the Son]. However, very often by the name of the Father, the person of the

are not compared with themselves. Rather, the Father is compared with all creatures, especially with the gods of the Gentiles. Therefore, [their argument denying the divinity of the Spirit] is the result of false reasoning. Otherwise we would be able to argue in this way from 2 Corinthians 13, "The grace of the Lord Jesus Christ," etc.: this grace is not ascribed to the Father or to the Holy Spirit; therefore, the Father and the Holy Spirit are excluded from this grace. And then in other passages grace is ascribed to the Holy Spirit without mentioning the Father or the Son—"You will receive the grace of the Holy Spirit"—therefore, is the Son not excluded by this? "The love of God has been poured into our hearts through the Holy Spirit." So then are the Father and Son excluded from this work? Not in the least! For what the Holy Spirit does the Father and the Son also do—indeed the Father works through the Son and Holy Spirit. On the Threefold Elohim.[25]

How Christians Should View Earthly "Lords." John Calvin: Now the Son of God, after he was manifested in the flesh, received from the Father dominion and power over all things, so that he alone might reign in heaven and on earth and that his Father might exercise authority through his hand. This is the reason he is called our "one Lord." But the fact that dominion is attributed to Christ alone does not mean that he has abolished all worldly orders. For Paul is here speaking about spiritual dominion; whereas the authorities of this world are political. . . . Therefore, although our religion acknowledges one Lord, this does not stand in opposition to the state having many lords, to whom honor and respect are due in that one Lord. Commentary on 1 Corinthians 8:6.[26]

Father is not indicated so much as simply the divine essence itself and Yahweh." Zanchi is making a distinction between talking about the persons in the divine essence and talking about the persons relationally; see further Zanchi, *De tribus Elohim*, 2:129-31, here p. 131.

[25]Zanchi, *De tribus Elohim*, 2:132; citing 2 Cor 13:14; Acts 2:38; Rom 5:5.

[26]CO 49:432 (cf. CTS 39:278).

8:7-13 *Protecting Those of Weak Conscience*

How Weak Consciences Are Wounded and Protected. Tilemann Hesshus: How, according to Paul, is the conscience of the weak wounded by the abuse of freedom? When people are weak, of course, they do not yet understand the teaching concerning Christian freedom, and they are fearful that they will harm their consciences by eating foods that have been sacrificed to idols. Nevertheless, they imitate the example of other people—people who understand that idols are nothing and feast on the food sacrificed to idols—and this wounds their consciences, for "whatever does not come from faith is sin." And those who feast contrary to their consciences also have doubts concerning religion and condemn God. Therefore care must be taken lest we offend a weaker brother or sister by an untimely use of freedom. Instead, through our moderation, let us strive to encourage them, instruct them in right doctrine, and strengthen them in the faith. . . .

There are many errors in the human mind. For people often do not recognize sins that, nevertheless, are very serious; and they often are fearful of wounds to the conscience when there is no danger. But whatever else people understand in matters of religion, they must be careful not to undertake anything against their conscience. For the person who judges something to be unclean—it is unclean for him. And it is a very serious sin to disregard God's wrath. First, therefore, we must consult the pure Word of God as to whether God prohibits something in it, for what we know God has forbidden should never be attempted. Second, if we should have any questions about something, it is better to abstain from it than to undertake something with a doubt-ridden conscience, for this would be to tempt God. But people often allege that they are restrained by conscience, so as perhaps to avoid performing their duty, although they are commanded to do it by the express Word of God. The brashness of such people must be vehemently reproached and explicitly refuted. For the conscience ought always to be governed by the Word of God. Explication of 1 Corinthians 8:7.[27]

Paul Defends God's Grace, Not Human Works. Jacques Lefèvre d'Étaples: Why [does Paul say] that food does not commend us to God, if it makes us more acceptable to God? And why [does he say that] we will not abound, if we receive more approval and grace from God? And why [does he say that] we will not suffer deprivation, if we receive less approval and grace from God? Thus one might say that the exploits and works of human beings are neither meritorious nor unmeritorious. We speak according to Paul, who attributes all things to the grace of God. It is almost wicked to speak about the merit of human works, especially in relation to God. For, strictly speaking, merit does not appear to require grace, but obligation; and merit is derived from human works. This way of thinking is very similar to those who believe that we can be justified by works, an error for which the Jews are especially condemned. Therefore let us be silent about the merit of our works, because they are insignificant, or rather of no account. Instead, let us exalt the grace of God, which is everything. People who defend human merit are concerned about human things. People who defend grace are concerned with God. O how much more beautiful is concern for God than people! Commentary on 1 Corinthians 8:8.[28]

Food Does Not Commend Us. Huldrych Zwingli: This word Paul speaks of the food that was offered to the idols, not now of daily food. Notice this, however, for a clearer understanding. At the time when Paul wrote the epistle there were still many unbelievers, more indeed, it seems to me, than Christians. According to custom, these unbelievers offered to other idols animals, such as calves, sheep, and also other forms of food; but at these same offerings, a great part, often all, was given to eat to those that made the offerings. And as unbelievers and Christians lived together, the Christians were often invited to partake of food or meat that had been sacrificed to the honor of the idols. Then some of the Christians were of the opinion that it was not proper to eat this food; but others thought that, if they ate the food of the idols but did not believe in them, such food could not harm them, and thought themselves stronger in their belief, because they had been free to do this thing than those who from faint-heartedness and hesitation did not venture to eat all kinds of food. To settle this difference Paul uses the above words: "No kind of food commends us to God." Even if one eats the food of the idols, they are not less worthy before God, nor yet more worthy, than one who does not eat it; and whoever does not eat it is no better. Indeed that will seem very strange to you, not only that meat is not forbidden, but also that even what has been offered to idols a Christian may eat. Liberty Respecting Food in Lent.[29]

Paul Neither Condones Gluttony nor Prescribes Fasting. John Calvin: "Nor, if we eat, are we the better." Paul is not speaking about well-filled stomachs, for the person who has eaten a meal has a fuller stomach than a person who is fasting. But Paul means by this that we neither gain nor lose righteousness by eating or abstaining from food. Moreover, he is not speaking about every kind of abstinence or every kind of eating. For overindulgence and extravagance for their own sake are displeasing to God, while sobriety and moderation are pleasing to him. But let us understand that the kingdom of God, which is spiritual, does not consist in the external practices, and therefore these neutral things are in themselves of no importance to God. Commentary on 1 Corinthians 8:8.[30]

Christian Freedom Subject to God's Truth. Balthasar Hubmaier: In those things that have to do with human practices, such as eating

[27]Hesshus, *Explicatio prioris epistolae ad Corinthios*, 125v-126r; citing Rom 14:23.
[28]Lefèvre d'Étaples, *Commentariorum in Epistolas Beati Pauli . . . Liber Secundus*, 113r-v.
[29]In Jackson, *Ulrich Zwingli's Early Writings*, 75.
[30]CO 49:434 (cf. CTS 39:281).

meat or not eating meat, holding or not holding holidays, etc., one may well forbear and do or admit something for the sake of the weak, but only for a time until our neighbor is better instructed in the Word of God, and so that Christian freedom should not be made into a new human law. But in true doctrine and in Christian deeds one must freely proclaim and do what God has commanded us and not otherwise, and trust again to the Word of God for its efficacy, even if the whole world were to fall away again. For it is much better that a person should fall than that the Word should fall, for by the Word it will be very easy for him . . . to be helped up again. A FORM FOR WATER BAPTISM.[31]

TWO SORTS OF STUMBLING BLOCKS. PETER MARTYR VERMIGLI: God wishes that we behave toward the weak so as to cause no scandal that might turn them away from the gospel or hold them back from beginning the Christian course. A scandal of word or deed occurs when the course of the gospel is hindered—the growth and transmission of this gospel should be the goal of our entire life and the North Star on which our eyes are constantly fixed. Scandals can be twofold: of life and of doctrine. Concerning stumbling blocks that proceed from corrupt morals, Tertullian says concerning the veiling of virgins that "a scandal is not an example of a good deed, but of an evil deed." And concerning perverse doctrines that cause scandal Augustine separated them into two categories. Belonging to the first category are those that pertain to the divine nature itself, as when the Father is considered greater than the Son, or when the Father is considered to be of a different nature or substance than the Son. The second category of scandals, to be sure, pertains to the church, as when it was said that the church was so rooted in one place that it could not be in another (as the Donatists were asserting at that time). . . . Different scandals are disseminated in different ways: some scandals have been established deliberately, as when laws are codified and decreed that oppose the gospel (which has often been done by the pope and many of the bishops); but other scandals are caused, not from an intentional or deliberate attempt to hinder the gospel, but out of either an effort to satisfy desires or an effort to purse delights and lusts, so that no consideration is given to religion and godliness. COMMENTARY ON 1 CORINTHIANS 8:9.[32]

IDOLATRY IS NEVER JUSTIFIED—EVEN OUT OF CONCERN FOR THE WEAK. ANDREAS BODENSTEIN VON KARLSTADT: It is unjust to use the pretext of not offending the weak and of brotherly love, and, under the appearance of not offending and of brotherly love, to practice idolatry. And to allow the Mass and other blasphemies to sprout and bloom. . . . Idols are more dangerous in Christendom than whorehouses, and more suitable for committing spiritual adultery than any whore or rogue. Therefore people do not practice brotherly love who, under the appearance of brotherly love, say that we should maintain idols (which the laity call saints) in the churches, on hills, in valleys, and at crossroads until the weak become strong. For they preach brotherly harm and not brotherly service or love. Such a pretext is nothing but a villain's cloak and a hidden snare for the destruction of poor souls—if God speaks truthfully and Paul teaches correctly. . . .

We should take such harmful things from the weak, tear them out of their hands, and not pay attention if they cry, scream, or curse about it. The time will come when they who now curse and damn us will thanks us. WHETHER ONE SHOULD PROCEED SLOWLY.[33]

[31]CRR 5:391.

[32]Vermigli, *In Selectissimam S. Pauli Priorem ad Corinth. Epistolam . . . Commentarii*, 204. For Tertullian's treatise *On the Veiling of Virgins*, see ANF 4:27-38. For Augustine, see his *Expositions of the Psalms* (NPNF 8:592). Donatus (died c. 355) was the leader of a schismatic Christian group that denied the sacramental power and authority of Catholic church leaders such as Felix of Aptunga, who had betrayed the faith during persecution but later returned to his ecclesiastical office. The Donatists were opposed in their views by Augustine, who appealed to the need for church unity and pointed out the sinfulness of all Christians and the need for God's grace.

[33]In Baylor, ed., *The Radical Reformation*, 64.

Consider Your Fellow Christian. Huldrych Zwingli: "And your brother will perish." Not only do you cause your brother to stumble, but you also destroy him for whom Christ died. There are two kinds of stumbling blocks. First there are the traps, snares, and nooses that are set up to harm us, by which simple and careless people are ensnared. Such are nearly all of the laws of the pope and the interdicts of wicked rulers, which surpass the laws of the Antichrist in their wickedness and cruelty. Second, when someone gives an opportunity and opening to their neighbor to commit evil, which Christ speaks of in Matthew 18 and Paul mentions here. Annotations on 1 Corinthians 8:11.[34]

To Injure the Weak Is to Wound Christ. Tilemann Hesshus: [Paul adds] that when you wound the conscience of a weak brother or sister, you not only injure a person who, indeed, has been redeemed by the blood of Christ (which is a very serious matter), but you also inflict a horrible wound on the Son of God himself, for Christ had already received the weak brother or sister into the faith; he had already engrafted the weak brother or sister into his body, and recognized them as members with him. Indeed, he had purchased them with his own precious blood and had transferred them to himself. Therefore, when by your rashness you cause ruin to a person so that they abandon the faith, do you not bring harm to the body of Christ and commit a terrible outrage against the Lord? In sum, therefore, in matters of religion, we should be careful lest, by an untimely use of our freedom, we cause offense to the weak. Rather, we ought to accommodate ourselves to the weak and seek their well-being rather than boast about our freedom, knowledge, and power that we possess in the Lord. This word of Paul corresponds to that lofty statement of Christ: "Whatever you have done for one of the least of these, you have done for me." And again, "Whatever you have not done for one of the least of these, you have not done for me." (Matt 25:40, 45). From this statement, we see that nothing is more important than to deter people from sin or excite them to virtue and love of neighbor. Exposition of 1 Corinthians 8:11.[35]

Sinning Against Christ Himself. Wolfgang Musculus: Paul deliberately draws out his discussion of this sin so that it might be recognized as an offense not only against a weak Christian but also against Christ himself. For he thought that those proud Corinthians did not adequately see the nature of their sin against the weak brothers, especially in this case, where they were pretending that they were promoting the knowledge and freedom of Christ. By means of irony, then, Paul proves them wrong to such an extent that, far from pleasing the redeemer Christ with their knowledge, they were actually sinning against him; and this was not some minor sin, but the most serious sin of all. For what more serious sin could be committed against Christ than to kill a person for whom Christ himself has died? A mother loves very deeply that son to whom she has given birth with great pain. If you should violently kill this son, have you not sinned grievously against the mother? And in this verse, Paul intensifies the evil deed even more. For he does not merely say: "In sinning, you sin against Christ," but "in sinning against your brothers, and piercing (rather than 'offending') their weak conscience, you sin against Christ." Commentary on 1 Corinthians 8:12.[36]

Love for God Requires Love of Neighbor. John Colet: In our actions we must always determine, not what we ourselves can do, but what others can bear, so that you measure your conduct by love and charity for your neighbor, not by your own knowledge and power, especially in irrelevant matters like food and drink. We do not gain anything if we eat, nor lose anything if we abstain. For food does not commend a person to God, but love of neighbor, along with a scrupulous care not

[34]Zwingli, *Annotatiunculae . . . ex ore Zvinglij*, 66; citing Mt 18:7-9.

[35]Hesshus, *Explicatio Prioris Epistolae ad Corinthios*, 127v-128r.

[36]Musculus, *Comm. 1 Cor.*, 261.

to offend anyone by your arrogance, since you ought to have the same compassion for another that you would wish Christ to have for you. They are fellow members of Christ: do not ruin their consciences by your recklessness. Abstain from everything rather than commit such an outrage. "If food scandalizes my brother, I shall never again eat meat," says Paul, "lest I scandalize my brother."

In conclusion, then, knowledge—however great—is condemned if it exists without the love of God. This love is recognized in love for your neighbor, if you love them as you wish to be loved; and if . . . you give no grounds for offense. Exposition of 1 Corinthians 8.[37]

Paul's Own Example of Self-Denial. The English Annotations: Here follows the conclusion Saint Paul inserts and states in the first person, so that he might not seem to demand from others what he will not first do himself. "I would rather," he says, "abstain forever from all kinds of meat than put a stumbling block before or give an occasion for sinning to any of my brothers and sisters; much less would I refuse, for their sake, to abstain from meat offered to idols at a certain time or place." Annotations on 1 Corinthians 8:13.[38]

People Abuse This Passage in Two Ways. John Calvin: There are foolish people who allow Christians scarcely any use of indifferent things lest they cause offense to superstitious persons. "Paul," they say, "prohibits here all things that might cause an offense. Now, to eat meat on Fridays will not fail to cause offense. Therefore we must abstain from eating meat, not only when weak persons are present, but without any exception, for it is possible that they might find out about it." I set aside their misinterpretation of the word *scandalizandi*.[39] But they are dreaming in not considering that Paul here is attacking those who rashly abuse their knowledge in the presence of weak persons, whom they do not bother to instruct. Hence, there will be no reason for criticism if teaching has been given beforehand. So too Paul is not commanding us to guess whether what we do might one day cause offense, but only when there is a present danger of doing so.

I come now to the other group of people. They are the pretended followers of Nicodemus, who under this pretext accommodate themselves to the wicked by participating in their idolatries. And rather than being content to excuse their evil deeds, they also want to compel other people to this same behavior. Nothing could be said more clearly to condemn their perverse dissimulation than what Paul here teaches—namely, that everyone who, by their example, encourages the weak to participate in idolatry inflicts a terrible injury on both God and human beings. Commentary on 1 Corinthians 8:13.[40]

[37]Colet, *Enarratio*, 202.

[38]Downame, *English Annotations*, DD4r*.

[39]Meaning, "To cause offense."

[40]CO 49:436 (cf. CTS 39:285-86). In the late 1530s and early 1540s, Calvin wrote three separate treatises condemning the so-called Nicodemites, that is, French Christians who privately affirmed Protestant teaching but, out of fear of persecution, continued to participate in the outward ceremonies of the Catholic Church.

9:1-27 Paul Surrenders His Rights

Am I not free? Am I not an apostle? Have I not seen Jesus our Lord? Are not you my workmanship in the Lord? 2If to others I am not an apostle, at least I am to you, for you are the seal of my apostleship in the Lord.

3This is my defense to those who would examine me. 4Do we not have the right to eat and drink? 5Do we not have the right to take along a believing wife,[a] as do the other apostles and the brothers of the Lord and Cephas? 6Or is it only Barnabas and I who have no right to refrain from working for a living? 7Who serves as a soldier at his own expense? Who plants a vineyard without eating any of its fruit? Or who tends a flock without getting some of the milk?

8Do I say these things on human authority? Does not the Law say the same? 9For it is written in the Law of Moses, "You shall not muzzle an ox when it treads out the grain." Is it for oxen that God is concerned? 10Does he not certainly speak for our sake? It was written for our sake, because the plowman should plow in hope and the thresher thresh in hope of sharing in the crop. 11If we have sown spiritual things among you, is it too much if we reap material things from you? 12If others share this rightful claim on you, do not we even more?

Nevertheless, we have not made use of this right, but we endure anything rather than put an obstacle in the way of the gospel of Christ. 13Do you not know that those who are employed in the temple service get their food from the temple, and those who serve at the altar share in the sacrificial offerings? 14In the same way, the Lord commanded that those who proclaim the gospel should get their living by the gospel.

15But I have made no use of any of these rights, nor am I writing these things to secure any such provision. For I would rather die than have anyone deprive me of my ground for boasting. 16For if I preach the gospel, that gives me no ground for boasting. For necessity is laid upon me. Woe to me if I do not preach the gospel! 17For if I do this of my own will, I have a reward, but if not of my own will, I am still entrusted with a stewardship. 18What then is my reward? That in my preaching I may present the gospel free of charge, so as not to make full use of my right in the gospel.

19For though I am free from all, I have made myself a servant to all, that I might win more of them. 20To the Jews I became as a Jew, in order to win Jews. To those under the law I became as one under the law (though not being myself under the law) that I might win those under the law. 21To those outside the law I became as one outside the law (not being outside the law of God but under the law of Christ) that I might win those outside the law. 22To the weak I became weak, that I might win the weak. I have become all things to all people, that by all means I might save some. 23I do it all for the sake of the gospel, that I may share with them in its blessings.

24Do you not know that in a race all the runners run, but only one receives the prize? So run that you may obtain it. 25Every athlete exercises self-control in all things. They do it to receive a perishable wreath, but we an imperishable. 26So I do not run aimlessly; I do not box as one beating the air. 27But I discipline my body and keep it under control,[b] lest after preaching to others I myself should be disqualified.

a Greek *a sister as wife* **b** Greek *I pummel my body and make it a slave*

Overview: Having established that Christian freedom with respect to neutral or indifferent matters must be accommodated to the consciences of weaker believers, Paul now illustrates in 1 Corinthians 9 how he applied this principle in the conduct of his own ministry among the Corinthians. Drawing on Paul's example, Reformation commentators describe at length the nature and priorities of the pastoral office. Protestant interpreters insist that the substance of faithful

Christian ministry is found in proclaiming the gospel of Jesus Christ—not in performing ceremonies or reciting Masses. True Christian pastors diligently seek lost people through the ministry of the Word; they adapt their sermons to the capacity of ordinary people; they hold indifferent ceremonies loosely so as to win men and women to the truth; they perform their pastoral duties with spiritual zeal and diligence to the very end. All commentators agree that ministers should receive adequate (neither too much nor too little) financial remuneration from their churches in return for their ministry labors. However, Protestant and Catholic interpreters draw very different conclusions as to Paul's meaning by the phrase *adelphēn gynaika* in 1 Corinthians 9:5 ("sister as a wife" or "sister as a woman"). For Protestant church leaders, this verse provides clear testimony that many of the original apostles had wives who accompanied them on their missionary journeys; consequently, in their view, the Roman Catholic Church perpetuates a great fraud in prohibiting marriage to bishops and priests.

Paul's Personal Example. Tilemann Hesshus: Since in chapter 8 Paul has taught that the consciences of the weak should be treated carefully in the use of personal freedom, so now in chapter 9 he sticks to the same topic, placing before the entire church his own personal example. He mentions with what faith and willingness of heart he behaves in the ministry, and that although he is free and possesses the power to do many things, nevertheless he has not made use of this power, but has accommodated himself to weaker brothers and sisters, and has always sought the salvation of his hearers and the edification of the church, even to his own inconvenience. Paul also takes the opportunity to add some instruction concerning the wage that ought to be given to ministers of the gospel. But the focus of the whole of chapter 9 is this: even though Paul had great freedom and power in eating and drinking, in taking a wife, in demanding wages according to the regulation of Jesus Christ, in foregoing circumcision, and in various other matters, yet he made use of none of these rights so as not to cause offense to anyone. And so too our affection for our brothers and sisters ought to be such that we would rather give up our right of freedom than cause anyone to stumble. Indeed, this is the spirit of true freedom: to be able to go without and abstain from all things when the situation demands it, so that we might win some people to Christ. Explication of 1 Corinthians 9.[1]

On Not Causing Offense. John Calvin: In the ninth chapter, Paul shows that he requires nothing more from the Corinthians than what he himself practiced, lest he seem to be unfair in placing a law on other people that he does not keep himself. For he reminds them how he voluntarily abstained from the freedom granted to him by the Lord so that he might not cause offense to anyone; and how, in indifferent matters, he had accommodated himself to everyone (as if he were taking on various appearances) so that they might learn from his example that no one should be so absorbed in themselves as not to endeavor to adapt themselves to their brothers and sisters for their edification. Introduction to Commentary on 1 Corinthians.[2]

9:1-6 *Paul's Self Defense*

Paul Set Aside His Freedom. John Colet: Paul was free, since he was an apostle, and the apostle of the Corinthians. Nevertheless, he judged that what was pure and lawful in itself was not lawful for him among the Corinthians, lest he should thereby abuse his authority, which was not intended for the destruction of the church, but for its construction. Consequently he was unwilling either to draw his livelihood from the gospel or to take women assistants around with him, although by the law of Christ and the example of other apostles these things were lawful. No, he was a man

[1]Hesshus, *Explicatio Prioris Epistolae ad Corinthios*, 129r-v.
[2]CO 49:301 (cf. CTS 39:44).

whose concern was, as it had to be, the advantage of Christ and of the gospel, and so he abstained from lawful things when he saw that it was not proper to use them lest he cause offense to the gospel of Christ. Exposition of 1 Corinthians 9.[3]

Why Does Paul Boast So Much? Philipp Melanchthon: Answer: First, the logic of his argument requires that he extol his right so that, by means of the comparison with him, he may shame those who, on account of their freedom, allow themselves to make all things lawful. Second, it is not just here but often elsewhere that he boasts so that the church may know that he is not proclaiming his own word but the word of him who called and sent him. Thus the church should listen not to him but to the God who sends him. Paul writes in all his epistles that he was called to be an apostle, so that the church might know with certainty that it is the Word of God which is proclaimed by him, because it is required of those who have been called that they should be certain that they are announcing the Word of God. Annotations on 1 Corinthians 9:1.[4]

Paul Appeals to His Apostolic Authority. Huldrych Zwingli: "Am I not an apostle?" Paul asserts his authority against the false apostles who defy him in all things, since this matter concerns the glory of God. For Paul was an apostle, sent by the command of Christ to the Gentiles (Acts 9). "Am I not free?" Since he asserts himself to be an apostle, he also claims for himself the rights and freedoms of the apostolic office. Even if he does not always take advantage of these rights, nevertheless he shows that they are permitted to him. "Have I not seen Jesus Christ, our Lord?" Only for this reason was anyone able to boast. For Paul had seen Christ in Damascus (Acts 9). Annotations on 1 Corinthians 9:1.[5]

Paul Had Seen Christ. Peter Martyr Vermigli: Paul discloses that he had seen the Lord, so that he might not be considered inferior to the other apostles who had fixed their eyes on the Lord Jesus during his lifetime. When Paul treats the subject of the resurrection at the end of this epistle, he says: "But afterward, he appeared also to me, as one untimely born." Now some people ask where the apostle saw the Lord. Some think that it was outside of Damascus, when he heard the voice, "Saul, Saul, why do you persecute me?" Ambrose thinks that it happened when Paul was praying in the temple. And so Paul saw the Lord after his resurrection, when he was already glorified, and he was sent by him to preach. Commentary on 1 Corinthians 9:1.[6]

Why Paul Appeals to Having Seen Christ. Giovanni Diodati: "Have I not seen [Christ]?" Namely, in the vision mentioned in Acts 22:18, or in the state of ecstasy reported in 2 Corinthians 12:2, 4. Now Paul adds this, because his adversaries were vilifying his ministry, claiming that he had not known Christ on the earth, and thus suggesting he lacked something either in the dignity of his person, or in his apostolic authority, or in the knowledge of those things that had been taught by the Lord. Annotations on 1 Corinthians 9:1.[7]

The Corinthians Are Paul's Workmanship. Wolfgang Musculus: With a great deal of boasting, Paul ascribes to himself a whole range of great human achievements that can be attributed to the power of God alone. But this was necessary because of the great shamelessness and wickedness of the false apostles that forced the

[3]Colet, *Enarratio*, 204. Colet renders the Greek term *adelphēn gynaika* ("a sister as a wife") with the Latin term *feminas ministras* ("women assistants"), suggesting that he did not believe that Paul was married. Early church fathers such as Clement and Eusebius, as well as later Protestant reformers, took this verse to mean that Paul had a wife.

[4]Melanchthon, *Annotationes in Epistolam priorem ad Corinthios*, 100.

[5]Zwingli, *Annotatiunculae . . . ex ore Zvinglij*, 67; citing Acts 9:15.

[6]Vermigli, *In Selectissimam S. Pauli Priorem ad Corinthios . . . Comentarii*, 213v-214r; citing 1 Cor 15:8; Acts 9:4. For Ambrose's (Ambrosiaster's) treatment of this verse, see his *Comment. in Epist. I ad Cor.*, in PL 17:241.

[7]Diodati, *Pious Annotations*, MM2v*.

apostle to engage in this boasting, as he also says in the next letter: "You forced me." Now we should not think that he attributed more to himself than is fitting for an apostle, since he was speaking as an apostle of Christ and as a minister of the Holy Spirit. Accordingly, Paul says: "Are you not my workmanship," that is, "the product of my apostleship, in the Lord?" It is as if he were saying, "Whatever you are in the Lord, you are through my apostleship. For you believed in Christ through me." Theophylact thinks that the clause "in the Lord" should be interpreted as "through the power of the Lord," lest it be supposed that Paul was ascribing so difficult a work to his own power. In my judgment the first interpretation is simpler, although the latter should not be dismissed entirely. Commentary on 1 Corinthians 9:1.[8]

The Corinthians Are the Seal of Paul's Apostleship. Peter Martyr Vermigli: By the word "seal" Paul means a "certain proof," just as letters are shown to be of firm authority by the seal, and many authors are accustomed to affix their seal to their completed writing as a sure mark of the finished work. In the same way, Paul testified that the Corinthians themselves were the sign and mark of his completed and perfect apostleship. It was necessary for them either to acknowledge that they had been converted to Christ or to deny it. If they were to deny it, he would protest that their church had not been planted or built up in Christ. But if they confessed that it was, then Paul was shown to be the apostle who had preached Christ to them. Nevertheless, it does not appear to be a convincing proof of apostleship when someone draws a crowd to himself and establishes an assembly under his leadership. For the Manichaeans had their leaders, and the Donatists theirs, and there were many leaders among the Arians—I said leaders, not pastors or bishops. But Paul's argument corresponds to those things that he had said previously, that he had seen the Lord and had been sent by him to confirm his sound teaching, which heretics were not declaring, although they had crowds of people following their teachings. Commentary on 1 Corinthians 9:2.[9]

Paul's Defense Before His Accusers. Tilemann Hesshus: Paul says, "This is my defense." It's as if here were saying: "I will not argue a lot with my accusers, for that church, built through my ministry, offers a living testimony on my behalf." And so he ties up the false apostles, for although they are accusing him of many things, are boasting greatly, and flaunting their freedom at inopportune times, nevertheless they are producing little fruit in the church. Explication of 1 Corinthians 9:3.[10]

Paul Had the Right to Eat, Drink, and Take a Believing Wife. John Calvin: Paul concludes from what was previously said, that he had the right to receive food and clothing from them. For Paul both ate and drank, but not at the church's expense. This, therefore, was one of the freedoms that he was giving up. The other was that he did not have a wife who was maintained at the people's expense. Eusebius concludes from these words that Paul was married, but that he left his wife in a particular place so as not to be a burden to the churches; but this is a false assumption, for a single person could have said the same thing. The fact that Paul honors a Christian wife with the

[8]Musculus, *Comm. 1 Cor.*, 265. For Theophylact's treatment of this verse, see his *Expositio in Epist. I ad Cor.*, in PG 124:663.

[9]Vermigli, *In Selectissimam S. Pauli Priorem ad Corinthios Epistolam . . . Comentarii*, 214r. The Manichaeans, with their leader Mani (c. 216–276), posited a dualistic cosmology in which the spiritual world of light battled against the evil material world of darkness. In their view, Christ was but one among a group of prophets who provided spiritual enlightenment. Donatus (died c. 355) was the leader of a schismatic Christian group that denied the sacramental power and authority of Catholic church leaders such as Felix of Aptunga who betrayed the faith during persecution but later returned to his ecclesiastical office. The Donatists were opposed in their views by Augustine, who appealed to the need for church unity and pointed out the sinfulness of all Christians and the need for God's grace. Arius (d. 336) was condemned at the Council of Nicaea (325) for affirming that the Son of God was a creature, thus denying the full divinity of Christ.

[10]Hesshus, *Explicatio Prioris Epistolae ad Corinthios*, 130v.

name of "sister" suggests first of all how firm and lovely the union between believing spouses should be, joined by a double bond. Second, this also suggests what modesty and consideration should exist between them. From this we can also conclude that it is not improper for church ministers to be married. I make no mention of the fact that the apostles employed this right [of being married], an example of which Paul will mention shortly. Commentary on 1 Corinthians 9:4.[11]

Women Accompanied the Apostles to Provide Necessary Resources. Cardinal Cajetan: Paul explains the way in which the other apostles were using this power, and this was their method: as the apostles were traveling about and preaching, they attracted around themselves some women who were assisting them by supplying necessary things. In so doing, they were following the example of Christ, who was accompanied by women who assisted by providing necessary resources. And Paul speaks of a "sister-woman" to indicate that the apostles had a woman who had the function of a "sister." I do not think that the woman who traveled with them was assisting out of her own resources (since outside the territory of the Jews this would have been difficult); rather, she was a woman to whom wealthy women would give money to provide necessary provisions for the apostles, both in the city and especially along the journey. Commentary on 1 Corinthians 9:5.[12]

Paul Here Is Referring to His Own Wife. Huldrych Zwingli: "To take along a sister as a wife." In Greek, *gynē* does not only mean "woman," but it can also mean "wife." So Paul is here speaking about his wife, whom he brought with him from time to time, though not always. As he said earlier, he wishes everyone to share his mindset, so that they would not be affected greatly by the passions of the flesh, controlling themselves amid their constant journeys, dangers, strife, and troubles. It is in this sense that Paul says: "I wish that all were as I myself am," that is, "I desire that everyone have a tranquil mindset—not overwhelmed with licentious passions—as was granted to me by the grace of God." But Paul does not condemn marriage, and he does not send away his wife. In fact, he calls her his "sister" on account of their common faith in Christ. Annotations on 1 Corinthians 9:5.[13]

The Apostles Were Married. Wolfgang Musculus: Recognize here what is said regarding the earthly provision of believers. For those people are completely inept who think this verse refers to wealthy women who followed the apostles and were providing financial support for their preaching. We read that this happened in the ministry of Christ, but not so among the apostles. People who defend virginity and sexual continence fabricate this false interpretation to hide the fact that the apostles were married. Now it is completely clear that when Paul here employs the term "sister-wife" (*adelphēn gynaika*), he uses "sister" in the sense of a believer in Christ. Moreover, he makes it clear in chapter 7 that the Greek word *gynē* signifies a wife. Now if Paul was only speaking about a female believer who was not married, why did he need to add the word "wife" after "sister"? For what sister is there who is not a woman? But it is possible for a woman to be a sister without being a wife. Therefore, since Paul added the word "wife" (*gynaika*) after the word "sister," I think that it is completely stupid for people not to recognize . . . that Paul was speaking about a believing wife, rather than merely a female believer. . . .

The fact that the apostles had wives is seen in the writings of both their contemporaries and their disciples. Ignatius, in his letter to the Philadelphians, wrote in this manner: "Now I do not disparage those other brothers of blessed memory who entered into marriage. For I hope God finds me worthy to follow in the footsteps of those who entered into the kingdom of God, men like

[11]CO 49:439 (cf. CTS 39:291). The Greek text reads literally "a sister as wife."

[12]Cajetan, *In Sacrae Scripturae expositionem*, 5:112.

[13]Zwingli, *Annotatiunculae . . . ex ore Zvinglij*, 69; citing 1 Cor 7:7.

Abraham, Isaac, and Jacob, as well as Joseph, Isaiah, and the other prophets, as well as Peter and Paul and the rest of the apostles, who joined themselves in marriage, not out of sexual appetite, but out of desire to propagate the human race."

Eusebius, in his *Ecclesiastical History*, also writes: "Indeed, Clement, whose words we have just quoted, wrote against those who rejected marriage. Among other things, he said this: 'Or will they reject even the apostles? For Peter and Philip had wives and they gave their daughters in marriage. And Paul does not hesitate, in one of his epistles, to greet his wife, whom he did not take about with him so as to make it easier for him to preach the gospel.'"

And so it is known, both from the words of the apostles themselves, and from the testimony of Ignatius and Clement (whom we can trust in this matter) that, first, the apostles, the brothers of the Lord, and Peter and Paul all had wives. Second, that their wives traveled about with them (with the exception of Paul). Third, it is proper for a minister of Christ to demand and receive from the church in which he proclaims the gospel the necessary financial provision to support not only himself but also his wife and children. This is his right, whether he wishes to demand it or not. Commentary on 1 Corinthians 9:5.[14]

Marriage Is Permissible for Christian Ministers. Tilemann Hesshus: From this passage it is clear that marriage is honorable for all people, and that it is prohibited to no class of people. For Paul testifies that many of the apostles, and especially the brothers of the Lord (James the Lesser, Simeon, and Judas Thaddeus) and Peter had wives and brought them along on their journeys and ministry. Therefore it is certainly the doctrine of demons when the Roman pontiff and his bishops prohibit legitimate marriage to priests. Explication of 1 Corinthians 9:5.[15]

Paul's Reference to Peter Does Not Lend Support to Papal Primacy. John Calvin: Now, those who wish to establish the papacy from this passage are making fools of themselves. We confess that Peter was recognized as first among the apostles, since it is always necessary in every assembly for there to be someone who presides over the others. And moreover, they respected Peter on account of the exceptional gifts with which he was endowed, for it is right to hold in high esteem and honor all those who excel in the graces of God. But Peter's primacy was not lordship; indeed, it had nothing to do with domination. For even though he stood out among the others, he was still subject to those who were his colleagues. Furthermore, it is one thing to hold primary place in a single church, but something else to claim for oneself sovereignty and dominion over the whole world. Even if we should grant all these things concerning Peter, what has this to do with the pope? For in the same way that Matthias succeeded Judas, so some Judas could succeed Peter. Indeed, we see that for almost the past nine hundred years, there has not been one from among his successors (or at least those who boast that they are his successors) who has been one whit better than Judas. Commentary on 1 Corinthians 9:5.[16]

Laborers Deserve Their Wages. Tilemann Hesshus: Now Paul adds that he has the power to abstain from working with his hands, and to receive his subsistence only from the ministry of the gospel. "For the laborer deserves his wages." Therefore, since the apostles and pastors are responsible for serving the entire church in the very difficult work of teaching and administering the sacraments, the rule of equity demands that they should receive their livelihood from the wages provided by the church. For our Lord Jesus Christ has also commanded this. And the apostles undoubtedly requested alms from their hearers so that they could have the time to study and preach, and abstain from working with their hands. Now,

[14]Musculus, *Comm.1 Cor.*, 269, 272-73. Ignatius of Antioch, "Letter to the Philadelphians," chap. 4, longer version, in ANF 1:81; Eusebius, *Eccl. History* 3:30, in NPNF 1:161-62.

[15]Hesshus, *Explicatio Prioris Epistolae ad Corinthios*, 131v.

[16]CO 49:440 (cf. CTS 39:292); citing Act 1:23-26.

Paul, so as to demonstrate with great transparency that he was not spreading the teaching of the gospel for the sake of personal gain but that he was only seeking the glory of God and the edification of the church, did not demand a wage nor do anything burdensome to the Christian assembly. Instead, he procured life's necessities by working with his own hands, and Barnabas followed Paul's example. Once again, by his example, Paul teaches that he did not use his rights, but preferred to use his freedom for the glory of God and the edification of the church. And he wants other teachers of the church to imitate this godly disposition. Explication of 1 Corinthians 9:6.[17]

The Challenges of Gospel Work. John Trapp: I agree with Melanchthon's opinion, who, when a person stated that Christian ministry was the art of arts and the science of sciences, said that if one added that it was the misery of miseries, then that person had hit the nail on the head. Commentary on 1 Corinthians 9:6.[18]

9:7-14 *Ministers of the Gospel Deserve Support*

Pastors Should Receive Sufficient Support. Guillaume Farel: We should feed [the pastor] who brings us the doctrine of life. For God commanded that he who evangelizes and preaches the gospel ought to live from the gospel. For this reason those who are taught and comforted by the Word of God should share all goods with him who serves them in the Word. Neither ought we to pay him an enormous amount, as we have fed the pompous in rubbish until now, nor leave him a pauper, but feed him and clothe him in such a way that he can duly perform his office. Without being puffed up by the abundance of riches, nor constrained by need to do otherwise than he should, he ought to have sufficient means to live. Summary and Brief Exposition.[19]

Ministers and Their Wages. Wolfgang Musculus: Paul drives his intense questioning to a simple conclusion. If no one ever fights at his own expense, if no one ever plants a vineyard without eating its fruit, if no one ever tends a flock without living off of the milk—thus it is a universal and perpetual law, recognized by all human beings and approved over time, that the person who works for the benefit of others should not be supported by his own resources but at the expense of those whom he serves. Now these examples beautifully accord with Paul's purpose: if you demand that the spoils of war be given to a solider, the fruit given to the farmer, the milk given to the shepherd, then it is equally appropriate that ministers who are proclaiming the gospel should not be expected to live at their own expense....

In the church of Christ, people sin in this matter in [four] ways. First, some ministers fulfill their pastoral duty, but, rather than being content with their basic wage, they seek wealth and luxury. Second, some ministers are lazy yet enjoy the wages that laborers deserve. Third, some ministers are not only lazy and take the wages that laborers deserve but also amass enormous wealth and live in extravagance. The fourth kind of minister is worst of all: they are the ones who are so unfit for fighting that they leave the people of the Lord desolate; they are so unfit for planting the vineyard of the Lord that they dissipate it; they are so unfit for tending the flock of the Lord that they destroy it. Commentary on 1 Corinthians 9:7.[20]

Paul's First Argument for Pastoral Support. Tilemann Hesshus: The first argument Paul gives is drawn from the example of human affairs. "No one serves as a soldier at his own expense." The pastor of the church is a soldier of Christ and the gospel. "The person who plants, enjoys its fruit." Therefore the pastor who plants the vineyard of the Lord should receive provisions from his labor. "The shepherd enjoys the milk of the flock," and receives a certain wage. Therefore

[17]Hesshus, *Explicatio Prioris Epistolae ad Corinthios*, 131v-132r; citing Lk 10:7.
[18]Trapp, *A Commentary or Exposition*, 679-80*.
[19]In Zuidema and Van Raalte, *Early French Reform*, 163.
[20]Musculus, *Comm. 1 Cor.*, 275-76.

the spiritual shepherd, who is in charge of the flock and the clergy of the Lord, ought to be entirely nourished and supported, together with his whole household. Explication of 1 Corinthians 9:7.[21]

Don't Butcher the Sheep. Huldrych Zwingli: "Who tends a flock and does not enjoy the milk of the flock?" Here Paul uses a vivid word picture. Now be on your guard against those who milk and shear the flock in the manner of the papists! You should recognize them as violent tyrants of the flock of God. They do not merely shear the sheep, but instead they flay them and strip away their skin. They do not merely enjoy the milk of the flock, but they very cruelly butcher the sheep and devour their fat. These are not shepherds; rather, I call them wolves! Annotations on 1 Corinthians 9:7.[22]

Ministers Should Receive Support. John Trapp: Ministers as they should be are as valiant as soldiers, as diligent as farmers, and as vigilant as shepherds; in the same way, they should live off their labor, as every tinker and tapster does. It is a sign of waning devotion when people are so close-fisted toward their ministers, whose very cold water does not go unrewarded. Commentary on 1 Corinthians 9:7.[23]

Human Experience Corroborates Scriptural Truth. Wolfgang Musculus: This present passage serves as proof for us that, in matters of religion, examples drawn from human experience should not be rejected. Everything that is right and fair in human experience is recognized as such in due time and place. But because of contentious and wicked people, we add the authority of holy Scripture to corroborate with the testimony of the Word of God those things that otherwise might seem to be human and uncertain from a worldly point of view. For all truth is in agreement with itself—as Paul shows. Indeed, the minister of Christ ought to be prepared to demonstrate from passages of holy Scripture how truth drawn from human experience is compatible with heavenly truth. The use of human examples should not be judged as vile and superfluous. . . . Ministers convey the brilliant light of heavenly truth—and a lot of power—when they demonstrate that what is found in the Word of God is consistent with what is found in the customs and experiences of human beings. Likewise, ministers of the Word need to show a lot of diligence . . . to listen, watch, observe, and pay attention to whatever is assumed to be just, fair, right, true, and useful in this age, whatever it may be, so that they can draw from them, for the purpose of teaching, proofs of heavenly truth, justice, equity, and usefulness. Commentary on 1 Corinthians 9:8.[24]

Interpreters Should Use Allegories Sparingly. William Perkins: It shall be lawful also to gather allegories: for they are arguments taken from things that are like, and Paul in his teaching often uses them (1 Cor 9:9). But they are to be used with these caveats: let them be used sparingly and soberly; let them not be far-fetched, but fitting to the matter in hand; they must be quickly dispatched; they are to be used for the instruction of the life and not to prove any point of faith. The Art of Prophesying.[25]

Paul's Second Argument for Pastoral Support. Tilemann Hesshus: Second, Paul argues from the testimony of God. He states that sacred Scripture itself—which ought to be the norm for all of our actions—commands that "an ox threshing [the grain] should not be muzzled." This shows that those who labor ought to be given a fair wage. Why does Paul say that oxen are of no concern to God? He is not denying that universal providence of God whereby God watches over every creature. This is known from the statement of Psalms 147: "He gives food to every creature, he

[21]Hesshus, *Explicatio Prioris Epistolae ad Corinthios*, 132v.
[22]Zwingli, *Annotatiunculae . . . ex ore Zvinglij*, 70.
[23]Trapp, *A Commentary or Exposition*, 680*.
[24]Musculus, *Comm. 1 Cor.*, 277-78.
[25]Perkins, *The Works of William Perkins*, 340-41.

gives horses their food as well as the young ravens that cry." Again: "Look at the birds of the heaven, they neither sow nor reap nor gather into barns, and yet your heavenly Father feeds them" (Matt 6:26). But Paul reminds his readers that that law was written not only for the sake of oxen, but even more for us, that we might learn from it that those who labor in the ministry should not be cheated of physical provision and a fair wage. If God wishes an ox threshing the grain to be fed, how much more is it God's will that farmers should plow with the expectation of reaping the fruit of their labor, and that reapers and threshers should be allowed to share in the crop. And so too it is completely fair that ministers of the gospel, who serve the church by means of the Word and are forced to disregard their private affairs, should be provided for with food and necessary support. Explication of 1 Corinthians 9:9-10.[26]

The Needs of Christian Teachers Must Be Provided. Menno Simons: Let all sincere and pious servants of Christ beware of this, and whatever they cannot earn by due labor and diligence will doubtlessly be provided for them as needed, not by the impenitent heathen, the drunkards, the usurers, the fornicators, but by the converted brethren who fear the Lord, for whom they sow spiritual things. For such teachers are the oxen that tread out the corn and are not to be muzzled. Brief Confession on the Incarnation.[27]

Gospel Laborers Deserve Financial Support. David Dickson: Paul appeals to the testimony of the law regarding giving food to the oxen that tread out the corn to show that it applied to those who labor for the benefit of others, especially in the ministry. Oxen are fed with the corn that they beat out with their feet. Therefore all laborers, plowers, threshers, and by consequence all laborers in the gospel ought to be maintained with the fruit of their own labors. For if those who plow and thresh in the hope of the reward are partakers of their hoped-for reward, then why should those who labor for the sake of the gospel not be partakers of the fruit of their own labors? Exposition of 1 Corinthians 9:10.[28]

The Value of the Gospel Justifies the Minister's Wage. Wolfgang Musculus: [An additional] argument that Paul gives for providing earthly wages to sustain the needs of the apostle (although these wages were small and of little significance) is adduced from the great value of the message announced to human beings through the ministry of the gospel. Paul uses a comparison to show that the support provided to the minister of Christ ought not to seem troublesome or extravagant. The benefits that are imparted by the minister of Christ are spiritual things that vivify the human spirit, bringing true happiness in this present life and, in the future life, promising eternal happiness for the body as well. By contrast, the wages that are owed to the minister are material in nature, that is, they are applicable to sustaining the human body. Since the spirit of a person is superior to their body, and since true life in heaven is more precious than this transitory life on earth, how much greater are those spiritual and eternal benefits than earthly and material wages! Thus that person is especially ungrateful of God's gifts who is unwilling to contribute earthly wages to a minister from whom they have received heavenly blessings. Commentary on 1 Corinthians 9:11.[29]

Paul's Third Argument for Pastoral Support. Tilemann Hesshus: Paul's third argument is derived from the comparison of greater things. For spiritual things—namely, the Word of God; knowledge of the true God; personal knowledge of the Mediator; consolation in the face of death, sin, and Satan; reception of the

[26] Hesshus, *Explicatio Prioris Epistolae ad Corinthios*, 132v-133r; citing Psalm 147:9.
[27] Simons, *Complete Writings*, 442.
[28] Dickson, *Exposition of St. Paul's Epistles*, 54*.
[29] Musculus, *Comm. 1 Cor.*, 279-81.

sacraments; absolution from sins; the doctrine of how one is able to arrive at eternal life and the kingdom of Christ—are infinitely more excellent than physical and earthly goods, such as friendship, food, drink, clothing, money, and the necessities of this life. "Since, therefore, we apostles impart spiritual things on you, the law of equity demands that you, in turn, share the necessities of life with us." This is a very weighty argument that all godly people ought seriously to consider and should awaken within them gratitude toward pastors. No human words can express how ungrateful are those persons who refuse to give fair wages to their pastors. Explication of 1 Corinthians 9:11.[30]

Paul's Fourth Argument for Pastoral Support. Tilemann Hesshus: The fourth argument is from the example of other teachers, who also received wages and support from the church—indeed, from the Corinthian church. From this, Paul infers that he was far more deserving of this support because he was . . . in a way the first builder, who laid the original foundation of this church. Paul then returns to his major principle: that he is not using that freedom and power as he certainly could have. And then, he adds this final reason why he has decided on this approach: not so as to chase after empty glory, but so that he might avoid in every way placing any obstacle to the gospel of Jesus Christ. Explication of 1 Corinthians 9:12.[31]

Paul's Fifth Argument for Pastoral Support. Tilemann Hesshus: The fifth argument is taken from the example of the priests and Levites who, whenever they were sacrificing, slaughtering sacrificial victims, and serving at the altar, were given their share of the sacrifice in accordance with the law. Now the glory of the new covenant is far greater and offers greater brightness than the old covenant. And pastors of churches, in teaching the people, undertake an office more difficult than the priests and Levites who slaughter sacrificial victims. It is only right, therefore, that pastors be sustained in the ministry. In the law of Moses, God carefully prescribes that provisions should be supplied to priests and Levites so that they might have leisure for the reading of Scripture. Now, Paul commands us to strive after teaching, and pastors and ministers in the new covenant are to be sustained to the extent of their devotion to it. Explication of 1 Corinthians 9:13.[32]

As with Levitical Priests, Modern Pastors Should Receive Support. John Calvin: The point is this: the Levitical priests were the ministers of the church of Israel; and the Lord established that provisions be given them for their ministry. Therefore the same principle of equity should be preserved with respect to ministers of the Christian church today. Now, ministers of the Christian church are those who proclaim the gospel. . . . Paul's reasoning is that pastors who labor at preaching the gospel should be supported, because the Lord once assigned sustenance to the priests because they were serving the church. Therefore a distinction must be maintained between the ancient priesthood and the priesthood of today. Priests under the law were set apart to preside over sacrifices, serve at the altar, and take care of the tabernacle and temple. Today they are set apart to proclaim the Word and dispense the sacraments. The Lord has not appointed his sacred ministers to be occupied with sacrifices; they are not appointed to stand at altars to offer sacrifices.

Therefore one sees how ridiculous those people are who apply this analogy, derived from sacrifices, to anything other than to the preaching of the gospel. And more than that, it is easily inferred from this passage that all those papal priests (from the head himself to the lowest clergy) are guilty of sacrilege, who devour the revenues appointed for true ministers, while they do not at all perform their duty. For what ministers does the apostle

[30]Hesshus, *Explicatio Prioris Epistolae ad Corinthios*, 133v.
[31]Ibid., 133v-134r.
[32]Ibid., 134r.

command that we support? Answer: those that apply themselves to preaching the gospel. Commentary on 1 Corinthians 9:13.[33]

Paul's Sixth Argument for Pastoral Support. Tilemann Hesshus: This sixth and most important argument comes from the authority and command of the Son of God, our Lord Jesus Christ. The person who dares to break or find fault with the command or ordinance of our Lord Jesus Christ is entirely wicked. For Jesus Christ himself, the head, redeemer, and Savior of the church, the author and judge of ministers, established this law and thus commanded it. "So that those who proclaim the gospel should get their living from the gospel"—that is, they should be supported by the church and their hearers with fair wages, by which they can support themselves and their households. Undoubtedly, Paul is looking back at the sermon of Christ in Matthew 10,[34] "For the laborer deserves his wages." And Christ several times repeated this law and decree in his sermons. It is therefore completely proper to seek decent and necessary wages from the ministry of teaching in the church so as to support one's household. Explication of 1 Corinthians 9:14.[35]

Christian Ministers Proclaim the Gospel. Wolfgang Musculus: "Those who proclaim the gospel." With these few words Paul expresses the substance and method of ministering for the Lord. The substance of Christian ministry is found in speaking the gospel—not in reciting and singing Masses. The method by which ministers serve the Lord is in announcing the Word. Notice here that Paul appropriately joins the gospel to proclamation—not making laws or issuing commands. The gospel is the good news of salvation provided to the whole world through Christ, and received by faith in Christ. The Lord wants this gospel to be proclaimed to people throughout the whole world, with great joy and gladness, in the same way that wonderful news is proclaimed with joyfulness to people who are miserable and afflicted. That is what we see in Romans 10: "How beautiful are the feet of those who proclaim peace," etc. Commentary on 1 Corinthians 9:14.[36]

The Spiritual Shepherd and His Provision. Michael Sattler: We have agreed as follows concerning the shepherds in the community of God.[37] According to Paul's prescription, the shepherd in God's community should be one who has a completely good reputation among those who are outside the faith. His duties should be to read, to admonish, to teach, to warn, and to punish or ban in the community; to lead all sisters and brothers in prayer and in breaking the bread; and to make sure that in all matters that concern the body of Christ the community is built up and improved. He should do this so that the name of God is praised and honored among us, and the mouths of blasphemers are stopped.

Should this pastor be in need, he should be provided for by the community that chose him, so that he who serves the gospel should also live from it, as the Lord has ordained. . . . But if a shepherd is banished or through the cross[38] brought to the Lord, another should be ordained in his place immediately so that God's little people are not destroyed, but maintained and consoled by the warning. The Schleitheim Articles.[39]

9:15-18 *Paul Proclaims the Gospel Free of Charge*

Why Does Paul Boast in Performing His Duty? Desiderius Erasmus: I am so resolute in this mindset [of not claiming my rights] that I would rather die of hunger than to begin to allow anyone to deprive me of this boasting, and having

[33]CO 49:444 (cf. CTS 39:298-99).
[34]*Sic*, Lk 10:7.
[35]Hesshus, *Explicatio Prioris Epistolae ad Corinthios*, 134v.
[36]Musculus, *Comm. 1 Cor.*, 285; citing Rom 10:15.
[37]That is, ministers.
[38]That is, martyrdom.
[39]In Baylor, *The Radical Reformation*, 176; citing 1 Tim 3:7.

once embraced it, I doggedly guard it. And I endure these things patiently, without any regret—and nothing brings me more pleasure or leads me to greater boasting—when I see that preaching the gospel free of charge is profitable to your salvation, and that by my example you are learning sometimes to avoid things that are permissible when the advantage of other people requires it.

Now if I should preach the gospel in the manner of other people, this would be no reason for boasting. The Lord has imposed it on me as a duty, and I am compelled to obey whether I want to or not. Therefore there is nothing praiseworthy when I perform my appointed duty; on the contrary, punishment awaits me if I should cease to preach the gospel. If I would have preached the gospel, freely, of my own will, then I would receive a reward from God for my prompt willingness; but even if unwilling, one must perform what has been commanded. I have been entrusted with the gospel, not so that I might keep it hidden to myself, but so that I might share it with the nations. When I communicate, I communicate the Lord's message, not my own. Otherwise, I cause injury to the Lord, whose talent—which he wanted me to multiply with interest—I kept unprofitably to myself. Now if you were to say, "Since God punishes those who do not perform their duty, and there is no reward for performing it, then what is the reason, O Paul, for your boasting?" The answer: praise is owed, if persons perform their duty beyond what is commanded of them. The Lord has commanded that the gospel be preached; but he has not commanded that we preach it for nothing. Rather, justice requires that we should eat and drink of that which is provided by those to whom we have announced the gospel. Therefore that which God granted as permissible, I did not wish to be permissible for myself. I did not use this power that was granted to me, because I recognized that, in your affairs and in the matter of the gospel, it was more important to communicate the gospel doctrine to you for free than that you should be admonished about my freedom. And it should be both plain and clear that I am not like certain people who teach for their own gain, looking after their own affairs rather than those of Jesus Christ. Paraphrase on 1 Corinthians 9.[40]

Paul Renounces His Rights. David Dickson: Hitherto Paul has defended his own rights. Now he shows the moderation that he has employed with his aforesaid freedom. First, with respect to physical sustenance he states his resolution to continue to do without it so as not to hinder the gospel—indeed, he would rather die by famine [than jeopardize the gospel]. The reason he gives for this is so that he can boast against those people who spoke evil of him, who might say that the apostle was preaching for hire. Exposition of 1 Corinthians 9:15.[41]

Paul's Ministry Was Above Reproach. Huldrych Zwingli: "It is better for me to die." "I place before you the good report of my life and the honor that I have obtained in preaching the gospel." This is what Paul boasts about, because he knows that no one is able to pass judgment on his ministry. For the fact that he has executed his office free from hindrance is visible to everyone, not only to those who support him, but also those who condemn him. Annotations on 1 Corinthians 9:15.[42]

Affliction Should Be Chosen Over Sin. John Trapp: [Paul] would rather starve than to do anything to prejudice the gospel. Affliction is to be chosen rather than sin, Job 36:21. As Zwingli said, "What death should not a person choose, nay what hell, rather than to sin against his conscience?" Daniel chose to be cast into the lions' den rather than to bear a lion within his own bosom. The primitive Christians thought it far better to be thrown to the lions without, rather than to endure lusts within. It is better to jump into a bonfire, said a good man once, than to commit any sin against God. The Armenian mouse would rather die than

[40]Erasmus, *Paraphrases*, 286-87; citing Mt 25:14-30.
[41]Dickson, *An Exposition of St. Paul's Epistles*, 54*.
[42]Zwingli, *Annotatiunculae . . . ex ore Zvinglij*, 70.

be defiled with any filth. If her hole is besmeared with dirt, she would rather choose to perish with hunger than to be polluted. Such was Paul here, and such we ought all to be. Commentary on 1 Corinthians 9:15.[43]

Unlike Jonah, Paul Willingly Preached the Gospel. Jacques Lefèvre d'Étaples: The necessity to preach to the Ninevites was laid on Jonah—whether he wanted to or not. Otherwise a curse was awaiting him for not complying with the divine command. If he did it willingly, he could expect a reward, that is, the granting of grace. But if he did it unwillingly, he was nevertheless fulfilling the duty that was commanded of him. And indeed, he carried out his assignment, though unwillingly, and so he was denied the grace that he might have received for this deed. [Similarly,] the necessity to preach the gospel was repeatedly given to Paul, whether he wanted to do so or not. Nevertheless, he freely and with much goodwill carried out the duty that was commanded of him, and for this reason he did not miss the expected reward (that is, of grace). But, even more, Paul was anticipating a grace of a different sort, namely, that the gospel of Christ might be manifested to those people without expense or inconvenience, but with the comfort and consolation of all. Commentary on 1 Corinthians 9:16.[44]

Ministers Are Compelled to Preach the Gospel. Martin Bucer: If we really love Christ, he is everything to us; therefore if anyone is called to this ministry, whatever unpleasantness, sufferings and crosses he may have to bear in the course of his ministry, he will be upheld and strengthened against all unpleasantness, sufferings, and crosses only by the fact that the Lord Jesus has commanded him to do this, and commanded it as the highest ministry of love that we can show him. Then each one will feel as Paul did when he writes about himself in 1 Cor. 9: "Yet when I preach the gospel, I cannot boast, for I am compelled to preach" . . .

"I am simply discharging the trust committed to me," says the dear apostle; for that should be more than enough for any Christian, if he is called to this ministry, to accept it and carry it out with all faithfulness, withstanding and suffering whatever trouble, labor, abuse, shame, suffering, and cross he may meet in the course of it. For the Lord will require the blood of his lambs at the hands of all those who either do not accept this ministry when they are called to it or are in some way neglectful in it. True Care of Souls.[45]

Paul's Memorable Instructions to Ministers. John Calvin: This is an extraordinary sentence. From it we learn, first of all, the nature of the call that ministers receive and how they are bound to it; and second, what the pastoral office involves and what responsibilities are included in it. Therefore, once a person has been called, let him not think that he is any longer free to draw back when he would like, if, for example, he is weighed down by burdensome and unpleasant problems. For ministers are devoted to the Lord and his church, bound to him with a sacred bond that would be sinful for them to break. As far as the second point is concerned, Paul says that the threat of a curse is on him if he does not proclaim the gospel. Why? Simply because he has been called to it, and therefore is constrained by necessity. How, therefore, will anyone who succeeds to this office avoid this same necessity? Commentary on 1 Corinthians 9:16.[46]

Ministers Must Teach the Simple Folk. Guillaume Farel: Nothing goes against the church of Jesus more than scorning the simple folk and not teaching or instructing them with all diligence. For the holy apostle said: "A curse be on me if I do not evangelize." For if those who have better understanding and the grace of our Lord do

[43]Trapp, *A Commentary or Exposition*, 680*.

[44]Lefèvre d'Étaples, *Commentariorum in Epistolas Beati Pauli . . . Liber Secundus*, 114v.

[45]Bucer, *Concerning the True Care of Souls*, 119-20.

[46]CO 49:45 (cf. CTS 39:300-301).

not teach doctrine to the ignorant, nor correct those in error, nor pick up those who have fallen, they will die in their sin. Their poor souls will be demanded from the hand of those to whom our Lord has given grace. On the contrary, those who, for the love of Christ, devote themselves to all will grow in virtue and will shine as the stars. Summary and Brief Exposition.[47]

Woe to Clergy Who Don't Preach the Gospel! Wolfgang Musculus: "Woe to me if I do not preach the gospel." The interjection of the word "woe" has two uses in Scripture. Sometimes it emphasizes a time of great calamity and misery, as in Matthew 24: "Woe to the women who are pregnant and nursing infants on that day!" Here, certainly, the Lord does not call pregnant and nursing women miserable, disastrous, and unfortunate except in so far as, in that future calamity, they will be hampered in their flight to safety on account of their heavy wombs and the infants nursing at their breasts. At other times, the word "woe" emphasizes eternal condemnation, as in Luke 6[:24]: "Woe to you who are rich, for you have received your consolation," and Matthew 23[:13]: "Woe to you scribes and Pharisees," etc. . . .

Today, woe should be ascribed to those who do not preach the gospel when it is their responsibility to do so. The bishops are like this, for they strenuously avoid preaching the gospel. [Here in this passage] the Apostle is using the word "woe" in the latter sense, showing that people who neglect performing the duties that have been commanded of them by the Lord should fear eternal condemnation and misfortune. We see here how unfortunate, or rather blind, are our modern-day bishops, because they have no sense of fear of this eternal curse. Commentary on 1 Corinthians 9:16.[48]

God's Ministers Must Serve Willingly. John Calvin: Now I understand the man who does something "willingly" to be he who acts with such cheerfulness and is so focused on the desire to edify others that he does not disparage anything that he knows will be useful for the church, just as, by contrast, he calls "unwilling" those people who do what necessity requires of them, but they do so grudgingly, because it conflicts with their desires. . . . However others might explain this passage, this (in my judgment) is the natural meaning: God does not approve the mere obedience of a person who performs an action grudgingly and with a reluctant mind. Therefore, whenever God has commanded something of us, we are deceived if we think we have discharged it rightly when we perform it grudgingly. For the Lord requires that his servants be cheerful and that they delight in obeying him and express their cheerfulness by acting without hesitation. In sum, Paul means that the only way he can satisfy his vocation would be by performing his duty willingly and with cheerfulness. Commentary on 1 Corinthians 9:17.[49]

Even Paul's "Reward" Was of God's Grace. John Trapp: "I have a reward"—yet not earned, but of free grace, God crowning his own works in us. He was a proud papist who said "I will not have heaven for nothing." And another who said, "Good works are the price of heaven." God will cast all such merit-merchants out of his temple. Commentary on 1 Corinthians 9:17.[50]

Four Kinds of Ministers. Wolfgang Musculus: We see in this passage . . . four kinds of ministers of Christ. The first are those who neglect their duty and do not proclaim the gospel. In the guise of his own person, the apostle threatens them with "woe." The second are those who preach the gospel, but do so against their will. These ministers are forced to do it by the necessity of their office. The third are those who preach the gospel willingly. This is their reward. The fourth are those who not only preach the gospel, and do it willingly, but also bestow the gospel of Christ without charge. Those ministers are especially

[47]In Zuidema and Van Raalte, *Early French Reform*, 133; alluding to Ezek 3.
[48]Musculus, *Comm. 1 Cor.*, 290-91; citing Mt 24:19.
[49]CO 49:445-46 (cf. CTS 39:301-2).
[50]Trapp, *A Commentary or Exposition*, 681*.

faithful who do this in various places and times for the progress of the gospel. Commentary on 1 Corinthians 9:18.[51]

Duties of a Bishop. Philipp Melanchthon: The epistles to Titus and Timothy teach what bishops ought to do. First they ought to teach the gospel, Matthew 10:7, 19ff. and Matthew 28, and here also, "Woe to me if I do not preach the gospel!" (1 Cor 9:16), that is, "I am damned if I do not preach the gospel." Second, the apostle prescribes them also to care for the poor lest they suffer want, as we see in 2 Corinthians 8. Now these are the primary aspects of a bishop's duties; to them is added a form of ruling, that they not rule tyrannically lest they burden the church with laws. This we see in 1 Peter 5: "Tend the flock of God that is under your care, exercising oversight not under compulsion, but willingly according to God, not for shameful gain, but eagerly, not domineering over those in your charge, but being examples to the flock," that is: "act as if you were the flock." Here the apostle describes the manner of ruling in this way: The bishop is responsible not only that there be no scandal among those of right judgment, but that even spiteful persons have no occasion or opportunity for scandal. Next, the bishop was to accommodate himself to the weakness of the brothers and sisters so that he wasn't a burden to anyone, either by his laws or in some other way. And so, Paul says, "What then is my reward?" Just this: "that in my preaching I may make the gospel free of charge, so as not to make full use of my right in the gospel." Annotations on 1 Corinthians 9:15-18.[52]

9:19-23 *Paul Became All Things to All People*

Four Grades of Christian Freedom. Tilemann Hesshus: True Christian freedom is that superior happiness and glory that comes from the fact that we have been freed by our Lord Jesus Christ from sin, from the wrath of God, from the curse of the law, from death, and from the tyranny of Satan; and also that we have been given the Holy Spirit, who inflames new light, righteousness, and life in us. Moreover, it restores lost men and women so that we might be able to serve God according to his Word, voluntarily and freely by his Spirit, and so that neither the law of Moses nor any human traditions as they relate to religion are able to bind our conscience before God. . . . Christ speaks about this spiritual freedom in John 8: "If the Son has freed you, you will be free indeed." And Paul states in Galatians 5: "Stand firm, therefore, in the freedom to which Christ has called you." And in 1 Corinthians 7, Paul states: "You were redeemed at a great price; do not become servants of human beings." And Isaiah 52 states: "You were sold for nothing, and you shall be redeemed without cost." For the sake of right teaching, we lay down four grades of freedom.

The first grade is freedom from sin, from the wrath of God, from the curse of the law, from death, from the tyranny of the devil and all his hellish servants. And instead, one receives the imputation of the righteousness of the Son of God, and reconciliation with the eternal Father. This freedom is far more precious than ruling many worlds and possessing fabulous riches. Scripture in various places speaks of this kind of liberty, such as Romans 6: "You are not under law, but under grace"; and in Romans 8: "The law of the Spirit of life has set me free in Christ Jesus from the law of sin and death."

The second grade is the gift of the Holy Spirit and, through him, the renovation of the Christian man or woman, whereby the Holy Spirit imparts new life and freedom. Consequently, our nature is no longer hostile to the compulsion of the law, but rather, with a prompt and willing spirit, we acknowledge, call on, revere, and love God. Paul speaks about this grade of freedom in Romans 8: "For you have not received the spirit of slavery to fall back into fear, but you have received the spirit

[51]Musculus, *Comm. 1 Cor.*, 292.
[52]Melanchthon, *Annotationes in Epistolam priorem ad Corinthios*, 100, 102; citing 1 Cor 8:4, 7-13; 1 Pet 5:2-3.

of adoption as sons, by whom we cry 'Abba! Father!'" And 2 Corinthians 3: "Where the Spirit is, there is freedom. And we all, with unveiled faces, beholding the glory of the Lord, are being transformed into the same image from glory to glory, for this comes from the Lord who is the Spirit."

The third grade is freedom from the legal and ceremonial laws of Moses. For after the Messiah appeared . . . the whole law of Moses was abrogated and no longer bound those born from the seed of Abraham. Paul speaks about this kind of freedom in Colossians 2: "Let no one judge you in questions of food or drink, or with regard to the function of feast days or Sabbaths, which are shadows of things to come." But the entire substance of the Law belongs to Christ, and pertains to his spiritual kingdom.

The fourth grade of freedom relates to the fact that no human traditions pertaining to religion can bind our conscience before God. Paul speaks about this grade in Colossians 2: "If, therefore, you died with Christ from the elemental spirits of the world, why, as if you were still alive in the world, do you submit to human regulations—'Do not handle, do not taste, do not touch' (which are all things that perish as they are used)—according to human precepts and teachings?" Therefore, when the Roman pontiff tries to bind and burden the consciences of people with his distinctions regarding foods, his prohibition of marriage, his obligations regarding prayers, his works of satisfaction—these chains must be broken asunder and Christian freedom must be recalled to memory, because all things in this world are clean. Explication of 1 Corinthians 9:19.[53]

Paul's Missionary Strategy. Peter Martyr Vermigli: To win someone to Christ means to make someone one's own property—and this occurs by faith, which comes from hearing. And people do not listen freely to someone unless they judge them to be their friend and concerned for their well-being. This was happening here, because Paul was making every effort to win the approval of the Corinthians. He became all things to all people—as far as ceremonies and neutral things were concerned. But in matters that were clearly prohibited by the Word of God, Paul did not seek to gratify people. As far as the Jews were concerned, he allowed Timothy to be circumcised; he shaved his head when he was at Cenchreae; he fulfilled his vow in Jerusalem. As for the Gentiles, he did not allow Titus to be circumcised and he opposed Peter to his face. Paul kept the law when he was with Jews, but not for the same reason, for they were insisting that it was required for them, while Paul obeyed it voluntarily and out of love for the salvation of others. Paul was eager to be considerate of those listeners who would have been immediately alienated from him if he had completely overturned the law and ceremonies in an instant. In the meantime, even as he was accommodating himself to their weaknesses, he was teaching them the primary doctrines of religion, bringing sin to their attention, and preaching to them of their need for righteousness, which external ceremonies cannot supply; and from this he concluded that righteousness must be sought from Christ alone. With these strategies, then, Paul was winning them. Commentary on 1 Corinthians 9:19.[54]

Preaching Must Be Accommodated to the Hearer. Wolfgang Musculus: With these words Paul gives a clear signal that the faithful minister of Christ must not simply preach and win over people by preaching the Word, but he must do it with exceptional zeal so as to accommodate his teaching to the understanding of his hearers. Those who would otherwise not be won over by preaching, he will win over by accommodating himself to them and tempting them. He will in no way be content to have won over some people,

[53]Hesshus, *Explicatio Prioris Epistolae ad Corinthios*, 137r-138v; citing Jn 8:36; Gal 5:1; 1 Cor 7:23; Is 52:3; Rom 6:14; 8:2, 15; 2 Cor 3:17-18; Col 2:16, 20.

[54]Vermigli, *In Selectissimam S. Pauli Priorem ad Corinth. . . . Commentarii*, 224r; citing Acts 18:18.

unless he acquires more people than usual. This passion to win over many people should never be absent from a minister of Christ. Commentary on 1 Corinthians 9:19.[55]

Winning the Lost. John Trapp: The Greek word for "gain" signifies among other things the joy and delight of the heart in gaining. It also signifies craft and guile, as is the case with the fox that, when he is very hungry after prey and can find none, lies down and pretends that he is a dead carcass. Thus when the birds light on him, he catches them. In the same way ministers must deny themselves to gain their hearers. Commentary on 1 Corinthians 9:19.[56]

Paul Accommodated His Freedom to Jews and Gentiles. John Calvin: To this point, Paul has used one particular example to demonstrate how diligently he had accommodated himself to the weak. Now, he adds a general statement, and then enumerates several examples. The general statement is this: that although he is under the authority of no one, nevertheless he has lived as if he were subject to the will of everyone, and has voluntarily subjected himself to the weak, to whom he was not bound in any way. And the particular examples are these, that among the Gentiles he was like a Gentile, and among the Jews he behaved as if he were a Jew. In other words, although he diligently followed Jewish ceremonies when he was among the Jews, he was very careful to avoid offending the Gentiles in his observance of them. . . . "To become all things" means to adopt every sort of appearance as the situation requires, or to assume different roles for the sake of peoples' differences. When Paul says that he became as one "outside the law" and "under the law," this should be understood to refer only to the ceremonial part of the law. For the moral part of the law applies to all in common, the Gentiles as well as the Jews; and Paul would not have been allowed to gratify humans to that extent. For this teaching was valid only for neutral things, as was said before. Commentary on 1 Corinthians 9:19-21.[57]

Ceremonial and Moral Law. David Dickson: In conforming himself to the Gentiles, who did not practice the Jewish law, Paul laid aside the use of those ceremonies as if he were without the law. In the meantime, he intimates that he did not mean the moral law, or the law of love, which is the perpetual law of God and Christ; from this he could not be freed. But Paul did free himself from the ceremonial law so that, for the sake of the gospel, he might choose whether to practice various ceremonies. Exposition of 1 Corinthians 9:21.[58]

Ministers Must Diligently Seek Lost People. Martin Bucer: The faithful ministers of Christ are not to give up lightly on anyone, as long as people are still people and God's creatures and have not shown themselves to be dogs by raging all the more against those who call them to the kingdom of heaven, the more faithfully such people want to assist them to find salvation; or in that the more attractively and gloriously the pearl of the holy gospel is presented to them, the more they despise it and trample it under foot. This is why the second point, the faithfulness, seriousness, and diligence with which the Lord desires his lambs to be sought, must be thoroughly taken to heart and faithfully considered. He desires that they should be sought wherever they are scattered, and sought with such seriousness and diligence that one should be ready to be all things to all people, as dear Paul was, and even to hazard one's own life, as the Lord himself did, so that the lost lambs might be found and won. True Care of Souls.[59]

Ministers Must Master Their People's Affections. John Trapp: St. Paul harps much on this string, out of a strong desire of winning

[55]Musculus, *Comm. 1 Cor.*, 293-94.
[56]Trapp, *A Commentary or Exposition*, 681*.
[57]CO 49:447 (cf. CTS 39:304-5).
[58]Dickson, *Exposition of St. Paul's Epistles*, 55*.
[59]Bucer, *Concerning the True Care of Souls*, 78.

souls to God. Ministers must turn themselves into all shapes and fashions both of spirit and speech to gain souls to God. Christ used every means of wisdom (said Clement of Alexandria) so as to convert some. Ministers should labor to be masters of their people's affections. COMMENTARY ON 1 CORINTHIANS 9:21.[60]

BEING ALL THINGS TO ALL PEOPLE. WOLFGANG MUSCULUS: "I have become all things to all people." Whereas Paul begins by speaking about specifics, in the end he concludes with a summary. It is as if he were saying: "What more? I have accommodated myself to all people. I have become all things to all people. I serve all people. I condemn no one. I wish my message to go forth in every way possible." Now the apostle should not be understood to be saying that he has accommodated himself to people outside the boundaries of the law of Christ, for then he would not be an apostle of Christ but an apostle of flatterers, and he would not be saving them but destroying them....

Who would not say that the apostle was the most inconsistent and changeable man (like Vertumnus, the god of changing seasons), turning himself into all different shapes, unless one considers Paul's goal? He was doing this, not so as to change his purpose, but so that he might turn people away from their error and win them to the knowledge of Christ. Consequently we must be cautious when judging ministers of Christ, lest we too easily call them two-faced when we see them following the example of Paul by being all things to all people. COMMENTARY ON 1 CORINTHIANS 9:22.[61]

PAUL WINS CONVERTS THROUGH AFFECTION, NOT DISSIMULATION. THE ENGLISH ANNOTATIONS: [Paul is saying that] in matters that are indifferent—things that may either be done or not done with a good conscience—I have changed myself in all fashions so as to comport with all, that I might win some of various kinds of people. St. Augustine, in his book *To Consentius: Against Lying*, illustrates this text very well: "The Apostle says, 'I have become everything to everyone' . . . not by deceit of dissimulation, but by the affection of compassion; for persons become like those whose infirmities they condescend to when they support and relieve someone else with the mercy they themselves would desire if they were in the same situation." ANNOTATIONS ON 1 CORINTHIANS 9:22.[62]

THAT I MIGHT SAVE SOME. JOHN TRAPP: This is the highest honor in the world, to have a hand in the saving of souls. Let us exercise our every ability toward this end. And if someone does not have fine wheat bread, then let them give barley bread to the poor, or whatsoever the Lord has committed to them. COMMENTARY ON 1 CORINTHIANS 9:22.[63]

PARTICIPANTS IN THE GOSPEL. PETER MARTYR VERMIGLI: Persons who share in [the blessings of] the gospel are those who cooperate in the salvation of those who hear. For the gospel is the power of God for salvation. They are the instruments through which God declares his power for delivering men and women. That is why people who overlook nothing that they think might serve the salvation of their neighbor are rightly called "participants" of the gospel. COMMENTARY ON 1 CORINTHIANS 9:23.[64]

PREACHERS MUST HEED THEIR OWN MESSAGE OF SALVATION. JOHN TRAPP: "That I may be saved together with you." For the bell may call men and women to church, though it never enters the church itself. The field may be well-sowed with a dirty hand. The well may yield excellent water, though it contains much mud. The builders of Noah's ark drowned. And the sign that tells the passenger that there is wholesome food or warm

[60]Trapp, *A Commentary or Exposition*, 681*.

[61]Musculus, *Comm. 1 Cor.*, 296. Vertumnus was an Etruscan god, a statue of whom stood in Rome.

[62]Downame, *English Annotations*, DD4v*. Augustine's statement is found in NPNF 3:493.

[63]Trapp, *A Commentary or Exposition*, 681*.

[64]Vermigli, *In Selectissimam S. Pauli Priorem ad Corinth. . . . Commentarii*, 225r-v.

lodging within may itself remain in the storms without. . . . Oh how many heavenly doctrines are in some people's ears that were never in the preacher's heart! So true is that statement of Hilary, "The ears of the people are more holy than the hearts of the priests." Commentary on 1 Corinthians 9:23.[65]

9:24-27 *The Need for Self-Discipline*

Our Goal Must Be Christ and His Salvation. John Colet: In the race of eternal life, just as in the stadium, there must be complete abstinence from whatever can either impede or defeat the gospel. Otherwise the Evangelist himself, even in his gospel ministry, risks perishing as an unprofitable servant. "I do everything for the sake of the gospel," says Paul, "so that I may be made a sharer in it." And he would have had no share in it, if he had not done all he could. . . .

With great care we must always do what profits others, not what we ourselves want. Our efforts must be aimed, not at what the body calls for, but at what the spirit desires. Finally, we must earnestly strive with all our strength, not for what we can do for ourselves, but for what helps Christ's church; and, setting aside all other considerations, we should contend for all men and women, thinking always that this alone is permitted: what is most useful for the church and the salvation of men and women in Christ.

But avoid like a dangerous cliff what is contrary to this while you are sailing to the harbor of everlasting rest. If you believe in Christ, if you hope in God, if you do everything in charity, if you keep your eyes unwaveringly fixed on the goal—for the goal is Christ, and the increase and perfecting of people's salvation in him—if, I say, with all faith, hope, and charity you aim at that and direct there all things, you cannot lose your way. Exposition of 1 Corinthians 9.[66]

What Is Paul Trying to Teach by This Racing Analogy? Johann Spangenberg: He wants to remind us of two things through this. First, those who have a calling and office and do not do what it requires are negligent, sluggish, and dull; these very same people stand in grave danger. Second, for the benefit of the weak we must abstain from many things that we consider good, right, and true, so that we—here on earth, on the path of faith—do not run futilely, but rather seize the true reward, eternal life. For it is not enough to begin; we must also finish the race. As Christ says in Matthew 24, "Whoever perseveres to the end will be blessed." Postil on the Epistle for Septuagesime.[67]

The Christian Life Requires Intense Exertion. Wolfgang Musculus: In a beautiful fashion, Paul likens the profession of the Christian faith, not to a lifestyle of leisure, suited for lazy and useless people, but to a race in which spiritual zeal is exercised by running and competing. It is a lifestyle of labor and zealous effort, not of torpor and neglect. In this race, we do not idly stand around, but, leaving behind the past, we hasten forward with sustained and intense effort so that we might finally cross the finish line reaching the heavenly prize. Somewhere Gregory of Nazianzus has rightly said . . . "He does not want you to remain in the same place in your learning, but rather always to be on the move; thus, if you have sinned, to return [to the right path], but if you have done rightly, to stretch forward to greater progress."[68] . . . Therefore, just as in a race where progress is made neither in standing still nor in going backward, so in Christianity the goal is no more reached without increase of faith and godliness and daily progress than if someone went backward and returned to their prior condition. Commentary on 1 Corinthians 9:24.[69]

[65]Trapp, *A Commentary or Exposition*, 681*.
[66]Colet, *Enarratio*, 206.
[67]Spangenberg, *Postilla Teütsch*, 4:109r-v; citing Mt 24:13.
[68]See *In novam Dominicam*, oratio 44.8 (PG 36:616-17).
[69]Musculus, *Comm. 1 Cor*, 300.

Running for the Crown. John Trapp: Ignatius said to Polycarp, "Here is the race, but the crown is above." "Run to win the race," the martyr Bradford[70] said to his fellow sufferers. "You are almost at your journey's end. I do not doubt but our Father will send to each of us, as he did to Elijah, a fiery chariot to convey us into his kingdom. Let us therefore not be dismayed to leave our cloaks behind us, that is, our bodies in ashes." Commentary on 1 Corinthians 9:24.[71]

Like Athletes of Old, Christians Must Practice Temperance. David Dickson: That the Corinthians might pursue temperance and not be so concerned about food that they offend others by eating meat offered to idols—to this end Paul shows them that they must run in the Christian race where all who run according to the laws of God will be crowned (rather than only one, as normally happens in sports). And how this occurs, Paul indicates as follows: In a manner similar to the runners and wrestlers who contended in those noble games usually celebrated near Corinth, they should not indulge themselves in gluttony and pleasures, but be temperate in all things, bearing all things so that they might win the conquering crown. In their Isthmian or Corinthian games, the runners and wrestlers disciplined themselves to follow a most temperate diet as they prepared for the race—just as horses are now trained for running. The victors in those games were crowned with laurel or ivy, or were honored with some such reward. In the same manner, the apostle calls Christians to exercise moderation in the use of the things of this world, and abstain from whatsoever may impede their race or hinder them in warfare, so that they might obtain an incorruptible prize, that is, an eternal crown, which is laid up in heaven for all those who strive lawfully and finish their race. Exposition of 1 Corinthians 9:24-25.[72]

[70] John Bradford was an English reformer who was executed during the reign of Mary Tudor (1553–1558) in 1555.
[71] Trapp, *A Commentary or Exposition*, 682*. For Ignatius's exhortation to Polycarp, see ANF 1:94.
[72] Dickson, *An Exposition of St. Paul's Epistles*, 55*.

The Dangers of Intemperance. John Trapp: These luxurious Corinthians were very much addicted to their stomachs; thus Paul calls them to temperance. It is ill-becoming of servants of the highest master to be slaves of their palates.... People may eat on earth what they must digest in hell. Commentary on 1 Corinthians 9:25.[73]

Christian Faith Means to Run with Certainty. Philipp Melanchthon: This then is Paul's meaning: "I run tenaciously because I know with certainty the promised prize and that I will gain it." So too in other things those people run more tenaciously who know they are going to win. Therefore you see the prize, which is the power of faith. For it is not faith but discouragement and despair when you are not driven by hope of gaining the prize. Moreover you will note this too: despair and unbelief is to think like this: "I will run indeed, but I do not know what will happen, I do not know what I will gain, because I am weak." This is the attitude of those who think they are saved by works. Likewise I am ignorant of God's judgment, for this is also to be ignorant of his mercy. Thus faith is to know with complete certainty God's goodwill toward us and by reflecting on that goodwill of God to be encouraged to do good works.... Annotations on 1 Corinthians 9:26.[74]

We Must Run and Fight to Obtain the Crown. Jacques Lefèvre d'Étaples: Why does it benefit you to announce the kingdom of God? Why should you run around proclaiming that God's commands (found in the writings of God) must be fulfilled through the spirit, not performed by the flesh? The flesh must be killed so that the spirit might live. If you break God's commands and live in a carnal fashion, neither running nor fighting, although you preach to others, will you be discovered to be among the condemned? We must follow

[73] Trapp, *A Commentary or Exposition*, 682*. See *Acts and Monuments* 7.244.
[74] Melanchthon, *Annotationes in Epistolam priorem ad Corinthios*, 106.

the example of Paul, truly running and truly fighting. If we do this, it is more than certain that Jesus Christ our king, who is blessed over all things, will give to us an immortal crown, for he wishes to give this crown not to one person alone but to all people for the sake of himself. The treasure of his goodness is infinite. May he receive honor and glory and thanks forever! Commentary on 1 Corinthians 9:26-27.[75]

Christian Preachers and Teachers Must Run Straight for the Goal. David Chytraeus: The ends of the ministry of the gospel are to teach rightly the true doctrine of the gospel, to administer the sacraments, and to perform the other parts of their office faithfully, for the glory of God and that many people might be saved. The ends of a scholar's life or our studies are wisdom and power of utterance, that is, wise and eloquent godliness, and perceiving and judging things rightly, speaking well, and living well. . . .

Therefore, just as runners always look to their mark, and champions employ all their skill and practice to defeat their adversaries . . . so let everyone in their vocations (and especially teachers and ministers of the church) choose wisely the means that lead to the righteous goal and, in performing these things, let them exhibit diligence and endurance so that they might attain in eternal life the promised reward of their diligence. Let them faithfully teach the pure doctrine of the gospel. Let them return regularly to those passages of doctrine that are necessary and most useful for the nourishment of true godliness, such as those treating repentance; faith; the person, office, and benefits of Christ; true prayer; the cross; good works; etc. Let them adjust their teaching to the capacity of their hearers. Let them examine, instruct, and strengthen those who are more ignorant. Let them constantly contend for the truth against heretics. Let them fight against their own natures and their sinful lusts. Let them bear with some infirmities and offenses for the sake of the common peace. Let them encourage their hearers with examples of all the virtues. Let them bridle ambition, wrath, desire for revenge, greed, and other affections lest they disfigure the doctrine of the gospel with scandals and themselves become castaways, losing the inheritance of eternal life. Postil on Septuagesima Sunday.[76]

Beware of Running Aimlessly! Tilemann Hesshus: There are many people in the church who embrace the church's doctrine, who undertake the work of the ministry, who subject themselves to severe dangers, and endure great troubles; yet they do not carefully seek the foundations of right teaching, nor adequately consider the goal of eternal life, nor employ lawful methods—and thus they undergo very difficult hardships in vain and without fruit.

The priests of Baal were running aimlessly, for they did not understand the foundations of right teaching, they did not join themselves to the church, they did not listen to the prophets, but instead they were serving in the worship of idols and were only seeking to satisfy their stomachs. The Pharisees were running aimlessly, about whom Paul testified that they had zeal for God, but not according to knowledge. For they were fervent in their religious zeal, but they did not understand the central message of Scripture, they were bewitched in errors, they were ignorant of the blessings of the Messiah, and they were waiting for everything in vain. So too, all heretics run aimlessly; that is, they are overtaken by a blind impulse, they do not focus on the certain end, they are not rooted in sound teaching, they do not employ lawful methods. . . .

Clearly, wicked men such as Arius, Nestorius, Macedonius, Pelagius, Aëtius, Thomas Müntzer, the Roman pontiffs, and the so-called king of Münster Jan van Leiden do *not* run aimlessly, for they sin against conscience—all these men were

[75]Lefèvre d'Étaples, *Commentariorum in Epistolas Beati Pauli . . . Liber Secundus*, 115r.

[76]Chytraeus, *Dispositio epistolarum*, 93-94.

knowingly fighting against the truth. Instead, Paul reproaches here those who have joined themselves to the church, and show a degree of zeal, and yet do not seek the truth, nor lean on a solid foundation, nor direct all their efforts to the glory of God and the salvation of the church. These people, when they experience sudden misfortune, are easily driven off course from their apparent piety. Therefore, by his own example, Paul warns that those who pursue godliness should take care lest they be overtaken by blind impulse, as one sees with the Anabaptists, or fanatics, or the ignorant multitude; instead, they should seek a sure foundation for their doctrine; they should keep in view the sure goal, namely, the glory of God, the edification of the church, and their own salvation. And they should see to it that, with godly fear, they choose lawful methods and the path demonstrated in the Word of God, so that they do not run off course or beat at the air. Explication of 1 Corinthians 9:26.[77]

What Prevents the Runner or Boxer from Winning the Reward? Johann Spangenberg: Two things. First, if they are too dull, sluggish, or unfit to run. Second, if they miss the goal and mark, wanting to busy themselves with other things beside the race or fight. Such people are too dull and unfit to run. They are weak in faith, too faint-hearted in hope, and do not direct their prayers according to God's Word. Nor do they allow Christ to be the way to heaven; instead they [try to] forge their own path.

Those who pursue other things beside the race or fight have a calling and office before God with pure doctrine and Christian living, but they abandon these things and instead chase after their own honor, glory, and praise, forgetting God's command and their neighbor's salvation and improvement. These people run and fight indeed, but they run an incomplete race and win nothing. Postil on the Epistle for Septuagesime.[78]

Paul Confident of His Election and Regeneration. David Dickson: If we should imagine that Paul is speaking here of the reprobate in an absolute sense, we should pay special attention to the necessary connection between a profane life (pursued to the end) and reprobation. For whoever dies in his sin demonstrates himself to be a reprobate. Now it is absurd, and completely contrary to Paul's writings, that he should raise doubts regarding his election, or suggest the decree of election to be changeable. On the other hand, because Paul was persuaded of his election and regeneration, which he demonstrated through the holiness of his life, he was careful to avoid evil deeds that would serve as signs of his hypocrisy, though not of his reprobation. Exposition of 1 Corinthians 9:27.[79]

The Meaning of the Word *Disqualified*. The English Annotations: The word "disqualified" does not signify a reprobate person, and the suggestion that Paul was uncertain of his election or of obtaining the prize is disproved by Romans 8:38 and 2 Timothy 4:7-8. Rather, the word means deserving reproach or guilty of fault. The Greek word *adokimos* is a metaphor either taken from those who are testing metals, who cast away the dross, or Paul continues to draw out his former metaphor of those who proved their physical mastery in those days when there were certain colleges or academies (like our Artillery Gardens) for martial exercise, where novices that refused to

[77]Hesshus, *Explicatio Prioris Epistolae ad Corinthios*, 141v-142v. Macedonius I, a mid-fourth-century bishop of Constantinople, was the leader of a heretical group known as the Macedonians, who denied the divinity of the Holy Spirit. The fourth-century theologian Aëtius founded the Anomean sect of Arians, which rejected as self-contradictory the orthodox statement that the Son ("the begotten one") was of the same divine essence with the Father. Jan van Leiden, or Jan Beukels (d. 1536), and Jan Matthijs (d. 1534), Anabaptist leaders and self-styled apocalyptic prophets, founded an Anabaptist kingdom in the German city of Münster in 1534 to prepare for Christ's return. See William R. Estep, *The Anabaptist Story: An Introduction to Sixteenth-Century Anabaptism* (Grand Rapids: Eerdmans, 1996), 152-60.

[78]Spangenberg, *Postilla Teütsch*, 4:109v-110v.

[79]Dickson, *Exposition of St. Paul's Epistles*, 55-56*.

submit themselves to rigorous discipline, or were found tardy in their trials, or possessed weak or sluggish bodies, were dismissed by their masters. Therefore the word *adokimos* does not signify being cast out forever from God's favor; rather, it means either to be rejected as worthless ore or dross; or it means to be cast out of the society and company of soldiers who wrestled or ran for the prize. Annotations on 1 Corinthians 9:27.[80]

[80]Downame, *English Annotations*, DD4v*. The author is referring to the Honorable Artillery Company, an elite English military organization that was established in 1537 by Henry VIII's royal charter, and originally trained at the Old Artillery Grounds in Spitalfields.

10:1-22 Warning Against Idolatry

For I do not want you to be unaware, brothers,[a] *that our fathers were all under the cloud, and all passed through the sea,* 2 *and all were baptized into Moses in the cloud and in the sea,* 3 *and all ate the same spiritual food,* 4 *and all drank the same spiritual drink. For they drank from the spiritual Rock that followed them, and the Rock was Christ.* 5 *Nevertheless, with most of them God was not pleased, for they were overthrown*[b] *in the wilderness.*

6 *Now these things took place as examples for us, that we might not desire evil as they did.* 7 *Do not be idolaters as some of them were; as it is written, "The people sat down to eat and drink and rose up to play."* 8 *We must not indulge in sexual immorality as some of them did, and twenty-three thousand fell in a single day.* 9 *We must not put Christ*[c] *to the test, as some of them did and were destroyed by serpents,* 10 *nor grumble, as some of them did and were destroyed by the Destroyer.* 11 *Now these things happened to them as an example, but they were written down for our instruction, on whom the end of the ages has come.* 12 *Therefore let anyone who thinks that he stands take heed lest he fall.* 13 *No temptation has overtaken you that is not common to man. God is faithful, and he will not let you be tempted beyond your ability, but with the temptation he will also provide the way of escape, that you may be able to endure it.*

14 *Therefore, my beloved, flee from idolatry.* 15 *I speak as to sensible people; judge for yourselves what I say.* 16 *The cup of blessing that we bless, is it not a participation in the blood of Christ? The bread that we break, is it not a participation in the body of Christ?* 17 *Because there is one bread, we who are many are one body, for we all partake of the one bread.* 18 *Consider the people of Israel:*[d] *are not those who eat the sacrifices participants in the altar?* 19 *What do I imply then? That food offered to idols is anything, or that an idol is anything?* 20 *No, I imply that what pagans sacrifice they offer to demons and not to God. I do not want you to be participants with demons.* 21 *You cannot drink the cup of the Lord and the cup of demons. You cannot partake of the table of the Lord and the table of demons.* 22 *Shall we provoke the Lord to jealousy? Are we stronger than he?*

a Or *brothers and sisters* **b** Or *were laid low* **c** Some manuscripts *the Lord* **d** Greek *Consider Israel according to the flesh*

Overview: Though Paul acknowledges that eating food sacrificed to idols is an indifferent matter, he in no way condones attending or participating in pagan sacrifices; thus, in this passage, he marshals powerful lessons from Israel's history and from the nature of the Lord's Supper to warn the Corinthians of the dangers of idolatry. For many Reformation commentators, Paul's treatment of Jewish history indicates the significant continuity between true believers in the old and new covenants: they share the same faith and the same mediator; they belong to the same church; they are the one people of God. Likewise, the Jews' escape from Egypt through the Red Sea and God's provision of manna and water ("spiritual food" and "spiritual drink") in the desert are viewed as types or figures of the Christian sacraments of baptism and the Lord's Supper. But do these Old Testament types contain the substance of the Christian sacraments? On this question, Lutheran, Reformed, and Anabaptist commentators express pointed disagreement with one another. The conundrum of the sacraments is treated in greater detail—and with somewhat more heat—as the commentators wrestle with Paul's language of participation and communion in his reference to the Lord's Supper in 1 Corinthians 10:16-17. Of course, the primary focus of this portion of Scripture is not the sacraments, but the dangers of idolatry, and thus Reformation commentators are quick to point out that Paul's discussion of sacramental participation and of Old Testament history is intended to remind the Corinthians of their spiritual union with Christ and God's fierce judgment against false worship. Though Christians inevitably face temptations of various kinds and intensity, they can find comfort in God's faithfulness and his sustaining grace.

A Life Worthy of Christ. Huldrych Zwingli: At the beginning of this chapter, almost like a concluding remark, Paul makes a general and emphatic exhortation to the Corinthians to abandon and set aside seeking knowledge that is foolish, worthless, and empty, and to focus instead on living a life worthy of Christ. Even as they boast in their Christian identity, at the same time they want to be slaves to evil deeds, shameful behavior, and scandals, and they do not expect divine retribution. The Israelites were once like this, for although they boasted that they were the people of God, nevertheless they did not at all control their filthy lusts and their shameful deeds. Thus the wrath of God raged among them to such an extent that they were afflicted with various plagues and perished in the desert. Examples like this are abundant throughout the accounts of Scripture. Moreover, lest the Gentiles think that the deeds of the Jews and the lessons of ancient history do not pertain to them, Paul demonstrates that both the Jews of old and Christians today share one and the same faith; they are one church, one people [of God]. For there is one God, one Mediator between God and humanity, Jesus Christ, who gave himself as the payment for the redemption of all people. Through him alone we are able to approach God—both those who came before him and those who come after him, the former because they believed in the promise, the latter because they believed in its fulfillment. Moreover, God has made the rites of Jews and Gentiles common and comparable: to the Jews he gave circumcision and the Passover, while to us he gave baptism and the Eucharist, as we see in Colossians 2 and 1 Corinthians 5. In all these ways, Paul shows that those who are under Christ and those who were under Moses are one and the same people of God, so that the Corinthians might understand that the punishments against the Jews also pertain to them. If they imitate them by their disgraceful lives, then everything that happened to the Jews they too will suffer. Annotations on 1 Corinthians 10.[1]

Magnifying God in All Things. Tilemann Hesshus: In chapter 10, Paul demonstrates through the example of the church in the old covenant that the sure proof that we are citizens of God, chosen to the fellowship of eternal life, is found in true godliness rather than an external title. And so, after rebuking several of their offenses, he adds a general admonition concerning avoiding security in carnal things, from which all sorts of wicked deeds customarily gush forth. However, he adds this extraordinary consolation: that because God is faithful, he will not allow us to be tempted beyond our strength. Finally, Paul exhorts the Corinthian church with the utmost seriousness to separate itself from all worship of idols and not to attend pagan sacrifices to idols. Instead, by its confession, the church should make clear that it condemns these things, and, in its whole life and in the use of its freedom, it should consider what contributes to magnifying God's glory and the building up of the church. Explication of Introduction to 1 Corinthians.[2]

10:1-5 *The Example of Israel*

Knowledge of the Scripture Essential. Wolfgang Musculus: Earlier [in chapter 9], Paul spoke concerning matters that were known and familiar to the Gentiles, when he said, "Do you not know that in a race all the runners compete, but only one receives the prize?" But here, he doesn't say, "Do you not know?," but rather "I do not want you to be ignorant brothers, that our fathers were all under the cloud and all passed through the sea, and

[1]Zwingli, *Annotatiunculae . . . ex ore Zvinglij*, 74-75; citing 1 Tim 2:5-6; Col 2:11-12; 1 Cor 5:7-8.

[2]Hesshus, *Explicatio Prioris Epistolae ad Corinthios*, 5v-6r.

all were baptized into Moses in the cloud and in the sea," etc. The example that Paul was appealing to was not drawn from the Gentile world but from the sacred history of the ancient Israelites, of which those Gentile Christians in Corinth had either no knowledge, or very modest and slight knowledge. Now since these examples were useful for their instruction and admonition, Paul urges them to acquire knowledge about these matters, from which they might see, as in a mirror, those things they should be on guard against and those things they should follow. People of prudence are made cautious by the dangers faced by others.... Paul counsels them to study the sacred Scriptures, recognizing that the Scriptures treat matters relevant to them. If only those who boast that they are the successors of the apostles were willing for believers to have the knowledge of the sacred Scriptures, so that the people of Christ might be made alive through them! ... Satan knows that ignorance of the Scriptures is the mother of all errors. Thus Christ said to the Sadducees: "You are in error because you do not know the Scriptures." And Chrysostom says: "This is the source of all evil: that they are ignorant of the Scripture." Commentary on 1 Corinthians 10:1.[3]

Paul Argues from Type to Reality. Jacques Lefèvre d'Étaples: Note how the types and figures pertain to the Jews. The Jews are a figure of the people of Christ; the clouds, a figure of the Holy Spirit; the sea, a figure of baptism; Moses, a figure of Christ as lawgiver; manna, a figure of the body of Christ as heavenly bread and life-giving food; water flowing from the rock, a figure of the blood of Christ as life-giving drink; the Rock, a figure of Christ, pierced on the cross; the desert, a figure of this world; the Promised Land, a figure of the heavenly kingdom; the serpents, a figure of demons; the Destroyer, a figure of the righteousness of God; the various punishments, a figure of the different eternal penalties; the end of the time of the Jews, a figure of the end of the ages.... Now Paul attaches each type to a particular thing and recalls a specific reality; and he sees the type in the reality, and the reality in the type just as one sees a shadow in the light and light in the shadow. The reality is the light, and the type is the shadow. Thus Paul's way of reasoning is from the type to the reality. Commentary on 1 Corinthians 10:1-11.[4]

The Example of Moses Foreshadows Christ. John Colet: The rebirth of the elect in Christ and their being nourished for eternal life—the nourishment being the body and blood of Christ—were prefigured in Moses by the sea and the cloud, which are the water and the Holy Spirit, and by the manna and the water flowing from the rock, which are the body and blood of Christ. For Christ is the rock that suffered steadfastly and was pierced on the cross, and poured forth his life-giving blood, quenching our thirst forever. Exposition of 1 Corinthians 10.[5]

Sacraments Do Not Guarantee an Eternal Crown. Jacques Lefèvre d'Étaples: Now someone might say: "We receive the Holy Spirit when we have been baptized in Christ [and] when we have participated in the body and blood of Christ. Therefore we are made participants of the gospel and receive the incorruptible crown." This is not at all correct: the truth ought to be recognized from the example [that follows]. For if we fall into the evil lusts of our carnal appetites; if we fall into greed, which is idolatry, or some other form of idolatry; if we fall into fornication; if we provoke Christ through our faithlessness; if we murmur against his providence and perform unlawful and criminal acts of this sort—even if we have been promised a crown through all those sacred mysteries—nevertheless, we will not receive this crown and will never enter into the kingdom

[3]Musculus, *Comm. 1 Cor.*, 306. See Chrysostom, *Homily 9* (Col 3:16-17), in NPNF 13:301.

[4]Lefèvre d'Étaples, *Commentariorum in Epistolas Beati Pauli ... Liber Secundus*, 115v-116r.

[5]Colet, *Enarratio*, 214.

of God, inasmuch as the sons of Israel in our example, who, although they participated in the sign of the Passover, fell into lawlessness ... [and] did not enter the land of promise. Because the disclosure of the secrets of Christ's sacraments are found in the old law, the apostle adds [the following discussion], saying, "Now I do not want you to be unaware, brothers...." Commentary on 1 Corinthians 10:1.[6]

Baptism and the Lord's Supper Represented in the Exodus. John Calvin: The apostle's object is to show that the Israelites were as much the people of God as we are, so that we might know that we will not escape unpunished the hand of God, which punished them so severely. For the point is this: if God did not spare the Israelites, he will not spare us, for our situation is the same as theirs. He proves this similarity from the fact that they had been endowed with the same signs of God's grace, for the sacraments are the marks by which the church of God is distinguished. First, he treats baptism, and teaches that the cloud (which protected the Israelites from the heat of the sun in the desert and directed them on their journey) along with their passage through the sea were an image of baptism for them. He also says that in the manna and the water flowing from the rock there was a sacrament, which corresponded with the sacred Supper. Commentary on 1 Corinthians 10:1.[7]

The Exodus Depicts Christian Baptism and Salvation. Wolfgang Musculus: The people of the old covenant were saved from Egypt by the blood of the lamb, and then, after coming through the cloud and the crossing of the sea, they were educated in Moses—that is, in the instruction of the Mosaic law—which he received on Mount Sinai. In such a way we have been liberated from the kingdom of Satan by the blood of a spotless lamb, and initiated into Christ through baptism. So too the clouds separated the Jews from the Egyptians and were a form of divine protection. So too in baptism we are separated from unbelievers and are received and initiated into heavenly grace. The sea drowned the Egyptians, but the Israelites, as the people of the Lord, crossed over from death to life and were purified for the journey to the Promised Land. Thus baptism, as the sacrament of the remission of sins, drowns our sins and, having snatched us from eternal death, purifies us for the journey to the heavenly country. Protected by the cloud and purified by the sea, the Jews shortly thereafter received heavenly teaching through Moses, through whose commandments all of the people faithfully and devotedly followed the Lord God and directed their lives. In a similar way, the doctrine of salvation is set before those initiated and baptized in the new covenant, and they follow this doctrine consistently. Whence Christ also, having said, "baptizing them in the name of the Father, and the Son, and the Holy Spirit," added "teaching them to observe all that I have commanded you." Commentary on 1 Corinthians 10:2.[8]

Children Are Included in the Old Testament Types of Baptism. Johann Oecolampadius: We find all the way through that the faith of the parents was profitably enjoyed by their children. In 1 Corinthians 10 the children also went through the Red Sea and participated in the faith of their parents.... At the time of the flood the children of the wicked perished with their parents. It was the same with Sodom and Gomorrah; the children suffered with their elders. Through the disobedience of their parents, children were led off as captives to Babylon and then again children were delivered from Babylon because of the faith of their parents. For children are in the same covenant with their parents. It is just as in Psalm 115:14. The Lord blesses the parents with their children. Antwort.[9]

[6]Lefèvre d'Étaples, *Commentariorum in Epistolas Beati Pauli ... Liber Secundus*, 115v.
[7]CO 49:451-52 (cf. CTS 39:313).
[8]Musculus, *Comm. 1 Cor.*, 309; citing Mt 28:19-20.
[9]Oecolampadius, *Antwort auff Balthasar Hübmaier büchlein wider*

Baptism into Moses. The English Annotations: Paul's meaning is that, as the deliverance out of Egypt was a figure of the redemption of Christ, and the wandering in the wilderness represented the life of the faithful in this world, and the land of Canaan was a shadow of the kingdom of heaven, so the passage through the Red Sea was a holy figure pointing to baptism, and the manna together with the water springing out of the Rock indicated the blessed Supper. Thus it appears that the fathers enjoyed the same spiritual benefits that the Christian church experiences. And yet, notwithstanding these benefits, many of them were punished, rooted out, and rejected by God because of their sins; so likewise, Christians ought to stand in fear of the similar judgment in case they profane the profession through similar transgressions. Annotations on 1 Corinthians 10:2.[10]

Baptism of Grief. Hans Hut: The water of every grief is the true essence and meaning of baptism, in which the person sinks in the death of Christ. It was not in Christ's time that this baptism was first established; it has existed from the beginning (Joel 3; Judg 8). All the elect friends of God have been baptized in it, from Adam down to the present, as Paul shows (1 Cor 10). So Christ also accepted this covenant from God in the Jordan River. And with it he testified that he was obedient to the father, in order to show love toward all people unto death, and as an example. For afterward he was richly endowed by the father with the baptism of every grief. . . . Whoever wants to be a disciple of the Lord must be baptized in this manner, and he will be cleansed in spirit through the bond of peace toward the one body [the community Christians]. On the Mystery of Baptism.[11]

Christ Is Spiritual Food and Drink. Philipp Melanchthon: The passing through the Red Sea was not only a figure of baptism but also the justification and the baptism itself of the fathers who had faith. Thus the cloud was not only a figure of the gospel but also an evangelical sign strengthening the faith of the fathers. So too the manna and the water from the rock were not only figures of the gospel but also evangelical signs strengthening the faith of the fathers, and in this way those who believed in God through these signs ate spiritually the manna; they drank spiritual water. This is why he says that it was not simply food and drink but "spiritual food" that those who believed ate spiritually. Second, manna certainly signifies nothing other than Christ's flesh eaten spiritually, as we see in John 6. Christ there compares the fleshly eating of the manna with the spiritual eating of his flesh: "Your fathers ate the manna in the wilderness, and they died. This is the bread that came down from heaven; if anyone eats of this bread, he will live forever." Now the dew is also Christ, who rained down from heaven laying "around the borders of the camp." Spiritual eating is to believe that in the flesh of Christ our sin is dead; and the mercy of God is signified no more clearly than in that flesh through which God sent down his Son, so that we might "have a high priest tempted in all things like us" so that he might be able to sympathize with us, etc. Hebrews 4. Hence the spiritual eating of Christ's flesh comes from the contemplation of his flesh, that is, the most despised form of Christ. Third, John 4 explains the water from the rock in this way: "Whoever drinks of the water that I shall give him will never thirst," and Psalm 22,[12] "He leads me besides still waters," etc. What he says of the rock that accompanied them should be understood in the same manner he explains about Christ, who keeps company with the people. For "Christ is the same yesterday, and today, and forever," Hebrews 13. Annotations on 1 Corinthians 10:3-4.[13]

der Predicanten gespräch zu Basel, von dem Kintertauff (Basel: Andreas Cratander, 1527), K ij v. In Old, *Shaping of the Reformed Baptismal Rite in the Sixteenth Century*, 121-22.

[10]Downame, *English Annotations*, DD4v*.

[11]In Baylor, *The Radical Reformation*, 163.

[12]*Sic*, Ps 23:2.

[13]Melanchthon, *Annotationes in Epistolam priorem ad Corinthios*,

Sacraments Bestow What They Signify. John Calvin: Further, when Paul says that the fathers ate "the same spiritual food," he first of all indicates what is the power and efficacy of the sacraments, and second, he shows that the old sacraments of the law had the same power as ours have today. For if the manna was *spiritual* food, it follows that bare symbols are not exhibited to us in the sacraments; rather the reality symbolized is at the same time truly given. For God is not a deceiver who nourishes us with empty symbols. A sign is indeed a sign and retains its own substance. But just as, on the one hand, the papists are ridiculous who imagine a (who knows what sort of) transformation of the symbols, so on the other hand, we have no business separating the reality and the symbol that God has conjoined. The papists confuse the reality and the symbol; wicked men such as Schwenckfeld and others like him tear apart the symbol from the reality. Let us preserve a middle course; that is, let us keep the union made by the Lord, but still keep them distinct from one another, lest we wrongly transfer to the one what belongs to the other.

It remains for us to consider the second point, namely, the resemblance of the old signs to ours. It is a well-known dogma of the schoolmen that "the sacraments of the old law merely symbolized grace, whereas our sacraments confer it." This passage is especially well-suited for refuting this error, for it proves that the reality of the sacrament was conveyed to the ancient people as much as to us. It is, therefore, wicked for the Sorbonnists to imagine that the holy fathers under the law were deprived of the reality of the signs. To be sure, I confess that the efficacy of these signs is both richer and more resplendent for us since the time of Christ's incarnation than what the ancient fathers possessed. And so the difference between us and them is only one of degree, or (as the common saying goes) one of "more and less," because we receive more fully what they received in smaller measure. But it is not the case that they received empty symbols while we obtain the reality.

112; citing Jn 6:49-59; Heb 4:15; Jn 4:14; Heb 13:8.

Some people explain these words as if the Israelites were eating the same food *among themselves*, not wishing to apply those things *to us*—but they are not paying attention to Paul's purpose. For what else does Paul mean here than this: that since the ancient people of God were endowed with the same blessings as us and shared in the same sacraments with us, we should not imagine that, due to some special privilege, we are going to be exempted from the punishment that they suffered. However, I do not wish to argue this point with anyone; I am simply stating what seems best to me. Commentary on 1 Corinthians 10:3.[14]

Sacraments Do Not Guarantee Salvation. John Trapp: The Jews fed on the sacraments [of manna and water], and yet they died in God's displeasure. The flesh of the sacrament cannot give life, but only the soul of it, which is the thing represented. It is well-observed that sacraments do not work physically, whether people sleep or wake, *ex opere operato*, by power inherent in them; rather, they work *ex opere operantis*, according to the disposition and qualification of the party that partakes of them. Commentary on 1 Corinthians 10:3.[15]

Jewish Sacraments and Christian Sacraments Are Different. Tilemann Hesshus: The godly reader must be expressly warned here about the enormous corruption of this passage of Paul that Calvin has brashly

[14]CO 49:453-54 (cf. CTS 39:316-18). The Sorbonne was the theological faculty at the University of Paris. Calvin is regularly critical of this theological body for its Catholic viewpoints and hostility to the progress of the Protestant Reformation.

[15]Trapp, *A Commentary or Exposition*, 682*. The Latin phrase *ex opere operato*, "by the work performed," affirmed the medieval Catholic view that the correct and priestly performance of the sacrament conveyed grace to the recipient unless the recipient placed an obstacle to grace. By comparison, *ex opere operantis*, "by the work of the worker," affirmed that the moral condition of the priest or the proper attitude of the recipient in the celebration of the sacrament would determine its efficacy. See Richard A. Muller, *Dictionary of Latin and Greek Theological Terms* (Grand Rapids, Baker Academic, 1985), 108.

attempted to force on the church of God. For when Paul says that all Israel ate the same spiritual food, Calvin explains this passage as follows: Since Paul compares the church in the old covenant with the church in the new covenant, and says that the Israelites ate the same spiritual food in the desert that we eat in the sacred Lord's Supper, from this Paul wanted it understood more fully that we are eating the flesh of Christ in the new covenant and in the Lord's Supper in the same manner that the fathers were eating it in the dessert—to be sure, by faith. But this is a clear and brash distortion of Paul's context. For Paul does not compare the Israelites in the desert with us, but with themselves. For he does not say that the Israelites ate the same spiritual food as we eat, for he was speaking about the eating of manna, which we have never seen or tasted. Therefore this is an enormous and clear deceit, since the phrase "all ate the same food" does not refer to the new covenant church, but only to all those whom Moses brought out of Egypt. And although all ate manna and the bread of angels, nevertheless all did not receive the manna without punishment, since some defiled it with their wickedness. (In the same way, you might say, that all those who were in Noah's ark during the flood were saved, and yet not all were pleasing to God.)

Second, although Paul mentions spiritual eating, he is not talking about the spiritual eating of Christ's body that happens by faith, but about the eating of manna, which was a physical eating that was nourishing the bodies of the Israelites. For that reason, Paul calls manna "spiritual eating" and water flowing from the rock "spiritual drink," because that food and drink were not bestowed through a universal natural law, but miraculously from heaven and by the power of Christ, whose presence was guiding that multitude. Ambrose could have taught Calvin concerning this meaning, for he explains very clearly the words of Paul in this fashion: "Paul calls the manna and the water that flowed from the rock 'spiritual' because they were not furnished by a law of this world, but by the power of God without any mixing of physical elements to suit the occasion, containing in themselves the figure of a future mystery, which we now lay ahold of in the commemoration of our Lord Christ." Therefore Ambrose eloquently states that Paul calls them "spiritual" because they were not created by the law of this world. Therefore no proof regarding either the presence or absence of the body of Christ in the sacred Supper can be adduced from this passage. Explication of 1 Corinthians 10:3-4.[16]

The Ancient Jews Partook of Christ's Flesh and Blood. John Calvin: We have already said that what was displayed in the old sacraments was united with the reality itself. Therefore, since these sacraments were symbols of Christ, it follows that Christ was joined to them, not locally, to be sure, and not in a union of nature or substance, but sacramentally. That is why the apostle says that "the Rock was Christ," for metonymy is commonly employed when speaking about the sacraments. . . . There remains another question: since we now eat of Christ's body and drink of his blood in heaven, how were the Jews partakers of the same spiritual food and drink, when the flesh of Christ was not yet in existence for them to eat? My answer is that his flesh, though it did not yet exist, was nevertheless food for them. And this is not a piece of empty sophistry, for their salvation was dependent on the benefit of his death and resurrection, and thus, on the flesh and blood of Christ. Therefore it was necessary for them to receive the flesh and blood of Christ so that they might partake in the blessing of redemption. The reception of it was the secret work of the Holy Spirit, who worked in them in such a manner that the flesh of Christ—although it had not yet been created—was made efficacious in them. Commentary on 1 Corinthians 10:4.[17]

[16]Hesshus, *Explicatio Prioris Epistolae ad Corinthios*, 146r-147r. For Ambrose's (Ambrosiaster's) treatment of this verse, see his *Comment. in Epist. I ad Cor.*, in PL 17:246-47.
[17]CO 49:455 (cf. CTS 39:319-20).

The Ancient Jews Partook of Christ Spiritually, by Faith. Andreas Bodenstein von Karlstadt: Note this, Luther . . . that both the food and drink of the fathers were spiritual, which they ate and drank from Christ. It wasn't a corporal drink or corporal food that they put in their external mouths, but spiritual, which one receives only in the inner person and in spirit (as Christ teaches, John 6). He rebukes the coarse bumpkins who want to eat or drink corporally from Christ when he says, "The flesh is of no use," for it is a spiritual food and a spiritual drink, and not a corporeal drink and food. You must have faith and the knowledge of Christ, not an external mouth and sharp teeth. You must extend the internal person if you want to drink from the blood of the spiritual rock (which is Christ), and you must whet and sharpen the powers of your faith and prepare rightly when you want to eat the spiritual food that is the flesh of Christ. If you come in another way, then you come as a mouth that has no understanding, and the closer you step bodily, the farther away you go with your heart. . . .

This is the summary: whoever wants to eat and drink of Christ must not eat and drink corporally from Christ, as our new papists claim, but spiritually in faith or in glorious, ardent, hearty, and loving knowledge of Christ the crucified. For our fathers Adam, Noah, Abraham, Isaac, Jacob, Moses, etc., ate and drank from Christ in their faith, through which they knew that Christ should come and be crucified, and woe to those who want to eat of Christ in any other way than spiritually . . . Explanation of 1 Corinthians 10.[18]

In What Sense Did the Rock "Follow Them"? Giovanni Diodati: The Rock refers to the water that came out of the rock that Moses struck. This is a very clear figure of Christ, who, when he was smitten by the Father in his death and suffering, poured out living springs of redemption, grace, and life to his whole church (Is 53:4, 6; Heb 5:9). The statement that the Rock "followed them" does not refer to the sign of the Rock, but to the sign of the water that came out of it, which pointed to the many running streams in the wilderness through which the people passed (see Deut 9:21; Ps 78:20; 105:41), although there were some interruptions of the supply of water, either as a trial or as punishment of the people (Num 20:2; 21:5, 16). This is very properly spoken of Christ, for not only are his benefits perpetual, but he himself, who is the source of these springs, is never separated from his people, but always resides in them and with them by his Holy Spirit. "And the Rock was Christ"—not in a substantial or material sense, but figuratively and sacramentally, which by virtue of God's command and covenant is joined to the real but spiritual fruition of Christ. Annotations on 1 Corinthians 10:4.[19]

God's Judgment Awaits Those Who Indulge Their Lusts. Tilemann Hesshus: From the example of the people of Israel, Paul now teaches that the external glory of the church is of no advantage unless you aim continually for godliness from the heart. Paul reminds them of this here by means of the story found in Numbers 11, where the people were burning with desire to eat meat—and Jesus Christ, indeed, gave them meat. But while they were still chewing the meat between their teeth, the wrath of God flared up and he killed the people with a very great slaughter. Those of us in the church should be careful that we don't indulge our lusts, therefore, lest we also provoke the severe wrath of God and bring a great punishment on us. Explication of 1 Corinthians 10:5.[20]

10:6-13 *The Jews Provide Us with Warnings*

Two Kinds of Examples. Wolfgang Musculus: There are two kinds of examples, those that ought to be avoided and those that ought to be

[18]Burnett, *The Eucharistic Pamphlets of Andreas Bodenstein von Karlstadt*, 221-22, 223; citing Jn 6:47-58, 63. Karlstadt's reference to "new papists" is his derogatory term for Luther and his followers.

[19]Diodati, *Pious Annotations*, Mm3*; referring to Ex 17:6.

[20]Hesshus, *Explicatio Prioris Epistolae ad Corinthios*, 147v.

imitated. The first kind serves as a deterrent, the second kind to encourage emulation. Paul introduces examples from [the history] of the Israelites that pertain to the first sort. He says: "Now all these things were figures for us, that we might not desire evil things as they did." . . . Why does Paul not say "that we might not do evil things"? Isn't it worse to do evil than to desire evil? My response is this: In the sight of God, desire is considered as the deed. So too desire is the root of a deed. "Each person," writes James, "is tempted when he is lured and enticed by his own desire. Then desire, when it has conceived, gives birth to sin, and when sin is fully grown brings forth death." And so we are warned to flee the desire of evil things for two reasons; because desire tempts us to commit sin and because, in the sight of God, desire is considered for sin (even if it is not acted on). Commentary on 1 Corinthians 10:6.[21]

Definition of Idolatry. David Chytraeus: Idolatry is not only the worship of images or of heathen gods. It is also employing human intelligence and willfulness without God's words, either to imagine something to be a god that is not a god; or to give to any creature the honor and service due to God alone (such as prayers and other sacrifices); or to worship God with the works of human hands, as Paul mentions in Acts 17, that is, with images and pictures, and to bind God to those images; or to willfully choose and establish services and ceremonies so as to please God and make him favorable to us; or to confirm other idolaters by our example, and by observation of outward ceremonies. . . . The virtue that counters idolatry is true godliness, or the true worship of God, or the Christian religion, which rightly acknowledges the one true God, the Father, the Son, and the Holy Spirit, the maker of heaven and earth, and calls on him and worships him with true faith and obedience, as he has revealed himself in his own Word of the law and the gospel. Postil for the Ninth Sunday After Trinity.[22]

The Sin of Idolatry. John Calvin: Paul is alluding to the history that is recorded in Exodus 32:7. For when Moses delayed on the mountain longer than the rude frivolity of the people could endure, Aaron was forced to make a golden calf and set it up for worship. He did this, not because he wanted the people to worship a different God, but to provide some visible sign of God's presence for the sake of their carnal minds. In punishing very severely this act of idolatry at that time, God showed by this example how much he abhors idolatry. Commentary on 1 Corinthians 10:7.[23]

The Sin of Fornication. John Calvin: Paul now speaks about fornication. From historical records it is clear that great licentiousness was common among the Corinthians, and one can readily infer from earlier chapters that those who had devoted themselves to Christ were not altogether free from this vice. Now the punishment of this vice should also frighten us and remind us how much God hates filthy passions. For in one day, 23,000—or, as Moses says, 24,000—people perished. But although they differ as to the number who died, the discrepancy is easily resolved. For it is not unheard of to give an approximate number when there is no intention of making an exact and detailed count of each person. For example, among the Romans there were those who were called the Hundred [*centumviri*], when in reality they numbered two men more than one hundred. Therefore about 24,000 people were killed by the hand of God; in other words, Moses has cited the upper limit, while Paul has cited the lower limit of 23,000 people—and thus there is no discrepancy in this matter. This history is recorded in Numbers 25:9.

Nevertheless, there is this one difficulty—why does Paul attribute this punishment to fornication, when Moses reports that the wrath of God was aroused from the fact that the people had initiated themselves into the sacred rites of Baal Peor? The answer is that the defection began with fornication. The children of Israel fell into that wickedness not

[21] Musculus, *Comm. 1 Cor.*, 318; citing Jas 1:14-15.
[22] Chytraeus, *Dispositio epistolarum*, 373-74.
[23] CO 49:457 (cf. CTS 39:322).

so much because they were deluded by false worship, but because they were seduced by the blandishments of prostitutes. Thus whatever evil things that followed from it ought to be attributed to fornication. Commentary on 1 Corinthians 10:8.[24]

Harmonizing Paul's Words with the Hebrew Text. Wolfgang Musculus: In this passage, the question arises why the apostle says that 23,000 people were killed [at Peor] when the Hebrew and Chaldean texts [of Num 25:9] report 24,000 people were killed, which the Septuagint also follows? Nicolas of Lyra defends the apostle by saying that the smaller number is included in the larger number, and what is true of the larger number is also true of the smaller number. In this way, Paul can be defended, even if he had said that 23,000 people were killed. Lyra's solution is not convincing to me. In my judgment, the apostle has not written anything that is not true history; in some way, the number 23,000 has crept into the text in place of 24,000. I suspect that either Paul or some other ancient wrote the abbreviation *eikositres* for the word *eikositessares*, and that afterward some negligent persons changed the abbreviation into the word *eikositreis*, and translated it into Latin as "23,000." I can't confirm this, but what I suspect happened is easily observed in the harmony of other passages.

But some people who are certain that the apostle wrote the number 23,000 refer this number only to those who were killed by the sword on the day following the hanging of the tribal chiefs. Hence Paul says that "they fell on a single day," while the remaining thousand refers to those chiefs who were hung on gibbets under the sun. And these chiefs were not alone, but their servants were no doubt punished as well. Thus, Moses is believed to have drawn the number 24,000 from the original history, including all those killed by hanging as well as the sword. Commentary on 1 Corinthians 10:8.[25]

Beware of Testing God! Philipp Melanchthon: To put God to the test is when either out of contempt for God or from unbelief we dare him, or through unbelief we are indignant at enduring the things the Lord imposes on us. The Scriptures generally call this murmuring or tempting God. There is no more common or more deadly plague among all peoples than to grow angry and grumble in this fashion, because of our adversities, as if God had forgotten us. We do not believe that God has brought such hardships on us; we do not believe that he will deliver us. The heart nurses within itself a perpetual anger, not only against people but also against God. This sort of unbelief is most clearly described in Exodus 17, "Is the Lord among us or not?" And in Numbers, chapter 14, "How long will this people despise me? How long will they not believe in me, in spite of all the signs I have done among them?" Annotations on 1 Corinthians 10:9.[26]

The Sin of Putting Christ to the Test. Tilemann Hesshus: When Paul says that "we must not put Christ to the test, as the Israelites were tempting Christ," he thereby sheds light for us on everything that Moses writes. For on the basis of his authority as an apostle, Paul points out that whatever Moses writes concerning Jehovah—who accompanied the camp of the Israelites and performed wondrous miracles among the people—ought to be understood of our Lord Jesus Christ, the perpetual guardian of the church. To put Christ to the test is to depart from the teachings of Christ; to undertake roles outside of our vocation; to disbelieve the miracles performed by Christ; to demand miracles from Christ out of sensual pleasure or curiosity. It is a great and perilous thing to put Christ to the test out of presumption, without God's command and without faith in Christ! Explication of 1 Corinthians 10:9.[27]

[24]CO 49:458 (CRS 39:324).
[25]Musculus, *Comm. 1 Cor.*, 322-23; referring to Num 25:4.
[26]Melanchthon, *Annotationes in Epistolam priorem ad Corinthios*, 114; citing Ex 17:7; Num 14:11.
[27]Hesshus, *Explicatio Prioris Epistolae ad Corinthios*, 148r-v.

The Deity of Christ Illustrated Here. Peter Martyr Vermigli: According to Paul, [the Israelites] are said to have put Christ to the test. This passage is powerful in the wonderful manner it proves his divinity as well as his eternal and perpetual nature. Some interpret this passage to refer to God, but Paul very clearly ascribes it to Christ, and rightly so. For, as we said earlier, [Christ] was the leader of the people of Israel in the desert; and the church [of the old covenant] considered him to be their Mediator in the same way we consider him as ours. And God does not impart his blessings to believers except through Christ. And so, we must believe that he was that angel who was going before the Israelites. Consequently, you see that angel called by the name YHWH more than once. It is necessary for us to be firmly established in this viewpoint so that we do not allow the divine nature of Christ to be wrested from us by the Arians. Commentary on 1 Corinthians 10:9.[28]

The Sin of Grumbling Against God. Tilemann Hesshus: The Israelites very frequently grumbled against the Lord, as is seen in Exodus 16, Numbers 11, Numbers 14, and elsewhere. But because Paul mentions here the "Destroyer," there is no doubt that he has in mind the history from Numbers 16, where Moses records how the earth opened up and swallowed Korah and Dathan, a band of seditious men, and the next day, the people grumbled against Moses, as if he had destroyed the people of God. And God's wrath burned hot, and he sent fire from the heavens that consumed 14,700 Israelites from the assembly. It should be noted from this passage that those who grumble against faithful pastors and ministers are grumbling against the Son of God, Jesus Christ. And by such grumbling, they demonstrate their impatience, mistrust, and hatred of Christ, and they call on themselves weighty punishments. Explication of 1 Corinthians 10:10.[29]

Israel's Idolatry Is an Example for Us. Huldrych Zwingli: These events were catastrophic! So how is it that these things are said to be an example, when so many thousands fell in a single day? These things actually happened, but they are also an example; that is, they signify something else to the future generations. Therefore these things were written down with human letters and entrusted to us for our benefit . . . so that we might guard ourselves against the sins for which they were punished. It is as if Paul were saying: "It is not at all true that these events do not pertain to you, because they were written chiefly for your benefit." Annotations on 1 Corinthians 10:11.[30]

God's Punishment of Israel Serves as a Timeless Example. Tilemann Hesshus: Now Paul applies these examples from the ancient church to the Corinthians and to each and every Christian. "All these things happened to the Israelites in the desert to serve as an example"; that is, they are examples of God's wrath against careless and wicked people in every age of the church, for that time when the people were brought out of Egypt was very illustrative. Now, if God did not spare those people to whom he imparted so much glory and so many miracles, but rather punished them most harshly, one can easily see that God will spare no one on account of the external reputation and glory of their church. Therefore let us often think about the history of the whole church and the history of the world, allowing the consideration of examples of God's wrath to incite us to the fear of God and godliness. God did not spare the most prosperous city of Jerusalem, which was the sole center for teaching and God's unique dwelling place on earth among humans; rather, he destroyed it completely because of its contempt for the Word and the murder of his Son. God did not spare the most prosperous kingdoms and nations, neither Asia, nor Greece, nor Egypt, nor Africa. He spared neither Antioch, nor Ephesus, nor Corinth, nor

[28]Vermigli, *In Selectissimam Priorem ad Corinthios Epistolam . . . Commentarii*, 249r.

[29]Hesshus, *Explicatio Prioris Epistolae ad Corinthios*, 148v-149r.

[30]Zwingli, *Annotatiunculae . . . ex ore Zvinglij*, 76.

Constantinople, nor Rome. Therefore let no one deceive themselves into false security or contempt of the Word of God, believing that God will spare them because of the reputation of their church or the dignity of their office. Instead, let this be fixed in their mind, that those who have received the greater gifts from God, those who have obtained the more respectable position in the church, will suffer the greater punishments if they provoke God's wrath by their false security and wickedness. Explication of 1 Corinthians 10:11.[31]

Christians Can Have Confidence in the Grace of God. Wolfgang Musculus: But here you might say: "Thus, if we listen to the apostle, we will not be secure in the grace of God, and no one will be confident of their salvation, since Paul warns so earnestly that those who think they stand (namely, in faith) should take heed lest they fall." What, therefore, do we teach concerning the certainty of God's grace in response to those who assert that no one is able to be certain of their salvation and the grace of God? And why is it that the apostle writes concerning himself, saying, "I know whom I have believed, and I am certain . . ." etc.

I respond as follows. In this matter there are two things to consider: first, when we look on the grace of God by faith, and second, when we look at ourselves. With respect to the first consideration, we are confident concerning the grace of God, which cannot be uncertain or changeable. The apostle does not impugn this certainty of salvation that faith produces by considering the truth and grace of God. Paul is not speaking about this kind of certainty in this passage, for how can he condemn in other people what he so openly proclaims about himself? With respect to the second consideration, we are not made secure when we gaze on ourselves, but become anxious and fearful that, through some powerful temptation on account of the corruption and weakness of our flesh, we will fall from the position of God's grace in which we have been received. And Paul recommends this kind of fear to the Corinthians—not doubting concerning the grace of God. For he was not speaking to people who were depending on the grace of God with an unshakeable faith, but rather to people who were bound in their false security, who were thinking that they (though filled with weaknesses) were standing and were secure with respect to their own strength, as if it was impossible for them to fall, who in the meantime were allowing those things that very easily could cause secure people to fall from a position of faith. That is why Paul does not say, "He who stands in the grace of God," or "he who has strong faith and hopes greatly in the certainty of the grace of God," but rather "he who thinks he stands should take heed lest he fall." Commentary on 1 Corinthians 10:12.[32]

We Must Persevere in Faith or Lose Salvation. Hans Denck: For one whom God has received through faith he can and will cast away once more should he not remain in the faith. For this reason he did not spare the angels even who were so sure of the matter that they gave way to delighting in themselves and in the process forgot God. Therefore Paul, the elect instrument of God, says not in vain, "let him who stands see to it that he does not fall." Did not God give his spirit to King Saul only to take it away again? It is true, nonetheless, that he never regrets his gifts. What is it to him? He might take away again the talent that he gave to us if we have nothing—that is, those to whom grace, too, means nothing at all. And yet he remains true and just. Speak, anyone who cares to, is it not to treat providence badly if we want to be sure of our recompense from God regardless of how we serve him? God have mercy! In short, we say that God has predestined his own for salvation, regardless of their works. In the same way we spoke, regardless of faith, so that Christ is fully removed as a means. For if works were really to be discarded without distinction, why then does Paul say so earnestly, "No fornicator, no adulterer,

[31]Hesshus, *Explicatio Prioris Epistolae ad Corinthios*, 149r-v.

[32]Musculus, *Comm. 1 Cor.*, 331-32; citing 2 Tim 1:12.

no greedy person, no drunkard, no blasphemer is able to inherit the kingdom of God"? And Christ says that one who does not lose himself is not worthy of him. Yet we want to be worthy by means of our garrulous faith, though we have not forsaken the smallest creaturely thing let alone ourselves on his account, and we do not expect God to be able to do it either. As a result, all of so-called Christendom is full of adulterers, greedy people, drunkards, and such like. Whether God Is the Cause of Evil.[33]

The Elect Are Targets of Satan. Simon Goulart: Both the elect and the reprobate are the target against which Satan shoots his arrows, and he hits them when God permits him to do so. Hence the elect must never think themselves exempt from such trials. Accordingly, Paul says in 1 Corinthians 10:12, "He who thinks he is standing, beware lest he fall." . . . Are not the moral failures of important people within the church of God proofs that they have been struck by the flaming arrows of the enemy? And the bitter torments that many of the elect suffer in their consciences, is this not a witness of this fact as well? On the other hand, those who want to see how Satan treats the reprobate, how he cruelly pierces their hearts with his flaming arrows, read the sad examples in Scripture of Cain, Saul, Ahithophel, Judas, and other desperate men like them. On Spiritual Flesh.[34]

Definition of Temptation. David Chytraeus: Temptation is a provocation or motion to sin and wretchedness that arises from human infirmity, that is, from the doubts and errors of the mind, and from the sinful inclinations and affections of the heart, or from the outward enticements and occasions, which stir up those sinful inclinations. Hence, David by looking on the beautiful shape of Bathsheba was tempted according to his own lust, and yet was not driven by the devil utterly to despise and hate God, as Nero, Saul, and Judas did. But to those who display the beginnings of true godliness, a true fear of God, and true faith, there is an exceedingly sweet comfort set forth in this statement: "God is faithful who does not allow us to be tempted beyond our strength." It's as if he were saying, "God loves us dearly, and with his steadfast goodness embraces all who display the beginning of true godliness, and he does not allow us to be overcome and to sink under the enticements of sin, nor does he lay a greater burden on us than we are able to bear." Rather, he distributes troubles by geometric proportion: on those saints who are great and strong (such as Jacob and David) he lays a heavier weight; and on those who are weaker he lays a lighter weight. Moreover, he strengthens and confirms our hearts with the Holy Spirit, so that we may be able to endure the pain. And he governs the outcome so that they may work for the welfare both of ourselves and others. Postil for the Ninth Sunday After Trinity.[35]

Paul Now Offers Comfort to Fearful Christians. John Calvin: I am of the opinion that [this verse] was intended for their consolation, lest on hearing so many terrible examples of the wrath of God (as he had previously reported), they might be discouraged, overwhelmed with dread. Hence, so that his exhortation might be useful, he adds that there is opportunity for repentance. It's as if he were to say: "There is no need to despair, and I do not wish to give you reason for losing heart. Indeed, that which has happened to you is what frequently happens to other people." Other interpreters are of the opinion that Paul is reprimanding them for their laziness in giving up when they encountered slight temptation. . . . According to these interpreters, therefore, the meaning would be this: "Was it proper for you to succumb to a slight temptation?" But because the context fits better if we take it as consolation, I prefer this interpretation.

[33]Denck, *Selected Writings*, 204-6; citing Mt 10:39.
[34]Goulart, *Seconde partie des Discours Chrestiens*, 274-75.
[35]Chytraeus, *Dispositio epistolarum*, 378.

"But God is faithful." Just as Paul commanded them to be of good cheer with respect to the past so as to spur them to repentance, so he also consoles them as to the future with a certain hope, because "God will not permit them to be tempted beyond their strength." But he warns them to look to the Lord, because a temptation, no matter how small it is, will immediately overwhelm us and finish us off if we depend on our own strength. Paul calls the Lord faithful not only because he keeps his promises; rather, his further meaning is this: "The Lord is the sure protector of his people, under whose care you are completely secure, for he never leaves his people destitute. Therefore, when he has taken you into his care, you have nothing to fear, provided you depend completely on him." Commentary on 1 Corinthians 10:13.[36]

Lead Us Not into Temptation. Balthasar Hubmaier: O heavenly Father! Behold the great anxiety, desolation, misery, persecution, and tribulation that is inflicted on us here on earth. Consider also our human weakness. Therefore, O sweet Father, we pray to you for the sake of your fatherly love that you might not abandon us in our pain and suffering and that we might not be overcome, nor fall away from your holy Word. Let us not be tested harder than we are able to bear. We are weak and impotent, and our enemies are strong, powerful, and cruel. You know that, O merciful Father. A Brief "Our Father".[37]

Christians Will Not Be Tempted Beyond Their Strength. Simon Goulart: As in the course of life, so also at the point of death, God does not permit that his children should be tempted beyond what they can endure, but provides a good way out of the temptation (1 Cor 10:13). An ancient writer once said that "some people die while laughing at it." But we would prefer to say that death is overcome by Christian constancy and magnanimity. It is necessary rather to aim to die in a holy and peaceable manner. And, according to the witness of St. Augustine, death cannot be judged bad that is preceded by a good life, and scarcely anyone dies well who has lived badly.

Death is never too early, whether with respect to the righteous or the wicked. Righteous people are gathered before their time, so as not to be any longer afflicted by perverse men. As for the wicked, God destroys them so that they might no longer torment the righteous. The present life is filled with such great evil that, in comparison, death can be judged a remedy, not a punishment. Some Thoughts on the End of Mortal Life.[38]

God Is Faithful to the End. John Trapp: When Mr. Latimer stood at the stake, and the tormentors about to set fire to him and Ridley, he lifted his eyes toward heaven with a friendly and comfortable countenance, saying "God is faithful!" etc. Ridley also at the stake, with a wondrous cheerful look, ran to Latimer, embraced, kissed, and (as those within earshot later reported) comforted him, saying, "Be of good heart, brother; God will either assuage the fury of the flame, or else will strengthen us to abide it." . . . God proportions the burden to the back, and the stroke to the strength of him that endures it. Commentary on 1 Corinthians 10:13.[39]

10:14-17 *Participation in the Body of Christ*

Paul Revisits Subject of Food Offered to Idols. Huldrych Zwingli: Above in chapter 8, when Paul scolded those so-called knowledgeable people who considered food offered to idols as an indifferent matter [*adiaphora*], he asserted that they were erring in two ways. First, because they act contrary to love of neighbor. For a Christian should show moderation for the sake of others. If their neighbor is offended, those who are free are guilty

[36]CO 49:462-63 (cf. CTS 39:331-32).
[37]CRR 5:243*.
[38]Goulart, *Seconde partie des Disours Chrestiens*, 315-16. See Augustine, *City of God* 1.11 (NPNF 2:9).
[39]Trapp, *A Commentary or Exposition*, 683*. The English martyrs Hugh Latimer and Nicholas Ridley were burned at the stake in 1555. See Foxe, *Acts and Monuments* 7.550.

of sin by not showing self-restraint. . . . Second, Paul demonstrates that they act contrary to conscience and piety. Although Paul treats other topics from chapter 9 through the middle of chapter 10, nevertheless he has not turned to something new. And so he returns to address this argument again. He discourages, therefore, the Corinthians from eating food sacrificed to idols, reproaching their wickedness and treachery. For he is confident that his argument, because it is derived from the law of love, is so solid and indestructible that he calls them as judges against those whose "knowledge" he was opposing. Thus he returns to his argument: "For this reason, my beloved, flee from idolatry." Annotations on 1 Corinthians 10:14.[40]

Idolatry Involves the Heart and External Actions. John Calvin: First of all, we must consider what Paul means by "idolatry." He certainly did not suspect the Corinthians of such ignorance or stupidity as to think that they worshiped idols in the heart. But as they had no scruple to attending the assemblies of the wicked, and observing with them certain ceremonies established in honor of idols, he condemns this license of theirs as being a very bad example. It is certain, therefore, that when he mentions "idolatry" here, he is speaking of outward idolatry, or if you prefer, the open profession of idol worship. For as God is said to be worshiped by kneeling and other signs of reverence (even though the principal and genuine worship of him is internal), the same is true of idols, for the same principle applies to opposites. There are many people today who attempt in vain to excuse their outward actions under the pretext that their heart is far removed from it; but Paul condemns these acts as "idolatrous," and rightly so. For, since we owe God not only the secret affections of the heart, but also outward praise, people who offer to an idol the appearance of adoration to that extent are depriving God of it. People can protest as much as they like that their heart is far from it, but they cannot hide the action itself, that they are transferring the honor God deserves to the idol. Commentary on 1 Corinthians 10:14.[41]

Idolatry Is Spiritual Adultery and Must Be Eradicated Without Delay. Andreas Bodenstein von Karlstadt: The father of each household should enjoin, repeat, and explain God's word to his children. From this it follows always that each community and household should pay attention, so that it understands God's commandment and acts accordingly. And God want us so little to wait until others follow and become pious that he has commanded that the godless be punished just as other vices are punished. And in addition he has commanded that whole cities that cultivate their idolatry or do not want to turn to the right path be killed and destroyed.

It is astonishing that our scripturally wise and our rulers punish carnal adultery and allow spiritual adultery[42] to go unpunished. They want to defeat spiritual adultery with their breath and to stave off carnal adultery with swords, iron, fire, and the executioner's wheel. But is this not miserable conduct among Christians? Is it not a devilish thing that they have more regard for, and punish more severely, the dishonoring of humankind than the dishonoring of God? Moses orders that idolatrous people or spiritual adulterers be killed no less than carnal adulterers. If they looked at their Paul correctly, they would certainly find that Paul did not punish the servants of idols less than the servants of whores. . . . Where we who believe in God's rule, and where we find images, we should remove them and deal with them as God commanded. We should also do this for our whole life, or every day. Yes, if we find images in our community—every community in every city—each community is in the same way responsible for distancing itself from images (Deut 14–15). Whether One Should Proceed Slowly.[43]

[40]Zwingli, *Annotatiunculae . . . ex ore Zvinglij*, 77-78.

[41]CO 49:463 (cf. CTS 39:333). Once again, Calvin is alluding to the Nicodemite "error." See above at 1 Cor 8:13.

[42]That is, idolatry.

[43]In Baylor, *The Radical Reformation*, 57-58, 61. Karlstadt here is

Religious Abuses Do Not Make Actions Themselves Idolatrous. John Donne: Because pictures have been adored, we do not abhor a picture; nor do we sit during the sacrament, because idolatry has been committed in kneeling. That church which they call "Lutheran" has retained more of these ceremonies than ours; and ours more than that which they call "Calvinist." But both the Lutheran and ours have done so without danger, because in both places we are diligent to preach to the people the right use of these indifferent things. For this is a true way of shutting out superstition, not always to abolish the thing itself—because, in the right use of it, the spiritual profit and edification may exceed the danger. Sermon on the Sunday of St. Paul's Conversion.[44]

Idolatry and the Lord's Supper. Dirk Philips: In these words we observe how Christians must flee from the service of idols because they are in the fellowship of Jesus Christ, and one body with all believers and saints, which they testify to and confirm with the Lord's Supper, just as the priests and children of Aaron who served the altar in the fleshly Israel and lived from it were in the fellowship of the altar. That is, they were partakers of all that God had attributed and given to the altar, Aaron, and his children. So it is also with those who, with the servants of idols, eat from their bread and drink from their cup. They are one body with them and are also in the fellowship of the servants of idols, yes, and of the devils themselves. For the unbelieving, idolatrous, and godless are one with the princes of this world whom they serve, and with the Babylonian harlot to whom they cling, and are also one body with her, and they carry on many spiritual harlotries, that is, idolatry with her (Rev 17:1). So now people who mingle with such and eat idolatrous sacrifices, that is, support her false worship, are in the same fellowship and must await the same punishment with her (Rev 18:4). Yes, they shall share from the plagues that shall come over Babylon, and shall be cast with the dragon into the fiery lake that burns with fire and sulfur (which is the second death; Rev 21:8), so long as they do not improve themselves and do not sincerely repent. An Apology or Reply.[45]

"Sensible" Christians Have the Right to Judge Doctrine. Tilemann Hesshus: Paul calls the members of the church "sensible ones," for true wisdom is only found in the church of Christ, in which the Holy Spirit illumines the minds of men and women, and shines forth the Word of God, the source of all wisdom. With insight and piety, Hilary said in *On the Trinity*: "The ungodly possess no wisdom in themselves. And when the fear of God (which is the beginning of wisdom) is absent, every beginning of good sense disappears with it."

The apostle Paul confers on the church the power of judging his teaching. Therefore it is permissible for the entire church of Christ—so-called laypersons in the assembly as well as clergy; common people as well as the greatest bishops—to examine the teachings of their pastors, and to pass judgment on controversial matters. In the same way, Christ teaches: "Beware of false prophets" (Matt 7). Explication of 1 Corinthians 10:15.[46]

Believers Are United in One Body Through the Supper. John Colet: In the cup that is blessed and the bread that is broken is a saving communion of the true body and blood of Jesus Christ himself, shared by many so that in it they may be one. The many are united as they partake of the One, and they are formed anew into it. In this partaking, to be sure, they are being conformed to Christ, and are in him. This is what is meant by the words: "Though many in number, all of us who participate in the one bread and the one cup are one bread and one body."

arguing against Luther, who insisted that the Reformation in Wittenberg (including removal of religious images) should be implemented slowly out of consideration for the consciences of weaker Christians.

[44]Donne, *Works*, 2:353*.

[45]CRR 6:184-85*.

[46]Hesshus, *Explicatio Prioris Epistolae ad Corinthios*, 152r-v; citing Mt 7:15. For Hilary's statement, see *On the Trinity*, book 5, in NPNF 9:85-97.

The food that we feast on is one, distributed to the whole fellowship as to one body, so that all people, nourished by the One, may be united in that by which they are nourished. . . . For from this comes the conformity and unity of all: that Christ, when he is shared by diverse people, does not enter into the nature of their diversity. For those who communicate are not stronger than he who is communicated to them, but being diverse, they are formed anew by the stronger one—that is, Christ—into one, and they happily pass from themselves into him by whom they are fed. Exposition of 1 Corinthians 10.[47]

The Cup and the Bread. Cardinal Cajetan: "The cup of blessing," that is, of gratitude, which is offered as an expression of gratitude to God; "which we bless," first when our priests consecrate it, and then when everyone offers praises to God. "Is it not communion in the blood of Christ?"—so that people participate in the substance communicated from the chalice. . . . Paul does not say "this signifies communion," but rather "this *is* communion," because partaking of the chalice is truly communion in the blood of Christ (not in wine). . . .

"And the bread that we break," that is, in the sacrificing and distribution of it. Just as Paul spoke of the "chalice" or "cup" to refer to the contents of the vessel, so now he says "bread" to refer to the physical appearance of bread. This interpretation is clearly proved by the word "is," when he adds "Is it not participation" (instead of "communion") "in the body of the Lord" (instead of "Christ"). Here Paul does not say *signifies*, but *is*. For, certainly, communion in the body of Christ does not consist in the substance of the bread eaten. Rather, the bread that we eat is only the *appearance* of bread, for it is true communion in the body of Christ, so that we are participating in the substance communicated, united with the thing itself. For the true body of Christ—not the substance of the bread—is communicated to all who are eating of it. Commentary on 1 Corinthians 10:16.[48]

Communion in the Blood of Christ. John Calvin: Now Paul says that the cup which has been blessed in this fashion is the communion of the blood of the Lord. What exactly does he mean? Get rid of the controversies, and everything will be clear. It is true that believers are united together through Christ's blood, so that they form a single body. It is also true that unity of this sort is properly called communion. The same thing can be said of the bread. Moreover, I note what Paul immediately adds by way of explanation, that we are all made one body, because "we all partake of the same bread together." But what, I ask, is the source of that communion [*koinōnia*] among us, if not because we have been united with Christ, so that we are "flesh of his flesh and bone of his bones"? For we must first be incorporated (so to speak) into Christ, so that we might be united to each other. Additionally, Paul is here not merely discussing human fellowship, but the spiritual union between Christ and believers so that he might thereby make it plain that it is an intolerable sacrilege for them to be polluted by fellowship with idols. Therefore, from the context of this passage, we can conclude that the communion of the blood is the fellowship that we have with the blood of Christ when he ingrafts us into his body, so that he might live in us and we in him.

Now when the cup is called a "communion," I confess that the expression is figurative, provided that the truth conveyed by the figure is not destroyed; or, in other words, provided that the reality itself is also present, and the soul partakes of communion in the blood, just as much as we drink wine with the mouth. But the papists are not able to say that the cup of blessing is the communion with the blood of Christ. For they possess a mutilated and mangled form of the Supper—if, indeed, that bizarre ceremony can be called a "Supper," which is a patchwork of various human inventions that barely retains the slightest trace of what our Lord instituted. Commentary on 1 Corinthians 10:16.[49]

[47]Colet, *Enarratio*, 216-18.

[48]Cajetan, *In Sacrae Scripturae expositionem*, 5:118.

[49]CO 49:464-65 (cf. CTS 39:335-36); citing Eph 5:30.

The Nature of Our Participation in Christ. Wolfgang Musculus: In order to instruct people who are more ignorant of these things, we must speak of various kinds of participation in the body and blood of Christ. I see four kinds of participation, namely natural, sacramental, spiritual, and celestial. First, there is a natural participation where we share the same nature, the same flesh and blood, since Christ is truly human and a son of Adam and shares the same essence with all of us, though without sin. And believers rejoice greatly in this participation. For though Christ sustains all people everywhere, he is nevertheless more precious to those good and honorable people who perceive by faith the fruit of his incarnation. . . .

Second, there is a sacramental participation where, in accordance with the Lord's instruction, the members of the church share together in the sacramental symbols of Christ's body and blood through bread and wine. The apostle speaks about this form of participation here in this passage, calling it "the participation in the body and blood of Christ," focusing not on the external symbols of bread and wine but on the intention of the Lord's institution and the meaning of the sacramental signs. . . .

Third, there is a spiritual participation where, through the Spirit, we participate by faith in the rich benefits of the flesh and blood of Christ, who was crucified for our sins, and we become partners of the same grace and redemption. People who participate spiritually . . . truly eat the flesh and drink the blood of Christ (though not in the sacrament itself); that is, they live by virtue of the merit and benefit of his death. In this way, that which the sacramental signs display is accomplished sacramentally through the church's external participation. This spiritual participation is not tied so closely to the sacramental participation that it cannot take place outside of it. . . .

Fourth, there is a celestial participation where our bodies become partners with and are conformed to the glorified Christ in the future age, which the apostle mentions in Philippians 3, saying, "But our citizenship is in heaven, and from it we await a Savior, the Lord Jesus Christ, who will transform our lowly bodies to be like his glorious body." . . . I see in Scripture these four kinds of participation in the body of Christ. The first is experienced by all human beings; the second is available to all Christians; the third and fourth are experienced only by elect believers. The first two kinds of participation do not save us without the third; our salvation and happiness is achieved in full by the fourth. Commentary on 1 Corinthians 10:16.[50]

Communion with Christ and One Another. Balthasar Hubmaier: As we now have communion with one another in this bread and drink of the Christ meal, so also should the body and blood of all of us be shared with each other, just as the body and blood of Christ are shared with us all. This is the meaning of the word *symbol* when we eat and drink together. Before eating from the table of the Lord, persons should test themselves and recollect whether they are so minded toward their neighbor. There is a great difference between the Christ meal and another meal, although all table meals should be accepted with thanksgiving. Nevertheless, in the Christ meal one should proclaim the death of Christ, and obligate and bind oneself together with body and blood in brotherly service through this visible word symbol and not come together merely for the sake of eating and drinking. Just this Paul calls a communion or fellowship. Several Theses Concerning the Mass.[51]

The Nature of Sacramental Participation. Tilemann Hesshus: The first argument by which Paul teaches that [the Corinthians] must flee idolatry is drawn from opposites. The person who participates in the body and blood of Christ ought to have nothing to do with idols. Christians are made participants of the body and blood of Christ. Therefore, they ought to have nothing in

[50]Musculus, *Comm. 1 Cor.*, 345-46; citing Phil 3:20-21.
[51]CRR 5:75-76.

common with idols, for there is no communion between Christ and Belial. This present passage is very significant, because it clearly explains the controversy concerning the presence of Christ's body in the sacred Supper, and very powerfully defends the true meaning against the tricks of the Calvinists, who shamefully corrupt Paul's words. Calvin contends that, with these words, Paul is engaging in a figure of speech: the bread is the communion of the body of Christ, that is, it is a *symbol* of the communion of the body of Christ. Other people corrupt Paul's statement thusly: "the bread is a thing through which fellowship with Christ occurs." Bullinger describes it this way: "When [Paul] says 'the body of Christ,' he indicates by allegory the church." And so one person twists Paul's words this way, someone else twists them a different way; but all Calvinists drive out and banish the body and blood of Jesus Christ from the sacred Supper. Therefore we must take great pains to guard this most precious treasure and preserve the truth of apostolic teaching.

Therefore, as far as language is concerned, it is certain that the word *koinōnia* does not mean "fellowship," but rather "communication" and "participation"—even Calvin conceded the obviousness of this fact. For Paul explains the word *koinōnia* with the term "partake" [*metochēn*] in verse 17. And Theophylact states: "*koinōnia* means something more significant than 'partake' [*metochē*], for it certainly indicates the most intimate union with Christ."

The term "body" in this passage does not simply mean "church" in an allegorical sense, but it means the very substance of the body of Jesus Christ, which hung on the cross for us and resurrected from the dead. For no one can deny that Paul here is speaking concerning the Eucharist, describing the body and blood of Jesus Christ, for he says, "the cup of blessing that we bless." And so the interpretation of Bullinger is stupid and impetuous when he says the body of Christ here signifies the church, for when Paul says that the cup is the participation of the blood of Christ, one must understand by this—not the church—but true participation in the blood of Christ. Therefore the apostle's words must be interpreted literally, not figuratively. Explication of 1 Corinthians 10:16-17.[52]

The Nature of True Christian Fellowship. Balthasar Hubmaier: This is the true fellowship of saints, 1 Cor 10:16. It is not a fellowship for the reason that bread is broken, but rather the bread is broken because the fellowship has already taken place and has been concluded inward in the spirit. . . . So every Christian speaks equally: "I have believed, therefore I have publicly confessed that Jesus is Christ, Son of the living God, and have thereafter had myself baptized according to the order of Christ, the high priest who lives in eternity." Or: "I have fellowship with Christ and all his members (1 Cor 10:16); therefore I break bread with all believers in Christ according to the institution of Christ." Without this inner communion in the spirit and in truth, the outward breaking of bread is nothing but an Iscariotic and damnable hypocrisy. It is precisely to this fellowship and commitment of love that the Supper of Christ points, as a living memorial of his suffering and death for us, spiritually signified and pointed to by the breaking of bread, the pouring out the wine, that each one should also sacrifice and pour out his flesh and blood for the other. Herein will people recognize that we are truly disciples of Christ. . . . All of the words that Christ spoke about the Last Supper tend toward this. For just as water baptism is a public testimony of the Christian faith, so is the Supper a public testimony of Christian love. Now he who does not want to be baptized or to observe the Supper, he does not desire to believe in Christ nor to practice Christian love and does not desire to be a Christian. A Form for Christ's Supper.[53]

Believers Partake Spiritually of Christ Through Faith. Andreas Bodenstein von Karlstadt: I fear that the new pope will do

[52]Hesshus, *Explicatio Prioris Epistolae ad Corinthios*, 153r-v. For Theophylact's treatment of this verse, see his *Expositio in Epist. I ad Cor.*, in PG 124:671.
[53]CRR 5:399.

greater violence to the gospel than the old if he compels us [to believe] that we should enter into the fellowship of the right body of Christ through the use of the Lord's Supper. For we eat the Lord's bread in remembrance . . . and we aren't incorporated through bread or made partakers of Christ's body. We partake of the body of Christ through knowledge . . . or through loving faith, which is the same thing. Through faith he cleanses the hearts, through love and faith Christ dwells in us, not in the belly or in the mouth but in the spirit, in the internal person, in the knowledge of the surpassing love of Christ; and through knowledge we have fellowship. Explanation of 1 Corinthians 10.[54]

Spiritual Fellowship with Christ. Dirk Philips: [True Christians] break the bread and drink out of the cup as a witness that they are in the fellowship of the body of Christ. They have come into this fellowship out of God's grace and election through faith, and they are established therein through true baptism. In this fellowship they are also preserved and established through the Supper of the Lord, through which fellowship they are also partakers of all that Christ has and are his, just as the children of Aaron in the fellowship of the altar were also partakers of all that Aaron their father had given and administered for them.

So also through the bread and through the wine of the Supper, the unity and the agreeableness and fellowship of believers is portrayed and testified. However, in order to signify this fellowship, the Lord has taken and ordained such symbols in the Supper that overall merge back and forth and with their forms arouse and motivate to such fellowship. For just as the bread is made of many grains, poured together and ground, and the many grains become one loaf in which each individual grain loses its body and form, and similarly with the grapes with the changing of their form become a common wine and drink's body, so also all Christians must be united with Christ and with each other. The Supper of Our Lord Jesus Christ.[55]

Anabaptists Abstain from the Supper of the Ungodly. Menno Simons: We learn from the Scriptures that the Holy Supper was instituted by the Lord as a sign and testimony and proof, not to the world but to the church of God, that all of us who partake of one bread are members of one body, namely, of the body of Christ. Since we see with our eyes and feel with our hands that both the dispensers and partakers of the worldly Supper are not true members of the Lord's body because the dispensers are all hirelings, thieves of the honor of God, and murderers of our souls, who sustain the thoughtless, reckless people in all manner of unrighteousness and blindness, and in a free and carnal life, by their promises, philosophy, and invention . . . and since the partakers are, speaking generally, an impenitent, willful, and vain people, yes, worldlings, who not only disrespect the Spirit, Word, and knowledge of the Lord, but for the most part trample it underfoot, as may be seen, therefore, we abstain from their supper. Reply to Gellius Faber.[56]

The Proper Use of the Lord's Supper. Martin Luther: To signify this fellowship, God has appointed such signs of this sacrament as in every way serve this purpose and by their very form stimulate and motivate us to this fellowship. For just as the bread is made out of many grains ground and mixed together, and out of the bodies of many grains there comes the body of one bread, in which each grain loses its form and body and takes on itself the common body of the bread; and just as the drops of wine, in losing their own form, become the body of one common wine and drink—so it is and should be with us, if we use this sacrament properly. Christ with all saints, by his love, takes on himself our form, fights with us

[54]In Burnett, *The Eucharistic Pamphlets of Andreas Bodenstein von Karlstadt*, 231; citing Eph 3:14-19.

[55]CRR 6:121-22*.

[56]Simons, *Complete Writings*, 717.

against sin, death, and all evil. This enkindles in us such love that we take on his form, rely on his righteousness, life, and blessedness. And through the interchange of his blessings and our misfortunes, we become one loaf, one bread, one body, one drink, and have all things in common. O this is a great sacrament, says St. Paul, that Christ and the church are one flesh and bone. Again through this same love, we are to be changed and to make the infirmities of all other Christians our own; we are to take on ourselves their form and their necessity, and all the good that is within our power we are to make theirs, that they may profit from it. That is real fellowship, and that is the true significance of this sacrament. The Sacrament of the Body of Christ.[57]

10:18-22 *The Cup of the Lord and the Cup of Demons*

The Example of Sacrifices in the Mosaic Law. John Calvin: Paul uses another example to prove that it is the nature of all sacred ceremonies that they bind us to a certain fellowship with God. For the law of Moses does not allow people to feast on a sacrifice unless they have prepared themselves properly. I am speaking not only about the priests but also about the common people who ate what was left over from the sacrifices. It follows from this that all who eat of the flesh of sacrificed animals are participants of the altar, that is, of that holiness with which God set apart his temple and the sacred rites that are performed in it. Commentary on 1 Corinthians 10:18.[58]

Pagan Sacrifices Are Offered to Demons. Tilemann Hesshus: Paul shows that what he is insisting on is drawn from the Lord's Supper and participation in the body of Christ: that the Corinthians should abstain from the sacrifices to idols lest they become participants with devils. Indeed, he says that idols are nothing and that whatever is sacrificed to idols is nothing. These things in themselves cannot help or harm us, but because those things that are offered to idols are offered to devils, they compel people to participate in idol worship—that is the reason these things should be avoided, lest people be participants with demons. Explication of 1 Corinthians 10:19-20.[59]

The Devil Is the Source of All Idolatry. Giovanni Diodati: These foods [sacrificed to idols] are not impure in their own substance, but in the way that they are used. And their use relates directly to the devil, who is the source of all idolatry and who is indirectly served by them (see Lev 17:7; Deut 32:17; Ps 106:37; Rev 9:20).... I grant that neither the idol nor the things that are sacrificed to it have any power to pollute God's creatures in their substance. Rather, it is the sin of idolatry that contaminates them; for idolatry is a revolt from the true God and his service that, in the end, leads people into the service of the devil, who is God's enemy. Hence, those who are present at these public feasts in honor of idols (since this is a notable part of idolatry) engage in the devil's service. People cannot give the excuse that this was not at all their intention, for when people participate publicly in a damnable rite like this, their particular intentions can neither excuse nor justify them from sin. For if not internally, at least externally, they are joining themselves to wicked people, strengthening them instead of condemning them. Annotations on 1 Corinthians 10:20.[60]

Participants with Demons. Wolfgang Musculus: I think the phrase "participants with demons" should be understood as follows. We cannot be united to demons through a natural participation. Wherefore all participation with demons is either sacramental, or spiritual, or penal. I call sacramental participation when a person participates in external worship and sacrifices. This

[57]LW 35:58.
[58]CO 49:465 (cf. CTS 39:336-37).
[59]Hesshus, *Explicatio Prioris Epistolae ad Corinthios*, 157r-v.
[60]Diodati, *Pious Annotations*, MM3v*.

pertains to all religious activities in which idols, shrines, sanctuaries, chapels, altars, images, feast days, sacrifices, mystical meals, and various rites and ceremonies are worshiped. Those who participate in these activities are participants with demons, even if they participate in only some of these activities. The apostle is here speaking about this kind of participation.

Spiritual participation with demons is, first of all, when the spirit of a person indulges in the errors of darkness related to superstition and wickedness, and then, with a malicious heart, participates with evil spirits so that he can rightly be called not only a slave of the devil but also the son of the devil. People who participate with demons in this way are all those wicked, superstitious, blind, proud, jealous, blasphemous, murderous, treacherous, shameful, hypocritical, scorners of God, etc. For they participate in a spirit of malice and wickedness. Today, people who are spiritual participants with demons rule in the church full of deceived people.

Penal participation with demons is when a person participates in eternal condemnation, which awaits all those who are participants with demons in this life (whether sacramentally or spiritually) without coming to their senses. Christ speaks about this kind of participation in Matthew 25, saying "Depart from me, you cursed ones, into the eternal fire prepared for the devil and his angels." Therefore the wicked will be participants with demons forever in eternal fire. Commentary on 1 Corinthians 10:20.[61]

Beware of Pagan Books! John Colet: Only with Christ, then, should we feast together at the splendid table of the Scriptures; and we should feast the more abundantly on the New Testament since there the Mosaic "water" has been changed by Christ himself into wine. At other tables, in other books—those of the pagans—where there is nothing with the savor of Christ and nothing without the savor of a demon—in those places, surely, Christians should not sit, unless they wish to appear a dinner guest of a demon rather than of the Lord. . . . If we seek to feed on the wisdom of pagans (which is demonic) rather than the Lord, we lose connection to the Lord. No one takes a meal at their tables—that is, in their books—unless they have no confidence in Scripture or are negligent toward it. Either is impious and execrable, and an abominable tempting of God.

Now if they should say, as they usually do, that the reading of pagan books helps our understanding of sacred Scripture, let them consider whether their confidence in them is not a greater obstacle. Because when you do this, you show that you have no confidence in your ability to understand holy writ through grace alone and prayer, through the help of Christ and of faith. Instead you put your trust in the principles and the assistance of the pagans. That is why Paul can say that "what pagans sacrifice they offer to demons and not to God. . . ." We must read only those books in which there is the saving taste of Christ; in which Christ is set forth for our feasting. Those in which there is no Christ are the table of demons. Exposition of 1 Corinthians 10.[62]

Table of the Lord and the Table of Demons. Tilemann Hesshus: Because it is so important, Paul sets down his argument at this point: Christians cannot at the same time be participants at the table of the Lord and at the table of devils. In the sacred Supper, the people were participants of Christ's body; but in their idol sacrifices, they were communing with devils. Therefore Christians ought to abstain completely from sacrifices to idols. This, then, is the apostle Paul's aim. Now if some Calvinist should object: "If Paul were speaking concerning *physical* participation in the body of Christ—and what participation is worthy or unworthy—a person could, at the same time, participate in the body of the Lord *and* participate in the table of a demon. But Paul denies that this can happen. Therefore he is

[61]Musculus, *Comm. 1 Cor.*, 352; citing Mt 25:41.

[62]Colet, *Enarratio*, 216, 218.

speaking about *spiritual* participation." We must answer that Paul's purpose is this: that this cannot happen with respect to the salvation of the soul. You cannot, at the same time, be a participant at the Lord's table and at the table of demons with respect to the salvation of your soul. For the person who eats the body of the Lord unworthily does something to the body of Christ. But the person who participates at the table of demons defiles himself with his foul idolatry. Thus we must beware lest we provoke the wrath of God. Explication of 1 Corinthians 10:21-22.[63]

Remembering Christ's Death Allows No Fellowship with the Devil. Andreas Bodenstein von Karlstadt: You should not be in the fellowship of devils; you cannot at the same time drink from the Lord's cup and the cup of the devil. Why? Because blood is in the cup? No, but because you should drink from the Lord's cup in remembrance of Christ's death. But such remembrance, if it is righteous, can neither allow nor see anyone drink from the devil's cup without horror. You cannot partake of the Lord's table and the devil's table at the same time. . . . Anyone who wishes to hear the external word rightly and partake of its contents must cast off all things that hinder or darken the word or that stop up the ears. . . . The sin of idolatry or sins against the love of neighbor aren't the only ones opposed to Christ's Supper, but so are many other sins, such as drunkenness, debauchery, blindness, etc., as Paul teaches in 1 Corinthians 11. This isn't because the body and the blood of Christ are in the sacrament, but because the Lord said, "Eat the bread and drink from the cup in remembrance of me." The remembrance of Christ's death can suffer no fellowship with the devil, and it also opposes the desires of the flesh. Explanation of 1 Corinthians 10.[64]

The Lord's Supper Is Antithetical to Works of Darkness. Anabaptists of Trieste: Concerning the memorial and Supper of the Lord Jesus Christ that he has ordered us to observe, we heartily confess and believe that all who desire to break the Lord's bread as the memorial of Christ's broken body, and all who desire to drink of this cup for the remembrance of the shed blood of Christ, must first be united by baptism to the one body of Christ of which Christ is the head. As Paul points out, we cannot at the same time participate in the Lord's cup and the cup of devils (1 Cor 10). This means that all those who have fellowship with the dead works of darkness have no part in the light. Those who follow the devil have no part with those who have been called out of the world by God (2 Cor 6). All who make their bed with evil have no part in the good. There is no possible alternative. Those who are not united by the call of God into one faith, to one baptism, in one Spirit, for one body with all the children of God, can also not be made one loaf with him. Confession.[65]

Do Not Provoke God. John Calvin: Paul warns how dangerous it is to provoke God—because no one can do this except to his own destruction. With human beings, the risk of war is uncertain (as they say). But to contend against God is nothing other than to call disaster on oneself. Therefore, if we are afraid to have God as our enemy, let us tremble at the thought of making excuses for flagrant sins, that is, whatever opposes his Word. Let us also tremble at the thought of calling into question those things that he has told us, because this is nothing less than to rise up against the heavens as the giants did. Commentary on 1 Corinthians 10:22.[66]

[63]Hesshus, *Explicatio Prioris Epistolae ad Corinthios*, 158r.
[64]In Burnett, *The Eucharistic Pamphlets of Andreas Bodenstein von Karlstadt*, 232-33; citing 1 Cor 11:21-22.
[65]CRR 10:270; citing 2 Cor 6:14-16.
[66]CO 49:467 (cf. CTS 39:341); referring to Gen 11:4.

10:23–11:1 Do All to the Glory of God

[23]*"All things are lawful," but not all things are helpful.*
"All things are lawful," but not all things build up.
[24]*Let no one seek his own good, but the good of his*
neighbor. [25]*Eat whatever is sold in the meat market*
without raising any question on the ground of
conscience. [26]*For "the earth is the Lord's, and the*
fullness thereof." [27]*If one of the unbelievers invites you*
to dinner and you are disposed to go, eat whatever is
set before you without raising any question on the
ground of conscience.[28]*But if someone says to you,*
"This has been offered in sacrifice," then do not eat it,
for the sake of the one who informed you, and for the
sake of conscience— [29]*I do not mean your conscience,*
but his. For why should my liberty be determined by
someone else's conscience? [30]*If I partake with thankful-*
ness, why am I denounced because of that for which I
give thanks?
[31]*So, whether you eat or drink, or whatever you do,*
do all to the glory of God. [32]*Give no offense to Jews or*
to Greeks or to the church of God,[33]*just as I try to*
please everyone in everything I do, not seeking my
own advantage, but that of many, that they may be
saved.
11 *Be imitators of me, as I am of Christ.*

Overview: In the final verses of this chapter, the apostle Paul returns one last time to the topic of Christian freedom, setting forth the foundational principle that Christians must exercise their freedom in a manner that promotes God's glory and edifies their neighbor. Protestant commentators attempt to hold in balance two important truths in this passage: first, that Christians, as recipients of God's grace, are free from the burden of the law and thereby empowered to enjoy God's good creation as free "kings" and "lords"; and second, that Christian freedom only applies to indifferent or neutral matters, and must always be exercised out of concern for God and neighbor. Characteristically, Protestant interpreters insist that believers must regularly consult the Word of God to determine whether an activity is required, permissible, or prohibited.

10:23-30 *Seeking the Good of One's Neighbor*

Paul Returns to the Matter of Brotherly Love. Wolfgang Musculus: Hitherto Paul has employed the fear of God's wrath to divert the Corinthians from sharing meals with unbelievers who are eating and drinking to idols. Paul now returns to the argument of brotherly love, which he has used in the two previous chapters 8 and 9, and he impresses on them again that those who eat everything indiscriminately are abusing their freedom and sinning against weaker brothers contrary to love. As is his custom, Paul considers not only what is permissible but also what is conducive to love. Commentary on 1 Corinthians 10:23.[1]

Churches Are Ruined by Self-Concern. John Colet: Again, everybody in the church should seek what benefits others, not themselves. This is what it means to love others, rather than ourselves: "love does not demand its own way." And here Paul says, "No one seeks his own good, but the good of others." The church's ruin lies in each person seeking their own personal advantage. Those who eagerly prioritizes the advantage of their neighbor—and of everyone in general—works for their own advantage, even when not seeking it. Exposition of 1 Corinthians 10.[2]

Paul Clarifies the Meaning of Christian Freedom. Tilemann Hesshus: Once again Paul responds here to the objection of those who

[1]Musculus, *Comm. 1 Cor.*, 356-57.
[2]Colet, *Enarratio*, 218; citing 1 Cor 13:5.

did not understand correctly his teaching concerning Christian freedom, and who were abusing godly opinion under the cloak of their wickedness and impurity. (He also sought to curb these things earlier, in chapter 6.) The Corinthians had heard "to the pure, all things are pure"; and "the earth belongs to the Lord"; thus "all things are lawful for Christians." From this they concluded that the worship of idols was among those things lawful. Therefore the apostle refutes this perverse opinion and tells them that the meaning of the doctrine of Christian freedom is very different.

First of all, it must be understood that what he said [regarding Christian freedom] does not pertain to behavior expressly prohibited in the Word of God. It is not at all permissible for godly people to worship idols, to swear false oaths, to spread false teaching, to stir up seditions, to associate with prostitutes, to steal, to lie. All people who do such things, Paul says, do not possess the kingdom of God (1 Cor 6:10). Rather, the doctrine of Christian freedom must be understood to refer to neutral and indifferent matters (since "to the pure in heart, nothing is impure")—that Christians are neither bound to the ceremonial laws of Moses, nor to the statutes and decrees of bishops. For Christians have been given freedom in Christ, and the "earth is the Lord's and the fullness thereof." Therefore it is lawful for godly people to enjoy various things with an attitude of thankfulness. We are not bound to certain kinds of food, nor to certain feast days, nor to certain types of political systems, nor to certain kinds of vestments, nor to certain ceremonies. Rather, for godly people, all things are lawful—that is, in matters that are neutral. But those who defiantly sin against the Decalogue are not godly people, but wicked despisers of God; for them, all things are impure, both in mind and conscience.

Second, although all things are lawful for Christians in neutral matters (for their consciences are free from all things by faith in the Word), nevertheless they should not abuse this freedom to the harm or detriment of anyone. For we ought not only to consider our own interests but also the church and our neighbor. That is why, if it seems that the untimely use of my freedom will be a hindrance to the edification of the church and cause scandal to my neighbor, I should rather set aside my right and abstain from using my liberty. Paul was free and could have omitted the circumcision of Timothy. But because he believed that it was useful for the church that Timothy be circumcised (so that the Jews might not shrink back from him), he circumcised him. Paul was free, and he could have demanded a salary from the churches that he was instructing. Nevertheless, he abstained from this, because he saw that the church would be edified by this. And so godly men and women ought to consider not only what would be lawful in itself from a good conscience, but also what would be expedient, what would build up the church, what would instruct and strengthen their fellow believers in the truth. Explication of 1 Corinthians 10:23-24.[3]

Three Crucial Questions. John Trapp: Is it lawful, is it appropriate, is it expedient?—these three are the most important questions. Things that are lawful in themselves may be inappropriate for our condition and calling, and not at all conducive to the benefit of others. You should consider unlawful for yourself whatsoever seems either inexpedient or inappropriate. Commentary on 1 Corinthians 10:23.[4]

Indifferent Things and the Law of Love. Simon Goulart: One calls "indifferent" those things that, considered simply in themselves, are by nature neither good nor bad, such as drinking, or eating, or other similar things that do not pertain to the kingdom of God, as the apostle says. Consequently, a person is able either to use it properly, or misuse it, or abstain from it altogether. . . . In general, the law of love (which is universal, encompassing all persons and things) explicitly prohibits that anything be done that scandalizes one's

[3]Hesshus, *Explicatio Prioris Epistolae ad Corinthios*, 159r-v; citing Tit 1:15; Ps 24:1.

[4]Trapp, *A Commentary or Exposition*, 684*.

neighbors or fails to edify them, even if it might be indifferent and permissible in itself. Nevertheless, it is necessary here to presuppose two things. First, that we should always allow the Word of God to guide us as to whether something is required, or permissible, or prohibited. Second, that each person should remain in their vocation. That is the sense in which we should understand St. Paul when he said that he had become all things to all people. As far as special laws that are established by political or ecclesiastical ordinances: even though it is strictly God alone who compels the conscience, nevertheless when the magistrate, who is a servant of God, judges that it is expedient for the public good that something (which would be lawful otherwise) should not be done, or when the church, out of concern for good order and to assure the common edification, establishes some laws touching indifferent matters, in these cases Christians ought to obey such laws. . . . But those who for any other than these three reasons—that is, who disregard the edification of their neighbor or despise a legitimate political or ecclesiastical constitution—sin grievously against God and their neighbor when they permit or prohibit according to their pleasure the free usage of indifferent things and rashly judge the consciences of other people in such matters. A Second Discourse on Christian Liberty.[5]

Meat Offered to Idols May Be Eaten. The English Annotations: Here the apostle permits that all things that are brought to market may serve us for food, even if it was well-known that the meat brought to market had previously been offered to idols, though not completely consumed in their idolatrous feasts. When brought to market . . . the meat did not honor the idol, but was to be taken for common meat. Annotations on 1 Corinthians 10:25.[6]

Christians Are a Race of Kings. Philipp Melanchthon: Paul proves our freedom from that passage in Psalm 9:[7] because if "the earth is the Lord's," it is necessary for it also to belong to Christ's children and to all who are in Christ. For, if they belong to the Lord of all, the heritage belongs to them, because they are his sons and daughters. Therefore neither creature, nor death, nor sin, nor food, nor drink can harm them, but they are able to use all things as their own according to the freedom of the Spirit. . . . Just as Christ is free and the Lord and king of all, so through faith we are free in him, lords and kings of life, death, sin, and (finally) all creatures. For we are a race of kings. Annotations on 1 Corinthians 10:26.[8]

The Bounty of the Earth. John Calvin: By the "fullness of the earth" the prophet means the abundance of good things with which the earth is furnished and adorned by the Lord. For if the earth was without trees, plants, animals, and other created things, it would be like a house without furniture and any utensils; or rather, it would be a thing mutilated and ugly. Now, if someone should object that the earth is cursed on account of sin, the answer is simple: Paul has in mind here its pure and unspoiled nature, because he is dealing with believers, for whom everything is sanctified through Christ. Commentary on 1 Corinthians 10:26.[9]

What God Has Created Is Holy and Good. Giovanni Diodati: Seeing that God is the Creator and Lord of all things, these [created] things are holy and good for human beings. Thus men and women should make use of them, acknowledging that they come from God's hands, with faith, invocation, and thanksgiving (1 Tim 4:3-4). The devil has no power to contaminate these [created things] with his idols, unless men and women themselves do it of their own accord through sin, and especially through the sin of idolatry. Annotation on 1 Corinthians 10:26.[10]

[5]Goulart, *Seconde partie des Discours Chrestiens*, 204-8.
[6]Downame, *English Annotations*, EE1r*.
[7]*Sic*, Ps 24:1.
[8]Melanchthon, *Annotationes in Epistolam priorem ad Corinthios*, 116.
[9]CO 49:469 (cf. CTS 39:344).
[10]Diodati, *Pious Annotations*, Mm4.*

Thinking About Your Neighbor's Good. Huldrych Zwingli: Paul does not say this to those so-called knowledgeable and curious people, but to the simple and devout people, when they are invited to the homes (not the temples) of unbelievers. For they were hesitant to go lest they be judged by others as friends of devils and supporters of idolatry. But they were also hesitant to decline lest the person who invited them think they despised them. Therefore Paul says: "If an unbeliever says to you, 'Come and eat,' it is not necessary for you to raise questions on account of your conscience. But if, during the course of the meal, someone says, 'This [food] was sacrificed to idols,' then do not eat it for the sake of conscience—not your conscience, but the conscience of the other person, who could be offended by your action." For if the person is a believer who says to you, 'This is food sacrificed to idols' (distinguishing this food from other kinds), he is warning you, and for that reason you should not eat. If the person is an unbeliever, he is already offended by your eating, for he is thinking or saying: "If it was so evil to worship idols or feast on food sacrificed to idols, then this Christian would never have engaged in such a huge wickedness but would have been adverse to this sacrificial food, etc." Annotations on 1 Corinthians 10:28.[11]

Liberty and Conscience. Wolfgang Musculus: "For why should my liberty be judged by someone else's conscience?" This statement is explained in various ways. First, some take this to be an objection of the Corinthians, who were eating various sorts of sacrifices without concern, and under the pretext of their freedom were rejecting this teaching of the apostle, saying: "Why should my freedom be subject to the judgment of another person's conscience? How is it fair that someone else's conscience should judge what I do with a clean conscience according to my freedom?" . . .

Second, some people think that this statement is in response to what Paul said above [in verse 27]: "Eat whatever is set before you without raising any question on the ground of conscience." To which the person responds, "But, in doing this, the believer will be judged by another, even if he eats with a clean conscience." To which the apostle answers, "Why should my liberty, by which I eat freely and give thanks for whatever is placed before me, be judged by someone else's conscience? What difference does it make if some people reproach me on account of something for which I give thanks?"

Third, some people think this statement is in response to what has come immediately before [in verses 28-29]: "Do not eat it, for the sake of the one who informed you and for the sake of conscience. I do not mean your conscience, but his." For why should it happen that our liberty should obey and answer to the judgment of another person's conscience, and be reproached for eating something for which I give thanks? This interpretation seems most likely to me. For Paul is speaking on his own behalf. Commentary on 1 Corinthians 10:29.[12]

The Other Person's Conscience. Tilemann Hesshus: Paul adds the explanation that he is speaking about the other person's conscience, which ought to be spared. And he adds the necessary instruction that our conscience should not depend on the judgment of other people. "You ought to abstain," he says, "from food sacrificed to idols, not for the sake of your conscience, which is free in the Lord, to whom belongs the whole earth, but for the sake of the other person's conscience, lest due to its weakness it should be scandalized by your example." "Why," he asks, "should my freedom be determined by someone else's conscience?" It's as if Paul were saying: "Our conscience and freedom should not depend on the judgment of another person's conscience, but rather on the Word of God, which displays that we are free in Christ. It is impossible for the judgment of another person's conscience either to wound or heal my conscience. Regardless of what others think of me, it is enough for me to know the blessing of Christ and to have the certainty of his Word. Explication of 1 Corinthians 10:29.[13]

[11]Zwingli, *Annotatiunculae . . . ex ore Zvinglij*, 86-87.

[12]Musculus, *Comm. 1 Cor.*, 365-66.

[13]Hesshus, *Explicatio Prioris Epistolae ad Corinthios*, 161v-162r.

We Must Avoid Intentionally Causing Offense to Others. John Calvin: Paul's argument [in verse 30] is the same as the one he just made, or nearly the same. Since it is God's blessing that all things are lawful for me, why should my behavior be interpreted as a sin on my part? Of course, we cannot prevent wicked people from maligning us, nor even the weak from sometimes being angry at us. But here Paul is rebuking those people who, through their excesses, willingly give grounds for offense and harm weak consciences when it is neither necessary nor expedient. Therefore Paul wishes us to make proper use of our blessings so that, by not indulging in thoughtless license, we might not give the weak opportunity to malign us. Commentary on 1 Corinthians 10:30.[14]

10:31–11:1 *Do Everything for the Glory of God*

Paul Sought to Please Others for Their Edification. Jacques Lefèvre d'Étaples: Here we have a holy command and a holy admonition: whatever we do should be done for the glory of God. It is certain, then, that we must abstain from all evil, for it is impossible to do evil things to the glory of God. And this is what it means to be holy: to conduct oneself without offense before all people, whether Jew or Gentile; all the more, to conduct oneself without offense in the household of faith and the assembly of believers, which is the church of God. Now Paul's desire to please everyone did not come from the carnal desire to please worldly flatterers, but from the desire to edify them and imitate the kindness of God derived from the Spirit. For we are responsible to please other people as long as we can edify and procure their salvation. Commentary on 1 Corinthians 10:31.[15]

Paul's General Principle. Wolfgang Musculus: Paul here places before all believers this general principle, summarizing what has been said before. For it wasn't possible for him to explain all those various circumstances that could be addressed in this regard. That is why Paul places before them, as it were, a general target they should aim for in all situations, saying: "So, whether you eat or drink, or whatever you do, do all to the glory of God." It is as if Paul were saying: "There are a countless number of dilemmas that you face as you live in the midst of unbelievers, both Jews and Greeks, for which there is no single rule. This is why you should resolve in your heart beforehand that in everything that you must do and endure, do it to the glory of God. Thus the Spirit of the Lord will be present with those of you who are inclined to direct all your affairs to the glory of God." Commentary on 1 Corinthians 10:31.[16]

The Central Principle for Christian Living. Tilemann Hesshus: This is the conclusion of Paul's entire discourse concerning the use of freedom, about which he has provided instruction in the course of three chapters. "This is the summary of everything," he says, "that not only in eating and drinking, but in every activity and endeavor of life, you direct all things to the glory of God and the good of your neighbor. Do not pursue your own advantage. Do not cause scandal to any person. But always seek the edification of the church of Jesus Christ, which is undoubtedly the greatest and most useful rule." This is the most certain standard by which the conscience can prove itself in every activity. For there are countless and infinite numbers of situations, and it is impossible for specific advice to be given for each and every situation. Paul therefore hands down this principle for the whole of life and every activity. "Do everything for the glory of God and for the advantage of the church and the neighbor." The Word of God teaches what conforms to the glory of God. The Word of God also teaches the

[14]CO 49:470-71 (cf. CTS 39:346-47).
[15]Lefèvre d'Étaples, *Commentariorum in Epistolas Beati Pauli . . . Liber Secundus*, 116v.
[16]Musculus, *Comm. 1 Cor.*, 367-68.

guiding principle, namely, what is useful for one's neighbor. Therefore it is not difficult for truly pious people to know what they should do, even when misfortune occurs: they should be far removed from all hypocrisy, and pray earnestly to Christ that he guide us by his Spirit. Explication of 1 Corinthians 10:31.[17]

Christ Should Be the Focus of Our Lives. John Trapp: It is said of a reverend divine from Scotland that he even ate, drank, and slept eternal life. In a similar fashion, these common actions should be as steps in our Christian walking. Do not despise them, therefore, but refer them to that supreme focus. . . . "Whatever you do, do it for the sake of God," one person has said. Another has stated: "For your sake, O Lord, for your sake." The glory of God ought to eat up all other ends, just as Moses's serpent ate up the sorcerers' serpents, or as the sun puts out the life of the fire. Emperor Jovinian's motto was this: "Christ is the focus of life." Commentary on 1 Corinthians 10:31.[18]

Offend Neither Jews nor Gentiles. Huldrych Zwingli: Arrange the whole of life so that you cause offense to neither Jews nor Gentiles—and you can do this easily if you are godly. Now, the Jews were especially attached to laws and ceremonies, while the Gentiles tasted of their superstitions and rites. The apostle advises, therefore, that among both groups, [Christians] should behave in such a way as to offend neither. They should not think the Jews doomed in their superstitions, nor should they discourage the Gentiles from the religion of Christ. They should not contend against the Gentiles for their empty wisdom, nor should they offend the godly among the Jews. "I present myself to you as an example," he says. "In all my dealings with everyone, I desire to please and accommodate myself to everyone." But recognize this only pertained to external matters, for in other respects Paul did not desire to please human beings, for if he had, he would not at all have been a servant of Christ. Annotations on 1 Corinthians 10:32-33.[19]

Imitators of Christ and Paul. John Calvin: "Be imitators of me." This shows how badly the chapters have been divided, because this sentence has been disjoined from the previous sentence (to which it should have been connected) and attached to the one that follows (to which it has nothing in common). Let us view this little sentence, then, as part of [chapter 10]. In verse 33, Paul had set forth his own example in confirmation of his teaching. Now he exhorts the Corinthians to imitate what he had done, even as he himself was imitating Christ, so that they might realize their need to agree with him in this. There are two things that must be observed here. First, that Paul prescribes nothing to others that he had not first practiced himself. Second, that Paul calls himself and others back to Christ as the only model of right action. For just as it is the quality of good teachers not to teach anything in word unless they are prepared to carry it out in action, so they should not be so exacting as to demand others to do immediately what they do all the time. This is what superstitious people usually do, for whatever they deem to be lovely, they also impose on other people, and they desire their example to be taken as an absolute rule. Worldly persons are also naturally inclined to follow the wrong sorts of examples, and, like apes, seek to copy whatever they see done by persons of great influence. Further, we see how many evils have been introduced into the church by this absurd eagerness to imitate all the actions of [Catholic] saints, without exception. That is why we must carefully hold on to this teaching of Paul—that we are to follow human beings only to the extent that they consider Christ as their prototype. Commentary on 1 Corinthians 11:1.[20]

[17]Hesshus, *Explicatio Prioris Epistolae ad Corinthios*, 162v.
[18]Trapp, *A Commentary or Exposition*, 685*; citing Ex 7:12.
[19]Zwingli, *Annotatiunculae . . . ex ore Zvinglij*, 88.
[20]CO 49:472 (cf. CTS 39:349-50).

This Verse Belongs to Chapter 11. John Trapp: This verse properly belongs to the previous chapter. The division of the books of Scripture into chapters is not very ancient. But the division of chapter verses was devised by Robert Estienne with good intent (as one person has stated), but with no great skill, as appears here and in various other passages. Commentary on 1 Corinthians 11:1.[21]

[21]Trapp, *A Commentary or Exposition*, 685*.

11:2-16 Head Coverings

2Now I commend you because you remember me in
everything and maintain the traditions even as I
delivered them to you. 3But I want you to understand
that the head of every man is Christ, the head of a
wife[a] is her husband,[b] and the head of Christ is God.
4Every man who prays or prophesies with his head
covered dishonors his head, 5but every wife[c] who prays
or prophesies with her head uncovered dishonors her
head, since it is the same as if her head were shaven.
6For if a wife will not cover her head, then she should
cut her hair short. But since it is disgraceful for a wife
to cut off her hair or shave her head, let her cover her
head. 7For a man ought not to cover his head, since he
is the image and glory of God, but woman is the glory
of man. 8For man was not made from woman, but
woman from man. 9Neither was man created for
woman, but woman for man. 10That is why a wife
ought to have a symbol of authority on her head,
because of the angels.[d] 11Nevertheless, in the Lord
woman is not independent of man nor man of
woman; 12for as woman was made from man, so man
is now born of woman. And all things are from God.
13Judge for yourselves: is it proper for a wife to pray to
God with her head uncovered? 14Does not nature itself
teach you that if a man wears long hair it is a disgrace
for him, 15but if a woman has long hair, it is her glory?
For her hair is given to her for a covering. 16If anyone
is inclined to be contentious, we have no such practice,
nor do the churches of God.

a Greek *gunē*. This term may refer to a woman or a wife, depending on the context **b** Greek *anēr*. This term may refer to a man or a husband, depending on the context **c** In verses 5-13, the Greek word *gunē* is translated *wife* in verses that deal with wearing a veil, a sign of being married in first-century culture **d** Or *messengers*, that is, people sent to observe and report

Overview: In the first half of 1 Corinthians 11, Paul addresses the subject of right order and decorum in public worship, rebuking the Corinthians for allowing women to prophesy and pray in church without head coverings. Reformation commentators believe that Paul's conception of spiritual headship—that husbands are the head of their wives, even as Christ is the head of the church—should serve as the guiding principle for public worship as well as gender relations in both the public sphere and household. Owing to the fact that Adam was created before Eve, and that the first woman was created from the first man, they maintain God has endowed men with special authority to teach and govern within church, society, and family. Men worship without head coverings in the Christian church to display the spiritual freedom and authority they possess *under Christ*. By contrast, the commentators assert that women are inferior to men in the created order and thus are required to respect their husbands and submit to their authority—a submission symbolized by women covering their heads in public worship. In what sense, then, do both men and women reflect the image of God? Reformation interpreters debate this question at length, drawing extensively from the opinions of early Christian authors such as Augustine. For those commentators who define the *imago Dei* primarily as dominion, women reflect the divine image in their authority over other creatures, but do not reflect the divine image in their relationships with men. Many commentators, however, believe that the *imago Dei* includes not only dominion but also spiritual or rational capacity, endowments that women share equally with men. Consequently, even though early modern interpreters affirm the superiority of men in the order of creation, they usually affirm the fact that men and women are joint heirs of grace, partakers together of eternal life, and daily partners in managing their households and raising children. Men and women need one another, and are called to lives characterized by mutual goodwill and sacrificial service.[1]

Correcting Their Abuses. John Calvin: In the eleventh chapter, Paul cleanses the public assemblies from certain corrupt practices that were not at all consistent with Christian decency and propriety, and reminds them of what great dignity and self-control should be exercised when we stand in the sight of God and angels. Now, he especially rebukes them for their corrupt administration of the Supper. And he adds the way for correcting the abuse that had crept into [the church], which is by calling them back to the Lord's first institution as the only sure rule and permanent law of right action. Introduction to Commentary on 1 Corinthians.[2]

Both Teaching and Rebukes. Tilemann Hesshus: As with the whole letter, so also this chapter contains both teaching and rebukes. Now there are two primary parts to this chapter. In part one, Paul praises the Corinthians for imitating and preserving the teaching and ceremonies that he had commended to them, and he urges them zealously to continue in it. But he reproaches them for sinning in outward discipline, because they allow women to pray with uncovered heads in the assembly of the faithful, while men pray with covered heads. Thus he instructs them as to what accords with decency, and what nature itself teaches. The second part of the chapter is a discourse on the Lord's Supper and its administration. Here, first of all, he rebukes an abuse in the Corinthian church whereby they receive the Eucharist in a disorderly fashion, without fearing God and drinking too much. Second, Paul passes on instruction regarding the Lord's Supper, and urges everyone to examine themselves before coming to the sacred Supper so that they do not eat the body of the Lord to their judgment. He also informs them that many people in the church, on account of this [false] security, are being punished with death. And finally, he urges the church to earnest repentance. Explication of 1 Corinthians 11.[3]

11:2-6 *Christian Headship*

Paul Begins with Praise. The English Annotations: As Paul is about to reprehend certain disorders in the church of Corinth, he begins notwithstanding with a general praise of them, which is the method the Spirit uses in the epistles to the seven churches of Asia (Rev 2:2, 9, 13, 19; 3:1, 8, 15). Similarly, Lactantius prescribes it as a rule for all discreet pastors, that they should follow the example of the ancient physicians who anointed the brim of the cup with honey when they were administering a bitter potion to the patient. Annotations on 1 Corinthians 11:2.[4]

Paul Is Not Defending Catholic Traditions. Wolfgang Musculus: [The Catholics] quote these words of Paul to confirm the authority of their traditions and ecclesiastical ceremonies, which we reject today as contrary to the Word of God. Behold, they say, it is good for believers to observe not only what is written but also those oral traditions that have been handed down from the apostles. First, they must prove that all those ceremonies that we reject were handed down from the apostles—which cannot be done. Second, they must prove that those ceremonies are not contrary to the Word of God. Third, they must prove that those ceremonies have been preserved to the present day as they were originally handed down from the apostles. Unless they prove these things, how can they defend from these words of the apostle so many and such manifest abuses? Commentary on 1 Corinthians 11:2.[5]

[1]For a more detailed discussion of the ways that Reformation-era exegetes treated 1 Cor 11:2-16, see John L. Thompson, *Reading the Bible with the Dead* (Grand Rapids: Eerdmans, 2007), 113-35.
[2]CO 49:302 (cf. CTS 39:44).
[3]Hesshus, *Explicatio Prioris Epistolae ad Corinthios*, 164r.
[4]Downame, *English Annotations*, EE1r*. Lucius Caecilius Firmianus Lactantius (c. 250–c. 325) was an early Christian author and an advisor to Emperor Constantine.
[5]Musculus, *Comm. 1 Cor.*, 375.

Method for Judging Human Traditions. Tilemann Hesshus: Because Paul says that the Corinthians are to "maintain the traditions" and established practices, the popes transform this into a fiction, by which they establish that there are two parts to the Word of God, namely, written teaching and unwritten tradition. And then they assert that we are required to obey with no less devotion the unwritten traditions as well the teaching expressed in the writings of the prophets and the apostles. If we should concede this to them, then they are, of course, very free and reckless in defining the apostolic traditions. For among the papists, there is no idolatry so foul, no ceremony so worthless and absurd, no abuse of the sacraments so revolting, no dogma so blasphemous, and (finally) no worship so impious that is not hidden under this subterfuge. To be sure, there is an apostolic tradition, although it can be established on the testimony of no human being. It must be understood, therefore, that by this statement [in verse 2], Paul does not in any way desire that the uncertain traditions of the ancients should be made equal to the Word of God. Rather, he warns elsewhere that we should beware of human traditions. Colossians 2 says, "Do not impose such things on yourself according to human traditions." But [the apostle] is speaking here about the traditions the Corinthians received either personally or by letter from Paul himself.

First of all, therefore, when people speak about traditions, it must be determined whether they are explicitly contained in the writings of the apostles; and even if you perceive this to be the case, the apostolic tradition must agree with these writings without any ambiguity. For the command of the Lord, which all human beings are required to obey, is immoveable. Thus [we read], "Listen!" Again, "Those who listen to you, listen to me."

Second, if the tradition is not stated in the apostolic writings, it must be determined whether it fights against the Word of God. . . . For it is wrong to think that the apostles have established a ceremony when it explicitly fights against the Word of God. Therefore, on this subject, the testimony of the church fathers should be brought forward for the good of all, that when a tradition disagrees with the writings of the prophets or apostles, it must be rejected and abolished without any hesitation. For the Holy Scripture is the most sure and certain norm for the whole of religion, for all articles of faith, for all controversies regarding ceremonies and worship. Cyprian once stated with piety and seriousness: "Whatever is established by human inspiration that violates a divine decree is adulterous, ungodly, and sacrilegious."[6]

Third, if any tradition is preached under the title of "apostolic authority," but is not expressly contained in the apostolic writings—even if it does not fight against the express Word of God—then we can establish with certainty that it must not be numbered among the articles of faith, nor even necessary for salvation. For all articles of faith, and whatever is acknowledged as necessary for salvation, have been clearly and fully set forth in the sacred writings of the Old and New Testaments. Therefore a tradition that is not contained in the apostolic writings, and does not fight against them, must be numbered among the neutral or indifferent things (*adiaphora*). Explication of 1 Corinthians 11:2.[7]

The Importance of Decorum in Public Worship. John Calvin: Paul now passes on to a different subject—namely, to instruct the Corinthians as to what decorum ought to be maintained in sacred assemblies. For, as people's clothing or attitude sometimes spoil, sometimes enhances their appearance, so decorum adorns all their actions, while indecency ruins it. Therefore a great deal depends on propriety, not only to unite grace and attractiveness to our actions but also to accustom our minds to what is honorable. While this is true generally in all things, it is particularly important in sacred matters. For if we do not maintain dignity in the church by conducting ourselves in a decent and honorable fashion, what scorn and (finally)

[6]Cyprian, *Epistle* 39.5 (ANF 5:318).
[7]Hesshus, *Explicatio prioris epistolae ad Corinthios*, 165r-166r; citing Col 2:22.

what great barbarism will be produced! Paul therefore prescribes some things related to public order, by which sacred assemblies are adorned. Commentary on 1 Corinthians 11:2.[8]

Head Coverings in Public Worship. Desiderius Erasmus: First of all, I praise you highly brothers and sisters because, in other matters, you remember me in everything and hold to that which I commanded and which I directed you to follow in your solemn assembly. . . . But, nevertheless, I do not want it to escape your notice that just as Christ is the head of every man, and the husband is the head of every wife, so God is the head of Christ. Although the man is master over his wife, nevertheless, he recognizes Christ as his master, and Christ himself recognizes the authority of the Father in all matters. It is proper that everyone who is subject to the Father should be devoted to his glory. You should behave in private in a way that appears profitable to each of you. But any man who prays or prophesies in a public assembly with his head covered dishonors his head as if he were a servant, since he should recognize no lord besides Christ. His uncovered head—that is, not only his cap removed but also his hair cut—[shows] that he is an equal with respect to the glory of Christ. . . . By contrast, if a woman prays or prophesies in the solemn assembly with her head uncovered, she shames her head, because it ought to be uncovered in private for the sake of her husband—not in a public assembly, where Christ is served, not her husband. Paraphrase on 1 Corinthians 11.[9]

Immodest Behavior Was a Problem in Corinth. Wolfgang Musculus: It is clear from the nature of the apostle's argument and reproof (which he treats for almost half of this chapter) that women in the church assembly had begun to pray and prophesy with heads uncovered, contrary to modesty befitting women, and men, contrary to proper order, had begun to pray and prophesy with their heads covered. It is known from various histories that among the Greeks—and especially among the Corinthians—men were effeminate and women immodest. And since this was considered the common custom among everyone in the country, no one considered anything wrong with either practice. That is why, when the Corinthians came to follow Christ, they initially did not understand how immodest the customary practices of their country were. And so they were behaving in the assembly of believers in the same way that they had previously behaved in the temples and worship services of their pagan gods. In order to correct them, Paul instructs them by means of this letter that the propriety and appropriate discretion of both men and women should be maintained in the church, such that the man should prophesy with his head uncovered, and the woman with her head covered or veiled. And Paul gives them this instruction, not simply as a bald command, but with accompanying reasons . . . as we will see in what follows. Commentary on 1 Corinthians 11:3.[10]

Reasons Why Women Must Cover Their Heads. John Colet: Now Paul is teaching the Corinthians a point of decorum and what is becoming in the style of dress of both sexes in the church. His teaching is that in a society composed of men and women, the latter should have their heads covered, the former uncovered, when praying or prophesying.

Attempting to give a reason why women should have their heads covered in church, he says that woman is from man, and is for the sake of man, and is the glory of man, and that her hair adorns her. He says that women are naturally inclined to take care of their hair, and that human customs ought to imitate nature, the best of teachers. Women should show diligence to cover what nature wishes to be covered.

Although he is making another point, and circles around it ambiguously with his words as though pretending not to see what he sees, Paul still seems by this careful reasoning to wish to extinguish or suppress something he very clearly saw in the Corinthian women, that is, their pride

[8]CO 49:472-73 (cf. CTS 39:350-51).
[9]Erasmus, *Paraphrases*, 301-2.
[10]Musculus, *Comm. 1 Cor.*, 376.

in their beautiful heads of hair. So he urges them to cover their heads up so as not to display their tresses, which easily lead women to false pride, and which easily captivate young men as though by seduction. Exposition of 1 Corinthians 11.[11]

Women Should Cover Their Heads. Martin Luther: One should govern wives not with great cudgels, flails, or drawn knives, but rather with friendly words, friendly gestures, and with all gentleness so that they do not become frightened and scared—as St. Peter says in 1 Peter 3—such that they no longer know what they should do. And so one must govern wives with reason and not with unreason, and give honor to the female sex as the weakest vessel, as well as coheirs of the grace of life, so that our prayers would not be hindered. And that's what St. Paul says in Ephesians 5: "You husbands, love your wives, as Jesus Christ loved his congregation" or church. . . .

"Wives should be subject to their husbands as to the Lord, for the husband is the wife's head"—also in Colossians 3. Because of this, the wife was not created from the head, so that she should govern over her husband, but rather should be subject and obedient to him. And so the wife wears a symbol of authority, that is, the veil on her head, as St. Paul writes in 1 Corinthians 11, that she is not free but rather is under obedience to her husband.

The wife veils herself with a fine, soft veil, spun and made from pretty, soft flax or linen, and she does not wrap a coarse bunch of woven fabric or a filthy cloth around her head or mouth. But why? For this reason: that she should speak fine, lovely, friendly words to her husband and not coarse, filthy, insulting words, as wicked wives do who carry a sword in their mouths and accordingly are struck on the mouth.[12] A Sermon on Marriage (1525).[13]

[11]Colet, *Enarratio*, 220-22.

[12]*Die bösen Weiber . . . das schwerdt im maul füren unnd werden darnach auff die scheiden geklopfft.* This proverb draws a parallel between sheath and mouth; to make that clear *auff die scheiden* has been rendered "on the mouth" rather than the more literal "on the sheath."

[13]WA 17,1:24, 26-27; citing 1 Pet 3:6-7; Eph 5:25, 22-23; Col 3:18 (cf. Karant-Nunn and Wiesner-Hanks, *Luther on Women*, 95).

Paul's First Explanation for Head Coverings. Tilemann Hesshus: Because the city of Corinth was wealthy and full of licentiousness, it is likely that the Corinthian women behaved very freely in the public assembly of the saints and some of them prayed bare-headed in the public meeting. The apostle reproves and corrects this wicked practice, and teaches that women ought to pray with their heads veiled, while men ought to pray with their heads uncovered. And he adds explanations for this command of his.

The first is because Christ is the head of the man, but the man is the head of the woman. Therefore, by means of his uncovered head, the man ought to profess his liberty and the dominion he possesses in Christ; while the woman ought to profess by means of her covered head that she is under her husband. To be sure, Christ is the head of the entire church—both of holy women as well as reborn men—and he gives life and the Spirit to all of its members. For in Christ, there is neither male nor female. The male does not have prerogative over the woman, but is saved [through her offspring]. But in this present passage Paul is speaking about the specific order that God has established whereby men should be responsible for the ministry of teaching and should hold public office and exercise authority in their marriages. He says that God is the head of Christ. Now, in the flesh, Christ receives from the eternal Father the rule and office of high priest, and so Christ attributes everything to the glory of the eternal Father. "The teaching that you hear," he says, "is not my own, but belongs to the one who sent me." "Christ is the head of man," that is, Christ has entrusted ministry to the man; he has established him as the leader in his family and has adorned him with glory, so that he represents the Lord Christ in his ministry and government. Thus he ought to ascribe everything to the glory of Christ, and his uncovered head attests to the fact that he is free in Christ. "The man is the head of the woman"; that is, the woman is drawn from the man and has glory and honor from her husband; for the wife shines from the beams of her husband. Thus by her veiled head she ought to profess that she is under her husband's authority and that she owes her husband modesty and reverence. Explication of 1 Corinthians 11:3-5.[14]

Defining "Prophesying" and "Praying." John Calvin: Now I take "prophesying" to mean here to declare the mysteries of God for the edification of the hearers (as we explain later in chapter 14). Likewise, "praying" means to prepare the form of a prayer, and taking the lead, so to speak, for all the people, which is the role of a public teacher. For Paul is not discussing prayers of every sort, but only solemn prayers in public. Commentary on 1 Corinthians 11:4.[15]

The Divinely Established Order in Christ's Body. David Dickson: To the previous admonition, Paul subjoins a maxim concerning the divinely established order in the mystical body of Christ, namely, that Christ is the nearest subordinate to God, as he is the God-man, the Mediator and head of the church, and that the man next succeeds in dignity unto Christ, and the woman to the man, who as far as it relates to the honor of her sex is made subordinate to the man as head. From this, the Corinthians will understand that order in church assemblies is to be observed.

It is apparent that the Corinthians did not sufficiently observe this order, because their women in the public assemblies (following the example of heathens) laid aside their veils, and the men covered their heads and faces.... This uncomeliness Paul reproves both in men and women in the arguments that follow. Exposition of 1 Corinthians 11:3-4.[16]

Exceptions When Men May Cover Their Heads in Worship. Huldrych Zwingli: This passage refers to either those teaching or listening to the Word of God. Paul wants men to uncover their heads in the public assembly. Let us discern whether they should follow this from general principal, or for a specific purpose. To be sure, Paul is not laying down everlasting and unchanging laws; instead he is giving instructions as to what is customary and honorable. Therefore this custom does not mandate that men must keep their heads completely bare during wintertime and frost, especially in cold regions or when the cold hurts the head. Naturally, people are free from certain external practices, but in such a way that the public custom is upheld. That which maintains public decency and is customary should not be defiantly disregarded. Commentary on 1 Corinthians 11:4.[17]

Different Countries Have Different Customs. John Trapp: "Dishonors his head"—as they understood it then and there. In other places it is otherwise. The French preach with their heads covered. The Turks neither kneel nor uncover their heads during public prayers, viewing these postures as unmanly. Various countries have various customs. Basiliades, the Duke of Muscovia, showed himself a tyrant when he nailed an ambassador's hat to his head for not uncovering it before him. Commentary on 1 Corinthians 11:4.[18]

Standards of Propriety Different for Men and Women. Wolfgang Musculus: There is no difference between man and woman as pertains to the grace of the kingdom of Christ by which we are saved by his blood. In this the man has no advantage, nor the woman disadvantage. But in matters of external government, not only in the world but also in the church, there is a great difference between the male and female sexes, so that what is permitted the man is not permitted to the woman, and what is proper for the woman is not appropriate for the man. Each sex has its own standard of propriety; in the world, this

[14]Hesshus, *Explicatio Prioris Epistolae ad Corinthios*, 166v-167r; citing Gal 3:28; Jn 7:16.
[15]CO 49:475 (cf. CTS 39:355).
[16]Dickson, *Exposition of St. Paul's Epistles*, 58*.
[17]Zwingli, *Annotatiunculae . . . ex ore Zvinglij*, 89.
[18]Trapp, *A Commentary or Exposition*, 685*. The nailing of ambassadors' hats to their heads is a habit attributed to Russian Tsar Ivan IV (1530–1584).

propriety is based on what agrees with public decency while in the church this propriety is based more on what agrees with divinely given wisdom and grace. . . .

Some people inquire here why Paul says that a woman dishonors her head if she prophesies with her head uncovered, when a little later, in chapter 14, he advises them to remain silent in church because it is shameful for a woman to speak in church. And in 1 Timothy 2, he says: "I do not permit a woman to teach others." What need is there, these people ask, to specify that a woman should not prophesy with her head uncovered, when it is not permissible for her to do it even with her head covered? I respond as follows: Paul is restraining female rashness, for women are frequently very talkative and, forgetting their place as women, burst forth with teaching and prophesying when it is absolutely forbidden them to speak in church. Nevertheless, Paul did not quench the spirit whereby some women, inspired to predict the future, were prophesying. Such women included the daughters of Philip the deacon, and many other women, who were prophesying according to the prophecy of Joel 2, where it is read: "After that time, I will pour out my spirit on all flesh, and your sons and daughters will prophesy." For this reason, Paul states that women dishonor their heads when they speak or prophesy with their heads uncovered . . . and when they rush to assume the teaching role, even with their heads covered. Commentary on 1 Corinthians 11:4-5.[19]

Women and Prophecy. Peter Martyr Vermigli: It is necessary for the woman to acknowledge her position, that is, that she is in subjection to the man. But what was the issue that concerned the apostle? For why is the woman here said to prophesy or pray when Paul gave instructions to Timothy and also states at the end of this letter that no means or opportunity should be given to women to speak in church, inasmuch as she should remain silent? We answer that, in this passage, Paul is only seeking to correct that particular vice whereby women were in public with their heads uncovered. But later in this letter, and also in his letter to Timothy, Paul will instruct them even to remain silent, for everything cannot be said all at once, given that the Corinthian women were struggling with a double vice, for they were strutting about bare-headed as well as speaking in public. Paul condemns one of the vices in this present passage, and addressed the other vice later on. Some people say that these things should be allowed to women since they can both pray and prophesy in private (which are not prohibited to them). It is also possible for us to explain this command of the apostle in another way: that it was established that women, under normal circumstances, should remain silent when a public function in the church was not entrusted to them—which was the ordinary and general pattern. Nevertheless, since occasionally the Spirit of the Lord has come upon them, it was not completely forbidden them to say something. We know that the prophetess Anna spoke in the temple concerning the Savior, at the purification of the blessed Virgin. Likewise, Deborah and Miriam, the sister of Moses, sang praises to God in public. And also, many passages testify that women in former times prophesied. The prophetess Huldah was consulted by King Josiah. Hannah, the mother of Samuel, brought forth a most beautiful song. Similarly, the Virgin Mary, the mother of Christ, sang a song. Philip, in the Acts of the Apostles, had several daughters who were prophesying. And the Lord instructed Mary Magdalene to announce his resurrection to the apostles. And one reads in the book of Joel: "I will pour out my Spirit on you, and your sons and daughters will prophesy."

There are some people who study this passage who think that the command for men to have uncovered heads and women to have covered heads pertains not only to those who publicly prophesy or pray but also to those who hear [words of prophecy and prayer]. But it does not seem that Paul's words agree with their opinion, since he is

[19]Musculus, *Comm. 1 Cor.*, 382, 384; citing 1 Cor 14:34; 1 Tim 2:12; Acts 21:9; Joel 2:28.

clearly speaking about women praying or prophesying. Commentary on 1 Corinthians 11:5.[20]

Paul's Second Explanation for Head Coverings. Tilemann Hesshus: The second reason that Paul adduces is from common understanding and the light of nature. Natural reason reminds us that it is disgraceful if a woman's hair is shaved or sheared, because, by nature, hair adorns women. And it is disgusting when a woman is seen with a shaved or sheared head. . . . Therefore nature itself teaches us what is proper and honorable. Thus, when a woman prays in a public assembly, she should cover her head and acknowledge with modesty that she is under the authority of her husband. Explication of 1 Corinthians 11:6.[21]

11:7-10 *The Image and Glory of God*[22]

Man Is an Intermediary Between God and Woman. Jacques Lefèvre d'Étaples: Man was created directly in the image and likeness of God and for his glory, but woman was created indirectly through the man. For man is a mediator, a kind of intermediary and veil, placed between a woman and God. This mystery is denoted when the man addresses God—especially when praying or prophesying—since he does it with a bare head, having no covering between himself and God. This he must do to give the honor of his creation to God, as is only right. But the woman, by covering her head, acknowledges her creation and so gives honor to God, as is proper. Commentary on 1 Corinthians 11:7.[23]

Men Are Like the Sun, Women Are Like the Moon. Martin Luther: In order not to give the impression that he was excluding the woman from all the glory of the future life, Moses [in Genesis 1] includes each of the two sexes; for the woman appears to be a somewhat different being from the man, having different members and a much weaker nature. Although Eve was a most extraordinary creature—similar to Adam so far as the image of God is concerned, that is, in justice, wisdom, and happiness—she was nevertheless a woman. For as the sun is more excellent than the moon (although the moon, too, is a very excellent body), so that woman, although she was a most beautiful work of God, nevertheless was not the equal of the male in glory and prestige.

However, here [in Genesis 1] Moses puts the two sexes together and says that God created male and female in order to indicate that Eve, too, was made by God as a partaker of the divine image and of the divine similitude, likewise of the rule over everything. Thus even today the woman is the partaker of the future life, just as Peter says that they are joint heirs of the same grace (1 Pet 3:7). In the household the wife is a partner in the management and has a common interest in the children and the property, and yet there is a great difference between the sexes. The male is like the sun in heaven, the female like the moon, the animals like the stars, over which sun and moon have dominion. In the first place, therefore, let us note from this passage that it was written that this sex may not be excluded from any glory of the human creature, although it is inferior to the male sex. Lecture on Genesis 1:27.[24]

Image of God Is Seen in the New Person. Philipp Melanchthon: There is a many-sided and varied controversy about the word *image*. Augustine felt humanity was the image of God because in the soul there is memory, intelligence, and will, which three represent the divine persons of the Father, Son, and Holy Spirit. This observation not only lacks the authority of Scripture but also has been invented without a basis. Here the

[20]Vermigli, *In Selectissimam Priorem ad Corinthios Epistolam . . . Commentarii*, 285r-v; citing 1 Cor 14:34; 1 Tim 2:11-12; Lk 2:36-38; Judg 5:1-31; Ex 5:20-21; 2 Chron 34:22;1 Sam 2:1-10; Lk 1:46-55; Acts 21:9; Jn 20:17-18; Joel 2:28.

[21]Hesshus, *Explicatio Prioris Epistolae ad Corinthios*, 167r.

[22]For a helpful interpretation of this pericope, see Thompson, *Reading the Bible with the Dead*, 126-35.

[23]Lefèvre d'Étaples, *Commentariorum in Epistolas Beati Pauli . . . Liber Secundus*, 117r.

[24]LW 1:68-69.

apostle calls humanity the image of God because just as God has dominion over the universe of things, so also inferior creatures are subject to humans, as seen in Genesis 1. Further, my view is that humans were made in the image and likeness of God in that they were to have a spirit and were to will and understand spiritual things. This is how the apostle uses the word for image in Colossians 3 . . . and more clearly in Ephesians 4, "Be renewed in the spirit of your minds, and put on the new person, who is created after the likeness of God in righteousness and the holiness of truth." Therefore the image of God is the new person who understands and wills things spiritual; wisdom, truth, and justice are the images by which God and humans come together in that the wisdom and justice in humans are nothing other than the overflow of the divine light poured out on us. Annotations on 1 Corinthians 11:7.[25]

Both Men and Women Created in Image of God. Huldrych Zwingli: "Man is the image and glory of God." Not because woman does *not* reflect the image of God; rather, Paul reveals the rank and precedence of the earliest creation and creature. For Adam was formed as a human being in the image and likeness of God first, and then the woman was formed from man. She also was formed in the image of God, but through the man. "Woman is the glory of man." When she enters the assembly and conducts herself honorably, the woman is the glory of her husband. For it is clear that the husband has her under his authority, and that she respects her husband. Thus she is the glory of her husband. But if she doesn't act honorably, then she brings shame on her husband. Commentary on 1 Corinthians 11:7.[26]

Paul's Meaning of "Image" Here. John Calvin: The same question can now be raised concerning "image" that was previously raised concerning "head." For both sexes were created in the image of God, and Paul exhorts women no less than men to be reformed according to that image. However, the "image" that he is now speaking about refers to the order of marriage, and hence it pertains to this present life, but has nothing to do with conscience. This is the simple solution: Paul here is not treating innocence and holiness, which are equally applicable to women and men. Rather, he is treating the preeminence that God has conferred on the man, so that he might be superior to the woman. The glory of God is evident in [man's] higher standing, as it is reflected in every superior authority. Commentary on 1 Corinthians 11:7.[27]

Women Don't Possess God's Image in the Same Way That Men Do. Peter Martyr Vermigli: How man is made in the image of God is explained in the beginning of Genesis, where it is written that God said: "Let us make man in our image and likeness, so that he might rule the birds of the heaven, the fish of the sea, and the beasts of the earth." Whereby in this passage the image of God is evident when man rules over all creatures, even as God governs everything. . . . Nevertheless the full expression of the image of God was not bestowed, for it is not enough to rule and guide created things well by means of memory, mind, and will, unless we understand and remember and desire what is pleasing to God. For though our soul remains, because it has been corrupted by sin, it will not govern created things properly, but rather practice tyranny against them. That is why the image of God refers to the new man, who understands divine truth, and whose desire is his righteousness, as Paul teaches us when he writes to the Colossians: "Put on the new man, which is being renewed in the knowledge of God, according to the image of its creator." From this we see that the true and efficacious knowledge of God is conducive to the perfection of the image. . . . When our soul both possesses the knowledge of God and is endowed with righteousness, then it

[25]Melanchthon, *Annotationes in Epistolam priorem ad Corinthios*, 118. See Augustine's statement in *De Trinitate*, PL 42:984-1044 (NPNF 3:143); Gen 1:26-27; Col 3:9-10; Eph 4:23-24.
[26]Zwingli, *Annotatiunculae . . . ex ore Zvinglij*, 90.

[27]CO 49:476 (cf. CTS 39:357).

truly reflects God, since righteousness and knowledge of divine things are nothing other than a certain outpouring of the divine nature into our soul. You will, perhaps, insist from this scriptural promise [in Gen 1:27] that the woman is also the image of God. Our response is this: if you compare her to other creatures, then she is the image of God, for she rules over them and has use of them. But here it is necessary to compare her to the man, and then she is said *not* to be the image of God, because she does not rule over the man, but rather is subject to him. Consequently, Augustine said in book three of *On the Trinity*: "If man and woman are treated with respect to their endowment of mind and reason, it is fitting to say that both are the image of God. But when the woman is contrasted to the man as far as activities and the affairs of this life, she is not the image of God, for she was created to be a helper for man." Commentary on 1 Corinthians 11:7.[28]

God's Image Shines More Obscurely in Women. The English Annotations: Here man is said to be the image and glory of God in regard to the rule that God gave him over the creatures. This image shines most brightly in man, who is immediately the image of God, but more obscurely in woman, who is the image of the man. If it be objected that the woman as well as the man were created according to God's image (Gen 1:27) and consequently that she as well as he is the image and glory of God, it may be answered that a woman may be considered either according to her special nature that she shares with man, and in that regard she was created according to the image of God in holiness and righteousness, or according to her sex as she was Adam's wife, and subject to him. In this latter sense, she does not bear the image of God, for subjection is not the image of God, but rather rule. Annotations on 1 Corinthians 11:7.[29]

Woman Is the Glory of Man. John Calvin: There is no doubt that the woman is an exceptional adornment of the man, for it is a great honor that God has appointed her as man's life partner and helper, and has made her subject to him as the body is subject to the head. For that which Solomon affirms regarding a diligent wife—that she is the "crown of her husband" (Prov 12:4)—is true of the whole sex, if we consider the ordering of God. This is what Paul commends here as he shows for what purpose the woman was created: to be an exceptional adornment of the man. Commentary on 1 Corinthians 11:7.[30]

Women Reflect the Glory of God in Their Spiritual States. David Dickson: The woman is the glory of the man or the image of his dignity; in her the excellence of man (for whose sake she was created) is reflected as in a mirror. She ought to profess her subjection to the man by covering herself. "Therefore," Paul says, "seeing that women behave otherwise among you Corinthians, they are guilty of uncomeliness." This in no way detracts from the fact that women are created, with respect to their souls and spiritual states, in the glory and image of God, just as men are. Exposition of 1 Corinthians 11:7.[31]

Men Are Like Kings of Their Households. Tilemann Hesshus: God has so ordained it that although both sexes have been created in the image and glory of God, nevertheless the man possesses authority within the family; he is like a king of his household, who acts as the deputy of God and Christ in his family. It is proper for the man, therefore, as the lord of his family, to display Christ's authority with his bare head. For he is the image and glory of God; that is, in his service and duty and authority over his family, he represents Christ and is the adornment of God, who created him and established him as lord. Paul is not speaking here about the spiritual image . . .

[28]Vermigli, *In Selectissimam Priorem ad Corinthios Epistolam . . . Commentarii*, 286r-v; citing Gen 1:26; Col 3:10.

[29]Downame, *English Annotations*, EE1v*.

[30]CO 49:476 (cf. CTS 39:357).

[31]Dickson, *Exposition of St. Paul's Epistles*, 58*.

but about order of the sexes, the glory of ministry, and ecclesiastical government. Explication of 1 Corinthians 11:7.[32]

Instructions to Women. David Joris: Make captive your understanding, you women, under the obedience of the Christian husband (Eph 5:22-24). Assent to his wise speech, which has been spoken from the fear of the Spirit. . . . Do not look after the husband to see that he fears the Lord; but let him look after you, for he was made first, then the woman (1 Cor 11:8; 1 Tim 2:13). He is also her head, but Christ is before and above all of these. Therefore he has the preeminence in all things. He precedes us in a legal and human fashion. Behind him follows the man, then the woman must follow the man. But she must attend to the children, so that they will learn correctly and properly from her and be maintained and taught to virtue in the fear of the Lord. But Christ attends to the man and the man to the woman, who is his concern. Pay attention and know what I say to you. Wonderful Working of God.[33]

Woman Was Made from Man. John Trapp: Woman was made from [Adam's] bone, but of one bone. . . . It was a bone from his side, not his head (she is not to be his mistress); nor his foot (she is not to be his handmaid); but his side, to show that she is a companion to her husband. It was a bone from under the arm, to remind the man to protect and defend the woman. It was a bone not far from his heart, to remind the man to love and cherish the woman. It was a bone from his left side, to remind the man that, due to her frailty and infirmity, the woman stands in need of both the one and the other from her husband. Commentary on 1 Corinthians 11:8.[34]

Reasons for Man's Excellence. Tilemann Hesshus: Many pagan writers, especially Euripides, attack [the female] sex with great insults. But they are insulting God (the author of women) and they are ungrateful to their relatives, who gave them birth. Now in the sacred Scripture, the Spirit customarily adorns God's more sacred works with various words of praise. Hence, the apostle demonstrates man's excellence with two arguments. The first is because woman was taken from man. Scripture says, "God took a rib from Adam's side, and he made the woman. And Adam said, 'this is now bone from my bones and flesh from my flesh,' for that reason she will be called a woman" (Gen 2). The second argument is because woman was created for the sake of man, not man for the sake of woman. For when God could not find a helper to be with Adam, he said: "It is not good for man to be alone, I will make a helper to be with him." Therefore man is the first in order and superior in excellence. Thus the woman ought to demonstrate by covering her head that she is under the authority of the man. The apostle next adds a third reason why women ought to cover their head with a head covering or veil in a public assembly, namely, "because of the angels." For the angels—since they are constant guardians of the godly, and especially delight in public gatherings where the Word of God is preached and God is worshiped with faithful prayer and words of thanksgiving—take great offense at the lascivious and disgusting customs of women, which nature itself abhors. Explication of 1 Corinthians 11:8-10.[35]

An Exception to the Rule. John Trapp: [Woman was created for man], unless it be some special women called and qualified to govern. Among whom Queen Elizabeth is famous for her female glory. A great French duchess said that Elizabeth was "the most glorious and happiest of all women who had ever held the scepter." Besides her sex, there was nothing in her woman-like or weak. Commentary on 1 Corinthians 11:9.[36]

[32]Hesshus, *Explicatio Prioris Epistolae ad Corinthios*, 167v.
[33]CRR 8:116.
[34]Trapp, *A Commentary or Exposition*, 686*.
[35]Hesshus, *Explicatio Prioris Epistolae ad Corinthios*, 168r; citing Gen 2:22-23, 18. Euripides (c. 480–406 BC) was one of the most influential tragedians of classical Athens.
[36]Trapp, *A Commentary or Exposition*, 686.* Queen Elizabeth, known as the Virgin Queen, ruled England from 1558 to 1603.

Mary Is Unique Among Women. Jacques Lefèvre d'Étaples: Now man and angels were created directly by God, and so, as a symbol of this reality, man should have no covering when he is turned toward God—just as with the angels. But the woman should have a covering, not only on account of her husband, but also on account of the angels. For she is guilty of pride if she considers her creation as equal to that of the angels, since she possesses this position through the mediation of the man. . . . But one should recognize how precious it is that just as the first Eve came from the first Adam and for the sake of the first Adam physically—which are types and figures—so the second Eve (who is the Virgin blessed among women) came from the second Adam and for the sake of the second Adam spiritually (who is the most blessed Christ Jesus)—which are archetypes and realities. And just as the first Adam is the head and source of all physical humanity (men as well as women), and so is called the father of all, so Christ is the father and head of all spiritual humanity. And just as Eve is the mother of all flesh and above all physical humanity (men as well as women), with the exception of Adam, so that most blessed Virgin is above all spiritual humanity (men as well as women), with the exception of Christ. For it was from Christ and for the sake of Christ that [the Virgin] alone was created—she is the mother of all spiritual humanity. Hence, it happens that the covering of Eve has been removed in the case of Mary, for no intermediary stands between Mary and the Lord Christ, from whom and on account of whom she exists. Commentary on 1 Corinthians 11:10.[37]

Because of the Angels. Wolfgang Musculus: This is the sense: Even if it were not shameful by custom for women to appear in public with their heads uncovered, and even if sexual propriety were not at issue, nevertheless it is shameful "because of the angels," whom Paul considers as spectators within the church. There is not general agreement with what Paul means by "angels" here, because this word *angelos* is interpreted in various ways. The word means "messenger" or "legate." Undoubtedly Paul is speaking here about those messengers of God whom he sends according to his will. In the law, the messenger of God is the priest, as we see in Malachi 2, where we read: "For the lips of the priest preserve knowledge and from his mouth men seek the law, because he has been appointed a messenger of the Lord." An apostle is also a messenger of God. Thus the apostles whom Christ is said to have sent before him are called "angels" in Luke 9; so also are the disciples of John in Luke 7. For that reason the celestial spirits are commonly called "angels," because they are sent from God to accomplish his ministry. As far as this present passage is concerned, some interpreters understand "angels" to mean ministers of the Word; others think this word refers to good spirits or bad spirits. I am favorable toward the explanation of those who understand "angels" to refer to good spirits, sent by God to the church, not only to the church as a whole, but also to individual believers. Given this interpretation, the apostle demands that both inside and outside the church, when we are not concerned about the scruples of human beings, we should at least be concerned to avert the gaze of angels by abstaining from everything that seems even the least bit dishonorable. Commentary on 1 Corinthians 11:10.[38]

Various Interpretations of "Angels." The English Annotations: Some take the word "angels" here to refer to the pastors of the congregation, who are termed "angels" in Malachi 2:7 and Revelation 1:20; in this view, the apostle seeks to enforce the modest behavior of women by appealing to the reverend respect that they should show, especially in the church, to these angels of the churches. Others take "angels" here in the proper sense for the celestial spirits, which always serve Christ, the head of the church. These angels

[37]Lefèvre d'Étaples, *Commentariorum in Epistolas Beati Pauli . . . Liber Secundus*, 117r-v.

[38]Musculus, *Comm. 1 Cor.*, 392; citing Mal 2:7; Lk 7:27.

are present in the congregation of the faithful and are offended at all disorder and uncomeliness that may occur there. Therefore, in this sense, the women should behave more modestly in the church out of regard for these spirits, lest they grieve them. . . . Others think that Paul speaks of "angels" not by way of aggravation, but by way of exhortation drawn from the example of the angels, who are careful to demonstrate their reverence for Christ, their head, covering their faces with two of their wings as a sign of their subjection to their head (Is 6:2). Similarly women should cover their heads and faces with a veil as a sign of subjection to *their* heads, namely, their husbands. Annotations on 1 Corinthians 11:10.[39]

11:11-16 *Mutual Dependence of Men and Women*

Men and Women Need Each Other. John Calvin: The statement "but neither is the man without the woman" is added in part to prevent men from scoffing at women, and in part as a consolation to women so that they may not be annoyed at their subjection. Paul is saying: "The male sex stands above the female sex, but with this exception, that they ought to be joined to one another in mutual goodwill, for the one cannot do without the other. For, if they should be separated, they would be like mutilated members of a mangled body. Let them, therefore, be closely tied to one another with the bond of mutual service." Commentary on 1 Corinthians 11:11.[40]

Men and Women Are Interdependent. John Trapp: This [verse] is added for the woman's comfort. There must be complete mutual respect and tenderheartedness between married couples that, when preserved fresh and fruitful, will immeasurably sweeten and beautify the estate of marriage. Love is a coin that must be exchanged between them, and returned in kind. In Colossians 3:16, Paul writes "Husbands, love your wives." He does not say, "Rule over your wives" . . . but "love your wives." Yes, let all your affairs be done in love. For the man cannot be without the woman, for he is not complete without her—he lacks a piece of himself. Neither can the woman be without the man, for she cannot subsist without him, as the vine cannot survive without a support rod. Commentary on 1 Corinthians 11:11.[41]

Don't Abuse Women! Tilemann Hesshus: Paul provides a clarification to his meaning by making clear the sense in which he wishes these things to be understood so that no one abuses his teaching. It's as if he were to say: "I am not saying these things so that men might proudly condemn women, or exalt themselves, or think that they have priority in inheriting salvation, but only so that order in discipline and church polity might be guarded in a decent and agreeable manner." Apart from this status, both women and men are creatures of God and are recipients by inheritance to the promise of eternal life. "Besides," Paul says, "in the Lord, man is not independent of the woman, nor the woman independent of the man." That is to say, neither sex can exist or procreate without the other. And so they ought to express mutual kindness and love to one another. Let the man piously consider that he was born from a woman and, by God's command, the woman was created to be his helper. Thus he should show honor to the female sex. Let the woman piously consider that she is from the man and was created for the sake of men, and that by God's command she is subject to her husband. That is why she should subject herself to him with a ready mind and exhibit reverence toward him. Paul adds "in the Lord," a phrase by which he indicates that this discretion and moderation and goodness is only evidenced in those who are members of Jesus Christ and led by the Holy Spirit. For wicked men, if they are unmarried, heap abuse on the female sex. If they are unable to keep themselves from marriage, they act like tyrants and get angry at women's natural requirements.

[39]Downame, *English Annotations*, EE1v*.
[40]CO 49:477 (cf. CTS 39:359-60).
[41]Trapp, *A Commentary or Exposition*, 686*.

Whereby the pagans have said, "A wife is a necessary evil." Or again, women, if they are not godly, either want to be masters over their husbands, thereby disturbing right order, or they obey their husbands with a reluctant spirit, because they do not acknowledge the Lord's will. Therefore Paul warns godly spouses to focus more intently on the Lord, the author of human beings who created the man and woman, and submit themselves to his will and plan. Exposition on 1 Corinthians 11:11-12.[42]

Human Procreation Comes from God. Menno Simons: That both man and woman are, by the saying "Be fruitful and multiply," made competent by God for procreation is too plain to deny. But each in his own ordained place: the man a sower and the woman as a receptive field, prepared by God for procreation, without which it is impossible for fruit to be born. This is God's ordinance that the Scriptures teach everywhere. Reply to Gellius Faber.[43]

Three Ways That Women and Men Are Equal. David Dickson: So that this comparison of men and women does not lead people to despise women, Paul highlights the equality of men and women in three respects. The first is in respect to Christ our Lord, or our state of grace in Christ. Men and women are equal in that both have been bought with the same price and are alike ordained to the service of Christ. The second is in respect to their common origins, for as the woman came from man in the creation, so in ordinary propagation the man comes from woman. The third is in respect to the first and principal efficient cause, that is, because God has made men and women and everything else, therefore men and women are equal. Exposition of 1 Corinthians 11:11-12.[44]

All Things Are from God. Peter Martyr Vermigli: But if "all things are from God," as Paul says, it should be evident that they are very useful for them. By this concluding statement of the apostle, the dogma of the Marcionites, Valentinians, and Manichaeans is utterly destroyed, for they stated that all things did not come from God, but that many things came from an evil principle. Commentary on 1 Corinthians 11:12.[45]

Do Not Fight Against Nature! Tilemann Hesshus: Paul repeats his argument, which he now draws from the judgment of nature. For nature itself teaches that both hair and the veil should be the adornment of the female sex. Therefore do not fight against nature. For the doctrine of the gospel has not extinguished or blotted out the remnant of natural judgment, but rather it restores the light of nature that has been obscured and makes it shine brightly again. And it adds from heaven a new light that was unknown to the whole of reason. Explication of 1 Corinthians 11:13-14.[46]

Paul Appeals to Contemporary Custom. John Calvin: Paul again sets before them nature as the teacher of propriety, and he calls natural that which had been received by universal consent and custom at that time—especially among the Greeks. For it was not always thought disgraceful for men to have long hair. Historical records report that long ago, that is, in ancient times, men everywhere had long hair. For this reason, even the poets were accustomed to call the ancients by the well-worn epitaph "unshorn." It was not until later that barbers began to be used in Rome, around the time of Africanus the Elder. And at the time when Paul wrote these things, the use of barbers was not yet popular in Gaul and Germany. Or rather, it would have been degrading for men as well as women to have been shaved or shorn. But since among the Greeks it was not considered very manly to have long hair (for those who did so were known as

[42]Hesshus, *Explicatio Prioris Epistolae ad Corinthios*, 168v-r.
[43]Simons, *Complete Writings*, 767-77*.
[44]Dickson, *Exposition of St. Paul's Epistles*, 59*.
[45]Vermigli, *In Selectissimam Priorem ad Corinthios Epistolam . . . Commentarii*, 288v. The heretical sects founded by Marcion (c. 85–c. 160), Valentinus (c. 100–c. 160), and Mani (c. 216–274) shared a dualistic cosmology that attributed the material world to an evil god or principle.
[46]Hesshus, *Explicatio Prioris Epistolae ad Corinthios*, 169r-v.

effeminate), Paul considers as "nature" a custom that was at that time confirmed. Commentary on 1 Corinthians 11:14.[47]

Paul Decries Long Hair in Men. John Trapp: [Long hair] are bushes of vanity . . . that they will never part with until the devil puts a candle into the bush. But our gallant young men object that the apostle here means only hair that is as long as women's hair. To which we answer that Homer called the Greeks "hair-nourishing men," even though they did not wear their hair as long as women. . . . And I think that these monstrous lovers of fashion—both men who nourish their horrid bushes of vanity, and women who most unnaturally crop their hair—should fear and tremble every hour, lest they bring [God's judgment] on their own heads, and on the whole kingdom. Commentary on 1 Corinthians 11:14.[48]

God's Word Is Superior to Nature's Proofs. Wolfgang Musculus: We should pay careful attention from this passage to what Paul says about the proof of nature. By observing these proofs, humans are able to gather many things useful for their lives, good reputation, a pleasant life, good manners, and also pious behavior. For nature, in so far as it is uncorrupted, is the very wise and orderly arrangement of divine providence, filled with wonderful works and examples. Some of these natural proofs are hidden, others are clearly seen. . . .

At the same time, we should note that Paul does not simply say, "Does not nature teach you?" but "Does not *even* nature teach you?" As Christians, the Corinthians had the teaching of the Word of God, from which they could be fully instructed. This Word is primary, and it has been given uniquely to the elect. But the proofs of nature hold second place, and serve those who are more ignorant. That is why in matters of piety, these proofs of nature should not be considered primary and should not be given weight without the Word. Thus we see here in this passage that the apostle does not draw his primary argument from nature, but only his secondary argument, which was more than enough to blunt the stupidity of the Corinthians. Commentary on 1 Corinthians 11:15.[49]

The Church Has the Right to Define Neutral Matters. Peter Martyr Vermigli: Some people were resisting this principle of the apostle, and did not think neutral and indifferent things should be defined in such a uniform and definite manner. But the church has the authority to determine these matters, provided that it always aims toward peace and edification and stretches toward the standard of the Word of God, which established it. And those who disagree with this conclusion are shown to be antisocial people, incapable of human interaction. This is the kind of sin that the Anabaptists commit most grievously. Paul says that godly people do not practice this sort of thing, where they argue or quarrel about these matters, because there is no end or limit to arguments over superfluous matters. The apostle saw that this regulation of his did not depend on human reason so much as on godly inference, and so he talked about these things. Nevertheless, what he related regarding the superiority of the man and the subjection of the woman—these things are firm. But what was written concerning the symbols [of this authority] was considered to be pleasing and in keeping with custom. I know that some people claim that the word "practice" [in verse 16] must refer to the veiling of women, a practice that happened among the Jews, and is now maintained in many churches. But it seems to me that this word is directed toward contention, that godly people should not be indulging in such arguments. Commentary on 1 Corinthians 11:16.[50]

[47]CO 49:478 (cf. CTS 39:361-62). Scipio Africanus Major (236–184/183 BC) was a famous Roman consul and general who defeated the Carthaginian general Hannibal at the Battle of Zama in 202 BC.
[48]Trapp, *A Commentary or Exposition*, 687*.
[49]Musculus, *Comm. 1 Cor.*, 396.
[50]Vermigli, *In Selectissimam Priorem ad Corinthios Epistolam . . . Commentarii*, 289v.

Paul Silences Contentious People. Tilemann Hesshus: Lest the Corinthians object with their sophisms and witty arguments (as was customary among the Greeks), and equally, lest they squabble over philosophical matters, Paul breaks off his argument and warns them to avoid being contentious. He says, "It is not pleasurable for me, nor is it my custom to argue with contentious people; and the churches of God do not practice this custom of arguing endlessly in the manner of contentious people. But when the church hears either the clear testimony of sacred Scripture or quietly acquiesces to weighty and godly reasons, it should have nothing more to do with those teachers or others like them. And so, disregarding contentious people, I desire you to agree to this godly and weighty opinion." Exposition on 1 Corinthians 11:16.[51]

May God Deliver Us from Contentious People! John Trapp: Luther said, "May the good Lord deliver his church from a vainglorious professor, from a contentious pastor, and from endless and needless controversies." . . . This is a foul fault in anyone, but especially in ministers, who must be careful (said Luther) that those three dogs do not follow them into the pulpit, namely, pride, covetousness, and contentiousness. A quarrelsome person is like a gambling cock, ever bloody with the blood of others and himself. And divisions are Satan's powder plot to blow up religion. Commentary on 1 Corinthians 11:16.[52]

[51]Hesshus, *Explicatio Prioris Epistolae ad Corinthios*, 169v.

[52]Trapp, *A Commentary or Exposition*, 687*.

11:17-34 The Lord's Supper

17 But in the following instructions I do not commend
you, because when you come together it is not for the
better but for the worse. 18 For, in the first place, when
you come together as a church, I hear that there are
divisions among you. And I believe it in part,[a] *19 for*
there must be factions among you in order that those
who are genuine among you may be recognized. 20
When you come together, it is not the Lord's supper
that you eat. 21 For in eating, each one goes ahead with
his own meal. One goes hungry, another gets drunk.
22 What! Do you not have houses to eat and drink in?
Or do you despise the church of God and humiliate
those who have nothing? What shall I say to you?
Shall I commend you in this? No, I will not.
23 For I received from the Lord what I also
delivered to you, that the Lord Jesus on the night
when he was betrayed took bread, 24 and when he had
given thanks, he broke it, and said, "This is my body,
which is for[b] *you. Do this in remembrance of me."*[c]
25 In the same way also he took the cup, after supper,
saying, "This cup is the new covenant in my blood.
Do this, as often as you drink it, in remembrance of
me." 26 For as often as you eat this bread and drink the
cup, you proclaim the Lord's death until he comes.
27 Whoever, therefore, eats the bread or drinks the
cup of the Lord in an unworthy manner will be guilty
concerning the body and blood of the Lord. 28 Let a
person examine himself, then, and so eat of the bread
and drink of the cup. 29 For anyone who eats and
drinks without discerning the body eats and drinks
judgment on himself. 30 That is why many of you are
weak and ill, and some have died.[d] *31 But if we judged*[e]
ourselves truly, we would not be judged. 32 But when
we are judged by the Lord, we are disciplined[f] *so that*
we may not be condemned along with the world.
33 So then, my brothers,[g] *when you come together to*
eat, wait for[h] *one another— 34 if anyone is hungry, let*
him eat at home—so that when you come together it
will not be for judgment. About the other things I will
give directions when I come.

a Or *I believe a certain report* **b** Some manuscripts *broken for* **c** Or *as my memorial;* also verse 25 **d** Greek *have fallen asleep* (as in 15:6, 20) **e** Or *discerned* **f** Or *when we are judged we are being disciplined by the Lord* **g** Or *brothers and sisters* **h** Or *share with*

Overview: Horrified that the celebration of the Lord's Supper in Corinth has become defiled by unseemly divisions, drunkenness, and neglect of the poor, Paul reminds his Christian readers of the purposes for which Christ instituted this sacred meal and calls them to remedy the situation through self-examination and heartfelt repentance. Perhaps no passage of Scripture sparked greater disagreement and more heated controversy among Reformation commentators than this one. Different interpretations of Christ's memorable statements "This is my body, which is for you," and "This cup is the new covenant in my blood" created major fault lines that separated traditional Catholic, Lutheran, Anabaptist, and Reformed Christians from one another. Whereas Protestant interpreters are united in their rejection of the Catholic doctrine of transubstantiation (i.e., that the substances of the sacramental elements, when consecrated, are miraculously changed into the body and blood of Christ), they fiercely disagree as to how—or whether—the sacramental signs of bread and wine communicate the true body of Christ to the believer. Martin Luther and his followers insist on Christ's real bodily presence in, with, and under the consecrated elements. By contrast, Huldrych Zwingli argues that the resurrected body of Christ remained in heaven, not on earth; hence, the Lord's Supper is primarily a memorial or commemoration service of Christ's death for sinners, though Christ is spiritually present among believers. Meanwhile, most

Anabaptists took a more strictly memorialist view.[1] In an effort to mediate these positions, John Calvin teaches that Christians feed on the very substance of Christ's body in the Lord's Supper through the power of the Holy Spirit, who unites believers to Christ's resurrected and ascended body in heaven. In their comments on these verses, Protestant authors address a variety of perceived abuses in the Catholic tradition. They speak against those medieval theologians who teach that the Mass is a bloodless sacrifice of Christ's body. So too they are highly critical of the traditional church for withholding the sacramental cup from lay participants, for encouraging the adoration of the consecrated host, and for teaching that the sacraments benefit recipients *ex opere operato*,[2] irrespective of personal faith. At the same time, Lutheran and Reformed commentators often cross swords over the practice of private communion and debate whether wicked persons feed on the body of Christ in the Supper. Ironically, while early modern interpreters agree that Christ instituted the Lord's Supper to foster godliness and communal affection, their polemical exchanges over this sacrament too often promoted neither.

11:17-19 *Divisions in Corinth*

THE CHURCH ON EARTH CONTAINS BOTH WHEAT AND WEEDS. TILEMANN HESSHUS: In this second part of the chapter, the apostle again rebukes and corrects another abuse that had crept into the Corinthian church, for some of them had turned the Lord's Supper into profane banquets and drinking parties, and were encouraging divisions among themselves. Moreover, the wealthy were welcomed in the church, and the poor were shamed, and so many of the Corinthians were receiving the body and blood of Christ to their judgment. Therefore the apostle strongly rebukes this abuse, and exhorts the church to true repentance and fear of the Lord. And by repeating the institution and teaching of the Lord's Supper, Paul is restoring its true and beneficial use.

When the apostle confesses that there are divisions within the Corinthian church (which had been founded by the apostle), he agrees with the Lord's parable concerning the enemy, who planted weeds in the Lord's field while the people were sleeping at night. It is for this reason that we must keep watch and pray against this enemy. Now the Donatists[3] are refuted by means of the apostle's testimony as well as this parable of Christ, for they imagine and demand the sort of church where evil people are not mixed in with the good, and where no divisions whatsoever exist—even though Christ clearly states, "Allow both [the weeds and wheat] to grow until the harvest, and at the harvest time God will command his angels to gather the weeds, and throw them into the fire, which will never be extinguished." . . .

Not all who join themselves to the church by their doctrinal confession are truly repentant, or continually call on God in Spirit and in truth. Instead, many people live careless lives; they are slaves of empty glory; they are concerned about their stomachs and hypocritically pretend to be religious people. When these conditions exist—namely, hatred, Satan's fury against the truth, superficiality, ambition, and wickedness—it cannot happen otherwise than that divisions and heresies should arise in the world. Nevertheless, Satan's efforts do not succeed, for the truth is not overthrown by heresies, nor is the church completely destroyed (which is Satan's chief aim). In fact, God knows how

[1]While Zwingli held to this "memorialist" view during most of his career, in the years after the Marburg Colloquy (1529) he did modify his position so as to affirm Christ's sacramental presence in the Lord's Supper. Thus in the appendix to his posthumously published *An Exposition of the Faith*, he writes, "We believe Christ to be truly present in the Supper, indeed we do not believe that it is the Lord's Supper unless Christ is present." Cited in W. P. Stephens, *Zwingli: An Introduction to His Thought* (Oxford: Oxford University Press, 2001), 105-6.

[2]Translated "by the work performed"—the teaching of the Roman Catholic Church that the sacraments convey grace to all recipients as long as they do not impede that grace through mortal sin.

[3]The Donatists were a schismatic Christian group led by Donatus (died c. 355) that denied the sacramental power and authority of Catholic church leaders such as Felix of Aptunga, who betrayed the faith during persecution but later returned to his ecclesiastical office.

to use such evil for his glory and the benefit of the church, and through these heresies, his people are made visible, and are both tested and established in true godliness. Thus when they are strongly opposed by false teachings, they persist constantly in the truth. Explication of 1 Corinthians 11:17.[4]

Not for the Better, but for the Worse. John Calvin: Paul accuses them, first of all, that they come together not for the better; and second, that they come together for the worse. To be sure, the second is more serious, but even the first is not to be endured, for if we are attentive to what should be done in church, there should be no public assembly where fruit is not borne. For there God's teaching is heard, prayers are made, the sacraments [*mysteria*] are celebrated. The fruit of God's Word is evident when we grow in our ability to trust in God and fear of him; when we make progress in the life of holiness; when we put off the old person more and more; when we make progress in newness of life. The purpose of the sacraments is to cultivate within us godliness and love. Prayers also ought to be used for these purposes. Besides all this, the Lord works efficaciously by his Spirit, because he does not want these things that he has instituted to be in vain. Therefore, if the sacred assemblies are of no benefit to us, and we are not made better by them, our ingratitude is to blame and we deserve to be reproved. . . .

The second [reason for reproof] follows—that [the Corinthians] come together for the worse. This is a far more serious matter, yet it almost always results from the first. For if we gain nothing from the benefits bestowed by God, the way he punishes our laziness is that we are rendered worse by them. Commentary on 1 Corinthians 11:17.[5]

Church Assemblies Can Be Edifying or Harmful. Wolfgang Musculus: Paul does not say, "You are not meeting together," or "You are meeting together only rarely," but "Your meeting together causes more harm than good." Indeed, the Corinthians were meeting together in sacred assembly, as they had been instructed, but this resulted more in the destruction than the edification of their consciences. For this reason, Paul does not praise the frequency of their assemblies. For how could he praise these assemblies when they resulted in the destruction of the body of Christ?

Thus in this passage we are warned to evaluate ecclesiastical assemblies. It is a good thing to gather together as one body of believers, indeed this has clearly been appointed by the wisdom of God. But if meeting together causes more destruction than edification, and if what could be good if it were rightly practiced begins to be evil, it is altogether appropriate for people to abstain from this type of assembly than to expose themselves to the destruction of their consciences. And this is the reason why people today should abandon those assemblies where no one is edified in the true faith, but everyone is drawn to superstitions and idolatrous worship (to say nothing about that foulest interaction with whores and simoniacs). Commentary on 1 Corinthians 11:17.[6]

Heresy and Division Can Demonstrate What Is True. John Colet: Heresy makes clear those who have been approved. When there is division and falling away, it is shown who is constant and self-consistent in the truth. . . . Fire proves gold, and within the jaws of falsehood, truth remains constant and is demonstrated. The weak sink down and are prone to division because of their lack of discretion. Discretion is found in truth, and the truth is established in unity, full of light in itself, and kindly and good toward all. It cannot be conquered; it cannot be extinguished; it cannot be deformed.

For the consolation of those Corinthians who were true and loyal, Paul points out that they can experience some good things from these false heresies: namely, a precise judgment and proof of

[4]Hesshus, *Explicatio Prioris Epistolae ad Corinthios*, 170r-v; citing Mt 13:24-30; 13:30.

[5]CO 49:480 (cf. CTS 39:364-65); citing Col 3:9.

[6]Musculus, *Comm. 1 Cor.*, 400-401.

who is true and sincere and sound in the sound Christ. Even the most violent winds overthrow only those trees whose roots are planted with too little depth and firmness in the earth. And our earth, our base, our rock, our steadfastness is Jesus Christ. Exposition of 1 Corinthians 11.[7]

Dissension in the Church Is Inevitable. Martin Luther: "There must be hordes among you." . . . Wherever God's Word is, the devil through his hordes always has to build his taverns and his whorehouses next to God's temple or church—just like he did in the beginning in Paradise and in Adam's house. . . . And so ever since he's always done the same, and he'll keep doing it. Now whoever is rankled by this and, wherever he sees it, immediately wants to judge that "this is no church," will ultimately be without the church and Christ altogether. For you'll find no church so pure that it teaches or believes and lives wholly in perfect harmony without any discord. Postil on the Epistle for the Tenth Sunday After Trinity.[8]

Schismatics and Heretics. John Calvin: It is well-known in what sense ancient writers used both of these terms, and how they distinguished between heretics and schismatics. They classified heresy as disagreement with regard to doctrine; schism, on the other hand, related to interpersonal conflict, as when a person left a church for such reasons as jealousy, hatred of their pastor, or ill-nature. Although it is true that the church cannot but be torn apart by false doctrine, and that heresy is the root and origin of schism, at the same time jealousy or pride is the mother of almost all heresies. Nevertheless, it is valuable to distinguish these two terms in this way. . . .

But observe that Paul says that "there must be [factions]," indicating by this phrase that this situation happens, not by chance, but by the sure providence of God. For he wishes to test his people, as gold is tested in the furnace, and since it is pleasing to God, it is therefore profitable. Nevertheless, we must not enter into thorny disputes—or rather, into labyrinths—concerning the necessity of fate. We know that there will never be a time when there are not many who are reprobates. We know that they are governed by the spirit of Satan and are effectively drawn to do evil. We know that Satan leaves no stone unturned to break the unity of the church. This is the source of that necessity which Paul is talking about—it is not fate. We also know that the Lord, by his marvelous wisdom, turns the pernicious machinations of Satan to the salvation of believers. Commentary on 1 Corinthians 11:19.[9]

Why Are Divisions Inevitable? Tilemann Hesshus: Paul's statement that "heresies are necessary" must not be understood to mean that they are God's will, or that fate is the cause of heresies or divisions. For his meaning must always be interpreted in light of [such passages as] "You are not a God who desires wickedness" (Ps 5). Again, "All these things I hate, says the Lord" (Zech 8). Instead, Paul means that, given corrupt human nature and the enduring tyranny of Satan in this world, it is inevitable for heresies and sects to arise. For Satan works tirelessly to incite a terrible hatred of Christ and the truth of his salvation, and he arouses people of petty, restless, and ambitious natures to sow false teaching and become authors of new factions. In this way he attacks Christ with insults, wounds the church, and prevents the salvation of many people. Explication of 1 Corinthians 11:19.[10]

Schisms and Heresies Are Necessary. John Trapp: [Paul means] schisms, divisions, yes, and that concerning the sacrament of the Lord's Supper (that bond of love) through Satan's malice. Now there can be no greater sin committed, Chrysostom once said, than to break the peace of

[7]Colet, *Enarratio*, 224.
[8]WA 22:171 (cf. LW 78:329).
[9]CO 49:480-81 (cf. CTS 39:366).
[10]Hesshus, *Explicatio Prioris Epistolae ad Corinthios*, 170v.; citing Ps 5:4; Zech 8:17.

the church. Cyprian also said it is an inexpiable blemish, which cannot be washed off with the blood of martyrdom. The error of it may be pardoned, Oecolampadius said in his epistle to the Lutherans of Swabia, if there is faith in Christ Jesus, but we cannot expiate the discord, even though we lay down our lives to do it. . . . Therefore all the more with schisms, which also, for the most part, degenerate into heresies, just as an old serpent degenerates into a dragon. In the time of Pope Clement V, Frederick the king of Sicily was so offended at the evil government of the church that he began to question the truth of the Christian religion. But Arnoldus de Villa Nova confirmed and settled his mind by this and other passages of Scripture, "Offenses must come, there must be heresies," etc., for God has decreed and foretold it. It is necessary for there to be heresies in the church, just as it is necessary that there are poisonous and venomous creatures in the world, because out of them God will work medicines. Commentary on 1 Corinthians 11:18-19.[11]

11:20-22 *The Corinthians Abuse the Lord's Supper*

The Corinthians Despised the Lord's Supper and One Another. Huldrych Zwingli: It appears that when the Corinthians came together in a public assembly, their custom was for all the people to gather together in the temple for a feast, both the wealthy, who brought their own food in abundance, and also the poor. For, even if they had nothing to eat, the poor were attending the public feast and the Lord's Supper on account of the symbolism and remembrance, and they waited until all had gathered. Over time, it happened that the wealthy did not wait for the poor; instead, they ate and drank, leaving nothing for the poor. Therefore Paul reproaches them for two things. First, that they are slaves of their stomachs, and only satisfy their own appetites. Second, that they do not wait for the poor. It is as if Paul were saying, "The fact that they have nothing to eat should make you ashamed! Yes, you are guilty of abuse if in this public and friendly banquet you fill your belly but ignore the poor. Do this in your homes, but not in the church! Now when you gather together for worship and thanksgiving, you should gather together as one body united in love so that, having set aside jealousy, envy, and hatred, you praise God with one mouth and heart! You, by contrast, are divided against one another, with everyone seeking their own self-interest. One person hates the other; the other person neglects and despises in return. And where people ought to serve God and their neighbors, instead they are slaves of their bellies and their own lusts. Thus you do not gather together to benefit each other; instead you leave worse off than before. Is this not to despise the church of God? This is not eating the *Lord's* Supper, but only one's *own* supper." Annotations on 1 Corinthians 11:20.[12]

The Corinthians Violated the Communal Nature of the Lord's Supper. Wolfgang Musculus: It is clear from Tertullian, for example, that it was the custom of the apostolic churches, as one body of believers, not only to devote themselves to prayers, teaching, fraternal correction, and the Psalms, but also, according to the example as well as the institution of Christ the Savior, to eat and drink together in this sacred assembly. And while sharing this meal, they celebrated the Eucharist and remembrance of the Lord's death by the breaking of bread and the passing of the cup. It was especially for that reason that they called it the Lord's Supper. They were admonished in the words of praise accompanying this sacred meal that it was not to be conducted in private and for the benefit of a single individual, but it was intended to be shared in public by all of the believers. For, since it pertained to the Lord

[11] Trapp, *A Commentary or Exposition*, 687*. Arnaldus de Villa Nova (c. 1240–1311) was a physician and religious reformer who served as the personal physician of the kings of Aragon and three popes, including Clement V.

[12] Zwingli, *Annotatiunculae . . . ex ore Zvinglij*, 92-93.

and was handed down by the Lord to the church, it should never be employed for private use or misused for the benefit of a faction. Therefore, since the Corinthians had begun to be divided into factions, Paul explicitly denies that they are eating the Lord's Supper, saying, "Therefore, when you come together in the same place, it is not the Lord's Supper that you eat." That is, "because you eat and drink, you cannot consider this the Lord's Supper." Why? Because, he says, "each person presumes to be eating their own supper. And one person remains hungry, and another person becomes drunk." The sectaries and wealthy people were not waiting until the whole company of believers gathered together so that all might eat and drink a common meal together. Instead, before the church had come together, they were eating and drinking privately, some out of zeal for their faction and others out of contempt for the church. Commentary on 1 Corinthians 11:20.[13]

The Corinthians Celebrate the Lord's Supper in a Faulty Manner. David Dickson: Paul demonstrates four notable faults among the Corinthians as they celebrate the Lord's Supper. First, all of them with their factions took the Lord's Supper schismatically (excluding other members of the church). Second, they mixed with the sacrament of the Lord's Supper their normal meal or their common feasts, which were called love feasts. Third, while the rich people feasted, the poor people were excluded. Fourth, in their feasts they drank to the point of drunkenness. Exposition of 1 Corinthians 11:21.[14]

The Integrity of Public Worship Must Be Preserved. John Calvin: "Do you not have houses?" From this we see that the apostle was entirely displeased with the custom of feasting, even if that aforementioned abuse had not existed. For although it seems quite acceptable for the whole church to share a common meal together, nevertheless it is wrong to transform a sacred assembly into practices foreign to its nature. We know what activities should occur when a church gathers together, namely, to hear teaching, to pour forth prayers and sing hymns to God, to celebrate the sacraments [*mysteria*], to profess the confession of faith, and to engage in religious ceremonies and other godly exercises. If anything else is done there, it is out of place. Everyone has a house of their own for eating and drinking; it is therefore improper to do these things in a sacred assembly. Commentary on 1 Corinthians 11:22.[15]

11:23-26 *The Institution of the Lord's Supper*

The Lord's Supper Is a Sacrifice That Unites Believers to God. John Colet: Now this Supper of the Lord, the eating of the bread and the drinking from the cup, contains a commemoration and a proclamation and a re-presentation of Christ's death, if in fact there is a breaking of his body, and a pouring out, as it were, of his blood. But the breaking and the pouring out exist so that God's elect may feed on that sacrifice, to the end that, with Christ dying in them, they may live anew in him; so that having Jesus wholly in themselves, they may be wholly and entirely in him, already incorporated and united with him in one body. This comes about by the participation of the unifying and life-giving body of him who gives himself wholly to us in his own Lord's Supper, so that he may transform us wholly into himself and make us fellow members with him, so that he may exist with his own as one body (with himself as head). Whereby we possess God wholly and are wholly in God, not only by the communication of the Divinity in our souls, but also by the communication of his body in our bodies, so that we may grow together into one body in him. . . .

Jesus Christ was slaughtered and sacrificed and put to death so that we might feed on him as our sacrifice until he comes, and, as we feed on

[13]Musculus, *Comm. 1 Cor.*, 409-10. For Tertullian's description of early Christian practice, see his *Apology* (especially chapter 39), in ANF 3:46-47.

[14]Dickson, *Exposition of St. Paul's Epistles*, 59*.

[15]CO 49:483 (cf. CTS 39:371).

him, that we might be mindful of his death on our behalf as participants in his death, so that we might live in him. And being participants in his life—though we are already dead in him—we are made alive in him, having been brought out of death. Our place is now in the temple, so that all of us may feed on the sacrifice, and all be partakers of God's altar—indeed, of God himself—offered on the altar of the cross. Thus, together with him, crucified and sacrificed with him, we too may be sacrifices pleasing to God. Exposition of 1 Corinthians 11.[16]

We Must Partake of the Sacrament by Faith. Martin Luther: So it is clear from all this that this holy sacrament is nothing else than a divine sign, in which are pledged, granted, and imparted Christ and all saints together with all their works, sufferings, merits, mercies, and possessions, for the comfort and strengthening of all who are in anxiety and sorrow, persecuted by the devil, sins, the world, the flesh, and every evil. And to receive the sacrament is nothing else than to desire all this and firmly to believe that it is done.

Here, now, follows the third part of the sacrament, that is, the *faith* on which everything depends. For it is not enough to know what the sacrament is and signifies. It is not enough that you know it is a fellowship and a gracious exchange or blending of our sins and suffering with the righteousness of Christ and his saints. You must also desire it and firmly believe that you have received it. Here the devil and our own nature wage their fiercest battle, so that faith may by no means stand firm. There are those who practice their arts and subtleties by trying [to fathom] what becomes of the bread when it is changed into Christ's flesh and of the wine when it is changed into his blood and how the whole Christ, his flesh and blood, can be encompassed in so small a portion of bread and wine. It does not matter if you do not see it. It is enough to know that it is a divine sign in which Christ's flesh and blood are truly present. The how and the where we leave to him. . . . Thus the sacrament is for us a ford, a bridge, a door, a ship, and a stretcher, by which and in which we pass from this world into eternal life. Therefore everything depends on faith. Blessed Sacrament of the Body of Christ.[17]

Christ Himself Is the One True Sacrament. Philipp Melanchthon: First, what is commonly called the sacrament we will call a sacramental sign because Paul calls Christ himself the sacrament in Colossians. Thus there is only one sacrament, namely, the faith of Christ. Second, the sacramental sign is the sign by which the divine promise has, as it were, been sealed by God, as seen in Romans 4. Third, there are altogether two sacramental signs: baptism and the Eucharist; the other sacraments listed are of human invention.

Fourth, baptism is the sign of death and new life. Thus John baptizes by water, while Christ baptizes by the Spirit and fire. And, strictly speaking, it is a sign of repentance; thus John said he was baptizing for repentance. To die is to be baptized in the baptism of John; to be brought back to life and know mercy is to be baptized in the baptism of Christ. Hence, at one time in the church baptism was presented to penitents for their consolation, and for them baptism was a sign of absolution, as penance is now treated. The sacrament of penance should not be distinguished from baptism, because baptism itself is a sacramental sign of repentance.

Fifth, those who have begun to be put to death and are already struggling with the flesh and its strong desires have need for encouragement; this comes about first, through the Word, and second, through the Eucharist—so that there might be some sensible sign of that Word by which we might be more certain about God's will.

Sixth, the Eucharist is thus a sign of new life that works on despairing consciences. Paul expresses the promise quite clearly: "This is my body which is broken for you," that is: See, this is

[16]Colet, *Enarratio*, 224, 226.

[17]LW 35:60-61, 66.

my body, which you are sharing among yourselves for your salvation. Now this is stated more clearly in what follows: "which is given for you" if you add the words that follow, "Do this in remembrance of me," that is, in memory of my death. It is necessary that you understand it this way: Behold, this body of mine should be a sign for you that admonishes you about my death and the benefits shared through my death. You see the most Christian of promises if you combine the words of the gospel narrative to this sacramental mode, from which you may understand that the Eucharist has been given to us as a sign, not a sacrifice.

Seventh, from this you can easily recognize those who are eating worthily and those who are eating unworthily. Those people eat unworthily who live in the flesh and are ruled by it; they are the sort of people who do not really repent of their sins. They regard the body of Christ as a joke; they crucify Christ for themselves, as Hebrews 6 says. People also approach [the table] unworthily who do not think they should come forward unless they have first been made pure and holy by confession and preparations. They are like fools who will not use medicine unless they are first healthy. Finally, people approach [the table] unworthily who do not believe that their sins are forgiven them. For these people are not mindful of the death of Christ. What the apostle says bears on this point: "Let a man examine himself, and so eat of the bread," that is: Let nobody approach [the table] with contempt for this food, but let them examine themselves, whether they also discern the body of the Lord. Now, what does it mean to "discern the body of the Lord?" I answer: To know for what use, for what reason, a person should come forward and eat. And so this must be believed as a sign that sins have been forgiven.

Eighth, those who approach [the table] worthily are only those who feel the burden of sin and believe that their sins are pardoned; hence it is not right to drive them from the Supper in fear . . . because the only truly appropriate way of preparing for Communion is if you believe. These are the people who announce the death of the Lord, that is, who give thanks for the death of the Lord, and who are strengthened and uplifted by the benefit of the Lord's death. This is not possible unless they sense how heavy the burden of sin is. Annotations on 1 Corinthians 11:17.[18]

The Meaning of the Lord's Supper. Balthasar Hubmaier: The Supper of Christ is a commemoration of his suffering and a proclamation of his death until he comes to us again. The breaking of his bread and the drinking of the wine in the Christ meal is an outward sign or symbol instituted by Christ before his death, which signifies to us how he offered his body for us and shed his blood so that we also do the same for the sake of our neighbor. . . .

When Christ commands, "Take, eat, this is my body given for you," he means his mortal body, for he himself suffered for us, and not the bread on the table that he gave them to eat. Likewise his blood, and not the wine in the chalice, was poured out for us. For just such a manner of speaking did Christ use when he said to Peter, "You are Peter and on this rock," meaning himself, "will I build my church" (Mt 16:18). And the rock was Christ (1 Cor 10:4). Accordingly, one should always pay more attention . . . to the things signified by the word symbols than to the symbols themselves. For outside of their signifying, the same mean nothing and are in vain. But the Spirit makes us alive, and the Spirit comes with the Word, which then assures the human being of eternal life, as the bread and wine are word symbols of his love, by which we remember how he, Christ, was our Christ, and how we also are always to be Christ to one another. We all are one bread and one body—we all, who have fellowship in one bread and in one drink. As one little kernel does not keep its own flour, but shares it with the others, and a single grape does not keep its juice for itself, but shares it with the others, so should we Christians

[18]Melanchthon, *Annotationes in Epistolam priorem ad Corinthios*, 118, 120, 122; citing Col 1:27; Rom 4:11; Heb 6:6. In this passage, Melanchthon follows the Vulgate reading of Col 1:27, where the Latin word *sacramentum* is used to describe the mystery of Christ in the believer.

also act—or we eat and drink unworthily from the table of Christ. For the bread we break means and commemorates the communion of the body of Christ with us, that he is our own, for he gave his body for us through the drink of the communion of his blood, which he poured out for the forgiveness of our sin. To All Christians Concerning the Instruction of the Mass.[19]

The History and Use of the Sacrament of Jesus' Body and Blood. Johann Spangenberg: In these words Paul indicates who established the sacrament of the altar, when, for whom, how—and with what words and why. Who established the exalted sacrament? Our Lord Jesus Christ, God's Son, the Savior of the world. Therefore it is in no way to be despised. At what time did he establish and institute it? On the night when he was betrayed by the betrayer Judas during their final meal, as Matthew, Mark, and Luke describe it. For whom did he institute it? For his disciples, that is, all who believe in Christ. For in the early church all Christians were called disciples; they were first named "Christians" in Antioch. Now whoever wants to go to the Sacrament must be Christ's disciple. They must believe what Christ says, and do what Christ commands.

How did he institute it? With bread and wine. We see bare external bread and wine, but for the sake of Christ's words that we hear—"Take and eat, this is my body; take and drink this is my blood"—we believe and confess that it is the body and the blood of Christ. But do not let yourself be worried how this happens. It is a work of faith. Let those curious minds [try to] figure it out; those who love to consider exalted matters without concern for their own destruction.

With what words did he institute it? He took the bread, gave thanks for it, and said: "Take and eat, this is my body, which is broken for you." And he took the cup and said: "This cup is the new covenant in my blood." This command is the true consecration. If we follow this command and believe his words, then such faith makes the bread the body of Christ and the wine the blood of Christ for us. The priest is only a servant who performs the command of Christ for us and who distributes the sacrament among the congregation.

Why did he institute it? "Do such," he said, "for my remembrance." He desires for us to come together as true brothers and sisters, eating and drinking the very best [food and drink], and talking with one another about things that make our heart joyous. We should, therefore, proclaim the Lord's death for the consolation of the afflicted heart and frightened conscience, for the strengthening of the weak in faith against all the devil's doctrine, human spittle, hypocrisy, and lies. Now isn't this a joyous little Supper, when we celebrate God's command and deal with divine matters, with the soul's salvation and sanctification? Woe to those who despise it! . . .

What are the fruits of the sacrament? That we accept each other, serve, help, and console each other. And as Christ offers himself to us as food and drink, so we too should offer ourselves as food and drink to our neighbors—that is, we should offer our goods and possessions for their enjoyment. That is to go to the sacrament as a Christian. Then God's blessing and favor, all grace, salvation, and sanctification will follow. Postil on the Epistle for Maundy Thursday.[20]

The Lord's Supper Established on Christ's Authority. John Calvin: "I received from the Lord." With these words, Paul indicates that no authority carries any weight in the church except the Lord's alone. For he might have put it this way: "I have not handed down to you something that I made up. When I came to you, I did not invent a new kind of Supper, according to my own imagination. Rather, I have Christ as my authority, and I received from him what I personally delivered to you. Return, therefore, to the original source." Therefore, saying goodbye to human laws, the authority of Christ

[19]CRR 5:75.

[20]Spangenberg, *Postilla Teütsch*, 4:185r-187r, 188v; citing Acts 11:26.

alone will remain, unshaken. Commentary on 1 Corinthians 11:23.[21]

For I Received from the Lord. Tilemann Hesshus: Now the first thing that must be carefully noted here is that the apostle Paul testifies that he did not learn about this ceremony from the other apostles, who were present at the final supper, nor from the Evangelists, but he received these things from our Lord Jesus Christ himself. For Paul (as he testifies on several occasions) was taken up into the third heaven, and he saw with his own eyes the Lord Jesus, who had risen from the dead. Therefore we ought to treat this description of the Lord's Supper as an important matter of faith, since Jesus Christ, the Son of God himself, has handed down to us this formula. And so that we may allow no uncertainty concerning the truth of the words of the Supper, and so that we may stir ourselves to frequent use of the sacred Supper, we ought always to look at the author of this Supper, Jesus Christ, full of majesty. Explication of 1 Corinthians 11:23.[22]

On the Night That He Was Betrayed. Peter Martyr Vermigli: This took place at night, since the [Passover] lamb had to be sacrificed "between the two evenings." The more learned of the Hebrews understood the "two evenings" as the twofold setting of the light—the setting of the sun and the setting of the moon—which marked the boundary of the night. The Jews had to sacrifice the paschal lamb in this middle space of time, and Christ followed this practice. Commentary on 1 Corinthians 11:23.[23]

He Took Bread in His Hands and Gave Thanks. Peter Martyr Vermigli: Because Christ "gave thanks" for the bread, we see that Paul instructed Timothy correctly when he wrote, "Consecrate food by the Word of God and prayer." The Hebrews had this custom (which they follow to this day) that, during religious feasts, the head of the household, after taking the cup and bread, would give thanks and distribute them to his family. Christ did not depart from this custom, because he wanted his sacraments to be employed in familiar and convenient ways. It is nowhere read that the Lord took food without offering prayers of thanksgiving, and we should be provoked by his example to do the same. Dionysius, in his *Ecclesiastical Hierarchies*, said that "prayers of thanksgiving both precede and follow holy mysteries." Moreover, sacred readings are introduced with prayers, so that souls might be won over and instructed in ways that must lead to giving thanks to God. Christ displayed this truth, for he both instructed the apostles concerning praying and then afterward (as the Evangelist asserts) they sang a hymn. Commentary on 1 Corinthians 11:24.[24]

The Body Broken for You. Cardinal Cajetan: Everything Paul has declared is found in the Gospels, except this clause, "which is broken for you," since Paul alone remembered this. There is no reason why this clause in the Latin should be rejected, since it would be very accurate that the true body of Christ was to be broken in various ways. For his skin was severely broken when he was flogged by Pilate's soldiers; his body was severely broken by the nails that affixed both his hands and feet to the cross; and, finally, his side was broken when one of the soldiers pierced his side with a spear. Commentary on 1 Corinthians 11:24.[25]

Corporeal Presence, Not Transubstantiation. Martin Luther: We maintain that the bread and the wine in the Supper are the true body and blood of Christ and that they are not only offered to and received by pious but also by evil Christians. And we maintain that we should

[21]CO 49:484 (cf. CTS 39:373).
[22]Hesshus, *Explicatio Prioris Epistolae ad Corinthios*, 254r.
[23]Vermigli, *In Selectissimam Priorem ad Corinthios Epistolam . . . Commentarii*, 297v; citing Ex 12:6.
[24]Vermigli, *In Selectissimam Priorem ad Corinthios Epistolam . . . Commentarii*, 297v; citing 1 Tim 4:5; Mt 26:30.
[25]Cajetan, *In Sacrae Scripturae expositionem*, 5:125.

not distribute only one kind. Nor do we need the lofty learning which teaches us that there is as much under one kind as under both—as the sophists and the Council of Constance teach. Even if it were true that there is as much under one kind as under both, one kind is still not the complete order and institution as established and commanded by Christ. . . .

Concerning transubstantiation, we have absolutely no regard for the subtle sophistry of those who teach that bread and wine surrender or lose their natural substances and that only the form and color of the bread remain, but it is no longer real bread. For it agrees best with Scripture to say that bread is and remains there, as St. Paul himself indicates: "The bread that we break" and "Eat of the bread." The Schmalkald Articles: Concerning the Sacrament of the Altar.[26]

Fanatics Distort the Clear Teaching of Christ. Martin Luther: [Vain fanatics] proceed to force the word of Christ open and shut like pincers. Indeed, they are arch-fanatics, and do not have a leg to stand on. . . . From the way in which the latter tear and twist the words, reason can well see that they are fools. There are only three words: "This is my body." So the one turns up his nose at the word "this" and severs it from the bread, claiming that one should interpret it thus: "Take, eat—this is my body"; as if I were to say: "Take and eat; here sits Hans with the red jacket." The second seizes on the little word "is"; to him it is the equivalent of "signifies." The third says, "this is my body" means the same as "this is a figure of my body." They set up these dreams of theirs without any scriptural basis. These fanatics do not disturb me, and are not worthy to be fought with. Some of them are crude, grammatical fanatics; the others are subtle, philosophical fanatics. Let them go, therefore, and let us adhere to the words as they read: that the body of Christ is present in the bread and that his body is truly present in the wine. This does not mean that he is not present in other places also with his body and blood, for in believing hearts he is completely present with his body and blood. But it means that he wishes to make us certain as to where and how we are to lay hold of him. There is the Word, which says that when you eat the bread you eat his body, given for you. If the Word were not there, I would not pay any heed to the bread. The Sacrament—Against the Fanatics.[27]

The Word *Is* Means "Signifies." Cornelis Hoen: Nor indeed did the apostles speak of the sacrament in this fashion [that is, as transubstantiation]; they *broke* bread, and *called* it bread: no word about this Roman belief. Nor is this contradicted by St. Paul who, although he says "The bread that we break, is it not a participation in the body of Christ?" does not say that the bread *is* the body of Christ. It is therefore obvious that in this text "is" [*est*] should be interpreted as meaning "signifies" [*significat*]; it is all the more clear from the comparisons St. Paul draws between our bread and the food offered to idols. Such food is, according to St. Paul, not changed in reality; notwithstanding this he can say: it "is" or "signifies" some sort of communion with the devil to whom the food is offered. . . . There were some in the time of Thomas Aquinas who said on this very issue that Christ was in the bread, but only as a sign, that Christ was present not corporeally but only sacramentally. And although Thomas rejected this position as heretical, the Romanists, who hand on his word as if they were an oracle, were not able to explain away Christ's assertion, "If anyone says to you that Christ is here do not believe him." . . .

[26]BoC 321* (WA 50:242, 243); citing 1 Cor 10:16. Luther is arguing against the Catholic doctrine of sacramental concomitance, articulated by the Council of Constance (1415), which asserted that "the whole body and blood of Christ are truly contained under both the form of bread and the form of wine." At the same time, the Council of Constance reaffirmed the church's requirement that laypeople only receive the bread (and not the wine) in the Eucharist. See Tanner, *Decrees of the Ecumenical Councils*, 1:418-19.

[27]LW 36:346*. The "fanatics" to whom Luther alludes here are (in order), Andreas Bodenstein von Karlstadt, Huldrych Zwingli, and Johannes Oecolampadius.

Neither the prophets foretold nor the apostles preached that Christ would daily become bread, so to speak, in the hands of any sacrificing priest. This idea is founded only on this saying of Christ, "This is my body, this do in remembrance of me." If Christ by these words intended what they say he did, certainly we do not doubt that just *one* word should suffice. But I wonder why they do not also say that John the Baptist was transubstantiated into Elijah, since Christ said to him, "He *is* Elijah"; or that John was transubstantiated into Christ when Christ said to him on the cross, "Woman, behold your son," or that Christ was transubstantiated into a stone when he, referring to himself, said, "Upon this rock I will build my church." A Most Christian Letter.[28]

The Literal Meaning of This Passage Teaches Remembrance of Christ. Andreas Bodenstein von Karlstadt: They break the Scripture who want to cite Christ's words, "The bread is the body," for Christ never said this. Instead, he said, "Take and eat. This is my body, which is given for you. Do this in my remembrance." From this, according to the literal understanding, nothing else follows but that Christ's body is the body that must be given for the world, and that we should take and eat his bread in his remembrance. But not only can one not understand from the literal contents that the bread was the body of Christ, but it is against the characteristics of the Greek language. First, it is against the punctuation, for this verse, "This is my body, which is given for you," etc. is separated from the previous verse by a period. In addition, it begins with a capital letter, as you can see in Luke. . . .

Thus one should pay attention to these words and observe that Christ gave his body for us. This is necessary, and the gospel and faith together require it. But the blind guides lead us to bread and say that we should take to heart that the bread is the body of Christ, although no Scripture shows this. They also make the simple pay much more attention to how the bread is the body of Christ than to eating the bread in ardent remembrance of Christ, to their judgment. Proving from Scripture.[29]

The Lord's Supper Is a Commemoration of Christ's Death. Huldrych Zwingli: Paul repeats the exact words of Christ, where it is clear (if we pay close attention) that we are not given his *body* in memory of his body, but bread [in memory of his body]. Now it is by metonymy that the bread is called his body and the wine his blood, by which the name of a thing assumes a symbolic figure and a designated sign. Since excellent books have been written about this matter, it is not necessary to write more here. Therefore this is the sense of the words "Take, eat, this is my body," that is, "this *represents* my body, or is a *remembrance* of my body, which is given for you." For it immediately follows, "Do this in remembrance of me." By this clause we perceive that this eating should not be understood as a feeding on the body of Christ for the strengthening of our soul or faith, but as a commemoration. Annotations on 1 Corinthians 11:24.[30]

Believers Feed On Christ's Body in Heaven. John Calvin: Let it be beyond controversy that Christ is speaking about the bread in this passage. Now we ask, in what sense? In order to arrive at the meaning, we must insist that the expression is figurative—for a person would have to be exceedingly wicked to deny that. Why then is the term "body" attributed to the bread? Everyone, I think, would agree that for the same reason John calls the Holy Spirit a dove. Thus far we are agreed. Further, the reason the Spirit was so-called was that he appeared under the form of a

[28]Hoen, "A Most Christian Letter," in Heiko A. Oberman, *Forerunners of the Reformation. The Shape of Late Medieval Thought* (New York: Holt, Rinehart and Winston, 1966), 269-70*.

[29]Karlstadt, *Proving from Holy Scripture That Christ Is in the Sacrament*, in *The Eucharistic Pamphlets of Andreas Bodenstein von Karlstadt*, ed. Amy Nelson Burnett (Kirksville, MO: Truman State University Press, 2011), 137-38; citing Lk 22:19-20.

[30]Zwingli, *Annotatiunculae . . . ex ore Zvinglij*, 93-94.

dove. Therefore the name Spirit is transferred to the visible sign. Why, then, should we not say that *metonym* is used in this passage in a similar fashion, and that the term body is attributed to the bread, because it is a sign and symbol of the body? . . . And so I take it as a settled point, that this is a sacramental way of speaking, when the Lord applies to the sign the name of the thing signified.

We must now proceed further and ask the reason for the metonym. My answer is that the name of the thing signified is not only applied to the sign because it represents it, but even more because it is a symbol by which the reality is presented to us. For I do not agree with those comparisons that some people borrow from secular or earthly things. The statue of Hercules is called Hercules, but what is this other than a bare and empty representation? But the dove is called the Spirit, because it is a certain pledge of the presence of the invisible Spirit. Therefore the bread is the body of Christ, because it testifies with certainty that the body it represents is offered to us. . . . Accordingly, it appears incontrovertible to me that the reality is here joined to the sign; that is, we really do become partakers in the body of Christ (as far as spiritual power is concerned) when we eat the bread. . . .

I conclude that Christ's body is really (as people commonly say)—that is, truly—given to us in the Supper as health-giving food for our souls. I am using the common expression, but my meaning is that our souls are fed on the substance of his body so that we are truly made one with him. Or, what amounts to the same thing, that a life-giving power from the flesh of Christ is poured into us by the Spirit, even though [his flesh] is a great distance from us and not mixed with us. . . .

But that participation in the Lord's body that (I maintain) is presented to us in the Supper does not demand a local presence, nor the descent of Christ, nor an infinite extension, nor anything of that sort. For since the Supper is a heavenly act, there is nothing absurd in saying that Christ, while remaining in heaven, is received by us. For the way that he communicates himself to us is by the secret power of the Holy Spirit, a power that is not only able to bring together, but also to join together, things that are separated by distance and are far from one other. Commentary on 1 Corinthians 11:24.[31]

Believers Commune on God's Grace in the Lord's Supper. Wolfgang Musculus: Someone might say here: So, then, in the Lord's Supper, we do nothing more than eat bread and drink wine, and by doing this we remember the Lord? I respond: We do indeed eat bread and drink wine, but not as ordinary physical food and drink, but as the bread and cup of the Lord (as it is called by the apostle and early church fathers), or as the sanctified bread and cup (as it is called by Cyprian), or as the sacrament of the body and blood of the Lord in which, as Augustine puts it, one thing is seen, another understood, as symbols and mysteries of grace of the new covenant, which we receive from the Lord's table. We chew and drink not only with our physical mouth but also with the mouth of faith, and in so doing we proclaim the death of the Lord with thanksgiving, and thereby our faith is strengthened. Thus in eating and drinking, we do not feed only on bread, but on mystical bread; we do not gaze on the outer shell, but we gaze on the inner substance of the sweetest thing of all, namely, the Lord's body crucified for us and his blood poured out for us. We feed on God's grace by faith and are renewed. Commentary on 1 Corinthians 11:24.[32]

The Sacrament Is a Holy Mystery. John Jewel: We affirm that bread and wine are holy and heavenly mysteries of the body and blood of Christ, and that by them Christ himself, being the true bread of eternal life, is so presently given to us that by faith we truly receive his body and blood. Yet we don't mean by this that the very nature of bread is changed and becomes nothing, as many have dreamed in these latter times—yet these people

[31]CO 49:486-88 (cf. CTS 39:366-78, 379, 380); citing Jn 1:32.
[32]Musculus, *Comm. 1 Cor.*, 428.

could never agree among themselves as to these dreams. For that was not Christ's meaning, that the wheaten bread should lay aside its own nature and receive a certain new divinity; rather, [Christ's meaning was] that he might change us, and (to use Theophylact's words) might transform us into his body. For what can be said more plainly than that which Ambrose said, "Bread and wine remain still the same as they were before, and yet changed into another thing"; or that which Gelasius says, "The substance of the bread, or the nature of the wine, do not cease to be." . . .

And in speaking in this way we do not mean to abase the Lord's Supper, or to teach that it is only a cold ceremony and nothing to be wrought therein (as many people falsely slander us to teach). For we affirm that Christ does truly and presently give himself wholly in his sacraments; in baptism, that we may put him on; and in his Supper, that we may eat him by faith and spirit and may have everlasting life by his cross and blood. And we do not say that this is done slightly and coldly, but effectually and truly. For, although we do not touch the body of Christ with teeth and mouth, yet we hold him fast and eat him by faith, by understanding, and by spirit. Apology.[33]

The Bread Is Not the Body of Christ. Balthasar Hubmaier: Here everybody can see that bread is bread and wine is wine, like other bread and wine. But it is instituted by Christ as a reminder and memorial. For as often as we break the bread together, distribute it, and eat, we should remember his body broken for us on the cross and distributed to all those who eat and enjoy it in faith. Here it is obvious that the bread is not the body of Christ but only a reminder thereof. Likewise, the wine is not the blood of Christ but also a memorial that he shed his blood and distributed it on the cross to all believers for the washing away of our sins, as the hoop in front of the tavern is not wine, but a remembrance thereof. It is fitting that we should remember and not forget his goodness but should proclaim, shout out, and be grateful for it to all eternity. Paul admonishes us very earnestly of this when he writes to the Corinthians in 1 Cor 11:26: "As often as you eat the bread (notice: he takes it as bread, and it is bread) and you drink the cup, that is, the wine (notice that it is wine which is drunk) you shall proclaim the death of the Lord until he comes." Notice: he says "until he comes." From this we hear that he is not present but will come only at the hour of the last judgment, in his great majesty and glory shining visibly to everybody as the lightning from east to west. Summa of the Entire Christian Life.[34]

Catholic Doctrine of Transubstantiation Is Ridiculous. John Trapp: Take note, says Beza, of this so-called holy consecration, concerning which the tonsured priests[35] say that they are more holy than the Virgin Mary, since Mary only conceived Christ, but they create him. To which the Virgin might reply that she carefully nourished the Christ, but they cruelly devour him. A professor said to a martyr, "Do you believe that Christ's body and blood are in the Eucharist really and substantially?" "I believe," he said, "that that is a real and substantial lie." Commentary on 1 Corinthians 11:24.[36]

Disagreements Over the Lord's Supper Do Not Empty It of Its Power. Valentin Weigel: Whoever has put on [Christ Jesus] through baptism is given food and drink through the very same Spirit with the flesh and blood of Christ to eternal life. He is unable to die eternal death, but temporal death he dies daily. Now such daily dying is his life. Such a person can truly say: "Christ is my life." That is, "Christ's death in me is my life, for without Christ's death in me I would have no life at all." Whoever is thus baptized and

[33]Jewel, *Apology of the Church of England*, 33, 34*. Theophylact's statement is found in his commentary *In Joannis* 16; Ambrose's statement is found in his *De sacramentis* 4.4; Gelasius's statement is found in his *Adversus Eutychetem et Nestorium*.

[34]CRR 5:88-89.

[35]Literally "shavelings."

[36]Trapp, *A Commentary or Exposition*, 688*.

fed through the Spirit of faith receives also the food of this commemoration.

In the Supper he receives the true body of Christ and drinks the blood of Christ. The body that was given for him on the cross; the blood that was poured out on the beam of the holy cross for his sins, as Christ says with explicit words: "This is my body; this is my blood," etc. In vain and for nothing is it that a sect persecutes and labels another as heretical on account of the sacraments. No Christian is entitled to this, nor does a true Christian do this; only false Christians establish themselves as masters over heretics and judges over their neighbors. For what do we battle and quarrel over the body and blood of Christ in the Supper [and] over holy baptism (even though they are the foremost articles)? All the same, for Christians, there is still one Supper, one bread, for everyone one baptism, one faith, etc.

I say through God's gracious gifting that I have no qualms with myself nor do I take offense with any other Christians. Be I wherever in the world I might be. Yes, I would receive among every sect in baptism and in the Supper nothing other than what Christ has granted and established. Some sects claim that in the bread and wine there is nothing, only bread and wine, merely a reminder of the absent body. What does it matter to me? If I am among them and participate in the Supper with them, I receive indeed the body and blood of Christ in the bread and wine. Their opinion does not affect what Christ has commanded to be established and received. Nor does it harm my faith.

Other sects claim transubstantiation. What does it matter to me? If I am among them, I receive in the bread and wine the true body and blood of Christ according to his command and institution. Another sect even claims that Christ's body and blood are received, many of them believe it will blot out their sins, but they do not repent, they do not die with Christ. Every one of them takes [the Supper] to their eternal death. What does it matter to me? If I am among them, the Spirit of Christ still teaches me that I am able in the bread and wine to take the body and blood of Christ for the commemoration of his death, so that I refresh and strengthen the eternal covenant; that I will be united with Christ and remain loved, persevering until death. POSTIL ON THE GOSPEL FOR QUINQUAGESIMAE.[37]

THIS CUP IS THE NEW COVENANT IN MY BLOOD. JOHN CALVIN: What Paul affirmed regarding the cup applies also to the bread. And so he expresses by this statement what he had previously stated more briefly—that the bread is his body. Therefore it is given to us for this reason, that it may be a covenant in his body, that is, a covenant that has been once for all ratified by the sacrifice of his body, and is now confirmed by eating, namely, when believers feast on that sacrifice. And so what Paul and Luke call the "covenant in my blood," and Matthew and Mark call the "blood of the covenant"—these amount to the same thing. For the blood was poured out to reconcile us to God, and now we drink it spiritually in order to be partakers of reconciliation. That is why, in the Supper, we have both the covenant and a confirmation of the covenant. COMMENTARY ON 1 CORINTHIANS 11:25.[38]

THE CUP REPRESENTS SUFFERING. ANABAPTISTS OF TRIESTE: A memorial sign or something by which one may remember is of two sorts. If Christ were always present in his body there would be no need to say that by [the Lord's Supper] they should remember him until he returned. He would not have spoken of coming again if he was always present. He said: you always have the poor with you, but you do not always have me (Mark 14). He said the same thing about the cup. They did not literally drink his blood. It would have been of no use since what goes into the mouth goes into the stomach and out again in the natural way. It does the soul no good. Rather, he instituted the chalice of the New Testament, which is suffering. As they received it from his hand and all drank of it, they

[37]Weigel, *Sämtliche Schriften* 12,1:140-42; citing 2 Cor 4:7-12.
[38]CO 49:489 (cf. CTS 39:382-83); citing Lk 22:20; Mt 26:28; Mk 14:24.

would be required to drink from the cup of the suffering of Christ with him. Confession.[39]

The Cup and the New Covenant. The English Annotations: As the bread is not the very body of Christ, but a sacrament thereof, so neither is the cup the new testament or covenant, but rather a sign and seal of it. As the covenant of God is renewed with his elect and ratified by his death and passion, so by the cup of the Lord it is also sealed to every faithful Christian. . . . By the word "cup," Paul is employing a common synecdoche[40] (as all grant) to refer to what is contained in the cup . . . which must be wine, not blood. For the apostle here says that the cup is the new testament in Christ's blood; that is, the wine in the cup is a sign and seal of the new testament that was confirmed by Christ's blood, which he shed on the cross, in the same way that the old testament or covenant was confirmed by the effusion of the blood of sacrificed animals, sprinkled on the people (Ex 24:8). Annotations on 1 Corinthians 11:25.[41]

The Lord's Supper Is a Memorial. Balthasar Hubmaier: "For so often as you eat of this bread, etc.": The sum and final cause of the Supper is briefly summarized in these words. Namely, that the Supper is a remembrance, a memorial sign, and a reminder of the suffering of Christ, and not a sacrifice. A Simple Instruction.[42]

For as Often as You Eat This Bread. Tilemann Hesshus: Therefore, Christ not only celebrated [this Supper] with his apostles, but he also wants us to imitate [his example] as we eat his body under the consecrated bread and drink his blood under the consecrated wine. For Paul here addresses the Corinthians and the entire church. The Lord's Supper is not an indifferent thing for us to use or abstain from. Rather, God sternly commands us through the words of the apostle to make frequent use of this Supper. Therefore those people who rarely approach the table of the Lord sin grievously against God. Let the reader take note here that, in the early church, the Lord's Supper was administered without mutilating the elements, with the blood of Jesus Christ being distributed to laypeople as well as to priests. For Paul is writing to the entire Corinthian church, and he commands that every person should frequently eat the Lord's body and drink from the Lord's cup. Therefore those wicked Roman popes ought to be cursed for having snatched the blood of Christ away from the people. Moreover, the apostle Paul tells us that in celebrating this Supper, we proclaim the Lord's death. He does not want the administration of the Supper to be a speechless spectacle that is conducted in profound silence. Rather, it ought to resound with a public confession concerning the crucified and resurrected Jesus Christ, so that the church might be gathered together and our faith might be aroused and confirmed by this public affirmation. Explication on 1 Corinthians 11:26.[43]

Until Christ Returns. Wolfgang Musculus: Paul indicates that this mystical Supper is also for proclaiming the Lord's death, and that this ceremony must not be abandoned or changed until he returns, which will happen at the end of the world. When Christ comes, there will be no further reason for celebrating this remembrance, because we will then be in his presence and will live together with him forever. While we are in this body, we are pilgrims from the Lord. For we walk by faith, not by sight. In this world, we do not enjoy the sight that we will enjoy in the future. Instead, we are sustained by faith, and we fellowship with the Lord through pious disciplines, deeds, and heartfelt devotion; this is where the ceremony of remembering the Lord is applicable. The Lord is certainly present with us through his Spirit, and through him this training of our faith is rendered effective. Nevertheless, the external appearance of the sacrament that is eaten is inferior to its full

[39]CRR 10:271; citing Mk 14:7.
[40] Synecdoche is a figure of speech in which a part is taken to represent the whole, or vice versa.
[41]Downame, *The English Annotations*, EE2r*.
[42]CRR 5:333.
[43]Hesshus, *Explicatio Prioris Epistolae ad Corinthios*, 256v.

delight, as Bernard says somewhere, in the same way that . . . faith is to sight, remembrance is to presence, eternity is to time, and the face is to a mirror. When by sight we delight in the glory of Christ's presence, the sacraments of this new covenant will find their fulfillment. The remembrance of Christ has been ordained for the present time, even as his presence will be ours in the future; for the former is of faith, and the latter of sight. Commentary on 1 Corinthians 11:26.[44]

11:27-34 *Eating in a Worthy—and an Unworthy—Manner*

The Best Preparation for Reception of the Sacrament. Johann Spangenberg: Whenever you find yourself weak in faith, cold in love, faint-hearted in hope, inclined to every sin; and you long to be strong in faith, ablaze in love, mighty in hope, and free from your sin; you long to be pious, humble, compassionate, at peace, righteous, gentle, sober, meek, faithful, and truthful—then you are the best prepared [for the sacrament]. The greater your hunger and thirst for righteousness, the better prepared you are. For this heavenly meal demands a hungry soul. Whoever is already full does not belong here. Mary sings in the Magnificat, "the hungry he has filled with good things and the rich he has left empty." So then, approach in faith and brotherly love with contemplation and sorrow for your sins, with sincere intention to shun sin and all its causes—with thanksgiving to God! And be sure that you receive the sacrament according to its fruits, as the signs of the sacrament—bread and wine—indicate. Certainly then you will find yourself in God's blessing, Christ's help and assistance, grace and lovingkindness, and finally eternal life. Help us to do this, God our Father, through your dear Son, Jesus Christ. Amen. Postil on the Epistle for Maundy Thursday.[45]

Different Degrees of "Unworthiness." John Calvin: To eat in an unworthy manner . . . is to pervert the pure and right use [of the sacrament] by our abuse of it. And so there are various degrees of unworthiness, so to speak. Some people sin more grievously, others less grievously. Some fornicators, perjurers, drunkards, or cheats may force their way in without repentance. Since reckless contempt like that is a sign of a cruel insult against Christ, there can be no doubt that these persons, whoever they are, receive the Supper to their own destruction. Other people will come [to the table] who are engaged in no obvious or flagrant vices, but nevertheless they have not prepared their hearts as they should have. Since this carelessness or negligence is a sign of irreverence, they also deserve punishment from God. Thus, just as there are various degrees of eating unworthily, so the Lord punishes some more lightly, while on others he inflicts more severe punishments. Commentary on 1 Corinthians 11:27.[46]

The Wicked Also Feed on Christ in the Lord's Supper. Tilemann Hesshus: Now, if, as the Calvinists contend, we only eat the flesh of Christ spiritually by faith; and if we receive in the sacred Supper only the power and efficacy of Christ's absent body; and if the consecrated bread is only a *symbol* of Christ's body, which has been carried into heaven and is located far from us, then one must necessarily conclude that people who are unworthy, negligent, hypocritical, or without saving faith are not made participants in the Lord's body and blood. For the unworthy and those who are outside the faith do not at all participate in the power and efficacy of the body of Christ; they are not freed from sin or made alive by the Spirit of Christ; instead, they remain in their sin and are under God's wrath, excluded from all participation in the benefits of Christ. "Those who do not believe in the Son will not see life, but God's wrath remains on them." But Paul clearly teaches that not only believers but also the unworthy and negligent

[44]Musculus, *Comm. 1 Cor.*, 432-33. See Bernard of Clairvaux, *Sermons on the Song of Songs* 33.3 (PL 183:952).
[45]Spangenberg, *Postilla Teüsch*, 4:189r-v; Lk 1:53.
[46]CO 49:491 (cf. CTS 39:385-86).

are made participants of Christ's body in the sacred Lord's Supper. For the apostle Paul warns the Corinthians with the severe statement that those who eat this bread in an unworthy manner are condemned on account of Christ's body. Paul states that people who eat this bread in an unworthy manner are those who do not examine themselves; that is, they thoughtlessly and boldly run up to the Lord's Table without being repentant, without true contrition or faith. He says that these people are condemned on account of Christ's body and blood. But this very serious condemnation will not be imposed unless a person ingests the Lord's body and blood. Now, if Christ's body and blood are absent [from the elements], and unworthy people only eat bread and drink wine, how are they condemned on account of Christ's body and blood? What the Calvinists assert is therefore frivolous. Explication of 1 Corinthians 11:27-28.[47]

The Wicked Do Not Receive Christ in the Sacrament. John Calvin: I take it as an axiom—and I will never allow myself to be diverted from it—that Christ cannot be separated from his Spirit. That convinces me that, when we receive his body, it is neither dead nor even passive, nor is his body divorced from the grace and power of his Spirit. (I shall not spend much time in proving this statement.) Now if a person is completely devoid of a living faith and repentance, since they do not have the Spirit of Christ, how can they receive Christ himself? Indeed, since they are completely under the influence of Satan and sin, how are they capable to receive Christ? Therefore, while I confess that there are some people who truly receive Christ in the Supper and yet, at the same time, do so unworthily—such is the case with many weak persons—nevertheless I do not admit that those who exercise only a faith in the historical events of the gospel, without a lively awareness of repentance and faith, receive anything but the sign. For I cannot bear to tear Christ apart, and I recoil from that absurd notion that Christ gives himself to be eaten by wicked people in a lifeless condition. Commentary on 1 Corinthians 11:27.[48]

Judas Ate Unworthily. Dirk Philips: From this it follows incontrovertibly that the unbelieving and evil ones have no part in the flesh and blood of Christ, so little as they are and abide in Christ, and Christ in them. Though they may eat the bread of Judas, they did not through this partake of the body and blood of Christ, but much more become guilty because of it. This is what Paul writes to the Corinthians: "Whoever therefore, eats unworthily from the bread and drinks the cup of the Lord, that one is guilty of the body and blood of the Lord" (1 Cor 11:27). For to be guilty of the body and blood of the Lord and to partake of the body and blood of Christ is not the same thing; they are far separated from each other. For through faith one becomes spiritually a partaker of Christ and his gifts, yes, of his flesh and blood. But through the abuse of the Supper one becomes guilty of the body and blood of the Lord and drinks judgment on himself, etc. (1 Cor 11:29).

We have an example of this in Judas, for even though he ate the bread and drank the wine with the apostles, nevertheless the bread was for him no fellowship of the body of Christ, and the cup no fellowship of his blood (as it was for the other apostles). For he was and remained before, in, and after the Supper in the fellowship of Satan. But all those who eat Christ are in his fellowship (just as he himself testified with the previously spoken words), and they may not be in the fellowship of Satan. . . .

[Therefore] Paul admonishes us that we must first test ourselves before eating the bread of the Supper and drinking from the cup (1 Cor 11:28). For whoever does not have a true faith in Jesus Christ, whoever is not incorporated into Christ, whoever does not want to die and live with Christ,

[47]Hesshus, *Explicatio Prioris Epistolae ad Corinthios*, 194r-195r; citing Jn 3:36.

[48]CO 49:491-92 (cf. CTS 39:386-87).

whoever does not have an upright love for Christ and neighbor, whoever is not one body with Christ and all the saints, that one may never more rightly use the Supper (which is, after all, a symbol of divine and brotherly love and unity) nor rightly distinguish the body of the Lord. The Supper of Our Lord Jesus Christ.[49]

Excommunication Protects People from Communing Unworthily. Martin Bucer: Now, since the holy Supper is the most glorious and joyful remembrance and communion of the Lord, in which there is given and imparted the highest pardon, complete peace, and perfect communion with Christ and all his members, the Holy Spirit has ordained and always maintained in his churches that, although those who repent are always to be comforted with the grace of God and salvation of Christ and are to be encouraged to share in the communion of Christ, which alone brings true atonement for sin, yet they are to be excluded and kept away from the holy Supper until such time as they have demonstrated their repentance in true humility so that the church may completely pardon them and forgive their sins. In the same way with the ancients, penitents were not admitted to the greater thank offerings until they had fulfilled their penance and purification, although in those offerings the communion of Christ and forgiveness of God were not so gloriously and actually imparted as they are in the holy Supper. This table is ordained for the disciples of Christ, who are, indeed, one body and one loaf in Christ; but those are not to be accepted who are bound to penance and have not yet been forgiven by the church. And it is not right for them to forgive someone as soon as they say, "I repent of my sins," when there is nothing to indicate that repentance. True Care of Souls.[50]

Self-Examination Is Necessary. David Dickson: Paul shows how easy it is to prepare to receive the sacrament in a worthy manner. He says that persons need only to examine themselves, being sensible of the greatness of their sin and misery so that they might recognize how much they need the remedy provided by Christ. And they should recognize their obligation to faith and commitment to holiness as they approach communing with Christ, and how they are lost a thousand times without him. And having examined themselves, then let them eat and drink in that holy banquet; that is, let them apply the thing signified by participating in the sign, so that they might recognize the need they have of it. Exposition of 1 Corinthians 11:28.[51]

Test Yourselves Before Eating. Balthasar Hubmaier: Before eating from the table of the Lord, people should test themselves and recollect whether they are so minded toward their neighbor. There is a great difference between the Christ meal and another meal, although all table meals should be accepted with thanksgiving. Nevertheless, in the Christ meal one should proclaim the death of Christ, and obligate and bind oneself together with body and blood in brotherly service through this visible word symbol and not come together merely for the sake of eating and drinking. . . .

We conclude that the bread and wine of the Christ meal are outward word symbols of an inward Christian nature here on earth, in which Christians obligate themselves to one another in Christian love with regard to body and blood. Thus as the body and blood of Christ became my body and blood on the cross, so likewise shall my body and blood become the body and blood of my neighbor, and in time of need theirs become my body and blood, or we cannot boast at all to be Christians. That is the will of Christ in the Supper. Whoever now rejects the will of Christ and does not do it and hardens themselves in all abuses shall rightly be punished with many plagues. Thenceforth come dearth, hail, pestilence, earthquakes, drought, dying, bloodshed, rebellion, and

[49]CRR 6:116-17, 129*.

[50]Bucer, *Concerning the True Care of Souls*, 135-36.

[51]Dickson, *Exposition of St. Paul's Epistles*, 60*.

all kinds of miseries and adversities. That is what I believe concerning the Christ meal. To All Christians Concerning the Instruction of the Mass.[52]

God Judges the Secrets of the Heart. Menno Simons: If anyone has a good appearance before other people, and is inwardly proud, avaricious, carnal, and without the Spirit of God, such a person is not judged by the church but by the Lord himself, the searcher of people's hearts and reins, as Scripture says. We therefore admonish all those who would go to the Lord's table to examine themselves before they go to this banquet, for all who eat unworthily of this bread and drink of this wine, eat and drink damnation to themselves. Foundation of Christian Doctrine.[53]

Infants Should Not Receive the Lord's Supper. Heinrich Bullinger: Augustine defends in more than one place the view that partaking of the Eucharist (that is, the sacrament of the Lord's Supper) is as necessary for newborn infants as is the sacrament of baptism. . . . But who in our day receives that ceremony as apostolic? Who doesn't see that those good [early church] fathers, who were otherwise very faithful pastors, in this matter allowed a human invention? The written doctrine of St. Paul deserves today to be more highly esteemed than the ancient traditions of the church. Paul writes: "Let everyone examine themselves, and so eat of this bread and drink of this cup." Whereby everyone should understand that the Eucharist, or sacrament of the Lord's Supper, should be received by people who are of mature age, and not infants. That is the reason it was permissible for our elders to forsake that tradition, and to draw closer to the [teaching of] Scripture. Decades.[54]

[52]CRR 5:76*.

[53]Simons, *Complete Writings*, 150.

[54]Bullinger, *Decades*, 3:398*. Augustine endorsed paedo-Communion in several places in his writings, including his treatise *On the Forgiveness of Sins and the Baptism of Infants* (1.26-27, 33).

To Commune Rightly We Must Be Imitators of Christ. John Colet: Those who abuse his kindnesses the Lord afflicts and punishes. All men and women, then, ought surely to punish themselves, to reprove and scrutinize and test and prove themselves, so that instead of God's punishment they may merit God's approval. Before people partake [of the Eucharist], they should put themselves to the test whether they are imitating Christ, lest they should die from that food that the sinner cannot endure. . . .

When Jesus was about to die, the disciples ate together of him; and they too would soon die so that they might rise with him when he returns. From that time on, all [Christians] take this very same sacrament; and all of them die together so that they all might rise again together when he comes. Exposition of 1 Corinthians 11.[55]

Worthy Reception of the Sacrament. Martin Luther: St. Augustine says, the sacrament seeks a hungry, thirsty, and desirous soul that yearns for it. But those who go only because of command or out of habit feel no desire or longing for it, but rather horror or dread, so that they would rather be away from it than near it. Persons with a yearning heart do not wait for a command, nor are they moved by precept or habit. They are driven by their need and their desire. They have their mind fixed only on the sacrament, which they desire. . . .

Such hunger and thirst are created not by compelling people, but by showing them their frailty and their need so that they will see their wretched condition and feel the desire to be delivered from it. This happens, for instance, when you recognize that you are weak in faith, cold in love, and faint in hope. You will find that you are disposed toward hatred and impatience, impurity, greed, and whatever other vice there is. This you will undoubtedly find and feel if you really look at yourself. All the saints have found this to be true about themselves. . . .

[55]Colet, *Enarratio*, 228.

The priest's elevation of the sacrament and the cup, together with the ringing of the bells, has no other purpose than to remind us of the words of Christ. It's as if the priest and the bell-ringer were saying to us all, "Listen, you Christians, and see, take and eat, take and drink, etc. 'This is the body and this is the blood of Christ,' spoken softly by the priest, but heard clearly and audibly by us." With these words you must now edify your hungry heart and rely on the truth of this divine promise, and then receive the sacrament, make your way to God, and say, "Lord, it is true that I am not worthy for you to come under my roof, but I need and desire your help and grace to make me godly. I do not come to you, trusting only in the wonderful words I just heard, with which you invite me to your table and promise me, the unworthy one, forgiveness of all my sins through your body and blood if I eat and drink them in this sacrament. Amen. Dear Lord, I do not doubt the truth of your words. Trusting them, I eat and I drink with you. Do unto me according to your words. Amen." ... Then you are indeed worthy of the sacrament. Sermon on the Worthy Reception of the Sacrament.[56]

A Prayer to Commune in a Worthy Fashion. Katharina Schütz Zell: O dear Father, grant that we may also be truly fed and strengthened with this bread so that we may not eat the bread of the Lord unworthily, to our judgment, and be guilty of the body and blood of Jesus Christ, but that we may be able to discern his body and not abandon or despise his members, but forgive, love, build up, help, and give them food and drink, as Christ has done for us. O dear Father, grant that we may well prove whether we have faith in the Son of God and the bond of a good conscience through the resurrection of Jesus Christ. Grant that we may make our election firm by showing whether the death of Christ Jesus lives in us and we are dead to sin; whether we also want to drink the cup with Christ and with him be baptized in the cross, in his death; and whether we love our neighbors as he loved us. That way we may show whether we have fellowship with all God's children in the blood of Christ and they have fellowship with us for Christ's sake: fellowship in our goods, assistance, counsel, teaching, honor, and life. That way we show that we discern the body of the Lord, we show what the power and nature of his fellowship are, and then we eat the fellowship of this bread. Our Father with Its Explanation.[57]

God's Table Is a Snare for Those Who Receive Unworthily. John Trapp: Paul says not "unworthy" (for so we all are) but "unworthily," that is, without preparation. For a good work may be spoiled in the doing, as many a good tale is marred in the telling, and many a good garment is ruined in the making. "Eat and drink judgment." He who entered without wearing a wedding garment went away not without fetters on his feet. He was taken from the table to the tormentors. God's table becomes a snare to unworthy recipients; they eat their bane and drink their poison. Emperor Henry VII of Germany was poisoned in the sacramental bread by a monk. Pope Victor II was poisoned by his subdeacon in the chalice. And one of our bishops of York was killed by poison put into the sacramental wine. [These examples show that] God will deal with ill-communicants. Commentary on 1 Corinthians 11:28-29.[58]

Averting God's Punishment. Tilemann Hesshus: The multitude of punishments that God is inflicting on the Corinthians demonstrates the seriousness of the sin and the magnitude of the guilt they are committing by their negligence and unworthy partaking [of the Lord's Supper]. Paul says, "Because you Corinthians are not sincerely repenting, but instead are living in a negligent

[56]LW 42:171-74*. Augustine's statement is found in his *Enarratio in psalmos* 21 (NPNF 8:60).

[57]In McKee, *Katharina Schütz Zell*, 166-67.

[58]Trapp, *A Commentary or Exposition*, 688*. Henry VII (b. 1275) was emperor of the Holy Roman Empire for barely a year, when he died (reportedly) of malaria in 1313. The German Pope Victor II occupied the papal office from 1055 to 1057.

fashion and profaning the Lord's Supper, for that reason God is afflicting you with various diseases and sternly reproving you in order to call you back to serious repentance." Life was shorter for many people because, by their negligence, they had provoked the wrath of God.

"For if we judged ourselves, we would not be judged by the Lord"; that is, if we were to seriously fear the wrath of God, we would sincerely repent and throw off our negligent attitude; we would seek to mitigate our punishment by truly fearing God and trusting in the Mediator. And God would no doubt bestow his divine blessing and a longer and happier life; even more, he would restrain his wrath. When the heathen repent, God not only pardons their sins and imputes righteousness to them but also mitigates temporal punishments and confers blessing on many of them in various ways. When Manasseh repented, God lessened his punishment and freed him from captivity. When the Ninevites repented, God spared them and altered his plan to destroy the city. And although David was severely punished by God with exile and various calamities—even though he returned to God in true repentance—yet God treated him much better than if he had persisted in that wickedness of his. Therefore Paul is here exhorting all Christians to repentance, and he assures those who repent a lessening of disaster, according to the promise of Joel 2: "Thus says the Lord: turn to me with all your heart, with weeping and fasting. Rend your heart, not your garments, and return to the Lord your God, for he is gracious, merciful, slow to anger, and rich in goodness, and he brings those who repent out of disaster." Commentary on 1 Corinthians 11:30-31.[59]

Adversities Are Works of God's Goodwill. Philipp Melanchthon: The one and only consolation in all adversities is that we are being tested by God's goodwill and for our salvation, according to that statement of Proverbs 3: "For the Lord reproves those whom he loves." And too this passage, "But when we are judged by the Lord, we are chastened so that we may not be condemned along with the world," because the wickedness within the human heart cannot be shown nor the mercy of God proclaimed unless it is tested by various temptations. Hence we must take the greatest care in all times of testing to embrace them as works of God's goodwill. Thus Proverbs 3 says, "Do not be weary when you are tested by God"; that is, do not lose confidence that all these things happen by God's goodwill. Also, in John 6 Christ beautifully teaches, saying to the fearful disciples, "It is I; do not be afraid." Annotations on 1 Corinthians 11:32.[60]

The Lord's Supper Is a Public Sacrament. Peter Martyr Vermigli: Following this general discussion, Paul now delivers specific instructions to the Corinthians . . . in order to correct the disorder surrounding their assemblies. "When you come together to eat," he says, "don't do it to watch or adore [the elements], or carry them around. For the purpose of the Lord's Supper is to eat the elements." Even though some people apply these words to feasts[61] as we have already said (which does not displease me entirely), this provides no relief for our adversaries, for those feasts were held in conjunction with the celebration of the Eucharist, and Paul is correcting in his discussion of the Eucharist the sins committed in those feasts. Thus what is said about the one applies to the other. "When you come together. . . ." Paul prescribes no specific time, since the sacraments are not restricted to times. "Wait for one another." Paul wants them to be very careful lest they perform in private what ought to be done in public. "If anyone is hungry, let them eat at home." The sacraments were not instituted to satisfy the needs of the body. The ancients considered the manna and water from the rock in that way, but the Gospels do not view the

[59]Hesshus, *Explicatio Prioris Epistolae ad Corinthios*, 260r-v; citing 2 Chron 33:13; Jon 3:1-10; Joel 2:12.

[60]Melanchthon, *Annotationes in Epistolam priorem ad Corinthios*, 126; citing Prov 3:12, 11; Jn 6:20.

[61]That is, the agape meals.

sacraments for this purpose. Nevertheless, as we said earlier, in the time of Tertullian . . . the Eucharist was eaten privately in households before the common meal. Cyprian remembers that it was permitted for Christians, after they had communed in the temple, to bring a portion of the sacraments home, which later on they shared with one another at the beginning of lunch or dinner. And at one time, these sacraments were brought to people who were absent, as Justin Martyr states clearly in his writings. But I do not think the apostle is saying here that he wishes the sacrament of the Eucharist to be eaten by them at home. Rather, as Chrysostom says, "In order to place greater emphasis on the seriousness of their sins, Paul sends them from the church to the household where they should satisfy both their thirst and hunger, on the grounds that such behavior would not now be fitting for people who were concerned with others in the church." Commentary on 1 Corinthians 11:33-34.[62]

Sharing the Lord's Supper Together. Wolfgang Musculus: Finally, after refuting the abuses that the Corinthians had brought into the Lord's Supper, Paul adds this conclusion. He criticizes the inequality among them, seeing that some of the Corinthians had assembled before the common people arrived and, bringing their own suppers and not waiting for the others, they were already filled while others remained hungry. Thus, in conclusion, he orders that, in the future, whenever they had to gather together for a meal, they should wait for one another. In other words, no one among them should eat the Supper by themselves, but everyone should eat and drink together in common, according to the Lord's institution. Commentary on 1 Corinthians 11:33.[63]

A Final Reminder. Tilemann Hesshus: Paul concludes this passage on the Lord's Supper and repeats by way of a reminder that they should gather together to celebrate the Eucharist in the fear of the Lord, so that they will not call God's judgment and punishment on themselves due to their negligence. The fact that he promises that he will give additional instructions when he comes, the papists—those perverters of Scripture—apply to their fictitious traditions, as if the apostle Paul imparted many things to the churches, the knowledge of which are necessary for salvation, which nevertheless are not commanded in his letters. But the papists cause injury to Paul's writings. For everything that is necessary to be known for salvation has been recorded in his letters. And the entire body of Christian teaching is comprised in his letters to the Romans, Galatians, and Ephesians. Paul is certainly referring here in this passage to indifferent matters concerning certain external ceremonies and customs, such as the order of readings and sermons, the method of convoking the assembly, and the order for distributing the Supper. For since a new church had been established in that place where, previously, the worship of idols had flourished, and since there was a need for some wise pastor who, in the midst of terrible confusion, could set in order various details, such as where and when to assemble, the order and method of conducting sermons and singing the Psalms, and distributing the Supper, these clever and proud Corinthians were undoubtedly arguing among themselves, with some of them approving this order, and others prescribing that. Therefore Paul promises that he will come and rightly arrange all things in the church, which certainly included the organization of gatherings, the order of readings, the collection of alms, the care for the poor, and other indifferent matters that don't have anything to do with salvation. Explication of 1 Corinthians 11:33-34.[64]

---

[62]Vermigli, *In Selectissimam Priorem ad Corinthios Epistolam . . . Commentarii*, 318r. For Tertullian's description of contemporary practice of the Eucharist, see his *Apology* 39, in ANF 3:47. For Justin Martyr's description, see his *First Apology* 65-67, in ANF 1:185-86. For Cyprian's counsel, see his letter to Caecilius (epistle 62), in ANF 5:358-64. For Chrysostom's treatment of this passage, see his *Homilies on 1 Corinthians* (homily 28), in NPNF 12:164-65.

[63]Musculus, *Comm. 1 Cor.*, 444.

[64]Hesshus, *Explicatio Prioris Epistolae ad Corinthios*, 262r-v.

12:1-11 Spiritual Gifts

Now concerning[a] spiritual gifts,[b] brothers,[c] I do not
want you to be uninformed. 2You know that when
you were pagans you were led astray to mute idols,
however you were led. 3Therefore I want you to
understand that no one speaking in the Spirit of God
ever says "Jesus is accursed!" and no one can say
"Jesus is Lord" except in the Holy Spirit.
4Now there are varieties of gifts, but the same
Spirit; 5and there are varieties of service, but the same
Lord; 6and there are varieties of activities, but it is the
same God who empowers them all in everyone. 7To
each is given the manifestation of the Spirit for the
common good. 8For to one is given through the Spirit
the utterance of wisdom, and to another the utterance
of knowledge according to the same Spirit, 9to another
faith by the same Spirit, to another gifts of healing by
the one Spirit, 10to another the working of miracles, to
another prophecy, to another the ability to distinguish
between spirits, to another various kinds of tongues,
to another the interpretation of tongues. 11All these
are empowered by one and the same Spirit, who
apportions to each one individually as he wills.

a The expression *Now concerning* introduces a reply to a question in the Corinthians' letter; see 7:1 b Or *spiritual persons* c Or *brothers and sisters*

Overview: In the first part of 1 Corinthians 12, Paul describes how the one true God bestows various spiritual gifts on his people; hence, the Corinthian believers should live in harmony with one another, using their gifts to serve the common good rather than to promote themselves. Protestant commentators share Paul's primary concern that spiritual gifts should be employed to glorify God and edify his church. At the same time, they find in these verses a strong warning against idolatry, a subtle affirmation of the doctrine of the Trinity, and a Pauline proof-text that counters Catholic confidence in the power of human free will in salvation. Reformation authors also give sustained attention to each of the nine spiritual gifts listed in this text. If some of these gifts, such as healing, miracles, and speaking in tongues, were particularly important for the advance of the gospel during the apostolic age, other gifts continue to be of crucial importance for the health of the present-day church. In this regard, Lutheran commentators extol the example of Martin Luther, who employed spiritual gifts such as wisdom, faith, prophecy, and the discernment of spirits to expose the error of Catholic doctrine and bring about the reformation of the church.

Not Exalting, but Serving. Martin Luther: In chapters 12 and 13 [St. Paul] discusses the many different gifts of God, among which love is the best. He teaches the people not to exalt themselves but to serve one another in unity of spirit, since there is one God, one Lord, one Spirit, and everything is one, however great the diversity. Preface to 1 Corinthians.[1]

One Body, One Spirit. Huldrych Zwingli: There were many abnormalities in the Corinthian church, as is clear enough from the preceding chapters, so that discord and jealousy arose among them even on account of the diversity of their gifts. Thus some were jealous of one another; others despised one another. And thereafter, everyone thoughtlessly and indiscriminately poured out abuse on whomever they could. Responding to this evil with a very powerful argument and exclamation, the apostle exhorts them to love one another, teaching that they are one body and one spirit, though with many different gifts. Therefore these gifts ought to be used in such a way that they might be seen to reflect their author: because [the Lord] is one and of the same mind, so he leads his

[1]LW 35:383.

people to unity and harmony. Annotations on 1 Corinthians 12.[2]

On Spiritual Gifts. Tilemann Hesshus: In this chapter, the apostle Paul teaches the Corinthian church what it should think about spiritual gifts, from where they originate, for what purpose they are given to the godly, what are the different kinds of gifts in the church, and how they ought to be used to shine forth the glory of God and to edify the church of Christ. Now, after the Corinthians had embraced the apostle's teaching and had been baptized in the name of Jesus Christ by the imposition of the hands of the apostles, they had received the visible outpouring of the Holy Spirit and been furnished with many excellent spiritual gifts so that they were speaking with various tongues, uttering prophecies, explaining sacred Scripture, and performing miracles. But some people among the Corinthians—and especially the false apostles—were exalting themselves with these gifts: They were attempting to display their knowledge of tongues in the assemblies. They were seeking popular favor with their eloquence. They were beginning to be haughty in their gifts and to look down on others in public. And they were aspiring to the highest place in the ministry so that they might be superior to others—as if the Holy Spirit had established a field for vainglory and had given his gifts for degrading and despising other people. Therefore, in this passage, the apostle Paul severely reproaches this great error and foul abuse of the gifts of the Spirit. And since God has conferred on godly people a very different purpose than that, Paul teaches that they should preserve the glory of God, that they should edify and enhance the church, and that they should do good to every person in the church. For pride, rivalry, contempt for weaker people, and envy must be completely absent from godly people, who are citizens in Christ's kingdom.

Paul uses four very weighty reasons so as to encourage piety and modesty among those Corinthians in the use of their gifts. First, he reminds them what sort of people they were before their conversion and illumination, that they were destitute of all knowledge of God and had defiled themselves with horrible idolatry. Thus they must not now flaunt their plumes. Second, Paul shows them that the source of the gifts is certainly not our free will, nor the keenness of our intellect, nor the excellence of our nature; rather, their source is the eternal God, the Father, Jesus Christ, and the Holy Spirit. It is only right, therefore, that we use gifts bestowed by God for the glory of God. Third, Paul teaches us that Christians are members of one body, whence he teaches that we should strive among ourselves with no rivalry and work with no jealousy, but instead should promote the common welfare of the whole body and encourage what is suitable and beautiful for everyone. Fourth, Paul explains the various levels and distinctions of offices and gifts that God has arranged in the church; for in the church he has assigned some to the position of apostles, others to the position of prophets, still others to the position of teachers. Therefore everyone ought to be content with their position and gift, and must apply themselves to adorning their station and demonstrating their faith to God and the church. Explication of 1 Corinthians 12.[3]

True Fellowship in the Church. Heinrich Bullinger: In the twelfth chapter of the first epistle to the Corinthians [Paul] expounds more fully and plainly the conjunction of the heads and members, and that mainly by the same parable of the members of the human body, expressing it very eloquently, and witnessing that between the highest members of the church and the lowest there is a great and fitting agreement, and also a diligent care, and assistance that is both continual and most faithful. From all this it appears that the marks of the true and lively church of Christ are the communion of the Spirit of Christ, sincere faith, and Christian charity, without which no one is a

[2]Zwingli, *Annotatiunculae . . . ex ore Zvinglij*, 98.

[3]Hesshus, *Explicatio Prioris Epistolae ad Corinthios*, 263v-264v.

partaker of this spiritual body. And by these things you may easily judge whether you are in the fellowship of the church or not. Decades.[4]

12:1-7 *The One True God Gives Different Gifts*

All Who Confess Jesus Christ as Lord Possess Spiritual Gifts. Jacques Lefèvre d'Étaples: The apostle has declared the great mystery of the Son of God, who is the hidden manna. Now he discusses the gifts of the Holy Spirit, which can only be possessed by those who believe in our Lord. Those who confess Jesus Christ to be Lord and God must necessarily possess these gifts. Those who blaspheme Christ Jesus and subject him to cursing do not possess these gifts. This is what those deceived people were doing who were following blind and mute idols. And this is what the Corinthians would now do if the grace of the Holy Spirit did not shine on them. Commentary on 1 Corinthians 12:1.[5]

Only the Righteous Possess Spiritual Gifts. Philipp Melanchthon: Besides faith, hope, and love, there are the gifts or *charismata*, namely, the twofold gifts, some natural such as eloquence, a retentive memory, civic prudence such as that found in Ahithophel. Other gifts are those of the work and efficacy of the Holy Spirit in the hearts of believers about which the apostle speaks here: "To each is given the manifestation of the Spirit for the common good." Also in Mark 16:17 we read, "And these signs will accompany those who believe: in my name they will cast out demons," etc. Also Matthew 21:21, "Truly, I say to you, if you have faith and do not doubt, . . . even if you say to this mountain, 'Be taken up and cast into the sea,' it will be done." These gifts, even if they are not righteousness, are still the works of the Spirit, as the apostle calls them, and generally works of faith.

Second: What, therefore? Do not such gifts always belong to the righteous? Does performing miracles belong only to the godly? Do not wicked people also have the gift of prophecy? I answer: It is certain that some miracles are tricks of demons, as was the case with Pharaoh's magicians and what Paul calls in 2 Thessalonians 2:9 "pretended wonders by the activity of Satan"—and also the miracles that now take place in those [Catholic] shrines to which the crowds and mob flock. But I do not recall in Scripture there being an example of some wicked person who truly performed miracles by divine power. Concerning prophecy, this is certain: that all true prophecy is the speech of the Holy Spirit. But the Holy Spirit sometimes speaks through the wicked, as through Balaam in Numbers 24:15-19 and Saul in 1 Samuel 19:23ff. I do not call prophecies such cases as that of Caiaphas (John 11:49-51), that is, those who prophesy without knowing it; rather, cases of prophesying occur when the person prophesying knows for certain that they are prophesying through the Holy Spirit, as Balaam and Saul. Annotations on 1 Corinthians 12.[6]

Paul Did Not Endorse Spiritual Ignorance. Wolfgang Musculus: The apostolic statement is clear: "I do not want you to be ignorant." The zeal of anti-Christians is not at all apostolic when they wish to subvert the church with the darkness of ignorance. We owe to them all that confusion, superstition, impiety, and corruption that persist now in some of the churches of our age. Here are the statements of those sons of darkness: "Laypeople should not be taught the holy Scriptures nor should they read them." "The biblical writings make heretics." "Those who walk simply, walk well"—as if to walk simply means to walk in ignorance, with one's eyes closed, rather than to live with sincerity, without deception and cunning. I beseech you, how will those people affirm with the apostle, "Concerning spiritual matters, brothers, I

[4]Bullinger, *Decades*, 4:25-26*.

[5]Lefèvre d'Étaples, *Commentariorum in Epistolas Beati Pauli . . . Liber Secundus*, 119r.

[6]Melanchthon, *Annotationes in Epistolam priorem ad Corinthios*, 136; citing 2 Sam 15:12, 31; 16:23.

do not want you to be ignorant"? If only the entire church might at last gain true knowledge of spiritual matters and spiritual people, and begin to discern between the true and false! Commentary on 1 Corinthians 12:1.[7]

The Scourge of Idolatry. Martin Luther: "Friends, think back each of you," he's saying. "What were you before you came to Christ? Nothing but blind heathens! You had no knowledge of God; instead you let yourselves be lead by the nose, wherever someone just said something about God. And your way of life was nothing other than completely fragmented worship—each person, wherever they turned, had to have their own idol, even the baby in the cradle, suckling his mother's milk." St. Augustine says that the city of Rome alone had more than four hundred gods. On top of that, Rome built a church, which still exists, formerly called the Pantheon, for all the gods in the world.

"You scampered with the masses wherever someone led you. You prayed, sacrificed, and fixed your hearts to absolutely speechless idols. They could neither teach nor advise nor comfort nor reward nor help you. And you got nothing out of this, beside that you were a blind, wretched, miserable, fragmented people. You could resist no error. You let yourselves be torn apart by everyone, like a poor flock of scattered sheep by wolves." Postil on the Epistle on the Tenth Sunday After Trinitys.[8]

The Corinthians Must Never Forget Their Pagan Past. Tilemann Hesshus: Paul adduces the first argument by comparing the blindness, ignorance, and wretched condition that the Corinthians experienced under paganism before their conversion with that light, knowledge, and those gifts with which they were endowed after they had been converted to God. . . . No language can express the wretched state of pagans and all human beings who do not know God and are outside of Christ's kingdom. For they live in horrible darkness; they defile themselves with terrible idolatry. Pagans worship as their gods Febris (the spirit of fever), Pallor (the god of fear), Bellona (the goddess of war), Priapus (the god of fertility), Boreas (the north wind), cats, and crocodiles. They perform the most disgustingly wicked deeds in their temples, by which they attempt to appease the deities—they even perform human sacrifices. They have experienced no great comfort in times of need; they have not understood the blessings of a mediator; and, in the end, they will be plunged screaming into eternal destruction. In a similar fashion, while in the papacy, we were ignorant of the true God and were led into error. Some people worshiped Anne, some worshiped Catherine, some worshiped Paul, some worshiped the three kings, still others worshiped the consecrated bread. Since God has rescued us from such darkness through the ministry of the Word and through the illumination of the Holy Spirit, it is proper for us always to remember this enormous blessing and, in modesty and true humility, demonstrate our gratitude toward God. For those who are haughty about their gifts have forgotten their previous condition. Explication of 1 Corinthians 12:2.[9]

The Folly of Idolatry. The English Annotations: Though the devil sometimes speaks in and through idols, yet the idols themselves "had mouths and speak not" (as the prophet David truly affirms of them in Ps 115:5). The craftsmen who made the mouths of the idol could not give them speech. Paul therefore speaks here in aggravation, to show what an absurd thing idolatry is. As Lactantius once observed, humans

[7]Musculus, *Comm. 1 Cor.*, 450.
[8]WA 22:172-73 (cf. LW 78:331).

[9]Hesshus, *Explicatio Prioris Epistolae ad Corinthios*, 265v-266r. Hesshus is referring here to two different practices of Catholic piety that were popular in the Middle Ages: the veneration of saints such as St. Anne (the mother of the Virgin Mary), St. Catherine of Alexandria (a fourth-century Christian martyr), Paul, and the three wise men (traditionally identified as Gaspar, Melchior, and Balthasar); and the adoration of the Communion wafer consecrated in the Eucharist.

are so foolish "that reasonable people worship unreasonable creatures, sensible people adore senseless animals, and those who can speak call on dumb images and pictures." Annotations on 1 Corinthians 12:2.[10]

The Ministry of the Holy Spirit. Martin Luther: Christ himself explains the Holy Spirit's office and preaching—what he should teach and say in the church. "The Spirit," he says, "will witness to me." Likewise: "He will glorify me, for he will take what is mine." He will have such a simple manner of speech that he knows how to preach nothing other than Christ alone. If he should witness to Christ and glorify him, then he must not elevate anything else that might obscure Christ and rob him of his glory. And whoever does this surely is not speaking from the Holy Spirit, even if he has great gifts and is called a teacher, bishop, pope, council, or even an apostle and angel from heaven. Among the Corinthians some neglected to preach Christ alone and instead pointed to the apostles themselves, choosing between them: one Cephas, another Apollos, the third Paul, etc. Postil on the Epistle for the Tenth Sunday After Trinity.[11]

The Work and Person of the Holy Spirit. Menno Simons: We believe the Holy Spirit to be the true, essential Holy Spirit of God, who adorns us with his heavenly and divine gifts, and through his influence, according to the good pleasure of the Father, frees us from sin, gives us boldness, and makes us cheerful, peaceful, pious, and holy. And so we believe and confess before God, before his angels, before all our brethren, and before all the world, that these three names, activities, and powers, namely, the Father, the Son, and the Holy Ghost (which the fathers called three persons, by which they meant the three, true, divine beings) are one incomprehensible, indescribable, almighty, holy, only eternal, and sovereign God. Confession of the Triune God.[12]

The Proof of the Spirit Is Within the Believer. Wolfgang Musculus: Paul begins to instruct them concerning spiritual matters. And first, he mentions that work of the Spirit which is universal among all believers. Then he adds those particular gifts that are not conferred to all people equally, but are distributed variously to different people. The universal work of the Spirit is that faith by which we call the crucified Jesus, "Lord." "Do you want evidence," Paul says, "that you are speaking in the Spirit of God? The fact that you call Jesus 'Lord' comes from the Spirit of God. If the Spirit were not in you, you would not be able to call Jesus 'Lord.' If he is in you, you will not call him accursed [*anathema*]." For it is the Spirit of God whom believers receive, the Spirit of truth, who bears witness that Jesus is Lord. That is why no one speaking through the Spirit calls Jesus accursed, and no one is able to call Jesus "Lord" except by him. . . .

We are warned by this passage that we should pay careful attention how we perceive Christ Jesus in ourselves, and what we say about other people. The Spirit proves, John says, whether we are from God. The Spirit's proof is necessary for us so that we are not deceived by others or deceive ourselves. Nothing can provide greater certainty than this: if we pay attention both to our own view and others' views concerning Christ. Thus words are not necessary for me to know that I have been filled with the Spirit. For, if I pay close attention, I can test from this how I feel about Christ in my heart. If I believe and feel strongly that Christ has been designated as Lord by God the Father, then I have this evidence of the Spirit of God, who performed this faith in me. However, to prove the work of the Spirit in other people, it is necessary for me to listen and identify how they speak and feel about

[10]Downame, *The English Annotations*, EE2v*. Contrary to this text, there is no evidence that Psalm 115 was written by David. Lactantius addresses the themes of human wisdom and idolatry in his *Treatise on the Anger of God*, in ANF 7:259-80.

[11]LW 78:336* (WA 22:178); citing Jn 15:26; 16:14; Gal 1:8; 1 Cor 1:12.

[12]Simons, *Complete Writings*, 496*.

Christ. If they confess that Christ is Lord, I know that the Spirit of God is in them. For no one is able to call Jesus "Lord," except by the Holy Spirit. Therefore the confession of this faith constitutes a sure proof of the Holy Spirit. Commentary on 1 Corinthians 12:3.[13]

Profession of Faith in Christ Is the Principal Gift of the Spirit. David Chytraeus: There is one chief and principal gift of the Holy Spirit that necessarily shines forth in all saints without fail: namely, the true recognition and profession of our Lord Jesus Christ, the Son of God; or, true faith that Jesus is the Lord, or truly in nature God, and that he is Christ our only Redeemer and Savior; and, at the same time, a rejection and avoidance of the worship of idols. Paul is speaking in this passage about this chief and principal gift that is common to all the saints: "No one speaking in the Spirit of God says 'Jesus is cursed.'" That is to say, all those who curse the Son of God as accursed or call him a plague condemned by God and as one who must be removed from the world (as the Jews, Turks, and heathen do in our day), or all those who blasphemously slander and corrupt the true doctrine concerning the person and work of Christ (as the Arians and papists do) are not members of the true church or governed by the Holy Spirit. "And no one can say 'Jesus is Lord' except by the Holy Spirit." That is to say, no one can rightly recognize and with firm faith embrace and constantly confess to the last gasp of life Jesus Christ as the only and true redeemer and giver of eternal life, unless they are governed and strengthened by the Holy Spirit. Paul is not speaking here of a mere profession of the name of Jesus, but of the whole teaching and confession of faith of Jesus Christ that perseveres, which John expounded in John 20: "These things are written so that you might believe that Jesus Christ is the Son of God and that, by believing, you might have life in his name." This faith is the chief and principal gift of the Holy Spirit, which must shine forth and appear in all godly people. Postil on the Epistle for the Tenth Sunday After Trinity.[14]

The Tongue Is an Instrument of the Holy Spirit. John Donne: The tongue is the fittest instrument for the Holy Ghost to work on and to work by. . . . The Son of God is the Word, and the Holy Ghost proceeds from him. And because that faith which unites us to God is expressed in the tongue, to the extent that the heart is the center in which the Holy Ghost rests, the tongue is the sphere in which he moves. And therefore St. Cyril says that as God set the cherubim with a fiery sword to keep us out of Paradise, so God has set the Holy Ghost in fiery tongues to let us in again. Sermon Preached on Whitsunday.[15]

True Christians Do Not Curse Christ. John Trapp: As the . . . Jews do today in their daily prayers and breviaries, and as the Gentiles used to do, including the Corinthians among them. But now they would rather die than curse Christ. Pliny wrote to Emperor Trajan that he could never force any that were truly Christians to invoke the gods or perform a sacrifice before the emperor's image or curse Christ. Commentary on 1 Corinthians 12:3.[16]

Jesus Is Lord. John Donne: When we say *Iesus est*, that "Jesus is," we thereby confess his eternity, and therein his Godhead. When we say *Iesus Dominus*, that "Jesus is a Lord," we thereby confess a dominion that he has purchased. And when we say *Iesum Dominum*, so that we profess him to be *the* Lord, then we confess a vigilance, a superintendence, a residence, and a permanence of Christ in his dominion, in his church, to the world's end. If he is the Lord in his church, there is no other who

[13]Musculus, *Comm. 1 Cor.*, 452-53; citing 1 Jn 4:13.

[14]Chytraeus, *Dispositio epistolarum*, 380-81; citing Jn 20:31.

[15]Donne, *Sermons of John Donne*, 6:122*. See Cyril, *Catechetical Lectures* (lecture xvi.15), in NPNF 7:128.

[16]Trapp, *A Commentary or Exposition*, 689*. Pliny the Younger's letter to Emperor Trajan was written c. 112. See Bettenson, *Documents of the Christian Church*, 3-4.

rules with him, there is no other that rules for him. . . . To say that "Jesus is the Lord" is to confess him as God from everlasting, who has been made man in the fullness of time and governs still that church which he has purchased with his blood. He therefore intends that we direct all our particular actions to his glory. Sermon Preached on Whitsunday.[17]

The Triune God Endows Gifts, Offices, and Activities. David Dickson: Paul ascribes gifts to the Holy Spirit, who distributes gifts both ordinary and extraordinary according to the needs of the church (verse 4). Paul ascribes the functions and offices to Christ, who being Lord in his house appoints what services he pleases, calls to offices whom he will, and employs those who are called in their functions as he will (verse 5). But various operations, or the exercise of various kinds of gifts, Paul ascribes in verse 6 to God the Father, who even as he is the beginning of all things, so he works efficaciously in all things. Now the apostle does not distinguish between these three categories of things (namely, gifts, offices, and operations) as if they come from one person of the Trinity rather than all persons of the Godhead. Rather, Paul makes this distinction . . . so that we might more easily be led by the hand to apprehend the distinction between the divine persons and their unity of essence; and so that we might observe the equality of the persons of the holy Trinity, and their unity in gifts, offices, and operation of gifts, and by observing this equality, might all together strive for the good of the church and the glory of God. Exposition of 1 Corinthians 12:4-6.[18]

The Same Spirit Works in Different Ways. John Colet: Human beings of themselves are powerless, and stupid, and wicked, and, finally, childish. But when they are called by grace to the all-powerful, all-wise, all-good Jesus Christ (who is the Word and the Eloquence of God), one and the same Spirit works all these things in these human beings, imparting as he desires to some the power to perform miracles through Christ. To others he imparts the ability to speak sparkling wisdom; to others the ability to perform acts of kindness; to others the ability to speak with diverse tongues; to others the ability to interpret sublime words from God as prophecy; to others the ability to speak forth the lofty truth of God's power. In power, wisdom, goodness, action, eloquence; in efficacy, multitude, variety, order, beauty; in goodness and kindness, in speech and truth; in erudition and instruction; in the purification, enlightenment, and perfection of humans in Christ; in the building and completion of Christ in God (which is the church)—truly, in all these ways, the Spirit of God is engaged and active and working in human beings. Exposition of 1 Corinthians 12.[19]

There Are Different Categories of Spiritual Gifts. Philipp Melanchthon: Paul has three categories in mind: gifts, ministries, and activities or powers. He calls "gifts" those things through which we work, such as utterance of wisdom and the utterance of knowledge. The apostle calls "ministries" those prophets and teachers, as he himself explains at greater length. He calls "activities" the power and ability to perform miracles such as healing, casting out demons, Peter's killing of Ananias (Acts 5:3ff.), etc. Moreover, these are part of the argument he began above: It is the same Spirit who pours himself on the church in many different ways; thus all of us who have been filled with the same Spirit should be in agreement. Annotations on 1 Corinthians 12:4.[20]

The Doctrine of the Trinity Taught Here. Martin Luther: Now here too he distinguishes the three—one God, Lord, and Spirit—and gives to each his own work, through

---

[17] Donne, *Sermons of John Donne*, 6:125*.

[18] Dickson, *Exposition of St. Paul's Epistles*, 61*.

[19] Colet, *Enarratio*, 232, 236*.

[20] Melanchthon, *Annotationes in Epistolam priorem ad Corinthios*, 142.

which he reveals himself. One person is God the Father, from whom as the source and first person all powers derive. The second is the Lord, that is, Christ, the Son of God, from whom as the head of the church all offices flow. The third is the Spirit, who produces and distributes all gifts in the church. Nevertheless, these three are all one divine, almighty, eternal essence. Accordingly all three are called and truly are one, since God must be one indivisible essence. . . . Nevertheless, these three—God, Lord, and Spirit—are not several gods, but the same divine essence. The Lord is no other God than God the Father; the Spirit is also none other than God and the Lord. Postil on the Epistle for the Tenth Sunday After Trinity.[21]

The Same Lord. John Calvin: The ancient fathers used these verses against the Arians to defend the Trinity of persons. For the Spirit is named here, then the Lord, and last God; and Paul ascribes one and the same activity to the three. Thus, by the name "Lord," they understood "Christ." But for my part, although I have no objection to understanding these verses this way, nevertheless I recognize that it is a weak argument if someone wants to close the mouth of the Arians. . . . "The ministries are different," Paul says, "but the Lord is the same, whom we must serve, whatever ministry we perform." This antithesis, then, demonstrates [Paul's] simple meaning, so that to restrict the title "Lord" to Christ is too forced. Commentary on 1 Corinthians 12:5.[22]

Salvation Comes from God's Grace *and* Human Effort. Desiderius Erasmus: Paul says to the Philippians, "Work out your salvation with fear and trembling," and the same, earlier to the Corinthians: "But it is the same God who works all things in everyone." There are hundreds more passages of this kind in Holy Scripture. If humans do nothing, why say, "Work out"? If humans do something, why say, "God works all things in everyone"? If you wish to twist the one passage to support a special interpretation, humans do nothing. On the other hand, if you wish to turn the other to your cause, humans do it all. If humans do nothing, there is no room for merits; where there is no room for merits, there is no room for punishments or rewards. If humans do it all, there is no room for grace, which Paul urges so many times. The Holy Spirit does not fight against himself, whose inspiration produced the canonical Scriptures. Both sides embrace and acknowledge the inviolable majesty of Scripture, but an interpretation must be found that will unravel the knot. . . . And so these passages, which seem to be in conflict with one another, are easily brought into harmony if we join the striving of our will with the assistance of divine grace. On the Freedom of the Will.[23]

Salvation Is by Grace Alone, Not by Human Works. Martin Luther: The protagonists of "free will" create difficulties where none exist, and dream contradictions for themselves. For instance: there is no conflict between: "If humans purify themselves," and: "God works all in all" (1 Cor 12:6); nor is it necessary to cut the knot by saying that God does something and humans do something. The former statement is hypothetical, and neither affirms nor denies any work or power in humans, but simply lays down what work and power there should be in humans. . . . The latter text, "God works all in all," is an indicative statement, declaring that all works and all power are in God. How then do these two passages conflict, when the one does not deal at all with the power of humans, and the other attributes all things to God? Do they not rather harmonize perfectly? But [Erasmus's] *Diatribe* is so ruinously sunk in, choked with, and stifled by this notion of its own carnal fancy—claiming that it is pointless to command impossibilities—that it cannot control itself; but

[21]LW 78:339, 340* (WA 22:181). Luther acknowledges that the external works of the Trinity are undivided. See Mickey L. Mattox, "From Faith to the Text and Back Again: Martin Luther on the Trinity in the Old Testament," *Pro Ecclesia* 15, no 3 (2006): 281-303.

[22] CO 49:498 (cf. CTS 39:399).

[23]LCC 17:73-74; citing Phil 2:12.

whenever it hears an imperative or hypothetical statement it straightaway tacks on its own indicative inferences: "something is commanded, therefore we can do it, else the command is stupid." The Bondage of the Will.[24]

The Triune God Bestows Different Gifts. Wolfgang Musculus: The diversity of gifts, Paul says, is not due to various spirits, but comes from exactly the same Spirit. And he does not consider the Lord's message different for different people because there are a variety of ministries in the church. For the Lord is the same, who is served by various kinds of ministries. In the same way, God should not be judged as changeable because there are different activities; rather, God should be recognized as one and the same in all of them. Among pagans, various activities were attributed to different gods, whether Jove, Neptune, Saturn, Apollo, or Mercury, etc., just as in the papacy different virtues are assigned to various saints. One saint is in charge of sailing in the sea, another for fighting wars, another for planting crops, etc. Another saint looks after various sicknesses. But the apostle ascribes the gifts, sent from heaven to the church, not to saints, nor to angelic spirits, but to God the Father, the Lord Christ, and the Holy Spirit. Thus it seems proper to recognize in this passage (following Chrysostom and Ambrose) the holy Trinity of divine persons—since I see nothing to prevent this interpretation. And when Paul speaks about those gifts in Ephesians 4, he says a similar thing: "One Spirit, one Lord, one God and Father of all." Now it should not be thought that Paul assigns gifts specifically to the Spirit, ministries to the Lord Christ, and activities to God the Father. All of God's gifts are from God the Father, through Christ, in the Holy Spirit. God performs his gifts in us by his Spirit, through Christ. Commentary on 1 Corinthians 12:6.[25]

The Purpose of the Spirit's Gifts. John Calvin: Paul now shows the purpose for which God has given his gifts, for he does not confer them on us in vain, nor does he intend them to be used for show. Therefore we must ask, what is their proper use? Paul answers *pros to sympheron*, that is, so that the church may gain benefit from them. "The manifestation of the Spirit" may be taken in a passive sense as well as an active sense: in a passive sense because wherever there is prophecy, or knowledge, or any other any gift, the Spirit of God manifests himself; in an active sense, because the Spirit of God, when he enriches us with any gift, unlocks his treasures, for the purpose of manifesting to us those things that would otherwise have been concealed and shut up. Commentary on 1 Corinthians 12:7.[26]

For the Common Good. John Trapp: We are neither born nor born again for ourselves. If we are not fit to serve the body, then neither are we fit to be of the body. They are not saints who do not seek the communion of the saints. . . . The Greek word [*to sympheron*] means to confer a benefit that redounds to the community. It appears to be a metaphor drawn from bees that bring all the honey they can find into the common hive. Commentary on 1 Corinthians 12:7.[27]

12:8-11 *Varieties of Gifts*

Nine Gifts That Benefit the Church. David Dickson: [Paul lists] nine kinds of gifts, which all tend to the good of the church. The first gift, the word of wisdom, is the seasonable application of sound doctrine to the hearers, which is the gift of a pastor. The second, the word of knowledge, is the gift of a teacher, who can give the general doctrine and meaning of the Scripture, although he does not have the gift to apply it. . . . The third gift is faith, which is the faith to

[24]Luther, *The Bondage of the Will*, 236-37.

[25] Musculus, *Comm. 1 Cor.*, 456-57. For Chrysostom's treatment of this passage, see his *Homilies on 1 Corinthians* (homily 29), in NPNF 12:170-71. For Ambrose (Ambrosiaster), see his *Comment. in Epist. I ad Cor.*, in PL 17:259.

[26]CO 49:499 (cf. CTS 39:400).

[27]Trapp, *A Commentary or Exposition*, 689-690*.

perform many famous miracles; in chapter 13 it is called "all faith." The fourth gift is that of healing diseases, one among the miraculous gifts that make up the list that follows. The fifth gift is that of working miracles and powerfully casting out devils and the enemies of the church, of which we have an example in Acts 13:11. The sixth gift is foretelling things to come, and revealing secrets. The seventh gift is distinguishing counterfeits from the gifts of the Spirit. The eighth gift is speaking with diverse kinds of tongues. The ninth gift is the interpretation of tongues, without the gift of speaking with those tongues; for it appears that some spoke with tongues who could not interpret them, and vice versa. In this way it seemed good to God to distribute his gifts. Exposition of 1 Corinthians 12:8-10.[28]

Luther Possessed the Gift of Wisdom. David Chytraeus: Paul in this passage lists nine kinds of gifts of the Holy Spirit, the first of which is *logos sophias*, or a word of wisdom, namely, a complete knowledge of all the articles of Christian doctrine, joined with a true and earnest godliness, or with a true fear of God and faith, where every decision and action coincides with the will of God. . . . Wisdom in this passage also includes . . . an exceptional and more perfect light, which not only understands true doctrine aright but also recognizes and ably discerns errors and false opinions. And such a kind of spiritual wisdom shone forth in Paul, Augustine, and Luther, as it was aroused by God through the experience of temptations and struggles, and confirmed through terrors and comforts. Postil on the Epistle for the Tenth Sunday After Trinity.[29]

Wisdom and Knowledge. Philipp Melanchthon: Wisdom is the experience of spiritual things; an example of this is found in the sermons of [Johannes] Tauler where he passes judgment on spiritual conditions. This wisdom understands what faith, hope, and sin are, while hypocrites understand absolutely nothing about these things. This is the way the apostle uses the word for wisdom elsewhere, as in Ephesians 1:17. Second, any other kind of comprehension is called knowledge, which pertains to knowing what should be done, what is lawful, what is unlawful. Of this sort is discussion about the power of the pope, the jurisdiction of magistrates, the sacraments, and other similar topics, which can be treated without any spiritual experience. Annotations on 1 Corinthians 12:8.[30]

The Difference Between Wisdom and Knowledge. John Calvin: As to the difference between these gifts, knowledge (or comprehension) and wisdom are taken in various ways in Scripture. But here I take them as expressing a degree of difference, as is found in Colossians 2:3, where they are joined together when Paul says that in Christ "are hidden all the treasures of wisdom and knowledge." Thus, in my opinion, knowledge indicates an understanding of holy things, whereas wisdom means a complete grasp of them. Sometimes prudence is placed in between them, as it were, in which case it indicates the skill of applying knowledge to some useful purpose. These two words are, indeed, very closely related; but still, you see a difference when they are compared to one another. Let knowledge therefore be understood as the ordinary comprehension of things, while the word wisdom includes revelations that are of a more secret and lofty nature. Commentary on 1 Corinthians 12:8.[31]

The Gift of Faith. Tilemann Hesshus: Paul is speaking here about a special kind of faith, whereby miracles are performed, or terrible and huge temptations are overcome, or special blessings are obtained from God. Now there is a

[28]Dickson, *Exposition of St. Paul's Epistles*, 61*; citing 1 Cor 13:2.
[29]Chytraeus, *Dispositio epistolarum*, 382-83.
[30]Melanchthon, *Annotationes in Epistolam priorem ad Corinthios*, 144. Johannes Tauler (c. 1300–1361) was a German Dominican preacher, writer, and mystic whose published sermons shaped Martin Luther's early theology.
[31]CO 49:499 (cf. CTS 39:401).

general kind of faith that is given by the Holy Spirit, by which we take hold of the promise of the gospel concerning the free remission of sins, granted to each and every person through the Mediator, Jesus Christ. And so Benjamin was living before God by his faith, as was Abraham, or Elijah, or David. But that special kind of faith—evidenced when either miracles are performed or some great deed undertaken—is not possessed by everyone. Special faith was seen when David entrusted himself to the Lord to win the victory over Goliath, and attacked this Philistine in full view of the entire army of the Israelites which was trembling with fear. Special faith was seen when Elisha raised the boy from the dead, whom Gehazi was not able to resuscitate. Special faith was seen when Isaiah obtained from the Lord that the sun's shadow would recede ten steps; and Joshua ordered the sun and moon to remain motionless in the middle of the sky for an entire day. Explication of 1 Corinthians 12:9.[32]

Luther Possessed the Gift of Faith. David Chytraeus: Faith [is] an assured trust fixed on God; the performance of great and wonderful things with a mighty and invincible courage; the gaining of freedom from grave dangers, which seem to defy human reason in situations no less difficult than the moving of mountains. Paul speaks about such faith in the following chapter: "If I have so great a faith as to remove mountains. . . ." Such faith was evident among the apostles, and in our days with Luther, who with a stout and unabashed courage of heart, spread abroad the doctrine of the gospel when all the world was against him. Postil on the Epistle for the Tenth Sunday After Trinity.[33]

The Spiritual Gifts of Faith and Healing. Wolfgang Musculus: Paul is not speaking here about the faith that justifies, which is common to all believers, without which God has ordained that we cannot be saved. Rather, he is speaking about faith in signs and miracles, as Chrysostom and Jerome recognized. . . . In the church of the elect, the Spirit of God does not give faith in Christ to some, hope to others, and love to still others. Rather, he enables all the elect to believe in Christ, hope in and anticipate the life to come, and love their brothers and sisters. Although he gives these things in different measures, to some more than others, nevertheless he gives as much as is necessary to everyone. Now the faith that Paul here classifies among the spiritual gifts, God does not give to everyone, but only to some. . . .

[Next], Paul speaks about the miraculous healing of diseases, which Christ promised in the last chapter of Mark to those who believed in him, saying: "These signs will accompany those who believe in me, etc., they will lay hands on the sick and they will be healed" (Mark 16:17-18). The apostles employed healing to great benefit in propagating faith in the name of Christ, as is seen in the story of the crippled man sitting at the gate of the temple, whom Peter restored to health and raised to his feet (Acts 3). Now, since there are many different kinds of diseases, Paul uses the plural, saying "to others, *gifts* of healing." He includes here not only people with fevers and bed-ridden paralytics but also those who are blind, deaf, mute, lame, etc. Gifts of healing were especially applied to people who had not yet come to faith in Christ, who, by this display of the miraculous power of God, and recognizing God's kindness in healing them, were encouraged to believe in the gospel. Miraculous signs like these were added to confirm God's grace. Commentary on 1 Corinthians 12:9.[34]

The Gift of Healing. Peter Martyr Vermigli: The gift of healing, by which various kinds of diseases were cured, was very common in

[32]Hesshus, *Explicatio Prioris Epistolae ad Corinthios*, 271v; citing 1 Sam 17:1-58; 2 Kings 4:1-37; Is 38:8; Josh 10:12-13.
[33]Chytraeus, *Dispositio epistolarum*, 383-84; citing 1 Cor 13:2.
[34]Musculus, *Comm. 1 Cor.*, 462-63; citing Acts 3:1-10. For Chrysostom's treatment of this passage, see his *Homilies on 1 Corinthians* (homily 29), in NPNF 12:172. For Jerome, see *Expositio in Primam Epistolam ad Corinthios*, in PL 30 (1865, ed.): 786.

the church at the beginning. This kind of blessing both attracted unbelievers to the gospel and was necessary for believers, because they often did not have access to doctors. For pagans generally did not hasten to their aid when believers were suffering maladies; rather, when persecution raged, the pagans wanted to kill them. Later on, believers were not always furnished with the leisure, healthy food, or money needed to regain their health. But now the situation is different, and thus miracles of this sort have been done away with. I know that it is mentioned by some people that Emperor Vespasian had in his finger the power to heal, and it is written that a very similar power belonged to Pyrrhus, king of the Epirus. But since those healings were performed by a certain power of nature, they achieved the healing of only one particular disease. But this gift of the Holy Spirit brought help to people with all kinds of diseases; indeed, God bestowed his power all the way to bringing the dead back to life. Irenaeus reported that this gift of the Holy Spirit continued in the church all the way to his time. Commentary on 1 Corinthians 12:9.[35]

Gifts of Healing and Miracles. John Calvin: Everyone knows what is meant by the gift of healing. There is more uncertainty about the power to effect miracles, or (as some would translate it) the "workings of powers." I am inclined, however, to think that what is meant here is the power that is employed against demons as well as against hypocrites. Therefore, when Christ and his apostles exercised authority to subdue demons or put them to flight, that was the gift of workings of powers [*energēma*]—and also when Paul inflicted the sorcerer with blindness and when Peter struck Ananias and Sapphira dead by his words alone. Therefore the gifts of healing and miracles are both expressions of God's goodness; but this latter gift expresses his severity for the destruction of Satan. Commentary on 1 Corinthians 12:10.[36]

The Great Works of God. The English Annotations: The gift of healing spoken of in the previous verse was miraculous, but here by the phrase *energēmata dynameōn* the apostle means the greater workings of God's mighty power, which surpassed and excelled among his miracles. Such miracles included the delivery of the people of Israel by the hand of Moses, and what God did by Elijah against the priests of Baal, in sending down fire from heaven to consume the sacrifice and licking up all the water [around the altar], and that which he did by Peter in the matter of Ananias and Sapphira, and similar such things. Annotations on 1 Corinthians 12:10.[37]

Miracles Don't Authenticate True Holiness. Guillaume Farel: Look at Judas, an apostle, preaching that which he learned from Jesus, doing all sorts of miracles, but being in the end nothing. For this reason those who have prophesied and done miracles but are not part of the elect will be rejected. By this the world is greatly abused, not having knowledge of the ordinance of God. These things are not possible to judge, for it is impossible to judge any being holy because of miracles or other things before the coming of our Lord. For by miracles or similar things we are not made holy. I do not even need to speak of miracles that are simply invented. For miracles are performed also by the reprobate. But those whom God loved greatly, like many prophets and John the Baptist, never performed any. Summary and Brief Exposition.[38]

Luther Possessed the Gift of Prophecy. David Chytraeus: Prophesying [is] the gift of foretelling things to come, as was evinced in Agabus (Acts 11 and 21) and in the daughters of

[35]Vermigli, *In Selectissimam Priorem ad Corinthios Epistolam . . . Commentarii*, 329r-v. Vespasian was Roman emperor from AD 70 to 79. Pyrrhus, king of Epirus, (c. 307–272 BC), is remembered for his invasion of Italy in 280 BC and his subsequent defeat at the hands of the Romans in 279 BC. In his book *Against Heresies* (2.32.4), Irenaeus (died c. 202) reports that gifts of healing were still being practiced in his day. See ANF 1:409.

[36]CO 49:500 (cf. CTS 39:402); citing Acts 13:11; 5:1-11.

[37]Downame, *English Annotations*, EE2v*.

[38]In Zuidema and Van Raalte, *Early French Reform*, 177.

Philip the evangelist (Acts 21), or it is a singular ability and fitness in expounding the prophecies of Scripture—that Luther possessed such a singular ability was witnessed even by Erasmus. Postil on the Epistle for the Tenth Sunday After Trinity.[39]

The Gifts of Prophecy and Distinguishing Spirits. Tilemann Hesshus: For the apostles, the word *prophecy* not only signified the preaching of future events, but more generally it was the function of teaching the gospel and explaining the holy Scripture, as Paul states in 1 Corinthians 14. Those who prophesy speak to men and women for their edification, encouragement, and consolation. Therefore a word of prophecy is employed in a twofold manner in holy Scripture. Sometimes it is employed for prediction, as Agabus predicted a famine, or when Athanasius predicted the death of Emperor Julian. Sometimes it indicates the skill of preaching to the people about God and eternal life.

Other people [have the gift] of distinguishing spirits. This gift is notable and is very necessary in the church, yet it is not given to everyone. For not all godly people—even if they understand the truth, are zealous to avoid error, and are governed by the Holy Spirit—are able to detect fanatical spirits and recognize their tricks and plots. For Satan transforms himself into an angel of light. Alexander and Athanasius were judging more accurately than many other bishops what a great blasphemy Arius was attempting to inflict on the church. Cyril judged the fanatical spirit of Nestorius far more correctly than John of Antioch or Theodoret. . . . Luther, of sacred memory, who was endowed with an extraordinary gift for discerning spirits, hereafter perceived the error of Karlstadt, Zwingli, Oecolampadius, Müntzer, Schwenckfeld, the Münsterites, and the Anabaptists. The fact that Luther detected and revealed to the world the Roman Antichrist was the gift of discerning spirits. . . . Since the church of Christ especially needs this notable gift so that the machinations of Satan can be disclosed and restrained from Christ's little ones, we must passionately pray to God that he will always provide some people in the church with this splendid gift of the Holy Spirit. Explication of 1 Corinthians 12:10.[40]

The Spiritual Gift of Tongues. Wolfgang Musculus: The gift of tongues was first poured out on the apostles by the Spirit of God shortly after the ascension of Christ, as they were undertaking their apostolic office of instructing people of all nations throughout the world. Afterward, the gift of tongues also began to be poured out on believers, as Christ had predicted in the last chapter of Mark: "These signs will accompany those who believe in me: in my name they will cast out demons; they will speak in new tongues, etc." The Corinthians became very proud of this type of gift, as will soon become clear. I understand the interpretation of tongues to have been not only the gift by which some people understood those speaking various languages but also the gift of explaining and proclaiming that which was said in a foreign tongue for the benefit of the church. This gift of interpretation is so necessary that the apostle does not wish any tongue to be spoken in church without it. Commentary on 1 Corinthians 12:10.[41]

The Gift of Tongues Not as Important Today. Peter Martyr Vermigli: This gift was especially necessary in the ancient world when only a few men were responsible for proclaiming the gospel throughout the whole world, which was hardly possible unless they had the capacity to

[39]Chytraeus, *Dispositio epistolarum*, 384; citing 1 Cor 14:6; Acts 11:27-28.

[40]Hesshus, *Explicatio Prioris Epistolae ad Corinthios*, 272r-273r. For Athanasius's prediction of Emperor Julian's death , see the appendix at NPNF 4:487. The "Münsterites" refers to the theocratic kingdom established in the German city of Münster by Jan Matthijs (d. 1534), Jan Beukels (d. 1536), and other Anabaptist radicals in 1534–1535. This radical experiment in theocratic communalism (including the practice of polygamy) and apocalyptic fervor ended when the city was conquered by Catholic and Protestant forces.

[41]Musculus, *Comm. 1 Cor.*, 464-65; citing Mk 16:17.

speak different languages. This gift is not as necessary today, since the church, which has now extended throughout the world, speaks in all languages and has its pastors and teachers everywhere. Nevertheless, the knowledge of the Greek and Hebrew tongues must by all means be preserved, because through them we have the Old and New Testament writings. The Corinthians were very pleased with themselves concerning this gift. In order to correct them, Paul does not list this gift among the first, but among the last—which you see not only here but also will see more clearly in the next chapter. Commentary on 1 Corinthians 12:10.[42]

The Spiritual Gift of Interpreting Tongues. John Calvin: The interpretation of tongues was different from the knowledge of tongues, for those who were endowed with the latter were often not acquainted with the language of the people with whom they were dealing. Interpreters translated foreign tongues into the native language. At that time they did not acquire these gifts by hard work or study, but they possessed them by a miraculous revelation of the Spirit. Commentary on 1 Corinthians 12:10.[43]

Luther Possessed the Gift of Interpreting Tongues. David Chytraeus: The interpretation of tongues [is] the ability to translate foreign languages clearly into our own tongue, as Luther, with singular clarity, translated the Psalms and the Prophets into the German language; or, more generally, it is an eloquence or gift of speaking, or of skillfully explaining entangled theological controversies, many of which arise only because of the ignorance of someone's choice of words and phrases. Postil on the Epistle for the Tenth Sunday After Trinity.[44]

Gifts Are Imparted by One Spirit, Not Many. Jacques Lefèvre d'Étaples: Christians do not perform these gifts from different spirits, but it is one and the same Spirit who descends invisibly and works all things in all God's people: many gifts in some people, few gifts in others; greater gifts in certain people, more humble gifts in others; all for the sake of his goodness and wisdom and for supporting the head. But there are many different spirits—not one and the same Spirit—who falsely distribute gifts. For this reason the pagans were deceived in error. They thought that Minerva distributes words of wisdom; that Mercury gives knowledge; that Apollo grants the power to heal; that Hecate bestows the power to predict the future; that Phoebe gives the power of divination; or again, that Mercury distributes the gifts of tongues and their interpretation. The spirits of error were diverse, dwelling prominently in their visible abode in heaven whence they had been invisibly driven. Therefore what Minerva inspired was not wisdom, but demonic messages (as I would call them), inimical to true wisdom. The books of Orpheus and Zoroaster, and certain ones of Proclus, Iamblichus, Porphyry, and some other Platonists contain such messages. The strength of Apollo was not real, but pretended. And what Hecates bestowed was not true power or wonders or miracles, but magical portents and tricks that were of no use—the kinds of things employed by the Docetists and Simon Magus. And the prophecies of Phoebe were not genuine, but ambiguous predictions whose meaning could be taken in different ways; generally, they were nothing but imposture, sophistry, and tricks intended to deceive people. As for the raging of the guardian Mercury: they were not true tongues nor true interpretations, but the deception of cunning eloquence for ruining the body and soul at the same time. Commentary on 1 Corinthians 12:11.[45]

[42]Vermigli, *In Selectissimam Priorem ad Corinthios Epistolam . . . Commentarii*, 329r-v.
[43]CO 49:500 (cf. CTS 39:403).
[44]Chytraeus, *Dispositio Epistolarum*, 385.
[45]Lefèvre d'Étaples, *Commentariorum in Epistolas Beati Pauli . . . Liber Secundus*, 119r-v. Docetism was the early Christian heresy that taught that Jesus Christ only appeared to have a human body.

Unity in the Spirit Precludes Self-Sufficiency. John Calvin: "One and the same Spirit who apportions. . . ." From this it follows that those people act wrongly who, without any concern for sharing, destroy that sacred unity where all the parts agree with one another and all act in harmony under the leading of the same Spirit. Paul again calls the Corinthians back to unity, when he reminds them that, whatever gifts they possess, they have obtained them from the same source. At the same time, he instructs them that no one possesses so much that they are sufficient in themselves and do not need the help of other people. For this is what he means by the phrase, "apportions to each one individually as he wills." The Spirit of God, therefore, distributes these gifts among us, in order that we all might contribute to the common good. He does not impart everything to a single individual, lest anyone become so satisfied with their portion that they cut themselves off from others, and live solely for themselves. Commentary on 1 Corinthians 12:11.[46]

Different People Have Different Gifts. John Trapp: It is reported that in Luther's house was found written: "Substance and eloquence, Philip Melanchthon. Substance without eloquence, Martin Luther. Eloquence without substance, Desiderius Erasmus." Every person has their own share, and all are not gifted alike. Commentary on 1 Corinthians 12:11.[47]

[46]CO 49:500 (cf. CTS 39:404).

[47]Trapp, *A Commentary or Exposition*, 690*.

12:12-31 One Body with Many Members

[12]For just as the body is one and has many members, and all the members of the body, though many, are one body, so it is with Christ. [13]For in one Spirit we were all baptized into one body—Jews or Greeks, slaves or free—and all were made to drink of one Spirit.

[14]For the body does not consist of one member but of many. [15]If the foot should say, "Because I am not a hand, I do not belong to the body," that would not make it any less a part of the body. [16]And if the ear should say, "Because I am not an eye, I do not belong to the body," that would not make it any less a part of the body. [17]If the whole body were an eye, where would be the sense of hearing? If the whole body were an ear, where would be the sense of smell? [18]But as it is, God arranged the members in the body, each one of them, as he chose. [19]If all were a single member, where would the body be? [20]As it is, there are many parts,[a] yet one body.

[21]The eye cannot say to the hand, "I have no need of you," nor again the head to the feet, "I have no need of you." [22]On the contrary, the parts of the body that seem to be weaker are indispensable, [23]and on those parts of the body that we think less honorable we bestow the greater honor, and our unpresentable parts are treated with greater modesty, [24]which our more presentable parts do not require. But God has so composed the body, giving greater honor to the part that lacked it, [25]that there may be no division in the body, but that the members may have the same care for one another. [26]If one member suffers, all suffer together; if one member is honored, all rejoice together.

[27]Now you are the body of Christ and individually members of it. [28]And God has appointed in the church first apostles, second prophets, third teachers, then miracles, then gifts of healing, helping, administrating, and various kinds of tongues. [29]Are all apostles? Are all prophets? Are all teachers? Do all work miracles? [30]Do all possess gifts of healing? Do all speak with tongues? Do all interpret? [31]But earnestly desire the higher gifts.

And I will show you a still more excellent way.

a Or *members*; also verse 22

Overview: Employing the analogy of the human body, Paul urges believers in Corinth to live in harmony with one another; members of the Christian church should think neither too highly nor too lowly of their gifts, but everyone should use their gifts for the common good. Reformation commentators find in these verses a beautiful picture of the church, where Christian believers of different ethnic and social backgrounds are united together in the body of Christ through the sacraments of baptism and the Lord's Supper. The reference to baptism in the text stirs a lively debate as to whether small children should be baptized into the body of Christ in the same manner as believing adults. Because God has sovereignly apportioned various spiritual gifts to every Christian man and woman, there is no place for pride, jealousy, or rivalry. Most Reformation interpreters argue (or assume) that a number of these spiritual gifts—such as predicting the future, the working of miracles, healing, and speaking in tongues—were important in the early church for validating the Christian faith, but are no longer needed or practiced in the present day. This conviction probably reflects, at least in part, Protestant skepticism regarding the putative "miracles" performed by Catholic saints and martyrs as well as deep-seated suspicions of radical end-times "prophets" such as Thomas Müntzer, Melchior Hofmann, and the Münster revolutionaries, Jan Matthijs and Jan Beukels.

12:12-13 *Unity in Diversity*

As the Body of Christ, the Church Is Called Heavenward. John Colet: That reason and wisdom by which the whole church is guided is in Jesus as its summit. As long as the church obeys it, the church is healthy, and beautiful, and effectual for some useful action. But if the opposite happens, if any human reason, wrath, and desire should break forth and too presumptuously transgress the bounds set by God's Spirit, then everything in God's church is wretchedly thrown into confusion and foully beset by disorders.

This is what has happened now, in our own age, because men and women have fallen away from the Spirit of God into their own reason, wrath, and unlawful desires. But when the Spirit keeps all things within himself and preserves each thing in its proper place, and composes all the members and people in the church in such a way that they flourish, and feel and do all things by the Spirit, then, in God, the church displays a beautiful form and countenance, and is entirely healthy, and pure, and alive, and vigorous, and radiant with a godly complexion. . . . For Christ is life itself in the life of God. In him all humanity is both drawn upward, as by a magnet, and sustained in God. And the same divinity, like a magnet, supports on high the rest of humanity who have a share in Christ, and at the same time keeps them close together on high and united with Jesus, as one member with another member. For humans are like iron who, by their own nature, are sure to fall to earth if deserted by the Spirit of God.

Therefore, on that precious stone, that most powerful rock, that heavenly and divine magnet, the whole church is supported and rests; above the valley of the world and wretchedness it shines forth radiant on the mountain, on Christ, as an object of admiration, looking upward to heaven and the glittering stars, looking down to earth and to dark humanity in their mist of gloom. Between heaven and earth [the church] stands on the summit of Christ, the towering mountain, but breathing in the clear and life-filled air of God's Spirit. From there they daily advance toward the same Christ, in their own purification by the divine fire, and finally they become in him altogether simple, pure, and united. Then, at the same time, they become clear and radiant by the light of the divine sun; and consumed by the love of God, they are made perfect in heaven, in Christ. Exposition of 1 Corinthians 12.[1]

Paul Uses the Similitude of the Human Body. John Calvin: Paul now draws a similitude from the human body, which he also makes use of in Romans 12:4, though for different reasons, as I have said previously. In that previous passage,[2] Paul exhorts everyone to be content with their own calling, and not to trespass on other people's territory, for ambition, curiosity, or some other passion drives many people to undertake more than is expedient. But in this passage, Paul exhorts believers to be in harmony with one another by the mutual sharing of their gifts, for they were not conferred on them by God to be enjoyed separately by themselves, but so that they might help one another. . . .

Therefore the meaning is this: although the members of the body are various and have different functions, they are nevertheless connected together in such a way that they are united as one. Therefore we who are members of Christ, although we are endowed with various gifts, ought nevertheless to focus on that union which we have in Christ. Commentary on 1 Corinthians 12:12.[3]

Infants Belong to the Body of Christ. Huldrych Zwingli: "We are all baptized into one body." Therefore baptism is nothing other than the sign of those who belong to the one body of Christ. The children of Christians also belong to the body and church of Christ, even before they

[1]Colet, *Enarratio*, 240.
[2]That is, Rom 12.
[3]CO 49:501 (cf. CTS 39:404-5).

are baptized. Who, therefore, will deny to them the sign of the people of God—that is, baptism—if they themselves belong to God? For no one is given the sign of God unless they are first part of the people of God. Now, this sign is given to them so that they might become known to others. Moreover, those who belong to the one body of Christ also have the same spirit; all of them focus on the same thing, namely, the glory of God and the advantage of the entire body. Therefore those who are eager to make a profit and are devoted to their own glory, who are animals to their own lusts because they are disciples of the Antichrist, do not have the spirit of Christ, no matter how much they echo the name "Christ" with their mouths. Annotations on 1 Corinthians 12:13.[4]

No Person Is Superior in Christ's Church. Wolfgang Musculus: Paul excludes every distinction within the universal fellowship of the whole church. He does this first by saying, not simply "we were baptized in one Spirit," but "we have *all* been baptized in one Spirit." Then, because he was not at all satisfied that this specific point would be observed by everyone, he adds the point of different races and conditions, saying, "whether Jews or Greeks, whether slave or free." Paul includes with these two races all other peoples, when he says, "whether Jews or Greeks." So too when Paul says, "whether slave or free," he includes in these two conditions people from all different sorts of social standings. Now Paul was applying his words to those quarrels that were then prevalent in the church. For first, there was an almost irreconcilable dispute between Jews and Greeks, that is, between races. Second, the prerogative of rich and free persons had begun to be considered greater than that of poor people and slaves. Therefore so as to point out that these prejudices should have no place in the church, Paul makes this specific reference to Jews and Greeks, slaves and free. . . .

Most despicable is the pride of the human heart, with which people despise what God does not despise—differences of race, or circumstance, or every sort of life condition—and do it in the name of God himself. God does not distinguish between Jews and Greeks, slaves and free people. Yet corruptible human beings made of dust, in matters of religion, distinguish one race from another, slaves from free people, the poor from the rich, the uneducated from the learned, and thus they wish to be associated with people of equal status, and separate themselves from those they consider to be inferior—though they all share the same divine dignity. I am not speaking here about the different social positions and ranks in the world, which Paul does not abolish on account of the kingdom of Christ. Rather, I am speaking about the pride by which one person does not associate with another person in religion on account of the humble state of his external circumstances. Commentary on 1 Corinthians 12:13.[5]

The Spiritual Benefits of Baptism and the Lord's Supper. Tilemann Hesshus: Let the godly reader observe in this passage the testimony of the final and effective cause of baptism and the Lord's Supper. Paul says, "in one Spirit, we were all baptized into one body." Therefore baptism has been instituted by God for this purpose, that through him we might be made members of the body of Christ, cleansed from sin, regenerated through the Holy Spirit, and established as heirs of eternal life, just as Paul also says elsewhere: "All of you who have been baptized into Jesus Christ have put on Jesus." Again, in Romans 6: "Do you not know that all who have been baptized in Christ Jesus have been baptized into his death? We have been baptized, therefore, with him by baptism into death, so that, just as Christ was raised from the dead by the glory of the Father, so too we might walk in newness of life."

Baptism, therefore, is not only an external sign that we are citizens of the church, but it is the means by which God works salvation in us and the Holy Spirit regenerates us to life. In the same

[4]Zwingli, *Annotatiunculae . . . ex ore Zvinglij*, 104.

[5]Musculus, *Comm. 1 Cor.*, 470.

fashion, Paul states concerning the Lord's Supper: "we have drunk of one Spirit." It's as if he were saying: "With this purpose in mind, the Son of God instituted his most sacred Supper, and he offers to everyone his flesh for eating and his blood for drinking, so that he might impart to us his Holy Spirit. And by this bond he unites us together with him as if members of one body. The Lord's Supper is not only an external sign that reminds us of the passion and death of Christ, but it is also the means and instrument by which the Son of God imparts to us his Spirit, confers life, nourishes and confirms our faith, and seals us as heirs of eternal life." Explication of 1 Corinthians 12:13.[6]

Infant Baptism Disproved. Menno Simons: Since Christ Jesus has commanded baptism on confession of faith and since the apostles have so taught and practiced it, and since the meaning of baptism according to 1 Corinthians 12:13 . . . cannot be construed except of believers, therefore it is sufficiently forbidden by this divine ordinance to baptize infants. . . . By these words of Paul believer's baptism is once more plainly taught and confirmed. On the other hand, anti-Christian infant baptism is rejected and denied because God the merciful Father in his holy gospel through Jesus Christ points us to faith alone, and to the new birth. Christian Baptism.[7]

Only Adult Believers Are Baptized in the Spirit. Dirk Philips: The apostle here writes primarily about the baptism of the Spirit and of the embodiment with the Christian congregation that takes place through the spirit of faith. For his words are thus: "We are all baptized by one Spirit into one body and all are refreshed by one spirit" (1 Cor 12:13). From these words it is easy to determine that Paul here speaks primarily of the baptism of adults, which occurs through the Spirit, and therefore [he] means only mature believers. For these are fit for such baptism and not the children. For what is the baptism of the Spirit other than that we receive the gift of the Holy Spirit from God, the heavenly Father, through Christ Jesus (Acts 2:38), through whom we truly confess God and truly believe in Jesus Christ. [This is] as the apostle testifies and says that "no one may call Jesus Christ Lord, except through the Holy Spirit" (1 Cor 12:3), who gives to each the gift of faith and apportions all spiritual gifts according to his will (1 Cor 12:11). Therefore faith is a gift of the Holy Spirit through which all believers are gathered into one body, and thereupon they are baptized as a sign and proof of a genuine inner being and the spiritual fellowship they have with Christ and all the saints.

Since then children do not have the spirit of faith, how shall they then through that same spirit be baptized into one body with all believers? Or if one after all wants (yet incorrectly and with force) to prove the gift of the Spirit and faith in children, then they must also through the same Spirit not only be baptized with the believers into one body but also receive the benefit of and participate in the Lord's Supper. For all those who through one Spirit have been baptized into one body and are refreshed with one Spirit (1 Cor 12:13), and have thus become one body and one loaf in Christ Jesus, these must also break bread with one another according to the institution of the Lord and according to the apostolic doctrine. The Baptism of Our Lord Jesus Christ.[8]

Believers Are United in the Sacraments. David Dickson: All the faithful are joined together in the sacraments of baptism and the Lord's Supper. That is, the union of all the faithful into one church, and partaking of one life, in one body, and one Spirit, is signified in the sacraments. Therefore, [Paul indicates], you ought not to disagree among yourselves about the diversity of gifts. Exposition of 1 Corinthians 12:13.[9]

[6]Hesshus, *Explicatio Prioris Epistolae ad Corinthios*, 274v-275r; citing Gal 3:27; Rom 6:3-4.
[7]Simons, *Complete Writings*, 264, 270.
[8]CRR 6:100.
[9]Dickson, *Exposition of St. Paul's Epistles*, 61*.

12:14-20 *Many Parts but One Body*

People Should Remain in Their God-Given Vocations. Martin Luther: Because the hands are compelled to work, they appear to be in a more troublesome situation than the eyes. But the feet support and carry the entire body, and if you consider the burden they bear, they are the most unfortunate members of the entire body. Better is the situation of the tongue, which tastes what is agreeable to it and is sumptuously fed. The gifts are of various kinds, but the burdens must be borne the way they have been laid on each person. God gives the ability to bear them, and one must keep in mind Paul's well-known statement (2 Cor 12:19): "My grace is sufficient for you." Although the feet alone support the bulk of the body, they nevertheless derive their power and healthy state from the body and enjoy all the benefits of the body. The eyes, precious members though they are, cannot assume this seemingly small and easy function; for they were created to be different and to serve a different purpose. Therefore it is necessary to observe the rule that everyone should remain in their calling and live content with their gifts but should not be inquisitive about other people. Lectures on Genesis 17:9.[10]

The Priesthood of All Believers. Martin Luther: Therefore, just as those who are now called "spiritual," that is, priests, bishops, or popes, are neither different from other Christians nor superior to them, except that they are charged with the administration of the Word of God and the sacraments, which is their work and office, so it is with the temporal authorities. They bear the sword and rod in their hand to punish the wicked and protect the good. A cobbler, a smith, a peasant—each has the work and office of their trade, and yet they are all alike consecrated priests and bishops. Further, everyone must benefit and serve every other by means of their own work or office so that in this way many kinds of work may be done for the bodily and spiritual welfare of the community, just as all the members of the body serve one another. Letter to the Christian Nobility.[11]

All Christians Are Important Members of Christ's Body. Tilemann Hesshus: Paul has explained at length and in detail each part of the similitude and comparison that he has provided. Thus there is no need for a detailed discussion here. But the summary of this whole comparison is this: just as God, in his marvelous wisdom, has established and combined different members in the human body, so too, in his wonderful wisdom and goodness, he has bestowed different gifts on the citizens of the church. That is why, even as there is no rivalry, no quarreling, no disagreement among the members of one human body, so too there ought to be no rivalry or disagreement among Christians. The bishop is like the eye of the church; ministers of the Word are like beautiful feet proclaiming the gospel of peace. The bishop cannot say that he doesn't need the service of ministers of the Word. Moreover, God confers more excellent gifts on the inferior citizens of his church in such a way that all the members of the body are made beautiful. Therefore, since one member in the body looks after another member, do not all members grieve and wither when one member is harmed? Such sympathy should also exist among Christians, and no one ought to be jealous either for a higher degree of honor or more excellent gifts, but should reflect on the fact that God has established all persons in their place, and that there is no one among the simple people of Christ whose lot in life is so unimportant that they do not serve the glory of God and bear fruit in the Lord. Hence we should despise no one. On the contrary, when one Christian suffers an injury, all grieve. When one person experiences glory and honor, everyone ought to rejoice. When such agreement and harmony is visible among all the members of Christ's body, then there will be no room for quarreling and disagreement. Explication of 1 Corinthians 12:14-20.[12]

---

[10]LW 3:130.

[11]LW 44:130.

[12]Hesshus, *Explicatio Prioris Epistolae ad Corinthios*, 276r-v.

The Dangers of Comparison and Envy. Peter Martyr Vermigli: "If the foot should say, 'Because I am not a hand'. . ." etc. Paul ascribes to members of the human body the words that were causing a commotion among the Corinthians. He does this so that the Corinthians would realize that it was not Paul now censuring them, but nature itself criticizing them. This is the nature of Christian freedom, to rebuke someone out of love, seasoning it with honey. It is as if Paul were saying: "If you find the law of nature concerning a living body convincing, why don't you find the law of love even more convincing?" The apostle enumerates four parts of the body—the eye, ears, hands, and feet—and he brings them together in such a manner that the foot speaks concerning the hand, but not the eye; and the ear speaks concerning the eye, but not any other member. He does this because it is the nature of envy to be jealous of good things that are close and near rather than far away. For you do not usually see common people envy the good fortune of a king, but rather they envy those who have a little more wealth than them. This is what Aristotle stated in his *Rhetoric* about envy. There are two vices that must be avoided: First, those who are endowed with lesser gifts should not think for that reason that they do not belong to the church. Second, those who are richly endowed with gifts should not think that weaker people and those with less-significant roles in the church are thereby not participants in the church, which is the body of Christ. Commentary on 1 Corinthians 12:15-16.[13]

Diversity of Gifts Should Be Welcomed, Not Despised. David Dickson: Seeing that the condition of the body requires a plurality and, consequently, a diversity of members, it follows that the lowest offices and the least-valued gifts are as important for the body as the most excellent offices and gifts. And if [those of low position] should exclude themselves, they would be doing so no less foolishly than if the foot should deny that it was the hand, or the ear deny that it was the eye—and for that reason, should conclude that it was not of the body. Therefore there should be no dissension among you, because of the diversity of gifts. Exposition of 1 Corinthians 12:16.[14]

The Necessity of Diverse Gifts in the Body. The English Annotations: Again, Paul is speaking to the same people who were discontented at the meanness of their gifts in comparison to others. He shows them that if what they desired were to come to pass, that is, that all should be equal to one another, there would follow the destruction of the whole body, and consequently themselves. For it could not be a body unless it were made of many members knit together, and diverse one from another. And so that no one should find fault with this division as unfair, Paul adds that God himself has united all these together; therefore, all must remain joined together so that the body may remain in safety. Annotations on 1 Corinthians 12:17.[15]

God Has Appointed Different Members in One Body. Wolfgang Musculus: God wished there to be a diversity of members, each uniquely distinct, and thus he appointed each one of them as he wished. That is why it would be incompatible with his divine intention if all the members of the human body were transformed into the same member, and the whole body comprised in that one member. Paul warns that we should think in a similar way about the members of the church and stop arranging them all into a single member. "For God arranged the members in the one body, each one of them as he chose." Therefore those who are "feet" in the body of the church, let them recognize that God has wished them to be "feet," and has placed them as "feet" in the body of the church. Consequently every member of the church should think this way. . . . Inasmuch as we are warned that God does all

[13]Vermigli, *In Selectissimam Priorem ad Corinthios Epistolam . . . Commentarii*, 340r. Aristotle discusses envy in *Rhetoric* 2.10.

[14]Dickson, *Exposition of St. Paul's Epistles*, 61*.

[15]Downame, *English Annotations*, EE2v*.

things according to his will, let us restrain our flesh from rash curiosity, lest we scrutinize the reasons for his works. For godly people, the pinnacle of goodness, righteousness, wisdom, and power is found in the will of God. Now Paul is not here violating this rule when he says that God appoints the members in the body. For although he speaks about the human body, nevertheless he is revealing to our eyes by means of this similitude the condition and nature of the true church of God. Commentary on 1 Corinthians 12:18.[16]

God Has Providentially Ordered All Things. John Calvin: "If all were one member." Paul means that God has not acted randomly, or without good reason, in assigning different gifts to the members of his body; but that it was necessary for him to do this for the preservation of the body. For if such an orderly arrangement were destroyed, confusion and disintegration of chaos would result. We ought to be all the more eager to submit ourselves to the providence of God, which has so suitably arranged everything for our common good. Commentary on 1 Corinthians 12:19.[17]

A Body with Only One Member Would Be Disastrous. David Dickson: If the body was only one member, three inconveniences would result. First, the rest of the members would be excluded, including the more noble senses (verse 17). Second, the change would be made contrary to the wise dispensation of God, who has otherwise appointed the diversity of members (verse 18). Third, the change would be contrary to the nature of living bodies, and would destroy them (verse 19). For this reason, God has made one living body out of many members (verse 20). In a similar fashion, in ecclesiastical matters, if there was only one function, three inconveniences would result. First, the other offices would be extinct. Second, the dispensation of God would be destroyed. Third, the church as a living body would be overthrown, since it now consists of many offices, united together in one body. Therefore harmony and agreement is to be protected. Exposition of 1 Corinthians 12:20.[18]

12:21-26 *Weak Members Deserve Special Honor*

Paul Now Addresses the Superior in the Church. Wolfgang Musculus: Paul continues with the similitude of the body as before. Hitherto he has discussed the unity of the body, how it consists in the multitude of members, and he has encouraged the hearts of believers who are humble and inferior in the church. Now he addresses the pride of those who are superior, calling them away from despising the humble to cultivating the unity and peace of this same body. "The eye," Paul says, "cannot say to the hand, 'I have no need of you.'" When encouraging those who were considered inferior, Paul expressed their thoughts by saying: "If the foot should say, 'because I am not a hand, I do not belong to the body,'" etc. Here, when he wishes to restrain the pride of those who considered themselves superior, he expresses their thoughts by saying: "Now the eye cannot say to the hand, 'I have no need of you.'" Paul describes them as "eyes" and "heads" within the church because, in the body, the head and eyes are like the teachers and governors. Commentary on 1 Corinthians 12:21.[19]

God Distributes Gifts and Offices According to His Wisdom. Tilemann Hesshus: This is the fourth argument whereby the apostle proves that there should not be haughtiness concerning gifts, nor fighting with others out of rivalry, nor deceiving anyone, nor jealousy of anyone else. For God himself did not establish only one sort of minister and office in the church, but has supplied the kingdom of his Son with various offices and gifts according to his wisdom and goodness. Human beings do not decide what gifts they will possess, nor do they station themselves at this or that place. Such

[16]Musculus, *Comm. 1 Cor.*, 475.
[17]CO 49:503-4 (CTS 39:410).
[18]Dickson, *Exposition of St. Paul's Epistles*, 61-62*.
[19]Musculus, *Comm. 1 Cor.*, 477.

decisions are determined only by the will and good pleasure of Almighty God, who understands clearly what is most useful for the church, and it is fitting that he alone distribute his gifts. Therefore we should gaze on the wisest plan of God and his most compassionate will with true humility and earnest expressions of gratitude, and faithfully serve in whatever place he has stationed us for the magnifying of God's glory and the edification of the church. Explication of 1 Corinthians 12:21-26.[20]

Superior People Need Inferior People. John Trapp: Those who are superior should not put down their inferiors, since they cannot live without them—a fact that they will be forced to acknowledge at one time or another. It was a saying of General Vere to the king of Denmark that kings did not care about their soldiers until that time when their crowns hung on the one side of their heads. Commentary on 1 Corinthians 12:21.[21]

People Adorn Their Less Honorable Members. Cardinal Cajetan: Paul calls "weaker" those members that are more feeble, such as the stomach, liver, and spleen; although they are more feeble (for they are easily wounded), they are more necessary than the eyes and hands. . . . Paul calls "less honorable members" the feet with respect to the hands, and the ears with respect to the eyes, for people who enjoy decorating their bodies are more accustomed to decorate these members. For in the ancient world, they covered up their feet with golden slippers, and even today people hang golden earrings on their ears. . . . Paul calls "shameful" those members that are dishonorable, or disgraceful, or unsightly. Even today, these members are covered with silken and golden trousers in many nations. Commentary on 1 Corinthians 12:22-23.[22]

No Member of the Body Is Naturally "Weak" or "Dishonorable." Peter Martyr Vermigli: "And on those parts we think less honorable," etc. Paul's reason rests on common sense, whereby we judge that less honorable members should be more carefully adorned. And it must be noted that when Paul mentions things that are "weak" and "dishonorable," we should remember the words that proceed it (i.e., "we think"). Because, if you evaluate those words according to the nature of things, there is no weak member, because its function has been appointed to it by nature. But the "weak" thing is determined by our opinion, and we think the same with regard to "honorable" things. God was the architect of all the members [of the body], and so none of the members should be called either shameful or dishonorable as to their natural constitution. That is why Augustine, in book four of his *Contra Julian*, sharply reproached Julian because he claimed that some members of our body were shameful before sin [entered the world], while other members were honorable or more free—and Julian cited this passage in Paul to defend his opinion. Augustine responded to him that Paul was not speaking about the human body insofar as it had been created by God, because God created nothing dishonorable. Commentary on 1 Corinthians 12:23.[23]

The Church's Unpresentable Parts. Wolfgang Musculus: I think that Paul means the same thing with the word *aschēmona* ("unpresentable parts") as the word *atimotera* ("less honorable parts"), for the latter refers to our buttocks, from which we expel excrement. As it relates to members of the church, Ambrose thought it referred to those brothers who are despised, going about in poverty and nakedness. I think the word refers to those who engage in less honorable duties, whether in the church or republic.

[20]Hesshus, *Explicatio Prioris Epistolae ad Corinthios*, 277r.
[21]Trapp, *A Commentary or Exposition*, 691*. Englishman Horace Vere, the first Baron Vere of Tilbury (1565–1635), was a distinguished military commander during the Thirty Years' War.
[22]Cajetan, *In Omnes Sacrae Scripturae expositionem*, 5:129.
[23]Vermigli, *In Selectissimam Priorem ad Corinthios Epistolam . . . Commentarii*, 341r-v. See Augustine, *Contra Julian* 4.16 (PL 44:779-82).

The apostle warns not only that these people should not be treated with contempt but, even more, that they should be carefully cherished and honored, lest the common body of the church dishonor them through neglect. We in no way agree with those who, under the pretext of celibacy, run after a life of unsettled lust and consider the married life of procreating children to be a less honorable and shameful way of life, an estate they even judge to be impure. For, in fact, the estate of marriage is honorable among all and the marriage bed undefiled (Hebrews 13:4). Commentary on 1 Corinthians 12:23.[24]

God's Purposes Are Not Always Hidden from Us. Peter Martyr Vermigli: "God has so composed the body, giving greater honor to the member that lacks it." These words are placed here by the apostle so that no one will think we have poor judgment when we treat with greater honor those members that seem more contemptible. He says that it is divine rather than human wisdom that God himself has composed the body in this fashion, conferring [honor] on the member that is lacking, and withdrawing [honor] from the one that abounds. And Paul adds the reason why God had done this: "that there be no division [*schisma*] in the body." This is the third reason that Paul proposes for not despising the weaker member, because divisions easily arise from such pride, and the body of Christ is thereby mangled. We learn from this passage that not every purpose of God is so hidden that its reason cannot be discerned. For we hear the reason for the divine purpose announced by Paul: "that there be no division in the body." In Exodus we see the same thing happening. For when the people came out of Egypt, they were led forty years through the desert, when they could have been brought quickly to the boundary of Palestine in the Promised Land. The Scripture says it happened this way so that, if Israel had been forced to fight immediately with the enemy, and was overcome with terror, she would not flee back to Egypt. Consequently, we will confess that the purpose of God is inscrutable in certain matters concerning predestination, the various apportionment of honors, and many other sorts of things God has determined to do on the basis of his supreme justice, although we do not understand his reason. But in certain other cases, we will not be prevented from being able to understand the reason for the divine purpose. Commentary on 1 Corinthians 12:24-25.[25]

The Importance of the Unity of the Body. Wolfgang Musculus: In the Greek, [this passage reads] "so that there might not be schism in the body," that is, so that some members are not divided from other members and the unity of the body torn apart. The reason Paul gives why God has composed the body in this way is so that it might remain in its unity and wholeness. For the body can hardly survive when the members are tearing each other apart. In truth, the members are torn apart when those parts thought of lesser value are forsaken for those deemed superior, and so mutual care and working with one another is abandoned. Hence Paul also adds "but that the members may have the same care for one another." Commentary on 1 Corinthians 12:25.[26]

Rejoicing Together and Grieving Together. John Calvin: "If one member suffers." In the human body, Paul says, there is seen such a sympathy that if one member suffers any misfortune, all the rest of the members grieve, just as when one member experiences something good, the rest rejoice. Hence there is no place for envy or contempt. "To be honored" is taken here in a broad sense, meaning to be in a good and happy state. For there is nothing better suited for promoting harmony than this shared concern for one another,

[24]Musculus, *Comm. 1 Cor.*, 479. For Ambrose's (Ambrosiaster's) treatment of this passage, see his *Comment. in Epist. I ad Cor.*, in PL 17:262.

[25]Vermigli, *In Selectissimam Priorem ad Corinthios Epistolam . . . Commentarii*, 342v.

[26]Musculus, *Comm. 1 Cor.*, 480-81.

where everyone recognize that they are enriched by the prosperity of others every bit as much as they, and similarly impoverished by their loss. Commentary on 1 Corinthians 12:26.[27]

When One Suffers, All Suffer. John Trapp: Luther, in a certain letter of his to Lambert Thorn, a prisoner for Christ, wrote, "I doubt (and this is grievous to me) that I shall ever have the honor of martyrdom as you have. But herein I can comfort myself, that your bonds are my bonds, your imprisonment and burning at the stake, mine. For, as long as I confess and extol them, so long I will both suffer with you and rejoice with you." Commentary on 1 Corinthians 12:26.[28]

12:27-31 *Desire the Higher Gifts*

The True Church Is One. Wolfgang Musculus: [Johann] Eck quotes this passage to prove that the church of Christ is one, and thus should not be torn part, and that no one can be saved outside of it. We do not deny this, as long as we recognize what the true church of Christ is. We know that the church is singular, just as the body of Christ is singular. We confess that it must not be torn apart, and we agree that, outside of it (just as outside of the body of Christ), no one can be saved—not because of their attachment to those other members, but because of their attachment to Christ, the head. But if the name "church" is maliciously ascribed to powerful people, to defects, adultery, and bloodthirstiness, and those defiled by idol worship, then we explicitly deny that this is the church; it is not the body of Christ, but a conspiracy of those who are deceiving others and are deceived themselves. Commentary on 1 Corinthians 12:27.[29]

Gifts Come Before the Ministry. John Calvin: At the beginning of the chapter, Paul spoke about gifts; now he begins to discuss offices—and this order of things we should carefully observe. For the Lord did not appoint ministers unless he had first equipped them with the necessary gifts and qualified them to perform their duty. Hence we must infer that those people who thrust themselves on the church without the necessary qualifications are fanatics and driven by an evil spirit. There are many people who boast that they are under the influence of the spirit and glory in a secret call from God, when all the time they are unlearned and completely ignorant. The natural order, on the other hand, is this: that the gifts come before the actual ministry. Therefore, just as Paul has taught above that everything a person has received from God should be devoted to the common good, so now he reminds them that offices are distributed in such a manner that, by their combined efforts, they may edify the church, each according to the proportion of their gifting. Commentary on 1 Corinthians 12:28.[30]

God Provides Different Ministries at Different Times. Martin Bucer: Thus our dear Lord Jesus exercises his rule in his church by calling everyone to it and ensuring that those who commit themselves to his church lack no good thing, either in spiritual or in temporal matters. That is why from the commencement of the church he has not only appointed and used one sort of minister to bring about the salvation of his people. There are some whom he used only at the beginning, to awaken the world to his Word and kingdom, such as prophets, who had the gift to declare those things that were hidden or in the future. Similarly those to whom he gave the gift of speaking immediately in many and foreign languages, and those who performed miracles and had the gift of bringing healing by calling on his name.

There are other ministries that the Lord still uses today, but not in so general or powerful a way

[27]CO 49:504-5 (cf. CTS 39:412).

[28]Trapp, *A Commentary or Exposition*, 691*. Lambert Thorn was executed by Catholic authorities in Brussels in July 1523 for his evangelical convictions.

[29]Musculus, *Comm. 1 Cor.*, 483. Johann Eck was a Catholic theologian, apologist, and Bible translator who opposed Martin Luther at the Leipzig Disputation (1519).

[30]CO 49:505-6 (cf. CTS 39:413-14).

as in the commencement of the church. Thus the apostles who bring the kingdom of Christ from one place to another, as the Lord's chief legates and ambassadors: at the beginning these spread the kingdom of Christ far and wide in a short time, setting up churches in every place. It may be that the Lord still provides this sort of ministry today and at all times, but we do not have so many of them, nor do they maintain in their apostolate so powerful a spirit and so exalted a role as the first apostles did. True Care of Souls.[31]

The Ministries of the Spirit. Desiderius Erasmus: How can it happen that nature is more important than grace? Are you not the body of Christ, or, to be sure, one part of its members, that he has arranged in his body (which is the church) so as to appoint to each its place and function? And in the first place, he has appointed apostles, who, as stewards of the gospel of grace, exercise the office of Christ. Next are prophets, who either lay bare the future or explain hidden things. Third are teachers, who, gifted in letters and the disciplines, share what they know for the common benefit. In the fourth place are those with powers, gifted to restrain the power of demons and display the name of Christ through miracles. Fifth are those who are able to heal diseases. Following this, those who are able to provide help to the afflicted by means of their judgment and discretion; those who, by their prudence, are very gifted in maintaining the multitude in their duty. And after that, those with a knowledge of languages that can be useful to other people. These various gifts not only encourage but also compel mutual harmony among you, as you in turn desire to help one another. Are all apostles? Are all prophets? Are all teachers? Are all equipped with power? Do all possess gifts of healing? Do all speak in various tongues? Do all have the gift of interpretation? Not at all! But to each person is given their own gift. No one should be despised, but everyone should strive to deserve to be joined to those things that are most excellent, and always make progress for the better. Paraphrase on 1 Corinthians 12.[32]

God Appointed Apostles and Prophets. Wolfgang Musculus: Paul says that God appointed in the church, not merely the apostle Peter, but apostles in general. He who appointed Peter also appointed Bartholomew, Andrew, Thomas, James, John, etc. And, as with Peter, he appointed them *in the church*. Was Peter the only one sent into the world to proclaim the gospel of the kingdom? . . . Since Paul assigns prophets to the second place between apostles and teachers, I think that the prophets mentioned here should be understood as those who were predicting the future. Subsequently, he also calls prophets those who speak to the people, either exhorting or reproaching them, or explaining the holy Scriptures. We learn more about these prophets below in chapter 14. Commentary on 1 Corinthians 12:28.[33]

Defining Apostles and Prophets. Tilemann Hesshus: In the New Testament, an apostle was a person called directly by Jesus Christ to give witness to the teaching, miracles, death, and resurrection of Jesus Christ. The apostle was not restricted to a certain place, but was sent into the whole world to preach the gospel of Jesus Christ, clearly equipped with the grace of the Holy Spirit and the gift of performing miracles as special testimony to the church that his teaching was without error.

The prophet in the Old Testament was a person called directly by God to purify the teaching of the church and propagate the promise concerning the Mediator. Prophets provided counsel to the governing authorities in the kingdom of Israel, and were endowed with the gift of predicting the future and performing miracles as testimony that they announced the certain teaching concerning God. The prophet in the New Testament was a person called directly by God, not for any political

[31]Bucer, *Concerning the True Care of Souls*, 25-26.

[32]Erasmus, *Paraphrases*, 315-16.

[33]Musculus, *Comm. 1 Cor.*, 486-87.

authority in a kingdom, nor restricted to a certain place, but sent into the world to purify the teaching of the church and shine forth the gospel of Jesus Christ. They were endowed by the Holy Spirit with the gift of predicting the future. Explication of 1 Corinthians 12:28.[34]

Special Roles. The English Annotations: The first and uppermost place is given to the apostles, because they were called to that office immediately by Christ, without any intermediate human authority (see Gal 1:1). They had manifold preeminence above other doctors and pastors; they could not err in matters of doctrine; their commission was general to preach to all nations; they were endued with special power to work miracles and punish the disobedient in an extraordinary manner. Secondarily, prophets were those who by a special and extraordinary gift interpreted in a prophetic manner the Scriptures for edification, exhortation, and consolation, cf. 1 Cor 14:3. Or they were those who infallibly foretold things to come, as Agabus in Acts 21:10 and the daughters of Philip the evangelist in Acts 21:9. Annotations on 1 Corinthians 12:28.[35]

The False Prophets of Münster. Obbe Philips: After this some others arose . . . who had been ordained by Jan Matthijs—such as Jacob van Campen, a teacher of Amsterdam, Damas of Hoorn, Leonard Boekbinder, Cornelius from the Brielle, Nicholas of Alkmaar, Maynard of Delft, and many others, with all of whom I have spoken and dealt much with—and such strange instruction was heard among them! One corrupted marriage. The second taught nothing but parables. The third would pardon no one nor recognize them as brother or sister who fell into apostasy after baptism and herewith referred to the willful and knowing sin unto death. The fourth would have the baptism of John before the baptism of Christ, etc. Others stood firmly by visions, dreams, and prophecies. Some also were of the opinion that when the brothers and teachers were put to death, they would immediately be resurrected and would rule on earth with Christ a thousand years, and all that they left behind them would be restored to them a hundredfold. Thus there were almost as many meanings as there were teachers, each comforting himself with lies and false promises, visions, dreams, and revelations. Some had spoken with God, others with angels—until they got a new trek underway to Münster. During this business, those at Münster accepted the teaching and commission of the apostles of Jan Matthijs, namely, Gerard Boekbinder and John of Leyden; and in time, with the message and their apostolic role, they took Münster with the sword and by force.

In this business, the most prominent in Münster were Jan Matthijs and John of Leyden, who later became king of Münster, also Bernard Rothmann. If one were to describe the beginning and end of all those events and how it all transpired, one would have to write a book about it—of the books, writings, and letters they daily sent to us, of the great signs, wondrous visions, and revelations they had daily. Since such highly celebrated prophets and prophecies came so quickly to an end and misrepresented themselves, one may perceive of which spirit they were the children and by which spirit they were led and driven. A Confession.[36]

Bishops Are Called to Teach the Gospel. Philipp Melanchthon: Nobody is unaware that those persons ought to teach who are called by God's clear revelation or through humans because they have a clear command to teach, "Woe to me if I do not preach the gospel." . . . [But] Paul did not want everyone to speak in the church; thus the function of those who are called to teach in the church should not be interrupted by those who have not been called—unless the speaker is teaching false doctrine. In that case, they should be interrupted by everyone. . . . Paul wants everyone to prophesy and commands them to be on guard lest

[34]Hesshus, *Explicatio Prioris Epistolae ad Corinthios*, 277v-278r.
[35]Downame, *English Annotations*, EE2v*.
[36]CRR 10:220-21*.

they extinguish the spirits. Therefore all who are able should teach, but everyone should attend to their own calling, to their own state, namely a father teaching his family, an instructor teaching his pupils, and those who are able teaching the people, provided that they act out of faith and seek the glory of the gospel. Such persons are undoubtedly called by the Spirit of God, because they have the grace to proclaim the gospel, which they ought to impart to the church. It is of these persons that the apostle speaks, "If anyone aspires to the office of bishop, he desires a noble task." Annotations on 1 Corinthians 12:28-29.[37]

The Office of Teacher Includes Pastors. Wolfgang Musculus: Paul does not fully enumerate all of the offices of ministers of Christ. For in Ephesians 4, along with prophets, he mentions evangelists and pastors, and then he places teachers. Now it appears that the teachers mentioned here are the same as those he calls pastors in Ephesians. It is clear that we should understand teachers to be those who instruct in the church. This function belonged to bishops and elders who, metaphorically speaking, were called pastors, whom the apostle appointed in the churches he established. In Acts 20, Paul said that these men had been appointed to this office by the Holy Spirit so that they might feed the church of God, which most certainly refers to teaching the Word.... In my opinion, it is somewhat of a stretch to refer this particular office to that of the catechists and teachers of students in the churches, as Origen once was. If a general definition of "teacher" is accepted, one can include this sense. But if we stick to a specific definition, I think that pastors, bishops, and elders should be understood here. This passage in no way refers to those papal doctors with their degrees, theologians, or our teachers, because it cannot be said that God appointed them in the church. For this reason I have frequently been surprised when ministers of Christ desire and even boast about some special title, like the degree of academic doctor, as if some authority for teaching might come from it. Commentary on 1 Corinthians 12:28.[38]

The Gift of Teaching. Tilemann Hesshus: The teacher in the church is a person called indirectly by God, that is, through other people, to spread the teaching concerning God among men and women, and to explain the holy and apostolic Scripture. Teachers are engaged with neither the governance of the church nor the administration of the sacraments, but only with the propagation of teaching drawn from the writings of the prophets and apostles, and with the faithful application of the same Scriptures for consolation and exhortation. Explication of 1 Corinthians 12:28.[39]

The Church Built Up by Sound Doctrine. Heinrich Bullinger: The last thing that is to be noted is this: that not only of old and up to the present time, but in these days too the Lord God gives doctors and pastors to the church: doctors, I say, and not governors and captains of hosts, not princes, not soldiers, not crafty men using deceitful means that nowadays they call practices. For by no other means and manner, by no other instrument than by the doctrine of truth and sound and simple godliness, is that holy catholic church of God built up, fenced, and preserved, of which at the beginning simple men and Christ's apostles laid the foundation. Decades.[40]

Miracles and Healing. Peter Martyr Vermigli: The word "powers" or "miracles" is in the Greek *dynameis*. People with this gift had the power to restrain wicked people. With this gift

[37]Melanchthon, *Annotationes in Epistolam priorem ad Corinthios*, 148, 150; 1 Cor 9:16; 1 Thess 5:19; 1 Tim 3:1.

[38]Musculus, *Comm. 1 Cor.*, 486-87; citing Eph 4:11; Acts 20:28. Origen (c. 184–253/254) was an early Christian exegete and theologian from Alexandria, remembered especially for his allegorical exposition of Scripture and his Platonic understanding of Christian theology. He was also a controversial figure, and his writings were later deemed heretical at the Second Council of Constantinople (553).

[39]Hesshus, *Explicatio Prioris Epistolae ad Corinthios*, 278r.

[40]Bullinger, *Decades* 4:33*.

they handed over excommunicated persons to be oppressed by Satan. Peter and Paul were chosen to use this gift. By means of this same gift, Elijah made fire come down from heaven. So too Elisha stirred up a bear against those boys who were mocking him, and, single-handedly and unarmed, brought the cavalry of the king of Syria into the city of Samaria. This gift from the Holy Spirit is the opposite of the gift of healing, for whereas by means of that former gift wicked people are restrained through punishments; with the latter gift people who have been oppressed by disasters and diseases are raised up again. Commentary on 1 Corinthians 12:28.[41]

Healings Validated the Faith of Early Christians. Heinrich Bullinger: There follows the gift of healing. We stated previously that some hold the view that medicine is also a gift of God—but Paul understood it as the gift of healing that was frequently practiced in the ancient church. On this subject, when Ambrose was asked why this gift did not also occur in his own day as it is known to have occurred in the past, he responded: "It was necessary for healings to occur in the church's beginning so that people might accept as valid the fundamentals of the faith. But now there is no need for healings, because people lead others to faith when their good works and simple proclamation are in evidence." Commentary on 1 Corinthians 12:28.[42]

The Offices of Helping and Government. John Calvin: Since the apostle here is enumerating [church] offices, I do not accept what Chrysostom says, that *antilēpseis*, that is, helps or assistance, consists in supporting the weak. What, then, does it mean? Certainly it either refers to an office and a gift of the church that once existed that is unknown to us today; or it pertains to the diaconate, that is, the care of the poor—and this latter interpretation is more pleasing to me. Now Paul mentions two kinds of deacons in Romans 12:7, which I have treated in my commentary on that passage.

I take "governments" to mean the elders, who were responsible for discipline. For the ancient church had its ruling council [*senatum*], which kept the people living honorably, as Paul indicates elsewhere (1 Tim 5:17), where he lists two kinds of elders. Therefore "government" consisted of those presbyters who excelled others in gravity, experience, and authority. Commentary on 1 Corinthians 12:28.[43]

The Office of Deacons. David Dickson: Paul lists the ordinary offices and gifts, namely, "helps," or the office of deacons, whose work it was to see to the maintenance of ministers, the necessities of the saints, and the dispensation of the public revenues of the church. Although this office may seem to be insignificant, Paul emphasizes its importance, and that it should not be given to men of inferior rank, but only to those who are trustworthy, and men of financial substance. . . . For without the help of this office, the work of ministry would be greatly hindered. Deacons, who undertook the responsibility of collecting stipends, enabled the ministers more freely to attend to the work of the Lord. Exposition of 1 Corinthians 12:28.[44]

Tongue-Speaking Includes Interpretation. John Calvin: By the phrase "various kinds of tongues" Paul includes both the knowledge of languages and the gift of interpreting them. But they were two distinct gifts, because sometimes a person who spoke many tongues did not, however, know the language of the actual church with which he had to deal. Interpreters compensated for this deficiency. Commentary on 1 Corinthians 12:28.[45]

[41]Vermigli, *In Selectissimam Priorem ad Corinthios Epistolam . . . Commentarii*, 346v.

[42]Bullinger, *In Priorem ad Corinthios Epistolam Commentarius*, 222-23. For Ambrose's (Ambrosiaster's) treatment of this verse, see his *Comment. in Epist. I ad Cor.*, in PL 17:263.

[43]CO 49:507 (cf. CTS39:416-17). For Chrysostom's treatment of this verse, see his *Homilies on 1 Corinthians* (homily 32), in NPNF 12:186-87.

[44]Dickson, *Exposition of St. Paul's Epistles*, 62*.

[45]CO 49:507 (cf. CTS 39:417).

Gift of Tongues Listed Last for a Reason. The English Annotations: Because the Corinthians were proud of this gift [of tongue-speaking], it appears that Paul names it last so as to humble them and lessen their self-conceit regarding this gift of the Spirit. For the way they used this gift made it least useful in the church. Annotations on 1 Corinthians 12:28.[46]

No Person Has All the Gifts. Peter Martyr Vermigli: Having set forth the different functions of the church, Paul now concludes that no one ought to imagine that all these gifts belong to a single person as if they were sufficient in themselves. It is true that the church has a sufficiency, as is clear from the aforementioned gifts. But this sufficiency must not be sought in a single member, for that would be like saying the entire welfare of a republic depended on a single magistrate or a single citizen. Commentary on 1 Corinthians 12:30.[47]

Eagerly Desire the Superior Gifts. Huldrych Zwingli: Paul is not speaking about gifts in their relation to one another, nor about the external function of the gifts, but about their internal function. For example: You are a bishop; someone else holds the consulship. Now Paul's intention is not that you who are consuls should also pursue the duties of a bishop. Instead, just as a bishop should exert all his energy to teach, to oppose wicked people, and to work for the benefit of the entire church, so also, even as you apply yourself to this responsibility alone—opposing vices and scandals, and restraining sinful people—you should not busy yourself with the affairs of your republic. Hence the meaning of "eagerly desire the superior gifts" is this: that you should eagerly desire that which is highest and best within the gifts. Therefore love is that highest and most excellent part among all the gifts that Paul is encouraging, for it is the life of all the virtues. As Paul demonstrates, love is that excellent way; it is the leader and guide of all the gifts. Now God alone arouses this love in our hearts through his Spirit. For at one time we were so corrupted by our carnal desires and so tainted with false opinions that it was not uncommon for us to cling to wickedness instead of the virtues, and we indulged in wickedness in the name of virtues. At that time, even if we were endowed with the aforementioned gifts, nevertheless we would use them for our own benefit and glory—if God, by his Spirit, did not stimulate our hearts and ignite the fire of love within us for another purpose. Therefore the gifts of the Spirit are neither useful nor blessings from God if there is no love within us. Commentary on 1 Corinthians 12:31.[48]

What Are the Superior Gifts? Wolfgang Musculus: What are the superior gifts? Recent interpreters refer this statement to what comes before, and relate it to the gifts of prophecy and teaching, which are more useful for the church than the gifts of healing or tongues—and thus they are superior. Jerome explains it this way, saying: "That is, earnestly desire prophecy." For truly, if prophecy is compared to the gift of tongues and gifts of healing, it is far more outstanding, which will be demonstrated in greater detail below in chapter 14. Since the gift of prophecy is not possessed by everyone, but is only bestowed on some, Paul has already said, "are all prophets?" I do not think that the apostle's intention is to encourage the Corinthians in general to pursue the gift of prophecy. . . . But I think it is simpler that, along with Chrysostom and Ambrose, we refer this passage to what follows, and that we understand faith, hope, and love as the gifts of God that are superior, because without them our salvation cannot stand. Commentary on 1 Corinthians 12:31.[49]

---

[46]Downame, *English Annotations*, EE2v-3r*.

[47]Vermigli, *In Selectissimam Priorem ad Corinthios Epistolam . . . Commentarii*, 346v.

[48]Zwingli, *Annotatiunculae . . . ex ore Zvinglij*, 106-7.

[49]Musculus, *Comm. 1 Cor.*, 489. For Jerome's treatment of this passage, see his *Against Jovinianus* 2.23, in NPNF 6:405-6. For Chrysostom, see his *Homilies on 1 Corinthians* (homily 32), in

A More Excellent Way. John Trapp: What was this "more excellent way"? Love for God and our fellow human beings (1 Cor 13:1). Graces are better than gifts. A shop full of barrels does not enrich unless they are full of commodities. Heavenly gifts are but the lumber of a Christian. It is grace that makes a man or woman rich toward God; for this reason, it is chiefly to be coveted. We should also be careful that we do not get spiritual rickets, growing big in the head (in our gifts) while decaying in our vitals, that is, in grace, and the exercise of it. Commentary on 1 Corinthians 12:31.[50]

NPNF 12:187-88. For Ambrose (Ambrosiaster), see his *Comment. in Epist. I ad Cor.*, in PL 17:264.

[50]Trapp, *A Commentary or Exposition*, 691*.

13:1-13 The Way of Love

If I speak in the tongues of men and of angels, but have not love, I am a noisy gong or a clanging cymbal. *2 And if I have prophetic powers, and understand all mysteries and all knowledge, and if I have all faith, so as to remove mountains, but have not love, I am nothing.* *3 If I give away all I have, and if I deliver up my body to be burned,*[a] *but have not love, I gain nothing.*

4 Love is patient and kind; love does not envy or boast; it is not arrogant 5 or rude. It does not insist on its own way; it is not irritable or resentful;[b] *6 it does not rejoice at wrongdoing, but rejoices with the truth. 7 Love bears all things, believes all things, hopes all things, endures all things.*

8 Love never ends. As for prophecies, they will pass away; as for tongues, they will cease; as for knowledge, it will pass away. 9 For we know in part and we prophesy in part, 10 but when the perfect comes, the partial will pass away. 11 When I was a child, I spoke like a child, I thought like a child, I reasoned like a child. When I became a man, I gave up childish ways. 12 For now we see in a mirror dimly, but then face to face. Now I know in part; then I shall know fully, even as I have been fully known.

13 So now faith, hope, and love abide, these three; but the greatest of these is love.

a Some manuscripts *deliver up my body* [to death] *that I may boast* **b** Greek *irritable and does not count up wrongdoing*

Overview: In 1 Corinthians 13 the apostle Paul reminds the proud Corinthians that Christian love is far superior to the spiritual gifts about which they boast; for, whereas love of God and neighbor is eternal, spiritual endowments such as prophecy, tongue-speaking, and knowledge are temporary and fleeting. In their comments on this passage, Protestant exegetes define Christian love and extol its beauty, even as they address a central problem raised by the text: Why does the apostle state that love is *greater* than faith and hope (1 Cor 13:13), when he argues elsewhere that men and women are justified by *faith* alone, rather than by faith and love? The majority of commentators resolve this apparent discrepancy by explaining that Paul is not speaking here about justifying faith, but about the *gift* of faith described in 1 Corinthians 12:9. Hence, rather than being a source of justification, love is the necessary fruit of the faith that justifies a Christian; as such, love must inform and guide the expression of all spiritual gifts. Reformation commentators are also intrigued by Paul's discussion of the imperfect and childlike quality of human knowledge. Christian men and women will only acquire a full and mature understanding of divine truth in heaven when they gaze on the glorious splendor of the triune God himself.

Love Is the Supreme Spiritual Gift. Jacques Lefèvre d'Étaples: The gifts of the Holy Spirit that have been enumerated are excellent, but they are specific and not necessary for the salvation of every member of the body of Christ. But there are three other gifts of the Holy Spirit that are necessary for every single member of Christ (those who have the capacity for reason): faith, hope, and charity, the latter of which is called love and love of God. For faith looks to God, as does hope; and charity especially looks to God. Now by means of this love God is especially loved for the sake of himself since all people are creatures of God and created in his image. However, all believers ought to be loved not only because they are creatures of God and reflect the image of God but also because they have been made sons and daughters of God through regeneration, because they are members of Christ, and because as brothers and sisters of Christ they, along with all believers, have the same father. . . . Nothing commends us more to God; nothing is more necessary for our salvation [than love]. We ought to be especially zealous for this love of God, preparing ourselves for it with all our strength, and begging God for it with our whole heart. Commentary on 1 Corinthians 13:1.[1]

Gifts Must Be Combined with Love. Martin Luther: St. Paul writes this chapter to silence and humble the arrogant among Christians, especially the teachers and preachers. The gospel gives great knowledge about God and Christ, in addition to many great gifts, which St. Paul lists (Romans 12; 1 Corinthians 12). Some have the gift of speaking, some of teaching, some of interpreting Scripture, some of ruling, and so forth. Thus among Christians there are great riches and treasures of spiritual knowledge and gifts, and all obviously know the meaning of God, Christ, human, conscience, sin, the present and the future life, devil, death, world, cross, etc. Nevertheless, we find few who correctly use those gifts and knowledge, who humble themselves to serve others, in accord with love. Rather, each one seeks their own honor, glory, and advantage, and wants to be seen as soaring over others. Postil on the Epistle for Quinquagesima Sunday.[2]

True Godliness. Tilemann Hesshus: In this chapter, Paul exhorts the Corinthians and the entire church to a true and genuine love of God and neighbor, for this is true godliness. This is the fountain, spring, and mother of all the virtues. This is the mistress of all gifts and duties. This alone is the goal toward which all things ought to be directed, to be sure, that we love both God and neighbor. This is the banner of Christ's kingdom, which all the citizens of the church ought to follow so as to subdue Satan together with all his machinations. And so Paul here commends love, and prefers it to all the gifts. And making a pretended comparison, he adds what will happen to those gifts and duties that in this life serve for the edification and propagation of the church, when God will be all in all. Explication of 1 Corinthians 13.[3]

Love Is the Business of a Christian. Martin Luther: Love, I say, is a fruit of this sacrament [of the Lord's Supper]. But this I do not perceive among you here in Wittenberg, even though you have had much preaching and, after all, you ought to have carried this out in practice. This is the chief thing, which is the only business of a Christian. But nobody wants to be in this, though you want to practice all sorts of unnecessary things, which are of no account. If you do not want to show yourselves Christians by your love, then leave the other things undone too, for St. Paul says in 1 Cor 13:1, "If I speak in the tongues of men and of angels, but have not love, I am a noisy gong or a clanging cymbal." This is a terrible saying of Paul. "And if I have prophetic powers, and understand all mysteries and all knowledge, and if I have all faith, so as to remove mountains, but have not love, I am nothing. If I give away all I have, and if I deliver my body to be burned, but have not love, I gain nothing" (1 Cor 13:2-3). Not yet have you come so far as this, though you have received great and rich gifts from God, the highest of which is the knowledge of the Scriptures. It is true, you have the true gospel and the pure Word of God, but no one as yet has given his goods to the poor, no one has yet been burned, and even those things would be nothing without love. You are willing to take all of God's goods in the sacrament, but you are not willing to pour them out again in love. Nobody extends a helping hand to another, nobody seriously considers the other person, but everyone looks out for themselves and their own gain, insists on their own way, and lets everything else go hang. If anybody is helped, well and good; but nobody looks after the poor to see how you might be able to help them. This is a pity. You have heard many sermons about it and all my

[1]Lefèvre d'Étaples, *Commentariorum in Epistolas Beati Pauli . . . Liber Secundus*, 121r.
[2]LW 76:339* (WA 17,2:162; E² 8:116).

[3]Hesshus, *Explicatio Prioris Epistolae ad Corinthios*, 279v-280r.

books are full of it and have this one purpose, to urge you to faith and love. Sermon on the Eve of the Sunday Before Reminiscere.[4]

13:1-3 *The Superiority of Love*

Love Is Superior to Eloquence. John Calvin: Paul begins by discussing eloquence, which, to be sure, is an admirable gift in itself, but in no way commends people to God when it is separated from love. When he speaks of "the tongues of angels," he is using hyperbole to denote what is unique or exceptional, although I prefer to construe it to mean a diversity of languages, which the Corinthians were holding in high esteem, judging everything by ambition—not by fruit. Commentary on 1 Corinthians 13:1.[5]

What Does "Speaking in Tongues" Mean? Johann Spangenberg: Nothing other than to read, sing, and exegete the Psalms, Prophets, and the holy Scriptures with clear words. Postil on the Epistle for Quinquagesima Sunday.[6]

The Tongues of Angels. The English Annotations: Since the angels are spirits (Heb 1:14), they do not technically have tongues as we do. This statement therefore must be understood to mean either the angels' faculty of expressing their conceptions to one another, employing their tongue as we use ours; or the apostle is referring to the variety of tongues that the angels may have used when they were sent to deliver messages to people of various nations and languages; . . . or else the apostle is referring not so much to the *variety* of tongues as to the *gift* of eloquence, and the exquisite nature of [angelic] speech. Annotations on 1 Corinthians 13:1.[7]

Clanging Cymbals. John Trapp: Sounding only for pleasure, but signifying nothing. Tiberius the emperor used to call the grammarian Apion the *cymbalum orbis*—the cymbal of the world—for his constant prattle. And Jerome inveighs against some people in his time that used only tinkling and tickling words, without weight or worth. Commentary on 1 Corinthians 13:1.[8]

Different Ministers Have Different Gifts. Martin Bucer: The churches have not taken their ministers all from the same type of person as far as outward things are concerned: indeed, in order that it may be seen that all Christians, high and low alike, are nonetheless one in Christ, ministers of the church have been taken from people of high, middle or lower classes, as each was found to excel in the necessary gifts for the care of souls.

For the sake of their recognition and approval by the people, and because of their geniality and good manners, it is often appropriate that many ministers are those born and brought up with respectable, capable people and friends: this was true of the majority of the ancient holy bishops, such as Ambrose, Augustine, Chrysostom, and others. When, however, those who possess these advantages and gifts do not have sufficient understanding of matters of the faith for themselves, let alone to be powerful in teaching and instruction of others, it is better for the churches to take those who excel in these necessary gifts of Christian understanding and zeal, even though they may not be so attractive and lovely from an outward point of view. Thus even though someone should come who is "able to speak in tongues of men and angels and fathom all mysteries," if they are not faithful and zealous in the affairs of the Lord, it is better to take those who may be lacking in eloquence and learning, but are genuinely concerned with the things of Christ. True Care of Souls.[9]

---

[4]LW 51:95-96.
[5]CO 49:508-9 (cf. CTS 39:419).
[6]Spangenberg, *Postilla Teütsch*, 4:128r.
[7]Downame, ed. *English Annotations*, EE3r*.
[8]Trapp, *A Commentary or Exposition*, 691*. Apion was a grammarian and teacher of rhetoric in Rome during the first half of the first century AD. He was infamous for his loquacious and boastful personality.
[9]Bucer, *Concerning the True Care of Souls*, 56-57*.

Prophecy, Mysteries, and Knowledge. Martin Luther: "To prophesy" is—as follows in chapter 14—when someone is able to understand and explain well the Prophets and Scriptures through the inspiration of the Holy Spirit. This is quite a fine gift. But "to know mysteries" means that we are able to interpret the Scriptures spiritually, as we say, through allegories, as Paul does in Galatians 4, when he says that Sarah and Hagar are two covenants, that Isaac and Ishmael are two peoples—Jews and Christians. Also that the bronze serpent of Moses is Christ on the cross (John 3), and that Isaac, David, Solomon, and similar historical characters were types of Christ. Such St. Paul calls a mystery, that is, a hidden, secret meaning beneath the superficial meaning of the narrative. "Knowledge," however, is the understanding of the external matters and Christian freedom, that we know that our conscience is bound to nothing, etc. So then St. Paul wants to say: "Now whoever is capable in the entire Scriptures, both the plain understanding of the Scriptures and the hidden understanding of its meaning, and knows everything about Christian freedom and how to conduct their external life, and does not have love—that is, they do not serve their neighbor with all this, but instead pursue their own honor and benefit—they are indeed lost and count for nothing before God." Postil on the Epistle for Quinquagesima Sunday.[10]

Defining Terms. Johann Spangenberg: [Prophesying means] nothing other than to preach and concentrate on the true understanding of God's Word. Now it is truly a glorious thing [only] on account of love—for the most holy office on earth is considered to be worthless by St. Paul if it does not walk in love. [To understand all mysteries means] that we can interpret the Scripture spiritually, and from the figures of the Old Testament we can draw out a fitting meaning that is presented according to Scripture. And by this we serve the Christian congregation. Postil on the Epistle for Quinquagesima Sunday.[11]

Paul Uses Hyperbole Here. Wolfgang Musculus: But someone will ask how it is possible for a person to understand all mysteries and have complete knowledge of both divine and human things, when God alone possesses these two things. I answer: the apostle is using hyperbole here, because it is not possible for anyone to know all mysteries and possess all knowledge. But he demonstrates by means of this hyperbolic fiction how all these gifts are nothing—even those that reach the highest status—if love is absent. Commentary on 1 Corinthians 13:2.[12]

Christians Are Justified by Faith Alone. Tilemann Hesshus: But why does Paul say: "And if I have all faith so as to move mountains, but have not love, I am nothing"? On the basis of this statement, first of all, the popes abuse Paul's intention, for they attempt to conclude from this that men and women are not justified by faith alone, but by both faith and love. And they argue that faith is only a preparation for justification, whereas love perfects it, and thus (they claim) we are formally righteous before God by means of love. And next, the followers of John Major seek to defend their error from this passage, as if Paul here were proposing that love is necessary for salvation, and that no one is able to be justified and saved apart from love; and moreover, that in the act of justification itself good works are especially necessary. These corruptions of Paul's statement must be completely refuted. Therefore we answer both the popes and the defenders of Major's error that in the apostolic writings one must always pay attention to what topic of doctrine is being explained. For the apostles do not teach everything in a confused fashion, but carefully distinguish subjects. Now, Paul is not referring in this passage to the justification of men and women before God,

[10]WA 17,2:163 (cf. E² 8:118; LW 76:340-41); citing Gal 4:24-31; Jn 3:14-15; Num 21:9.

[11]Spangenberg, *Postilla Teütsch*, 4:128r-v.

[12]Musculus, *Comm. 1 Cor.*, 496-97.

a doctrine that he explains in Romans 3 and 4, and Galatians 3, where he has clearly shown that men and women are justified by faith alone apart from works. Instead, in this present passage, Paul is referring to the good works of those who have been born again and justified, namely, that love which ought to be the guide of all the gifts—this passage, therefore, is not treating the article of justification. Note how Augustine distinguishes between *being* justified and the justified: "Good works," he says, "do not precede justification, but come after one has been justified."[13] And so we distinguish between the act of justification itself of men and women, and the judgment of those people who have been justified. When treating justification itself, good works must not be combined with it. For humans beings are justified freely before God by faith alone, without the works of the law. In other words, good works are not the cause, nor the reason, nor the source, nor one of the sources of justification. Good works are not the means for taking hold of justification. They are not even a necessity that must be present for justification to occur; rather, without any condition and necessity of good works, men and women are justified before God by faith on account of the Mediator Jesus Christ. The death of Jesus Christ alone is the sole and sufficient cause of our justification. And faith alone is the means by which we appropriate to ourselves the benefits of the Mediator. . . . But after a man or woman has been justified freely by faith, then the fruit of good works ought certainly to follow faith, for it is impossible for those who have experienced the remission of all their sins, who have been established as heirs of eternal life, not to begin to love the merciful God. Explication of 1 Corinthians 13:2.[14]

What Paul Intends by "Faith." Wolfgang Musculus: Paul moves on to faith, by which he means not that faith which is common to all Christians, by which we are rendered Christian and justified before God, and by which our hearts are purified, without which no one is able to please God. Rather, he intends the faith that he mentioned among the spiritual gifts in the previous chapter, saying: "to another, faith by the same Spirit." This kind of faith is miraculous; it is not given to all people any more than the other gifts of wisdom, knowledge, prophecy, tongues, healing, etc. We spoke about this in the previous chapter. Commentary on 1 Corinthians 13:2.[15]

Both Faith and Love Are Necessary. Hans Denck: Food and drink cannot be separated from each other if they are to be of any benefit. Food without drink constipates and does not nourish. This is what Paul means to say when he writes: "If I had faith to remove mountains but lacked love, it would be nothing." Drinking without food softens and intoxicates. Love without faith cheats itself in its presumptuous claim that it loves everything for God's sake. While this may appear to be so for a while, it is nonetheless untrue. Suddenly it breaks out for everyone to see that love will love only that which love loved before, even though that were evil, and that love always hates that which speaks the truth to love, even if that were good. Food and drink, if taken together, are useful indeed. Food comforts and strengthens; drink kindles love and perfects that for which Christ came, which is the washing away of sin, a task that has been accomplished in the shedding of Christ's blood. Confession Addressed to the City Council of Nuremberg.[16]

Religious Behavior Without Love Is Nothing. John Trapp: The same is true of all other parts of Christian obedience, whether active or passive. If we attended church as frequently as Anna the prophetess was in the temple (Lk 2:36-38), so that our ears were nailed to the church doors (as someone once said); if our knees were as calloused as a camel's knees with our kneeling before the Lord; if our faces were furrowed with continual

[13]Augustine, *Exposition of the Psalms* (NPNF 8:545).
[14]Hesshus, *Explicatio Prioris Epistolae ad Corinthios*, 280v-281v.
[15]Musculus, *Comm. 1 Cor.*, 497; citing 1 Cor 12:9.
[16]Denck, *Selected Writings*, 22.

weeping, as Peter's was said to be—but we lacked love—then all would be nothing. Commentary on 1 Corinthians 13:2.[17]

Motives Behind Almsgiving Important. Menno Simons: But as to the alms and support of the poor, I would say that it is a good and praiseworthy work, and I heartily approve of it. Many pious heathen philosophers, such as Aristotle, Plato, etc., have also considered it just. But that sincere and true repentance, or the true kernel and basis of sincere love that is a fruit of true faith, consists therein, this we deny; for we may give in hypocrisy, as well as in love, as may be witnessed in the scribes and Pharisees, by manifest heathen, and daily still in the case of the papists.... Therefore let everyone take heed as to the purpose and mind with which they give alms. For the love that is of God and is of a divine nature hates all boasting and hypocrisy, and does not know them. Of this I am sure. Reply to Gellius Faber.[18]

Good Works Must Be Wedded to Christian Love. Tilemann Hesshus: The apostle teaches that all the other duties of a Christian man or woman—such as extraordinary generosity toward the poor, constancy in enduring dangers, confessions, and other such things—are without any benefit if they do not originate from true love, which is the source, parent, and goal of all virtues and duties. The reason for this is clear, since virtues that are void of love are also devoid of faith; and because they are performed only out of human power, they are not aroused by the Holy Spirit. As a result, such so-called virtues are nothing but a pretense, for they are not directed toward the glory of God and the good of neighbor, but only strive after the shadow of glory before people. Therefore such so-called virtues do not please God and are not true virtues; they do not receive any reward from God. Instead they belong to that category of works about which Christ said: "Truly I say to you, they have already received their reward." Explication of 1 Corinthians 13:3.[19]

13:4-7 *The Nature of Love*

Love Makes Us Coworkers with the Spirit. John Colet: Now love makes us cohelpers and coworkers with the Spirit of Christ, and makes us the living bearers of the flowers and fruits of righteousness in Christ, who is the fruit-bearing tree of righteousness. Because if having been loved, we love in return, then we are not jealous, we are not envious, we rejoice in the good everywhere and grieve at evil. It is always by love in the Spirit that we do good. Then we are not puffed up nor swollen with pride, but in humility and lowliness we willingly and kindly serve all for good. Then we are not ambitious and eager for honor, but holding ourselves in low esteem and elevating others above ourselves, we seek the honor and glory of God in all things. We strive after nothing for ourselves but after everything for God and for the good of all. We seek other people's advantage, not our own, desiring to abound more in others than in ourselves, and being satisfied that we are doing good to others, and in so doing imitating God. And when we become like him in this way, we judge that we have found sufficient reward.

For what could be better or richer for us than to become like God? And this happens in us especially when we are generous and give bountifully to others—which is the only way we are seen to be able to imitate God. For the other qualities that are in God, such as wisdom and power, we cannot imitate. But his goodness, his Spirit of love, we are able to imitate through generosity and almsgiving. Exposition of 1 Corinthians 13.[20]

Love Is Patient. Wolfgang Musculus: The Greek word here is *makrothymei*, which means "to

[17]Trapp, *A Commentary or Exposition*, 692*.
[18]Simons, *Complete Writings*, 657.
[19]Hesshus, *Explicatio Prioris Epistolae ad Corinthios*, 283r-v; citing Mt 6:5, 16.
[20]Colet, *Enarratio*, 266.

be long-suffering." Many interpreters choose to render this clause "Love is patient." The particle *thymos* (passion) is related to the heart; but it denotes the heart considerably moved and disturbed, as when blood begins to bubble within the chest and boil forth into wrath.

Whether we take *thymon* to refer to the heart simply, or to the movement of the heart, *makrothymia* is the virtue of self-control that keeps us from growing hot with anger and suddenly flying into a rage. Thus those who translate this phrase "Love is patient" do so correctly. For that reason, Paul ascribes this virtue to love because love renders a person patient and slow to anger.

Scripture states that God is long-suffering toward sinners. When we consider Paul's words "Love is patient," we should be warned by this passage. God is love; therefore, it follows that he is slow to anger and patient. Who has considered adequately what a great blessing this is given what will one day happen? Take hold of the patience of God now, for it is inevitable that the world will soon be destroyed. Commentary on 1 Corinthians 13:4.[21]

Love Is Kind. Tilemann Hesshus: The second fruit is kindness, that is, the virtue aroused by the Holy Spirit by which persons with an eager heart assist and run to help their neighbors (both friends and enemies) in all their needs and through every sort of responsibility in which we are involved. A remarkable example of kindness shone forth in Joseph, who was kind to his brothers, although they had attempted to destroy him. Obadiah, the minister of King Ahab, exemplified kindness when he protected the prophets of the Lord, even though he feared danger to his life. Barzillai the Gileadite was kind, who, although he feared exile, followed the king into exile with his entire family. Explication of 1 Corinthians 13:4.[22]

[21]Musculus, *Comm. 1 Cor.*, 504-5.

[22]Hesshus, *Explicatio Prioris Epistolae ad Corinthios*, 285r-v; citing Gen 50:19-21; 1 Kings 18:3-16; 2 Sam 19:31-40.

Love Does Not Envy. David Chytraeus: [Love is characterized by] friendliness and modesty, which acknowledges and loves God's gifts in other people, and desires the well-being of good people and rejoices in their prosperity. Against this virtue stands envy, which is grieved that another person should excel us or be preferred before us, and desires to have that person removed or set aside so that we might not be considered inferior to them. Thus Saul envied the glory of David; Pompey envied the power of Caesar; and Marius was incited to rivalry against Sulla. Postil on the Epistle for Quinquagesima Sunday.[23]

Love Is Not Boastful or Arrogant. David Chytraeus: [Love is characterized by] humility, repressing pride, acknowledging our own weakness, submitting ourselves to others, and employing our gifts on behalf of others without contempt. Humility is related to the first and fourth commands. The opposites of [such humility] are vaunted pride; admiration of oneself; trusting in one's own virtue, wisdom, wealth, and other gifts; and despising other people. Each one of us can discern an example of such pride in our own hearts. Postil on the Epistle for Quinquagesima Sunday.[24]

Love Is Not Arrogant or Rude. Tilemann Hesshus: The third vice that wages war against love is pride and arrogance, by which persons are haughty against their neighbor, attributing more to themselves than is proper, setting themselves before others, and despising others. Pride had to be detested in Nestorius, who made this proud and wicked statement before the public assembly: "Give me, O emperor, the earth cleansed from heretics, and I will bestow heaven on you." John of Antioch was puffed up with pride against Cyril, and thus became a prominent source of horrible and pernicious disagreement in the Synod of Ephesus—for there is always strife among proud people.

[23]Chytraeus, *Dispositio epistolarum*, 119-20.

[24]Ibid., 120.

The arrogance that puffed up Karlstadt against Luther sadly aroused a quarrel in the church.

"Does not act rudely." People who are swollen with pride do not preserve either moderation or propriety. Instead, they pour forth their foolishness by means of dishonorable deeds and arrogant words, and lose all the favor that they might otherwise receive from their gifts. For any indication of a soul that is haughty and proud destroys all favor and creates envy and hatred toward God and other people, but the ability of modesty to bring forth human kindness is astonishing. Samosata[25] behaved in an improper manner as he paraded his arrogance here and there, strutting about in an improper fashion and reading his letters in public so as to show that he was involved in many affairs. I hardly doubt that he would bother or offend the Corinthians even a little, since they were struggling with this same vice. They did not apply themselves to either patience or kindness. They were burning with envy, they behaved rudely, they were puffed up with pride, and they conducted themselves indecently in public. Therefore Paul instructs them to struggle against these things by means of love and that it is necessary for all godly people to keep as far from these sorts of vices as possible. Explication of 1 Corinthians 13:5.[26]

Love Is Not Self-Serving. John Calvin: "Does not seek its own." From this we may infer how far love is from our human nature, for all of us are naturally disposed to love and care for ourselves, and strive for our own advantage. Indeed, to speak more accurately, we rush headlong into it. The remedy for such a perverse inclination is love, which causes us (against our natural reason) to be concerned for our neighbors, loving them and being concerned for their welfare. Moreover, "to seek one's own things" is to be devoted to oneself, and to be completely absorbed with caring for one's own advantage. This definition resolves the question of whether it is permissible for Christians to be concerned for their own advantage. For Paul does not here reprove every kind of care or concern for ourselves, but only that excessive concern that arises from an immoderate and blind love of ourselves. Now the excess consists in this: if we think so much about ourselves that we ignore other people; or if the desire for our own advantage distracts us from expressing that concern that God commands us to have for our neighbor. Commentary on 1 Corinthians 13:5.[27]

Love Is Not Irritable. Martin Luther: "[Love] does not act rudely," as the angry, impatient, and obstinate people do, who always and contrary to everyone want to be right. They yield to no one, and yet insist that everyone should yield to them. If that does not happen, then they set the world on fire, and they fume and rage with screams and complaints and vengefulness. That follows from the puffing up and pride we just spoke about. Postil on the Epistle for Quinquagesima Sunday.[28]

Love Keeps No Record of Wrongs. Martin Luther: [Love] is not suspicious, it interprets everything for the best and takes everything in simplicity. But the arrogant are exceedingly suspicious. They always worry that they are not regarded as great enough. They interpret all they see and hear in the worst way, as Joab explained Abner's action (2 Samuel 3). That is a shameful vice, and it is very difficult to deal with such people. Postil on the Epistle for Quinquagesima Sunday.[29]

Love Is Not Resentful. Tilemann Heshus: That is, love does not suspect others of evil or harbor evil. People commonly sin through their

[25] Paul of Samosata was bishop of Antioch from 260 to 268. He was accused and later deposed for heretical ideas concerning the person of Christ.

[26] Hesshus, *Explicatio Prioris Epistolae ad Corinthios*, 286r-v. Cyril of Alexandria opposed John the patriarch of Antioch over his support for Nestorius, and excluded John from the Council of Ephesus (431) for arriving late.

[27] CO 49:510-12 (cf. CTS 39:423-24).

[28] LW 76:340-41* (WA 17,2:167; E² 8:123).

[29] LW 76:344* (WA 17,2:167; E² 8:123); citing 2 Sam 3:25. Luther alludes here to his explanation of the eighth commandment in the *Small Catechism*.

false suspicions. For while they correctly desire to be on their guard, they go overboard. Theodosius II was suspicious of his wife Eudocia on account of the gift of fruit that Paul Rhetorem gave her, and he indulged this suspicion to such a degree that he saw to it that Paul was killed. Constantine the Great, having been incited by calumnies and suspicion, commanded that his son Crispus—an outstanding man—be killed. In a similar fashion, many people in the church suspect that others are grasping for their authority and position so that they prematurely guard themselves and attack others. Love is foreign to this vice; it does nothing out of perverse suspicion. The second statement is also fitting, that love does not harbor evil; that is, even if godly people recognize that they have received some sort of injury, nevertheless, they do not make so much of it that they desire to break the bonds of love or act against the duty of love. Instead, they overlook this injury and ignore the harm done them—unlike those who stir up the crowd by vindicating their rights. Explication of 1 Corinthians 13:5.[30]

Love Rejoices in Truth and Righteousness. Wolfgang Musculus: Faithful persons, endowed with true Christian love, do not rejoice when they see injustice practiced between brothers and sisters, as when one acts wickedly and wrongfully toward another. But more than being greatly saddened and aggrieved by injustice, they also delight in the faith and integrity of their brothers and sisters, and rejoice together with everyone when things are done in accordance with truth, sincerity, and faithfulness. And so they are sorrowful with those who are sad, and rejoice with those who are joyful. This kind of sadness and joy does not occur when heresies and schisms prevail in the church, for it is the nature of schismatics to experience much sadness if others (out of good judgment) do not join their faction. . . . No doubt this was happening in the church of Corinth on account of the enthusiasm of the sects. For when the poor were being despised in the Lord's Supper, this didn't bother the sectarians for they despised the poor. When that fornicator was living with his stepmother, the sectarians were not sorrowful, but instead were filled with pride (as we have seen in chapter 5). This sort of attitude is foreign to Christian love, which does not rejoice, but is saddened, sorrowful, and mourns from the heart when wickedness, injustice, jealousy, scandals, schisms, false teaching, and false worship appear in the church. But Christian love rejoices when the truth flourishes in the church and reigns in the mind, devotion, and behavior of everyone. Commentary on 1 Corinthians 13:6.[31]

Love Rejoices in Truth. Dirk Philips: Therefore the apostle says love does not rejoice at unrighteousness, but rejoices with the truth (1 Cor 13:6). Therefore love does not act hypocritically and does not deal deceitfully. Love does not transgress the teaching and rule of Christ. It shuns all false worship, all idolatry, ceremonies, and institutions of humans that are contrary to God. It does not seek the friendship of this world; it does not desire to please people. It knows well that all which is regarded as high among people is an abomination before God. It does not adorn the flesh; it does not seek what is temporal and perishable. It does not fear the cross of Jesus Christ but it rejoices in the same (Gal 6:16). An Apology or Reply.[32]

Love Bears All Things. John Calvin: Paul indicates by all these statements that love is neither impatient nor malicious. For it is the essence of forbearance to bear and endure all things, while it

[30]Hesshus, *Explicatio Prioris Epistolae ad Corinthios*, 287r-v. Married to Emperor Theodosius II in 421, Eudocia fell from favor in 441 when she was falsely accused of committing adultery with Paulinos, the master of the offices. Theodosius had Paulinos murdered and banished Eudocia from the empire. Though the reasons why Emperor Constantine I ordered the execution of his son Crispus in 326 are not entirely clear, one popular theory is that Constantine's wife Fausta falsely accused her stepson of attempting to rape her—in an effort to strengthen the political position of her own sons.

[31]Musculus, *Comm. 1 Cor.*, 512.
[32]CRR 6:192-93*.

is the essence of kindness and humanity to believe and hope all things. For we are by nature too devoted to ourselves, and this vice makes us irritable and complaining. The result of this is that everyone wants other people to carry them on their shoulders, while refusing to assist them in any way. The remedy for this disease is love, which causes us to be subject to one another, and teaches us to lend our shoulders to their burdens. Again, because we are naturally malicious, we are also suspicious, and assume the worst of nearly everything. But love calls us back to kindness, so that we may think favorably and sincerely of our neighbors. Commentary on 1 Corinthians 13:7.[33]

The Fourfold Fruit of Love. Tilemann Hesshus: "Bears all things." [The Greek word] *stegein* means to hold up something, as a column holds up a building. Thus it is necessary for godly and wise rulers to hold up many things that would otherwise collapse. Paul, that wise apostle, put up with many weaknesses and pretended not to see many things among his colleagues. He appeased and quieted the disturbed minds of many people. And from time to time, when he noticed that the building of the church was threatened with ruin, he himself carried the church on his shoulders. Jerome, that hot-tempered and impatient man, would have instigated great conflicts in the church if Augustine had not counteracted him by his moderation and wisdom.

"Believes all things." Paul here is not speaking about the ease or futility of believing something without solid evidence. Rather, he is indicating here the exceptional virtue that true love produces, namely, that kindness by which we interpret disputed things in the most charitable light and do not yield to blind suspicions. For when we do not have certain proof of maliciousness, we should conclude that our neighbor wishes us well. And though Saul was the most bitter enemy of David, nevertheless Jonathan, the son of Saul, believed David because he loved him and had no reason to suspect him of evil toward him. King Joash trusted the priests and entrusted money to them for the repair of the temple, since he did not have reason to suspect them of wrongdoing. But although kindness is an exceptional virtue, without which it is impossible for groups of people to cultivate peace among one another, so too this virtue must be joined to prudence, lest our gullibility catapult us into danger. In this way, the brother of Judas Maccabeus was ruthlessly cut down when he too easily trusted Tryphon; and Abner, having once trusted Joab, was killed by him. . . .

"Hopes all things." Love hopes for the improvement of one's neighbor, and so treats them gently and does not immediately rush to conclusions. Just as parents who, though they detect negligence and brashness in their son and do not want to allow it, nevertheless do not immediately drive him out of the house, but hope that he will be restored to better judgment—and thus, due to this hope, the parents act more leniently than the delinquent son deserves. In this way, David firmly endured Joab and Abishai, hoping for their improvement. Similarly, when the senator Symmachus had sung the praises of the tyrant Maximus and was charged with high treason, Theodosius acquitted and tolerated him, hoping for his improvement.

"Endures all things." Just as the commendation of love began with patience, so now at the end Paul repeats this same virtue, so as to remind us that patience is necessary in every observance of love. For the weaknesses of people are various and manifold. Many colleagues are fastidious and difficult. Many things happen daily contrary to our expectation and against our wishes. Patience must be exhibited in all these circumstances, lest by our impatience we disturb the general peace. However, this patience must be directed in a wise manner, for rulers should not close their eyes to all sins, nor should pastors always ignore the sins of their hearers and remain silent. Grave vices must especially be reproached and notorious sins punished sharply. And that patience is inappropriate and pernicious which overlooks false teaching and allows the minds of simple people to be

[33]CO 49:511 (cf. CTS 39:424).

infected with error, for fear of disturbing the peace. Explication of 1 Corinthians 13:7.[34]

Love Produces Trust. Jörg Haug: Now then, when true love has come out of proper discernment and understanding and has driven out fear, then faith or trust is added; for if one loves someone, then one believes that person; thus love gives birth to trust or faith. . . . One cannot believe or trust a person totally in earthly matters unless one first knows and loves that person. How then should I trust and hope in the eternal God, whom I do not see without first knowing and loving him, trusting and hoping for all the best from him? But when I know him in truth as my highest and only good, then I cannot help but love him in truth with my whole heart as my noblest treasure. For I know with certainty that he is faithful and just and the only singular good. Such love forces me out of experience to trust him and to expect all the best from him. A Christian Order of a True Christian.[35]

Love Believes, Hopes, and Endures All Things. The English Annotations: These actions of love, namely, that it believes, hopes, and endures all things, may either refer to God or to our neighbor. If they refer to God, then Paul's meaning is this: that love believes every word of God, hopes for all the good things he promises, and patiently awaits the accomplishment of all his gracious promises and meekly endures all his chastisements. If they refer to our neighbor, then Paul's meaning is this: that love believes and hopes all good for our neighbor, and patiently bears all wrongs, even death itself, if such afflictions accord with the will of God. Now we should not infer from this that a charitable person does not seek to prevent evil, or is careless to defend himself (Prov 14:15). For all that the apostle here affirms regarding love comes to this, that a charitable person seeks to construe all things to the best, and hopes for the best where there is no clear reason to the contrary. Such persons are more willing to suffer the greatest wrong than desire revenge or cause the least injury; they endure all things they can with a good conscience; and they seek only those things that they are confident contribute to the glory of God or the advantage of the truth. Annotations on 1 Corinthians 13:7.[36]

13:8-13 *Faith, Hope, and Love*

Love Never Passes Away. John Colet: Prophecy, tongues, and knowledge can perish, and perish they will, since they belong only to this life, which shall come to an end. But love, by which we are rooted in Christ, by which we grow, flower, and bear fruit for life everlasting, by which we are alive in oneness and purity, in the strength and beauty of faith, by which we are, so to speak, one nature and one essence with the immortal Christ—this shall never pass away. It is our perfection, and it will not be brought to nothing; by it we shall be recognized and accepted. . . . Therefore, as we are loved, let us love so that we might not fall away by not loving. Let us by love benefit others, lest we ourselves fail. As we make others rich, we ourselves are most greatly enriched. When you love others the most, and seek in God and Christ the well-being of others, then you are most loving of yourself and seek the greatest things for yourself. Exposition of 1 Corinthians 13.[37]

Miraculous Gifts Have Now Ceased—but That Isn't Paul's Point Here. Wolfgang Musculus: Seeing that some people were treating the gifts of prophecy, tongues, knowledge,

[34]Hesshus, *Explicatio Prioris Epistolae ad Corinthios*, 289v-291r; citing 2 Chron 24:1-27; 2 Sam 3:37; 18:1-33. Jonathan Apphus, the youngest brother of Judas Maccabeus, was tricked by the general Diodatus Tryphon to attend a conference in 143 BC, and was subsequently captured and executed. When Theodosius I rose to the imperial office in AD 379, he both pardoned and restored the Roman statesman Quintus Aurelius Symmachus (c. 345–402), who had temporarily supported an imperial rival named Magnus Maximus.

[35]CRR 10:8-9.

[36]Downame, ed., *English Annotations*, EE3r*.

[37]Colet, *Enarratio*, 268, 270.

etc. as more important than love, and that some were becoming proud because of these gifts, Paul again teaches that they are inferior to love. He does this through a comparison, contrasting gifts that are temporary and will one day end with love, which is everlasting and will never end. Thus, when he has said "love never fails," he adds the phrase "prophecies will be abolished, tongues will cease, and knowledge will be abolished." . . .

Certainly those former miraculous gifts of prophecy, tongue-speaking, healing, etc. have now ceased in the church because there was no purpose or reason for them after the gospel of the kingdom of God had been proclaimed, confirmed, and received throughout the world. But the apostle is not speaking here about this cessation, but about what will happen to gifts of all sorts after this life, as is clear from what follows. Prophecy, the gift of tongues, and knowledge all have their place in this present world, as is required by the situation and condition of our pilgrimage here on earth. But in the future that will not be the case. Commentary on 1 Corinthians 13:8.[38]

The Life of Faith Contrasted with the Heavenly Life. Martin Luther: Here St. Paul begins to speak about the distinction between this life in faith and that life of divine seeing in heaven. . . . It is the same God and all good that we believe here and will see there, without distinction. But there is a distinction in the knowledge we have of that same God—in one way here in this life, and in another way in that life. In this life, we do not see him but believe him. Now faith is an imperfect, dark seeing for which the Word is necessary, which is promoted through the preaching office, tongues, and prophecy. Without the Word, faith cannot exist. In that life, we do not believe him but see him, which is a perfect knowledge, for which neither the Word nor preaching nor tongues nor prophecy is necessary. For that reason, these all must cease. Thus, he says, "our knowing" (that is, in this life) "is partial," that is, imperfect, for it is based on believing, not on seeing. "And our prophesying is partial," that is, imperfect, for it is based on the Word and preaching. Both our knowledge and prophesying point to nothing less or less significant than the angels see, namely, the same God. Postil on the Epistle for Quinquagesima Sunday.[39]

Prophecy and Knowledge Necessary Because of Our Imperfection. John Calvin: This passage is interpreted incorrectly by most people, as if it meant that our knowledge, and also our prophecy, are not yet perfect, but we are daily making progress in them. But the true meaning of Paul is that it is *because* of our imperfection that we now possess knowledge and prophecy. Thus the phrase "in part" means "because we are not yet made perfect." Knowledge and prophecy remain a part of us as long as imperfection clings to us, for which they provide support. It is indeed true that we ought to make progress throughout our lives, and that whatever we possess is only beginning. But we must recognize what Paul wishes to prove here: namely, that the gifts in question are only temporary. But the reason why he points this out is that their usefulness is only effective so long as we make daily progress toward the goal. Commentary on 1 Corinthians 13:9.[40]

Human Knowledge Is Imperfect. Tilemann Hesshus: "For we know in part." Paul is not speaking about the imperfection of doctrine, as if everything has not been revealed to us as far as our salvation is concerned. Rather, he is speaking about *our* weakness and imperfection, since we are imperfect and not able to endure the splendor of God's presence. And so, for this reason, we need prophets, academic studies, the knowledge of the languages, and other sorts of knowledge. Nevertheless, all these things are obscure, and weak, and mixed with our doubts. Consequently these things will be abolished in the next life, when, in the presence of God, we will gaze on the Father, Son,

[38]Musculus, *Comm. 1 Cor.*, 517.

[39]LW 76:346-47* (WA 17,2:169-70; E[2] 8:126-27).

[40]CO 49:513 (cf. CTS 39:428).

and Holy Spirit; we will understand the truth in all its clarity, without any obscurity, without any doubt, without any error. For we recognize a man or woman at noon and in full light far better than when we look at them in the darkness. Explication of 1 Corinthians 13:9-10.[41]

Human Knowledge Is Partial. John Trapp: We therefore know things but imperfectly, because we are taught imperfectly. "My greatest knowledge," said Chytraeus, "is to know that I know nothing." And Augustine said: "I am ignorant not only in most other things, but even the Scriptures, which are my chief study and trade of life." . . . The rabbis in their comments on Scripture, when they encounter difficult passages they cannot explicate, solve it by saying, "When Elijah comes, he shall resolve all our doubts." Erastus, at the point of death, said that he was happy to die because now he would fully understand an answer to all those hard questions, for which he could now find no satisfaction. Commentary on 1 Corinthians 13:9.[42]

When Will the Perfect Come? John Calvin: It's as if Paul were saying, "When the goal has been reached, then the things that helped us during the race will be finished." But Paul retains the mode of speech that he has previously used, when he contrasts "perfection" to that which is partial. Now when will the perfection come? To be sure, it begins at death, for at that time we put off our many weaknesses, along with our body. But it will not be completely established until the day of judgment, as we shall presently hear. Commentary on 1 Corinthians 13:10.[43]

Comparisons to Childhood. Wolfgang Musculus: Paul compares this present life to childhood, the future life to adulthood. Certainly, children possess gifts of mind and intellect, but imperfectly. Children also possess the capacity for speech, but in a manner that is more babbling than speaking appropriately on account of the immaturity of their understanding as well as the fact that their stuttering tongues have not yet been fully trained. Such imperfection clings to childhood until it is effaced through the maturity of adulthood, when both understanding and speech acquire their perfection. For adults both think with a power of reason more perfect and speak more skillfully than children. Clearly such is the nature of this present life that all those things that we recognize for God's gifts—our feeling, speaking, and behaving—are imperfect and (as it were) childish, and will not reach full maturity and perfection before we are transferred to the adulthood of the future life. . . .

Why, therefore, are we proud in our reputation for wisdom or wealth or superior power, when we are no wiser than children, when we speak in a childish manner, when we delight in childish things, and when we act in childish ways? Who does not laugh at children with their inability to consider things seriously, and the way they show off all the things they know and do? And do we act any differently when we are inflamed by a high opinion of our own wisdom and power? For this reason, those who accept something for wisdom and knowledge recognize that it is still childish and imperfect, and in this way they imitate the apostle, since the perfect things are prepared for us in heaven. Commentary on 1 Corinthians 13:11.[44]

Knowledge of God on Earth Is Incomplete. Huldrych Zwingli: "In a mirror." Paul makes himself even clearer, for the meaning here is the same as before, but more explicit. While we are here on earth, we see all things imperfectly, as happens when someone looks through spectacles. But in our [heavenly] homeland, we will see clearly and plainly all those things that now appear as shadows. "Now I know in part." "I know [says Paul] that there are some who esteem me too highly, as if I lack nothing. I say to them that I too have imperfect knowledge. As much as I know now, how

[41]Hesshus, *Explicatio Prioris Epistolae ad Corinthios*, 292r-v.
[42]Trapp, *A Commentary or Exposition*, 693*.
[43]CO 49:513 (cf. CTS 39:428).
[44]Musculus, *Comm. 1 Cor.*, 520-21.

much more God himself will one day make plain to me, for knowledge of God is from God alone." Annotations on 1 Corinthians 13:12.[45]

The Christian's Knowledge of God Is Imperfect. Philipp Melanchthon: The comparison between a perfect knowledge of God and an imperfect one is above and beyond all natural power of comprehension. For nature is completely ignorant of God, as is said above, "The unspiritual person does not perceive the things that belong to the Spirit." Hence Paul does not ascribe natural knowledge to the knowledge of blessed things, but of spiritual things. Second, Paul mentions the mirror and dimness. The mirror is knowledge; the dimness is the hidden or obscure form of God, by which he is known. The mirror or knowledge is not sophistical faith, but that truthful faith that is in the heart, which glorifies God. In other words, it fears God, and guides us with confidence to God's mercy or grace. Third, faith, insofar as it is not in the heart, consists of darkness and hypocrisy; but, on the other hand, where true faith exists, it glorifies God from the heart and does not despise him, and it seeks God—it is there that light exists along with life and the certain knowledge of God. Psalm: "They walk, O Lord, in the light of your countenance." For, having full confidence in [God's] mercy, they live in such a way that they know whom they fear, and they know to whom they can entrust and commit themselves—but wicked hypocrites have nobody either to fear or to trust in. Therefore the faithful know God, while the wicked do not know him. When Paul says "dimly," he denotes the word of that faith, or the form of that knowledge, by which God is known—though the word is obscure. I call the word of faith and God that which is effective in our hearts by God's Spirit. God's justice and wrath are known when the law terrifies. The mercy and riches of his goodness are known when the evangelical word of grace touches the heart—though that knowledge is still obscure. Hitherto those forms of God are obscure because they are not entirely understood. They are the sum of the firstfruits of the Spirit, not the fullness. Now it seems that Paul alluded to that passage in Numbers 12:8, when he recalls dimness and images, "With him I speak mouth to mouth, and not in riddles; he does not see God in figures." Annotations on 1 Corinthians 13:12.[46]

Differences Between Our Present and Future Knowledge of God. David Chytraeus: Paul shows three differences between our present knowledge of God and the knowledge that is to come. First, our knowledge of God in this life is partial or imperfect, obscure, mixed with darkness and doubting. But in eternal life it shall be perfect, full of light, clear, without any darkness and imperfection. Second, employing a simile, [Paul shows that] in this life we are like children that are beginning to prattle and learn the ABC's of heavenly wisdom. But in the future life we shall be grown adults, we shall speak perfectly, and shall be pastors and doctors of divinity in the heavenly university. Third, in this life, we see God's essence and will in a riddle, that is to say, wrapped up in his Word; and in a mirror, that is to say, by the light kindled in us by the Holy Ghost. "But then we shall see him face to face." That is to say, we shall behold God without any darkness. "Then I shall know him as I am known." That is to say, I shall have a clear and transparent knowledge of God, even as God has knowledge of me. Postil on the Epistle for Quinquagesima Sunday.[47]

Taking on the Image of Christ. John Colet: Therefore, thanks to an unwavering faith in Christ (who has revealed the future truth), and to a steadfast hope and expectation of what will be, and, finally, to a love both of him whom by faith we already know as through a glass darkly, and of him whom we shall hereafter know fully, face to face,

[45]Zwingli, *Annotatiunculae . . . ex ore Zvinglij*, 113-14.

[46]Melanchthon, *Annotationes in Epistolam priorem ad Corinthios*, 150, 152; citing 1 Cor 2:14; Ps 89:15.

[47]Chytraeus, *Dispositio epistolarum*, 123-24.

when it will appear what we are to be, when (as John declares) we shall see God as he is—we are rescued by these three virtues and this threefold cord from this wicked, dark, and murderous world, and are swept up by God's grace (if only we wish to obey it) so that we may live forever in the kingdom of goodness and of light. And if, in the meantime, during this present life, we devote ourselves as much as we can to the instructions of Christ, the Gospels, and the apostles, so that we advance step by step in virtue and righteousness, and approach daily, closer and closer to our ideal of righteousness, Jesus Christ (being drawn from glory into glory by the Spirit of the Lord), then we will finally be changed into the same image (2 Cor 3:18).... Now all people to whom this threefold cord of gold is thrown down to draw them to God are advised and instructed to draw near to God and, as much as they can, asking God constantly by faith, seeking him in hope, and knocking on his door in love. They should run along the path of Christ so that they may find what they have asked for, may receive what they have sought, and may have opened to them the things for which they knocked. Exposition of 1 Corinthians 7.[48]

Seeing as If Through a Glass. The English Annotations: There is such a difference between our present knowledge and that which we shall enjoy hereafter in the life to come. [It is as different] as seeing human images in a glass and looking at them full in the face. At this time we see God in the Word and sacraments, and in his works; in these there is revealed to us by a kind of reflection the image of those things whereof we cannot directly see the original truth and proper essence in this world. Annotations on 1 Corinthians 13:12.[49]

Seeing Christ Face to Face. John Trapp: That is, distinctly, clearly, immediately, beatifically. And surely, if Lipsius, when he read Seneca, thought that he had reached the summit of Mt. Olympus, above mortality and human things, then what state shall we be in when we behold Christ in his glory and consider that every vein in that blessed body bled to bring us so great a bliss? If mathematics are so delightful that people think it sweet to live and die in those studies, what shall we think of heaven's happiness, which we shall one day clearly apprehend—though not fully comprehend? Commentary on 1 Corinthians 13:12.[50]

Our Knowledge of God Is Different from His Knowledge of Us. John Donne: What is it to "know him, as he is known"? . . . It cannot be a comprehensive knowledge of God. To comprehend is to know a thing as well as that thing can be known; and we can never know God so much, but that he will know himself better. Our knowledge cannot be so expanded, nor God so condensed and contracted, that we can know him that way, i.e., comprehensively. It cannot be such a knowledge of God as God has of himself, nor as God has of us. For God comprehends us, and all this world, and all the worlds he could have made, and himself.... As God knows me, so I shall know God; but I shall not know God in the same way that God knows me.... As the fire does truly shine like the sun shines, though it does not shine out as far, nor for as many purposes, in the same way then, I shall know God.... And so my knowledge will be so like his knowledge as it shall produce love, like his love, and we shall love him as he loves us. Sermon Preached at St. Paul's for Easter.[51]

Faith, Hope, and Love All Reflect Confidence in God. Huldrych Zwingli: "Now faith, hope, and love abide, these three, but the greatest of these is love." It should be noted that the word *faith* is understood in various ways throughout holy Scripture. First, it means belief. Second, it means firmness. Third, it means a strong

[48]Colet, *Enarratio*, 156, 158; citing 1 Jn 3:2.
[49]Downame, *English Annotations*, EE3r*.

[50]Trapp, *A Commentary or Exposition*, 693*. Justus Lipsius (1547–1606) was a Flemish humanist who attempted to show the compatibility of ancient Stoicism with Christianity.
[51]Donne, *Sermons of John Donne*, 8:235*.

and unwavering confidence in God, and this alone should be understood as the faith that justifies and brings salvation. Now those who do not understand that faith, hope, and love are the same thing, namely, this confidence in God, frequently struggle to understand many passages. For if you have faith in Christ, but do not have hope in him or love him in return, then your faith is worthless (Jas 1). If you say that you have hope in God, but do not love, then you make yourself a liar. For if you have been instructed concerning God in such a fashion that you know that your hope should be in him alone, then it is impossible for you not to recognize him as your greatest good. And if you recognize him as your greatest good, then it is impossible not to love him. . . . For no one is able to love the God in whom they do not believe. Annotations on 1 Corinthians 13:2.[52]

Love Abides into Eternity. Jacques Lefèvre d'Étaples: No one should be surprised if today there are no prophets or tongues, no gifts of healing, no wonders, and if so few possess wisdom and knowledge—because the salvation of believers does not depend on these. But these gifts were necessary for the conversion of unbelievers. What, then, is necessary for believers? Faith, hope, and love. And God be praised that he does not cease pouring out these three necessary gifts on believers until the end of the age! It is through these divine gifts, therefore, that we are able to serve him in this present age, just as in the next age we will be able to praise him with unfailing love forever along with all of the angels and saints. Commentary on 1 Corinthians 13:13.[53]

Is Love Greater Than Faith? Johann Spangenberg: On account of its properties and domain, love is greater than faith. Faith only reaches out to God; love, however, reaches out to God and all human beings. Faith ends here on earth; love, however, begins here and remains eternal. But on account of its dignity, faith is above love; faith makes us pious, righteous, and holy before God. Habakkuk: "The righteous shall live by faith." St. Paul describes faith as justification, the forgiveness of sins, righteousness, and sanctification. Love he allows to remain a fruit and consequence of faith. He values it highly on account of the false apostles and hypocrites who boast about their faith and yet do not have even a flicker of love in their heart. God grant us his grace, so that we might be found upright in both things, in faith and love. Amen. Postil on the Epistle for Quinquagesima Sunday.[54]

Why Is Charity More Excellent Than Faith or Hope? David Dickson: Charity is more excellent than faith or hope . . . because charity shall never fail, but shall also continue in the life to come, when faith and hope shall cease. In the meantime, let us remember that faith in some respects is more excellent than charity, because faith is the cause of love (Gal 5:6). We are justified by faith, and have peace with God (Rom 5:1). And Christ dwells in our heart by faith, which works charity in us (Eph 3:17). But the apostle, in treating the concord and edification of the church, rightfully extols charity, as much as it relates to this purpose. He also knew that no one can endeavor to grow in Christian charity who does not also labor after growth in faith, which is the cause of love. Exposition of 1 Corinthians 13:13.[55]

Christian Teachers Must Teach in Word and Example. Menno Simons: It becomes the evangelical teacher to set before himself nothing except the most illustrious precepts of the gospel—such as faith, charity, patience, spirituality, gentleness, peace, mildness, truth, moderation, etc., so that no one will be able with justice to thrust any aspersions against him with any taint of baseness. He must teach not only by word, but

[52]Zwingli, *Annotatiunculae . . . ex ore Zvinglij*, 108; citing Jas 1:22-25.

[53]Lefèvre d'Étaples, *Commentariorum in Epistolas Beati Pauli . . . Liber Secundus*, 121v.

[54]Spangenberg, *Postilla Teütsch*, 4:132v-133r; citing Hab 2:4.

[55]Dickson, *Exposition of St. Paul's Epistles*, 63*.

also by example, following the teachings of Paul. CHRISTIAN BAPTISM.[56]

LOVE'S SUPERIORITY. JOHN TRAPP: [Love is the greatest of these] because it is longest-lasting. Gifts that presume imperfections in us (such as faith and hope) or misery in others (such as pity, etc.) shall pass away. Second, [love is the greatest] because love is diffusive of itself and benefits others, whereas faith and hope are private goods; that is, they are confined to the person of the believer. The statement of the martyr Elizabeth Folkes,[57] when she was at the stake, was momentous: "Farewell all the world; farewell faith; farewell hope." And so, taking the stake in her hand, she said, "Welcome love." COMMENTARY ON 1 CORINTHIANS 13:13.[58]

CHRISTIAN MINISTERS MUST MODEL FAITH, LOVE, AND ZEAL. RICHARD BAXTER: Content not yourselves with being in a state of grace, but be also careful that your graces are kept in vigorous and lively exercise, and that you preach to yourselves the sermons that you study before you preach them to others. . . . We are the nurses of Christ's little ones. . . . If we feed on unwholesome food, either errors or fruitless controversies, our hearers are like to fare the worse for it. Whereas, if we abound in faith, and love, and zeal, how would it overflow to the refreshing of our congregations, and how would it appear in the increase of the same graces in them! O brethren, watch therefore over your own hearts: keep out lusts and passions and worldly inclinations; keep up the life of faith, and love, and zeal: be much at home, and be much with God. REFORMED PASTOR.[59]

[56]Simons, *Complete Writings*, 229.

[57]Elizabeth Folkes a Protestant who was executed at the stake during the reign of Mary Tudor in 1557. See John Foxe, *Acts and Monuments* (1583), 12.2032.

[58]Trapp, *A Commentarie or Exposition*, 693*.

[59]Baxter, *Reformed Pastor*, 61-62.

FAITH, HOPE, AND LOVE ABIDE. THE ENGLISH ANNOTATIONS: [There are two possible meanings of this verse.] Either it means that while we are in this life, it is very necessary that all three graces of faith, hope, and charity should be and abide in us; for without faith we cannot be justified nor made acceptable to God, without hope faith cannot subsist, and by love faith must be working. But after this life faith shall be turned into vision, hope into fruition, but then love shall be in greatest perfection. Or the apostle's meaning is that faith, hope, and charity are virtues that are to abide and continue in the church militant, and be working in and possessed by true believers at all times and ages, whereas the gift of tongues and miracles were necessary in the first planting of the church but afterward were to cease, as they have now done so for many ages. ANNOTATIONS ON 1 CORINTHIANS 13:13.[60]

PAUL'S BEAUTIFUL DISCOURSE ON LOVE SHAMES FALSE TEACHERS. MARTIN LUTHER: Here you see what a little word "love" is and how quickly it is uttered! But among so much vice, who would have sought so much precious virtue and excellence in that one virtue as St. Paul here ascribes to love? I think that here love is praised and portrayed better than in anything the heathen have written about virtues and vices. He presents a pattern of which all false teachers must be ashamed, who say much about love, but not one of these points is found in them.

It truly only stings and storms against the false teachers whenever he lists one of the virtues of love. Whenever he so praises love and points out its nature, at the same time he always wants to target them as the ones who have none of these, so that you might well add a little gloss next to each attribute of love, saying: "But you act very differently." POSTIL ON THE EPISTLE FOR QUINQUAGESIMA SUNDAY.[61]

[60]Downame, *English Annotations*, EE3v*.

[61]LW 76:348-49* (WA 17,2:171-72; E^2 8:129).

14:1-25 Prophecy and Tongues

Pursue love, and earnestly desire the spiritual gifts, especially that you may prophesy. [2]For one who speaks in a tongue speaks not to men but to God; for no one understands him, but he utters mysteries in the Spirit. [3]On the other hand, the one who prophesies speaks to people for their upbuilding and encouragement and consolation. [4]The one who speaks in a tongue builds up himself, but the one who prophesies builds up the church. [5]Now I want you all to speak in tongues, but even more to prophesy. The one who prophesies is greater than the one who speaks in tongues, unless someone interprets, so that the church may be built up.

[6]Now, brothers,[a] if I come to you speaking in tongues, how will I benefit you unless I bring you some revelation or knowledge or prophecy or teaching? [7]If even lifeless instruments, such as the flute or the harp, do not give distinct notes, how will anyone know what is played? [8]And if the bugle gives an indistinct sound, who will get ready for battle? [9]So with yourselves, if with your tongue you utter speech that is not intelligible, how will anyone know what is said? For you will be speaking into the air. [10]There are doubtless many different languages in the world, and none is without meaning, [11]but if I do not know the meaning of the language, I will be a foreigner to the speaker and the speaker a foreigner to me. [12]So with yourselves, since you are eager for manifestations of the Spirit, strive to excel in building up the church.

[13]Therefore, one who speaks in a tongue should pray that he may interpret. [14]For if I pray in a tongue, my spirit prays but my mind is unfruitful. [15]What am I to do? I will pray with my spirit, but I will pray with my mind also; I will sing praise with my spirit, but I will sing with my mind also. [16]Otherwise, if you give thanks with your spirit, how can anyone in the position of an outsider[b] say "Amen" to your thanksgiving when he does not know what you are saying? [17]For you may be giving thanks well enough, but the other person is not being built up. [18]I thank God that I speak in tongues more than all of you. [19]Nevertheless, in church I would rather speak five words with my mind in order to instruct others, than ten thousand words in a tongue.

[20]Brothers, do not be children in your thinking. Be infants in evil, but in your thinking be mature. [21]In the Law it is written, "By people of strange tongues and by the lips of foreigners will I speak to this people, and even then they will not listen to me, says the Lord." [22]Thus tongues are a sign not for believers but for unbelievers, while prophecy is a sign[c] not for unbelievers but for believers. [23]If, therefore, the whole church comes together and all speak in tongues, and outsiders or unbelievers enter, will they not say that you are out of your minds? [24]But if all prophesy, and an unbeliever or outsider enters, he is convicted by all, he is called to account by all, [25]the secrets of his heart are disclosed, and so, falling on his face, he will worship God and declare that God is really among you.

a Or *brothers and sisters;* also verses 20, 26, 39 **b** Or *of him that is without gifts* **c** Greek lacks *a sign*

Overview: Given that spiritual gifts are bestowed for the glory of God and the edification of one's neighbor (and *not* for self-promotion), Paul now shows the Corinthians how the gift of prophecy is more profitable than speaking in tongues for building up the church. With rare exceptions, Reformation commentators equate the gift of prophecy in their day with the preaching office of the Christian minister, who instructs the people of God through the exposition of Scripture. Faithful Christian preaching must be clear, plain, and simple; it is intended for the edification, encouragement, and consolation of the Christian assembly. For Protestant interpreters, the fact that Paul gives priority to prophecy over tongue-speaking constitutes a strong rebuke of the traditional Catholic Church, which mandates that the Mass be celebrated in the "foreign tongue" of Latin. Their unwavering commitment to the intelligibility of the proclaimed Word even causes several Reformed church leaders to question whether instrumentation and congregational singing belong in the Christian worship service. To be sure, Reformation commentators recognize that tongue-speaking is a gift of the Holy Spirit that has a rightful place in the church—though that place is now primarily circumscribed to the knowledge and interpretation of the biblical languages of Greek and Hebrew. What ultimately builds up the body of Christ, therefore, is not the chattering of foreign tongues, but the prophetic gift of Christian preaching as it strengthens believers, convicts and converts unbelievers, refutes false teaching, and announces the glory of God.

The Orderly Use of Gifts. Martin Luther: In chapter 14 [St. Paul] teaches the preachers, prophets, and singers to use their gifts in an orderly manner; they are to display their preaching, skill, and understanding for edification only, and not in order to gain honor for themselves. Preface to 1 Corinthians.[1]

The Main Concern Is Edification. John Calvin: In chapter 14, Paul begins to give more specific details of how the Corinthians have erred in their use of spiritual gifts. And since they placed so much value on ostentation, he teaches them that edification should be their central concern in all things. For this reason he prefers prophecy to all other gifts, because it is more useful; whereas the Corinthians were valuing tongues more highly, purely on the grounds of their empty show. He also lays down the right order for doing things, and at the same time reproaches them for the fault of shouting forth in unknown tongues without fruit. For as they were doing so, they were neglecting teaching and exhortations, which always ought to have the priority. After that, he forbids women from teaching in public, because it is unseemly. Preface to the Commentary on 1 Corinthians.[2]

Zealous to Love. Tilemann Hesshus: Paul is still instructing the Corinthians concerning spiritual gifts, and promptly impresses on them that they should be especially zealous to love, which serves everyone, everywhere, and always promotes the edification of the church. Then he states that those gifts should especially be sought and exercised that are the most beneficial for the church, that is, prophecy—which is the faculty of explaining sacred Scripture and instructing the people concerning God and the benefits of the Mediator. The Corinthians greatly admired the gift of various tongues and displayed that gift in their public assemblies, as if the purpose for which the Holy Spirit had adorned the church with the gift of tongues was so that godly people might regard themselves as superior in the presence of the church or pagans. Therefore Paul refutes this error in detail and with many arguments. He teaches that the gift of prophesying, that is, expounding the holy Scripture and instructing the people, is far more necessary and more profitable than the gift of tongues—although tongue-speaking is also excellent and important, provided that a person employs it for the benefit of the church and not for a mere show. Next, Paul establishes the order with which prophets or teachers ought to teach in the church. He forbids women from being given the authority of preaching in public. Finally, he concludes this passage with this notable rule: that they should take pains that all things in the church should be done decently and in order. Explication of 1 Corinthians 14.[3]

[1]LW 35:383.

[2]CO 49:302 (cf. CTS 39:45).

[3]Hesshus, *Explicatio Prioris Epistolae ad Corinthios*, 298v-299v.

14:1-5 *Prophecy Edifies the Church*

Speech Must Be Based on Spiritual Understanding. John Colet: From the passage where it is written "Now concerning spiritual gifts . . ." all the way to the end of this fourteenth chapter, the subject matter is continuous and uninterrupted instruction about the better spiritual gifts, and an exhortation to seek them. The most beneficial thing of all in the church is wisdom along with love. Now, the Corinthians were arrogant, and they prided themselves on their skill of tongue-speaking. Previously Paul has exhorted them on to love, to the point of telling them that without love, nothing else can profit men and women in spiritual matters. Now he commands them to direct their minds to the spiritual understanding of what is read or spoken in church, in such a way that if they do not properly understand what is being spoken from heavenly revelation (even if it is spoken with the greatest of eloquence) they should be completely silent and say nothing in the church. Let them talk to themselves when alone—and to God, if they wish. Skillful speech is a good thing, but without understanding it is empty noise; those who speak in this manner are speaking into the air. They are like foreigners.

Even with the gift of tongues itself, therefore, Paul wants the Corinthians to strive for things that are spiritual. The Spirit speaks mysteries; and the prophecy and spiritual interpretation of the learned and wise speak both to God and to other people by means of the Spirit of prophecy, and build up the church, especially if the speakers exhibit the insight of their words through their examples and actions. For just as understanding is the life of speech, so action is the life of understanding. Understand, then, what you speak. Pray that you may understand. Put into practice what you understand, so that action may give life to your understanding, and understanding may enlighten your speech. Exposition of 1 Corinthians 14.[4]

[4]Colet, *Enarratio*, 272; citing 1 Cor 12:1.

Follow the Way of Love. John Trapp: That is, follow it hot-foot, as they say, pursue and practice it. It is more than to desire or to be zealous for something, as is clear from the next words, "Be zealous for spiritual gifts." Follow love closely, as the hunter does with the prey, or as the persecutor does with the martyr, who wants to hide or escape if they can. Love may be compared to the precious stone called pantarb, spoken of by Philostratus; it is a stone of great beauty and of strange properties, so bright and radiant that it gives light in the darkest midnight. And its light possesses that wondrous power that it attracts other stones and draws them into heaps, as if they were so many beehives. But lest so precious a gift should be undervalued, nature has not only hidden this stone in the secret bowels of the earth but has also put into it a property of slipping out of the hands of those that hold it . . . unless they hold it fast indeed. Commentary on 1 Corinthians 14:1.[5]

Prophecy Is Superior to Tongue-Speaking. Jacques Lefèvre d'Étaples: The person who prophesies speaks edifying words to the people, now exhorting them, now consoling them. For those who follow the encouraging words of the prophet avoid eternal death; they long for heaven and despise earthly things. They encourage others in these things as well. Second, prophecy is better than the pure gift of tongues, for it is better to edify the church and the company of believers than to edify only oneself. For those who prophesy edify a large number of people, but those who possess only the gift of tongues edify only themselves. Commentary on 1 Corinthians 14:1.[6]

The Nature and Importance of Prophecy. Philipp Melanchthon: "To speak in tongues" is to announce a Scripture text or prayers in some tongue or other; prophecy is the explanation of Scripture. And here is the occasion for this chapter: Those who possessed the gift of tongues were each

[5]Trapp, *A Commentary or Exposition*, 694*.

[6]Lefèvre d'Étaples, *Commentariorum in Epistolas Beati Pauli . . . Liber Secundus*, 122r.

saying their prayers in a different tongue when they came to the church wherever it was meeting. And the knowledge of all tongues gave childish pleasure as something marvelous to inquisitive heathen. Everybody gave time for tongues so that prophecy (that is, the interpretation of Scripture) was neglected. Now it was only for the sake of hearing Scripture that Christ established these assemblies: "As often as you do this, do this in remembrance of me." And Colossians 3: "Let the Word of Christ dwell in you richly." And Psalm 102: "That men and women may declare in Zion the name of the Lord and in Jerusalem his praises, when people gather together," etc. Therefore Paul scolds the Corinthians for devoting so much of their effort to tongues that they were neglecting something better and more necessary. The zeal for tongues was praiseworthy, but useless without prophecy, that is, without the explanation of Scripture. What if, in our day, Paul was to observe that nothing rang forth in our churches except foreign tongues and the bellowing of singers? What if he heard those sophist preachers who primarily taught in foreign tongues, that is, men arguing over obscure and stupid questions? Now, in summary, he teaches in this chapter both what should be the primary concern of Christians and what is the order of teaching in the church. No other passage so directly attacks the tyranny of the popes. Annotations on 1 Corinthians 14:1.[7]

Solemn Speech. William Perkins: The art or faculty of prophesying is a sacred doctrine of exercising prophecy rightly. Prophecy (or prophesying) is a public and solemn speech of the prophet, pertaining to the worship of God and the salvation of our neighbor (1 Cor 14:3, 24; Rom 1:9).... There are two parts to prophecy: preaching of the word and conceiving of prayers. For in speaking there are only two duties of the prophet (that is, of the minister of the Word), namely, the preaching of the Word and praying to God in the name of the people (Rom 12:6; Gen 20:7). For this reason the word "prophecy" is also used to describe prayers (1 Chron 25:1; 1 Kings 18:26, 29). And every prophet is partly the voice of God, that is, in preaching; and partly the voice of the people in the act of praying (Jer 15.19). Preaching of the Word is prophesying in the name and room of Christ, whereby men and women are called to the state of grace and preserved in it. The Art of Prophesying.[8]

The Nature of the Gift of Prophecy. The English Annotations: The apostle is not speaking here about the gift of the Holy Spirit by which people were inspired to foretell future things, as the word was used in the Old Testament. Rather, he is speaking about the gift of the Holy Spirit whereby people were enabled to expound the Scriptures, given by divine inspiration, and apply them to the benefit of their hearers, for their edification, instruction, and comfort. Annotations on 1 Corinthians 14:1.[9]

Interpreting the Spirit's Mysteries. Martin Luther: We cannot resist taking histories and drawing out hidden interpretations from them, which Paul calls "mysteries." Let me give a coarse example: Isaac was sacrificed on the alter and, nevertheless, remained alive, so that it indicates that Christ must die and rise again and be alive. This we must allow. For Paul says the Holy Spirit "utters mysteries." That is his office. He can also find and interpret mysteries.... This does not mean that we should suffer that just anyone should fall into the holy Scriptures and speculate and dream whatever they want. We should resist no one, if they have the Holy Spirit. And St. Paul said in Romans 12: "If anyone brings out prophecies, they should resemble the faith." The analogy of faith. Whoever wants to bring out hidden meanings must be sure that he interprets according to the faith—that these interpretations fit the faith. Sermon on Exodus 1.[10]

[7]Melanchthon, *Annotationes in Epistolam priorem ad Corinthios*, 156; citing 1 Cor 11:25; Col 3:16; Ps 102:21-22.

[8]Perkins, *The Works of William Perkins*, 333*.

[9]Downame, *English Annotations*, EE3v*.

[10]WA 16:28; citing Rom 12:6.

Paul Mandates Worship in the Vernacular. Wolfgang Musculus: Note here that Paul does not say "not everyone understands him," but "no one understands him." It is possible when you speak German to a German audience that you are not understood by everyone because of various dialects, as would occur if you spoke in Low German to people who understood High German. In this case, even if everyone could not understand you, nevertheless most could, so that you would not be speaking entirely in vain. But if a person spoke a completely foreign and unknown tongue in church, since no one could understand it, he would not be speaking to people but to God. Such is the case in German churches when everything is spoken and sung in Latin, which is so foreign to the German language that nothing of it can be understood by a native German. . . . This is what the Roman Church has ordained, whereby Satan has wished directly to contradict this apostolic teaching and prevent the building up of Christ's churches. Commentary on 1 Corinthians 14:2.[11]

Prophets Edify the Church. Huldrych Zwingli: It happens that some people utter mysteries in foreign tongues that not even they themselves understand, or at least they pay little attention to what their words mean. Now since they do not provide fruit to themselves or to anyone else, are they not spewing forth only empty wind? But even if a prophet completely understands and pays attention to what he is saying, and yet those hearing do not understand anything he says, then how does this build up the church? Therefore to prophesy, that is, to reveal the meaning of Scripture to the people, is certainly a distinguished office and very useful, for it builds up. Therefore, unless the one who speaks in tongues at the same time prophesies, little benefit will result; but if the person who possesses the gift of tongues also has the gift of prophecy, then great good will result. We have stated elsewhere that the name "prophet" is variously interpreted in the Scripture. Among the Jews, prophets were understood to be those who, inspired by the Spirit, possessed detailed knowledge of the speech and will of God. Their office was to be experts of the divine word, which had been given by God himself and taken down for the people. Further, they pulled down and demolished whatever had been raised up against God; they planted and built whatever pleased God. The prophets were vigilant lest harmful things attack the people of God.

This is the same office that bishops, pastors, and evangelists have in the church of Christ. Still, the ancient prophets do differ from ours, because hidden beneath their words the prophets of old by the revelation of the Spirit prophesied and predicted the future—although in the beginning of the church there were also prophets of this kind, as seen in Acts 13 and 21, and also in Acts 11. But between the apostles and prophets there is this difference: the apostles were sent first and foremost to unbelievers, but the prophets were not. For the prophets were sent to believers. Annotations on 1 Corinthians 14:3.[12]

The Gift of Prophecy Superior to Tongues. David Dickson: Those who speak in an unknown tongue, although it is by the gift of the Spirit, speak the mysteries of God, yet speak without profit, because they are understood by God alone, and not by other people. But a prophet or pastor who speaks in a known tongue, teaches, exhorts, [and] comforts their hearers, and so speaks profitably. Therefore prophecy is more excellent than the gift of tongues. Exposition of 1 Corinthians 14:3.[13]

The Three Functions of the Gift of Prophecy. Wolfgang Musculus: Prophets, therefore, are those who teach in the church; they accomplish much more than if they were singing and praying in a miraculous language. In fact, observe Paul's brief and splendid description of

[11]Musculus, *Comm. 1 Cor.*, 532.

[12]Zwingli, *Annotatiunculae . . . ex ore Zvinglij*, 115-17.

[13]Dickson, *Exposition of St. Paul's Epistles*, 64*.

this prophetic gift: "the one who prophesies," he says, "speaks to people for their edification, encouragement, and consolation." Therefore there are three functions of the prophet in the church: to edify, encourage, and console.

"Edification" is a metaphorical term for building through instruction. Those who teach ignorant and unlettered persons construct them into the building of the Lord's house. This pertains to all things that concern the planting of faith and piety in the hearts of the elect, by which, like living stones, we are constructed into the temple of God on the foundation that is Christ. . . . The second function is encouragement, in Greek *paraklēsis*. In this function, the prophet diligently exhorts those who already believe and profess devotion to Christ to continue steadfastly in faith and true piety. . . . This function of prophecy is of the greatest importance for all those who are acquainted with the truth of Christ and all piety, but who do not imitate it adequately in their behavior and lifestyle. The apostle Paul diligently performed this function of prophecy at Ephesus, when for three years, night and day, he did not cease warning and exhorting with tears all of the believers (Acts 20).

The third function of the prophet is consolation, in Greek *paramythia*. Consolation is to lovingly address those who are suffering, afflicted, sad (such as the poor), abandoned, imprisoned, impoverished—especially for the sake of Christ—and to offer them such encouragement that they receive consolation and are strengthened in a spirit of endurance. This practice of *paramythia* is the responsibility of all Christians, but especially of prophets, the ministers of the Word of God. Taken as a group, the people of Christ are ignorant; they are idle and lazy; they are downhearted. The gift of prophecy is thus given to the church so that the ignorant might be instructed, the idle might be warned, and the downhearted might receive consolation. Commentary on 1 Corinthians 14:3.[14]

The Threefold Fruit of Preaching. The English Annotations: Those who expound the Scriptures in a known tongue . . . speak in such a manner that people may understand them, and receive fruit and benefit by them. This fruit is stated in the following words, "edification, exhortation, and comfort." By edification he means the confirmation of faith and instruction of the ignorant. By exhortation he means inciting to virtue and reproof of the unruly. By comfort he means applying the promises of God to the consolation of the afflicted. And these are the three uses to which all expositors of the Word ought to apply the doctrine they deliver. Annotations on 1 Corinthians 14:3.[15]

People Need Different Kinds of Preaching. Tilemann Hesshus: "The one who prophesies speaks to people"; that is, the person who explains the holy Scripture to everyone in a vernacular and known language, and who instructs the people concerning God and eternal life (for this is what Paul means by "prophesy")—that person is the one who bears extraordinary fruit when they speak to the church. That person instructs many people and contributes to the salvation of many people. That person speaks for edification, encouragement, and consolation.

The church has need for different kinds of preaching. Paul calls "edification" the instruction in the principal points of godliness. This is when a pastor instructs the people concerning God, the three persons of the divinity, the two natures united in the single person of Jesus Christ, the law, the fall of our first parents, human powers, sin, the gospel, justification of men and women before God, the office of the Mediator, repentance, good works, the church, eternal life, and all the remaining articles concerning our faith in which our salvation consists. For the knowledge of these things is necessary for all Christians anticipating eternal salvation. And these things are learned only by the preaching of the gospel. These things, therefore, must not

[14]Musculus, *Comm. 1 Cor.*, 535-36.

[15]Downame, *English Annotations*, EE3v*.

only be transmitted to each person clearly, plainly, simply, in a known language, and with appropriate words without any ambiguity, but also they must be confirmed and established by testimonies from the holy Scriptures. Thus this office entails great effort; but its usefulness is immeasurable.

Second, the church is in need of encouragement. For through the sermon, people must be aroused to have enthusiastic devotion for heavenly teaching, for earnest godliness, for prayer, for words of thanksgiving, for eager confession of the divine name, for continual repentance, for faith, for works of charity, for zealous peace, for patience, and for all other kinds of virtues. In this regard, divine threats must be set forth, by which God deters us from our sins; and God's most illustrious promises must be impressed [on the congregation], by which God encourages men and women to obedience.

Moreover, from time to time, consolation is necessary for the entire church and for individual godly persons. For the church in this life is afflicted with the cross and afflictions, and in this world she is subject to various dangers and injuries. In this regard, unless the church is sustained by consolation from the divine Word, she cannot endure in the faith. Now the Word of God furnishes the most powerful and effective consolations in every trial, whether it be a physical trial or a spiritual one. Therefore pastors ought diligently to announce these things to their congregations and encourage those whose minds are terrified. Explication of 1 Corinthians 14:3.[16]

All Scripture Is for the Church's Benefit. Martin Luther: To speak with tongues is to read or sing the Psalms or Prophets in the congregation, and not to exegete them—even if the reader understands them. To prophesy is to take the sense [of the passage] from God and to offer it to others. To exegete is to hand on the meaning to others. Thus St. Paul means that to speak with tongues does not improve the congregation; however, to prophesy and to exegete improve the congregation. In the Spirit, God commands by the Spirit. German Bible (1546): Marginalia on 1 Corinthians 14:5.[17]

Foreign Languages Do Not Edify the Church. Tilemann Hesshus: "The one who speaks in a tongue edifies himself; but the one who prophesies, edifies the church." This is the same thing that Paul has said above. People who use a foreign language serve themselves, for since they understand the language, they are able to instruct themselves, confirm themselves in the faith, console themselves, and be encouraged. But the church is harvesting no fruit from it, for she cannot be instructed, nor aroused, nor encouraged to take hold of consolation by a language that is not understood. Explication of 1 Corinthians 14:4.[18]

Paul Does Not Disparage the Gift of Tongues. Peter Martyr Vermigli: [Paul says this] in an effort to defend himself from calumny, for he might have appeared to some people, perhaps, to be either envious of the common people among the Corinthians or disparaging God's gifts. He removes both of these calumnies when he says that he wishes that they speak in tongues. He doesn't degrade the gifts, which he knew were gifts of God and not given to people in vain. "As far as I'm concerned," he says, "I would like all of you to speak in tongues, if God should grant this to all of you." We have already noted this same construction of speech in this epistle, where Paul referred to his celibacy: "I wish that all of you," he said, "were just as I am." It had to be added: "If your weakness would permit it, and if God would have given the gift of celibacy to everyone." He does a similar thing here. And immediately after this Paul encourages and demonstrates that he has a greater desire that they prophesy, and he announces the reason for his desire: because the gift of prophecy is more important and more excellent than the gift of tongues.

---

[16]Hesshus, *Explicatio Prioris Epistolae ad Corinthios*, 300v-301r.

[17]WADB 7:125.

[18]Hesshus, *Explicatio Prioris Epistolae ad Corinthios*, 301r-v.

"All of you." Paul doesn't desire for two or three or four people to speak in tongues and prophesy, but that all people equally display these gifts—so far was he from envying the Holy Spirit's gifts in them! This sort of envy is prevalent in the political calculating of this world, where those who have obtained any honor rarely want to allow others to participate who are not of their rank. . . . But in the church of Christ this must not happen. For, as Paul demonstrates, we ought to desire that those gifts of God that are most excellent be shared by as many people as possible. Commentary on 1 Corinthians 14:5.[19]

Tongues Are Important for Proclaiming the Gospel to the Nations. John Calvin: "Now I want all of you to speak in tongues." Again, Paul declares that he does not esteem prophecy so highly that he does not leave some place for tongues. This must be carefully noted, for God has bestowed nothing on his church in vain, and there was some use for tongues. Therefore, although the Corinthians, out of their misguided zeal for showiness, had turned that gift into something that was partly useless and worthless, and partly even harmful, by correcting this fault Paul is nevertheless commending the use of tongues—so far is he from wishing that they be abolished or belittled.

In our own day, when the knowledge of tongues is more than necessary, and when God in his wonderful kindness has brought them forth from darkness into the light, there are now some great theologians who rage and bluster against them. Since it is certain that the Holy Spirit has adorned tongues with undying honor in this verse, it is easy to deduce by what spirit those critics are moved who do everything they can to stir up insults against those who study the languages. Yet they are dealing with different things. For Paul here means languages of any sort, which were so important in proclaiming the gospel among all nations. Those theologians, on the other hand, condemn those languages, from which the pure truth of Scripture is to be drawn, as from a fountain. Paul adds an exception, that we should not be so mesmerized by tongues that we neglect prophecy, which ought to have the priority. Commentary on 1 Corinthians 14:5.[20]

14:6-12 *Unintelligible Tongues Do Not Edify the Church*

Ministers Must Be Useful in Their Churches. Wolfgang Musculus: "If I come to you . . . how will I benefit you?" Therefore it is required of ministers who come to a church that they should be useful, bear fruit, and benefit those to whom they come. . . . But today, church leaders do not come to their dioceses, their parishes, their canonical offices, their prelacies so that they might benefit the church. Instead, they come more for honor and privilege, so as to profit only themselves—in so doing, they destroy both themselves and the church. Commentary on 1 Corinthians 14:6.[21]

Revelation, Knowledge, Prophecy, and Teaching. Tilemann Hesshus: The second argument [proving the superiority of prophecy for building up the church] comes from the example of Paul himself. "If I should wish to display my gift of various languages among you," Paul says, "and should preach to you in Greek or Hebrew or Latin or Spanish, you would comprehend nothing useful from it unless at the same time I was explaining it to each one of you. Note, therefore, that the display of foreign languages in the church without interpretation is void of all fruit." Paul here sets forth four kinds of fruitful speech in the church, that is, through revelation, through knowledge, through prophecy, or through teaching. Revelation is when it is explained to the church what has been revealed and disclosed to us from heaven. Thus, in Acts 22, Paul explains in his sermon the revelation that the Lord Jesus had shown to him. Again, Paul

[19]Vermigli, *In Selectissimam Priorem ad Corinthios Epistolam . . . Commentarii*, 374v; citing 1 Cor 7:8.

[20]CO 49:518 (cf. CTS 39:436-37).

[21]Musculus, *Comm. 1 Cor.*, 540.

relates a revelation in Acts 23, where the Lord Jesus encouraged him in the barracks. And the apostle Peter relates in Acts 11 a revelation that he saw in an ecstatic state. Again, in 2 Peter 1, Peter relates that he saw by a revelation the glory of Jesus Christ on Mount Tabor.

Knowledge or learning is when we point out to people correct and wholesome advice from the Word of God on obscure and dangerous subjects. It is when we teach men and women what they should consider regarding political government; how those who govern can be successful; for what reason a husband should be separated from his wife; how godly couples can experience happiness; how every facet of human life ought to be directed to the standard of the divine Word. Paul speaks with knowledge in 1 Corinthians 7, where he furnishes advice on a variety of situations the church was wondering about. Again, Paul imparts knowledge to the church in Ephesians 5 and 6 when he instructs fathers and mothers of households, children, and servants as to the nature of their duties. Solomon, in his proverbs, speaks with knowledge to the entire church, teaching all men and women how they ought to walk wisely in their vocations and in all life's activities.

I understand prophecy in this verse (as I stated previously) as the explanation of the prophecies of the Scriptures. Now Paul is speaking prophecy for the church in Romans 4, where he explains the statement of Moses in Genesis 15: "Abraham believed God and he credited it to him as righteousness."

Teaching is when a chief point of godliness is explained, as in [Paul's] letter to Rome, which first accuses human beings of sin; then explains the principle article of faith, how men and women are justified before God; and then shows the effects of faith. Paul thereby teaches what sin is, what grace is, what the law is. He hands down the teaching concerning election. Again, he spoke to the church by way of teaching concerning good works. Paul's intention is that, whatever kind of instruction we use in the church, it is necessary that we use the language and type of speech that can be understood by everyone. Explication of 1 Corinthians 14:6.[22]

Flutes, Harps, and Trumpets. Tilemann Hesshus: This third argument [for proving the superiority of prophecy for building up the church] is drawn from musical instruments, whereby [Paul] demonstrates that the use of foreign tongues that are not understood by the people achieve nothing—there is a clear similarity. No one takes delight in a flute or a harp producing a confused sound, for there is no way to know what one should sing. In the same way, a foreign and unknown tongue neither instructs nor influences the human mind, but remains only sound. . . . [Paul's] mention of the trumpet is very appropriate, since the trumpet calls soldiers to battle. In a similar way, the Word of God, which is the trumpet of the Holy Spirit, arouses the minds of godly people so that they might eagerly join hands and, with the help of the Holy Spirit, energetically fight against Satan, the world, and the flesh. Explication of 1 Corinthians 14:7-8.[23]

The Power of Music. John Calvin: Paul introduces examples, first from musical instruments, and then from the general nature of things. For there is no sound that does not have its own particular quality by which it is distinguished. "Even inanimate things," Paul says, "teach us something." There are, of course, many noises or crashes that occur randomly without any melody. But Paul is speaking here about sounds that are produced by human artistry, as if he were saying, "People cannot give life to a harp or flute, but nevertheless they make it give forth a sound that is regulated in such a manner that it can be discerned. How absurd then for human beings, who are endowed with intelligence, to utter confused and unintelligible sounds!" . . . Finally, we all know from experience the power music has to excite the

[22]Hesshus, *Explicatio Prioris Epistolae ad Corinthios*, 301v-302v; citing Acts 22:7-10; 23:11; 11:5-10; 2 Pet 1:17.
[23]Hesshus, *Explicatio Prioris Epistolae ad Corinthios*, 303r.

emotions of men and women. That is why Plato teaches, with good reason, that music is of great value in shaping the customs of the state. Commentary on 1 Corinthians 14:7-8.[24]

An Illustration from Musical Instruments. David Dickson: As a trumpet, or any other instrument touched or blown, that is played in a confused fashion makes an unprofitable and ungrateful sound, so also a tongue that is not understood gives nothing but an uncertain and useless sound. But prophets utter their prophecies in a known tongue. Therefore the gift of tongues is inferior to the gift of prophecy. Exposition on 1 Corinthians 14:7-9.[25]

Is Paul Endorsing Congregational Music? Peter Martyr Vermigli: It now seems appropriate, by way of conclusion, to examine whether in fact musical voices and musical instruments ought to be permitted in our temples. Though the apostle does not touch on this matter in this present passage (for he has deduced his argument only from the similitude of music), nevertheless if we consider the purpose of the apostle's reasoning, it will not be strange, perhaps, to introduce a discussion of this matter for the common good. For often those harmonies prevent the comprehension of words and the understanding of meaning. And so I will briefly touch on what should be affirmed in the present matter. Those who defend the use of music in temples, bring up the words of the apostle to the Ephesians: "Singing songs, hymns, and spiritual songs." They also cite David, who calls us to worship God, not only with a voice of song, but with practically all musical instruments. And David adds this reason: Since it is necessary to devote ourselves to praising and glorifying God with all our strength and all our members, there is no reason why our voice and our musical talents should not be raised to that same purpose. For this reason Paul and Silas are reported in Acts 16 to have been praying and singing praises to God in prison. So too the three young men sang hymns to the Lord when they were not burned up in the fiery furnace. They also hold up as an example for us the savior Lord Jesus, who, after he had sung a hymn at supper along with his apostles, withdrew to the Mount of Olives. But whether these are solid reasons [for congregational music] we will make evident at the end of this discussion. . . .

In the ancient church, the office of singers and readers was delegated to the humblest of people. But now one sees that the most prestigious people perform these duties. Moreover, a second vice ought to have been guarded against so that the office of divine worship focuses on the greatest and most important things. . . . For today we often see it happen in major festivals that, on account of the multitude of ceremonies and lengthy music, it is necessary to put off preaching until midday, when people are drowsy and inattentive. In addition, it should be clear that a song should not be so choppy and rough that its meaning cannot be understood. Nor should it be permissible that cantors be paid so much money as to deplete church funds, from which one needs to pay ministers (who are more useful) and poor people. Now concerning organs and strange musical instruments, I do not see how they can be retained in the temples when, on account of their blaring, nothing of the Word of God is understood. Even though the Roman Church has fallen into many abuses, nevertheless, instruments of this sort are never permitted when the Roman pontiff celebrates the Mass!

What I said a little earlier, namely, that it is not easy to prove from the testimony of sacred writ whether the singing of songs in sacred assemblies is permissible, will be made clear by responding to those opposing arguments that were made at the beginning [of this excursus]. The passage from Ephesians is weak, for if the entire text is considered, it will be clear what Paul has in mind. Thus he states: "Do not get drunk with wine, for that is debauchery, but be filled with the Spirit, addressing

[24]CO 49:519-20 (cf. CTS 39:439-40). See Plato, *The Republic* IV, 424b-424e. LCL 237:330-34.
[25]Dickson, *Exposition of St. Paul's Epistles*, 64*.

yourselves in psalms and hymns and spiritual songs, singing and making melody in your hearts." From this you see that Christians are admonished to sing to *themselves* and in their hearts—nothing is mentioned here regarding sacred assemblies. I suppose that Christians, especially when they gather for God-honoring activities and recreation, might sing together now and then, as long as these songs are neither lewd nor worldly, but holy. Second, regarding those passages drawn from the Old Testament, they must not be strictly applied to the New Testament, unless we want to resume practicing the ceremonies and sacrifices of the ancient law. Concerning Paul and Silas, when they were imprisoned, it is not clearly stated that they were singing. For prayers and praises to God could be recited through speaking, that is, in a loud voice. And what are we to make of the hymn that the apostles and Savior recited at the Last Supper? It is evident that they did this in private—not in a sacred assembly. And the hymn that Christ sang with his apostles is known to have been associated with a Jewish custom that is still observed today in the Jewish Passover—and thus this practice should not now be repeated. As far as organs or musical instruments are concerned, if they are employed with the safeguards noted previously, then they can be used as long as they accompany human voices that are singing in such a way that the words of God and praise are intelligible. But as they are used today, I don't know how they can be tolerated. Commentary on 1 Corinthians 14:7-8.[26]

God's Word Must Be Intelligible in the Church. Wolfgang Musculus: Paul writes, "How will anyone know what is said?" . . . Paul says he cannot see how a person can understand an unintelligible tongue that is spoken in church. Catholic priests ask: "Why is it necessary for the people to understand the Latin words with which we pray, consecrate, and sing in the church? The ignorant multitude ought to adore these words with wonder and devotion—not understand them." The apostle was not unfamiliar with such an argument. Other people, with no less seriousness, say, "Why must what is spoken be understood when the words are in accordance with the apostolic authority of Rome?" . . . The reason Paul gives to those who ask these sorts of things . . . is "because you will be speaking into the air." Thus the person who speaks unintelligibly is speaking into the air. To speak into the air is to speak empty words in such a way that no understanding of the words is grasped by the audience. Commentary on 1 Corinthians 14:9.[27]

Pray for the Gift of Interpretation! Desiderius Erasmus: There are clearly many kinds of languages in the world that are spoken—that can be seen by everyone. But if nothing were added to the sound, then our speech to one another would be in vain. For although both persons would correctly speak their languages, nevertheless neither would understand the other. So it happens that I who speak Greek am like a barbarian to the person from Africa; and, likewise, that person from Africa who does not understand is like a barbarian to me. So then, you Corinthians, because you eagerly chase after and exalt the gifts of those who possess miraculous tongues, you will encourage me by paying attention to those greater gifts that are useful to the whole congregation. And so persons who have the gift of tongues should request in their prayers that God might bestow the gift of interpretation. Paraphrase on 1 Corinthians 14.[28]

---

[26]Vermigli, *In Selectissimam Priorem ad Corinthios Epistolam . . . Commentarii*, 377v-378r; citing Eph 5:19; Acts 16:25; Dan 3:1-30; Eph 5:18-19. Modern translations of Daniel 3 make no mention of the young men singing hymns during their time in the fiery furnace. Congregational singing was not practiced in Zurich's reformed liturgy until the end of the seventeenth century. For more, see Roland Diethelm, "Bullinger and Worship: 'Thereby one does not plant and sow,'" in *Architect of Reformation: An Introduction to Heinrich Bullinger, 1504-1575*, ed. Bruce Gordon and Emidio Campi (Grand Rapids: Baker Academic, 2004), 135-58.

[27]Musculus, *Comm. 1 Cor.*, 545.

[28]Erasmus, *Paraphrases*, 322-23.

Interpretation of Tongues Should Be Sought. Jacques Lefèvre d'Étaples: Because the gift of tongues by itself is among the less important gifts from the Holy Spirit, Paul instructs the Corinthians that those who have only tongues from among the gifts of the Holy Spirit, should entreat the same Spirit to confer on them the gift of understanding and interpreting tongues for the greater edification of themselves and the church. Nebuchadnezzar is an example of a person who has only a tongue. He had a vision from God but he did not understand it; thus he did not even know who was speaking. He prays and utters words of praise through the Holy Spirit, but his mind does not receive it. Daniel is an example of a person who has both the gift of tongues and their interpretation. He had a vision from God *and* received the ability to interpret it. It is a good thing to see visions of God. It is a good thing to pray and give praise to God through the Holy Spirit. But it is better to see visions *and* receive understanding of them. It is better to pray in the Spirit and utter inspired words of praise, *and* to understand them with both intelligence and mind. Commentary on 1 Corinthians 14:10-11.[29]

All Things Should Serve the Edification of the Church. Tilemann Hesshus: Paul adduces this conclusion from the previous arguments: that a person should not display knowledge of a foreign tongue without interpretation. Instead, all things must be established for the building up of the church, and we should be eager for spiritual gifts so that we are better prepared to instruct others. This principle must be imprinted on our deepest consciousness and must always be kept before our eyes so that we direct all things, and especially the labors of ministry, to magnifying the glory of God and edifying the church. The pastor should always deal with subject matter that is useful and necessary. He should see to it that he instructs his people in the catechism, delivering it to them faithfully, repeating it continually, impressing on them the necessary articles of faith, encouraging with all seriousness his hearers to repent. He should vehemently reproach the sins and errors that attack the church. He should strengthen those who are feeble; he should offer consolation to those wasting away from sorrow; he should arouse those who are lazy; he should refute the sophists. He should not chase after the applause of people; he should not adapt his sermons to the will of the powerful; he should not introduce empty subtleties from the pulpit; he should not engage in joking in the presence of the church of Jesus Christ. He should not be zealous for subjects that are uncertain, but in everything he should seek to build up of the church. Explication of 1 Corinthians 14:12.[30]

14:13-19 *Tongues Must Be Interpreted*

Public Prayers Must Be in the Vernacular. Tilemann Hesshus: Paul's fifth argument [for proving the superiority of prophecy for building up the church] is drawn from the practice of public prayer, which, unless it is uttered in a vernacular tongue known to all, does nothing to edify the church. "If anyone," he says, "is endowed with the gift of tongues, let them pray to the Lord that they might also receive the gift of interpretation." Unless they have obtained this from the Lord, they should not exhibit the gift of a foreign tongue in the church. For public prayers that are uttered in a foreign tongue have no place in the church. Explication on 1 Corinthians 14:13.[31]

God's Word Must Edify God's People. John Trapp: Unfruitful, that is, in regard to other peoples' edification. "It would be a great grace," said the martyr Lambert, "if we might have the Word of God diligently and often spoken and sung to us in such a way that people might understand it. Then it would happen that craftsmen would sing spiritual psalms while sitting at their work benches,

[29]Lefèvre d'Étaples, *Commentariorum in Epistolas Beati Pauli . . . Liber Secundus*, 122r; citing Dan 2; Dan 7.

[30]Hesshus, *Explicatio Prioris Epistolae ad Corinthios*, 304r.

[31]Ibid., 304v.

and husbandmen at their plows"—as St. Jerome desired it. Pavier, the town clerk in London during the reign of Henry VIII, was a man who could not bear to have the gospel written in English. Consequently he once swore a great oath that he would rather cut his own throat than to live long enough to see the king's highness approve the translation of Scripture into English and allow it to be read to the people by his authority. But Pavier broke his promise, for shortly thereafter he hanged himself. Commentary on 1 Corinthians 14:14.[32]

People Must Be Instructed to Pray in the Vernacular. Guillaume Farel: Until now the sheep of God have had very poor instruction in this, through the great negligence of the pastors, who need to instruct them to pray in a language they comprehend, and not merely to mutter from the lips without any understanding. For, as saint Paul says, "If I pray in a tongue, my understanding is unfruitful." And therefore he commands that whatever is spoken in the assembly of believers, which is the church, be spoken in a language that all can comprehend; otherwise we should remain silent. Now if we had observed this command, never would such dark times have come on us, for we should have prayed more in spirit and truth to the celestial Father himself in heaven, and not to creatures on earth, carnal and vain. The Lord's Prayer and Apostles' Creed.[33]

True Prayer Comes from Our Hearts, Not Merely from Our Lips. John Calvin: We should observe here that Paul thinks it a great fault if our understanding plays no role in prayer. And no wonder, for what else do we do in prayer except pour out our thoughts and desires before God? And too, given that prayer is the spiritual worship of God, what is more out of keeping with its very nature than to proceed merely from the lips, and not from the innermost reaches of the soul? And these things would have been completely familiar to everyone had not the devil dulled the senses of the world to such an extent that people thought they were praying properly when they were moving their lips. Commentary on 1 Corinthians 14:14.[34]

Should We Sing in Church? Balthasar Hubmaier: Yes, with my mouth I sing understandable words, and with my spirit I reflect on the words, so that I do not honor my God with my lips while my heart is far from it, as the Pharisees did. It is also better to speak or sing five words understandably before the church than ten thousand that cannot be understood. A Christian Catechism.[35]

Musical Instruments in Worship. Wolfgang Musculus: "I will sing praise with my spirit, but will sing praise with my mind also." The Greek word here is *psalō*, that is, praise (*Psallam*). It is possible that some people in the Corinthian church were singing the Psalms of David in the Hebrew language. Speaking from his own authority, Paul advises them to sing the Psalms in their own language so they can be understood in the church. Whether the Corinthians were singing the Psalms of David or some other songs, I think all agree that it was the custom in this church to sing songs to God. Now we should not restrict the word "making praise" to those songs that some are accustomed to sing with musical instruments, whether zither, harp, or lyre. For although the word "making praise" properly refers to singing with musical accompaniment, nevertheless this in no way prohibits the use of whatever sort of songs, especially in the church. For in truth, the first Christians did not use musical instruments in church. Commentary on 1 Corinthians 14:15.[36]

The Public Sermon Must Edify the People. Heinrich Bullinger: Paul points out more clearly how we can benefit from the diversity

[32]Trapp, *A Commentary or Exposition*, 695.* John Lambert's deposition and martyrdom are described in Foxe, *Acts and Monuments* 5.181-236. Pavier's oath and subsequent death are found in ibid., 5.63, 65; 8.635.

[33]In Zuidema and Van Raalte, *Early French Reform*, 105*.

[34]CO 49:522 (cf. CTS 39:446).

[35]CRR 5:359.

[36]Musculus, *Comm. 1 Cor.*, 551.

of tongues, namely, if we interpret them. He does not say, "we condemn speaking and singing in tongues," but rather, "we wish that an interpretation be added in an ordinary (rather than foreign) language, especially in all affairs conducted in the church, so that prophecy may not be harmed in any way, but maintain first place in all matters." To "pray in the spirit" is to pray only with our spirits, without any breath or words; but to "pray in the mind" is to pray with our very understanding, laying bare our minds through prayer. . . . "To bless" (*benedicere*) is to praise and honor God. Now, on the basis of this passage, Priscus thought that there was a custom that the whole church would respond "Amen" to the words of the preacher. And echoing this response, Jerome says, "Amen" in one of his letters to Marcella. . . . And Paul states that a person cannot respond "Amen"—that is, to affirm what has been proclaimed—unless that person has understood the sermon. . . . But if someone should object, "But these are sacred words that the preacher is speaking," Paul responds: "That doesn't mean you are instructing the people. What is proclaimed is holy, but meanwhile the people in the congregation, when they return to their homes after the discourse of the teacher, are in no way made better, and they have not learned in this public sermon how they ought to live privately." Commentary on 1 Corinthians 14:15-16.[37]

Praying with Understanding. John Trapp: For a prayer to be effectual there must be both intention of the mind and affection of the heart; otherwise it is not praying, but parroting. I have read that a parrot in Rome could distinctly repeat the Apostles' Creed. Commentary on 1 Corinthians 14:15.[38]

Agreement in Prayer. Wolfgang Musculus: "How will someone say, 'Amen'?" It is altogether necessary for there to be harmony and agreement in the prayers of believers, since prayer is directed toward God. In the church, it is not at all unusual for one person to pray publicly on behalf of everyone. And there are many shared concerns that are properly presented to God through the voice of one person. But now, in this present passage, the apostle suggests that prayers of this sort should be concluded and strengthened by the common people, that is, by the acclamation of those listening, so as to affirm for themselves those prayers that one person has prayed to God on their behalf. But today, neither the person who prays nor the people who listen to the prayer put any thought into the words that have been expressed in the prayer. In the church, after the minister and the altar attendant have recited a prayer, how few people respond with the word "Amen," agreeing from the heart with what was said? In the papacy, priests shout "Amen" loudly enough. But meanwhile they do not do this out of agreement and knowledge of heart, but out of long-standing custom; they shout "Amen" more to give thanks for the end of their prayers than for the substance of their prayers. . . . How astonishing it is, therefore, that for so many centuries the majority of us were praying to God in vain! Commentary on 1 Corinthians 14:16.[39]

Paul Is Not Jealous of Other People's Gifts. John Calvin: "I thank," etc. Since people commonly belittle other people's abilities in which they themselves do not excel, and since Paul does not wish to be seen to belittle the gift of tongues out of spite or envy, he anticipates such suspicion by showing that he is, in this respect, superior to them all. "See," he says, "how what I am saying gives you no reason for suspicion, as if I would depreciate what I don't possess. For if we were to have a competition over tongue-speaking, not one of you could compete with me. But while I might be able to make a good showing in this sort of thing, I am more concerned about edification." Paul's teaching derives no small weight from the fact that he is not

[37]Bullinger, *In omnes apostolicas epistolas . . . commentarii*, 231-32. Priscus was a Greek historian of the fifth century who wrote the influential *Byzantine History* (published around 476).
[38]Trapp, *A Commentary or Exposition*, 695*.

[39]Musculus, *Comm. 1 Cor.*, 553.

thinking about his own reputation. However, so that he doesn't appear excessively arrogant, he ascribes the whole thing to God. Thus he tempers his boasting with modesty.

"I would rather speak five words." This is hyperbole, unless you understand "five words" to mean "five sentences." Now since Paul, who could have otherwise dazzled everyone by his tongue-speaking, voluntarily refrains from doing so and without any ostentation makes edification his only aim, he clearly shows the inflated ambition of those who are very eager to show off with empty jingling. At the same time, the authority of the apostle ought to have no small influence in calling them back from vanity of this sort. Commentary on 1 Corinthians 14:18-19.[40]

14:20-25 *Tongues Are a Sign for Unbelievers, Prophecy for Believers*

We Must Avoid Childish Thinking. Philipp Melanchthon: "Childish Thinking." Childish thinking is when people lack a spiritual priority in things, and cling to those things that they feel instead of progressing from the gifts to cling to God alone, not his gifts. As Proverbs 22 says: "Folly is bound up in the heart of a child, but the rod of discipline drives it far from him."

"Be children in evil." A child in evil is, in the strict sense, contrasted to that which is spiteful or worthless; or it is characterized by what is simple and straightforward. Jeremiah 4 speaks in this way about such an attitude: "For my people are foolish; they know me not; they are stupid children; they have no understanding. They are 'wise' in doing evil! But how to do good they know not." Annotations on 1 Corinthians 14:20.[41]

Be Mature in Your Thinking. Tilemann Hesshus: Paul inserts a reminder concerning the use of gifts—that they should not be expressed in a childish or foolish manner, but ought to be employed with wisdom. "Do not be childish in your thinking." It's as if Paul were saying, "Do not be so crazy, and do not indulge in such childish imagination as to suppose that religion and Christian happiness consists only in this, that you can exhibit spiritual gifts without any fruit. Even common sense recognizes that it is foolish to exercise a foreign tongue among people who do not understand it. Those of you who are illumined by the Holy Spirit, therefore, ought to be wiser than other people who are outside the church." "Be children in evil"; that is, "Be innocent and ignorant in things that are evil and forbidden. Do not seek to be cunning or shrewd in evil arts or tricks, but be mature in your thinking"; that is, "Always make progress in wisdom and in the knowledge of God's will. To the extent that it is possible, establish yourself in spiritual truth and mature wisdom." The word "mature" here does not mean perfect in every detail, but that which is genuine, pure, and trustworthy. To this Paul contrasts what is corrupt, fake, deceitful, and mutilated. The wisdom of the flesh is imperfect and defiled with foolishness and error. But the Spirit's wisdom is perfect, although it continues to grow in the lives of godly people. Thus it is Paul's meaning that spiritual gifts ought to be used wisely, not for empty show, nor so that we might win the applause of people (as stupid pagans are accustomed foolishly to do), but for magnifying the glory of God and the edification of the church. In this way genuine glory will be accomplished, not only in the world, but in all of eternity, when we attribute everything to the glory of God. For this promise is most true and illustrious: "The person who glorifies me, I will glory." Explication of 1 Corinthians 14:20.[42]

This Passage in Isaiah Is Rightly Called "The Law." Wolfgang Musculus: Paul says, "In the law it is written." You will never find in the books of Moses what Paul here quotes. In fact, if

[40]CO 49:524 (cf. CTS 39:450); citing 1 Cor 13:1.

[41]Melanchthon, *Annotationes in Epistolam priorem ad Corinthios*, 158; citing Prov 22:15; Jer 4:22.

[42]Hesshus, *Explicatio Prioris Epistolae ad Corinthios*, 306r-307r; citing 1 Sam 2:30.

you search for these exact words, you will not find any passage in all of Scripture where it is written: "By people of foreign tongues and lips will I speak to this people, and even then they will not listen to me." Nevertheless, it must be that the apostle drew these words from somewhere out of the law, unless we conclude that he quoted from the law things that were never written in the law. Now, I do not find any passage from which it seems likely these words were drawn, except the passage in Isaiah 28. We should not think it unusual that Paul describes the writings of the prophets as "law." . . . For in fact, when speaking of the law, Paul sometimes refers in general to those things that pertain to the Old Testament, or to the Pentateuch, or to the book of Judges, or Samuel, or the book of Kings, or the Psalms, or the Prophets, etc. Commentary on 1 Corinthians 14:21.[43]

God's Wrath Expressed Against Those Who Despise Prophecy. John Calvin: Now the meaning [of this passage from Isaiah] is that the people have been afflicted with so much blindness and folly that when God speaks to them they understand him no better than any barbarian or foreigner, babbling in an unknown tongue—which is a terrible curse. Now, Paul has not quoted the prophet's words exactly, because he thought it adequate to point out the passage so that the Corinthians, being warned, might consider it more carefully. . . .

Now from this Paul concludes the following: "Brothers, beware of being like a child, which the prophet rebukes so severely, lest the voice of God resound in your ears without fruit. For when you reject prophecy, which is given to you, and you prefer to be dazzled by empty sounds, is this not willfully to incur the curse of God?" Moreover, lest the Corinthians should say in reply that elsewhere in Scripture it is praiseworthy to be children spiritually, Paul anticipates them and indeed urges them to be "children in evil," but to beware of being "children in their thinking." We may infer from this how foolish those people are who make Christian simplicity consist in ignorance. Paul would wish, as much as possible, that all believers be mature [*perfectus*] in thinking. Commentary on 1 Corinthians 14:21.[44]

Foreign Tongues Cannot Convert the Sinner. Giovanni Diodati: "In the Law," referring to the Old Testament (as we see in John 15:25). Now the passage from Isaiah, which is a reproof of the people's willful stupidity, relates to the subject at hand in this way. Just as God did not cease propounding his Word to his people (though they had hardened themselves against understanding it to their salvation) and it served only to reprove them and seal their condemnation, so when the Word is taught and comes in a language that they do not understand, it is a sign that God will not make it an instrument of conversion and enlightenment, but of conviction, so as to harden unbelievers. "And even then," namely, they will not be influenced in the slightest with this clear token of divine wrath (as if a father were muttering to his children) to shake off their stupidity. Annotations on 1 Corinthians 14:21.[45]

Tongues Are a Sign for Unbelievers—Prophecy a Sign for Believers. Cardinal Cajetan: After quoting this statement of Isaiah, Paul draws out the difference between prophecy and tongues for those to whom they have been given as a sign from God. And he asserts, literally, that the gift of tongues was given by God to the Jewish people, at a period when they were unfaithful, as a sign to confute their disbelief; and likewise prophecy was given to the same people when they were faithful. If you were to compare the situation of the Jewish people when they had true faith to their situation when they passed from faithfulness to unfaithfulness, you would perceive this: that numerous prophecies were given to the people when they were in a state of faith. But

[43]Musculus, *Comm. 1 Cor.*, 561-62; citing Is 28:11.

[44]CO 49:525 (cf. CTS 39:452-53).

[45]Diodati, *Pious Annotations*, Nn2r*.

when they killed Christ out of unbelief and passed over into the company of the unfaithful, the Holy Spirit came through gifts of various tongues on the day of Pentecost. And so the difference between tongues and prophecy that Paul establishes here is understood with regard to the situation of the Jewish people. And he said this so that the Corinthians (being mature rather than children in their thinking) might learn from the different conditions of the Jews the different reasons that prophecy and the gift of tongues are given, [and] how much prophecy surpasses tongues. For he portrays prophecy as fruitful to the people, inasmuch as they are faithful; but the gift of tongues is unfruitful to the same group of people, inasmuch as they did not believe in the Messiah, or rather as they were crossing over to a state of unbelief at that time. Commentary on 1 Corinthians 14:22.[46]

Paul Here Condemns the Abuse of Tongues. Huldrych Zwingli: "Will they not say that you are out of your minds?" Paul sails between Scylla and Charybdis in that he entirely prohibits speaking in languages that are not understood in the church, but nevertheless, he does not condemn speaking in tongues. It is difficult to condemn the *abuse* of a practice, while commending and praising the practice itself—which is what Paul does here. Therefore Paul turns his attention to the disagreement and afterward responds to the objections of the Jews. For someone might say, "Paul, why do you despise tongues? Did God not once furnish his people with these weapons?" Paul answers: "I am not condemning tongue-speaking entirely, nay rather, I praise them exceedingly. But on the other hand, I warn you to be careful with tongues. For when you cry out in tongues that are not understood by simple folk, they will think you are out of your mind." Annotations on 1 Corinthians 14:23.[47]

Decorum Must Be Preserved in Worship. Wolfgang Musculus: Paul describes the outcome that will result from such confusion. As if to say: "Come now, if you all speak various tongues in church what use will this be to you, or to the common ignorant folk or unbelievers, who come into your assembly? Judge for yourself, will you not be considered insane?" . . . Therefore believers in the church should beware lest it erect an obstruction for common people and unbelievers by allowing things with any appearance of foolishness and insanity. Indeed, our faith in Christ, our hope, our endurance of the cross and tribulation, our renunciation of the world and our flesh—all these things are condemned as foolishness by the sons of this world, and we should bear such reproach patiently and bravely. But in other matters that can be done with reason, decorum, and usefulness, we should be careful not to act so irrationally and unprofitably that we are more deserving of ridicule and contempt than praise and commendation. Commentary on 1 Corinthians 14:23.[48]

Limitations of Tongues and Prophecy. Peter Martyr Vermigli: Paul has already laid out the strength and main point of his argument. But it might be possible for the Corinthians to object: "If tongues have been given as a sign to unbelievers, then why isn't it useful for us to employ them in our assemblies? For when unbelievers come, at least they will see this sign, which will move them to wonder and perhaps compel them to receive the gospel." But it must be considered that this sign of tongues often causes people to ridicule when they hear it—this is the danger that Paul is presently warning the church about. We do not deny that whenever people listen to the teaching of Christ, they are brought to a state of wonder by means of a kind of miracle. But in this present passage, Paul is not referring to this precedent. And he states additionally that the gift of tongues cannot advance further than to excite confusion and wonder. But prophecy does more than cause wonder; it also has the ability to impart

[46]Cajetan, *In omnes Sacrae Scripturae expositionem*, 5:137.
[47]Zwingli, *Annotatiunculae . . . ex ore Zvinglij*, 120.
[48]Musculus, *Comm. 1 Cor.*, 566.

power. Paul refers to this when he says that an unbeliever who enters the church will conclude that those who speak various tongues are insane. . . .

Here's another question: Since prophecy is said to pertain to believers, why does it sometimes happen that prophecy leads to the conversion of unbelievers, who, when they hear someone prophesying in church, feel themselves condemned and their views refuted, fall prostrate and worship God, and confess that he is present in the church? In response, we say this: Paul does not deny that unbelievers sometimes receive benefit from and are converted through prophecy. But he wishes to say only this, that unbelievers do not derive usefulness from prophecy when they assemble together. And so as to make the matter clearer, let us observe that prophecy and tongues are not always equally beneficial for unbelievers. Isaiah's prophecies did not preserve King Ahaz. And Jeroboam was not converted from his idolatry through the prophecy of the man of God, who not only prophesied before him but also restored the king's shriveled arm to its original health. Nor was King Ahab prompted by the preaching of Elijah to turn to the Lord. For this reason, just as tongues do not always move people to wonder and prepare them for the gospel, so too prophecy does not always call wicked people back to the right path. Commentary on 1 Corinthians 14:23-25.[49]

The Word of God Penetrates the Mind. John Calvin: But we shall find it much easier to understand this passage if we compare it with another passage, from Hebrews 4:12: "The Word of God is living and active, sharper than any two-edged sword, piercing to the division of soul and spirit, of joints and marrow, and discerning the thoughts of the heart." For in both passages, the same efficacy of the Word of God is spoken of, though the passage from Hebrews is fuller and clearer. As far as the present passage is concerned, it is not difficult to understand what is meant by "convinced" and "judged." People's consciences are in a stupefied condition, and they are not troubled by a sense of displeasure with their wickedness as long as they are shrouded in the darkness of ignorance. In short, unbelief is like lethargy that makes us insensitive. But the Word of God penetrates into the deepest recesses of the mind, and dispersing the darkness with a shining light, as it were, it drives away the deadly lethargy. Commentary on 1 Corinthians 14:24.[50]

The Power of Prophecy to Convict and Convert the Sinner. Tilemann Hesshus: "But if all prophesy," that is, if each one of you has been equipped with the gift of explaining the sacred Scripture and passing on the teaching about God and eternal life, then unbelievers will be refuted and judged by everything. That is, they will be convinced in their hearts of their errors, for a great light shines forth in the church. If some unbelievers come to worship services and assemblies of the godly, and hear a hymn or preaching in a foreign language, they will not be converted by it nor edified; instead, they will laugh at the barbarous noise. But if they hear many people in the assembly explaining doctrines concerning God, the law, the fall of humankind, the reasons for death and disasters, the benefits of the Mediator, good works, the church, and eternal life; and if they hear idolatry vehemently refuted, lust and wickedness reproached, people called to repentance, violent threats and examples of divine wrath discussed, and the most wonderful promises explained—then they will be refuted and convinced in their hearts that the church's teaching is more reasonable than that of the pagans. For pagans defile themselves with shameful lusts and wickedness; they fabricate filthy idols; they live in terrible darkness of error and blasphemies, and, destitute of all consolation, they are finally thrown into the destruction of despair.

And if God, through his Spirit, converts unbelievers in the assembly—because the Word of God cannot go forth without fruit—then they will freely reveal the secret thoughts of their hearts and they will acknowledge that they have

[49]Vermigli, *In Selectissimam Priorem ad Corinthios Epistolam . . . Commentarii*, 384v-385; citing Is 7; 1 Kings 13; 17.

[50]CO 49:526-27 (cf. CTS 39:456).

been convicted by the evidence of the truth. They will detest the idols that they previously worshiped; they will wonder at the darkness in which they previously lived when they were pagans; they will cast off the wicked deeds with which they previously defiled themselves. And falling down on their faces, they will adore the God who has revealed himself through so many clear testimonies in the church. And they will confess that God is truly present in the church and that the idols of the pagans are nothing. Certainly this outstanding fruit—the refutation of idols, the manifestation of God's glory, the conversion of unbelievers, the strengthening of believers—is produced through prophecy and the explanation of sacred Scripture. Therefore it is far more profitable to be zealous for the gift of prophecy than to display knowledge of foreign tongues. Explication of 1 Corinthians 14:23-25.[51]

[51]Hesshus, *Explicatio Prioris Epistolae ad Corinthios*, 309v-310v.

The Power of Prophecy to Humble Us. John Calvin: "Falling on his face, he will worship." Now it is the knowledge of God alone that is able to bring down the pride of the flesh. Prophecy causes that to happen to us. Hence the proper effect and nature of prophecy is to bring people down from their lofty perch so that, lying prostrate, they might worship God. But even prophecy is useless to many people—or rather, they are made even worse by hearing it. But Paul does not wish to attribute this function to prophecy, as if it always produces this result. Rather, he only wishes to show how much usefulness is derived from it, and how it functions. Thus it is exceptional praise that prophecy forces unbelievers to confess that God is present and that his majesty shines forth in the midst of their assembly. Commentary on 1 Corinthians 14:25.[52]

[52]CO 49:527-28 (cf. CTS 39:457).

14:26-40 ORDERLY WORSHIP

*[26]What then, brothers? When you come together,
each one has a hymn, a lesson, a revelation, a
tongue, or an interpretation. Let all things be done
for building up. [27]If any speak in a tongue, let there
be only two or at most three, and each in turn, and
let someone interpret. [28]But if there is no one to
interpret, let each of them keep silent in church and
speak to himself and to God. [29]Let two or three
prophets speak, and let the others weigh what is
said. [30]If a revelation is made to another sitting
there, let the first be silent. [31]For you can all
prophesy one by one, so that all may learn and all
be encouraged, [32]and the spirits of prophets are
subject to prophets. [33]For God is not a God of
confusion but of peace.*

*As in all the churches of the saints, [34]the women
should keep silent in the churches. For they are not
permitted to speak, but should be in submission, as
the Law also says. [35]If there is anything they desire to
learn, let them ask their husbands at home. For it is
shameful for a woman to speak in church.*

*[36]Or was it from you that the word of God came?
Or are you the only ones it has reached? [37]If anyone
thinks that he is a prophet, or spiritual, he should
acknowledge that the things I am writing to you are a
command of the Lord. [38]If anyone does not recognize
this, he is not recognized. [39]So, my brothers, earnestly
desire to prophesy, and do not forbid speaking in
tongues. [40]But all things should be done decently and
in order.*

Overview: In an effort to correct the disorder and dissensions accompanying the practice of prophecy and tongue-speaking in the Corinthian church, Paul gives detailed instructions regarding the priority and practice of prophecy, the role of women in public assemblies, and the crucial importance of preserving decorum and good order in Christian worship services. As noted above, Reformation commentators believe that the gift of prophecy is expressed primarily (or even entirely) through Christian preaching, where faithful gospel ministers explain the genuine sense of a Scripture text and apply its message to their congregations for their instruction and edification. Compared to prophecy, the gift of foreign tongues is nearly useless in public worship, unless these languages enhance faithful exposition of the biblical text. Protestant interpreters find special significance in Paul's requirement that prophets must defer to one another as well as submit to the judgment of others—clearly, no church officer (not even the pope!) can demand unquestioning obedience; *all* Christians have the responsibility to judge right doctrine by the standard of God's Word; *all* Christians are "priests" in the sight God. With that said, however, the magisterial reformers insist that only a select group of men—called by God and appointed by his church—are permitted to preach, administer the sacraments, and oversee discipline in the Christian church. Likewise, women may not teach or preach in the Christian assembly; their God-given role requires them to submit to their husbands and instruct their children in God's Word privately at home. A number of commentators, including Katharina Schütz Zell of Strasbourg, propose an important exception to this general rule, however: in emergency situations, women may teach men when it involves refuting false doctrine. Reformation exegetes agree that Paul's particular censure of the Corinthian church points to a larger principle that is relevant for every Christian assembly, namely, that Christian worship should be conducted with propriety and decorum so as to glorify God and edify his people.

14:26-33a *Judging Prophecies*

All Christians Edify the Church. Wolfgang Musculus: All things should be done for edification. This relates to the purpose for everything that is performed in the assembly of the church. That is, that all things should be done for the building up of believers (namely, those who are in the church). In other words, that all might be strengthened more and more in the faith and knowledge of Christ, and grow in true piety and righteousness. This is the true building up of the Lord's temple. Now, who are the builders of this temple? Paul says, "each one of you." Thus all who were then members of the church were at the same time its builders. . . . Paul does not simply admonish the Corinthians that "when you come together, do everything for edification," but rather he says, "when you come together let each of you bring a psalm, a teaching, a tongue, a revelation, and an interpretation." Therefore the instruments of this edification are psalms, teaching, tongues, revelations, and interpretations. . . . Paul does not attribute all of these to a single person, because the Holy Spirit does not so distribute these gifts that all of them are conferred on a single person. Instead, each person receives their own gift, as is mentioned in chapter 12. Commentary on 1 Corinthians 14:26.[1]

Church Singing and Reading Must Be in the Spirit. Balthasar Hubmaier: I am well satisfied with singing and reading in the church, but not as it has hitherto been practiced—only if it is done in the spirit and from the heart and with understanding of the words and for the edifying of the church, as Paul teaches. A Brief Apologia.[2]

The Right Order of Tongue-Speaking. Tilemann Hesshus: Paul now teaches the Corinthians in what order and for what purpose they ought to employ and rightly arrange the various gifts with which God has adorned his church. The practice of the early church is made clear in this passage. Whenever the church had assembled, some passage from the prophetic writings was read aloud, and then several people delivered an explanation to the rest of the congregation. If anyone came forward who was endowed with the gift of preaching, he would be given the opportunity to speak. Thus, in Luke 4, Christ requested the book, read a passage from Isaiah, and then demonstrated that this prophecy had been fulfilled. So too in Acts 13, after they read in Moses and the Prophets, the rulers of the synagogue sent for Paul, asking whether he wished to offer any word of teaching or consolation to the people. This was the custom in the early church. Therefore Paul warns the Corinthians that they also should preserve this kind of order in their gatherings, lest they be filled with noisy confusion: "If anyone has either a Psalm, or a tongue, or a lesson, or a revelation, let them share it for the common good, so that it might edify the church"—they should not use their gift foolishly, without benefiting others. "If anyone speaks in a tongue, let there be two, or three at the most, and let each speak in turn." That is to say, if anyone endeavors to offer a reading from the prophets, whether in Hebrew or another foreign language, only two or at the most three persons are permitted to speak in turn. "And let someone else interpret." Following the Hebrew practice, after reading the passage from the prophetic writings, an interpretation should immediately be added, so that the church can be edified. But if there is no interpreter present, the foreign tongue should not be permitted in the assembly, for the church would glean no fruit from it, since no one would understand it. Nevertheless, lest people who possess a foreign tongue think that their gift is useless, they can speak to themselves and to God with their tongue, to arouse themselves to prayer, thanksgiving, hope, and patience. But the church of God must not be bothered with unknown tongues that are not interpreted. Explication of 1 Corinthians 14:26-28.[3]

Public Worship Must Edify the Assembly. David Dickson: If the Spirit shall suggest to any of the prophets any godly psalm to praise God, or

[1]Musculus, *Comm. 1 Cor.*, 573-74.
[2]CRR 5:300.
[3]Hesshus, *Explicatio Prioris Epistolae ad Corinthios*, 311r-312r.

any doctrine, or an expression of a foreign tongue for the benefit of the church, or a revelation of things to come, or a mystery not observed before, or the interpretation of a foreign tongue, or of Scripture, Paul commands that the exercise of all these gifts be suited to the edification of the church, so that all may go out of the assembly better than they came. Exposition of 1 Corinthians 14:26.[4]

Paul Permits, but Does Not Require, Speaking in Tongues. John Calvin: Now, it should be observed that Paul is not making a command, but only giving permission. For the church can do without tongues without inconvenience, except insofar as they are helpful to prophecy—as is the case with Hebrew and Greek today. But Paul makes this concession so that it might not seem that he is withholding any spiritual gift from the assembly of believers. . . . Therefore, when Paul corrects the fault of the Corinthians, he does so with the greatest moderation. On the one hand, he in no way rejects any gift of God, so that all his benefits might be clearly seen among the believers. But, on the other hand, he imposes restrictions, lest human ambition secretly usurp the place of the glory of God, and so that less important gifts do not stand in the way of those that are superior. Commentary on 1 Corinthians 14:27.[5]

Tongues and Prophecy in Zurich. Heinrich Bullinger: We will now say a word by way of digression to clarify the meaning of this present passage. We will briefly describe the arrangement of tongues and prophecy in the Zurich church since its restoration by Huldrych Zwingli, of happy memory. First of all, he did away with those hours that are called "canonical," along with the incantations in foreign languages and the noisy ceremonies and music. It was not that he was displeased with sacred reading and prayer, for he especially wanted to restore those things. Rather, he did this because there were many singers and readers in public worship who were opposed to the teachings of the Christian faith, and who were very superstitious and only interested in making money. And also because those who were responsible for reading the Bible completely picked it apart and abused it in exactly the same way that those pseudo-teachers of the Corinthians were known to have handled sacred things in the holy assembly. Thus all these practices have been abolished, and more useful things substituted in their place.

First of all, the people assemble daily solely for prayers and public sermons, where God is entreated concerning those matters dictated by the present needs of the church, and where a pious message, drawn from a certain passage of Scripture, is delivered in the vernacular tongue without any concealed language. Second, as far as the languages and the more profound matters of prophecy are concerned, they are reserved for the time previously devoted to singing. The assembly of those who teach God's Word now convenes daily at the canonical hours. In this meeting, they treat the most important matters in the Old Testament books with diligence and reverence (for portions of the New Testament are explained each day in the public sermons)—however, nothing is discussed here in a confused or thoughtless manner. The Scripture is studied book by book, chapter by chapter, and no passage is begun that is not finished. Indeed, nothing is lectured on that can't be examined in a leisurely and very diligent fashion, with a concern for the weightiness of the subject and the benefit of the hearers. Now this assembly begins with holy prayers. Everyone repeats general prayers to the all-powerful and merciful God (whose Word is a lamp for our feet and a light to our path) that he might open and illumine our minds to have a pure and holy understanding of his oracles, and be transformed according to what we have rightly understood, so that we might displease no part of his majesty, through Christ our Lord. Once these prayers are completed, a young man who is a stipendiary of the church reads in the Vulgate version (as they call Jerome's edition) the passage that the prophet arrives at in the flow and

[4]Dickson, *Exposition of St. Paul's Epistles*, 65*.
[5]CO 49:528-29 (cf. CTS 39:459).

sequence of his interpretation. For young men of exceptional character and promise are supported with a stipend from the church treasury and are educated in the liberal arts, the languages, and the sacred writings so that someday they might pay back the churches that supported them and be very profitable in the holy ministry. . . . Now, once the young man has recited the passage in the Latin language, the Hebrew reader stands up and rereads the same passage in the Hebrew language, noting here and there common idioms and peculiarities of the language, rehearsing their meaning, at different times interpreting word for word, but also reading aloud the opinions of the grammarians and rabbis. Today, Dr. Konrad Pellikan—who is a man exceptionally gifted in the languages, in piety, and in the humane letters—fulfills this role with diligence, erudition, and piety. The Greek reader follows the reading of the Hebrew and treats in succession the Greek text (whether the Septuagint or some other Greek version), comparing it to the Hebrew, showing how the Greek is different from it, and being attentive to when it restores something. Finally, after this comparison is made and the Greek version interpreted, the person who has made the interpretation discharges the office of prophet. And the passage that has already been read in Latin, Greek, and Hebrew is explained in detail with all diligence and the utmost care, showing how that present passage was treated by the ancient writers, what the Jewish and Catholic interpreters judged concerning it—regarding the agreement of the sacred words; the coherence, structure, and meaning of the words; the authority and distinctiveness of their conclusions; and the strength and propriety with which everything must be presented. In brief, [the prophet sets forth] the genuine sense of the passage, as well as its use and application, showing what ought to be learned from it regarding faith, godliness, holiness, righteousness, and perseverance. Commentary on 1 Corinthians 14:27.[6]

Long Sermons Can Be Onerous. John Trapp: "Or at the most three"—lest the hearers be tired out. Our infirmity will not permit any long intention, either of body or mind. Long services can hardly maintain their vigor, just as in tall bodies the spirits are diffused. Erasmus has observed that Origen never preached more than an hour, and often but half an hour. "He considered it better to preach often than long," Erasmus stated. Commentary on 1 Corinthians 14:27.[7]

Let Him Speak to Himself and God. John Calvin: "Let him enjoy," Paul says, "his gift in his own conscience, and give thanks to God." For I take "speaking to himself and God" to mean thinking silently about the gift graciously conferred, with gratitude, and to enjoy it privately, since there is no opportunity to express it publicly. For Paul contrasts this secret way of speaking from public speaking in Church—the latter of which he forbids. Commentary on 1 Corinthians 14:28.[8]

God's People Can Discern Right Teaching. Huldrych Zwingli: But on what basis will unlearned persons and the well-educated judge? How can a mortal human judge the eternal Word of God? This is my answer: The spiritual person judges all things. Therefore, whoever hears the heavenly Word of Scripture explicated by a prophet in church, that person is to judge what he hears. Nevertheless, the prophet's word that is heard is not the word itself by which we believe. For if we were made believers by hearing the word, then clearly all of us would be believers, for today all the prophets proclaim the gospel. But on the contrary, we see today that many people hear and see who nevertheless do not have faith. Therefore it is clear that we are made believers by that word which the heavenly Father places in our hearts, not that external word

[6]Bullinger, *In Priorem ad Corinthios Epistolam Commentarius*, 235. The *Prophezei* was founded by Zwingli in 1525 to provide training in biblical exegesis, interpretation, and proclamation for Zurich's pastors and theological students.

[7]Trapp, *A Commentary or Exposition*, 696*. See Erasmus, "De Vita, Phrasi, docendi ratione and Operibus Origenis" in *Desiderii Erasmi Roterodami operamonia* (Leiden, 1703–1706), 8:438.

[8]CO 49:529 (cf. CTS 39:459-60).

that the prophet preaches, but the word by which God both illuminates us so that we might understand and draws us so that we might follow. Those who have been imbued by that word judge the word that rings forth in the congregation and strikes the ears of those listening. At the same time, the word of faith, which resides in the mind of believers, is judged by no one, but by it the external word is judged. God has ordained that this word be proclaimed in the midst of his people, even though faith does not come from the external word—as Christ explains elsewhere in the parable of the seed. For believers judge not according to their own opinions, but according to the divine Spirit. Therefore the judge of the preached word is not a human being, but rather the divine Spirit that dwells in the heart of the righteous person—this Spirit is easily able to discern the disposition of what is taught. . . .

For it belongs to the sheep to judge whether it is a shepherd or a thief who has come to them, and whether they are listening to the voice of a shepherd or a villain. The sheep recognize, listen to, and follow their shepherd. They will not even listen to a stranger, much less follow them. Now, how is it that the sheep are so knowledgeable and so shrewd that they are never deceived? It is because the shepherd knows his sheep and the sheep know their shepherd—because they have been known by God. The Father has drawn them to himself inasmuch as all have been taught by God, for no one comes to Christ unless the Father has drawn him. Thus the sheep are not able to err, since they know the voice of the shepherd so well that they would never receive a stranger. Annotations on 1 Corinthians 14:29.[9]

Paul Is Not Saying *Everyone* Can Preach. Martin Luther: Undoubtedly some maintain that in 1 Corinthians 14, St. Paul gave anyone liberty to preach in the congregation, even to bark against the established preacher. . . . What a fine model I imagine that would be, for anyone to have the right to interrupt a preacher and begin to argue with him! Soon another would join in and tell the other two to hush up. Perchance a drunk from the tavern would come in and join the trio calling on the third to be silent. At last the women too would claim the right of "sitting by," telling the men to be silent. Then one woman silencing the other—oh what a beautiful holiday, auction, and carnival that would be! What pigsties could compare in goings-on with such churches? Infiltrating and Clandestine Preachers.[10]

All Christians Have the Right to Judge Doctrine. Philipp Melanchthon: In commanding that others judge [what has been said], Paul wants the authority of judging doctrine to be in the hands of the church. And he adds that "you all can prophesy," by which he establishes the right of every individual in the church to judge concerning doctrine and to teach; indeed, he also commands those teaching that, if something is revealed to a person seated, they should listen quietly to the person seated. The same thing is said in 1 Thessalonians 5: "Do not quench the Spirit. Do not despise prophesying, but test everything; hold fast to what is good." That is, all are free to teach, and all are to be heard and judged by everyone. And 1 Peter 3 states, "Always be prepared to make a defense to anyone who calls you to account for the hope that is in you." . . . And so anybody has the right to judge about matters of faith, and Matthew 7 says: "Beware of false prophets"; therefore, true prophets should be judged from false prophets. This accords very closely with what is in Numbers 11: "Would that he grant that all the people were prophets and the Lord might place his spirit on them." Therefore the popes are acting very wickedly in usurping to themselves alone the power of judging concerning doctrine. And it is even more wicked that they have decreed that they are not required to give the reason for their judgment. Annotations on 1 Corinthians 14:29.[11]

[9]Zwingli, *Annotatiunculae . . . ex ore Zvinglij*, 121-22; citing Mt 13:18-23; Jn 6:65.

[10]LW 40:388-89; citing 1 Cor 14:34.

[11]Melanchthon, *Annotationes in Epistolam priorem ad Corinthios*,

Judge According to the Word and Truth. Menno Simons: I ask that you do not measure and judge in a carnal way with dialectics and similar human wisdom. But I ask you to examine it and judge it according to the Word and truth of the Lord, as those who understand spiritual matters; as unblamable, regenerate Christians, who are full of the knowledge and fear of God, driven by the Holy Spirit, who do not seek human favor, praise, and honor, their own advantage and carnal welfare, but only the honor and glory of God, and the eternal salvation of their brethren. For to such alone belongs the judgment in spiritual matters, and not to the carnally minded. Brief Confession on the Incarnation.[12]

Pastors' Sermons Should Be Tested and Obeyed. Guillaume Farel: Those who hear good pastors should test and judge that which they say and seek diligently to know if it is of the word of God. Once they have tested it, they should hold to it and believe it, not because of the pastor who bears it, but because it is the word of God.

If they find that the pastor bears something other than the word of God, they ought to guard themselves not to trust in it or believe it. Even if one of the greatest apostles of God or an angel of heaven came to teach something else than the pure word of God, we should not hold to any of it or believe it. For we should have no other nourishment than the pure word of God. Scripture clearly testifies that whatever is not clearly proved by Scripture should not be received. Summary and Brief Exposition.[13]

Christians Have the Right to Judge Prophets' Teaching. Wolfgang Musculus: By "the others," Paul understands the entire multitude of the church assembly that hears those words of prophecy. He distinguishes those who speak and those who hear; and lest those who hear should seem like logs, he assigns to them the responsibility of judging what is spoken. Paul does not say, "let the others listen," nor does he say, "let the others agree," nor "let the others applaud"; rather, he says, "let the others judge." Thus Paul requires that people in the assembly listen attentively to the words of prophecy, and test with their minds the soundness of the things spoken, whether they are true, imparted from the Spirit of God, or false, coming from a human source. And so those things that are true should be accepted, and those things that are false should be condemned. If only the discretion of this sort of judgment were permitted to the auditors in the church! . . . For a person is a legitimate church officer if he is a brother speaking in the midst of brothers, a prophet in the midst of those freely judging him, a minister of Christ in the midst of the members of Christ. But a person is not a legitimate church officer if he is a great lord in the midst of servants, a wolf in the midst of sheep, a cunning and shrewd sophist in the midst of foolish folk. It is tyrannical not to allow people the freedom of judgment. All tyrants hate legitimate freedom; they act wickedly, loving the darkness and hating the light. Commentary on 1 Corinthians 14:29.[14]

True Ministers Receive Divine Revelations. Thomas Müntzer: Therefore, as long as heaven and earth stand, these villainous and treacherous parsons are of no use to the church in even the slightest matter. For they deny the voice of the Bridegroom, which is a truly certain sign that they are a pack of devils. How could they then be God's servants, bearers of this word, which they shamelessly deny with their whore's brazenness? For all true parsons must have revelations, so that they are certain of their cause, 1 Corinthians 14. But the parsons, with their stubborn hearts, say that this is impossible. Because they are convinced of this—after they presume to have devoured the whole of Scripture—they shall be struck down with the words of St. Paul, 2 Corinthians 3, just

160, 162; 1 Thess 5:19-21; 1 Pet 3:15; Mt 7:15; Num 11:29.

[12]Simons, *Complete Writings*, 425.

[13]In Zuidema and Van Raalte, *Early French Reform*, 162-63*.

[14]Musculus, *Comm. 1 Cor.*, 580-81.

like thunder and lightning, for there Paul makes the distinction between the elect and the damned. The Prague Protest.[15]

Allowing the Spirit Freedom to Speak. John Calvin: Now Paul requires this discretion of everyone—that each person in turn shall defer to another who has something better to impart. For, certainly, this is the true freedom of the Spirit—not that everyone be permitted to babble rashly whatever they wish, but that everyone, from the highest to the lowest, voluntarily allow themselves to be put in their place, and that the one Spirit be listened to, by whatever voice he speaks. Commentary on 1 Corinthians 14:30.[16]

God's Word Has Priority in the Church—Even When Spoken by Humble People. Tilemann Hesshus: There is a great diversity of gifts in the church, some more illustrious and others less so. The mysteries of the Spirit are not immediately understood by all; God does not give all the gifts to one person. The Holy Spirit is not restricted by place, or rank, or person; he freely imparts his heavenly gifts, and he often grants more light in spiritual matters to those of lower rank than to those possessing the highest episcopal authority. So too he often gives a clearer knowledge of Christ and his kingdom to young people and children than to those who are wise. Therefore the Holy Spirit's grace and divine counsel must be recognized and received with a grateful heart, however God chooses to reveal his will to us. People who occupy the highest rank in the church should not exercise tyranny: they should not want to be the only ones heard, nor should they stubbornly defend their opinions when they announce in public an opinion that is inferior. If a person who occupies a lower position in the church understands a passage of Scripture more clearly and correctly through the illumination of the Holy Spirit, he should be given an opportunity to speak. However famous a doctor of the church he might be, he should not be ashamed to learn from a humble Christian, or even a child, the illustrious truth from the clear testimony of the sacred Scripture. The great teacher Paul was not ashamed to learn from Ananias of Damascus. The prophet Nathan was not ashamed to retract his advice concerning building the temple in Jerusalem. Moses was not ashamed to receive a prophecy from a prophet, even if it was the wicked Balaam, for the authority of revelations and doctrine are not dependent on the person of the minister, but on the Holy Spirit. Therefore Paul here prohibits anyone from exercising tyranny in the church; he prohibits anyone from babbling whatever they wish, even if their judgment is considered superior to everyone else's; he prohibits people from despising the Word of God on account of the lowliness of the person. Explication of 1 Corinthians 14:30.[17]

The Priesthood of All Believers. Wolfgang Musculus: This passage clearly supports that doctrine by which the restoration of our religion began to be taught, namely, that all Christians are priests. Even if they do not belong to the office of minister, nevertheless they possess the dignity of the heavenly calling, as we read in 1 Peter: "But you are a chosen race, a royal priesthood, a holy nation, and people for his own possession, that you may proclaim the power of him who called you out of darkness into his marvelous light." Because of this dignity, the authority to proclaim the power of God and prophesy in the midst of the church belongs to all believers, regardless of the protests of the pseudo-bishops. Yes indeed, Paul's statement to the Corinthians, "all have the authority to prophesy," pertains to all Christians.

Nevertheless, the office of minister (without which a church cannot exist) is not thereby rendered null and void, because no person should

[15]Baylor, *The Radical Reformation*, 4; citing 2 Cor 3:3. The "villainous and treacherous parsons" to whom Thomas Müntzer refers are undoubtedly Martin Luther and other evangelical clergymen who rejected Müntzer as a false prophet.
[16]CO 49:530 (cf. CTS 39:461-62).

[17]Hesshus, *Explicatio Prioris Epistolae ad Corinthios*, 315r-v.

usurp this general authority except in urgent cases when bishops, pastors, and professors do not perform their duties or when they act in a manner opposed to their duties, and when the Spirit has revealed it with certainty, which was the situation the apostle speaks of here. In situations like this, those whose hearts have been inspired by the Spirit of God can prophesy. But if all are permitted to prophesy, then all are also permitted to perform the remaining duties within the church that are of less importance, such as administering the sacraments of both baptism and the Lord's Supper, singing Psalms, praying and giving thanks in church, visiting and consoling the sick, catechizing the ignorant, etc. . . .

When ministers are faithful to the Lord and duly perform the ministry of the kingdom of God, it is not permissible for a person who is not in the ministerial office to seize the role of prophesying to the believers—unless that person has received some exceptional revelation from the Spirit that must be reported to the church. But when there are no ministers, or when there are some, but they do not perform their duties or do so dishonestly, deceiving and seducing the people of the Lord—in such cases, the authority to prophesy and perform the remaining pastoral duties in the church belongs to all believers. But if some common person remains uncorrupted, and is still pure of faith and godliness, it is permissible to choose him as pastor and minister that he might serve the Lord faithfully. Commentary on 1 Corinthians 14:31.[18]

Judging the Prophets. Huldrych Zwingli: Paul always anticipates objections. Someone might say: "If the prophet is subject to a tribunal, then contentions will crop up. For a prophet will speak reluctantly if he is found guilty of error by ignorant people." Paul responds, "By no means! For the spirit of the prophets should be listened to by the prophets." For God is not a God of contention and disagreement, but a God of unity and peace. Therefore, wherever true faith is, there also the Spirit of heaven will be recognized. Additionally, wherever the Spirit of heaven is, there the pursuit of unity and peace will be, with no wrangling. Therefore it is the case that whoever is a faithful prophet—whenever he is ignorant or errs—will gladly welcome correction and instruction, even from the lowest person. The church is not in danger of falling into confusion. For, if the church has been brought together by God, then he himself is in their midst. And all who are faithful strive toward peace and unity. And if they begin to disagree strongly or bitterly, they will immediately discern those who are gifted, who speak according to love and the Spirit of God, and will curb those babblers. Annotations on 1 Corinthians 14:32.[19]

Spirits of the Prophets. Cardinal Cajetan: The word "spirit" is in the plural, and does not mean the Holy Spirit, but signifies the particular spirit, that is, the prophets' particular gifts that are received from the Holy Spirit. For true prophets are not frenzied and out of their minds when they prophesy; rather, the gifts of the Holy Spirit that they receive are subject to the freedom of the Holy Spirit as far as their use is concerned. For, as is characteristic of gifts, they can be used or not used—one can speak or remain silent. And Paul has said this to answer the objection of those who maintain that people uttering prophecies are not able to control themselves, but must finish the message they have begun.

"For God is not a God of confusion, but of peace." If the spirits of the prophets were *not* subject to the prophets, then God—who inspires the prophets—would be the author of dissension. For he would be the cause of disorder and confusion, with many people prophesying at the same time against their wills. Indeed, when many people prophesy without taking turns, then there is confusion and an opportunity for dissension. For this reason Paul gives this explanation for his statement: because God is not a God of dissension,

[18]Musculus, *Comm. 1 Cor.*, 581-82; citing 1 Pet 2:9.

[19]Zwingli, *Annotatiunculae . . . ex ore Zvinglij*, 123.

disorder, and confusion, but of peace. Commentary on 1 Corinthians 14:32-33.[20]

Christians Must Be Zealous for Peace. John Calvin: Here we have a most valuable statement, for it teaches us that we do not serve God unless we are lovers of peace and eager to promote it. Therefore, whenever there is a love of quarreling, we can be quite certain that God is not ruling there. But how easy it is to say this! How continually we talk about it! Yet, in the meantime, most people fly into a rage about nothing, or they disturb the church out of their desire to be conspicuous and promote themselves by some means or other.

Let us bear in mind, therefore, that in judging the servants of Christ we should keep in view this standard—whether they are zealous for peace and concord, and whether they conduct themselves peacefully and avoid quarreling as much as they can. Nevertheless we understand this to be a "peace" that is bounded by God's truth. For if we are called to fight against wicked doctrines, even if heaven and earth are turned upside down, yet we must persevere in this battle. We must, indeed, make it our special concern to preserve the truth of God without contention; but if the wicked resist, we must struggle against them, and not be afraid of being blamed for the disturbances. For cursed is that peace which is a token of our defection from God; and blessed are those struggles with which God's kingdom must be defended. Commentary on 1 Corinthians 14:33.[21]

14:33b-35 *Women in Worship*

Women Instructed Women in The Early Church. Jacques Lefèvre d'Étaples: But did not Priscilla and many other holy women also receive responsibility for public instruction? They were especially given responsibility to instruct women—even as men were to instruct men. But when the church was established and gathered together, women were not rashly to speak in the presence of men, but were to serve in the church with holy silence (as was proper for them). Commentary on 1 Corinthians 14:34.[22]

Women Should Remain Silent in Church. Martin Luther: The church is recognized externally by the fact that it consecrates or calls ministers, or has offices that it is to administer. There must be bishops, pastors, or preachers who publicly and privately give, administer, and use the aforementioned four things or holy possessions[23] in behalf of the name of the church. . . . It is, however, true that the Holy Spirit has excepted women, children, and incompetent people from this function, but chooses (except in emergencies) only competent males to fill this office, as one reads here and there in the epistles of St. Paul that a bishop must be pious, able to teach, and the husband of one wife—and in 1 Corinthians 14 he says, "The women should keep silence in the churches." In summary, it must be a competent and chosen man. Children, women, and other persons are not qualified for this office, even though they are able to hear God's Word, to receive baptism, the sacrament, absolution, and are also true, holy Christians. On the Councils and the Church.[24]

The Role of Women in Church. Martin Luther: We shall for the present not be concerned about the right of these women[25] of the Old Testament to teach and to rule. But surely they did not act as the infiltrators [in Corinth] do, unauthorized and out of superior piety and wisdom. For then God would not have confirmed their ministry and worked by miracles and great deeds. But in the New Testament the Holy Spirit, speaking through St. Paul, ordained that women

[20]Cajetan, *In Sacrae Scripturae expositionem*, 5:139.

[21]CO 49:532 (cf. CTS 39:466).

[22]Lefèvre d'Étaples, *Commentariorum in Epistolas Beati Pauli . . . Liber Secundus*, 122v.

[23]That is, the holy Word of God, the sacrament of baptism, the sacrament of the Lord's Supper, and the exercise of the keys.

[24]LW 41:154-55.

[25]That is, Deborah, Sarah, Hagar, and Hannah.

should be silent in churches and assemblies, and said that this is the Lord's commandment. Yet he knew that previously Joel had proclaimed that God would pour out his Spirit on his handmaidens. Furthermore the four daughters of Philip prophesied (Acts 21). But in the congregations or churches where there is a ministry women are to be silent and not to preach. Otherwise, they may pray, sing, praise, and say "Amen," and read at home, teach each other, exhort, comfort, and interpret the Scriptures as best they can. Infiltrating and Clandestine Preachers.[26]

Even Common People and Women Can Find the Meaning of Scripture. François Lambert: Because to discern the divine meaning of the Scriptures, or the literal meaning of the Scriptures (for it is the same), depends on God, we declare that common people can attain to it because they can discern the sense by training [themselves] in the Scriptures even if they cannot read. Truly on the contrary, they often come to it more easily than those greatly learned, who are accustomed to produce faith by human and natural erudition or experience. Truly the common people are unlearned according to the flesh, for as those who are capable of divine learning and enlightenment, they do not believe anything strange.

It is also not enough if they are unable to read. Even now they faithfully hear the word and the Scriptures, and besides, they hear without rashness, but with either proper understanding by faith, or with pure and humble faith in God also ponder diligently with meditation. True prayer should be a continual companion.

Nevertheless, no one should think that I want to grant opportunity to certain proud common people who presently think that they understand something from those things which they either hear or read from the holy Scriptures, [and] elevate themselves above, wanting presently to philosophize. But these proud ones are easily taken. Once before I saw another one unable to read even an iota, who afterwards, in order to comprehend something, was instructed orally and deemed learned, or otherwise seemed to be good. The same, however, would forthrightly claim opposition against all, however greatly pious and truly exercised in the Scriptures, by affirming his own false ideas. I often had conference with him so that I may curb his insanity, but in vain.

These are those, who on account of such, badly hear the word of the Lord. Immediately they consider themselves learned, and do not understand what they are talking about. Against them, if, for instance, you adduce ten texts of Scripture, indeed, according to their actual meaning, they say that you do not understand anything, and that you have perversely lifted those texts. Hence, those must often be repressed, and separated from the church who thus want to discuss the holy word without restraint. I am for all common people who sincerely seek God, but I strive against the haughty "learned" ones for this reason: I truly refuse to aid impiety and to give opportunity to those proud and thoughtless people. Learning must be loved if piety is not to be spurned also with unbelief by a godly simple person who is blessed by knowledge of the truth. For the truth must be equally venerated by all, and also the insolence of falsehood must be condemned in all.

If therefore common people of both sexes are pious and humble, and desire to be taught from the Lord, and to teach the truth of his word, we intend for them to speak about such things, so that those who are able to attain to it alone from common people may, as we also predicted, possess understanding by having been exercised in the word of God. Because they attain to this, they must preserve it with all diligence. On Prophecy 5.15.[27]

Women Should Not Speak in a Properly Organized Congregation. John Calvin: It appears that the Corinthian church was also defiled with this fault, that the chattering of

[26]LW 40:390-91; citing Joel 2:28-29; Acts 21:9; 1 Tim 2:12.

[27]François Lambert, *Commentarii Prophetia, Eruditione et Linguis, deque Litera et Spiritu* (Argentorati, 1526), 100r-101r.

women was permitted in the sacred assembly, or rather, was given full liberty. Hence Paul forbids them from speaking in public for the purpose of teaching or prophesying. Now, this must be understood as referring to ordinary practice, or where the church is duly constituted. For a situation may arise that requires a woman to speak in public. Paul here is considering only what is proper in a properly organized congregation. Commentary on 1 Corinthians 14:34.[28]

These Are Social Norms, Not Permanent Sanctions. John Calvin: What sort of freedom of conscience could there be in such attentiveness and caution? Indeed, it will be very clear when we consider that these are no fixed and permanent sanctions by which we are bound, but outward rudiments for human weakness. Although not all of us need them, we use them, for we are mutually bound, one to another, to nourish mutual love. . . . What? Does religion consist in a woman's shawl, so that it is unlawful for her to go out with a bare head? Is that decree of Paul's concerning silence so holy that it cannot be broken without great offence? Is there in bending the knee or in burying a corpse any holy rite that cannot be neglected without offence? Not at all. For if a woman needs such haste to help a neighbor that she cannot stop to cover her head, she does not offend if she runs to her with head uncovered. And there is a place where it is no less proper for her to speak than elsewhere to remain silent. Also, nothing prohibits a man who cannot bend his knees because of disease from standing to pray. Finally, it is better to bury a dead man in due time than, where a shroud is lacking, or where there are no pallbearers to carry him, to wait until the unburied corpse decays. Nevertheless the established custom of the region, or humanity itself and the rule of modesty, dictate what is to be done or avoided in these matters. In them a man commits no crime if out of imprudence or forgetfulness he departs from them; but if out of contempt, this willfulness is to be disapproved. Institutes 4.10.31.[29]

Even Submissive Women Must Sometimes Speak in Church. Katharina Schütz Zell: I have exercised myself in the holy Scriptures and godly matters for more than forty-eight years now and never abandoned the grace of God; I have heard the old teachers and let them be my counselors and made the wine new (to put in new skins) since I was ten years old. I never got bogged down hearing, learning, and following until the day (sad to me but happy to him) of the death of my dear and good husband. I could now teach others and with the elderly Anna prophesy about Christ to those who are waiting for redemption and praise the Lord. But considering that I must appropriately be submissive under the man's office, according to the teaching of St. Paul, I myself seek to hear others and to be exhorted as far as they speak the truth! But where that is not so, then I would tell you and not keep silent, but speak, point out, and answer your wrong preaching and insulting words about the innocent. Letter to Caspar Schwenckfeld.[30]

Women Can Teach and Profess Their Faith in Private. Tilemann Hesshus: Thus far Paul has described the ministry and taught the people concerning the judgment and organization of public preaching. Now he adds instruction concerning women, forbidding that women should preach in public. For the Scripture states that the woman is under the authority of her husband, "your desire shall be for your husband, and he shall rule over you" (Gen 3:16). For the woman sinned first, and then she seduced her husband. For that reason God has imposed on her this punishment that she should be perpetually under her husband's authority. Thus, since a large part of governing consists in public speaking, the Holy Spirit teaches that it is not proper in the church of God for

[28]CO 49:532-33 (cf. CTS 39:467-68).

[29]LCC 20:1209 (CO 2:890).

[30]In McKee, *Katharina Schütz Zell*, 196-97; citing Mt 9:16, 17; Mk 2:22; Lk 2:36-38.

women to have the authority to speak in public, lest it appear that some measure of governing is being imparted to them. To be sure, it is lawful for them to learn from their husbands and instruct their children at home. It is also lawful for them to make a profession of faith: Hannah, the mother of Samuel, testified to her faith as an expression of gratitude, and offered her example to the church. The prophetess Deborah revealed the command of God, judged, and instructed Israel—but she did so in her home, like a mother instructing her children. She did not disclose these things in public through a sermon; it is true that she accompanied the army, urging Barak to lead—but she refrained from making a public speech (Judg 7). So too the prophetess Huldah gave advice in her home, and explained the oracles of God, but she did not preach in the church (2 Kings 22).

In the New Testament, Mary the mother of our Lord made an extraordinary profession of faith concerning God's immeasurable mercy toward her and the coming of the Messiah—but she did this in the privacy of the home of Elizabeth and Zechariah and other relatives. In this fashion, it is permissible for holy women to instruct their children and families at home, and to console and instruct on the Word of God those who are sick and wasting from disease in their homes as well. So too, when necessity demands it, women can make a godly confession of faith and refute false teaching. Concerning such a situation Paul speaks in 1 Corinthians 11: "Every wife who prays or prophesies with her head uncovered dishonors her head." Of course, Paul is speaking about when she prophesies—that is, teaches the Word of God—in the privacy of her home among children and relatives, exhorting them to godliness, instructing them, and comforting other people. But in public Christian assemblies, she must abstain from preaching, lest it appear that she is usurping the authority of her husband, contrary to Scripture. Explication of 1 Corinthians 14:34-35.[31]

[31]Hesshus, *Explicatio Prioris Epistolae ad Corinthios*, 320r-v; citing 1 Cor 11:5.

A Defense of Women on the Basis of Scripture. Marie Dentière: However, my most honored Lady, [I write] not to teach you, but so that you might take pains with the King, your brother, to obviate all these divisions which reign in the places and among the people over whom God commissioned him to rule and govern. And also over your people, whom God gave you to provide for and to keep in order. For what God has given you and revealed to us women, no more than men, should we hide it and bury it in the earth? And even though we are not permitted to preach in public in congregations and churches, we are not forbidden to write and admonish one another in all charity. . . . Not only will certain slanderers and adversaries of truth try to accuse us of excessive audacity and temerity, but so will certain of the faithful, saying that it is too bold for women to write one another about matters of Scripture. We may answer them by saying that all those women who have written and have been named and praised in holy scripture should not be considered too bold. Several women are named and praised in holy scripture, as much for their good conduct, actions, demeanor and example as for their faith and teaching: Sarah and Rebecca, for example, and first among all the others in the Old Testament; the mother of Moses, who, in spite of the king's edict, dared to keep her son from death and saw that he was cared for in the Pharaoh's house . . . , and Deborah, who judged the people of Israel in the time of the Judges, is not to be scorned. Must we condemn Ruth, who, even though she was of the female sex, had her story told in the book that bears her name? I do not think so, seeing that she is numbered among the genealogy of Jesus Christ. What wisdom had the Queen of Sheba, who is not only named in the Old Testament, but whom Jesus dared to name among the other sages! If we are speaking of the graces that have been given to women, what greater grace has come to any creature on earth than to the virgin Mary, mother of Jesus, to have carried the son of God? It was no small grace that allowed Elizabeth, mother of John the Baptist, to have born a son miraculously after having been sterile. What woman was a greater preacher than the Samaritan woman, who was not ashamed to preach Jesus and his word, confessing him openly before everyone, as soon as she heard Jesus say that we must adore God in spirit and truth? Who can boast of having the first manifestation of the great mystery of the resurrection of Jesus, if not Mary Magdalene, from whom he had thrown out the seven devils, and the other women, to whom, rather than to men, he had earlier declared himself through his angel and commended them to tell, preach, and declare it to others?

Even though in all women there has been imperfection, men have not been exempt from it. Why is it necessary to criticize women so much, seeing that no woman ever sold or betrayed Jesus, but a man named Judas? Who are they, I pray you, who have invented and contrived so many ceremonies, heresies and false doctrines on earth if not men? And the poor women have been seduced by them. Never was a woman found to be a false prophet, but women have been misled by them. While I do not wish to excuse the excessively great malice of some women that goes far beyond measure, neither is there any reason to make a general rule of it, without exception, as some do on a daily basis. . . . Therefore, if God has given grace to some good women, revealing to them by his holy scriptures something holy and good, should they hesitate to write, speak, and declare it to one another because of the defamers of truth? Ah, it would be too bold to try and stop them, and it would be too foolish for us to hide the talent God has given us, God who will give us the grace to persevere to the end. Amen. Epistle to Marguerite de Navarre.[32]

Women Must Not Speak in Public Deliberations. Wolfgang Musculus: Paul gives the reason for this regulation, not because this truth (which popular opinion everywhere approves) requires it, but because of the frivolity and vanity being displayed by the Corinthians. Now Paul gives a twofold reason: first, it is unlawful; second, it is disgraceful. Paul says that it is unlawful for women to speak, saying: "They are not permitted to speak." It is not lawful because it is not permitted to them. Now, there are two reasons that they are not permitted to speak. First, because the opposite practice has been prescribed by the divine law, which Paul expresses by saying, "but they must be submissive, as the law says." Second, so that some sense of public decency and the propriety of maleness and femaleness is preserved when women are removed from public deliberations, as happens in all nations. I know what some philosophers write on this subject, but nothing here is prejudicial against the common customs of nations and people. . . . Now the apostle has plainly not disallowed the speaking of words generally, as if women were permitted to say nothing whatsoever. Rather, he has disallowed that kind of speaking where public deliberations or judicial cases are officially discussed and treated in assemblies of men in the churches and in the marketplace, where men come together, not women. Commentary on 1 Corinthians 14:34-35.[33]

Some Women Are Appointed to Speak in the Assembly. François Lambert: Understand that it is not only a man who can speak. Indeed, certainly at that time it was a lawful thing for women to be prophets. Thus, the four daughters of Philip the Evangelist prophesied in Acts 21, and [so did] Anna the widow of Phanuel in Luke 2. The universal law is that the woman in the congregation be silent, and that [women] should ask their husbands at home. [Yet] truly this law is not broken when the Lord specially works in some women who rather ought to ask some men concerning these things rather than their own husbands. I speak concerning carnal and stupid men who are without the spirit, and concerning truly holy women who are also full of the Spirit of

[32]Dentière, *Epistle to Marguerite de Navarre*, 53-56; citing Gen 11–22; 24–28; Ex 2; Judg 4–5; Mt 1; 1 Kings 10; Mt 12:42; Lk 1; Jn 4; Lk 23–24; Mt 28:1-10; Mk 16:9; Jn 20:1-18.

[33]Musculus, *Comm. 1 Cor.*, 590.

God. Thus it is what Paul himself says in 1 Corinthians 7: the bad husband is saved through the good of his wife. Nevertheless, holy women always do it so that with all reverence they may teach their unbelieving husbands, and not with dominion. On Prophecy 23.5.[34]

Some Women Are Exceptions to the Rule. John Trapp: Husbands must dwell with their wives according to knowledge (1 Pet 3:7), and be as guides for them in the way to heaven. The master's breast must be the household's treasury. . . . Olympia Fulvia Morata, an Italian from the city of Ferrara, was a singular example in that she taught Greek and Latin at Heidelberg in the year 1554. Indeed ancient histories make mention of a woman named Aratha, who read openly in the schools at Athens for twenty-five years, wrote forty books, and had one hundred philosophers among her students. Likewise, Leoptia wrote against Theophrastus, and Corinna often contended with Pindarus in writing verse. Commentary on 1 Corinthians 14:35.[35]

God Is Not Absent in the Words of Women. Argula von Grumbach: I had to listen for ages to your decretal preacher crying out in the Church of Our Lady: "Heretic, heretic!" . . . But if they are to prove their case they'll have to do better than that. I always meant to write to him, to ask him to show me which heretical articles the loyal worker for the gospel, Martin Luther, is supposed to have taught.

However I suppressed my inclinations; heavy of heart, I did nothing. Because Paul says in 1 Timothy 2: "The women should keep silence, and should not speak in church." But now that I cannot see any man who is up to it, who is either willing or able to speak, I am constrained by the saying: "Whoever confesses me." And I claim for myself Isaiah 3: "I will send children to be their princes; and women, or those who are womanish, shall rule over them." And Isaiah 29: "Those who err will know knowledge in their spirit, and those who mutter will teach the law." And Ezekiel 20: "I raise up my hand against them to scatter them. They never followed my judgments, they rejected my commandments, and their eyes were on the idols of their fathers. Therefore I gave them commandments, but not good ones; and judgments by which they could never live." And Psalm 8: "You have ordained praise out of the mouth of children and infants at the breast on account of your enemies." And Luke 10: "Jesus rejoiced in the Spirit, and said 'Father, I give you thanks that you have hidden these things from the wise, and revealed them to the little ones.'" Jeremiah 3: "They will all know God, from the least to the greatest." John 6 and Isaiah 54: "They will all be taught of God." Paul in 1 Corinthians 12: "No one can say 'Jesus' without the spirit of God." Just as the Lord says of the confession of Peter in Matthew 16: "Flesh and blood has not revealed this to you, but my heavenly Father." To the University of Ingolstadt.[36]

14:36-40 *Decency and Order*

Paul Chastises the Proud Corinthians. Huldrych Zwingli: "But we," the Corinthians say, "will not practice this custom." Paul responds by saying, "On what basis are you so arrogant and so insolent? Did the gospel originate with you? Did you forget that you learned it from me? Why, therefore, are you now so proud? Why do you not submit willingly to correction? Why do you refuse to gather in an orderly fashion? Why do you not accommodate yourselves to other churches?" Annotations on 1 Corinthians 14:36.[37]

[34]François Lambert, *Commentarii Prophetia, Eruditione et Linguis, deque Litera et Spiritu*, Argentorati, 1526, 111r-v.

[35]Trapp, *A Commentary or Exposition*, 696*. Olympia Fulva Morata (1526–1555) was an Italian classical scholar who converted to Protestantism in the 1540s, and thereafter sought refuge in her husband's natal city of Heidelberg in 1554.

[36]Argula von Grumbach, *A Woman's Voice in the Reformation*, edited by Peter Matheson (Edinburgh: T&T Clark, 1995), 79-80*; citing Mt 10:32; 1 Tim 2:11; Isaiah 3:4,12; 29:24; Ezek 20:23-26; Ps 8:2; Lk 10:21; Jer 31:34; Jn 6:45; Is 54:13; 1 Cor 12:3; Mt 16:17.

[37]Zwingli, *Annotatiunculae . . . ex ore Zvinglij*, 124.

Paul Insists That His Message Is from God. Heinrich Bullinger: Having concluded his discussion of the genuine use of tongues and prophecy as well as describing their abuse, Paul turns his attention to the false apostles—or rather to all of the Corinthians—by raising rhetorical objections as warnings to them . . . saying, "Now why is it, O Corinthians, that you refuse to observe the customs practiced by other churches? Did the preaching of the gospel originate first with you, so that other churches must be forced to follow your practice? Are you alone wise and the other churches foolish? Now since you received the gospel first from me, why do you not carefully obey my warning?" "But we would obey," the Corinthians say, "if only our teachers recognized what you are proposing." "But," Paul says, "this matter has been sufficiently debated. I am very annoyed and will not dispute with those contentious people. However, on this matter I have complete certainty, that if there are any prophets among you who are duly instructed in the good through the Spirit of God, they will easily recognize and confess that in this matter I have conveyed to you the Lord's instructions rather than my own. But these instructions will no doubt be despised by those who do not wish to obey these restrictions of ours. If any of those people are so wicked that they either do not or cannot see this fact—very well then, let them remain blind to their danger!" Commentary on 1 Corinthians 14:36-38.[38]

We Must Avoid Unteachable and Quarrelsome People. Tilemann Hesshus: In conclusion, Paul applies a sharp rebuke so as to restrain those people who were defending their opinions so proudly and stubbornly, and to turn them toward greater modesty. Undoubtedly, the apostle recognized that the Corinthians were consumed with the vice of pride, chasing after pleasure, and stubbornness. And so he employs a harsher reproof in order to call them back to a sounder mind. He wanted them to recall that they were Gentiles and had received the teaching of the gospel from other people, namely, from Jews and the apostles; for this reason, they should allow themselves to be instructed, receive the laws of godliness, and not order other people around. The Corinthians are not the only church of God. Therefore they should consider what honorable customs have also been established in other churches of the saints. And so as to remove any doubt that they should now pay attention to his warning, he adds that what he has proposed has been commanded by the Lord, and that those who are spiritual should be able to recognize this. But if anyone should have stubbornly opposed themselves to it, their judgment is certain, since they are hostile to the Spirit and treat the Lord's commandments with contempt.

"If anyone fails to understand, let him misunderstand." Paul here drives away those who dispute endlessly, because they are people of contentious and fastidious natures who never allow themselves to be satisfied, now raising new questions, now introducing new glosses, now devising new ways to avoid the truth—while condemning and ignoring those foundational truths that are demonstrated to them. Paul commands that unteachable people of this sort should be forsaken and condemned. They should say goodbye (he says) to such people, who never stop debating and asking questions. This is not because we might be influenced by the stubbornness and brashness of people of this sort, for they do not seriously examine the truth, but instead take pains to chase after stupid things and take pleasure in darkness. Therefore we should not weary ourselves in vain because of these people.

Paul mentions, finally, that we ought especially to desire the gift of prophecy, and zealously strive for it, as most useful and necessary for the church. But the gift of tongues should neither be condemned, nor hindered, nor begrudged to anyone, but ought to be held in high esteem in its place. Explication of 1 Corinthians 14:38-39.[39]

[38]Bullinger, *In Omnes Apostolicas Epistolas . . . Commentarii*, 237.

[39]Hesshus, *Explicatio Prioris Epistolae ad Corinthios*, 321r-v.

Right Worship. John Calvin: This conclusion is more general; it briefly sums up not only the whole matter but also the various parts. Even more, it is also the rule by which we must regulate everything that has to do with external polity. Since in various passages Paul has treated the subject of rites, he wanted at this point to summarize everything briefly, namely, that decorum should be preserved, and disorder should be avoided. . . . The Lord grants us freedom regarding external rites, so that we might not imagine that his worship is confined to such things. However, at the same time, he has not permitted us an unsettled and unbridled liberty, but he has provided boundaries for us (as one might say); or, he has limited the freedom he gives us in such a way that it is finally only from his Word that we can determine what is right. Therefore, when this passage is rightly considered, it shows the difference between the tyrannical edicts of the pope, which oppress people's consciences in cruel servitude, and the godly laws of the church, by which discipline and right order are maintained. Commentary on 1 Corinthians 14:40.[40]

Discipline Must Be Done in an Orderly Way. Second Helvetic Confession: And seeing that there must be discipline in the church, and that among the ancient Fathers excommunication was in use, and there were ecclesiastical judgments among the people of God, wherein this discipline was exercised by godly men, it belongs also to the minister's duty, for the edifying of the church, to moderate this discipline according to the condition of the time and public estate and according to necessity. Wherein this rule is always to be held, that "all things ought to be done to edification, decently, and in order," without any oppression or tumult. Of the Ministers of the Church.[41]

Right Worship Must Be Purged of Vain Ceremonies. John Jewel: Regarding the multitude of vain and superfluous ceremonies, we know that Augustine complained grievously about them in his own time; and therefore we have cut off a great number of them, because we know that people's consciences were encumbered by them and the churches of God overladen with them. Nevertheless, we keep still and esteem, not only those ceremonies that we are sure were delivered to us from the apostles, but also some other ceremonies that we thought might be endured without harm to the church of God, because we had a desire that all things in the holy congregation might, as Paul commanded, "be done in a fitting and orderly way." But as for all those things that we saw were either very superstitious, or unprofitable, or annoying, or mocking, or contrary to holy Scriptures, or else inappropriate for sober and discreet people—of which there are an infinite number nowadays in the Roman religion—these, I say, we have utterly refused without all manner of exception, because we would not have the right worshiping of God any longer defiled with such follies. Apology.[42]

Public Worship Must Be Conducted with Gravity and Modesty. David Dickson: [Paul states] that decency should be observed by persons coming to the public assembly of the church, and that in things necessary for worship, all things should be performed with gravity and modesty, without superstition and indecency. And the parts of divine worship should be ordered and disposed in their times as to best serve the glory of God and the edification of the church. Exposition of 1 Corinthians 14:40.[43]

Order Must Be Observed in the Church. John Trapp: "Let all things be done." This is a general rule of great importance. In matters both real and ritual, decency, and order must be observed

[40]CO 49:535-36 (cf. CTS 39:474).
[41]*Creeds* 3:883*.

[42]Jewel, *Apology of the Church of England*, 37*. Augustine, *Ad Inquisitiones Januarii*, lib. 2, epist. 55. ch.19; NPNF 1:315.
[43]Dickson, *Exposition of St. Paul's Epistles*, 66*.

in church meetings. For this the Colossians were much commended (2:5). So too our Savior ordered the people whom he fed to keep order in their sitting on the grass; they sat down by rank, just as rows or borders of garden beds. . . . In regard to this an expositor notes: "Order must be observed in the church." Commentary on 1 Corinthians 14:40.[44]

[44]Trapp, *A Commentary or Exposition*, 697*.

15:1-11 The Resurrection of Christ

Now I would remind you, brothers,[a] *of the gospel I*
preached to you, which you received, in which you
stand, 2and by which you are being saved, if you hold
fast to the word I preached to you—unless you
believed in vain.
3For I delivered to you as of first importance what
I also received: that Christ died for our sins in
accordance with the Scriptures, 4that he was buried,
that he was raised on the third day in accordance
with the Scriptures, 5and that he appeared to Cephas,
then to the twelve. 6Then he appeared to more than
five hundred brothers at one time, most of whom are
still alive, though some have fallen asleep. 7Then he
appeared to James, then to all the apostles. 8Last of all,
as to one untimely born, he appeared also to me. 9For
I am the least of the apostles, unworthy to be called an
apostle, because I persecuted the church of God. 10But
by the grace of God I am what I am, and his grace
toward me was not in vain. On the contrary, I
worked harder than any of them, though it was not I,
but the grace of God that is with me. 11Whether then
it was I or they, so we preach and so you believed.

a Or *brothers and sisters*; also verses 6, 31, 50, 58

Overview: Because some members of the Corinthian church harbored doubts regarding the future resurrection of the dead, Paul now turns his attention to this fundamental teaching of the Christian faith. Before doing so, however, he lays the groundwork by reminding the Corinthians of the gospel that he had taught them as well as the nature and fruitfulness of his apostleship. Reformation commentators emphasize that these verses contain the foundation of Christian doctrine and the heart of their evangelical message: that the Lord Jesus Christ died for sinful human beings and rose again on the third day for their justification. This glorious gospel continues to produce bountiful fruit in the lives of Christians, as they experience remission of sins, reconciliation with God, daily consolation, freedom from the law, a new spiritual existence, and hope for the future resurrection—all thanks to Christ's work on their behalf. Many commentators find special significance in the fact that the Lord's resurrection was both prophesied in Scripture *and* testified to by the early church. To be sure, God's scriptural revelation bears the greatest authority, but the experience of early Christians who encountered Christ alive after his crucifixion is also convincing evidence for his resurrection. Early modern commentators describe in detail the various eyewitnesses who beheld Christ after his resurrection, though a number of questions remain unanswered: *When* and *where* did Jesus appear to the five hundred disciples? And *who* exactly was the disciple James, mentioned in 1 Corinthians 15:7—was he the brother of Jesus, or the son of Mary's sister, or someone else? Finally, Reformation commentators present the apostle Paul as both a compelling witness to Christ's resurrection and a beautiful example of the power of the gospel. When Christians are tempted to despair on account of the enormity of their sins, they do well to consider God's marvelous grace and mercy expressed toward Paul, who was a persecutor of Christians before he met the resurrected Christ. For nearly all Protestant commentators, Paul's biography—as well as his statement in 1 Corinthians 15:10—makes it abundantly clear that salvation comes from God's grace alone, apart from human cooperation or merit.

On the Resurrection. Martin Luther: This chapter deals throughout with our article of faith concerning the resurrection of the dead. This theme was occasioned by the fact that a number of factious spirits had arisen among the Corinthians who were ruining their faith and teaching that the resurrection of the dead is nothing. And there were others, as St. Paul states elsewhere, who tried to be clever and subtle and alleged that the resurrection had taken place a long time ago. As they interpreted it, we arose from sin through baptism and entered into a new spiritual life, etc. Matters finally came to such a pass that people believed (as in the case of the Sadducees in the days of Christ) that a person's years did not extend beyond this life, that their life was comparable to that of a cow or of other animals, and that they were created for no other purpose than to live blamelessly here on earth. And thus this doctrine gave birth to many impertinent fellows who believed absolutely nothing regarding the resurrection or a future life, who only ridiculed this doctrine and mocked the Christians in every way. They acted like real heathen. St. Paul quotes their words, as they said: "What kind of bodies will we have if we all rise again? Where will we all find room? If we all live at the same time, how can we find sufficient food and drink? How can we all have wives and beget children and perform other natural functions of this body and this life? etc." And thus others too now began to affect wisdom.... And unfortunately today we have again arrived at the point where many, both peasants and townspeople, and particularly Junker Hans of the nobility, prate so absurdly, shamelessly, and heathenishly about this when they presume to be so smart and stick their nose into the Scriptures. COMMENTARY ON 1 CORINTHIANS 15.[1]

THE USEFULNESS OF THIS CHAPTER. PHILIPP MELANCHTHON: This chapter is useful in a number of ways. For Paul discusses the resurrection of the dead, the fruit of Christ's resurrection, Christ's kingdom, the power of death, the power of sin, and the power of the law. Second, the occasion for this chapter was the error and wickedness of some Corinthians, who doubted the resurrection of the dead and the immortality of the soul; and he condemns this error with many varied arguments. He immediately begins his argument without an explicit proposition. And he draws out his argument from the example of Christ in this manner: If Christ has risen, then there is a resurrection of the dead. He proves the premise that Christ has risen in many ways. ANNOTATIONS ON 1 CORINTHIANS 15:1.[2]

PAUL TREATS THE DOCTRINE OF RESURRECTION LAST FOR A REASON. JOHN CALVIN: In chapter 15, Paul attacks that very pernicious error which, although we can scarcely believe it to have won over most of the Corinthians, nevertheless had taken over some of them to such a degree that a remedy was clearly necessary. Now, it appears that he deliberately postponed mentioning this matter until the end of his letter. For if he had started off with it, or turned immediately to it after he had begun, they would have thought that he was accusing all of them. Thus he demonstrates that the hope of the resurrection is so necessary that, if it is taken away, the whole gospel falls into ruins. Having demonstrated this doctrine through powerful arguments, he goes on to show the principle and rationale of it. In a word, he carefully provides a detailed discussion of this subject. ARGUMENT OF 1 CORINTHIANS.[3]

REJECTING THEIR DENIALS. WOLFGANG MUSCULUS: The argument of this chapter is clear. Some among the Corinthians were denying the resurrection of the dead. Paul strongly opposes this evil teaching lest, if he were delayed in coming, it should infect the whole church and undermine the sum of our salvation. We are not going to explore from whence this evil teaching sprouted in that church, whether from the Sadducees or some philosophers, and to what extent they rejected the resurrection. Other interpreters comment on these matters. The apostle simply says: "But if Christ is

[1]LW 28:59.

[2]Melanchthon, *Annotationes in Epistolam priorem ad Corinthios*, 162.
[3]CO 49:302-3 (cf. CTS 39:45-46).

proclaimed to have risen from the dead, how can certain people among you say that there is no resurrection of the dead?" On the basis of the resurrection of Christ, Paul declares that the dead will be resurrected; and Paul applies this assertion against those who deny the resurrection of the body.

There are seven parts to this chapter. First, Paul reminds them of the doctrine of the gospel that he taught them. Second, as elsewhere, he commends the toil and fruitfulness of his apostleship. Third, from the resurrection of Christ, he refutes those who were denying the resurrection of the dead. Fourth, he asserts the resurrection of the dead from the power of Christ's resurrection. Fifth, he argues that all piety is in vain if the dead do not rise. Sixth, he explains the manner, order, and glory of the future resurrection. Seventh, he concludes with a few recommendations. Commentary on 1 Corinthians 15:1.[4]

The Resurrection Is the Goal of the Gospel Story. David Chytraeus: The most joyful resurrection of the Son of God, our Lord Jesus Christ, is the foundation of our faith and salvation, the end and goal of the whole evangelical history, and the chief comfort and harbor in which our hearts alone may rest in all troubles and in death. As the conqueror that has vanquished sin, death, hell, and Satan, he has achieved a glorious triumph and imparts righteousness and eternal salvation on those of us who flee to him, even calling back our bodies from death to life. Since we should always remember this exceedingly great and wonderful work of God and its benefit for us, let us embrace it with burning faith and announce it continually with thankful hearts and voices.

This epistle [lesson] is intended to convince us of these things, exhorting us to the true celebration of the feast of Easter, that is to say, to the true confession of the person and benefits of the sacrificial Lamb Christ, sacrificed for us on the altar of the cross; to true repentance or acknowledgement of our sins and of God's wrath placed on this Lamb; and to true faith . . . assuredly believing that our Passover Lamb has been slain and offered up for us, and that our sins are taken away by this Lamb of God, and that even when we experience death, life, and everlasting joy will most certainly be restored to us with Christ who has risen again. Postil for Easter Day.[5]

Heretics Have Often Questioned Scripture's Teaching on the Resurrection. John Donne: As there have been more heresies about the humanity of Christ than about his divinity, so there have been more heresies about the resurrection of his body, and consequently of ours, than about any other particular article that concerns Christ's humiliation or exaltation. Simon Magus was the first to strike deep at the root, [claiming] that there was no resurrection at all. The Gnostics . . . acknowledged a resurrection, but they said it was of the soul only, and not of the body, for they thought that the soul lay dead (at least in a dead sleep) till the resurrection. Those heretics that are called the Arabians did (as the Gnostics) affirm the temporary death of the soul, as well as of the body, but then they allowed a resurrection for both soul and body after that death, contrary to the Gnostics, who believed in the resurrection of the soul only. Hymeneus and Philetus (of whom St. Paul speaks) limited the resurrection to the soul, but then they restricted the resurrection of the soul to *this* life, [claiming] that the resurrection was accomplished already for those who were baptized. . . . The Armenian heretics said that it was not the human body, but the *masculine* body—that all should rise in the more perfect sex, and none as women. Origen allowed a resurrection, and allowed the body to be a natural body. But he contracted the time, saying that when we rose we should enjoy the benefits of the resurrection, even in bodily pleasures, for a thousand years, and then be annihilated, or absorbed and swallowed up into the nature and essence of God himself. Sermon Preached at Lincoln's Inn.[6]

[4]Musculus, *Comm. 1 Cor.*, 603.

[5]Chytraeus, *Dispositio epistolarum*, 177-78.

[6]Donne, *Sermons of John Donne* , 3:115*; citing 2 Tim 2:18.

15:1-2 *The Good News Proclaimed by Paul*

The Fruit of Paul's Gospel. Martin Luther: For here you hear what fruit this gospel of St. Paul produced among them and what fruit it still produces, namely, that all became Christians through it and were saved and that people must still be saved by it. And since this fruit is ours by virtue of the gospel, why should we search further or permit ourselves to be diverted from this and be directed and led to other things? For whatever directs us otherwise can surely not be as good, but it must be false and sheer seduction, since it pretends to have something that we already have by means of this gospel; and thereby it denies all this or disdains it utterly. Therefore Paul addresses the Corinthians as though it were unnecessary to admonish them beyond asking them to recall and observe what they received and how they became Christians. . . . And let us note here that Paul is speaking of the oral presentation of the gospel preached by him and that he assigns to it such a claim and such praise, that they "stand in it and are saved by it" alone. Commentary on 1 Corinthians 15:1.[7]

The Gospel Message Must Be Guarded. Tilemann Hesshus: Wishing to refute those who were denying the resurrection of the dead, and wanting to explain this article of faith, Paul leads the Corinthians to the original and unchanging source of all the articles of faith, namely, the gospel of Jesus Christ, which God announced to the world through the prophets and apostles. For this alone is the foundation of all of our salvation, as Paul eloquently teaches: "No one can lay a foundation other than that which is laid, which is Jesus Christ." There is no other principle more suitable and more powerful for refuting all kinds of corruption than if we oppose them with the gospel of Jesus Christ, revealed to the world through the prophets and apostles. And in particular, Paul teaches us the rule for confirming our faith and refuting deceptive errors. Paul binds the entire church to this gospel, and he wishes that all the dogmas related to this gospel that he has taught to be considered.

When he says that "I would remind you of the gospel I proclaimed," he shows that it is not sufficient for right doctrine to be proclaimed in the church and the articles of the faith explained correctly one time only. Rather, due to the indifference and negligence of men and women, as well as the scheming of Satan, who frequently spreads tares among the wheat, it is necessary frequently to repeat teachings and to recall to memory and confirm the articles of faith through the testimony of Scripture so that godly people might persevere steadfastly with an informed faith. When Paul says, "Do not neglect the gift that was given to you through prophecy," he indicates that Timothy should not busy himself preaching novel sermons nor be enslaved to the new opinions of curious people. Instead, he should always repeat and impart the same teaching concerning Jesus Christ, and apply himself fully to this one thing: that he might instill in his hearers sound faith in Jesus Christ.

The "gospel" does not signify here a single article of the faith, but the whole doctrine of the prophets and apostles concerning Jesus Christ, which Paul had faithfully proclaimed to the Corinthians. The sum of this doctrine is especially this, that Jesus Christ died for our sins in accordance with the Scriptures, and that he rose from the dead on the third day for our justification in accordance with the Scriptures. This is the essential point of the whole of religion that must be guarded with the greatest diligence. Explication of 1 Corinthians 15:1-2.[8]

Christians Are Being Saved by the Gospel. Wolfgang Musculus: Consider this, reader, that Paul did not employ the past tense, "by which you have been saved"; rather, he employed the present-tense *sōzesthe*, that is, "by which you

[7]LW 28:67.

[8]Hesshus, *Explicatio Prioris Epistolae ad Corinthios*, 324r-325r; citing 1 Cor 3:11; 1 Tim 4:14.

are being saved." For even though, by the death of Christ, complete salvation has been given to us—a salvation that was proclaimed by the gospel and embraced by faith—nevertheless we do not yet take possession of that salvation perfectly as long as we are living in faith and hope. That is why we have not yet been saved perfectly, but are being saved daily as in the case of a disease. For while persons are under the care of physicians, they are *being* cured and healed; the efficacy of their healing (whereby they feel that, having been delivered from death, they are now being cured) gives them hope of a perfect cure. And for that reason they in no way resist the treatment of physicians, and do nothing whatsoever against their instructions. Similarly, with this word *sōzesthe*, the apostle is reminding the Corinthians to persevere in the gospel of salvation that they have received, lest they wish to render void this work of salvation that has begun in them and lose all hope of perfecting this salvation. As with a disease, it is most pleasing of all when the physician says, "Be of good cheer, you are healed." In the same way, it is fitting that nothing more acceptable can happen to us than when the apostle of Christ—the greatest physician—affirms to believers that we are being saved by the gospel that we have received. Commentary on 1 Corinthians 15:2.[9]

Paul Exhorts the Corinthians to Persevere in the Truth. Tilemann Hesshus: Paul encourages the Corinthians with this most weighty of all exhortations to persevere in the truth, since they would obtain salvation through this gospel that they were receiving. For they have been reconciled to God through faith in Christ. They have been liberated from the power of Satan. They have obtained peace of conscience. They have been given the Holy Spirit. They have been designated heirs of eternal life. And having already been established in this salvation, which was sealed on their conscience, they were certainly able to judge that the gospel of Jesus Christ which they had learned from the apostle Paul was both true and salvific. Therefore they must not abandon this teaching, whose saving power they had already experienced. Paul also indicates that they are not able to throw away this true and eternal gospel teaching without endangering their eternal salvation. This, therefore, is a most weighty argument for the Corinthians to hold on to the knowledge of the truth. Explication of 1 Corinthians 15:2.[10]

Unless You Believed in Vain. Martin Luther: Paul appends a warning by way of precaution, saying: "If you hold it fast—unless you believed in vain." Those are hard and sharp words, and yet they are spoken in a friendly and winning tone, so that the Corinthians might see how faithfully and fatherly he is disposed toward them and how concerned he is about them. . . . For Paul is speaking as a faithful pastor, who must do both, that is, hope for the best regarding them and simultaneously be concerned about them. Thus he wants to comfort them lest they despair and to admonish them to return and cling to this firmly when they are tempted to fall away. . . . Therefore faith is not such a slight object as one assumes but a valiant hero who is to hold to the Word; this appears so insignificant and as nothing so that all the world would not give a penny for it. And yet it is so active and so mighty that it tears heaven and earth apart and opens all graves in the twinkling of an eye. Commentary on 1 Corinthians 15:2.[11]

15:3-7 *The Gospel of Jesus Christ*

The Christian's Confession. Guillaume Farel: I believe that [Jesus Christ] bore his torment and his cross for my sins and the sins of all believers. By his torment and pain he has blessed, sanctified, and made highly meritorious and beneficial all the torments, sufferings, tribulations, and adversities that we would suffer in this world. Indeed, a good Christian must now long for

[9]Musculus, *Comm. 1 Cor.*, 606.

[10]Hesshus, *Explicatio Prioris Epistolae ad Corinthios*, 325v.

[11]LW 28:67-68, 73*.

suffering and tribulations in this mortal life, honoring them as most holy relics, soaked and dripping with the precious blood of your blessed Son Jesus Christ.

I believe that he died and was buried to slay, destroy, and bury all my sins, and the sins of all believers, by which he has moreover killed and made harmless bodily death, even making it beneficial and consecrated. For I know with certainty that my death will be the entrance into eternal life.

I believe that he descended into hell, to destroy and imprison the subtlety, violence, and perversity of the devil, so that from now on the enemy cannot overwhelm me. He has delivered me from the sorrows of hell, so that they too cannot overwhelm me.

I believe that on the third day he arose from the dead, to give new life to all believers. By this new life he has raised us with him by his mercy and Spirit, so that from now on we may nevermore sin but serve you alone with all power.

I believe that he ascended into heaven and that he has received from you, O my most blessed heavenly Father, all power and honor, above all the angels and all other creatures. He sits at your right hand, that is to say, he is King and Lord over all your possessions in heaven and on earth, and likewise in hell. And for this reason he is able to help me, and will help me and all believers, in all our need, and will deliver us from all our opponents and enemies. Lord's Prayer and Apostles' Creed.[12]

A Matter of First Importance. Cardinal Cajetan: "For I delivered to you as of first importance." Paul is going to show that the future resurrection of the dead is contained in the gospel that he preached and received. And so he mentions again those things contained in the gospel which he preached to them that served as the basis for their faith in the future resurrection of the dead, namely, the mystery of the death and resurrection of Christ. And Paul says that he had imparted these things of greatest importance in the order of doctrine. For when announcing the gospel, he began with the mystery of Christ as man, that he might thereby deduce from it the mystery of Christ as God. "Which I also received"—"I did not invent this gospel, but I received it through a revelation from Jesus Christ." As far as the clause "that Christ died for our sins": As had been promised in the Law and the Prophets, the Messiah truly died according to the flesh, not for the sake of his own sin (whether actual or original), but for the sake of our sins. "According to the Scriptures": Lest they object that it was a fanciful idea of the Jews that the Messiah died for our sins, Paul says that this had been predicted in the writings of the prophets. As far as that clause "he was buried": Paul mentioned this both to show the reality of his death and the solid fact of his resurrection. For a person is not buried unless they are truly dead; and to rise from the grave is most miraculous. Commentary on 1 Corinthians 15:3.[13]

Christ Died for Our Sins. John Calvin: By taking upon himself our curse, he might redeem us from it. For what else was Christ's death than a sacrifice for expiating our sins; an atoning punishment by which we might be reconciled to God; the condemnation of one person for the purpose of obtaining forgiveness for us? Paul speaks in a similar fashion in Romans 4:25, though in that passage he ascribes another effect to the resurrection, namely, that it confers righteousness on us. For, as sin was destroyed through the death of Christ, so righteousness is procured through his resurrection. This distinction must be carefully observed, so that we might understand how we are benefited from his death as well as from his resurrection. Now, when other passages of Scripture only make mention of his death, we know that his resurrection is included in the reference to his death. But when the two are mentioned separately, the beginning of our salvation is in his death (as we see here) and its completion is in his resurrection. Commentary on 1 Corinthians 15:3.[14]

---

[12]In Zuidema and Van Raalte, *Early French Reform*, 114.

[13]Cajetan, *In Sacrae Scripturae expositionem*, 5:140.

[14]CO 49:538 (cf. CTS 40:10).

The Central Tenet of the Christian Faith. Tilemann Hesshus: The central tenet and foundation of our entire religion is that our Lord Jesus Christ died for our sins and rose again for our justification. All of our comfort, salvation, and hope rest on this foundation. From this is derived that greatest comfort concerning the resurrection of the dead and the future life of eternal glory. Therefore Paul rightly begins in this way his refutation of the error of Epicurus, who denied the resurrection of the dead. For it is necessary that this foundation be thoroughly secured—that Jesus Christ the Son of God died for the sins of the world and rose again for the sake of our justification—in order to defeat the blasphemy of the Sadducees or Epicureans, as well as all heresies. Therefore let this notable and highest head of our religion constantly be in view. Because Jesus Christ, the Son of God, died and was buried for our sins, it is certain that we have been satisfied from the judgment of the law and the justice of God; it is certain that the kingdom of Satan and sin has been overturned; it is certain that the wrath of God has been appeased and the righteousness of Jesus Christ before God rightly accomplished for us. Moreover, because Jesus Christ did not remain dead, but rose from the dead on the third day by the power of God, and thus introduced us to a new and heavenly life, it is necessary that the dominion of death be destroyed. It is necessary that human beings do more than drown in the miseries of this life. It is necessary that an eternal and heavenly life remains after this life. It is necessary that believers do more than hope in Christ for this life. It is necessary that our bodies, which are engrafted into Christ by faith, not remain forever in the dust of death, but someday rise again to life, so that they might take hold of the fruit of their faith and live with Christ forever. All of these enormous consolations necessarily follow from that good news (*evangelium*), that Jesus Christ died for our sins and rose again on the third day. Explication of 1 Corinthians 15:3.[15]

Paul Establishes His Argument on Scripture and Experience. Martin Luther: Paul adduces two kinds of proof (in refutation of their false teaching) in support of his message, or gospel, which he has preached concerning Christ's resurrection. First, he points out that he took this from Scripture and that he proves this with Scripture. In the second place, he cites his own experience and that of many others who saw the resurrected Christ. For it is the mark of a fair man to prove and attest what he proclaims and says, not only with words but also with deed and example both of himself and others.... And note how Paul again extols and exalts the testimony of Scripture and the external Word as he emphasizes and repeats the phrase "in accordance with the Scripture." To be sure, he does not do this without reason. He does this in the first place to resist the mad spirits who disdain Scripture and the external message and in place of this seek other secret revelation. And today, every place is also teeming with such spirits, confused by the devil, who regard Scripture a dead letter and boast of nothing but the Spirit, although these people retain neither Word nor Spirit. But here you notice how Paul adduces Scripture as his strongest proof, for there is no other enduring way of preserving our doctrine and our faith than the physical or written Word, poured into letters and preached orally by him or others; for here we find it stated clearly: "Scripture! Scripture!" But Scripture is not all spirit, about which they drivel, saying that the Spirit alone must do it and that Scripture is a dead letter that cannot impart life. But the fact of the matter is that, although the letter by itself does not impart life, yet it must be present, and it must be heard or received. And the Holy Spirit must work through this in the heart, and the heart must be preserved in the faith through and in the Word against the devil and every trial. Commentary on 1 Corinthians 5:3.[16]

The Scriptures Announced the Death of Christ. Wolfgang Musculus: Paul says that

[15]Hesshus, *Explicatio Prioris Epistolae ad Corinthios*, 326v-327v.

[16]LW 28:76-77.

[Christ's] death was for our sins "in accordance with the Scriptures." Now Paul does not mean the New Testament, which at that time was not yet in existence, but the Old Testament Scriptures, in which the oracles of God, through the prophecies of the prophets and shadow-like future types, both predicted and foreshadowed many years before the death of Christ for us. . . .

Now the [Old Testament] Scriptures that predict the death of Christ can easily be collected from the writings of the Gospel writers and the apostles, the more illustrious of these prophecies being Isaiah 53, Daniel 9, and Psalm 22. They also employ figures, as in the paschal lamb in Exodus 12, in the sacrifice of Isaac in Genesis 22, in the red heifer offered for sins according to the law in Numbers 19, and in the lifting up of the bronze serpent in Numbers 21 and John 3. Commentary on 1 Corinthians 15:3.[17]

Christ's Death Predicted. John Donne: The apostle thought it a hard, a heavy, and incredible thing to say that this person, this Christ, this man and God, was dead. And therefore . . . that he might mollify the hardness of that saying and defend the hearer from being scandalized with that saying . . . he adds this, Christ is dead "according to the Scriptures." If the Scriptures had not told us that Christ should die, and told us again that Christ did die, it would be hard to conceive how this person, in whom the Godhead dwelt bodily, should be submitted to death. But therein principally is he *Christus*, as he was capable of dying. Sermon Preached on Trinity Sunday.[18]

According to the Scriptures. John Trapp: [Scripture] both foreshowed and foreshadowed [Christ's death and resurrection] in Adam's waking; Isaac's reviving, as it were from the dead; Joseph's abasement and advancement; Sampson's breaking the bars and bearing away the gates of Gaza; David's being drawn out of the deep; Daniel's out of the lion's den; Jeremiah out of the dungeon; Jonah out of the belly of hell. Commentary on 1 Corinthians 15:4.[19]

Did Christ Appear to Eleven or Twelve Disciples? Jacques Lefèvre d'Étaples: The Vulgate edition reads "after this to the Eleven." In the Greek one reads "then to the Twelve." I think "eleven" stands correct, based on the testimony of the Gospels of Matthew and Luke, and the Acts of the Apostles. For Matthias was the twelfth disciple: after the ascension, he was accepted into the number of the Twelve. To be sure, Matthias saw Jesus following his resurrection, for he was one of his followers. But he was not yet among the number of the Twelve. Commentary on 1 Corinthians 15:5.[20]

Scripture Does Not Err in Referring to the "Twelve." John Calvin: Now how can Paul say that [Jesus] appeared to the Twelve, when only eleven remained after the death of Judas? Chrysostom thinks that this happened after Matthias had already been elected as a substitute. Other interpreters preferred to correct this verse, as if it were mistaken. But when we realize that there were twelve in number set apart by Christ's command, even though one of them would be expunged from the list, there is nothing absurd about the fact that the title "twelve" remained. It was for the same reason that the body of Roman men were known as the hundred men (*Centumviri*), though they were 102 in number—for the use of this particular title predominated. By the Twelve, therefore, one should simply understand here the chosen apostles. Commentary on 1 Corinthians 15:5.[21]

Jesus' Resurrection Appearances. Tilemann Hesshus: Paul proves the resurrection of Christ by the testimony of the weightiest of authority, since the resurrected Christ was seen by

[17]Musculus, *Comm. 1 Cor.*, 611.
[18]Donne, *Sermons of John Donne*, 3:300*.
[19]Trapp, *A Commentary or Exposition*, 697*.
[20]Lefèvre d'Étaples, *Commentariorum in Epistolas Beati Pauli . . . Liber Secundus*, 126v.
[21]CO 49:539 (cf. CTS 40:10-11). Chrysostom treats this passage in his *Homilies on 1 Corinthians* (homily 38), in NPNF 12:229.

the same apostles who witnessed him hanging and dying on the cross. Paul does not rehearse every testimony of Christ's resurrection, but only some of the most important ones . . . so that they might strengthen our faith. On the day of his resurrection, he allowed himself to be seen five times. First, he appeared to Mary Magdalene in the garden (John 20; Mark 16). Second, he appeared to the other women who came to anoint the Lord (Matthew 28). Third, he appeared to Peter (Luke 24). Paul reminds us of this story here. Fourth, he appeared to Cleopas and Nathanael as they were traveling to Emmaus (Luke 24). Fifth, on the evening of the day of resurrection, he appeared to a gathering of the disciples (Luke 24; Mark 16; John 20)—the apostle Paul recalls this story again here. Sixth, Christ appeared to a gathering of the apostles and Thomas on the eighth day after the resurrection (John 20). Next, Paul adds several other testimonies of the resurrected Christ, which are very worthy of note. For he says that Christ Jesus was seen resurrected from the dead by more than five hundred brothers at one time. This is Christ's seventh appearing. Paul does not say exactly when this appearing occurred, but I think it was at that time reported in Matthew 28, which took place on the mountain of Galilee, when the apostles gathered in obedience to the command delivered by Christ and the angels at the Passover feast—no doubt, many of Christ's disciples and apostles were with them. Paul here recalls this extraordinary history as the clearest and most critical testimony of the resurrected Christ. The greater part of the disciples, who were eyewitnesses, were still alive and were able to give a verbal testimony that they had seen Christ. Eighth, Christ appeared to Simon Peter, Thomas, Nathanael, the sons of Zebedee, and two others from the apostles at the Sea of Tiberius—this appearing is described in John 21. Ninth, as Paul indicates here, Christ was seen by James, who was called the brother of the Lord because he had been born of the sister of Mary, the aunt of Christ. He was the first bishop of the church of Jerusalem. Where and when this appearing occurred, however, is not recorded. Tenth, Christ appeared to all the apostles, as Paul testifies here, no doubt on the day of the Lord's ascension, near Bethany on the Mount of Olives (Luke 24; Acts 1), where, in the sight of the apostles and many disciples, Christ ascended into heaven. These appearances are described in the Gospel histories so that, being strengthened by these testimonies, we might have confidence that Jesus Christ was truly resurrected from the dead and now reigns at the right hand of the Eternal Father. . . .

Indeed, Paul testifies that he himself saw Jesus Christ raised from the dead—how many times Paul saw the Lord can be gathered from various passages. For when he was traveling along the road to Damascus, he saw the Lord Jesus, as Ananias testified. Paul is speaking here about this revelation. Then, as he was proceeding into the temple at Jerusalem, Paul saw the Lord Jesus in a trance, instructing him to depart. Thereafter Paul saw the Lord Jesus in the barracks at Jerusalem (Acts 23). And without a doubt, he also saw the Lord Jesus when he was caught up into the third heaven, and remembered this revelation in Paradise (2 Cor 12). Therefore it is proper to consider Paul to be a faithful eyewitness. Paul made himself equal with the apostles, considering the greatness of the blessing with which Jesus Christ, the Son of God, had blessed him, and given that he had allowed Paul to see him many times after his resurrection and ascension into heaven. At the same time, however, Paul confessed himself unworthy that God should express such evident mercy and kindness toward him. Explication of 1 Corinthians 15:5-8.[22]

James's Role in the Early Church. Peter Martyr Vermigli: James, who was the Lord's brother, is enumerated; he was not regarded among the twelve apostles. Chrysostom said that James was mentioned here because Christ established him as the bishop of Jerusalem, but I don't think

[22]Hesshus, *Explicatio Prioris Epistolae ad Corinthios*, 328r-329v; citing Jn 20:11-18; Mk 16:9-11; Mt 28:9-10; Lk 24:1-52, 13-35, 36-49; Mk 16:14-18; Jn 20:19-23, 24-29; Mt 28:16-20; Jn 21:1-14; Lk 24:50-53; Acts 1:6-11; 22:17-18; Acts 23:11; 2 Cor 12:1-4.

this is very likely, since the sacred writings would have revealed such a thing. I think it preferable to say, therefore, that this happened by the election of the apostles. For it is clear from Scripture that James was not numbered among the apostles, but that he held a certain office and was appointed to a particular city, which was never fitting for an apostle. For those called to the apostolic office traveled throughout the world preaching and planting churches—they were not bound to one group of people more than another. Paul is the only one who mentions this appearance to James; the other Evangelists are silent about it. Some have written that James was the companion of Cleopas, when the Lord appeared in the guise of a traveler along the road to Emmaus, but no evidence supports this. Commentary on 1 Corinthians 15:7.[23]

To Which James Does Paul Refer? Wolfgang Musculus: Since there were two men named James among the apostles, the first [the son of] Zebedee, the brother of John; the second [the son] of Alphaeus, and thereafter a third was added, surnamed Justus, whom they called the brother of the Lord because he was the son of Mary (the sister of the mother of the Lord) and who was established as bishop of Jerusalem—it is uncertain which of these men the apostle means here. Chrysostom indicated the third of these men. But he made this suggestion as a conjecture, since none of the Gospel writers makes any reference to this appearance. Commentary on 1 Corinthians 15:7.[24]

15:8-11 *Paul, the Least of the Apostles*

Before His Conversion, Paul Was Like a Premature Baby. Martin Luther: Using figurative language, Paul calls himself "one untimely born," that is, a child born prematurely, before it is fully matured and, as we say, remains unbaptized. Paul wants to say: "I was just like a child that comes into the world before its due time, that cannot survive and 'never sees the sun,' as Ps 58:8 puts it, that cannot enjoy this life. I came from my mother virtually as a premature or untimely, aborted fruit. This mother was the synagogue, or Jewry, in which I lived and had my being, which was to give me spiritual life and bring me into the kingdom of God, so that I might live to God and bear fruit and also beget spiritual children from the Jewish nation, as the other apostles did. But I came to be a premature and dead child that persecuted Christ and his Christendom." . . . Thus Paul rejects all his previous holiness with these words. It is as though he were saying: "To be sure, I was a pious Jew and conducted myself blamelessly in the law like no other in my generation, etc. And yet I regard all of that as an unripe and decayed fruit, without purpose and never beholding the sun until I was reborn by Christ. Just as such a child is cast forth from its mother's womb and is buried forthwith and thus passes from one place of darkness to another, so all my righteousness in the law is also nothing but a rejected thing that serves no purpose in the sight of God and is assigned to damnation. Now I am ashamed of it and must condemn it myself. Yet I formerly esteemed it highly and supposed that I merited much with it before God." Commentary on 1 Corinthians 15:8.[25]

Paul's Untimely Birth. Tilemann Hesshus: It's as if Paul were saying: "I was not chosen along with the other apostles to the apostolic office. I was not present at Christ's sermons and miracles. I was not born again by the Word before the death of Christ, as was the case with the other apostles, who saw Christ for forty days. Instead, after his ascension, I was like an untimely birth—a disgusting mass of flesh, without life and without light. I was not reborn by the Spirit; I was not made new in Christ; I was destitute of all life and righteousness; I was a most disgusting mass of flesh in the sight of God—in fact, I was persecuting the church of God.

[23]Vermigli, *In Selectissimam Priorem ad Corinthios Epistolam . . . Commentarii*, 400v.

[24]Musculus, *Comm. 1 Cor.*, 616. Note here that Musculus holds to the perpetual virginity of Mary, and thus believes that James (surnamed Justus) was the son of Mary's *sister*, also named Mary.

[25]LW 28:83.

But God's mercy toward me was so great and so immense that he not only imparted life to me, received me by grace, and regenerated me as a son of God, but also allowed me to see Christ Jesus, resurrected from the dead, and he appointed me as an apostle." Explication of 1 Corinthians 15:8.[26]

Paul, the Persecutor of the Church. Wolfgang Musculus: Observe the sort of persecution that Saul employed against the church of God. Israel was still the church of God when Saul persecuted the faithful of Christ. Israel was the universal [*catholica*] church, and had the temple, the priesthood, the worship, and law of God; it possessed the patriarchs, it possessed the promises, it possessed the title of "antiquity." Saul was a member of this church, raised up in the law of God, more vehement in his jealousy for the traditions of the fathers than others his age. Meanwhile, to Israel, the Christians seemed to promote nothing other than a schismatic church, smelling like a new heresy that deserved to be extirpated through any means possible. From this perspective, the leaders of the universal church were persecuting all those whom they condemned as a new sect, and they believed that their cause was the most righteous of all and represented allegiance to God. With zeal of this sort Saul was persecuting the Christians, ignorant of the fact that he was persecuting the church of God, a fact that he afterward recognized and often confessed.... And so we see from this example that it is neither new nor unusual that today, those who want to be seen as the head of the universal church are persecuting the church of Christ, hurling [against the Protestants] the name "church," the patriarchs, the title of antiquity, the universal tradition, and other things like that. Commentary on 1 Corinthians 15:9.[27]

Paul's Life Illustrates God's Vast Mercy. Tilemann Hesshus: Paul mentions further his unworthiness so that he might extol and illustrate all the more the kindness and mercy of God, who had conferred on him so many great gifts. Indeed, this is the most convincing argument and clearest testimony that the mercy of God toward unworthy and wretched sinners is immense: that a cruel and violent persecutor of the church not only converted to the faith and received grace but also that he was adorned with so many remarkable gifts that he was numbered among the apostles of Jesus Christ. Therefore we should always consider this remarkable example of God's mercy when the knowledge of the enormity of our offenses frightens us and attempts to drive us to despair. Explication of 1 Corinthians 15:9-10.[28]

God's Grace Alone. John Calvin: "Not I but the grace." The Vulgate, by leaving out the article (i.e., *the* grace), permits people who don't know the Greek language an opportunity for error. For since it renders this passage "Not I, but God's grace with me," they thought that only half the credit belongs to the grace of God, and the remaining half belongs to human beings. Therefore they understand the meaning to be that Paul did not work on his own, because he could do nothing without cooperating grace, but nevertheless he acted out of his own free will by means of his own strength. But his words have a very different meaning, for what he [initially] ascribed to himself, by way of correction, he ascribes entirely to the grace of God—*entirely*, I say, not partly. For whatever he appeared to have done, he testifies that it was entirely the work of grace. This is certainly a remarkable passage, both for overthrowing the pride of human beings and for making clear how divine grace works in us. For Paul, as if he had improperly made himself the author of any good work, corrects what he had said and testifies that the grace of God is the efficient cause of everything. We should not imagine that Paul is merely feigning humility here, for he is speaking from the heart and knows that it is the truth. Let us learn, therefore, that the only good we have is that which the Lord graciously bestows, and that the only good things

[26]Hesshus, *Explicatio Prioris Epistolae ad Corinthios*, 329v.
[27]Musculus, *Comm. 1 Cor.*, 619-21.
[28]Hesshus, *Explicatio Prioris Epistolae ad Corinthios*, 330r.

that we perform are done by God himself in us—not because we do nothing ourselves, but because we do nothing unless acted on, that is, by the guidance and prompting of the Holy Spirit. Commentary on 1 Corinthians 15:10.[29]

I Worked Harder Than Any of Them. Peter Martyr Vermigli: As a metaphor, this manner of speaking can indicate the fruit of his labor, for Paul planted many churches, and he won more people to Christ than others. Chrysostom has annotated thusly: "Paul had diminished himself greatly when he called himself 'untimely born,' 'unworthy,' and a 'persecutor'—without any excuse. But now, since he commends himself somewhat for his labors, he immediately adds by way of correction, 'but it was not I, but the grace of God that is with me.'" Commentary on 1 Corinthians 15:10.[30]

God's Grace and Human Activity. Balthasar Hubmaier: "However, not I, but the grace of God that is in me" (1 Cor 15:10). My dear Eliphas, as you think that not I but the grace of God is working, so I think: with me and not without me. For the Scripture does not say, "I without the grace" nor "the grace without me." But it says: "The grace of God with me." Therefore also the saying of Paul should be understood: "I can do all things in him who strengthens me" (Phil 4:13). Freedom of the Will.[31]

Not I, but God's Grace. Heinrich Bullinger: Again, lest Paul should seem to be attributing anything to his own powers, he adds by way of correction: "Though it was not I, but the grace of God that is with me." For God uses men and women as instruments; nevertheless, all the glory and praise for good deeds ought to be ascribed to God, who sometimes ascribes to us what he himself works through us, and that by grace. For he punishes our evil within us, and crowns his gifts in us. Commentary on 1 Corinthians 15:10.[32]

There Is Only One Gospel. Tilemann Hesshus: Paul warns the Corinthians not to suppose that there are different gospel doctrines given the diversity of ministers and gifts. For there is one celestial truth in which our salvation is comprised, regardless of whether it is preached by a prophet, an apostle, an angel, or a bishop. And whether the herald of the truth is equipped with great or mediocre gifts, that person intends to announce the same gospel doctrine. For the gospel was not invented or thought up by humans or angels, but God alone revealed his will through the Son concerning the salvation of humans and the gathering of the church. No angel is permitted to change this gospel. Thus Paul says, "If an angel from heaven should teach another gospel, let him be accursed." Therefore we should not focus on the various gifts in the ministers; rather, we should always focus on the author of the sacred gospel, that is, the eternal God. Explication of 1 Corinthians 15:11.[33]

[29]CO 49:541 (cf. CTS 40:15-16).
[30]Vermigli, *In Selectissimam Priorem ad Corinthios Epistolam . . . Commentarii*, 402v-403r. Chrysostom treats this passage in his *Homilies on 1 Corinthians* (homily 38), in NPNF 12:231.
[31]CRR 5:487.
[32]Bullinger, *In Priorem ad Corinthios Epistolam Commentarius*, 241.
[33]Hesshus, *Explicatio Prioris Epistolae ad Corinthios*, 331r; citing Gal 1:8.

15:12-34 The Resurrection of the Dead

12Now if Christ is proclaimed as raised from the dead,
how can some of you say that there is no resurrection
of the dead? 13But if there is no resurrection of the
dead, then not even Christ has been raised. 14And if
Christ has not been raised, then our preaching is in
vain and your faith is in vain. 15We are even found to
be misrepresenting God, because we testified about
God that he raised Christ, whom he did not raise if it
is true that the dead are not raised. 16For if the dead
are not raised, not even Christ has been raised. 17And
if Christ has not been raised, your faith is futile and
you are still in your sins. 18Then those also who have
fallen asleep in Christ have perished. 19If in Christ we
have hope[a] *in this life only, we are of all people most*
to be pitied.

20But in fact Christ has been raised from the dead,
the firstfruits of those who have fallen asleep. 21For as
by a man came death, by a man has come also the
resurrection of the dead. 22For as in Adam all die, so
also in Christ shall all be made alive. 23But each in his
own order: Christ the firstfruits, then at his coming
those who belong to Christ. 24Then comes the end,
when he delivers the kingdom to God the Father after
destroying every rule and every authority and power.
25For he must reign until he has put all his enemies
under his feet. 26The last enemy to be destroyed is
death. 27For "God[b] *has put all things in subjection*
under his feet." But when it says, "all things are put in
subjection," it is plain that he is excepted who put all
things in subjection under him. 28When all things are
subjected to him, then the Son himself will also be
subjected to him who put all things in subjection
under him, that God may be all in all.

29Otherwise, what do people mean by being
baptized on behalf of the dead? If the dead are not
raised at all, why are people baptized on their behalf?
30Why are we in danger every hour? 31I protest,
brothers, by my pride in you, which I have in Christ
Jesus our Lord, I die every day! 32What do I gain if,
humanly speaking, I fought with beasts at Ephesus? If
the dead are not raised, "Let us eat and drink, for
tomorrow we die." 33Do not be deceived: "Bad
company ruins good morals."[c] *34Wake up from your*
drunken stupor, as is right, and do not go on sinning.
For some have no knowledge of God. I say this to
your shame.

a Or *we have hoped* **b** Greek *he* **c** Probably from Menander's comedy *Thais*

Overview: Having established the historical reliability of Christ's resurrection, Paul now proceeds to show the Corinthian believers that their own future bodily resurrection is inextricably tied to Christ's resurrection. Reformation commentators follow Paul's argument closely as they demonstrate how this chief article of the Christian faith constitutes a necessary foundation for gospel ministry—to deny this doctrine is to destroy the Christian religion and render Christian discipleship absurd. The fact that Christ conquered death and now reigns with God in heaven justifies bold gospel witness; it also empowers believers in their daily service, comforts them in the midst of suffering, and fills them with hope, joy, and courage as they confront death. More fundamentally, because Jesus Christ now reigns in heaven as the victor over sin and death, Christians have full confidence that the curse of Adam has been reversed; that God will decisively judge and punish the wicked; and that one glorious day the Lord will bring his chosen people into his glorious presence where, adorned with perfect righteousness, they will experience God as their highest good, their greatest happiness, and their eternal joy. For Luther, this magnificent resurrection hope is already becoming a reality for Christians here and now, since only their "left foot" remains in the grave.

Though Reformation commentators insist that Paul's overall meaning is clear, they do encounter several interpretive minefields in this passage. In response to the question "Why does Paul quote the Greek poet Menander?" (1 Cor 15:33), most interpreters remind their readers that all truth comes from God, even if it is found in the mouth of a pagan author. The question of when—or whether—Paul fought wild beasts in Ephesus (1 Cor 15:32) also invites lively discussion. Far more difficult to understand is Paul's cryptic reference to people "being baptized on behalf of the dead" in 1 Corinthians 15:29, which elicits detailed explanations and substantial disagreement among the commentators. Notwithstanding these debates, the reformers share a common concern that many people in their congregations continue to diminish the doctrine of Christ's resurrection, whether out of doubt, presumption, or spiritual laziness. Consequently the reformers conclude this passage by echoing Paul's strong censure of the Corinthians, calling them to repent of their moral lethargy and seek spiritual renewal through study, meditation, prayer, and concentrated struggle against Satan and his minions. As one commentator notes, Christian soldiers either advance or retreat—there is no middle way.

15:12-19 *Christ's Resurrection and Our Resurrection*

Paul Adduces Six Arguments for the Resurrection. Simon Goulart: St. Paul rests the doctrine of the resurrection on six arguments, namely, (1) the preaching of the gospel; (2) the resurrection of Christ; (3) the power of our Savior; (4) the deposit of the Holy Spirit; (5) the testimony of many things that appear in nature; (6) the perpetuity of the kingdom of Jesus Christ. On the Resurrection of the Dead.[1]

Our Resurrection and Christ's Resurrection Are Interdependent. Martin Luther: Paul stakes everything on the basic factor with which he began, namely, that Christ arose from the dead. This is the chief article of the Christian doctrine. No one who at all claims to be a Christian or a preacher of the gospel may deny that. With this he wants to confront them and force them to the conclusion that their denial of the resurrection of the dead denies even more definitely that Christ rose from the dead; for if the former is not true, the latter must be fabricated also. And since all Christians must believe and confess that Christ has risen from the dead, it is easy to persuade them to accept also the resurrection of the dead; or they must deny in a lump the gospel and everything that is proclaimed of Christ and of God. For all of this is linked together like a chain, and if one article of faith stands, they all stand. Therefore Paul also makes all things interdependent here, and he always deduces one thing from the other. Commentary on 1 Corinthians 15:12.[2]

Christ's Resurrection Assures the Believer's Resurrection. Huldrych Zwingli: What Paul says here regarding the resurrection, "I understand the life of the soul after the death of the body," he now explains and argues for its immortality in this chapter. "How can some of you say that souls do not remain alive after death, when Christ himself still lives?" Now Paul proves it with this twofold proposition. Christ is the spirit and life of our souls. If he was raised from the dead, that is, after the death of his body his soul continued to live, our souls also will remain alive after the death of our bodies. On the other hand, if Christ was not raised from the dead, then neither will we arise again, that is, we will not live. Therefore Paul shows that both our body and soul were in Christ, and that everything pertaining to death and resurrection that was accomplished in Christ's body and soul must also be accomplished in us. For Christ, who has become ours entirely,

[1]Goulart, *XXVIII Discours Chrestiens*, 308-9; citing 1 Thess 4:14; Phil 3:10; Eph 1:14; 1 Cor 15:36, 27.

[2]LW 28:94.

did all these things for us. And so Christ's resurrection is the consolation of our souls. That is, his resurrection reveals that another life follows after death. If there is truly no such thing as the immortality of souls, then Christ has not arisen; that is, his spirit does not live. Annotations on 1 Corinthians 15:12.[3]

The Doctrine of the Resurrection Should Convince and Transform Us. John Donne: All of St. Paul's words are like lightning, which affects and leaves some mark on everything it touches. And if he has touched you now, he desires not only to make you believe in the resurrection of the body, but to feel a present resurrection in your soul, and to cause *me* to believe that *you* feel it, as you express it in life and conversation. Sermon Preached at Saint Paul's Church.[4]

Christ's Resurrection Is the Power and Cause of Our Resurrection. Wolfgang Musculus: Christ died not only as a human being but also as a mediator between God and humanity, and he did not die without sin. For although in his person he was free from all sin, nevertheless he took on himself all of our offenses and sins, together with the condemnation from all our debts. And he bore them in his body on the tree so that he might satisfy God the Father for them, and he liberated us from eternal death and condemnation and brought us reconciliation with God as partners of eternal life. And because Christ has risen from the dead, he has risen not only as a man but also as a mediator, redeemer, and savior of all human beings. He is the one who has erased the written record of our sins on the cross; he is the victor over sin and death, and the restorer of eternal life that was lost through Adam. But if our sins were not able to hold him in death, which he submitted to on account of our sin . . . how much less are they able to hold us down, against whom they no longer hold any jurisdiction? That is why the resurrection of Christ is not only an example of our future resurrection, but it is the very potency and cause of it. Therefore it is inevitable that we will rise from the dead. Commentary on 1 Corinthians 15:13.[5]

Christ's Resurrection Means That He Reigns. Philipp Melanchthon: Christ's resurrection is Christ's being glorified and reigning, as Ephesians 1 says: "He raised him from the dead and seated him at his right hand in the heavenly places." Moreover, Christ's reigning means that he fills all things. And so to believe in Christ's resurrection is to believe in Christ reigning. But to believe that Christ is reigning is to believe that he cannot be harmed by death or sin or any creature, and that he cannot be stripped of God's favor. This resurrection is the knowledge of which Paul speaks in Philippians 3: "That I may be found in him, not having a righteousness of my own that comes from the law, but that which comes through faith in Christ, the righteousness from God that depends on faith—that I may know him and the power of his resurrection and may share in his sufferings." And this view of Christ arising and reigning brings peace, life, joy, etc. It is not enough to gaze on Christ suffering and dying unless you also gaze on him as risen. And so, just as he says here that we are still in our sins if Christ has not risen, so those people are still in their sins who do not believe Christ has risen; that is, those who do not believe that he is reigning and who do not believe that he has received such good things, righteousness and life; [instead], they still behave before God with a faithless, sad, bitter, and contemptuous heart. Annotations on 1 Corinthians 15:14.[6]

The Entirety of Gospel Preaching Hangs on the Resurrection. Wolfgang Musculus: Now if Christ has not risen, Paul says, our preaching is thus in vain. By this he means not only that

[3]Zwingli, *Annotatiunculae . . . ex ore Zvinglij*, 128-29.
[4]Donne, *Sermons of John Donne*, 7:211*.
[5]Musculus, *Comm. 1 Cor.*, 630.
[6]Melanchthon, *Annotationes in Epistolam priorem ad Corinthios*, 164; citing Eph 1:20; Phil 3:9-10.

part of the gospel whereby Christ is proclaimed to have risen but the entire proclamation and teaching of the gospel. Paul states that the entire sum of gospel preaching is void if Christ has not risen. For then it is preached in vain concerning God, concerning the incarnate Word, his only-begotten Son, concerning his teaching and miracles, concerning his death and burial, concerning forgiveness and remission of sins, and those other things contained in the teaching of the gospel. For all these things depend on the resurrection of a mediator, through whom death has been conquered and our justification procured. If Christ has not risen, then he is still held captive in death; he is not the victor over death, but has been conquered by death. If Christ has not risen, then, the Father has deserted his Son, and permitted him to see corruption; and David was a false prophet when he spoke in his own person about him: "You will not abandon my soul to Sheol nor will you allow your holy one to see corruption." Commentary on 1 Corinthians 15:14.[7]

The Absurdity of Denying the Resurrection. Tilemann Hesshus: Paul summarizes all the absurd things that necessarily follow from that deceitful and wicked teaching [that there is no resurrection] so as to demonstrate its worthlessness and falsehood. For hypotheses that are drawn from absurd and erroneous arguments must necessarily be false, whereas a hypothesis drawn from what is true must necessarily be true. Nothing is more absurd than to say that all the apostles' preaching was worthless and without any fruit. One of the most excellent blessings that God, out of his great kindness, bestows on humanity is to establish the gospel ministry through human agency. He raised up apostles and endowed them with illustrious gifts so that they might explain to the world the benefits of the Mediator and teach the way to eternal life. Without a doubt, this here is the greatest treasure given to human beings: the preaching of the gospel, by which we obtain the true knowledge of God, are called to repentance, are born anew to eternal life, and are given the Holy Spirit, and from which we draw the most efficacious consolations in the face of every kind of need. Therefore it is the height of absurdity and wickedness—and completely contrary to whole of sacred Scripture—to call "vain" this most healthful and salvific preaching, which is both the most necessary and most precious thing in the world.

So too it would be absurd to say that your faith is in vain. For it was through faith that you were freed from the idolatry and raging of the pagans and arrived at the knowledge of the true God. It was through faith that you were reconciled to God, obtained the remission of all sins, and were rescued from the power of darkness and the tyranny of Satan. Through faith you have peace of conscience, are endowed with the Holy Spirit, are adorned with a multitude of extraordinary gifts, and experience unwavering consolation in every trial. Through faith you have free access daily to the throne of God, and possess sure hope in the inheritance of eternal life. Therefore it is completely absurd and insane to call "vain" and "futile" this faith whose extraordinary fruit and power we experience daily in our heart. But this necessarily follows if Christ did not rise again from the dead. Explication of 1 Corinthians 15:14.[8]

Paul Lists Seven Absurdities of Denying the Resurrection. David Dickson: The first absurdity: It follows from their doctrines that Christ is not risen. Therefore it is false, since between the Christ (who is the Head) and believers (who are the members) there is such a union that if we deny the resurrection of the one, we deny the resurrection of the others, and vice versa. . . . The second absurdity: By consequence it follows from their tenets that the preaching of the apostles is in vain. Therefore it is false. The third absurdity: It will follow (Paul says) that your faith is in vain. Therefore their doctrine is false, for unless Christ has arisen, neither righteousness, nor eternal life, nor any other effects of Christ's

[7]Musculus, *Comm. 1 Cor.*, 631; Ps 16:10.

[8]Hesshus, *Explicatio Prioris Epistolae ad Corinthios*, 333v-334v.

resurrection would have been expected.... The fourth absurdity: It would follow that we spoke a false testimony, not only about Christ, but also about God, who was the raiser of Christ. He would not be the raiser of Christ if there were no resurrection. Therefore their doctrine is false.... The fifth absurdity: It would follow also from their doctrine that besides your faith being in vain, you still remain in your sins without redemption. Therefore it is false, for our redemption, and the taking away of our sins, is dependent on Christ's resurrection. The sixth absurdity: It will follow from those who deny the resurrection that the saints who are dead have perished. Therefore it is false. The seventh absurdity: It would follow from their opinion that Christians were of all people most miserable, because their error not only cuts off the hope of happiness in the life to come but also in this present life. Because, if there were no future resurrection, then Christians would willingly subject themselves most foolishly to many inconveniences, and deprive themselves of many advantages for the sake of religion. Therefore the opinion of those who deny the resurrection is false and absurd. Exposition of 1 Corinthians 15:14-19.[9]

The Doctrine of the Resurrection Emboldens Believers. Martin Luther: This text serves both to strengthen the believers and to frighten the others that they may know what a great blasphemy those who deny this article are committing. It is as though Paul were saying: "Dear Corinthians, this is not a matter for jest or ridicule; for if you deny this article, you are not denying anything trivial, nor for that matter a single article, but you are actually giving God the lie to his face, saying: 'God is not God, Christ is nothing, etc.' But if you have any regard for God and Christ—and you surely must have if you want to be Christians and have us preach to you—you cannot deny this article. For the inference will constrain you to say: 'In truth, if Christ has his apostles proclaim this and, in addition, has proved this by deeds, there can be no doubt regarding it.'" Therefore venture forth and depart this life boldly in faith in this article, convinced that after we are long in our graves and are decomposed, and the beautiful trumpet will sound and say, as Christ did to Lazarus: "Peter, Paul, come forth!"—that we will then come forth in a moment like a spark, more resplendent than the entire heaven, with our whole body and all our members again completely intact, even though we may now be burned to ashes, consumed in the water, torn to bits by wolves, or eaten by ravens. Commentary on 1 Corinthians 15:14-15.[10]

The Resurrection Gives Hope to Suffering Christians. Tilemann Hesshus: If Christ has not been raised, then he was not the victor over sin and Satan. Nor was he the true Messiah, since Scripture promised that the Messiah would rise from the dead. Nor has he freed you from sin and death. Thus it necessarily follows that you still remain in your sins—which is the utmost calamity—if the dead do not rise. Moreover, those who sleep in Christ would then perish. The Corinthians were receiving great comfort from Christ, that those who would fall asleep in Christ would be blessed, since he would preserve them into eternal life and glory. Now, Paul says, should you accept that wicked error of the Sadducees, then all hope for the blessing of these things is lost; they have not slept happily in Christ Jesus. Indeed, he says, not only do you lose your hope in the blessing of the dead, but the entire faith of Christians will be condemned as complete folly. For there is no human group or sect in the world that has faced so much hatred, such diverse dangers, so many calamities, and such dreadful punishments on account of their religious devotion than we Christians, as the history of the church, and especially the history of the apostles and martyrs, demonstrates. The world can endure all sorts of different sects, errors, blasphemies, and wicked deeds, but it cannot endure Christians. It

[9]Dickson, *Exposition of St. Paul's Epistles*, 66*.

[10]LW 28:99-100.

harbors extreme hatred for those who sincerely profess the truth of Christ; it detests those apostles as *katharmata kai peripsmata*.[11] Isaiah was executed by the sword. Jeremiah was stoned to death in Egypt. Paul was beheaded. Polycarp was burned to death. Ignatius was torn to pieces by wild animals. Blandina was laid out on a red-hot iron grate. The world was so madly cruel against the Christians that the tyrants and executioners exhausted themselves as they invented new ways to kill and torture the Christians. And so, if there is no resurrection of the dead and no blessedness remains after this life, then Christians would certainly be the most miserable, ill-starred, and even foolish of all human beings—Christians, I say, who should be the wisest and happiest of all people, because they alone are enlightened by the light of the divine Word. They are governed by the command of the Holy Spirit; they alone practice true worship of God; and they are nurtured by God's mercy more than all the people in the whole world. . . . Therefore it is necessary that another life and the resurrection of the dead await us so that God might fulfill according to his promises the true life that, though postponed to the saints in this life, is found in the resurrection of the dead and the next life. And so, in this manner, Paul teaches here that godly people are afflicted in this life with all kinds of difficulties and often experience sadness, so that such suffering of his innocent people might shine forth as a testimony of the future resurrection of the dead and the life to come. Explication of 1 Corinthians 15:15-19.[12]

What Is the Condition of "Those Who Have Fallen Asleep"? John Calvin: From this passage, some fanatics conclude that there is not life in the intermediate period between death and resurrection; but this crazy notion is easily disproved. For although the souls of the dead are now living and enjoy a blessed rest, nevertheless the whole of their happiness and comfort depends exclusively on the resurrection. For the only ground of their well-being is the anticipation of that day when they will be called to take possession of the kingdom of God. Hence, as far as the hope of the dead is concerned, there is no real hope unless that day [of resurrection] comes sooner or later. Commentary on 1 Corinthians 15:18.[13]

Christianity Would Be Foolish Apart from the Hope of Resurrection. Martin Luther: The sixth and final point with which St. Paul concludes is: "If in this life only we have hoped in Christ, we are of all people most to be pitied." That is tantamount to saying: "If it were true that there is no life after the present one, I should gladly forgo baptism, pulpit, and all of Christianity." For observe Christians and compare them with people who do not believe. The latter live in a whirl of pleasure; they have and they do what they please, and when they have lived their life, "they perish forever without any regarding it," as Job 4:20 says. They never experience what real suffering or sadness, misery and grief are. In contrast to them, we who want to be Christians endure all kinds of troubles and misfortunes, so that people despise and vilify, revile and slander us. The world is so hostile to us; it begrudges us our very life on earth. Daily we must be prepared for the worst that devil and world can inflict on us. In the face of this, who would be stupid enough to be a Christian if there were nothing to a future life? . . .

Such people must be comforted with this message: "My dear man, you may feel this very much, and it may pain you uninterruptedly to live thus, and, admittedly, you are a poor, miserable person; but be patient and be assured that this must be because you are a Christian. Otherwise you would not be so tormented. However, you must fend this off and cling with a firm faith to the fact that your Christ has risen from the dead. He

[11] Refuse and dirt.

[12] Hesshus, *Explicatio Prioris Epistolae ad Corinthios*, 336r-337r. Both Protestants and Catholics viewed martyrs such as Ignatius bishop of Antioch (d. c. 110), Polycarp bishop of Smyrna (d. c. 155/156), and Blandina of Lyons (d. 177) as spiritual examples of Christian faith and fortitude in the face of suffering and death.

[13] CO 49:543 (cf. CTS 40:20-21).

too suffered such anguish and fear of hell, but through his resurrection he has overcome all. Therefore, even though I am a sinner and deserving of death and hell, this shall nonetheless be my consolation and my victory, that my Lord Jesus lives and has risen so that he, in the end, might rescue me from sin, death, and hell." With such faith Christians must soothe and assuage their suffering and check their unhappiness. Commentary on 1 Corinthians 15:19.[14]

Christians Would Be People Most Miserable. The English Annotations: In the sense that Christians not only forsake the pleasures of this world but are subject also to a great many crosses, tribulations, and persecutions for their profession of the truth—therefore, if there is no resurrection, Christians would necessarily be most miserable. For then they would enjoy no good or comfort at all, neither here in this world nor hereafter in eternity. The ground of Paul's argument is this: that the perfect felicity of the soul and the immortality thereof are by God's order inseparable from the resurrection of the body. Wherefore people who deny the one also overthrow the other. Annotations on 1 Corinthians 15:19.[15]

15:20-24 *Christ, the Second Adam*

Jesus Is Life and Light. John Colet: There will take place hereafter, by that Life itself who is the light of humanity, a certain wonderful revivification of created things and mortal creatures. He who created the world from nothing shall re-create the ruins—not because of any human merits whatsoever. The pure will and goodness of God, which was the cause of the first creation, will in the same way be the only and exclusive cause of the re-creation.

This vivifying of death starts with human beings. The angels sinned first; but mercy and grace take hold of humans who were seduced due to their weakness and ignorance. Human beings were wicked, full of darkness, dead. From wickedness came darkness; from darkness came death. But he who is Life itself mercifully took on himself wickedness, darkness, and death, so that by this Life humanity might be made warm again and enlightened, and restored to spiritual life. And further, so that humans might grow from day to day in spiritual stature, and might finally become completely spiritual beings.

Beginning with human beings, this living force that makes things good, bright, and alive will press onward and will continue to restore to life as long as there are objects in the creation to renew. But those creatures that are beyond restoration, whose sin is excused neither by weakness nor ignorance, but who are damned by their own wicked wills that reject divine grace (among which are the fallen angels and also people who have rejected Christ), by that same powerful Life will be cast away beyond the boundaries of life, into that eternal misery of death. But those who . . . are warmed and enlightened by God's rays, they are marked for eternal life, having goodness, wisdom, and life from God in Christ. Exposition of 1 Corinthians 15.[16]

Christ's Resurrection Was Unique. Jacques Lefèvre d'Étaples: But you might ask: Why is Christ called the firstfruits of those who have fallen asleep and the first who has risen from the dead? For before Christ, the son of the widow of Zarephath was resurrected from the dead, having been resuscitated by the prophet Elijah. And was not Lazarus also resurrected, along with those whom the Lord resuscitated before his passion? It is necessary to recognize a twofold resurrection: the first, perfect, the second imperfect; the first, the reality, the second, a shadow; the first, unchanging; the second, changeable. I say "unchanging" because what was mortal put on immortality and was produced by the immortal. Now, Christ was the very first person to have risen

[14]LW 28:103, 105.
[15]Downame, *English Annotations*, EE4r*.
[16]Colet, *Enarratio*, 276.

from the dead, having accomplished a true resurrection that was unchanging. Paul says that Christ, when he rose from the dead, did not die a second time; death did not control him any longer. But other people who arose from the dead before Christ arose through an imperfect resurrection, one that was shadowy and impermanent. Commentary on 1 Corinthians 15:20.[17]

For Christians, Their Resurrection Has Already Begun. Martin Luther: And what is more than that, by calling Christ "the firstfruits of those who have fallen asleep" Paul wishes to signify that the resurrection is to be viewed and understood as having already begun in Christ, indeed, as being more than half finished, and that this remnant of death is to be regarded as no more than a deep sleep, and that the future resurrection of our body will not differ from suddenly awaking from such a sleep. . . . Now if I know this and believe it, my heart or conscience and soul have already passed through death and grave and are in heaven with Christ, dwell there and rejoice over it. And in that way we have the two best parts, much more than half, of the resurrection behind us. And because Christ animates and renews the heart by faith, he will also surely drag the decomposed rascal after him and cloth him again, so that we can behold him and live with him. For that is his Word and work on which we are baptized and live and die. Therefore this will surely not fail us, as little as it failed him. No matter when or how God ordains that we die, whether in bed or in the fire, in the water, by the rope or by sword, the devil, death's master and butcher, will surely see to killing us and carrying out his trade, so that we will not be able to choose or select a mode of death. But no matter how he executes us, it shall not harm us. He may give us a bitter portion, such as is administered to put people to sleep and make them insensitive, but we will wake up again and come forth on that Day, when the trumpet will sound. That the devil shall not prevent, because even now we are more than halfway out of death in Christ, and he will not be able to hold back this poor belly and bag of maggots either. Commentary on 1 Corinthians 15:20.[18]

Christ's Resurrection and Our Resurrection. John Donne: Christ's resurrection, even after it was fully accomplished, was still a mystery, outside the compass of reason. And then, even as it was above our reason (although it was the proof and the pattern of our resurrection), nevertheless it is above our imitation. For our resurrection will not be like his. As Bernard says, "All of us shall be raised from the dead, but only Christ arose from the dead." We shall be raised by a power working on us; he rose by a power inherent and resident in himself. Sermon Preached at Saint Paul's on Easter Day Evening.[19]

Christ Has Restored Life to Humanity. Huldrych Zwingli: "For as by a man came death, by a man has come also the resurrection from the dead." Here again the resurrection of the dead is obtained on behalf of the living. By Adam we were hurled down into death; by Christ we have been restored to life—understand that this always includes both the body and the soul. By death, understand all the necessities of both body and soul. For death is the final evil. Annotations on 1 Corinthians 15:21.[20]

Restoring What Was Lost Through Adam. John Calvin: The point to be proved is that Christ is the firstfruits and that not merely as an individual was he raised from the dead. Paul proves this from contraries, because death is not from nature, but is the consequence of human sin. Therefore, just as Adam did not die for himself alone, but for all of us, so it follows that Christ (who is the antitype) did not rise from the dead for himself alone. For he came so that he might restore everything that had been ruined in Adam.

[17]Lefèvre d'Étaples, *Commentariorum in Epistolas Beati Pauli . . . Liber Secundus*, 124v; citing 1 Kings 17.

[18]LW 28:110-11.

[19]Donne, *Sermons of John Donne*, 7:100*.

[20]Zwingli, *Annotatiunculae . . . ex ore Zvinglij*, 129-30.

The force of the argument should be noted, however, for Paul does not contend by means of a similitude, nor by an example, but he finds recourse in opposite causes to prove opposite effects. The cause of death is Adam, and we die in him. Therefore Christ, whose role it was to restore to us what we had lost in Adam, is the cause of providing life to us, and his resurrection is the assurance and guarantee of ours. And just as Adam was the origin of death, so Christ was the source of life. Paul makes the same comparison in the fifth chapter of Romans, but there is this difference: for in that passage he is examining spiritual life and death, while here he is discussing the resurrection of the body, which is the fruit of the spiritual life. Commentary on 1 Corinthians 15:21.[21]

Christ is the Opposite of Adam. The English Annotations: Christ is to be considered as opposite to Adam in respect of the contrary effects that the sin of the one and the merits of the other produced. For as from the one man, Adam, sin came over all, because by nature all were born of him, so from the one man, Christ, life comes to all (that is to say, all that are faithful) because in Christ they are made children of God by grace, and are quickened and restored to life by him. Annotations on 1 Corinthians 15:21.[22]

Paul Is Not Teaching Universal Salvation. Wolfgang Musculus: But here one may ask why the apostle says that all are made alive through Christ just as all died through Adam, when it is known from other passages of Scripture that not all, but only the elect and those who believe, are made alive and saved through Christ? . . . I answer: the apostle does not mean by this that all people in the world will be saved. Rather, since in this present discussion he has established belief in the resurrection of the dead on the resurrection of Christ, now he illustrates this by using a comparison between Adam and Christ, teaching that Christ is the author of life just as Adam was the author of death. So that, just as no human being dies outside of Adam (and all humans situated in Adam die), so no one is made alive outside of Christ (and all who are in him will be made alive). It was not convenient here for Paul to say, "so also in Christ some, a few, or many will be made alive"—this can be inferred from what follows. Thus Christ is not the life-giver of all people in general. Commentary on 1 Corinthians 15:22.[23]

Why Do the Elect in Christ Die? Theodore Beza: Question [number 33]: Why, then, do the elect still die, if death was conquered for them by Christ? Answer: Because Christ did not come to restore us into the station of this world that was lost in Adam, but in order to transfer us into a far better immortality; but that is not able to happen unless we migrate from this world. Therefore, although this separation of body and spirit, which is called the first death, arises from sin, whose remnants are even in the most holy people, nevertheless, if you consider the counsel and plan of God, death is not imposed on the elect by God as judge, but was sent by a most kind Father calling his own nearer to himself. Thus envisioned, it not only does not frighten believers, it actually renews and refreshes them. Christian Questions and Responses.[24]

The Firstborn from the Dead. Tilemann Hesshus: Immediately afterward Paul emphasizes the privileged position and preeminence of Christ, just as he does in Colossians 1, where Paul calls him *prōtotokon ek tōn nekrōn*, "the beginning and firstborn from the dead, that in everything he might be preeminent." For Paul desires that the source of our resurrection always be before our eyes. Now, if anyone objects that Enoch and Elijah were translated alive into heaven, and Moses was resuscitated before the time of Christ, we respond as follows: these things happened by the merit and

[21]CO 49:545-46 (cf. CTS 40:25).

[22]Downame, ed., *English Annotations*, EE4v*.

[23]Musculus, *Comm. 1 Cor.*, 644-45.

[24]Beza, *A Little Book of Questions and Responses*, 12.

power of the Mediator, the Son of God, in whom they believed. For the death and resurrection of Christ, which occurred at a specific time, was applicable to all times. Now, lest someone be surprised by the fact that our bodies rot in the grave, when we do not see the corruption of Christ's flesh, Paul teaches that God has established the following order: that Christ is preeminent in all things, and is the firstborn from the dead; then, that each of us who in this life believe in Christ will be resuscitated at his glorious coming. Explication of 1 Corinthians 15:23.[25]

In the End, God Alone Will Rule. Martin Luther: When the hour strikes, [Paul] wishes to say, in which we who are Christ's are to rise and follow him, then all is accomplished, and the end to which Scripture points is at hand. This earthly life with all its misery and misfortune will cease, the vile devil with his rule will come to an end, yes, also both the secular and the spiritual offices will terminate. In sum, all things on earth will come to an end, and that which we together with all saints have desired and waited for since the beginning of the world will be ushered in, namely, that God himself will be Lord alone and rule alone in us, his children. To this rule there will be no end. He Himself explains what he means with the end when he says that he will abolish every rule and power and will alone be all in all. Commentary on 1 Corinthians 15:24.[26]

Christians Must Eagerly Anticipate the End. John Calvin: Paul previously put a bridle on people's impatience when he warned them that the suitable time for the new resurrection life would not be before Christ's coming. But since this world is like a stormy sea in which we are constantly tossed, and our life condition is so uncertain—or rather so turbulent and all things are subject to sudden changes—this could disturb the weak of heart. Hence, Paul now reminds them of that day, saying that all things will be put in order. "Then," therefore, "the end comes," that is, the goal of our race—the quiet harbor—a condition no longer subject to changes. And at the same time, Paul admonishes us that that end must be anticipated, because it is not proper that we should be crowned in the middle of the race. Commentary on 1 Corinthians 15:24.[27]

The End of All Principalities and Authorities. Wolfgang Musculus: Paul explains how and when Christ is going to hand over the kingdom to God the Father: "when he will have destroyed," he says, "every principality, authority, and power." That is, when he will have accomplished that there is no longer any prince, any authority, any power, either in heaven or on earth, except God alone, reigning over all and in all. Different [passages] explain the ranks of archangels and angels; the principality, dominion, and power of evil spirits; the principalities, authorities, and powers of this world. What is going to happen to all of these authorities at the end of the world is completely clear to believers. Indeed, angels will remain, but their role will be different than in this life. Evil spirits will be given over to eternal punishment. Some of the princes and authorities of this world are enemies and adversaries of God's kingdom; others preserve magisterial authority as constituted by the Lord. In the end of the world, neither righteous nor wicked princes and magistrates will remain; they will all be abolished. There will no longer be any need for justice, because there will be no evil people to punish, and no need for magistrates to defend the cause of good people. The wicked, along with Satan their prince, will be exterminated. Therefore, all principalities, all authorities, all powers in the world will be abolished. But in my judgment, the apostle in this passage is speaking about the principalities, authorities, and powers that are adversaries and enemies of the kingdom of God, such as the principalities of

[25]Hesshus, *Explicatio Prioris Epistolae ad Corinthios*, 339v-340r; citing Col 1:18.
[26]LW 28:123-24.
[27]CO 49:546 (cf. CTS 40:26).

evil spirits and wicked tyrants—the adversaries of God and Christ—whose rebellion and final destruction Psalm 22 sings about and prophesies. Commentary on 1 Corinthians 15:24.[28]

Christ Will Never Cease to Reign. David Dickson: Having completed all things that his Father committed to him to finish, Christ shall hand over to the Father the kingdom committed to him, that is, the kingdom over all things that are in the world for the purpose of perfecting the work of our redemption. Christ shall (I say) deliver the kingdom to God, according to his humanity, and to his Father, according to his divinity. That doesn't mean that Christ will cease to reign immediately, but rather, he will cease to reign mediately as previously. Christ will not cease to reign with the Father, but shall cease to reign as the Father's deputy for the purpose of warring against his enemies or engaging in the laborious and painful work of gathering his church. Thus there will be no true end of his kingdom. He shall indeed reign much more gloriously than he presently does, when his adversaries are conquered . . . [and] he shall govern together with the Father, and fill all things with his light, love, and life through his immediate powers. Annotations on 1 Corinthians 15:24.[29]

Not Fodder for Arians. Peter Martyr Vermigli: These words are added to cheer up the spirits of the Corinthians, who might have been discouraged because they saw this resurrection long delayed. And so he consoles them, and says that the resurrection cannot happen until Christ has first vanquished all things and subjugated all things to himself. Then it will be the end of death and all our misfortunes. Here some people are troubled when they hear that Christ will hand over his kingdom to God the Father. For they imagine that on account of these things that he is far inferior to the Father. Hence, Arians everywhere abused these words to confirm their dogma. But they did so shamelessly. For since there are two natures in Christ, it should be seen according to which nature these words are said. And surely, if the context is considered, these words should be ascribed to his humanity—to which the resurrection properly fits. In this sense Christ is said to be the firstfruits [of those who have fallen asleep]; his divinity does not rise again, for it never died.[30] But let him be considered the Word according to his divine nature. Surely they don't think that the Son handed over the kingdom to his God and Father in such a way that he didn't keep it for himself? If they want to argue this, by the same reasoning they would also be compelled to think that the Father abdicated all his power, because the Son says: "All power has been given to me," and "All things have been handed over to me by my Father." But if the Father can hand over such things to the Son, but it is not therefore held that he is inferior to the Son, why should we regard the Son as inferior to the Father, because it is said that at some time he will hand over the kingdom to the Father? According to his human nature Christ has God in authority over him, hence he said: "I am ascending to my God and to your God." And because he has God as his Father, according to both natures, for that reason he adds in that passage, "My father and your Father." And here it is said that he hands over the kingdom not only to God but also to his Father. For this reason there's nothing ambiguous in this phrase, nor is it absurd. Commentary on 1 Corinthians 15:24.[31]

15:25-28 *All Things Are Subject to Christ*

Christ's Present Kingdom. Tilemann Hesshus: "For he must reign until he has put all his enemies under his feet"; that is, for the time

[28]Musculus, *Comm. 1 Cor.*, 655.

[29]Dickson, *Exposition of St. Paul's Epistles*, 68*.

[30]This sounds unfitting, but Vermigli means, "According to his divinity he does not rise again, for according to his divinity he never died." See further, Donald Fairbairn, *Life in the Trinity: An Introduction to Theology with the Help of the Church Fathers* (Downers Grove, IL: IVP Academic, 2009), 168-79.

[31]Vermigli, *In Slectissimam Priorem ad Corinthios Epistolam . . . Commentarii*, 411v-412r; citing 1 Cor 15:20; Mt 28:18; 11:27; Jn 20:17.

being this form of Christ's kingdom remains until the coming of Christ and the universal resurrection of the dead. Christ is seated at the right hand of the eternal Father; he is Priest, King, and Mediator of the church; he governs his church by the Word; he calls men and women to repentance; he gives them new birth through the sacraments; he comforts them in their afflictions; he defends them from various dangers; he protects them against the furies of the world and Satan; he sanctifies them through the Holy Spirit; from that time forward he increases in them the knowledge of God; he sustains them in the faith; he allows them to be swallowed up in death; he preserves them for the future resurrection. It is necessary for Christ to exercise this sovereign reign until he has gathered together the entire church, which the Father has chosen in the Son from eternity, and has triumphed over all his enemies in the whole world. For the Father has delegated this kingdom to his Son: "I will put enmity," he says, "between you and the woman, between your offspring and her offspring. He shall crush your head. . . ." (Gen 3). And Psalm 110: "The Lord sends forth from Zion the scepter of your kingdom, to rule in the midst of your enemies." Explication of 1 Corinthians 15:25.[32]

Paul Answers Several Objections. Heinrich Bullinger: Now, you may ask, "why did the Lord not initiate this eternal happiness immediately upon Christ's resurrection?" Because, according to the prophecy of David in Psalm 110, it is necessary for him to rule until he can place all his enemies under his feet. For it was necessary before the judgment that the glory of Christ should become known throughout the world so that all the sons of God dispersed throughout the whole earth might be gathered together, and that the Lord Jesus might also reveal himself to all the devil's allies and finally conquer them, vindicating both his own blood and the blood of his saints, poured out by the hands of the wicked. And, in a manner of speaking, he will triumphantly trample on them on that day.

After having added this detail, Paul returns to his description of the judgment and kingdom of God, which was also mentioned in the prophetic passage of Psalm 110. "Truly," I say, "at that time of judgment and the end of all things, the final enemy—that is, death itself, which to the very end constantly afflicts humanity—will be abolished and slain by the thrust of the divine sword." Thus Paul employs personification when speaking about death, as if it were a person. "No one," he says, "will die after the day of judgment. For the godly will live forever, while the wicked will be tormented forever." Now all these things Paul says are closely related to the prophecy of Psalm 9: that all that is opposed to God will be subjected to the Lord Jesus; that is, they will be swept away from his presence by the power of God, and he will confer on the saints everything they need to enjoy true happiness, joy, and pleasure. Moreover, in this passage Paul responds a second time to a scoffing objection, saying, "Truly, when the prophet says that all things would be placed under the Lord's feet, he meant created things—not the creator himself." For Christ himself is inseparable from the one God; and all things are subject to him except that which is God and one with the Father. Commentary on 1 Corinthians 15:25-27.[33]

The Last Enemy Is Death. Martin Luther: It is an especially fine and appealing text and a comforting note that he calls death the last enemy of Christ. I could never have extended the meaning of this text so and interpreted the word "enemies" as referring to death, as St. Paul does here. For at first sight these words apply solely to the Jews and the Gentiles who torment the Christians on earth. But like a true painter and carver, St. Paul fashions a lovely picture and portrays death as it must be portrayed. He refers to death as the words of the psalm do, which read (Ps 110:1): "Till I make your

[32]Hesshus, *Explicatio Prioris Epistolae ad Corinthios*, 341v-342r; citing Gen 3:15; Ps 110:2.

[33]Bullinger, *In Priorem ad Corinthios Epistolam Commentarius*, 245-46; citing Ps 110:1.

enemies your footstool." In that way we might learn to know and regard our Lord as an enemy of death; his kingdom is intent on engaging death in combat, in putting him in subjection under his feet, until he has utterly destroyed him. I am fond of having Christ depicted and proclaimed thus, showing that he is not a man who delights in wrath and punishment and who deals unmercifully with people, but as one who is a king and who has occupied his kingdom for the purpose of battling with all his might against his last enemy until he has cast death under his feet. Therefore it would be proper to inscribe this verse with golden letters and to hold it before the eyes of Christians constantly. . . .

But Christian have already been thrust into death by the very fact that they became Christians. Wherever they may be, they occupy themselves with this hourly. They expect death any moment so long as they sojourn here, because devil, world, and their own flesh give them no rest. However, they enjoy the advantage of already being out of the grave with their right leg. Moreover, they have a mighty helper who holds out his hand to them, namely, their Lord Christ; he has left the grave entirely a long time ago, and now he takes the Christian by the hand and pulls them more than halfway out of the grave; only the left foot remains in it. For their sin is already remitted and expunged, God's wrath and hell are extinguished, and they already live fully in and with Christ with regard to their best part, which is the soul, as they partake of eternal life. Therefore death can no longer hold them or harm them. Commentary on 1 Corinthians 15:26.[34]

Death No Longer Reigns Over Christians. John Calvin: We see that there are still many enemies that resist Christ and continue to oppose his reign. But death will be the last enemy to be destroyed. Thus Christ must still be the administrator of the Father's kingdom. Let believers, therefore, be of good courage and not give up hope until all things that must precede the resurrection are accomplished. Now it is asked why Paul says that death shall be the final enemy destroyed, since it has already been destroyed by Christ's death, or rather, by his resurrection, which is the victory over death and the attainment of life. I answer that it *was* destroyed in such a way that it is no longer deadly for believers, but not in such a way that it causes them no annoyance. It is true that the Spirit of God dwells within us, yet we still carry about a mortal body. The source of death will one day be removed, but that has not yet happened. We have been born again from incorruptible seed, but we have not yet become perfect. Or, to express the matter briefly in a similitude, the sword of death, which could penetrate even to the heart, has become dulled. Though it still wounds, yet it does so without danger, for we die, but in dying we enter life. In summary, we should feel about death just as Paul teaches elsewhere concerning sin (Rom 6:12)—that it indeed dwells within us, but it does not rule over us. Commentary on 1 Corinthians 15:26.[35]

God's Kingdom of Grace and Glory. Philipp Melanchthon: The kingdom is twofold: one of grace, the other of glory. The kingdom of grace is the kingdom of Christ. For Christ has been put forward as a propitiatory offering and a sign of grace. Those who believe in him are certain that they have been justified by faith before God and have grace. Likewise, the kingdom of Christ includes judgment, John 5:22: "The Father judges no one, but has given all judgment to the Son." Therefore for Christ to reign is for him to judge the saints, that is, to protect them against injury from all creatures. But the kingdom of glory is nothing but the revelation of the glory of God's children. It is called the kingdom of God, where God is now "all in all"; that is, he is manifested and revealed as doing all things in all people. Hence to hand over the kingdom to the Father is to render glory to the Father and reveal that glory to the elect so that the elect may recognize that the glory of God is that which belongs to Christ. Or even better: The

[34]LW 28:131-32, 133*.

[35]CO 49:547-48 (cf. CTS 40:28-29).

kingdom of God is the same in both pilgrims and the blessed, namely, righteousness, peace, life, etc. But the kingdom of God among the pilgrims is called the kingdom of Christ for this reason: because among the pilgrims God reigns through Christ. For the will of the Father cannot be known except in Christ, who was offered as the sign and pledge of the Father's mercy, as he himself says in John 14: "I am the way, the truth, and the life; no one comes to the Father, but by me. If you had known me, you would have known my Father also." Therefore, as longs we are pilgrims, we know God's glory in that sign that he has offered to us; through it we believe, and we trust in it against all creatures. That knowledge of Christ or knowledge of the Father's glory in Christ is the kingdom of God for those traveling as pilgrims. . . . But among the blessed in heaven God reigns not through Christ but through himself; that is, the blessed know the glory of God not just in a sign in Christ but in the Father himself. Second, after the final resurrection Christ will hand over the kingdom to God his Father; that is, he will present the elect to the Father, among whom the Father himself will then reign through himself without a sign; he will reveal to them his glory through himself, not only in Christ. And Christ will subject himself to the Father; that is, he will give glory to the Father and reveal that glory to the elect so that they may recognize that Christ's glory does not belong to Christ but to the Father. Third, when he shall have subjected himself to the Father, all things are still subjected to Christ, as the text here says in verse 28: "Then the Son himself will also be subjected to him who put all things under him," hence all things are still subjected to the Son. Annotations on 1 Corinthians 15:28.[36]

The Son Will Be Subject to the Father. Tilemann Hesshus: When Christ, the God-man, will have brought the church into the Father's presence, then it will be disclosed that he received the kingdom from the Father in eternity, that he honored the Father with ineffable reverence and obedience, that all things were achieved by him, that he accomplished all his commands, that he ascribed all things to his glory. However, this subjection of the Son does not refer to the equality of essence of the Father and Son, for that title "Son" teaches us that he is of the same essence with the Father and that he is very closely united to the Father in reverence. Explication of 1 Corinthians 15:28.[37]

The Submission of the Son. The English Annotations: The Son shall be subject to his Father as a man with respect to his mystical body. This does not mean that the Son was not subject to his Father previously. Rather, it is because on that day, in the sight of human beings and angels, he will most manifestly declare his subjection to his Father by surrendering his kingdom to him. . . . For this reason his mystical body, that is to say, the church, which is presently in distress and does not yet partake wholly of his glory, is not yet fully perfect. This is also the reason that the bodies of the saints that lie in the grave will not be glorified until the resurrection. But since Christ is God, we are subject to him. . . . But as our Priest, Christ is subject to his Father, as we are as well. Annotations on 1 Corinthians 15:28.[38]

God Will Satisfy All Our Desires. Martin Luther: Then, says St. Paul, God will be "everything to everyone"; that is, everybody will find all wants that are now satisfied by all things satisfied in God himself. When he will reveal himself, we will be satisfied in body and soul and will no longer stand in need of so many things as we now do here on earth. In the first place, for the sustenance and preservation of body and life, father and mother, meat and drink, house and home, clothing and shoes, in addition, princes and masters who protect us and provide

[36]Melanchthon, *Annotationes in Epistolam priorem ad Corinthios*, 166, 168; citing Jn 14:6-7.

[37]Hesshus, *Explicatio Prioris Epistolae ad Corinthios*, 342v.
[38]Downame, *English Annotations*, EE4v*.

the peace; then in the spiritual realm pastors and preachers who teach us and administer the sacraments, who comfort in times of distress and counsel in matters of conscience, etc. Also sun and moon, air, fire, and water for the entire world. Who can enumerate all the items that men and women require here on earth for the wants of the body? But over there all of this will cease; none of these wants will any longer exist. We will have so much in God that no food, no drink, no malmsey can be so precious or feed us or quench our thirst as well as God himself will do with the sight of himself. You will always be strong and vigorous, healthy and happy, also brighter and more beautiful than sun and moon, so that all the garments and the gold bedecking a king or emperor will be sheer dirt in comparison with us when we are illumined by but a divine grace. Nor will we need a patron or any government, money or goods, house or home, or other physical possessions, but we will have sufficient of everything in him. Similarly, we will have all spiritual gifts, eternal righteousness, comfort and joy of conscience, that no one will be able to terrify us or confuse us or disquiet us any longer. In short, in place of whatever we must now derive from all creatures here and there singly and piecemeal—although this, too, comes from him and is given by him—we shall have him directly, without any flaw and without ceasing. Commentary on 1 Corinthians 15:28.[39]

The Joy of God's Presence. Tilemann Hesshus: "So that God might be all in all," that is, that his divine majesty might shine forth in the Son and in the whole church. At that time God will no longer reign in the church through the ministry of the gospel and sacraments, but his divinity will impart heavenly blessings directly; he will fill us with his penetrating light; he will adorn us with complete righteousness; he will drench us with pure joy; he will raise us up to eternal life. No infirmity will hinder us; we will be in need of no spiritual props; we will lack nothing that we desire. Seeing God will be our highest goodness, our greatest happiness, our eternal joy. We will learn the wisdom of God without weariness. We will show forth righteousness without haughtiness. We will enjoy gladness without confusion. The glory of those blessed of God will be diverse, but there will be no room thereby for envy or rivalry. For the Lord will satisfy the desire of everyone, and God himself will be all things to everyone. No one will desire anything more as long as they are permitted to enjoy God's presence. "O Lord Jesus, when we will have happily finished the race that you ordained for us, with the help of your Spirit, guide us to this highest and singular happiness and eternal joy, so that the fruit of your death might also shine forth in us, and that we might love you forever, eternal Father, Son, and Holy Spirit, and never grow weary of worshiping you. Amen." Explication of 1 Corinthians 15:28.[40]

God Working All in All. John Donne: Here God does all in all, but he does it all through instruments. Even in the infusion of faith, he works by the ministry of the gospel. But [in the resurrection] he shall be all in all, doing all in all, immediately, by himself, for Christ shall deliver up the kingdom to God, that is, to his Father. His kingdom is the administration of his church by his ordinances in the church. At the resurrection there shall be an end of that kingdom: there shall be no more church, no more working on people through preaching, but God himself shall be all in all. "Ministers are like masks (*larvae*) of God," Luther says. Sermon Preached at St. Paul's on Easter.[41]

Union with God Through Christ. John Trapp: Until sin and death are abolished, we have no access to God but by Christ. But after all Christ's enemies are trod underfoot, then we shall have an immediate union with God. Nevertheless, it shall be the proper and everlasting praise of

[39]LW 28:141-42.

[40]Hesshus, *Explicatio Prioris Epistolae ad Corinthios*, 342v-343r.
[41]Donne, *Sermons of John Donne*, 8:233*.

Christ that he is the one who procured that union. Commentary on 1 Corinthians 15:28.[42]

15:29 *The Baptism of the Dead*

Early Christians Baptized Catechumens on the Graves of the Deceased. Martin Luther: But Paul adds a phrase to the word "baptize," *pro mortuis*. This has been interpreted to mean—and so it reads in Latin—that they had themselves baptized "for the dead," that is, for the unbelievers in heathendom. Then they would have been baptized twice, once for themselves and the second time for members of their family. But that cannot be. For in Acts 2:38 Peter says: "Be baptized everyone of you in the name of Jesus Christ," etc. This does not mean that one should be baptized for another. It is the same as that everyone must repent, believe, and profess faith for themselves. Therefore I adhere to the meaning, in concurrence with the old Greek teachers. . . . In St. Paul's day this article [regarding the resurrection] was still novel and was just being spread. It was unheard of among the heathen, also among the most erudite in Greece, although they did advance to the point where they assumed that the soul lived after the death of the body, without being able to prove this conclusively. However, that human beings would rise again and that body and soul would be reunited, of that they knew nothing at all. In view of this, it was hard for them at first to believe the apostles' proclamation; and those who believed it had to endure much ridicule. And so, in order to strengthen this article among the people, they had themselves baptized at the graves of the dead in token of their firm conviction that the dead who lay buried there and over whom they were being baptized would rise again. . . . For that reason they baptized people here at the graves, as though to say: "Here I am having myself baptized in proof of my faith and conviction that these deceased people lying here will all arise." . . .

So you see that it is all-important that this article [regarding the resurrection of the body] be firmly maintained among us; for if it begins to totter or is no longer regarded as valid, all the other articles will also be useless and invalid, because all that Christ did in coming to earth and establishing his kingdom in the world was done for the sake of the resurrection and the future life. Commentary on 1 Corinthians 15:29.[43]

Why Does Paul Speak of the Baptism of the Dead? Huldrych Zwingli: This meant either that they sprinkled the graves of the dead with water, or perhaps that they were baptized on behalf of those who had died. By this comparison Paul proves that the soul continues to live after the death of the body. It's as if he were saying: "By baptizing on behalf of the dead you demonstrate that their souls are alive. For if they were not still alive, why is it necessary for them to be baptized? Without a doubt, you believe that by doing this they are granted freedom from misery and affliction, transferring them to a better life. Clearly this demonstrates that their souls continue to live. Why then do you deny that there is life after death?" By this argument Paul reveals that those who teach otherwise are false teachers. Paul does not defend this rite of baptism, but he says this with a grimace and a look of contempt on his face. Annotations on 1 Corinthians 15:29.[44]

Paul May Be Referring to Pagan Burial Practices. Heinrich Bullinger: Paul once again returns to the main topic and demonstrates the resurrection of the dead by means of several arguments. The first he adduces from their superstition—which he doesn't approve of, but which it appears was customarily practiced there. Certain people were being baptized *hyper tōn nekrōn*, that is, on behalf of, or for the advantage and benefit (as it seemed to them) of those who were dead, since they had been preceded in death. Those people, indeed, believed that the souls of the dead were immortal; it followed, therefore, that they were baptizing for the

[42]Trapp, *A Commentary or Exposition*, 699*.

[43]LW 28:149-51.

[44]Zwingli, *Annotatiunculae . . . ex ore Zvinglij*, 131-32.

sake of those buried corpses (which would not have happened without an awareness of resurrection). "It is necessary," Paul says, "either that there is a resurrection of the dead, or that your practice of baptism for the dead is completely superfluous. But you will not grant that it is superfluous. Therefore, you indicate by this rite of sprinkling that there is a resurrection of the dead." Now, all those sacred commentators that I have consulted interpret this passage in this fashion, including Tertullian, Theophylact, the Paraphraser,[45] the schoolmen, and also Ambrose. The latter states explicitly, "By this example, Paul is not approving of what they were doing, but he demonstrates their unshakeable confidence in the resurrection."

But if we change the words, and read this passage as follows: "If the dead are not raised at all, why are they baptizing over the dead?"—changing the verb from being passive to active, and changing the phrase "on behalf of the dead" to "over the dead"—the passage conveys this more simple meaning, namely, that ceremony by which almost all pagans baptize by washing (that is, soaking and sprinkling with water) the bodies of the dead at burial to testify publicly that those feeble bodies, sown in the earth, will once again be resuscitated. . . . Hence it seems that the apostle has drawn his argument from this present ceremony of the pagans, of which, nevertheless, he does not approve. Indeed, he has demonstrated the attitude with which the Corinthians have advanced their argument, exposing their impiety. It's as if he were saying, "Are you not ashamed to deny what even pagans affirm in their burial rites?" Commentary on 1 Corinthians 15:29.[46]

Catechumens Sought Baptism When Death Was Imminent. John Calvin: Now, let us seek the meaning [of this verse]. . . . I say that those who are "baptized for the dead" are people already thought of as dead who have altogether despaired of life. And thus the particle *hyper* will have the force of the Latin word *pro*, as when we say, "to consider one to be abandoned"—an interpretation not forced. Or if you would prefer a different interpretation, the phrase "baptized for the dead" will mean to be baptized for the good of the dead, not the living. Now, it is well known that, from the very beginning of the church, those who were still catechumens, when afflicted with disease, if the threat of death seemed likely, would customarily seek baptism so that they would not depart from this world before they had surrendered themselves to Christ—and they did this so that they might carry with them the seal of their salvation. It appears from the writings of the church fathers that, later on, superstition intruded into this practice, for the Fathers attack those who were delaying their baptisms until the point of death so that they might face the judgment of God with all their sins expiated once and for all. This was certainly a gross error, which proceeded partly from great ignorance and partly from hypocrisy. But Paul in this passage is only addressing a custom that was sacred and in accordance with the Lord's instruction—that if catechumen, who had already embraced in their hearts the Christian faith, perceived that death was imminent, they would seek baptism, partly for their own comfort, and partly for the edification of their fellow believers. For it is no small consolation to wear a token of salvation stamped in one's body. There is another source of edification to be mentioned, namely, that it serves as a confession of his faith. Therefore they were baptized on behalf of the dead because it was not at all profitable for this present world; and so the fact that they were seeking baptism was because they had despaired of life. We now see that Paul had good reason to ask the Corinthians what they would do if no hope remained after death. Commentary on 1 Corinthians 15:29.[47]

"Baptism of the Dead"—Two Possible Interpretations. John Donne: We find

[45]That is, Erasmus.

[46]Bullinger, *In Priorem ad Corinthios Epistolam Commentarius*, 246-47. For Ambrose's [Ambrosiaster's] treatment of this verse, see his *Comment. in Epist. I ad Cor.*, in PL 17:279-80.

[47]CO 49:551-52 (cf. CTS 40:36-37).

among our own expositors since the Reformation two senses of these words, either of which may be taken, for both capture the purpose and intention of the apostle, which is to prove the resurrection.... The first is that this was a baptism of those people who, in order to provide a special testimony of their faith in the resurrection ... administered or received baptism atop the tombs and graves of other Christians who had already departed this life, thereby declaring their opinion that those who were buried would receive a resurrection, and that they themselves were baptized into the same faith, and so were part of the communion of the saints. And in this sense, the original [text] would be preserved, which is best translated, not *for* the dead (*pro mortuis*), but *on* the dead (*super mortuos*), i.e., on the graves of the dead.... This is the interpretation of Luther, who is powerful in the interpretation of every Scripture passage that he undertakes. And Melanchthon, a man of more learning and temperance than probably anyone of us has met in our perverse times, follows this same interpretation. ... [Luther and Melanchthon] may have seen early authors [who testified to this practice] whom I have not. For my part, I confess that I never remember seeing a reference to this practice in ecclesiastical histories.

There is an additional interpretation, which is ... subject to no such objection, and is therefore the best to be embraced, which is founded on a custom that began very early in the church of God.... Based on the belief that, at the time of baptism, sinners experienced a complete washing away and deliverance from their sins, people regularly—or at least, very often—deferred their baptisms until their death beds, so that they might migrate and pass out of this world in that restored purity provided by baptism, without contracting any more sins after baptism. We are convinced of this early practice, for ecclesiastical history is full of examples of it. Thus St. Paul argues in accordance with this custom [that] ... if people desire baptism at the very end of their lives, when they are judged no better than dead (*pro mortuis*) and when they have had no fellowship with the church militant here in this life, does not this very desire imply a confession of the resurrection? Sermon Preached at Saint Paul's.[48]

False Baptism Was an Ancient Problem. Menno Simons: And so, dear children, because the learned ones have always sought righteousness in infant baptism and still seek it, therefore you can easily surmise that these proponents of infant baptism have because of this consideration gained entrance [into the church]. With the earliest ancients it was not the common practice, I say common practice, as may be learned from Tertullian, Rufinus, and others; but as it appears immediately after the demise of the apostles, or perhaps while they were still alive, people began to abuse the true Christian baptism, which belongs to believers only, even as some of the Corinthians already in the days of Paul suffered themselves to be baptized for the dead. Christian Baptism.[49]

15:30-34 *Paul Endures Danger for Resurrection Hope*

Seeking a Better Life After Death. John Calvin: [Paul is arguing:] "If our resurrection and ultimate happiness is in this world, why on our own accord do we abandon it and voluntarily submit ourselves to death?" The argument might be laid out in this fashion: "We would face danger each and every hour in vain if we did not look ahead to a better life after death." Paul is speaking, however, about voluntary dangers, to which believers expose their lives for the purpose of confessing Christ. Commentary on 1 Corinthians 15:30.[50]

A Second Proof for the Resurrection. Peter Martyr Vermigli: "Why are we in danger all the time?" Another absurd conclusion

[48]Donne, *Sermons of John Donne*, 7:206-9*.

[49]Simons, *Complete Writings*, 279-80. In his treatise *On Baptism* (early third century), Tertullian acknowledged the practice of infant baptism among contemporaries, while at the same time condemning it.

[50]CO 49:552 (cf. CTS 40:38).

that Paul shows—demonstrated from his own situation—is that the suffering which the apostles and holy people endured for the resurrection of the dead is superfluous. Indeed, it served as very convincing evidence to see that the apostles suffered so many painful and harsh situations, as Paul mentions earlier in his letter, that it seemed that God had appointed them as those sentenced to death; they were hungry, thirsty, naked, buffeted with blows, etc. And let no one object to us that some of them endured such grave dangers out of a desire for fame and glory, for that is pure foolishness. . . . But if you say, "Do not many people suffer death very gloriously for the sake of their country and virtue?"—I confess that's true. In such situations one sees the kind of virtue and honor about which Paul speaks in Romans: "For the sake of a righteous person someone might die, and perhaps for a good person someone might dare to die," where you see that it can happen for a person to die for the sake of fame or for country and virtue, if they consider these things important. But as far as the apostles and martyrs are concerned, would they not be insane to wish to die for a lie for the sake of achieving a resurrection that did not exist? Commentary on 1 Corinthians 15:30.[51]

In What Way Was Paul in Danger Every Hour? Tilemann Hesshus: The second argument [for the resurrection] comes from the testimony and authority of the apostles and all the martyrs. If there is no resurrection of the dead, then the apostles and martyrs are the most stupid of people. If in fact there is no reason why they expose themselves every hour to the danger of death by their confession of the truth, then, after this life, they will harvest no fruit from their perseverance and purpose—except that their lives are cut short all the more quickly. But it would be pure folly to condemn the apostles and martyrs—in whom so much wisdom and the light of the Spirit shines—of foolishness or stupidity. Therefore the resurrection of the dead is an actual fact. And recognizing this, the apostles and martyrs endure every torture and torment and, by their steadfast will, disregard the threats of all tyrants as well as all the good things of this life. For they stand with complete confidence that they will be resurrected from the dead with glorious bodies and will enjoy a bountiful reward for their labors.

Why does Paul testify on oath that he dies daily? He does this to indicate that he is afflicted with constant calamities, dangers, and terrors for the sake of the gospel ministry. He is speaking of outward battles and inner terrors. For not only were tyrants, heretics, and false brothers afflicting Paul, but even evil spirits were harassing him with terrors, and an angel of Satan was striking him with blows. Hence he was daily reminded about the nearness of death, and considered death preferable to life. Certainly he endured these incessant tortures patiently out of hope for the resurrection of the dead, which freed him from all troubles and terrors. Therefore people who are suffering for the sake of the gospel can learn and be strengthened from Paul's testimony (which shines forth in his patience amid so many troubles and terrors), that they will surely be resurrected from the dead; and, with this hope, all the martyrs constantly endure sufferings of every sort. Explication of 1 Corinthians 15:30-31.[52]

Paul Here Is Making a Solemn Oath. Wolfgang Musculus: *By our boasting.* The Greek is *nē tēn ēmeteran kauchēsin*, by which Paul confirms what he says with a solemn oath. Now he swears by his boasting or pride—however, not what he had in himself but what he had in Christ Jesus, of whom he boasted that he was an apostle, and on account of whom he was enduring all those dangers. For Paul knows that he is the Lord of life and death, reigning at the right hand of the Father, and that he will return to destroy all the wicked, and even death itself, and to raise them from the

[51]Vermigli, *In Selectissimam Priorem ad Corinthios Epistolam . . . Commentarii*, 418r-v; citing 1 Cor 4:9-11; Rom 5:7.

[52]Hesshus, *Explicatio Prioris Epistolae ad Corinthios*, 344r-v; citing 2 Cor 12:7.

dead, etc. I think that Paul was referring to that sort of boasting which was so certain and firm in itself that he did not hesitate to swear by it. What mind would not be receptive to such boasting for the sake of Christ? Who would refuse to undergo dangers for the sake of this truth?

Chrysostom reads this passage *nē tēn hymeteran kauchēsin*—that is, by *your* boasting—but I don't think this reading is correct. For, first of all, it is not very likely that the apostle wished to swear by that boasting that he had in Christ concerning the Corinthians, whom he remembered in 2 Corinthians 7, saying, "I have great confidence in you; I have great pride concerning you"—for that fact was uncertain. Second, Paul does not say "that *you have*," but "that *I have* in Christ Jesus our Lord." Whereby Paul isn't speaking about the boasting that the Corinthians had in Christ Jesus, and he quite correctly does not swear by that inasmuch as he is uncertain of it. Therefore, since Paul necessarily swears by his boasting that he had in Christ, I think it abundantly clear that Chrysostom's reading does not agree with the apostle's intention.

We learn from this passage that swearing an oath is permissible for Christians—though only when undertaken in an appropriate circumstance—seeing that the apostle did not hesitate to use an oath both in this and other passages. Commentary on 1 Corinthians 15:31.[53]

Paul Dies Every Day. The English Annotations: "I die daily"; that is, death hangs over me continually, and I daily prepare myself for it; or, I am not only in danger of my life every day, but I am continually afflicted with so many crosses and tribulations that my life is more like death than life. Annotations on 1 Corinthians 15:31.[54]

Ancient Arena Games. John Calvin: Now the phrase "they fought with wild beasts" does not refer to those who were thrown to wild beasts in the arena, as Erasmus has falsely supposed. Rather, it refers to those who were condemned to be handed over to fight with wild beasts to provide entertainment for the people. Thus there were two kinds of punishment that were totally different: to be thrown to the wild beasts and to fight wild beasts. For those who were thrown to wild beasts were straightaway torn to pieces; but those who fought wild beasts went forth into the arena armed so that, if they were endued with strength, courage, and agility, they might be able to escape by killing the wild beast. Indeed, there was even a sport in which those who fought wild beasts were trained like gladiators. Usually, however, very few escaped since the fighter who killed one wild beast was required to face a second, and so forth, until the cruelty of the spectators was satiated, or at least their mercy evoked. . . .

We see to what extremes God allowed his servant [Paul] to come, and also how miraculously he rescued him. No mention of this fight, however, appears in Luke. Hence we may infer that Paul endured many things that have not been written down. Commentary on 1 Corinthians 15:32.[55]

No Reason to Doubt That Paul Battled Beasts at Ephesus. Wolfgang Musculus: This is Paul's sense: "When I was at Ephesus, where I proclaimed Christ and fought with wild beasts, if I had not been aided by the spirit and power of God, and compelled by confidence in his truth . . . what advantage would I have expected from such horrible dangers . . . if indeed the dead are not raised? For even if by doing this I was hoping for a perfect kingdom, why would I allow myself to be mangled and eaten by beasts for a human kingdom (indeed, of this whole world), if in fact nothing could be expected after this life?"

That Christians were often condemned to wild beasts is plain in the writings of Tertullian. Since any general disaster was assumed by the pagan world to be a punishment, Christians were blamed

[53]Musculus, *Comm. 1 Cor.*, 671; citing 2 Cor 7:4. Chrysostom's treatment of this passage is found in his *Homilies of 1 Corinthians* (homily 40), in NPNF 12:245-46.
[54]Downame, *English Annotations*, FF1r*.

[55]CO 49:553 (cf. CTS 40:40). For Erasmus's translation of this verse, see his *Paraphrases*, 339.

for such disasters, and the people would shout: "The Christians to the lions!" From Tertullian [we learn that] believers were thrown to the wild beasts and thereafter mangled—with no one to plead their case, unarmed to protect themselves, often nude. From other authors, [we learn that] believers were sent as armed gladiators into the arena to fight wild beasts in front of spectators. But as far as Paul is concerned, it is debated whether he truly battled with wild beasts, lions, leopards, bears, etc., or whether he was speaking of his struggles for the truth of Christ against wicked men who *acted like* ferocious beasts. Theophylact follows the latter interpretation, attributing the beasts to the unbelieving Jews and the goldsmith Demetrius, who mangled and completely devoured Paul as if they were lions. Those who draw this conclusion are compelled by the fact that no mention is ever made in Acts that Paul was thrown to the wild beasts in Ephesus. On the other hand, those who hold to the prior sense think that metaphorical interpretations ought not to be rashly foisted on the plain meaning of a passage unless one is forced to do so by the absurdity, the impossibility, or the clear error of the plain meaning. The fact that Luke makes no mention of beasts does not prevent the plain sense here any more than the fact that, in Acts, no mention is made of the catalog of very grave dangers that Paul lists in 1 Corinthians 11. That is why it is recognized that Acts does not describe everything that the apostle experienced and suffered. If Luke would have reported that the apostle battled wild beasts in Ephesus, we would have believed it happened, even if Paul remained silent about it. So when Paul himself writes about something he experienced, why should I not believe that it happened, even if Luke wrote nothing about it? For this reason, I think that there is not sufficient reason to deviate from the simple and plain meaning of the words in this passage. Commentary on 1 Corinthians 15:32.[56]

[56]Musculus, *Comm. 1 Cor.*, 672-73. See Tertullian, *Apology* 40, in ANF 3:47.

Did Paul Actually Fight Wild Beasts? The English Annotations: Either the words are spoken figuratively or literally. If taken figuratively, Paul speaks of beasts to indicate beastly minded men, such as the Cretans, whom he calls "evil brutes, lazy gluttons" (Tit 1:12), or the kinds of men Ignatius of Antioch says he fought from Syria to Rome. . . . "not being bitten," he says, "by brute beasts, but by savage creatures in the shape of men." Or the words may be taken literally, as Chrysostom, Ambrose, and others understand the words. Nicephorus, in his *Ecclesiastical History*, reports it as literal, for it is certain that the Christians at that time were often condemned to the beasts. Likewise, it was common for people in Tertullian's day to say, "The Christians to the lions!" This literal interpretation affords a stronger argument for the resurrection, which is the scope of the text; and it better accords with the sense of Paul's previous argument than if we understand the words to mean a metaphorical fight. Annotation on 1 Corinthians 15:32.[57]

The Wicked Will Always Mock. Martin Luther: Here St. Paul is speaking in the role of the mockers who ridiculed and derided his preaching with these words. He quotes this saying from the prophet Isaiah (Is 22:13), who had had the same experience. . . . Undoubtedly St. Paul, too, had to hear something similar from his mockers. For this is a common saying that the world and all peasants and burghers and Sir Braggart[58] quote when God's Word is used to frighten them with death and hell: "Oh, the parsons tell us much about death; they paint a gruesome picture of the devil and make hell hot for us. Well, let us have a good drink together while life lasts. When we die, we are dead." . . . All right, Christians must listen to such

[57]Downame, *English Annotations*, FF1r*. See Ignatius of Antioch, *Letter to the Romans* 5, in ANF 1:75; Chrysostom's treatment of this verse is found in his *Homilies on 1 Corinthians* (homily 40), in NPNF 21:246. For Ambrose (Ambrosiaster), see his *Comment. in Epist. I ad Cor.*, in PL 17:281. For Nicephorus, see his *Ecclesiastical History* 2.25.

[58]Literally *Junker Scharrhans*.

mockery. They have to let these mockers have their say until things are cleared up and the time comes when these people will not despise death as they do now. For, praise be to God, I and others have often experienced and witnessed that our prophecy and preaching was borne out and that neither peasant nor junker was ever so impudent and proud when death confronted them as not to be frightened and angered by it. Then their previous mockery and defiance did not help them against death. For death is adept at making the proudest and the jolliest dejected and cowardly when he greets them but a little with pestilence. Then their heart and courage droop as they think of leaving their goods and their splendor behind. But if those who do not believe can be frightened so by death, there will surely be far more to frighten them in hell. There they will no longer say as they do now: "When we are dead, we are dead." But they will lie in eternal flames and lament and bewail the fact that they were ever born. They will have to curse and damn themselves for having heard God's Word and for having despised and derided it so blasphemously. Commentary on 1 Corinthians 15:32.[59]

Eat, Drink, for Tomorrow We Die! Heinrich Bullinger: But if the dead do not rise again, or if all human hope ends in death, what remains except to repeat the speech of those wicked people found in Isaiah 22, "Let us eat and drink, for tomorrow we die!" In this way the prophet describes the speech of the wicked, who were satiated by wealth, among whom there was nothing but joy and gladness, who were butchering young calves, cutting the throats of rams, eating their flesh and getting completely drunk, and then, at their banquets, between drinks, shouting out this song full of wickedness, "Let us eat and drink, for tomorrow we die!" This phrase appears to have been taken up either by an Egyptian ceremony where, during the banquet, they passed around a human skull, encouraging the dinner guests to live merrily since they would one day finally pass away from the human race; or, by the statement of Sardanapalus, the most wicked of men, whose epitaph the Latin translator of Strabo rendered with this verse: "Since you know that you are mortal, fill up on the present delights of the soul, for after death there are pleasures no more. For surely, I am now dust who recently controlled so much. . . ." Even today, many people recite brief verses of this sort; and they were also pompously sung back then by those very licentious people in Corinth. Commentary on 1 Corinthians 15:32.[60]

Bad Company Ruins Good Morals. Jacques Lefèvre d'Étaples: Naturally, all the words and carnal acts of the wicked corrupt good morals. Christ requires pure morals. Why do I force the prostitutes and pimps of Tibullus, Catullus, and Terence on the ears of adolescents and those having tender and unspoiled souls? Why do I force on impressionable people Ovid's heroes and those kinds of Siren songs that are deadly as well as poisonous? All such things prudent people avoid; how much more the Christian men and women, who will avoid them like rocks that cause shipwreck. Those who do such things, don't you know that they allure to corruption the tender souls of young people, marked by the Holy Spirit, and young virgins committed to Christ? Nevertheless, for those who destroy even one person, it is appointed (according to God's Word) that a millstone should be hung around their neck and they be thrown into the depths of the sea. "Do not be deceived: 'Bad company ruins good morals.'" Now if you do not wish to believe Menander, who first made this statement, then believe Paul, who now repeats the same thing. Christ wants pious people. He wants faithful people. Commentary on 1 Corinthians 15:33.[61]

[59]LW 28:157-59.

[60]Bullinger, *In Priorem ad Corinthios Epistolam Commentarius*, 248; citing Is 22:13. The Greek historian and geographer Strabo (born c. 64 BC) reported this epitaph of the infamously wicked king of Assyria Sardanapalus in his *Historical Sketches*.

[61]Lefèvre d'Étaples, *Commentariorum in Epistolas Beati Pauli . . . Liber Secundus*, 125v. Sixteenth-century church leaders frequently censored the licentious writings of ancient Latin authors such as the poets Tibullus (born c. 55 BC) and Catullus (born c. 87 BC),

Do Not Be Deceived! John Calvin: Since nothing is easier than to slip into profane speculation under the appearance of asking questions, Paul resists this danger by warning them that wicked conversations have greater effect than we might suppose in defiling our minds and corrupting our morals. To show this, Paul uses a quotation of the poet Menander, for we are at liberty to borrow from everywhere whatever comes forth from God. And since all truth is from God, there is no doubt that the Lord has placed in the mouth of even wicked people every doctrine that is true and salvific. However, I prefer the discussion of this matter found in Basil's oration *Address to Young Men*. Since Paul, therefore, knew that this proverb was well-known among the Greeks, he preferred to employ it so as to penetrate more quickly to their minds, instead of expressing the same idea in his own words. . . .

Here, therefore, Paul . . . warns that we must guard against all evil conversations, as we would against the most deadly poison, for they slip secretly into our minds and soon corrupt our entire life. Thus let us take note that nothing is more pestilential than wicked doctrines and profane arguments, which lure us even a little from the right and simple faith. It is not without good reason that Paul warns us not to be deceived. Commentary on 1 Corinthians 15:33.[62]

Christians Must Be Vigilant in Their Battle Against Sin. Martin Luther: Such diligent occupation and concern with God's Word St. Paul expresses with the words "wake up" or "be vigilant." He does not speak merely of waking up but of waking up fully, or being so wide awake that it can really and blessedly be called that, that is, according to God's Word. The world, too, is vigilant with regard to its affairs, but not with regard to God's Word. . . . But here, St. Paul says, we must watch so as not to sin. The world must watch against poverty, against disturbance of the peace, or against enemies, so that all may be well with people and country. But our watching serves to end sin and to prosper and preserve righteousness; it serves the reign of faith and of love and the extermination of unbelief. This demands that we earnestly occupy ourselves with and cultivate God's Word always and everywhere, snatch it up avidly, hear it, sing it, speak and read it gladly against the despicable satiety and indolence of which I have spoken. Then we will have our castle and fortress well-guarded and all holes closed to keep the devil from stealing in. Otherwise, if I or others fail to preach with diligence and if you don't hear it or are practiced in it, imagining that you are well acquainted with it—that is not watching or warding off but slumbering, letting your head droop; indeed, it is snorting right in the midst of the devil's guns and spears and affording him a good and safe place for breaking in and ascending into the castle without difficulty. This is what happened also to the Corinthians. Commentary on 1 Corinthians 15:34.[63]

Christian Soldiers Either Advance or Retreat. Tilemann Hesshus: Paul has interjected a sharp rebuke in order to shake the grogginess from the drowsy and presumptuous Corinthians, arousing them to seek the truth diligently and constantly defend it. He does this also to induce them to true fear, deep repentance, and training in true piety. Paul could easily see that there was a great and detestable presumption among the Corinthians, since they were so easily listening to the profane and wicked error that destroyed the whole Christian religion with one smear. And so he shakes them, as from the sleep of presumption, and urges them to take care lest they

and the playwright Terence (born c. 190 BC).

[62]CO 49:554 (cf. CTS 40:42-43). In his *Address to Young Men on the Right Use of Greek Literature*, Basil the Great (c. 329–379) notes, "Since we must need attain to the life to come through virtue, our attention is to be chiefly fastened upon those many passages from the poets, from the historians, and especially from the philosophers in which virtue itself is praised." In Frederick Morgan Padelford, *Essays on the Study and Use of Poetry by Plutarch and Basil the Great* (New Haven, CT: Yale University Press, 1902), 106.

[63]LW 28:166-67.

slip back into sin. For the Holy Spirit's gifts would gradually diminish and be forgotten unless they were enlivened by persistent repentance, study, meditation, prayer, and struggles against Satan's insults and schemes. The Christian soldier always either advances or retreats. But when they surrender themselves to inactivity and careless presumption, they are exposed to the various traps of Satan, who is intent either to seduce Christians into error or throw them headlong into sin and, in so doing, to overpower and extinguish faith from them.

Paul mentions that some of the Corinthians are ignorant of God. Surprisingly, the Corinthians were pleased with themselves on account of their wisdom and learning, but Paul finds fault with them because they did not yet know God as they should have. For those who allow themselves to be convinced that the dead do not arise again do not actually know God, nor believe the gospel; nor are they worthy of the name Christian. And so the Corinthians should rightly be filled with shame, because, although they were boasting of their great knowledge of religion, they were overturning the chief foundation of the Christian name and the sole object of all of our hope. Explication of 1 Corinthians 15:34.[64]

[64]Hesshus, *Explicatio Prioris Epistolae ad Corinthios*, 345v-346r.

15:35-49 The Resurrection Body

35 But someone will ask, "How are the dead raised?
With what kind of body do they come?" 36 You foolish
person! What you sow does not come to life unless it
dies. 37 And what you sow is not the body that is to be,
but a bare kernel, perhaps of wheat or of some other
grain. 38 But God gives it a body as he has chosen,
and to each kind of seed its own body. 39 For not all
flesh is the same, but there is one kind for humans,
another for animals, another for birds, and another
for fish. 40 There are heavenly bodies and earthly
bodies, but the glory of the heavenly is of one kind,
and the glory of the earthly is of another. 41 There is
one glory of the sun, and another glory of the moon,
and another glory of the stars; for star differs from
star in glory.

42 So is it with the resurrection of the dead. What is
sown is perishable; what is raised is imperishable. 43 It is
sown in dishonor; it is raised in glory. It is sown in
weakness; it is raised in power. 44 It is sown a natural
body; it is raised a spiritual body. If there is a natural
body, there is also a spiritual body. 45 Thus it is written,
"The first man Adam became a living being";[a] the last
Adam became a life-giving spirit. 46 But it is not the
spiritual that is first but the natural, and then the
spiritual. 47 The first man was from the earth, a man of
dust; the second man is from heaven. 48 As was the man
of dust, so also are those who are of the dust, and as is
the man of heaven, so also are those who are of heaven.
49 Just as we have borne the image of the man of dust,
we shall[b] also bear the image of the man of heaven.

a Greek *a living soul* **b** Some manuscripts *let us*

Overview: In this section, the apostle Paul anticipates objections from the Corinthians by explaining how material bodies subject to weakness, sin, disease, death, and decay can be raised incorruptible, immortal, and sinless. Reformation commentators endorse with enthusiasm Paul's use of illustrations drawn from everyday life, such as germinating seeds and the splendor of heavenly bodies, to demonstrate the reality of the resurrection of the body. Even as God gives life to tiny dry seeds that, after being "buried" in the earth, spring to life to produce an abundant harvest, so too God will resurrect the Christian dead from the grave and bestow on them new and glorious bodies. This raises difficult questions, however, about the nature of resurrection bodies and how they differ from earthly bodies. For the magisterial reformers, the *substance* of humans' bodily existence will not change in the future resurrection: men and women will still be clothed in bodies. But whereas the earthly body is animated by the human soul, is subject to corruption and death, and is dependent on food, drink, clothing, and sleep for its existence, the heavenly or spiritual body will be empowered by the Holy Spirit and thus be immortal, incorruptible, glorious, and strong. Following Paul's argument, Reformation commentators conclude this section by showing that Christian hope in a future resurrection is predicated on the life, death, and resurrection of Jesus Christ, the second Adam or the Second Man, who, having reversed the curse of the first Adam, remains the source and author of resurrection life. Paul's description of Christ as "the second man from heaven" encourages several interpreters to probe matters of high Christology. At the same time, the magisterial reformers explicitly repudiate the doctrine of the celestial flesh of Christ, taught by Dutch Anabaptist leaders such as Melchior Hoffman and Menno Simons, which stated that Jesus Christ's human body came from heaven rather than from the womb of the Virgin Mary.

15:35-38 *The Example of the Seed*

Paul Uses Similitudes to Shed Light on Lofty Secrets. Simon Goulart: [Another] proof is taken from several created objects that somewhat represent the resurrection to come. They are presented to us by way of a similitude so as to make this lofty secret somewhat more familiar to us. St. Paul in 1 Corinthians 15 uses the examples of grain, various bodies, the sun, moon, and stars. To these examples we can add that each day is like a picture of our life, with the night and sleep representing death. When we awake, we return from death to life; this is an ordinary sign of the resurrection of the body. Several ancient and contemporary writers have also pointed to other similitudes, such as the sun rising on our horizon, the stages of the moon, the phoenix rising out of the ashes, and many sorts of birds that, having become dull in the winter, return to vigor in the springtime. On the Resurrection of the Dead.[1]

Paul Addresses Three Main Objections. David Dickson: The third part of this chapter follows in which Paul answers three objections of his adversaries. The first objection is this: It seems impossible that the dead should arise, for how can this happen? The second objection: No one can describe with what bodies they shall arise. The third objection: What shall become of those people who are alive at the coming of the Lord; since they have not died, how can they rise again? Annotations on 1 Corinthians 15:35.[2]

Seed-Sowing as an Image of Resurrection. Desiderius Erasmus: Now since there will be a future resurrection, more inquisitive persons will ask how this will happen, or what sort of body will they have when they arise from the dead, inasmuch as these present bodies of ours are changed into ashes, or earth, or something more disgusting. You are a fool who wonders whether God is able at some time to resuscitate bodies, since nature does this daily when it germinates a seed. For after a dry and dead seed is planted into the earth, it seems to rot there, and so finally when it comes forth from the earth, it is as if it is reborn and restored to life—indeed, it is revivified in a manner just as if it were previously dead and buried. And the appearance of the plant that is reborn through the seed is very different from what was planted in the furrow. A tiny, contemptible, dark, and dry little seed is buried in the soil, it decays in the mud, and then, as if coming back to life, it springs forth as a tender seedling, and soon as a stalk and then with an ear of grain. But none of these were visible in that tiny seed that you entrusted to the earth. . . . And look at what a small seed sprouts into such a great tree, with its powerful trunk, its winding roots, its broadly dispersed branches, its lush canopy of leaves, its pleasant blossoms, its abundant fruit. None of these things was present when you buried that contemptible, tiny seed in the earth. And yet you dared to hope for all these things, depending on the power of nature—and do you not dare to expect the same from God, depending on him who is all-powerful? Paraphrases on 1 Corinthians 15.[3]

The Value of Using Illustrations to Teach Doctrine. Martin Luther: What a precious artist St. Paul becomes here, painting and carving the resurrection into everything that grows on earth! He encompasses everything with the words "what you sow," namely, all sorts of grains and plants. He employs all of this as an illustration or a painting with which to inculcate this article and everywhere to illustrate it visually. This he does despite the fact that he has already proved it mightily with Scripture and God's Word; that might have sufficed. For whoever will not believe or cannot be persuaded by God's Word and the example or experience of the resurrection initiated in Christ will very likely be preached to in vain by illustrations and examples. It should suffice for Christians to hear God's Word declare that they will come forth from the earth alive, with body, soul, and all senses. They should regard that as true and certain because God said it. They should not inquire

[1]Goulart, *XXVIII Discours Chrestiens*, 308-9.
[2]Dickson, *Exposition of St. Paul's Epistles*, 68*.
[3]Erasmus, *Paraphrases*, 339-40.

further how this will happen but should leave that to God. For He who is able to raise all the dead from the earth with one word will surely also know how to bestow a form and an essence that will serve and be appropriate to the heavenly, eternal life. . . .

Those who believe God's Word that Christ has risen and that we shall rise with him are well served by such illustrations. They are like silk kerchiefs or paper bags into which they can place this article to carry it with them. For this is what we use allegories and illustrations for, to lay hold of doctrine better and always to bear it in mind. In that way we have it before our eyes daily and are constantly reminded of it. Commentary on 1 Corinthians 15:35-38.[4]

Paul Answers Scoffers Who Deny the Resurrection. Tilemann Hesshus: This is the sixth section of the chapter, where Paul describes the mode of the future resurrection and refutes the blasphemies of those who were criticizing the doctrine of the resurrection of the dead as an absurd fable and something completely impossible. In the same way, the Sadducees were drawing many absurd conclusions from the resurrection of the dead. "A woman," they were saying, "was married to seven brothers in turn; whose wife, therefore, will she be at the resurrection of the dead?" (see Mt 22:28). In a similar fashion, the Epicureans were throwing out their objections: "We see that human bodies are reduced to dust and scattered; how then is it possible for bodies to be resurrected? And what will be the form and activities of bodies in the next life? Won't they require food and drink, rest and sleep? Won't they engage in work? Won't they be exposed to diseases and sorrows?" They found enormous pleasure in heaping ridicules of this sort. But Paul, endowed with the apostolic spirit, condemns as complete foolishness these sorts of wicked arguments of human reason and mocking against the clear Word of God, and he shows that God places before our eyes each and every year the image of resurrection through the natural world. Indeed, by the very food that nourishes us, we can refute the insanity of those who mock that it is impossible for bodies that have been reduced to dust to rise again. For we scatter seeds over the earth and watch them decay and die in the ground, yet we have no doubt that, after several months, an abundant harvest will be gleaned when they grow larger. Why, therefore, do you doubt that our bodies, which are scattered and decay in a similar fashion, can rise from the dead? He who gives life to dead seed and produces a plentiful harvest from them is the same God who is able both to bring life to the bodies of dead human beings and bring them forth from the earth. . . .

And the seed that you sow is not the body that is produced. Instead, once a plain seed of grain is planted in the earth, God, according to his marvelous wisdom, then produces first the shoot, then the stem, then an ear of grain, then many ears bursting with abundant grain. And God gives to each and every kind of grain its own body. The same thing will be true in the resurrection of the dead. For the bodies that rise again will not have the same stench and weakness with which they were entrusted to the earth, but God will bring forth from the earth altogether new and glorious bodies. That is not to say that different bodies will be resurrected; rather, this same body, which we now possess, will be made alive again. As Job says, "After my skin shall be destroyed, then in my flesh I will see God" (Job 19:26).

But the condition of that future body will be very different from our present bodies. For our bodies now require food, drink, sleep, rest, and clothing. They become hungry. They are subject to disease and sickness, and they suffer from various difficulties. But in the future, our bodies will be glorified, living forever without food or drink, just like the Spirit. They will experience no evil; they will be full of splendor. Thus people are altogether foolish when they employ human reason to ridicule the doctrine of the resurrection of the dead. Explication of 1 Corinthians 15:35-38.[5]

[4]LW 28:175.

[5]Hesshus, *Explicatio Prioris Epistolae ad Corinthios*, 346v-347v. The Epicureans, followers of the Greek philosopher Epicurus

Death Does Not Destroy Our Bodies. John Trapp: Paul here provides an answer to the Epicureans' second question, "With what body do they come? With a dead, diseased, rotten body, etc.?" No, no says the apostle. Sin is only rotted with its accompanying infirmities. But the rotting of the body is only like the rotting of corn under the dirt, that it may arise incorruptible; or like the melting of an old metal plate in the fire to bring it out in a better condition. Christ was buried in a garden to demonstrate that death does not destroy our bodies, but only to sow them, for the dew of the grass will revive them again. Commentary on 1 Corinthians 15:37.[6]

15:39-41 *Earthly and Heavenly Bodies*

The Resurrected Body Will Be a Fleshly Body. Cardinal Cajetan: Paul introduces his second illustration from the universality of bodies, since every sort of physical body belongs to one of four species, namely, creatures that fly, creatures that swim, human beings, and the rest of those creatures that walk (by which it is understood also those creatures that slither or crawl). And Paul wishes to make clear from this that the future body in the resurrection will be from flesh, a point that was not made evident in his first example [of the seed]. Paul wishes it to be understood from the great diversity of bodies—or rather, from the fact that every possible bodily difference is found in this world—that one will also find established in the future new world a body suitable to that new world, with every bodily difference suitable to that newness. Commentary on 1 Corinthians 15:39.[7]

Will There Be Differences Among Resurrected Bodies? Wolfgang Musculus: Various interpreters explain this passage in different ways. Some relate this comparison of flesh and bodies to the difference of glory that will exist among resurrected bodies after the resurrection, by which some will be more distinguished in accordance to the superiority of their merits. Hence, in this sense: Not only will the nature of our body in the resurrection be different from that nature it has in death and the grave, but also, when we are resurrected, there will be a great difference between those who have been resurrected as it relates to the splendor of the glorified bodies. For just as in this life, some creatures possess the body of a human, others of an animal, others of a fish, others of a bird, although all are of the same flesh (as it pertains to its substance); and just as bodies differ among themselves, some of which are celestial bodies and others earthly bodies, although they all share a bodily nature; and just as glory differs among celestial bodies, so that one star differs from another in splendor, and the moon is brighter than the stars, and in truth the sun surpasses the moon in its splendor, though they share the same celestial substance—so it will be in the resurrection of the dead. Some, like the sun, will reflect the glory of Christ; others will reflect the glory of the patriarchs; others the glory of the prophets; others the glory of the apostles; others the glory of pastors and doctors; still others the glory of the rest of the faithful—although all will share in the joy and immortality of the future resurrection. This interpretation is followed by church fathers such as Chrysostom, Ambrose, and Augustine. . . .

Other interpreters do not think this text refers to the difference between resurrected bodies, whereby either the elect are distinguished from the reprobate, or the elect are distinguished among themselves on the basis of different splendor. Rather, they think that this text refers to the same difference mentioned in the previous example, where the body produced from its seed indicates how a body springs forth with different qualities. This explanation is most acceptable to me also. Commentary on 1 Corinthians 15:39.[8]

(c. 341–270 bc), believed that humans should strive for emotional tranquility by avoiding pain and pursuing pleasure, especially the pleasure of contemplation.

[6]Trapp, *A Commentary or Exposition* 700*.

[7]Cajetan, *In Sacrae Scripturae expositionem*, 5:145.

[8]Musculus, *Comm. 1 Cor.*, 687-88. Chrysostom's treatment of this verse is found in his *Homilies of 1 Corinthians* (homily 41), in

The Glory of Heavenly and Earthly Bodies. Cardinal Cajetan: Paul introduces his third illustration from the difference between heavenly bodies and earthly bodies. The sun, moon, and stars are called heavenly bodies. On the other hand, earthly bodies are trees and other plant life and minerals that are fixed on the earth. "But the glory of heavenly bodies is of one kind, and the glory of earthly bodies is of another." Paul is attributing glory to bodies metaphorically, in proportion to how much they possess in themselves that is worthy of praise (and, in that sense, glorified). Whence their disposition or quality that renders them praiseworthy is called their glory, because it is the source of glory. But Paul notes that the disposition or quality by which heavenly bodies are praised is different from and far superior to that by which earthly bodies are praised. Commentary on 1 Corinthians 15:40.[9]

More Like Spirits Than Bodies. John Trapp: The glory of our terrestrial bodies shall, at the resurrection, be celestial. They shall be more like spirits than bodies, so clear and transparent (said Aquinas) that all the veins, humors, nerves, and bowels shall be seen as in a glass. They shall be conformed to the glorified body of Christ, as to the standard. Commentary on 1 Corinthians 15:40.[10]

Despite Differences in Glory, Heavenly Bodies Share the Same Essence. Martin Luther: In the third place, after Paul has spoken of all kinds of living bodies, he also speaks of other bodies in general. Thus he briefly mentions all the physical or visible creatures, gold, silver, fire, water, stone, wood, iron, and whatever other terrestrial things there may be. And then he also mentions everything up in the heavens, sun, moon, planets, and other stars, which he calls "celestial bodies." There are so very many terrestrial or celestial bodies, and yet each one is distinguished in kind from the other. The one is always more glorious and precious than the other: gold is better than lead; silver is better than straw; jewels are better than fieldstones. And among the celestial bodies the sun is more resplendent and beautiful than the moon, and one star is more beautiful and brighter than another. And yet all stars have one nature or body. And everything on earth is also God's creature, the least as well as the greatest and the most precious. Similarly, in the life to come, too, there will be various differences with regard to brightness and glory. And yet all will be of one heavenly essence as one body and as members of Christ. So there are many and various members in one natural body, each bearing its own name and fulfilling its own functions or offices, and yet all partake of the one essence and nature of the one body. Commentary on 1 Corinthians 15:39-42.[11]

Future Glory in Heaven Not Derived from Our Merits. Wolfgang Musculus: The church fathers, since they believe that the glory of the future life will be different according to the diversity of merits of righteousness, explain this passage as follows: There is one glory of the sun, and another glory of the moon, and another glory of the stars; and indeed, stars differ from others stars in glory. Thus it will also be in the resurrection of the dead. There is one glory of the sun, that is, of Christ; another glory of the moon, that is of the blessed Virgin (according to Nicolas of Lyra); another glory of the stars, that is, of the saints. And stars differ from other stars in glory; that is, some saints were more illustrious than others on account of the merits they performed. This conclusion holds more that is debatable than certain and useful, especially because they measure the difference of the future glory of the sons of God according to the good works of this present life—a view that I do not know how it can be reconciled to the glory of the grace of God. If the glory of the

NPNF 12:251-52. For Ambrose (Ambrosiaster), see his *Comment. in Epist. I ad Cor.*, in PL 17:282-83.

[9]Cajetan, *In Sacrae Scripturae expositionem*, 5:145.

[10]Trapp, *A Commentary or Exposition*, 700*. See Aquinas, *Summa Theologica*, Supplement, Q. 85.

[11]LW 28:183-84.

future life is distributed according to the merits we perform, the apostle should not have said in the previous analogy, "Truly, God gives it a body as he wishes," but rather "God gives it a body as it deserves." Thus, as others have noted, unless eternal life should be distinguished from God's glory, so that the *gift* of God is eternal life, but human merit is the *glory* of eternal life, then how can this opinion be reconciled with sacred Scripture? And though without a doubt it should be conceded that some people will be more illustrious than others in the future life, nevertheless it is a very dangerous doctrine to attribute it to our merits. Peter Martyr Vermigli, a man especially well-trained in the sacred Scriptures, has treated this question in detail in his locus on this present passage, to which I refer the reader. Commentary on 1 Corinthians 15:41.[12]

The Christian's Great Hope. Balthasar Hubmaier: I believe and confess the resurrection of the body. Yea, of this very body that now clothes me. Even if it should be consumed by worms, drowned, decomposed, burned; yea and even if my temporal honor, property, body, and life are taken away, I will still first receive the true honor that is valid before God, imperishable possessions, and impassable, transfigured, immortal body, and eternal life on the day of the joyous resurrection of my flesh. O my mild Lord Jesus Christ, strengthen and preserve me in faith! Twelve Articles of the Christian Faith.[13]

15:42-44 *The Body Sown Perishable Will Be Raised Imperishable*

The Superiority of Our Future Spiritual Bodies. Tilemann Hesshus: Paul provides examples to illustrate the doctrine of the resurrection of the dead. And he demonstrates how much more excellent and illustrious our bodies will be in the resurrection of the dead than in this present life. When our bodies are committed to the earth—this is likened to sowing. For the heavenly Father is like a farmer, and we are God's wheat and agriculture. "Our bodies are sown perishable"; that is, they are subject to corruption for as long as we dwell in this life, until we are swallowed up in death. But in the resurrection, our bodies will be subject to no corruption or change; instead, they will be immortal. "Our bodies are sown in dishonor; they are raised in glory." Our bodies are dishonorable in the sense that they are polluted with many sins, deprived of that purity with which they were adorned at the beginning of creation, and because of this sin they are subject to God's wrath and death and necessarily return to the dust. . . . Thus our bodies endure the disgrace of the grave because, on account of our sins, we are swallowed up in death. "But they are raised in glory." Our bodies will be adorned with their original purity; no filth of sin will be seen in them. Their purity will shine forth brightly, and they will be clothed in beauty and glory. "It is sown in weakness," for our bodies in this life are subject to a variety of diseases and accidents. We are in need of food and drink, clothing and shelter. We suffer hunger. And we find it difficult to protect ourselves from the cold, storms, heat, and wild beasts. Without warning we are exposed to a thousand dangers; a grape seed, a fly, or a morsel of bread can kill a person. Thus the weakness of our bodies in this life is enormous, and in the end they must necessarily rot in the grave. But these same bodies "are raised in power." At that time, Paul says, they will be endowed with renewed strength; they will not grow weary from labor; they will not be afflicted by disease; they will not be exposed to dangers; they will not experience any difficulties. Explication of 1 Corinthians 15:42-43.[14]

The Nature of the Resurrection Body. Simon Goulart: As for the corruption that now presses down the soul, and the vices by which the flesh lusts against the spirit, such flesh shall cease to be, because it could not be able to possess the

[12]Musculus, *Comm. 1 Cor.*, 691. For Vermigli's interpretation, see *Common Places*, 327-50

[13]CRR 5:240.

[14]Hesshus, *Explicatio Prioris Epistolae ad Corinthios*, 349r-v.

kingdom of God. In regard to the substance of the same flesh, it shall not be abolished, but still remain, but everlastingly glorified. For this reason, St. Paul said, "That body, being sown a fleshly body, shall rise again as a spiritual body." Because there shall be so strong a union between the soul and the body that the soul making the body to live without any supply of nourishment, and having no more combat and striving within us between the spirit and the flesh, all being then spirit, we shall not feel any enemies, assaults, or dangers whatsoever—without or within—but shall be filled, compassed about, satiated, crowned with permanent glory. . . . The belief of this article encourages all Christians, but particularly wise old men, to bear patiently their infirmities and maladies. The Wise Vieillard.[15]

Our Bodies Raised in Honor and Power. Martin Luther: No matter how dishonorable or worthless [our body] is at present, it will return in a form so honorable and precious that its future honor and glory will surpass the present shame and dishonor many thousand times. Every creature will be amazed over it, all the angels will sing praises and smile admiringly at it, and God himself will take delight in it. This is why it is described as "sown." It is like the seed. That too must submit to being cast away so shamefully, to being scraped into the ground, and to having feet tread over it at the place where it will later grow again. The same process is experienced here, because it is really the work of God. He himself wants to create it anew, so that it no longer remains frail and filthy as it is now but becomes perfectly pure and precious.

We . . . know that later and at the proper time the body, weak and devoid of all strength and power though it may be when it lies in the grave, will be so strong that with one finger it will be able to carry this church, with one toe it will be able to move a tower and play with a mountain as children play with a ball. And in the twinkling of an eye it will be able to leap to the clouds or traverse a hundred miles. For then the body will be sheer strength, as it is now sheer feebleness and weakness. Nothing that it decides to do will be impossible for it. It will be able to defeat the whole world alone. It will become so light and nimble that it will soar both down here on earth and up above in the heavens in a moment. Commentary on 1 Corinthians 15:43.[16]

The Difference Between Natural and Spiritual Bodies. John Calvin: Paul sums up everything in a word by saying that the body that is now natural [*animale*] will at that time be spiritual. Now the one is called natural [*animale*] because it is fashioned by the soul [*anima*], and the other is called spiritual because it is fashioned by the Spirit [*spiritu*]. At present, it is the soul [*anima*] that gives life to the body, preventing it from becoming a corpse—hence, the natural body takes its name very appropriately from it. But after the resurrection, the power that gives life to the body will be the Spirit—which is more excellent. Let us always keep in mind what we have previously noted, that there is but one and the same substance of the body and that it is only the quality that is being referred to here. To make things clear, let the present quality of the body be called *animation*, and the future quality be called *inspiration*. For the soul now gives life to the body by means of many intervening supports; for we are in need of drink, food, clothing, sleep, and other such things. Hence the weakness of *animation* is clearly demonstrated. But the power of the Spirit for giving life will be much more complete, exempt from all necessities of this sort. This is the simple and straightforward meaning of the apostle. Commentary on 1 Corinthians 15:44.[17]

The Natural Body Becomes a Spiritual Body. Wolfgang Musculus: "It is sown a natural body, and raised a spiritual body." In sum, this body of ours, which dies and is buried, is a natural [*animale*] body; but when it is raised, it will

[15]Goulart, *The Wise Vieillard*, 187-88*.

[16]LW 28:187-88.

[17]CO 40:557 (cf. CTS 30:50-51).

no longer be a natural body, but a spiritual one. The natural body is corruptible, inglorious, and weak; but the spiritual body is incorruptible, glorious, and strong. Commentary on 1 Corinthians 15:44.[18]

Resurrection of Our Bodies, Made Better. John Donne: God shall not give me another, a better body at the resurrection, but the same body made better. For . . . if the flesh of human beings was not to be saved, the Author of salvation would never have taken the flesh of human beings on himself. Sermon Preached at Whitehall.[19]

Meaning of the "Spiritual Body." The English Annotations: "Raised a spiritual body"—not in regard to substance or being, but in regard to those qualities of which glorified bodies shall partake, that is, that besides the life they have by their souls, they shall be sustained without any bodily means, and kept in an eternal, incorruptible, blessed, and glorious life by the supernatural power of the Holy Spirit, infused into them by Jesus Christ. Or, by "spiritual body," Paul may mean (as some ancient interpreters affirm) a body free from carnal desires, being wholly subject to and ruled by the Spirit. Annotations on 1 Corinthians 15:44.[20]

15:45-49 *The First and Last Adam*

Adam, the First Man. Wolfgang Musculus: Paul calls Adam the "first man" not only by virtue of time and rank in which he was formed by God first (in the same way that people are accustomed to speak of the first day in the week, or the first year of some reign) but also for being the original starting point, who was created as head and source of all human posterity. The first tree in a garden is the first one planted in it. It is first in a twofold sense: first in time and first in propagation, so that all other trees are propagated from it. Adam is the first man in this twofold manner. Commentary on 1 Corinthians 15:45.[21]

The Nature of the Human Soul. John Calvin: Lest it appear that what he said about the natural [*animali*] body was a newly invented idea, Paul quotes Scripture, which states that "Adam became a living soul," meaning that his body was quickened by the soul, so that he became a living human being. It is asked what the meaning of the word "soul" is here. It is well-known that the Hebrew word *nepeš* [soul], which Moses employs, has a variety of meanings. But in this present passage, it means either the life principle or the very essence of life itself. The second of these senses I greatly prefer. I observe that the same thing is said about the animals, that they became a living soul, but while the soul of every living creature ought to be judged according to its kind, there is nothing to prevent a soul—that is to say, the life principle—from being common to all of them. And yet there remains something peculiar and distinct to the human soul, namely, that which is essentially immortal, such as the light of intelligence and reason. Commentary on 1 Corinthians 15:45.[22]

Adam Was Created to Live a Natural Life. Tilemann Hesshus: Paul demonstrates the phrase "natural body" [*animalis corporis*] from the testimony of sacred Scripture, Genesis 2, "And God breathed into his face the breath of life, and the man became a living soul." Here Moses states in a concise fashion both that God breathed on and imparted to the man a rational soul, and that, from the union of the soul with the body, he gave him a natural life [*vitam animalem*], which was in need of food, drink, sleep, and clothing. And Paul teaches that, even if Adam had not sinned, but had persisted in that purity and righteousness in which he was created, nevertheless he would have lived a natural life that was in need of nourishment until God transferred him to that celestial and spiritual

[18]Musculus, *Comm. 1 Cor.*, 697.
[19]Donne, *Sermons of John Donne*, 4:61*.
[20]Downame, *English Annotations*, FF1r*.
[21]Musculus, *Comm. 1 Cor.*, 699.
[22]CO 49:558 (cf. CTS 40:51); citing Gen 2:7; 1:20, 24.

life. There is no doubt that Adam, created in the image of God, was indwelt by the Holy Spirit and was created in righteousness and true holiness. But this righteousness and holiness did not exist apart from the Holy Spirit. And thus Adam was influenced by the Holy Spirit, but he did not live a fully spiritual or celestial life, but rather a natural [*animalem*] life, which was in need of food and drink. Therefore Paul teaches from the testimony of the Scripture that the first man was created for a natural life [*vitam animalem*], from which proceeded the natural life of all human beings. Explication of 1 Corinthians 15:45.[23]

Jesus Christ Is the Second Adam. The English Annotations: The second Adam, that is, Jesus Christ the head of all the elect, is ordained by God to be the fountain and author of spiritual and eternal life by the communication of the Spirit, who restores life unto the dead, and preserves them in life forever. Just as Christ after his resurrection now has a spiritual body, immortal and incorruptible (Phil 3:21), so also shall he give similar bodies to all who descend from him, not by way of any natural propagation, but by spiritual regeneration. For each Adam communicates to his offspring that which he possesses, the one by nature, the other by grace. Annotations on 1 Corinthians 15:45.[24]

Adam's Creation Proves That God Can Resurrect Us. Martin Luther: St. Paul says: "The first man was from the earth, a man of dust; the second Man is from heaven." That is to say that we are, beginning with the birth of the first man Adam, nothing but flesh and blood and entirely earthly; for as Scripture says (Gen 2:7), he was "formed of dust from the ground." Paul here refers to that statement. If you have read that in Scripture and are able to believe such a miracle, that God made that Adam from and of the earth, then you can surely also believe that he will make a celestial body from the other, the heavenly Adam. Just place a clod of earth next to a living human being. Then ask yourselves what comparison there is between that clod of dirt and that beautiful living picture that is Adam? Yet the latter is nothing more than that same clod of dirt converted into blood, flesh, veins, bone, eyes, ears, head, etc. If God can make a living person with all his members and powers from this dirt, should he not be able to form a spiritual, celestial body from the present natural body, which already possesses the nature or the essence of the body? Commentary on 1 Corinthians 15:47.[25]

The Breadth of God's Gracious Plan. John Donne: God began the first world with only two people, Adam and Eve. The second world, after the flood, he began with a greater number, the eight people preserved on the ark. But when he establishes the last and everlasting world in the final resurrection, he will admit such a great number that none of us who are here now, or have been, or will be on the face of the earth, will be denied in that resurrection, if we have truly felt this grace. For grace accepted is the infallible earnest of glory. Sermon Preached on Easter Day Evening.[26]

The Celestial Flesh of Christ. Menno Simons: The heavenly Seed, namely, the Word of God, was sown in Mary, and by her faith, being conceived in her by the Holy Ghost, became flesh, and was nurtured in her body; and thus it is called the fruit of her womb, the same as a natural fruit or offspring is called the fruit of its natural mother. For Christ Jesus, as to his origin, is no earthly man, that is, a fruit of the flesh and blood of Adam. He is a heavenly fruit or man. For his beginning or origin is of the Father, like unto the first Adam, sin excepted. Brief Confession on the Incarnation.[27]

[23]Hesshus, *Explicatio Prioris Epistolae ad Corinthios*, 350v; citing Gen 2:7.
[24]Downame, *English Annotations*, FF1r*.
[25]LW 28:194.
[26]Donne, *Sermons of John Donne*, 7:117.
[27]Simons, *Complete Writings*, 437. As this quotation indicates, Menno Simons rejected the idea that Christ received his human nature from Mary since, he believed, that would taint him with

The Earthly Adam and the Heavenly Adam. Heinrich Bullinger: The first Adam is of the earth; therefore, all those who are born from him are of the earth. In addition, Paul has called "earthly" those who are subject to corruption and affected by death. For it is written, "You are dust and to dust you will return." The second Adam, the Lord Christ, the true Man, has been made celestial by the resurrection; therefore, all those who will be raised by his power will be of heaven. Now, Paul compares the celestial to the earthly so that we might understand that people who have abandoned the senses and affections of this earthly body have now been made immortal and heavenly. Paul is saying nothing here about the Lord's incarnation, as if Jesus did not take on true human flesh from the Virgin Mary through the Holy Spirit, but brought an imaginary flesh with him from heaven. Commentary on 1 Corinthians 15:47.[28]

The Man from Heaven. Tilemann Hesshus: In order to demonstrate the extraordinary difference between the future and present life, Paul again compares the two "roots" to each other: Adam who was the originator of the human race, and Christ who was the originator of the church. The natural life was produced from Adam, while the spiritual life was given to us by Christ. And it is possible to see how great a difference there is between them by considering their persons. Adam was created from the dust of the earth and was earthly—a creature of God. But the second man, Christ, is the Lord from heaven; that is, he is not only a true human being, having assumed our flesh, which he acquired from the Virgin Mary, but at the same time he is also Lord Jehovah himself, the eternal and omnipotent God, who descended from heaven and was made a human being. Therefore the author of the future life, the second Adam, is superior to and more powerful than the first Adam, who is under the control of the natural life. We should not be surprised that the life which comes from God's Christ is superior to that which comes from Adam. Let the reader take note here of the singular testimony of both natures of Jesus Christ. As to his human nature, he was named Jesus Christ, for he received true human flesh from the Virgin Mary. Second, Paul confirms that this Jesus is the Lord from heaven. Hence it is testified that Christ is the eternal and omnipotent Jehovah God, who descended from heaven for the sake of our salvation. Nevertheless, there are not two Christs, but one Christ, who is both man and the Lord from heaven. On the basis of this passage, the Valentinians and Anabaptists attempt to prove that the flesh of Christ was brought down from heaven and was not of the same kind as our human nature. But Paul is not saying this. Rather he wishes to show that Christ is not only a human, as Adam was a genuine human, but at the same time he is the eternal Lord Jehovah God from heaven. Christ's divine nature is from heaven, for indeed, the Son was begotten from the essence of the Father from eternity. Christ's humanity comes from the womb of the Virgin Mary. Certainly, because the two natures are joined in the union of the one person, Paul rightly stated that the Second Man is Lord from heaven, just as it is rightly stated that the human Christ is from eternity. For though Christ's humanity has not existed from eternity, nevertheless, through the communication of the attributes, that which is proper to one nature is attributed to the entire person *in concreto* because of the hypostatic union. For that person, who is human, is the Lord from heaven. And that person is from eternity, namely, according to his divine nature. Explication of 1 Corinthians 15:48.[29]

Adam's original sin. Instead, Simons followed Melchior Hoffman in arguing for the "celestial flesh" of Christ, a doctrine that became distinctive of early Dutch Anabaptists. Modern-day Mennonites no longer hold this view. See Timothy George, *Theology of the Reformers*, 289-93.

[28]Bullinger, *In Priorem ad Corinthios Epistolam Commentarius*, 253; citing Gen 3:19.

[29]Hesshus, *Explicatio Prioris Epistolae ad Corinthios*, 351v-352r. Hesshus here addresses an ancient christological controversy over how the properties of Christ's human and divine natures communicate in the unity of his person. This controversy was revisited by Lutheran and Reformed theologians in the sixteenth century, in large part as it related to Christ's corporal presence in the Lord's Supper. See Muller, *Dictionary of Latin and Greek Theological Terms*, 72-74.

Paul Is Not Teaching the Celestial Flesh of Christ. Wolfgang Musculus: Now note carefully, reader, how foolish those people are who conclude from the fact that the apostle here calls Christ the Lord from heaven . . . that his flesh was not received from the virgin mother, but brought down from heaven. If they conclude consistently, then *our* flesh is not from the earth, but has its origin in heaven. For thus we would be celestial, just as the Lord himself existed in heaven. Commentary on 1 Corinthians 15:47-48.[30]

Christ's Body Did Not Come from Heaven. The English Annotations: The meaning is not that Christ brought his body from heaven, because Adam received his body from the earth. Rather, as John's baptism is said to be from heaven (though neither he nor the water with which he baptized descended from heaven, but because he received it from God, who is in heaven), so also Christ our Lord, according to human nature, is said to be from heaven because his human nature was formed by the Holy Spirit, and united to the divine. In this regard his generation was divine and heavenly. Annotations on 1 Corinthians 15:47-48.[31]

Image Bearers of the First and Second Adam. Huldrych Zwingli: If at the present time we bear the image of an earthly human being, made of dust, we will one day bear the image of the heavenly Adam. For, just as Christ initially carried around an earthly body, later, after his resurrection, he had a heavenly, spiritual, and immortal body. And so also we who believe in Christ initially bear this earthly and corruptible body, but will one day bear a spiritual and heavenly body. And just as Christ died in the body—and yet his soul lived on—so too we also will sleep in the body, that is, we will die but our souls will live on. This is how those people understood that article of faith in the Apostles' Creed, which stated: "I believe in the resurrection of the flesh and the life everlasting." Now by this confession they not only understood the life that would come after the judgment day, but also the life believers in Christ experience immediately after death. For Christ says: "Those who believe in me will have eternal life." But this life is not eternal sleeping—it is not sleep—but perpetual laughter, rejoicing, and indescribable gladness. Therefore God the Father wished to show us these things in the death and life of his Son so that we might have certainty that—being finally united with Christ—he who took on flesh for us was born for us, lived for us, died for us, and at last was resurrected and brought back to life for us. This is what Irenaeus says: "Christ's body feeds our bodies to immortality," namely, that our souls will certainly be rendered victorious, just as was the soul of Christ.[32] And also that our flesh will arise to immortality, just as our flesh has been united with the divine Christ. Therefore, as the first body that dies and decays comes from Adam, so the second body that rises again resplendent, glorious, and immortal is from Christ—for we bear the image of both. And both are our parents: the first is the source of corruption and sin; the second is the source immortality and grace. In the former, we live with affliction and trouble; in the latter we experience neither trouble nor difficulties. That is the reason Christ has united with our flesh and blood. Annotations on 1 Corinthians 15:49.[33]

Image of the Man of Heaven. John Trapp: Our bodies shall be fashioned like that of Christ's glorious body in beauty, brightness, incorruption, immortality, grace, favor, agility, strength, and other unspeakable qualities and excellencies. Whether they shall have that power as to toss the greatest mountains like a ball, indeed, to shake the whole earth at their pleasure (as Anselm and Luther think), I cannot say. Commentary on 1 Corinthians 15:49.[34]

[30]Musculus, *Comm. 1 Cor.*, 708.
[31]Downame, *English Annotations*, FF1r*.
[32]Irenaeus, *Against Heresies* 5.2.3 (ANF 1:528).
[33]Zwingli, *Annotatiunculae . . . ex ore Zvinglij*, 136-37; citing Jn 3:16.
[34]Trapp, *A Commentary or Exposition*, 701*. For Anselm's comment, see Eadmer, *Liber de S. Anselmi Similitudinibus*. Ch. 52. PL 159:631.

15:50-58 Mystery and Victory

*[50]I tell you this, brothers: flesh and blood cannot
inherit the kingdom of God, nor does the perishable
inherit the imperishable. [51]Behold! I tell you a mystery.
We shall not all sleep, but we shall all be changed, [52]in
a moment, in the twinkling of an eye, at the last
trumpet. For the trumpet will sound, and the dead
will be raised imperishable, and we shall be changed.
[53]For this perishable body must put on the imperishable, and this mortal body must put on immortality.
[54]When the perishable puts on the imperishable, and
the mortal puts on immortality, then shall come to
pass the saying that is written:*

"Death is swallowed up in victory."
[55]"O death, where is your victory?
O death, where is your sting?"

*[56]The sting of death is sin, and the power of sin
is the law. [57]But thanks be to God, who gives us the
victory through our Lord Jesus Christ.*
*[58]Therefore, my beloved brothers, be steadfast,
immovable, always abounding in the work of the
Lord, knowing that in the Lord your labor is not
in vain.*

Overview: Paul concludes this magnificent chapter by describing the glorious moment at the end of human history when Christ will decisively achieve the resurrection of his blood-bought people—an event so awesome that the apostle can't help but burst forth in a beautiful song celebrating Christ's victory over sin and death. Rather than speculating about the precise time of Christ's bodily return to earth, Reformation commentators concern themselves with harmonizing 1 Corinthians 15:51-54 with other eschatological passages in the New Testament, as well as explaining the ways that Christ's resurrection has satisfied God's law, broken the power of sin, vanquished the grave, and destroyed death forever. Yet again the commentators emphasize that the final resurrection involves the salvation of our present bodies transformed—not, as the "new Manichaeans" argue, the creation of entirely new bodies. At the same time, Paul's allusion to several Old Testament passages in his song of triumph (1 Cor 15:55-56) causes Reformation authors to discuss the proper method of gleaning the plain, simple, and clear meaning of prophetic texts. More than a doctrine simply to be confessed, the future resurrection of believers offers extraordinary comfort and joy to Christians as they mourn the death of loved ones, struggle with sin, and encounter intense suffering in this present life. Hence, among the practical entailments of resurrection hope, the commentators emphasize the need for steadfast courage and godly labor in the service of the risen Christ, for those who labor in the Lord will bear lasting fruit and enjoy eternal glory.

15:50-53 *The Dead Will Be Raised Imperishable*

Paul Speaks Against "Flesh and Blood" Reasoning. Martin Luther: St. Paul has almost finished his sermon now. He has said enough about this article. However, he adds another item, by way of supplement as it were. He wants to confide a secret to them, revealing how things will be on the Last Day when we are to rise. But he prefaces this with a brief warning, as though he were to say: "You heard the wiseacres and factious spirits preaching against this article and asked derisively: 'How will this take place? What sort of bodies will we have?' Therefore I counsel and warn you faithfully to be on your guard against flesh and blood and whatever human wisdom and ideas may suggest. Do not suppose that you will obtain or retain this article in that way. For it is not recognized otherwise than from heaven by faith, which the Holy Spirit must bestow. In short, be governed by that, lest you think and live as flesh and blood does, which believes nothing at all and lives as though we would remain here forever. Strive to obtain the resurrection. For such carnal, worldly ways and thoughts do not belong in heaven; they must all cease and vanish." Commentary on 1 Corinthians 15:50.[1]

Flesh and Blood Cannot Inherit the Kingdom of God. Tilemann Hesshus: Paul makes clear by way of explanation why we must long for the image of the heavenly human being—no doubt because human nature, infected and corrupted by sin, is not suited for the heavenly and eternal kingdom, for there is no place in God's sight and in the spiritual and eternal kingdom for sin and death, or corruption. Therefore the image of the earthly Adam must be cast aside; our flesh must be purged, illuminated, and restored; our nature must be wiped clean of sin and death, and righteousness and spiritual life must be ignited within it. That is why Paul says, "Flesh and blood cannot inherit the kingdom of God," that is, without such a transformation. . . .

The ancient Manichaeans and Marcionites wickedly and shamelessly abused this passage of Paul, for they wanted to establish from Paul's statement here that there would be no resurrection of our bodies. The person who is truly godly will curse such a debased and shameless heretical teaching! For in this remarkable sermon, Paul very sharply refutes this monstrous error that denies the resurrection of bodies, and he demonstrates with very clear arguments that our bodies are also going to be resurrected. And yet, those shameless Manichaeans dared to find a pretext for their fictitious doctrine in this passage. But the ancients vehemently refuted them. Irenaeus and others teach that Paul was not denying the salvation of the flesh; rather, he was expecting a change in its characteristics. Flesh and blood cannot possess the kingdom of God without changing. Indeed, when flesh and blood will have been resuscitated from the dead and vivified by the Spirit, then they will certainly possess an inheritance in the kingdom of God. For Job says, "In my flesh I will see God." And Christ Jesus will make our wretched bodies conform to his glorious body.

Matthias Flacius Illyricus follows the Manichaeans rather than the orthodox church when he distorts this passage and contends that this "flesh" indicates original sin and sinful corruption, and that this "flesh" must in a way be destroyed and transformed into a new kind of thing in essential righteousness. These Manichaean monstrosities are alien to Paul's way of thinking. Paul does not say that flesh and blood are characterized by original sin; rather, he says that flesh and blood are corrupted so that they cannot possess the kingdom of God. . . . Paul does not say that the essence of flesh and blood must be destroyed, but that their conditions and qualities must be changed, no doubt referring to their mortality, filthiness, and pollution. Illyricus overturns the foundation of our salvation when he argues that the essence of the flesh, which is original sin, must be destroyed, for Jesus Christ did not come to destroy human flesh, but to destroy sin and death in the flesh, and to save the flesh. Explication of 1 Corinthians 15:50.[2]

Who Inherits the Kingdom of God? John Donne: This then is the blessed state that we aspire to, in the kingdom of God in this life; peace in the state, peace in the church, peace in our conscience. In this [present condition] we answer the motions of his blessed Spirit here in this ordinance, and endeavor to be conformed to him in our life and conversation. In this [present condition] he is our King, and we are his subjects, and this is the kingdom of God, the kingdom of grace. Now the title by which we make claim to this

[1]LW 28:197.

[2]Hesshus, *Explicatio Prioris Epistolae ad Corinthios*, 354v-355v; citing Job 19:26. The Lutheran theologian Matthias Flacius argued that original sin belonged to the substance rather than the accidents of the human being. Orthodox Lutherans rejected this position in the first article of the *Formula of Concord* (1577).

kingdom is found here in our text: *Inheritance.* Who can and who cannot inherit the kingdom of God? I cannot have it by purchase, by my own merits and good works. It is neither my former good disposition nor God's foresight of my future cooperation with him that is the cause of his giving me his grace. I cannot have this by covenant, or by the gift, or bequeathing of another, by works of supererogation (as if a martyr of the primitive church should send me a vial of his blood, a splinter of his bone, a slice of his flesh, wrapped up in a half-sheet of paper, in an imaginary six-penny indulgence from Rome, and bid me receive grace and peace of conscience through it).... I have no title to this kingdom of God, but through inheritance. And from where does my inheritance come? From the seed of God; because I am born of the seed of God I inherit this peace.... But what is that seed? The Word of God. The seed is the Word of God. Sermon at Lincoln's Inn.[3]

Two Kinds of Mysteries. Wolfgang Musculus: "Behold," Paul says, "I tell you a mystery." This "mystery" is hidden and secret. It is not accessible to general knowledge, not even to believers, but is revealed only to a select number of people through revelation. There are two kinds of mysteries. The first kind of mystery pertains to those things that everyone must understand and believe for salvation. The apostles are stewards of these kinds of mysteries. To this category belong all the chief teachings of the Christian faith that are mysteries on account of the fact that they are incomprehensible to human reason. The testimonies and prophecies of sacred Scripture say a lot about these mysteries. Mysteries of the second kind are not necessary for salvation and are not known by believers; concerning these mysteries nothing is clearly taught in Scripture. The resurrection of the dead concerns that first kind of mystery, which all must believe and about which the Scriptures bear testimony. But this present mystery concerning the manner of the future resurrection and the future transformation [of the world] is of the second kind, of which no mention is made in Scripture. It is possible to be ignorant of this mystery without harm to our salvation. Commentary on 1 Corinthians 15:51.[4]

The Christian's Blessed Hope. John Colet: He who will come like lightning breaking forth from the east and spreading rapidly to the west will gather his people to himself in an instant and unite them into his own likeness, at the same time scattering and dispersing the darkness, driving death away and banishing it, so that life and light may possess all things. Most blessed will be those who are in that light and that life, in our Lord of Glory, Jesus Christ. Most wretched will be those who are not: they will be without our Lord Jesus Christ, and in cold, darkness, and never-ending death. Exposition of 1 Corinthians 15.[5]

The Glorious Return of Christ. Guillaume Farel: I believe that he will come down again from heaven in the last day of the judgment to judge the living and the dead, who from the beginning of the world until that day shall have been dead. All people, all the angels, and all the devils must appear before his throne of judgment, and they must see him there bodily, as he delivers both me and all his believers from bodily death, and from all imperfections and miseries, as he corrects and punishes eternally our enemies and opponents, and as he delivers us forever from their violence. All this he will do if we are found among the number of those chosen, as I fully expect to be. Lord's Prayer and Apostles' Creed.[6]

This Hope of Christ's Return Should Strengthen Our Faith. Tilemann Heshus: With incredible speed, God will reveal the coming of his Son in the clouds; angels will gather all the saints from the four corners of the world; the Son of God will quickly perform his judgment

[3]Donne, *Sermons*, 3:127-28*.

[4]Musculus, *Comm. 1 Cor.*, 712.

[5]Colet, *Enarratio*, 278; citing Mt 24:27.

[6]In Zuidema and Van Raalte, *Early French Reform*, 115.

and transfer them into the heavenly and eternal kingdom. Paul makes mention of the last trumpet also in 1 Thessalonians 4, "For the Lord will descend from heaven with a shout, with the voice of the archangel, and with sound of the trumpet of God." And Christ says in John 5, "All who are in the tombs will hear the voice of the Son of God." Let us strengthen our faith, therefore, with these so remarkable testimonies in which the circumstances of the resurrection of the dead are described, and let us prepare ourselves with earnest repentence for this glad day when Christ comes in the clouds. Explication of 1 Corinthians 15:51-52.[7]

Not Everyone Will Sleep. Huldrych Zwingli: On that Last Day, when our Lord will come in judgment, not everyone will be dead. Indeed, on that day when he suddenly appears, he will find some people who are still living and surviving. But these people who are left must also die and be transformed. That is, they will cast aside mortality and corruption (for flesh and blood will not inherit the kingdom of God) in exchange for immortality and glory. This change and transformation will take place suddenly and unexpectedly. Annotations on 1 Corinthians 15:51.[8]

Those Who Are Alive When Christ Returns. David Dickson: What shall become of those people who are alive at the coming of our Lord? How shall those who have not died, who are found alive by the Judge at his coming, rise from the dead? Paul answers by revealing a mystery, namely, that all shall not die, nor rise again. For those people who are alive at the coming of our Lord will be taken, and they will be changed into an eternal state of immortality, either in glory or in torment. This change will be instead of death and a resurrection. Annotations on 1 Corinthians 15:51.[9]

In a Moment, in the Twinkling of an Eye. John Calvin: Paul is still speaking generally—that is, all people[10] are included here. For change will be sudden and instantaneous for everyone, because Christ's second coming will be sudden. And to convey the idea of a moment, Paul states "in the blink (or flicker) of an eye," for there are two readings in the Greek, *ropē* or *ripē*—whichever word is chosen doesn't affect the sense of the verse. Paul has chosen to use the movement of a body that surpasses all in quickness; for nothing is more rapid than the movement of an eye, and at the same time he has made an allusion to sleeping, to which the blinking eye is contrasted. Commentary on 1 Corinthians 15:52.[11]

The Last Trumpet. Huldrych Zwingli: "At the last trumpet." Paul understands this trumpet call to be when Christ summons the dead through his angels. He calls this a "shout" in 1 Thessalonians. In John 6[12] Christ calls this "the voice of the Son of God." They all mean the same thing, and each is explained by the other. Annotations on 1 Corinthians 15:52.[13]

The Meaning of the Last Trumpet. The English Annotations: By the last trumpet some understand the voice of the archangel, or Christ's proclamation for the raising of the dead. But it seems more probable as the people of God were assembled in their solemn feasts and fasts by the sound of a trumpet, and as on Mount Sinai the law was delivered with a most loud and dreadful sound, so also the summons of all the dead shall be with a similar sound, which is here called the last trumpet. Annotations on 1 Corinthians 15:52.[14]

We Shall Be Changed. Martin Luther: The Greek word [*allagēsometha*] found here means

[7]Hesshus, *Explicatio Prioris Epistolae ad Corinthios*, 357v-358r; citing 1 Thess 4:16; Jn 5:28.
[8]Zwingli, *Annotatiunculae . . . ex ore Zvinglij*, 138.
[9]Dickson, *Exposition of St. Paul's Epistles*, 69*.
[10]That is, both the elect and reprobate.
[11]CO 49:562 (cf. CTS 40:59).
[12]*Sic*, Jn 5:25, 28.
[13]Zwingli, *Annotatiunculae . . . ex ore Zvinglij*, 138-39; citing 1 Thess 4:16.
[14]Downame, *English Annotations*, FF1r*.

chiefly to change so as to be moved from one place to another, for instance, from the water to dry land, from the earth into the air. Similarly, then we too will be found elsewhere and in a different condition in the twinkling of an eye. The very hour before we were here on earth in a house or on a field. Suddenly we are removed from table or bed or from our work, as we happen to be walking, standing, sitting, or lying, so that we are dead and alive again in a moment, changed in every way, and soaring up in the clouds. Those are the changes Paul has in mind here. To be sure, he encompasses also the other qualitative changes. Of these he already remarked earlier that the body will put on a different dress, that is, that it will be glorified and bright, much more resplendent and beautiful than the sun. But that will not happen while the body is still sojourning in this inn and garbed in this dress. No, it will first be divested of everything and become naked in the same moment and be burned to powder and be carried away.... All that is on earth will be consumed in a moment. The whole world will lie in ruins and be changed. We will be near and with Christ forever. The others, however, who did not believe will be thrust into eternal torment. And this God will do, Paul says, through the last trumpet. For prior to this, "the Lord himself will descend from heaven with a cry of command," as 1 Thessalonians 4:16 declares, and he will bid the archangel blow the trumpet, which will resound through heaven and earth. This will cause everything to fall into ruin and all the dead to be awakened. Commentary on 1 Corinthians 15:52.[15]

The Elect and Damned Will Be Changed—but in Different Ways. Cardinal Cajetan: Please note, prudent reader, that Paul states in the third person "the dead will be raised imperishable," so that we will understand this to be common to all dead human beings, the elect as well as the damned. But he states in the first person, "*we* shall be changed," so that we will understand what will be peculiar to the elect (among whom Paul numbers himself). And the fact that he repeats what he said earlier—"we shall all be changed" (verse 51)—is not due to wordiness, for when he said this earlier he was referring specifically to those elect who are still alive, that they too are going to be changed. In the same way, here in verse 52, he is speaking specifically of all the dead to distinguish them from the damned. And so we learn that there are differences between those things experienced by all the dead and those things particular to the elect. For that which pertains to incorruptibility will be common to all the dead, but that which pertains to glory will be particular to the elect. Paul calls the transformation to the state of glory a "change" in the pure and absolute sense; whereas we should understand the transformation that occurs to the body of the damned to be a "change" in a secondary sense. The damned will at least be transformed from a state of corruptibility to one of incorruptibility. But the elect will be transformed to an incorruptible, impassible, living, glorious state, and to a state of supreme happiness in everything. For this reason they are rightly said to be changed in a pure and absolute sense. Commentary on 1 Corinthians 15:52.[16]

Why Is Paul Silent Regarding the Resurrection of the Wicked? Wolfgang Musculus: It should be noted once again that when Paul speaks in the first person, saying, "*We* will be changed," he is speaking about believers. For he explains these mysteries for the benefit of these believers, just as he did in his previous letter to the Thessalonians. And he does this for good reason. For from the order of resurrection (which he describes in that previous letter), Paul indicates that the Lord will be very concerned to defend his glory by discriminating between the righteous and the wicked; and thus he will first separate the righteous from the presence of the wicked. This is the reason, therefore, why the apostle does not mention even once the resurrection of the wicked; not because they will not also be resurrected, but

[15]LW 28:200-201.

[16]Cajetan, *In Sacrae Scripturae expositionem*, 5:148.

because he believes it sufficient if believers understand correctly this mystery, how those who have died in Christ will be resurrected first, and then those believers still living will suddenly be changed, and then they will be taken up together to meet the Lord in the sky. That is why people are too curious who anxiously wonder about the reprobate, asking, "What sort of resurrected bodies will they have?" They are like those people who (when the right and proper use of the Lord's Supper is being taught for the edification of believers) contentiously debate concerning the wicked, asking, "What do the wicked receive and eat from the Table of the Lord?" . . . Believers understand the calling and hope that they have as believers; they entrust judgment of the reprobate to the righteous judge. Commentary on 1 Corinthians 15:52.[17]

Resurrection Hope for a Deceased Husband. Katharina Schütz Zell: With my husband and all believers, I hope to obtain that costly resurrection of Jesus, through the resurrection of Jesus Christ, who could not experience corruption. We must experience corruption, but we will not remain in it. For the Spirit of God will bring our flesh and bones together again, signal the dawn, and make us alive, as the prophets Ezekiel and Daniel and also our holy Christ himself have testified: that the hour will come when the dead who are in the grave will hear the voice of the Lamb of God and go forth. St. Paul also says this. I hope to obtain and see that resurrection with my dear husband, along with our dear children. (Together we had two, and they lie in this graveyard.) It is now in the twenty-first year since—with great pain!—we carried our first child and trod this place with him; he was the first person buried in this graveyard, where with such fitting earnestness he[18] so often longed to come. Therefore just as he desired to be buried in this place with his and my children, so I hope that this place will also be my abiding place until the trumpet and voice come: "Rise up, you dead, for the judgment." Then my good husband and all the believing dead will hear the happy voice of our worthy Lord Jesus Christ: "Come here, you blessed, into the kingdom that was prepared for you from the beginning; you have fed me, sheltered me, given me drink, clothed me, and comforted me." Lament and Exhortation.[19]

Resurrection Life in God's Presence. Simon Goulart: [Christians] will receive eternal life in body and soul, the body being glorified, protected from all evils, and no longer assaulted by sin, ignorance, errors, illnesses, sorrow, perplexity, fear, anguish, or enemies. Delivered from all pains and sorrows, they will enjoy fully and completely the Lord their God, the fountain and inexhaustible treasure of all good things, who will pour out on them all his goodness, his infinite joy, with which he will satisfy all their thoughts and desires. They will see him and contemplate him face to face, without any clouds to obscure him. . . . The eternal Father will disclose his burning and unspeakable love for them, which he demonstrated by sending his Son into the world to draw them from death into eternal life. His children will be moved by such graciousness, filled with wonder, contentment, and ineffable delight, and they will love their heavenly Father with a burning love, submitting themselves fully to his wisdom with eager joy. . . . And they will rejoice with continuous joy in his presence, magnifying his glory, singing of his goodness along with the holy angels and the entire church triumphant. . . . This entire company together, with one heart and voice, recalling the goodness and infinite blessings God has shown them, will celebrate with songs of thanksgiving the praises of the Father, the Son, and the Holy Spirit. On Eternal Life.[20]

[17]Musculus, *Comm.1 Cor.*, 719.

[18]That is, her husband.

[19]McKee, *Katharina Schütz Zell*, 117; Acts 2:27, 31; Ezek 37:7-10; Dan 12:2; Jn 5:25, 28-29. Katharina delivered this address at the graveside of her deceased husband, Matthias Zell, in January 1548.

[20]Goulart, *XXVIII Discours Chrestiens*, 323-24.

The Mortal Body Will Put On Immortality. Tilemann Hesshus: Paul repeats and explains what he said above concerning this transformation. As long as this flesh is subservient to corruption, disease, and death, it is not able to experience the heavenly kingdom. Therefore we will be changed, and indeed, in such a way that the substance of our body and soul will be preserved. But this body will take off all infirmity, mortality, and corruption, for Christ will wipe clean our nature of sin and death, since these are separable from it. On the other hand, the substance of our body and soul will put on heavenly light, perfect righteousness, and unending life. Therefore the doctrine of the resurrection of the dead should be understood to include not only renewal in this life and the beginning of new obedience but also the resuscitation of bodies from the dead and the transformation, glorification, and transition of our whole nature to the heavenly life. Explication of 1 Corinthians 15:53.[21]

Our Victory Concealed in Christ. David Joris: Therefore be understanding. Know your blessed teaching and the hiddenness of the kingdom. For when it appears that your wisdom, understanding, and spirit have been lost, by such faith in the promises of God you will receive again the imperishable for the perishable (1 Cor 15:53), the heavenly in place of the earthly, light for darkness, good for evil, truth for lies. Otherwise, people are led into deception. When it appears you have lost your life or yourself, you will be preserved. When it appears you are dishonored, he brings you to honor. When you appear to become sick and weak, you will become strong. When you appear poor of spirit or understanding, behold, you will become rich therein. You appear to become foolish and childish, but you become wise and a truly perfect person in Christ Jesus. In him our wisdom, salvation, righteousness, and victory is completely concealed. This is the truth of the Holy Spirit, God's testimony, in which all things will be restored correctly. Hear and follow his teaching, his advice and testimony, so that you will be blessed. O pay attention and observe closely what is written or spoken to you from this Spirit. Blessed Instruction.[22]

15:54-58 *Death Is Swallowed Up in Victory!*

Paul Quotes from the Old Testament. John Calvin: Furthermore, it is not completely clear from which Old Testament passage Paul has drawn this quotation, for many statements occur in the prophets that relate to this. Most likely the first clause is taken either from Isaiah 25:8, where it is said "The Lord has destroyed death forever," or (and this is the preference of many, indeed, nearly everybody) from Hosea 13:14, where the prophet, deploring the obstinate wickedness of Israel, complains that Israel was like a premature child that struggles against the efforts of his mother in labor, so as not to emerge from the womb. And from this the prophet concludes that Israel had no one but himself to blame that he was not liberated from death. He says, "I will ransom them from the power of the grave, I will rescue them from death." It is of little importance whether one takes that verb in the future indicative mood, or in the subjunctive mood. For in either mood, the meaning amounts to this: that God was prepared to confer salvation on them, if they were willing to accept his blessing; and that it was their own fault if they perished.

Afterward, Hosea adds, "I will be your ruin, O death! I will be your destruction, O grave!" By these words God indicates that he will finally save his people only when death and the grave are reduced to nothing. For nobody will deny that in this passage there is a description of completed salvation. Therefore since we do not yet see death destroyed, it follows that we do not yet possess that complete salvation which God promises to his people, and consequently is delayed until the last day. At that time, then, death will be swallowed up—that is, reduced to nothing—so that we may

[21]Hesshus, *Explicatio Prioris Epistolae ad Corinthios*, 358r.

[22]CRR 8:259*.

have a complete and thorough victory over it. Commentary on 1 Corinthians 15:54.[23]

Paul Quotes Isaiah's Prophecy. Tilemann Hesshus: The first testimony that Paul chose was from Isaiah 25: "On this mountain the Lord will lift from the face the veil that covers all peoples, and the covering that envelops all nations. And death will be swallowed up with victory, and the Lord God will wipe away the tears from all faces, etc." It is clear that the prophet's entire sermon speaks about this immeasurable blessing of the Mediator Jesus Christ, that he would destroy sin and death, demolish the works of Satan, and restore righteousness and eternal life. "On this mountain"—that is, in this kingdom, or, in this church (which is gathered together by the gospel)—God will remove the veil that covers the face. This is what he calls death, for dead corpses are usually wrapped in linen and then buried in the earth, and all nations are at the mercy of this wretched condition. Thus, by metonymy, Isaiah calls death a "covering," because it covers all nations, as he himself soon explains with his own words. Now, the Son of God, Jesus Christ, by undergoing death for us, has swallowed up death in victory; and, rising on the third day, he has broken the entire power of death, destroyed its tyranny, and opened up for us the way to eternal life. "Whoever believes in me," Jesus says, "will not come under condemnation, but will cross over from death into life. And I will revive them on the very last day." And it is clear that the prophet was speaking about the resurrection of all the dead, because he adds, "And the Lord God will wipe away the tears from the faces of everyone." Commentary on 1 Corinthians 15:54.[24]

Our Victory Song over Death. Martin Luther: Then we will really begin to glory joyfully and defiantly and say and sing: "O death, where is thy sting? O hell, where is thy victory?" That is really snapping one's fingers at death and hell and saying: "Dear death, do not bite me, but show your anger with me and kill me. I defy death and hell and challenge them to touch a hair on my head! Where are you now, you vile maneaters?" Then there will be nothing but making game of death, hell, and the devil. And as they now boast and jeer at the world, saying, "We defy you to escape us!" the tables will then be turned. . . . This has already begun through Christ on his own body. He sings this song of defiance against death and hell uninterruptedly: "Dear death, once upon a time you crucified and buried me too; and you trampled me underfoot. You assumed that you had gained the victory and had devoured me. But where are you now? I defy you to pursue me further!" For death has already been drowned and swallowed up entirely on his body, with not as much as a speck of death's dust remaining on him. Now we who believe in him share in this when the hour comes in which we see and feel how death and hell are entirely swallowed up and exterminated. At present, however, we await the hour, assured that this will surely come to pass and that we can already defiantly rely on Christ by faith over against sin, death, and hell. Commentary on 1 Corinthians 15:55.[25]

The Death of the Body Will Be Destroyed. Wolfgang Musculus: "O death, where is your victory?" In Hebrew "death" is *sheol*, a word that means grave and sepulcher; this is different from hellish *gehenna*, which will never have an end. . . . And that *gehenna* has been defeated through Christ, though not for everyone, but it pertains only to the elect and believers, while the wicked and reprobate will endure *gehenna* forever. But the death and corruption of our bodies will be thoroughly taken away and reduced to nothing, as much from the elect as the reprobate. Commentary on 1 Corinthians 15:55.[26]

[23]CO 49:563 (cf. CTS 40:62-63).
[24]Hesshus, *Explicatio Prioris Epistolae ad Corinthios*, 359r-v; citing Is 25:8; Jn 3:18; 5:24.
[25]LW 28:207.
[26]Musculus, *Comm. 1 Cor.*, 724.

Like Hosea, Paul Ridicules Death. Tilemann Hesshus: The other testimony is drawn from the prophet Hosea, chapter 13. And both testimonies have the same meaning, that the power of death has been destroyed through the crucifixion, death, and resurrection on the third day of our Lord Jesus Christ, who has conquered the grave and made a way for us to eternal and heavenly life. Because of the fall of Adam and the sin of humanity, death had dominion over all people. No one was spared—no one was safe from the tyranny of death, no matter their noble stock, no matter how gifted they were in wisdom or strength. All were forced to obey this master, and it would have held us in its bondage for all eternity had not a liberator come to us. But the Son of God, Jesus Christ our Lord, has been given to us, who by experiencing death and rising again through his divine power has broken, demolished, and destroyed the dominion of death and has completely swallowed up death. And thus it is no longer able to exercise its power over godly people, nor hold our bodies in the grave, for Christ, the Captain and Author of Life, will bring our bodies back to life and bathe us with eternal life. Therefore godly people rightly follow the example of the prophet [Hosea] and Paul (who are both inspired by the Spirit) in taunting that most cruel and savage tyrant who has been disarmed and defeated, and is now paraded as a captive in triumph by Christ. "O death, where now is your sting? O grave, where now is your victory? Previously you taunted us and ridiculed our strength and the stratagems that we brandished in an effort to stave off death, for you knew we were wasting our effort because you were more powerful than all of us. But now everything has changed. We taunt and ridicule your threats and appearance, for we know that you have been disarmed, and that all your power has been broken by Jesus Christ. We dare you now to cause us any harm! Rather, your efforts will only serve to our advantage. And Jesus Christ is our resurrection, through whom we ridicule you, and we tread you underfoot by the Spirit. O grave! Previously you stretched wide your terrifying jaws and devoured everything with your unquenchable appetite. Where now is that vast abyss of yours? Where now is your monstrous tyranny and victory, by which you prevailed over even the most powerful human monarchs? For certainly Jesus Christ has torn apart your jaws and led out the captive prisoner; thus you are forced in disgrace to release those godly people who believe in Christ. For Christ is bringing our souls back from hell, resurrecting our bodies from the grave, and transferring us to eternal life and the heavenly kingdom." Explication of 1 Corinthians 15:55.[27]

Where, Death, Is Your Sting? John Trapp: This is the sharpest and shrillest note, the boldest and bravest challenge that a human being ever rang in the ears of death.... Death is here out-braved, called craven to its face and bidden, "Do your worst!" Ambrose was bold to say, "I am neither ashamed to live nor afraid to die." The martyr Anne Askew undersigned her confession in this way: "Written by me, Anne Askew, who neither wishes for death nor fears its power—who is merry as one that is bound for heaven." Mr. Bradford, having been told that he would be burned the next day, took off his cap and, lifting up his eyes, praised God for it. Commentary on 1 Corinthians 15:55.[28]

Usefulness of the Doctrine of the Resurrection. Simon Goulart: This doctrine of the resurrection is of excellent use. (1) It supports our faith in the midst of miseries, dangers, and terrible accidents to which our poor bodies are exposed in this present life. (2) It softens the sadness that results from the death of our parents, friends, and neighbors. (3) It diminishes the fear of death, showing us that at the end of this earthly race a better life awaits us.... (4) This doctrine makes us careful and prompts our service to God.

[27]Hesshus, *Explicatio Prioris Epistolae ad Corinthios*, 360r-361r; citing Hos 13:14.

[28]Trapp, *A Commentary or Exposition*, 701*. The martyrdom of Anne Askew in 1546 appears in Foxe, *Acts and Monuments* 5.549-50. John Bradford was an English reformer who was executed during the reign of Mary Tudor (r. 1553–1558) in 1555.

It also encourages us to live in an edifying manner with those whom we expect will be companions with us in eternal life. (5) It draws us back from sin, restraining us from defiling our soul that is so excellent and our body that is sanctified by the precious blood of Jesus Christ. For this body, I say, will live in incomprehensible joy and holiness; it will converse with God, along with the holy angels, patriarchs, prophets, apostles, martyrs, and all the other elect, who have left the world with their thoughts lifted up and focused on their Savior. On the Resurrection of the Dead.[29]

The Gospel Declares Victory Over Death. Philipp Melanchthon: Here is a splendid comparison of death, sin, and the law: sin causes shame, and shame is death. But sin brings shame through the law. For the specific duty of the law is to show sin and judge what has been exposed. Sin brings shame, and as Romans 4 says "The law brings wrath." For the law shows what ought to be done but does not furnish the power to do it. So it condemns us since we are not able to do it. Moreover, just as the law is a sentence of death, so the gospel is the promise of life. It is nothing else than a proclamation of this verdict: "Death is swallowed up in victory." Annotations on 1 Corinthians 15:55-56.[30]

Christ Is Victorious over Hell, Sin, and the Law. Heinrich Bullinger: The apostle explains how victory over sin, death, and the grave . . . has been achieved through Christ—not from the strength or merits of the saints. For it is to Christ that the saints will render all glory, praise, and thanksgiving, singing a new song to him in the resurrection, and even now here on earth they offer to him hymns of glory and praise. Now, Paul's explanation involves three very beautiful levels. The first level is the grave, namely, eternal punishment, by which they are condemned to death in the second death. In the second level there is sin—that power of death and hell—for on account of sin there is death. For this reason, it is called "the sting of death," no doubt as an allusion to the fact that poisonous animals inject their venom by the wound of a sting. . . . And so those who sin, infected by the poison of concupiscence, are like those who die from puncture wounds of lethal poison. Perhaps the apostle has made an allusion either to that serpent whom Moses mentions in Genesis 3, or to those poisonous snakes that are described in Numbers 21, which were biting people with a fire of burning poison. And once bitten, the people moved quickly to drink water and, drinking it all up, they were soon bursting—but no remedy for this evil could be found except the bronze serpent, lifted up in the air, which was a figure of Christ. For by the grace of Christ, the power was taken away from the deadly poison so that thereafter it did not kill. Now there is no condemnation for those who are incorporated into Christ Jesus. The third level is the law, which is the power of sin. For at the right time, the law incites the desire for sinning, as it is written: "The law brings wrath," or again, "I would not have known what sin is except by the law."

Now what is the reason for these three levels? The reason is this: to explain Christ's grace and victory, but now, in reverse order, summed up from the end to the beginning. When the law is endured, the strength of sin is weakened. When sin is endured, the power of death ceases. And with death disarmed, hell itself is crushed. But how can this happen? Even as Christ set us free, he took the form of a servant, and ransomed us from the curse of the law, while he was made a curse for us. But when he endured the curse of the law, he also endured sin; and, truly, when he endured sin, he disarmed death; and, truly, when death was overthrown and conquered, hell was overcome and left desolate. What else, then? The saints, therefore, who perish along with other people, live in Christ's grace and victory. And thus honor and praise and glory should be given to Christ; in him the saints live and are resurrected;

[29]Goulart, *XXVIII Discours Chrestiens*, 321-22.
[30]Melanchthon, *Annotationes in Epistolam priorem ad Corinthios*, 174; citing Rom 4:15.

to him the saints will sing praises forever. Commentary on 1 Corinthians 15:56.[31]

Christ's Victory Has Become the Christian's Victory. Martin Luther: This is the beautiful sermon for Christians that shows us how we, through Christ's victory, rid ourselves of sin's sting, which kills us, and the power of the law, which drives this sting into us. And it shows us that in the end this sting will be completely destroyed in us. And now St. Paul appropriately concludes with a song that he sings: "Thanks and praise be to God, who gave us such a victory!" We can join in that song and in that way always celebrate Easter, praising and extolling God for a victory that was not won or achieved in battle by us—it is far too sublime and great for that—but was presented and given to us by the mercy of God. He had compassion with our misery, from which no one could rescue us, and he sent his Son and let him enter the battle. He laid these enemies, sin, death, and hell, low and retained the victory. He transferred this victory to us, so that we may say it is our victory. It is just as if it had been gained by us. The only condition is that we must accept this sincerely and not give God the lie, as they do who presume to overcome their sin and death by themselves. Nor dare we be found ungrateful for this, as vulgar false Christians do, but we must keep this in our heart in firm faith and confirm ourselves in this and always be engrossed in such a message of thanks and sing of this victory in Christ. And in faith in this we must cheerfully depart this life, until we experience this victory also in our own body. May God help us to that end through the same dear Son. To him be glory and honor forever. Amen. Commentary on 1 Corinthians 15:56-57.[32]

The Victory Is Close at Hand. Guillaume Farel: O true champions and warriors of the Word of God, have courage: the victory is close at hand, the triumph ordained with the great captain Jesus. Do not turn your backs in this mighty battle! Enter forcefully into it for the honor of such a good Father and great king who looks on us to see what the battle is and who battles in us. He leads us and directs us by his Spirit so that all will be well. Give to him alone the glory. Do not rest with visible and present things, but with the invisible and with those things that are promised to us! Summary and Brief Exposition.[33]

The Use We Should Make of Christ's Victory. David Dickson: Paul shows a twofold use of Christ's victory. The first is that thanks may be given to God, who has given us victory through Christ over death, sin, and the law. Yes, truly, God has imputed the victory of Christ to us and has made it ours; for he has died for us, and by his resurrection has obtained for us victory over death, that he might make us conquerors. . . . Another use of this doctrine is that under hope of the free gift at the day of resurrection we would persevere constantly in the faith of the gospel and diligently endeavor to bring forth the fruits of faith. Because in the resurrection the Lord will give us whatever we have lost with humans, namely, the reward of good works. Annotations on 1 Corinthians 15:57-58.[34]

Living in the Light of the Future Resurrection. Desiderius Erasmus: Because the future resurrection is certain, and because so great a happiness is guaranteed as certain through it—though, this will be true only for those who have been planning for the heavenly life here and now by their innocence and avoidance of sin—do not waiver from that which you once believed, and do not allow yourselves to be lured away from right opinion by associating with wicked people. But instead, pay careful attention to make daily progress in those things that draw you close to God; see to it

[31]Bullinger, *In Priorem ad Corinthios Epistolam Commentarius*, 258-59; citing Rom 4:15; 7:7.
[32]LW 28:212-13.

[33]In Zuidema and Van Raalte, *Early French Reform*, 175.
[34]Dickson, *Exposition of St. Paul's Epistle*, 70*.

that you always prove yourselves gracious to others, preparing yourselves for the future resurrection. Do not be annoyed by any labor, since you can be certain that, with the help of Christ, you will achieve eternal joy after your temporary troubles. Paraphrases on 1 Corinthians 15.[35]

Hope of the Resurrection Motivates Christians to Persevere. John Calvin: Having satisfied himself that he had proved the doctrine of the resurrection, Paul now concludes his discussion with a word of exhortation, and this is much more effective than if he had made use of a simple conclusion with an assertion. "Since your labor," he says, "is not in vain in the Lord, be steadfast and abound in good works." Now, he says that their labor is not in vain because God has stored up for them a reward. This is the singular hope that encourages believers at the outset, and afterward sustains them to persevere in the race. Hence, he exhorts them to remain steadfast, because they are resting on an unshakeable foundation, since they know that a better life is prepared for them in heaven. Paul adds "abounding in the work of the Lord"—for the hope of the resurrection keeps us from growing weary in well-doing, as he teaches in Colossians 1:10. For in the face of so many obstacles that continually oppose us, who would not lose heart or withdraw from the course, were it not that, by thinking about that better life, they are by this means kept in the fear of God? Now, on the other hand, Paul intimates that if the hope of the resurrection were taken away, it would be as if the foundations were overturned, and the whole basis of godliness destroyed. Without a doubt, if the hope of reward is taken away and destroyed, then enthusiasm for running the race would not only wane but would end altogether. Commentary on 1 Corinthians 15:58.[36]

Bearing Fruit That Will Last Forever. Tilemann Hesshus: "Abounding in the work of the Lord." After having proved the resurrection of the dead, Paul urges the Corinthians to progress energetically in the ministry of the Word, in confession, in love of neighbor, in patience, and to build up the Lord's church in every good work, and shine forth the glory of God. And Paul briefly mentions a most delightful and very noteworthy promise: "In the Lord your labor will not be in vain." The doctrine that denies the resurrection of the dead is blasphemy, because it takes away all comfort and thus destroys all zealousness, the desire to work on behalf of the church, and hard work. For all our duties, all our struggles, all our labors bear no fruit if there is no resurrection of the dead. . . . Moreover, Paul significantly adds: "In the Lord." All our labors, exertions, efforts, struggles, duties, illustrious deeds, troubles, and punishments that are experienced apart from faith in Jesus Christ are going to perish forever and are fruitless. Hercules undertook immense tasks, but in vain, for he perished forever along with his labors. Hector laid down his life for his country; Miltiades exposed himself to dangers; Scipio, having performed illustrious deeds based on his excellent judgment, endured the ingratitude of his country; Camillus brought help to an ungrateful country; Regulus preferred to suffer horrible tortures than to break his word. All of these labors were futile and worthless, therefore, because they were not undertaken through faith in Jesus Christ. That very sad statement of Cicero is not only very true for him but also for all the wicked in the world: "O the deceitful hope and uncertain fortune of human beings, and our worthless contentions, which are shattered and wrecked in midcourse"—he should also have added that all these things are altogether without fruit. But the labors of Moses, David, and Jehoshaphat; the struggles endured by Hezekiah, Jeremiah, and Paul; the exiles of Athanasius; the tortures experienced by Ignatius, Polycarp, Vincent, and Blandina; the dangers faced by Luther; and the duties, devotion, and efforts of all the saints, whatever they discharge diligently and endure patiently—this in no way disappears without fruit, but will be compensated with eternal

[35]Erasmus, *Paraphrases*, 346-47.
[36]CO 49:565 (cf. CTS 40:66).

and immortal glory. Those who instruct many people in righteousness will shine forth as stars in the firmament of heaven. Explication of 1 Corinthians 15:58.[37]

Our Labor Is Not in Vain. Wolfgang Musculus: This statement is very important. The labor of believers in the Lord is of three sorts: first, there is the labor of ministers of the gospel; the second and third are the ministries to all believers and to people in general. The first labor is expressed in preaching the gospel; the second is expressed in brotherly love; the third is expressed in maintaining the purity of faith and the sanctity of the Christian life. Neither the first, second, nor third sort of labor is worthless. Our labor is worthless when we labor in vain. To labor in vain is to fail to achieve the goal of our labor, or to work in such a way that no fruit can come from our labor. The labor of ministers and believers of the Lord is necessarily fruitful, not due to the merit of the laborers, nor to the kind of labor performed, but on account of the goodness and truth of the Lord, who is unable to disregard and disappoint their labors. That is why this passage here does not consider who produces faithful works and labors in the church. The apostle ascribes the fact that our labor is not in vain *to the Lord,* not to us. . . . Therefore the apostle attributes nothing to our labors because everything depends on the grace and power of the Lord. Commentary on 1 Corinthians 15:58.[38]

The Glorious Goal of Eternal Life. Simon Goulart: The eternal and blessed life with God in heaven, accompanied by rest and unspeakable glory, is the goal of the Christian's faith. This is the harbor of their hope, the refuge of all their desires, the crown of their consolation that they will certainly enjoy, having escaped from the travails of this miserable and fleeting earthly life, indeed, from death itself. . . . Thus eternal life is the end and fulfillment of all good things, for which God has purchased us through his Son. This is the goal on which our gaze should be fixed throughout our earthly pilgrimage. This is the treasure that we should unceasingly desire. This is the hour and the blessing to which all the plans and efforts of our lives should be inclined. . . . This is our true country, our permanent city, in which our citizenship has been acquired by the merit of the death of Jesus Christ. This is the home that we long for, amid the banishments, the weariness, the dangerous fears of this valley of misery and the shadow of death. This is the safe refuge and the beautiful harbor toward which we sail amid so many waves and storms that constantly trouble the world. This is the blessed land where we will dwell by means of death. On Eternal Life.[39]

[37]Hesshus, *Explicatio Prioris Epistolae ad Corinthios,* 364r-365r. The Athenian citizen Miltiades the Younger (c. 550–489 BC) was famous for his courageous role in the Battle of Marathon (490 BC) against the Persians. Through the leadership of the Roman general Scipio Africanus (236–183 BC), the Romans successfully defeated Carthage in the Second Punic War (202 BC); upon returning to Rome, however, Scipio was accused of bribery and misappropriation of funds. Similarly, the Roman general and dictator Marcus Furius Camillus (c. 446–365 BC) was impeached by his enemies for embezzlement in the aftermath of his successful military campaign against the Etruscan city of Veii. Following his defeat by Carthaginian armies during the First Punic War (255 BC), the Roman general Marcus Atilius Regulus was paroled on condition that he return home to negotiate a peace; instead of supporting the peace, however, he urged the Roman Senate to reject it, and then fulfilled the terms of his parole by returning to Carthage, where he was tortured to death. The Alexandrian bishop and theologian Athanasius was exiled five times for his support of the doctrine of the Trinity codified at the Council of Nicaea (325). Ignatius bishop of Antioch (died c. 110), Polycarp bishop of Smyrna (died c. 155/156), Vincent of Saragossa (died c. 304), and Blandina of Lyons (died 177) all suffered martyrdom for their Christian faith.

[38]Musculus, *Comm. 1 Cor.,* 729.

[39]Goulart, *XXVIII Discours Chrestiens,* 322-23, 326-27.

16:1-4 The Collection for the Saints

Now concerning[a] *the collection for the saints: as I directed the churches of Galatia, so you also are to do.* [2]*On the first day of every week, each of you is to put something aside and store it up, as he may prosper, so that there will be no collecting when I come.* [3]*And when I arrive, I will send those whom you accredit by letter to carry your gift to Jerusalem.* [4]*If it seems advisable that I should go also, they will accompany me.*

a The expression *Now concerning* introduces a reply to a question in the Corinthians' letter

Overview: As Paul prepares to conclude his letter to the Corinthians, he encourages them to organize a collection for the needs of poor believers in Jerusalem. Reformation commentators discover in Paul's counsel a number of important principles for Christian benevolence: almsgiving should be a voluntary act of generosity rather than a mandatory payment of a debt; churches need to discriminate between the deserving poor and lazy freeloaders; and Christian workers must avoid all appearance of greed or financial misconduct. Drawing on these principles, Protestant interpreters lodge specific criticisms against the forced communalism of the Anabaptists, the mendicancy and laziness of the monastic orders, and the shocking fiscalization of the papal church. Even the Catholic commentator Cardinal Cajetan joins his voice to this chorus of protest by speaking against the traditional church's penchant for fundraising and extracting money through indulgences and various ecclesiastical taxes. The shared view of the commentators, whether Catholic or Protestant, is that as Christians show mercy and generosity toward the poor, they are imitating their Father in heaven.

16:1-4 *Faithful Giving*

Supporting the Church. John Calvin: Chapter 16 has two parts. In the first part, Paul exhorts them to relieve the need of their brothers and sisters in Jerusalem. They were at that time weighed down with famine and were being treated cruelly by wicked people. The apostles had given Paul this responsibility to encourage the Gentile churches to provide assistance to them. Therefore he exhorts them to lay aside whatever was in their heart to contribute so that it might be delivered to Jerusalem without delay. Finally, Paul concludes his letter with a friendly exhortation and words of thanksgiving. Introduction to 1 Corinthians.[1]

Persevere in the Faith. Tilemann Hesshus: In this final chapter, Paul treats three subjects. First, he urges the Corinthians to contribute alms to alleviate the needs of the Jerusalem church, and he explains to them his plan for his journey. And he reminds them to receive Timothy with compassion and not despise him; and he makes an excuse for Apollos because he will not come to them. Second, Paul repeats a weighty and very necessary reminder that they should not be careless or indifferent as they teach doctrine to the church, but they should always be alert and continuously persevere in the faith. So too they should strongly endure dangers and troubles, and stand like men against Satan's insults and tricks. The final part of the chapter is devoted to greetings. Explication of 1 Corinthians 16.[2]

Paul Combines Encouragement with Correction. Wolfgang Musculus: To this point, the apostle has removed through careful correction the evils sprouting in the church of the

[1]CO 49:303-4 (cf. CTS 40:46).
[2]Hesshus, *Explicatio Prioris Epistolae ad Corinthios*, 369r-v.

Corinthians related to lifestyle, sacred worship, spiritual gifts, and belief in the resurrection of the dead. Now, consequently, he goes on to give directions regarding works of brotherly love, saying, "Concerning the collection for the saints. . . ." Although that church was struggling with many problems, nevertheless Paul was not content only to give them criticism and correction. Instead he adds words of encouragement in which he rightly directs those believers to pursue deeds of Christian love. Commentary on 1 Corinthians 16:1.[3]

Works of Charity Display God's Gracious Character. Jacques Lefèvre d'Étaples: Having treated more profound mysteries, the apostle goes on to the more familiar topic of giving alms to the poor saints who were in Jerusalem, who had nothing because of Christ. Or, more precisely, that those who possessed such alms should see to it that they brought to completion the work of charity that they had intended. Those who perform works of charity emulate the providence, mercy, grace, and blessing of God. The providence of God is the general and particular good of each and every person, which God distributes to each and every person; in this way, one sees that he displays his marvelous care for each and every person at the same time. Mercy is also mentioned, because all creatures are so needy in themselves that they will perish on the spot unless God's mercy should support them by coming to their aid. Grace is mentioned because it is not a debt owed, but a pure gift of divine liberality. Blessing is mentioned because it is by the blessing of God that all things abound, all things are made joyful, and all needs satisfied. For this reason those who attend to works of mercy in God's name are said to be sharing his providence, mercy, liberality, and blessing by imitation. Commentary on 1 Corinthians 16:1-4.[4]

True and False Almsgiving. Guillaume Farel: Almsgiving is mercy and compassion; it is to save and help another because we are inwardly moved with pity when we see their poverty and needs. When a father sees his son in great need, his heart and bowels are moved and warmed with compassion, and he goes straightaway to help and save his son. Likewise, a mother's love for her child is so heated that she would pass through fire and her enemies to save him. This also happens between brothers and between friends. . . .

But it certainly is not almsgiving to give to those who can work, who have abandoned some or all of their belongings, have abandoned their work (even though they could live without relying on anyone), and have done this to be without work and at their leisure, without the trouble that comes with living in the world, to live in laziness in a monastery or other place where they only serve to burden the poor people and poor laborers, as are the churchmen, monks, and nuns, who by their rules and statutes are separated from others. Rather, it is to give them a noose to hang themselves and a sword to pierce themselves by feeding their wickedness. Summary and Brief Exposition.[5]

Two Kinds of Alms. Wolfgang Musculus: There are two kinds of alms by which the church supports the needy poor. The first of these is ecclesiastical; the second is private. Paul is speaking about ecclesiastical alms in this passage. This demands the common contribution of each and every person and involves a common regulation and arrangement. The other kind of alms is voluntary, and depends on the will of the contributors, what, how much, to whom, how, and when they wish to give. . . . Since, therefore, ecclesiastical and public collections should be taken in all churches (so that the sustenance of the faithful poor does not depend on private contributions to the poor), we can hardly approve the negligence of those churches in which there is no ecclesiastical collection, and only a very small number of people

[3]Musculus, *Comm. 1 Cor.*, 730-31.

[4]Lefèvre d'Étaples, *Commentariorum in Epistolas Beati Pauli . . . Liber Secundus*, 128v.

[5]In Zuidema and Van Raalte, *Early French Reform*, 143, 144.

are supported by the private beneficence to the poor. Even if, on certain occasions, some money from a death tax is bequeathed to the crowd of paupers, nevertheless this cannot be reckoned as generosity of the living. Finally, even if from time to time something is given from the public chest, it is not possible that alms of this sort that are given by individuals in the church should be considered as the fruit of love. That the apostle in this passage is asking not so much for some public welfare, as a collection from each and every believer, is clear when he says "each of you." Commentary on 1 Corinthians 16:1-2.[6]

The Needs of the Jerusalem Church. Tilemann Hesshus: Several Scripture passages testify to the fact that the Jerusalem church was suffering under great poverty. For in the epistle to the Galatians, the apostles ask Paul to exhort the Gentiles to assist in the church collection for the Jews (Gal 2). And in Romans 15, Paul commends the godly in Macedonia and Achaia for having alleviated the need of the saints in Jerusalem, and he adds that the Gentiles owe this duty to the Jews since the Gentiles received the gospel from the Jews. No doubt, the severe persecutions that arose in Jerusalem after Christ's resurrection, and the famine that afflicted the world under Claudius (which the prophet Agabus had foretold in Acts 11), had reduced the saints in Judea to great poverty. And so, by his example, Paul teaches that it is the duty of godly pastors to provide care for the poor and diligently encourage those who hear the Word to provide aid for the needs of those in distress. Now whoever is oppressed by poverty and exile on account of professing the gospel is worthy of financial aid and support. And even as generosity toward destitute persons is a necessary virtue in the church that is frequently afflicted by exile and poverty, so too it is a quality of godly people.... Now, those in whom the light of sincere faith shines, and who are led by the Holy Spirit—these people are moved by mercy, and they are zealous to imitate the heavenly Father, from whom they receive countless blessings. Therefore godly people should always remember Christ's powerful promise: "Truly, truly I say to you, if anyone will give a cup of cold water to one of these little ones, they will not lose their reward." Explication of 1 Corinthians 16:1.[7]

The Collection for the Poor Jews. David Dickson: Regarding the collection, the famine that was prophesied by Agabus (Acts 11:28), along with the persecution, caused much distress to the churches of Judea, so that the apostles living in Jerusalem exhorted Paul and Barnabas to arrange for a collection among the Gentiles to supply the need of the poor Jews. In Galatians 2:20 Paul speaks about this contribution, commanding that on the Lord's day (which was when all Christians ceased from their labors and met publicly to worship God) everyone should throw something into the treasury according to their ability, without vainglory.... We may imagine that they imitated the example of the ancient church, in which a bored chest was placed in the entrance to the house where they met for the worship of God. Annotations on 1 Corinthians 16:1-2.[8]

"On the First Sabbath" Does Not Mean the Lord's Day. John Calvin: What Paul is getting at is this—that they should have their alms prepared in time. Therefore he exhorts them not to wait until he comes, because anything that is done suddenly and in a hurry is not done well, but to contribute what they thought proper, each person according to their capacity, on the Sabbath—that is, on the day when they were holding their sacred assemblies. Chrysostom interprets this clause *kata mian sabbatōn* to mean "on the first Sabbath." I do not agree with him, for Paul means instead that one person should contribute on one Sabbath, another person on another, or even that

[6]Musculus, *Comm. 1 Cor.*, 734.

[7]Hesshus, *Explicatio Prioris Epistolae ad Corinthios*, 367v-368v; citing Gal 2:10; Rom 15:26-27; Acts 11:28; Mt 25:24.

[8]Dickson, *Exposition of St. Paul's Epistles*, 70*. Referring to 2 Kings 12:9.

everyone might contribute on every Sabbath if they should wish to do so. For Paul's primary concern is convenience, and second, that the sacred assembly, when believers celebrate the communion of the saints, might serve as an additional stimulus to them.

Nor do I accept Chrysostom's view that the term "Sabbath" is employed here to mean the Lord's day. For it is very likely that, in the beginning, the apostles retained the Sabbath day already in use, but that afterward they were forced by Jewish superstition to abrogate that day and substitute it with another. Moreover, the Lord's day was chosen primarily because our Lord's resurrection put an end to the shadows of the law. And so the day itself reminds us of our Christian liberty. We can, however, easily infer from this passage that believers have always had a particular day for resting from their work—not because the worship of God allows for idleness, but because it is important for common harmony that a particular day be designated for holding sacred assemblies, as they cannot be held daily. Commentary on 1 Corinthians 16:2.[9]

On the First Day of the Week. Theodore Beza: The Greek is *kata mian sabbatōn*.[10] The Vulgate renders this clause "during each Sabbath." Erasmus renders it "on one of the Sabbaths." In fact, it is correct to give distributive force (as they call it) to the word *kata*; thus there is no doubt that the clause *mian sabbatōn* signifies the first day of the week, as we show [in our annotations] on Matthew 28:1 and explain in detail at Mark 16:9. Annotations on 1 Corinthians 16:2.[11]

From Sabbath to Lord's Day. Peter Martyr Vermigli: From ancient times, the Sabbath was observed by the orderly arrangement of the law as a remembrance of the creation of the world. But now the Lord's day is in use as a remembrance of Christ's resurrection and so as to strengthen hope in our future resurrection. When this transition happened has not been described in the sacred writings. Yet in the book of Revelation, we have John's explicit mention of the Lord's day, and it is probable that for some time the first Christians retained this Jewish custom so that they assembled together on the day of the Sabbath; but afterward, as we see, the practice changed. Commentary of 1 Corinthians 16:2.[12]

The Christian's Sabbath. John Trapp: The Greek scholiast appropriately renders this verse as the Christian Sabbath, the Lord's day. In ancient times, to sanctify this day was a badge of Christianity. When the question was asked, "Have you kept the Lord's day?" the answer was given, "I am a Christian, I can do no less than to keep the Lord's day." But the world has now grown perfectly profane (as someone has said) and one can play on the Lord's day without books. The Sabbath of the Lord, the holy day of his rest, is shamelessly troubled and disquieted. Commentary on 1 Corinthians 16:2.[13]

Paul Was Not a Professional Fundraiser. Cardinal Cajetan: Paul arranges that the alms given for the saints in Jerusalem should not be collected from the common fund, or from certain people chosen for this, but that everyone should decide in their own mind what they should contribute, so that the Lord might be the trustee of all the money that was given. And it is believed that the reason for this arrangement was so that no one could accuse Paul of being a professional fundraiser [*quaestor*] or that priests, preachers, or Christians in general should be fundraisers. Since profit significantly denigrates and compromises the

[9]CO 49:566-67 (cf. CTS 40:68-69). Chrysostom's treatment of this verse is found in his *Homilies on 1 Corinthians* (homily 43), in NPNF 12:259.

[10]Literally "every one of a week."

[11]Beza, *Annotationes Maiores*, 248. Beza's interpretation of this clause is shared by most modern exegetes. See, for example, Fee, *The First Epistle to the Corinthians*, 813.

[12]Vermigli, *In Selectissimam Priorem ad Corinthios Epistolam . . . Commentarii*, 444v; citing Rev 1:10.

[13]Trapp, *A Commentary or Exposition*, 702*.

Christian church, why is the church today filled with indulgences, crusade taxes, Hospitaller taxes, etc.? Commentary on 1 Corinthians 16:2.[14]

Whomever You Will Approve. Wolfgang Musculus: Since the financial contribution to be sent to Jerusalem would be collected from the generosity of all, Paul relinquished authority to those men by whom the Corinthians wished to send it. Paul does not say, "whoever I will have approved"; but "whomever you will have approved." Thus Paul is exercising great caution so that the Corinthians won't perceive anything suspicious in this matter, as if he were acting for his own benefit rather than the needs of the saints. . . . And note how prudent Paul is: he does not say: "whomever you will have wanted"; nor "I will send whichever of you want to go"; but "whomever you will have approved." In Greek this word is *dokimasēte*, which signifies something that is proved and known through extensive experience. It's as if Paul were saying: "Whichever men you will have recognized and indicated are trustworthy and suitable for undertaking this business—I will send them." Therefore Paul grants to them the authority to choose those men who were going to be sent to Jerusalem, although at the same time he requires prudence and diligence so that not anyone might undertake the task, but that they might choose men of proved judgment. Naturally this affair required men who were both trustworthy and energetic. Trustworthy men, who would not treacherously embezzle any of the money entrusted to their care, but who would faithfully deliver it to those needy saints according to the wishes of those who made the contribution. Energetic men, who would conduct themselves prudently during the long and dangerous journey that was approaching, lest they by their lack of wisdom might bring danger on themselves and cause troubles for the saints. Commentary on 1 Corinthians 16:3.[15]

The Corinthian Gift Was a Special Grace. The English Annotations: In the original, it is *tēn karin hymōn*, that is, your grace, or free gift . . . because this was a kind of holy offering to the saints, and not a work of ordinary charity toward the poor. And hereby Paul also signifies that their pious and generous inclination to contribute to the saints was an effect of God's grace in the Corinthians, as he expressly affirms in 2 Corinthians 8:1-2. Annotations on 1 Corinthians 16:3.[16]

Almsgiving Should Not Be Mandated. Peter Martyr Vermigli: People are not usually easily influenced to give alms generously when it depends on them to distribute them in good faith. Second, let us note that those alms are called "grace," because those contributing the alms were providing a testimony by them of the favor and grace with which they were moved toward the people of Jerusalem. Or rather, Paul says this to remind them that "we possess none of those alms contributed except from the grace of God, for we brought nothing into this world and will take nothing from it."

Now from this present and similar passages are refuted the Anabaptists who preach that all things ought to be held in common among Christians. For according to their view, there would be no need to encourage believers to contribute alms, for each person would know how they should contribute. But since the sacred writings recommend alms to us, they clearly demonstrate that each person is the owner of his own possessions, although the fruit and use coming from them should be possessed to share with our neighbors who are in need. We see in this passage that the Corinthian church does not resist Paul, saying, "Why are you telling us about the people in Jerusalem? Do we not have our own paupers whom we must nourish? We should give alms to our own poor!" Instead, when they heard Paul stating that it was not enough for them to feed those of their own church, without also considering to support those brothers and sisters who were

[14]Cajetan, *In Sacrae Scripturae expositionem*, 5:149-50.
[15]Musculus, *Comm. 1 Cor*, 738-39.
[16]Downame, *English Annotations*, FF1v.

from other churches when the opportunity permitted, they promptly agreed with him. For even when charity must be organized, nevertheless it must not be carried out in such a way that people are forced to do it. Commentary on 1 Corinthians 16:3-4.[17]

[17]Vermigli, *In Selectissimam Priorem ad Corinthios Epistolam . . . Commentarii*, 444v.

16:5-12 Plans for Travel

5I will visit you after passing through Macedonia, for
I intend to pass through Macedonia, 6and perhaps I
will stay with you or even spend the winter, so that
you may help me on my journey, wherever I go. 7For
I do not want to see you now just in passing. I hope to
spend some time with you, if the Lord permits. 8But I
will stay in Ephesus until Pentecost, 9for a wide door
for effective work has opened to me, and there are
many adversaries.

10When Timothy comes, see that you put him at
ease among you, for he is doing the work of the Lord,
as I am. 11So let no one despise him. Help him on his
way in peace, that he may return to me, for I am
expecting him with the brothers.

12Now concerning our brother Apollos, I strongly
urged him to visit you with the other brothers, but it
was not at all his will[a] *to come now. He will come*
when he has opportunity.

a Or *God's will for him*

Overview: In this passage, Paul briefly explains to the Corinthians his future ministry plans as well as the travel plans of his colleagues Timothy and Apollos. Reformation commentators highlight for their readers Paul's unflagging zeal to spread the gospel message, his passion for God's glory, and his evident pastoral concern for the churches. Paul's remarkable example demonstrates that the "work of the Lord" (1 Cor 16:10) consists primarily in the proclamation of the gospel and the building up of the church—ministries that invariably require personal sacrifice and entail (more often than not) intense spiritual conflict. The fact that Paul decides to prolong his stay in Ephesus illustrates this principle: where there is the greatest opportunity for gospel advance, there Satan and his minions are particularly active to obstruct it. Several Reformation commentators are also impressed by the fact that Paul qualifies his travel itinerary with the phrase "if the Lord permits" (1 Cor 16:7), an apt reminder that Christians must always submit themselves to God and entrust their future plans to his providence.

16:5-9 *Paul's Itinerary*

Paul Wants to Spend Extended Time in Corinth. Peter Martyr Vermigli: Earlier, Paul had threatened to come and visit the Corinthians to punish those who were filled with proud conceit. Now he again promises to come to them, but he says it more gently. The Vulgate's inscription to this epistle states that it was written in Philippi. And certainly the apostle could have gone from there to Corinth by a brief shortcut, if he had not resolved to cross through Macedonia. But other people think that this epistle was written in Ephesus, which Chrysostom and the Greek schoolmen confirm. And this was certainly the case because, among his greetings, Paul adds the name of all the churches of Asia, and Ephesus was a major city in Asia Minor. And so Paul is very specific in explaining that he will pass through Macedonia. Then he says, "perhaps." For although he was endowed with the prophetic spirit, yet (since prophets are not always moved by divine inspiration) he speaks hypothetically—which ought to be understood as, "If it should please the Lord." For, in his second epistle, Paul is even forced to apologize [to the Corinthians] for not visiting them at the arranged time. And he promises that he wants to stay for some time among them, and not merely see them in passing—which is proof that he greatly desired their salvation. In the meantime, there were many things at Corinth in need of improvement and correction that could not be resolved very quickly. Now, Paul was not expecting to remain in Macedonia for very long, for things were going very well there. Indeed, the apostle gives a singular commendation to the churches of Macedonia. And so Paul is behaving like a doctor, who spends his time in the place where the disease is most virulent. Commentary on 1 Corinthians 16:5-7.[1]

Paul Seeks to Encourage the Corinthians. Tilemann Hesshus: Paul promises that he will come to Corinth so that his presence might encourage them. And he explains the reasons for his departure in order to demonstrate his zeal for spreading the gospel of Jesus Christ and to enlighten others by his example. He also mentions the fruitful outcome with which the Lord had adorned his preaching, so as to teach that the church was gathered and the gospel spread far and wide, not by human diligence or wisdom or effort, but by God. . . . Therefore Paul rejoices that a door has been opened to him by God to spread far and wide the light of the gospel, and God has worked powerfully through his preaching. In the meantime, enemies are always present who either attempt to turn the minds of simple people from the purity of Christ's teaching to illusions, or who attempt to subvert faithful ministers and extinguish the light of the divine Word by their tyranny. But followers of Christ have dominion in the midst of their enemies. Explication of 1 Corinthians 16:5-9.[2]

The Gospel Did Not Hibernate During Paul's Visit to Corinth. Wolfgang Musculus: "But I will spend the winter." . . . It is troublesome and inconvenient to journey, sail, and go on military campaigns during the winter because of the cold, snow, and rain. That is why it was customary for people to spend the winter indoors and, after having endured the inconvenience of winter, they were able to complete the journey they had begun. Therefore do the apostles also spend the winter in one place so as to avoid winter's troubles? To be sure, they spend the winters this way, but with this concern, that nothing should impede the spread of the gospel by doing so. For if acquiring possessions is as important as guarding them, so watering the gospel is as important as planting it. For the apostle Paul, the winter spent in residence among the Corinthians was not a break from gospel ministry, but was busy with spreading the gospel. Just as when the apostle was taken captive, the gospel was not captive, so when the apostle was hibernating for the winter, the gospel was not hibernating. Commentary on 1 Corinthians 16:6.[3]

If the Lord Permits. John Calvin: Now when Paul has said everything, he adds this limitation, "If the Lord permit." The saints should conclude all their plans and deliberations with this reservation. For it is most foolhardy to undertake and arrange many things in the future when, indeed, not even a moment is in our power. Now, the principle thing is, in the inward disposition of our minds, to submit to God and his providence in whatever we resolve to do. But at the same time, it is proper that we accustom ourselves to such forms of expression, so that whenever we must deal with the future, we entrust everything to God's will. Commentary on 1 Corinthians 16:7.[4]

Divine Permission. Wolfgang Musculus: Now when we read "if the Lord permits" three kinds of permission should be recognized. The first kind is when we freely concede those things that we are able to reject (unless we are agreeing to the wishes of those more powerful than us). Thus it is read that the Lord permitted the unclean spirits that entreated him to migrate into the flock of swine in Matthew 8. The second kind is when, being coerced and forced against our will, we concede to more powerful people those things that

[1]Vermigli, *In Selectissimam Priorem ad Corinthios Epistolam . . . Commentarii*, 447v; citing 1 Cor 16:19.
[2]Hesshus, *Explicatio Prioris Epistolae ad Corinthios*, 369r.
[3]Musculus, *Comm. 1 Cor.*, 744.
[4]CO 49:568 (cf. CTS 40:71).

we are not able to prevent. Thus all of us hand over our goods to the enemy when we have lost the power to resist them. The third kind is when, though we do not approve, but are not coerced, we permit things to happen for certain reasons that, at other times, we might have rejected (or we reject those things that we might have been seen to concede). Now nobody in their right mind will deny that the first kind of permission can pertain to God. For who is so stupid as to deny that God grants many of those prayers that it was entirely possible for him to justly and freely deny? In a similar fashion, I think that it is without controversy that the third kind of permission also pertains to God, because he not only allows certain things to happen that he could prevent for various reasons but also prevents good things from happening, which by all appearances he could rightly have permitted. That God allows evil to happen is clearly demonstrated from the words of the apostle found in Acts 14, "In past ages, [God] allowed all Gentiles to walk in their own ways." God was certainly able to restrain them and turn them away from their sinful lives, but there were reasons why he allowed all of these people to be confined to their unbelief, which he could have prevented with no trouble. . . . No one in their right mind will attribute to the invincible and omnipotent God the second kind of permission, which is due to lack of power and coercion. Therefore, when the apostle says here, "I hope to spend some time with you, *if the Lord permits*," in my judgment this refers to the first kind of permission. Commentary on 1 Corinthians 16:7.[5]

Why Did Paul Remain in Ephesus Until Pentecost? John Calvin: "I will remain." From this statement I have theorized above that this epistle was sent from Ephesus rather than from Philippi. . . . Paul therefore predicts that he will remain at Ephesus until Pentecost, adding the reason—so that they might wait for him more patiently. Erasmus prefers the translation "until the fiftieth day," influenced by a frivolous conjecture rather than by any solid argument. He argues that the day of Pentecost had not yet been established among Christians, as it is now celebrated. I grant this. He says that it ought not to be understood as referring to the Jewish festival, because in various places Paul abrogates and disapproves of the superstitious observance of days. But I do not concede to him that Paul was celebrating that day in Ephesus because of superstition with regard to the day, but instead because there would be more people assembled on that day, and so he was hoping that it would afford him an opportunity to spread the gospel. In the same way, when Paul was traveling quickly to Jerusalem, he reported that the reason for his hurry was so that he "might arrive there by Pentecost." But while other people presented themselves at the sacrifice according to the ritual of the law, Paul had in mind a different end, that his ministry might be more useful amid a larger audience. Commentary on 1 Corinthians 16:8.[6]

A Wide Door of Opportunity. John Calvin: Paul gives two reasons for remaining longer in Ephesus: because an opportunity is there for him to further the gospel, and, owing to a multitude of enemies, his presence there was particularly required. Therefore it's as if he were saying: "I will accomplish much good by remaining here for a little while, and Satan would cause a lot of harm if I were absent." In the first clause, Paul uses a common metaphor when he employs the term "door" for an opportune moment. For the Lord was opening a doorway for him to advance the gospel. He calls this a "great door" because he was able to win many people. He calls the door "effective" because the Lord was blessing his labors and was making his teaching efficacious through the power of his Spirit. We see, therefore, how this holy man pursued Christ's glory everywhere, and did not strive for his own convenience or his own pleasure. Instead, he focused simply on this: where he might do the greatest good and serve his Lord with the greatest fruit. And he adds to this that he

[5]Musculus, *Comm. 1 Cor.*, 748-49; citing Acts 14:16.

[6]CO 49:568-69 (cf. CTS 40:72-73); citing Acts 20:16.

by no means ran away from troubles, but voluntarily stationed himself where he saw that the fighting would be most fierce and difficult. For he was remaining [in Ephesus] because there were so many enemies threatening, and since he was so well equipped to withstand their attack, he had to be all the more prepared and resolute. Commentary on 1 Corinthians 16:9.[7]

Reasons for Paul's Delay. David Dickson: Paul gives two reasons why he deferred his coming until the time of the Jewish feast (deciding to stay longer at Ephesus). First, because God had opened a great door, or offered an abundant occasion for the winning of many people and converting them to the gospel. God had clearly given a blessing to his labors, which he calls an "effectual door." Second, because the tumult of his adversaries was so great that his presence was required and Satan, in his absence, did much harm. Annotations on 1 Corinthians 16:9.[8]

Opportunities and Adversaries. The English Annotations: Paul recognizes a great occasion or opportunity for doing much good in his ministry. For Ephesus was a very populated city, well-known for the famous temple of Diana and also diverse schools and nurseries of learning. Or the apostle may be intimating that some great advantage was gained for the gospel by the conversion of some notable men or women in that city. Where there is greatest opportunity for doing good, there the devil and his agents work most busily to stop and hinder it. For, as St. Chrysostom aptly observes, the devil works the hardest where he is most likely to lose the most. And it is no wonder that the gospel finds many enemies, since the Truth is a stranger on the earth; Christ causes the falling and rising of many people, and serves as a sign that many shall speak against (Lk 2:34). Annotations on 1 Corinthians 16:9.[9]

16:10-12 *Timothy and Apollos, the Lord's Workmen*

Godly Ministers Need Encouragement. Tilemann Hesshus: Paul urges the Corinthians to welcome his coworker Timothy with kindness, and to hold him with respect on account of the Lord's work, that is, on account of the preaching of the gospel. And Paul forbids that they should either despise him because of his age or frighten him by their arrogance. Now the preaching of the gospel is difficult work; thus those who serve in that capacity ought to be strengthened with encouragement rather than frightened by contempt and harshness in order that their holy zeal and godly efforts to spread the gospel might not be extinguished. We should consider neither the person nor the age of ministers, but the ministry that they exercise, which does not originate from them, but from the almighty and omnipotent God, who has commissioned them to look after our salvation. Next, Paul makes an excuse for Apollos, since he will not be coming to Corinth. Explication of 1 Corinthians 16:10-11.[10]

The Nature of the Lord's Work. Wolfgang Musculus: What is the work of the Lord that must be undertaken by a faithful minister? Is it to wear a two-horned miter? To have rings encircling one's fingers? To exhibit the shepherd's crook? To be draped in a pallium like a rain jacket? To dress the loins in the manner of grazing sheep? And once or twice in the course of a year to amuse oneself with theatrical displays, anointing walls, chalices, altars, and bells? This trash has nothing to do with the work of the Lord. The work of the Lord is the ministry of proclaiming the gospel, planting and nourishing the church, and applying oneself tirelessly to care for the salvation of believers. This is the work of the Lord, which was not invented by human beings, but was imposed by the Lord himself on the apostles and their successors. And this work the apostles faithfully performed. Commentary on 1 Corinthians 16:10.[11]

---

[7]CO 49:569 (cf. CTS 40:73-74).

[8]Dickson, *Exposition of St. Paul's Epistles*, 70*.

[9]Downame, *English Annotations*, FF1v*. For Chrysostom's comment, see Homily I on the Statutes, NPNF: 9:334

[10]Hesshus, *Explicatio Prioris Epistolae ad Corinthios*, 369v-370r.

[11]Musculus, *Comm. 1 Cor.*, 757.

Calming Timothy's Fear. Peter Martyr Vermigli: "That he has nothing to fear among you." Some interpreters take these words to mean external persecutions—and they say that for a good reason—remembering that Paul was devoted not only to the safety of his disciple [Timothy] but also to the well-being of the entire church, for whom he would make a great sacrifice lest a member of Christ so noble should be lost. Nevertheless, it does not appear that Paul wrote these things about the persecutions of tyrants, but about those persecutions that the Gentiles were stirring up, seeing that the Corinthians were not able to calm them. Perhaps he is referring to the dangers stirred up by the false apostles and Paul's enemies, which could have been threatening Timothy. If we accept this explanation, we will see that the safety of ministers ought to be the concern of their churches. When Peter was held in prison, the church was praying for him without ceasing. So too Ambrosius reports in his *Sermon Against Auxenium* that a Christian plebe, when he saw that grave danger was threatening Peter at Rome, begged him to allow him to serve him, which he did for a while, standing by him as a witness to the people of Christ. But I think this statement is referring to a fear of a different sort. True pastors especially fear that they are wasting their efforts and that greater and more severe blindness will arise when they speak regarding judgment and the condemnation of their hearers. Consequently Paul is going to exhort the Corinthians to be eager to listen and perform those things that Timothy has announced for their improvement and correction. In this way Timothy would be free from fear. Commentary on 1 Corinthians 16:10.[12]

Modest Ministers Must Work. John Trapp: Every faithful minister works, even those of a meaner sort. The vine is the weakest of trees, but full of fruit. A little hand may thread a needle. A little boat may do best in a low river. The church in Philadelphia had but little strength (Rev 3:8), and yet it kept God's word. Commentary on 1 Corinthians 16:10.[13]

Paul Commends Both Timothy and Apollos. Heinrich Bullinger: Paul enthusiastically commends the brothers Timothy and Apollos with words full of love and respect. We learn from these words how much we owe to ministers of the Word of God who are holy, learned, and faithful; and also how much those people sin who despise and constantly abuse such ministers. There are indeed deceivers who shout, "Those who listen to you, listen to me. Those who despise you, despise me." And so, under the pretext of these words, they feign a certain authority . . . and pursue their own affairs. Of course, everyone condemns those kinds of people. Yes, indeed, because of such people, Paul himself has clearly said, "Let no one despise him. For he does the Lord's work just as I do." Therefore all who do the work of the Lord should not be despised; for those who despise them despise the Lord. Thus those who pursue their own affairs should not be listened to, for they seek their own good, not the Lord's good. In the first chapter of this epistle, and also in Acts 19, we heard some things about Apollos, who at one time was preaching at Corinth. It appears that he had been called to Corinth, and yet, since certain circumstances prevented him from coming, Paul mentions it briefly in this passage, excusing both himself and Apollos. Commentary on 1 Corinthians 16:11-12.[14]

Apollos's Delay. John Calvin: Apollos had succeeded Paul in the task of building up the Corinthians; for this reason, Paul earlier attributes to Apollos the role of watering. He now apologizes for Apollos's not coming with the others, and he does so lest the Corinthians suspect that Paul had impeded him from coming. For Apollos was better known to the Corinthians, and so they were more

[12]Vermigli, *In Selectissimam Priorem ad Corinthios Epistolam . . . Commentarii*, 449r-v; citing Acts 12.

[13]Trapp, *A Commentary or Exposition*, 702*.

[14]Bullinger, *In Priorem ad Corinthios Epistolam Commentarius*, 261.

favorable toward him; and they would be inclined to conjecture that, because Paul was offended at them, it had been decided that Apollos would not come to them. They would certainly have been asking each other: "Why did he send these men to us rather than Apollos?" Paul replies that it was not at all his fault, because he had urged Apollos to go. But he promises that Apollos will come as soon as he has the opportunity. COMMENTARY ON 1 CORINTHIANS 16:12.[15]

[15]CO 49:570 (cf. CTS 40:74-75); citing 1 Cor 3:6.

16:13-18 FINAL INSTRUCTIONS

[13]Be watchful, stand firm in the faith, act like men, be
strong. [14]Let all that you do be done in love.
[15]Now I urge you, brothers[a]—you know that the
household[b] of Stephanas were the first converts in
Achaia, and that they have devoted themselves to the
service of the saints— [16]be subject to such as these,
and to every fellow worker and laborer. [17]I rejoice at
the coming of Stephanas and Fortunatus and
Achaicus, because they have made up for your absence,
[18]for they refreshed my spirit as well as yours. Give
recognition to such people.

a Or *brothers and sisters*; also verse 20 **b** Greek *house*

Overview: Having explained his travel plans, Paul now provides final words of instruction to the Corinthian Christians, exhorting them to persevere in faith and love and to submit to the godly leaders appointed over them. Reformation commentators devote considerable space to Paul's succinct summary of Christian ethics in 1 Corinthians 16:13-14. In the face of Satan's relentless attacks, Christian "soldiers" must remain armed for battle by being vigilant, firm of faith, full of courage, strong of spirit, and motivated by love. Likewise, Paul's warm commendation of the household of Stephanas gives Protestant commentators one last opportunity to articulate the qualities of Christian leadership and the respect those leaders deserve. The fact that Paul praises the household of Stephanas for being "devoted to the service of the saints" has nothing to do with the Catholic cult of saints, but illustrates that *all* Christian believers, whether they be princes or paupers, are the "saints" of God in need of pastoral care. Finally, several commentators point out the various intense emotions that Paul displays in this passage and throughout his writings—clear proof that Christian life and ministry does not require a kind of Stoic indifference, but engages the full spectrum of human feelings, including joy and sadness, hopefulness and disappointment.

16:13-14 *Stand Firm in the Faith!*

Godly Disciplines. Desiderius Erasmus: Watch out for the snares of wicked desires. Persevere in the faith once for all entrusted to you. With a broken spirit, oppose those things that stand in the way of the gospel, and be strong. And in everything that you undertake, do it in love rather than with quarreling. Paraphrase on 1 Corinthians 16.[1]

Gospel Ministry Requires Vigilance and Steadfastness. Huldrych Zwingli: Vigilance, steadfastness, and perseverance are necessary in every endeavor, but especially in the affairs of the gospel. Those who are negligent will suffer very harsh punishments for their negligence. Now, it is especially incumbent on bishops, pastors, and prophets to be vigilant and steadfast, and then also for those who govern the republic. Faith is often attacked. Therefore it is important that we stand and fight strongly. Annotations on 1 Corinthians 16:13.[2]

Corinthians Must Stand Guard Like Soldiers. Wolfgang Musculus: As Paul concludes his letter—before adding his commendation of certain select believers along with his official greetings—he offers concise words of advice that are especially necessary for that church. First, he says, "be watchful." That is, beware lest your soul becomes drowsy; be watchful for the sake of your salvation; be attentive and cautious. If they are watchful, then scarcely any seductive

[1]Erasmus, *Paraphrases*, 349.
[2]Zwingli, *Annotatiunculae . . . ex ore Zvinglij*, 141.

persons will creep into their church. If they are watchful, then they will hardly ever permit a foothold for factions and false apostles. . . . Then, drawing out the metaphor further, Paul adds, "Stand firm in the faith." One does not stand guard by lying prostrate on the ground, or by sitting in a leisurely fashion, but by standing, prepared to detect and expose the plots of the enemy . . . they must not disagree among themselves with hatred and jealousy, but have a loving and harmonious disposition toward one another. Thus, developing the metaphor of standing guard, Paul says: "Be watchful, stand firm in the faith, act like men, be strong, let all of your actions be done in love." Commentary on 1 Corinthians 16:13.[3]

The Christian's Warfare Against Satan. Tilemann Hesshus: This is the second part of the chapter, in which Paul repeats and emphasizes an exhortation that is especially necessary. Satan incessantly sets up his traps against us to throw careless and thoughtless people headlong into errors or wickedness. We must be watchful, therefore, in zeal and prayer. We must continually hold sacred Scripture in our hands. We must inquire into the fundamental truths of our religion and ponder the Holy Spirit's oracles. Satan's tricks must be carefully avoided, and God continually petitioned to direct us in the truth by his Holy Spirit. We must stand fast in the knowledge of the truth lest we invent new doctrines through our weak character or ambition, or we approve thing invented by other people. With manly courage and the Spirit's strength, we must excel in enduring the troubles, dangers, abuses, miseries, and temptations that godly people are in the habit of experiencing. For in this battle, no one is crowned and will have attained the victor's wreath except the person who will have fought strongly and constantly. Then Paul repeats the command to exercise love in every kind of duty. For this ought to be the guide of all our actions and decisions. And though Paul emphasized this command above with many words, he repeats it here at the end of the epistle to root it deep into our memory. Explication of 1 Corinthians 16:13-14.[4]

Five Duties of Christian "Soldiers." David Dickson: Paul then exhorts the Corinthians to five military duties of Christian soldiers. First, that even if he and Apollos are slow in coming to them that they should in the meantime keep continual watch lest Satan should come on them while they are secure and drunk with worldly cares. Second, that they should be constant in the faith, firmly holding the truth of the gospel, being united to Christ by faith. Third, that they should show themselves to be courageous in every combat against the adversaries of faith and their salvation. Fourth, that they should be strong in the power of God, and not faint under the evils that they encounter. Fifth, that they should make love the arbitrator of all things, both ecclesiastical and civil, serving the common good in everything. Annotations on 1 Corinthians 16:13-14.[5]

Love Necessary for True Christian Fellowship. Martin Luther: True fellowship is divine and heavenly; it is the noblest, surpassing all the others as gold surpasses copper or lead; it is the communion of saints, in which we all are brothers and sisters, so near to one another that greater nearness could never be conceived. For there is *one* baptism, *one* Christ, *one* sacrament, *one* meal, *one* gospel, *one* faith, *one* Spirit, *one* spiritual body, and each one is a member of the other; no other brotherhood is so deep and close.

But if you say, "Unless I get something through the fellowship, of what use is it?" The answer is, "You serve the community and other peoples as love does, and you will have your reward without any seeking or desiring it." Love serves freely, which is why God in return also gives to it every blessing, freely and without charge. Because all things must be done in love if they are to be well pleasing to

[3]Musculus, *Comm. 1 Cor.*, 764.

[4]Hesshus, *Explicatio Prioris Epistolae ad Corinthios*, 370r-v.
[5]Dickson, *Exposition of St. Paul's Epistles*, 71*.

God, the community must also be in love. Yet what is done in love can by its nature not seek its own; instead it seeks the benefit of others, and especially the congregation. As you find your trust in Christ and his dear saints growing in strength, your certainty grows of their love toward you, and how they will stand by you in all the troubles of life and death. Therefore your love goes out to each one and you desire to help everyone, hate no one, suffer with all, and pray for all. Again, if you take to heart the shortcomings and lapses of all Christians and of the whole church, or the fall of any one, and your love is given to them all, so that you would readily help anyone, hate none, sympathize with all, and pray for them, then all is well. The Sacrament of the Body of Christ.[6]

A Family of Love. John Trapp: Love is the saints' insignia (John 13:35). The heathen acknowledged that no people in the world loved as the Christians did. In primitive times, as Tertullian said, Christians were united with one another in mind and spirit. But now, alas, it is far otherwise. Love began to grow cold among the Corinthians. That is why Paul here gives this sweet and savory counsel. Love in Christ's day was much decayed; in Basil's time it had dried up. Bishop Latimer saw such a lack of it that he thought the last days were at hand. One would wish that this apostolic precept were well practiced, and that we were all (in a sober sense) members of the family of love. Commentary on 1 Corinthians 16:14.[7]

16:15-18 *The Godly Example of Stephanas*

Stephanas and His Household. John Calvin: We know from daily experience how advantageous it is that those whom God has endowed with the most excellent gifts should have the highest authority. Accordingly, if we want to look after the welfare of the church, let us always take care that honor is conferred on good people. Let their advice have the greatest weight; let others submit to them and allow themselves to be governed by their good judgment. Paul is doing this very thing when he admonishes the Corinthians to show respect to the house of Stephanas (some codices add "and Fortunatus"[8]). For God manifests himself to us when he shows us the gifts of his Spirit. Therefore, lest we wish to appear to be despisers of God, let us freely submit ourselves to whomever God has conferred the superior gifts.

Now, so that they might be more inclined to honor that house . . . Paul reminds them that they were the firstfruits of Achaia, that is, that the household of Stephanas was the first to have embraced the gospel. That's not because the one that precedes temporally is always better than the others, but where there is perseverance, honor is rightly bestowed on those who have paved the way (as it were) for the gospel through readiness of faith. But let us note that the people whom Paul has honored with such a complimentary title are those who had dedicated their service and resources to the believers. And a little later, Paul commends Fortunatus and Achaicus for the same reason, namely, that the better a person is, the more he or she should be held in high esteem in order that they might be able do even more good. Commentary on 1 Corinthians 16:15-18.[9]

The Household of Stephanas. Menno Simons: I say that the Holy Spirit has testified in clear print that the three families of which the Scriptures make mention in particular, saying they were baptized, were all believing persons as may be plainly understood from reading Acts 10:33-34 as to the household of Cornelius; Acts 16:15, of the household of the [Philippian] jailer; 1 Corinthians 16:15, of the household of Stephanas in good clear report. . . . I repeat it, to serve the saints is a work of

[6]LW 35:70, 72.

[7]Trapp, *A Commentary or Exposition*, 703*. See Tertullian's statement in his *Apology*, ANF 3:46.

[8]An early version of the Latin Vulgate followed the Alexandrian and Coptic manuscript traditions in adding "and Fortunatus" to verse 15. Calvin and Erasmus follow the more authoritative manuscript tradition that reads simply "household of Stephanas."

[9]CO 49:571 (cf. CTS 40:76-77).

faith. Since the house of Stephanas served the saints, as Paul writes, therefore they showed by their fruits that they had faith. Christian Baptism.[10]

Worshiping the Saints Is Blasphemy. Guillaume Farel: The worship, adoration, and prayers done for saints, and for all others who are out of this world, is a thing done without faith, against the Word of God. In this God is dishonored, because his honor is given to the creature. In fact, one also dishonors saints, because one appeals to them despite that which they did, said, and taught. For the saints do not want us to trust in them, but in God. . . .

Those blaspheme who say that the saints are our intercessors, advocates, and mediators between God and us, the way, the life, and the hope. Their treatment of the saints is outrageous, and they dishonor our Lord Jesus, who alone is mediator, who intercedes for us with the Father. He is our advocate, who speaks for us, the only way, life, and truth, and no other. Our hope is in God alone: those who put their trust in him are happy; those who put their trust in another are cursed. Summary and Brief Exposition.[11]

The True Cult of Saints. Wolfgang Musculus: Paul not only commends [the members of the household of Stephanas] because they were the first to believe the gospel of God, but he also proposes this for consideration: that after they began to believe, they devoted all possible strength to ministering to their believing brothers, with holy and devout zeal. Those who were believing in Christ—paupers, refugees, and the downhearted—Paul now in the second place calls "saints," as a reminder both of the high status they possessed and for what purpose this household of Stephanas was ministering among them. Stephanas and his household reckoned and acknowledged those people to be saints of God, and for this reason they were offering them hospitality, feeding them, clothing them, treating them with every kind of refreshment and consolation (as much as they were able), and encouraging them in the Christian faith. All of these acts of service Paul includes under the word "ministry," so that no one might imagine that anything is exempt from such service. We learn here the true meaning of the term "cult of saints" [*cultores divorum*], as the papacy calls it, for the apostolic doctrine teaches us who the saints are and with what kind of service they minister. Worship God by faith, O brothers and sisters, and serve him alone; but minister to the saints (that is, believers in Christ) who are afflicted in this age through necessary acts of charity. In so doing, you will be the legitimate worshipers and servants of God, and genuine ministers of the saints. Commentary on 1 Corinthians 16:15.[12]

Showing Deference to Spiritual Men. Cardinal Cajetan: Rather than commanding them, Paul implores the Corinthians to be morally subject not only to those who were part of the household of Stephanas but to all those who were cooperating and laboring in the ministry to the saints. From this we learn that we should exhibit deference and reverence toward those men who are more proven and more spiritual—though not with that legal subjection which we owe to bishops. Commentary on 1 Corinthians 16:16.[13]

Stephanas, Fortunatus, and Achaicus. Heinrich Bullinger: Paul gives thanks that the Corinthians had sent these men. What he is saying is this: "I was longing for you, namely, for your presence, which those men have supplied by their arrival. And so they have refreshed my spirit, or rather, your spirit, because I am entirely one with you." On the other hand, you see that the apostles were also sad, joyful, and refreshed. We say this for the sake of those who believe that our religion is some sort of Stoicism. Moreover, Paul says: "Give recognition to people of this sort," which is to say,

[10]Simons, *Complete Writings*, 281-82.
[11] In Zuidema and Van Raalte, *Early French Reform*, 145, 146*.
[12]Musculus, *Comm. 1 Cor.*, 770.
[13]Cajetan, *In Sacrae Scripturae expositionem*, 5:150.

"hold them in honor." Commentary on 1 Corinthians 16:17-18.[14]

The Ministry of Stephanas, Fortunatus, and Achaicus. Cardinal Cajetan: So that we might understand in what way the presence of those three men was an encouragement, Paul explains that they refreshed, not the body, but both "my spirit" and "your spirit." By informing Paul of the Corinthians' disposition, the men did two good things: first, they comforted the spiritual affections of Paul, which had been saddened on account of the Corinthians' many faults; second, they provoked Paul to instruct and exhort the Corinthians. That is the reason they are said to have refreshed the spirit of both Paul and the others. And since those three men exercised such a useful role, Paul advises that the Corinthians should hold these men with affection, adding the phrase "Give recognition, therefore, to such people." Commentary on 1 Corinthians 16:18.[15]

Refreshment for Paul's Spirit. Wolfgang Musculus: In Greek, we read *anepausan gar*, that is, "they once more brought rest." When an exhausted soul is given an interval of rest, either by the cessation or easing of work, this is called *anapauesthai*. The spirit of Paul was refreshed by this kind of rest with the coming of Stephanas, Fortunatus, and Achaicus. Now even if Paul's longing for the Corinthian church was not entirely removed by the presence of those men, nevertheless it was lightened somewhat. Thus the spirits of godly people are refreshed in this life by other people who (even if they do not take away the labor to which they are called by divine providence) promptly provide them with an interval of rest, so that they do not completely collapse. Even so, the time draws near when the spirits of godly people will obtain full and complete refreshment and rest from their work for eternity. The spirit of the apostle was burdened with his concern for all the churches. His worry was not entirely removed by the arrival of these three men, but it was relieved in part and for a time.... In this way, God has provided for the refreshment of godly people whereby they might be renewed in this life. Commentary on 1 Corinthians 16:18.[16]

[14]Bullinger, *In Priorem ad Corinthios Epistolam Commentarius*, 261.
[15]Cajetan, *In Sacrae Scripturae expositionem*, 5:150.
[16]Musculus, *Comm. 1 Cor.*, 774-75.

16:19-24 GREETINGS IN CHRIST

[19]The churches of Asia send you greetings. Aquila and Prisca, together with the church in their house, send you hearty greetings in the Lord. [20]All the brothers send you greetings. Greet one another with a holy kiss.

[21]I, Paul, write this greeting with my own hand. [22]If anyone has no love for the Lord, let him be accursed. Our Lord, come![a] [23]The grace of the Lord Jesus be with you. [24]My love be with you all in Christ Jesus. Amen.

a Greek *Maranatha* (a transliteration of Aramaic)

Overview: Paul concludes his long epistle by passing along his own greeting as well as the greetings of foreign churches, warning hypocrites of God's judgment, and assuring the Corinthians of his unwavering love for them. Reformation commentators devote space to several of the peculiar details of this passage, including the references to the church in Aquila and Priscilla's home (1 Cor 16:19), the "holy kiss" (1 Cor 16:20), and Paul's signing the letter in his own hand (1 Cor 16:21). A far thornier problem is posed by the Aramaic phrase *maran atha*, which invites prolonged exegetical discussions of Hebrew and Aramaic philology as well as the history of Christian interpretation of this passage. With some nuance of difference, the majority of Reformation commentators believe that the phrase *anathema maran atha* constitutes a twofold banning formula by which Paul formally excommunicates those hypocrites who teach false doctrine and degrade the church with their scandalous behavior.[1] At the same time, Paul's concluding words provide important lessons for the contemporary church. Commentators praise the unity and mutual concern that existed between different local churches in Paul's day. Moreover, Paul's fervent and stubborn love for *all* of the Corinthians—even those whom he has strongly rebuked in the course of his epistle—should serve as a powerful reminder that Christian ministers are called to sacrifice everything for the good of the faithful in the Lord Jesus Christ.

16:19-20 *The Churches Send Their Greetings*

Paul's Final Greetings. Desiderius Erasmus: The congregations in Asia greet you. Aquila and Priscilla, and the rest of the Christian congregation that they have in their home, send warm greetings to you with godly affection. All those here who profess the name of Christ send their greetings to you. Be united among yourselves with mutual goodwill and greet one other with a holy and pure kiss as a symbol of true harmony. I, Paul, greet you. I have signed this greeting in my own hand to demonstrate both my affection for you and that this letter is not spurious. If anyone does not love the Lord Jesus, let them be cursed—Maranatha!—inasmuch as they are rejecting him from whom salvation alone can be obtained, and denying the fact that he has come to bestow great blessing on believers, but terrible punishment on unbelievers. May the favor and kindness of the Lord Jesus Christ be with you. I pray that even as I love you with Christian affection, so you too might love one another with that pure love with which Christ Jesus has united you together. Amen. Paraphrase on 1 Corinthians 16.[2]

Christian Greetings Help Unite the Church. Peter Martyr Vermigli: To greet

[1]Most modern English translations, including the ESV, understand the phrase *Maran atha* in verse 22 to be an eschatological prayer, "O Lord, come!"

[2]Erasmus, *Paraphrases*, 349-50.

someone is to wish them well, which is a duty that Christians should not at all be adverse to, though they should be careful not to do it in a hypocritical manner. Paul desires to join together members of Christ's body everywhere, for which purpose those mutual greetings are very powerful. Anabaptists reject those sorts of greetings and fiercely cling to what Christ said: "Greet no one on the road." They do not pay attention to the fact that, with that statement, Christ was prescribing that no delay or hesitation should interfere with the gospel. Besides, Christ himself greeted the disciples by saying, "Peace be with you." Likewise, Paul and the other apostles prefix greetings to their letters. Commentary on 1 Corinthians 16:19.[3]

Mutual Love Should Unite Various Churches. Wolfgang Musculus: Paul sent ahead a more general greeting, which was something even more precious. It is a great thing when a Christian brother greets another brother from the heart and looks on him with true love in the Lord. But it is greater still when churches display loving affection for other churches—not only churches of one and the same nation, which can possibly happen out of love for the same *patria* and language, but churches of various regions and nations, as when German churches love from the heart the churches of France, Italy, England, and Spain for the sake of Christ, and they share mutual love one with another. The profession of one and the same faith in Christ, sealed with the same sacraments; the common union under the headship of Christ; the regeneration and guidance that is from the same Spirit—all these things demand this common and general church love (*philekklēsian*). That such mutual love existed in the apostle's day is certain given this general greeting of the churches that he delivered. Thus he admonishes all churches that they should be united and joined together with affection, if indeed they want to be considered churches not only in appearance and in name but truly for the sake of Christ. Commentary on 1 Corinthians 16:19.[4]

Aquila and Priscilla. Peter Martyr Vermigli: From this passage one can conclude that Paul was probably writing this letter from Ephesus, which was the capital city of Asia. This also seems to be the case from what he adds: "Greet Aquila and Priscilla." For Paul spent time with them in Ephesus when he was their guest—indeed, they were of the same craft with him, for they were tent makers. And they were so zealous for the gospel that they brought Apollos to their home and were teaching him, for he had not yet fully been instructed in Christ (as is described in the Acts of the Apostles). And Paul gives them a warm commendation in the final chapter of Romans, when he says that they risked their necks for him, and that all the Gentile churches are obliged to them. Commentary on 1 Corinthians 16:19.[5]

Christian Families Should Function as Little Churches. John Calvin: "With the church in their house." What a wonderful expression, since it attributes the name "church" to a single family. And yet it is fitting that all the families of godly people should be organized in such a way as to be so many little churches. As to the term "congregation," which Erasmus prefers—this is alien to Paul's intention. For it was not Paul's intention to designate a mere crowd of people, using a common term, but to speak with great respect about the Christian household. That Paul sends greetings in the name of Aquila and Priscilla confirms that this epistle was written at Ephesus rather than Philippi, as we noted earlier. Commentary on 1 Corinthians 16:19.[6]

---

[3]Vermigli, *In Selectissimam Priorem ad Corinthios Epistolam . . . Commentarii*, 454r-v; citing Lk 10:4; Jn 20:21, 26.

[4]Musculus, *Comm. 1 Cor.*, 776.

[5]Vermigli, *In Selectissimam Priorem ad Corinthios Epistolam . . . Commentarii*, 454v; citing Acts 18:24-28.

[6]CO 49:571-72 (cf. CTS 40:77-78). For Erasmus's use of congregation (*congregatio*) to describe the church in the home of Aquila and Priscilla, see the excerpt from his *Paraphrase* included above.

The Holy Kiss. John Calvin: The custom of kissing was very common among the Jews, as is clear from Scripture. In Greece, though, it was not so common and popular—but it was not unknown. It is probable that Paul is speaking here about a solemn kiss, by which people greeted one another in their sacred assemblies. For I could easily believe that a kiss was used in connection with the Lord's Supper already during the age of the apostles—in place of which, in certain countries that were somewhat adverse to the custom of kissing, the practice of kissing the patina crept in. Whatever the case, since this was a symbol of mutual love, I have no doubt that Paul meant to encourage them to cultivate goodwill among themselves—not only in their hearts and as they performed necessary duties but also with the sign of a kiss, as long as it was "holy," that is, not immodest or deceptive, though it is possible to take the word "holy" in the sense of "sacred." Commentary on 1 Corinthians 16:20.[7]

Greet with a Holy Kiss. The English Annotations: "Greet one another with a holy kiss," not with a hypocritical kiss, as with Judas, nor out of carnal affection, as mentioned in Proverbs 7:13. Rather, express your unfeigned love to those who are called to be saints and fellow members of one holy, mystical body, whereof Christ is the head. Annotations on 1 Corinthians 16:20.[8]

16:21-24 *Final Exhortations*

Paul's Hand-Written Greeting Authenticates His Letter. Wolfgang Musculus: There are two things to note. First, Paul himself also greets the Corinthians. And second, he writes down this greeting in his very own handwriting without the help of an amanuensis (which he often used) so that the Corinthians might have certainty concerning both that greeting and the entire letter, and so as to take away every opportunity for deceivers lest they thrust on the churches some false and corrupt substitution under Paul's name. And Paul uses such caution not only in this letter but in all his other letters, as one can see from his second letter to the Thessalonians, where he says the following: "I Paul write this greeting in my own hand, which is the sign in all my letters." Commentary on 1 Corinthians 16:21.[9]

Paul Pronounces an Anathema on Hypocrites. Tilemann Hesshus: Now [hypocrites] are completely alien from the true love of Christ, for they do not help build up the church, they do not shine forth the glory of Christ. Instead, they stir up divisions, they promote false doctrines, they attack godly teachers, they deform the church with scandals—such people Paul threatens with *anathema*, that is, excommunication, a curse, and eternal damnation. Now the anathematized person has no place in Christ's kingdom, but is weighed down under God's curse. And so the apostle Paul teaches here that people anathematized before God are not only those who are excommunicated by the public judgment and decision of the church but also those who hide their godlessness under the outer appearance of religion, and skillfully feign zeal for piety, since they are completely offensive to Christ and the truth. . . . Although these people advertise themselves to be, or are even considered, leaders of the church, nevertheless because they lack a sincere love for Christ, they are anathematized by the judgment of the apostle, that is, they are objects condemned by God and destined for eternal torment, unless they are converted to God.

Interpreters variously dispute the word *maran atha*, which Paul adds. Many follow Ambrose's interpretation, which says that the word *maran atha* in the Syriac language means "Our Lord is coming." But it seems to me that this reading does not sufficiently agree with the preceding sentence. And why did Paul need to speak Syriac among the Corinthians? Therefore I find much more pleasing

[7]CO 49:572 (cf. CTS 40:79-80). The *patina* is the dish used to serve the consecrated bread during the Catholic Mass.
[8]Downame, *English Annotations*, FF1v*.
[9]Musculus, *Comm. 1 Cor.*, 777-78; citing 2 Thess 3:17.

the interpretation of Theodor Bibliander, Wolfgang Capito, and Paul of Burgos, who read *mecherem atha*, and assert that this word is the same as the Hebrew word ḥērem, that is, anathema. Therefore Paul repeats the same thing: anathema, and *maran atha* or *mecherem atha*. "Whoever you are, you who do not love Jesus Christ, the savior of the world, you are anathema, excommunicated, and cursed." There is nothing surprising for a foreign word to be written differently by the apostle, or corrupted by scribes. Explication of 1 Corinthians 16:22.[10]

The Meaning of the Phrase *Maran atha*. Heinrich Bullinger: Paul adds . . . that powerful statement: "If anyone does not love the Lord Jesus Christ, let him be anathema. *Maran atha*." Concerning this statement, Saint Jerome writes in a certain letter to Marcella: "*Maran atha* is more Syriac than Hebrew, although to some degree it is from the overlapping of both languages, and it sounds like Hebrew. It is interpreted 'Our Lord has come.' Now, this is the meaning: If anyone does not love the Lord Jesus Christ, let him be anathema—and, once that is accomplished, the statement is then inserted "Our Lord has come" because it would be hopeless to want to strive with stubborn insolence against one who was known already to have come." That is what Jerome says. Others explain this passage, "If anyone does not love our Lord Jesus Christ, they will die in utter destruction." But Theodor Bibliander, interpreter of sacred letters in our church, thinks that the word *Maran atha* was drawn from the Hebrew term *ḥērem* (accursed), and rendered *mecherem atha* in Chaldean; and then, through the fault of scribes, the term *meḥerem atha* was corruptly written as *maran atha*. Commentary on 1 Corinthians 16:22.[11]

[10]Hesshus, *Explicatio Prioris Epistolae ad Corinthios*, 371r-372r. The biblical scholars Theodor Bibliander (1509–1564) and Wolfgang Capito (c. 1478–1541) provided leadership of the Protestant churches in Zurich and Strasbourg (respectively). The Spanish archbishop Paul of Burgos (c. 1351–1435) was a Jewish convert to Christianity whose biblical scholarship included his *Additiones* to Nicholas of Lyra's *Postilla*.

[11]Bullinger, *In Priorem ad Corinthios Epistolam Commentarius*, 262.

A Final Apostolic Curse. The English Annotations: *Anathema, maran atha*. The former word is Greek, meaning "accursed" (Rom 3:9; Gal 1:8). The latter word is a Syriac word, and means "our Lord comes." For *maran* means "our Lord," and *atha* means "comes." It was a word used in the greatest excommunication among Christians, implying that they summoned the excommunicated person before the dreadful tribunal at the second coming of the Son of God. See Jude 14-15, "Behold the Lord comes with ten thousands of his saints, to execute judgment on all," etc. Other interpreters expound this passage in this way: "Let him be accursed even until the coming of the Lord to his death day, indeed, forever." This dreadful kind of excommunication, which the apostle here calls *maran atha*, the Jews called *Shammatha*: *Sham* signifies the Tetragrammaton, Jehovah, and *atha* means "he comes." . . . Now the apostle thunders forth this dreadful sentence of excommunication here against those who willfully oppose the gospel and are impenitent haters of Christ, not out of any evil passion of mind but out of his apostolic spirit and holy zeal. Annotations on 1 Corinthians 16:22.[12]

Paul Curses Atheists and All Non-Christians. John Donne: If a man or woman does not love the Lord; if they do not love the God who is, who was, and who is to come, what will please them? Whom will they love? If they love the Lord, but do not love Christ, and so love a God in general, but lay no hold to a particular way of his salvation, then the words of the apostle to the Ephesians apply: "When you were without Christ, you were without God" (Eph 2:12). Non-Christians are atheists in Paul's sense of the word. . . . From presumptuous atheists who do not believe in God; from reserved atheists who do not believe that Christ was God; from melancholic atheists who do not believe that [the death of] Jesus applies

[12]Downame, *English Annotations*, FF1v*. The Hebrew word *Shammatha* was the highest form of Jewish excommunication. See Robertson and Plummer, *1 Corinthians*, 400-401.

to them; from those of no religion; from those of no Christian religion; from those that err fundamentally in the Christian religion—the apostle commands a separation . . . until the Lord comes with his declaration of judgment, "If anyone does not love the Lord Jesus Christ, let them be accursed. Amen." Sermon on Trinity Sunday.[13]

Paul's Pure Love for the Faithful. Wolfgang Musculus: Observe how Paul joins his love to the grace of Christ to demonstrate his immense love for those who are true Christians, that is, those who not only make an outward profession, but are also participants of that grace. It is for good reason that, after he has reproached so many serious corruptions throughout the course of this letter, Paul has placed this affirmation of his love at the final finish line (as it were), so that they might understand that he wrote nothing from wrongful desire, but from every impulse of love. And lest it appear that he loved only some from among them—a group distinct from those other people whom he has reproached—Paul does not say simply "my love be with you," but, more universally, "my love be with you all." Thus he excludes none of them, and meanwhile reminds them to remain united so that, just as he himself embraces all of them with the bond of his love without distinction, so too they themselves, rejecting all zeal for factions, should desire to be one in the Lord and harmoniously embrace one another with mutual love. Paul adds the words "in Christ," that is, "on account of Christ," "to the extent that you are in Christ," "those who faithfully cling to him."

The Roman pontiff also boasts about his love for the faithful so as to pretend that he possesses the apostolic spirit. But the tree is known by its fruit. To be sure, he loves—but as a wolf loves the sheep. The statement "my love be with you all" can also be a wolf's words to the sheep. But this is not the love of a Lover, but more the love of a devourer. Apostolic love expends everything on behalf of the faithful, but the wolf's love devours everything that everyone possesses. Commentary on 1 Corinthians 16:24.[14]

Paul's Unbroken Love. Peter Martyr Vermigli: "My love be with you all." Paul, in a sense, stretches out his hand to the Corinthians and embraces them, though he's absent from them. And because this letter could have offended some of them, given that he had written some very harsh things, he soothes them with that final statement, saying: "My love toward you is inviolate and unbroken, and it is in Christ Jesus our Lord." Commentary on 1 Corinthians 16:24.[15]

A Final Prayer. Tilemann Hesshus: Grace signifies God's mercy and all the Mediator's blessings. Paul testifies that since he is an apostle on account of Jesus Christ, he embraces with a burning love everyone who is in Christ Jesus. "You, Lord Jesus, eternal God, Redeemer of the world, lift up our hearts by your Holy Spirit so that we might love you with a pure faith—lest we be condemned—and, being joined to you through the most intimate bond of the Spirit, that we might see your heavenly glory, live with you, and worship you for all eternity. Amen." Explication of 1 Corinthians 16:24.[16]

---

[13]Donne, *Sermons of John Donne*, 3:311-12*.

[14]Musculus, *Comm. 1 Cor.*, 781-82; referring to Mt 12:33.

[15]Vermigli, *In Selectissimam Priorem ad Corinthios Epistolam . . . Commentarii*, 457v.

[16]Hesshus, *Explicatio Prioris Epistolae ad Corinthios*, 372r.

Map of Europe at the Time of the Reformation

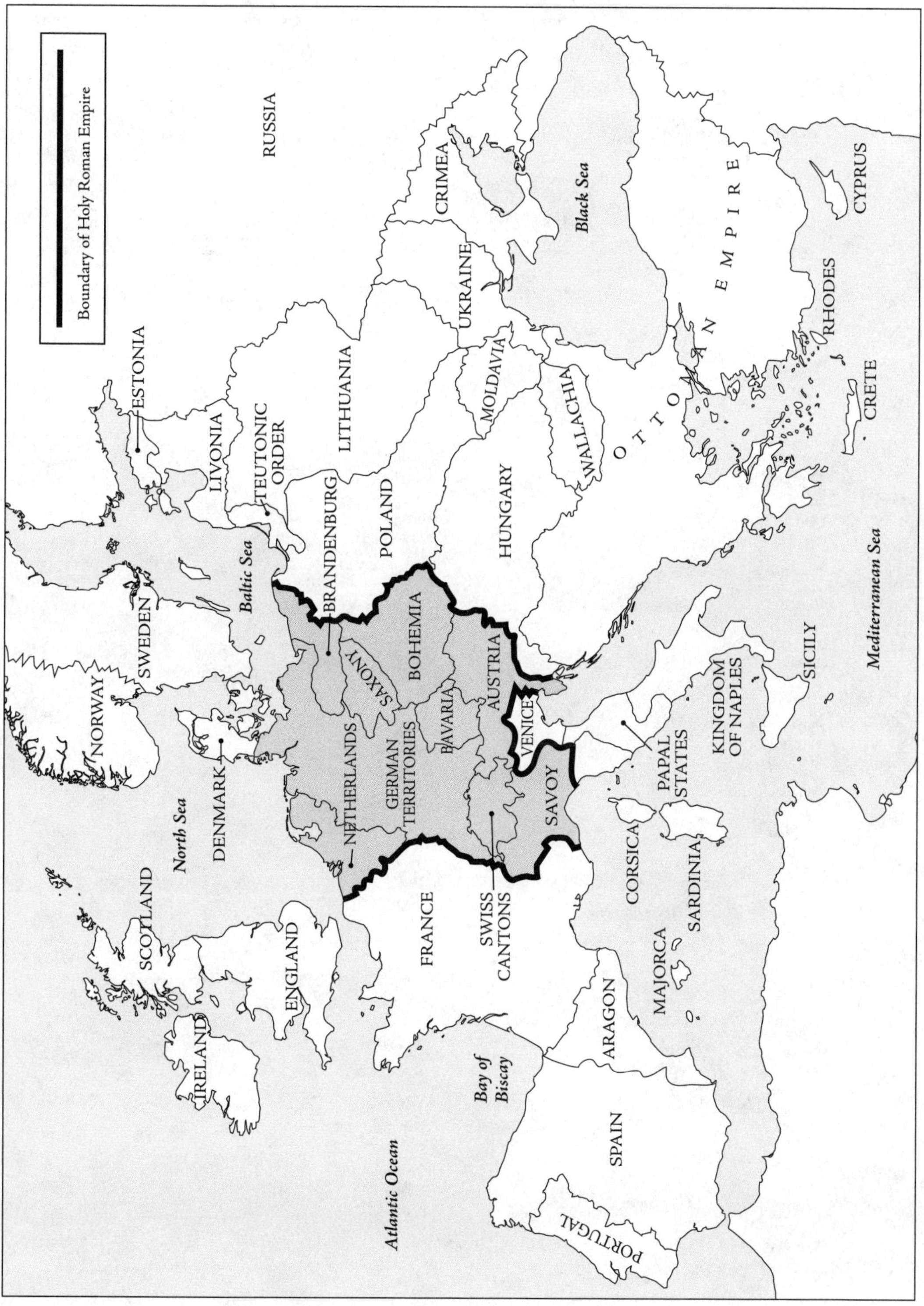

Timeline of the Reformation

	German Territories	France	Spain	Italy	Switzerland	Netherlands	British Isles
1309–1377		Babylonian Captivity of the Papacy					
1337–1453		d. Nicholas of Lyra Hundred Years' War	b. Paul of Burgos (Solomon ha-Levi)(d. 1435) Alonso Tostado (1400–1455)				Hundred Years' War
1378–1415		Western Schism (Avignon Papacy)		Western Schism			
1384							d. John Wycliffe
1414–1418					Council of Basel (1431–1437)		
1415				Council of Constance; d. Jan Hus; Martin V (r. 1417–1431); Council of Florence (1438–1445)			
1450	Invention of printing press						
1452				b. Leonardo da Vinci (d. 1519)			
1453				Fall of Constantinople			
1455–1485	b. Johannes Reuchlin (d. 1522)						War of Roses; rise of House of Tudor
1456	Gutenberg Bible						
1460				Pope Pius II issued *Execrabilis*			
1466		b. Jacques Lefèvre d'Étaples (d. 1536)					
1467						b. Desiderius Erasmus (d. 1536)	b. John Colet (d. 1519)
1469	b. Antoius Broickwy von Königstein (d. 541)						
1470				b. Santes Pagninus (d. 1541)			b. John (Mair) Major (d. 1550)
1475				b. Michelangelo (d. 1564)			
1478	b. Wolfgang Capito (d. 1541)		Ferdinand and Isabella	b. Jacopo Sadoleto (d. 1547)			b. Thomas More (d. 1535)

	German Territories	France	Spain	Italy	Switzerland	Netherlands	British Isles
1480	b. Balthasar Hubmaier (d. 1528); b. Andreas Bodenstein von Karlstadt (d. 1541)						
1481–1530			Spanish Inquisition				
1482					b. Johannes Oecolampadius (d. 1531)		
1483	b. Martin Luther (d. 1546)						
1484	b. Johann Spangenberg (d. 1550)				b. Huldrych Zwingli (d. 1531)		
1485	b. Johannes Bugenhagen (d. 1554)						b. Hugh Latimer (d. 1555)
1486	r. Frederick the Wise, Elector (d. 1525); b. Johann Eck (d. 1543)						
1488	b. Otto Brunfels (d. 1534)						b. Miles Coverdale (d. 1568)
1489	b. Thomas Müntzer (d. 1525); b. Kaspar von Schwenckfeld (d. 1561)						b. Thomas Cranmer (d. 1556)
1491	b. Martin Bucer (d. 1551)		b. Ignatius Loyola (d. 1556)				
1492			Defeat of Moors in Grenada; Columbus discovers America; expulsion of Jews from Spain	Alexander VI (r. 1492–1503)			
1493	b. Justus Jonas (d. 1555)						
1494							b. William Tyndale (d. 1536)
1496	b. Andreas Osiander (d. 1552)					b. Menno Simons (d. 1561)	
1497	b. Philipp Melanchthon (d. 1560); b. Wolfgang Musculus (d. 1563) b. Johannes (Ferus) Wild (d. 1554)						

	German Territories	France	Spain	Italy	Switzerland	Netherlands	British Isles
1498				d. Girolamo Savonarola	b. Conrad Grebel (d. 1526)		
1499	b. Johannes Brenz (d. 1570) b. Justus Menius (d. 1558)			b. Peter Martyr Vermigli (d. 1562)			
1500			b. Charles V (–1558)				
1501	b. Erasmus Sarcerius (d. 1559)						
1502	Founding of University of Wittenberg			Julius II (r. 1503–1513)		b. Frans Titelmans (d. 1537)	
1504					b. Heinrich Bullinger (d. 1575)		
1505	Luther joins Augustinian Order			b. Benedict Aretius (d. 1574)			
1506		b. Augustin Marlorat (d. 1562)		Restoration of St. Peter's begins			
1507				Sale of indulgences approved to fund building			
1508	b. Lucas Lossius (d. 1582)						
1509		b. John Calvin (d. 1564)					r. Henry VIII (–1547)
1510	Luther moves to Rome			b. Immanuel Tremellius (d. 1580)			b. Nicholas Ridley (d. 1555)
1511	Luther moves to Wittenberg						
1512				Sistine Chapel completed			
1512–1517				Fifth Lateran Council; rejection of conciliarism			
1513	Luther lectures on Psalms			r. Pope Leo X (–1521)			b. John Knox (d. 1572)
1515	Luther lectures on Romans	r. Francis I (–1547); b. Peter Ramus (d. 1572)					
1516		Est. French National Church (via Concordat of Bologna)		Concordat of Bologna		Publication of Erasmus's Greek New Testament	
1517	Tetzel sells indulgences in Saxony; Luther's Ninety-five Theses						

	German Territories	France	Spain	Italy	Switzerland	Netherlands	British Isles
1518	Heidelberg Disputation; Luther examined by Cajetan at Diet of Augsburg			Diet of Augsburg			
1519	Leipzig Disputation	b. Theodore Beza (d. 1605)	Cortés conquers Aztecs; Portuguese sailor Magellan circumnavigates the globe		Zwingli appointed pastor of Grossmünster in Zurich; b. Rudolf Gwalther (d. 1586)		
1520	Publication of Luther's "Three Treatises"; burning of papal bull in Wittenberg		Coronation of Charles V	Papal Bull v. Luther: *Exsurge Domine*			
1521	Luther excommunicated; Diet/Edict of Worms—Luther condemned; Luther in hiding; Melanchthon's *Loci communes*	French-Spanish War (–1526)	French-Spanish War; Loyola converts	Papal excommunication of Luther			Henry VIII publishes *Affirmation of the Seven Sacraments* against Luther; awarded title "Defender of the Faith" by Pope
1521–1522	Disorder in Wittenberg; Luther translates New Testament						
1521–1525		First and Second Habsburg–Valois War					
1522	Luther returns to Wittenberg; Luther's NT published; criticizes Zwickau prophets; b. Martin Chemnitz (d. 1586)		Publication of Complutensian Polyglot Bible under Cisneros		Sausage Affair and reform begins in Zurich under Zwingli		b. John Jewel (d. 1571)
1523	Knight's Revolt	Bucer begins ministry in Strasbourg	Loyola writes Spiritual Exercises	r. Pope Clement VII (–1534)	Iconoclasm in Zurich		
1524	Luther criticizes peasants; d. Johann von Staupitz					Erasmus's disputation on free will	
1524–1526	Peasants' War						
1525	Luther marries; execution of Thomas Müntzer; publication of Luther's *Bondage of the Will*				Abolition of mass in Zurich; disputation on baptism; first believers' baptism performed in Zurich		

	German Territories	France	Spain	Italy	Switzerland	Netherlands	British Isles
1526					Zurich council mandates capital punishment of Anabaptists	Publication of Tyndale's English translation of NT	
1527	d. Hans Denck (b. c. 1500) d. Hans Hut (b. 1490) b. Tilemann Hesshus (d. 1588)			Sack of Rome by mutinous troops of Charles V	First Anabaptist executed in Zurich; drafting of Schleitheim Confession		
1528	Execution of Hubmaier						
1529	Second Diet of Speyer; evangelical "protest"; publication of Luther's catechisms; Marburg Colloquy; siege of Vienna by Turkish forces	Abolition of mass in Strasbourg			d. Georg Blaurock (b. 1492)		Thomas More appointed chancellor to Henry VIII
1530	Diet of Augsburg; Confession of Augsburg	d. Francois Lambert (Lambert of Avignon) (b. 1487)	Charles V crowned Holy Roman Emperor				
1531	Formation of Schmalkaldic League				d. H. Zwingli; succeeded by H. Bullinger		
1532		Publication of Calvin's commentary on Seneca; conversion of Calvin	b. Francisco de Toledo (d. 1596)				
1533	b. Valentein Weigel (d. 1588)	Nicholas Cop addresses University of Paris; Cop and Calvin implicated as "Lutheran" sympathizers	b. Juan de Maldonado (d. 1583)				Thomas Cranmer appointed as Archbishop of Canterbury; Henry VIII divorces
1534	First edition of Luther's Bible published	Affair of the Placards; Calvin flees d. Guillame Briçonnet (b. 1470)		Jesuits founded; d. Cardinal Cajetan (Thomas de Vio) (b. 1469)			Act of Supremacy; English church breaks with Rome
1535	Bohemian Confession of 1535; Anabaptist theocracy at Münster collapses after eighteen months				b. Lambert Daneau (d. 1595)		d. Thomas More; d. John Fisher

	German Territories	France	Spain	Italy	Switzerland	Netherlands	British Isles
1536	Wittenberg Concord; b. Kaspar Olevianus (d. 1587)				First edition of Calvin's *Institutes* published; Calvin arrives in Geneva (–1538); First Helvetic Confession	Publication of Tyndale's translation of NT; d. W. Tyndale	d. A. Boleyn; Henry VIII dissolves monasteries (–1541)
1537					Calvin presents ecclesiastical ordinances to Genevan Council		
1538					Calvin exiled from Geneva; arrives in Strasbourg (–1541)		
1539		Calvin publishes second edition of *Institutes* in Strasbourg		d. Felix Pratensis			Statute of Six Articles; publication of Coverdale's Great Bible
1540				Papal approval of Jesuit order			d. Thomas Cromwell
1541	Colloquy of Regensburg	French translation of Calvin's *Institutes* published	d. Juan de Valdés (b. 1500/1510)		d. A. Karlstadt; Calvin returns to Geneva (–1564)		
1542	d. Sebastian Franck (b. 1499)			Institution of Roman Inquisition			War between England and Scotland; James V of Scotland defeated; Ireland declared sovereign kingdom
1543	Copernicus publishes *On the Revolutions of the Heavenly Spheres*; d. Johann Eck (Johann Maier of Eck) (b. 1486)						
1545–1547	Schmalkaldic Wars; d. Martin Luther			First session of Council of Trent			b. Richard Bancroft (d. 1610)
1546	b. Johannes Piscator (d. 1625)						
1547	Defeat of Protestants at Mühlberg	d. Francis I; r. Henri II (–1559)					d. Henry VIII; r. Edward VI (–1553)
1548	Augsburg Interim (–1552) d. Caspar Cruciger (b. 1504) b. David Pareus (d. 1622)						

	German Territories	France	Spain	Italy	Switzerland	Netherlands	British Isles
1549	d. Paul Fagius (b. 1504)	d. Marguerite d'Angoulême (b. 1492)			Consensus Tigurinus between Calvin and Bullinger		First Book of Common Prayer published
1550	b. Aegidius Hunnius (d. 1603)						
1551–1552				Second session of Council of Trent			
1552	d. Sebastian Münster (b. 1488) d. Friedrich Nausea (b. c. 1496)						Book of Common Prayer revised
1553	d. Johannes Aepinus (b. 1449)				Michael Servetus executed in Geneva		Cranmer's Forty-Two Articles; d. Edward VI; r. Mary I (d. 1558)
1554							Richard Hooker (d. 1600)
1555	Diet of Augsburg; Peace of Augsburg establishes legal territorial existence of Lutheranism and Catholicism b. Johann Arndt (d. 1621)	First mission of French pastors trained in Geneva				b. Sibbrandus Lubbertus (d. 1625)	b. Lancelot Andrewes (d. 1626) b. Robert Rollock (d. 1599); d. Hugh Latimer; d. Nicholas Ridley d. John Hooper
1556	d. Pilgram Marpeck (b. 1495) d. Konrad Pellikan (b. 1478) d. Peter Riedemann (b. 1506)		Charles V resigns			d. David Joris (b. c. 1501)	d. Thomas Cranmer
1557							Alliance with Spain in war against France
1558			d. Charles V				b. William Perkins (d. 1602); d. Mary I; r. Elizabeth I (–1603)
1559		d. Henry II; r. Francis II (–1560); first national synod of French reformed churches (1559) in Paris; Gallic Confession		First index of prohibited books issued	Final edition of Calvin's *Institutes*; founding of Genevan Academy	b. Jacobus Arminius (d. 1609)	Elizabethan Settlement

	German Territories	France	Spain	Italy	Switzerland	Netherlands	British Isles
1560	d. P. Melanchthon	d. Francis II; r. Charles IX (1574); Edict of Toleration created peace with Huguenots	d. Domingo de Soto (b. 1494)		Geneva Bible		Kirk of Scotland established; Scottish Confession
1561-1563				Third session of Council of Trent			
1561						Belgic Confession	
1562	d. Katharina Schütz Zell (b. 1497/98)	Massacre of Huguenots begins French Wars of Religion (–1598)					The Articles of Religion—in Elizabethan "final" form (1562/71); publication of Latin edition of Jewel's *Apology*
1563	Heidelberg Catechism						
1564				b. Galileo (d. 1642)	d. J. Calvin		b. William Shakespeare (d. 1616); publication of Lady Ann Bacon's English translation of Jewel's *Apology*
1566	d. Johann Agricola (b. 1494)			Roman Catechism	Second Helvetic Confession		
1567						Spanish occupation	Abdication of Scottish throne by Mary Stuart; r. James VI (1603–1625)
1568						d. Dirk Phillips (b. 1504) Dutch movement for liberation (–1645)	*Bishops' Bible*
1570		d. Johannes Mercerus (Jean Mercier)		Papal Bull *Regnans in Excelsis* excommunicates Elizabeth I			Elizabeth I excommunicated
1571	b. Johannes Kepler (d. 1630)		Spain defeats Ottoman navy at Battle of Lepanto				b. John Downame (d. 1652)
1572		Massacre of Huguenots on St. Bartholomew's Day		r. Pope Gregory XIII (1583–1585)		William of Orange invades	b. John Donne (d. 1631)
1574		d. Charles IX; r. Henri III (d. 1589)					

	German Territories	France	Spain	Italy	Switzerland	Netherlands	British Isles
1575	d. Georg Major (b. 1502); Bohemian Confession of 1575						
1576		Declaration of Toleration; formation of Catholic League		b. Giovanni Diodati (d. 1649)		Sack of Antwerp; Pacification of Ghent	
1577	Lutheran Formula of Concord						England allies with Netherlands against Spain
1578	Swiss Brethren Confession of Hesse d. Peter Walpot		Truce with Ottomans				Sir Francis Drake circumnavigates the globe
1579			Expeditions to Ireland			Division of Dutch provinces	
1580	Lutheran Book of Concord						
1581			d. Teresa of Avila				Anti-Catholic statutes passed
1582				Gregorian Reform of calendar			
1583							b. David Dickson (d. 1663)
1584		Treaty of Joinville with Spain	Treaty of Joinville; Spain inducted into Catholic League; defeats Dutch at Antwerp			Fall of Antwerp; d. William of Orange	
1585	d. Josua Opitz (b. c. 1542)	Henri of Navarre excommunicated		r. Pope Sixtus V (–1590)			
1586							Sir Francis Drake's expedition to West Indies; Sir Walter Raleigh in Roanoke
1587	d. Johann Wigand (b. 1523)	Henri of Navarre defeats royal army					d. Mary Stuart of Scotland
1588		Henri of Navarre drives Henri III from Paris; assassination of Catholic League Leaders	Armada destroyed				English Navy defeats Spanish Armada
1589		d. Henri III; r. Henri (of Navarre) IV (–1610)	Victory over England at Lisbon				Defeated by Spain in Lisbon
1590		Henri IV's siege of Paris		d. Girolamo Zanchi (b. 1516)			Alliance with Henri IV

	German Territories	France	Spain	Italy	Switzerland	Netherlands	British Isles
1592	d. Nikolaus Selnecker (b. 1530)						
1593		Henri IV converts to Catholicism					Books I-IV of Hooker's *Laws of Ecclesiastical Polity* published
1594		Henri grants toleration to Huguenots					
1595		Henri IV declares war on Spain; received into Catholic Church		Pope Sixtus accepts Henri IV into Church			Alliance with France
1596		b. René Descartes (d. 1650) b. Moïse Amyraut (d. 1664)					
1597							Book V of Hooker's *Laws of Ecclesiastical Polity* published
1598		Edict of Nantes; toleration of Huguenots; peace with Spain	Treaty of Vervins; peace with France				
1600	d. David Chytraeus (b. 1531)						
1601							b. John Trapp (d. 1669)
1602					d. Daniel Toussain (b. 1541)		
1603							d. Elizabeth I; r. James I (James VI of Scotland) (–1625)
1604	d. Cyriacus Spangenberg (b. 1528)						d. John Whitgift (b. 1530)
1605						b. Rembrandt (d. 1669)	Guy Fawkes and gunpowder plot
1606							Jamestown Settlement
1607							b. John Milton (d. 1674)
1608							
1610		d. Henri IV; r. Louis XIII (–1643)	d. Benedict Pererius (b. 1535)			The Remonstrance; Short Confession	

	German Territories	France	Spain	Italy	Switzerland	Netherlands	British Isles
1611							Publication of Authorized English Translation of Bible (AV/KJV); George Abbot becomes Archbishop of Canterbury (–1633)
1612							b. Richard Crashaw (d. 1649)
1616							b. John Owen (d. 1683)
1617							b. Ralph Cudworth (d. 1689)
1618–1619						Synod of Dordrecht	
1618–1648	Thirty Years' War						
1620							English Sepratists land in Plymouth, Massachusetts
1621							d. Andrew Willet (b. 1562)
1628							Puritans establish Massachusetts Bay colony
1633	d. Christoph Pelargus (b. 1565)						Laud becomes Archbishop of Canterbury
1637	d. Johann Gerhard (b. 1582)					*Statenvertaling*	
1638							d. Joseph Mede (b. 1638)
1640				Diodati's Italian translation of Bible published			
1642–1649							English civil wars; d. Charles I; r. Oliver Cromwell (1660)
1643		d. Louis XIII; r. Louis XIV (–1715)					
1643–1649							Westminster Assembly
1645							d. William Laud (b. 1573)

	German Territories	France	Spain	Italy	Switzerland	Netherlands	British Isles
1648		Treaty of Westphalia ends Thirty Years' War					Books VI and VIII of Hooker's *Laws of Ecclesiastical Polity* posthumously published
1656	d. Georg Calixtus (b. 1586)						
1658							d. Oliver Cromwell
1659							Richard Cromwell resigns
1660							English Restoration; r. Charles II (–1685)
1662							Act of Uniformity; Book VII of Hooker's *Laws of Ecclesiastical Polity* posthumously published
1664						d. Thieleman Jans van Braght (b. 1625)	d. John Mayer (b. 1583)
1671							d. William Greenhill (b. 1591)
1677							d. Thomas Manton (b. 1620)
1678						d. Anna Maria von Schurman (b. 1607)	
1688							Glorious Revolution; r. William and Mary (-1702); d. John Bunyan (b. 1628)
1691							d. Richard Baxter (b. 1615)

BIOGRAPHICAL SKETCHES OF REFORMATION-ERA FIGURES AND WORKS

For works consulted, see "Sources for Biographical Sketches," p. 489.

Thomas Adams (1583–1653). English Puritan pastor in Buckinghamshire and London. A popular and eloquent Calvinist preacher, many of his sermons were published during his lifetime; his sermons were collected into three volumes after his death.

Johannes Aepinus (1499–1553). German Lutheran preacher and theologian. Aepinus studied under Martin Luther,* Philipp Melanchthon* and Johannes Bugenhagen* in Wittenberg. Because of his Lutheran beliefs, Aepinus lost his first teaching position in Brandenburg. He fled north to Stralsund and became a preacher and superintendent at Saint Peter's Church in Hamburg. In 1534, he made a diplomatic visit to England but could not convince Henry VIII to embrace the Augsburg Confession.* His works include sermons and theological writings. Aepinus became best known as leader of the Infernalists, who believed that Christ underwent torment in hell after his crucifixion.

Johann Agricola (c. 1494–1566). German Lutheran pastor and theologian. An early student of Martin Luther,* Agricola eventually began a controversy over the role of the law, first with Melanchthon* and then with Luther himself. Agricola claimed to defend Luther's true position, asserting that only the gospel of the crucified Christ calls Christians to truly good works, not the fear of the law. After this first controversy, Agricola seems to have radicalized his views to the point that he eliminated Luther's *simul iustus et peccator* ("at the same time righteous and sinful") paradox of the Christian life, emphasizing instead that believers have no need for the law once they are united with Christ through faith. Luther responded by writing anonymous pamphlets against antinomianism. Agricola later published a recantation of his views, hoping to assuage relations with Luther, although they were never personally reconciled. He published a commentary on Luke, a series of sermons on Colossians, and a massive collection of German proverbs.

Henry Ainsworth (1571–1622/1623). English Puritan Hebraist. In 1593, under threat of persecution, Ainsworth relocated to Amsterdam, where he served as a teacher in an English congregation. He composed a confession of faith for the community and a number of polemical and exegetical works, including annotations on the Pentateuch, the Psalms and Song of Songs.

Henry Airay (c. 1560–1616). English Puritan professor and pastor. He was especially noted for his preaching, a blend of hostility toward Catholicism and articulate exposition of English Calvinism. He was promoted to provost of Queen's College Oxford (1598) and then to vice chancellor of the university in 1606. He disputed with William Laud* concerning Laud's putative Catholicization of the Church of England, particularly over the practice of genuflection, which Airay vehemently opposed. He also opposed fellow Puritans who wished to separate from the Church of England. His lectures on Philippians were his only work published during his lifetime.

Alexander (Ales) Alesius (1500–1565). Scottish Lutheran theologian. Following the martyrdom of his theological adversary Patrick Hamilton (c. 1504–1528), Alesius converted to the Reformation and fled to Germany. In 1535 Martin Luther* and Philip Melanchthon* sent him as an emissary to Henry VIII and Thomas Cranmer.* He taught briefly at Cambridge, but after the Act of Six Articles reasserted Catholic sacramental theology he returned to Germany, where he lectured at Frankfurt an der Oder and Leipzig. Alesius composed many exegetical, theological and polemical works, including commentaries on John, Romans, 1–2 Timothy, Titus and the Psalms.

Moïse Amyraut (1596–1664). French Reformed pastor and professor. Originally intending to be a lawyer, Amyraut turned to theology after an encounter with several Huguenot pastors and having read Calvin's* *Institutes*. After a brief stint as a parish pastor, Amyraut spent the majority of his career at the Saumur Academy. He was well known for his irenicism and ecumenicism (for example, in advocating intercommunion with Lutherans). Certain aspects of his writings on justification, faith, the covenants and especially predestination proved controversial among the Reformed. His doctrine of election is often called hypothetical universalism or Amyraldianism, stating that Christ's atoning work was intended by God for all human beings indiscriminately, although its effectiveness for salvation depends on faith, which is a free gift of God given only to those whom God has chosen from eternity. Amyraut was charged with grave doctrinal error three times before the National Synod but was acquitted each time. Aside from his theological treatises, Amyraut published paraphrases of almost the entire New Testament and the Psalms, as well as many sermons.

Anabaptists of Trieste (1539). Following a meeting between Swiss Brethren and the Hutterites at Steinabrunn on December 6, 1536, around 140 radicals were arrested and imprisoned in Falkenstein Castle. After six weeks in captivity, the ninety men of the group were forced to march to Trieste to be sold as galley slaves. Twelve days after arrival, all but twelve prisoners managed to escape and return to Moravia, where they published a confession of their beliefs.

Jakob Andreae (1528–1590). German Lutheran theologian. Andreae studied at the University of Tübingen before being called to the diaconate in Stuttgart in 1546. He was appointed ecclesiastical superintendent of Göppingen in 1553 and supported Johannes Brenz's* proposal to place the church under civil administrative control. An ecclesial diplomat for the duke of Württemberg, Andreae debated eucharistic theology, the use of images and predestination with Theodore Beza* at the Colloquy of Montbéliard (1586) to determine whether French Reformed exiles would be required to submit to the Formula of Concord.* Andreae coauthored the Formula of Concord. He and his wife had eighteen children.

Lancelot Andrewes (1555–1626). Anglican bishop. A scholar, pastor and preacher, Andrews prominently shaped a distinctly Anglican identity between the poles of Puritanism and Catholicism. He oversaw the translation of Genesis to 2 Kings for the Authorized Version.* His eight-volume collected works—primarily devotional tracts and sermons—are marked by his fluency in Scripture, the Christian tradition and classical literature.

Benedict Aretius (d. 1574). Swiss Reformed professor. Trained at the universities of Bern, Strasbourg and Marburg, Aretius taught logic and philosophy as well as the biblical languages and theology. He advocated for stronger unity and peace between the Lutheran and Reformed churches. Aretius joined others in denouncing the antitrinitarian Giovanni Valentino Gentile (d. 1566). He published commentaries on the New Testament, as well as various works on astronomy, botany and medicine.

Jacobus Arminius (1559–1609). Dutch Remonstrant pastor and theologian. Arminius was a vocal critic of high Calvinist scholasticism, whose views were repudiated by the Synod of Dordrecht. Arminius was a student of Theodore Beza* at the academy of Geneva. He served as a pastor in Amsterdam and later joined the faculty of theology at the university in Leiden, where his lectures on predestination were popular and controversial. Predestination, as Arminius understood it, was the decree of God determined on the basis of divine foreknowledge of faith or rejection by humans who are the recipients of prevenient, but resistible, grace.

Johann Arndt (1555–1621). German Lutheran pastor and theologian. After a brief time teaching, Arndt pastored in Badeborn (Anhalt) until 1590, when Prince Johann Georg von Anhalt (1567–1618) began introducing Reformed ecclesial policies. Arndt ministered in Quedlinberg, Brunswick, Eisleben and Celle. Heavily influenced by medieval mysticism, Arndt centered his theology on Christ's mystical union with the believer, out of which flows love of God and neighbor. He is best known for his *True Christianity* (1605–1609), which greatly influenced Philipp Jakob Spener (1635–1705) and later Pietists.

John Arrowsmith (1602–1659). English Puritan theologian. Arrowsmith participated in the Westminster Assembly, and later taught at Cambridge. His works, all published posthumously, include three sermons preached to Parliament and an unfinished catechism.

Articles of Religion (1562; revised 1571). The Articles underwent a long editorial process that drew from the influence of Continental confessions in England, resulting in a uniquely Anglican blend of Protestantism and Catholicism. In their final form, they were reduced from Thomas Cranmer's* Forty-two Articles (1539) to the Elizabethan Thirty-Nine Articles (1571), excising polemical articles against the Anabaptists and Millenarians as well as adding articles on the Holy Spirit, good works and Communion. Originating in a 1535 meeting with Lutherans, the Articles retained a minor influence from the Augsburg Confession* and Württemberg Confession (1552), but showed significant revision in accordance with Genevan theology, as well as the Second Helvetic Confession.*

Anne Askew (1521–1546). English Protestant martyr. Askew was forced to marry her deceased sister's intended husband, who later expelled Askew from his house—after the birth of two children—on account of her religious views. After unsuccessfully seeking a divorce in Lincoln, Askew moved to London, where she met other Protestants and began to preach. In 1546, she was arrested, imprisoned and convicted of heresy for denying the doctrine of transubstantiation. Under torture in the Tower of London she refused to name any other Protestants. On July 16, 1546, she was burned at the stake. Askew is best known through her accounts of her arrests and examinations. John Bale (1495–1563), a bishop, historian and playwright, published these manuscripts. Later John Foxe (1516–1587) included them in his *Acts and Monuments*, presenting her as a role model for other pious Protestant women.

Augsburg Confession (1530). In the wake of Luther's* stand against ecclesial authorities at the Diet of Worms (1521), the Holy Roman Empire splintered along theological lines. Emperor Charles V sought to ameliorate this—while also hoping to secure a united European front against Turkish invasion—by calling together another imperial diet in Augsburg in 1530. The Evangelical party was cast in a strongly heretical light at the diet by Johann Eck.* For this reason, Philipp Melanchthon* and Justus Jonas* thought it best to strike a conciliatory tone (Luther, as an official outlaw, did not attend), submitting a confession rather than a defense. The resulting Augsburg Confession was approved by many of the rulers of the northeastern Empire; however, due to differences in eucharistic theology, Martin Bucer* and the representatives of Strasbourg, Constance, Lindau and Memmingen drafted a separate confession (the Tetrapolitan Confession). Charles V accepted neither confession, demanding that the Evangelicals accept the Catholic rebuttal instead. In 1531, along with the publication of the Augsburg Confession itself, Melanchthon released a defense of the confession that responded to the Catholic confutation and expanded on the original articles. Most subsequent

Protestant confessions followed the general structure of the Augsburg Confession.

Authorized Version (1611). In 1604 King James I* commissioned this new translation—popularly remembered as the King James Version—for uniform use in the public worship of the Church of England. The Bible and the Apocrypha was divided into six portions and assigned to six companies of nine scholars—both Anglicans and Puritans—centered at Cambridge, Oxford and Westminster. Richard Bancroft, the general editor of the Authorized Version, composed fifteen rules to guide the translators and to guard against overly partisan decisions. Rather than offer an entirely fresh English translation, the companies were to follow the Bishops' Bible* as closely as possible. "Truly (good Christian Reader)," the preface states, "we neuer thought from the beginning that we should need to make a new Translation, nor yet to make of a bad one a good one . . . but make a good one better, or out of many good ones, one principall good one, not iustly to be excepted against: that hath bene our endeauour, that our mark." Other rules standardized spelling, dictated traditional ecclesial terms (e.g., *church*, *baptize* and *bishop*), and allowed only for linguistic marginal notes and cross-references. Each book of the Bible went through a rigorous revision process: first, each person in a company made an initial draft, then the company put together a composite draft, then a supercommittee composed of representatives from each company reviewed these drafts, and finally two bishops and Bancroft scrutinized the final edits. The text and translation process of the Authorized Version have widely influenced biblical translations ever since.

Robert Bagnall (b. 1559 or 1560). English Protestant minister. Bagnall authored *The Steward's Last Account* (1622), a collection of five sermons on Luke 16.

John Ball (1585–1640). English Puritan theologian. Ball was a respected educator. He briefly held a church office until he was removed on account of his Puritanism. He composed popular catechisms and tracts on faith, the church and the covenant of grace.

Thomas Bastard (c. 1565–1618). English Protestant minister and poet. Educated at Winchester and New College, Oxford, Bastard published numerous works, including collections of poems and sermons; his most famous title is *Chrestoleros* (1598), a collection of epigrams. Bastard was alleged to be the author of an anonymous work, *An Admonition to the City of Oxford*, which revealed the carnal vices of many clergy and scholars in Oxford; despite denying authorship, he was dismissed from Oxford in 1591. Bastard was recognized as a skilled classical scholar and preacher. He died impoverished in a debtor's prison in Dorchester.

Jeremias Bastingius (1551–1595). Dutch Reformed theologian. Educated in Heidelberg and Geneva, Bastingius pastored the Reformed church in Antwerp for nearly a decade until the Spanish overran the city in 1585; he later settled in Dordrecht. He spent the last few years of his life in Leiden on the university's board of regents. He wrote an influential commentary on the Heidelberg Catechism that was translated into English, Dutch, German and Flemish.

Johann (Pomarius) Baumgart (1514–1578). Lutheran pastor and amateur playwright. Baumgart studied under Georg Major,* Martin Luther* and Philipp Melanchthon* at the University of Wittenberg. Before becoming pastor of the Church of the Holy Spirit in 1540, Baumgart taught secondary school. He authored catechetical and polemical works, a postil for the Gospel readings throughout the church year, numerous hymns and a didactic play (*Juditium Salomonis*).

Richard Baxter (1615–1691). English Puritan minister. Baxter was a leading Puritan pastor, evangelist and theologian, known throughout England for his landmark ministry in Kidderminster and a prodigious literary output, producing 135 books in just over forty years. Baxter came to faith through reading William Perkins,* Richard Sibbes* and other early Puritan writers and was the first cleric to decline the terms of ministry in the national English church imposed by the 1662 Act of Uniformity; Baxter wrote on behalf of the more than 1700 who shared ejection from the national church. He hoped for restoration to national church ministry, or toleration, that would allow lawful preaching and pastoring. Baxter sought unity in theological, ecclesiastical, sociopolitical and personal terms and is regarded as a forerunner of Noncomformist ecumenicity, though he was defeated in his efforts at the 1661 Savoy Conference to take seriously Puritan objections to the revision of the 1604 Prayer Book. Baxter's views on church ministry were considerably hybrid: he was a paedo-baptist, Nonconformist minister who approved of synodical Episcopal government and fixed liturgy. He is most known for his classic writings on the Christian life, such as *The Saints' Everlasting Rest* and *A Christian Directory*, and pastoral ministry, such as *The Reformed Pastor*. He also produced *Catholick Theology*, a large volume squaring current Reformed, Lutheran, Arminian and Roman Catholic systems with each other.

Thomas Becon (1511/1512–1567). English Puritan preacher. Becon was a friend of Hugh Latimer,* and for several years chaplain to Archbishop Thomas Cranmer.* Becon was sent to the Tower of London by Mary I and then exiled for his controversial preaching at the English royal court. He returned to England upon Elizabeth I's accession. Becon was one of the most widely read popular preachers in England during the Reformation. He published many of his sermons, including a postil, or collection of sermon helps for undertrained or inexperienced preachers.

Belgic Confession (1561). Written by Guy de Brès (1523–1567), this statement of Dutch Reformed faith was heavily reliant on the Gallic Confession,* although more detailed, especially in how strongly it distances the Reformed from Roman Catholics and Anabaptists. The Confession first appeared in French in 1561 and was translated to Dutch in 1562. It was presented to Philip II (1527–1598) in the hope that he would grant toleration to the Reformed, to no avail. At the Synod of Dordrecht* the Confession was revised, clarifying and strengthening the article on election as well as sharpening the distinctives of Reformed theology against the Anabaptists, thus situating the Dutch Reformed more closely to the international Calvinist movement. The Belgic Confession in conjunction with the Heidelberg Catechism* and the Canons of Dordrecht were granted official status as the confessional standards (the Three Forms of Unity) of the Dutch Reformed Church.

Theodore Beza (1519–1605). French pastor and professor. Beza was compatriot and successor to John Calvin* as moderator of the Company of Pastors in Geneva during the second half of the sixteenth century. He was a noteworthy New Testament scholar whose *Codex Bezae* formed the basis of the New Testament section of later English translations. A leader in the academy and the church, Beza served as professor of Greek at the Lausanne Academy until 1558, at which time he moved to Geneva to become the rector of the newly founded Genevan Academy. He enjoyed an international reputation through his correspondence with key European leaders. Beza developed and extended Calvin's doctrinal thought on several important themes such as the nature of predestination and the real spiritual presence of Christ in the Eucharist.

Theodor Bibliander (1504?–1564). Swiss Reformed Hebraist and theologian. Professor of Old Testament at the Zurich Academy from 1531, Bibliander published two Hebrew grammars, a collection of letters by Zwingli* and Oecolampadius*, commentaries on Isaiah, Ezekiel, and Nahum, a Latin translation of the Qur'an, and a tract warning Christians against the threat of Islam. He taught a universalist view of predestination, arguing that God saved all people unless they rejected divine grace. Following a dispute with double-predestinarian Peter Martyr Vermigli*, he was forced into retirement in 1560.

Hugh Binning (1627–1653). Scottish Presbyterian theologian. At the age of eighteen, Binning became a professor of philosophy at the University of Glasgow. In his early twenties he left this post for parish ministry, and died of consumption a few years later. His commentary on the Westminster Confession and a selection of his sermons were published after his death.

Bishops' Bible (1568). Anglicans were polarized by the two most recent English translations of the Bible: the Great Bible (1539) relied too heavily on the Vulgate* and was thus perceived as too Catholic, while the Geneva Bible's* marginal notes were too Calvinist for many Anglicans. So Archbishop Matthew Parker (1504–1575) commissioned a new translation of Scripture from the original languages with marginal annotations (many of which, ironically, were from the Geneva Bible). Published under royal warrant, the Bishops' Bible became the official translation for the Church of England. The 1602 edition provided the basis for the King James Bible (1611).

Georg Blaurock (1492–1529). Swiss Anabaptist. Blaurock (a nickname meaning "blue coat," because of his preference for this garment) was one of the first leaders of Switzerland's radical reform movement. In the first public disputations on baptism in Zurich, he argued for believer's baptism and was the first person to receive adult believers' baptism there, having been baptized by Conrad Grebel* in 1525. Blaurock was arrested several times for performing mass adult baptisms and engaging in social disobedience by disrupting worship services. He was eventually expelled from Zurich but continued preaching and baptizing in various Swiss cantons until his execution.

Bohemian Confession (1535). Bohemian Christianity was subdivided between traditional Catholics, Utraquists (who demanded Communion in both kinds) and the *Unitas Fratrum*, who were not Protestants but whose theology bore strong affinities to the Waldensians and the Reformed. The 1535 Latin edition of this confession—an earlier Czech edition had already been drafted—was an attempt to clarify and redefine the beliefs of the *Unitas Fratrum*. This confession purged all earlier openness to rebaptism and inched toward Luther's* eucharistic theology. Jan Augusta (c. 1500–1572) and Jan Roh (also Johannes Horn; c. 1490–1547) presented the confession to King Ferdinand I (1503–1564) in Vienna, but the king would not print it. The *Unitas Fratrum* sought, and with slight amendments eventually obtained, Luther's advocacy of the confession. It generally follows the structure of the Augsburg Confession.*

Bohemian Confession (1575). This confession was an attempt to shield Bohemian Christian minorities—the Utraquists and the *Unitas Fratrum*—from the Counter-Reformation and Habsburg insistence on uniformity. The hope was that this umbrella consensus would ensure peace in the midst of Christian diversity; anyone who affirmed the 1575 Confession, passed by the Bohemian legislature, would be tolerated. This confession was, like the Bohemian Confession of 1535, patterned after the Augsburg Confession.* It emphasizes both justification by faith alone and good works as the fruit of salvation. Baptism and the Eucharist are the focus of the sacramental section, although the five traditional Catholic sacraments are also listed for the Utraquists. Though it was eventually accepted in 1609 by Rudolf II (1552–1612), the Thirty Years' War (1618–1648) rendered the confession moot.

Book of Common Prayer (1549; 1552). After the Church of England's break with Rome, it needed a liturgical manual to distinguish its theology and practice from that of Catholicism. Thomas Cranmer* drafted the Book of Common Prayer based on the medieval Roman Missal, under the dual influence of the revised Lutheran Mass and the reforms of the Spanish Cardinal Quiñones. This manual details the eucharistic service, as well as services for rites such as baptism, confirmation, marriage and funerals. It includes a matrix of the epistle and Gospel readings and the appropriate collect for each Sunday and feast day of the church year. The 1548 Act of Uniformity established the Book of Common Prayer as *the* authoritative liturgical manual for the Church of England, to be implemented everywhere by Pentecost 1549. After its 1552 revision, Queen Mary I banned it; Elizabeth reestablished it in 1559, although it was rejected by Puritans and Catholics alike.

The Book of Homilies (1547; 1563; 1570). This collection of approved sermons, published in three parts during the reigns of Edward VI and Elizabeth

I, was intended to inculcate Anglican theological distinctives and mitigate the problems raised by the lack of educated preachers. Addressing doctrinal and practical topics, Thomas Cranmer* likely wrote the majority of the first twelve sermons, published in 1547; John Jewel* added another twenty sermons in 1563. A final sermon, *A Homily Against Disobedience*, was appended to the canon in 1570. Reprinted regularly, the *Book of Homilies* was an important resource in Anglican preaching until at least the end of the seventeenth century.

Martin (Cellarius) Borrhaus (1499–1564). German Reformed theologian. After a dispute with his mentor Johann Eck,* Borrhaus settled in Wittenberg, where he was influenced by the radical Zwickau Prophets. He travelled extensively, and finally settled in Basel to teach philosophy and Old Testament. Despite his objections, many accused Borrhaus of Anabaptism; he argued that baptism was a matter of conscience. On account of his association with Sebastian Castellio (1515–1563) and Michael Servetus (1511–1553), some scholars posit that Borrhaus was an antitrinitarian. His writings include a treatise on the Trinity and commentaries on the Torah, historical books, Ecclesiastes and Isaiah.

John Boys (1571–1625). Anglican priest and theologian. Before doctoral work at Cambridge, Boys pastored several parishes in Kent; after completing his studies he was appointed to more prominent positions, culminating in his 1619 appointment as the Dean of Canterbury by James I. Boys published a popular four-volume postil of the Gospel and epistle readings for the church year, as well as a companion volume for the Psalms.

Thieleman Jans van Braght (1625–1664). Dutch Radical preacher. After demonstrating great ability with languages, this cloth merchant was made preacher in his hometown of Dordrecht in 1648. He served in this office for the next sixteen years, until his death. This celebrated preacher had a reputation for engaging in debate wherever an opportunity presented itself, particularly concerning infant baptism. The publication of his book of martyrs, *Het Bloedigh Tooneel of Martelaersspiegel* (1660; *Martyrs' Mirror*), proved to be his lasting contribution to the Mennonite tradition. *Martyrs' Mirror* is heavily indebted to the earlier martyr book *Offer des Heeren* (1562), to which Braght added many early church martyrs who rejected infant baptism, as well as over 800 contemporary martyrs.

Johannes Brenz (1499–1570). German Lutheran theologian and pastor. Brenz was converted to the reformation cause after hearing Martin Luther* speak; later, Brenz became a student of Johannes Oecolampadius.* His central achievement lay in his talent for organization. As city preacher in Schwäbisch-Hall and afterward in Württemberg and Tübingen, he oversaw the introduction of reform measures and doctrines and new governing structures for ecclesial and educational communities. Brenz also helped establish Lutheran orthodoxy through treatises, commentaries and catechisms. He defended Luther's position on eucharistic presence against Huldrych Zwingli* and opposed the death penalty for religious dissenters.

Guillaume Briçonnet (1470–1534). French Catholic abbot and bishop. Briçonnet created a short-lived circle of reformist-minded humanists in his diocese under the sponsorship of Marguerite d'Angoulême. His desire for ecclesial reform developed throughout his prestigious career (including positions as royal chaplain to the queen, abbot at Saint-Germain-des-Prés and bishop of Meaux), influenced by Jacques Lefèvre d'Étaples.* Briçonnet encouraged reform through ministerial visitation, Scripture and preaching in the vernacular and active study of the Bible. When this triggered the ire of the theology faculty at the Sorbonne in Paris, Briçonnet quelled the activity and departed, envisioning an ecclesial reform that proceeded hierarchically.

Thomas Brightman (1562–1607). English Puritan pastor and exegete. Under alleged divine inspiration, Brightman wrote a well known commentary on Revelation, influenced by Joachim of Fiore (d. 1202). In contrast to the putatively true churches of Geneva and Scotland, he depicted the Church of England as a type of the lukewarm Laodicean church. He believed that the Reformation would result in the defeat of the Vatican and the Ottoman Empire and that all humanity would be regenerated through the spread of the gospel before Christ's final return and judgment.

Otto Brunfels (c. 1488–1534). German Lutheran botanist, teacher and physician. Brunfels joined the Carthusian order, where he developed interests in the natural sciences and became involved with a humanist circle associated with Ulrich von Hutten and Wolfgang Capito.* In 1521, after coming into contact with Luther's* teaching, Brunfels abandoned the monastic life, traveling and spending time in botanical research and pastoral care. He received a medical degree in Basel and was appointed city physician of Bern in 1534. Brunfels penned defenses of Luther and Hutten, devotional biographies of biblical figures, a prayer book, and annotations on the Gospels and the Acts of the Apostles. His most influential contribution, however, is as a Renaissance botanist.

Martin Bucer (1491–1551). German Reformed theologian and pastor. A Dominican friar, Bucer was influenced by Desiderius Erasmus* during his doctoral studies at the University of Heidelberg, where he began corresponding with Martin Luther.* After advocating reform in Alsace, Bucer was excommunicated and fled to Strasbourg, where he became a leader in the city's Reformed ecclesial and educational communities. Bucer sought concord between Lutherans and Zwinglians and Protestants and Catholics. He emigrated to England, becoming a professor at Cambridge. Bucer's greatest theological concern was the centrality of Christ's sacrificial death, which achieved justification and sanctification and orients Christian community.

Johannes Bugenhagen (1485–1558). German Lutheran pastor and professor. Bugenhagen, a priest and lecturer at a Premonstratensian monastery, became a city preacher in Wittenberg during the reform efforts of Martin Luther* and Philipp Melanchthon.* Initially influenced by his reading of Desiderius Erasmus,* Bugenhagen grew in evangelical orientation through Luther's works; later, he studied under Melanchthon at the University of Wittenberg, eventually serving as rector and faculty member there. Bugenhagen was a versatile commentator, exegete and lecturer on Scripture. Through these roles and his development of lectionary and devotional material, Bugenhagen facilitated rapid establishment of church order throughout many German provinces.

Heinrich Bullinger (1504–1575). Swiss Reformed pastor and theologian. Bullinger succeeded Huldrych Zwingli* as minister and leader in Zurich. The primary author of the First and Second Helvetic Confessions,* Bullinger was drawn toward reform through the works of Martin Luther* and Philipp Melanchthon.* After Zwingli died, Bullinger was vital in maintaining adherence to the cause of reform; he oversaw the expansion of the Zurich synodal system while preaching, teaching and writing extensively. One of Bullinger's lasting legacies was the development of a federal view of the divine covenant with humanity, making baptism and the Eucharist covenantal signs.

John Bunyan (1628–1688). English Puritan preacher and writer. His *Pilgrim's Progress* is one of the best-selling English-language titles in history. Born to a working-class family, Bunyan was largely unschooled, gaining literacy (and entering the faith) through reading the Bible and such early Puritan devotional works as *The Plain Man's Pathway to Heaven* and *The Practice of Piety*. Following a short stint in Oliver Cromwell's parliamentary army, in which Bunyan narrowly escaped death in combat, he turned to a preaching ministry, succeeding John Gifford as pastor at the Congregational church in Bedford. A noted preacher, Bunyan drew large crowds in itinerant appearances and it was in the sermonic form that Bunyan developed his theological outlook, which was an Augustinian-inflected Calvinism. Bunyan's opposition to the Book of Common Prayer and refusal of official ecclesiastical licensure led to multiple imprisonments, where he wrote many of his famous allegorical works, including *Pilgrim's Progress*, *The Holy City*, *Prison Meditations* and *Holy War*.

Jeremiah Burroughs (c. 1600–1646). English Puritan pastor and delegate to the Westminster Assembly. Burroughs left Cambridge, as well as a rectorate in Norfolk, because of his nonconformity. After returning to England from pastoring an English congregation in Rotterdam for several years (1637–1641), he became one of only a few dissenters from the official presbyterianism of the Assembly in favor of a congregationalist polity. Nevertheless, he was well known and respected by presbyterian colleagues such as Richard Baxter* for his irenic tone and conciliatory manner. The vast majority of Burroughs's corpus was published posthumously, although during his lifetime he published annotations on Hosea and several polemical works.

Cardinal Cajetan (Thomas de Vio) (1469–1534). Italian Catholic cardinal, professor, theologian and biblical exegete. This Dominican monk was the leading Thomist theologian and one of the most important Catholic exegetes of the sixteenth century. Cajetan is best-known for his interview with Martin Luther* at the Diet of Augsburg (1518). Among his many works are polemical treatises, extensive biblical commentaries and most importantly a four-volume commentary (1508–1523) on the *Summa Theologiae* of Thomas Aquinas.

Georg Calixtus (1586–1656). German Lutheran theologian. Calixtus studied at the University of Helmstedt where he developed regard for Philipp Melanchthon.* Between his time as a student and later as a professor at Helmstedt, Calixtus traveled through Europe seeking a way to unite and reconcile Lutherans, Calvinists and Catholics. He attempted to fuse these denominations through use of the Scriptures, the Apostles' Creed, and the first five centuries, interpreted by the Vincentian canon. Calixtus's position was stamped as syncretist and yielded further debate even after his death.

John Calvin (1509–1564). French Reformed pastor and theologian. In his *Institutes of the Christian Religion,* Calvin provided a theological dogmatics for the Reformed churches. Calvin's gradual conversion to the cause of reform occurred through his study with chief humanist scholars in Paris, but he spent most of his career in Geneva (excepting a three-year exile in Strasbourg with Martin Bucer*). In Geneva, Calvin reorganized the structure and governance of the church and established an academy that became an international center for theological education. He was a tireless writer, producing his *Institutes,* theological treatises and Scripture commentaries.

Wolfgang Capito (1478?–1541). German Reformed humanist and theologian. Capito, a Hebrew scholar, produced a Hebrew grammar and published several Latin commentaries on books of the Hebrew Scriptures. He corresponded with Desiderius Erasmus* and fellow humanists. Capito translated Martin Luther's* early works into Latin for the printer Johann Froben. On meeting Luther, Capito was converted to Luther's vision, left Mainz and settled in Strasbourg, where he lectured on Luther's theology to the city clergy. With Martin Bucer,* Capito reformed liturgy, ecclesial life and teachings, education, welfare and government. Capito worked for the theological unification of the Swiss cantons with Strasbourg.

Thomas Cartwright (1535–1606). English Puritan preacher and professor. Cartwright was educated at St. John's College, Cambridge, although as an influential leader of the Presbyterian party in the Church of England he was continually at odds with the Anglican party, especially John Whitgift.* Cartwright spent some time as an exile in Geneva and Heidelberg as well as in Antwerp, where he pastored an English church. In 1585, Cartwright was arrested and eventually jailed for trying to return to England despite Elizabeth I's refusal of his request. Many acknowledged him to be learned but also quite cantankerous. His publications include commentaries on Colossians, Ecclesiastes, Proverbs and the Gospels, as well as a dispute against Whitgift on church discipline.

Mathew Caylie (unknown). English Protestant minister. Caylie authored *The Cleansing of the Ten Lepers* (1623), an exposition of Luke 17:14-18.

John Chardon (d. 1601). Irish Anglican bishop. Chardon was educated at Oxford. He advocated Reformed doctrine in his preaching, yet opposed those Puritans who rejected Anglican church order. He published several sermons.

Martin Chemnitz (1522–1586). German Lutheran theologian. A leading figure in establishing Lutheran orthodoxy, Chemnitz studied theology and patristics at the University of Wittenburg, later becoming a defender of Philipp Melanchthon's* interpretation of the doctrine of justification. Chemnitz drafted a compendium of doctrine and reorganized the structure of the church in Wolfenbüttel; later, he led efforts to reconcile divisions within Lutheranism, culminating in the Formula of Concord*. One of his chief theological accomplishments was a modification of the christological doctrine of the *communicatio idiomatium*, which provided a Lutheran platform for understanding the sacramental presence of Christ's humanity in the Eucharist.

David Chytraeus (1531–1600). German Lutheran professor, theologian and biblical exegete. At the age of eight Chytraeus was admitted to the University of Tübingen. There he studied law, philology, philosophy, and theology, finally receiving his master's degree in 1546. Chytraeus befriended Philipp Melanchthon* while sojourning in Wittenberg, where he taught the *Loci communes*. While teaching exegesis at the University of Rostock Chytraeus became acquainted with Tilemann Heshusius,* who strongly influenced Chytraeus away from Philippist theology. As a defender of Gnesio-Lutheran theology Chytraeus helped organize churches throughout Austria in accordance with the Augsburg Confession.* Chytraeus coauthored the Formula of Concord* with Martin Chemnitz,* Andreas Musculus (1514–1581), Nikolaus Selnecker* and Jakob Andreae.* He wrote commentaries on most of the Bible, as well as a devotional work titled *Regula vitae* (1555) that described the Christian virtues.

David Clarkson (1622–1686). English Puritan theologian. After his dismissal from the pastorate on account of the Act of Uniformity (1662), little is known about Clarkson. At the end of his life he ministered with John Owen* in London.

John Colet (1467–1519). English Catholic priest, preacher and educator. Colet, appointed dean of Saint Paul's Cathedral by Henry VII, was a friend of Desiderius Erasmus,* on whose classical ideals Colet reconstructed the curriculum of Saint Paul's school. Colet was convinced that the foundation of moral reform lay in the education of children. Though an ardent advocate of reform, Colet, like Erasmus, remained loyal to the Catholic Church throughout his life. Colet's agenda of reform was oriented around spiritual and ethical themes, demonstrated in his commentaries on select books of the New Testament and the writings of Pseudo-Dionysius the Areopagite.

Gasparo Contarini (1483–1542). Italian statesman, theologian and reform-minded cardinal. Contarini was an able negotiator and graceful compromiser. Charles V requested Contarini as the papal legate for the Colloquy of Regensburg (1541), where Contarini reached agreement with Melanchthon* on the doctrine of justification (although neither the pope nor Luther* ratified the agreement). He had come to a similar belief in the priority of faith in the work of Christ rather than works as the basis for Christian life in 1511, though unlike Luther, he never left the papal church over the issue; instead he remainied within it to try to seek gentle reform, and he adhered to papal sacramental teaching. Contarini was an important voice for reform within the Catholic Church, always seeking reconciliation rather than confrontation with Protestant reformers. He wrote many works, including a treatise detailing the ideal bishop, a manual for lay church leaders, a political text on right governance and brief commentaries on the Pauline letters.

John Cosin (1594–1672). Anglican preacher and bishop. Early in his career Cosin was the vice chancellor of Cambridge and canon at the Durham cathedral. But as a friend of William Laud* and an advocate for "Laudian" changes, he was suspected of being a crypto-Catholic. In 1640 during the Long Parliament a Puritan lodged a complaint with the House of Commons concerning Cosin's "popish innovations." Cosin was promptly removed from office. During the turmoil of the English Civil

Wars, Cosin sojourned in Paris among English nobility but struggled financially. Cosin returned to England after the Restoration in 1660 to be consecrated as the bishop of Durham. He published annotations on the Book of Common Prayer* and a history of the canon.

Council of Constance (1414–1418). Convened to resolve the Western Schism, root out heresy and reform the church in head and members, the council asserted in *Sacrosancta* (1415) the immediate authority of ecumenical councils assembled in the Holy Spirit under Christ—even over the pope. Martin V was elected pope in 1417 after the three papal claimants were deposed; thus, the council ended the schism. The council condemned Jan Hus,* Jerome of Prague (c. 1365–1416) and, posthumously, John Wycliffe. Hus and Jerome, despite letters of safe conduct, were burned at the stake. Their deaths ignited the Hussite Wars, which ended as a result of the Council of Basel's concessions to the Bohemian church. The council fathers sought to reform the church through the regular convocation of councils (*Frequens*; 1417). Martin V begrudgingly complied by calling the required councils, then immediately disbanding them. Pius II (r. 1458–1464) reasserted papal dominance through *Execrabilis* (1460), which condemned any appeal to a future council apart from the pope's authority.

Council of Trent (1545–1563) Convoked by Pope Paul III (r. 1534–1549) with the support of Charles V*, the nineteenth ecumenical council was convened in the northern Italian city of Trent. Attended primarily by Italian clerics, it met in three distinct phases. Beginning in December 1545, during its first eight sessions, the council issued doctrinal decrees, asserting the authority of tradition alongside Scripture, the authenticity of the Vulgate, the prerogative of the church in interpretation, and the necessity of human cooperation in the work of salvation. Ecclesial abuses were also addressed, as attempts were made to eliminate absenteeism and pluralism and devolve power from Rome to bishoprics and parishes. The council was suspended following the outbreak of the plague in Trent in March 1547. A number of Protestant delegates were present during the second phase of the council, which met between May 1551 and April 1552 under the supervision of Pope Julius III (r. 1550–1555). The primary achievement of this period of the council was the clarification of teachings on the seven sacraments, with transubstantiation, the objective efficacy of the Eucharist, and the necessity of auricular confession confirmed as dogma. Reconvened by Pope Pius IV (r. 1559–1565) in 1561, the third phase of the council addressed the relationship between bishops and Rome, resulting in affirmations of the divine appointment of the church hierarchy and the obligation of bishops to reside in their dioceses. Clerical education, the regulation of marriage, and teachings on purgatory, indulgences, the use of images, and the saints were also addressed.

Miles Coverdale (1488–1568). Anglican bishop. Coverdale is known for his translations of the Bible into English, completing William Tyndale's* efforts and later producing the Great Bible commissioned by Henry VIII (1539). A former friar, Coverdale was among the Cambridge scholars who met at the White Horse Tavern to discuss Martin Luther's* ideas. During Coverdale's three terms of exile in Europe, he undertook various translations, including the Geneva Bible*. He was appointed bishop of Exeter by Thomas Cranmer* and served as chaplain to Edward VI. Coverdale contributed to Cranmer's first edition of the Book of Common Prayer.*

William Cowper (Couper) (1568–1619). Scottish Puritan bishop. After graduating from the University of St. Andrews, Cowper worked in parish ministry for twenty-five years before becoming bishop. As a zealous Puritan and advocate of regular preaching and rigorous discipline, Cowper championed Presbyterian polity and lay participation in church government. Cowper published devotional works, sermon collections and a commentary on Revelation.

Thomas Cranmer (1489–1556). Anglican archbishop and theologian. Cranmer supervised church reform and produced the first two editions of the

Book of Common Prayer.* As a doctoral student at Cambridge, he was involved in the discussions at the White Horse Tavern. Cranmer contributed to a religious defense of Henry VIII's divorce; Henry then appointed him Archbishop of Canterbury. Cranmer cautiously steered the course of reform, accelerating under Edward VI. After supporting the attempted coup to prevent Mary's assuming the throne, Cranmer was convicted of treason and burned at the stake. Cranmer's legacy is the splendid English of his liturgy and prayer books.

Richard Crashaw (1612–1649). English Catholic poet. Educated at Cambridge, Crashaw was fluent in Hebrew, Greek and Latin. His first volume of poetry was *Epigrammatum sacrorum liber* (1634). Despite being born into a Puritan family, Crashaw was attracted to Catholicism, finally converting in 1644 after he was forced to resign his fellowship for not signing the Solemn League and Covenant (1643). In 1649, he was made a subcanon of Our Lady of Loretto by Cardinal Palotta.

Herbert Croft (1603–1691). Anglican bishop. As a boy Croft converted to Catholicism; he returned to the Church of England during his studies at Oxford. Before the English Civil Wars, he served as chaplain to Charles I. After the Restoration, Charles II appointed him as bishop. Croft ardently opposed Catholicism in his later years.

John Crompe (d. 1661). Anglican priest. Educated at Cambridge, Crompe published a commentary on the Apostles' Creed, a sermon on Psalm 21:3 and an exposition of Christ's passion.

Caspar Cruciger (1504–1548). German Lutheran theologian. Recognized for his alignment with the theological views of Philipp Melanchthon,* Cruciger was a scholar respected among both Protestants and Catholics. In 1521, Cruciger came Wittenberg to study Hebrew and remained there most of his life. He became a valuable partner for Martin Luther* in translating the Old Testament and served as teacher, delegate to major theological colloquies and rector. Cruciger was an agent of reform in his birthplace of Leipzig, where at the age of fifteen he had observed the disputation between Luther and Johann Eck.*

Ralph Cudworth (d. 1624) English Protestant minister. Father of noted Cambridge Platonist Ralph Cudworth (1617–1688), the elder Cudworth was a fellow of Emanuel College, Cambridge and rector of Aller in Somersetshire.

Marguerite d'Angoulême (1492–1549). French Catholic noblewoman. The elder sister of King Francis I of France, Marguerite was the Queen of Navarre and Duchess of Alençon and Berry. She was a poet and author of the French Renaissance. She composed *The Mirror of a Sinful Soul* (1531)—condemned by the theologians of the Sorbonne for containing Lutheran ideas—and an unfinished collection of short stories, the *Heptaméron* (1558). A leading figure in the French Reformation, Marguerite was at the center of a network of reform-minded individuals that included Guillame Briçonnet,* Jacques Lefèvre d'Etaples,* Gérard Roussel (1500–1550) and Guillame Farel (1489–1565).

Jakob Dachser (1486–1567). German Anabaptist theologian and hymnist. Dachser served as a Catholic priest in Vienna until he was imprisoned and then exiled for defending the Lutheran understanding of the Mass and fasting. Hans Hut* rebaptized him in Augsburg, where Dachser was appointed as a leader of the Anabaptist congregation. Lutheran authorities imprisoned him for nearly four years. In 1531 he recanted his Radical beliefs and began to catechize children with the permission of the city council. Dachser was expelled from Augsburg as a possible insurrectionist in 1552 and relocated to Pfalz-Neuberg. He published a number of poems, hymns and mystical works, and he versified several psalms.

Jean Daillé (1594–1670). French Reformed pastor. Born into a devout Reformed family, Daillé studied theology and philosophy at Saumur under the most influential contemporary lay leader in French Protestantism, Philippe Duplessis-Mornay (1549–1623). Daillé held to Amyraldianism—the belief that Christ died for all humanity inclusively, not particularly for the elect who would inherit salvation (though only the elect are in fact saved). He wrote a controversial treatise on the church fathers that aggravated many Catholic and Anglican scholars because of Daillé's apparent demotion of patristic authority in matters of faith.

Lambert Daneau (1535–1595). French Reformed pastor and theologian. After a decade of pastoring in France, following the St. Bartholomew's Day Massacre, Daneau fled to Geneva to teach theology at the Academy. He later taught in the Low Countries, finishing his career in southern France. Daneau's diverse works include tracts on science, ethics and morality as well as numerous theological and exegetical works.

John Davenant (1576–1641). Anglican bishop and professor. Davenant attended Queen's College, Cambridge, where he received his doctorate and was appointed professor of divinity. During the Remonstrant controversy, James I sent Davenant as one of the four representatives for the Church of England to the Synod of Dordrecht.* Following James's instructions, Davenant advocated a *via media* between the Calvinists and the Remonstrants, although in later years he defended against the rise of Arminianism in England. In 1621, Davenant was promoted to the bishopric of Salisbury, where he was generally receptive to Laudian reforms. Davenant's lectures on Colossians are his best-known work.

Defense of the Augsburg Confession (1531). See *Augsburg Confession.*

Hans Denck (c. 1500–1527). German Radical theologian. Denck, a crucial early figure of the German Anabaptist movement, combined medieval German mysticism with the radical sacramental theology of Andreas Bodenstein von Karlstadt* and Thomas Müntzer.* Denck argued that the exterior forms of Scripture and sacrament are symbolic witnesses secondary to the internally revealed truth of the Sprit in the human soul. This view led to his expulsion from Nuremberg in 1525; he spent the next two years in various centers of reform in the German territories. At the time of his death, violent persecution against Anabaptists was on the rise throughout northern Europe.

Stephen Denison (unknown). English Puritan pastor. Denison received the post of curate at St. Katherine Cree in London sometime in the 1610s, where he ministered until his ejection from office in 1635. During his career at St. Katherine Cree, Denison waded into controversy with both Puritans (over the doctrine of predestination) and Anglicans (over concerns about liturgical ceremonies). He approached both altercations with rancor and rigidity, although he seems to have been quite popular and beloved by most of his congregation. In 1631, William Laud* consecrated the newly renovated St. Katherine Cree, and as part of the festivities Denison offered a sermon on Luke 19:27 in which he publicly rebuked Laud for fashioning the Lord's house into a "den of robbers." Aside from the record of his quarrels, very little is known about Denison. In addition to *The White Wolf* (a 1627 sermon against another opponent), he published a catechism for children (1621), a treatise on the sacraments (1621) and a commentary on 2 Peter 1 (1622).

Marie Dentière (1495–1561). Belgian Reformed theologian. Dentière relinquished her monastic vows and married Simon Robert (d.1533), a former priest, in Strasbourg. After Robert died, she married Antoine Froment (1508–1581), a reformer in Geneva, and became involved in the reform of that city. Her best-known writings are a tract addressed to Marguerite d'Angoulême,* the *Very Useful Epistle* (1539), in which she espoused the evangelical faith and the right of women to interpret and teach scripture, and a preface to Calvin's sermon on 1 Timothy 2:8-12. Dentière is the only woman to have her name inscribed on the International Monument to the Reformation in Geneva.

David Dickson (1583?–1663). Scottish Reformed pastor, preacher, professor and theologian. Dickson defended the Presbyterian form of ecclesial reformation in Scotland and was recognized for his iteration of Calvinist federal theology and expository biblical commentaries. Dickson served for over twenty years as professor of philosophy at the University of Glasgow before being appointed professor of divinity. He opposed the imposition of Episcopalian measures on the church in Scotland and was active in political and ecclesial venues to protest and prohibit such influences. Dickson was removed from his academic post following his refusal of the oath of supremacy during the Restoration era.

Veit Dietrich (1506–1549). German Lutheran preacher and theologian. Dietrich intended to study medicine at the University of Wittenberg, but Martin Luther* and Philipp Melanchthon* convinced him to study theology instead. Dietrich developed a strong relationship with Luther, accompanying him to the Marburg Colloquy (1529) and to Coburg Castle during the Diet of Augsburg (1530). After graduating, Dietrich taught on the arts faculty, eventually becoming dean. In 1535 he returned to his hometown, Nuremberg, to pastor. Later in life, Dietrich worked with Melanchthon to reform the church in Regensburg. In 1547, when Charles V arrived in Nuremberg, Dietrich was suspended from the pastorate; he resisted the imposition of the Augsburg Interim to no avail. In addition to transcribing some of Luther's lectures, portions of the Table Talk and the very popular *Hauspostille* (1544), Dietrich published his own sermons for children, a manual for pastors and a summary of the Bible.

Giovanni Diodati (1576–1649). Italian Reformed theologian. Diodati was from an Italian banking family who fled for religious reasons to Geneva. There he trained under Theodore Beza;* on completion of his doctoral degree, Diodati became professor of Hebrew at the academy. He was an ecclesiastical representative of the church in Geneva (for whom he was a delegate at the Synod of Dordrecht*) and an advocate for reform in Venice. Diodati's chief contribution to the Italian reform movement was a translation of the Bible into Italian (1640–1641), which remains the standard translation in Italian Protestantism.

John Dod (c. 1549–1645). English Puritan pastor. Over the course of his lengthy pastoral career (spanning roughly sixty years), Dod was twice suspended for nonconformity and twice reinstated. A popular preacher, he published many sermons as well as commentaries on the Ten Commandments and the Lord's Prayer; collections of his sayings and anecdotes were compiled after his death.

John Donne (1572–1631). Anglican poet and preacher. Donne was born into a strong Catholic family. However, sometime between his brother's death from the plague while in prison in 1593 and the publication of his *Pseudo-Martyr* in 1610, Donne joined the Church of England. Ordained to the Anglican priesthood in 1615 and already widely recognized for his verse, Donne quickly rose to prominence as a preacher—some have deemed him the best of his era. His textual corpus is an amalgam of erotic *and* divine poetry (e.g., "Batter My Heart"), as well as a great number of sermons.

Dordrecht Confession (1632). Dutch Mennonite confession. Adriaan Cornelisz (1581–1632) wrote the Dordrecht Confession to unify Dutch Mennonites. This basic statement of Mennonite belief and practice affirms distinctive doctrines such as nonresistance, shunning, footwashing and the refusal to swear oaths. Most continental Mennonites subscribed to this confession during the second half of the seventeenth century.

John Downame (c. 1571–1652). English Puritan pastor and theologian. See *English Annotations*.

Charles Drelincourt (1595–1669). French Reformed pastor, theologian and controversialist. After studying at Saumur Academy, Drelincourt pastored the Reformed Church in Paris for nearly fifty years. He was well known for his ministry to the sick. In addition to polemical works against Catholicism, he published numerous pastoral resources: catechisms, three volumes of sermons and a five-volume series on consolation for the suffering.

The Dutch Annotations (1657). See *Statenvertaling*.

Daniel Dyke (d. 1614). English Puritan preacher. Born of nonconformist stock, Dyke championed a more thorough reformation of church practice in England. After the promulgation of John Whitgift's* articles in 1583, Dyke refused to accept what he saw as remnants of Catholicism, bringing him into conflict with the bishop of London. Despite the petitions of his congregation and some politicians, the bishop of London suspended Dyke from his ministry for refusing priestly ordination and conformity to the Book of Common Prayer.* All of his work was published posthumously; it is mostly focused on biblical interpretation.

Johann Eck (Johann Maier of Eck) (1486–1543). German Catholic theologian. Though Eck was not an antagonist of Martin Luther* until the dispute over indulgences, Luther's Ninety-five Theses (1517) sealed the two as adversaries. After their debate at the Leipzig Disputation (1519), Eck participated in the writing of the papal bull that led to Luther's excommunication. Much of Eck's work was written to oppose Protestantism or to defend Catholic doctrine and the papacy; his *Enchiridion* was a manual written to counter Protestant doctrine. However, Eck was also deeply invested in the status of parish preaching, publishing a five-volume set of postils. He participated in the assemblies at Regensburg and Augsburg and led the Catholics in their rejection of the Augsburg Confession.

Elizabeth I of England (1533–1603) English monarch. The daughter of Henry VIII (r. 1509–1547) and Anne Boleyn (c. 1501–1536), Elizabeth outwardly conformed to Catholicism during the reign of her sister Mary I (r. 1553–1558), but her Protestant upbringing encouraged the hopes of many reformers upon her accession in 1558. With the 1559 Elizabethan Settlement, Elizabeth redefined England as a Protestant country, with the Act of Supremacy asserting the monarch as the head of the English church, and the Act of Uniformity establishing the 1559 *Book of Common Prayer** as the valid order of service within the realm. However, Elizabeth resisted the aggressive persecution of Catholics for political reasons, while also allowing some traditional vestments, furniture and ceremonies to be retained. Her moderate and pragmatic reforms frustrated many who wished for more thorough change and led to the emergence of the Puritan movement. Elizabeth faced numerous threats during her reign, including the machinations of Scottish Catholics and claims to the throne of Mary Stuart (1542–1547), leading to her rival's imprisonment and execution in 1587; the attempted invasion of England by Spain, which culminated in the celebrated defeat of the Spanish Armada in 1588; and a Catholic rebellion in Ireland that was suppressed during the Nine Years War (1594–1603). Elizabeth never married, and was succeeded on the throne by James I* following her death in 1603.

English Annotations (1645; 1651; 1657). Under a commission from the Westminster Assembly, the editors of the English Annotations—John Downame* along with unnamed colleagues—translated, collated and digested in a compact and accessible format several significant Continental biblical resources, including Calvin's* commentaries, Beza's* *Annotationes majores* and Diodati's* *Annotations.*

Desiderius Erasmus (1466–1536). Dutch Catholic humanist and pedagogue. Erasmus, a celebrated humanist scholar, was recognized for translations of ancient texts, reform of education according to classical studies, moral and spiritual writings and the first printed edition of the Greek New Testament. A former Augustinian who never left the Catholic Church, Erasmus addressed deficiencies he saw in the church and society, challenging numerous prevailing doctrines but advocating reform. He envisioned a simple, spiritual Christian life shaped by the teachings of Jesus and ancient wisdom. He was often accused of collusion with Martin Luther* on account of some resonance of their ideas but hotly debated Luther on human will.

Paul Fagius (1504–1549). German Reformed Hebraist and pastor. After studying at the University of Heidelberg, Fagius went to Strasbourg where he perfected his Hebrew under Wolfgang Capito.* In Isny im Allgäu (Baden-Württemberg) he met the great Jewish grammarian Elias Levita (1469–1549), with whom he established a Hebrew printing press. In 1544 Fagius returned to Strasbourg, succeeding Capito as preacher and Old Testament lecturer. During the Augsburg Interim, Fagius (with Martin Bucer*) accepted Thomas Cranmer's* invitation to translate and interpret the Bible at Cambridge. However, Fagius died before he could begin any of the work. Fagius wrote commentaries on the first four chapters of Genesis and the deuterocanonical books of Sirach and Tobit.

Guillaume Farel (1489–1565) French Reformed preacher and theologian. At the vanguard of the French Reformation, Farel was a student of Jacques Lefèvre d'Étaples* and member of Archbishop Briçonnet's* circle in Meaux until his desire for more rapid change saw him depart in 1523 to preach the Protestant message in Basel, Montbéliard, Strasbourg, Bern, and Aigle. During this period of his ministry, he composed the first French Protestant book, an evangelical commentary on the Lord's Prayer and the Apostle's Creed, as well as the first French Confession of Faith. A catalyst in Geneva's acceptance of the Reformation in 1536, it was Farel who persuaded Calvin* to settle in the city. After he and Calvin were banished from Geneva in 1538, Farel accepted the pastorate in Neuchâtel, a position he held until his death while continuing to travel and support the Reformation in the French-speaking lands.

John Fary (unknown). English Puritan pastor. Fary authored *God's Severity on Man's Sterility* (1645), a sermon on the fruitless fig tree in Luke 13:6-9.

William Fenner (1600–1640). English Puritan pastor. After studying at Cambridge and Oxford, Fenner ministered at Sedgley and Rochford. Fenner's extant writings, which primarily deal with practical and devotional topics, demonstrate a zealous Puritan piety and a keen interest in Scripture and theology.

First Helvetic Confession (1536). Anticipating the planned church council at Mantua (1537, but delayed until 1545 at Trent), Reformed theologians of the Swiss cantons drafted a confession to distinguish themselves from both Catholics and the churches of the Augsburg Confession.* Heinrich Bullinger* led the discussion and wrote the confession itself; Leo Jud, Oswald Myconius, Simon Grynaeus and others were part of the assembly. Martin Bucer* and Wolfgang Capito* had desired to draw the Lutheran and Reformed communions closer together through this document, but Luther* proved unwilling after Bullinger refused to accept the Wittenberg Concord (1536). This confession was largely eclipsed by Bullinger's Second Helvetic Confession.*

John Fisher (1469–1535). English Catholic bishop and theologian. This reputed preacher defended Catholic orthodoxy and strove to reform abuses in the church. In 1521 Henry VIII honored Fisher with the title *Fidei Defensor* ("defender of the faith"). Nevertheless, Fisher opposed the king's divorce of Catherine of Aragon (1485–1536) and the independent establishment of the Church of England; he was convicted for treason and executed. Most of Fisher's works are polemical and occasional (e.g., on transubstantiation, against Martin Luther*); however, he also published a series of sermons on the seven penitential psalms. In addition to his episcopal duties, Fisher was the chancellor of Cambridge from 1504 until his death.

John Flavel (c. 1630–1691). English Puritan pastor. Trained at Oxford, Flavel ministered in southwest England from 1650 until the Act of Uniformity in 1662, which reaffirmed the compulsory use of the Book of Common Prayer. Flavel preached unofficially for many years, until his congregation was eventually allowed to build a meeting place in 1687. His works were numerous, varied and popular.

Giovanni Battista Folengo (1490–1559). Italian Catholic exegete. In 1528 Folengo left the Benedictine order, questioning the validity of monastic vows; he returned to the monastic life in 1534. During this hiatus Folengo came into contact with the Neapolitan reform-minded circle founded by Juan de Valdés.* Folengo published commentaries on the Psalms, John, 1–2 Peter and James. Augustin Marlorat* included Folengo's comment in his anthology of exegesis on the Psalms. In 1580 Folengo's Psalms commentary was added to the Index of Prohibited Books.

Formula of Concord (1577). After Luther's* death, intra-Lutheran controversies between the Gnesio-Lutherans (partisans of Luther) and the Philippists (partisans of Melanchthon*) threatened to cause a split among those who had subscribed to the Augsburg Confession.* In 1576, Jakob Andreae,* Martin Chemnitz,* Nikolaus Selnecker,* David Chytraeus* and Andreas Musculus (1514–1581) met with the intent of resolving the controversies, which mainly regarded the relationship between good works and salvation, the third use of the law, and the role of the human will in accepting God's grace. In 1580, celebrating the fiftieth anniversary of the presentation of the Augsburg Confession to Charles V (1500–1558), the *Book of Concord* was printed as the authoritative interpretation of the Augsburg Confession; it included the three ancient creeds, the Augsburg Confession, its Apology (1531), the Schmalkald Articles,* Luther's *Treatise on the Power and Primacy of the Pope* (1537) and both his Small and Large Catechisms (1529).

Sebastian Franck (1499–1542). German Radical theologian. Franck became a Lutheran in 1525, but by 1529 he began to develop ideas that distanced him from Protestants and Catholics. Expelled from Strasbourg and later Ulm due to his controversial writings, Franck spent the end of his life in Basel. Franck emphasized God's word as a divine internal spark that cannot be adequately expressed in outward forms. Thus he criticized religious institutions and dogmas. His work consists mostly of commentaries, compilations and translations. In his sweeping historical *Chronica* (1531), Franck supported numerous heretics condemned by the Catholic Church and criticized political and church authorities.

Leonhard Frick (d. 1528). Austrian Radical martyr. See *Kunstbuch*.

Gallic Confession (1559). This confession was accepted at the first National Synod of the Reformed Churches of France (1559). It was intended to be a touchstone of Reformed faith but also to show to the people of France that the Huguenots—who faced persecution—were not seditious. The French Reformed Church presented this confession to Francis II (1544–1560) in 1560, and to his successor, Charles IX (1550–1574), in 1561. The later Genevan draft, likely written by Calvin,* Beza* and Pierre Viret (1511–1571), was received as the true Reformed confession at the seventh National Synod in La Rochelle (1571).

Geneva Bible (originally printed 1560). During Mary I's reign many English Protestants sought safety abroad in Reformed territories of the Empire and the Swiss Cantons, especially in Calvin's* Geneva. A team of English exiles in Geneva led by William Whittingham (c. 1524–1579) brought this complete translation to press in the course of two years. Notable for several innovations—Roman type, verse numbers, italics indicating English idiom and not literal phrasing of the original languages, even variant readings in the Gospels and Acts—this translation is most well known for its marginal notes, which reflect a strongly Calvinist theology. The notes explained Scripture in an accessible way for the laity, also giving unlearned clergy a new sermon resource. Although controversial because of its implicit critique of royal power, this translation was wildly popular; even after the publication of the Authorized Version (1611) and James I's 1616 ban on its printing, the Geneva Bible continued to be the most popular English translation until after the English Civil Wars.

Johann Gerhard (1582–1637). German Lutheran theologian, professor and superintendent. Gerhard is considered one of the most eminent Lutheran theologians, after Martin Luther* and Martin Chemnitz.* After studying patristics and Hebrew at Wittenberg, Jena and Marburg, Gerhard was appointed superintendent at the age of twenty-four. In 1616 he was appointed to a post at the University of Jena, where he reintroduced Aristotelian metaphysics to theology and gained widespread fame. His most important work was the nine-volume *Loci Theologici* (1610–1625). He also expanded Chemnitz's harmony of the Gospels *(Harmonia Evangelicae)*, which was finally published by Polykarp Leyser (1552–1610) in 1593. Gerhard was well-known for an irenic spirit and an ability to communicate clearly.

George Gifford (c. 1548–1600). English Puritan pastor. Gifford was suspended for nonconformity in 1584. With private support, however, he was able to continue his ministry. Through his published works he wanted to help develop lay piety and biblical literacy.

Anthony Gilby (c. 1510–1585). English Puritan translator. During Mary I's reign, Gilby fled to Geneva, where he assisted William Whittingham (c. 1524–1579) with the Geneva Bible.* He returned to England to pastor after Elizabeth I's accession. In addition to translating numerous continental Reformed works into English—especially those of John Calvin* and Theodore Beza*—Gilby also wrote commentaries on Micah and Malachi.

Bernard Gilpin (1517–1583). Anglican theologian and priest. In public disputations, Gilpin defended Roman Catholic theology against John Hooper (c. 1495-1555) and Peter Martyr Vermigli.* These debates caused Gilpin to reexamine his faith. Upon Mary I's accession, Gilpin resigned his benefice. He sojourned in Belgium and France, returning to pastoral ministry in England in 1556. Gilpin dedicated himself to a preaching circuit in northern England, thus earning the moniker "the Apostle to the North." His zealous preaching and almsgiving roused royal opposition and a warrant for his arrest. On his way to the queen's commission, Gilpin fractured his leg, delaying his arrival in London until after Mary's death and thus likely saving his life. His only extant writing is a sermon on Luke 2 confronting clerical abuses.

Glossa ordinaria. This standard collection of biblical commentaries consists of interlinear and marginal notes drawn from patristic and Carolingian exegesis appended to the Vulgate*; later editions also include Nicholas of Lyra's* *Postilla*. The *Glossa ordinaria* and the Sentences of Peter Lombard (c. 1100–1160) were essential resources for all late medieval and early modern commentators.

Simon Goulart (1543–1628) French Reformed pastor, translator, and theologian. Goulart spent most of his career as a pastor in Geneva and its surrounds, particularly at the city parish of St. Gervais, and was the leader of the Company of Pastors during the last decades of his life. A prolific translator, he published numerous French editions of classical, patristic, and contemporary works from diverse authors including Plutarch, Seneca, Chrysostom, Cyprian, Tertullian, Beza*, Perkins* and Vermigli*. He also composed numerous devotional writings, important histories of early French Protestantism, and polemical treatises supporting the Huguenot cause.

Conrad Grebel (c. 1498–1526). Swiss Radical theologian. Grebel, considered the father of the Anabaptist movement, was one of the first defenders and performers of believers' baptism, for which he was eventually imprisoned in Zurich. One of Huldrych Zwingli's* early compatriots, Grebel advocated rapid, radical reform, clashing publicly with the civil authorities and Zwingli. Grebel's views, particularly on baptism, were influenced by Andreas Bodenstein von Karlstadt* and Thomas Müntzer.* Grebel advocated elimination of magisterial involvement in governing the church; instead, he envisioned the church as lay Christians determining their own affairs with strict adherence to the biblical text, and unified in volitional baptism.

William Greenhill (1591–1671). English Puritan pastor. Greenhill attended and worked at Magdalen College. He ministered in the diocese of Norwich but soon left for London, where he preached at Stepney. Greenhill was a member of the Westminster Assembly of Divines and was appointed the parliament chaplain by the children of Charles I. Oliver Cromwell included him among the preachers who helped draw up the Savoy Declaration. Greenhill was evicted from his post following the Restoration, after which he pastored independently. Among Greenhill's most significant contributions to church history was his *Exposition of the Prophet of Ezekiel*.

Catharina Regina von Greiffenberg (1633–1694). Austrian Lutheran poet. Upon her adulthood her guardian (and half uncle) sought to marry her; despite her protests of their consanguinity and her desire to remain celibate, she relented in 1664. After the deaths of her mother and husband, Greiffenberg abandoned her home to debtors and joined her friends Susanne Popp (d. 1683) and Sigmund von Birken

(1626–1681) in Nuremberg. During her final years she dedicated herself to studying the biblical languages and to writing meditations on Jesus' death and resurrection, which she never completed. One of the most important and learned Austrian poets of the Baroque period, Greiffenberg published a collection of sonnets, songs and poems (1662) as well as three sets of mystical meditations on Jesus' life, suffering and death (1672; 1683; 1693). She participated in a society of poets called the Ister Gesellschaft.

Argula von Grumbach (c. 1490–c. 1564) German Lutheran noblewoman. Grumbach, an attendant of Queen Kunigunde of Austria (1465–1520), was one of the first women to publish in support of the Reformation. She is best known for letters from 1523 and 1524 written in defense of Arsacius Seehofer (1503–1545), a lecturer at the university of Ingolstadt accused of Lutheranism. For unknown reasons, Grumberg ceased to publish after 1524, although her private correspondence after this time demonstrates a continued effort to support evangelical reform.

Rudolf Gwalther (1519–1586). Swiss Reformed preacher. Gwalther was a consummate servant of the Reformed church in Zurich, its chief religious officer and preacher, a responsibility fulfilled previously by Huldrych Zwingli* and Heinrich Bullinger.* Gwalther provided sermons and commentaries and translated the works of Zwingli into Latin. He worked for many years alongside Bullinger in structuring and governing the church in Zurich. Gwalther also strove to strengthen the connections to the Reformed churches on the Continent and England: he was a participant in the Colloquy of Regensburg (1541) and an opponent of the Formula of Concord.*

Hans Has von Hallstatt (d. 1527). Austrian Reformed pastor. See *Kunstbuch*.

Henry Hammond (1605–1660). Anglican priest. After completing his studies at Oxford, Hammond was ordained in 1629. A Royalist, Hammond helped recruit soldiers for the king; he was chaplain to Charles I. During the king's captivity, Hammond was imprisoned for not submitting to Parliament. Later he was allowed to pastor again, until his death. Hammond published a catechism, numerous polemical sermons and treatises as well as his *Paraphrase and Annotations on the New Testament* (1653).

Jörg Haug (Unknown) German Anabaptist leader. Haug was a radical preacher during the 1525 Peasant's Revolt and composed a tract entitled *A Christian Order of a True Christian* (1524) enumerating seven degrees of faith reached by Christians.

Peter Hausted (d. 1645). Anglican priest and playwright. Educated at Cambridge and Oxford, Hausted ministered in a number of parishes and preached adamantly and vehemently against Puritanism. He is best known for his play *The Rival Friends*, which is filled with invective against the Puritans; during a performance before the king and queen, a riot nearly broke out. Haustead died during the siege of Banbury Castle.

Heidelberg Catechism (1563). This German Reformed catechism was commissioned by the elector of the Palatinate, Frederick III (1515–1576) for pastors and teachers in his territories to use in instructing children and new believers in the faith. It was written by theologian Zacharias Ursinus (1534–1583) in consultation with Frederick's court preacher Kaspar Olevianus* and the entire theology faculty at the University of Heidelberg. The Heidelberg Catechism was accepted as one of the Dutch Reformed Church's Three Forms of Unity—along with the Belgic Confession* and the Canons of Dordrecht—at the Synod of Dordrecht,* and became widely popular among other Reformed confessional traditions throughout Europe.

Niels Hemmingsen (1513–1600). Danish Lutheran theologian. Hemmingsen studied at the University of Wittenberg, where he befriended Philipp Melanchthon.* In 1542, Hemmingsen returned to Denmark to pastor and to teach Greek, dialectics and theology at the University of Copenhagen. Foremost of the Danish theologians, Hemmingsen oversaw the preparation and publication of the first Danish Bible (1550). Later in his career he became embroiled in controversies because of his Philippist theology, especially regarding the Eucharist. Due to rising tensions with Lutheran nobles outside of Denmark, King Frederick II (1534–1588) dismissed Hemmingsen from his university post in 1579, transferring him to a prominent but less internationally visible Cathedral outside of Copenhagen. Hemmingsen was a prolific author, writing commentaries on the New Testament and Psalms, sermon collections and several methodological, theological and pastoral handbooks.

Tilemann Hesshus (1527–1588). German Lutheran theologian and pastor. Hesshus studied under Philipp Melanchthon* but was a staunch Gnesio-Lutheran. With great hesitation—and later regret—he affirmed the Formula of Concord.* Heshuss ardently advocated for church discipline, considering obedience a mark of the church. Unwilling to compromise his strong convictions, especially regarding matters of discipline, Hesshus was regularly embroiled in controversy. He was expelled or pressed to leave Goslar, Rostock, Heidelberg, Bremen, Magdeburg, Wesel, Königsberg and Samland before settling in Helmstedt, where he remained until his death. He wrote numerous polemical tracts concerning ecclesiology, justification, the sacraments and original sin, as well as commentaries on Psalms, Romans, 1–2 Corinthians, Galatians, Colossians and 1–2 Timothy, and a postil collection.

Cornelis Hoen (c. 1460–1524). Dutch humanist, jurist, and theologian. A lawyer at the Court of Holland at the Hague, Hoen was prosecuted in 1523 over his sympathy for the evangelical message. He proposed a symbolic interpretation of Christ's presence in the Eucharist justified with reference to Matthew 24:23 in an influential, posthumously-published treatise.

Christopher Hooke (unknown). English Puritan physician and pastor. Hooke published a treatise promoting the joys and blessings of childbirth (1590) and a sermon on Hebrews 12:11-12. To support the poor, Hooke proposed a bank funded by voluntary investment of wealthy households.

Richard Hooker (c. 1553–1600). Anglican priest. Shortly after graduating from Corpus Christi College Oxford, Hooker took holy orders as a priest in 1581. After his marriage, he struggled to find work and temporarily tended sheep until Archbishop John Whitgift* appointed him to the Temple Church in London. Hooker's primary work is *The Laws of Ecclesiastical Polity* (1593), in which he sought to establish a philosophical and logical foundation for the highly controversial Elizabethan Religious Settlement (1559). The Elizabethan Settlement, through the Act of Supremacy, reasserted the Church of England's independence from the Church of Rome, and, through the Act of Uniformity, constructed a common church structure based on the reinstitution of the Book of Common Prayer.* Hooker's argumentation strongly emphasizes natural law and anticipates the social contract theory of John Locke (1632–1704).

John Hooper (d. 1555). English Protestant bishop and martyr. Impressed by the works of Huldrych Zwingli* and Heinrich Bullinger,* Hooper joined the Protestant movement in England. However, after the Act of Six Articles was passed, he fled to Zurich, where he spent ten years. He returned to England in 1549 and was appointed as a bishop. He stoutly advocated a Zwinglian reform agenda, arguing against the use of vestments and for a less "popish" Book of Common Prayer.* Condemned as a heretic for denying transubstantiation, Hooper was burned at the stake during Mary I's reign.

Rudolf Hospinian (Wirth) (1547–1626). Swiss Reformed theologian and minister. After studying theology at Marburg and Heidelberg, Hospinian pastored in rural parishes around Zurich and taught secondary school. In 1588, he transferred to Zurich, ministering at Grossmünster and Fraumünster. A keen student of church history, Hospinian wanted to show the differences between early church doctrine and contemporary Catholic teaching, particularly with regard to sacramental theology. He also criticized Lutheran dogma and the Formula of Concord*. Most of Hospinian's corpus consists of polemical treatises; he also published a series of sermons on the Magnificat.

Caspar Huberinus (1500–1553). German Lutheran theologian and pastor. After studying theology at Wittenberg, Huberinus moved to Augsburg to serve as Urbanus Rhegius's* assistant. Huberinus represented Augsburg at the Bern Disputation (1528) on the Eucharist and images. In 1551, along with the nobility, Huberinus supported the Augsburg Interim, so long as communion of both kinds and regular preaching were allowed. Nevertheless the people viewed him as a traitor because of his official participation in the Interim, nicknaming him "Buberinus" (i.e., scoundrel). He wrote a number of popular devotional works as well as tracts defending Lutheran eucharistic theology against Zwinglian and Anabaptist detractions.

Balthasar Hubmaier (1480/5–1528). German Radical theologian. Hubmaier, a former priest who studied under Johann Eck,* is identified with his leadership in the peasants' uprising at Waldshut. Hubmaier served as the cathedral preacher in Regensberg, where he became involved in a series of anti-Semitic attacks. He was drawn to reform through the early works of Martin Luther*; his contact with Huldrych Zwingli* made Hubmaier a defender of more radical reform, including believers' baptism and a memorialist account of the Eucharist. His involvement in the Peasants' War led to his extradition and execution by the Austrians.

Aegidius Hunnius (1550–1603). German Lutheran theologian and preacher. Educated at Tübingen by Jakob Andreae (1528–1590) and Johannes Brenz,* Hunnius bolstered and advanced early Lutheran orthodoxy. After his crusade to root out all "crypto-Calvinism" divided Hesse into Lutheran and Reformed regions, Hunnius joined the Wittenberg theological faculty, where with Polykarp Leyser (1552–1610) he helped shape the university into an orthodox stronghold. Passionately confessional, Hunnius developed and nuanced the orthodox doctrines of predestination, Scripture, the church and Christology (more explicitly Chalcedonian), reflecting their codification in the Formula of Concord.* He was unafraid to engage in confessional polemics from the pulpit. In addition to his many treatises (most notably *De persona Christi*, in which he defended Christ's ubiquity), Hunnius published commentaries on Matthew, John, Ephesians and Colossians; his notes on Galatians, Philemon and 1 Corinthians were published posthumously.

Jan Hus (d. 1415). Bohemian reformer and martyr. This popular preacher strove for reform in the church, moral improvement in society, and an end to clerical abuses and popular religious superstition. He was branded a heretic for his alleged affinity for John Wycliffe's writings; however, while he agreed that a priest in mortal sin rendered the sacraments inefficacious, he affirmed the doctrine of transubstantiation. The Council of Constance* convicted Hus of heresy, banned his books and teaching, and, despite a letter of safe conduct, burned him at the stake.

Hans Hut (1490–1527). German Radical leader. Hut was an early leader of a mystical, apocalyptic strand of Anabaptist radical reform. His theological views were shaped by Andreas Bodenstein von Karlstadt,* Thomas Müntzer* and Hans Denck,* by whom Hut had been baptized. Hut rejected society and the established church and heralded the imminent end of days, which he perceived in the Peasants' War. Eventually arrested for practicing believers' baptism and participating in the Peasants' War, Hut was tortured and died accidentally in a fire in the Augsburg prison. The next day, the authorities sentenced his corpse to death and burned him.

George Hutcheson (1615–1674). Scottish Puritan pastor. Hutcheson, a pastor in Edinburgh, published commentaries on Job, John and the Minor Prophets, as well as sermons on Psalm 130.

Roger Hutchinson (d. 1555). English reformer. Little is known about Hutchinson except for his controversies. He disputed against the Mass while at Cambridge and debated with Joan Bocher (d. 1550), who affirmed the doctrine of the celestial flesh. During the Marian Restoration he was deprived of his fellowship at Eton because he was married.

Andreas Hyperius (1511–1564). Dutch Protestant theologian. A peripatetic student, Hyperius moved through Germany, France, Italy and England until settling in Marburg as professor of theology in 1541. Alongside commentaries on Romans and Hebrews, he composed texts on homiletics, the use of the church fathers, practical piety, and church administration.

Abraham Ibn Ezra (1089–c. 1167). Spanish Jewish rabbi, exegete and poet. In 1140 Ibn Ezra fled his native Spain to escape persecution by the Almohad Caliphate. He spent the rest of his life as an exile, traveling through Europe, North Africa and the Middle East. His corpus consists of works on poetry, exegesis, grammar, philosophy, mathematics and astrology. In his commentaries on the Old Testament, Ibn Ezra restricts himself to *peshat* (see *quadriga*).

Valentin Ickelshamer (c. 1500–1547). German Radical teacher. After time at Erfurt, he studied under Luther,* Melanchthon,* Bugenhagen* and Karlstadt* in Wittenberg. He sided with Karlstadt against Luther, writing a treatise in Karlstadt's defense. Ickelshamer also represented the Wittenberg guilds in opposition to the city council. This guild committee allied with the peasants in 1525, leading to Ickelshamer's eventual exile. His poem in the Marpeck Circle's *Kunstbuch** is an expansion of a similar poem by Sebastian Franck.*

Thomas Jackson (1579–1640). Anglican theologian and priest. Before serving as the president of Corpus Christi College at Oxford for the final decade of his life, Jackson was a parish priest and chaplain to the king. His best known work is a twelve-volume commentary on the Apostles' Creed.

King James I of England (VI of Scotland) (1566–1625). English monarch. The son of Mary, Queen of Scots, James ascended to the Scottish throne in 1567 following his mother's abdication. In the Union of the Crowns (1603), he took the English and Irish thrones after the death of his cousin, Elizabeth I. James's reign was tumultuous and tense: Parliament and the nobility often opposed him, church factions squabbled over worship forms and ecclesiology, climaxing in the Gunpowder Plot. James wrote treatises on the divine right of kings, law, the evils of smoking tobacco and demonology. His religious writings include a versification of the Psalms, a paraphrase of Revelation and meditations on the Lord's Prayer and passages from Chronicles, Matthew and Revelation. He also sponsored the translation of the Authorized Version*—popularly remembered as the King James Version.

John Jewel (1522–1571). Anglican theologian and bishop. Jewel studied at Oxford where he met Peter Martyr Vermigli.* After graduating in 1552, Jewel was appointed to his first vicarage and became the orator for the university. Upon Mary I's accession, Jewel lost his post as orator because of his Protestant views. After the trials of Thomas Cranmer* and Nicholas Ridley,* Jewel affirmed Catholic teaching to avoid their fate. Still he had to flee to the continent. Confronted by John Knox,* Jewel publicly repented of his cowardice before the English congregation in Frankfurt, then reunited with Vermigli in Strasbourg. After Mary I's death, Jewel returned to England and was consecrated bishop in 1560. He advocated low-church ecclesiology, but supported the Elizabethan Settlement against Catholics and Puritans. In response to the Council of Trent, he published the *Apoligia ecclesiae Anglicanae* (1562), which established him as the apostle for Anglicanism and incited numerous controversies.

Justus Jonas (1493–1555). German Lutheran theologian, pastor and administrator. Jonas studied law at Erfurt, where he befriended the poet Eobanus Hessus (1488–1540), whom Luther* dubbed "king of the poets"; later, under the influence of the humanist Konrad Muth, Jonas focused on theology. In 1516 he was ordained as a priest, and in 1518 he became a doctor of theology and law. After witnessing the Leipzig Disputation, Jonas was converted to Luther's* cause. While traveling with Luther to the Diet of Worms, Jonas was appointed professor of canon law at Wittenberg. Later he became its dean of theology, lecturing on Romans, Acts and the Psalms. Jonas was also instrumental for reform in Halle. He preached Luther's funeral sermon but had a falling-out with Melanchthon* over the Leipzig Interim. Jonas's most influential contribution was translating Luther's *The Bondage of the Will* and Melanchthon's *Loci communes* into German.

David Joris (c. 1501–1556). Dutch Radical pastor and hymnist. This former glass painter was one of the leading Dutch Anabaptist leaders after the fall of Münster (1535), although due to his increasingly radical ideas his influence waned in the early 1540s. Joris came to see himself as a "third David," a Spirit-anointed prophet ordained to proclaim the coming third kingdom of God, which would be established in the Netherlands with Dutch as its *lingua franca*. Joris's interpretation of Scripture, with his heavy emphasis on personal mystical experience, led to a very public dispute with Menno Simons* whom Joris considered a teacher of the "dead letter." In 1544 Joris and about one hundred followers moved to Basel, conforming outwardly to the teaching of the Reformed church there. Today 240 of Joris's books are extant, the most important of which is his *Twonder Boek* (1542/43).

Andreas Bodenstein von Karlstadt (Carlstadt) (1486–1541). German Radical theologian. Karlstadt, an early associate of Martin Luther* and Philipp Melanchthon* at the University of Wittenberg, participated alongside Luther in the dispute at Leipzig with Johann Eck.* He also influenced the configuration of the Old Testament canon in Protestantism. During Luther's captivity in Wartburg Castle in Eisenach, Karlstadt oversaw reform in Wittenberg. His acceleration of the pace of reform brought conflict with Luther, so Karlstadt left Wittenberg, eventually settling at the University of Basel as professor of Old Testament (after a sojourn in Zurich with Huldrych Zwingli*). During his time in Switzerland, Karlstadt opposed infant baptism and repudiated Luther's doctrine of Christ's real presence in the Eucharist.

Edward Kellett (d. 1641). Anglican theologian and priest. Kellett published a sermon concerning the reconversion of an Englishman from Islam, a tract on the soul and a discourse on the Lord's Supper in connection with Passover.

David Kimchi (Radak) (1160–1235). French Jewish rabbi, exegete and philosopher. Kimchi wrote an important Hebrew grammar and dictionary, as well as commentaries on Genesis, 1–2 Chronicles, the Psalms and the Prophets. He focused on *peshat* (see *quadriga*). In his Psalms commentary he attacks Christian interpretation as forced, irrational and inadmissible. While Sebastian Münster* censors and condemns these arguments in his *Miqdaš YHWH* (1534–1535), he and many other Christian commentators valued Kimchi's work as a grammatical resource.

Moses Kimchi (Remak) (1127–1190). French Jewish rabbi and exegete. He was David Kimchi's* brother. He wrote commentaries on Proverbs and Ezra-Nehemiah. Sebastian Münster* translated Kimchi's concise Hebrew grammar into Latin; many sixteenth-century Christian exegetes used this resource.

John Knox (1513–1572). Scottish Reformed preacher. Knox, a fiery preacher to monarchs and zealous defender of high Calvinism, was a leading figure of reform in Scotland. Following imprisonment in the French galleys, Knox went to England, where he became a royal chaplain to Edward VI. At the accession of Mary, Knox fled to Geneva, studying under John Calvin* and serving as a pastor. Knox returned to Scotland after Mary's death and became a chief architect of the reform of the Scottish church (Presbyterian), serving as one of the authors of the Book of Discipline and writing many pamphlets and sermons.

Antonius Broickwy von Königstein (1470–1541). German Catholic preacher. Very little is known about this important cathedral preacher in Cologne. Strongly opposed to evangelicals, he sought to develop robust resources for Catholic homilies. His postils were bestsellers, and his biblical concordance helped Catholic preachers to construct doctrinal loci from Scripture itself.

Kunstbuch. In 1956, two German students rediscovered this unique collection of Anabaptist works. Four hundred years earlier, a friend of the recently deceased Pilgram Marpeck*—the painter Jörg Probst—had entrusted this collection of letters, tracts and poetry to a Zurich bindery; today only half of it remains. Probst's redaction arranges various compositions from the Marpeck Circle into a devotional anthology focused on the theme of the church as Christ incarnate (cf. Gal 2:20).

Osmund Lake (c. 1543–1621). English Pastor who ministered at Ringwood in Hampshire.

François Lambert (Lambert of Avignon) (1487–1530). French Reformed theologian. In 1522, after becoming drawn to the writings of Martin Luther* and meeting Huldrych Zwingli,* Lambert left the Franciscan order. He spent time in Wittenberg, Strasbourg, and Hesse, where Lambert took a leading role at the Homberg Synod (1526) and in creating a biblically based plan for church reform. He served as professor of theology at Marburg University from 1527 to his death. After the Marburg Colloquy (1529), Lambert accepted Zwingli's symbolic view of the Eucharist. Lambert produced nineteen books, mostly biblical commentaries that favored spiritual interpretations; his unfinished work of comprehensive theology was published posthumously.

Hugh Latimer (c. 1485–1555). Anglican bishop and preacher. Latimer was celebrated for his sermons critiquing the idolatrous nature of Catholic practices and the social injustices visited on the underclass by the aristocracy and the individualism of Protestant government. After his support for Henry's petition of divorce he served as a court preacher under Henry VIII and Edward VI. Latimer became a proponent of reform following his education at Cambridge University and received license as a preacher. Following Edward's death, Latimer was tried for heresy, perishing at the stake with Nicholas Ridley* and Thomas Cranmer.*

William Laud (1573–1645). Anglican archbishop, one of the most pivotal and controversial figures in Anglican church history. Early in his career, Laud offended many with his highly traditional, anti-Puritan approach to ecclesial policies. After his election as Archbishop of Canterbury in 1633, Laud continued to strive against the Puritans, demanding the eastward placement of the Communion altar (affirming the religious centrality of the Eucharist), the use of clerical garments, the reintroduction of stained-glass windows, and the uniform use of the Book of Common Prayer.* Laud was accused of being a crypto-Catholic—an ominous accusation during the protracted threat of invasion by the Spanish Armada. In 1640 the Long Parliament met, quickly impeached Laud on charges of treason, and placed him in jail for several years before his execution.

Ludwig Lavater (1527–1586). Swiss Reformed pastor and theologian. Under his father-in-law Heinrich Bullinger,* Lavater became an archdeacon in Zurich. In 1585 he succeeded Rudolf Gwalther* as the city's Antistes. He authored a widely disseminated book on demonology, commentaries on Chronicles, Proverbs, Ecclesiastes, Nehemiah and Ezekiel, theological works, and biographies of Bullinger and Konrad Pellikan.*

John Lawson (unknown). Seventeenth-century English Puritan. Lawson wrote *Gleanings and Expositions of Some of Scripture* (1646) and a treatise on the sabbath in the New Testament.

Jacques Lefèvre d'Étaples (Faber Stapulensis) (1460?–1536). French Catholic humanist, publisher and translator. Lefèvre d'Étaples studied classical literature and philosophy, as well as patristic and medieval mysticism. He advocated the principle of *ad fontes*, issuing a full-scale annotation on the corpus of Aristotle, publishing the writings of key Christian mystics, and contributing to efforts at biblical translation and commentary. Although he never broke with the Catholic Church, his views prefigured those of Martin Luther,* for which he was condemned by the University of Sorbonne in Paris. He then found refuge in the court of Marguerite d'Angoulême, where he met John Calvin* and Martin Bucer.*

Edward Leigh (1602–1671). English Puritan biblical critic, historian and politician. Educated at Oxford, Leigh's public career included appointments as a Justice of the Peace, an officer in the parliamentary army during the English Civil Wars and a member of Parliament. Although never ordained, Leigh devoted himself to the study of theology and Scripture; he participated in the Westminster Assembly. Leigh published a diverse corpus, including lexicons of Greek, Hebrew and juristic terms, and histories of Roman, Greek and English rulers. His most important theological work is *A Systeme or Body of Divinity* (1662).

John Lightfoot (1602–1675). Anglican priest and biblical scholar. After graduating from Cambridge, Lightfoot was ordained and pastored at several small parishes. He continued to study classics under the support of the politician Rowland Cotton (1581–1634). Siding with the Parliamentarians during the English Civil Wars, Lightfoot relocated to London in 1643. He was one of the original members of the Westminster Assembly, where he defended a moderate Presbyterianism. His best-known work is the six-volume *Horae Hebraicae et Talmudicae* (1658–1677), a verse-by-verse commentary illumined by Hebrew customs, language and the Jewish interpretive tradition.

Lucas Lossius (1508–1582). German Lutheran teacher and musician. While a student at Leipzig and Wittenberg, Lossius was deeply influenced by Melanchthon* and Luther,* who found work for him as Urbanus Rhegius's* secretary. Soon after going to work for Rhegius, Lossius began teaching at a local gymnasium (or secondary school), *Das Johanneum*, eventually becoming its headmaster. Lossius remained at *Das Johanneum* until his death, even turning down appointments to university professorships. A man of varied interests, he wrote on dialectics, music and church history, as well as publishing a postil and a five-volume set of annotations on the New Testament.

Sibrandus Lubbertus (c. 1555–1625). Dutch Reformed theologian. Lubbertis, a key figure in the establishment of orthodox Calvinism in Frisia, studied theology at Wittenburg and Geneva (under Theodore Beza*) before his appointment as professor of theology at the University of Franeker. Throughout his career, Lubbertis advocated for high Calvinist theology, defending it in disputes with representatives of Socinianism, Arminianism and Roman Catholicism. Lubbertis criticized the Catholic theologian Robert Bellarmine and fellow Dutch reformer Jacobus Arminius*; the views of the latter he opposed as a prominent participant in the Synod of Dordrecht.*

Martin Luther (1483–1546). German Lutheran priest, professor and theologian. While a professor in Wittenberg, Luther reinterpreted the doctrine of justification. Convinced that righteousness comes only from God's grace, he disputed the sale of indulgences with the Ninety-five Theses. Luther's positions brought conflict with Rome; his denial of papal authority led to excommunication. He also challenged the Mass, transubstantiation and communion under one kind. Though Luther was condemned by the Diet of Worms, the Elector of Saxony provided him safe haven. Luther returned to Wittenberg with public order collapsing under Andreas Bodenstein von Karlstadt;* Luther steered a more cautious path of reform. His rendering of the Bible and liturgy in the vernacular, as well as his hymns and sermons, proved extensively influential.

Georg Major (1502–1574). German Lutheran theologian. Major was on the theological faculty of the University of Wittenberg, succeeding as dean Johannes Bugenhagen* and Philipp Melanchthon.* One of the chief editors on the Wittenberg edition of Luther's works, Major is most identified with the controversy bearing his name, in which he stated that good works are necessary to salvation. Major qualified his statement, which was in reference to the totality of the Christian life. The Formula of Concord* rejected the statement, ending the controversy. As a theologian, Major further refined Lutheran views of the inspiration of Scripture and the doctrine of the Trinity.

John (Mair) Major (1467–1550). Scottish Catholic philosopher. Major taught logic and theology at the universities of Paris (his alma mater), Glasgow and St Andrews. His broad interests and impressive work drew students from all over Europe. While disapproving of evangelicals (though he did teach John Knox*), Major advocated reform programs for Rome. He supported collegial episcopacy and even challenged the curia's teaching on sexuality. Still he was a nominalist who was critical of humanist approaches to biblical exegesis. His best-known publication is *A History of Greater Britain, Both England and Scotland* (1521), which promoted the union of the kingdoms. He also published a commentary on Peter Lombard's *Sentences* and the Gospel of John.

Juan de Maldonado (1533–1583). Spanish Catholic biblical scholar. A student of Francisco de Toledo,* Maldonado taught philosophy and theology at the universities of Paris and Salamanca. Ordained to the priesthood in Rome, he revised the Septuagint under papal appointment. While Maldonado vehemently criticized Protestants, he asserted that Reformed baptism was valid and that mixed confessional marriages were acceptable. His views on Mary's immaculate conception proved controversial among many Catholics who conflated his statement that it was not an article of faith with its denial. He was intrigued by demonology (blaming demonic influence for the Reformation). All his work was published posthumously; his Gospel commentaries were highly valued and important.

Thomas Manton (1620–1677). English Puritan minister. Manton, educated at Oxford, served for a time as lecturer at Westminster Abbey and rector of St. Paul's, Covent Garden, and was a strong advocate of Presbyterianism. He was known as a rigorous evangelical Calvinist who preached long expository sermons. At different times in his ecclesial career he worked side-by-side with Richard Baxter* and John Owen.* In his later life, Manton's Nonconformist position led to his ejection as a clergyman from the Church of England (1662) and eventual imprisonment (1670). Although a voluminous writer, Manton was best known for his preaching. At his funeral in 1677, he was dubbed "the king of preachers."

Augustin Marlorat (c. 1506–1562). French Reformed pastor. Committed by his family to a monastery at the age of eight, Marlorat was also ordained into the priesthood at an early age in 1524. He fled to Geneva in 1535, where he pastored until the Genevan Company of Pastors sent him to France to shepherd the nascent evangelical congregations. His petition to the young Charles IX (1550–1574) for the right to public evangelical worship was denied. In response to a massacre of evangelicals in Vassy (over sixty dead, many more wounded), Marlorat's congregation planned to overtake Rouen. After the crown captured Rouen, Marlorat was arrested and executed three days later for treason. His principle published work was an anthology of New Testament comment modeled after Thomas Aquinas's *Catena aurea in quatuor Evangelia*. Marlorat harmonized Reformed and Lutheran comment with the church fathers, interspersed with his own brief comments. He also wrote such anthologies for Genesis, Job, the Psalms, Song of Songs and Isaiah.

Pilgram Marpeck (c. 1495–1556). Austrian Radical elder and theologian. During a brief sojourn in Strasbourg, Marpeck debated with Martin Bucer* before the city council; Bucer was declared the winner, and Marpeck was asked to leave Strasbourg for his views concerning paedobaptism (which he compared to a sacrifice to Moloch). After his time in Strasbourg, Marpeck traveled throughout southern Germany and western Austria, planting Anabaptist congregations. Marpeck criticized the strict use of the ban, however, particularly among the Swiss brethren. He also engaged in a christological controversy with Kaspar von Schwenckfeld.*

Johannes Mathesius (1504–1565). German Lutheran theologian and pastor. After reading Martin Luther's* *On Good Works*, Mathesius left his teaching post in Ingolstadt and traveled to Wittenberg to study theology. Mathesius was an important agent of reform in the Bohemian town of Jáchymov, where he pastored, preached and taught. Over one thousand of Mathesius's sermons are extant, including numerous wedding and funeral sermons as well as a series on Luther's life. Mathesius also transcribed portions of Luther's Table Talk.

John Mayer (1583–1664). Anglican priest and biblical exegete. Mayer dedicated much of his life to biblical exegesis, writing a seven-volume commentary on the entire Bible (1627–1653). Styled after Philipp Melanchthon's* *locus* method, Mayer's work avoided running commentary, focusing instead on textual and theological problems. He was a parish priest for fifty-five years. In the office of priest Mayer also wrote a popular catechism, *The English Catechisme, or a Commentarie on the Short Catechisme* (1621), which went through twelve editions in his lifetime.

Joseph Mede (1586–1638). Anglican biblical scholar, Hebraist and Greek lecturer. A man of encyclopedic knowledge, Mede was interested in numerous fields, varying from philology and history to mathematics and physics, although millennial thought and apocalyptic prophesy were clearly his chief interests. Mede's most important work was his *Clavis Apocalyptica* (1627, later translated into English as *The Key of the Revelation*). This work examined the structure of Revelation as the key to its interpretation. Mede saw the visions as a connected and chronological sequence hinging around Revelation 17:18. He is remembered as an important figure in the history of millenarian theology. He was respected as a mild-mannered and generous scholar who avoided controversy and debate, but who had many original thoughts.

Philipp Melanchthon (1497–1560). German Lutheran educator, reformer and theologian. Melanchthon is known as the partner and successor to Martin Luther* in reform in Germany and for his pioneering *Loci communes*, which served as a theological textbook. Melanchthon participated with Luther in the Leipzig disputation, helped implement reform in Wittenberg and was a chief architect of the Augsburg Confession.* Later, Melanchthon and Martin Bucer* worked for union between the reformed and Catholic churches. On account of Melanchthon's more ecumenical disposition and his modification of several of Luther's doctrines, he was held in suspicion by some.

Justus Menius (1499–1558). German Lutheran pastor and theologian. Menius was a prominent reformer in Thuringia. He participated in the Marburg Colloquy and, with others, helped Martin Luther* compose the Schmalkald Articles.* Throughout his career Menius entered into numerous controversies with Anabaptists and even fellow Lutherans. He rejected Andreas Osiander's (d. 1552) doctrine of justification—that the indwelling of Christ's divine nature justifies, rather than the imputed alien righteousness of Christ's person, declared through God's mercy. Against Nikolaus von Amsdorf (1483–1565) and Matthias Flacius (1520–1575), Menius agreed with Georg Major* that good works are necessary to salvation. Osiander's view of justification was censored in Article 3 of the Formula of Concord*; Menius's understanding of the relationship between good works and salvation was rejected in Article 4. Menius translated many of Luther's Latin works into German. He also composed a handbook for Christian households and an influential commentary on 1 Samuel.

Johannes Mercerus (Jean Mercier) (d. 1570). French Hebraist. Mercerus studied under the first Hebrew chair at the Collège Royal de Paris, François Vatable (d. 1547), whom he succeeded in 1546. John Calvin* tried to recruit Mercerus to the Genevan Academy as professor of Hebrew, once in 1558 and again in 1563; he refused both times. During his lifetime Mercerus published grammatical helps for Hebrew and Chaldean, an aid to the Masoretic symbols in the Hebrew text, and translated the commentaries and grammars of several medieval rabbis. He himself wrote commentaries on Genesis, the wisdom books, and most of the Minor Prophets. These commentaries—most of them only published after his death—were philologically focused and interacted with the work of Jerome, Nicholas of Lyra,* notable rabbis and Johannes Oecolampadius.*

Ambrose Moibanus (1494–1554). German

Lutheran bishop and theologian. Moibanus helped reform the church of Breslau (modern Wroclaw, Poland). He revised the Mass, bolstered pastoral care and welfare for the poor, and wrote a new evangelical catechism.

Thomas More (1478–1535). English Catholic lawyer, politician, humanist and martyr. More briefly studied at Oxford, but completed his legal studies in London. After contemplating the priesthood for four years, he opted for politics and was elected a member of Parliament in 1504. A devout Catholic, More worked with church leaders in England to root out heresy while he also confronted Lutheran teachings in writing. After four years as Lord Chancellor, More resigned due to heightened tensions with Henry VIII over papal supremacy (which More supported and Henry did not). Tensions did not abate. More's steadfast refusal to accept the Act of Supremacy (1534)—which declared the King of England to be the supreme ecclesial primate not the pope—resulted in his arrest and trial for high treason. He was found guilty and beheaded with John Fisher (1469–1535). Friends with John Colet* and Desiderius Erasmus,* More was a widely respected humanist in England as well as on the continent. Well-known for his novel *Utopia* (1516), More also penned several religious treatises on Christ's passion and suffering during his imprisonment in the Tower of London, which were published posthumously.

Sebastian Münster (1488–1552). German Reformed Hebraist, exegete, printer, and geographer. After converting to the Reformation in 1524, Münster taught Hebrew at the universities of Heidelberg and Basel. During his lengthy tenure in Basel he published more than seventy books, including Hebrew dictionaries and rabbinic commentaries. He also produced an evangelistic work for Jews titled *Vikuach* (1539). Münster's *Torat ha-Maschiach* (1537), the Gospel of Matthew, was the first published Hebrew translation of any portion of the New Testament. Despite his massive contribution to contemporary understanding of the Hebrew language, Münster was criticized by many of the reformers as a Judaizer.

Thomas Müntzer (c. 1489–1525). German Radical preacher. As a preacher in the town of Zwickau, Müntzer was influenced by German mysticism and, growing convinced that Martin Luther* had not carried through reform properly, sought to restore the pure apostolic church of the New Testament. Müntzer's radical ideas led to expulsions from various cities; he developed a highly apocalyptic theology, in which he heralded the last days that would establish the pure community out of suffering, prompting Müntzer's proactive role in the Peasants' War, which he perceived as a crucial apocalyptic event. Six thousand of Müntzer's followers were annihilated by magisterial troops; Müntzer was executed.

John Murcot (1625–1654). English Puritan pastor. After completing his bachelor's at Oxford in 1647, Murcot was ordained as a pastor, transferring to several parishes until in 1651 he moved to Dublin. All his works were published posthumously.

Simon Musaeus (1521–1582). German Lutheran theologian. After studying at the universities of Frankfurt an der Oder and Wittenberg, Musaeus began teaching Greek at the Cathedral school in Nuremberg and was ordained. Having returned to Wittenberg to complete a doctoral degree, Musaeus spent the rest of his career in numerous ecclesial and academic administrative posts. He opposed Matthias Flacius's (1505–1575) view of original sin—that the formal essence of human beings is marred by original sin—even calling the pro-Flacian faculty at Wittenberg "the devil's latrine." Musaeus published a disputation on original sin and a postil.

Wolfgang Musculus (1497–1563). German Reformed pastor and theologian. Musculus produced translations, biblical commentaries and an influential theological text, *Loci communes Sacrae Theologiae* (*Commonplaces of Sacred Theology*), outlining a Zwinglian theology. Musculus began to study theology while at a Benedictine monastery; he departed in 1527 and became secretary to Martin Bucer* in Strasbourg. He was later installed as a pastor in Augsburg, eventually performing the first evangelical liturgy in the city's cathedral. Displaced by the Augsburg Interim, Musculus ended his career as professor of theology at Bern. Though Musculus was active in the pursuit of the reform agenda, he was also concerned for ecumenism, participating in the Wittenberg Concord (1536) and discussions between Lutherans and Catholics.

Friedrich Nausea (c. 1496–1552). German Catholic bishop and preacher. After completing his studies at Leipzig, this famed preacher was appointed priest in Frankfurt but was run out of town by his congregants during his first sermon. He transferred to Mainz as cathedral preacher. Nausea was well connected through the German papal hierarchy and traveled widely to preach to influential ecclesial and secular courts. Court preacher for Ferdinand I (1503–1564), his reform tendencies fit well with royal Austrian theological leanings, and he was enthroned as the bishop of Vienna. Nausea thought that rather than endless colloquies only a council could settle reform. Unfortunately he could not participate in the first session of Trent due to insufficient funding, but he arrived for the second session. Nausea defended the laity's reception of the cup and stressed the importance of promulgating official Catholic teaching in the vernacular.

Melchior Neukirch (1540–1597). German Lutheran pastor and playwright. Neukirch's pastoral career spanned more than thirty years in several northern German parishes. Neukirch published a history of the Braunschweig church since the Reformation and a dramatization of Acts 4–7. He died of the plague.

Nicholas of Lyra (1270–1349). French Catholic biblical exegete. Very little is known about this influential medieval theologian of the Sorbonne aside from the works he published, particularly the *Postilla litteralis super totam Bibliam* (1322–1333). With the advent of the printing press this work was regularly published alongside the Latin Vulgate and the *Glossa ordinaria*. In this running commentary on the Bible Nicholas promoted literal interpretation as the basis for theology. Despite his preference for literal interpretation, Nicholas also published a companion volume, the *Postilla moralis super totam Bibliam* (1339), a commentary on the spiritual meaning of the biblical text. Nicholas was a major conversation partner for many reformers though many of them rejected his exegesis as too literal and too "Jewish" (not concerned enough with the Bible's fulfillment in Jesus Christ).

Johannes Oecolampadius (Johannes Huszgen) (1482–1531). Swiss-German Reformed humanist, reformer and theologian. Oecolampadius (an assumed name meaning "house light") assisted with Desiderius Erasmus's* Greek New Testament, lectured on biblical languages and exegesis and completed an influential Greek grammar. After joining the evangelical cause through studying patristics and the work of Martin Luther,* Oecolampadius went to Basel, where he lectured on biblical exegesis and participated in ecclesial reform. On account of Oecolampadius's effort, the city council passed legislation restricting preaching to the gospel and releasing the city from compulsory Mass. Oecolampadius was a chief ally of Huldrych Zwingli,* whom he supported at the Marburg Colloquy (1529).

Kaspar Olevianus (1536–1587). German Reformed theologian. Olevianus is celebrated for composing the Heidelberg Catechism and producing a critical edition of Calvin's *Institutes* in German. Olevianus studied theology with many, including John Calvin,* Theodore Beza,* Heinrich Bullinger* and Peter Martyr Vermigli.* As an advocate of Reformed doctrine, Olevianus oversaw the shift from Lutheranism to Calvinism throughout Heidelberg, organizing the city's churches after Calvin's Geneva. The Calvinist ecclesial vision of Olevianus entangled him in a dispute with another Heidelberg reformer over the rights of ecclesiastical discipline, which Olevianus felt belonged to the council of clergy and elders rather than civil magistrates.

Josua Opitz (c. 1542–1585). German Lutheran pastor. After a brief stint as superintendent in Regensburg, Opitz, a longtime preacher, was dismissed for his support of Matthias Flacius's (1520–1575) view of original sin. (Using Aristotelian categories, Flacius argued that the formal essence of human beings is marred by original sin, forming sinners into the image of Satan; his views were officially rejected in Article 1 of the Formula of Concord.*) Hans Wilhelm Roggendorf (1533–1591) invited Opitz to lower Austria as part of his Lutheranizing program. Unfortunately Roggendorf and Opitz never succeed in getting Lutheranism legal recognition, perhaps in large part due to Opitz's staunch criticism of Catholics, which resulted in his exile. He died of plague.

Lucas Osiander (1534–1604). German Lutheran pastor. For three decades, Osiander— son of the controversial Nuremberg reformer Andreas Osiander (d. 1552)—served as pastor and court preacher in Stuttgart, until he fell out of favor with the duke in 1598. Osiander produced numerous theological and exegetical works, as well as an influential hymnal.

John Owen (1616–1683). English Puritan theologian. Owen trained at Oxford University, where he was later appointed dean of Christ Church and vice chancellor of the university, following his service as chaplain to Oliver Cromwell. Although Owen began his career as a Presbyterian minister, he eventually departed to the party of Independents. Owen composed many sermons, biblical commentaries (including seven volumes on the book of Hebrews), theological treatises and controversial monographs (including disputations with Arminians, Anglicans, Catholics and Socinians).

Santes Pagninus (c. 1470–1541). Italian Catholic biblical scholar. Pagninus studied under Girolamo Savonarola* and later taught in Rome, Avignon and Lyons. He translated the Old Testament into Latin according to a tight, almost wooden, adherence to the Hebrew. This translation and his Hebrew lexicon *Thesaurus linguae sanctae* (1529) were important resources for translators and commentators.

David (Wängler) Pareus (1548–1622). German Reformed pastor and theologian. Born at Frankenstein in Lower Silesia, Pareus studied theology at Heidelberg under Zacharias Ursinus (1534–1583), the principal author of the Heidelberg Catechism.* After reforming several churches, Pareus returned to Heidelberg to teach at the Reformed seminary. He then joined the theological faculty at the University of Heidelberg, first as a professor of Old Testament and later as a professor of New Testament. Pareus edited the *Neustadter Bibel* (1587), a publication of Martin Luther's* German translation with Reformed annotations—which was strongly denounced by Lutherans, especially Jakob Andreae* and Johann Georg Sigwart (1554–1618). In an extended debate, Pareus defended the orthodoxy of Calvin's exegesis against Aegidius Hunnius,* who accused Calvin of "judaizing" by rejecting many traditional Christological interpretations of Old Testament passages. Towards the end of his career, Pareus wrote commentaries on Genesis, Hosea, Matthew, Romans, 1 Corinthians, Galatians, Hebrews and Revelation.

Paul of Burgos (Solomon ha-Levi) (c. 1351–1435). Spanish Catholic archbishop. In 1391 Solomon ha-Levi, a rabbi and Talmudic scholar, converted to Christianity, receiving baptism with his entire family (except for his wife). He changed his name to Paul de Santa Maria. Some have suggested that he converted to avoid persecution; he himself stated that Thomas Aquinas's (1225–1274) work persuaded him of the truth of Christian faith. After studying theology in Paris, he was ordained bishop in 1403. He actively and ardently persecuted Jews, trying to compel them to convert. In order to convince Jews that Christians correctly interpret the Hebrew Scriptures, Paul wrote *Dialogus Pauli et Sauli contra Judaeos, sive Scrutinium Scripturarum* (1434), a book filled with vile language toward the Jews. He also wrote a series of controversial marginal notes and comments on Nicholas of Lyra's* *Postilla,* many of which criticized Nicholas's use of Jewish scholarship.

Christoph Pelargus (1565–1633). German Lutheran pastor, theologian, professor and superintendent. Pelargus studied philosophy and theology at the University of Frankfurt an der Oder, in Brandenburg. This irenic Philippist was appointed as the superintendent of Brandenburg and later became a pastor in Frankfurt, although the local authorities first required him to condemn Calvinist theology, because several years earlier he had been called before the consistory in Berlin under suspicion of being a crypto-Calvinist. Among his most important works were a four-volume commentary on *De orthodoxa fide* by John of Damascus (d. 749), a treatise defending the breaking of the bread during communion, and a volume of funeral sermons. He also published commentaries on the Pentateuch, the Psalms, Matthew, John and Acts.

Konrad Pellikan (1478–1556). German Reformed Hebraist and theologian. Pellikan attended the University of Heidelberg, where he mastered Hebrew under Johannes Reuchlin. In 1504 Pellikan published one of the first Hebrew grammars that was not merely a translation of the work of medieval rabbis. While living in Basel, Pellikan assisted the printer Johannes Amerbach, with whom he published some of Luther's* early writings. He also worked with Sebastian Münster* and Wolfgang Capito* on a Hebrew Psalter (1516). In 1526, after teaching theology for three years at the University of Basel, Huldrych Zwingli* brought Pellikan to Zurich to chair the faculty of Old Testament. Pellikan's magnum opus is a seven-volume commentary on the entire Bible (except Revelation) and the Apocrypha; it is often heavily dependent upon the work of others (esp. Desiderius Erasmus* and Johannes Oecolampadius*).

Benedict Pererius (1535–1610). Spanish Catholic theologian, philosopher and exegete. Pererius entered the Society of Jesus in 1552. He taught philosophy, theology, and exegesis at the Roman College of the Jesuits. Early in his career he warned against neo-Platonism and astrology in his *De principiis* (1576). Pererius wrote a lengthy commentary on Daniel, and five volumes of exegetical theses on Exodus, Romans, Revelation and part of the Gospel of John (chs. 1–14). His four-volume commentary on Genesis (1591–1599) was lauded by Protestants and Catholics alike.

William Perkins (1558–1602). English Puritan preacher and theologian. Perkins was a highly regarded Puritan Presbyterian preacher and biblical commentator in the Elizabethan era. He studied at Cambridge University and later became a fellow of Christ's Church college as a preacher and professor, receiving acclaim for his sermons and lectures. Even more, Perkins gained an esteemed reputation for his ardent exposition of Calvinist reformed doctrine in the style of Petrus Ramus,* becoming one of the first English reformed theologians to achieve international recognition. Perkins influenced the federal Calvinist shape of Puritan theology and the vision of logical, practical expository preaching.

François Perrault (1577–1657). French Reformed pastor for over fifty years. His book on demonology was prominent, perhaps because of the intrigue at his home in 1612. According to his account, a poltergeist made a commotion and argued points of theology; a few months later Perrault's parishioners slew a large snake slithering out of his house.

Dirk Philips (1504–1568). Dutch Radical elder and theologian. This former Franciscan monk, known for being severe and obstinate, was a leading theologian of the sixteenth-century Anabaptist movement. Despite the fame of Menno Simons* and his own older brother Obbe, Philips wielded great influence over Anabaptists in the Netherlands and northern Germany where he ministered. As a result of Philips's understanding of the apostolic church as radically separated from the children of the world, he advocated a very strict interpretation of the ban, including formal shunning. His writings were collected and published near the end of his life as *Enchiridion oft Hantboecxken van de Christelijcke Leere* (1564).

Obbe Philips (1500–1568) Dutch radical leader. Trained as a physician, Philips was drawn to mystical Anabaptism, as taught by Melchior Hoffman (1495–1543) in his hometown of Leewarden. After adult rebaptism and ordination, he preached in Amsterdam, Delft, Appingedam, and Grongen, and he ordained other leaders including his brother Dirk Philips*, David Joris*, and Menno Simmons*. Disillusioned with the growth of revolutionary, enthusiastic, and apocalyptic elements within Anabaptism and unable to reconcile any visible church with the church of God, Philips withdrew from the radical movement in 1540, after which nothing is known of his life. His only extant writing, entitled *The Confession of Obbe Philips*, was published after his death and recounts elements of the history of the Anabaptist movement and defends his departure from the movement.

Johannes Piscator (1546–1625). German Reformed theologian. Educated at Tübingen (though he wanted to study at Wittenberg), Piscator taught at the universities of Strasbourg and Heidelberg, as well as academies in Neustadt and Herborn. His commentaries on both the Old and New Testaments involve a tripartite analysis of a given passage's argument, of scholia on the text and of doctrinal loci. Some consider Piscator's method to be a full flowering of Beza's* "logical" scriptural analysis, focused on the text's meaning and its relationship to the pericopes around it.

Felix Pratensis (d. 1539). Italian Catholic Hebraist. Pratensis, the son of a rabbi, converted to Christianity and entered the Augustinian Hermits around the turn of the sixteenth century. In 1515, with papal permission, Pratensis published a new translation of the Psalms based on the Hebrew text. His *Biblia Rabbinica* (1517–1518), printed in Jewish and Christian editions, included text-critical notes in the margins as well as the Targum and rabbinic commentaries on each book (e.g., Rashi* on the Pentateuch and David Kimchi* on the Prophets). Many of the reformers consulted this valuable resource as they labored on their own translations and expositions of the Old Testament.

Quadriga. The *quadriga*, or four senses of Scripture, grew out of the exegetical legacy of Paul's dichotomy of letter and spirit (2 Cor 3:6), as well as church fathers like Origen (c. 185–254), Jerome (c. 347–420) and Augustine (354–430). Advocates for this method—the primary framework for biblical exegesis during the medieval era—assumed the necessity of the gift of faith under the guidance of the Holy Spirit. The literal-historical meaning of the text served as the foundation for the fuller perception of Scripture's meaning in the three spiritual senses, accessible only through faith: the allegorical sense taught what should be believed, the tropological or moral sense taught what should be done, and the anagogical or eschatological sense taught what should be hoped for. Medieval Jewish exegesis also had a fourfold interpretive method—not necessarily related to the *quadriga*—called *pardes* ("grove"): *peshat*, the simple, literal sense of the text according to grammar; *remez*, the allegorical sense; *derash*, the moral sense; and *sod*, the mystic sense related to Kabbalah. Scholars hotly dispute the precise use and meaning of these terms.

Petrus Ramus (1515–1572). French Reformed humanist philosopher. Ramus was an influential professor of philosophy and logic at the French royal college in Paris; he converted to Protestantism and left France for Germany, where he came under the influence of Calvinist thought. Ramus was a trenchant critic of Aristotle and noted for his method of classification based on a deductive movement from universals to particulars, the latter becoming branching divisions that provided a visual chart of the parts to the whole. His system profoundly influenced Puritan theology and preaching. After returning to Paris, Ramus died in the Saint Bartholomew's Day Massacre.

Rashi (**Shlomo Yitzchaki**) (1040–1105). French Jewish rabbi and exegete. After completing his studies, Rashi founded a yeshiva in Troyes. He composed the first comprehensive commentary on the Talmud, as well as commentaries on the entire Old Testament except for 1–2 Chronicles. These works remain influential within orthodox Judaism. Late medieval and early modern Christian scholars valued his exegesis, characterized by his preference for peshat (see quadriga).

Remonstrance (1610). See *Synod of Dordrecht*.

Johannes Reuchlin (1455–1522). German Catholic lawyer, humanist and Hebraist. Reuchlin held judicial appointments for the dukes of Württemberg, the Supreme Court in Speyer and the imperial court of the Swabian League. He pioneered the study of Hebrew among Christians in Germany, standing against those who, like Johannes Pfefferkorn (1469–1523), wanted to destroy Jewish literature. Among his many works he published a Latin dictionary, an introductory Greek grammar, the most important early modern Hebrew grammar and dictionary (*De rudimentis hebraicis*; 1506), and a commentary on the penitential psalms.

Edward Reynolds (1599–1676). Anglican bishop. Reynolds succeeded John Donne* as the preacher at Lincoln's Inn before entering parish ministry in Northamptonshire. During the English Civil Wars, he supported the Puritans because of his sympathy toward their simplicity and piety—despite believing that Scripture demanded no particular form of government; later he refused to support the abolition of the monarchy. Until the Restoration he ministered in London; afterward he became the bishop of Norwich. He wrote the general thanksgiving prayer which is part of the morning office in the *Book of Common Prayer.**

Urbanus Rhegius (1489–1541). German Lutheran pastor. Rhegius, who was likely the son of a priest, studied under the humanists at Freiburg and Ingolstadt. After a brief stint as a foot soldier, he received ordination in 1519 and was made cathedral preacher in Augsburg. During his time in Augsburg he closely read Luther's* works, becoming an enthusiastic follower. Despite his close friendship with Zwingli* and Oecolampadius,* Rhegius supported Luther in the eucharistic debates, later playing a major role in the Wittenberg Concord (1536). He advocated for peace during the Peasants' War and had extended interactions with the Anabaptists in Augsburg. Later in his career he concerned himself with the training of pastors, writing a pastoral guide and two catechisms. About one hundred of his writings were published posthumously.

Lancelot Ridley (d. 1576). Anglican preacher. Ridley was the first cousin of Nicholas Ridley,* the bishop of London who was martyred during the Marian persecutions. By Cranmer's* recommendation, Ridley became one of the six Canterbury Cathedral preachers. Upon Mary I's accession in 1553, Ridley was defrocked (as a married priest). Ridley returned to Canterbury Cathedral after Mary's death. He wrote commentaries on Jude, Ephesians, Philippians and Colossians.

Nicholas Ridley (c. 1502–1555). Anglican bishop. Ridley was a student and fellow at Cambridge University who was appointed chaplain to Archbishop Thomas Cranmer* and is thought to be partially responsible for Cranmer's shift to a symbolic view of the Eucharist. Cranmer promoted Ridley twice: as bishop of Rochester, where he openly advocated Reformed theological views, and, later, as bishop of London. Ridley assisted Cranmer in the revisions of the Book of Common Prayer.* Ridley's support of Lady Jane Grey against the claims of Mary to the throne led to his arrest; he was tried for heresy and burned at the stake with Hugh Latimer.*

Peter Riedemann (1506–1556). German Radical elder, theologian and hymnist. While traveling as a Silesian cobbler, Riedemann came into contact with Anabaptist teachings and joined a congregation in Linz. In 1529 he was called to be a minister, only to be imprisoned soon after as part of Archduke Ferdinand's efforts to suppress heterodoxy in his realm. Once he was released, he moved to Moravia in 1532 where he was elected as a minister and missionary of the Hutterite community there. His *Account of Our Religion, Doctrine and Faith* (1542), with its more than two thousand biblical references, is Riedemann's most important work and is still used by Hutterites today.

John Robinson (1576–1625). English Puritan pastor. After his suspension for nonconformity, Robinson fled to the Netherlands with his congregation, eventually settling in Leiden in 1609. Robinson entered into controversies over Arminianism, separation and congregationalism. Most of his healthy congregants immigrated to Plymouth in 1620; Robinson remained in Leiden with those unable to travel.

Nehemiah Rogers (1593–1660). Anglican priest. After studying at Cambridge, Rogers ministered at numerous parishes during his more than forty-year career. In 1643, he seems to have been forced out of a parish on account of being a Royalist and friend of William Laud.* Rogers published a number of sermons and tracts, including a series of expositions on Jesus' parables in the Gospels.

Robert Rollock (c. 1555–1599). Scottish Reformed pastor, educator and theologian. Rollock was deeply influenced by Petrus Ramus's* system of logic, which he implemented as a tutor and (later) principal of Edinburgh University and in his expositions of the Bible. Rollock, as a divinity professor and theologian, was instrumental in diffusing a federalist Calvinism in the Scottish church; he lectured on theology using the texts of Theodore Beza* and articulated a highly covenantal interpretation of the biblical narratives. He was a prolific writer of sermons, expositions, commentaries, lectures and occasional treatises.

Jacopo Sadoleto (1477–1547). Italian Catholic Cardinal. Sadoleto, attaché to Leo X's court, was appointed bishop in 1517, cardinal in 1536. He participated in the reform commission led by Gasparo Contarini.* However, he tried to reconcile with Protestants apart from the commission, sending several letters to Protestant leaders in addition to his famous letter to the city of Geneva, which John Calvin* pointedly answered. Sadoleto published a commentary on Romans that was censored as semi-Pelagian. His insufficient treatment of prevenient grace left him vulnerable to this charge. Sadoleto emphasized grammar as the rule and norm of exegesis.

Heinrich Salmuth (1522–1576). German Lutheran theologian. After earning his doctorate from the University of Leipzig, Salmuth served in several coterminous pastoral and academic positions. He was integral to the reorganization of the University of Jena. Except for a few disputations, all of Salmuth's works—mostly sermons—were published posthumously by his son.

Robert Sanderson (1587–1663). Anglican bishop and philosopher. Before his appointment as professor of divinity at Oxford in 1642, Sanderson pastored in several parishes. Because of his loyalty to the Crown during the English Civil Wars, the Parliamentarians stripped Sanderson of his post at Oxford. After the Restoration he was reinstated at Oxford and consecrated bishop. He wrote an influential textbook on logic.

Edwin Sandys (1519–1588). Anglican bishop. During his doctoral studies at Cambridge, Sandys befriended Martin Bucer.* Having supported the Protestant Lady Jane Grey's claim to the throne, Sandys resigned his post at Cambridge upon Mary I's accession. He was then arrested and imprisoned in the Tower of London. Released in 1554, he sojourned on the continent until Mary's death. On his return to England he was appointed to revise the liturgy and was consecrated bishop. Many of his sermons were published, but his most significant literary legacy is his work as a translator of the Bishop's Bible (1568), which served as the foundational English text for the translators of the King James Bible (1611).

Erasmus Sarcerius (1501–1559). German Lutheran superintendent, educator and pastor. Sarcerius served as educational superintendent, court preacher and pastor in Nassau and, later, in Leipzig. The hallmark of Sarcerius's reputation was his ethical emphasis as exercised through ecclesial oversight and family structure; he also drafted disciplinary codes for regional churches in Germany. Sarcerius served with Philipp Melanchthon* as Protestant delegates at the Council of Trent, though both withdrew prior to the dismissal of the session; he eventually became an opponent of Melanchthon, contesting the latter's understanding of the Eucharist at a colloquy in Worms in 1557.

Michael Sattler (c. 1490–1527). Swiss Radical leader. Sattler was a Benedictine monk who abandoned the monastic life during the upheavals of the Peasants' War. He took up the trade of weaving under the guidance of an outspoken Anabaptist. It seems that Sattler did not openly join the Anabaptist movement until after the suppression of the Peasants' War in 1526. Sattler interceded with Martin Bucer* and Wolfgang

Capito* for imprisoned Anabaptists in Strasbourg. Shortly before he was convicted of heresy and executed, he wrote the definitive expression of Anabaptist theology, the Schleitheim Articles.*

Girolamo Savonarola (1452–1498). Italian Catholic preacher and martyr. Outraged by clerical corruption and the neglect of the poor, Savonarola traveled to preach against these abuses and to prophesy impending judgment—a mighty king would scourge and reform the church. Savonarola thought that the French invasion of Italy in 1494 confirmed his apocalyptic visions. Thus he pressed to purge Florence of vice and institute public welfare, in order to usher in a new age of Christianity. Florence's refusal to join papal resistance against the French enraged Alexander VI (r. 1492–1503). He blamed Savonarola, promptly excommunicating him and threatening Florence with an interdict. After an ordeal by fire turned into a riot, Savonarola was arrested. Under torture he admitted to charges of conspiracy and false prophecy; he was hanged and burned. In addition to numerous sermons and letters, he wrote meditations on Psalms 31 and 51 as well as *The Triumph of the Cross* (1497).

Leupold Scharnschlager (d. 1563). Austrian Radical elder. See *Kunstbuch*.

Leonhard Schiemer (d. 1528). Austrian Radical martyr. See *Kunstbuch*.

Hans Schlaffer (c. 1490–1528). Austrian Radical martyr. See *Kunstbuch*.

Schleitheim Articles (1527). After the death of Conrad Grebel* in 1526 and the execution of Felix Manz (born c. 1498) in early 1527, the young Swiss Anabaptist movement was in need of unity and direction. A synod convened at Schleitheim under the chairmanship of Michael Sattler,* which passed seven articles of Anabaptist distinctives—likely defined against both magisterial reformers and other Anabaptists with less orthodox and more militant views (e.g., Balthasar Hubmaier*). Unlike most confessions, these articles do not explicitly address traditional creedal interests; they explicate instead the Anabaptist view of the sacraments, church discipline, separatism, the role of ministers, pacifism and oaths. Throughout the document there is a resolute focus on Christ's example. Also referred to as the Schleitheim Confession and the Schleitheim Brotherly Union, the Schleitheim Articles are considered the definitive statement of Anabaptist theology, particularly regarding separatism.

Schmalkald Articles (1537). In response to Pope Paul III's (1468–1549) 1536 decree ordering a general church council to solve the Protestant crisis, Elector John Frederick (1503–1554) commissioned Martin Luther* to draft the sum of his teaching. Intended by Luther as a last will and testament—and composed with advice from well-known colleagues Justus Jonas,* Johann Bugenhagen,* Caspar Cruciger,* Nikolaus von Amsdorf (1483–1565), Georg Spalatin (1484–1545), Philipp Melanchthon* and Johann Agricola*—these articles provide perhaps the briefest and most systematic summary of Luther's teaching. The document was not adopted formally by the Lutheran Schmalkald League, as was hoped, and the general church council was postponed for several years (until convening at Trent in 1545). Only in 1580 were the articles officially received, by being incorporated into the *Book of Concord* defining orthodox Lutheranism.

Anna Maria van Schurman (1607–1678). Dutch Reformed polymath. Van Schurman cultivated talents in art, poetry, botany, linguistics and theology. She mastered most contemporary European languages, in addition to Latin, Greek, Hebrew, Arabic, Farsi and Ethiopian. With the encouragement of leading Reformed theologian Gisbertus Voetius (1589–1676), van Schurman attended lectures at the University of Utrecht—although she was required to sit behind a wooden screen so that the male students could not see her. In 1638 van Schurman published her famous treatise advocating female scholarship, *Amica dissertatio . . . de capacitate ingenii muliebris ad scientias*. In addition to these more polemical works, van Schurman also wrote hymns and poems, including a paraphrase of Genesis 1–3. Later in life she became a devotee of Jean de Labadie (1610–1674), a former Jesuit who was also expelled from the Reformed church for his separatist leanings. Her *Eucleria* (1673) is the most well known defense of Labadie's theology.

Kaspar von Schwenckfeld (1489–1561). German Radical reformer. Schwenckfeld was a Silesian nobleman who encountered Luther's* works in 1521. He traveled to Wittenberg twice: first to meet Luther and Karlstadt,* and a second time to convince Luther of his doctrine of the "internal word"—emphasizing inner revelation so strongly that he did not see church meetings or the sacraments as necessary—after which Luther considered him heterodox. Schwenckfeld won his native territory to the Reformation in 1524 and later lived in Strasbourg for five years until Bucer* sought to purify the city of less traditional theologies. Schwenckfeld wrote numerous polemical and exegetical tracts.

Scots Confession (1560). In 1560, the Scottish Parliament undertook to reform the Church of Scotland and to commission a Reformed confession of faith. In the course of four days, a committee—which included John Knox*—wrote this confession, largely based on Calvin's* work, the Confession of the English Congregation in Geneva (1556) and the Gallic Confession.* The articles were not ratified until 1567 and were displaced by the Westminster Confession (1646), adopted by the Scottish in 1647.

Second Helvetic Confession (1566). Believing he would soon die, Heinrich Bullinger* penned a personal statement of his Reformed faith in 1561 as a theological will. In 1563, Bullinger sent a copy of this confession, which blended Zwingli's and Calvin's theology, to the elector of the Palatinate, Frederick III (1515–1576), who had asked for a complete explication of the Reformed faith in order to defend himself against aggressive Lutheran attacks after printing the Heidelberg Confession.* Although not published until 1566, the Second Helvetic Confession became the definitive sixteenth-century Reformed statement of faith. Theodore Beza* used it as the organizing confession for his *Harmonia Confessionum* (1581), which sought to emphasize the unity of the Reformed churches. Bullinger's personal confession was adopted by the Reformed churches of Scotland (1566), Hungary (1567), France (1571) and Poland (1571).

Obadiah Sedgwick (c. 1600–1658). English Puritan minister. Educated at Oxford, Sedgwick pastored in London and participated in the Westminster Assembly. An ardent Puritan, Sedgwick was appointed by Oliver Cromwell (1599–1658) to examine clerical candidates. Sedgwick published a catechism, several sermons and a treatise on how to deal with doubt.

Nikolaus Selnecker (1530–1592). German Lutheran theologian, preacher, pastor and hymnist. Selnecker taught in Wittenberg; Jena and Leipzig, preached in Dresden and Wolfenbüttel, and pastored in Leipzig. He was forced out of his post at Jena because of suspicions that he was a crypto-Calvinist. He sought refuge in Wolfenbüttel, where he met Martin Chemnitz* and Jakob Andreae.* Under their influence Selnecker was drawn away from Philippist theology. Selnecker's shift in theology can be seen in his *Institutio religionis christianae* (1573). Selnecker coauthored the Formula of Concord* with Chemnitz, Andreae, Andreas Musculus (1514–1581), and David Chytraeus.* Selnecker also published lectures on Genesis, the Psalms, and the New Testament epistles, as well as composing over a hundred hymn tunes and texts.

Short Confession (1610). In response to some of William Laud's* reforms in the Church of England—particularly a law stating that ministers who refused to comply with the Book of Common Prayer* would lose their ordination—a group of English Puritans immigrated to the Netherlands in protest, where they eventually embraced the practice of believer's baptism. The resulting Short Confession was an attempt at union between these Puritans and local Dutch Anabaptists ("Waterlanders"). The document highlights the importance of love in the church and reflects optimism regarding the freedom of the will while explicitly rejecting double predestination.

Richard Sibbes (1577–1635). English Puritan preacher. Sibbes was educated at St. John's College,

Cambridge, where he was converted to reforming views and became a popular preacher. As a moderate Puritan emphasizing interior piety and brotherly love, Sibbes always remained within the established Church of England, though opposed to some of its liturgical ceremonies. His collected sermons constitute his main literary legacy.

Menno Simons (c. 1496–1561). Dutch Radical leader. Simons led a separatist Anabaptist group in the Netherlands that would later be called Mennonites, known for nonviolence and renunciation of the world. A former priest, Simons rejected Catholicism through the influence of Anabaptist disciples of Melchior Hoffmann and based on his study of Scripture, in which he found no support for transubstantiation or infant baptism. Following the sack of Anabaptists at Münster, Simons committed to a nonviolent way of life. Simons proclaimed a message of radical discipleship of obedience and inner purity, marked by voluntary adult baptism and communal discipline.

Henry Smith (c. 1550–1591). English Puritan minister. Smith stridently opposed the Book of Common Prayer* and refused to subscribe to the Articles of Religion,* thus limiting his pastoral opportunities. Nevertheless he gained a reputation as an eloquent preacher in London. He published sermon collections as well as several treatises.

Domingo de Soto (1494–1560). Spanish Catholic theologian. Soto taught philosophy for four years at the University in Alcalá before entering the Dominican order. In 1532 he became chair of theology at the University of Salamanca; Soto sought to reintroduce Aristotle in the curriculum. He served as confessor and spiritual advisor to Charles V, who enlisted Soto as imperial theologian for the Council of Trent. Alongside commentaries on the works of Aristotle and Peter Lombard (c. 1100–1160), Soto commented on Romans and wrote an influential treatise on nature and grace.

Cyriacus Spangenberg (1528–1604). German Lutheran pastor, preacher and theologian. Spangenberg was a staunch, often acerbic, Gnesio-Lutheran. He rejected the Formula of Concord* because of concerns about the princely control of the church, as well as its rejection of Flacian language of original sin (as constituting the "substance" of human nature after the fall). He published many commentaries and sermons, most famously seventy wedding sermons (*Ehespiegel* [1561]), his sermons on Luther* (*Theander Luther* [1562–1571]) and Luther's hymns (*Cithara Lutheri* [1569–1570]). He also published an analysis of the Old Testament (though he only got as far as Job), based on a methodology that anticipated the logical bifurcations of Peter Ramus.*

Johann Spangenberg (1484–1550). German Lutheran pastor and catechist. Spangenberg studied at the University of Erfurt, where he was welcomed into a group of humanists associated with Konrad Muth (1470–1526). There he met the reformer Justus Jonas,* and Eobanus Hessius (1488–1540), whom Luther* dubbed "king of the poets." Spangenberg served at parishes in Stolberg (1520–1524), Nordhausen (1524–1546) and, by Luther's recommendation, Eisleben (1546–1550). Spangenberg published one of the best-selling postils of the sixteenth century, the *Postilla Teütsch*, a six-volume work meant to prepare children to understand the lectionary readings. It borrowed the question-answer form of Luther's *Small Catechism* and was so popular that a monk, Johannes Craendonch, purged overt anti-Catholic statements from it and republished it under his own name. Among Spangenberg's other pastoral works are *ars moriendi* ("the art of dying") booklets, a postil for the Acts of the Apostles and a question-answer version of Luther's *Large Catechism*. In addition to preaching and pastoring, Spangenberg wrote pamphlets on controversial topics such as purgatory, as well as textbooks on music, mathematics and grammar.

Georg Spindler (1525–1605). German Reformed theologian and pastor. After studying theology under Caspar Cruciger* and Philipp Melanchthon,* Spindler accepted a pastorate in Bohemia. A well-respected preacher, Spindler published postils in 1576 which some of his peers viewed as crypto-Calvinist. To investigate this allegation Spindler read John Calvin's* *Institutes*, and subsequently converted to the Reformed faith. After years of travel, he settled in the Palatinate and pastored there until his death. In addition to his Lutheran postils, Spindler also published Reformed postils in 1594 as well as several treatises on the Lord's Supper and predestination.

Statenvertaling (1637). The Synod of Dordrecht* commissioned this new Dutch translation of the Bible ("State's Translation"). The six theologians who undertook this translation also wrote prefaces for each biblical book, annotated obscure words and difficult passages, and provided cross-references; they even explained certain significant translation decisions. At the request of the Westminster Assembly, Theodore Haak (1605–1690) translated the *Statenvertaling* into English as *The Dutch Annotations Upon the Whole Bible* (1657).

Johann von Staupitz (d. 1524). German Catholic theologian, professor and preacher. Frederick the Wise summoned this Augustinian monk to serve as professor of Bible and first dean of the theology faculty at the University of Wittenberg. As Vicar-General of the Reformed Augustinian Hermits in Germany, Staupitz sought to reform the order and attempted unsuccessfully to reunite with the conventional Augustinians. While in Wittenberg, Staupitz was Martin Luther's* teacher, confessor and spiritual father. He supported Luther in the early controversies over indulgences, but after releasing Luther from his monastic vows (to protect him), he distanced himself from the conflict. He relocated to Salzburg, where he was court preacher to Cardinal Matthäus Lang von Wellenburg (d. 1540) and abbot of the Benedictine monastery. Staupitz wrote treatises on predestination, faith and the love of God. Many of his sermons were collected and published during his lifetime.

Michael Stifel (1486–1567). German Lutheran mathematician, theologian and pastor. An Augustinian monk, Stifel's interest in mysticism, apocalypticism and numerology led him to identify Pope Leo X as the antichrist. Stifel soon joined the reform movement, writing a 1522 pamphlet in support of Martin Luther's* theology. After Luther quelled the fallout of Stifel's failed prediction of the Apocalypse—October 19, 1533 at 8 a.m.—Stifel focused more on mathematics and his pastoral duties. He was the first professor of mathematics at the University of Jena. He published several numerological interpretations of texts from the Gospels, Daniel and Revelation. However, Stifel's most important work is his *Arithmetica Integra* (1544), in which he standardized the approach to quadratic equations. He also developed notations for exponents and radicals.

Viktorin Strigel (1524–1569). German Lutheran theologian. Strigel taught at Wittenberg, Erfurt, Jena, Leipzig and Heidelberg. During his time in Jena he disputed with Matthias Flacius (1520–1575) over the human will's autonomy. Following Philipp Melanchthon,* Strigel asserted that in conversion the human will obediently cooperates with the divine will through the Holy Spirit and the Word of God. In the Weimar Disputation (1560), Strigel elicited Flacius's opinion that sin is a substance that mars the formal essence of human beings. Flacius's views were officially rejected in Article 1 of the Formula of Concord*; Strigel's, in Article 2. In 1567 the University of Leipzig suspended Strigel from teaching on account of suspicions that he affirmed Reformed Eucharistic theology; he acknowledged that he did and joined the Reformed confession on the faculty of the University of Heidelberg. In addition to controversial tracts, Strigel published commentaries on the entire Bible (except Lamentations) and the Apocrypha.

Johann Sutell (1504–1575). German Lutheran pastor. After studying at the University of Wittenberg, Sutell received a call to a pastorate in Göttingen, where he eventually became superintendent. He wrote new church orders for Göttingen (1531) and Schweinfurt (1543), and expanded two sermons for publication, *The Dreadful Destruction of Jerusalem* (1539) and *History of Lazarus* (1543).

Swiss Brethren Confession of Hesse (1578). Anabaptist leader Hans Pauly Kuchenbecker penned this confession after a 1577 interrogation by Lutheran authorities. This confession was unusually amenable to Lutheran views—there is no mention of pacifism or rejection of oath taking.

Synod of Dordrecht (1618–1619). This large Dutch Reformed Church council—also attended by English, German and Swiss delegates—met to settle the theological issues raised by the followers of Jacobus Arminius.* Arminius's theological disagreements with mainstream Reformed teaching erupted into open conflict with the publication of the *Remonstrance* (1610). This "protest" was based on five points: that election is based on foreseen faith or unbelief; that Christ died indiscriminately for all people (although only believers receive salvation); that people are thoroughly sinful by nature apart from the prevenient grace of God that enables their free will to embrace or reject the gospel; that humans are able to resist the working of God's grace; and that it is possible for true believers to fall away from faith completely. The Synod ruled in favor of the Contra-Remonstrants, its Canons often remembered with a TULIP acrostic—total depravity, unconditional election, limited atonement, irresistible grace, perseverance of the saints—each letter countering one of the five Remonstrant articles. The Synod also officially accepted the Belgic Confession,* Heidelberg Catechism* and the Canons of Dordrecht as standards of the Dutch Reformed Church.

Arcangela Tarabotti (1604–1652). Italian Catholic nun. At the age of eleven, Tarabotti entered a Benedictine convent as a student-boarder; three years later her father forced her to take monastic vows. The dignity of women and their treatment in the male-controlled institutions of early modern Venice concerned Tarabotti deeply. She protested forced cloistering, the denial of education to women, the exclusion of women from public life and the double standards by which men and women were judged. Tarbotti authored numerous polemical works and an extensive correspondence.

Johannes Tauler (c. 1300–1361) German mystical theologian. A Dominican friar and disciple of Meister Eckhart (c. 1260–c. 1328), Tauler spent most of his career as a mendicant preacher in Strasburg and Basel. Known through a collection of about eighty German sermons, Tauler taught a practical spirituality, accessible to those outside the cloister and intended to draw his audience to deeper contemplation of the divine nature.

Richard Taverner (1505–1575). English Puritan humanist and translator. After graduating from Oxford, Taverner briefly studied abroad. When he returned to England, he joined Thomas Cromwell's (1485–1540) circle. After Cromwell's beheading, Taverner escaped severe punishment and retired from public life during Mary I's reign. Under Elizabeth I, Taverner served as justice of the peace, sheriff and a licensed lay preacher. Taverner translated many important continental Reformation works into English, most notably the Augsburg Confession* and several of Desiderius Erasmus's* works. Some of these translations—John Calvin's* 1536 catechism, Wolfgang Capito's* work on the Psalms and probably Erasmus Sarcerius's* postils—he presented as his own work. Underwritten by Cromwell, Taverner also published an edited version of the Matthew Bible (1537).

Thomas Thorowgood (1595–1669). English Puritan pastor. Thorowgood was a Puritan minister in Norfolk and the chief financier of John Eliot (1604–1690), a Puritan missionary among the Native American tribes in Massachusetts. In 1650, under the title *Jews in America, or, Probabilities that Americans be of that Race*, Thorowgood became one of the first to put forward the thesis that Native Americans were actually the ten lost tribes of Israel.

Frans Titelmans (1502–1537). Belgian Catholic philosopher. Titelmans studied at the University of Leuven, where he was influenced by Petrus Ramus.* After first joining a Franciscan monastery, Titelmans realigned with the stricter Capuchins and moved to Italy. He is best known for his advocacy for the Vulgate and his debates with Desiderius Erasmus* over Pauline theology (1527–1530)—he was deeply suspicious of the fruits of humanism, especially regarding biblical studies. His work was published posthumously by his brother, Pieter Titelmans (1501–1572).

Francisco de Toledo (1532–1596). Spanish Catholic theologian. This important Jesuit taught philosophy at the universities of Salamanca and Rome. He published works on Aristotelian philosophy and a commentary on Thomas Aquinas's work, as well as biblical commentaries on John, Romans and the first half of Luke. He was also the general editor for the Clementine Vulgate (1598).

Alonso Tostado (1400–1455). Spanish Catholic bishop and exegete. Tostado lectured on theology, law and philosophy at the University of Salamanca, in addition to ministering in a local parish. Tostado entered into disputes over papal supremacy and the date of Christ's birth. Tostado's thirteen-volume collected works include commentaries on the historical books of the Old Testament and the Gospel of Matthew.

Daniel Toussain (1541–1602). Swiss Reformed pastor and professor. Toussain became pastor at Orléans after attending college in Basel. After the third War of Religion, Toussain was exiled, eventually returning to Montbéliard, his birthplace. In 1571, he faced opposition there from the strict Lutheran rulers and was eventually exiled due to his influence over the clergy. He returned to Orléans but fled following the Saint Bartholomew's Day Massacre (1572), eventually becoming pastor in Basel. He relocated to Heidelberg in 1583 as pastor to the new regent, becoming professor of theology at the university, and he remained there until his death.

John Trapp (1601–1669). Anglican biblical exegete. After studying at Oxford, Trapp entered the pastorate in 1636. During the English Civil Wars he sided with Parliament, which later made it difficult for him to collect tithes from a congregation whose royalist pastor had been evicted. Trapp published commentaries on all the books of the Bible from 1646 to 1656.

Immanuel Tremellius (1510–1580). Italian Reformed Hebraist. Around 1540, Tremellius received baptism by Cardinal Reginald Pole (1500–1558) and converted from Judaism to Christianity; he affiliated with evangelicals the next year. On account of the political and religious upheaval, Tremellius relocated often, teaching Hebrew in Lucca; Strasbourg, fleeing the Inquisition; Cambridge, displaced by the Schmalkaldic War; Heidelberg, escaping Mary I's persecutions; and Sedan, expelled by the new Lutheran Elector of the Palatine. Many considered Tremellius's translation of the Old Testament as the most accurate available. He also published a Hebrew grammar and translated John Calvin's* catechism into Hebrew.

William Tyndale (Hychyns) (1494–1536). English reformer, theologian and translator. Tyndale was educated at Oxford University, where he was influenced by the writings of humanist thinkers. Believing that piety is fostered through personal encounter with the Bible, he asked to translate the Bible into English; denied permission, Tyndale left for the Continent to complete the task. His New Testament was the equivalent of a modern-day bestseller in England but was banned and ordered burned. Tyndale's theology was oriented around justification, the authority of Scripture and Christian obedience; Tyndale emphasized the ethical as a concomitant reality of justification. He was martyred in Brussels before completing his English translation of the Old Testament, which Miles Coverdale* finished.

Juan de Valdés (1500/10–1541). Spanish Catholic theologian and writer. Although Valdés adopted an evangelical doctrine, had Erasmian affiliations and published works that were listed on the Index of Prohibited Books, Valdés rebuked the reformers for creating disunity and never left the Catholic Church. His writings included translations of the Hebrew Psalter and various biblical books, a work on the Spanish language and several commentaries. Valdés fled to Rome in 1531 to escape the Spanish Inquisition and worked in the court of Clement VII in Bologna until the pope's death in 1534. Valdés subsequently returned to Naples, where he led the reform- and revival-minded Valdesian circle.

Peter Martyr Vermigli (1499–1562). Italian Reformed humanist and theologian. Vermigli was one of the most influential theologians of the era, held in common regard with such figures as Martin Luther* and John Calvin.* In Italy, Vermigli was a distinguished theologian, preacher and advocate for moral reform; however, during the reinstitution of the Roman Inquisition Vermigli fled to Protestant regions in northern Europe. He was eventually appointed professor of divinity at Oxford University, where Vermigli delivered acclaimed disputations on the Eucharist. Vermigli was widely noted for his deeply integrated biblical commentaries and theological treatises.

Vulgate. In 382 Pope Damasus I (c. 300–384) commissioned Jerome (c. 347–420) to translate the four Gospels into Latin based on Old Latin and Greek manuscripts. Jerome completed the translation of the Gospels and the Old Testament around 405. It is widely debated how much of the rest of the New Testament was translated by Jerome. During the Middle Ages, the Vulgate became the Catholic Church's standard Latin translation. The Council of Trent recognized it as the official text of Scripture.

Peter Walpot (d. 1578). Moravian Radical pastor and bishop. Walpot was a bishop of the Hutterite community after Jakob Hutter, Peter Riedemann* and Leonhard Lanzenstiel. Riedemann's *Confession of Faith* (1545; 1565) became a vital authority for Hutterite exegesis, theology and morals. Walpot added his own *Great Article Book* (1577), which collates primary biblical passages on baptism, communion, the community of goods, the sword and divorce. In keeping with Hutterite theology, Walpot defended the community of goods as a mark of the true church.

Valentin Weigel (1533–1588). German Lutheran pastor. Weigel studied at Leipzig and Wittenberg, entering the pastorate in 1567. Despite a strong anti-institutional bias, he was recognized by the church hierarchy as a talented preacher and compassionate minister of mercy to the poor. Although he signed the Formula of Concord,* Weigel's orthodoxy was questioned so openly that he had to publish a defense. He appears to have tried to synthesize several medieval mystics with the ideas of Sebastian Franck,* Thomas Müntzer* and others. His posthumously published works have led some recent scholars to suggest that Weigel's works may have deeply influenced later Pietism.

Hieronymus Weller von Molsdorf (1499–1572). German Lutheran theologian. Originally intending to study law, Weller devoted himself to theology after hearing one of Martin Luther's* sermons on the catechism. He boarded with Luther and tutored Luther's son. In 1539 he moved to Freiburg, where he lectured on the Bible and held theological disputations at the Latin school. In addition to hymns, works of practical theology and a postil set, Weller published commentaries on Genesis, 1–2 Samuel, 1–2 Kings, Job, the Psalms, Christ's passion, Ephesians, Philippians, 1–2 Thessalonians and 1–2 Peter.

John Whitgift (1530–1604). Anglican archbishop. Though Whitgift shared much theological common ground with Puritans, after his election as Archbishop of Canterbury (1583) he moved decisively to squelch the political and ecclesiastical threat they posed during Elizabeth's reign. Whitgift enforced strict compliance to the Book of Common Prayer,* the Act of Uniformity (1559) and the Articles of Religion.* Whitgift's policies led to a large migration of Puritans to Holland. The bulk of Whitgift's published corpus is the fruit of a lengthy public disputation with Thomas Cartwright,* in which Whitgift defines Anglican doctrine against Cartwright's staunch Puritanism.

Johann Wigand (1523–1587). German Lutheran theologian. Wigand is most noted as one of the compilers of the *Magdeburg Centuries*, a German ecclesiastical history of the first thirteen centuries of the church. He was a student of Philipp Melanchthon* at the University of Wittenberg and became a significant figure in the controversies dividing Lutheranism. Strongly opposed to

Roman Catholicism, Wigand lobbied against innovations in Lutheran theology that appeared sympathetic to Catholic thought. In the later debates, Wigand's support for Gnesio-Lutheranism established his role in the development of confessional Lutheranism. Wigand was appointed bishop of Pomerania after serving academic posts at the universities in Jena and Königsburg.

Thomas Wilcox (c. 1549–1608). English Puritan theologian. In 1572, Wilcox objected to Parliament against the episcopacy and the Book of Common Prayer,* advocating for presbyterian church governance. He was imprisoned for sedition. After his release, he preached itinerantly. He was brought before the courts twice more for his continued protest against the Church of England's episcopal structure. He translated some of Theodore Beza* and John Calvin's* sermons into English, and he wrote polemical and occasional works as well as commentaries on the Psalms and Song of Songs.

Johann (Ferus) Wild (1495–1554). German Catholic pastor. After studying at Heidelberg and teaching at Tübingen, this Franciscan was appointed as lector in the Mainz cathedral, eventually being promoted to cathedral preacher—a post for which he became widely popular but also controversial. Wild strongly identified as Catholic but was not unwilling to criticize the curia. Known for an irenic spirit—criticized in fact as *too* kind—he was troubled by the polemics between all parties of the Reformation. He preached with great lucidity, integrating the liturgy, Scripture and doctrine to exposit Catholic worship and teaching for common people. His sermons on John were pirated for publication without his knowledge; the Sorbonne banned them as heretical. Despite his popularity among clergy, the majority of his works were on the Roman Index until 1900.

Andrew Willet (1562–1621). Anglican priest, professor, and biblical expositor. Willet was a gifted biblical expositor and powerful preacher. He walked away from a promising university career in 1588 when he was ordained a priest in the Church of England. For the next thirty-three years he served as a parish priest. Willet's commentaries summarized the present state of discussion while also offering practical applications for preachers. They have been cited as some of the most technical commentaries of the early seventeenth century. His most important publication was *Synopsis Papismi, or a General View of Papistrie* (1594), in which he responded to many of Robert Bellarmine's critiques. After years of royal favor, Willet was imprisoned in 1618 for a month after presenting to King James I his opposition to the "Spanish Match" of Prince Charles to the Infanta Maria. While serving as a parish priest, he wrote forty-two works, most of which were either commentaries on books of the Bible or controversial works against Catholics.

Thomas Wilson (d. 1586). English Anglican priest. A fellow of St John's, Cambridge, Wilson fled to Frankfurt to escape the Marian Persecution. After his return to England, he served as a canon and Dean of Worcester.

John Woolton (c. 1535–1594). Anglican bishop. After graduating from Oxford, Woolton lived in Germany until the accession of Elizabeth I. He was ordained as a priest in 1560 and as a bishop in 1578. Woolton published many theological, devotional and practical works, including a treatise on the immortality of the soul, a discourse on conscience and a manual for Christian living.

Girolamo Zanchi (1516–1590). Italian Reformed theologian and pastor. Zanchi joined an Augustinian monastery at the age of fifteen, where he studied Greek and Latin, the church fathers and the works of Aristotle and Thomas Aquinas. Under the influence of his prior, Peter Martyr Vermigli,* Zanchi also imbibed the writings of the Swiss and German reformers. To avoid the Inquisition, Zanchi fled to Geneva where he was strongly attracted to the preaching and teaching of John Calvin.* Zanchi taught biblical theology and the *locus* method at academies in Strasbourg, Heidelberg, and Neustadt. He also served as pastor of an Italian refugee congregation. Zanchi's theological works, *De tribus Elohim* (1572) and *De* *natura Dei* (1577), have received more attention than his commentaries. His commentaries comprise about a quarter of his literary output, however, and display a strong typological and christological interpretation in conversation with the church fathers, medieval exegetes, and other reformers.

Katharina Schütz Zell (1497/98–1562). German Reformed writer. Zell became infamous in Strasbourg and the Empire when in 1523 she married the priest Matthias Zell, and then published an apology defending her husband against charges of impiety and libertinism. Longing for a united church, she called for toleration of Catholics and Anabaptists, famously writing to Martin Luther* after the failed Marburg Colloquy of 1529 to exhort him to check his hostility and to be ruled instead by Christian charity. Much to the chagrin of her contemporaries, Zell published diverse works, ranging from polemical treatises on marriage to letters of consolation, as well as editing a hymnal and penning an exposition of Psalm 51.

Huldrych Zwingli (1484–1531). Swiss Reformed humanist, preacher and theologian. Zwingli, a parish priest, was influenced by the writings of Desiderius Erasmus* and taught himself Greek. While a preacher to the city cathedral in Zurich, Zwingli enacted reform through sermons, public disputations and conciliation with the town council, abolishing the Mass and images in the church. Zwingli broke with the lectionary preaching tradition, instead preaching serial expository biblical sermons. He later was embroiled in controversy with Anabaptists over infant baptism and with Martin Luther* at the Marburg Colloquy (1529) over their differing views of the Eucharist. Zwingli, serving as chaplain to Zurich's military, was killed in battle.

SOURCES FOR BIOGRAPHICAL SKETCHES

General Reference Works

Allgemeine Deutsche Biographie. 56 vols. Leipzig: Duncker & Humblot, 1875–1912; reprint, 1967–1971. Accessible online via deutsche -biographie.de/index.html.

Baskin, Judith R., ed. *The Cambridge Dictionary of Judaism and Jewish Culture*. New York: Cambridge University Press, 2011.

Bettenson, Henry and Chris Maunder, eds. *Documents of the Christian Church*. 3rd ed. Oxford: Oxford University Press, 1999.

Betz, Hans Dieter, Don Browning, Bernd Janowski and Eberhard Jüngel, eds. *Religion Past & Present: Encyclopedia of Theology and Relgion*. 13 vols. Leiden: Brill, 2007–2013.

Bremer, Francis J. and Tom Webster, eds. *Puritans and Puritanism in Europe and America: A Comprehensive Encyclopedia*. 2 vols. Santa Barbara, CA: ABC-CLIO, 2006.

Haag, Eugene and Émile Haag. *La France protestante ou vies des protestants français*. 2nd ed. 6 vols. Paris: Sandoz & Fischbacher, 1877–1888.

Hillerbrand, Hans J., ed. *Oxford Encyclopedia of the Reformation*. 4 vols. New York: Oxford University Press, 1996.

Kolb, Robert, and Timothy J. Wengert, eds. *The Book of Concord: The Confessions of the Evangelical Lutheran Church*. Translated by Charles Arand et al. Minneapolis: Fortress, 2000.

McKim, Donald K., ed. *Dictionary of Major Biblical Interpreters*. Downers Grove, IL: InterVarsity Press, 2007.

Müller, Gerhard, et al., ed. *Theologische Realenzyklopädie*. Berlin: Walter de Gruyter, 1994.

Neue Deutsche Biographie. 28 vols. projected. Berlin: Duncker & Humblot, 1953–. Accessible online via deutsche-biographie.de/index.html.

New Catholic Encyclopedia. 15 vols. New York: McGraw-Hill, 1967; 2nd ed., Detroit: Thomson-Gale, 2002.

Oxford Dictionary of National Biography. 60 vols. Oxford: Oxford University Press, 2004.

Pelikan, Jaroslav. *The Christian Tradition*. 5 vols. Chicago: University of Chicago Press, 1971–1989.

Stephen, Leslie, and Sidney Lee, eds. *Dictionary of National Biography*. 63 vols. London: Smith, Elder and Co., 1885–1900.

Terry, Michael, ed. *Reader's Guide to Judaism*. New York: Routledge, 2000.

Wordsworth, Christopher, ed. *Lives of Eminent Men connected with the History of Religion in England*. 4 vols. London: J. G. & F. Rivington, 1839.

Additional Works for Individual Sketches

Akin, Daniel L. "An Expositional Analysis of the Schleitheim Confession." *Criswell Theological Review* 2 (1988): 345-70.

Bald, R. C. *John Donne: A Life*. Oxford: Oxford University Press, 1970.

Bireley, Robert, *The Refashioning of Catholicism, 1450–1700*, Washington, DC: Catholic University of America Press, 1999.

Burke, David G. "The Enduring Significance of the KJV." *Word and World* 31, no. 3 (2011): 229-44.

Campbell, Gordon. *Bible: The Story of the King James Version, 1611–2011*. Oxford: Oxford University Press, 2010.

Doornkaat Koolman, J ten. "The First Edition of Peter Riedemann's 'Rechenschaft.'" *Mennonite Quarterly Review* 36, no. 2 (1962): 169-70.

Fischlin, Daniel and Mark Fortier, eds. *Royal Subjects: Essays on the Writings of James VI and I*. Detroit: Wayne State University Press, 2002.

Fishbane, Michael A. "Teacher and the Hermeneutical Task: A Reinterpretation of Medieval Exegesis." *Journal of the American Academy of Religion* 43, no. 4 (1975): 709-21.

Friedmann, Robert. "Second Generation Anabaptism as Illustrated by the Walpot Era of the Hutterites." *Mennonite Quarterly* 44, no. 4 (1970): 390-93.

Frymire, John M. *The Primacy of the Postils: Catholics, Protestants, and the Dissemination of Ideas in Early Modern Germany*. Leiden: Brill, 2010.

Furcha, Edward J. "Key Concepts in Caspar von Schwenckfeld's Thought, Regeneration and the New Life." *Church History* 37, no. 2 (1968): 160-73.

Gordon, Bruce, *The Swiss Reformation*. Manchester: Manchester University Press, 2002.

Greaves, Richard L. *Society and Religion in Elizabethan England*. Minneapolis: University of Minnesota, 1981.

Greiffenberg, Catharina Regina von. *Meditations on the Incarnation, Passion and Death of Jesus Christ*. Edited and translated by Lynne Tatlock. The Other Voice in Early Modern Europe. Chicago: University of Chicago Press, 2009.

Grendler, Paul. "Italian biblical humanism and the papacy, 1515-1535." In *Biblical Humanism and Scholasticism in the Age of Erasmus*. Edited by Erika Rummel, 225-76. Leiden: Brill, 2008.

Heiden, Albert van der. "Pardes: Methodological Reflections on the Theory of the Four Senses." *Journal of Jewish Studies* 34, no. 2 (1983): 147-59.

Hendrix, Scott H., ed. and trans. *Early Protestant Spirituality*. New York: Paulist Press, 2009.

Hvolbek, Russell H. "Being and Knowing: Spiritualist Epistelmology and Anthropology from Schwenckfeld to Böhme." *Sixteenth Century Journal* 22, no. 1 (1991): 97-110.

Kahle, Paul. "Felix Pratensis—a Prato, Felix. Der Herausgeber der Ersten Rabbinerbibel, Venedig 1516/7." *Die Welt des Orients* 1, no. 1 (1947): 32-36.

Kelly, Joseph Francis. *The Ecumenical Councils of the Catholic Church: A History*. Collegeville, MN: Liturgical Press, 2009.

Lake, Peter. *The Boxmaker's Revenge: "Orthodoxy", "Heterodox" and the Politics of the Parish in Early Stuart London*. Stanford, CA: Stanford University Press, 2001.

Lockhart, Paul Douglas. *Frederick II and the Protestant Cause: Denmark's Role in the Wars of Religion, 1559–1596*. Leiden: Brill, 2004.

Lubac, Henri de. *Medieval Exegesis: The Four Senses of Scripture*. 3 vols. Translated by Mark Sebanc and E. M. Macierowski. Grand Rapids: Eerdmans, 1998–2009.

Manetsch, Scott, *Calvin's Company of Pastors: Pastoral Care and the Emerging Reformed Church, 1536–1609*. Oxford: Oxford University Press, 2013.

Matheson, Peter, *Argula von Grumbach: A Woman's Voice in the Reformation*. Edinburgh: T&T Clark, 1995.

McKinley, Mary B. "Volume Editor's Introduction." In *Epistle to Marguerite of Navarre and Preface to a Sermon by John Calvin*, edited and translated by Mary B. McKiney. Chicago: University of Chicago Press, 2004.

Norton, David. *A Textual History of the King James Bible*. New York: Cambridge University Press, 2005

Packull, Werner O. "The Origins of Peter Riedemann's Account of Our Faith." *Sixteenth Century Journal* 30, no. 1 (1999): 61-69.

Papazian, Mary Arshagouni, ed. *John Donne and the Protestant Reformation: New Perspectives*. Detroit: Wayne State University Press, 2003.

Paulicelli, Eugenia. "Sister Arcangela Tarabotti: Hair, Wigs and Other Vices." In *Writing Fashion in Early Modern Italy: From Sprezzatura to Satire*, by idem, 177-204. Farnham, Surrey, UK: Ashgate, 2014.

Pragman, James H. "The Augsburg Confession in the English Reformation: Richard Taverner's Contribution." *Sixteenth Century Journal* 11, no. 3 (1980): 75-85.

Rashi. *Rashi's Commentary on Psalms*. Translated by Mayer I. Gruber. Atlanta: Scholars Press, 1998.

Reid, Jonathan A. *King's Sister—Queen of Dissent: Marguerite of Navarre (1492–1549) and her Evangelical Network*. Leiden: Brill, 2009.

Schmidt, Josef, "Introduction" in Johannes Tauler, *Sermons*. New York: Paulist Press, 1985, 1-34.

Spinka, Matthew. *John Hus: A Biography*. Princeton, NJ: Princeton University Press, 1968.

———. *John Hus at the Council of Constance*. New York: Columbia University Press, 1968.

———. *John Hus and the Czech Reform*. Hamden, CT: Archon Books, 1966.

Steinmetz, David C. *Reformers in the Wings: From Geiler von Kayserberg to Theodore Beza*. Oxford: Oxford University Press, 2000.

———. "The Superiority of Pre-Critical Exegesis." *Theology Today* 37, no. 1 (1980): 27-38.

Synder, C. Arnold. "The Confession of the Swiss Brethren in Hesse, 1578." In *Anabaptism Revisited: Essays on Anabaptist/Mennonite Studies in Honor of C. J. Dyck*. Edited by Walter Klaassen, 29-49. Waterloo, ON; Scottdale, PA: Herald Press, 1992.

———. "The Schleitheim Articles in Light of the Revolution of the Common Man: Continuation or Departure?" *Sixteenth Century Journal* 16, no. 4 (1985): 419-30.

Todd, Margo. "Bishops in the Kirk: William Cowper of Galloway and the Puritan Episcopacy of Scotland." *Scottish Journal of Theology*, 57 (2004): 300-312.

Van Liere, Frans. *An Introduction to the Medieval Bible*. New York: Cambridge University Press, 2014.

Voogt, Gerrit. "Remonstrant-Counter-Remonstrant Debates: Crafting a Principled Defense of Toleration after the Synod of Dordrecht (1619–1650)." *Church History and Religious Culture* 89, no. 4 (2009): 489-524.

Wallace, Dewey D. Jr. "George Gifford, Puritan Propaganda and Popular Religion in Elizabethan England." *Sixteenth Century Journal* 9, no. 1 (1978): 27-49.

Wengert, Timothy J. "'Fear and Love' in the Ten Commandments." *Concordia Journal* 21, no. 1 (1995): 14-27.

———. "Philip Melanchthon and John Calvin against Andreas Osiander: Coming to Terms with Forensic Justification." In *Calvin and Luther: The Continuing Relationship*, edited by R. Ward Holder, 63-87. Göttingen: Vandenhoeck & Ruprecht, 2013.

Wilkinson, Robert J. *Tetragrammaton: Western Christians and the Hebrew Name of God*. Leiden: Brill, 2015.

BIBLIOGRAPHY

Primary Sources and Translations Used in the Volume

Baxter, Richard. *The Reformed Pastor*. Puritan Paperbacks. Edited by William Brown. Carlisle, PA: Banner of Truth Trust, 2007.

Baylor, Michael, ed. *The Radical Reformation*. Cambridge Texts in the History of Political Thought. New York: Cambridge University Press, 1995.

Beza, Theodore. *A Little Book of Christian Questions and Responses*. Translated by Kirk M. Summers. Allison Park, PA: Pickwick, 1986.

———. *Theodori Bezae Annotationes Maiores in Novum Domini Nostri Iesu Christi Testamentum*. Geneva: J. Des Planches, 1594. Digital copy online at www.e-rara.ch.

Bromiley, G. W., ed. and trans. *Zwingli and Bullinger*. LCC 24. Philadelphia: Westminster, 1953.

Bucer, Martin. *Concerning the True Care of Souls*. Translated by Peter Beale. Edinburgh: Banner of Truth Trust, 2009.

Bullinger, Heinrich. *The Decades of Henry Bullinger*. Edited by Thomas Harding. 2 vols. Grand Rapids: Reformation Heritage Books, 2004.

———. *In priorem D. Pauli ad Corinthios epistolam commentarius*. In *In omnes apostolicas epistolas, divi videlicet Pauli XIIII. Et VII. canonicas, commentarii*. Zurich: Christoph Froschauer, 1549. Digital copy online at www.e-rara.ch.

Cajetan, Cardinal (Thomas de Vio). *Epistolae Pauli et Aliorum Apostolorum. Ad graecam veritatem castigate, & per reverendissimum dominum dominum Thomam de vio, Caietanum, Cardinalem sancti Xisti, iuxta sensum literalem enarratae. Recens in lucem editae*. Paris: Jehan Petit, 1540.

———. *Opera omnia qvotqvot in Sacrae Scripturae expositionem reperiuntur*. 5 vols. Lyon: Jean & Pierre Prost, 1639. Digital copy online at books.google.com.

Calvin, John. *Commentaries on the Epistles of Paul the Apostle to the Corinthians*. 2 vols. Translated and edited by John Pringle. CTS 39–40. Edinburgh: Calvin Translation Society, 1848–1849. Digital copy online at archive.org.

———. *Ioannis Calvini Opera quae supersunt omnia*. 59 vols. Corpus Reformatorum 29-88. Edited by G. Baum, E. Cunitz and E. Reuss. Brunswick and Berlin: C. A. Schwetschke, 1863–1900. Digital copy online at archive-ouverte.unige.ch/unige:650.

———. *Institutes of the Christian Religion* (1559). Edited by John T. McNeill. Translated by Ford Lewis Battles. LCC 20–21. Philadelphia: Westminster, 1960. Latin text available in CO 2 (1864). Digital copy online at archive-ouverte.unige.ch/unige:650.

Chytraeus, David. *Dispositio epistolarum, quae diebus dominicis et aliis in ecclesia usitate populo proponi solent*. Wittenberg: Johannes Crato, 1563. Digital copy online at www.gateway-bayern.de.

———. *A Postil or orderly disposing of certeine Epistles usually red in the Church of God, uppon the Sundayes and Holydayes throughout the whole yeere*. London: Henrie Bynnemann, for Lucas Harrison and George Bishop, 1570. Digital copy online at EEBO.

Colet, John. *John Colet's Commentary on First Corinthians*. Edited and translated by Bernard O'Kelly and Catherine A. L. Jarrott. Medieval and Renaissance Texts and Studies. Binghamton, NY: Center for Medieval and Early Renaissance Studies, 1985.

Denck, Hans. *Selected Writings of Hans Denck*. Edited and translated by Edward J. Furcha and Ford Lewis Battles. Pittsburgh Original Texts and Translation Series. Pittsburgh, PA: Pickwick, 1975.

———. *Selected Writings of Hans Denck, 1500–1527*. Edited and translated by Edward J. Furcha. Texts and Studies in Religion Series. Lewiston, NY: Edwin Mellen, 1989.

Dickson, David. *An exposition of all St. Paul's epistles, together with an Explanation of those other Epistles . . . Wherein the sense of every Chapter and Verse is Analytically unfolded*. London: Eglesfield, 1659. Digital copy online at EEBO.

Diodati, Giovanni. *Pious Annotations Upon the Holy Bible*. London: Nicolas Fussell, 1651. Digital copy online at EEBO.

Donne, John. *The Sermons of John Donne*. Edited by George R. Potter and Evelyn M. Simpson. 10 vols. Berkeley: University of California Press, 1953–1962.

Downame, John, ed. *The English Annotations*. 2nd ed. London: John Legatt, 1651. Digital copy online at EEBO.

Erasmus, Desiderius. *Erasmus' Annotations on the New Testament. Acts—Romans—1 and 2 Corinthians*. Edited by Anne Reeve and M. A. Screech. Leiden: Brill, 1990.

———. *Novum Testamentum ab Erasmo Recognitum III, Epistolae apostolicae (prima pars)*. Opera Omnia Desiderii Erasmi Roterodami 6,3. Edited by Andrew J. Brown. Amsterdam: Elsevier, 2004.

———. *Paraphrases des Erasmi Roterodami in epistolas Pauli apostoli ad Rhomanos, Corinthios & Galatas, quae commentarii uice esse possunt*. Basel: Johann Froben, 1520. Digital copy online at www.gateway-bayern.de.

Erasmus, Desiderius, and Martin Luther. *Luther and Erasmus: Free Will and Salvation*. Edited and translated by E. Gordon Rupp and Philip S. Watson. LCC 17. Louisville, KY: Westminster John Knox, 1969.

Estep, William R. *The Anabaptist Story: An Introduction to Sixteenth-Century Anabaptism*. Grand Rapids: Eerdmans, 1996.

Foxe, John. *Actes and Monuments of these Latter and Perillous Days, Touching Matters of the Church*. London: 1583. Digital copy online at www.johnfoxe.org.

Gordon, Bruce and Emidio Campi, eds. *Architect of Reformation: An Introduction to Heinrich Bullinger, 1504–1575*. Grand Rapids: Baker Academic, 2004.

Goulart, Simon. *Seconde partie des Discours Chrestiens. Contenant XX Traitez divers, pour l'instruction & consolation des fideles*. Geneva: Iacob Stoer, 1595. Digital copy online at www.e-rara.ch.

———. *XXVIII Discours Chrestiens. Touchant l'estat du Monde & de l'Eglise de Dieu. Nouvellement mis en lumiere, pour l'instruction & consolation des fideles affligez, & qui aspirant à la vie eternelle*. Geneva: Iacob Stoer, 1591. Digital copy online at www.e-rara.ch.

———. *The Wise Vieillard or Old Man*. London: John Dawson, 1621. Digital copy online at EEBO.

Hesshus, Tilemann. *Explicatio prioris epistolae ad Corinthios & proposita piae iuuentuti in Academia Ienensi*. Jena: Ernst von Gera, 1573. Digital copy online at www.gateway-bayern.de.

Hubmaier, Balthasar. *Balthasar Hubmaier: Theologian of Anabaptism*. Edited and translated by H. Wayne Pipkin and John H. Yoder. CRR 5. Scottdale, PA: Herald, 1989.

———. *A Christian Catechism Which Every Person Should Know Before He Is Baptised in Water* (1526). In *Three Reformation Catechisms: Catholic, Anabaptist, Lutheran*. Translated by Denis Janz, 131-78. Texts and Studies in Religion Series. New York: Edwin Mellen, 1982.

Jewel, John. *An Apology of the Church of England*. Edited by John E. Booty. New York: Church Publishing, 2002.

Joris, David. *The Anabaptist Writings of David Joris: 1535–1543*. Edited and translated by Gary K. Waite. CRR 7. Scottdale, PA: Herald, 1994.

Karlstadt, Andreas. *The Eucharistic Pamphlets of Andreas Bodenstein von Karlstadt*. Edited and translated by Amy Nelson Burnett. Kirksville, MO: Truman State University, 2011.

Lambert, François. *Commentarii Prophetia, Eruditione et Linguis, deque Litera et Spiritu*. Argentorati: 1526.

Lefèvre d'Étaples, Jacques. *Jacobi Fabri Stapulensis in omnes D. Pauli epistolas commentariorum libri XIII. Commentariorum in Epistolas Beati Pauli . . . Liber Secundus. Qui est in Primam Epistolam ad Corinthios*. Cologne: Eucharii, 1531. Digital copy online at www.gateway-bayern.de.

Luther, Martin. *D. Martin Luthers Werke, Kritische Gesamtausgabe: [Schriften]*. 73 vols. Weimar: Hermann Böhlaus Nachfolger, 1883–2009. Digital copy online at archive.org.

———. *D. Martin Luthers Werke, Kritische Gesamtausgabe: Deutsche Bibel*. 12 vols. Weimar: Böhlaus Nachfolger, 1906–1961. Digitial copy online at archive.org.

_________. *D. Martin Luthers Werke, Kritische Gesamtausgabe: Tischreden*. 6 vols. Weimar: Hermann Böhlaus Nachfolger, 1912–1921. Digital copy online at archive.org.

———. *Luther's Works [American edition]*. 82 vols. planned. St. Louis: Concordia; Philadelphia: Fortress, 1955–1986, 2009–.

Melanchthon, Philipp. *Annotations on the First Epistle to the Corinthians[Annotationes in Epistolam priorem ad Corinthios]*. Edited and translated by John Patrick Donnelly. Milwaukee: Marquette University Press, 1995.

Muller, Richard A. *Dictionary of Latin and Greek Theological Terms*. Grand Rapids: Baker Academic, 1985.

Musculus, Wolfgang. *In Ambas Apostoli Pauli ad Corinthios Episolas Commentarii*. Basel: Johannes Herwagen, 1566. Digital copy available online at www.gateway-bayern.de.

Oberman, Heiko A. *Forerunners of the Reformation*. New York: Holt, Rinehart and Winston, 1966.

Old, Hughes Oliphant. *The Shaping of the Reformed Baptismal Rite in the Sixteenth Century*. Grand Rapids: Eerdmans, 1992.

Perkins, William. *The Work of William Perkins*. Edited by Ian Breward. Appleford, UK: Sutton Courtenay Press, 1970.

Philips, Dirk. *Writings of Dirk Philips*. Edited and translated by Cornelius J. Dyck, William E. Keeney and Alvin J. Beachy. CRR 6. Scottdale, PA: Herald, 1994.

Robinson, Hastings,ed. *Original Letters Relative to the English Reformation*. Cambridge: Cambridge University Press, 1850.

Schaff, Philip, ed. *The Creeds of Christendom: With a Critical History and Notes*. 3 vols. New York: Harper & Row, 1877. Reprint, Grand Rapids: Baker, 1985. Digital copy online at ccel.org

Simons, Menno. *The Complete Writings of Menno Simons, c. 1496–1561*. Edited by J. C. Wenger. Scottdale, PA: Herald, 1984.

Snyder, Arnold C., ed. *Sources of South German/Austrian Anabaptism*. Translated by Walter Klaasen, Franck Friesen and Werner O. Packull. CRR 10. Kitchener, ON: Pandora, 2001.

Spangenberg, Johann. *Der Apostel Geschichte: Kurtze auslegung Fur die jungen Christen inn Frage verfasset*. Wittenberg: Georg Rhau, 1545. Digital copy online at www.gateway-bayern.de.

———. *[Postilla Teütsch:] Auslegung der Episteln, so auff die Sonntage vom Advent biß auff Ostern in der Kirchen gelesen werden*. Postilla Teütsch 4. Magdeburg: Michael Lotter, 1544. Digital copy online at www.gateway-bayern.de.

Tanner, Norman P., ed. *Decrees of the Ecumenical Councils*. 2 vols. Washington, DC: Georgetown University Press, 1990.

Tierney, Brian. *Origins of Papal Infallibility, 1150–1350: A Study of the Infallibility, Sovereignty, and Tradition of the Middle Ages*. Leiden: Brill, 1972.

Trapp, John. *A Commentary or Exposition upon all the Books of the New Testament*. London: Ekins, 1656. Digital copy online at EEBO.

Vermigli, Peter Martyr. *The Peter Martyr Reader*. Edited by John Patrick Donnelly, SJ, Frank A. James III, and Joseph C. McLelland. 5 vols. Kirksville, MO: Truman State University Press, 1999.

———. *In Selectissimam S. Pauli Apostoli Priorem ad Corinth. Epistolam . . . Commentarii doctissimi*. Zurich: Christoph Froschauer, 1551. Digital copy online at www.e-rara.ch.

Weigel, Valentin. *Valentin Weigel Sämtliche Schriften*. 14 vols. Stuttgart-Bad Constatt: Frommann-Holzboog, 1996–.

Williams, George H., and Angel M. Mergal, eds. *Spiritual and Anabaptist Writers*. LCC 25. Philadelphia: Westminster, 1957.

Zanchi, Girolamo. *De tribus Elohim, aeterno Patre, Filio, et Spiritu sancto, uno eodemque IEHOVA*. 2 vols. Frankfurt am Main: Georg Rab, 1572–1573. Digital copy online at books.google.com.

Zell, Katharina Schütz. *Katharina Schütz Zell, Church Mother*. Edited and Translated by Elsie McKee. Chicago: University of Chicago Press, 2006.

Zuidema, Jason, and Theodore Van Raalte. *Early French Reform: The Theology and Spirituality of Guillaume Farel*. Burlington, VT: Ashgate, 2011.

Zwingli, Huldrych. *Annotatiunculae per Leonem, ex ore Zwinglij in utranue Pauli ad Corinthios Epistolam publice exponentis conceptae*. Zurich: Christoph Froschauer, 1528. Digital copy online at www.e-rara.ch.

———. *Ulrich Zwingli Early Writings*. Edited by Samuel Macauley Jackson. Durham, NC: Labyrinth Press, 1987.

Other Works Consulted

Augustijn, Cornelis. *Erasmus: His Life, Works, and Influence*. Translated by J. C. Grayson. Toronto: University of Toronto Press, 1991.

Bettenson, Henry, and Chris Maunder, eds. *Documents of the Christian Church*. 4th ed. New York: Oxford University Press, 2011.

Brecht, Martin. *Martin Luther*. 3 vols. Translated by James Schaaf. Minneapolis: Fortress, 1985–1993.

Burnett, Amy Nelson. *Karlstadt and the Origins of the Eucharistic Controversy*. New York: Oxford University Press, 2011.

Calvin, John. *Selected Works of John Calvin: Tracts and Letters*. 7 vols. Edited by Henry Beveridge. Reprint, Grand Rapids: Baker, 1983.

Chambers, Bettye Thomas. *Bibliography of French Bibles: Fifteenth- and Sixteenth-Century French-Language Editions of the Scriptures*. Geneva: Droz, 1983.

Croce, Benedetto. *Galéas Caracciolo, Marquis de Vico*. Geneva: Droz, 1965.

Cross, F. L., and E. A. Livingstone. *The Oxford Dictionary of the Christian Church*. 3rd ed. New York: Oxford University Press, 2005.

Duffy, Eamon. *Saints and Sinners. A History of the Popes*. New Haven, CT: Yale University Press, 1997.

Fairbairn, Donald. *Life in the Trinity: An Introduction to Theology with the Help of the Church Fathers*. Downers Grove, IL: IVP Academic, 2009.

Farmer, Craig S. *The Gospel of John in the Sixteenth Century: The Johannine Exegesis of Wolfgang Musculus*. Oxford Studies in Historical Theology. New York: Oxford University Press, 1997.

Fee, Gordon. *The First Epistle to the Corinthians*. New International Commentary on the New Testament. Grand Rapids: Eerdmans, 1987.

Fitzgerald, Alan D., ed. *Augustine Through the Ages: An Encyclopedia*. Grand Rapids: Eerdmans, 1999.

Fox, Michael V. *Proverbs 10–31*. Anchor Yale Bible 18b. New Haven, CT: Yale University Press, 2009.

Foxe, John. *The Acts and Monuments of John Fox*. 8 vols. 4th ed. London: Religious Tract Society, 1877.

Frymire, John. *The Primacy of the Postils: Catholics, Protestants, and the Dissemination of Ideas in Early Modern Germany*. Leiden: Brill, 2010.

George, Timothy. *Theology of the Reformers*. Rev. ed. Nashville: B&H Academic, 2013.

Gerrish, Brian A. *Grace and Gratitude: The Eucharistic Theology of John Calvin*. Minneapolis: Fortress, 1993.

Greenslade, S. L., ed. *The Cambridge History of the Bible*. 3 vols. Cambridge: Cambridge University Press, 1963–1970.

Greschat, Martin. *Martin Bucer: A Reformer and His Times*. Translated Stephen E. Buckwalter. Louisville, KY: Westminster John Knox, 2004.

Hagen, Kenneth. "What Did the Term *Commentarius* Mean to Sixteenth-Century Theologians?" In *Théorie et pratique de l'exégèse: Actes du troisième colloque international sur l'histoire de l'exégèse biblique au XVIe siècle*, edited by Irena Backus and Francis Higman, 13-38. Geneva: Droz, 1990.

Hains, Todd R. "Luther and the Bound Conscience in His German Church Postils." MA thesis, Trinity Evangelical Divinity School, 2007.

Horace. *Satires, Epistles, Ars Poetica*. Translated by H. Rushton Fairclough. LCL 194. Cambridge, MA: Harvard University Press, 1929.

Kingdon, Robert M. *Adultery and Divorce in Calvin's Geneva*. Cambridge, MA: Harvard University Press, 1995.

Krans, Jan. *Beyond What Is Written: Erasmus and Beza as Conjectural Critics of the New Testament*. Leiden: Brill, 2006.

Krey, Peter D. S., and Philip D. W. Krey, eds. *Romans 9–16*. RCS NT 8. Downers Grove, IL: IVP Academic, 2016.

Luther, Martin. *The Bondage of the Will*. Translated by J. I. Packer and O. R. Johnston. New York: Fleming H. Revell, 1957.

———. *Martin Luther's Basic Theological Writings*. 2nd ed. Edited by Timothy F. Lull. Minneapolis: Fortress, 2005.

———. *Martin Luther: Selections from His Writings*. Edited by John Dillenberger. New York: Doubleday, 1962.

———. *Luther on Women: A Sourcebook*. Edited by Susan Karant-Nunn and Merry Wiesner-Hanks. Cambridge: Cambridge University Press, 2003.

———. *Sermons of Martin Luther*. Edited and translated by John Nicholas Lenker. 8 Vols. Grand Rapids: Baker, 1983.

———. *Works of Martin Luther*. 6 vols. Philadelphia: Muhlenberg, 1932.

Manetsch, Scott M. *Calvin's Company of Pastors: Pastoral Care and the Emerging Reformed Church, 1536–1609*. New York: Oxford University Press, 2013.

———. "(Re)constructing the Pastoral Office: Wolfgang Musculus's Commentaries on 1 and 2 Corinthians." In *On the Writing of New Testament Commentaries*, edited by Stanley Porter and Eckhard Schnabel, 253-66. Leiden: Brill, 2013.

Mattox, Mickey L. "From Faith to the Text and Back Again: Martin Luther on the Trinity in the Old Testament." *Pro Ecclesia* 15, no. 3 (2006): 281-303.

McIndoe, John. "John Calvin: Preface to the Homilies of Chrysostom." *Hartford Quarterly* 5 (1965): 19-26.

McKim, Donald K., ed. *The Cambridge Companion to John Calvin*. Cambridge: Cambridge University Press, 2004.

———, ed. *Dictionary of Major Biblical Interpreters*. Downers Grove, IL: IVP Academic, 2007.

Meylan, Henri. "Professeurs et Étudiants, Questions d'Horaires et de Leçons." In *La Réforme et l'éducation*, edited by Jean Boisset, 67-85. Toulouse: Privat, 1974.

Morris, Leon. *1 Corinthians*. Tyndale New Testament Commentaries. Grand Rapids: Eerdmans, 1998.

Muller, Richard A. *Dictionary of Latin and Greek Theological Terms: Drawn Principally from Protestant Scholastic Theology*. Grand Rapids: Baker, 1985.

Muller, Richard A., and John L. Thompson, eds. *Biblical Interpretation in the Era of the Reformation: Essays Presented to David C. Steinmetz in Honor of His Sixtieth Birthday*. Grand Rapids: Eerdmans, 1996.

———. "The Significance of Precritical Exegesis: Retrospect and Prospect." In *Biblical Interpretation in the Era of the Reformation: Essays Presented to David C. Steinmetz in Honor of His Sixtieth Birthday*, edited by Richard A. Muller and John L. Thompson, 335-45. Grand Rapids: Eerdmans, 1996.

Olin, John, ed. *John Calvin—Jacopolo Sadoleto: A Reformation Debate*. Grand Rapids: Baker, 1987.

Ozment, Steven. *Protestants: The Birth of a Revolution*. New York: Doubleday, 1993.

Padelford, Frederick Morgan. *Essays on the Study and Use of Poetry by Plutarch and Basil the Great*. New Haven, CT: Yale University Press, 1902.

Parker, T. H. L. *Calvin's New Testament Commentaries*. Louisville, KY: Westminster John Knox, 1993.

Pelikan, Jaroslav. *The Reformation of the Bible, the Bible of the Reformation*. New Haven, CT: Yale University Press, 1996.

Pervo, Richard I. *The Acts of Paul: A New Translation with Introduction and Commentary*. Cambridge: James Clarke, 2014.

Puyroche, M. "La bibliothèque d'un Pasteur à la fin du XVIe siècle." *Bulletin de la société de l'histoire du Protestantisme français* 21 (1872): 327-37.

Schilling, Heinz. "Confessional Europe." In *Handbook of European History 1400–1600*, edited by Thomas Brady, Heiko A. Oberman and James Tracy, 2:641-82. Leiden: Brill, 1994.

Sheridan, Mark. *Language for God in the Patristic Tradition: Wrestling with Biblical Anthropomorphism*. Downers Grove, IL: IVP Academic, 2015.

Stephens, W. P. *The Theology of Huldrych Zwingli*. Oxford: Oxford University Press, 1986.

———. *Zwingli: An Introduction to His Thought*. Oxford: Oxford University Press, 2001.

Strauss, Gerald. "The Mental World of a Saxon Pastor." In *Reformation Principle and Practice*, edited by Peter Newman Brooks, 161-70. London: Scolar Press, 1980.

Tappert, Theodore G., ed. *The Book of Concord*. Philadelphia: Fortress, 1959.

Thompson, John. "Calvin as a Biblical Interpreter." In *The Cambridge Companion to John Calvin*, edited by Donald McKim, 58-73. Cambridge: Cambridge University Press, 2004.

———. *Reading the Bible with the Dead*. Grand Rapids: Eerdmans, 2007.

———. "Rules Proved by Exceptions: The Exegesis of Paul and Women in the Sixteenth Century." In *A Companion to Paul in the Reformation*, edited by R. Ward Holder, 501-540. Leiden: Brill, 2009.

Thompson, Mark. *A Sure Ground on Which to Stand: The Relation of Authority and Interpretive Method in Luther's Approach to Scripture*. Eugene, OR: Wipf & Stock, 2006.

Vogler, Bernard. *Le Clergé Protestant Rhénan au Siècle de la Réforme (1555–1619)*. Paris: Éditions Ophrys, 1976.

Wengert, Timothy J. "The Rhetorical Paul: Philip Melanchthon's Interpretation of the Pauline Epistles." In *A Companion to Paul in the Reformation*, edited by R. Ward Holder, 129-64. Leiden: Brill, 2009.

Other Reformation Commentary on Scripture Volumes Consulted

Beckwith, Carl L., ed. *Ezekiel, Daniel*. RCS OT 12. Downers Grove, IL: IVP Academic, 2012.

Bray, Gerald L., ed. *Galatians, Ephesians*. RCS NT 10. Downers Grove, IL: IVP Academic, 2011.

Cooper, Derek, and Martin J. Lohrmann, eds. *1–2 Samuel, 1–2 Kings, 1–2 Chronicles*. RCS OT 5. Downers Grove, IL: IVP Academic, 2016.

Chung-Kim, Esther, and Todd R. Hains, eds. *Acts*. RCS NT 6. Downers Grove, IL: IVP Academic, 2014.

Farmer, Craig S., ed. *John 1–12*. RCS NT 4. Downers Grove, IL: IVP Academic, 2014.

Kreitzer, Beth, ed. *Luke*. RCS NT 3. Downers Grove, IL: IVP Academic, 2015.

Selderhuis, Herman J., ed. *Psalms 1–72*. RCS OT 7. Downers Grove, IL: IVP Academic, 2015.

Thompson, John L, ed. *Genesis 1–11*. RCS OT 1. Downers Grove, IL: IVP Academic, 2012.

Tomlin, Graham, ed. *Philippians, Colossians*. RCS NT 11. Downers Grove, IL: IVP Academic, 2013.

Author and Writings Index

Subject Index

Scripture Index

2 Corinthians

Galatians

Ephesians